D0151089

ENCYCLOPEDIA OF CONTEMPORARY RUSSIAN CULTURE

This addition to the highly successful Contemporary Cultures series covers the period from 1953, with the death of Stalin, to the present day. Both 'Russian' and 'Culture' are defined broadly. 'Russian' refers to the Soviet Union until 1991 and the Russian Federation after 1991. Given the diversity of the Federation in its ethnic composition and regional characteristics, questions of national, regional, and ethnic identity are given special attention. There is also coverage of Russian-speaking immigrant communities. 'Culture' embraces all aspects of culture and lifestyle, high and popular, artistic and material: art, fashion, literature, music, cooking, transport, politics and economics, film, crime – all, and much else, are covered, in order to give as full a picture as possible of the Russian way of life and the experience throughout the extraordinary changes undergone since the middle of the twentieth century.

The *Encyclopedia of Contemporary Russian Culture* is an unbeatable resource on recent and contemporary Russian culture and history for students, teachers and researchers across the disciplines.

Entries include extensive cross-references and the longer entries carry short bibliographies.

There is a full index.

Tatiana Smorodinskaya is Associate Professor of Russian, Middlebury College, Vermont, USA.

Karen Evans-Romaine is Associate Professor of Russian, Ohio University, USA.

Helena Goscilo is Professor of Slavic Languages and Literatures, University of Pittsburg, USA.

ENCYCLOPEDIA OF CONTEMPORARY RUSSIAN CULTURE

Edited by
Tatiana Smorodinskaya
Karen Evans-Romaine
Helena Goscilo

Routledge
Taylor & Francis Group

LONDON AND NEW YORK

First published 2007
by Routledge
2 Park Square, Milton Park, Abingdon, Oxon OX14 4RN
www.routledge.co.uk

Simultaneously published in the USA and Canada
by Routledge
270 Madison Avenue, New York, NY 10016
www.routledge-ny.com

Routledge is an Imprint of the Taylor and Francis Group, an informa business

© 2007 Routledge

Typeset in Baskerville and Optima by Taylor & Francis Books
Printed and bound in Great Britain by MPG Books Ltd, Bodmin, Cornwall

British Library Cataloguing in Publication Data
A catalogue record for this book is available from the British Library

Library of Congress Cataloging-in-Publication Data
A catalog record for this book has been requested

ISBN10: 0-415-32094-1
ISBN13: 978-0-415-32094-8

Contents

Consultant editors

Birgit Beumers (Theatre, Cinema)
University of Bristol

Alison L. Hilton (Art History, Folk Art)
Georgetown University

Louise McReynolds (History, Popular Culture)
University of North Carolina at Chapel Hill

Donald J. Raleigh (History)
University of North Carolina at Chapel Hill

Harlow L. Robinson (Music, Film)
Northeastern University

Maya Turovskaya (Russian Cinema, Culture)
Film Institute, Moscow

Andrei Zorin (Media, History of Ideas)
Russian State University for the Humanities,
Moscow

Contributors

Laura Adams
Princeton University

Barbara C. Allen
La Salle University, Philadelphia, PA

Anthony Anemone
College of William and Mary

Nadezhda Azhgikhina
Moscow State University

Marina Balina
Illinois Wesleyan University

Marjorie Mandelstam Balzer
Georgetown University

Elena Baraban
University of Victoria, British Columbia

Emily B. Baran
University of North Carolina at Chapel Hill

Henryk Baran
State University of New York at Albany

Jennifer B. Barrett
University of Texas at Austin

Djurdja Bartlett
London College of Fashion

Michele Berdy
The Moscow Times

Birgit Beumers
University of Bristol

Angela Brintlinger
The Ohio State University

Avram Brown
University of California at Davis

Samuel Brown
Davis Center for Russian Studies, Harvard
University/Harvard Medical School

Philip Ross Bullock
University College, London

Alexander Burry
The Ohio State University

Vitaly Chernetsky
Miami University, Ohio

Edward Alan Cole
Grand Valley State University, Allendale, MI

Susan Corbesero
University of Pittsburgh

Alexander Domrin
University of Iowa College of Law and Institute of
Legislation and Comparative Law, Russia

Marko Dumančić
University of North Carolina at Chapel Hill

Karen Evans-Romaine
Ohio University

Benjamin Forest
Dartmouth College, Hanover, NH

Sibelan Forrester
Swarthmore College, Swarthmore, PA

John Freedman
The Moscow Times

Nila Friedberg
Portland State University, OR

David J. Galloway
Hobart and William Smith Colleges, Geneva, NY

Elena Gapova
Centre for Gender Studies, European Humanities
University - International, Minsk/Vilnius

David Gillespie
University of Bath

Bella Ginzbursky-Blum
The College of William and Mary

David Gompper
University of Iowa

Helena Goscilo
University of Pittsburgh

Seth Graham
University College London

Dmitry Gravin
Independent scholar, Moscow

Gasan Gusejnov
University of Bonn, Germany

Alya Guseva
Boston University

Andrew Gustafson
Independent scholar, Moscow

Edythe C. Haber
Harvard University

Erika Haber
Syracuse University

Karl Hall
Central European University

Kristen M. Harkness
University of Pittsburgh

Yana Hashamova
The Ohio State University

Patrick Henry
University of California, Berkeley

Vicki L. Hesli
University of Iowa

Katharine Hodgson
University of Exeter

Beth Holmgren
Duke University

Yvonne Howell
University of Richmond, VA

George E. Hudson
Wittenberg University, Springfield, OH

Natalia Ivanova
Znamya, Moscow

Emily D. Johnson
University of Oklahoma

Juliet Johnson
McGill University

Vida Johnson
Tufts University

Polly Jones
School of Slavonic and East European Studies,
University College, London

Katia Kapushesky
Independent scholar, Cambridge, UK

Janet E. Kennedy
Indiana University, Bloomington

Stephen T. Kerr
University of Washington

Lisa A. Kirschenbaum
West Chester University of Pennsylvania

Nadieszda Kizenko
State University of New York at Albany

Laura Kline
Wayne State University, Detroit, MI

Jane E. Knox-Voina
Bowdoin College, Brunswick, ME

Diane P. Koenker
University of Illinois at Urbana-Champaign

Sergei Kokovkin
Middlebury College, Middlebury, VT

Natasha Kolchevska
University of New Mexico

Natalia Kolodzei
Kolodzei Art Foundation, Inc., Highland Park, NJ

Ann Komaromi
University of Toronto

Sharon A. Kowalsky
University of North Carolina at Chapel Hill

Regina Kozakova
Independent scholar, New York

Dasha Krijanskaia
GITIS-Scandinavia Theatre School, Denmark

James Krueger
University of Iowa

Konstantin Kustanovich
Vanderbilt University

Andrea Lanoux
Connecticut College

Alexander Ledenev
Lomonosov Moscow State University

Tatyana Ledeneva
Moscow Institute of International Relations

Sunghae Anna Lim
Princeton University

Byron Lindsey
University of New Mexico

Mark Lipovetsky
University of Colorado, Boulder

Emily Lygo
Wolfson College, Oxford

David MacFadyen
University of California, Los Angeles

Irina Makoveeva
University of Pittsburgh

Fran Markowitz
Ben-Gurion University, Israel

Daniel J. McCarthy
Northeastern University

Olga Medvedkov
Wittenberg University, Springfield, OH

Yelena Mingonok
Institute of World Literature, Academy of Science, Moscow

Yuri Medvedkov
The Ohio State University

Olga Mesropova
Iowa State University

Vladimir Morosan
Musica Russica, Inc., Guilford, CT

Miriam Neirick
University of California, Berkeley

Kira Nemirovskaia
Institute of History of Arts, St. Petersburg, Russia

Catharine Nepomnyashchy
Columbia University

Valeria Z. Nollan
Rhodes College, Memphis, TN

Stephen M. Norris
Miami University, Ohio

Tatyana Novikov
University of Nebraska at Omaha

Mike O'Mahony
University of Bristol

Elena Omelchenko
Ulianovsk State University, Russia

Serguei A. Oushakine
Princeton University

Elena Oznobkina
Institute of Philosophy of the Russian Academy of
Sciences

Vladimir Paperny
University of California, Los Angeles

Olga Partan
Wellesley College, Wellesley, MA

Lyudmila Parts
McGill University

Nadya Peterson
Hunter College, City University of New York

Petre Milltchov Petrov
University of Pittsburgh

Rachel S. Platonov
University of Manchester

Teresa L. Polowy
University of Arizona

Alexander Prokhorov
The College of William and Mary

Elena Prokhorova
The College of William and Mary

Sheila M. Puffer
Northeastern University

Susan E. Reid
University of Sheffield

Ona Renner-Fahey
University of Montana

Harlow Robinson
Northeastern University

Anna Rodionova
Washington and Lee University

Andrei Rogatchevski
University of Glasgow

Peter Rollberg
The George Washington University

Edward E. Roslof
Director, Fulbright Program in the Russian
Federation

Jeanmarie Rouhier-Willoughby
University of Kentucky

Maria Rubins
University College, London

Larissa Rudova
Pomona College, Claremont, CA

Karen Ryan
University of Virginia

Christine A. Rydel
Grand Valley State University, Allendale, MI

Shawn Salmon
University of California, Berkeley

Rimgaila Salys
University of Colorado at Boulder

Stephanie Sandler
Harvard University

Karin Sarsenov
Lund University, Sweden

Timothy M. Schlak
University of Pittsburgh

Tim J. Scholl
Oberlin College, Oberlin, OH

Andreas Schonle
Queen Mary, University of London

Anatole Senkevitch
University of Michigan

Tatiana Senkevitch
The Getty Research Institute, Los Angeles, CA

Timothy D. Sergay
Independent scholar, Worthington, OH

David Shneer
University of Denver

Elena Skipetrova
Moscow State University

Alexandra Smith
University of Canterbury, New Zealand

David Hunter Smith
Independent scholar, New Canaan, CT

Tatiana Smorodinskaya
Middlebury College, Middlebury, VT

Ivor Stodolsky
Helsinki University

Vladimir Strukov
University of London

Susmita Sundaram
The Ohio State University

Benjamin Sutcliffe
Miami University, Ohio

Sergei Tarkhov
Russian Academy of Sciences

Jennifer Ryan Tishler
University of Wisconsin, Madison

Ivan Titkov
Moscow State University

Svetlana Titkova
Moscow State University

Julia Trubikhina
New York University

Irina Udianskaya
Moscow State University

Dan Ungurianu
Vassar College, Poughkeepsie, NY

Ilia Utekhin
European University at St. Petersburg, Russia

Michael Wachtel
Princeton University

Christopher J. Ward
Clayton State University, Morrow, GA

Bob Weinberg
Swarthmore College, Swarthmore, PA

Boris Wolfson
University of Southern California

Josephine Woll
Howard University

Yuri Zaretsky
Russian State University of the Humanities,
Moscow

Olga Zaslavsky
Independent scholar, Providence, RI

Vladimir Zubok
Temple University

List of entries

Thematic list of entries

private property
privatization
ruble
shabashnik
shock therapy
shortages (defitsit)
U.E.
underground economy
voucher

Education

academic degrees
academic titles
academic year, Soviet and post-Soviet
acting schools
akademgorodok
All-Russian (All-Union) State Institute of
    Cinematography (VGIK)
art schools and academies
cheating (shpargalka)
educational stipends, Soviet/post-Soviet
    (stipendiia)
educational system, post-Soviet
educational system, Soviet
Encyclopedia, Soviet
ideological education, Soviet
Literary Institute (named after A.M.Gorkii)
Moscow State Institute (University) of Foreign
    Relations (MGIMO)
Moscow State University (Moskovskii
    gosudarstvennyi universitet imeni Lomonosova)
Novosibirsk State University
pedagogy, Soviet
Russian Academy of Theatre Arts (RATI, formerly
    GITIS)
Russian People's Friendship University
Russian State University for the Humanities
    (Rossiiskii Gosudarstvennyi Gumanitarnyi
    Universitet, RGGU)
scientific organizations (nauchnye obshchestva)
St. Petersburg State Academy of Theatre Arts
    (SPGATI, formerly LGITMiK)
St. Petersburg State University (Sankt-Peterburgskii
    gosudarstvennyi universitet, SPGU)
State Attestation Commission
Tatianin den
vocational education

Fashion and design

Burda
coats
costume design, theatre
denim

dublenka
fashion industry, post-Soviet
fashion industry, Soviet
fashion magazines
felt boots (valenki)
folk costume
footwear
garderob
headgear
Iudashkin, Valentin
tapochki (slippers)
vatnik
Zaitsev, Viacheslav (Slava) Mikhailovich

Film

Abdrashitov, Vadim Iusupovich
Abuladze, Tengiz
Adabashian, Aleksandr Artemovich
Alov and Naumov
Arabov, Iurii Nikolaevich
Askoldov, Aleksandr Iakovlevich
Balabanov, Aleksei Oktiabrinovich
Balaian, Roman Gurgenovich
Banionis, Donatas Iuozovich
Beloe solntse pustyni (*White Sun of
    the Desert*)
Bodrov, Sergei Sergeevich
Bodrov, Sergei Vladimirovich
Bondarchuk, Sergei Fedorovich
Bykov, Rolan Anatolevich
cameramen
Cheburashka
chernukha
Chukhrai, Grigorii Naumovich
Chukhrai, Pavel Grigorevich
Daneliia, Georgii Nikolaevich
Dykhovichnyi, Ivan Vladimirovich
Eralash
Ezhov, Valentin Ivanovich
film, animation
film, auteur
film, children's
film, comedy
film directors, 1950s and 1960s
film, documentary
film, educational (nauchno-populiarnoe kino)
film, festivals and prizes
film, Georgian
film, literary adaptation (ekranizatsiia)
film, post-Soviet
film, Soviet – Stagnation period
film, Soviet – Stalin era
film, Soviet – Thaw period
film studios

film, television
film, World War II
Fitil
Gabrilovich, Evgenii Iosifovich
Gaidai, Leonid Iovich
Gerasimov, Sergei Appolinarevich
German, Aleksei Iurevich
Goblin
Gogoberidze, Lana Levanovna
Goldovskaia, Marina Evseevna
Govorukhin, Stanislav Sergeevich
Ibragimbekov, Rustam
Ilenko, Iurii Gerasimovich
Ioseliani, Otar
Iusov, Vadim Ivanovich
Ivanov-Vano, Ivan Petrovich
Kalatozov, Mikhail
Karmen, Roman Lazarevich
Kazakh film
Kheifits, Iosif Efimovich
Khitruk, Fedor Savelevich
Khotinenko, Vladimir Ivanovich
Khrzhanovskii, Andrei Iurevich
Khutsiev, Marlen
Klimov, Elem Germanovich
Konchalovskii (Mikhalkov-Konchalovskii), Andrei
    Sergeevich
Kotenochkin, Viacheslav Mikhailovich
Kozintsev, Grigorii Mikhailovich
Kulidzhanov, Lev Aleksandrovich
Lebeshev, Pavel Timofeevich
Lioznova, Tatiana Mikhailovna
Livnev, Sergei Davidovich
Lotianu (Loteanu), Emil Vladimirovich
Lungin (Lounguine), Pavel Semenovich
Mamin, Iurii Borisovich
Masiania
Menshov, Vladimir Valentinovich
*Mesto vstrechi izmenit nelzia (The Meeting
    Place Cannot Be Changed)*
Mikhalkov, Nikita Sergeevich
Mindadze, Aleksandr Anatolievich
Mitta, Aleksandr Naumovich
Motyl, Vladimir Iakovlevich
Muratova, Kira Georgievna
Norshtein, Iurii Borisovich
Nu pogodi! (Just You Wait!)
Panfilov, Gleb Anatolievich
Paradzhanov, Sergei Iosifovich
Petrov, Aleksandr Dmitrievich
Pichul, Vasilii Vladimirovich
Poloka, Gennadii Ivanovich
Proshkin, Aleksandr Anatolievich
Riazanov, Eldar Aleksandrovich
Rogozhkin, Aleksandr Vladimirovich
Romm, Mikhail Ilich

scriptwriters
Selianov, Sergei Mikhailovich
*Semnadtsat mgnovenii vesny (Seventeen
    Moments of Spring)*
Shakhnazarov, Karen
Shepitko, Larisa Efimovna
Shveitser, Mikhail Abramovich
Sokurov, Aleksandr Nikolaevich
Solovev, Sergei Aleksandrovich
Tarkovskii, Andrei Arsenievich
Todorovskii, Petr Efimovich
Todorovskii, Valerii Petrovich
Trus, Balbes, Byvalyi
Uchitel, Aleksei Efimovich
Urusevskii, Sergei Pavlovich
Zalakavicius, Vitautas
Zarkhi, Aleksandr Grigorevich
Zeldovich, Aleksandr Efimovich

Film/theatre actors

Abdulov, Aleksandr Gavrilovich
Akhedzhakova, Liia Medzhidovna
Andreev, Boris Fedorovich
Androvskaia, Olga Nikolaevna
Aroseva, Olga
Artmane, Vija
Babochkin, Boris Andreevich
Baltic actors in Soviet cinema
Basilashvili, Oleg Valerianovich
Basov, Vladimir Pavlovich
Batalov, Aleksei Vladimirovich
Bogatyrev, Iurii Georgievich
Boiarskii, Mikhail Sergeevich
Borisov, Oleg Ivanovich
Borisova, Iuliia Konstantinovna
Bronevoi, Leonid Sergeevich
Burliaev, Nikolai Petrovich
Churikova, Inna Mikhailovna
Dal, Oleg Ivanovich
Demidova, Alla Sergeevna
Durov, Lev Konstantinovich
Dvorzhetskii, Vladislav Vatslavovich
Dzhigarkhanian, Armen Borisovich
Etush, Vladimir Abramovich
Evstigneev, Evgenii Aleksandrovich
Freindlikh, Alisa Brunovna
Gaft, Valentin Iosifovich
Garin, Erast Pavlovich
Gerdt, Zinovii Efimovich
Giatsintova, Sofia Vladimirovna
Gluzskii, Mikhail Andreevich
Gribov, Aleksei Nikolaevich
Gundareva, Natalia Georgievna
Gurchenko, Liudmila Markovna

Food and drink

zelenyi zmii
zephyr (zefir)

Geography

administrative structure, Russian Federation
administrative structure, Soviet Union
Armenia
Arzamas-16 (Sarov)
Azerbaidzhan
Babii Iar
Baikal
Baikonur
Baltic Sea region (Pribaltika)
BAM (Baikal-Amur Railroad)
Bashkortostan (Bashkiria)
Belarus
Black Earth region (Chernozemnaia zona)
blizhnee zarubezhe (near abroad)
Buriatia
Caucasus
Central Asia
Chechnia
Chernobyl
Chukchi
Cossacks
Crimea
Dagestan
Ekaterinburg
Estonia
ethnic minorities (malye narody)
Evenki
Far East (Dalnii vostok)
Far North (Krainii sever)
Finno-Ugric
Georgia
Gypsy/Roma
Iakutia (Sakha)
Jews
Kalmykia (Kalmyk)
Kamchatka
Karelia
Kazakhstan
Kiev
Kolyma
Koriak
Kuzbas
Kyrgyzstan (Kirgizia)
Lake Ladoga
Latvia
Lezgins
Lithuania
Magadan
Mamaev Kurgan
Mari

Moldova (Moldavia, Moldava)
Mordva
Moscow
Nenets (Samoeds)
Nizhnii Novgorod (Gorkii)
Norilsk
Novgorod
Odessa
Ossetia
Podmoskove
Pomore
Primorskii krai
Provincial Russia
Russian Federation
Russians
Saami (Lopars, Lapps)
Siberia
Solovki
St. Petersburg
Stalingrad
steppe
taiga
Tajikistan (Tadzhikistan)
Tatars
territorial conflicts
tselina
tundra
Turkmenistan (Turkmenia)
Ukraine
Urals
USSR (Union of Soviet Socialist Republics, Soviet Union)
Uzbekistan
Valdai
Volga region (Povolzhe)
white nights
White Sea Canal (Belomorkanal)

Language

dictionaries
mat
names and renaming, Soviet
names, personal
neologisms
Old Church Slavonic (Old Church Slavic)
proverbs (poslovitsy)
rhetoric, Soviet
slang

Literature

adventure novel (prikliuchencheskii roman)
awards, literary, post-Soviet
awards, literary, Soviet

Music

Performing arts

Philosophy and intellectual life

Politics and history

Religion

Society

blat
byt (everyday life)
communal apartment (kommunalka)
crime
dacha
day care, Soviet and post-Soviet
death
environment
families
feminism
games
health
holidays, post-Soviet
holidays, Soviet
homelessness
homosexuality
hotels
housing, Soviet and post-Soviet
Interdevochka
izba
joke (anekdot)
market (rynok)
Maslenitsa
medical system
migration, post-Soviet
name day celebration (imeniny)
national myths (narodnye mify)
New Russians (Novye russkie)
nomenklatura
oligarkh
poshlost
putevka
queue (ochered)
railroads
Registration of Civil States (ZAGS)
Russian roulette (Russkaia ruletka)
Russian soul (Russkaia dusha)
sanatoria (sanatorii)
sex and sexuality
smoking
social stratification, post-Soviet
social stratification, Soviet
superstitions, Russian
toska
toys
traditions and customs
transportation system
transportation, inner city
troika
wedding ceremony
women
work
youth culture

Sports and leisure

bania
basketball
Brumel, Valerii Nikolaevich
Bure, Pavel Vladimirovich
chess
club (kruzhok)
Dinamo
fan (bolelshchik)
figure skating
fitness (fizicheskaia kultura)
fitness test (GTO)
gymnastics
hockey
Iashin, Lev
Kafelnikov, Evgenii Aleksandrovich
Karelin, Aleksandr Aleksandrovich
Kasparov, Garri Kimovich
Kharlamov, Valerii Borisovich
Kurnikova, Anna Sergeevna
Rodnina, Irina Konstantinovna
soccer
Spartak
sport clubs and teams
sports education
sports, post-Soviet
sports, Soviet
Torpedo
track and field
Tretiak, Vladislav Aleksandrovich
TsSKA
vacations, Soviet and post-Soviet
Vlasov, Iurii Petrovich
Zarnitsa

Visual arts

Academy of Arts
Antoshina, Tatiana Konstantinovna
Apt-Art
art market
art, abstract (abstraktnoe iskusstvo)
art, informal
art, nonconformist
art, post-Soviet
art, Soviet
Beliutin, Elii Mikhailovich
Bogatyr, Svetlana Zakharovna
Brenner, Aleksandr Davidovich
Bruskin, Grisha
Bulatov, Erik Vladimirovich
Bulgakova, Olga Vasilevna
Bulldozer Exhibition (buldozernaia vystavka)
Chagall, Mark
Conceptualism, art

Writers

Acknowledgements

We are indebted to the board of editorial consultants listed at the beginning of this volume. Their expertise enabled us to expand our original list of entries and contributors, and their individual and collective input has resulted in a more informative encyclopedia than otherwise would have been possible. We are enormously grateful to the authors who contributed entries and conscientiously answered our numerous queries. A number of individuals deserve special thanks for the generous collegiality that prompted them to write a large number of entries, to step in graciously when we needed help with particularly difficult or lesser-known topics, or to submit excellent entries at short notice. These staunch colleagues are Samuel Brown, Philip Ross Bullock, Aleksandr Domrin, Seth Graham, Gasan Gusejnov, Stephen Kerr, Tatiana Ledeneva, Alexander Prokhorov, Elena Prokhorova, Tim Scholl, Vladimir Strukov, and Josephine Woll. Our greatest debt is to John Freedman, who accomplished truly extraordinary feats of scholarly heroism. We also acknowledge the anonymous reviewers of our initial proposal, from whose comments we benefited substantially.

Finally, we render thanks to our editors at Routledge: Gerard Greenway, who saw us through the challenging initial stages of this project; Kate Aker, who helped us through the middle, the incomparable Jason Mitchell, who kept us on track, and above all Susan Cronin, whose unobtrusive vigilance, remarkable efficiency, and patient encouragement ensured our completion of the volume.

Tatiana Smorodinskaya
Karen Evans-Romaine
Helena Goscilo

Introduction

The *Encyclopedia of Contemporary Russian Culture*, like its German counterpart, published in the same series several years ago, reflects the accelerating interdisciplinary trend in Russian studies. Russian historians and anthropologists are increasingly engaging culture in its many facets, from the interrelationship of politics and the arts – film, literature, the visual and performing arts – to various forms of everyday or 'small-c' culture. By the same token, scholars and teachers of Russian language and literature are crossing the traditional boundaries of philology just as frequently, to study the same materials as historians and anthropologists, but from the perspective of language, literature, and the arts. Nowadays teachers in the language classroom regularly incorporate 'content', which necessitates broader knowledge of politics, economics and business, journalism and the media, and 'high' and 'low' culture. This blurring of conventional demarcations between sub-disciplines in Russian studies requires that scholars and teachers become generalists while remaining specialists in their chosen fields. Accordingly, this volume offers an introduction to myriad aspects of Russia's political and cultural life, both for specialists unfamiliar with related sub-disciplines, and for the general reader interested in contemporary Russia.

Several factors make an encyclopedia of contemporary Russian culture particularly important in the first decade of the twenty-first century. The Russian Federation as a successor state to the former Soviet Union soon will have existed for two decades. More than twenty years have passed since the inception of Mikhail Gorbachev's policies of perestroika (restructuring) and glasnost (openness). These innovations reverberated throughout the world: they brought independence and, in most cases, freedom to republics of the Soviet Union and satellite nations in the Eastern Bloc, and palpably affected the economies and political alignments of nations geographically remote from, but with close ties to, the Soviet Union. Despite Russia's dramatically altered status in the world today, it continues to play a vital role in global politics, economics, science, research, and cultural development. Within Russia, the radical political changes and economic reforms of the past two decades have profoundly transformed society and culture. The 1990s–2000s witnessed the birth of new concepts and the revival of formerly proscribed ideas from the past; the social structure of the Russian Federation underwent a startling metamorphosis; and the realia of a new way of life partly displaced a long-familiar mode of existence. The most productive way of examining these upheavals and the current state of affairs is in the context of both Russian and Soviet culture.

The editors of this volume have defined 'contemporary' as post-Stalinist, with Stalin's death in 1953 as the watershed date. Although in Western Europe the end of World War II (1945) arguably marked the birth of contemporary culture, in the Soviet Union, the imperative of post-war recovery subordinated culture to the exigencies of reconstruction, though the repression of cultural producers continued until Stalin's death. Thus the volume omits major representatives of Soviet culture, such as Sergei Eisenstein, because their main contributions belong to the Stalin era. Given the ill-advisedness of analyzing contemporary culture without taking historical context into account, the encyclopedia provides entries on Lenin, Stalin, World War II, Socialist Realism, etc., for these key figures, events, and concepts shaped contemporary Soviet and post-Soviet Russian culture.

The encyclopedia approaches Russian culture from a consciously practical, rather than theoretical, standpoint. Entries encompass both 'high' and 'low' culture: literature, scholarship, science, and the visual and performing arts, on the one hand, and, on the other hand, the everyday life of the Russian Federation's citizens, represented by entries ranging from food, clothing, habits, and customs, to the folk cultures of Russians and some of the Russian Federation's ethnic minorities. In addition, the encyclopedia addresses aspects of culture that defy categorization as 'high' or 'low', for instance, such facets of Russia's political and economic life as geographical divisions and their effect on politics, economics, and culture; biographies of important politicians; administrative structures; political parties; and social categories. Longer entries on journalism and the media provide an overview that touches on issues of censorship and philosophy, while shorter pieces illustrate how these are manifested in specific periodicals and media personalities. The contents are grouped in broad categories so as to facilitate readers' use of the encyclopedia: architecture, cultural policy and institutions, economics, education, fashion and design, film, film and theatre actors, food and drink, geography, language, literature and writers, mass media, music, performing arts, philosophy and intellectual life, politics and history, religion, society, sports and leisure, and the visual arts.

This volume defines 'Russian' from various points of view, best clarified by the entry on the word 'Russian', embracing ethnic Russians and citizens and residents of both the Russian Federation and the former Soviet Union. Although the encyclopedia focuses on the culture of the Russian-speaking majority in the Russian Federation, it contains entries on each of the republics of the former Soviet Union, on major non-Russian regions within and bordering on the Russian Federation, and on ethnic minorities in Russia. The inclusion of ethnic minorities in a reference work on 'Russian' culture

springs not from the desire to erase differences, but to acknowledge historical events and their effects on individuals who were the victims of war, occupation, forced migration, political realignments, and organic or cataclysmic phenomena that have yielded a rich diversity of cultures in the Russian Federation and the former Soviet Union.

The 154 contributors to this volume come from Canada, Denmark, Finland, Germany, Hungary, Israel, New Zealand, the Russian Federation, Sweden, the United Kingdom, and the United States. The name of each author appears directly under that author's entry.

Structure and organization

The encyclopedia contains 1,272 alphabetically arranged entries from 50 to 2,000 words in length. Entries cover major events, concepts, and historical periods; biographies of both key and lesser-known figures in Russian and Soviet contemporary history; and terms defining unique aspects of Russian culture, from clothes and drinks to sundry rituals. Occasionally, entries are listed by their Russian title, as in the case of periodicals, which readers are likely to encounter in the Russian original or in translations so varied that to provide one Anglophone rendition as a heading could be misleading (e.g., *Ogonek* or *Pravda*). For the most part, however, entries appear under their English equivalents, as in the case of objects (felt boots rather than *valenki*) and concepts (developed socialism rather than the less familiar *razvityi sotsializm*). The Russian term frequently appears in parentheses following the English translation in the entry title or in text of the entry. To minimize confusion and frustration in cases of organizational or political name changes over time, we have supplied blind entries under former names or acronyms that direct readers to the entry: for example, under Leningrad, a blind entry directs the reader to St. Petersburg. Extensive cross-referencing, indicated by 'See also' at the end of each entry and preceding the list of Further Reading, identifies both connections explicitly identified in the text and links between topics that may not be obvious to the non-specialist. The thematic list of entries at the beginning of the volume, and the thorough, analytical index at the end, should help readers quickly find the required entry.

The list of Further Reading accompanies only entries of 500 or more words, with a few exceptions whose logic is self-evident. Whenever possible, the editors have opted for print sources rather than Internet sources, as Internet sites (and perhaps especially in/on Russia) can quickly become obsolete, unreliable, or short-lived.

We have followed the Library of Congress system of transliteration, using -kii instead of -sky, -kh for the Russian letter 'x', and so forth. For the sake of readability we have dropped the Russian soft and hard signs, usually transliterated by apostrophes in the Library of Congress system. Thus names ending in a soft sign plus -ev are spelled without either the widely used 'i' or the apostrophe, yielding Vasilev rather than the more familiar Vasiliev or Vasil'ev. The unorthodox decision to render names in Library of Congress transliteration without the apostrophe avoids the complication arising in transliterations of Russian words that could be spelled with either the letter 'i' or a soft sign (i.e. Vasilev vs. Gergiev). We have made a few exceptions to this transliteration system for the most famous and established transliterations, including Tchaikovsky (rather than Chaikovskii), Prokofiev (rather than Prokofev), Eisenstein and Yeltsin (rather than Eltsin).

Abdrashitov, Vadim Iusupovich

b. 19 January 1945, Kharkov, Ukrainian SSR

Film director

Together with his scriptwriter, Aleksandr Mindadze, Abdrashitov explores moral and spiritual problems of late Soviet society. *Slovo dlia zashchity* (*A Word for the Defence*, 1976) is set during a murder inquiry, where the accused and her lawyer grow closer as they reflect on male–female relationships. *Parad planet* (*Parade of the Planets*, 1984) offers a surreal meditation on growing old, and *Sluga* (*The Manservant*, 1988) examines a 'cult of personality' and its disastrous psychological effects. In post-Soviet times, *Vremia tantsora* (*Time of the Dancer*, 1997) is set during a period of civil strife, suggesting that Russia itself is set on a tragic historical course.

See also: cult of personality; Mindadze, Aleksandr

DAVID GILLESPIE

Abdulov, Aleksandr Gavrilovich

b. 29 May 1953, Tobolsk, Russia

Film and theatre actor, film director

Trained at GITIS, Abdulov has worked at the Lenkom Theatre in Moscow since 1975, but is best known for his film roles. During the late 1970s and 1980s, Abdulov became a sex symbol, embodying the romantic, self-reflexive, slightly ironic anti-establishment hero in such films as *Obyknovennoe chudo* (*An Ordinary Miracle*), *Karnaval* (Carnival), and *Ubit drakona* (*To Kill a Dragon*). In 2000, Abdulov directed his first film, the lavish but undistinguished musical *Bremenskie muzykanty & Co* (*The Musicians of Bremen & Co*), in which he plays the jester-narrator, an older, wiser version of his Stagnation-era heroes. People's Artist of the RSFSR.

See also: Lenkom Theatre; Russian Academy of Theatre Arts

RIMGAILA SALYS

Abramov, Fedor Aleksandrovich

b. 29 February 1920, Verkola; d. 14 May 1983, Leningrad

Writer

One of the 'village prose' writers of the 1960s and 1970s. Abramov's works are distinguished by their stark social realism and gallery of resilient peasant characters. His credo of artistic honesty can be traced to a *Novyi mir* article of 1954, in which he criticized post-war literature for its idealized picture of Russian village life. His most ambitious work is the tetralogy *Bratia i sestry* (*Brothers and Sisters*, 1959–78), depicting life in a northern Russian village throughout World War II to the mid-1970s. His most uncompromising work is that published posthumously, such as the short story *Poezdka v proshloe* (*A Journey into the*

Past, 1989), a withering critique of collectivization.

See also: collective farms; *Novyi mir*; village prose; World War II (Great Patriotic War)

DAVID GILLESPIE

Abrau-Diurso

Abrau-Diurso is the name of two villages, Abrau and Diurso, in the south of Russia (in the Novorossiisk region on the Black Sea) where they produce high quality wines and champagne under the brandname of 'Abrau-Diurso'. The vineyards and trade were damaged severely as a result of Mikhail Gorbachev's anti-alcohol campaigns in 1986.

See also: alcoholism

VLADIMIR STRUKOV

Abuladze, Tengiz

b. 31 January 1924, Kutaisi, Georgian SSR;
d. 6 March 1994, Tbilisi, Georgia

Director, writer

After graduating from the All-Russian (All-Union) State Institute of Cinematography (VGIK) in 1953, Abuladze returned to Tbilisi to make his films. His first, *Skhvisi shvilebi* (*Chuzhie deti*; *Someone Else's Children*, 1958), drew official displeasure for its lack of broad social resonance; his second, a humorous coming-of-age story set during World War II, *Me, bebia, Iliko da Ilarioni* (*Ia, babushka, Iliko i Ilarion*; *Iliko, Ilarion, Grandmother and I*, 1963), proved safer. Abuladze's reputation rests on his Georgian trilogy: *Vedreba* (*Molba*, *The Prayer*, 1968), a morality play set in medieval Georgia; *Natvris khe* (*Drevo zhelaniia*, *Tree of Desire*, 1977), portraying the conflict between individual happiness and community welfare during the turn-of-the-twentieth-century; Georgia and *Monanieba* (*Pokaianie*, *Repentance*, 1984, released 1986), a surrealistic exploration of the nature and legacy of tyranny that both heralded

and contributed to the transformation of Soviet society under Gorbachev.

See also: All-Russian (All-Union) State Institute of Cinematography (VGIK); film, Georgian

JOSEPHINE WOLL

academic degrees

The post-graduate academic degrees of *kandidat nauk* (candidate of science) and *doktor nauk* (doctor of science) differentiate academic qualification in a given discipline. The *kandidatskaia* and *doktorskaia* degrees were introduced in 1934 and replaced the master and doctor degrees awarded in Russia from 1819 to 1917.

The *kandidat nauk* degree is awarded to individuals who have completed a higher education (with a diploma from a post-secondary institution), have completed academic requirements in *aspirantura* (graduate school), have passed candidacy exams, and have defended a *kandidatskaia dissertatsiia* (candidate of science dissertation). The dissertation must make a significant theoretical contribution to a field of study. Before the defence of the dissertation, a graduate student presents his/her research at scholarly conferences and publishes at least two works. The dissertation must be publicly defended and approved by an academic council that consists of about twenty leading specialists in the field from different universities and research institutes. After the academic council approves the thesis, it is submitted for final approval to the Higher Attestation Commission (VAK) at the Ministry of Education. This committee granted all post-graduate academic degrees in the USSR and continues to do so in post-Soviet Russia. The final approval takes several months and may involve an additional anonymous examination of the thesis. As a regular university degree requires five–six years of highly specialized training, *aspirantura* (graduate school) involves at least three years of independent research leading to the completion of the dissertation (*kandidatskaia dissertatsiia*), the requirements for which are similar to those for a PhD thesis, the *kandidat nauk* degree is recognized frequently in the West as equivalent to the doctoral degree. In 2003, Russia and France signed an agreement recognizing the *kandidatskaia* degree as equivalent to the French doctorate.

The *doktor nauk* (doctor of science) degree is awarded to individuals who hold the *kandidatskaia* degree, have completed academic requirements in *doktorantura* (post-graduate school), have supervised graduate research, published monographs and articles, and have publicly defended a *doktorskaia dissertatsiia* (doctor of science dissertation). The *doktorskaia dissertatsiia* must be a major contribution to the field. In scope, it is similar to the German *Habilitation* dissertation; in the United States, it can be considered roughly equivalent to the rank of full professor, as it requires the defence and publication of what is in essence a second book. The approval procedures for a *doktorskaia* dissertation are similar to those for *kandidatskaia*.

See also: educational system, post-Soviet; educational system, Soviet; State Attestation Commission

ELENA BARABAN

academic titles

The academic titles of *dotsent* and professor are awarded to instructors who teach in institutions of higher education or to scientists and scholars in research institutes. These titles and the academic structure of which they are a part were adopted from the Prussian system. In Russia, the title *dotsent* (docent, from the Latin *docens*, 'teaching'), introduced in 1863, designated full-time university instructors who had a master's degree, but was replaced in 1884 with the title *privat-dotsent*. The USSR re-established the title *dotsent*, normally awarded to instructors with the academic degree of Candidate of Science and at least one year's fulfilment of a *dotsent*'s duties, though occasionally a university instructor without that degree but with extensive teaching experience may be awarded the title. Similarly, the title of professor (from Latin *professor*, 'instructor') normally requires the academic degree of Doctor of Science and at least one year's work in the position of professor. Since 1992, both titles have been conferred by the Attestation Commission for Higher Education

of the Ministry of Education upon the recommendation of the academic council of the university or institute employing the candidate.

A faculty member who has not yet been granted either title is generally called *prepodavatel* (instructor) or *starshii prepodavatel* (senior instructor, roughly equivalent to Assistant Professor in the American system).

See also: academic degrees; educational system, post-Soviet; educational system, Soviet

ELENA BARABAN

academic year, Soviet and post-Soviet

The Soviet and post-Soviet academic year generally comprises two semesters at university level (September–December and February–May) and four quarters (*chetvert*) at schools, followed by examination periods (January and June). Instruction lasts approximately 25–30 hours a week. About ten weeks of the year are allocated as holiday.

Study in the USSR involved numerous extracurricular activities (including labour projects, sports and cultural events, field trips, summer camp programmes, and others) aimed at political education.

Den znanii (Day of Learning, 1 September) honours the beginning of a new academic year, commemorating the philosophical underpinnings and goals of the educational system, expressed through two Russian words: *vospitanie* (upbringing) and *obrazovanie* (formal education). Celebrations include official gatherings of both students and teaching staff; in school, parents come with pupils, who bring flowers to their teachers. In Soviet times, celebrations included formal salutations, parades, and ceremonies, and other expressions of respect for the authorities and political system.

In the 1990s, the pre-revolutionary tradition of celebrating Student Day on St. Tatiana's Day (25 January, the day Moscow University was founded in 1755) was revitalized to reinstate the status of students and promote their social links outside the ideological agenda.

In the USSR, the State Planning Committee directed universities to admit a limited number of students for study in each specialty. Candidates had to pass entrance examinations consisting of oral and written tests in three to five subjects related to the projected area of study. The inclusion of examinations in the history of the Communist Party maintained ideological integrity. The university faculty composed and administered the examinations, and supplied tutoring for them, which encouraged cheating, grade inflation, and bribery.

In the 1990s, the Russian government waived the quota for student admissions and in 2000–3, following European integration initiatives, implemented a new examination system, known as the *EGE* or *Edinyi gosudarstvennyi ekzamen* (Comprehensive State Examination): pupils in secondary schools take a predetermined set of comprehensive examinations composed and administered by the Ministry of Education with the help of external staff; institutions of advanced and higher education accept these grades for admission. In spite of its obvious benefits, this system advocates centralization and standardization – traditionally, insurmountable obstacles to the genuine reform of education in Russia.

See also: educational system, post-Soviet; educational system, Soviet

VLADIMIR STRUKOV

Academy of Arts

The Russian (previously Imperial) Academy of Arts was founded in St. Petersburg in 1857 by decision of the Senate. The focus of the academy's activity was the enactment of state policy in art, architecture, and art education. The academy remained faithful to its original principles under all regimes throughout its history, and it demonstrated intolerance to non-official aesthetic and ideological programmes, such as the Itinerants (*Peredvizhniki*), a group representing realist artists in the late nineteenth century.

Today the Academy is a powerful structure with 150 acting members and corresponding members, numerous divisions, two art lyceums, two famous higher educational institutions (the Surikov Moscow State Academic Art Institute and the Repin St. Petersburg State Academic Institute of Painting, Sculpture, and Architecture), studios, research institutions, and exhibition halls. In its educational institutions the Academy offers classical art education, organizes internships abroad, and assists artists and sculptors in the exhibition and sale of their works through state commissions.

Among the members of the Academy of Art are outstanding artists, art scholars, architects and designers who represent various trends in modern Russian art. In recent years under the aegis of the Academy major programmes have been carried out in Moscow, such as the reconstruction of the Cathedral of Christ the Saviour, the construction of the architectural-sculptural ensemble to commemorate the Second World War on *Poklonnaia gora*, and the *Okhotnyi riad* (Hunters' Row) and Manezh Square commercial and entertainment centre next to Red Square. Since 1997, the President of the Academy has been the well-known sculptor Zurab Tsereteli.

See also: Cathedral of Christ the Saviour; Moscow; Tsereteli, Zurab.

YURI ZARETSKY

Academy of Sciences (Akademiia nauk SSSR, Rossiiskaia Akademiia Nauk)

In July 1925, The Imperial Academy of Sciences and Arts, established in 1724 by Peter the Great, became the USSR (and in December 1991, the Russian) Academy of Sciences. Unlike Western European academies, it originally combined the functions of research and education, engaging prominent foreign scholars, then Russian specialists, including Mikhail Lomonosov, the founder of Moscow University. After publishing the first maps of Russia, partly based on expeditions to remote areas of the country, in the late eighteenth century the Academy abandoned education and delegated arts to the newly established Academy of Arts. It subsequently expanded the scope of its research, particularly in the humanities, creating a department of Russian language and literature. Vladimir Dal (Dahl), author of the first comprehensive Russian dictionary, and Lev Tolstoi numbered among its members. Scientists in the Academy included such figures as mathematician Nikolai Lobachevskii, chemist Dmitrii Mendeleev, and biologists Vladimir Vernadskii and Ivan Pavlov, the latter awarded the Nobel Prize in 1904 for his work in the physiology of digestion. By October 1917, the Academy boasted 220 members.

After the October Revolution, which drastically changed the academic community through members' death or emigration, the Academy supervised expeditions to explore natural resources, elaborated economic development plans, and trained specialists in new branches of economics and culture. In 1934, the Academy was transferred from St. Petersburg to Moscow, where it still is located.

In tune with the Communist Party's insistence that the academic community conform to ideological doctrine, the infamous 'case of the Academy of Sciences' was fabricated in 1929–31, and over 100 scientists were arrested. In the mass repressions of the 1930s, purges of many academic institutions involved entire staff, from the director to rank-and-file workers. After World War II, these repressions continued: the government eradicated many scientific schools and replaced many prominent scientists with dogmatic younger researchers.

During the 1950s, new institutes and research centres established in provincial centres developed scholarship. In 1957, the Siberian Division of the Academy of Sciences was founded in Novosibirsk, and by the early 1960s every Soviet republic had its own Academy of Sciences. Official figures for 1975 show 42,500 Academy researchers, including 678 full (as opposed to corresponding) Academy members. Devoting great resources to the training of young scientists, the Academy also had members who continued to win Nobel Prizes, including chemist Nikolai Semenov (1956), physicists Nikolai Basov, Aleksandr Prokhorov (1964), and Petr Kapitsa (1978).

In the 1990s, the Academy of Sciences suffered tremendous budget cuts, demoralization, and severe reductions in its ranks, as salaries and prestige plummeted and outstanding scholars fled to the West or left the Academy for more lucrative work. Its future remains uncertain.

See also: Nobel Prize winners, non-literary; science and technology

ALEXANDER LEDENEV

acting schools

The leading Russian theatre schools that offer degrees in stage and film acting are located in Moscow and St. Petersburg and attract a geographically diverse body of Russian-speaking applicants. The oldest of these schools, the St. Petersburg Academy of Theatre Arts (formerly LGITMiK), was founded in 1779. Moscow houses several renowned acting schools: the Shchepkin Theatre School (founded in 1809), affiliated with the Malyi Theatre; the Russian Academy of Theatre Arts, formerly GITIS (1878); the Boris Shchukin Theatre Institute (1914), affiliated with the Vakhtangov Theatre; and the Moscow Art Theatre School-Studio (1943).

Most acting schools follow a similar admissions process and educational curriculum. Admission into the leading schools is highly competitive and selective, since entrance classes are small: 20–30 students each year. To demonstrate their acting potential, applicants must participate in several stages of auditions, reciting prose and poetry before committees that include actors, directors, professors, etc. The most gifted students then take written and oral exams in the humanities and social sciences and are admitted upon successful performance.

During their four years of study, acting students divide their time between acting and academic coursework, and are expected to commit themselves to a challenging schedule of 10–12 hours a day, six days a week. At the foundation of the acting classes is the famous Konstantin Stanislavskii acting method, which focuses on theatrical verisimilitude, achieved through a display of psychological 'truthfulness' and the recreation of real life on stage. Throughout their course of study, students take dancing, fencing, gymnastics, voice, and speech training classes. They are also required to complete arts and humanities courses such as History of Russian and Western Theatre and Drama, Art History, Philosophy, and Foreign Languages. Their education culminates in auditions at various theatre companies that recruit fresh talent, and many students go on to become film actors, and television personalities.

See also: Moscow Art Theatre; Russian Academy of Theatre Arts; St. Petersburg State Academy of Theatre Arts; Vakhtangov Theatre

OLGA PARTAN

Adabashian, Aleksandr Artemovich

b. 10 August 1945, Moscow

Actor, director, artist

A graduate of the Moscow High Arts College (Stroganovka), Adabashian is a man of many talents. Artist; actor (*Hound of the Baskervilles*, 1981, *Nastia*, 1993, *Prezident i ego vnuchka* [*The President and His Granddaughter* 2000]); screenwriter (*Trans-Siberian Express*, 1977, *Ochi chernye* [*Dark Eyes*, 1987]); and director, he became famous as a long time co-author (with Pavel Lebeshev, cameraman) of the first seven films directed by Nikita Mikhalkov (*Raba liubvi* [*Slave of Love* 1977], *Piat vecherov* [*Five Evenings*, 1979], *Rodnia* [*Relatives*, 1981]). In 1992, he released his directorial debut film, *Mado, Poste Restante* in France; in 2002, he directed the TV series *Azazel*, based on the popular mystery by Boris Akunin.

See also: Akunin, Boris; Lebeshev, Pavel; Mikhalkov, Nikita

ALEXANDER DOMRIN

administrative structure, Russian Federation

The administrative structure of the Russian Federation, according to the 1993 Constitution, combines the republican form of government with the federal form of democracy. The president, elected for four years (up to eight years in succession), is the head of state and commander-in-chief of the armed forces. The three branches of government (executive, legislative, and judicial) are formally separated. A 2004 law has streamlined the government, leaving it with eleven subordinated federal ministries; the president directly guides the five most powerful ministries and five major federal services.

The federation comprises 89 self-governed, sub-national jurisdictions. Each delegates two representatives (senators) to the federal chamber of parliament (*Federalnoe sobranie*). By population numbers, the sub-national units vastly differ. The homelands of minorities, mostly in peripheral or sub-Arctic areas, constitute thirty-two members of the federation, including twenty-one ethno-republics and ten less populous autonomous regions (*okrug*), as well as the Jewish Autonomous unit at the rank of *oblast* (also known as Birobidzhan, the name of its capital city). Only ethno-republics have the right to institute state languages, in addition to the federation-wide status of the Russian language. Six territories (*krai*) and forty-nine provinces (*oblast*) complement the ethnically identified jurisdictions. Both Moscow and St. Petersburg are also federation members, independent of surrounding provinces.

In 2001–5 President Vladimir Putin strengthened presidential control over parliament, regional jurisdictions, and civil society, suppressing demands in the republics agitating for greater sub-unit rights. Most notable were assaults on ethnic separatism in Chechnia. The administrative structure of the federation was modified in 2001 by a decree that grouped the federation members into seven Federal Districts (FD, *Federalnyi okrug*), under the supervision of governor-generals who are presidential appointees. The federal districts have created new geopolitics inside Russia. In particular, federal districts have boundaries to ensure that ethnic homelands are outvoted in each case. Ethnic homelands are absent in the most populous and politically strong Central FD (18 members of the federation and 37.7 million residents in 2004). The Northwest FD has a population of 12.1 million in Russian *oblasts*, compared to 1.7 million in the ethno-republics. The corresponding numbers in the Southern FD are 15.9 million and 7 million; in the Povolzhe (Volga region) FD, 18.6 million and 12.3 million; and in the Ural FD, 10.3 million and 2 million. Russian *oblasts* in the Siberian FD have 12.4 million residents, compared to 7.5 million in ethno-republics. In the Far Eastern FD, the equivalent numbers are 5.4 million and 1.2 million.

In 2005, Putin further centralized the administrative organization of Russia by introducing a law that permits him to nominate governors in the federation members. The pro-centralization lobby and the United Russia Party propose to eliminate smaller ethnic jurisdictions and advocate merging the Komi Republic, Arkhangelsk Oblast, Vologda Oblast and the Nenets Autonomous Okrug.

See also: Putin, Vladimir; Russian Federation

YURI MEDVEDKOV AND OLGA MEDVEDKOV

administrative structure, Soviet Union

From 1956 until 1991 the Soviet Union consisted of fifteen Soviet Socialist Republics (SSR) or union republics: the Russian Republic, also known as the Russian Soviet Federative Socialist Republic (RSFSR), and the Lithuanian, Latvian, Estonian, Belorussian, Ukrainian, Moldavian, Georgian, Azerbaidzhani, Armenian, Kazakh, Uzbek, Turkmen, Kirgiz, and Tadzhik Soviet Socialist Republics. A union republic was the largest administrative and political unit. Nationality, population, and location determined republic status. Most union republics were subdivided into autonomous republics, *oblasts*, autonomous *oblasts*, *krais*, and *raion*.

An Autonomous Soviet Socialist Republic (ASSR) was a territorial and administrative subdivision of an SSR, such as the RSFSR, Georgia, Azerbaidzhan, and Uzbekistan, created to grant a degree of administrative autonomy to some major ethnic minorities. Autonomous Republics had their own Constitution and laws, but were directly subordinate to their union republic, with no right to secede from it. In 1989, the Soviet Union had twenty autonomous republics.

An autonomous *oblast* was a territorial and administrative subdivision of a union republic (or of a *krai* in the Russian Republic), created to grant a degree of autonomy to a national minority within the *krai* or Republic. It had neither a constitution nor laws of its own. In 1989, the Soviet Union had eight autonomous *oblasts*.

A *krai* was a large territorial and administrative subdivision thinly populated and found only in the Russian Republic. There were six *krais*: Krasnodar, Stavropol, Altai, Krasnoiarsk, Khabarovsk, and Primore. The *oblast*, the main territorial and administrative subdivision of an SSR, had existed since the 1920s. Ten of the fifteen union republics were subdivided into *oblasts*. There was no difference in legal status between a territorial *krai* and an *oblast*. Historical reasons explain the difference in terms. In 1989, there were 127 *krais* and *oblasts*. In terms of political and administrative authority, they resembled counties in the United States and Great Britain. Many *oblasts*, however, were (and still are) about the size of American states. For example, Tiumen *oblast*, the storehouse of Russian oil and natural gas, is only slightly smaller than Alaska.

A territorial and administrative subdivision of a *krai* or *oblast* in the Russian Republic, the autonomous *okrug* granted a degree of administrative autonomy to an ethnic minority, usually located in large, remote areas with sparse populations. In 1989, the Soviet Union had ten autonomous *okrugs*, found only in the Russian Republic.

In terms of area, a more appropriate comparison with counties would be the more than 3,200 *raions* (regions or districts), the Soviet Union's smallest territorial and political subdivision with rural or municipal administration. Every *krai*, *oblast* and city was divided into districts (*raion*) with its own local authorities. A rural *raion* was a county-sized district within a *krai*, *oblast*, autonomous republic, autonomous *okrug*, or SSR. A city *raion* was similar to a borough in some large cities of the United States.

Further reading

Pipes, R. (1968) *The Formation of the Soviet Union: Communism and Nationalism, 1917–1923*. New York: Atheneum.

TATYANA LEDENEVA

adventure novel (prikliuchencheskii roman)

This term refers to various genres within popular fiction: the travelogue, science fiction, fantasy, and detective and mystery novels. The Russian adventure novel gained popularity in the nineteenth century due to translations of such foreign writers as Sir Walter Scott, James Fenimore Cooper, Robert Louis Stevenson, Jules Verne, Alexandre Dumas *fils*, and Jack London. From the 1920s to the 1940s Soviet critics lambasted adventure novels, labelling them a 'great bourgeois evil', and they were rehabilitated only after World War II. The best-known Soviet adventure novels are Aleksandr Grin's *Alye parusa* (*Scarlet Sails*, 1921); Veniamin Kaverin's *Dva kapitana* (*Two Captains*, 1936–44), adapted in the early twenty-first century into the hit musical *Nord-Ost*; and Vladimir Obruchev's *Zemlia Sannikova* (*Sannikov's Land*, 1926). The most popular Soviet comic adventure novels are *Dvenadtsat stulev* (*The Twelve Chairs*, 1927) and *Zolotoi telenok* (*The Golden Calf*, 1930) by Ilia Ilf and Evgenii Petrov; their hero, the con artist Ostap Bender, became the most famous trickster in Soviet literature and remains a popular hero today.

Since the 1990s, Russia has witnessed a new fashion in fantasy novels, including those of Vladislav Krapivin and Sviatoslav Loginov, as well as Mikhail Uspenskii and Maria Semenova, who introduce motifs from Slavonic folklore into the genre. Max Frei (the pen-name of Svetlana Martynchik and Igor Stepin) leads in the Russian postmodern adventure novel. Dmitrii Emets has published a number of parodies on the *Harry Potter* series by J. K. Rowling, with the orphan Tania Grotter, who studies at magic school, as the protagonist.

See also: detective fiction; humour and satire, Soviet; *Nord-Ost*; postmodernism; science fiction

TATYANA LEDENEVA

advertising

The concept of advertising contradicted the spirit of the Soviet economy, which excluded branding and competition. Rather than selling a product, advertisements functioned as educational spots to explain how to use products, introduce new inventions, and guide the viewer. Moreover, since the majority of foods were sold unwrapped, there was no space for branding.

Advertising entered Soviet culture with Gorbachev. The first ad featured Michael Jackson advertising Pepsi Cola (May 1988). The spot was of symbolic value: advertising was viewed as part of Western culture and most advertising spots served to reveal the dream world of Western consumerism. Full-blown advertising started after the state's price fixing had ceased, on 1 January 1992.

Banks commissioned the first major televised advertising campaigns in Russia. The MMM campaign (1992–94) is the most significant advertising campaign in Russian history. MMM was a pyramid scheme invented by Sergei Mavrodi; its success was created exclusively through its advertising campaign, which featured the fictional characters Lenia (Leonid) Golubkov, his wife Rita, and his brother, Ivan. Lenia, an unassuming, small, uneducated, working-class man, and lower in social rank than any likely owners of television sets, was elevated to the status of a hero in the best socialist tradition. Clip-maker Bakhyt Kilibaev created a series of ads, telling a full-blown story of the impact of MMM on three generations: a young student couple; a middle-aged single woman; and an elderly couple. The business finance corporation Bank Imperial had its ad series *World History* (*Vsemirnaia istoriia*, 1993–97), created by film-maker Timur Bekmambetov (*Nochnoi dozor* [*Night Watch*, 2004]). The ads draw on figures of world history, all absolute rulers endowed with wisdom, humour, and benevolence.

Adverts for alcohol glorified the delirium tremens induced by excessive vodka consumption (Smirnoff) and associated vodka with Russian pride and moral standards (Russkii Standart, Flagman). A range of original Russian beer labels appeared on the market in the 1990s, the brand names betraying their indigenous Russian character: Afanasii is an old Russian Christian name; Krasnyi Byk (Red Bull) is a parody on the alcoholic drink of the same name; Tolstiak (Fatso) and Tri medvedia (Three Bears) allude to Russian folktales; Staryi melnik (Old Miller) and Sibirskaia korona (Siberian Crown) assume an ancient history. Russian cigarette brands also draw on the Russian and Soviet past to give their products a pseudo-history (Fabergé, Russian Style [Russkii stil], Iava).

The return to nineteenth-century Russia is a widespread tendency in advertising for Russian products. Several milk and dairy products brands, such as Milaia Mila (Dear Mila), Doiar-ushka (Milkmaid), and Domik v derevne (House in the village) heavily rely on folk themes and the memory of an idealized past for their campaigns.

Social advertising deploys the method of pleading for support of the Russian economy (e.g., tax payment, purchase of home-grown produce). The new Russia still lacks confidence in its products and its industry, highlighting its own weaknesses. Russia advertises itself as a society that responds to pleading rather than seduction and that prefers to reinvent the past rather than dream of the future.

See also: drinks, alcoholic; economic system, post-Soviet; folktales; Gorbachev, Mikhail; per-estroika and glasnost; vodka

BIRGIT BEUMERS

Aguzarova, Zhanna

b. 7 July 1967, Novosibirsk oblast

Singer

After coming to Moscow in 1983, Aguzarova joined the rock'n'roll band Post Scriptum, sub-sequently renamed Bravo, as its singer, and enjoyed immense popularity. In 1989, she quit Bravo and moved to Los Angeles, where she performed in a restaurant, then returned to Russia in 1996. She released ten albums, solo and with Bravo and the group Nochnoi Prospekt.

ALEXANDER DOMRIN

AIDS (SPID)

AIDS, Acquired Immune Deficiency Syndrome, or SPID (*Sindrom priobretennogo immunnogo defitsita*) is a global pandemic infection. The virus HIV (*VICh*) was first recognized in the 1980s and AIDS has progressed worldwide at an explosive rate. While the Soviet Union, which criminalized IV drug abuse and homosexuality, was relatively free of AIDS, the rupture of society that occur-red with its collapse has seen the rise of sexual indiscretion and drug abuse. Concomitantly SPID has proliferated in Russia. Initial attempts to control the spread by universal testing and visa limitations for foreigners have proved ineffective. SPID is still stigmatized as a sign of moral decay, and a group of Russian physicians even proclaimed SPID a divine punishment.

Misperceived as a homosexual disease in the West, in Russia SPID is primarily spreading through the sexual networks of usually male drug users. Many authorities feel that a window of opportunity was missed, and attempts to limit the epidemic in the Former Soviet Union will now likely fail. As of 2004, Russia has reached the pivotal 1 per cent infection rate and will likely proceed to a full epidemic. The bulk of the disease affects the young: 80 per cent of the infected are under 30 years of age, an ominous demographic sign. Unfortunately, aside from an array of unproved therapies (Armenium, most notoriously), there is a limited supply of antiviral medications available at urban AIDS centres. Outside large cities, the situation is worse.

Though Russian estimates in 2004 are 250,000 infected, UN estimates are three–four times higher. Some believe that 15 million (10 per cent of the population) will be living with HIV by 2020, with over 20 million dead. Some authors have raised concerns about the territor-ial integrity of the Russian Federation by 2050 on the basis of native depopulation.

Further reading

Field, M. (2004) 'HIV and AIDS in the Former Soviet Bloc', *New England Journal of Medicine* 351: 117–20.

SAMUEL BROWN

Aigi, Gennadii Nikolaevich

b. 21 August 1934, Shaimurzino village, Chuvashia, USSR (now Russia); d. 21 February 2006, Moscow

Poet, translator

While studying at Moscow's Literaturnyi institut, Aigi received early encouragement from Boris

Pasternak. His first publications were poems in and translations into Chuvash. Aigi's original Russian poetry is in free verse (unrhymed, though relatively strict rhythmically), which made it suspect to the Soviet literary establishment. His incantatory, mystical poetic voice was as distinctive as his form. The themes are universal (nature and time being particularly prominent), but his poetry looks and sounds unique, with sparse and evocative words, often one to a line, as if suspended in space. Admirers considered him a genius (as numerous prizes attest), while detractors dismissed him as a fraud.

See also: Literary Institute; Pasternak, Boris

MICHAEL WACHTEL

Aitmatov, Chingiz Terikulovich

b. 12 December 1928, Sheker, Kirovskii district, Kyrgyz SSR

Writer

One of the major figures in Russian and Kyrgyz literature, Aitmatov writes both in Kyrgyz and in Russian. Aitmatov trained as veterinarian (1953) and worked as a livestock specialist in his native Kyrgyzstan. In 1958, he graduated from the *Literaturnyi Institut* (Gorkii Literary Institute) and published the novella *Dzhamilia* (Jamila), a beautiful love story that brought Aitmatov international acclaim. Most of Aitmatov's short stories and novels are set in Central Asia. During the Soviet period, he wrote according to the accepted method of Socialist Realism, but he combined an in-depth psychological analysis with a highly original use of folklore, parables, myths, and fantasy to explore issues of social problems, gender, national identity, history, and ethics. The novels *Belyi parokhod* (*The White Ship*, 1970) and *I dolshe veka dlitsia den* (*The Day Lasts Longer Than A Hundred Years*, 1980) both have elements of magic realism. Aitmatov's works have been translated into more than 150 languages. He was awarded the Lenin Prize for Literature (1963) and the USSR State Prize (1968, 1977, and 1983). He received the titles of National Writer of the Kyrgyz Republic (1968) and Hero of Socialist Labour (1978). Since 1990, Aitmatov has served in a number of ambassadorial positions in the Benelux countries.

See also: awards, literary, Soviet; Central Asia; Kyrgyzstan; Literary Institute; literature, Soviet Republics; Socialist Realism

ELENA BARABAN

akademgorodok

The *akademgorodok* (academic town) is a planned community of researchers, generally located in a suburban setting near a major university or research institute. This phenomenon dates from 1957, when the Siberian branch of the USSR Academy of Sciences was created as part of Khrushchev's drive to establish world-class research centres beyond the Urals to facilitate exploitation of rich Siberian natural resources. The most famous *akademgorodok* is a suburb of Novosibirsk and the site of Novosibirsk State University. Vasilii Aksenov's *Zolotaia nasha zhelezka* (*Our Golden Ironburg*) (1988) recreates the *akademgorodok* atmosphere, with its cult of all things intellectual and its moderate opposition to the regime.

See also: Academy of Sciences; Aksenov, Vasilii; Novosibirsk State University

Further reading

Aksenov, V. (1989) *Our Golden Ironburg*, trans. Ronald E. Peterson, Ann Arbor, MI: Ardis.

ANDREI ROGATCHEVSKI

Akhedzhakova, Liia Medzhidovna

b. 9 July 1938, Dnepropetrovsk, Ukraine

Theatre, film, and television actress

Akhedzhakova made her stage debut in the Moscow Theatre for Young Viewers in 1961. She joined the Moscow Sovremennik Theatre in 1977, becoming one of its leading stars. Since 1973, Akhedzhakova has appeared in more than thirty-five films. A gifted character actress, she has played an array of supporting and leading roles, frequently appearing in the melodramas and comedies directed by Eldar Riazanov, including *Ironiia sudby* (*Irony of Fate*, 1975), *Garazh* (*Garage*, 1979), and *Nebesa obetovannye* (*The Promised Heavens*, 1991). Akhedzhakova often plays exaggerated, larger-than-life characters, whom she makes endearing by giving them a strong emotional foundation.

See also: Riazanov, Eldar; Sovremennik Theatre

JENNIFER RYAN TISHLER

Akhmadulina, Bella (Isabella) Akhatovna

b. 10 April 1937, Moscow

Poet, translator, prose writer

A voice of conscience in Russian life since she began her career in 1956, Akhmadulina has always championed truth, justice, and friendship in art and her own life. After her expulsion from the Institute of World Literature for refusing to sign a denunciation of Pasternak, she worked as a journalist in Siberia. At times in official disfavour, she then earned her living by translating poetry, mainly from Georgian. After graduating from the institute, she began her poetic career and became one of the most popular poets of the Thaw era, reading her poems to large, appreciative crowds in arenas. With maturity, her poetry became more difficult and less accessible, although she has retained a loyal following. Her major theme remains poetry in all of its manifestations and forms. She acknowledges her poetic debt to her predecessors, especially Aleksandr Pushkin, Mikhail Lermontov, Anna Akhmatova, and Marina Tsvetaeva. Always experimental with form, in the 1980s she turned to prose and since then has often incorporated poetry into her stories as formal and thematic elements. Akhmadulina's youthful whimsy has turned into mature contemplation, yet she has not lost her wonder at the world around her.

See also: Akhmatova, Anna; literature, Thaw; Pasternak, Boris; Pushkin, Aleksandr; sixties generation

CHRISTINE A. RYDEL

Akhmatova, Anna Andreevna

(née Anna Gorenko)

b. 11 June 1889, Bolshoi Fontan (near Odessa), Ukraine; d. 5 March 1966, Domodedovo (near Leningrad)

Poet, literary scholar, translator

Akhmatova is hailed as an icon of twentieth-century Russian literature and culture. Born Anna Gorenko, she later adopted the name Akhmatova from her Tatar great-grandmother. She spent much of her childhood in Tsarskoe Selo, a suburb of St. Petersburg known for its superb lycée, where her future husband, poet Nikolai Gumilev, studied and their poetic mentor, Innokentii Annenskii, taught. Akhmatova studied law and, later, literature. Through Gumilev, whom she married in 1910, she joined a literary group called *Tsekh poetov* (The Guild of Poets). A number of these poets, chiefly Gumilev, Sergei Gorodetskii, and Osip Mandelstam, developed a school of poetics called Acmeism, whose principles of craft and clarity developed in reaction to the mysticism of Symbolist poetry. Akhmatova remained faithful to Acmeist principles throughout her career.

She first used the name Akhmatova in 1912 for her debut book of verse, *Vecher* (*Evening*), which met with enormous success. Akhmatova's next four books, likewise popular, resembled her first in style and themes: *Chetki* (*Rosary*) in 1914, *Belaia staia* (*The White Flock*) in 1917, *Podorozhnik* (*Plantain*) in 1921, *Anno Domini* in 1922. These five volumes represent the first and most prolific period in her literary career.

Akhmatova gave birth to a son, Lev, in 1912, but the two poets' marriage ended in divorce in 1918; three years later Gumilev was executed by the Bolsheviks. In 1918, Akhmatova married Assyrologist Vladimir Shileiko, and while still married to him began her long relationship with the art historian Nikolai Punin.

The Soviets unofficially banned Akhmatova's poetry from 1925 until 1940. Unable to publish her verse, she turned to translation and literary criticism. In 1946, she was denounced by the Central Committee and expelled from the Writers' Union. Her son was arrested for the second time in May 1937, and sentenced to a Soviet labour camp. Though he volunteered for the front in 1944, he was arrested again in 1949. Akhmatova's attempts to mollify the Communist government by writing poetry in praise of Stalin proved fruitless; her son was not released until 1956. Akhmatova's late cycle *Rekviem* (*Requiem, 1935–40*) and *Poema bez geroia* (*Poem Without a Hero*) are her most important works. The former addresses the tragedy and horror of Stalin's purges; the latter, on which she worked from 1940 until the end of her life, is a complex triptych devoted to Russian literary culture.

The only surviving great poet of her generation, during the 1950s and 1960s Akhmatova was deemed the reigning authority on poetry. A group of gifted young poets, including Anatolii Naiman and Evgenii Rein, gathered around her and were nicknamed her 'orphans'. Of these, she distinguished a rare talent in Iosif Brodskii and, it is often said, handed the torch over to him. Only towards the end of her life was Akhmatova officially rehabilitated by the Soviet government.

See also: Brodskii, Iosif; corrective labour institutions; unions, creative, Soviet

Further reading

Akhmatova, A. (1992) *The Complete Poems of Anna Akhmatova*, trans. and ed. Judith Hemschemeyer, Boston, MA: Zephyr Press.

Naiman, A. (1991) *Remembering Anna Akhmatova*, trans. and ed. Wendy Rosslyn, New York: Henry Holt and Co.

Reeder, R. (1995) *Anna Akhmatova: Poet and Prophet*, New York: Picador.

ONA RENNER-FAHEY

Akimov, Nikolai Pavlovich

b. 3 [16] April 1901, Kharkov; d. 6 September 1968, Moscow

Director, stage designer

Educated as a stage designer in Petrograd, Akimov created sets for several major Moscow and Leningrad productions of the 1920s and 1930s. His controversial directing debut at Moscow's Vakhtangov Theatre (1932) ironically posited the title character of *Hamlet* as an affirmative activist. He was artistic director of the Leningrad *Teatr komedii* (Comedy Theatre) from 1935 until 1949 and 1955 until 1958, and chief director of the Lensovet Theatre in Leningrad from 1951 until 1955. He was an important interpreter of Evgenii Shvarts's satirical plays, and his marginally surrealistic, fairy-tale-like set designs for these and other plays influenced Soviet theatre design in the 1950s and 1960s.

See also: theatre, Soviet; Vakhtangov Theatre

JOHN FREEDMAN

Aksenov, Vasilii Pavlovich

b. 20 August 1932, Kazan

Writer

Prose writer, playwright, and scriptwriter, Aksenov belongs to the generation of writers whose literary careers started during the Thaw and who represented the new liberal wave in Russian literature. His first novels, *Kollegi* (*Colleagues*) and *Zvezdnyi bilet* (*A Ticket to the Stars*) appeared in the journal *Iunost* (Youth) in 1960 and 1961, respectively, winning immediate success with the liberal intelligentsia and young, educated readers. In style, language, and characters, the novels marked a clear departure from the mandatory tenets of Socialist Realism. Although official critics chastised Aksenov for using slang and deviating from the canon in his portrayal of Soviet youth, he managed to balance his writings within the confines of Soviet ideology. In March 1963, however, Nikita Khrushchev attacked him and other liberal artists for transgressing ideological boundaries. In response, Aksenov discontinued his 'balancing act' between ideological demands and his own objectives, switching to the genre of fantastic satire. He wrote five plays and several novels as allegorical fantasies exposing the oppressive Soviet regime. Only two of these works were published; others, including one of his most important works, the novel *Ozhog* (*The Burn*, 1975), appeared in the West.

In 1978, Aksenov, with Viktor Erofeev and others, initiated the unauthorized, uncensored publication of the anthology *Metropol'*, released by the American publisher Ardis in 1979. In 1980, the USSR stripped Aksenov, then on a lecture tour in the United States, of his Soviet citizenship, forcing him to remain in the USA. Thereafter Aksenov remained a prolific writer and teacher of Russian literature at George Mason University.

After Gorbachev's government restored his citizenship in 1990, many of Aksenov's works appeared in Russia for the first time. Upon retiring from his professorship at George Mason in 2004, Aksenov moved back to Moscow, where he actively participates in Russian literary life. He remains highly popular, and one of his novels, *Moskovskaia saga* (*Generations of Winter*, 1992), was serialized on Russian television.

See also: Erofeev, Viktor; *Metropol*; Thaw

Further reading

Dalgård, P. (1982) *The Function of the Grotesque in Vasilij Aksenov*, Aarhus: Arkona.

Kustanovich, K. (1992) *The Artist and the Tyrant: Vassily Aksenov's Works in the Brezhnev Era*, Columbus, OH: Slavica.

Mozejko, E. *et al.* (eds) (1986) *Vasiliy Pavlovich Aksënov: A Writer in Quest of Himself*, Columbus, OH: Slavica.

KONSTANTIN KUSTANOVICH

Akunin, Boris

(né Grigorii Shalvovich Chkhartishvili)

b. 20 May 1956, Zestafoni, Georgia

Writer

A scholar, critic, and translator of English, American, and Japanese literature, Boris Akunin has lived in Moscow since 1958. In 1998, he began writing mystery novels about an elegant, witty nineteenth-century detective, Erast Fandorin. Engaging plots, masterful stylizations of nineteenth-century language, and numerous allusions to literary classics quickly earned Akunin the reputation of a detective writer for intellectuals. In 2000, he was named Russian Writer of the Year. Begun in 1998, *Prikliucheniia Erasta Fandorina* (*Adventures of Erast Fandorin*) is

Akunin's longest series. The *Prikliucheniia sestry Pelagei* trilogy (*Adventures of Sister Pelageia*) (1999–2003), set in the Russian hinterland of the nineteenth century, features crimes investigated by a nun. Akunin's third detective series, *Prikliucheniia magistra* (*Adventures of Nicholas*) begun in 2000, recounts the adventures of Nicholas Fandorin, grandson of the famous Erast Fandorin, and those of Nicholas's seventeenth- and eighteenth-century ancestors. Akunin's mysteries have been translated into many languages, including English (*The Winter Queen* (2003), *Turkish Gambit* (2004), and *Murder on the Leviathan* (2004)).

See also: detective fiction

ELENA BARABAN

Akvarium

Founded in 1972 by Boris Grebenshchikov, Akvarium emerged as one of Russia's most influential rock bands, long dominating the Leningrad/St. Petersburg rock music scene. Their playful lyrics combine references to mundane daily life with subversive puns, allusions to spiritual and philosophical traditions, and deliberately esoteric and at times nonsensical elements. These traits, the wide use of classical string instruments, and an openness to eclectic musical experimentation make Akvarium's songs instantly recognizable. The band's influence on Russian music and youth culture peaked during the 1980s and early 1990s, but Akvarium retains an active and prominent presence in Russia to this day.

See also: Grebenshchikov, Boris; rock music

VITALY CHERNETSKY

alcoholism

In Russia, alcohol (and particularly the indigenous Russian drink, vodka) have always been a control lever over the nation and its citizens. Since the times of Ivan the Terrible, vodka has been an attribute of statehood and a symbol of Russia. In the USSR, alcoholism was considered a heritage of capitalist exploitation and alien to the socialist way of life.

Soviet authorities maintained a constant policy of alcohol prohibition, including a ban on the production of home-distilled vodka as both harmful to health and damaging to the economy. Beginning in 1919, the production, purchase, and sale of home-distilled vodka, consumption of which increased after the Civil War, were punishable by law. In 1924, the state established a monopoly on the production of alcoholic drinks, and vodka sales increased by 40 per cent. Since 1945, the consumption of alcohol has sharply increased. The state police (*militsiia*) and newly-established special health protection units became engaged in the battle with alcoholism. Clinics devoted to the treatment of alcoholism appeared, and both public drunkenness and involving minors in alcohol-consumption became criminal offenses. In the mid-1960s, data on the production and consumption of alcohol were classified as secret, and in state budgets, alcohol-related expenses were transferred to the category of food expenses. The production and sale of alcohol and alcoholic drinks fell under direct state control, and in various periods income from the state wine monopoly has constituted between 15 and 40 per cent.

The struggle with alcoholism was conducted through the mass media, with posters and wall newspapers in workers' clubs, libraries, and sports and amateur arts clubs; anti-alcohol agitation also was included in films and theatre productions. Trade unions and health departments were similarly engaged in education against alcohol abuse.

The Soviet legal system developed institutions to punish alcoholics, such as *medvytrezviteli*, sobering-up stations where those arrested for public drunkenness and disorderly behaviour were briefly held; and *Lechebno-trudovye profilaktorii* (LTP, labour treatment centres). The latter institutions were established in 1974 for the forced medical treatment and re-education (for one to two years) of chronic alcoholics who avoided medical treatment and violated labour discipline and the social order. These were *de facto* prisons, and the method of treatment entailed subjecting the incarcerated 'patients' to forced labour and depriving them of all civil rights. This system disappeared in 1994.

In 1985, Gorbachev launched a new campaign against alcohol abuse. His government issued a decree, 'On measures to prevent hard drinking and alcoholism and the eradication of bootlegging'. A society for the struggle for sobriety was created, with obligatory membership for all Communist Party and Komsomol personnel. While vodka production was virtually liquidated, low-quality alcohol products were imported, and fights occurred in queues for alcohol, the purchase of which was limited through the introduction of ration cards (*talony*) to one bottle a month per person. The wine-making industry suffered enormous damage: over one-third of vineyards in the USSR were destroyed and more than a thousand wine-making factories were closed. The so-called 'Gorbachev experiment' led to the loss of one of the most profitable items in the state budget and actually increased alcoholism and the number of alcohol-related deaths.

Currently there is no state monopoly on liquor sales or production; domestic production of vodka and beer by private companies has increased, and a significant amount of alcohol is imported. Hard liquor can be purchased everywhere, even in small street kiosks; beer is regarded by some Russians as a soft drink and is consumed in public places, such as metro trains. In spite of state attempts to control production quality and fight the sale of counterfeit spirits, there is considerable risk of buying products hazardous to one's health. Teenage drinking is a significant problem, while the legal drinking age of 18 has not been strictly enforced in post-Soviet Russia. Recently the Duma has tried to address the problem of alcoholism by adopting laws introducing restrictions in beer advertising (2004) and limiting the sale of hard liquor to the hours of 8 a.m. to 11 p.m. (2006). Nevertheless, alcoholism continues to be a significant health hazard and social problem in Russia, contributing to short life-expectancy and the misdemeanor rate.

See also: advertising; amateur cultural activity; crime; drinks, alcoholic; Duma; economic system, Soviet; fitness; Gorbachev, Mikhail; health; legal system, Soviet; perestroika and glasnost; propaganda; queue; Soviet and post-Soviet; unions, professional; vodka

ELENA OMELCHENKO

Aleksandrov Soviet Army Song and Dance Ensemble

Founded in 1928 on the initiative of Marshal Kliment Voroshilov and under the direction of General Aleksandr Aleksandrov (1883–1943), professor at the Moscow Conservatory, this twelve-person ensemble burgeoned in Stalinist times into a popular, officially promoted, 200-strong military chorus accompanied by a folk dancing troupe. The ensemble has performed extensively in the Soviet Union and abroad; it toured the frontlines exhaustively in World War II and continues to give concerts at Russian military bases in the post-Soviet period. The ensemble is world-renowned as an outstanding purveyor of officially processed Soviet Russian folk and military music, a repertoire that includes such old chestnuts as 'Kalinka', 'Katiusha', and 'Poliushko, pole'.

See also: folk music; Moscow Conservatory

BETH HOLMGREN

Aleshkovskii, Iuz Efimovich

(né Iosif Efimovich Aleshkovskii)

b. 21 September 1929, Krasnoiarsk

Writer

Although he wrote officially approved screenplays and children's fiction, Iuz Aleshkovskii is best known for his underground songs and his satirical prose. He spent four years in the GULag (1950–53) for breach of military discipline. The labour camp experience resonates strongly in his songs, which he began performing unofficially in the mid-1950s and contributed to the almanac *Metropol* (1979).

In his prose, Aleshkovskii refused to make any concessions – thematic, ideological, or stylistic – necessary for publication in the USSR. In short works such as *Nikolai Nikolaevich* and *Maskirovka* (Camouflage), and in the novels *Kenguru* (Kangaroo) and *Ruka* (The Hand), Aleshkovskii focuses on lower social strata, makes liberal use of *mat* (unprintable obscenities), and combines ruthless satire of Soviet reality with the grotesque.

Aleshkovskii emigrated in 1979, first to Vienna and then to the USA. His literary output since emigration includes the novel *Karusel* (The Carousel) and a number of shorter pieces; these and his earlier works are set in Russia and involve characters of low social status. His works been published in his native land only since 1990.

See also: GULag; literature, émigré; mat; *Metropol*

RACHEL S. PLATONOV

Aliev, Geidar

b. 10 May 1923, Nakhychevan, Azerbaidzhan; d. 12 December 2003, Cleveland, Ohio

Politician

Born into a worker's family, Aliev graduated from university as a historian and started working for national security in the Azerbaidzhan Soviet Socialist Republic (1944–69), and in 1967–69 as head (Major General) of the Azerbaidzhani KGB. After thirteen years (1969–82) as First Secretary of the Azerbaidzhani Communist Party, Aliev left for Moscow, where he became a Member of the Politburo and First Deputy Chairman of the USSR Council of Ministers. In 1990, he retired voluntarily and returned to Azerbaidzhan, where he was elected president in 1993. He held that office until 2003, when his eldest son, Ilham Aliev, was elected to succeed him. Aliev died at the Cleveland Clinic while under treatment for a heart ailment.

See also: Azerbaidzhan

TATYANA LEDENEVA

All-Russian (All-Union) State Institute of Cinematography (VGIK)

The All-Russian State Institute of Cinematography (VGIK), called the All-Union State

Institute of Cinematography (*Vsesoiuznyi gosu-darstvennyi institut kinematografii*) until 1992, was the world's first state film school: it was officially founded on 1 September 1919 in Moscow under the directorship of renowned film-maker Vladimir Gardin. The same year, avant-gardist Lev Kuleshov joined the school's faculty, forming his own workshop and developing innovative approaches to all aspects of cinema. VGIK has departments of direction, acting, cinematography, animation, production design, criticism, and economics (production). From the beginning, the majority of the school's faculty have been leading Soviet film artists. In the 1930s and 1940s, Sergei Eisenstein (Eisenstein) formulated the basic pedagogical principles and shaped a generation of Soviet film-makers. Other influential teachers at VGIK were Ihor Savchenko, Mikhail Romm, Sergei Bondarchuk, and Sergei Gerasimov, after whom VGIK was named in 1986.

See also: Bondarchuk, Sergei; Gerasimov, Sergei; Romm, Mikhail

PETER ROLLBERG

Alov and Naumov

Alov, Aleksander Aleksandrovich

b. 26 September 1923, Khar'kov; d. 12 June 1983, Moscow

Film-maker, screenwriter

Naumov, Vladimir Naumovich

b. 6 December 1927, Leningrad

Film-maker, screenwriter

Alov and Naumov graduated in 1952 from VGIK, where they studied under Igor Savchenko. Like the Russian avant-garde film-makers of the 1920s, they collaborated on films until Alov's death. The major theme of their Thaw-era films is the Russian Revolution (*Trevozhnaia iunost* [*Restless Youth*, 1955], *Pavel Korchagin*, 1956, *Veter* [*Wind*, 1959]). In 1966, the authorities banned their adaptation of Dostoevskii's story *Skvernyi anekdot* (*A Nasty Story*). Their adaptation of Mikhail Bulgakov's play *Beg* (*Flight*, 1970) recalls the epic style of Stalinist

cinema. Beginning with *Teheran 43* (1980), and especially after Alov's death, the recurring theme of Naumov's films is the growing distance between the present and the time of the film-maker's tumultuous youth.

See also: All-Russian (All-Union) State Institute of Cinematography (VGIK); film, Soviet – Thaw period

ALEXANDER PROKHOROV

amateur cultural activity (samodeiatelnost)

The term *samodeiatelnost* refers to amateur artistic activity, as distinguished both from professional artistic activity and from folklore. *Samodeiatelnost* encompasses a broad range of creative spheres, including theatre, music, dance, poetry, and the visual arts.

Lenin himself actively promoted the connection between socialism and the mass participation of the working class in various forms of creative activity. From the beginning, amateur cultural activity was not simply a means of popular artistic self-expression; rather, it was imbued with a significant political aspect, being viewed as an instrument for the artistic and ideological education of the masses. As such, cultural authorities paid particular attention to the regulation of amateur cultural activity, for example, through professional and material aid given to clubs and through the judging of competitions and exhibitions.

Samodeiatelnost underwent a particular flowering, starting in the late 1950s. Amateur song became especially popular, at first spontaneously and later through organized clubs. By the mid-1970s, when the first all-Union amateur artistic festival was held, approximately 25 million people across the Soviet Union were engaged in *samodeiatelnost*; subsequently, this number is estimated to have grown by 1.5–2 million participants per year. Many forms of organized amateur cultural activity continue in the post-Soviet period.

See also: bards; Communist Youth League; *kapustnik*; KSP; Pioneer organization; Thaw

RACHEL S. PLATONOV

Amber Room

The Amber Room is a room in the enfilade of state apartments in the Catherine Palace, a royal summer residence designed by Bartolomeo Rastrelli and located in Tsarskoe Selo, outside St. Petersburg. The walls of this 96 sqm room are decorated with amber panels, which were presented to Peter I by King Friedrich-Wilhelm I of Prussia in 1716. First installed in Peter's Summer Palace and in the Winter Palace of Empress Elizabeth, the panels were moved to Tsarskoe Selo around 1750, where they were put in place by architect A. Martelli, along with mirrors, Florentine mosaics, chandeliers, and painted imitations of amber. When the room was opened in the mid-1750s, many observers dubbed it the 'eighth wonder of the world'. The amber panels are sensitive to temperature and humidity, and require permanent maintenance. The Amber Room has been restored several times, including 1830–33, 1893, and 1933–35. On 17 September 1941, the Nazis occupied the Catherine Palace, dismantled the panels, and presumably moved them to Germany. During the war, several amber panels were shown at the Amber Museum in Königsberg, but they disappeared before the Soviet Army occupied the city. After 1945, Soviet authorities searched in vain for the Amber Room in Germany, and ultimately decided to recreate it. In 1980, the partially restored Amber Room was opened to visitors. The restoration was completed in time for the tercentenary of St. Petersburg, in May 2003.

See also: St. Petersburg; World War II (Great Patriotic War)

MARIA RUBINS

Andreev, Boris Fedorovich

b. 9 February 1915, Saratov, d. 25 April 1982, Moscow

Film actor

Andreev catapulted to fame in the late 1930s portraying ne'er-do-well workers who reform under Party guidance: Balun in *Bolshaia zhizn'* (*The Great Life*), Duma in *Traktoristy* (*Tractor Drivers*). He typically played the strong, somewhat awkward, good-hearted giant with a bass voice. This man-of-the-people role was the Soviet hypostasis of the medieval *bogatyr* (Russian knight), whom Andreev portrayed literally in the title role of the 1956 film *Ilia Muromets*. Svintsov in the war film *Dva boitsa* (*Two Fighting Men*) was one of his best dramatic roles. People's Artist of the USSR (1962), and USSR State Prize (1948, 1950).

RIMGAILA SALYS

Andropov, Iurii Vladimirovich

b. 15 June 1914, Stavropol; d. 9 February 1984, Moscow

Political leader

Iurii Andropov succeeded Leonid Brezhnev as General Secretary of the Communist Party of the Soviet Union (CPSU), serving from November 1982 until his death in 1984. Appointed to the Politburo in 1973, Andropov chaired the Committee for State Security (KGB) (1967–82). Although his service as General Secretary was short, Andropov initiated programmes to revive the Soviet economy through campaigns against corruption and alcoholism and reintroduced several strict bureaucratic measures. He also retired many older government and party officials, promoting younger men, including Mikhail Gorbachev, to positions of authority.

See also: Brezhnev, Leonid; Communist Party; Federal Security Service; Gorbachev, Mikhail

Further reading

Solovyov, E. (1983) *Yuri Andropov: A Secret Passage into the Kremlin*, New York: Macmillan.

VICKI HESLI AND JAMES KRUEGER

Androvskaia, Olga Nikolaevna

(née Shults)

b. 21 July 1898, Moscow; d. 31 March 1975, Moscow

Stage and film actress

Androvskaia began her acting career at the famous Korsh Theatre (1918) before joining the 2nd Studio of the Moscow Art Theatre (MKhAT) in 1919 and MKhAT's main troupe in 1924. Androvskaia's elegance and charm were particularly valued in comedies, from Beaumarchais to Wilde; among her legendary accomplishments were the roles of Liza in Griboedov's *Gore ot uma* (*Woe from Wit*) and Varvara in Aleksandr Ostrovskii's *Groza* (*The Thunderstorm*). The actress also won praise for her superb screen performances in popular Chkehov adaptations, such as *Medved* (*The Bear*, 1938) and *Chelovek v futliare* (*The Man in the Shell*, 1939). People's Artist of the USSR (1948).

See also: Moscow Art Theatre

PETER ROLLBERG

anti-Semitism

Despite the end of the fear and uncertainty that marked life for Jews during the final years of Stalin's rule, anti-Semitism has continued to play a role in post-Stalinist politics and culture. While its expression took different forms and had varying levels of intensity, anti-Semitism was invariably linked to the ideological and political concerns of the Kremlin and enjoyed strong roots in popular attitudes and behaviour.

Under Khrushchev and Brezhnev, the Kremlin focused on limiting (and, in some cases, denying) the admission of Jews to certain fields of study and employment, such as the diplomatic corps, foreign trade, the humanities and social sciences, the secret police, and the higher ranks of the party. Other state policies possessed undeniable anti-Semitic motivation and character, though officials tried to mask the anti-Semitism through specious arguments and

language. From the mid-1950s to the mid-1980s the campaign against Soviet Jewry relied on well-established themes and caricatures that condemned Judaism as the promoter of capitalism and the unbridled economic exploitation of non-Jews. One notable example is Trofim Kichko's book *Iudaizm bez prikras* (*Judaism without Embellishment*, 1963), where the author calls Jews Nazi collaborators. When Khrushchev tried to root out corruption in the economy in the early 1960s, Jews occupied a prominent place among the ranks of persons arrested and executed for crimes that included currency speculation, bribery, and embezzlement. Once again, the argument relied on the purported link between Judaism and the ideologically suspect nature of Jewish life and society. Similarly, the Kremlin couched its pro-Arab, anti-Israeli diplomacy in terms of anti-Zionism, though the media campaign against Israel portrayed Zionists in the most unflattering terms and images and did not distinguish between Zionists and Jews. These anti-Jewish campaigns served the Cold War diplomacy of the Soviet Union.

The message of these policies and pronouncements was clear: Jews were an unpatriotic and unassimilable minority who owed greater loyalty to the enemies of the Soviet Union and whose shortcomings stemmed from their ethno-religious characteristics. This official anti-Semitism found fertile soil among the non-Jewish populace, which, for the most part, was a wellspring of anti-Jewish attitudes and beliefs, thereby ensuring that the government's policy would find a welcome reception. Government policies against the Jews only confirmed the worst suspicions that Jews were subversives intent on destroying the Soviet Union. Since 1991, Russian hyper-nationalism and patriotic fervor have drawn sustenance from the legacy of these anti-Semitic policies and attitudes. But the grip of anti-Semitism on society has diminished as society has become more urban, educated, and literate in the past few decades – traits that tend to be associated with the generations born after 1953. In addition, the post-1991 governments have abandoned the anti-Semitic policies of their Communist predecessors, and anti-Semitism as an open force in politics and culture has weakened.

See also: Brezhnev, Leonid; Cold War; Jews; Judaism; Khrushchev, Nikita;

Further reading

Brym, R. J. (2003) 'Russian Antisemitism, 1996–2000', in Z. Gitelman (ed.) *Jewish Life after the USSR*, Bloomington, IN: Indiana University Press, pp. 99–116.
Brym, R. J. and Degtyarev, A. (1993) 'Antisemitism in Moscow: Results of an October 1992 Survey', *Slavic Review* 52, 1: 1–12.
Gitelman, Z. (2001) *A Century of Ambivalence*, 2nd edn, Bloomington, IN: Indiana University Press, Chapters 5–9.

BOB WEINBERG

Antoshina, Tatiana Konstantinovna

b. 5 January 1956, Krasnoiarsk

Multimedia artist

Antoshina received her graduate degree in Art History from the Stroganov Art Institute in 1991. Active since the early 1990s, she explores and playfully subverts gender roles in her art. Her early ceramic works include *Poet and Speaker* and *Chimeras, Come Here*, which freezes the ephemeral, radical performance acts by the Actionist Aleksandr Brener in the traditional media of porcelain. In her photographic series *Museum of a Woman* (*Muzei zhenshchiny*, 1997), she replaces world-famous artworks showing female nudes with male figures. Antoshina's major preoccupation is the representation, or the construction, of maleness in modern and contemporary art. Her works have been shown in numerous international exhibitions, including *After the Wall*, Moderna Muzeet in Stockholm (1998). In 2002, she was a special prizewinner, and a prizewinner (Silver Camera) in 2003 at the Moscow House of Photography.

See also: photo-art

NATALIA KOLODZEI

APN (Agenstvo Pechati Novosti)

See: RIA Novosti

appetizers (zakuski)

Appetizers (*zakuska*, pl. *zakuski*), which may be hot or cold, are an integral part of any Russian festive meal and, often, also of everyday meals. Preceding soup and the main course, they may range from a piece of herring or a pickle to an elaborate variety of delicacies, including caviar.

Appetizers are rarely consumed without alcohol, constituting part of the drinking ritual and intended to follow each glass of vodka or another alcoholic drink. In practical terms, they serve two purposes: killing the bad taste of low-quality vodka (or enhancing the taste of good vodka) and filling a stomach to alleviate the effect of liberally consumed alcohol. Best to satisfy these requirements are salty and fatty foods, hence the most popular cold *zakuski* are pickles, pickled wild mushrooms, sauerkraut, sausages, hams, tongue, home-made pâtés, *studen* and *zalivnoe* (meat and fish in aspic, respectively), herring, smoked salmon and sturgeon, salmon and sturgeon ('red' and 'black') caviar, and cheese – all accompanied by white or brown (called black) bread. Salads supplement the *zakuski* menu. The two most common are *vinegret* (a beet and potato salad) and a potato salad, *olive*.

Virtually any hot and spicy dish can be used as a hot *zakuska*, but most of the latter require some sort of meat. Fried eggs with ham or sausage, hotdogs in a spicy tomato sauce, wild mushrooms sautéed with onions and sour cream, as well as various meat and fish *pirogi* (pies) in bite-sized portions are popular hot appetizers. In home cuisine, however, hot appetizers have become rare. Ordinary Russians hardly ever serve a complete traditional meal consisting of hot and cold *zakuski*, soup, main course, and dessert. On social occasions hot appetizers and soup are usually omitted.

The *zakuski* table is often decorated with plates of unchopped dill, parsley, cilantro, and scallions, which the diners pick at from time to time as finger food.

See also: caviar; drinks, alcoholic; pirog/
pirozhki; salads; vodka

KONSTANTIN KUSTANOVICH

April Factory (Aprelevskaia fabrika)

The April Factory (*Aprelevskaia fabrika*, also
known as the *Aprelevka*, founded in 1910, has
mass-produced recordings of Soviet songs since
1917; productions have included the 'Internationale'. In 1919, under the auspices of Tsen-
tropechat, the factory produced thousands of
records of an agitprop nature, with speeches by
Lenin, Kollontai, Lunacharskii, and others.
During World War II, the factory issued a
recording of the patriotic song *Sviashchennaia
voina* (*The Sacred War*). At the same time, it began
issuing recordings of lighter genres – *estrada*
(variety) and Soviet jazz. The April factory currently produces CDs on commission.

See also: House of Recordings; popular music,
Soviet; recording studios; World War II (Great
Patriotic War)

OLGA ZASLAVSKY

Apt-Art

Apt-Art ('apartment art') is a term invented by
the Moscow artist Nikita Alekseev in 1982 to
describe the new practice of exhibiting art works
using private apartments as Galleries. The first
Apt-Art show took place in Alekseev's own
apartment, known as the Apt-Art gallery (1982–
84). Apt-Art works did not embrace a unified
artistic style, but were associated with a distinct
trend of Moscow Conceptualism. In contrast to
the Conceptualists' intellectual and analytical
aesthetics, Apt-Art adopted an ironic attitude to
art, emphasizing spontaneity, playfulness, and
buffoonery. Among the most frequent participants of Apt-Art shows were the group Mukhomor (Toadstool), Konstantin Zvezdochetov,
Georgii Kizevalter, the brothers Vladimir and
Sergei Mironenko, and Andrei Fillipov. The

tradition of Apt-Art exhibits was continued by
Galereia Vrubel (Vrubel Gallery, 1986–96) and
the gallery Escape (1998–) in Moscow.

See also: Conceptualism, art; Zvezdochetov,
Konstantin

LARISSA RUDOVA

Arabov, Iurii Nikolaevich

b. 25 October 1954, Moscow

Screenwriter, poet, novelist, essayist

Arabov is best known as the screenwriter for
nearly all of director Aleksandr Sokurov's feature films, including *Molokh* (*Moloch*), for which
Arabov received the prize for best screenplay at
the 1999 Cannes Film Festival. Arabov heads
the screenwriting department at VGIK (the All-
Russian State Institute of Cinematography),
from which he graduated in 1980. The author
of four volumes of poetry, most recently *Vozdukh*
(*Air*, 2003), he has identified himself as a
metarealist poet. In 2004, Arabov was awarded
the Apollon Grigorev prize for his second novel,
Big-bit, published in the thick journal *Znamia*
(*The Banner*) the previous year. His essays, stories
and articles have appeared in numerous publications.

See also: All-Russian (All-Union) State Institute
of Cinematography (VGIK); film, festivals and
prizes; poetry, post-Soviet; Sokurov, Aleksandr;
thick journals

PATRICK HENRY

Arbat

Arbat is a kilometre-long cobbled street in west-
central Moscow, between *Smolenskaia* and
Arbatskaia metro stations. A must-see tourist
attraction, Arbat is a pedestrian-only street with
museums, souvenir shops, street performers,
roadside restaurants, and portrait artists. The
Vakhtangov Theatre is located off Arbat Street,
and at one end of Arbat is the restaurant Praga.

The city of Moscow celebrated the 500th anniversary of the street in 1993. A cultural symbol of the city, Arbat has been immortalized in the works of the two Soviet writers, Bulat Okudzhava and Anatolii Rybakov.

See also: Moscow; Okudzhava, Bulat; Rybakov, Anatolii; Vakhtangov Theatre

SUSMITA SUNDARAM

Arbatova, Mariia Ivanovna

(née Mariia Gavrilina)

b. 17 July 1957, Murom, Russia

Writer

A writer, politician, human rights activist, and leading feminist in post-Soviet Russia, Arbatova has written fourteen plays staged in both Russia and abroad and has published numerous books. She received the Cambridge Bibliographical Centre gold medal (1991) for her contribution to twentieth-century culture and the *Literaturnaia gazeta* (Literary Gazette) prize (2002). For five years, Arbatova co-hosted the women's talk show *Ia sama* (By Myself) on the now defunct channel TV 6. As leader of *Klub zhenshchin, vmeshivaiushchikhsia v politiku* (Club of Women Who Interfere in Politics) and co-chair of *Partiia prav cheloveka* (Human Rights Party), Arbatova operates as an advocate for women in Russia's social and political life.

YANA HASHAMOVA

Arbuzov, Aleksei Nikolaevich

b. 13 [26] May 1908, Moscow; d. 20 April 1986, Moscow

Playwright

Arbuzov's plays have happy endings. Even so, many of his public, at home and abroad, wanted to see in Arbuzov a 'Soviet Chekhov'. Without straying from the thematic canon (the exploration of the Far East, the siege of Leningrad),

Arbuzov's consistently successful works posited on stage the existence of a vibrant private sphere in everyday Soviet life. From his first hit, *Tanya* (1939), to the popular *Irkustkaia istoriia* (*It Happened in Irkutsk*, 1959) and *Moi bednyi Marat* (*The Promise*, 1964), Arbuzov kept the focus on his characters' intimate relationships, using the device of the love triangle to construct a world in which ideology seemed reduced to a mere footnote to experience.

See also: drama, Soviet

BORIS WOLFSON

architecture, Soviet and post-Soviet

When the Bolshevik Revolution broke out in 1917, few progressive artists and architects failed to embrace its ideals, welcoming what they perceived as the Revolution's profoundly regenerative capacity to rid society of debilitating exploitation and to generate the socio-economic wherewithal to build a new egalitarian society. Sustained by their vision of an egalitarian society, Soviet avant-garde artists and architects pursued new strategies and modes of expression innately capable of embodying and communicating the ideals of the new revolutionary order.

Throughout the 1920s, groups of architects experimenting with a variety of approaches were active in the Soviet Union. The Rationalists, led by Nikolai Ladovskii, explored visual and perceptual means of determining the expressive qualities of spatial form, which they regarded as the ultimate sensate material of architecture. They experimented with ways of manipulating the heightened geometrical properties of form and its designed expressive attributes, or motifs, that could activate the perceptual mechanisms of the observer's body, thereby facilitating their interaction with space and orientation to their physical and spatial settings. The Constructivists, with Moisei Ginzburg and Aleksandr Vesnin at the helm, theorized a purposeful architecture aimed at facilitating a life-enhancing 'mechanization of life' by harnessing the civilizing force of the machine. Their design method called for analyzing the social and technical demands of a building and its role in society in order to arrive empirically at forms innately capable of satisfying those demands and fulfilling the ideals of the emerging Socialist society. Notable examples include Ginzburg's Narkomfin Apartment House (1928–30), designed with Ivan Miliis, and the Vesnin brothers' Palace of Culture for the Proletarian Region (1931–37), both in Moscow.

Several architects embraced Modernism without joining either movement. Konstantin Melnikov was known for the originality of his designs, exemplified by the perceptually energized Rusakov Club (1927–28) in Moscow. Ilia Golosov, who designed the Zuev Workers' Club of 1929 in Moscow, analyzed the symbolism of geometrically organized volumes and their direct effect on perception; his brother Panteleimon designed the Pravda Building (1930–34) in Moscow. Grigori B. Barkhin likewise expanded upon the Modernist project in a number of his designs, including his Izvestiia Building in Moscow (1925–27). Other architects, who did not pursue Modernism but whose work evinced innovative trends, were Lev Rudnev, Andrei Belogrud, and Ivan Fomin, whose concept of 'proletarian classicism', also known as Red Doric, inspired his impressive Dynamo Club (1928) and Mossoviet (1928) Buildings, both in Moscow.

The competition for the Palace of Soviets in Moscow (1931–34) signaled the demise of Modernist architecture and the complete transformation of Soviet architectural theory and practice under the Stalinist regime. Boris Iofan's final design for the Palace, executed in collaboration with Vladimir Shchuko and Vladimir Gelfreikh and far more rhetorical and colossal in scale than his earlier variants, was a multi-tiered trophy building, topped by a 328-ft statue of Lenin that would have soared to a height of 1,400 feet, exceeding that of the Empire State Building. Though never built, its mammoth tower was the central landmark adopted in the general plan of Moscow (1935) by Vladimir Semenov and Sergei Chernyshev.

Socialist Realism, which restricted the accepted means of expression to those of a figurative architecture that was realist in style and socialist

in content, dictated the mandated new tendency in Soviet architecture. The Stalinist regime repudiated the stark, abstract forms of Soviet Modernism as incomprehensible, thus alienating, to the masses. Socialist Realist architecture was intended to inspire pride in the Soviet state's accomplishments and projected grandeur and to utilize a style accessible to the populace. Accessibility necessitated a familiar, rhetorical, and monumental style executed on a scale calculated to awe and to inspire the New Soviet Man. The adaptation of the classical tradition was the preferred option for supplying Soviet architecture with its requisite broad base of popular support.

The emphasis on classical expression in the 1930s, however, was interpreted pluralistically. Ivan Zholtovskii championed a direct return to the Palladian model, as for example, in his apartment house (1933–34, later, the Intourist Building) on Mokhov Street (Moscow). Andrei Burov incorporated classicist allusions into modular systems. Rudnev created Romantic compositions, combining classicism with formal avant-garde principles, as in the Frunze Military Academy (1932–37, Moscow). Golosov returned to the classical underpinnings of romantic symbolism, as in the housing block (1936–38) in the Avtozavodsk region of Gorkii (now Nizhnii Novgorod). Evgenii Levinson and Fomin in Leningrad achieved a synthesis of the methods of St. Petersburg classicism with the tectonics of reinforced-concrete structures in their apartment block (1931–35) on the Karpovka Embankment. Karo Arabian and Vladimir Simbirtsev aimed at integrating the expressive power of architecture with the Classical tradition to convey socialist symbolism in their Red Army Theatre in Moscow (1924–40): the floor plan of the building is a five-pointed star, the emblem of the Red Army, while the whole structure is encased in a colossal Corinthian colonnade.

With the growth of nationalist sentiment in the late 1930s came a perceptible shift toward the expression of national forms in Soviet architecture. Extensive use was made of national motifs in some of the Moscow subway stations. This tendency culminated in the designs of the various pavilions at the All-Union Agricultural Exhibition in Moscow (1939–40), with those of the Uzbek, Georgian, Armenian, and Ukrainian republics being the most distinctive. The originality of form and richness of ornament reflected the architectural traditions as well as the folk arts of the various republics. Finally, a trend towards official showcase monumentality also emerged, pointing the way to the post-war period. That trend's most extreme expression was the new public centre in Leningrad, whose main building, with its gigantic geometric colonnade, was built by Noi Trotskii (1937–41). With the outbreak of World War II, all building activity ceased.

By the end of the war, Soviet architecture had come fully to reflect the definition of Stalinism as the 'russification of Marxism'. This tendency is most apparent in the monumental style in the design of the seven tall buildings for post-war Moscow, aiming for an epic transformation of the Soviet capital's traditional skyline. Long enriched by an array of such vertical elements as towers, church cupolas, and belfries, that traditional skyline had become obliterated by the more cosmopolitan reconstruction of urban ensembles undertaken just prior to the war, in accordance with the 1935 plan. Erected on strategic sites to form a ring around the centre of Moscow, with the projected Palace of Soviets at its core, the ensemble effectively simulated, on a cosmic scale, the traditional spatial configuration and pyramidal silhouette of medieval Russian kremlins and monasteries, whose enclosing ring of wall towers and cathedral cupolas were dominated by a tall central belfry. This ensemble, which raised the height of the central portion of Moscow's skyline, discussed above, recaptures tradition yet projected a new paradigm for post-war Stalinist urbanism.

The end of the Stalinist regime (1953) ushered in a limited thaw in Soviet architecture. Late in 1954, Nikita Khrushchev criticized the decorative excesses and high building costs of the seven-tower ensembles. The 20th Party Congress followed suit in 1955, declaring that these excesses had distorted the country's architectural legacy and sapped its budget. The Congress announced that a top national priority was the improvement of the country's housing and building industries, the replacement of traditional construction methods with standardized mass-production techniques utilizing large-scale

pre-cast concrete panel construction. In the early 1960s, five-storey housing blocks sprang up on the outskirts of cities; these pre-cast large-panel (*krupno-panelnye*) developments were conceived as a Soviet alternative to the prosperity of post-war suburban America. Arranged to loosely frame a series of gardens planted with birch trees, these were the first apartments a young Soviet couple could afford to buy on a worker's yearly salary. Though small, they offered an alternative to cramped communal living. Termed *khrushcheby* by their detractors (a play on words combining the first part of Khrushchev's name with the last part of the Russian word *trushcheby*, meaning slums), these prefab modular units eventually became a standardized model for social housing throughout the East Bloc.

The Khrushchevian reforms also propelled Soviet architecture into the arena of Late Modern architecture. The Palace of Congresses in the Moscow Kremlin (1959–61), known today as the State Kremlin Palace and designed by Mikhail Posokhin, affirmed Khrushchev's mandate for a return to Modernism. Built to host Communist Party congresses as well as musical and theatrical performances, the stark, 394ft-long glass and marble-faced concrete and glass edifice became a building model in the 1960s, but never found favour with most Muscovites, who found it an affront to the Kremlin and to personal enjoyment. The work of Posokhin, who became the chief architect of Moscow, tellingly reflects the changes that had occurred in Soviet architecture in the space of a decade. After the Palace of Congresses, Posokhin created, with Mdoiants and Svirskii, the most famous urban development project under Khrushchev – the multi-block Kalinin Avenue complex (1962–68), now generally known as the New Arbat. Khrushchev, shortly after returning from his stopover in New York while on a trip to America, ordered that the thoroughfare, planned since 1935, finally be constructed and lined with restaurants, stores, and buildings towering in the American style. This monumental complex, which established a major new shopping artery for Moscow, comprised four identical 25-storey concrete-and-glass office buildings in the shape of an open book. The original complex included a 55ft promenade protected from the traffic by the 17m green area between the prospect and the row of two-storey stores. Terminating the avenue complex at the Moscow River is the 32-storey Building for the Council for Mutual Economic Assistance, or CMEA (1963–70). The spacious promenades and sleek façades were meant to evoke the era's progressive values. The ensemble's ideological potential was especially evident during festive illuminations, when bright lights in windows in the book-shaped blocks would form the letters USSR or the digits of the coming new year. The construction of this expansive complex involved the demolition of part of the pre-Revolutionary neighbourhood around the Old Arbat, and many Muscovites considered it alien to the city. The complex currently is undergoing a $2.8 million remodelling to recapture and enhance the harmony of the pedestrian zone and the street's role as an upmarket shopping and entertainment centre.

In the 1970s and 1980s, Soviet architects resumed their intense collaboration with artists while evincing an emerging post-modern sensibility inspired by readings of Western post-modern texts. Rejecting the legacy of the country's early avant-garde, they were rediscovering the legacy of indigenous Stalinist 'post-modern' aesthetics, which many considered the original episode of the genre. In the late 1970s, disillusioned with the bureaucratic, moribund state of architectural practice and tedious standardized production, a group of young architects banded together, to create, in the late 1980s, the so-called 'Paper Architecture' movement. Unconcerned with producing anything that could be built, these 'paper architects' re-asserted the image of the visionary artist in Russian society.

After the collapse of the Soviet Union in 1991, architecture initially continued in a post-modern vein. Yeltsin's fleeting call for the country to reinvest in its national legacy and cultural traditions helped rekindle interest in Stalinist buildings, which ultimately inspired the construction of such vapid landmarks as Triumph Palace, a 61-storey luxury apartment house rendered as a pseudo-Stalinist set-back skyscraper in the Sokol region. The rediscovery of Russian architecture had actually occurred earlier, and at a more modest and genuine level in reaction to the international modernism that had been mass-produced under Khrushchev.

City neighbourhoods and discrete, intimate urban settings were appreciated anew as repositories of the familiar, intimate, and reassuring, but this brief respite ended with a return to large-scale reconstruction and development.

The real mover behind that development was Moscow's mayor, Iurii Luzhkov, who determined to reconstruct Moscow and eliminate its Stalinist stamp. The extravaganza of ceremonies Luzhkov masterminded to commemorate Moscow's 850th anniversary did not aim to destabilize familiar monumental propaganda, but to create its post-Soviet rival. Luzhkov began modestly, tidying up the city, resurfacing crumbling sidewalks, repaving rutted roads, and rebuilding the Moscow beltway into a ten-lane superhighway. He also developed the Russian Bistro fast-food restaurant, where the food was cheap, the service quick, and the menu and motif thoroughly Russian. He subsequently embarked on 'grand projects': in the tradition of Robert Moses, who had shaped much of twentieth-century New York, Luzhkov devised major projects that reshaped the Moscow skyline. These include the reconstruction of the Cathedral of Christ the Saviour; the reconstruction of the Kazan Cathedral and the Trinity Gates and Iberian Chapel on Red Square, which Stalin had demolished as part of the regime's offensive against the Orthodox Church; the construction of the largest underground shopping mall in Europe, near Red Square, three stories of underground space decorated with banal statuary and details by Luzhkov's court sculptor, Zurab Tsereteli; the great expansion of the Tretiakov Library; a major addition to the Bolshoi Theatre, mired in problems; the restoration of Quarengthi's eighteenth-century Gostiny Dvor and recreation of its original function as a commercial and public building in Kitai-Gorod; and the addition of a 140ft-high, 12-acre sliding roof of glass-reinforced plastic to cover Luzhniki Stadium, making it Europe's largest stadium. Rulings of official architectural commissions, the results of official competitions, and growing criticism of the demolition of countless historic landmarks have not deterred Luzhkov, whose plans have been realized by his coterie of architects and artists, particularly Posokhin and Tsereteli.

Luzhkov's latest, high-profile projects, centred on the construction of skyscrapers include the

New Ring of Moscow, which entails building a second ring of soaring skyscrapers beyond the city's centre. Some sixty skyscrapers, spaced in a series of discrete building zones, are to be erected over the next fifteen years, with affluent individuals and businesses from Russia and elsewhere bidding to acquire options for constructing the structures. The second project, Moscow-City, is a huge complex along the Krasnopresnenskii Embankment northwest of the city centre, designated as the capital's future administrative and financial centre. The largest investment and construction project in Russia and Europe today, it involves the construction of a series of soaring high-tech towers and a modern infrastructure

These projects attest to Luzhkov's determined pursuit of a new generation of sleek, super-tall skyscrapers, with signature designs increasingly produced by leading Western architects to enhance marketability, impress the sceptics, and signal that Moscow is an economic and cultural force to be reckoned with. The objective is nothing less than to raise the city's skyline and transform the capital into a world-class metropolis that would rival the leading towered cities of the world.

Over ten years in the making, the Moscow-City project was slowed by the 1998 economic crisis and the consequent difficulty of attracting investors and secondary developers. Until a few years ago, only the Tower 2000 Office Complex and Bagration Pedestrian Bridge had been completed. At this point, the project has come alive as a result of the new building boom and massive, unprecedented transformation sparked by the recent high profits from oil and gas exports and the city's burgeoning real-estate and building markets. The latter are managed by Capital Group, a high-profile conglomerate development company that is the first to commission foreign architects, with a growing preference for 'star' architects, who can deliver a readily marketable commodity.

Key complexes planned for the rejuvenated Moscow-City complex project have been designed by leading Western architectural firms. Norman Foster has recently been commissioned to design Russia Tower, the centrepiece of Moscow-City, projected at a height exceeding 2,000 feet, to be the tallest building in the world.

Zaha Hadid is slated to design a complex of residential towers. Two signature complexes are now under construction. The first is the Capital Cities Towers, designed by NBBK, the US-based international architectural firm, whose workmanlike 73-storey Moscow Tower and 62-storey St. Petersburg Tower are slated to be Russia's tallest buildings and the highest residential towers in the world. The second, Federation Towers, designed by German-based architects Peter Schweger and Sergey Tchoban, encompasses two soaring glass skyscrapers, 794 and 1,161 ft high respectively and linked to a taller transparent mast. From the latter's observation deck, visitors will be able to view a city being transformed by a feverish quest for cosmic, ever taller skyscrapers – the latest generation of Muscovite *vysotki*.

See also: architecture, visionary; architecture, wooden; Armenia; art museums; Bolshoi Theatre; Cathedral of Christ the Saviour; church architecture, Russian Orthodox; Dinamo; economic system, post-Soviet; economic system, Soviet; fast food; Georgia; Golden Ring; housing, Soviet and post-Soviet; Khrushchev, Nikita; kremlin; Kremlin (Moscow); Luzhkov, Iurii; Manezh; Moscow; nationalism; Nizhnii Novgorod (Gorkii); *Pravda*; Red Square; Russian Orthodox churches; Socialist Realism; Stagnation; Stalin, Iosif; St. Petersburg; Thaw; Tretiakov Gallery; Tsereteli, Zurab; Ukraine; Uzbekistan; VDNKh/VVTs; vysotka; World War II (Great Patriotic War); Yeltsin, Boris

Further reading

Ikonnikov, A.V. (1988) *Russian Architecture of the Soviet Period*, trans. L. Lyapin, Moscow: Raduga Publishers.

Paperny, V. (2002) *Culture Two: Architecture in the Age of Stalin*, trans. J. Hill and R. Barris, Cambridge: Cambridge University Press.

Proekt Rossiia [*Project Russia*], Issue 5 (1997).

Proekt Rossiia [*Project Russia*], Issue 34 (2005).

Senkevitch, A. Jr. (1983) 'Aspects of Spatial Form and Perceptual Psychology in the Doctrine of the Rationalist Movement in Soviet Architecture in the 1920s', *VIA*, 6 (University of Pennsylvania Graduate School of Fine Arts): 78–115.

—— (1990) 'The Sources and Ideals of Constructivism in Soviet Architecture', in *Art into Life: Russian Constructivism 1914–1932*, New York: Rizzoli, pp. 169–91.

ANATOLE SENKEVITCH

architecture, visionary

Visionary architecture encompasses theoretical, speculative, and imaginary products of creative thinking by architects. Visionary thinking and architectural fantasies are particularly important in times of political, economic, or cultural uncertainty for their capacity to challenge hidebound conventions and reveal new modes of innovation. In the early post-Revolutionary years, the Russian avant-garde challenged conventions in its unwavering pursuit of dynamic new forms and strategies for a new architecture capable of embodying the ideals of a new revolutionary order. The results yielded a phenomenal array of visionary architecture.

Few visionary projects can compare to Vladimir Tatlin's 1920 design for the Monument to the Third International, intended to surpass the height of the Eiffel Tower, then the tallest structure in the world. The spiraling steel superstructure of Tatlin's tower was conceived as both a monument to the soaring progress of a society liberated by the Communist International and a symbolic visualization of a new ultra-modern type of kinetic structure intended to fulfil both artistic and utilitarian purposes.

Iakov Chernikhov was perhaps the pre-eminent avant-garde master of visionary architectural fantasies. His meticulous compositions, ranging from abstract dematerializations of pure primary forms to more overtly architectural delineations of 'fantasies on an industrial theme' and dynamic renderings of 'scientific research institutes', were proposals for a new world of architectural form and a new language of vision for expressing fresh narratives of a vibrant socialist culture. At times, Chernikhov's field became a space of collisions, deconstructions, and dematerialized events, embodying a dynamic formal strategy that anticipated and subsequently inspired such contemporary architects as Zaha Hadid, Daniel Libeskind, and Bernard Tschumi. Chernikhov's brand of visionary architecture put him on a par with Piranesi as one of the great architectural fantasists of the time.

In the late 1970s, a group of young graduates at the Moscow Architectural Institute, disheartened by the stagnation of the Soviet architectural profession during the Brezhnev regime, founded the so-called 'Paper Architecture' movement; this loosely organized group of 'paper architects' included Iosif Brodskii, Ilia Utkin, Iurii Avvakumov, and Mikhail Belov. Their visionary designs, teeming with ironic narratives, sprang from an instinctive opposition to Soviet totalitarian culture, evincing what the architect-turned-poet Andrei Voznesenskii termed 'the sublimation of despair'. Brodskii and Utkin's etchings portrayed a unique vision of unusual, often impossible, allegorical structures and cityscapes aimed at reviving people's fragmentary memories of Russia's rich classical legacy and once proud urban culture. Their project for a 'Museum of Contemporary Architectural Art' (1987), comprising an empty shell of a Pantheon-like dome flanked by interminable silhouettes of moribund skyscrapers, is emblematic of their strategy, as is 'Bridge Above the Precipice' (1987), with a chapel shaped like a glazed dome hovering above a limitless precipice. Underlying their fresh, witty designs was a biting critique of the toll exacted by the dehumanizing architecture prevalent in Soviet cities.

Avvakumov's architectural fantasies were conceived not as didactic alternatives to established Soviet architectural practice, but simply as intriguing options for enhancing contemporary architectural expression. His Perestroika Tower (1991), offering ironic commentary on the impending shift from a Soviet to a post-Soviet order, juxtaposed a reproduction of Tatlin's avant-garde tower with a replica, engulfed within it, of Mukhina's monumental sculpture, *Rabochii i krestianka* (*Worker and Peasant Woman*), an icon of Socialist Realism that had crowned Iofan's Soviet pavilion at the 1937 Exposition des Arts et Techniques dans la Vie Moderne in Paris.

Belov's dichotomous narrative of text and form resonates in his ironic conception of a 'Cocktail Museum' of Architecture (1988). His visionary project divided the museum into two discrete but connected parts comprising 'rational' and 'irrational' forms and spaces, respectively, to signify the radically contrasting poles of contemporary architecture. Observers were to be encouraged to examine the constructed physical embodiment of their preferred kind of architecture and to digest the 'cocktail' of its corresponding styles, fashions and genres, while implicitly comparing these manifestations to their 'opposite'.

The brilliant, short-lived successes of the postmodern Paper Architecture phenomenon on the world stage affirmed the enormously creative power of its proponents, while in the process reiterating the pervasive cultural and architectural malaise they were inherently powerless to overcome.

See also: architecture, Soviet and post-Soviet; Socialist Realism; Stagnation; Voznesenskii, Andrei

Further reading

Klotz, H. (ed.) (1990) *Paper Architecture: New Projects from the Soviet Union*, New York: Rizzoli.
Thomsen, C.W. (1994) *Visionary Architecture: From Babylon to Virtual Reality*, New York: Prestel.

ANATOLE SENKEVITCH

architecture, wooden

Wooden architecture illustrates how accomplished but anonymous Russian master builders achieved richly complex ends with simple means. They perfected basic forms and techniques that enabled them to develop an architecture distinguished by continuity, vertical accents, picturesque profiles, and rich decoration. Log houses or *izby* (singular: *izba*), constructed from a sturdy framework of interlocking axe-hewn logs; log churches; and assorted log buildings dotted the countryside for centuries and even today remain an integral part of the Russian landscape. In the late nineteenth century, members of the artists' colonies at Abramtsevo and Talashkino studied and drew inspiration from popular wood architecture and folk crafts, generating a reflective 'neo-Russian' style.

In the initial post-Revolutionary years, buildings were erected of wood chiefly to conserve exceedingly scarce resources. Architects exploited the opportunity to experiment freely in the construction of wooden structures. Ivan Zholtovskii's entrance gate at the All-Russian Agricultural and Craft Industry Exhibition (1923) in Moscow ingeniously reduced the solid mass of the classical triumphal arch to an openwork structure that exposed its skeletal timber construction. Konstantin Melnikov's first erected works were also wooden: the Makhorka Tobacco Pavilion at the same All-Russian Agricultural Exhibition, the New Sukharev market (1924) in Moscow, and the Soviet Pavilion (1924–25) at the Exposition Internationale des Arts Décoratifs et Industriels Modernes in Paris were all striking compositions that propelled Melnikov to the forefront of Russian avant-garde architecture.

In later Soviet times, however, successive regimes were embarrassed by the number of wooden religious and secular buildings still populating major Russian towns – particularly those open to foreign tourists. By the eve of the October Revolution, Arkhangelsk, the leading base of Russia's timber industry, boasted the world's largest ensemble of wooden architecture. Ivanovo-Voznesenk (now Ivanovo), the 'proletarian capital' of the fledgling Soviet state, likewise had many wooden structures, residential complexes, and modern workers' villages. Still, the capital cities of Moscow and Leningrad were particularly susceptible to demolition campaigns aimed at eradicating these unsightly wooden 'ideological embarrassments'.

The subsequent growth of the Soviet preservation movement and the foreign tourists' heightened interest in wooden architecture in the 1960s compelled Soviet authorities, desperate for hard currency, to feature wooden buildings in concentrated preserves called open-air museums. Inspired by the pioneering museum at Skansen, Sweden, these museums were created by moving an assortment of wooden structures, ranging from churches to peasant houses, cattle sheds, haylofts, storage rooms, and windmills from their original settings and re-assembling them on the museum site to simulate a generic village indigenous to a given area. Conceived as both educational sites and tourist attractions, open-air museums continue to be popular with Russian and foreign tourists alike.

Following the collapse of the USSR, some Russian architects rediscovered and began to exploit the expressive power of wooden buildings, exemplified by the striking contemporary work of architects Evgenii Asse and Totan Kuzembaev. Kuzembaev's series of houses and public facilities at the Kliazma Reservoir Resort display an exquisite mastery of material, form, and expressive spontaneity, overlaid with subtle evocations of Russian avant-garde designs.

See also: architecture, Soviet and post-Soviet; folk art; Golden Ring; izba; Russian Orthodox churches

Further reading

Opolovnikov, A. and Opolovnikova, Y. (1989) *Wooden Architecture of Russia: Houses, Fortifications, Churches*, New York: H. N. Abrams.
Proekt Rossiia [Project Russia], Issue 33 (2005).
Voronin, N.N. (1965) *Palaces and Churches of the Kremlin*, London: P. Hamlyn.
Voyce, A. (1954) *The Moscow Kremlin: Its History, Architecture, and Art Treasures*, Berkeley, CA: University of California Press.

ANATOLE SENKEVITCH

archives

After the October Revolution, a 1918 reform in the system of archives merged the holdings of liquidated ministries and organs of government into one state archival fund. The central archival department of the USSR, formed in 1929, oversaw national, republican, and local archives, and in 1938 transferred state archives to the NKVD. The centralized system of selection and storage of documents required that the most important ones be placed in the central state archives in Moscow and Leningrad, and less important ones in republic, regional, city, and district state depositories (subsequently to be destroyed). Each ministry and department had its own archive. In all archives, some documents were classified as secret and given out only with special permission. In 1960, the state archival department was placed under the direct command of the Soviet Council of Ministries. State archives housed documents to be permanently preserved, while city and district archives retained materials of lesser significance. A wide and heavily financed network of Communist Party archives preserved documents about revolutionary events and the Communist Party. Archives independent of state and Party included many holdings, which specialized in documents on foreign politics, on the Ministry of Defence, the KGB, and the USSR Academy of Science.

After the Soviet Union's collapse in 1991, the system of party archives was liquidated, their holdings transferred to state archives, with some previously classified documents made available. Replacing the main archival department, a Russian Committee on Archives (Roskomarkhiv) was formed, and reorganized in 2004 into the Federal Archival Agency (FAA) at the Ministry of Culture and Mass Communications of the Russian Federation. In 1992, documents of the Politburo of the CPSU Central Committee and similarly important state documents were transferred to the newly formed Russian President's Archive. Archives of the Russian President and of special and secret state services that collect and keep documents discourage access. Russia also has archives of religious organizations, private companies, banks, and other NGOs.

Russian archives *in toto* house about 460,000,000 items. Access to documents requires a letter from the researcher's institutional affiliation or a personal written application to the director of the relevant archive. The archival depository is organized into separate 'funds' or divisions (*fondy*), according to institution, organization, or individual. There are card catalogues (personal and systemic), indices and directories describing the contents of the *fond*. Major Federal Archives in Russia are located in Moscow and St. Petersburg, including the State Archive of the Russian Federation (GARF), the Russian State Archive of Ancient Acts (eleventh–nineteenth centuries) (RGADA), the Russian State Historical Archive (RGIA), the Russian State Military-Historical Archive (RGVIA), the Russian State Archive of Literature and Arts (RGALI), the Russian State Archive of Audio Documents (RGAFD), the

Russian State Archive of Film- and Photo-Documents (RGAKFD), and others.

See also: Academy of Sciences; Communist Party; Federal Security Service (FSS/FSB)

SERGEI TARKHOV

Argumenty i fakty

Nationally published tabloid

The newspaper was born in 1978 of official statistical surveys that by 1980 had become weekly pamphlets. With perestroika, *AiF* (as it is affectionately known) became a key source of previously censored information and by 1990 enjoyed circulation among 33.5 million readers. A decade later, that number had inevitably dropped, yet remained remarkably healthy at approximately 10 million. Keen to embrace stories both serious and light, the paper enjoys an extensive émigré readership and includes substantial regional inserts for subscribers in Moscow, St. Petersburg, Rostov, the Kuban region, and elsewhere.

DAVID MACFADYEN

Arkhipova, Irina Konstantinovna

b. 2 December 1925, Moscow

Opera singer

Mezzo-soprano Arkhipova initially trained as an architect while taking singing lessons. After her graduation from the Moscow Conservatory, she began her operatic career in Sverdlovsk, but in 1956 moved to the Bolshoi Theatre, where she débuted as Carmen. There, she took part in premières of operas by Khrennikov, Prokofiev and Shchedrin, as well as playing the Kostelnička in Janáček's *Jenůfa*. She has performed the more traditional Russian and Italian operatic repertoire in the Soviet Union and abroad, and her solo recitals typically including songs by Russian and Soviet composers.

See also: Bolshoi Theatre; Khrennikov, Tikhon; Moscow Conservatory; opera singers, Bolshoi Theatre; Prokofiev, Sergei; Shchedrin, Rodion

PHILIP ROSS BULLOCK

Armenia

The Republic of Armenia is located in Southwestern Transcaucasia, east of Turkey. Capital: Erevan. Population: 2,982,904 (2005), 97.9 per cent of whom are ethnic Armenians. Heirs to one of the oldest civilizations, Armenians formed a concentrated population, respected as artisans, scientists, and merchants. Despite periods of autonomy, over the centuries Armenia was subordinated by various empires, including the Roman, Byzantine, Arab, Persian, and Ottoman, in a bloody history of massacres, deportation, and tremendous suffering. The slaughter of 1.5 million Armenians by Ottoman Turks in 1915–22 led to emigration and the emergence of an Armenian diaspora in Syria, Greece, other European countries, and the United States. Modern Armenia owns only a part of its historical territory, and even its main symbol – Mount Ararat – is now on Turkish territory.

Incorporated into Russia in 1828 and into the USSR in 1920, Armenia gained its independence from the Soviet Union on 21 September 1991. Soviet Armenia developed a modern industrial sector, supplying manufactured goods to other Soviet republics in exchange for raw materials and energy. The ongoing conflict with Azerbaidzhan over the ethnic Armenian-dominated region of Nagorno-Karabakh and the break-up of the centrally directed economic system of the former Soviet Union contributed to its severe economic decline in the early 1990s. Armenia has few natural resources: the country is a food importer, and its mineral deposits (copper, gold, bauxite) are small. Armenia's severe trade imbalance has been offset somewhat by international aid and foreign investment. Economic ties with Russia remain close, especially in the energy sector. Ties to and support from the Armenian diaspora remain strong.

Armenia prides itself on being the first nation to adopt Christianity (in the early fourth century). Some 94 per cent of the population still belongs to the Armenian Apostolic Catholic Church. The Armenian language, whose alphabet was created in 406 AD, constitutes a separate branch of the Indo-European family. The Armenian Church still uses the ancient *Grabar* language, while modern Armenian, known as *Ashkharapar*, is spoken by 2.5 million in Armenia and by 1.2 million abroad. Armenian history and culture, including a literary tradition dating back over 1,500 years, had a great impact on such prominent Russian writers as Valerii Briusov, Sergei Gorodetskii, Andrei Belyi, Osip Mandelshtam, Vasilii Grossman, and Andrei Bitov.

Armenian cultural figures who have achieved international fame include landscape painter Martiros Sarian (1880–1972) and composer Aram Khachaturian (1903–78), who composed the ballets *Gaian* and *Spartak* (*Spartacus*), the 'Saber Dance', and incidental music to Lermontov's *Masquerade*.

See also: Bitov, Andrei; Khachaturian, Aram

Further reading

Hovannisian, R. (1978) *The Armenian Holocaust: A Bibliography Relating to the Deportations, Massacres and Dispersion of the Armenian People, 1915–1923*, Cambridge, MA: Armenian Heritage Press.

——— (1993) *Looking Toward Ararat: Armenia in Modern History*, Bloomington, IN: Indiana University Press.

Suny, R. (1983) *Armenia in the Twentieth Century*, Chico, CA: Scholars Press.

TATYANA LEDENEVA

Aroseva, Olga

(née Varvara Aleksandrovna Aroseva)

b. 21 December 1925, Moscow

Actress

Daughter of a Bolshevik functionary, writer, and diplomat (purged in 1937), Aroseva spent her early years in Prague. She began her professional life as an actress in the late 1940s in Nikolai Akimov's Theatre of Comedy in Leningrad. In the 1960s and 1970s, she became famous after

playing eccentric roles in Eldar Riazanov's films and in a popular TV comedy series, *Kabachok 13 stulev* (*Thirteen Chairs Café*). A leading actress at the Satire Theatre in Moscow, on her 70th birthday, Aroseva was awarded the Order of Honour by President Yeltsin and a silver-coated Buick by Boris Berezovskii.

See also: Akimov, Nikolai; Berezovskii, Boris; *Kabachok 13 stulev* (*Thirteen Chairs Café*); Riazanov, Eldar; Satire Theatre

ALEXANDER DOMRIN

art, abstract (abstraktnoe iskusstvo)

Abstract art is generally defined as a twentieth-century manifestation that rejects figural representation as the basis of art. Vasilii Kandinskii is customarily credited with creating the first completely abstract painting (1910), although abstraction had been developing in Europe, particularly France, since the 1870s.

Abstract art became significant in Russia shortly before the Revolution with the avant-garde movements Rayonism (particularly in the work of Mikhail Larionov and Natalia Goncharova), Suprematism (developed by Kazimir Malevich), and Constructivism (represented in the work of Vladimir Tatlin and others). After the Revolution, the state promoted avant-garde art partly as a rejection of what were considered bourgeois values inherent in traditional art. The primary goal was to create an art for the proletariat that would transform the viewer by radically changing the environment.

After the official declaration 'On the Reorganization of Literary and Artistic Organizations' in 1932, which ushered in Socialist Realism as the mandatory mode of artistic production, abstract art was forced underground. Creators of abstract works were labelled 'formalists' – dedicated merely to aesthetics and not to approved socialist content.

Abstract art officially reappeared only during the Thaw. In 1959, the Moscow 'Exhibition of American Painting and Sculpture' introduced many Soviet artists to major Western schools such as Abstract Expressionism. Other exhibitions of modern Western art followed, and selected works by early Soviet avant-gardists were reintroduced for artists' study. The influx of information about Western and Russian abstract art continued until the infamous 'Thirty Years of Moscow Art' exhibition in 1962, during which Khrushchev denounced Ernst Neizvestnyi and other young abstract artists. By then, however, Russian artists had gained some international attention and continued to push back the boundaries of official art.

During the Stagnation era, Soviet art institutions cautiously allowed the publication of some books on movements such as Cubism. A few official exhibitions also showed abstract art. Artists working in abstract styles gained limited official recognition, especially after the 1974 Bulldozer Exhibition. In addition, artists increasingly gained public attention, for the authorities generally overlooked small unofficial shows in apartments and clubs.

Nonconformist artists produced abstract art for various reasons, including self-expression, spirituality, and opposition to Socialist Realism. Their styles are likewise varied: Lidiia Masterkova produces rhythmic combinations of colour and line; Elii Beliutin's and Valerii Volkov's works recall New York Action Painting of the 1950s; Francisco Infante concentrates on the rotations of geometric objects, colour, and light through space.

See also: Apt-Art; Beliutin, Elii; Bulldozer Exhibition; Infante, Francisco; Masterkova, Lidiia; Neizvestnyi, Ernst

Further reading

Barabanov, Y. (1998) 'Art in the Delta of Alternative Culture', in *Forbidden Art: The Postwar Russian Avant-Garde*, New York: Distributed Art Publishers.
Kornetchuk, E. (1990) 'Soviet Art and the State', in J. Bowlt, E. Kornetchuk, and N. Roberts (eds) *The Quest for Self-Expression*, Columbus, OH: Columbus Museum of Art.
Moszynska, A. (1990) *Abstract Art*, London: Thames and Hudson.
Tuchman, M., Freeman, J. and Blotkamp, C. (1996) *The Spiritual in Art: Abstract Painting 1890–1985*, New York: Abbeville Press.

KRISTEN M. HARKNESS

art galleries and exhibition halls
Moscow

A small number of galleries opened in modest facilities in Moscow during the late 1980s, when artists still exhibited in their cramped studios. With the opening of the First Gallery (1989), the first private gallery in Moscow dealing exclusively with contemporary art, artists discovered a home venue. During its short-lived existence, the gallery, founded by Aidan Salakhova with Aleksandr Iakut and Evgenii Mittoi, arranged a number of exhibitions of famous artists (Ilia Kabakov, Eric Bulatov, Ivan Chuikov) and conducted projects with the renowned artists Francesco Clemente and Robert Rauschenberg. Following the collapse of the USSR, Salakhova opened the Aidan Gallery, which continued her interest in conceptual and New Russian Classicist art, inspired by the Neo-academist St. Petersburg artist Timur Novikov.

The Marat Guelman (Gelman) Gallery, one of Moscow's first and most influential galleries, began to work with young and starting artists who have since developed into leading participants in the Moscow art scene and represent Russia at the largest world forums of contemporary art. Guelman acquired enormous clout through active collaboration with foreign as well as Moscow and St. Petersburg galleries. He continues to curate major, provocative exhibitions and participate in numerous leading events. The Regina Gallery, founded during perestroika, was one of the first to deal with the then-discredited art of Socialist Realism and the first to master the art of publicity and provocation. Famous for its shocking performances, the gallery showcased the installation artist Oleg Kulik milking a dog and had gynaecological texts read in detail to the audience. The XL Gallery, founded in 1993 by Elena Selina, promotes Conceptual and post-Conceptual art, but basically projects itself as a 'homeopathic remedy' enabling the art organism to heal itself. From its inception, the gallery has mounted frequent exhibitions of cutting-edge works of contemporary art, and its exhibition catalogues read like ongoing conversations with friends and family, chronicling the conflicts, rivalries, and controversies in Moscow's contemporary art world. The gallery's pioneering *XL Forum*, an online chat room on the gallery's ground-breaking web page, maintains similarly open discussions of varied art topics.

These galleries initially sold to a handful of Western collectors, but subsequently to local private buyers and corporate collections, a radically new but flourishing breed in Russia. Large banks and firms began developing their corporate collections in the 1990s: Inkombank bought contemporary Russian Conceptualist and avant-garde art; Stolichnyi Bank collected antique glass, Western European painting from the sixteenth–nineteenth centuries and eighteenth–twentieth-century Russian art; Markon acquired Soviet art from the 1950s until the 1970s. Corporate collectors turned to Moscow galleries for Western as well as Russian art, displayed in their offices to impress Western visitors. In 1993, Aidan Salakhova sold four prints by Andy Warhol to a corporate collector, a purchase attracting enormous media attention in Russia.

The financial crisis of 1998 precipitated a major setback in the art market and the virtual collapse of the country's funding support for art. The Soros Centre for Contemporary Art, which previously had financed a significant number of art projects in Russia, proved largely unresponsive this time around, closing down in 2000. In the first years of the twenty-first century, however, the market began to develop virtually anew, its economic boom driven by the high concentration of billionaires in Moscow. Russia's new rich wanted to acquire authentic art for their offices and homes. Having already spent millions building collections of art and antiques mainly from the nineteenth and twentieth centuries, they now are moving into contemporary art.

To meet the growing demand, in the past few years, several world-class galleries have opened in and near Moscow, housed in chic contemporary facilities with the latest technical amenities that compare favourably with those in Chelsea, London, and Paris. The RuArts Gallery, in a new, elegant building in the historic Ostozhenka district of old Moscow near the Pushkin Fine Arts Museum, promotes the work of young Russian artists, especially those experimenting with new media. Its owner is Marianna Sardarova, the wife of a businessman with interests in natural gas, who has a sizeable personal collection of contemporary and Soviet-era non-conformist art.

The Stella Art Gallery, named after its Russian owner, Stella Kay, opened in 2003, investing enormous resources in the business and surrounding herself with leading experts in contemporary Russian and Western art. The Gallery aims to serve as a gateway for bringing works of international masters to Russia while simultaneously enhancing the image of Russian contemporary artists abroad. It has two exhibition halls: one exhibits international contemporary art; the other represents projects by recognized and beginning Russian artists. Stella Art Gallery recently signed an exclusive contract with the Robert Mapplethorpe Foundation for the sale of the late artist's works in Russia and brokered the sale of three Kabakov works for a tidy sum.

Gary Tatintsian, an accomplished art dealer who owns a gallery in New York, recently opened his Gary Tatintsian Gallery on Ilinka Street near Red Square. Drawn by the growing interest of Russia's private and corporate collectors in contemporary Western art, Tatintsian is continuing his practice of presenting young, cutting-edge Western artists working in diverse media. His inaugural exhibition featured eight contemporary artists (including Tony Matelli, Peter Halley, and Tony Ausler) whose works reflect the new, multifaceted landscape of contemporary visual culture. The lower gallery is used by gallery director Marina Loschak for exhibitions that continue a project she had initiated as director of the celebrated but now-closed Moscow Art Centre.

Another recent addition to the Moscow gallery scene is Our Artists (*Nashi Khudozhniki*) Gallery, owned by Natalia Kurnikova and housed in a striking new building located in the village of Borki, an oasis of New Russian inhabitants in the Rublev region outside Moscow. An authority on Russian émigré artists in Paris, Kurnikova had acquired ten years of gallery experience and had organized two exhibitions at the Tretiakov Gallery before opening her gallery in 2005 with personal capital. Her gallery specializes in the work of early and mid-twentieth-century Russian émigré artists, supplemented by artists in Kurnikova's personal collection, ranging from

Petr Konchalovskii, Robert Falk, and Ilia Mashkov to the Sixties Group.

Apart from private commercial galleries, another significant venue is the network of non-profit and artist-run initiatives that surfaced in the 1990s and continue to create and promote original work by cutting-edge artists. The non-profit-making TV Gallery promotes time-based video art, produces cultural programming about art for television, and maintains a lively pro-gramme of exhibitions, media production, single-channel and video installations. The Spider & Mouse Gallery, founded by Igor Ioganson (spider) and Marina Perchikhina (mouse), has a strong identity as a video gallery but also presents mixed media projects, reflect-ing the curators' support of fresh, innovative work both in Russia and internationally. The Escape Gallery, created in reaction to the growing dominance of a narrow circle of gallerists, curators, and critics, aims to disrupt the artistic status quo and to help artists experi-ment, present, and promote their work. These 'off-beat' galleries play an important role in facilitating and assuring the development of a robust, multifaceted contemporary art in Russia.

Another fresh venue in the Moscow art scene is the ARTStrelka Arts Centre, which opened in October 2004 in the complex of former garages of the Red October chocolate factory. Con-ceived by curators Olga Lopukhova and Vladi-mir Dubosarskii as an upbeat combination of art fair and art market, this complex attempts to forge a viable partnership between Moscow's contemporary artists and the new Russian busi-ness community. The ARTStrelka complex includes ten galleries, studios, and offices housed in the former factory garages: the XL Gallery, the Club of Collectors Gallery, the Viktor Freidenberg Design Studio, the Liza Plavinskii Gallery, the James Gallery, the Reflex Photo-graphy Gallery, the Art Business Consulting office and gallery, the David Ter-Oganian Showcase Gallery, the Electroboutique View Station and Gallery, and Lopukhova's ART-Strelka Projects Gallery. The complex, which also has become a lively centre of bohemian art life in Moscow, has attracted thousands of visitors and prospective buyers to its ongoing exhibitions and art fairs. In seeking to develop an active centre for various contemporary arts

by rehabilitating a former industrial site near the Kremlin and connected by a footbridge to the nearby site of the Cathedral of Christ the Saviour, the complex's founders have followed an important European model for the cultural revitalization of urban space. However, the centre may yet be swept away by Mayor Iurii Luzhkov's plans for redeveloping this area into an exclusive multi-use complex of hotels, luxury housing, offices, restaurants, and designer boutiques.

Although exhibition halls of varying scope and size exist in most Russian towns, the major facilities are concentrated in Moscow and St. Petersburg. The most prominent and esteemed exhibition hall in Moscow is the Manège (*Manezh*) Gallery, known officially as the Central Exhibition Hall (*Tsentralnyi vystavochnyi zal*), erected in 1817 as the Royal Cavalry Riding School by the engineer Augustin Béthencourt and the architect Osip Bove. Its steady stream of expositions is devoted to art, architecture, photos, and computer technologies. Moscow's Photo-biennale also takes place at the Manège, as does the annual Art-Manège exhibition of art gallery collections.

The main centre for major public art exhibi-tions in Moscow is the Central House of Artists (*Tsentralnyi dom khudozhnikov*, 1979), one of Rus-sia's largest exhibition halls, in a building on the Crimean Embankment (*Krymskii val*) that it shares with the New Tretiakov Gallery. The facility was designed to accommodate sizable art exhibitions with large canvasses and public functions in seven exhibition halls. Commercial galleries, subsequently added, mount their own shows. The Art Moscow art fair, which high-lights current directions in contemporary art in Russia, takes place here.

The New Manège, an exhibition hall that opened in 1996, is located not far from the ori-ginal Manège. It hosts significant temporary exhibitions of contemporary art along with con-certs, auctions, symposiums, press conferences and other art-related events.

St. Petersburg

Unlike Moscow, Russia's second capital has few world-class private galleries and no active, viable art market due to insufficient capital flow. St. Petersburg's enduring legacy as an imperial *Gesamtkunstwerk* appears inimical to the creation of a vigorous money-driven art market. However, keen, informed, and creative entrepreneurship is transforming the once-imperial museum enterprise competitive in today's global art market. The Russian Museum (*Russkii muzei*), the only established, published institution in Russia actively collecting contemporary Russian art, is developing both a market and an audience for contemporary art in St. Petersburg by dedicating several rooms in its Benois Wing to changing exhibitions of both Russian and foreign contemporary projects.

St. Petersburg's leading art galleries include Gallery D-137, the Marina Gisich Gallery, and the NoMI Gallery, all owned by women determined to establish a viable contemporary art market in the northern capital. Gallery D-137 on Nevskii prospect (Neva Avenue), founded in 1996 by Olga Kudriavtseva, deals with graphic art, painting, sculpture, and photography by contemporary Russian and foreign artists. The gallery also promotes New Russian Classicism, the Neo-academist tendency associated with St. Petersburg artist Timur Novikov. The Marina Gisich Gallery, founded in 2001, emphasizes Conceptual contemporary art, represents some of Russia's leading contemporary artists, such as Oleg Bogomolov and Georgii Gurianov, and promotes robust art criticism. The NoMI Gallery, which opened in 2001 in the building of its sponsor, the journal *New World of Art – NoMI* (*Novyi mir iskusstva*-NoMI), is owned by Vera Bibinova, the journal's editor. It promotes promising young contemporary artists not only from St. Petersburg and Moscow, but also from the Baltic states.

Although there are several exhibition halls of varying scope in St. Petersburg, the most important and prominent is also a former cavalry riding school (1805–7), designed by the architect Giacomo Quarenghi and called the Manège Central Exhibition Hall (*Tsentralnyi vystavochnyi zal 'Manezh'*). Having functioned as an exhibition hall only since the 1970s but predating its Moscow counterpart by only a few years, Quarenghi's facility hosts leading art and architectural exhibitions and events, and is the centre of art and cultural life in St. Petersburg.

See also: art museums; art, post-Soviet; art, Soviet; Baltic Sea region; Cathedral of Christ the Saviour; Conceptualism, art; Kabakov, Ilia; Kulik, Oleg; Moscow; New Russians; Novikov, Timur; oligarkh; Red Square; Russian Museum; St. Petersburg

Further reading

Moscow: Treasures and Traditions, exhib. cat. 1990 (Washington, DC: Smithsonian Institution Traveling Exhibition Service in association with University of Washington Press, c.1990).

Nikonova, I. I. (ed.) (1989) *The State Tretyakov Gallery: Its History and Collections*, Leningrad: Aurora Art Publishers.

Norman, G. (1998)*The Hermitage: The Biography of a Great Museum*. New York: Fromm International.

Piotrovsky, M.B. and Neverov, O.O. (1997) *Hermitage: Essays on the History of the Collection*, trans. L.N. Lezhneva, St. Petersburg: Slavia Art Books.

Prilutskaya, T. (1992) *Pushkin Museum of Fine Arts, Painting*, trans. A. Bloch and L. Tomasson, St. Petersburg: Aurora.

Proekt Rossiia [*Project Russia*], Issue 36 (2005).

The State Russian Museum: From the Icon to Modernism; trans. K. MacInnes, Bad Breisig: Palace Editions, 2005.

ANATOLE SENKEVITCH

art, informal

Russian non-professional art has a complex history; its practitioners have included serfs who were master artists and nobles who were amateurs. This complexity was compounded in the Soviet era by the suppression of non-official art forms. In the post-Stalin era, a loosening and degeneration of Socialist Realist doctrines allowed a 'flourishing of naïve art' from the 1960s to the 1980s (Bogemskaia 1999: 391). The official mass institutions of amateur art (*samodeiatelnost*) began to tolerate instances of self-taught art (previously disparaged as *liubitelstvo*), such as the works of peasant-philosopher Ivan Selivanov. This took place in the context of an interest in all forms of 'primitive' art, harking back to the early avant-garde (especially Kandinskii, Goncharova, and Larionov), which invigorated the emerging non-conformist underground. The interests of the intelligentsia extended well beyond folk art and naïve art, to illegal spheres such as the ex-convict Efrosiniia Kersonovska's graphic depiction of the GULag. However, it was only in the post-Soviet era that the concepts of *Art Brut*, *Neuve Invention*, and *Outsider Art* (*Iskusstvo postoronnikh*) gained currency, legitimizing the study of a wide range of creative works – from the elaborate codes of Russian prison tattoos to the spiritualism of hermit-artists or the private iconographies of those with a 'non-standard psyche'. Although more willingly accepted internationally than in Russia, the most widely recognized such 'outsiders' include Aleksandr Lobanov, Roza Zharkikh, Pavel Leonov, and Vasilii Romankov. With the formation of new institutions such as the Moscow Museum of Outsider Art (1996), the spectrum has further widened in recent years, fostering public recognition of 'environments' such as the eccentric fairy-tale sculptural ensembles of Aleksei Rudov near Laduga, or lift-engineer Gennadii Prokoshin's folk-surrealist children's playground in Moscow.

See also: amateur cultural activity; art, non-conformist; folk art; GULag; Socialist Realism

Reference and further reading

Bogemskaia, K.G. *et al.* (1999) in *Samodeiatelnoe khudozhestvennoe tvorchestvo v SSSR. Ocherk istorii: konets 1950-kh – nachalo 1990-kh godov*, St. Petersburg, Omitrii Bulanin.
—— (2001) *Poniat primitiv*, St. Petersburg.

IVOR STODOLSKY

art market

After decades of stifling oppression, a vibrant contemporary art scene has emerged in the New Russia, thanks to a booming economy, the establishment of commercial galleries, the formation of contemporary art centres, and participation by Russian artists in international art exhibitions such as the Venice Biennale and the first Moscow Biennale of Contemporary Art, which opened in January 2005. As the capital of the Russian Federation and thus the country's centre of political, economic, and cultural power, Moscow is the most fertile – indeed, currently the only – Russian city capable of supporting a thriving art market.

Prior to the late nineteenth century, art collecting in Russia was a privilege principally confined to emperors, their entourage, and wealthy noble families. The great reforms following the abolition of serfdom in 1861 that gave rise to the country's rapid industrialization also engendered a new breed of entrepreneurs who, having aspired to become art collectors, were poised to rouse the public with their taste for the new and the unconventional.

The rising importance of urban mercantile patronage during that period placed Moscow at the forefront of such artistic patronage. The textile magnate Pavel Tretiakov amassed a collection of Russian art that would shortly form the nucleus of the Tretiakov Gallery. Other important entrepreneurs, including Tretiakov's brother Sergei, specialized in collecting Western art. Moscow merchants Sergei Shchukin and Ivan Morozov similarly assembled celebrated collections of Impressionist and Post-Impressionist art. In St. Petersburg, smaller but important collections belonged to Aleksei Musin-Pushkin, the Vorontsov-Dashkovs, and others.

After the Revolution, private art collections were nationalized and their holdings apportioned among the country's major museums, particularly the Hermitage, the Russian Museum, and the Tretiakov Gallery. Collecting *per se* was banned, though several collections were later brought to light: Pavel Korin's collection of icons, Ilia Zilberstein's collection of Russian and Western European realist paintings, and especially George Costakis's splendid collection of Russian avant-garde art, which played a decisive role in the rediscovery and recognition of many avant-garde artists.

Although throughout the 1920s groups of artists working in various styles and pursuing different modes of expression were active in the Soviet Union, by the early 1930s, the increasingly authoritarian Stalinist regime had curtailed freedom of artistic expression. The official art mandated by the doctrine of Socialist Realism, which supplanted modernism with a representational art realist in style and Socialist in content, was regulated by the Union of Soviet Artists. Dictating accepted art practices, it controlled all state galleries, and monopolized what then passed for an art market. Stalin's death in 1953 and the ensuing Thaw paved the way for a tentative liberalization in the arts. Artists began to experiment with the basic parameters of Socialist Realism, and the more permissive atmosphere yielded an 'unofficial' art encompassing diverse styles, including abstractionism and postmodernism. Official tolerance of 'unofficial' art by succeeding Soviet regimes vacillated until the waning days of the USSR. Liberalization suffered a blow in December 1962, when Khrushchev rejected the abstract art by Ernst Neizvestnyi and Vladimir Iankilevskii in an exhibition at the Manège Exhibition Hall in Moscow. The crowning confrontation occurred at the Bulldozer Exhibition (1974), the outdoor display of unofficial art held in Izmailov Park on the outskirts of Moscow, which drove unofficial art and artists further underground.

The unofficial art movement in the Soviet Union was thus forged by the enforced absence of an art market. Its members produced artworks and showed them to each other, in their apartments and studios, and were little concerned about an audience. When Mikhail Gorbachev first came to power, the Moscow art world was still populated by heirs of the ill-fated Bulldozer Exhibition. Nevertheless, perestroika sparked an international boom in contemporary Russian art, stirred by Sotheby's landmark 1988 auction in Moscow, which fetched sensational prices for twentieth-century Russian art and made instant celebrities of many modern and contemporary artists. Soviet artists not only could finally exhibit and sell their work in the West, but also could create with a Western audience in mind: if their work was to go to Western museums, it had to speak in an international language. With the ensuing collapse of the Soviet Union, the new market economy enabled the development of a gallery system. Artists now could create work according to their own taste and the tastes of their private patrons.

Government funding for art virtually collapsed in the meantime, and the funding programmes at the Soros Centre for Contemporary Art established by the financier George Soros took up the slack, financing up to 50 per cent of the actual realized art projects in Russia; 'unofficial' art thus could survive and flourish, though opening a gallery in privately rented space was prohibitively expensive.

See also: art, post-Soviet; art, Soviet; art galleries and exhibition halls; art museums; Bulldozer Exhibition; economic system, post-Soviet; Gorbachev, Mikhail; Iankilevskii, Vladimir; Krushchev, Nikita; Manezh exhibition of 1962; Neizvestnyi, Ernst; perestroika and glasnost; Russian Museum; Socialist Realism; Stalin, Iosif; Thaw; Tretiakov Gallery

ANATOLE SENKEVITCH

art museums

Moscow and St. Petersburg boast some of the greatest museums in the world. St. Petersburg's Hermitage, the product of a sustained imperial project, is a preeminent art museum; the Russian Museum, born of the royal family's attempts to counter the intrusive cosmopolitanism of the capital's emerging bourgeois culture, has one of the largest, most comprehensive holdings in Russian art. In contrast, Moscow's museums were the result of municipal rather than imperial initiatives: the Tretiakov Gallery's incomparable original collection of early Russian art was a gift to the city of Moscow, while the Pushkin Fine Arts Museum began as an art museum at Moscow University.

The first modern museum of art to emerge in Russia, the Hermitage was founded in 1764 by Catherine the Great, whose indefatigable activities as an art collector account for the phenomenal collection of paintings that formed its nucleus. When the Hermitage opened to the public in 1852, it contained only the imperial collections. It now houses more than 40,000 drawings, 500,000 engravings, and 8,000 paintings of the Flemish, French, Dutch, Spanish, and Italian Schools, including many by Rembrandt, Rubens, Picasso, and Matisse, which represent only a fraction of the museum's riches. The collections include the art of India,

China, Egypt, pre-Columbian America, Greece, and Rome, as well as Scythian art from the Eurasian steppe.

The Hermitage occupies five magnificent buildings erected especially for the Russian royal family's ever-increasing art gallery along the Neva River Embankment in the very centre of St. Petersburg: the Winter Palace (*Zimnii dvorets*), the Small Hermitage (*Malyi Ermitazh*), the Large Hermitage (*Bolshoi Ermitazh*), the New Hermitage (*Novyi Ermitazh*), and the Hermitage Theatre (*Teatr Ermitazha*). The Baroque Winter Palace (1754–62), the official residence of Russian emperors, designed by architect Bartolomeo Rastrelli, is the centrepiece of the Hermitage ensemble. The Small Hermitage (1764–66), the long, narrow structure standing next to the Winter Palace, was added by Jean-Baptiste Vallin de la Mothe and Iurii Velten as Catherine's private residence when she assumed the throne. As her art collection grew, Catherine commissioned Velten to design the Great Hermitage (1774) to consolidate her vast art holdings, and Giacomo Quarenghi to design the Hermitage Theatre (1783–87), connected to the Great Hermitage by an arched elevated gallery over the Winter Canal. Nicholas I, confronted with the need to house the ever-growing Hermitage art collection, commissioned German architect Leo von Klenze to build the New Hermitage (1842–51). Opened in 1852, it was Russia's first public museum, though initially admission was by royal invitation only. After the October Revolution (1917), the Hermitage became a public museum, its treasures open to the general public.

Reforms sparked by the abolition of serfdom (1861) bred a museum movement that resulted in the establishment of Russia's great public museums in St. Petersburg and Moscow, and important regional museums in major provincial and district centres such as Kazan, Nizhnii Novgorod, Iaroslavl, Penza, Viatka, Ufa, Simbirsk, Kaluga, Serpukhov, and Perm. Based on private gifts and miscellaneous de-accessioned items conveyed by the Hermitage and the Academy of Fine Arts in St. Petersburg, these regional museums housed significant art works, but lacked clear areas of specialization. Some included ethnographic material and were combined with museums of local history.

The Russian Museum (*Russkii muzei*), originally called the Russian Museum of Emperor Alexander III, in honour of the late emperor's efforts to promote the creation of a national museum of Russian art in St. Petersburg, opened its doors to the public in 1898 as the county's first state museum of Russian fine art. Its original collection encompassed paintings donated by the Hermitage, the Academy of Fine Arts, and the various royal palaces surrounding St. Petersburg. The Michael Palace (*Mikhailovskii dvorets*, 1819–25), built by architect Carlo Rossi for Grand Duke Michael, was the museum's main building and the country's showcase of Russian art. As additional works were donated after 1898, a large wing was added in 1914–16, later named the Benois Wing after Russian artist Alexandre Benois, to accommodate the museum's growing collection.

Today the collection of the Russian Museum numbers some 400,000 works and covers the entire history of Russia's fine arts, from the tenth century to the present day. It reflects virtually every form and genre of art in Russia, including a unique collection of Old Russian icons, paintings, graphic art and sculpture, decorative and applied art, folk art and numismatics, as well as the world's finest collection of Russian avant-garde art. The Benois Wing houses the Museum's unique collection of twentieth-century and contemporary Russian art.

In 1992, Russian President Boris Yeltsin signed a decree declaring the Russian Museum an invaluable component of the nation's cultural heritage, an act that paved the way for the museum's subsequent acquisition of three additional properties in the historic core of the city: the Stroganov Palace (*Stroganovskii dvorets*, 1853), designed by architect Bartolomeo Rastrelli; the Marble Palace (*Mramornyi dvorets*, 1768–85), designed by architect Antonio Rinaldi; and the St. Michael's (Engineering) Castle (*Mikhailovskii [inzhenernyi] zamok*, 1797–1800), designed by architects Vincenzo Brenna and Vasilii Bazhenov. Restoration work is under way at all these facilities, but it is far enough along to permit each one to begin mounting exhibitions with materials and artifacts from the Museum's collections.

The turn of the twentieth century brought two major museums to Moscow: the Tretiakov

Gallery (*Tretiakovskaia galereia*) and the Museum of Fine Arts (*Muzei izobrazitelnykh iskusstv*). The Tretiakov Gallery opened its doors in 1906 on a site not far from the Kremlin. Regarded today as *the* national treasury of Russian art, the Gallery's collection consists entirely of Russian works and artists crucial to the history of Russian art. The gallery was named after entrepreneur and textile manufacturer Pavel Tretiakov, who in 1892 donated to the city of Moscow approximately 2,000 works of Russian art from his private collection, his own house, and the surrounding buildings in which he had displayed his collection. These buildings were incorporated into the gallery's initial structure, featuring a neo-Russian façade designed by Viktor Vasnetsov. Between 1981 and 1997, the gallery was expanded into its current extended complex, of which Vasnetsov's signature façade remains the crowning feature. The complex includes the Church of St. Nicholas at Tolmachi, a landmark of Muscovite architecture, housing a collection of icons that include the twelfth-century Icon of the Virgin of Vladimir.

In the mid-twentieth century, the works of Soviet art that the Tretiakov Gallery (now renamed the New Tretiakov Gallery) had collected since the 1920s were moved into new facilities on the Crimean Bank (*Krymsky val*), to a huge building shared with the Central House of Artists (*Tsentralnyi dom khudozhnika*), one of the largest exhibition halls in Russia. The New Tretiakov opened in 1979. Its unrivalled Soviet-era collection ranges from paintings by world-famous Russian avant-garde artists of the early 1920s to art works embodying the official style of Socialist Realism, promulgated by the Stalinist regime from the 1930 until the 1950s, and the underground art of the Second Wave of the 1960 until the 1980s. The adjacent sculpture park, originally conceived of as a Graveyard to Fallen Monuments of the Soviet era (including statues of Stalin and Feliks Dzerzhinskii), now is largely devoted to sculptural works by contemporary Russian artists

The Pushkin Museum of Fine Arts, Russia's second largest collection of Western European art after the Hermitage, opened in 1912 as the Alexander III Fine Arts Museum. It was founded by Ivan Tsvetaev, father of Russian poet Marina Tsvetaeva and a Professor of Art History at Moscow University, where the museum had originated as the Museum of Fine Arts and Antiquities. The museum's building (1898–1912), designed by Moscow architect Roman Klein, was financed by public subscription and a generous donation from wealthy benefactor, Iurii Nechaev-Maltsev. Famous for its collections of Impressionist and post-Impressionist paintings, it also houses works by old masters, including Rubens, Rembrandt, and Botticelli, and examples of Egyptian and Hellenistic art and Roman antiquities.

During the Soviet period, museums were turned into public institutions supported by the state and open to the general public. They came under centralized control and private collections were nationalized. Once Moscow became the Soviet capital in 1918, the status of the Pushkin Museum and the Tretiakov Gallery notably improved, while that of the Hermitage and the Russian Museum declined. The Alexander III Fine Arts Museum, initially renamed the Museum of Fine Arts, then finally, the Pushkin State Museum of Fine Arts (*Gosudarstvennyi muzei izobrazitelnykh iskusstv imeni A. S. Pushkina*) in 1937, was the beneficiary of thousands of paintings expropriated from the Hermitage and confiscated from private collections. In 1924, it established a special department of sculpture, to accommodate the transfer of sculpture collections from the Rumiantsev Museum and the museum of the former Stroganov Art School. Similarly, the nationalized Tretiakov Gallery gained increasing stature and support as the country's leading museum of Russian art, acquiring nationalized collections from the Rumiantsev Museum, the Tsvetkov Gallery, the Ostroukhov Museum of Icons and Paintings, and several private collections from surrounding estates of the former nobility.

In contrast, the Hermitage experienced a number of de-accessions, especially between 1928 and 1933, when the Soviet government sold off some 2,880 major paintings from its collection to raise much-needed hard currency. Many were sold to 'friends of the Soviet Union' at cut-rate prices. The greatest beneficiary of this clandestine effort was US Secretary of the Treasury, Andrew Mellon, who then conveyed 21 paintings acquired from the Hermitage to the National Gallery of Art in Washington, DC.

In 1948, the Shchukin and Morozov pre-Revolutionary collections of French Impressionist and post-Impressionist paintings, which had been expropriated in 1928 to form the Museum of Modern Western Art, were divided up between the Pushkin Museum and the Hermitage. The Pushkin also received additional paintings from the former Rumiantsev Museum.

During détente, the Pushkin Fine Arts Museum acquired its international reputation, propelled by initiatives of the Soviet regime. It proved the logical site for a series of newsmaking blockbuster exhibits, including the immensely popular 'Moscow-Paris' and the 'Moscow-Berlin' shows.

Following the collapse of the Soviet Union in 1991, museums found themselves in dire financial straits. Economic disarray and massive reduction in governmental support forced them to seek funding from alternative sources abroad and face the need for marketing and fund-raising expertise. The Pushkin, the Tretiakov, and the Russian Museum have been able to establish beneficial affiliations with New Russian financiers and foreign investors. Mikhail Piotrovskii, the Hermitage's entrepreneurial director since 1992, has been able to trade on the incomparable calibre of the Hermitage's holdings and its international acclaim to launch several ambitious projects that are transforming the Hermitage into an innovative global force envied by its international peers.

The Hermitage's $2 million joint venture with IBM, which began in late 1997, has made it one of the best-computerized cultural institutions in the world. IBM has given the museum an award-winning web site and digital library, and has created a computer information centre for visitors to the museum. The path-breaking Education and Technology Centre is also a significant part of the Hermitage/IBM alliance.

In June 2000, the Hermitage Museum signed a long-term cooperation agreement with the Solomon R. Guggenheim Foundation, which aims to make each museum's respective collections accessible to broader audiences through an array of joint ventures. Its centrepiece is the Guggenheim's partnership in the $100 million transformation of the east wing of the General Staff Building, facing the Winter Palace across Palace Square, into an effective museum space.

The transformed building will house the Hermitage's collection of Impressionist and post-Impressionist paintings, together with loans of twentieth- and twenty-first-century art from the Guggenheim Museum in New York and other private and public institutions.

Inspired by the Guggenheim Foundation's global expansion project, Piotrovskii also instituted a bold programme of 'cultural expansion' aimed at opening branches abroad to facilitate the Hermitage's fuller integration into the global cultural scene. These branches include the Hermitage Rooms in London's prestigious Somerset House, featuring selections from Catherine the Great's collection; Las Vegas's Guggenheim-Hermitage Museum, designed by Dutch architect Rem Koolhaas in the Venetian Resort Hotel Casino and conceived to appeal to a different kind of audience; and the latest branch, the Hermitage Amsterdam Museum, located in a historic building on the banks of the Amstel River, which displays exhibitions of works selected from the Hermitage.

Two new museums appeared in Moscow during the 1990s: the Museum of Private Collections (*Muzei chastnykh kollektsii*) opened in 1994 as part of the Pushkin Museum of Fine Arts in Moscow. The brainchild of Realist painter Ilia Zilverstein, who in 1985 bequeathed his extensive collection to the future museum, it now holds more than twenty collections, including Sergei Solovev's collection of graphic art, Evgenii Stepanov's collection of animalistic sculpture, and Lidiia Delektorskaia's collection of paintings and graphic art by Henri Matisse.

The Museum of Contemporary Art (*Muzei sovremennogo iskusstva*, 1999) was established by Zurab Tsereteli, the controversial Moscow sculptor and president of the Russian Academy of Arts, whose private collection supplied the core of the Museum's holdings. The Museum, the first in Russia devoted exclusively to contemporary art, is housed in the Gubin Manion, designed by Moscow architect, Matvei Kazakov. The Museum's focus is the development of its collections of early twentieth-century European and Russian avant-garde art.

The phenomenal recent changes in the dynamic worlds of art galleries and museums, wrought by an infusion of New Russian and foreign capital, have shaken the art worlds of

Moscow and St. Petersburg out of their Soviet-era complacency and launched them on a contemporary trajectory that stands to propel them toward the cutting edge of twenty-first-century global artistic development.

See also: art, post-Soviet; art, Soviet; art galleries and exhibition halls; Hermitage; Moscow; Moscow State University; Nizhni Novgorod (Gorkii); Russian Museum; St. Petersburg; Socialist Realism; Solovev, Sergei; Stalin, Iosif; Tretiakov Gallery; Tsereteli, Zurab; Urals; Volga region; Yeltsin, Boris

ANATOLE SENKEVITCH

art, nonconformist

Nonconformist art emerged in the USSR during the Thaw, when Russian artists became acquainted with the early Soviet avant-garde and such twentieth-century Western styles as Surrealism and Abstract Expressionism. This material inspired many artists to explore new modes of art production. The limited freedom of the Thaw ended in 1962 with the notorious 'Thirty Years of Moscow Art' exhibition, at which Khrushchev denounced the 'new' art and its creators. After this explosive confrontation, any artists deviating from the tenets of Socialist Realism were driven underground.

Labelling artists as nonconformist is problematic, for many who rejected Socialist Realism did not work in explicitly avant-garde styles. Moreover, many so-called nonconformists had official positions as illustrators or graphic designers. Less to do with style than with attitudes toward the function of art, Soviet nonconformist art supported free self-expression, multiple interpretations, and diversity of media in art – precisely what Socialist Realism rejected. During Stagnation, many nonconformist artists passionately committed to the value of 'authentic' art adopted the avant-garde narrative of the artist-genius who passes moral judgment on all things official, even if their own art did not differ substantially from a social, if not Socialist, realism.

Nonconformist art was diverse in its style and philosophy. In the 1960s, its representatives gravitated toward an exploration of contemporary Western artistic styles and the formation of groups such as the Lianozovo School and Stretenskii Boulevard. Eli Beliutin's and Valerii Volkov's works recall the Action Painting of Wilem de Kooning and Franz Kline. Francisco Infante's paintings echo 1960s Op Art. Lidiia Masterkova, a member of the Lianozovo School, produced canvases that draw upon geometric abstraction, colour field painting, and Abstract Expressionism. Ernst Neizvestnyi, a direct target of Khrushchev's attacks in 1962, created expressive sculpture inspired by Henri Matisse's late work. Since official permission for exhibitions had become impossible, these artists turned their apartments into temporary galleries, creating the Apt-Art movement.

The 1970s were marked by rich diversity among nonconformist artists, partly owing to a less stringent supervision by the authorities, which also affected official art. The semi-tolerance of non-conformism during Stagnation peaked with the 1974 Bulldozer Exhibition, where the Soviet authorities destroyed an unofficial open-air exhibition by bulldozing it. The ensuing international scandal resulted in a situation beneficial to nonconformist artists: Soviet authorities pretended to tolerate the occasional unofficial exhibition, while maintaining a close watch on its participants and a readiness to punish anyone who stepped beyond the boundaries of the permissible.

Some artists in the 1970s continued to experiment with Western trends and adapt them to Soviet conditions. Conceptualism proved particularly fruitful for artists such as Ilia Kabakov, Vitalii Komar and Aleksandr Melamid, Irina Nakhova, Dmitrii Prigov, and Svetlana Kopystianskaia. Oleg Tselkov and Leonid Purygin mined Surrealism. Oskar Rabin worked with the spatial distortions of Cubism and combined them with the distortions of Surrealism to express the harshness of Soviet life.

Other artists worked with endemic traditions, particularly icons and folk art. Some nonconformists perceived the use of folk art as a mark of authenticity and integrity. Since early Soviet avant-garde artists such as Natalia Goncharova had used the 'primitive' qualities of folk art in their work, nonconformist artists' references to folk art subtly declared an allegiance to the avant-garde and with it a belief, however naïve, in 'pure art' devoid of ideology. Purygin's art makes many clear references to Russian folk art, especially the decorative patterning and 'primitive' figuration of *lubok*. (A form of medieval folk art that endured to the eighteenth century, *lubok* was a woodcut or metal engraving devoted to religious, satirical, or amusing topics.) These 'primitive features' have also been exploited by Elena Figurina, Natalia Nesterova, and Arkadii Petrov.

New art forms also emerged in the 1970s. Performance art proved particularly fruitful for Komar and Melamid, The Red Star Group, and the Collective Actions Group. Their performances often concentrated on the ritualization of space and thought both in and outside of Soviet society. Artists such as Aleksandr Kosolapov and Evgenii Rukhin experimented with collages comprising textiles and found objects.

Sots-art is probably the best-known nonconformist movement to have developed in the 1970s. Inverting the standard language and imagery of Soviet propaganda and Socialist Realism, Sots-art produced a highly ironic interpretation of Soviet culture. Komar and Melamid, the leaders of the movement, are best known for producing meticulously painted, highly naturalistic lampoons of Socialist Realism. Leonid Sokov's sculptures literally construct an alternative view of the 'correct' processes of perception, while Kosolapov's transformation of Soviet icons into capitalist mass marketing points to how both systems control 'the masses'.

The nonconformist art of the 1980s reflected the impact of glasnost and the wave of emigration among the arts community in the mid-1970s. The artists who had begun their explorations in the 1970s continued to develop their art, consolidating their aesthetics and increasing their productivity as they gained international recognition. Sots-art and Conceptualism remained strong movements, but were joined by a reinvigorated realism known as photorealism (or hyperrealism). Semen Faibisovich, Aleksandr Petrov, and Sergei Sherstiuk led attempts to establish an art that worked with photography, especially the distortions and imperfections of the casual snapshot. Sotheby's sale of contemporary Soviet art in 1988 radically changed art production in the USSR. It instantly exposed these artists to an international art market and a degree of fame and wealth they had never experienced, while effectively ending the concept of nonconformist art.

See also: Apt-Art; Bulldozer Exhibition; Conceptualism, art; Lianozovo School; Socialist Realism; Sots-art

Further reading

Bown, M. (1989) *Contemporary Russian Art*, New York: Phaidon.
Rosenfeld, A. and Dodge, N. (eds) (1995) *Nonconformist Art: The Soviet Experience 1956–1986*, New York: Thames and Hudson.
Tamruchi, N. (1995) *An Experience of Madness: Alternative Russian Art in the 1960s–1990s*, New South Wales: Craftsman House.
White, G. (ed.) (1998) *Forbidden Art: The Postwar Russian Avant-Garde*, New York: Distributed Art Publishers.

KRISTEN M. HARKNESS

art, post-Soviet

Post-Soviet art has experienced a somewhat artificial division into two camps, based on and located in Russia's two contrasting capitals. Art of the 1990s in St. Petersburg consolidated around Timur Novikov's New Academy of Fine Arts (Neo-academism), while Moscow shuttled between Conceptualism and the modernist aesthetics of the early-twentieth-century avant-garde.

Moscow art of the 1990s elaborated on the Conceptualist principles established by its originators, Ilia Kabakov and Dimitrii Prigov, while the related movement of Sots-art, with its reconfigurations of communist propaganda, gradually redirected its attention to capitalist advertising, especially in the works of Aleksandr Kosolapov and Leonid Sokov. In diverse ways, Kosopalov, Olga Bulgakova, Elena Figurina, and others revived the early Soviet avant-garde, which Neo-academists rejected for its capitalist associations, preferring a resuscitation of the distant past to a revision of the too-recent utopian culture of the future.

In 1989, Timur Novikov's New Academy of Every Kind of Art became the New Academy of Fine Arts and embarked on a programme of rededicating arts to classical aesthetics. By the early 1990s, young St. Petersburg-based artists such as Viktor Kuznetsov, Oleg Maslov, Bella Matveeva, Andrei Medvedev, Egor Ostrov, and Olga Tobreluts began to study under the Academy's professors – including Denis Egelskii and Georgii Gurianov – and to exhibit with the Neo-academists (so renamed in 1991). The movement reached its zenith in the mid-1990s, when its members frequently exhibited in museums and galleries throughout Russia, Europe, and the United States, and adopted the movement's key ideas as a lifestyle dedicated to specific aestheticized mores. Since the late 1990s, and particularly since Novikov's death in 2002, Neo-academism's visibility has diminished.

Neo-academists' works reflect the movement's close association with St. Petersburg's history and European traditions: a nostalgia for the neo-classicism of the tsarist empire, a fascination with classical antiquity via the Silver Age, an embrace of the city's distinctly European façade and myth of a pan-European culture, and a rejection of anything explicitly Russian. Neo-academists' enthusiasm for neo-classical aesthetics, domestically identified with Socialist Realism, alienates those who wish to disengage from the Soviet past; yet Neo-academists' recuperation of classical aesthetics differs from Socialist Realism's. The artists work in diverse media, including performance and digital imaging. They produce art that evokes nostalgia for a lost culture that struggled with its greatness and its decadence – though the question of which lost culture is at issue remains open.

Moscow artists such as Kabakov, Prigov, and Irina Nakhova continue to work within Conceptualism. As émigrés (seasonally so in Prigov's case), however, they have gradually moved away from the specifics of Soviet ideology and everyday life that earlier informed their art towards the more universal questioning of Western Conceptualism. Vitalii Komar and Aleksandr Melamid likewise, while continuing to lampoon society in their highly naturalistic style, have broadened their purview to include cultures other than Russian.

Drawing on the actions begun by non-conformist artists in the 1970s, Moscow-based artists during the 1990s turned to performance as a significant aspect of their production. Aleksandr Brenner, Oleg Kulik, and Oleg Mavromati have become notorious for their outrageous performances, which test the limits of the human body and the art world's tolerance. Brenner in particular is fond of confrontational actions. Violently anti-capitalist, he is perhaps best known for spray-painting a dollar sign on a Malevich painting in a Dutch museum – an action that resulted in his arrest. Following the tradition of Chris Burden, Mavromati has had himself crucified several times, ostensibly to draw attention to the current status of art. Oleg Kulik, similarly concerned with the changing social functions of art throughout history, has found inspiration in the performances of the renowned German Conceptualist Joseph Beuys (1924–86), known for his theory and practice of a 'social sculpture' grounded in political involvement. Infamous for a number of performances in which he interacted with dogs and simulated canine identity and behaviour, Kulik recently has turned to installations and video.

As for post-modernists in the West, identity is a central focus for many Moscow-based artists. A number of young female artists have explored issues of gender in Soviet and post-Soviet culture. Working in various media, including the gender-specific 'genres' of quilting, embroidery, cooking, and cleaning, Maria Konstantinova, Vera Khlebnikova, and Maria Chuikova have mined their personal histories to produce provocative works. Tatiana Antoshina works in digital imaging and installations to create images that question both male–female relations and the representation of women throughout art history. Anna Abazieva and Elena Kovylina have also embraced digital media, producing, among other works, a reinterpretation of the Cold War battles between East and West.

After 2000, the division between Moscow and St. Petersburg artists began to dissolve. While St. Petersburg artists still lean toward academic figuration and Moscow artists toward the exploration of art history, Russian artists of the early twenty-first century often cross those boundaries in order to grapple with issues of identity other than those addressed by their predecessors.

See also: Antoshina, Tatiana; art, non-conformist; Brenner, Aleksandr; Conceptualism, art; Kabakov, Ilia; Komar and Melamid; Kulik, Oleg; Matveeva, Bella; Nakhova, Irina; Novikov, Timur; Prigov, Dmitrii; Sots-Art

Further reading

Andreeva, E. (2000) 'O kulturnoi situatsii 1990-kh godov, kak my v nee voshli i kuda my iz nee vyshli' (On the Cultural Situation of the 1990s: How We Got into It and for What We Left It), *Moscow Art Magazine* 28–9: 18–21.

Manovich, L. (1997) 'Behind the Screen: Russian New Media', *Art/Text* 58: 40–2.

Osmolovskii, A. (2001) 'Neoakademizm i protsedura opoznaniia [Neo-academism and the Process of Identification]', *Khudozhestvennyi zhurnal/Moscow Art Journal* 40: 52–5.

Turkina, O. and Mazin, V. (1999) 'In the Time When the Great Stories Collapse', in *After the Wall: Art and Culture in Post-Communist Europe*, vol. 1, Stockholm: Moderna Museet, pp. 74–9.

KRISTEN M. HARKNESS

art schools and academies

Most of the fine art institutes, art schools and colleges in Russia were established in the mid-eighteenth to the early nineteenth centuries and represent an important artistic educational tradition. The art schools and colleges mainly provide training in graphic, industrial, set, and interior design; applied arts and crafts; and conservation, whereas the fine art institutes (accredited by the state as institutions of higher, post-graduate, and supplementary professional artistic education) specialize in painting, sculpture, architecture, graphic art, and theory and history of the arts.

Many of the art schools are based on local artisanship, including production of lacquered miniatures and terracotta toy figurines, wood-carving and painting, lace-making, and golden-thread embroidery. The Fedoskino Art College, the Abramtsevo School of Design, the Stroganov State Art School, and the Moscow State Academic Art School in Memory of 1905 are the major prestigious art schools. They frequently provide a basis for students who intend to study further at the Russian Academy of Arts. In the 1990s, some of the art schools and colleges, especially those with great traditions, such as the Mukhina Industrial Art School in St. Petersburg or the Stroganov Industrial Art School in Moscow, widened their scope of disciplines and have been offering students subjects similar to those of the fine art institutes.

The Repin State Academic Institute of Painting, Sculpture, and Architecture (St. Petersburg) and Moscow's State Academic Surikov Art Institute are the largest institutions in art education and important research centres in Russia. Both operate within the structure of the Russian Academy of Arts. The Repin Institute first opened its doors to students in 1758, a year after the Academy of Arts was officially founded. In 1944, the Institute was named after Ilya Repin, a former professor and a member of the Itinerants (*Peredvizhniki*), a group representing realist artists in the late nineteenth century.

The Surikov Art Institute dates from 1843, when the Moscow College of Painting, Sculpture, and Architecture was established. During the early twentieth century the college underwent a series of transformations and in 1939 became the Moscow State Fine Art Institute, since 1947 a part of the Russian Academy of Arts. In 1948, the Institute took the name of former professor and influential Russian artist Vasilii Surikov, also a member of the Itinerants, to celebrate the centenary of his birth.

The classical education offered in the eighteenth century under the Academy's first presidents (Ivan Shuvalov and Ivan Betskoi) has survived until today. The training is based on strictly organized, gradually progressing tasks in drawing and composition, complemented by compulsory copying of classic specimens of universally recognized masters. The Academy Institutes organize prestigious competitions for students' graduation projects, and the first prize affords the possibility to travel abroad to further their study of the arts.

See also: Academy of Arts; art, post-Soviet; art, Soviet

KATIA KAPUSHESKY

art, Soviet

The definition of Soviet art as that produced during the existence of the Soviet Union (1922–91) and on its territory begs many questions as to whether 'Soviet' is a chronological, geographical, or qualitative term. A first step towards the formation of a Soviet state art in Russia was Lenin's Plan for Monumental Propaganda of 1918, a state-funded public art project intended to replace the monuments of the former tsarist regime with commemorations of new heroes. By providing artists with state commissions, it established a relationship between artists and the new state whereby art became a public matter with a social responsibility to address the masses, educate them in the values of the October Revolution, and thus help bring about a new socialist society.

In the course of the 1920s many different answers were proffered to the question, 'What is Soviet art?' The Constructivists proposed that 'Soviet art' was an oxymoron, for Art was a capitalist commodity and a smokescreen for bourgeois ideology. They determined instead to take the skills of the artist into the factory and into the life of the masses through the rational re-formation of objects and environments of everyday life. Some abandoned what they now considered the atavistic, individualistic, and pre-industrial craft of easel painting for the use of the camera and photomontage. As a technological and seemingly objective medium, they found it more appropriate for the new society based on industrial progress and rationality. Others rejected easel painting but not painting altogether, turning instead to murals on the grounds that their mass address rendered them more socialist. One of the most notable movements in mural painting was the Ukrainian group, the Boichukisty. The Society of Easel Painters (*Obshchestvo stankovogo tvorchestva* [OST], founded in 1925), meanwhile, maintained the continued viability of painting as a cultural form under socialism, although they rejected abstract painting. Taking as their subject matter icons of Soviet modernity that accorded with the Party's vision of progress – the new woman, new forms of transportation, etc. – they sought to depict these in appropriately contemporary and expressive forms. Their diverse styles were informed by recent developments in Western European art, such as Cubism, Expressionism, and *Neue Sachlichkeit*. Other groups of the 1920s continued to develop the Cézannist tradition, one of the most significant developments in Russian in painting since the early twentieth century.

In terms of its size, monopoly of resources and commissions, and its power to define 'Soviet art' and set the future course of its development, the most important group in the 1920s was the Association of Artists of Revolutionary Russia, (*Assotsiatsiia khudozhnikov revoliutsionnoi Rossii* [AKhRR]), founded in the same year as the Soviet Union, 1922. Its declared aim was to depict Revolutionary Russia, the life of the proletariat, the Red Army, and the peasantry in an accessible, realistic manner derived from nineteenth-century Russian realism. AKhRR established direct links with powerful Soviet state institutions such as the Red Army and trade unions, seeking their patronage and cultivating a mass audience among factory workers and soldiers. They also sought the Party's recognition of their programme as the sole official Soviet art, but were denied an official monopoly. AKhRR established what became a defining practice of Soviet state art: thematic exhibitions for which artists were commissioned to produce works on assigned themes, such as 'The Life and Customs of the Workers' and 'Peasants' Red Army' (1922). AKhRR created a network of affiliated associations throughout Russia and also in some non-Russian republics, rendering the organization not just Russian but Soviet in the territorial sense.

The formation of the Soviet Union in December 1922 represented the integration of many peoples and territories of the former tsarist empire under the control of the Soviet government. Reflecting the Soviet Union's composition, the formation of Soviet art entailed integrating the art of diverse peoples and places into a single cohesive culture, but one that at least nominally embraced national diversity. In 1925 and again in 1930, Stalin promulgated the principle that Soviet culture must be 'socialist in its content and national in form, having the aim of educating the masses in the spirit of socialism and internationalism' (Stalin, [1953] 1988: 367).

In practice, however, the introduction of Socialist Realism – favouring media and practices such as figurative oil painting that were fundamental to the Western European tradition but alien in parts of Central Asia, along with the growing hegemony of AKhRR's definition of realism derived from nineteenth-century Russian models – belied the ecumenism of official claims to embracing national diversity.

The Party's 'Decree on the Reconstruction of Literary and Artistic Organizations' in 1932 disbanded independent artistic associations and called for 'the integration of all writers who support the platform of the Soviet government and who aspire to participate in socialist construction in a single union of Soviet writers (artists) with a communist faction therein' (Bowlt, 1988: 290). The decree obliged artists to join a regional Artists' Union (a USSR Artist Union was not established until 1957) and to pledge adherence to the sole approved method of Soviet art, Socialist Realism. Aspects of the state patronage and management of art were developed on the basis of AKhRR's practices, including the production of thematic exhibitions sponsored by a major state organization, such as 'Industry of Socialism' in 1939. Artists were now to be organized professionals with a public mandate as 'engineers of the human soul'. Failure to join the union and to pledge adherence to Socialist Realism implied exclusion from the ranks of accredited, professional Soviet artists. 'Private' or alternative practices such as intimate painting did not cease, but circulated only among close acquaintances and did not form a part of public Soviet culture.

After Stalin's death in 1953, artists and critics began to disaggregate the concepts of socialist, realist, and Soviet hitherto welded into the unitary 'Socialist Realism'. While continuing to seek a civic form of art addressed to contemporary reality and possessing a fundamental optimism, some artists challenged the stylistic norms of Stalinist painting and the taboo on modernist devices, such as expressive colour and brushstroke, intensified and simplified tonal contrasts, and deformation; they sought a contemporary style of Soviet art.

Beginning in the Thaw and continuing in the Brezhnev era, the concept of 'national form' increasingly served as a real force to diversify Soviet art, referred to as 'multinational Soviet art', although this entailed a degree of stereotyping of national schools.

One of the most significant artistic and social developments of the Thaw was the emergence of a 'nonconformist' or 'underground' art world in parallel with the official Soviet institutions. The boundary between unofficial and more experimental permitted art was undefined and unstable in the climate of radical re-examination of Soviet institutions and practices of the late 1950s and early 1960s, but was rendered more concrete by 1963 (though still not impermeable) as a result of the Manezh Affair of 1962. Despite the reassertion of ideological control represented by this event, the parameters of official or permitted Soviet art continued to broaden during the Brezhnev era, with the officially endorsed concept of 'Socialist Realism as a historically open system'. The coexistence of a parallel, nonconformist art world was tacitly accepted as long as the boundary was not breached, though periodically major harassments such as the 1974 Bulldozer Exhibition reminded such artists that their work did not have the rights of citizenship as 'Soviet art'. Ironically, when the Soviet Union opened up during perestroika, it was avant-garde tendencies such as Sots-Art and Moscow Conceptualism, formed in the ambience of unofficial culture, that came most successfully to represent 'Soviet art' on the international art market.

See also: Brezhnev, Leonid; Bulldozer Exhibition; Communist Party; Conceptualism, art; Khrushchev, Nikita; Lenin, Vladimir Ilich; Manezh exhibition of 1962; Socialist Realism; Sots-Art; Stagnation; Thaw

References

Bowlt, J. (1988) *Russian Art of the Avant-Garde*, rev. edn, London: Thames & Hudson.

Stalin, I. ([1953] 1988) *Sochineniia*, vol. 12, Moscow: Gosudarstvennoe izdatelstvo politicheskoi literatury, p. 367.

Further reading

Chen, J. (1944) *Soviet Art and Artists*, London: Pilot Press.

Cullerne Bown, M. and Taylor, B. (1993) *Art of the Soviets*, Manchester: Manchester University Press.

Elliott, D. (1992) *Soviet Socialist Realist Painting*, exhibition catalogue, Oxford: Museum of Modern Art.

Golomstock, I. and Glezer, A. (1977) *Soviet Art in Exile*, New York: Random House.

Kornetchuk, E. (1990) *The Quest for Self-Expression: Painting in Moscow and Leningrad 1965–1990*, exhibition catalogue, Columbus, OH: Columbus Museum of Art.

Sopotsinsky, O. (1978) *Soviet Art*, Leningrad: Aurora.

SUSAN E. REID

Artek

Founded in 1925 by Vladimir Lenin, this was the first and most elite summer camp for Pioneers. Its location in the Crimea and its foreign guests made visits to Artek an honour usually granted only to the children of the powerful. During the Soviet era Artek symbolized the state's alleged support for peace and friendship among nations. In May 1991, the camp became the *Mezhdunarodnyi detskii tsentr* (International Children's Centre) and children had to pay for their stay. Like the rest of the Crimea, Artek is now part of Ukraine.

See also: Crimea; Lenin, Vladimir Ilich; Pioneer organization; Ukraine

BENJAMIN SUTCLIFFE

Artmane, Vija

b. 21 July 1929, Tukuma, Latvia

Latvian stage and screen actress

Artmane studied in the drama studio of the Rainis Academic Theatre in Riga, which hired her upon graduation in 1949. The film role of a dying mother in the melodrama *Rodnaia krov* (*Kindred Blood*, 1963) brought her national stardom. For the next twenty-five years, Artmane's warm femininity, dignity, and natural elegance made her the Baltic darling of Russian directors, who featured her in numerous films, albeit of uneven quality. After Latvia's independence, Artmane was publicly blamed for political opportunism during the Soviet period and vir-

tually left without roles. Only in 2000 did Russian television producers remember the still-popular actress and cast her in several mini-series. People's Artist of the USSR (1969).

See also: Baltic actors in Soviet cinema; Latvia

PETER ROLLBERG

arts administration and management, Soviet and post-Soviet

Arts administration in the Soviet era must be viewed in light of the gradual consolidation of Communist Party ruling structures. All governmental activity worked by Party decree; the Communist Party Central Committee members responsible for cultural activity developed Soviet cultural policy, to be carried out by local Party authorities. The Leninist notion of *partiinost* in the arts saw them as expressions of class warfare, in which socialist and bourgeois culture existed in a constant and irreconcilable state of antagonism and mutual hostility. Given this starting point, the basic principle of arts administration was vigilant political and ideological control over all cultural activity, and thus over the nation's intellectual and cultural life.

Although the 1920s allowed for avant-garde experiment, as seen in the work of poet Vladimir Maiakovskii, theatre director Vsevolod Meierkhold, and artists Vasilii Kandinskii and Mark Shagal (Chagall), supported by the Bolshevik Narkompros (*Narodnyi kommissariat prosveshcheniia* [People's Commissariat of Enlightenment]), beginning in the early 1930s under Stalin, cultural authorities distanced themselves from such 'fellow travellers'. The creation of artistic unions (1932–65), whose policy was founded on the principles of Socialist Realism, solidified the feudal relationship between the state and artists of all kinds: writers, artists, musicians, and filmmakers. Union membership did not protect artists from repressions or executions during the Stalinist terror; prominent victims included Meierkhold, writers Boris Pilniak and Isaak Babel, and actor Veniamin Zuskin. Composers Dmitrii Shostakovich and Sergei Prokofiev were accused of 'formalist distortion' and 'anti-democratic', 'anti-Soviet' tendencies in their work, of a 'purposeful complexity' that made their works unclear to the masses. Official tastes were regulated by Party leaders and members of the Party's Committee on Artistic Activity (*Komitet po delam iskusstv*), under the leadership of the Soviet of People's Commissars (1936–47), and, later, under the USSR Soviet of Ministries (1946–53). This body was the predecessor of the Ministry of Culture.

On 15 March 1953, ten days after Stalin's death, the regulation of cultural activity reached its apogee with the creation of a special ministry. Cultural life became even more ideologized and standardized, artistic production became clichéd, directed toward the creation of a unified image of *homo Sovieticus*. Anything that did not support this standard image was labelled hostile and was mercilessly suppressed. The newly created USSR Ministry of Culture was administered by Party officials who had no relationship to the arts; for many years the music department did not have a single employee with an advanced degree in music. Early Ministers of Culture included a machinist and a weaver. The latter, Ekaterina Furtseva, remained in her position for fourteen years and proved to be the most unconventional and decisive Minister of Culture in the Soviet era.

During the Thaw, the practice of creating pro-Stalinist works of art, sculpture, theatre, and film gradually disappeared; however, pressure on the creative intelligentsia increased. The Party announced Soviet art's messianic role: to struggle to 'save world culture from bourgeois decadence, dissolution, and death'. This new struggle required experimentation, the limits of which were strictly controlled. Such artistic phenomena as abstractionism and formalism were subjected to the harshest criticism. Khrushchev, fearing revisionism, called for tight control of the arts, so that, as he put it, people's brains would be 'washed', not 'soiled'. The scandal over the Manezh exhibition of 1962 was merely the outer manifestation of the irritation that Party authorities felt toward the arts. Khrushchev described abstract art as 'drawn by a donkey's tail'. Art that promoted universally human ideals was seen as 'abstract humanism'. Exhibitions destroyed by bulldozers were characterized as 'stubborn subjectivity'. At subsequent meetings with representatives of the creative intelligentsia, the cultural authorities mentioned the work of writers, film-makers, theatre workers, and composers. Ministry of Culture functionaries arranged such meetings upon orders of the Communist Party Central Committee's ideological commission, which felt that in order to avoid mental 'fermentation', the 'screws' on literature and the arts had to be 'tightened'. This ruling tendency led to a crisis of stagnation in all arts.

Perestroika and glasnost demanded the reorganization of the Party's entire system of cultural administration and greater artistic independence. The Party moved from ideological to economic principles. Artistic leaders, for example at the Fifth Congress of the Cinematographers' Union, limited the government's managerial role and for a time even banned the authorities from engagement in artistic administration. Such reforms led to a normalization of artistic life. In these conditions, new theatres, galleries, and publishing houses appeared. However, the principle of competition, which replaced state commissions, led to rapid commercialization. Economic laws did not take into account the specificities of artistic life; without governmental support, some artistic enterprises did not survive market conditions. In these new conditions artists need to seek financial support from outside traditional channels, to exist on contributions from the private sector, and thus to face a new kind of dictatorship – economics. These issues led to the creation in 2004 of a new Ministry of Culture and Mass Communications, and two federal agencies: one for Culture and Cinematography, the other for Press and Mass Communications. The responsibility of these agencies include the support of culture, film, and other arts, and the preservation of the nation's artistic treasures. Governmental support carries certain dangers, however, a return to the feudal relationship of the previous era and the subjection of the artist to new bureaucratic strictures. The question of hard-won artistic freedom in the new era remains open.

See also: art galleries and exhibition halls; art museums; Bulldozer Exhibition; censorship; Communist ideology; Communist Party; economic system, post-Soviet; economic system, Soviet; intelligentsia; Khrushchev, Nikita; Manezh exhibition of 1962; partiinost; perestroika and glasnost; philosophy, Soviet (Marxist-Leninist); propaganda, Soviet and post-Soviet; Socialist Realism; Stagnation; Stalin, Iosif; Thaw; unions, creative, post-Soviet; unions, creative, Soviet

SERGEI KOKOVKIN AND ANNA RODIONOVA

Arzamas-16 (Sarov)

Arzamas-16 was the code name for a closed city in the Nizhnii Novgorod region. Founded in 1946 in the thick forest near the old Orthodox Serafim Sarovskii monastery, it housed the research centre that designed the first Soviet nuclear bomb (tested in 1949) and hydrogen bomb (tested in 1953). From 1946–1959 it was also known as KB-11 (*konstruktorskoe biuro* [construction office]), and after 1960, as VNIIEF (*Vsesoiuznyi iaderno-fizicheskii nauchno-issledovatelskii institut* [All-Union Nuclear Physics Experimental Research Institute]), and after 2003 as Sarov. Pavel Mikhailovich Zernov, Iulii Borisovich Khariton, and Andrei Dmitrievich Sakharov lived and worked there. Arzamas is also the name given in 1779 to a small town (famous for its breed of geese) in the Nizhnii Novgorod region.

See also: closed city; Nizhnii Novgorod (Gorkii)

Further reading

Kocharyants, N. and Gorin, S. (1993) *Arzamas-16 (Sarov): From the History of the USSR Nuclear Centre Establishment*, Arzamas-16: VNIIEF

TATYANA LEDENEVA

Arzhak, Nikolai

See: Daniel, Iulii Markovich.

Ashkenazii, Vladimir Davidovich

b. 6 July 1937, Gorkii (Nizhnii Novgorod)

Pianist, conductor

Considered one of the best virtuoso pianists of his generation, Ashkenazii established his career with first prizes in both the Queen Elisabeth Competition in Brussels (1956) and the second Tchaikovsky Competition (1962). He has recorded major works in the piano solo and concerto repertoire (Melodia, Decca). In 1963, he defected to the West, settling in London and, subsequently, Switzerland. Once abroad, he started to conduct and established a successful recording and touring career with major European (Czech, Berlin, Royal Philharmonic), American (Boston, Cleveland), and Asian (NHK) orchestras, specializing in the music of Rachmaninov, Prokofiev, Sibelius, and Shostakovich.

See also: classical music, Soviet; piano performance, Russian/Soviet; Prokofiev, Sergei; Shostakovich, Dmitrii; Tchaikovsky Competition

DAVID GOMPPER

Asian cuisine

Nomadic tribes and caravans along the Silk Road brought ethnic diversity to the culinary traditions of Central Asian cuisine. Nevertheless, *non* (large circular bread) and lamb are the basic staples of the area. The richness of the region boasts grapes, apricots, almonds, pistachios, pumpkins, figs, pomegranates, the fabled apples of Kazakhstan, and over a thousand varieties of Uzbekistan melons.

Fresh and dried fruit, dozens of varieties of raisins, and pale jade radishes adorn the stalls at fruit and spice bazaars, where vendors sell *samsa* – fried, round pies filled with scallions or herbs, lamb, pumpkin, and mashed chick peas. *Chaikhana* (teahouses) greet patrons with the ancient Muslim hospitality ritual of *dastarkhan*: *piala* (hot green tea), accompanied by a tray of raisins, dried apricots, dried chick peas, pistachios, almonds, and *khalva* (halva).

The nomadic people of Turkmenistan rely on the meat and milk of camels, horses, sheep, and mountain goats; *kavardak*, lamb chunks simmered in huge clay pots; and *chal*, fermented milk of camels and sheep. In Kazakhstan and Kyrgyzstan, *kazi*, highly spiced horsemeat sausage; and *besh barmak*, homemade noodles and lamb, with broth in a separate bowl, are highly prized. The most sophisticated cooking appears in Tadjikistan and Uzbekistan, where the influences of Persia, Turkey, Afghanistan, and India prevail. The Uzbeks learned to steam buns and dumplings, especially *manty* (filled with lamb) from China; to bake in a *tandir* (clay oven) from India, and to cook kebabs on iron grills from Mongols.

On the most important occasions, men assemble rice pilafs. *Zirvak* (rice topping) in Uzbekistan usually consists of lamb, carrots, onions, and pungent spices; the Tadzhik *zirvak* normally employs nuts, chicken, candied orange peel, and raisins. Salads and pickles accompany the pilafs. Tea and milk drinks like *ayran*, akin to yoghurt, provide a cooling complement to the meals.

See also: Central Asia; Kazakhstan; Kyrgyzstan; Tajikistan; Turkmenistan; Uzbekistan

CHRISTINE A. RYDEL

Askoldov, Aleksandr Iakovlevich

b. 17 June 1932, Moscow

Film director

Askoldov studied film at the All-Russian (All-Union) State Institute of Cinematography (VGIK). He adapted Vasilii Grossman's 1934 short story, *V gorode Berdicheve* (*In the Town of Berdichev*), for his only film, *Komissar* (*The Commissar*, 1967). Askoldov's visual boldness, his ambiguous portrayal of the film's Bolshevik protagonist, who is seduced by the warmth and humanity of the Jewish household where she awaits her child's birth, and his flash-forward to Jewish victims of the Holocaust (a subject rarely depicted on Soviet screens) resulted in a ban on the film and the effective end of Askoldov's film career. *The Commissar* reached Soviet audiences at the Moscow Film Festival in July 1987, and quickly achieved international celebrity.

See also: All-Russian (All-Union) State Institute of Cinematography (VGIK)

JOSEPHINE WOLL

Astafev, Viktor Petrovich

b. 1 May 1924, Ovsianka, Krasnoiarsk region; d. 29 November 2001, Krasnoiarsk

Writer

Astafev wrote in various genres, including village prose, war prose, and crime dramas. His career lasted for more than half a century. A front-line soldier wounded in World War II, Astafev wrote combat stories distinguished by their harsh realism and informed by his experience. *Pastukh i pastushka* (*The Shepherd and Shepherdess*, 1971) remains one of the most hard-hitting pictures of war published in the Soviet Union, and *Prokliaty i ubity* (*The Cursed and the Slain*, 1992–97) is uncompromising in its attention to the everyday details of the ordinary soldier's life. Although he has published works about the Russian countryside, he has avoided the glorification of the peasant character that is a feature of many works of village prose. Instead, *Tsar-ryba* (*Tsar-Fish*, 1976) speaks to modern environmental concerns in its criticism of the destruction of nature and of man's desire to impose his will on the natural world despite catastrophic consequences. Many of his short stories are based on his own village childhood and contain some of the most evocative descriptions of the Russian countryside in twentieth-century literature. His novella *Pechalnyi detektiv* (*The Sad Detective*, 1986) caused controversy with its relentless picture of crime and its anti-modern tone, purporting to show late Soviet society approaching meltdown.

See also: village prose; World War II (Great Patriotic War)

DAVID GILLESPIE

Averintsev, Sergei Sergeevich

b. 10 December 1937, Moscow; d. 21 February 2004, Vienna

Philologist, translator, poet

Averintsev graduated from the Moscow State University Department of Classical Philology and subsequently worked as a research fellow at the Institute of World Literature of the Soviet (later Russian) Academy of Sciences. During perestroika he was elected Deputy of the First People's Congress of the USSR. In the last decade of his life Averintsev was Professor at the Department of Slavonic Studies at the University of Vienna (Austria). He combined studies of antiquity with an interest in early Christian literature and theology and German philosophy of the nineteenth and twentieth centuries. In addition, Averintsev translated German poetry and published his own poems of a largely spiritual character. Since the 1970s Averintsev has earned the profound respect of the Soviet intelligentsia. He is buried in Moscow.

See also: intelligentsia; Moscow State University

GASAN GUSEJNOV

aviation, Soviet and post-Soviet

Russian naval officer Aleksandr Mozhaiskii invented the first Russian airplane in 1885, which was abandoned after its failure during the test flight. Engineer Igor Sikorskii (1889–1972), who created the 'Russian vitiaz' airplane in 1913, subsequently emigrated to the United States and designed the first modern helicopter.

In 1924, the first metal Russian airplane, a model ANT-2, was constructed by Andrei Nikolaevich Tupolev, the foremost aircraft designer in the USSR, who in 1918 helped organize the first national aerodynamics research institution and later designed several jet-propelled military and commercial airplanes. His son, Andrei Andreevich Tupolev (1925–2001), also designed a number of Soviet planes, including its first jetliner, its first supersonic passenger jet, and a long-range supersonic bomber.

The first international flight (Moscow to Koenigsberg, Germany) opened to the public on 1 May 1922, the first local flight (Moscow to Nizhnii Novgorod) on 15 July 1923. In 1928, Nikolai Polikarpov created the first training airplane, the U-2, used in agriculture and, in 1941–45, as both a sanitation plane and night-time bomber.

The Soviet aircraft industry emerged in 1929–32. Soviet pilots who achieved world records for flight height and range became national heroes (Valerii Tchkalov, Anatolii Serov) and heroines (Valentina Grizodubova, Polina Osipenko, Maria Raskova). In 1934, the pilots who saved the polar expedition from the steamship *Cheliuskin* became the first Heroes of the Soviet Union (the highest Soviet military award).

In the first German-Soviet air battle during the Spanish Civil War of 1936–39, Soviet planes performed poorly, and Stalin imprisoned some of his best engineers, including Andrei Tupolev, in a *sharashka*, a scientific research institute within the GULag, where all 'employees' were political convicts (Aleksandr Solzhenitsyn depicts this environment in *V kruge pervom* [*First Circle*]). Tupolev's design of the Tu-2 bomber prompted his release.

During World War II, Soviet aircraft development made great progress, with 7,900 warplanes produced in 1941 and over 40,000 in 1944. The best Soviet airplane in World War II was the IL-2 (*Shturmovik*), designed by Sergei Iliushin. Pilots who became Soviet legends included Aleksandr Pokryshkin, Ivan Kozhedub, Viktor Talalikhin, and Nikolai Gastello. Boris Polevoi's *Povest o nastoyashchem cheloveke* (*A Story about a Real Man*, 1946) narrates the legendary exploits of a Soviet pilot in World War II.

During the war, the two main design bureaus were headed by Pavel Sukhoi and Aleksandr Yakovlev. After 1945, a third bureau came to the forefront, directed by Artem Mikoian and Mikhail Gurevich. The Mikoian-Gurevich MiG-15, invented in 1947, was the first Soviet jet fighter to challenge American jets during the Korean War (1950–53). MiG fighters of increasingly advanced design continued to be the main source of Soviet fighter power, from the MiG-29 (Fulcrum), to the Su-27UB (Pugachev's Cobra), the Su-30M (MK-export version), and the Su-37, with numerous models in between.

To meet post-war challenges, new design bureaus, headed respectively by Nikolai Kamov and Mikhail Mil, began to construct helicopters. Another bureau, under Oleg Antonov, dealt with cargo aircraft designs. It also became possible to build civilian airliners, such as Tupolev's: the jet-powered Tu-104 and Tu-114, with enough range to cover the vast distances of the Soviet heartland.

From the 1960s until the 1980s, Soviet state-owned civil aircraft flew to 3,600 cities in the USSR and to 84 foreign countries. The Soviet airline Aeroflot, founded in 1932, had a monopoly on Soviet international air transportation. In the 1990s Russian aircraft were in crisis: passenger turnover declined by 300 per cent, half of Soviet airports ceased to operate, factories lacked orders, and airlines desperate for new planes had no means to purchase them. As a result of spontaneous privatization, only 25 per cent of aircraft companies remained under state ownership. In the 2000s the urgent objective of the existent 200 Russian airlines is to update the pool of old aircraft manufactured in the 1960s until the 1980s with new planes that meet stringent international noise and emission requirements. Though unable to export civil planes, Russia makes substantial profits on military aircraft export to developing countries, particularly India and China.

See also: defence industry

Further reading

Belyakov, R. and Marmain, J. (1993) *MiG: Fifty Years of Secret Aircraft Design*, Annapolis, MD: Naval Institute Press.

Boyd, A. (1977) *The Soviet Air Force Since 1918*, New York: Stein and Day Publishers.

Butowski, P. with Miller, J. (1991) *OKB MiG: A History of the Design Bureau and Its Aircraft*, Leicester: Aerofax, Inc.

Duffy, P. and Kandalov, A. (1996a) *Tupolev: The Man and His Aircraft*, Shrewsbury: Airlife.

——— (1996b) *The Osprey Encyclopedia of Russian Aircraft, 1875–1995*, London: Osprey Aerospace.

Higham, R., Greenwood, J. and Hardesty, V. (1998) *Russian Aviation and Air Power in the Twentieth Century*, London: Frank Cass.

Kerber, L. (1996) *Stalin's Aviation Gulag: A Memoir of Andrei Tupolev and the Purge Era*, Washington, DC: Smithsonian Institution Press.

TATYANA LEDENEVA

avos/avoska

Avos means 'perhaps', 'it may happen'; '*na avos*' means 'just in case', 'in case something comes up'. The *avoska* is a woven string bag (*setka* or *setochka* ['net']), small enough to fold into a purse or pocket but large enough to contain several kilos of produce. People in the Soviet Union routinely carried these bags in case stores or street stalls unexpectedly offered something desirable for sale. Plastic bags (*pakety*) are now available in most Russian stores; although they usually cost a small amount, they are increasingly replacing the traditional bag or container shoppers used to supply themselves.

SIBELAN FORRESTER

avtoritet

The standard meaning of *avtoritet* (an authority) is a person or thing (such as a source of information) that is universally accepted or influential. In prison camp slang, *avtoritet* is either an inmate respected by the other prisoners or a third party asked to mediate between two fighting gangs. In the post-Soviet period, it has acquired the meaning of a crime boss.

See also: crime; prison system, Soviet and post-Soviet; slang

MICHELE BERDY

awards, cultural, post-Soviet

Since 1992, the State Prize of the Russian Federation (*Gosudarstvennaia premiia Rossiiskoi Federatsii*) has been awarded for achievements in science, technology, literature, and the arts, succeeding the analogous prize awarded by the Soviet government in preceding decades. With the awarding of the 2004 State Prizes, presented to their recipients by President Vladimir Putin on Russia Day, 12 June 2005, the number of those honoured sharply decreased and the amount of the award substantially increased to 250,000 rubles. The collapse of state control over Russian culture in the post-Soviet period has also spurred the appearance of privately sponsored prizes, and the change in the terms of the State Prizes may be designed to bring them more in line with the private ones. The most prominent of these private initiatives is the Triumph Prize, conceived by the writer Zoia Boguslavskaia and underwritten by the Triumph Foundation, chaired by the financier Boris Berezovskii. The Triumph Prize may be awarded to a practitioner of any art form and of any nationality who has made a significant contribution to Russian culture. Laureates of the Triumph Prize include composers, ballerinas, pianists, choreographers, artists, actors, filmmakers, writers, and rock stars. Each year the Triumph Foundation awards five prizes totalling $250,000. There are also prizes bestowed by more specialized cultural institutions, such as the Golden Sofit which is awarded annually by the St. Petersburg Division of the Union of Theatrical Workers for achievement in any profession or genre of the theatrical arts. The prize was first awarded on 24 June 1995. The Union of Theatrical Workers also gives the Golden Mask award for achievement in all aspects of theatrical activity. Notable among film prizes are the St. George Awards conferred at the annual Moscow Film Festival.

See also: awards, literary, post-Soviet; awards, state and government, Soviet and post-Soviet; Berezovskii, Boris; film, festivals and prizes; holidays, post-Soviet; Putin, Vladimir; unions, creative, post-Soviet

CATHARINE NEPOMNYASHCHY

awards, cultural, Soviet

The Soviet state recognized its distinguished citizens from its earliest days, rewarding military valour and feats of labour with awards such as the Red Banner (*orden Krasnogo znameni*) and Order of Lenin (*orden Lenina*). Achievements in culture were slower to be recognized; the Stalin Prizes (*Stalinskie premii*) were created in honour of Stalin's 60th birthday in December 1939, to honour cultural achievements and advances in invention and engineering.

The prizes' creation at one of the key junctures of the Stalin cult indicated the degree to which they would be linked to Stalin's leadership. The limited memoir material about the Stalin Prizes (Dmitrii Shepilov, Konstantin Simonov) suggests that Stalin had the final word on the prizes, although formally this task fell to the Stalin Prize Committee, comprising favoured writers and artists, such as Aleksandr Fadeev, which in its turn was advised by departments of the Central Committee.

Perhaps because of the variety of people involved, the Stalin prizes were not consistent, either officially or unofficially, in their selection criteria. Archival materials from the Stalin Prize Committee reveal complex discussions about the prizes, yet also a growing tendency, particularly in the post-war period, to reward works of art that were effectively paeans to Stalin. Yet other Stalin-era winners included the relatively 'un-Stalinized' works of Viktor Nekrasov, Aleksandr Tvardovskii, and Dmitrii Shostakovich. In both cases, Stalin's sometimes capricious personal tastes seem to have played a decisive role.

The Stalin Prizes fell into disuse and disrepute in the Khrushchev era; they attracted the opprobrium of the Party and numerous writers, especially after the 'secret speech' (1956), when the Lenin Prizes replaced them. There were attempts to make the selection process more transparent and democratic, but the limits of the Lenin Prizes' boldness were shown in 1964 when the committee refused to honour Aleksandr Solzhenitsyn's *Odin den Ivana Denisovicha* (*One Day in the Life of Ivan Denisovich*). The Soviet State Prizes were established in 1966 and functioned alongside, and in much the same way as, the Lenin Prizes.

See also: awards, state and government, Soviet and post-Soviet; Communist Party; cult of personality; Khrushchev, Nikita; Nekrasov, Viktor; Shostakovich, Dmitrii; Simonov, Konstantin; Solzhenitsyn, Aleksandr; Stalin, Iosif; Thaw; Tvardovskii, Aleksandr

POLLY JONES

awards, literary, post-Soviet

Three main factors have shaped the history of literary awards in post-Soviet Russia: (1) the state's lack of interest in literature; (2) the relative insignificance of once-powerful literary institutions such as the fractious and fragmented writers' unions; and (3) the logic of the emerging literary market. Where once the state had doled out a limited number of awards to writers, in the 1990s an array of new, independent awards began to appear. The Booker Russian Novel Prize, created by Booker plc, which also sponsors the British Booker Prize, was first awarded in 1992 and remains arguably the most important literary award in Russia. Three years later, Boris Berezovskii's newspaper *Nezavisimaia gazeta* launched a Russian-funded alternative, the Anti-Booker Prize for prose, drama, and poetry. The new awards range from the highbrow Apollon Grigorev Prize, first presented in 1998 and selected by professional literary critics, to the National Bestseller Prize, which is oriented more toward the mass market. A few awards, such as the Andrei Belyi Prize, originated in the late Soviet underground. The government has continued to present awards to writers, though they carry little cachet. On the whole, literary awards have proven only moderately successful in enhancing writers' reputations or their sales.

See also: awards, literary, Soviet; Berezovskii, Boris; *Nezavisimaia gazeta*; poetry, post-Soviet

PATRICK HENRY

awards, literary, Soviet

From 1939 until the 1960s, the highest governmental literary award was the Stalin Prize (*Stalinskaia premiia*), first awarded by Stalin himself and granted primarily for a writer's political loyalty. Konstantin Simonov won this prize six times. Renamed the State Prize (*Gosudarstvennaia premiia*) in 1961, it ranks second, after the Lenin Prize (*Leninskaia premiia*), and is estimated at 5,000 roubles.

The Lenin Prize (10,000 roubles), established as the highest Soviet literary prize in 1957, likewise favoured political conformity over artistic merits. Its recipients included Leonid Leonov (1957), Mikhail Sholokhov (1960), Aleksandr Tvardovskii (1961), Kornei Chukovskii (1962), Sergei Smirnov (1965), Mikhail Svetlov (1967),

and many representatives of union republics. The political nature of the Lenin Prize nakedly manifested itself when Leonid Brezhnev received it for his memoirs in 1979. From 1967 until the fall of the Soviet Union the Lenin Prize was awarded biannually.

In 1947, the Belinskii Prize for literary criticism, theory, and history – named after the liberal nineteenth-century literary critic – was established. Since 1949, the International Stalin Prize (renamed the International Lenin Prize in 1956) 'for strengthening peace among nations' was often bestowed upon foreign writers loyal to the Soviet Union. Every union republic also had its own literary awards named after prominent writers in the respective republics.

See also: Brezhnev, Leonid; Sholokhov, Mikhail; Simonov, Konstantin; Tvardovskii, Aleksandr

ALEXANDER LEDENEV

awards, state and government, Soviet and post-Soviet

The Soviet state rewarded its citizens' military valour, labour achievements, and professional service with orders, medals, honorary titles, and other marks of distinction, most accompanied by various privileges. The highest honorary title awarded for outstanding heroic deeds performed for the socialist state was Hero of the Soviet Union (*Geroi Sovetskogo Soiuza*, established in 1934; from 1939, that title also carried with it the Gold Star medal). Recipients of the award automatically received an Order of Lenin in addition. The Hero award could be conferred more than once (a practice abolished in 1988), and those who were awarded the Hero twice were entitled to a bronze bust in their home town. Approximately 12,600 people got this award more than once – Leonid Brezhnev, four times. People distinguished for feats of labour were decorated with a Gold Star called the Hammer and Sickle of a Hero of Socialist Labour (1938). Heroes of Socialist Labour were stakhanovites who over-fulfilled assigned work, invented new ways to increase labour productivity, or otherwise significantly contributed to the development of socialist economy, science, and culture. Stalin became the first Hero of Socialist Labour (1939). Special privileges attached to these titles included an increased retirement pension, priority in services, housing privileges, and free annual round-trip, first-class tickets and travel packages (*putevki*) to a sanatorium or house of rest.

The highest Soviet decorations included the Red Banner (*Krasnoe znamia*, 1924), awarded to military personnel and units for exceptional courage during combat; the Red Star (*Krasnaia zvezda*, 1930), awarded to all ranks and units for outstanding service in defence of the Soviet Union; Orders of Suvorov, Kutuzov, Aleksandr Nevskii, and of the Patriotic War (1942); Order of Victory (1943), awarded only to highly ranked military commanders; Order of Bogdan Khmelnitskii (1943); and the Orders of Nakhimov and Ushakov (1944). The Order for Service to the Motherland in the Armed Forces of the USSR, introduced in 1974, was reserved for military veterans. Heroism on the battlefield and in extraordinary situations was also distinguished by various medals, such as those for the Defence of Leningrad (1942) and the Capture of Berlin (1945). Honorary military titles were also granted: Pilot-Cosmonaut of the USSR (1961, to cosmonauts who flew into space), Distinguished Military Pilot of the USSR (1965), and others.

Outstanding service to the state was awarded by the Order of Lenin (1930), of the October Revolution (1967), and of the Friendship of Peoples (1972, for strengthening friendship among socialist nations). Those orders were bestowed upon individuals (military or civilian), organizations, unions, collective groups of workers, military units, regions, cities, etc.

In order to increase the national birthrate at the end of World War II, the Order of Mother-Heroine was established (1944), given to mothers of ten or more children and carrying many privileges. Mothers of five or more children were awarded Motherhood medals. Heroic exploits in peacetime and labour were acknowledged with various medals and diplomas: for rescuing a drowning person (1957), maintaining public order (1950), heroism in labour (1938), restoration of the Donbass coal mines (1947),

development of the virgin lands (*tselina*, 1956), construction of the Baikal-Amur Railroad (1976), etc. Veterans of the armed forces and labour also received special honorary titles and medals, e.g., Veteran of Labour (1974), for many years of impeccable service and dedicated work for the Soviet economy, culture, science, medicine, and education. Jubilee medals were used to distinguish various accomplishments and services, such as the medal commemorating the 100th anniversary of Lenin's birth (1969), awarded to advanced workers and specialists, veterans, members of the international workers' movement, and foreign Communist Party members.

Scientists and scholars likewise received orders and medals for achievements in labour and advancement in research: *Gospremiia* (State Prize), Lenin Prize (the former Stalin Prize), and various prizes established by other Soviet institutions and organizations (Academy of Sciences, Council of Ministers, Komsomol, or one of the Soviet republics). In 1956, a gold medal named after Mikhail Lomonosov was established by the order of the USSR Council of Ministers, to be awarded once every three years for outstanding achievements in natural and technical sciences. Achievements in culture and arts were deemed achievements in labour and were rewarded with orders and medals; State, Lenin and other prizes; as well as other honorary titles: People's Artist (*Narodnyi artist*) of the USSR, People's Architect, and so forth.

Each Soviet republic awarded its own titles (e.g., People's Artist of the Belorussian SSR, Distinguished Artist of the RSFSR). Honorary titles existed for every profession and occupation in the country: distinguished lawyer, journalist, veterinarian, driver, geologist, teacher, doctor, economist, etc. Athletes received honorary titles based on their competitive or testing results: Master of Sports Candidate, Master of Sports, Distinguished Master of Sports, Distinguished Coach, etc.

In post-Soviet Russia, awards and titles institutionalized during the Soviet era continue to be honoured; however, some old awards were abolished, others changed, and new ones were established. Hero of the Soviet Union became Hero of the Russian Federation (1992). The highest new state awards include the Order of

St. Andrew the First-Called (*Sv. Apostola Andreia Pervozvannogo*, the patron saint of Russia), established in 1998 and awarded to outstanding citizens of the Russian Federation for exceptional service that promotes the greatness and glory of Russia. Its military version is Andrew the First-Called with Swords. The pre-Revolutionary order of St. George was reinstated for military valour. The military Orders of Suvorov, Ushakov, Nakhimov, Aleksandr Nevskii, and Kutuzov were preserved, and a new Order of Zhukov introduced (1995). The Order of Courage (1994) is awarded for bravery and self-sacrifice in saving lives during natural disasters, protecting social order, and law enforcement. A new Order and medal for Service to the Fatherland (*Za zaslugi pered Otechestvom*, 1994) recognizes distinguished service to the country – in industry and agriculture, construction and transport, education and sciences, culture and medicine, defence and law enforcement, state security and military service. One of the new medals, to a Defender of Free Russia (*Zashchitniku svobodnoi Rossii*), appeared a year after the 1991 August coup to commend Russian and foreign citizens for defending constitutional order and implementing democratic political and economic reforms. The Russian state continues to reward citizens for various accomplishments with Jubilee medals: the 60th Anniversary of the Victory in World War II (the Great Patriotic War) 1941–45 (2004), 300th anniversary of the Russian Navy (1996), and in commemoration of the 850th Anniversary of Moscow (1997).

Honorary professional titles, including those in arts and culture, remained essentially the same, with USSR replaced by Russian Federation. The Academy of Sciences now annually awards two major Lomonosov gold medals on 19 November – one to a Russian, the other to a foreign scientist or scholar, for outstanding achievements in the fields of the natural sciences and humanities (1993). In 1999, the Pushkin Medal was introduced for accomplishments in culture, education, the humanities, literature and the arts, and significant contributions to the preservation and study of Russia's cultural heritage and the mutual enrichment of national cultures.

See also: Academy of Sciences; awards, cultural, post-Soviet; awards, cultural, Soviet; awards, literary, post-Soviet; awards, literary, Soviet; BAM (Baikal-Amur Railroad); Brezhnev, Leonid; Communist Youth League; Moscow State University; mother-heroine; Pushkin, Aleksandr; sanatoria; Stakhanovism; Stalin, Iosif; tselina; vacations, Soviet and post-Soviet; World War II (Great Patriotic War)

TATIANA SMORODINSKAYA

Azerbaidzhan

Azerbaidzhan is located in Transcaucasia, South-western Asia, bordering the Caspian Sea. Its capital is Baky, spelled Baku in Russian. In ancient times the region was a crossroads for trade routes and thus suffered many invasions. It came under the cultural influence of Persia and Turkey.

Russia conquered Azerbaidzhan in the early nineteenth century. The exploitation of oil brought an influx of Russians into Baku. Armenians also became important as merchants and local officials. In 1913, Baku was the largest city in the Caucasus. The first independent Democratic Republic of Azerbaidzhan emerged in 1918–20. In 1920, Azerbaidzhan was occupied by the Red Army and came under the Soviet Union's political and economic control. During Stalin's dictatorship, Azerbaidzhan suffered from forced collectivization and widespread purges, while simultaneously undergoing industrialization and a significant increase in literacy.

On 30 August 1991, Azerbaidzhan became an independent nation, headed by a unicameral National Assembly and president. Azerbaidzhan shares all the formidable problems of the former Soviet republics in making the transition from a command to a market economy, but its considerable energy resources (oil and gas) brighten its long-term prospects. In 1991–94, the country became involved in a military conflict with Armenia over the disputed territory of Nagorny Karabakh.

Only about 40 per cent of ethnic Azeris live in the country (7,868,385 in 2004). The rest are scattered round the world. Most Azerbaidzhanis speak the Turkic language Azeri. The language switched from the Arabic to the Latin alphabet (1923), then to the Cyrillic alphabet (1939), and in the 1990s returned to a modified Latin alphabet. The national religion is Islam; Azerbaidzhan is one of the most liberal Muslim-majority states.

Azerbaidzhanis are grounded in both Islamic and European cultures, mostly Turkish and Russian, best reflected in their rich literary heritage, much of which derives from an oral tradition of poems and ancient epics. Azerbaidzhan is also famous for its embroidered textiles and musical traditions.

The region in Iran south of the Araks River is also known as Azerbaidzhan. The people on both sides of the border speak the same Turkic language, share the religion of Islam, and had a common history until the Russian conquest. Under this pretext Soviet forces occupied the northern part of Iran during World War II, but had to withdraw in 1946. From that time until the late 1980s, contacts between Azerbaidzhanis north and south of the Iranian-Soviet border were severely limited.

Further reading

Akinea, S. (1986) *Islamic Peoples of the Soviet Union*, 2nd edn, London: Routledge and Kegan Paul.

——. (1992) *The Azerbaijani Turks: Power and Identity under Russian Rule*, Stanford, CA: Hoover University Press.

Bennigsen, A., Broxup, M. and Wimbush S. (1986) *Muslims of the Soviet Empire: A Guide*, Bloomington, IN: Indiana University Press.

TATYANA LEDENEVA

B

Babii Iar

At this ravine on the outskirts of Kiev, Ukraine, the Nazis murdered approximately 200,000 people, mostly Jews, during World War II. Anti-Semitism among Soviet leaders delayed acknowledgement of the true scale of events at Babii Iar until the Thaw (1960s). In 1961, Evgenii Evtushenko published a poem memorializing the victims. Dmitrii Shostakovich set this poem to music in his Symphony no. 13, op. 113, in B flat minor (1962). Other accounts of the brutality at Babii Iar include a poem by Ilia Erenberg (1945) and a documentary novel by Anatolii Kuznetsov (1966). A memorial was erected at the site in 1976.

See also: anti-Semitism; Erenberg, Ilia; Evtushenko, Evgenii; Jews; Shostakovich, Dmitrii; Thaw; Ukraine; World War II (Great Patriotic War)

SHARON A. KOWALSKY

Babkina, Nadezhda Georgievna

(née Nadezhda Georgievna Zasedateleva)

b. 19 March 1950, Akhtubinsk, Astrakhan oblast

Folk singer

Born into a Cossack family, Babkina is a well-known Russian folk singer with a rare voice: a low alto with bass overtones. In 1975, she founded the vocal ensemble Russian Song (*Russkaia pesnia*), with six young female singers, soon joined by six males. The group is strong in improvisation within authentic and stylized folk genres and has toured numerous countries. Babkina has arranged more than a hundred folk songs, and released successful albums and videos. People's Artist of the Russian Federation (1992).

See also: folk music

ALEXANDER DOMRIN

Babochkin, Boris Andreevich

b. 18 January 1904, Saratov; d. 17 July 1975, Moscow

Actor, director

Babochkin is remembered primarily for his legendary performance as the earnest, gruff peasant-general in the 1934 film *Chapaev*, although his career began in 1921 and spanned over fifty years. Though he occasionally expressed frustration that *Chapaev* had typecast him, his entire body of work testifies to his dramatic range. He has appeared in over twenty films, and in most of the classic roles of Russian theatre, including Griboedov's *Gore ot uma* (*Woe from Wit*), Gogol's *Revizor* (*The Inspector General*), and Pushkin's *Boris Godunov*. Babochkin taught acting at VGIK from 1944 until his death.

See also: All-Russian (All-Union) State Institute of Cinematography (VGIK)

SETH GRAHAM

babushka

A diminutive form of *baba* (old woman, or (married) peasant woman); *babka* (grandmother; midwife); *babushka* means 'grandmother' or 'old woman' (of sufficient age to be a grandmother). Accordingly, the word is used in the West for a headscarf like those traditionally worn by Russian village women. Grandmothers often live with their grown children and play an important role in the family, especially that of childminder for children when their mothers are working. In addition, the Russian *babushka* traditionally has been a crucial institution of social control, even in large cities, taking it upon herself to give advice to neighbours, acquaintances, even strangers: it is not uncommon to see a *babushka* tell a stranger to dress properly in cold weather, not to sit on a cold surface, or to close a window to avoid draughts.

See also: families; women

SIBELAN FORRESTER

Baikal

Lake Baikal, in Eastern Siberia, is the deepest lake in the world (1,620 m), and contains approximately 20 percent of the world's fresh water. Among its many endemic species are the *epishura*, tiny crayfish that clean the lake and make it possible to see to a depth of 40 m, and the *nerpa*, the world's only freshwater seal. Suffering pollution from a pulp and paper mill on its shores since 1957, Baikal is now threatened by the oil industry. Despite its addition to the UNESCO list of world heritage endangered sites, Baikal continues to be polluted and threatened.

See also: Buriatia; Siberia

EMILY LYGO

Baikonur

Also known as Tiuratam, Baikonur is the oldest space launch facility (cosmodrome) in the world. Founded on 2 June 1955 in Kazakhstan, this Soviet top-classified military site got its misleading name after a remote Kazakh town in 1957, when the USSR launched the world's first

man-made satellite, or *sputnik*. Used for all Soviet, CIS, and most international manned, lunar, planetary, and geostationary orbit launches, Baikonur has been a symbol of national success and technological innovation. Since 1994, Russia has been renting Baikonur from Kazakhstan for an annual fee. Besides Baikonur, Russia also has the cosmodromes Plesetsk and Svobodnyi.

See also: Kazakhstan; space programme and exploration

Further reading

Canby, T. (1986) 'A Generation After Sputnik', *National Geographic*, October: 420–65.

TATIANA LEDENEVA

Bakhtin, Mikhail Mikhailovich

b. 16 November 1895, Orel; d. 7 March 1975, Moscow

Writer, philosopher

Philosopher, literary critic, and cultural historian Mikhail Bakhtin is the author of highly influential works including *Problemy poetiki Dostoevskogo* (*Problems of Dostoevskii's Poetics*), *Formy vremeni i khronotopa v romane* (*Forms of time and chronotope in the novel*), and *Tvorchestvo Fransua Rable i narodnaia kultura srednevekoviia i Renessansa* (*Rabelais and His World*). Important critical studies such as *Formalnyi metod v literaturovedenii* (*The Formal Method in Literary Scholarship*) and *Marksizm i filosofiia iazyka* (*Marxism and the Philosophy of Language*), published under the names of Pavel Medvedev and Valentin Voloshinov, respectively, are now widely, if not definitively, accepted as Bakhtin's works.

Bakhtin was a student in St. Petersburg during the revolutions of 1917. From 1930 to 1934, he was in exile in Kazakhstan. Bakhtin spent the following thirty years in obscure provincial towns, struggling to find employment, holding minor academic positions, giving private lessons and public lectures. Unknown to all but a small circle of friends and intellectual associates, his writings remained largely unpublished. The only major work to appear under his name in the first seventy years of his life – the book on Dostoevskii – was rediscovered in the early 1960s by a group of graduate students from the Gorkii Institute of World Literature in Moscow and opened the door to its author's rehabilitation. In the last decade of his life Bakhtin finally found scholarly recognition, resulting in the publication of his book on Rabelais and some of his main contributions to the theory of the novel. Most of his works were published only after his death in 1975.

Covering diverse areas such as ethics, theology, literary criticism, rhetoric, and cultural studies, Bakhtin's work is unified by recurrent themes and concerns, most significantly a certain type of consciousness, in which the boundaries between the 'self' and the 'other' are radically unstable, permeable, incessantly negotiated through signs and acts. He searched for manifestations of this consciousness on several cultural levels, from the micro-level of language's semantic units, through the realm of speech genres and literary forms, to the macro-level of societies, historical periods, and cultural traditions. In all these spheres, Bakhtin sought to demonstrate the inherently dialogic, unfinalized nature of identities and meanings. For language, this meant underscoring the 'interrelatedness', the 'addressivity' of the spoken or written word, its dependence on and determination by the social context in which it appears. Bakhtin's fascination with the novel stemmed from his understanding of the genre as a unique space of contested meaning, a dialogic environment for multiple social voices and ideologies. An inheritor of all anti-canonical tendencies from previous ages, the novel perpetuated through modern times a spirit of healthy irreverence and joyous relativity that Bakhtin considered inherent in folk culture. A celebration of this spirit, *Rabelais and His World* presents the Renaissance folk carnival as a time–space (chronotope) of inverted hierarchies, iconoclastic licence, and travestied identities, thus translating Bakhtin's conceptions of language and textuality into a vision of redemptive social dynamics.

See also: literary criticism

Further reading

Bakhtin, M. (1968) *Rabelais and His World*, trans. H. Iswolsky, Cambridge, MA: MIT Press.

—— (1981) *The Dialogic Imagination: Four Essays by Mikhail Bakhtin*, trans. C. Emerson and M. Holquist, Austin, TX: University of Texas Press.
—— (1984) *Problems of Dostoevsky's Poetics*, trans. C. Emerson, Minneapolis, MN: University of Minnesota Press.
Clark, K. and Holquist, M. (1984) *Mikhail Bakhtin*, Cambridge, MA: Harvard University Press.
Todorov, T. (1984) *Mikhail Bakhtin: The Dialogical Principle*, trans. W. Godzich, Minneapolis, MN: University of Minnesota Press.

PETRE MILLTCHOV PETROV

Balabanov, Aleksei Oktiabrinovich

b. 25 February 1959, Sverdlovsk

Screenwriter, director, producer

Screenwriter, director, and co-founder of STV Film Studio in St. Petersburg, Balabanov is one of the most successful, versatile, and influential film makers of the post-Soviet era. His films, whether literary adaptation (*Zamok* [*The Castle*, 1994]), urban gangster thriller (*Brat* [*Brother*, 1997], *Brat-2* [*Brother 2*, 2000]), art house cinema (*Pro urodov i liudei* [*Of Freaks and Men*, 1998]), or nationalist blockbuster (*Voina* [*War*, 2002]), reflect the social breakdown and ideological anarchy of post-Communist Russia. Winners of numerous prizes at national and international film festivals, e.g., *Brother* won the FIPRESCI at Torino, they have consistently led in the domestic box office and video rental markets.

See also: film, festivals and prizes; film, post-Soviet; film studios

ANTHONY ANEMONE

Balaian, Roman Gurgenovich

b. 15 April 1941, Nerke Oratag, Azerbaidzhani SSR

Film director

Balaian is most famous for *Polety vo sne i naiavu* (*Flights in Dream and in Reality*, 1983), starring

Oleg Iankovskii. Balaian has also made acclaimed adaptations of Russian literary classics. *Ledi Makbet Mtsenskogo uezda* (*Lady Macbeth of Mtsensk*, 1989) is a faithful rendering of Leskov's 1865 story; it is distinguished by its attention to detail and sexual frankness. In post-Soviet Russia he has examined human relationships against a background of professional killings, as in *Dve luny, tri solntsa* (*Two Moons, Three Suns*, 1998), starring Vladimir Mashkov, and in a school for deaf mutes, as in *Noch svetla* (*The Night is Bright*, 2004), with Irina Kupchenko.

See also: Azerbaidzhan; film; literary adaptation; Iankovskii, Oleg; Mashkov, Vladimir

DAVID GILLESPIE

ballet, post-Soviet

In the late 1980s and early 1990s, several important changes occurred in Russian ballet that reflected the sociopolitical and cultural situation in the country. New artistic trends largely resulted from contact with the West, acquaintance with the creative activity of European and American choreographers, and with contemporary dance. During the Soviet era, classical Russian ballet was isolated from Western influences and modern trends, its generation of dancers confident of its worldwide supremacy. The 'golden age' of the Bolshoi Theatre (the 1960s–the 1970s) boasted such superb dancers as Maia Plisetskaia, Vladimir Vasilev, Ekaterina Maksimova, Natalia Bessmertnova, Mikhail Lavrovskii, and Marina Kondrateva; Iurii Grigorovich's arresting performances and stagings; and sensational tours in the West. At the beginning of the 1990s, however, the Bolshoi rarely mounted original productions (*La Bayadère*, 1991, *The Corsair*, 1994), while the Mariinskii Theatre in St. Petersburg restored Grigorovich's old ballets, such as *The Legend of Love* (1992).

A major tendency in post-Soviet ballet was the effort to acquire active mastery of the Western ballet repertoire and new forms of choreography. For the first time Russian dancers performed neoclassical plotless ballets of the best twentieth-century American choreographer, George Balanchine (1904–83): *Tema s variatsiiami*

(*Theme and Variations*, 1989), *Apollon* (*Apollo*, 1992) at the Mariinskii Theatre, and *Bludnyi syn* (*The Prodigal Son*, 1991) at the Bolshoi. These productions made clear that dancers raised on Marius Petipa's classics and Grigorovich's *tants-simfonizm* (dance-symphonism) had difficulties mastering a new style. Problems in assimilating the creative heritage of leading Western choreographers – George Balanchine, Roland Petit, Jerome Robbins, Maurice Béjart, John Neumayer, William Forsythe – still plague large Russian ballet companies. Recent premieres of this repertoire, such as Neumayer's *Son v letniuiu noch* (*Midsummer Night's Dream*, 2004), Balanchine's *Koncherto Barokko* (*Baroque Concerto*) at the Bolshoi (2004); Forsythe's *Steptext* (2002), and Balanchine's *Serenade* at the Perm Theatre (2004), however, show that younger dancers have learned a new idiom and style. Since the end of the 1980s Russian actors have had the opportunity to work on contract in western companies and participate in premieres of new ballets, which opportunities have given them the chance to become international ballet super-stars (Nina Ananiashvili, Irek Mukhamedov, Vladimir Malakhov, Igor Zelenskii).

The other recent trend – interest in authentic classical productions – manifests itself in reconstructions of Marius Petipa's choreography: *Sleeping Beauty* in the 1890 version (1999), and the four-act *Bayadère* of 1877 (2002) mounted at the Mariinskii, as well as *Doch faraona* (*The Pharaoh's Daughter*) of 1862, reconstructed by Pierre Lacotte at the Bolshoi (2000). The most successful Russian choreographers of the post-Soviet period are Boris Eifman, Dmitrii Briantsev, and, in the last few years, the Moldavian Radu Poklitaru, who staged an ultramodern *Romeo and Juliet* at the Bolshoi (2003), and that theatre's artistic leader, Aleksei Ratmanskii, known for his *Sny o Iaponii* (*Dreams about Japan*, 1998), *Lea* (2001), and others. The best dancers of the new generation include Uliana Lopatkina, Diana Vishneva, Svetlana Zakharova, Maria Aleksandrova, Ekaterina Shipulina, Nina Kaptsova, Natalia Ledovskaia, Nikolai Tsiskaridze, Andrei Uvarov, Sergei Filin, Adrian Fadeev, and Leonid Sarafanov. All possess vivid presence and virtuoso technique, and perform in both classical and modern ballets, often abroad.

Post-Soviet ballet has witnessed the appearance of small ballet companies, many of them driven by commercial considerations, many modern-dance groups, and studios of expressive and free dance. Whereas in the early 1990s modern-dance groups largely imitated European and American choreographic practices, nowadays Russian companies have their own style, characterized by an unusual choreographic lexicon and interesting stage design: *Provintsialnye tantsy* (Provincial Dances), with choreographer Tatiana Baganova; *Nezavisimaia tantsevalnaia komanda 'Kipling'* (Independent 'Kipling' Dance Team) in Ekaterinburg, *Teatr sovremennogo tantsa* (Theatre of Modern Dance), with choreographer Olga Pona, in Cheliabinsk, *Balet Evgeniia Panfilova* (Eugene Panfilov's Ballet) in Perm, and *Kineticheskii teatr Sashi Pepeliaeva* (Aleksandr Pepeliaev's Kinetic Theatre) in Moscow.

See also: ballet dancers, Bolshoi Theatre; ballet dancers, Mariinskii Theatre; ballet, Soviet; Bolshoi Theatre; choreographers, Soviet; Eifman, Boris; Mariinskii Theatre; Plisetskaia, Maia

Further reading

Encyclopedia (1997) *Russkii balet: Entsiklopediia*, Moscow: Soglasie.

IRINA UDIANSKAYA

ballet, Soviet

Ballet represented one of the Soviet Union's most awkward inheritances from the imperial period. As ballet was inextricably linked to the tsarist court, its survival was widely questioned in the early Soviet period. The situation remained precarious until the 1930s, when ballet, like champagne and caviar, lent the young Soviet state valuable cultural capital and its ruling elite a newfound and necessary sense of status. An art form with obvious origins in court ceremonial and Renaissance spectacle should not have survived the Soviet cultural revolutions of the 1920s, but arguments advanced by People's Commissar for Enlightenment Anatolii

Lunacharskii and others advocated the preservation of the past's cultural heritage. The establishment of 'academic' theatres, meant to preserve the cultural inheritance of the past after the October Revolution (1917), afforded ballet ample time to adapt to new, ever-changing ideologies. During this time, Soviet ballet pioneered a number of innovations, beginning with its advocacy in the 1930s of a new type of ballet that would dispense with conventional pantomime gestures (another legacy of the nineteenth century). Called *drambalet* (a contraction of 'dramatic ballet'), new works such as Rostislav Zakharov's *Bakhchisaraiskii fontan* (*Fountain of Bakhchisarai*, 1934) and Leonid Lavrovskii's *Romeo i Dzhulietta* (*Romeo and Juliet*, 1940) typified the new trend: these are works on a grand scale adapted from literary monuments, set to music in late-romantic style and with choreography that would violate no nineteenth-century norms. Movement and meaning were to fuse into a dance of lyric expression, an updated version of the ballet's ongoing fascination with movement that could advance narrative.

During the inter-war period, important artists, choreographers, and ballets were 'transferred' from the Leningrad stage to Moscow – effectively a promotion accorded the Bolshoi Theatre as well as the artists and new repertory it featured. The Leningrad (Kirov) ballet remained the more conservative company, mostly tending its legacy of 'classic' works from the nineteenth century. The Moscow ballet developed a somewhat acrobatic, bombastic style of dancing that both shocked and awed Western audiences when cultural exchanges began in the 1950s. Outside the capitals, the gospel of Russian/Soviet ballet was spread from the 1930s onward, when 'national' ballets were developed throughout the Soviet Union. Both the Bolshoi and Kirov troupes passed the war years in the Urals, and the Kirov's internment in Perm resulted in the rise of a third ballet centre in that city, still powerful in the post-Soviet period.

Cultural agreements signed between the Soviet Union and Western governments in the 1950s resulted in a sudden wave of tours to and from Russia. Though Soviet officials maintained an air of confidence in the superiority of their ballet companies and the new works created for them, the Soviet tours of the Paris Opera Ballet in 1958, American Ballet Theatre in 1960, and the New York City Ballet in 1962 shook the Soviet ballet to its foundations: not only had these 'bourgeois' ballet troupes produced talented dancers, but their innovative repertories revealed the puritanical, hidebound quality that characterized the greater share of the Soviet repertory.

Iurii Grigorovich, then a young choreographer intent on modernizing the Soviet canon, created versions of nineteenth-century classics starkly different from the traditional versions on view in Leningrad. Together with leading Soviet scenographer Simon Virsaladze, he created re-stagings that cleared the stage of the props and Victorian sumptuousness that still characterized the Leningrad versions, and gave the classics a modern, if vacuous, look. Grigorovich's own ballets, including *Legenda o liubvi* (*Legend of Love*, 1961) and *Spartak* (*Spartacus*, 1968), epitomized a new style of dancing for the coming decades. The new, athletic performance of Moscow dancers such as Maia Plisetskaia and Vladimir Vasilev characterized the Soviet style in ballet until the system's collapse in the 1980s.

The Bolshoi and Kirov ballets were led by artistic directors with long tenures in the second half of the twentieth century: Konstantin Sergeev and Oleg Vinogradov in Leningrad, Grigorovich in Moscow. Each was responsible for maintaining and restaging classic works, adding new works to the repertory, and quelling the troupe's growing revolt against the blandness of the Soviet repertory, particularly as touring began to reveal its artistic inadequacies. A series of defections to the West beginning in the 1960s infused Western companies with talented stars such as Rudolf Nureev, Natalia Makarova, Mikhail Baryshnikov, and Aleksandr Godunov, but left voids in Soviet troupes. Nina Ananiashvili, the Bolshoi's most promising ballerina of the 1980s, brokered the first agreement to appear on both Western and Soviet stages, just as the disintegration of the Soviet Union and the ballet system it had carefully tended rendered this revolutionary gesture almost meaningless.

See also: ballet dancers, Bolshoi Theatre; ballet dancers, Mariinskii Theatre; Baryshnikov, Mikhail; Bolshoi Theatre; choreographers, Soviet; Godunov, Aleksandr; Grigorovich, Iurii; Lavrovskii, Leonid; Mariinskii Theatre; Nureyev (Nureev), Rudolf; pantomime; Plisetskaia, Maia; Urals; Vasilev, Vladimir; World War II (Great Patriotic War)

Further reading

Krasovskaia, V. (1971) *Russkii baletnyi teatr nachala XX veka* [Russian Ballet Theater of the Beginning of the Twentieth Century], Leningrad.

Roslavleva, N. (1966) *Era of the Russian Ballet*, London.

Souritz, E. (1990) *Soviet Choreographers in the 1920s*, ed. Sally Banes, trans. Lynn Visson, Durham, NC: Duke University Press.

TIM J. SCHOLL

ballet dancers, Bolshoi Theatre

A pleiad of extraordinarily talented Moscow dancers emerged in the late 1950s and early 1960s: Maia Plisetskaia, Vladimir Vasilev, Ekaterina Maksimova, and Natalia Bessmertnova represented the Bolshoi Theatre's first group of home-grown stars. Their remarkable careers coincided with celebrated, and unprecedented, foreign tours that introduced the world to an emerging and energetic Bolshoi style. Their tenures also coincided with a relatively creative phase in the company's history: Iurii Grigorovich's artistic direction, and the new, more contemporary ballets he created for the company such as *Spartak* (*Spartacus*), and *Legenda o liubvi* (*Legend of Love*) featured stellar roles for the company's young stars.

Moscow's Bolshoi Ballet had long occupied a secondary position relative to Petersburg's Mariinskii Ballet and its first Soviet successors. The transfer of the capital from Petrograd to Moscow would gradually shift the ballet's balance of power as well, and mostly by an analogous system of 'transferring' the dancers, choreographers, directors, and repertory from Leningrad to Moscow. Ballerina Marina Semonova joined the company in 1930; Galina Ulanova moved to Moscow in 1944. Both reigned as the company's stars and later as esteemed pedagogues. Semonova danced in a mostly

Petersburg repertory and style; Ulanova created a number of new roles, Juliet in the acclaimed Lavrovskii/Prokofiev ballet among them. She starred in a number of feature films made from ballets, and she led the first, triumphant tours of London and New York in the 1950s.

Plisetskaia was the inheritor of a Moscow theatrical family tradition: her Uncle Asaf and Aunt Sulamith were leading Bolshoi dancers and teachers. Plisetskaia had already achieved fame as a dancer in the late 1940s, but the varied impediments to her early career delayed her worldwide celebrity by at least a decade. Yet of the next, equally celebrated generation of Bolshoi dancers, only Plisetskaia, considered headstrong and untrustworthy by Party officials, managed to create roles with famed Western choreographers (Roland Petit, Maurice Béjart) and foreshadowed the détente with Western ballet managed by late Soviet dancers, such as Nina Ananiashvili, the first Bolshoi dancer who managed to appear with Western companies as a guest artist rather than as a defector.

See also: ballet, post-Soviet; ballet, Soviet; ballet dancers, Mariinskii Theatre; Bolshoi Theatre; Grigorovich, Iurii; Lavrovskii, Leonid; Mariinskii Theatre; Plisetskaia, Maia; Prokofiev, Sergei; Ulanova, Galina; Vasilev, Vladimir

TIM J. SCHOLL

ballet dancers, Mariinskii Theatre

A group known best for its famous defectors to the West in the 1960s and 1970s, the dancers who left the Kirov Ballet (as it was then known) in the 1960s and 1970s followed paths blazed by St. Petersburg dancers of the early 1900s. Anna Pavlova, Vatslav Nijinsky, Michel Fokine, Bronislava Nijinska, George Balanchine, and Alexandra Danilova were the most celebrated of the exodus of Mariinskii dancers and choreographers who spread the gospel of Russian ballet to Western Europe and the Americas in the early twentieth century. A second set of defectors decamped to Moscow once state power and cultural prestige shifted to the Soviet capital: Marina Semenova, Galina Ulanova, and Iurii Grigorovich were each instrumental in

raising pedagogical, performance, and choreographic standards in Moscow when they left the former Mariinskii for careers in the Bolshoi Theatre. The defectors of the third wave – Rudolf Nureev, Natalia Makarova, and Mikhail Baryshnikov – briefly revived the star touring circuit their predecessors had invented in the early twentieth century. Those who remained in Leningrad faced stale repertories but enjoyed the dwindling glories of the former Imperial Theatre system: first-rate pedagogy and coaching, an established dance academy, and performance tradition. Most formidable among them were Natalia Dudinskaia and her husband, Konstantin Sergeev. She was the prima ballerina and pupil of famed pedagogue Agripina Vaganova; he, the *jeune premier* of the 1940s and director of the ballet from 1951 to 1956 and from 1960 to 1970. His restaged versions of the nineteenth-century classics became definitive and marked the company as the conservator of Marius Petipa's choreographic bequest. Irina Kolpakova combined their two functions into one: like Dudinskaia, she excelled in the most exacting of the nineteenth-century's ballerina roles, and like Sergeev, in party politics. This apotheosis of talent wed with power signalled the company's creative stagnation, but less conventional Mariinskii dancers sought careers abroad. Nonetheless, a small group of talented dancers brightened an otherwise bleak late Soviet landscape: Iurii Solovev's untimely death ended a dynasty of extraordinary male dancing at the Kirov; the affiliated Perm School furnished the Kirov's most finished ballerinas of the 1970s and 1980s: Liubov Kunakova and Olga Chenchikova. Yet the resilience of the Leningrad/St. Petersburg ballet academy became apparent in the post-Soviet years, as Vaganova's institution produced an astonishing annual crop of ballerinas, including Uliana Lopatkina, Diana Vishneva, and Daria Pavlenko.

See also: ballet, post-Soviet; ballet, Soviet; Baryshnikov, Mikhail; Bolshoi Theatre; choreographers, Soviet; Grigorovich, Iurii; Mariinskii Theatre; Nureyev (Nureev), Rudolf

TIM J. SCHOLL

Baltic actors in Soviet cinema

In late Soviet culture, the Baltic republics (Estonia, Latvia, and Lithuania) played the role of the USSR's most Westernized outpost, reassuring Soviet ideologues that Western cultures could be tamed and controlled. During the Cold War, films about the West were usually shot in Tallinn or Riga. Actors from the Baltic republics, such as Regimantas Adomaitis, Donatas Banionis, Juozas Budraitis (all three from Lithuania), Ivars Kalnins and Vija Artmane (both from Latvia) were usually cast in the roles of Westerners. Soviet film makers and viewers perceived these actors' non-Slavic features, body language, and slightly accented Russian speech as an 'authentic' representation of Western-ness. For example, almost the entire Soviet career of Banionis was devoted to playing a palette of Western types: from a self-reflective intellectual loner (*Solaris*, Tarkovskii 1972) to a middle-class philistine (*Begstvo mistera Mak-Kinli* [*The Escape of Mr. McKinley*], Shveitser 1975). Baltic actors also played Westerners in Soviet television films of the 1970s and the 1980s. In the 1978 adaptation of Somerset Maugham's *Theatre*, Viya Artmane as Julia Lambert and Ivars Kalnins as Tom Fennel became iconic Western characters on the Soviet television screen. Ideologically the Western types played by these actors signified the decadence of bourgeois life, while visually they were part of the coveted Western *mise-en-scène*. This fashion of casting actors from Baltic countries as the domesticated Western 'other' continues in post-Soviet Russian cinema with Lithuanian Ingeborga Dapkunaite playing a British hostage in Chechen captivity in Aleksei Balabanov's 2002 film *Voina* (*War*).

See also: Balabanov, Aleksei; Baltic Sea region; Estonia; film, Soviet – Thaw period; Latvia; Lithuania; Tarkovskii, Andrei

ELENA PROKHOROVA AND ALEXANDER PROKHOROV

Baltic Sea region (Pribaltika)

The Baltic region (or *Pribaltika*) encompasses three states (Estonia, Latvia, and Lithuania) on the Eastern coast of the Baltic Sea. Established in 1918, the Baltic States were independent until 1940 when they became incorporated into the USSR (during World War II), and were occupied by Germany in 1941. Recaptured by the USSR in 1944, they remained part of the Soviet Union until 1991. The region is mostly a low-lying plain with some hills and highlands in the south-east.

The region had a primarily agricultural economy before Soviet annexation and, in the next fifty years, was completely integrated into the Soviet system. While lacking natural resources, the Baltic region possessed a highly skilled workforce and an excellent transport location. During the period of Soviet centralized economy, the region was a large supplier of tools; it was also a large resort area, outdone only by the Black Sea and the Caucasus

The total population of the region is less than 7.5 million: Estonia – 1.4; Latvia – 2.35; Lithuania – 3.6. The level of urbanization is quite low, approximately 70 per cent. The largest cities are the capitals: Estonia's Tallinn – 400,000; Latvia's Riga – 790,000; Lithuania's Vilnius – 570,000. In the post-Soviet era, both Estonia and Latvia, unlike Lithuania (where all residents were allowed to apply for naturalization regardless of ethnic origin), still have significant problems with citizenship legislation. Russians constitute approximately 30 per cent of the population (and about 60 per cent of residents with higher education), but only those citizens who lived there before 1940 and their descendants were eligible for citizenship in 1991. In 2004, the Baltic countries joined NATO and EU.

See also: Estonia; Latvia; Lithuania

IVAN TITKOV

BAM (Baikal-Amur Railroad)

The Baikal-Amur Mainline (BAM) is a 3,115-km-long railroad line stretching from East Siberia to the Pacific Coast across some of Russia's harshest terrain. Conceived as a titanic project to mobilize Soviet youth, it came to embody the stagnation of the Brezhnev era. The project was launched in 1974, supposedly to provide an alternative to the Trans-Siberian railroad, to open access to the region's rich mineral resources, and to develop industry in the vast, sparsely populated area. Thousands of Komsomol (Communist Youth League) youths flocked to the region to work on the railroad, but the harsh environment and terrible planning proved insurmountable obstacles. By the time the BAM officially opened in 1984, it was full of gaps and rife with technical problems. To this day it is not fully operational and remains of little commercial or strategic value.

See also: Communist Youth League; railroads; Stagnation; transportation system

ANDREW GUSTAFSON

bania

The *bania* (bathhouse) has an important cultural function in Russian life, providing not only hygiene, but also opportunities for relaxation, socializing, and healing. Whether public or private, a *bania* has a *parnaia* (steam room), in which one reaches the desired, sometimes unbearably high, temperature and humidity by throwing water on the hot *kamenki* (stones). Indispensable for washing in the *bania* is a *venik* (a bunch of dry twigs with leaves), usually made of birch twigs, with which bathers flog themselves or each other to open the pores and induce intense sweating. In a private *bania* in the country, one may jump naked into a nearby body of water or snow for momentary relief from heat.

Bathers not only use different infusions and solutions to create steam with medicinal properties or a desired fragrance, but also apply various lotions or ointments to face and body. Herbal, fruit, and black teas, imbibed during or immediately after the *bania*, are believed to alleviate a cold, soothe stomach spasms, or simply intensify healthy sweating.

Russians used to visit the *bania* once a week, usually on Saturdays. In large urban centres the *bania* tradition is gradually dying out as a people increasingly acquire non-communal apartments

with private bathtubs and showers and use the *bania* exclusively for relaxation. In the country, bathroom plumbing is still scarce, and people wash in either public or private *banias*. In post-perestroika Russia luxurious *banias* or saunas have become the spas of choice for the mafia and New Russians, who often supplement the pleasure of steam with women and alcohol.

See also: communal apartment; health; New Russians

Further reading

Giliarovskii, V. (1983) 'Bani', in *Moskva i moskvichi*, Moscow: Moskovskii rabochii.
Prudius, S. (ed.) (2004) *Entsiklopediia bani*, Moscow: EKSMO.

KONSTANTIN KUSTANOVICH

Banionis, Donatas Iuozovich

b. 28 April 1924, Kaunas, Lithuania

Theatre and film actor and director

Banionis's theatre career is connected with the Panevezhis Drama Theater in Lithuania. His cinematic debut was in the films of Vitautas Zhalakiavichus (*Nikto ne khotel umirat, Nobody Wanted to Die*, 1963), which marked the rise of national cinema in Lithuania during the Thaw. The role of Kris Kelvin in Andrei Tarkovskii's *Solaris* (1972) established Banionis's reputation as an 'intellectual actor', capable of expressing complex thoughts and emotions in a reserved manner. This quality, highly valued during Brezhnev's Stagnation, coupled with Banionis's 'Western' (i.e., Baltic) appearance, determined his casting in roles of Soviet spies (e.g., Ladeinikov in Savva Kulish's *Mertvyi sezon, The Dead Season*, 1968) and Westerners (e.g., Mr. McKinley in Mikhail Shveitser's *Begstvo mistera Mak-Kinli* (*The Escape of Mr. McKinley* 1975)).

See also: Baltic actors in Soviet cinema; Tarkovskii, Andrei

ELENA PROKHOROVA

baranka

A hard, ring-shaped roll, usually made of wheat flour. The rolls can be sweet or savoury, are sometimes dried to the consistency of pretzels, and are traditionally served with tea. *Baranka* is also slang for the steering wheel of a car.

See also: bread

MICHELE BERDY

Baranskaia, Natalia Vladimirovna

b. 18 December 1908, St. Petersburg

Writer

Baranskaia's fiction addressed women's problems from the 1960s till the 1980s. Her novella *Nedelia kak nedelia* (*A Week Like Any Other*, 1969), internationally acclaimed by feminists, depicts the hectic routine of an educated Moscow working mother. In a more subjective vein, her only novel, *Den' pominoveniia* (*Remembrance Day*, 1989), describes loss and women's struggle to survive during the Nazi invasion. Baranskaia inclines to idealize female characters dedicated to unreflecting self-sacrifice and the imperatives of maternity and responsibility – tendencies that run counter to Western feminism.

See also: literature, women's

BENJAMIN SUTCLIFFE

bards

This term refers to poets who became popular as singer-songwriters during the Thaw (late 1950s–1960s), singing their own lyrics and accompanying themselves on the guitar. The genre of the bards' works is called *samodeiatelnaia pesnia* ('amateur song'), *avtorskaia pesnia* ('author's song'), or *bardovskaia pesnia* ('bard song'). Its stylistic deviation from official norms, its questionable ideological orientation, and its rapid, uncontrolled dissemination all posed serious problems for the Soviet authorities. Accordingly, the bard movement had a complicated legal status, which fluctuated in response to political developments.

Bard song was an unofficial, acoustic, solo genre that emphasized simple melodies, untrained singing voices, and unpolished guitar-playing technique. It represented a reaction against not only the complicated staging and slick professionalism of Soviet 'mass' and variety stage songs, but also the ideological and linguistic clichés found therein. Bard songs circulated widely via *magnitizdat* ('magnetic publication'), that is, through home-made tape recordings that were passed from hand to hand.

The roots of bard song can be found in nineteenth-century Russian musical and literary culture (particularly the *romans*); in the late-nineteenth- and early-twentieth-century variety stage (especially as represented by Aleksandr Vertinskii); and also in student and, arguably, labour camp songs of the pre-1953 period. Parallels also exist with the traditions of German cabaret song (e.g., Bertolt Brecht) and French *chanson* (e.g., Yves Montand and Georges Brassens). Drawing on this complex genealogy, bard song nonetheless appeared during the Thaw as a qualitatively new cultural phenomenon. The patriarch of bard song is Bulat Okudzhava, who began performing his songs for circles of friends in the late 1950s. As Okudzhava's works spread through *magnitizdat* and his popularity increased, a pleiad of other bards began to emerge. Next to Okudzhava, the best-known and most highly regarded bards are Aleksandr Galich and Vladimir Vysotskii; other leading figures include Mikhail Ancharov, Novella Matveeva, Iurii Vizbor, and Iulii Kim.

The bards are commonly divided into two groups, the *bardy-romantiki* ('romantic bards') and the *bardy protesta* ('protest bards'). The numerically superior former group includes Okudzhava, Aleksandr Gorodnitskii, Evgenii Kliachkin, Iurii Kukin, Matveeva, Vizbor, and countless others. A lyrical tone predominates in their works, and common themes include love, friendship, and the romanticism of the road. The last theme is sometimes combined with hints of exoticism or fantasy (for example, images of foreign or imaginary lands), and in this fashion manifests a strongly escapist strain. The latter group includes Galich, Vysotskii, and, to a lesser extent, Kim. The works of these 'protest bards' are often openly political, sharply criticizing the Soviet regime and Soviet society at large. Politically sensitive topics such as the GULag, anti-Semitism, and rampant alcoholism are addressed unsparingly. Sometimes muted and at other times outspoken, alienation from the image of reality presented in official sources is an undercurrent present in both groups' songs. Another commonality is the concept of bard songs as a means of communication or as intimate conversations among friends.

Official responses to the genre were initially fairly positive. Bards' lyrics were compared favourably with those of 'mass' and variety stage songs; songs were discussed in the local and national press, played on the radio, and sometimes published, though in modest numbers and in censored form. As bard song became a mass phenomenon, largely through the uncontrolled medium of *magnitizdat*, official attitudes changed. Soviet authorities, startled and concerned by the wildfire spread of the bard movement, soon tried to bring it under control. Beginning in the early 1960s, the Komsomol took action, organizing or regularizing amateur song clubs and playing a major role in the management of local, regional, and national song competitions and festivals. Club activities were monitored by the KGB, contest juries were stacked with representatives of various official organs, and certain bards and songs were virtually barred from the stage.

From the late 1960s–1970s, the bards' existence was more precarious, as the authorities simultaneously suppressed the bard song movement and co-opted or commissioned songs for use in approved settings (such as films, theatre, and television productions). If the works of the 'protest bards' were almost never published, during these years even publication of works by the apolitical 'romantic bards' was severely curtailed. In short, the bard movement gradually became a type of underground culture. During perestroika the situation changed once again: publication of bards' works was resumed and expanded, and official recordings of bards' performances were issued. Bard song is intimately linked to the particular circumstances of its genesis; in the post-Soviet period, dramatic political, social, and technological changes have led some to argue that, despite the continued popularity of bard song festivals and KSPs (*Kluby samodeiatel'noi pesni* [Clubs of Amateur Songs]),

the genre is now dead. The success of Timur Shaov's recordings alone argues against a premature burial.

See also: amateur cultural activity; anti-Semitism; Federal Security Service (FSS/FSB); Galich, Aleksandr; GULag; kapustnik; KSP (Klub samodeiatelnoi pesni; amateur song club); music in film; music in theatre; Okudzhava; perestroika and glasnost; romance; samizdat; sixties generation; song, Soviet popular; Stagnation; Thaw; Vizbor, Iurii; Vysotskii, Vladimir

Further reading and discography

Andreev, I. and Boguslavskii, I. (*c*.1990) *Vladimir Vysotsky: Hamlet with a Guitar*, Moscow: Progress.

Galich, A. (*c*.1983) *Songs and Poems*, Ann Arbor, MI: Ardis.

Okudzhava, B. (1982) *65 Songs*, Ann Arbor, MI: Ardis.

Novikov, V. and Basovskaia, E. (2000) *Avtorskaia pesnia*, Moscow: Olimp.

Shipov, R. (ed.) (2000) *Piat'desiat rossiiskikh bardov: Spravochnik*, Moscow: Vagant.

Smith, G. S. (1984) *Songs to Seven Strings: Russian Guitar Poetry and Soviet 'Mass Song'*, Bloomington, IN: Indiana University Press.

Sosin, G. (*c*. 1975) 'Magnitizdat: uncensored songs of dissent', in R. Tokes (ed.) *Dissent in the USSR: Politics, Ideology, and People*, Baltimore, MD: Johns Hopkins University Press.

Vishevsky, A. (1993) 'The Bards', in A. Vishevsky *Soviet Literary Culture in the 1970s: The Politics of Irony*, Gainesville, FL: University Press of Florida.

Vysotsky, V. (2000) *Vladimir Vysotskii*, Moscow, Moroz Records (32 CDs).

RACHEL S. PLATONOV

Baryshnikov, Mikhail Nikolaevich

b. 27 January 1948, Riga

Dancer, actor, choreographer, director

After early training at the Riga Ballet School, in 1964, Baryshnikov transferred to the Leningrad Ballet School (now the Academy of the Russian Ballet), to become a principal dancer at the Kirov (now Mariinskii) Ballet in 1967; there he performed leading male parts in the classical

repertoire. While touring Canada in 1974, Baryshnikov defected to the West, where his career
took off. He was named principal dancer with
the American Ballet Theater. His versatile ballet
technique, plasticity, musicality, and performing
acumen enabled him to cover a wide repertoire,
ranging from traditional roles in classical ballets
to collaboration with innovative American
choreographers such as Alvin Ailey, John Butler,
Twyla Tharp, Mark Morris, Merce Cunning-
ham, Yvonne Rainer, Trisha Brown, and Paul
Taylor. George Balanchine invited Baryshnikov
to perform with his company, the New York
City Ballet, in 1978–79, including the leading
roles in Balanchine's *Midsummer Night's Dream*,
Symphony in C, *Union Jack*, and *Apollo*. Baryshnikov later returned to the American Ballet
Theatre as principal dancer and artistic director
(1980–89). After numerous guest appearances
with the major European ballet companies, in
1990, together with Mark Morris, he founded a
modern dance company, the White Oak Dance
Project. Currently, he heads the Baryshnikov
Arts Center (BAC), a creative laboratory for the
performing and visual arts in New York.

Baryshnikov's filmography includes leading
roles in such movies as *The Turning Point* (1977)
and *White Nights* (1985) and numerous television
appearances. He is the recipient of the Gold
Medal at the First International Ballet Competition in Moscow (1969), the Nijinsky Prize in
Paris (1970), an Emmy Award (1979), and
Kennedy Center Honors (2000).

See also: ballet dancers, Mariinskii Theatre;
emigration

TATIANA SENKEVITCH

Bashkortostan (Bashkiria)

Republic on the territory of the Russian Federation, with a Bashkor(t) ethnic population. In
pre-revolutionary and Soviet Russia the name of
the autonomous republic was Bashkiria, the
name of the nationality was Bashkir. The capital is
Ufa. After 1991, the republic renamed itself Bashkortostan and its nationality Bashkor(t). An ethnic
group of 1,345,000 people constituting 0.9 per
cent of the Russian Federation's population,
Bashkors belong to a sub-Uralic ethnic type,

traceable to Turkic nomadic tribes who had travelled to the southern Urals in the fourth century.
The Bashkir language belongs to the Turkic group
of the Altai family. The language was originally
written in the Arabic alphabet; the Latin alphabet
was adopted in 1929, and the Cyrillic in 1939. The
predominant religions of the republic are Sunni
Islam and paganism. The best-known Bashkor
poet is Salavat Yulayev (1754–1800).

Further reading

Smith, G. (ed.) (1990) *The Nationalities Question in
the Soviet Union*, London: Longman.

TATYANA LEDENEVA

Bashlachev, Aleksandr Nikolaevich

b. 27 May 1960, Cherepovets; d. 17
February 1988, Leningrad

Poet, singer

A graduate of the Journalism Department of
Urals State University in Ekaterinburg (1983), in
1984, Bashlachev moved to Moscow, then to
Leningrad. 'SashBash' conquered both capitals
with his unique combination of rock energy,
refined poetry, and deep exploration of Russian
national themes, myths, and images. From 1983
to 1987, he wrote about sixty-five songs, recorded
four studio albums, and gave numerous concerts. Probably the most significant Russian poet
of the 'generation of yardkeepers and watch-
men', Bashlachev committed suicide, aged 28.
The most complete collection of his songs was
released by *Otdelenie Vykhod* on seven CDs.

See also: bards; Ekaterinburg; rock music

ALEXANDER DOMRIN

Bashmet, Iurii Abramovich

b. 24 January 1953, Rostov-na-Donu

Violist, conductor, professor

A graduate of the Moscow Conservatory (1978),
Bashmet   won   the   Munich   International

Competition in 1976. He constantly performs with world-renowned artists and is considered one of the leading violists in the world – an achievement all the more important, given the limited concerto repertoire for viola and thus the instrument's relatively low profile. Bashmet has been a strong advocate of contemporary music, promoting the works of Shnittke, Gubaidulina, and others, many of whom have written pieces for him. He founded the Moscow Soloists Chamber Orchestra (*Kamernyi orkestr 'Solisty Moskvy'*) in 1986, which tours and records regularly. Bashmet has taught at the Moscow Conservatory since 1978. USSR State Prize (1986), Russian State Prize (1994, 1996).

See also: Gubaidulina, Sofiia; Moscow Conservatory; Shnittke, Alfred; violin performance, Russian/Soviet

DAVID GOMPPER

Basilashvili, Oleg Valerianovich

b. 26 September 1934, Moscow

Theatre, film, and television actor

Basilashvili made his theatre debut in 1956 at the Leningrad Lenin Komsomol Theatre; in 1959, he joined the Leningrad Large Dramatic Theatre, where he gained fame for his performances in Anton Chekhov's plays. Basilashvili made his film debut in 1957 and throughout his long career gained a reputation for playing conflicted intellectuals, exemplified in his nuanced portrayal of the gentle, wavering translator Buzykin in O*sennii marafon* (*Autumn Marathon*, 1979). He frequently appeared in Eldar Riazanov's films, including *Vokzal dlia dvoikh* (*Train Station for Two*, 1982) and *Nebesa obetovannye* (*The Promised Heavens*, 1991).

See also: Riazanov, Eldar

JENNIFER RYAN TISHLER

basketball

The basketball rulebook appeared in Russian in 1901. Moscow's *Dinamo* won the first USSR championship (1923); however, *TsSKA* gradually became the strongest Russian basketball team, with the Lithuanian SSR's *Zhalgiris* its principal rival during the Soviet years. In the 1980s this rivalry acquired political implications: *Zhalgiris's* fans generally supported political freedom, while TsSKA was associated with totalitarianism. The Soviet basketball team's top achievements include Olympic titles in 1972 and 1988. (Both times they defeated the US team in the finals.) In the 1990s, Arvidas Sabonis became an NBA star. The brightest Russian basketball star of the 2000s is Andrei Kirilenko of the Utah Jazz.

See also: Dinamo; TsSKA

ALEXANDER LEDENEV

Basov, Vladimir Pavlovich

b. 28 July 1923, Urazov, Kursk province;
d. 17 September 1987, Moscow

Film director, screenwriter, actor

After graduating from VGIK in 1952, Basov became a prolific director of such Thaw dramas as *Bitva v puti* (*Battle Underway*, 1961), of such mildly anti-Stalinist tales as *Tishina* (*The Silence*, 1963), and of Second World War spy thrillers, especially the super-hit *Shchit i mech* (*Shield and Sword*, 1968). A moderate social critic but far from dissident, Basov was a solid storyteller, content with achieving domestic resonance. He carved out a parallel career for himself as an actor, gaining popularity with dozens of scene-stealing supporting roles, especially in comedies by Georgii Daneliia and Leonid Gaidai. People's Artist of the USSR (1983).

See also: All-Russian (All-Union) State Institute of Cinematography (VGIK); Daneliia, Georgii; dissident; film, Soviet – Thaw period; Gaidai, Leonid; Thaw; World War II (Great Patriotic War)

PETER ROLLBERG

Batalov, Aleksei Vladimirovich

b. 20 November 1928, Vladimir

Actor, director, teacher

Scion of an acting family, Batalov first charmed audiences as the young worker-hero of *Bolshaia semia* (*The Big Family*, 1954), and again in *Delo Rumiantseva* (*The Rumiantsev Case*, 1955). His mobile, eloquent features added credibility to the soldier Boris in *Letiat zhuravli* (*The Cranes are Flying*, 1957), as they did to the brilliant, doomed scientist Gusev in *Deviat dnei odnogo goda* (*Nine Days of a Year*, 1962), two of the Thaw's most important films. As a director, Batalov adapted Gogol's *Shinel* (*The Overcoat*) and Dostoevskii's *Igrok* (*The Gambler*) for the screen. He starred in *Moskva slezam ne verit* (*Moscow Doesn't Believe in Tears*, 1979), Best Foreign Film Oscar-winner for 1980.

See also: film, Soviet – Thaw period

JOSEPHINE WOLL

BDT

See: Tovstonogov Bolshoi Drama Theatre

beef Stroganov

A gourmet dish dating back to the second half of the nineteenth century and associated with various branches of the illustrious Stroganov clan, beef Stroganov is made of fillet strips sautéed with onions and simmered in sour cream sauce with mustard, tomato paste, or mushrooms. Soviet *obshchepit* versions use cheaper cuts of meat, which produces vastly inferior results. Popular in the Soviet Union, beef Stroganov is also widespread in the West, where it became one of the symbols of Russian cuisine, although it can be best described as an eclectic Russo-French concoction typical of the late Imperial period.

See also: meat dishes

DAN UNGURIANU

Belarus

The Republic of Belarus (formerly called Belorussia) is located in Eastern Europe, bordering Russia, Ukraine, Poland, Lithuania, and Latvia. Its population approximates 10 million, about twice that of Finland or Denmark. Its territory covers 207,595 sq km, comparable to the size of Portugal, Greece, and Austria, and is divided into six regions (*oblasts*). The capital is Minsk, its official languages are Belarussian and Russian.

Populated by the Krivichi Slavic tribe, the oldest city in Belarus, Polacak, was first mentioned in the Primary Chronicle (*Povest vremennykh let*) in 862 AD. Under attack by Crusaders and Mongol-Tatars, some territories of the current Belarus joined the Grand Duchy of Lithuania. Belarus became part of the Russian Empire (and subsequently, of the USSR) after the partition of the Commonwealth of Poland in 1772. Occupation by Nazi Germany had devastating consequences, killing a quarter of the Belarussian population. In 1945, Belarus became a founding member of the United Nations. During the Soviet era, Belarus was one of the most prosperous and industrially advanced republics of the USSR.

Following its adoption of the Declaration of State Sovereignty in Russia on 12 June 1990, the Belarussian parliament (Supreme Soviet) declared state sovereignty on 27 July 1990. Unlike most other former Soviet republics, in the post-Soviet era Belarus prevented de-industrialization of its economy and preserved machinery, chemical, and petroleum products as its main exports. Since the disintegration of the USSR, Belarus has experienced a steady growth of its per capita GDP (from $4,957 in 1994 to $8,790 in 2002) and a rise in its Human Development Index (from 0.679 in 1994 to 0.797 in 2002). Life expectancy at birth in Belarus is 68.1 years (in Russia, 65). In 2004, the GDP of Belarus increased by 11 percent, as compared with the previous year's, one of the highest growth rates in the Commonwealth of Independent States; its industrial output rose by 15.6 per cent against 2003.

On 2 April 1996, Belarus and Russia signed a treaty creating a Commonwealth; on 23 May 1997, they adopted the Union Statute; and on 8 December 1999, they signed the Treaty on the

Establishment of the Union State of Russia and Belarus. The Constitution of the Union is expected to be drafted by the end of 2005. The constitution of Belarus was adopted in 1994 under significant influence of the Russian constitutional model and was further amended by the 1996 referendum.

See also: administrative structure, Soviet Union

Further reading

United Nations (2003) *Human Capacity of Belarus: Economic Challenges and Social Responses*, UN Development Programme.

ALEXANDER DOMRIN

Beliutin, Elii Mikhailovich

b. 10 June 1925, Moscow

Painter, teacher

A pioneer of Nonconformist art, Beliutin established a Studio of Experimental Painting and Graphic Arts in Moscow (1948). He and his students were among those denounced by Khrushchev at the Manezh exhibition of 1962. Although Beliutin's painterly abstractions reveal the impact of American Abstract Expressionism, his artistic philosophy is not one of individual expression. He views art as a medium for emotional communication and collective experience, able to overcome the divisiveness of modern life.

See also: Khrushchev, Nikita; Manezh exhibition of 1962

JANET E. KENNEDY

bells

The bell tower is an essential part of Christian and especially Russian Orthodox church architecture. Even in the Soviet period, the huge 'Tsar-bell' was a favourite Moscow Kremlin tour stop. Bells (*kolokol*, plural *kolokola*) ring the call to worship in rhythms that vary with the liturgical year and maintain a religious and traditionally civic role as timekeeper. Russian cathedrals and monasteries assembled choirs of unique, anthropomorphized bells, which created a distinctive auditory landscape, especially in larger cities. Church bells, and church property in general, were subject to confiscation after 1917, when the state nationalized churches and monasteries and banned or restricted ringing. By 1928–29, churches and cathedrals were rapidly losing their bells. Local museums sometimes saved smaller or older bells (some from the fifteenth and sixteenth centuries), but most of the huge bells were taken down regardless of historical significance and melted for use in industry; a few were sold overseas for hard currency. Popular lore recalls misfortunes that struck local people who agreed to remove or break bells. By 1930, the remaining church bells in the USSR were silent.

Post-Soviet churches are buying bells, and some sets have been returned from overseas. Special schools teach the traditional art of bell ringing, and the huge demand for new bells makes their manufacture a growth industry in Russia.

See also: church architecture, Russian Orthodox

SIBELAN FORRESTER

Beloe solntse pustyni (*White Sun of the Desert*)

A cult classic, this film (Mosfilm, 1969), directed by Vladimir Motyl and featuring a popular song by Bulat Okudzhava, is the definitive Soviet 'eastern'. In the waning months of the Civil War, a Red Army soldier, on his way back to his wife after many years on the Front, is drafted for one final mission: to protect and safely convey to the nearest town a harem abandoned by a Central Asian warlord who is trying to dodge the advancing Bolsheviks. Stylish and sly, the film earned its near-universal popularity by mediating skilfully between the ideologically safe aesthetic of 'revolutionary romanticism' and the irreverent sensibility of a 'spaghetti western'.

See also: Okudzhava, Bulat

BORIS WOLFSON

Belov, Vasilii Ivanovich

b. 23 October 1932, Timonikha, Vologda region

Writer

One of the major village prose writers of the 1960s and the 1970s, whose *Privychnoe delo* (*That's How It Is*, 1966) remains a major work in its affirmation of the link between humans and the natural world. *Plotnitskie rasskazy* (*Carpenters' Stories*, 1968), *Bukhtiny vologodskie* (*Tall Tales from Vologda*, 1969), and *Lad* (*Harmony*, 1979–81) celebrate the inner strength of the peasant and peasant culture. In 1972, he began publishing a cycle of novels, beginning with *Kanuny* (*Eves*), about collectivization, but by the 1990s historical accuracy had been replaced by chauvinistic attack on all things non-Russian. His novel *Vse vperedi* (*The Best Is Yet to Come*, 1986) was criticized for its anti-Semitism.

See also: anti-Semitism; collective farms; nationalism ('the national question'); village prose

DAVID GILLESPIE

Belza, Igor Fedorovich

b. 26 January [8 February] 1904, Kielce, Russia (now Poland); d. 5 January 1994, Moscow

Musicologist, composer, literary scholar

Belza graduated as a composer from Kiev conservatory (1925), where he subsequently taught composition, instrumentation, polyphony, and the history of music. From 1941, he was a professor at the Moscow Conservatory, Senior Scholar at the Institute of Art History, and the Institute of Slavic and Balkan Studies at the Academy of Sciences of the USSR. His major works cover the musical culture of Poland, the Czech and Slovak republics, and Russian classics. The author of five symphonies and other musical compositions, he also wrote music for films. Awards include medals from Poland and the USSR; the titles Doctor of Art (1954) and

Honorary Doctor of Philosophy of Prague University (1967).

YURI ZARETSKY

Berezovskii, Boris Abramovich

b. 23 January 1946, Moscow

Businessman, political figure

The most notorious of the oligarchs – Russian businessmen who gained extensive political and economic power in the 1990s. Berezovskii founded the automobile resale company LogoVAZ in 1989. By the mid-1990s he controlled the oil company Sibneft, the state airline Aeroflot, the ORT television network, and several other business and media holdings. Berezovskii was close to Russian President Boris Yeltsin, and served as the Deputy Secretary of Yeltsin's National Security Council in 1996. Elected to the Duma in 1999, he came into conflict with President Vladimir Putin and moved to London in 2000, where he was granted political asylum.

See also: Duma; oligarkh; television channels; television, post-Soviet; Putin, Vladimir; Yeltsin, Boris

JULIET JOHNSON

Berggolts, Olga Fedorovna

b. 16 May 1910, St. Petersburg; d. 13 November 1975, Leningrad

Writer

A Communist Party member, Berggolts, known for the poetry she wrote during the Leningrad Siege of World War II, struggled to reconcile her political ideals with personal and artistic integrity. She was active in the post-Stalin Thaw, promoting the revival of lyric poetry and autobiographical prose, and was an outspoken supporter of greater literary freedom. Poems related to her imprisonment of 1938–39 first appeared in a 1965 collection; posthumous publications show that an apparently 'official' writer was no mere conformist but questioned some of the regime's more reprehensible programmes and activities.

KATHARINE HODGSON

Bernes, Mark Naumovich

b. 8 [21] September 1911, Nizhin, Ukraine; d. 17 August 1969, Moscow

Actor, singer

After working in theatres in Kharkov and Moscow, Bernes made his film debut in the demagogical GULag picture *Zakliuchennye* (*Convicts*, 1936). He gained national fame during World War II, when his sincere, charming portrayals of Soviet soldiers (e.g., in *Dva boitsa* [*Two Soldiers*, 1943]) won the hearts of millions. A number of films profited from the actor's characteristic soft, hoarse voice, accompanied by guitar – a gift that eventually helped him launch a parallel career as a singer with concert tours both in the USSR and abroad. In later years, Bernes demonstrated his potential as a versatile character actor. People's Artist of the RSFSR (1965).

See also: GULag; World War II (Great Patriotic War)

PETER ROLLBERG

berries (iagody)

For centuries the berries that grow in the forests and swamps of northern Russia have been a crucial source of vitamin C, antioxidants, and other micronutrients that would otherwise be lacking in the locally-based diet of most Russians. Berries are gathered during the short sub-Arctic summer, and then preserved for use the year round as *varene* (a thick jam of whole berries), compotes, and raw preserves (fresh fruit ground with sugar). In the more temperate zones of European Russia, strawberries, gooseberries, black and red currants, and other cultivated berries are also important for their culinary, medicinal, and cosmetic benefits. *Malina* (raspberry) is used like aspirin to break fevers; *moroshka* (an apricot-coloured swamp berry with sour nectarine taste) is noted for its overall tonic effects; *brusnika*, *chernika*, and *kliukva* are all similar in tartness and medicinal properties to the American cranberry. The *oblepikha* (sea buckthorn) berry is an orange oblong fruit that grows on a silvery-leafed bush native to the Altai Mountains. It is a prized ingredient in rejuvenating skin creams. Traditional Russian beverages made from berries include the alcoholic *nalivka*, an intensely flavoured berry liqueur; and *mors* and *kisel*, both made from red berries (usually cranberries) that have been boiled in water, filtered, and sweetened to provide a nutritious red juice. *Kisel* is thickened with cornstarch for added bulk, and is remembered now as the ubiquitous drink in Russian daycare, school, and hospital cafeterias. The initial appeal of carbonated, artificially-sweetened Western sodas that flooded the market after the collapse of the USSR has waned somewhat in the second post-Soviet decade, as Russian brands of native berry drinks, such as *mors*, have regained popularity among a new generation of health-conscious consumers. Berry-picking and production are also on the rise as an alternative source of private enterprise in economically depressed rural areas.

See also: drinks, alcoholic; drinks, non-alcoholic; varene

YVONNE HOWELL

Bichevskaia, Zhanna Vladimirovna

b. 17 June 1944, Moscow

Singer

Trained at the State College of Circus and Stage Arts, Zhanna Bichevskaia debuted as a singer in the late 1960s. Under the influence of Joan Baez, Pete Seeger, and Bulat Okudzhava, she became famous for performing Russian folk songs, ballads, *romansy*, and also contemporary bard songs, in a pioneering 'country-folk' style. She is the winner of numerous song competitions and awards, both Soviet and international. Baptized in 1988, Bichevskaia has since devoted herself to spiritual music and to promoting Russian Orthodoxy in increasingly nationalistic terms.

See also: bards; folk song; Okudzhava, Bulat; romance; Russian Orthodoxy

RACHEL S. PLATONOV

Bitov, Andrei Georgievich

b. 27 May 1937, Leningrad

Prose writer, essayist, poet

Trained as a geologist, Bitov has been writing and publishing since 1960. His œuvre includes short stories and novellas (mostly focused on a central urban hero who bears a distinct resemblance to the author), a novel, travelogues, and essays. Dating his interest in art to a screening of Fellini's *La Strada* in 1954, Bitov is perhaps best known in the West for his novel *Pushkinskii dom* (*Pushkin House*, 1971), published in Russian in the US in 1978 and in the Soviet Union a year later. One of the participants in the samizdat literary almanac *Metropol* in 1979, Bitov was forbidden to publish in the USSR until perestroika. Though he was drawn into writing via poetry in the 1950s, he published his first volume of verse on the occasion of his sixtieth birthday.

Though in many ways Bitov's works chronicle the existential problems of his – the first post-Stalin – generation, he also addresses universal issues, exploring the meaning of writing, history, and creativity. *Pushkin House*, arguably his most important work, confronts the meaning of Soviet history of the Stalin period through the lens of Russian literary history. Bitov's travelogues (such as *Uroki Armenii* [*Lessons of Armenia*, 1978]) and critical essays are as interesting as his fiction. His position in Russian letters of the second half of the twentieth century is that of an independent, thoughtful, creative, and complex writer, concerned about the environment, the meaning of man's existence in a compromised universe, and the lessons of history.

See also: literature, Soviet; literature, post-Soviet; *Metropol*; samizdat

Further reading

Bitov, A. (1978) *Pushkinskii dom*, Ann Arbor, MI: Ardis; *Novyi Mir*, 1987, Nos 10–12.

Chances, E. (1993) *Andrei Bitov: The Ecology of Inspiration*, Cambridge: Cambridge University Press.

Spieker, S. (1996) *Figures of Memory and Forgetting in Andrej Bitov's Prose*, Frankfurt: Peter Lang.

ANGELA BRINTLINGER

Black Earth region (Chernozemnaia zona)

The Black Earth region, located in the southwestern Russian steppes, includes Belgorod, Kursk, Lipetsk, Tambov, and Voronezh Oblasts. It has an estimated population of 8 million. Its cultural and educational centre is the city of Voronezh (population 1 million). Part of the Central Federal District and the Communist-leaning 'Red Belt', it lies on the border with Ukraine. The name derives from the black colour of this region's extremely fertile soil (praised in the lyrics of poet Osip Mandelshtam), which accounts for agriculture as the area's major industry. The Black Earth region was home to a number of writers and artists in the nineteenth and twentieth centuries, including writers Ivan Turgenev, Nikolai Leskov, Ivan Bunin, Andrei Platonov, poet Fedor Tiutchev, artist Ivan Kramskoi, and others.

See also: Red Belt; steppe

VLADIMIR STRUKOV

black market

The process of de-Stalinization initiated by Khrushchev after Stalin's death in March 1953 made the borders that for approximately two decades had isolated the USSR from the West more porous. Although freedom of travel across the Soviet borders was still strictly limited, foreign tourists and students increasingly visited the Soviet Union. In 1957, Moscow hosted the World Youth Festival, which exposed young Soviets to Western culture and fashions. Commercial and art exhibits from the United States and other countries followed. These developments awakened Russians' taste for Western goods and bred the *fartsovshchik* – a new kind of black marketer. *Fartsovshchiki* bought various items, ranging from chewing gum and clothes to electronic and hard currency, from foreigners and sold them for profit to other Soviets. The occupation was illegal, and if caught, a *fartsovshchik* could face a long prison term for 'speculation'; dealing in particularly large amounts of hard currency risked capital punishment. *Fartsovshchiki* also traded in icons and other Russian antiques. Black market activity has been portrayed in literature and popular culture, for example, in Sergei Dovlatov's story 'Finskie krepovye noski' (Finnish Crepe Socks, 1999).

See also: crime; economic system, Soviet

Further reading

Beliaev, I. (1994) *Zhil byl fartsovshchik*, TV film.

KONSTANTIN KUSTANOVICH

blat

An informal network-based system of reciprocal access to goods and services, in which both consumers and those in official positions participate. A widespread feature of the Soviet economy, it was rooted in two phenomena: constant shortages of foodstuff, consumer goods, and supplies for industrial production and numerous rigid but often contradictory and poorly enforced regulations. *Blat* provided access to items in short supply: scarce goods, services (especially those available free of charge, such as health care and education) and favours (such as jobs, promotions, and kindergarten vacancies). Those in official positions in the state hierarchy or the state distribution system provided access to such scarce items. The nature of *blat* relations has changed in post-communist Russia, and some observers suggest that its significance has

declined. Consumer goods are no longer in short supply, and the monetization of the economy shifted the emphasis from reciprocal exchange of favours to straightforward bribery. Nevertheless, influence and information remain difficult to procure, and access to them is still often regulated through *blat*. In particular, *blat* is often used in business relations as a way to receive benefits in the form of state subsidies, loans, contracts, reduced import duties or tax breaks. Moreover, *blat* and bribery have become fused, with *blat* serving as an introduction to the bribe-taker.

See also: economic system, Soviet; shortages

Further reading

Ledeneva, A. (1998) *Russia's Economy of Favours: Blat, Networking and Informal Exchange.* Cambridge: Cambridge University Press.

ALYA GUSEVA

bliny

Russian version of crepes. Although there are several varieties of *bliny*, the most common consist of all-purpose wheat flour, eggs, milk, and butter. *Bliny* are often served on festive occasions such as Maslenitsa (Russian Mardi Gras) and are eaten with a variety of fillings, such as meat or herring, caviar, and fruit jams. In post-Soviet Moscow roadside *bliny* stands sell freshly made crepes.

See also: Maslenitsa

SUSMITA SUNDARAM

blizhnee zarubezhe (near abroad)

This term currently refers to the fourteen former USSR republics, which in 1990 became independent states bordering Russia: Armenia, Azerbaidzhan, Belarus, Estonia, Georgia (Gruziia), Kazakhstan, Kyrgyzstan, Latvia, Lithuania (Litva), Moldova, Tadzhikistan, Turkmenistan, Ukraine, and Uzbekistan. The term 'near abroad' has a broader meaning than the CIS, for the latter excludes Estonia, Latvia, Lithuania, and Georgia. Most Russians disapprove of the 'near abroad' countries' desire to achieve independence from the 'imperial centre', worrying about such possible negative consequences as economic decline and the deterioration of conditions for the Russian-speaking population residing in these countries.

In the Soviet era, the term referred to 'friendly' East bloc countries bordering the USSR, such as Bulgaria, Czechoslovakia, East Germany, Hungary, Poland, Romania, and Yugoslavia.

See also: Armenia; Azerbaidzhan; Belarus; Estonia; Georgia; Kazakhstan; Kyrgyzstan; Latvia; Lithuania; Moldova; Tajikistan; Turkmenistan; Ukraine; Uzbekistan

TATYANA LEDENEVA

Bodrov, Sergei Sergeevich

b. 27 December 1971, Moscow; d. 19 September 2002, Northern Osetiia

Actor, film director

Son of the screenwriter/director by the same name, Bodrov achieved cult status in post-Soviet film. His Danila Bagrov in Aleksei Balabanov's *Brat* (*Brother*, 1997) and *Brat-2* (*Brother 2*, 2000) introduced a new cinematic hero and launched the Bodrov myth, sealed by his death in a glacier avalanche while directing his second film, *Sviaznoi* (*Messenger*). A non-professional actor, Bodrov received awards for his role in *Kavkazskii plennik* (*Prisoner of the Mountains*), directed by Bodrov Sr. (1996). Subsequently, he worked as a leading journalist in the television programme *Vzgliad*, completed a doctorate (*kandidatskaia*) in art history at Moscow State University, directed a sequel to the *Brat* series, titled *Sestry* (*Sisters*, 2001), and hosted the television programme *Poslednii geroi* (*The Last Hero*, 2002).

See also: Balabanov, Aleksei; film, post-Soviet; *Vzgliad*

IRINA MAKOVEEVA

Bodrov, Sergei Vladimirovich

b. 28 June 1948, Khabarovsk

Film-maker, scriptwriter, producer

After graduating in scriptwriting from VGIK (1974), Bodrov worked as special correspondent for the satirical magazine *Krokodil* (*Crocodile*, 1975–80), and wrote scripts for over twenty films. Since 1984 he has lived and worked in both Moscow and Los Angeles. Bodrov's early films addressed issues of youth and crime: *Svoboda – eto rai* (*Freedom Is Paradise*, 1989); *Katala* (*The Swindler*, 1989); *Belyi korol, krasnaia koroleva* (*White King, Red Queen*, 1992); and *Ia khotela uvidet angelov* (*I Wanted to See Angels*, 1992). International success came with his anti-war film, *Kavkazskii plennik* (*Prisoner of the Mountains*, 1996), which explores the psychology of people devoid of political ideals.

See also: All-Russian (All-Union) State Institute of Cinematography (VGIK); Bodrov, Sergei Sergeevich; Caucasus; *Krokodil*; War, Chechen

BIRGIT BEUMERS

Bogatyr, Svetlana Zakharovna

b. 24 June 1945, Kiev, Ukraine

Artist

A graduate from the applied arts faculty of the Moscow Textile Institute (1968) and member of the USSR Artists' Union since 1969. After 1974, when she could no longer participate in officially endorsed exhibitions, Bogatyr joined Moscow's artistic underground; her attic studio quickly became an active intellectual forum for many Russian dissidents. Bogatyr works in oil and counts light and transparency as major features of her paintings, which often address spiritual issues. Resident in France since 1991, she has works exhibited in major Russian galleries (Moscow's Tretiakov and St. Petersburg's State Russian Museum) and abroad (Russian House in Washington, DC).

See also: art, Soviet; dissident; Tretiakov Gallery

KATIA KAPUSHESKY

Bogatyrev, Iurii Georgievich

b. 2 March 1947, Riga; d. 2 February 1989, Moscow

Stage and screen actor

Bogatyrev graduated from the Shchukin Theatre studio in 1971, then joined the troupe of the Sovremennik (Contemporary) Theatre, and in 1977 switched to the Moscow Art Theatre (MKhAT), where he excelled in contemporary drama and Bulgakov's plays. Nikita Mikhalkov included Bogatyrev in his core group of actors, featuring him in virtually all of his pictures; Bogatyrev was particularly effective as Andrei Shtolts in *Neskolko dnei iz zhizni I. I. Oblomova* (*Oblomov*, 1979). The actor's strengths – dynamic body language, extreme concentration, and a somewhat enigmatic presence – were superbly used in his portrayal of Manilov in the adaptation of Gogol's *Mertvye dushi* (*Dead Souls*, 1984). People's Artist of the RSFSR (1988).

See also: Mikhalkov, Nikita; Moscow Art Theatre (MKhAT); Sovremennik Theatre

PETER ROLLBERG

Boiarskii, Mikhail Sergeevich

b. 26 December 1949, Leningrad

Actor, singer

After graduating from the actors' section of the Leningrad State Institute of Theatre, Music, and Cinematography (LGITMiK, 1972), Boiarskii worked in the Leningrad Lensovet Theatre (1972–86). In 1988, he founded and became the artistic director of the Benefis (Benefit) musical-dramatic theatre. As a screen actor (since 1973) he is known for musicality, expressiveness, and an explosive temperament. In films, he has played the roles of daredevils, adventurers, scoundrels, and charming and sexy heroes: *Solomennaia shliapka* (*The Straw Hat*, 1974); *Sobaka na sene* (*A Dog in the Hay*, 1977); *D'Artanian i tri mushketera* (*D'Artagnan and the Three Musketeers*, 1978); *Koroleva Margo* (*Queen Margo*, 1996) and others. His popularity as a pop singer is based on his performance of songs from his films in

concerts and on TV. He was the co-author and MC of the TV show *Domino* (1995–97). People's Artist of Russia (1990).

See also: St. Petersburg State Academy of Theatre Arts; theatre, Soviet

IRINA UDIANSKAYA

Bolshoi Drama Theatre

See: Tovstonogov Bolshoi Drama Theatre

Bolshoi Theatre

Moscow's Bolshoi ('Large' or 'Grand') Theatre was founded in 1776, although its present building dates from 1825. Once the flagship opera and ballet company of the Soviet Union, it has seen its status challenged by the Mariinskii Theatre in St. Petersburg in the post-Soviet era.

In the field of opera, the Theatre's most influential director was Boris Pokrovskii, whose productions of Prokofiev's *Igrok* (*The Gambler*, 1974) and Shchedrin's *Mertvye dushi* (*Dead Souls*, 1977) were notable successes. Lavish and traditional accounts of the Russian classics, often remaining in the repertoire for many years, have largely characterized the Bolshoi's creative development. Soviet operas were also an important feature of the company's activity; Shaporin's *Dekabristy* (*Decembrists*, 1953), Khrennikov's *Mat* (*Mother*, 1975), Prokofiev's *Voina i mir* (*War and Peace*, 1959) and *Povest o nastoiashchem cheloveke* (*Story of a Real Man*, 1960), and Shchedrin's *Ne tolko liubov* (*Not for Love Alone*, 1961) were important productions in the decade after Stalin's death. As director of the Bolshoi ballet between 1964 and 1995, Iurii Grigorovich cultivated a muscular and energetic style of performance (long seen as typically Muscovite), best represented by his productions of Khachaturian's *Spartak* (*Spartacus*, 1968) and the three Tchaikovsky ballets staged in the 1960s. Given Soviet central planning, talented artists from across the Soviet Union almost invariably found their way to the Bolshoi: singers Galina Vishnevskaia, Irina Arkhipova, Elena Obraztsova and Evgenii Nesterenko, conductors Aleksandr

Melik-Pashaev and Gennadii Rozhdestvskii, and dancers Maia Plisetskaia (whose husband, Rodion Shchedrin, composed several important ballet scores, as well as the above-mentioned opera, for the theatre) and Galina Ulanova all excelled here.

The Bolshoi played an important part in cultural exchange between the Soviet Union and the countries of both Eastern Europe and the capitalist West. Tours by and collaboration with visiting companies introduced Russian audiences to such operas as Janáček's *Jenůfa*, Bartók's *Bluebeard's Castle*, and Britten's *Midsummer Night's Dream*. In return, the opera and ballet troupes of the Bolshoi toured extensively abroad, appealing to foreign audiences' taste for the old-fashioned and the exotic, as well as earning valuable currency (both economic and cultural) for the Soviet Union. Occasional attempts to export 'Soviet' art met with failure, as in the case of the disastrous reception of Molchanov's opera *Zory zdes tikhie* (*The Dawns Are Quiet Here*) in New York in 1975.

Glasnost, perestroika, and the collapse of the Soviet Union posed serious challenges for the Bolshoi Theatre. Outdated productions, uninspiring singing and playing, poor administration, and frequent personality clashes have undermined the company's accustomed hegemony. Amidst the general crisis, however, there have been signs of hope. Productions by foreign directors such as Francesca Zambella and Peter Ustinov have been much admired. A smaller, second stage was opened, which has already been graced by acclaimed productions of Shostakovich's *Svetlyi ruchei* (*The Limpid Stream*) and Stravinskii's *Rake's Progress*. The timely prospect of a new opera by Leonid Desiatnikov with a libretto by Vladimir Sorokin is as curious as it is inspiring.

See also: Arkhipova, Irina; ballet dancers, Bolshoi Theatre; Desiatnikov, Leonid; Khachaturian, Aram; Khrennikov, Tikhon; Mariinskii Theatre; Nesterenko, Evgenii; Obraztsova, Elena; opera singers, Bolshoi Theatre; Plisetskaia, Maia; Prokofiev, Sergei; Rozhdestvenskii, Gennadii; Shchedrin, Rodion; Shostakovich, Dmitrii; Sorokin, Vladimir; Stravinskii, Igor; Ulanova, Galina; Vishnevskaya, Galina

Further reading

Bartlett, R. (2001) 'Moscow: since 1918', in S. Sadie and J. Tyrell (eds) *New Grove Dictionary of Music and Musicians*, 2nd edn, London: Grove.

Pokrovsky, B. A. and Grigorovich, Yu. N. (1979) *The Bolshoi: Opera and Ballet at the Greatest Theater in Russia*, London: B. T. Batsford.

Vishnevskaya, G. (1984) *Galina: A Russian Story*, trans. G. Daniels, London: Hodder & Stoughton.

PHILIP ROSS BULLOCK

BOMZh

See: homelessness

Bondarchuk, Sergei Fedorovich

b. 25 September 1920, Belozerka, Ukraine; d. 20 October 1994, Moscow

Screenwriter, director, actor

Bondarchuk studied acting at VGIK and first appeared in Sergei Gerasimov's *Molodaia gvardiia* (*Young Guard*, 1948). In 1959, Bondarchuk's directorial debut, *Sudba cheloveka* (*A Man's Fate*), won the Grand Prize at the Moscow Film Festival. A milestone of de-Stalinization, the film was one of the first to deal with the fate of Soviet POWs during World War II, a topic previously banned, because Stalin had declared them traitors. Bondarchuk directed the four-part film epic *Voina i mir* (*War and Peace*, 1965–67), which brought him an Oscar (1969) and international acclaim. Bondarchuk's last project, a Russian–Italian film adaptation of Sholokhov's *Tikhii Don* (*Quiet Flows the Don*), was never released.

See also: All-Russian (All-Union) State Institute of Cinematography (VGIK); film, festivals and prizes; film, literary adaptation; film, World War II; Gerasimov, Sergei; Sholokhov, Mikhail.

ALEXANDER PROKHOROV

Borisov, Oleg Ivanovich

(né Albert Borisov)

b. 8 November 1929, Privolzhsk, Ivanovo district; d. 28 April 1994, Moscow

Stage and screen actor

A graduate of the studio school of the Moscow Art Theatre (MKhAT, 1951), Borisov became a leading star of the Grand Dramatic Theatre (BDT) in Leningrad (1964–83) and MKhAT (1983–90). On screen, he demonstrated his comedic potential in *Daite zhalobnuiu knigu* (*Give Me the Complaint Book*, 1964), among others. One of the finest method actors of his generation, Borisov made a lasting impression in adaptations of Russian literary classics, such as *Podrostok* (*The Adolescent*, 1983), as well as subversive socio-psychological dramas, including *Ostanovilsia poezd* (*The Train Has Stopped*, 1982) and *Sluga* (*The Servant*, 1988), in which the actor's ascetic, pain-ridden features reflect the inner turmoil of dogmatic characters. People's Artist of the USSR (1978)

See also: complaints book; Moscow Art Theatre (MKhAT); Tovstonogov Bolshoi Drama Theatre (BDT)

PETER ROLLBERG

Borisova, Iuliia Konstantinovna

b. 17 March 1925, Moscow

Stage and film actress

Borisova studied at the Shchukin Theatre School in Moscow, graduating in 1949, and joined the troupe of the Vakhtangov Theatre. She became a star in contemporary Soviet comedies, but made the most lasting impressions with classical interpretations of such roles as Princess Turandot in Carlo Gozzi's play. Two of Borisova's few film roles also brought her fame: Nastasia Filippovna in Ivan Pyrev's adaptation of Dostoevskii's *Idiot* (*The Idiot*, 1958), and the Soviet ambassador to Sweden, modeled after Aleksandra Kollontai, in Aleksandr

Zarkhi's *Posol Sovetskogo Soiuza* (Ambassador of the Soviet Union, 1970). People's Artist of the USSR (1969).

See also: Vakhtangov Theatre; Zarkhi, Aleksandr

PETER ROLLBERG

bread

One of the main staples of the Russian diet, *khleb* (bread) is eaten at virtually every meal. White bread (*belyi khleb*) is traditionally baked in oblong loaves; brown bread (called *chernyi* [black]), in varieties close to rye and pumpernickel, is either round or shaped in bread pans. In St. Petersburg, *khleb* refers only to brown breads; white bread is called *bulka* ('roll' in other parts of Russia) or *baton* (loaf). *Bublik* is a ring-shaped, soft roll, similar to *baranka*, but much thicker and made of a softer, usually yeast, dough. *Kolach* is a small, soft bread, shaped in the form of a key. *Lavash* is a thin white bread from the Caucasus. Traditional Russian breads are dense and sold unsliced, but a variety of European and sliced breads have appeared in the post-Soviet period. In literature and conversational speech, bread is used to mean the basic food necessary for survival, hence the expression 'Khleb – vsemu golova' (Bread is the head of everything).

See also: baranka; Caucasus

MICHELE BERDY

Brenner, Aleksandr Davidovich

b. 1957 (date unknown), Alma-Ata, Kazakhstan

Artist, writer

A graduate of the Philology Department of the Leningrad State Pedagogical Institute (1980), from 1988 Brenner worked in Israel as a street performance artist and as an art critic for the weekly magazine *Beg vremeni* (*The Race of Time*). During the 1990s, as one of the leaders of the group Moscow Actionists, he transformed performance into a means of resisting dogmatism in art. His art-actions were eccentric, provocative, and often extreme. The most notorious occurred in the Stedelijk Museum (Amsterdam, 1997), when he spray-painted a dollar sign over Kazimir Malevich's *White Cross*, which cost him six months in a Dutch prison. A participant in numerous exhibitions of modern art in Russia and abroad, Brenner has authored over twenty books of poetry and prose.

See also: Moscow Actionism

YURI ZARETSKY

Brezhnev, Leonid Ilich

b. 12 December 1906, Kamenskoe, Ukraine; d. 10 November 1982, Moscow

Political leader

General Secretary of the Communist Party of the Soviet Union (CPSU), 1964–82, after 1977, Leonid Ilich Brezhnev concurrently held the position of Chairman of the USSR Supreme Soviet. A political commissar during World War II, after the war he headed the Communist Party organization in the Soviet republic of Moldavia, which in 1952 he left for Moscow to serve under Iosif Stalin in the Secretariat of the Central Committee of the Communist Party. Following Stalin's death in 1953, Brezhnev was temporarily removed from the Secretariat and assigned to lesser posts, but was recalled to Moscow in 1956 to join the Secretariat again, and advanced to the position of General Secretary of the CPSU in 1964.

Under Brezhnev, the Soviet Union experienced stability, then stagnation. In contrast to his predecessor, Nikita Khrushchev, with his shifting policy, Brezhnev credited technical progress and scientific management with ensuring economic growth. This approach initially produced positive results in the economy and improved relations with the West. Brezhnev also expanded the economic and social security programmes available to Soviet citizens. In exchange for certain political and cultural freedoms the public received government-subsidised services, including housing, education, medical care, and state pensions.

Whatever 'thaw' in cultural policies the Brezhnev regime appeared to support abruptly ended in 1966, when the Committee of State Security (KGB) cracked down on dissidents. Although the KGB's use of terror hardly matched that under Stalin, the threat of arrest or deportation controlled their numbers.

Under Brezhnev the Nuclear Nonproliferation Treaty was signed in 1970, and the Anti-Ballistic Missile Treaty in May 1972. In 1975, the USSR became a signatory of the Helsinki Accords. The Brezhnev Doctrine, which stipulated that threats to any communist government were a threat to all, rationalized the 1968 Soviet invasion of Czechoslovakia. When a wave of strikes inundated Poland in 1981 and a 'counter-revolution' threatened to overturn that country's communist system, Brezhnev decided not to invade Poland, but installed a repressive pro-Soviet government that established 'martial law'.

Serious problems in the Soviet developmental model emerged during the Brezhnev era. These included widespread alcoholism and absenteeism from work, a general decline in the economy, dependence on oil exports, reliance on foreign grain and manufactured goods, and aging leadership. Dissidence grew as people became disgruntled with economic conditions and limited freedoms. The highest government and party officials kept their positions until death or infirmity, which near the end of Brezhnev's rule contributed to limited innovation in policy, characterized by the term 'stagnation'.

See also: Communist Party; dissident; Khrushchev, Nikita; Stagnation; Stalin, Iosif; Thaw; World War II (Great Patriotic War)

Further reading

Navazelskis, I. (1988) *Leonid Brezhnev*, New York: Columbia University Press.

VICKI L. HESLI AND JAMES KRUEGER

broadcasts, foreign

Vrazheskie golosa (enemy voices) is what official Soviet propaganda labelled the foreign radio stations that used to broadcast in Russian: the

BBC, Radio Liberty, Deutsche Welle, Voice of America, and Voice of Israel. These stations provided uncensored information about life outside the Soviet Union and covered events within the Soviet Union bypassed by official Soviet mass media. *Spidola* brand portable radios, manufactured in Riga, Latvia, could be bought and the frequency bands retuned to receive these broadcasts, also called *golosa iz-za kuchi* (voices from behind the heap) by Soviet propaganda. The International Service of Voice of America launched its Russian-language broadcasts in February 1951, while the BBC has been broadcasting in Russian since January 1941. Though doing so constituted a punishable crime, close friends would gather to listen either at someone's dacha or in the woods outside big cities, where (owing to limited funds) the broadcasts were not jammed.

Starting in 1955, two generations of fans would glue themselves to their *Spidolas* to hear the latest in jazz news on the broadcast 'This Is Will Conover: Jazz Hours, USA', at a time when jazz was banned in the Soviet Union.

See also: censorship; radio, Soviet

Further reading

Nelson, M. (1997) *War of the Black Heavens: The Battles of Western Broadcasting in the Cold War*, Syracuse, NJ: Syracuse University Press.

Puddington, A. (2000) *Broadcasting Freedom: The Cold War Triumph of Radio Free Europe and Radio Liberty*, Lexington, KY: University Press of Kentucky.

Rawnsley, G. D. (1996) *Radio Diplomacy and Propaganda: The BBC and VOA in International Politics, 1956–64*, New York: St. Martin's Press.

REGINA KOZAKOVA

Brodskii, Iosif Aleksandrovich

b. 24 May 1940, Leningrad; d. 28 January 1996, New York

Poet

Nobel Prize laureate (1987), Poet Laureate of the United States (1991–92), Leningrad-born Brodskii was once called a 'Yankee in Russian poetry' (Kublanovsky, in Polukhina, 1992). Brodskii himself claimed that English-speaking poets were his 'mental family – far more so than anybody among [his] own contemporaries, inside or outside of Russia'. Whatever the validity of this statement, Brodskii's poetry certainly conveyed a sense of internal emigration even before the poet left Russia, which led to persecution from the Soviet authorities: on 13 March 1964, an infamous trial took place in Leningrad, where Brodskii was accused of parasitism (*tuneiadstvo*) and sentenced to five years' hard labour in the Northern Russian village of Norenskaia in the Archangelsk region, later shortened to a year and a half. This period proved extremely prolific, resulting in many poems devoted to the poet's beloved Marina Basmanova.

Although Brodskii's mentor was Anna Akhmatova, the poets he considered his major sources of influence are Marina Tsvetaeva, W. H. Auden, and Robert Frost. Brodskii taught himself English and Polish, and devoted poems to many foreign poets or translated them into Russian. During his exile he studied English by translating and memorizing John Donne's verses: as a result, Brodskii introduced Baroque-style metaphors into Russian. His poetry also includes recurring biblical motifs, images of antiquity, and references to music, especially jazz.

While in the USSR, Brodskii published only four original poems, while his work widely circulated in *samizdat*. In 1965–72, he published three books in the West: *Stikhotvoreniia i poemy* (*Short and Long Poems*, 1965), *Elegy to John Donne and Other Poems* (1967), and *Ostanovka v pustyne* (*A Halt in the Desert*) (1970). Attention by the West aggravated Brodskii's relationship with Soviet authorities, which in 1972 forced him to leave the USSR. He landed in Vienna, and immigrated to the United States the same year.

Brodskii taught at the University of Michigan, Columbia University, New York University, Queens College, Mount Holyoke College, and elsewhere. In 1977, he started writing essays in English and thereafter regarded himself as a Russian poet and American essayist. His books of English prose include *Less Than One* (1986),

Watermark (1992), and *On Grief and Reason* (1995). Other collections include *Selected Poems* (1973), *A Part of Speech* (1980), *To Urania* (1988), *Marbles* (1989), *So Forth* (1996), and *Collected Poems in English* (2000).

Brodskii died in New York and was buried at the St. Michele cemetery in Venice.

See also: Akhmatova, Anna; literature, émigré; parasitism; poetry, Soviet; samizdat

Further reading

Bethea, D. (1994) *Joseph Brodsky and the Creation of Exile*, Princeton, NJ: Princeton University Press.

Loseff, L. and Polukhina, V. (eds) (1990) *Brodsky's Poetics and Aesthetics*, New York: Macmillan.

—— (eds) (1999) *Joseph Brodsky: The Art of a Poem*, New York: St. Martin's Press.

MacFadyen, D. (2000) *Joseph Brodsky and the Soviet Muse*, Montreal: McGill-Queen's University Press.

Polukhina, V. (ed.) (1992) *Brodsky through the Eyes of his Contemporaries*, New York: St. Martin's Press.

NILA FRIEDBERG

Brodsky, Joseph

See: Brodskii, Iosif Aleksandrovich

Bronevoi, Leonid Sergeevich

b. 17 December 1928, Kiev, Ukraine

Actor

Bronevoi graduated from the Tashkent Theatre Institute (1950) and the Moscow Art Theatre Studio School in Moscow (1955). After working in the Russian provinces, he joined the Malaia Bronnaia Theatre (1961), where he played in Anatolii Efros productions including Shakespeare's *Romeo and Juliet* (1970) and Gogol's *Marriage* (*Zhenitba*, 1985). Since 1988, Bronevoi has worked at the Lenkom Theatre. A master of expressionist portrayal, Bronevoi has been a star on the Russian screen since 1965. His master-piece was his performance as Gestapo Chief Heinrich Müller in Tatiana Lioznova's television series *Semnadtsat mgnovenii vesny* (*Seventeen Moments of Spring*, 1973). In 1987, Bronevoi was awarded the title of People's Artist of the USSR.

See also: Efros, Anatolii; Lenkom Theatre; Malaia Bronnaia Theatre (Teatr na Maloi Bronnoi); Moscow Art Theatre (MKhAT); *Semnadtsat mgnovenii vesny* (*Seventeen Moments of Spring*)

ELENA BARABAN

Brumel, Valerii Nikolaevich

b. 14 April 1942, Razvedki; d. 26 January 2003, Moscow

Athlete

A legendary Soviet high jumper, who held the world record from 1961 (2.23 m) to 1971 (2.28 m), Brumel won the gold medal at the 1964 Olympic Games. After a motorcycle accident in 1965 put him out of commission, his determination to jump again added to his heroic image. The Soviet public and fans abroad passionately followed the athlete's courageous struggle against physical limitations. After numerous operations and intensive rehabilitation, Brumel returned to jumping, though he never managed to match his previous heights.

IRINA MAKOVEEVA

Bruskin, Grisha

(né Grigorii Davidovich Bruskin)

b. 21 October 1945, Moscow

Artist

A painter and sculptor educated at the Moscow Textile Institute, during the early 1980s Bruskin courted controversy as a dissident artist when the Soviet authorities prematurely closed two of his solo exhibitions, in Vilnius and Moscow. He is best known for his figurative paintings and sculptures, many of which combine such incongruous references as the alphabet primer of Russian schools, Socialist Realism, and the Kabbalah. Bruskin's reputation soared following the sale of his *Fundamentalnyi leksikon* (*Fundamental Lexicon*, 1980) at Sotheby's famous sale of contemporary Russian art in 1988. The following year he moved to New York and subsequently has exhibited widely in the international arena. In 1999, he was commissioned to produce a permanent monumental work for the redesigned Reichstag building in Berlin.

MIKE O'MAHONY

Buddhism

The Russian Federation's roughly one million Buddhists live predominantly in traditionally Buddhist (Tibetan Gelug school) regions: Buryatia, Tuva, and Europe's only Buddhist territory, Kalmykia.

Buddhism penetrated Buryatia 150 years before Empress Elizaveta Petrovna decreed it the area's religion in 1741. Though Stalinist repressions of Buddhist clergy peaked in 1940, present-day major centres of Russian Buddhist education, the Aga and Ivolga monasteries, opened in 1946, and a decade later Kalmyks returned from Stalin's Siberian deportation for 'disloyalty'. In an anti-dissident crackdown, in 1972 authorities arrested the Buryat Tantric revivalist Bidiia Dandaron (d. 1974), who maintained Buddhist traditions during Stalin-era imprisonments and instructed numerous non-Buryat disciples.

Buddhist revivalism since 1990 has restored, along with monasteries, such figures and teachings to national memory. Buddhism and shamanism shape post-Soviet Buryat and Tuvan identity, and Kalmykia's general cultural reclamation continues with the widespread post-Soviet construction of Buddhist institutions, though the republic's Buddhist revival has been complicated by President Kirsan Iliumzhinov's patronage of religious edifices to cover his regime's authoritarianism.

Non-Asiatic Soviet interest in Buddhism grew in the 1960s with the religious revival among the intelligentsia. The 1980s and 1990s witnessed the revival of the Russian Academy of Science's century-old *Bibliotheca Buddhica*, authoritative Buddhist texts edited by renowned Russian Buddhologists. Interest in Buddhism among contemporary Russian writers and intellectuals is reflected, for example, in the work of Viktor Pelevin.

With the disintegration of the Soviet Union, representation and ownership have become key issues in Russian Buddhism. The Dalai Lama, admitted into the Soviet Union but banned from Russia in post-Soviet times owing to pressure from the People's Republic of China, advocates 'indigenous' Buddhism and proselytizes through permanent representatives of the Tibetan government in exile. In December 2004, he visited Kalmykia, a Buddhist republic within the Russian Federation, the first visit to the Russian Federation since 1992.

Many regional temples in Russia have dissociated themselves from the Soviet-era Buryatia-based national Buddhist organization (now called the Buddhist Traditional Sangha of Russia). Since 1998 'indigenous' Buddhists and non-Sangha believers have waged a legal (and even physical) struggle over St. Petersburg's Kalachakra Temple.

See also: Buriatia; Kalmykia; Lamaism (Buddhism)

Further reading

Zhukovskaia, N. L. (2000–01) 'The revival of Buddhism in Buryatia: problems and prospects', *Anthropology and Archeology of Eurasia* 39, 4: 23–47.

AVRAM BROWN

Bulatov, Erik Vladimirovich

b. 5 September 1933, Sverdlovsk

Artist

Frequently linked to Sots-Art and Conceptualism, today Bulatov is one of the most successful former Soviet painters working in the West. He grew up in Moscow and attended the

Moscow School of Art (1947–52) and the Surikov Art Institute (1952–58). Bulatov's artistic development was influenced by mentors Robert Falk and Vladimir Favorskii. In the USSR, Bulatov earned a living illustrating children's books while privately painting unconventional works at odds with Soviet aesthetics. His now famous *Gorizont* (*Horizon*, 1972) drew attention at the 1977 Venice Biennale, and since 1988 his work has been exhibited at the Zurich Kunsthalle, Paris Centre Pompidou, and other venues. He lives and works in Paris and Moscow.

See also: Conceptualism, art; Sots-Art

ANN KOMAROMI

Bulgakova, Olga Vasilevna

b. 30 January 1951, Moscow

Artist

Bulgakova graduated from the Surikov Art Academy in 1975. A member of the USSR Artists' Union, Bulgakova pushed the boundaries of official art early in her career. Influenced by Surrealism, her paintings often include theatrical and carnival images that suggest delicate balances between opposing metaphorical forces. Her use of richly layered symbolism and allegory is common to artists of the Stagnation era.

KRISTEN M. HARKNESS

Bulldozer Exhibition (buldozernaia vystavka)

On 15 September 1974, a group of dissident artists, including Oskar Rabin, Evgenii Rukhin, Vladimir Nemukhin, Lidiia Masterkova, Aleksandr Melamid, and Vitalii Komar, organized an open-air art show on a vacant lot in the outskirts of Moscow. KGB agents, pretending to be gardeners and construction workers, dispersed the crowd and crushed some of the art pieces with bulldozers. The effect of the repression was the opposite of what the authorities wanted to achieve: the event and the participants received wide publicity in international media. The publicity created a demand for Soviet unofficial art among Western art dealers and eventually led to Sotheby's auction of 1988 in Moscow, where previously unknown artists' works were sold at much higher prices than expected. The publicity also helped to launch careers of artists who emigrated in the 1970s, especially that of Komar and Melamid.

See also: Federal Security Service (FSS/FSB); Komar and Melamid; Masterkova, Lidiia; Nemukhin, Vladimir; Rabin, Oskar; Rukhin, Evgenii

Further reading

Rosenfeld, A. and Dodge, N. T. (eds) (1995) *From Gulag to Glasnost: Nonconformist Art from the Soviet Union*, New York: Thames and Hudson.

VLADIMIR PAPERNY

Buratino

Buratino (from Italian for 'wooden doll', marionette), a long-nosed, wooden troublemaker, is the protagonist of Aleksei Nikolaevich Tolstoi's fairy-tale novel for children, *Zolotoi kliuchik, ili Prikliucheniia Buratino* (*The Golden Key, or The Adventures of Buratino*, 1935), based on Carlo Collodi's *Pinocchio*, from which it largely deviates. Tolstoi's play version (1936) was produced at the Central Children's Theatre in Moscow (1937) and at numerous Theatres of Young Spectators. Tolstoi's film script (1937) and Aleksandr Ptushko's film (1939) launched screen versions, from 1959 (Ivan Ivanov-Vano's animated film, scripted by Nikolai Erdman) to 1997, including the 1975 musical version (director Leonid Nechaev), with songs composed by Bulat Okudzhava. The numerous reproductions of Buratino in the media and the numerous products called Buratino (including lemonade, toys, even a rocket launcher) make him comparable to Mickey Mouse in American culture. Eventually Buratino and other characters from Tolstoi's book became proverbial figures and subjects of jokes. Predominantly erotic in the Soviet period, Buratino folklore entered jokes about the New Russians during the 1990s. Contemporary artists (Igor Makarevich, Maksim Smagin) use the image of Buratino in their works; Izhevsk boasts a monument to Buratino; and Moscow has an interactive Children's Museum of Buratino/Pinocchio (1997). As a positive manifestation of non-ideological freedom, Buratino challenges Soviet culture by undermining officially approved, 'serious' values.

See also: Ivanov-Vano, Ivan; joke; New Russians; Okudzhava, Bulat; theatre, Soviet

MARK LIPOVETSKY

Burda

German magazine that features sewing and knitting patterns, recipes, and advice on beauty and cosmetics. Long before its first publication in Russian (1987), Soviet women eager to keep up with Western fashions perused it for information unattainable in the Soviet press or stores.

IRINA MAKOVEEVA

Bure, Pavel Vladimirovich

b. 31 March 1971, Moscow

Hockey player

Nicknamed 'the Russian Rocket', Bure is a quick-skating, high-scoring right-winger who began his career with TsSKA in 1987. Having defected to North America over a contract dispute, Bure debuted with the NHL's Vancouver Canucks in 1991–92. He has earned numerous accolades despite a spate of injuries (NHL's top rookie in 1992, best forward at the 1998 Olympics, NHL's leading goal scorer in 2000 and 2001, several-time NHL All-Star Team member), but hockey's ultimate prizes, the Stanley Cup and Olympic gold, have proved more elusive.

See also: hockey; TsSKA

RACHEL S. PLATONOV

bureaucracy

Russian bureaucracy has long historical roots, for contemporary government officials inherited all the notorious traits of Imperial Russia's bureaucrats satirized in the works of Gogol, Goncharov, Dostoevskii, Chekhov, and Belyi: obstructionism, nepotism, corruption, and perceived omnipotence. The Soviet system also bred fear, rigidity, and incompetence among those empowered to make decisions, who frequently were appointed on the basis not of professional merit but of connections and Party membership. Low-ranking Soviet officials tried to avoid any responsibility, passing decisions on to their superiors, and doggedly followed established practices, in the fear of taking initiative or risks. A plethora of rules, contradictory regulations, and numerous prohibitions made for endless, redundant paperwork and red tape, with bribes as the only viable solution to a problem. Even such everyday processes as obtaining a simple certificate or registering one's residence could take several days. The *nomenklatura* (the highest officials in the Soviet and post-Soviet hierarchy) continues to be the Russian elite, and its power in contemporary Russia is unchallenged, for all attempts to reduce the role of bureaucracy in post-Soviet Russia have failed. Putin's construction of an 'administrative vertical' and the reestablishment of state control over the most profitable natural resource companies can only contribute to the prosperity and power of Russian bureaucrats. Bribes and connections continue to be the only 'solutions' to many bureaucratic problems in post-Soviet Russia.

See also: blat; natural resources; nomenklatura; oligarkh; privatization; Putin, Vladimir

TATIANA SMORODINSKAYA

Buriatia

Buriatia is a republic in the Russian Federation inhabited by the Buriat ethnic minority. This ethnic group belongs to the Central-Asian Mongoloid anthropological type. Buriats have lived in the Lake Baikal area in southern Siberia for about 1000 years. Russian colonization occurred in the seventeenth century. Administrative territories are the Republic of Buriatia (capital Ulan-Ude) and two Buriat autonomous *okrugs* (Aga Buryat in the Irkutsk *oblast* and Ust-Orda in the Chita *oblast*). Some 86.6 percent of the republic's population (421,000) speaks either Buriat (in the Mongolian group of the Altai family) or Mongolian. Historically the native population's main occupation was nomadic cattle breeding, supplemented by hunting, fishing, and agriculture. The traditional dwelling was a nomad's *yurta*: a tent or octagonal timber cabin. The ancient native religion of Shamanism has been superseded by Lamaism.

See also: Baikal; ethnic minorities; Lamaism (Buddhism); Siberia

Further reading

Chaussonnet, V. (1995) *Crossroads Alaska: Native Cultures of Alaska and Siberia*, Washington, DC: Smithsonian Institution Press.

Forsyth, J. (1999) *A History of the Peoples of Siberia: Russia's North Asian Colony 1581–1990*, Cambridge: Cambridge University Press.

TATYANA LEDENEVA

Burliaev, Nikolai Petrovich

b. 3 August 1946, Moscow

Actor, director, screenwriter, cultural activist

As a child actor, Burliaev stunned international audiences in the title role of *Ivanovo detstvo* (*Ivan's Childhood*, 1962), conveying youthful idealism along with tenderness and vulnerability. After studying acting at the Shchukin Theatre School and directing at VGIK, Burliaev gave his best screen performances in literary adaptations, including *Igrok* (The Gambler, 1972) and *Malenkie tragedii* (Little Tragedies, 1979). He directed several ideologically-charged features, most infamously the cumbersome biopic *Lermontov* (1986). In the 1990s, Burliaev became a prominent cultural voice with strong Slavophile leanings and created a film festival for Slavic and Orthodox nations, 'The Golden Knight' (Zolotoi Vitiaz). He has also published poetry and prose. People's Artist of Russia (1996).

See also: All-Russian (All-Union) State Institute of Cinematography (VGIK); Slavophiles

PETER ROLLBERG

Bykov, Rolan Anatolevich

b. 12 November 1929, Kiev; d. 6 October 1998, Moscow

Film-maker, screenwriter, actor

Bykov graduated from the Shchukin Theatre Institute in 1951 and in 1956 founded the Moscow State University Student Theatre. After 1960, Bykov directed films at Mosfilm Studios. Most of his pictures were about and for children, including *Aibolit-66* (*Doctor Ouch-66*, 1966) and *Avtomobil, skripka i sobaka Kliaksa* (*The Car, the Violin, and Kliaksa the Dog*, 1974). Bykov's films set in Soviet schools (*Vnimanie, cherepakha!* [*Watch Out, a Turtle!* 1969] and *Chuchelo* [*Scarecrow*, 1983]) criticized a society based on hypocrisy and violence. Among Bykov's most memorable cinematic roles are Efim in Aleksandr Askoldov's *Kommissar* (*Commissar*, 1967) and the jester in Andrei Tarkovskii's *Andrei Rublev* (1969). In the 1990s, Bykov headed Russian federal programmes dealing with children's creative development, such as 'Children–Screen–Culture' and 'Culture and Childhood'.

See also: Askoldov, Aleksandr; film, children's; Tarkovskii, Andrei

ALEXANDER PROKHOROV

Bykov, Vasilii Vladimirovich

(né Vasil Vladimirovich Bykau)

b. 19 June 1924; Vitebsk Region, Belorussia; d. 22 June 2003, Minsk

Writer

A distinguished war writer, Bykov started his literary career after fighting in World War II as an infantry lieutenant. Most of his prose was written in both Belarussian and Russian. Bykov won popularity in the Thaw period with the novellas *Tretia raketa* (*The Third Flare*, 1962), *Alpiiskaia ballada* (*Alpine Ballad*, 1964), and *Mertvym ne bolno* (*The Dead Feel No Pain*, 1966), followed in the 1970s by *Sotnikov* (1970), *Obelisk* (1974), and *Poiti i ne vernutsia* (*To Go and Not to Return*, 1978). Bykov's œuvre focuses on the behaviour of two or three main characters in identical circumstances during a limited time period, usually in extreme war conditions that test individual morality. Since his protagonists face comrades' cruelty and betrayal as well as death, deprivation, famine, and cold, Soviet critics accused him of compromising the heroic Soviet past. In 1974, nevertheless, Bykov was awarded the USSR State Prize for *Hold Out Till Dawn*, and in 1986 the Lenin Prize for *Znak bedy* (*Sign of Misfortune*). After the disintegration of the USSR Bykov appeared in political opposition to Belarus authorities. From the middle of the 1990s he lived abroad in Finland, Germany, and the Czech Republic.

See also: literature, World War II; World War II (Great Patriotic War)

Further reading

Dedkov, I. (1980) *Vasil Bykov*, Moscow: Sovremennik.
Lazarev, L. (1986) *V. Bykov: On Craftsmanship*, trans. A. Calvert, Moscow: Raduga.

ALEXANDER LEDENEV

byt (everyday life)

Linguist Roman Jacobson insisted that *byt* was 'culturally untranslatable' into Western languages. The word is sometimes understood as 'everyday existence', 'everyday routine', or 'stagnation'. The Bolsheviks inherited their negative attitude toward *byt* from the avant-garde: '*Liubovnaia lodka razbilas o byt*' ('Love's boat has crashed against *byt*') wrote the Futurist poet Vladimir Maiakovskii in his suicide note in 1930. The Soviet state's early decrees were aimed at freeing the workers from *byt* by promoting communal living, collective child rearing, and industrialized food preparation. The Stalinist epoch reversed this trend by advocating family values, individualism in housing, customized tailoring (which in practice was available to the chosen few), and other traditional ways of life. Under Khrushchev, there was a brief attempt to revive the anti-*byt* strivings of the 1920s, even as mass housing development helped to free residents from the unbearable conditions of communal apartments.

See also: communal apartment; Khrushchev, Nikita

VLADIMIR PAPERNY

C

calendars, old and new

The Russian Empire used the 'old' Julian calendar, not the 'new' calendar introduced by Pope Gregory XIII in 1582 (and adopted by England and the American colonies in 1752). In the nineteenth century, Russia was twelve days behind the 'new' calendar, and thirteen days behind in the twentieth century. Thus, the February Revolution began on 8 March 1917, and the October Revolution occurred on 7 November 1917, according to the new calendar. The Bolsheviks banned the old calendar, although the Russian Orthodox Church continued to use it, celebrating Christmas on 7 January (25 December, old calendar). The difference between the two calendars is critical in using the time machine in Iurii Mamin's film *Okno v Parizh* (*Window to Paris*, 1993).

See also: holidays, Russian Orthodox; holidays, Soviet; Mamin, Iurii; Russian Orthodoxy

NADIESZDA KIZENKO

cameramen

Russian cinematography began when professional photographers mastered the new technology in order to film newsreels, initially for foreign companies (e.g., Pathé Frères), and, after 1908, for Russian producers. In the 1910s, cameramen such as Fedor Burgasov (1890–1944) added subtle, psychological details to Protazanov's and Bauer's melodramas by introducing close and tracking shots and by refining lighting techniques.

The emergence of Soviet avant-garde cinema in the 1920s went along with innovative approaches to cinematography that self-consciously departed from the unhurried rhythm of bourgeois cinema. The so-called 'Russian montage' and its supreme masters Eduard Tissé (1897–1961) and Anatolii Golovnia (1900–82) who worked for Eisenstein and Pudovkin, respectively, became household names in international cinema. Distinctly poetic approaches were characteristic of Ukrainian Danylo Demutskii (1893–1954), who gave Dovzhenko's revolutionary meditations radiance and fluidity, and Andrei Moskvin (1905–74), the creative partner of the FEKS group in Leningrad.

The introduction of sound film in the 1930s necessitated slower editing and de-emphasized camera work. Among the prominent cameramen of early sound film were Arkadii Koltsatyi (1905–?) and Leonid Kosmatov (1901–77), who took Stalinist picturesque grandiosity to its extreme. The subsequent Thaw was marked by neo-realist sobriety, visual expressiveness, and rejection of static, hierarchical compositions, especially in the groundbreaking work of Sergei Urusevskii (1908–74) in Mikhail Kalatozov's pictures. The 1960s saw the emergence of a multitude of styles, including the baroque imagery of Vadim Iusov (b. 1929), who worked for Tarkovskii and Bondarchuk, Lithuanian Jonas Gricius (b. 1928), whose fame rests on Grigorii Kozintsev's Shakespeare adaptations, and Georgian Levan Paatashvili (b. 1926), among others.

See also: Bondarchuk, Sergei; Kalatozov, Mikhail; Kozintsev, Grigorii; Tarkovskii, Andrei; Urusevskii, Sergei

PETER ROLLBERG

cars, Soviet and post-Soviet

The car industry in Russia before and after the Soviet Union has relied on several plants: e.g., GAZ, ZIS/ZIL, UAZ, AZLK, and especially VAZ (the Volga automobile factory [*Volzhskii avtomobilnyi zavod*]), the largest and most famous, thanks to subsidies from Fiat (Italy). Construction began in Togliatti (near Samara) in 1967, enabling the annual manufacture of 220,000 units by 1971. The first classic VAZ model was the boxy VAZ-2101 or *Zhiguli*, clearly based upon the Fiat 124, later known as *Lada* for export markets. With a top speed of 140 km/h, the *Zhiguli* was designed as the people's car, but rising costs over nine Soviet versions kept it unaffordable. Yet purchasers were willing to wait several years for a *Zhiguli*, despite its high price.

The late 1970s witnessed the appearance of the 4x4 *Niva*, popular in Western Europe and on tough Russian roads (after tests in Uzbekistan) because substandard asphalt could ruin VAZ Wankel engines cased in cheap Soviet alloys as well as small urban models like *Lada's Cheburashka* or the inexpensive *Oka* of the 1970–80s, the Russian equivalent of Fiat's *Cinquecento*. With help from Porsche, front-wheel-drive and family hatchbacks such as the *Samara* marked the1980s. In 1995, VAZ unveiled its 16 millionth car, while experiments yielded the mini-van *Nadezhda*, echoing the VIS subsidiary that manufactures pick-ups.

The Gorkii automobile factory GAZ (*Gorkovskii avtomobilnyi zavod*) in what is now Nizhnyi Novgorod began work on 1 January 1932 producing trucks and, with American assistance, automobiles resembling the Ford Model A of the late 1920s. During World War II, efforts concentrated on 4x4 jeeps; however, it was the sleek, 105 km/h *Victory* (*Pobeda*) of 1946 that instituted a GAZ mythology. Larger, more elegant models, such as the 12-ZIM (1950) and *Chaika* M-13 (1959) underscored the enduring influence of American designs (Buick and Packard), favoured by politicians. From the mid-1950s until the late 1960s the Volga developed as a variation upon the limousine aesthetic, just as the modern 4x4 *Ataman* recalls Mercedes jeeps. Attempts by the ZIL limousine manufacturers to match Western standards even moved into racing cars during the 1960s, albeit with scant success; today politicians prefer a BMW or Mercedes to a ZIL pastiche.

Moscow's Lenin Komsomol Automobile Factory, AZLK (*Avtomobilnyi zavod imeni leninskogo komsomola*), established in November 1930, until 1933 undertook production of Ford A/AA designs, followed in the next decade by Opel Kadett imitations (the K38). The renowned and rotund *Moskvich* enjoyed healthy exports from 1948–60s, though the UAZ 469 and *Niva* are the two Soviet cars to have had genuine success abroad. The Ulianovsk Automobile Factory UAZ (*Ulianovskii avtomobilnyi zavod*) was founded in 1941–42 to develop a tradition of 4x4s, jeeps, vans, and trucks. Martial connections to civilian cars were clearest at the Izhevsk Mechanical Factory IZH (*Izhevskii mekhanicheskii zavod*), which produced military hardware and after 1966 embarked upon *Moskvich* adaptations.

After 1991, low incomes (allowing for a mere 14 cars per 100 citizens), wasted state subsidies, ruinous privatization, and embezzlement wreaked havoc with the car industry as domestic companies struggled against cheap Asian alternatives, luxury models from BMW, Mercedes, and even Rolls Royce, and Ford returned to build cars within Russia. New tax legislation made purchasing foreign brands prohibitively expensive for the ordinary citizen; however, luxury models remain evident in Russia's capital cities. Today there is a thriving black market in cars stolen in Russia or imported from abroad, resulting in countless humorous comparisons between a slick Mercedes 600 and the 'hunchbacked', 'big-eared' *Zaporozhets*, an unsightly variation on the Fiat 600 or German *Trabant*.

In the past ten years, with the growth of the middle class and the wealthy 'new Russians', automobiles have become increasingly popular, and the roads in Moscow and St. Petersburg, as well as several other large cities, are clogged with traffic that has more than doubled during the decade. Parking in the capital cities' downtown areas – not planned for automobile traffic – has become such a problem that many new architectural projects in Moscow include plans for underground parking garages. In addition, Russia's legendarily poor road conditions present an acute problem for a population increasingly dependent on automobiles. The limited improvements in the Ring highway around Moscow and the exponential increase in the number of petrol stations in the capital cities are but the first in many crucial steps taken to improve Russia's automobile infrastructure.

See also: black market; kopeika; New Russians

Further reading

www.autodux.ru (Russian)
www.automarket.ru (Russian)
www.autosoviet.altervista.org (English and Italian)

DAVID MACFADYEN

cathedral (sobor)

A sizable church (*sobor* in Russian) that serves as a bishop's headquarters. Any large city or monastery has a cathedral where a patriarch, bishop, or head priest conducts religious services. Russian Orthodox cathedrals have two or three altars, are massive, domed, and richly decorated with icons, corbels, ceramic and coloured glazed tiles. Among the most important Russian cathedrals are Moscow's Cathedrals of Christ the Saviour (*Khram Khrista Spasitelia*), of the Annunciation (*Blagoveshchenskii sobor*), of the Archangel (*Arkhangelskii sobor*), the Assumption/Dormition (*Uspenskii sobor*), and St. Basil's Cathedral (*Sobor Vasiliia Blazhennogo*); St. Petersburg's St. Isaac's Cathedral (*Isaakievskii sobor*), Peter and Paul Cathedral (*Petropavlovskii sobor*), Cathedral of Our Lady of Kazan (*Kazanskii sobor*); Assumption Cathedral (*Uspenskii sobor*) in Vladimir; and St. Sophia Cathedrals (*Sofiiskii sobor*) in Kiev and Novgorod.

The Russian word for cathedral bred the term *sobornost* (collectivity), supposedly coined by Russian philosopher Aleksei Khomiakov, and referring to Russian Orthodoxy's commonality through voluntary participation based on love of God and one's neighbour.

Many ancient Russian cathedrals were closed or destroyed by Soviet authorities. Since the USSR broke up, countless cathedrals have been restored.

See also: Cathedral of Christ the Saviour; church architecture, Russian Orthodox; Moscow; Russian Orthodoxy; St. Petersburg

ELENA SKIPETROVA

Cathedral of Christ the Saviour (Khram Khrista Spasitelia)

The Cathedral, or Temple, of Christ the Saviour, commissioned by Tsar Alexander I and designed by Konstantin Ton, commemorates the 1812 expulsion of Napoleon from Moscow. The construction, begun in 1831 just upriver from the Moscow Kremlin, proved difficult, and the huge, golden-domed edifice was not consecrated until 1889. In 1931, the Soviet government destroyed the enormous building – possibly because it overshadowed the Government House complex across the river – and eventually replaced it with a swimming pool. Following the 1991 Soviet collapse, reconstruction began, and in 1996 the Cathedral of Christ the Saviour reopened.

See also: church architecture, Russian Orthodox; Kremlin (Moscow)

EDWARD ALAN COLE

Caucasian

The phrase '*litso kavkazskoi natsionalnosti*' (literally 'an individual of Caucasian nationality') was coined in the 1990s in political and media discourse to refer to migrants from either the Transcaucasian states (Armenia, Azerbaidzhan, and Georgia) or regions in the south of Russia populated by ethnic minorities (i.e. Adigeia, Chechnia, Dagestan, North Osetia, etc.). The implications of this term quickly changed from legalistic to pejorative after terrorist attacks in Moscow during the early 1990s, in which Chechens were the main suspects. Its usage reveals xenophobia and rising nationalism in Russia.

See also: Armenia; Azerbaidzhan; Chechnia; Dagestan; ethnic minorities; Georgia; nationalism ('the national question'); Ossetia

VLADIMIR STRUKOV

Caucasian cuisine

The cuisines of Armenia, Azerbaidzhan, and Georgia are famed for their meat kabobs and breads. Typical Armenian dishes include *lavash* (flat bread) wrapped around herbs, *chanakh* (sheep cheese), or grilled meats; *dolma* (stuffed vegetables); *keufta* (bulgur and ground lamb balls); and *bourek* (flaky, savoury-filled pastries). Persian influence appears in sumptuous, saffron-flavoured pilafs accompanied by chicken, meat, or game in Azerbaidzhan. In Georgia, *tabaka* (grilled flattened chicken), *chakhokhbili* (tomato chicken stew), *khachapuri* (cheese bread), *kharcho* (spicy beef soup), and *khashi* (tripe soup) – a reputed hangover cure – are perennial favourites.

Abundant use of herbs and spices enhances dishes in all cuisines. Georgians like fresh cilantro, tarragon, parsley, dill, mint, and basil to flavour dishes and to garnish them; *khmeli-suneli* (seasoning mix) consists of ground dried coriander seed, basil, dill weed, summer savoury, parsley, mint, fenugreek, imereti saffron (marigold flowers), and bay leaf. Armenians prefer a milder, sweeter mix that includes allspice, cumin, and cinnamon. Azerbaidzhanis flavour their foods with a delicate sweet-and-sour sauce made from pomegranates, dried lemons, sour plums, and the juice of unripe grapes; they also sprinkle stews with bright purple sumac powder for extra tartness. Georgians use *adzhika*, a red peppery condiment; *tkemali*, green plum sauce; and *satsivi* (aromatic walnut) sauce for chicken or turkey.

Georgians rely heavily on vegetables such as beans (both kidney and green), eggplant, and tomatoes. *Lavash* is popular in all three countries, but Armenians and Georgians also bake round bread loaves, the latter in a *toné* (clay oven). All cuisines use nuts extensively: walnuts in Georgia, pine nuts in Armenia, and pistachios and almonds in Azerbaidzhan. For dessert, Georgians love fresh apricots and peaches, Armenians revel in succulent local grapes, and Azerbaidzhanis prefer dried apricots, quince, sour cherries, and persimmons or pistachio *pakhlava* (baklava). Georgian wines and Armenian cognac are world-renowned.

See also: Armenia; Azerbaidzhan; Caucasus; dining, Soviet; Georgia; tabaka

CHRISTINE A. RYDEL

Caucasus

The Caucasus, located in the south-west of the former Soviet Union between the Black and Caspian Seas, is named after the Caucasus mountains (the Greater Caucasus, which stretch from West to East for 1250 km, with the highest peaks Elbrus 5633 m, Dykhtau 5203 m, Shkhara 5058 m, and Kazbek 5047 m, and the Lesser Caucasus). The Caucasus includes the Northern Caucasus (within the Russian Federation), the northern slopes of the Greater Caucasus, and Transcaucasia (Georgia, Armenia, Azerbaidzhan), and the southern slopes of the Greater and Lesser Caucasus. The area of 440,000 sq. km has a population of 30.7 million. In altitudes higher than 4000 m, there is year-round snow; there are also 1,400 glaciers. The region is subject to frequent earthquakes. The climate in the mountains varies according to elevation; the climate is temperate in the Northern Caucasus and subtropical in Transcaucasia.

The most unstable and conflict-ridden area of the former USSR, the Caucasus is extremely diverse ethnically and culturally, with inhabitants falling into three language families: Ibero-Caucasian (Georgian or Kartvelian, Abkhaz/Adygh, Nakh, and Dagestanian); Indo-European (Armenian, Greek, Russian, Ukrainian, Kurdish, and Ossetian); and Turkic (Azeri, Kumyk, Nogai, Tatar, Balkar, Turkmen, and Karachai).

Throughout history, numerous states and empires have tried to take over the Caucasus because of its advantageous geographical position.

It was conquered by Persians, Romans, Byzantines, Arabs, Khazars, Mongols, and Ottoman Turks. From the sixteenth to the eighteenth centuries, parts of the Northern Caucasus were annexed by Russia, which built a fortified line along the rivers Terek and Kuban that was guarded by Cossacks. The main competitors for the territory of the Caucasus in the eighteenth century were Persia, Russia, and the Ottoman Empire. Russia was the most active and gradually during the nineteenth century conquered almost the entire Caucasus region. From 1817 to 1864 in the east of Northern Caucasus, Russian troops waged a long-lasting war with the Caucasian mountain peoples of Chechnia, Dagestan, and Adygea, who passionately resisted Russian rule.

In the Soviet era, Georgia, Armenia, and Azerbaidzhan became Soviet republics. The Northern Caucasus went through numerous administrative divisions and reorganizations before several autonomous republics (Dagestan, Kabardino-Balkaria, Checheno Ingushetia, and Northern Ossetia) and autonomous oblasts (Karachai-Cherkessia and Kalmykia) were established. In 1942, during World War II, German troops occupied the western regions of the Northern Caucasus. After the liberation, many peoples (Kalmyks, Chechens, Ingushs, Balkars, Karachais, Meskhetian Turks, and Greeks) were accused of collaboration with the enemy and deported to Kazakhstan and elsewhere in Central Asia, and Siberia. In 1956, Khrushchev returned them to their historical 'motherland'. After the collapse of the USSR in 1991, Georgia, Azerbaidzhan, and Armenia became independent states, while in the Northern Caucasus, Adygea, Karachai-Cherkessia, Kabardino-Balkaria, Northern Ossetia, Dagestan, Chechnia, and Ingushetia were established as autonomous republics within the Russian Federation. The 1990s brought armed conflict to the Caucasus. Under Soviet rule, Armenians living contiguously in Azerbaidzhan had their own autonomous *oblast* of Nagorno-Karabakh, as did Abkhaz and Ossetians in Georgia. After the USSR disintegrated, those regions declared their independence, which went unacknowledged internationally and triggered military conflict. Within the territory of the Russian Federation a similar conflict took place between the Ingush and the Ossetians (1992–93). In 1994, Chechen nationalists announced Chechnia's (Ichkeria's) secession from Russia, which led to the Chechen War and frequent terrorist attacks.

The population of the Caucasus has doubled in the past fifty years, due to a high birth rate, related to local demographic and religious traditions. High population density (mostly rural) and economic turmoil have caused high rates of unemployment and poverty, which in turn have led to the migration of Caucasians into Russia, Ukraine, and Kazakhstan, particularly to large cities and other areas with many construction sites, and regions of oil and gas drilling. Civil wars and ethnic conflicts contributed to the rise in emigration during the 1990s. The percentage of Caucasians in the populations of large Russian cities and wealthy regions is constantly growing. In Moscow, Caucasians are the second largest ethnic group after Russians (3.19 per cent in 2002). Russians have a negative attitude toward the number of Caucasian ethnic groups in Russian cities, and demonstrate extreme forms of intolerance towards these migrants, who control fruit markets, casinos, and the automobile trade.

In the Soviet era, the beautiful Caucasus attracted large numbers of tourists; it offered sea resorts on the Black and Caspian Seas, ski resorts and mountain climbing in the Northern Caucasus and Georgia, and rafting. Owing to the unstable political situation in the region, however, tourism is currently in decline.

See also: administrative structure, Soviet Union; Armenia; Azerbaidzhan; Caucasian; Caucasian cuisine; Chechnia; Dagestan; Georgia; vacations, Soviet and post-Soviet; War, Chechen

SERGEI TARKHOV

caviar

A nutritious, high-calorie fish product, caviar (*ikra*) is one of the most prestigious appetizers in Russian cuisine. Black caviar from sturgeon, the rarest and the most expensive variety, originates mainly in the Caspian Sea. The larger its size and lighter the colour of its grains, the higher the quality. White sturgeon (*beluga*) is the Queen of caviar, with second place belonging to regular sturgeon (*osetr*), and third to tostellate sturgeon (*sevruga*). Quality depends on the age of the fish. Red caviar is the roe of salmon (*keta*, hunchback salmon, red salmon) coming from the Far East, and tastes soft and delicate; black is usually more expensive. Generally pasteurized and canned today, caviar is one of Russia's chief symbols and exports.

See also: appetizers; dining, Russian

ELENA SKIPETROVA

cemeteries

Cemeteries have remained important features of Russian settlements since the burial mounds of prehistoric times. Russians lavish care and attention on the graves not only of ancestors and relatives, but also of outstanding persons in all walks of life, unknown peoples of the remote past, and even fallen soldiers of invading enemies. In general, cemeteries fall into three categories: ordinary, honorific, and memorial. Ordinary cemeteries range from small burial plots under village church windows to vast urban necropolises, such as the Smolensk Cemetery in St. Petersburg, which contains graves dating from the foundation of the city right up to the present day. Honorific cemeteries may be devoted to specific elites, such as the Communist and Soviet heroes buried near Lenin's Tomb and in the front wall of the Moscow Kremlin, or just to famous people in general, such as those entombed in the Novodevichii and Donskoi cemeteries in Moscow, or in the Tikhvin Cemetery in St. Petersburg. Memorial cemeteries usually preserve the memory of great historical events; for example, at the Piskarev Cemetery in St. Petersburg, the mass graves of an estimated half a million victims preserve the memory of the terrible Siege of Leningrad in World War II

See also: Kremlin (Moscow); Piskarev Cemetery; St. Petersburg; World War II (Great Patriotic War)

EDWARD ALAN COLE

censorship

Soviet literature and arts of the post-Stalin period were shaped by the experience and institutional structures of censorship inherited from earlier Soviet culture. Yet the final decades of Soviet cultural life witnessed a much increased struggle between conservative bureaucracy and repressive leadership, on the one hand, and, on the other, writers, practitioners of the various arts, and scholars who employed various strategies to challenge the limitations placed on their activity by the organs of censorship more or less openly. As the pendulum shifted back and forth between relaxation and restriction, 'thaws' alternated with 'freezes' in Soviet cultural policy.

Censorship accompanied the development of secular literature and arts in Russia almost from the beginning. Alexander I issued the first censorship statute in 1804, and virtually all of Russia's greatest writers experienced harsh censorship under Nicholas I's reign (1825–55) as a formative influence. Censorship relaxed after the death of Nicholas I, during the first period of 'glasnost' preceding the reforms of Alexander II in the early 1860s. A 1906 statute abolished preliminary censorship in the wake of the revolution of 1905, prompting a growth in popular entertainment, including more explicit treatment of sexuality.

Censorship was reinstituted immediately after the Bolshevik Revolution (1917), and historians continue to debate the extent to which Soviet censorship was a continuation or legacy of the tsarist system. Certainly, the tsarist and Soviet regimes shared the problem of controlling a vast and ethnically diverse empire; both distrusted open discussion and artistic portrayal of topics perceived as threatening to political and social stability. Yet in its fully developed form, Soviet censorship constituted a system of state control over the arts unprecedented in its complexity and invasiveness.

The main censorship agency, *Glavlit*, assumed its final form during the first decade of Soviet power. A statute signed by Lenin two days after the Bolshevik takeover closed down anti-Bolshevik newspapers. The Main Administration for Literary and Publishing Affairs (*Glavnoe upravlenie po delam literatury i izdatelstva*) or Glavlit was established in 1922, and in the course of the Soviet period evolved into an enormous bureaucracy with representatives in every publishing enterprise in the USSR. Glavlit censors were guided by a list (*perechen*) of forbidden topics ranging from labour camps to natural disasters. All Soviet cultural production was subject to both preliminary and post-publication/performance censorship; the latter could include the closing down of journals or plays and the removal of books from libraries.

The line between censorship and self-censorship could become indistinct. The very existence of Glavlit pressured writers and editors to forestall censors' objections by internalizing them in the processes of writing and editing. Moreover, the pervasive control of the educational system, press, and arts inevitably shaped the tastes, expectations, and interpretive strategies of readers and producers of culture. On the one hand, readers learned to read between the lines of the censored text, seeking Aesopian meanings behind politically correct facades – hence the widely used expression *ezopovskii iazyk* (Aesopian language). On the other hand, while a small, highly educated group of the population had private libraries or access to restricted texts within public libraries, the cultural horizon of the majority was fixed by what was allowed, promoted, and filtered by the state.

Socialist Realism in the arts constituted an aggressive form of censorship that dictated not only what stories could be told, but how they should be told. Formal experimentation, including the use of idiosyncratic vocabulary, slang, and expletives, was proscribed and termed 'formalism'. The most virulent stage of Stalinist cultural control was what is termed *zhdanovshchina*, after Stalin's cultural henchman Andrei Zhdanov. Attacks on Anna Akhmatova, Mikhail Zoshchenko, and Dmitrii Shostakovich crippled their careers and set the stage for the post-Stalin years.

During the post-Stalin period, as de-Stalinization followed Khrushchev's 'secret speech' (1956), the Soviet leadership continued to intervene in the censorship process. After Khrushchev authorized the publication of Aleksandr Solzhenitsyn's *One Day in the Life of Ivan Denisovich* (*Odin den Ivana Denisovicha*) in the journal *Novyi mir* (*New World*) in November 1962, conservatives

engineered Krushchev's visit to an exhibit of abstract art at the Manège exhibition hall (December 1962). The tactic was successful: an appalled Khrushchev would not repeat his 'error'.

Throughout the post-Stalin period, writers and artists found ways to circumvent censorship. In the mid-1950s, the first Soviet works began to appear in *tamizdat* – published abroad. In 1957, Boris Pasternak's *Doctor Zhivago* was published in Italy by Feltrinelli, reputedly against the author's wishes, after the editorial board of *Novyi mir* rejected the manuscript. The campaign of opprobrium to which Pasternak was subjected was clearly intended to discourage other writers from challenging the authority of official censorship. In 1966, the writers Andrei Siniavskii and Iulii Daniel were placed on trial, convicted, and sentenced to terms of hard labour for publishing literary works abroad under the pseudonyms Abram Terts and Nikolai Arzhak. The strategy of using a Stalin-era show trial to assert cultural control backfired when the writers pleaded not guilty, and outrage over this single instance of Soviet writers placed on trial for their writings fuelled the growth of the dissident movement.

Just as literature produced 'for the drawer' or published in *tamizdat* and smuggled back into the USSR could be circulated in *samizdat*, so the songs of bards like Vladimir Vysotskii, Aleksandr Galich, and Bulat Okudzhava could be disseminated as *magnitizdat* on homemade tapes for reel-to-reel players. Arts that required performance or exhibition space were clearly more vulnerable to being denied an audience. Even those films and theatrical performances that had been passed by preliminary censorship could be shelved or shut down after production or opening. Nonconformist artists, with restricted access to state-owned studio and gallery space and materials, had to find ways of creating and storing works in cramped Soviet apartments. One of the most creative strategies for circumventing censorship was the 'paper architecture' movement. More public and confrontational attempts to expand the boundaries of the acceptable in the arts are the so-called Bulldozer Exhibition in 1974 and the 1979 presentation of the uncensored *Metropol* literary anthology. The government ultimately suppressed both.

During the Thaw, the uneven process of censorship and rehabilitation of previously banned works resulted in their entrance into Soviet literature long after they had been written and in many cases after their authors' deaths. Works by long-prohibited writers – from Modernist poets to émigrés to suppressed Soviet writers – made their way to the pages of contemporary journals. The most prominent example of this anachronistic reclamation was the posthumous publication of Mikhail Bulgakov's *Master i Margarita* (*The Master and Margarita*) in the journal *Moskva* (*Moscow*) in 1966–67, over a quarter of a century after the author's death. This process of 'returning literature' would become a hallmark of censorship's weakening during glasnost in the late 1980s.

Following the example of Alexander II over a century earlier, Mikhail Gorbachev initiated a policy of glasnost (openness) as a prelude to reform. Shortly after his rise to the position of General Secretary of the Communist Party in April 1985, Gorbachev began a relaxation of censorship that steadily eliminated long-standing taboos. In 1987, works of literature and film either produced 'for the drawer' or shelved, appeared: notably, Anatolii Rybakov's novel *Deti Arbata* (*Children of the Arbat*) and Tengiz Abuladze's film *Pokaianie* (*Repentance*). The following year witnessed the publication of previously banned works by 'safely dead' Soviet and émigré writers, such as Pasternak's *Doctor Zhivago* and Evgenii Zamiatin's dystopian novel *My* (*We*). The year 1989 marked a watershed, seeing the publication of works by living émigré writers, including Aleksandr Solzhenitsyn. The publication in *Novyi mir* of Solzhenitsyn's monumental exposé of the labour camp system, *Arkhipelag GULag* (*The Gulag Archipelago*) in early 1989 to all intents and purposes marked the end of cultural censorship in the USSR.

Through most of Soviet history, all mention of the existence of censorship was banned in works published in the USSR. Yet the topic left its trace on a number of prominent works, both censored and uncensored. A hint at the existence of censorship may be found, for instance, in the fact that Zhivago's poetry remains in manuscript at the end of *Doctor Zhivago*. Siniavskii's novella *Liubimov* (translated as *The Makepeace Experiment*) and such short stories as *Pkhents* evoke the plight of the underground writer. Vladimir Voinovich in his dystopian *Moscow 2042* satirizes the institution of censorship by envisaging writers typing away on keyboards hooked to a computer that is merely a façade, sending their words into oblivion. The Master in Bulgakov's *Master and Margarita* is a victim of censorship when his novel about Pontius Pilate is denied publication by reviewers. The novel's most-quoted line, 'Manuscripts don't burn', challenges the institution of censorship on metaphysical grounds, suggesting that higher truths of art, history, and the spirit transcend the censor's purview.

To what extent the press and the arts have achieved freedom from censorship in post-Soviet Russia remains an open question. The rise of the market and the strengthening of the legal system have prompted the state to adopt new strategies in harnessing wayward voices. Attention has focused on a number of high-profile cases, notably the state's takeover of control over television and the writer Vladimir Sorokin's trial in 2002 for disseminating pornography. These cases complicate the perceived changes in the cultural process since the collapse of the USSR.

See also: Abuladze, Tengiz; Akhmatova, Anna; art, nonconformist; bards; Bulldozer Exhibition; Daniel, Iulii; dissident; Galich, Aleksandr; Glavlit; Gorbachev, Mikhail; GULag; Khrushchev, Nikita; legal system, post-Soviet; Manezh exhibition of 1962; *Master i Margarita* (*The Master and Margarita*); *Metropol*; NTV; Okudzhava, Bulat; Pasternak, Boris; perestroika and glasnost; Rybakov, Anatolii; samizdat; Shostakovich, Dmitrii; Siniavskii, Andrei; Socialist Realism; Solzhenitsyn, Aleksandr; Sorokin, Vladimir; Stalin, Iosif; tamizdat; television, post-Soviet; Thaw; Voinovich, Vladimir; Vysotskii, Vladimir

Further reading

Dewhurst, M. and Farrell, R. (1973) *The Soviet Censorship*, Metuchen, NJ: The Scarecrow Press.

Ermolaev, H. (1997) *Censorship in Soviet Literature 1917–1991*, New York: Rowman & Littlefield.

Loseff, L. (1984) *On the Beneficence of Censorship: Aesopian Language in Modern Russian Literature*, trans. J. Bobko, Munich: Otto Sagner in Kommission.

Tax Choldin, M. and Friedberg, M. (eds) (1989) *The Red Pencil: Artists, Scholars, and Censors in the USSR*, Boston, MA: Unwin Hyman.

CATHARINE NEPOMNYASHCHY

Central Asia

Central Asia (*Sredniaia Aziia*) is a landlocked region bordered by Russia, China, Afghanistan, and Iran. Central Asian countries include Kazakhstan, Kyrgyzstan, Tajikistan, Turkmenistan, and Uzbekistan. Northern Afghanistan and the Xinjiang region of China, and sometimes Mongolia and Tibet, are also considered part of Central Asia. Central Asia's history and culture can be divided by the two main ways of life of its inhabitants. Nomadic people such as the Kazakhs, Kyrgyz, and Turkmen lived mainly in the steppes, mountains, and deserts, while settled peoples such as the Tajiks, Uzbeks, and Uighurs lived in the oasis areas. Throughout history Central Asia has been a cultural crossroads. At the beginning of the twenty-first century this region is one of the most developed yet impoverished parts of the world.

Central Asia covers more than 1.5 million square miles, with a population of more than 60 million, and the Fergana Valley is one of the most densely populated places on earth. Central Asia is bordered by the steppe of Siberia in the north, the Tien Shan, Alay, and Pamir Mountains in the south-east, and the Caspian Sea in the west. It has two of the highest mountain peaks in the world: Ismail Samani peak (formerly Communism Peak) and Pobedy (Victory) Peak, both exceeding 24,000 feet. The climate of Central Asia is continental and arid, characterized by hot summers and cold winters. Several major deserts are located in Central Asia: the Kyzyl Kum, the Kara Kum, and the Taklamakan. The area's major rivers include the Syr, the Amu, and the Ili. Major bodies of water include the Caspian Sea, the Aral Sea, and Lake Balkhash. Central Asia's agriculture is devoted mainly to cotton and food crops. The region has a wealth of natural resources, including oil, natural gas, and gold. Central Asia has two cities with a population exceeding 1 million: Tashkent (Uzbekistan) and Almaty (Kazakhstan).

Evidence of human settlements in Central Asia goes back to the Stone Age, but recorded history begins with settlements of Iranian groups such as the Soghdians, whose civilization dates back to the beginning of the first millennium BCE. During this era, Central Asia was invaded from the south-west by conquerors such as Alexander the Great. All of the great world religions found adherents in Central Asia: Buddhism, Christianity, Judaism, Zoroastrianism, and various animistic religions were practised before the arrival of Islam in the eighth and ninth centuries CE. Islam slowly spread from the oases to the nomadic tribes, many of whom also continued to practise shamanism.

From the tenth century on, Turkic and Mongol tribes from the north-east invaded in waves, conquering the predominantly Iranian cities, and assimilating to the Iranian culture. The most famous of these nomadic conquerors was Chenggiz Khan, who conquered Central Asia in the thirteenth century. Another famous Central Asian leader was Amir Temur (known as Tamerlane in Europe), who ruled his vast fourteenth-century territories from the city of Samarkand (now in Uzbekistan). For centuries Central Asia was a crossroads for trade: the Great Silk Road connected China and the Mediterranean, traversing Central Asian cities such as Kashgar (now in China) and Bukhara (now in Uzbekistan). During the fifteenth and sixteenth centuries, the oasis cities of Central Asia were universally renowned for their sophisticated institutions of art, Islamic education, and Sufi mysticism.

Central Asia in the nineteenth and early twentieth centuries was the site of the so-called 'Great Game', the battle for influence between the British and Russian empires. From the eighteenth century onwards, Russian colonialism expanded southward into Kazakhstan and Turkestan, while British control expanded northward, towards Afghanistan. In 1917, the Russian Revolution prompted several independence movements in Central Asia, but by the 1920s Afghanistan rid itself of the British, while the territory formerly under Russian influence became part of the Soviet Union.

During the twentieth century, Central Asia underwent rapid modernization and profound cultural transformations. The nomadic populations were forced to settle, the farmers were forced to collectivize, and in the cities former merchants and clerics were persecuted as enemies of the people. During World War II, Stalin deported entire nations (such as the Crimean Tatars, Volga Germans, and Koreans) from the Soviet Union's borders to the heartland of Central Asia, and many people died on route. Many of the Russians, Ukrainians, and other Europeans who were evacuated from war zones to Central Asia stayed after the war. This multiethnic population contributed to industrialization and economic growth in Central Asia during the latter half of the twentieth century. It also contributed to the spread of Russian language and culture in a process often referred to as russification.

During the Brezhnev era, the Soviet Central Asian republics had stable political leaderships that were seen as promoting local economic interests as much as Communist ideology. The Soviet invasion of Afghanistan in 1979 and Moscow's crackdown on corruption among Central Asian officials in the early 1980s led to the growth of national assertiveness. However, even during the Gorbachev era, few Central Asians had any desire for independence from the Soviet Union. Nonetheless, in 1991 the five Soviet Central Asian republics became independent nations. During the 1990s, these new countries struggled with economic and political reforms, while their neighbours in Afghanistan suffered years of violence and civil war. Meanwhile, Uighurs in Xinjiang became increasingly active in agitating for independence from China.

See also: Kazakhstan; Kyrgyzstan; Tajikistan; Turkmenistan; Uzbekistan

Further reading

Bacon, E. (1978) *Central Asia Under Russian Rule: A Study in Culture Change*, Ithaca, NY: Cornell University Press.
Jones Luong, P. (2003) *The Transformation of Central Asia: States and Societies from Soviet Rule to Independence*, Ithaca, NY: Cornell University Press.
Roy, O. (2000) *The New Central Asia: The Creation of Nations*, New York: New York University Press.
Soucek, S. (2000) *A History of Inner Asia*, Cambridge: Cambridge University Press.

LAURA ADAMS

Central House of Journalists (Dom Zhurnalistov, DomZhur)

The Central House of Journalists (*Dom Zhurnalistov* or, commonly, *DomZhur*), located at Nikitskii Bulvar, 8a, has a rich literary past. During the 1830s, D. N. Sverbeev held literary evenings there that included Pushkin, Gogol, and Chaadaev. In 1920, it was turned into the House of Press, where writers such as Maiakovskii, Briusov, and Blok read their verses. In 1938, it was renamed the House of Journalists, and its restaurant was a popular spot for journalists throughout the Soviet period, and the subject of parody in Mikhail Bulgakov's novel *The Master and Margarita*. Now it is the venue for press conferences, working groups, events of the Moscow Section of the Journalists' Union, and memorial services for distinguished journalists.

See also: death; journalism; journalists, post-Soviet; *Master i Margarita* (*The Master and Margarita*); unions, creative, Soviet

MICHELE BERDY

Central House of Writers (TsDL)

The Central House of Writers (*Tsentralnyi dom literatorov*), founded in 1934 as a club for Soviet writers. Located in an Art Nouveau mansion, the club became the hub of official literary life, hosting everything from readings to funerals. The club's café and its formal restaurant in the elegant 'oak hall' were popular meeting spots for Writers' Union members, parodied in Mikhail Bulgakov's novel *Master and Margarita*. In 1959 an addition was built, which contained a large auditorium as well as a smaller hall and a billiard room. The mansion quickly passed into private hands after 1992, and a top-class restaurant has occupied the 'oak hall' ever since. The newer half of the building continues to hold literary events on a regular basis.

See also: *Master i Margarita (The Master and Margarita)*; unions, creative, Soviet

PATRICK HENRY

Chagall, Marc

(né Mark Zakharovich Shagal)

b. 1887, Vitebsk [Viciebsk], Belarus; d. 1985, Saint-Paul-de-Vence

Artist

Born in Belarus to a Hassidic family, Chagall became a major force in twentieth-century art. Known for his brilliant colour, themes from Jewish and Russian folk mythology, and proto-surrealistic imagery, Chagall produced an enormous œuvre that influenced generations of artists.

Chagall began his artistic training in Vitebsk before moving to St. Petersburg in 1907. The anti-Semitism he encountered there prevented him from entering the Art Academy, but he quickly found support among the intelligentsia. Chagall relocated to Paris in 1910, where he soon gained fame in the arts community and the media. By 1914, he was well known in European art circles and had had his first retrospective exhibition.

At the outbreak of World War I, Chagall returned to Belarus. He became the Commissar of Arts in Vitebsk after the Revolution. Due to friction with fellow artist Kazimir Malevich, then teaching in Vitebsk, Chagall moved to Moscow in 1920 and accepted commissions to design sets for the Jewish and Kamernyi (Chamber) theatres. In 1922, Chagall left the USSR, settling in France in 1923, where he lived for the remainder of his life, with the exception of 1941–46, which he spent in the United States.

In spite of his dreamlike spaces through which humans, animals, and objects float in states varying from reverie to horror, Chagall strongly denied any association with the Surrealists. Throughout his career he emphasized his Jewish and Russian identity, grounding his artwork in lived experience. The last thirty years of his life were occupied with public commissions; the most famous are his ceiling for the Paris Opera and his stained-glass windows in Jerusalem.

See also: anti-Semitism; Belarus; folk mythology; intelligentsia; Jews; Judaism

Further reading

Ayrton, M. (1948) *Chagall*, London: Faber and Faber.
Chagall, M. (1960) *My Life*, New York: Orion.
Compton, S. (1985) *Chagall*, New York: H. N. Abrams.
Haftmann, W. (1998) *Chagall*, New York: H. N. Abrams.
Venturi, L. (1956) *Marc Chagall: His Life and Work*, New York: Skira.

KRISTEN M. HARKNESS

chastushka

A genre of musical folk culture, *chastushki* (pl.) are short (usually four-line) rhyming verses sung to the accompaniment of an accordion or balalaika. They appeared in the late nineteenth century and became particularly widespread during the twentieth, especially in rural areas. *Chastushki* can be lyrical, but are more often jocular, topical, or obscene. In the Soviet period, they were often anti-Soviet, and they continue to appear as critical commentary on social and political life. A typical *chastushka* of the late Soviet period was: *Moia mila podo mnoi/ Sdelala dvizhenie/ To li khochet perestroiku/ To li uskorenie!* (My beloved under me/Gave some indication/But does she want perestroika?/Or acceleration?)

See also: folk song

MICHELE BERDY

cheating (shpargalka)

Shpargalka may be translated almost perfectly as 'cheat sheet'. Cheating is much more common in the Russian school and university system than in the American and British systems; it is one aspect of corruption that is manifested in many facets of society and reflects a general distrust of authority. What Americans would call academic dishonesty functions both as a shortcut in a demanding and sometimes arbitrary examination system and as an expression of a greater sense of collectivity in the Russian school and university systems, especially in the latter, where for years a given group of students takes required classes together. Like term papers, standard *shpargalki* are now for sale online. *Shpargalka* also describes a study aid, especially in small writing on a single page, or (with a touch of irony) a speaker's notes. The word refers to a brief summary of the most important facts in news programmes, or information sections of student publications.

SIBELAN FORRESTER

Cheburashka

Cartoon character

Cheburashka, created by writer Eduard Uspenskii, is the furry, saucer-eared protagonist of four stop-motion animated shorts made by Roman Kachanov between 1969 and 1983. A paragon of the naïve positive hero of Soviet children's culture, Cheburashka is an animal of indeterminate species who comes to the USSR inside a crate of oranges. He and his worldlier partner, Gena the Crocodile, inspired innumerable jokes that satirically invert the duo's loyal friendship and sense of civic duty. Both the jokes and animations remain popular, as evidenced by the DVDs and stuffed Cheburashka dolls readily available in Russian stores and kiosks.

See also: film, animation; film, children's; literature, children's; Uspenskii, Eduard

SETH GRAHAM

chebureki

Chebureki are deep-fried lamb dumplings. Originally a Crimean Tatar dish, *chebureki* became popular in other regions of the former USSR. A kind of Soviet fast food sold in special snack bars called *cheburechnaia*, they are semi-circular and can fit in one's palm. The traditional filling is made of ground lamb mixed with chopped onions and parsley and seasoned with salt and coriander.

ELENA BARABAN

Chechnia

The Chechen Republic of Ichkeria borders Dagestan, Stavropol Krai (region), Ingushetia, North Ossetia, and Georgia in the North Caucasus region of Russia. In 2005, the population of 1.3 million includes Chechens, Ingush, Russians, and other North Caucasians. Rich oil resources, a mountainous landscape, and mineral waters made Chechnia a spa centre of Imperial Russia and a highly exoticized locale. The Chechens (Nokhchi in their native language) are ethnically and linguistically very similar to the neighbouring Ingush people. They have traditionally lived as stateless clans (*teips*) of fighters. Originally pagan, they were converted to Islam in the late eighteenth century by Sufi missionaries.

For over two centuries, Chechens have resisted Russian rule. In the early 1900s, General Aleksei Ermolov, who founded the capital city of Groznyi, pursued brutal means to subdue Chechens and other Caucasians, frequently burning down entire villages. The Dagestanian rebel Imam Shamil led a war against Russia from 1834 to his defeat in 1859. Following Chechen support for the Reds in the Civil War, the Bolsheviks created an autonomous Chechen-Ingush republic in 1922. However, in 1944, Stalin deported about 500,000 Chechens and Ingush to Kazakhstan and Siberia. Nearly 80,000 died on the way, and the survivors were not allowed to return until 1957. Various Chechens achieved high military and political positions in the Soviet Union. In 1991, one of them, Jokhar Dudaev, declared independence from Russia and became the first president of Chechnia. Russia intervened in 1994, and the resulting First Chechen War ended in Russia's defeat. Hostilities were renewed in 1999, and the Second Chechen War continues. The conflict has made a shambles of the Chechen economy and infrastructure, with the oil industry producing at a much lower rate than before 1991. Unemployment exceeds 75 per cent, and organized crime is rampant.

See also: Caucasus; Dagestan; Georgia; Kazakhstan; Siberia; Stalin, Iosif; War, Chechen

ALEXANDER BURRY

chelnok

Since the 1990s the words *chelnok* (or *chelnochnik*) and *chelnochnitsa* (female), from an old word for a canoe-like boat, refer to 'shuttle traders' who buy inexpensive consumer goods in Turkey, China, Indonesia, and other countries so as to sell them in Russia, often at booths in flea markets.

See also: economic system, post-Soviet

MICHELE BERDY

Chernobyl

The explosion at Reactor Number Four at the Chernobyl Atomic Power Station in Ukraine on 26 April 1986 spurred glasnost – the first time an environmental and technological catastrophe of that magnitude was discussed in the Soviet press. Two explosions during a routine test destroyed the reactor core and the roof, releasing radioactive contamination over much of Europe, with the highest concentrations in Belarus, Ukraine, and Russia. Soviet authorities immediately began emergency firefighting and clean-up operations, but initially tried to keep the disaster a secret. Only when elevated levels of radiation were detected at a nuclear power station in Sweden did the Soviet leadership acknowledge the accident. During the spring of 1986, about 200,000 people took part in the clean-up efforts, while roughly 116,000 residents

of the contaminated zone were evacuated and resettled. The legacy of Chernobyl continues in the former Soviet Union in terms of health, energy policy, food production, and housing, although the issue of long-term effects of radiation from the Chernobyl disaster on those living in the affected regions remains highly controversial. Under international pressure, in December 2000, Ukraine decommissioned and shut down the remaining reactors at the Chernobyl Atomic Power Station.

See also: environment; health; housing, Soviet and post-Soviet; Ukraine

Further reading

Marples, D. (1988) *The Social Impact of the Chernobyl Disaster*, London: Macmillan.
Petryna, A. (2002) *Life Exposed: Biological Citizens after Chernobyl*, Princeton, NJ: Princeton University Press.
http://www.iaea.org/NewsCenter/Focus/Chernobyl/pdfs/05-28601_Chernobyl.pdf

JENNIFER RYAN TISHLER

Chernomyrdin, Viktor Stepanovich

b. 9 April 1938, Orenburg oblast, Russia

Politician

After graduating from the Kuibyshev Industrial Institute, Chernomyrdin worked in the Orsk City Committee of the Communist Party (KPSS), then as director of the Orenburg Gas Refinery, before working in the Central Committee of the KPSS. He was Minister of the Gas Industry of the USSR 1985–89, and then Chairman of the Board of Gasprom (1989–92). After his stint as Prime Minister (1992–March 1998), he served as Acting Prime Minister in August and September 1998. From 1995 to 1999 he headed the movement *Nash dom – Rossiia* (Our Home – Russia), and was appointed Russian Ambassador to Ukraine in 2001. He is best known for his colourful speech and is credited with the phrase 'Khotelos kak luchshe, a poluchilos kak vsegda' (we wanted the best, but it turned out as usual).

See also: political parties, post-Soviet; Yeltsin, Boris

MICHELE BERDY

chernukha

Chernukha is a term derived from the Russian word for 'black' (*chernyi*). Since the late 1980s it has been widely used, usually pejoratively, to describe films and literature that employ a dark, naturalistic style to depict the most negative aspects of Russian life, especially alcohol abuse, poverty, domestic conflict, and violent crime. The *chernukha* trend emerged during perestroika, when official proscriptions no longer restricted cultural producers in the graphic portrayal of societal ills. Initially applied mostly to prose fiction (particularly the work of Liudmila Petrush-evskaia), the *chernukha* label is now most commonly associated with film. Some examples of films considered *chernukha* are Vasilii Pichul's *Malenkaia Vera* (*Little Vera*, 1988) and Pavel Lounguine's *Taksi-bliuz* (*Taxi Blues*, 1990).

See also: perestroika and glasnost; Petrush-evskaia, Liudmila

SETH GRAHAM

chess

Introduced into Russia in the tenth century, chess became widely popular in the nineteenth and twentieth centuries. Such celebrities as Peter the Great, Mikhail Lomonosov, Lev Tol-stoi, and Vladimir Lenin were lovers of chess, which in the USSR achieved the status of a prestigious intellectual game, combining ele-ments of art, science, and sports. Chess tourna-ments have always received mass media attention in Soviet and post-Soviet Russia, with most periodicals running special chess sections. Chess became a favourite hobby among differ-ent social groups of all ages, from schoolchildren to pensioners. Literature reflects Russians' love for the game, mentioned in Aleksandr Pushkin's *Evgenii Onegin*, Ilf and Petrov's *Twelve Chairs*, and Boris Pasternak's poetry. It figures centrally in Vladimir Pudovkin's film comedy *Chess Fever*, Mikhail Bulgakov's *Master and Margarita*, and Vladimir Nabokov's novel *Defense*. Nabokov's *Poems and Problems* (1971) calls chess a poetic art.

Emigré Aleksandr Alyokhin became the first Russian world champion in 1927. In the second half of the twentieth century the Soviet govern-ment monitored the development of chess, establishing a wide network of chess schools and organizing a system of competitions. The best Soviet/Russian chess players (including Mikhail Botvinnik, Vasilii Smyslov, Mikhail Tal, Tigran Petrosian, Boris Spasskii, Anatolii Karpov, Garri Kasparov, and Vladimir Kramnik) attained movie-star status, their records equated with Soviet achievements in space exploration. Some world tournament finals were politicized: in 1972 for the first time the Soviet grand master was defeated by an American (Spasskii/Fisher), and in Karpov's matches (Karpov/Korchnoi [1978, 1981], Karpov/Kasparov [1984–90]) the government's favourite was Karpov, while the intelligentsia favoured his rivals. By the twenty-first century, chess in Russia, as in the rest of the world, has lost its former popularity, though it still enjoys high cultural status in Russia.

See also: Kasparov, Garri; *Master i Margarita* (*The Master and Margarita*); Nabokov, Vladimir

Further reading

Plisetsky, D. and Voronkov, S. (eds) (1994) *Russians versus Fischer*, Moscow: Chess World.

ALEXANDER LEDENEV

choral music

Choral music is performed by a choir or inten-ded for performance by a choir. Depending on the performing forces, choral music typically divides into two categories: folk choral music – performed by informally or spontaneously con-stituted vocal ensembles, who perform without the benefit of music notation; and 'professional' choral music – performed by vocal ensembles specially selected and trained for that purpose, who usually sing from some type of written musical notation. Whereas folk choral music is transmitted primarily by means of the oral tradition, the development of professional choral music can be charted through surviving written texts.

In Russia, choral music represents the oldest type of music, traceable to the medieval origins of Russian culture in Kievan Rus. For the first six centuries of Russian history, choral music, or, more properly, choral singing (*penie*), was intimately connected with the liturgical services of the Russian Orthodox Church. The term 'music' (*musikiia, muzyka*) entered the lexicon only in the second half of the seventeenth century, and then only in reference to instrumental music.

During the initial six hundred years, 'professional' choirs in Russia were no bigger than three to five adult male singers. The first such choir with a continuous history was the Tsar's Singing Clerics, established in the late fifteenth or early sixteenth century. This choir eventually became known as the Imperial Court Chapel in St. Petersburg (today called the Glinka Cappella). Similarly, the establishment of the Russian Patriarchate in 1589 enabled the formation of the choir of Patriarchal Singing Clerics, eventually known as the Moscow Synodal Choir (disbanded following the October Revolution of 1917). In the mid-seventeenth century, these choirs, initially comprising only adult men's voices, were augmented by boy sopranos and altos, and grew in number to several dozen singers, eventually increasing to a staff of 80–100 singers. The formation of church choirs became particularly widespread in the nineteenth century, as larger churches were constructed. Alexander II's reforms in the 1860s, allowing freedom of assembly, led to the formation of civic choral societies, which included women's voices. Women's voices were admitted to church choirs in the 1880s, following the initiative of composer and conductor Aleksandr Arkhangel'skii. In the early years of the twentieth century, Mitrofan Piatnitskii organized a choir of Russian peasant singers and began to concertize with them in cities; this pioneering enterprise led to the formation of Russian folk choirs and folklore ensembles, which consciously replicated the village folk song repertoire and folk manner of performance (bright, forward vowel placement, use of chest register by the women, a high, narrow range for the men) in a concert setting. By contrast, the majority of Russian church choirs and 'academic' concert choirs employ a manner of vocal production that is grounded in Italian *bel canto*, which stems from the predominant influence of visiting Italian musicians in the eighteenth century.

See also: church music; Russian Orthodoxy

Further reading

Morosan, V. (ed.) (1991) *One Thousand Years of Russian Church Music: 988–1988*, vol. 1 (Musica Russica).

—— (1994) reprint edition, corrected and revised, *Choral Performance in Pre-Revolutionary Russia* (Musica Russica).

VLADIMIR MOROSAN

choreographers, Soviet

Soviet choreography enjoys neither the acclaim accorded the dancers who appeared in the monuments created for Soviet ballet, nor the reputations of the companies that commissioned them. Like other sectors of the planned economy, Soviet ballet was meant to produce a quota of cultural capital (especially as, from the 1950s on, it functioned as one of the state's most successful export items), yet an industrial sameness characterized much of its output. Innovative choreographers, such as Kasian Goleizovskii and Leonid Iakobson, had few opportunities to work on the main Soviet stages. Productions of new works for the Bolshoi and Kirov ballets were mostly left to artistic directors with long tenures – Konstantin Sergeev and Oleg Vinogradov in Leningrad, Iurii Grigorovich in Moscow – who devoted significant portions of their choreographic energies to restaging nineteenth-century classics. The most successful Soviet choreographers were those who managed to create works that suited the shifting ideologies of Soviet art. Rostislav Zakharov's *Bakhchisaraiskii fontan* (*Fountain of Bakhchisarai*, 1934), based on the Pushkin poem and set to music by Boris Asafev, answered the call for a 'dramatic' ballet that could convey its narrative in movement alone, without the aid of conventional pantomime. Leonid Lavrovskii's version of *Romeo and Juliet* (*Romeo i Dzhuletta*, to music by Prokofiev, 1940), expanded upon this *drambalet* formula, resulting in a work of epic sweep well suited to the pompous grandeur of Stalin-era aesthetics. Grigorovich's thirty-year career at the head of the Bolshoi Ballet allowed him the unique opportunity to develop as a choreographer and refine a dance aesthetic he pioneered in Leningrad in the late 1950s. His early works for the Kirov Ballet (*Kamennyi tsvetok* [*Stone Flower*, 1957], *Legenda o liubvi* [*Legend of Love*, 1961]) attracted attention for their emotional sweep and the choreographer's facility with large ensembles. Grigorovich's *Spartak* (*Spartacus*, 1968) remains the most plausible Soviet ballet of the post-war era and exemplifies the unique style the choreographer developed in Moscow. In Leningrad, Boris Eifman established a company that functioned largely as an alternative to the dominant state companies, and he pioneered a highly theatrical, bombastic style of choreography that won admirers in the late Soviet era. The movement idioms developed by Goleizovskii and Iakobson are notable for their originality and enrichment of the classical ballet vocabulary. The more famous Soviet-era choreographers were better at adapting literary monuments to grandly-scaled works, building upon the legacy of Marius Petipa's nineteenth-century masterpieces, though rarely approaching that choreographer's skill or originality.

See also: ballet, Soviet; ballet dancers, Bolshoi Theatre; ballet dancers, Mariinskii Theatre; Bolshoi Theatre; economic system, Soviet; Eifman, Boris; Grigorovich, Iurii; Iakobson, Leonid; Lavrovskii, Leonid; Mariinskii Theatre; pantomime; World War II (Great Patriotic War)

TIM J. SCHOLL

Christmas, Orthodox

Officially banned by the Soviets after the 1917 Bolshevik Revolution, in the post-Soviet era Russian Christmas has returned as a state-sponsored holiday celebrated on 7 January, mainly in accordance with the Julian calendar, though some adhere to the Western (Gregorian) date.

While the Orthodox Christmas service is one of the most resplendent of the liturgical calendar year, secular observation is second to the New Year holiday, which the Soviets promoted while ignoring Yule. Similarities with the West include the Christmas tree (*elka*), gift-giving, and a jolly grandfatherly figure, known as Grandfather Frost (*Ded Moroz*), dressed in blue and accompanied by the Snow Maiden (*Snegurochka*).

See also: holidays, Russian Orthodox

TIMOTHY M. SCHLAK

Chto? Gde? Kogda? (What? Where? When?)

Television game show

Since its debut on 4 September 1975, *Chto? Gde? Kogda?* (What? Where? When?) has been one of the most popular game shows on Russian television. Teams of intellectuals answer complex questions sent in by television viewers and picked up from the game table randomly. Hundreds of *Chto? Gde? Kogda?* clubs across the former USSR and abroad compete for the right to participate in the games broadcast on television. The game was invented by Vladimir Voroshilov (1930–2001). He was also the show's host and President of the *Chto? Gde? Kogda?* Clubs Association until his death.

See also: television, post-Soviet; television, Soviet

ELENA BARABAN

Chubais, Anatolii Borisovich

b. 16 June 1955, Barysau, Belarus

Politician

Chubais graduated from the Leningrad Economic Engineering Institute (1977). After serving in Mayor Sobchak's 'reformist' government in St. Petersburg, Chubais headed the Russian Federation's State Property Committee under

Vice-Premier Egor Gaidar. He became the main driving force in the privatization of state assets, also known as the 'piratization' of the Russian economy. In the 1990s, he also served as First Vice-Premier, Minister of Finance, and the head of Yeltsin's administration. A co-leader of the Union of Rightist Forces (SPS, badly defeated in 2003), he currently heads the second largest state monopoly, Unified Electrical Systems (RAO-EES).

See also: economic system, post-Soviet; Gaidar, Egor; political parties, post-Soviet; privatization; Sobchak, Anatolii; Union of Rightist Forces (Soiuz pravykh sil; SPS); Yeltsin, Boris

ALEXANDER DOMRIN

Chukchi

The Chukchi are one of several ethnic groups indigenous to the arctic, northeastern-most corner of Russia. Related to the Eskimos across the Bering Strait, they number only about 13,000, but have had a disproportionate presence in the Russian cultural consciousness since the 1970s, primarily because of a large cycle of *anekdoty* (jokes) satirizing their perceived linguistic shortcomings and cultural backwardness. The impetus behind the *anekdoty* is not exclusively ethnic, however; they also satirized state propaganda that held up the Chukchi as an example of the far-reaching, civilizing effects of Soviet ideology on even the most 'primitive' peoples within the USSR.

See also: ethnic minorities; Far North; joke

SETH GRAHAM

Chukhrai, Grigorii Naumovich

b. 23 May 1921, Melitopol; d. 29 October 2001, Moscow

Director, screenwriter

Grigorii Chukhrai graduated in 1953 from VGIK, where he studied with Mikhail Romm and Sergei Iutkevich. His first two films, *Sorok pervyi* (*1941*, 1956) and *Ballada o soldate* (*Ballad of a Soldier*, 1959), won prizes at Cannes and restored the reputation of Soviet cinema for originality and formal innovation. Chukhrai's *Chistoe nebo* (*Clear Sky*, 1961) was the first Soviet film to deal with the Stalinist purges. His films are usually melodramas that depict a vulnerable hero who faces difficult choices during a major social upheaval. From 1965 until 1975, Chukhrai headed the Experimental Creative Studio at Mosfilm, a successful attempt to introduce market incentives to the Soviet film industry.

See also: All-Russian (All-Union) State Institute of Cinematography (VGIK); film, Soviet – Thaw period; Romm, Mikhail

ALEXANDER PROKHOROV

Chukhrai, Pavel Grigorevich

b. 14 October 1946, Bykovo, Moscow region.

Film director

Son of director Grigorii Chukhrai (1921–2003). Pavel Chukhrai's most celebrated film is undoubtedly *Vor* (*The Thief*, 1997), starring Vladimir Mashkov, which was nominated for an Oscar for Best Foreign Language Film. *Vor* is set in post-war Soviet Russia; it examines human relationships and the disastrous psychological effects of Stalinism, a theme it shares with one of Chukhrai's earliest films, *Zapomnite menia takoi* (*Remember Me This Way*), made for television in 1988. In 2004, he returned to recent history with *Voditel dlia Very* (*A Driver for Vera*), set in 1962, which again presents human relationships in a clearly defined socio-political context.

See also: Chukhrai, Grigorii; Mashkov, Vladimir; Stalin, Iosif; World War II (Great Patriotic War)

DAVID GILLESPIE

Chukovskaia, Lidiia Korneevna

b. 24 March [7 April] 1907, St. Petersburg;
d. 7 February 1996, Moscow

Editor, prose writer

Daughter of writer, children's poet, and critic
Kornei Ivanovich Chukovskii, Chukovskaia
bore witness to the Stalinist era in her writings
and defended Soviet writers, worked as an
editor in the children's literary division of the
Leningrad State Publishing House until 1930,
when the section was closed. At the height of the
Stalinist Terror in 1937, Chukovskaia's husband
was arrested and killed; she captured the
experiences of the Stalinist era in her novellas
Sofia Petrovna and *Spusk pod vodu (Going Under)*.
Starting in 1938 and continuing for three decades, Chukovskaia kept a detailed journal of her
conversations with the poet Anna Akhmatova, a
record that is the basis for her *Zapiski ob Anne
Akhmatovoi (Notes on Anna Akhmatova)*. In the 1960s
and 1970s, Chukovskaia grew more outspoken,
openly criticizing Mikhail Sholokhov for his
attacks on Siniavskii and Daniel and defending
Solzhenitsyn, Sakharov, and Pasternak. Her
activity led in 1974 to her expulsion from the
Writers' Union, a process she described in the
volume *Protsess iskliucheniia (The Process of Expulsion)*. Her membership in the Union was
restored in 1988, the year that *Sofia Petrovna* was
published in the Soviet Union.

See also: Akhmatova, Anna; Daniel, Iulii; dissident; Pasternak, Boris; Sholokhov, Mikhail;
Siniavskii, Andrei; Solzhenitsyn, Aleksandr;
unions, creative, Soviet

Further reading

Holmgren, B. (1993) *Women's Works in Stalin's
Time: Lidiia Chukovskaia and Nadezhda Mandel-
stam*, Bloomington, IN: Indiana University
Press.

Sandler, S. (1990) 'Reading Loyalty in Chukovskaia's *Zapiski ob Anne Akhmatovoi*', in W.
Rosslyn (ed.) *The Speech of Unknown Eyes: Akhmatova's Readers on Her Poetry*, Nottingham:
Astra Press.

JENNIFER RYAN TISHLER

church architecture, Russian Orthodox

Russian Orthodox church architecture is a bar-
ometer of national identity, dating from the
Christianization of Rus in 988 AD. For centuries,
its forms reflected the nation's religious connection to Byzantium. Three major centres of early
Rus architecture would influence most subsequent Russian churches: Kiev, Novgorod and
Pskov, and Vladimir-Suzdal.

After the Mongol invasion in 1240 – the first
war to destroy many church monuments – the
art of stone building was largely lost. When
Moscow emerged as the new centre of Russia,
its rulers invited Italian architects to rebuild the
Kremlin for the glory of both church and state.
Nevertheless, as Fioravanti's Dormition Cathedral (1475–79) shows, church forms and idioms
were still distinctively Russian. Perhaps the best-
known Muscovite-era church is the Cathedral of
the Intercession on the Moat, popularly known
as St. Basil's, built by the Pskov architects
Barma and Postnik on Red Square (1555–60).

Peter I marked a revolution in church architecture. For the first time, Russian churches
used Western forms. From their putti to their
spires, Trezzini's Cathedral of Saints Peter and
Paul (1717–32), Rastrelli's Smolnyi Cathedral
(1748–74), Voronikhin's neo-classical Kazan
Cathedral (1801–11), and Montferrand's St.
Isaac's Cathedral (1818–58) exemplify the
notion of St. Petersburg as a window onto
Europe.

But, along with political russification, a celebration of indigenous forms triumphed with the
Russian style and the *style moderne* in the
second half of the nineteenth century. New
church buildings (over 5,500 between 1906
and 1912 alone) arose not only across the
entire empire, but also everywhere the Russian
empire wanted to assert its presence – the
United States, the Holy Land, and Western
Europe.

October 1917 halted these trends as new
churches stopped being built and existing churches
and monasteries were declared the property of
the state. Some were turned to different purposes, converted into cinemas, petrol stations, or
warehouses. Many were destroyed: both in the
Soviet Union and in Poland, the previous

century's Russian-style churches were singled out for their associations with the empire.

The goal was not only to undercut people's religious beliefs and practices, but also to transform historic memory and the experience of public space. The periods of greatest destruction were 1928–37, under Stalin, and under Khrushchev in the early 1960s. From 1917 to 1988, Russian Orthodox architecture was built only outside Russia.

Perestroika applies to few things as literally as to architecture: the building of new churches and the restoration of old ones in Russia has exploded since 1991. The massive Cathedral of Christ the Saviour, originally built to commemorate the War of 1812 and blown up at Stalin's orders in 1931, was entirely rebuilt at huge cost in 2000. New churches, usually in suburban workers' districts, almost exclusively follow the historicist neo-Russian style of the late nineteenth and early twentieth centuries. Polianskii's St. George Memorial Church (1995) in Moscow, commemorating World War II, is novel inasmuch as it successfully blends traditional forms with such new elements as windowed walls.

See also: Kiev; Khrushchev, Nikita; Moscow; perestroika and glasnost; Russian Orthodoxy; Thaw; World War II (Great Patriotic War)

Further reading

Brumfield, W. (1997) *A History of Russian Architecture*, Cambridge: Cambridge University Press.

NADIESZDA KIZENKO

church bells

See bells

church hierarchy

This term refers collectively to all bishops in the Russian Orthodox Church. Only men can be admitted into the three ranks of Orthodox clergy: bishops, priests, and deacons. Anyone who seeks to become a clergyman must marry before being ordained. Married clergymen are called white clergy because of their white liturgical robes; they can serve only as priests or deacons in parish churches. Unmarried clergymen, known as black clergy because they wear black robes, are monks and can be deacons, priests, or bishops. Clergy cannot marry after ordination. A married parish clergyman who becomes a widower is required to take monastic vows and enter the black clergy. Only unmarried clergy can be consecrated as bishops.

The church hierarchy is composed entirely of bishops who are part of the apostolic succession (the unbroken line of church leaders that began with Jesus's apostles). Two or more bishops must participate in the ordination of a new bishop in order for it to be valid. Every bishop is the main Christian leader in his geographical region (diocese [*eparkhiia*]). He oversees all priests and deacons in his diocese. A priest administers the sacraments and conducts church services in the parish assigned by his bishop. A deacon (*diakon*) assists the priest in these duties. All bishops together are the defenders of Orthodox tradition and practice. The four levels of bishops in ascending order are bishop (*episkop*), archbishop (*arkhiepiskop*), metropolitan (*mitropolit*), and patriarch (*patriarkh*). Lower-ranking bishops respect those who are higher in the church hierarchy, but Orthodox doctrine states that every bishop is equal to every other bishop. This doctrine was ignored in the Soviet period, when the church hierarchy adopted secular top-down decision-making. Since 1991, the number of Orthodox bishops has increased while the ability of the patriarch and metropolitans to demand unconditional obedience from other bishops has decreased.

See also: monastic life; Russian Orthodoxy

EDWARD E. ROSLOF

church music (tserkovnaia muzyka)

Russian church music, more properly, church singing (*penie*), forms an inherent, essential aspect of Russian Orthodox liturgical worship.

No Orthodox church service takes place without singing, which is typically divided among the celebrating clergy, a designated chanter (*psalomshchik*) or choir, and, for certain elements of the service, the entire assembly of worshippers.

Following the examples of liturgical singing brought to Kiev and Novgorod by Bulgarian and Greek singers, all early Russian church singing was in the form of chant, performed either in unison or, according to the recent suggestions of Russian musicologists, with an *ison* or sustained drone, following Byzantine models. There are two basic types of melodic-textual relationships: a more or less syllabic or neumatic structure, found in *znamennyi* chant, and a more florid, melismatic structure, characterizing chants known as *kondakarian* (eleventh–twelfth centuries) and *demestvennyi* chant and *putevoi* chant (fifteenth century and later).

In the latter half of the sixteenth century, surviving written monuments begin to display evidence of polyphonic performance, typically in three (more rarely, in two or four) parts moving largely in parallel motion (linear polyphony – *strochnoe penie*). Starting in the mid-seventeenth century, this indigenous Russian style of polyphony, as well as unison singing, ceded to harmonic-style singing based on Western European models, which came to central and northern Russia (Muscovy) via Ukraine. Beginning in the late seventeenth and early eighteenth centuries, church singing in Russia began to reflect stylistically the developments in Western European choral music, ranging from the Baroque concerted style (Diletskii, Titov), through the Italian 'classical' style (Berezovskii, Bortnianskii, Degtiarev, Vedel'), and the Romantic style (Glinka, L'vov, Arkhangel'skii). Towards the end of the nineteenth century, Russian composers, starting with Tchaikovsky, turned for inspiration to the early chants, giving rise to the 'new Russian choral school' of choral composition, exemplified by the Moscow Synodal School of Church Singing and its choir. This group of composers, including Chesnokov, Kalinnikov, Kastalaskii, Grechaninov, Ippolitov-Ivanov, Nikolaskii, and Rakhmaninov, created a vast repertoire of unaccompanied sacred choral music based on texts of the Orthodox liturgical services.

During the Soviet era, church singing in Russia, along with the rest of the Orthodox Church, was severely suppressed. Since the fall of Communism, church singing has experienced a vigorous restoration.

See also: choral music; Russian Orthodoxy

Further reading

Morosan, V. (ed.) (1991) *One Thousand Years of Russian Church Music: 988–1988*, vol. 1 (Musica Russica).
—— (1994) reprint edition corrected and revised, *Choral Performance in Pre-Revolutionary Russia* (Musica Russica).

VLADIMIR MOROSAN

Churikova, Inna Mikhailovna

b. 1943, Belebei, Bashkiria (Bashkorkostan), Russia

Actress, screenwriter

Churikova has been one of Russia's most acclaimed actresses since the 1960s, when she drew raves as the eccentric, sensitive heroines of the films *V ogne broda net* (*No Ford Through the Fire*) and *Nachalo* (*The Debut*), both directed by her husband, Gleb Panfilov. They have collaborated on several other films, including *Tema* (*The Theme*), and *Romanovy: Ventsenosnaia semia* (*The Romanovs: Imperial Family*), for which they co-wrote the screenplay. Introduced to Western audiences through her role in Viacheslav Khristofovich's *Rebro Adama* (*Adam's Rib*), Churikova is also well known for her work on stage at Moscow's Lenkom Theatre.

See also: Lenkom Theatre; Panfilov, Gleb

SETH GRAHAM

cinematography

See: cameramen

circus

Circuses have always been one of the favourite forms of popular entertainment in Russia, with Russian circuses having roots in eleventh-century performances of wandering medieval minstrels (*skomorokhi*), who travelled in small groups, entertaining spectators with song, dance, and comic performances as well as trained bears and other animals. Starting in the eighteenth century, circus performances were staged in *balagans* – temporary wooden buildings constructed during marketplace festivities.

The oldest permanent Russian circuses are located in St. Petersburg and Moscow. The first permanent circus was wooden, built in St. Petersburg in 1827. The Italian circus performer and entrepreneur G. Ciniselli then promoted construction of the first stone circus in St. Petersburg, which opened in 1877 and is known as the Circus on the Fontanka. The first permanent circus in Moscow – the Salamonskii Circus – opened in 1880 and is now known as the Iurii Nikulin Circus; it accommodates more than 2,000 spectators.

Soviet circuses were known for the virtuosity of their highly-trained performers. Generously supported by the government, they were controlled and directed by a state agency, *Soiuzgostsirk*, which made the circus a leading cultural export by allowing leading circus troupes to travel abroad for long periods of time. Circuses from Soviet republics enriched the Soviet circus with the distinctive originality of various national traditions, adding a multi-cultural flavour. Most large Soviet cities had permanent circuses, and travelling companies toured the towns and provinces of the Soviet Union. The State Circus and Estrada School was the leading institution that recruited and trained new talent in various circus genres.

Like their Western counterparts, Soviet and Russian circus performances traditionally include numerous acts: clowning, magic, acrobatics, trained animals, horse-riding, aerial acts, pantomimes, juggling, tightrope walkers, athletics, etc. Many Soviet circus performers achieved international recognition and greatly contributed to the development of circuses around the world. Several prolific dynasties of circus performers, which handed down skills from one generation to another, include the Durovs and the Filatovs, famous for their trained animal acts; the Kios, renowned for their magic art; and the Zapashnys, known for their aerial acrobatics. Famous Soviet clowns included Karandash (which means pencil) – a Russian version of Charlie Chaplin, whose real name was Mikhail Rumiantsev; the energetic and optimistic Oleg Popov, easily recognizable with his red wig and checkered hat; and Iurii Nikulin, a clown and movie star who became legendary for his satirical clowning and exquisite sense of humour.

After the fall of the Soviet Union, circuses in Russia encountered great financial difficulties owing to lack of government support. These economic problems and the removal of travel restrictions led many of the best performers to move abroad and perform for leading world circuses. For example, the Cirque du Soleil, one of the most famous international circuses, heavily relies on performers from Russia and other former Soviet republics. While the exodus of circus performers from Russia has contributed to the fame of Russian circus training, it has also deprived Russian spectators of the chance to see the best performers.

See also: Durov Animal Theatre; folk dance; folk music; Nikulin, Iurii

Further reading

Lipovsky, A. (ed.) (1967) *The Soviet Circus: A Collection of Articles*, trans. F. Glagoleva, Moscow: Progress Publishers.

Nordbye, M. (2004) 'The Magical World of the Russian Circus', *Russian Life* 47:1.

OLGA PARTAN

CIS (SNG)

The Commonwealth of Independent States (*Sodruzhestvo nezavisimykh gosudarstv*, SNG) is a post-Soviet political union of twelve states (formerly republics of the USSR) officially created on 8 December 1991 by the presidents of Russia, Ukraine, and Belorussia (Belarus). The formation of the CIS led to the final dissolution

of the USSR on 25 December 1991. By the end
of that year Armenia, Azerbaidzhan, Kazakhstan,
Kyrgyzstan, Moldova, Tajikistan, Turkmenistan, and Uzbekistan had joined the Union, as
did Georgia in 1992. Of the former Soviet
republics, only the Baltic states (Estonia, Latvia,
and Lithuania) did not join.

The CIS coordinates the activity of its
member states in political, economic, cultural,
military, and other spheres. The Union's major
body is a coordination-consultation committee,
with an executive secretariat headquartered in
Minsk, Belarus. Other bodies of the Commonwealth include many councils – of heads of state,
prime ministers, foreign affairs ministers, ministers of defence, and commanders of frontier
troops – as well as a court on economics and a
commission on human rights. Various regional
links were forged on the territory of the CIS: the
United State of Russia and Belarus; the Eurasian Economic Association (EvrazES), encompassing Belarus, Kazakhstan, Kyrgyzstan,
Russia, and Tajikistan; the Central Asian economic association, comprehending Kazakhstan,
Kyrgyzstan, Tajikistan, Uzbekistan; and
GUAM, which unites Georgia, Ukraine, Azerbaidzhan, and Moldova. In 2002, the new
Organization of the Treaty of Collective Security (Organizatsiia Dogovora o kollektivnoi bezo-
pasnosti, ODKB) included among its members
Armenia, Belorussia, Kazakhstan, Kyrgyzstan,
Russia, and Tajikistan, with Moldova and
Ukraine as participating observers.

See also: administrative structure, Soviet
Union; Armenia; Azerbaidzhan; Baltic Sea
region; Belarus; Estonia; Georgia; Latvia;
Lithuania; Kazakhstan; Kyrgyzstan; Moldova;
Russian Federation; Tajikistan; Turkmenistan;
Ukraine; Uzbekistan

SERGEI TARKHOV

classical music, post-Soviet

During the Soviet era, classical music occupied
the top rung in a hierarchical music world, and
knowledge of it was deemed an obligatory part
of a well-bred Soviet citizen's education. Both
structurally and financially, classical music was

supported by the state, which maintained strict
control over it. Largely left to its own devices in
the post-Soviet era, classical music has moved
away from the monolithic. Although the state
continues to provide significant financial support
for its institutions (conservatories and other
musical institutes, as well as many orchestras
and opera houses), neither the government nor
official ideology bears responsibility for the
status of classical music in the popular consciousness, nor for the system of values within
the world of classical music.

Revision

Perestroika witnessed a significant revision of
music history, as of other disciplines: previously
banned works of unofficial and émigré composers and performers were performed in Soviet
concert halls; previously sealed historical
archives were opened; the iron curtain separating Soviet and Western music was lifted, allowing greater exchange between Soviet and
foreign composers and performers; the ban on
religious music was eliminated; and political
ideology was no longer a criterion for judging a
work or performance. Names from the avant-
garde suppressed from Soviet music returned:
Aleksandr Molosov, Nikolai Roslavets, Vladimir
Deshevov, and Artur Lure (Lourie). The work of
émigrés was reclaimed as part of Russia's music
history – not only the work of major composers
such as Igor Stravinskii, Sergei Rakhmaninov,
and Sergei Prokofiev, but also lesser-known but
significant figures in Russian emigration: Nikolai
Cherepnin, Serge Kusevitskii (Koussevitzky),
and Petr Suvchinskii. Sacred music was incorporated into the concert repertoire and attracted
scholarly attention. Works by composers who
had lived under the ever-watchful eye of Soviet
cultural authorities and under constant pressure
to conform started being evaluated according to
their merits, including compositions by Alfred
Shnittke (1934–98), Edison Denisov, Sofiia
Gubaidullina and others from the 1960s, the so-
called *shestidesiatniki*, frequently performed today.
In contrast, the 'generals' of Soviet music now
receive little attention on concert stages or in
scholarly publications. Finally, twentieth-century
Russian music can be placed in a proper
context, since Russian musicians, concert-goers,

and music historians can now hear classical music from all over the world.

One of the most significant subjects of post-Soviet musical revisionism is Dmitrii Shostakovich, whose life developed in synchrony with Soviet cultural history. His œuvre is being rediscovered by Russian composers and performers, as well as concert-goers and the wider reading public. Many of his compositions, perceived as an anthology of Soviet-era 'Aesopian language', are receiving unprecedented attention on Russian stages, particularly his previously banned 1932 opera *Lady Macbeth of Mtsensk* (*Ledi Makbet Mtsenskogo uezda*). His personality and life have been carefully examined and reconstructed: he is seen as one of the pillars of Soviet music history and as one of the greatest victims of the Soviet cultural establishment. While his life has thus become a monument to a bygone era, at the end of the twentieth century his music seemed current as never before. His neoclassicist structure as a background to expressionist experiment, his pre-postmodernist work with 'others' text', the novelistic dramatism of his music have contributed to Shostakovich's reputation as one of the twentieth century's musical geniuses.

Alongside the reevaluation of Russian and Soviet musical history has appeared a new criticism with fresh views on contemporary music. Reflections on musical life of the 1990s have fallen into the hands of a new generation, of whom the best known are Petr Pospelov, Olga Manulkina, Iuliia Bederova, Boris Filanovskii, and Mikhail Fikhtengolts. Their publication forum is no longer scholarly journals, but popular periodicals, including *Kommersant*, *Russkii telegraf* (Russian Telegraph), and *Izvestiia*. The main values in this new criticism are a fluent command of various aspects of musical culture, a lack of cultural bias, the ability to speak freely, and a lively, humorous style.

Composition

The co-existence of several generations of composers has led to the simultaneous development of contrasting trends in composition. Every generation carries its greatest names like a banner. Among traditionalists in Russia, the greatest names include Georgii Sviridov and Valerii Gavrilin, 'Russianist' composers whose work develops independently of Western trends and fashions; they have created a profoundly Russian minimalism and new simplicity. Among modernists the most famous are Galina Ustvolskaia and Alemdar Karamanov, the creators of original musical conceptions outside the bounds of the avant-garde. Their work has received recognition only in the post-Soviet era. The development of modernism has become something of a rarity: composers well known in the Soviet era, such as Sofia Gubaidullina, Sergei Slonimskii; Boris Tishchenko, and Aleksandr Knaifel opted for more conservative forms during the last two decades of the twentieth century; they operate on 'neo'-styles and on the authority of texts both sacral and culturally sacralized. This tendency among modernists has provided a natural background for the development of musical postmodernism and enabled the co-existence of wildly different approaches and musical methods. In Moscow, chief representatives of postmodernism include Vladimir Martynov, Vladimir Tarnopolskii, Viktor Ekimovskii, and Tatiana Sergeeva; in St. Petersburg, Leonid Desiatnikov, Anatolii Korolev, and Aleksandr Popov. If one can identify a general tendency among the younger generation, it is the blurring of borders between classical and popular music, high and low art, and lively contact with diverse contemporary musical forms, aided by a demand for the work of such authors as Anton Batagov, Pavel Karmanov, and Aleksei Aigi in Russian film and television.

Institutions and audiences

The renewal of classical musical culture is closely linked with the emergence of new, independent musical institutions. Whereas this process has hardly touched musical education, apart from that in schools, it has radically changed concert life, for new orchestras, chamber ensembles, and opera troupes have appeared, and new philharmonics and promotion companies have undertaken new projects. The commercialization of classical music can be seen in the greater percentage of 'pop' performances than in the Soviet era, when 'strict' public tastes were cultivated. Musical stars play a greater role, especially in 'crossover' performances, which have brought classical music to new audiences. The most successful post-Soviet musical ensembles have acquired the ability to work simultaneously with public financing and private sponsorship, and to appeal to audiences while remaining in touch with current developments in classical music. A good example is St. Petersburg's Mariinskii Theatre, Russia's most important opera and ballet theatre during the 1990s, which works with both state and vast private financing provided by both Russian and Western sponsors. Able to earn money through tours; it has a more active world touring schedule than any troupe its size. The Mariinskii Theatre presents about fifteen premieres per season (not unlike Western opera houses), while also maintaining the principle of a repertory theatre, offering one to two performances a day and a different performance daily. The Mariinskii's repertoire is free of stylistic biases, presenting both traditional and contemporary works and following both 'Slavophile' and 'Westernizer' lines.

One of the moving forces of post-Soviet musical life has been the activity of Western cultural foundations, including Germany's Goethe-Institut, the British Council, the Institut français and the Dutch Institute – all of which bring their own soloists, chamber ensembles, choirs, and orchestras to Russia on cultural missions. They introduce both contemporary music and the 'other' contemporary music: early music on authentic instruments, which enjoys great popularity in Russia.

See also: classical music, Soviet; classical musicians/performers, post-Soviet; Denisov, Edison; Desiatnikov, Leonid; educational system, post-Soviet; educational system, Soviet; Gubaidulina, Sofiia; *Kommersant*; Mariinskii Theatre; orchestras, Soviet and post-Soviet; perestroika and glasnost; periodicals, post-Soviet; popular music, post-Soviet; Prokofiev, Sergei; Shnittke, Alfred; Shostakovich, Dmitrii; sixties generation; Slavophiles; Slonimskii, Sergei; Socialist Realism; Stravinskii, Igor; Sviridov, Georgii; Tarnopolskii, Vladimir; Tishchenko, Boris; Ustvolskaia, Galina; Westernizers

Further reading

Cherednichenko, T. (2002) *Muzykalnyi zapas: 70-e*, Moscow.
Novaia kritika: 1991–2001, 3 vols, St. Petersburg: Pro arte. In press.
(1994, 1996) *Muzyka iz byvshego SSSR. Sbornik statei*, 2 vols, Moscow.
(1996) *Shostakovich. K 90-letiiu so dnia rozhdeniia. Sbornik statei*, St. Petersburg.
(2001) *Shostakovich: mezhdu mgnoveniem i vechnostiu. Sbornik statei*, St. Petersburg.

KIRA NEMIROVSKAIA

classical music, Soviet

Soviet classical music was subjected to the same political scrutiny and control as the other art forms. Refusing to allow music to follow an autonomous course, cultural bureaucrats assigned it the task of celebrating and teaching the principles of socialism. However, the extent of government intrusion varied depending on the period.

Already in the 1920s, a decade of relative freedom and experimentation, warring ideas on what constituted socialist music had led to the creation of numerous factions. In 1932, the Union of Soviet Composers was established to control the splintered music world. Its resolution, 'On the Reformation of Literary and Artistic Organizations', espoused the doctrine of Socialist Realism, a term that acquired ever-changing meanings. According to the Socialist Realist aesthetic, music should serve the proletariat, be accessible upon first hearing to workers, and have a subject matter glorifying workers' deeds. Because instrumental compositions (in contrast to literature, theatre, and ballet) lacked a clear narrative, it was difficult to define precisely how to apply Socialist Realism to music. This problem was to plague both composers and bureaucrats throughout the history of the Soviet Union. For all of the difficulty in determining what Soviet music should be, it was clear early on what it should not be: Modernist and experimental. Music of composers such as Arnold Schoenberg, Anton Webern, and Igor Stravinskii, which had been performed in the 1920s, was officially banned in the 1930s.

In this period of increasing surveillance and conformism, simple, melody-driven works ('song operas') such as Ivan Dzerzhinskii's *Tikhii Don* (*Quiet Flows the Don*) and Tikhon Khrennikov's *V buriu* (*Into the Storm*) were upheld as models of Soviet music.

The treatment of Dmitrii Shostakovich parallels the development of official Soviet attitudes towards music; the USSR's most renowned composer, he was alternately championed and punished according to the needs of the regime. Shostakovich's early works were received with great fanfare in part because he belonged to the first generation of composers educated in the Soviet Union. But in 1936, as Stalin tightened the reins on the arts, Shostakovich was severely disciplined in a *Pravda* review denouncing his opera *Ledi Makbet Mtsenskogo uezda* (*Lady Macbeth of Mtsensk*). The article, *Sumbur vmesto muzyki* ('Muddle instead of Music') sounded an alarm not only for Shostakovich but for all composers with any interest in individualized expression. The war brought some respite for Shostakovich in the clamorous reception of his Seventh Symphony (Leningrad), but this reprieve was short-lived. In 1948, Stalin's cultural emissary, Andrei Zhdanov, denounced all adherents to 'Formalism' (officially, the separation of form and content, but in practical terms anything straying from Socialist Realism as defined by the Party at any given moment) and deemed their music unsuited for performance in the Soviet Union. This denunciation was directed at Vano Muradeli for his ideologically innocuous opera *Velikaia Druzhba* (*The Great Friendship*), but Shostakovich, Sergei Prokofiev, Aram Khatchaturian, Nikolai Miaskovskii, and others were implicated as well.

Stalin's death in 1953 and Khrushchev's subsequent rise ushered in an era of greater leniency. After decades of isolation, contacts were again forged with Western composers such as Luigi Nono and Stravinskii, and with iconoclastic Western performers such as Leonard Bernstein and Glenn Gould (the latter's performances earning him an enormous following in the Soviet Union). The music of the Second Viennese School, formerly dismissed as Formalist and decadent, began to attract Russian composers. Andrei Volkonskii, a Geneva-born Russian repatriated in 1947, and

Filip Gershkovich, a student of Berg and Webern, led the new interest in serialism. In 1956, Volkonskii wrote 'Musica Stricta' for solo piano, the first attempt at a twelve-tone work by a Soviet composer. Alfred Shnittke, Arvo Pärt, Edison Denisov, and others experimented with dodecaphonic techniques in part as a rebellion against the strictures of Socialist Realism. Paradoxically, while serialism was becoming a new kind of orthodoxy in Western contemporary music, it symbolized artistic resistance in the Soviet Union.

The appeal of the Second Viennese School was partly linked to its perception as forbidden fruit. For a few, the serialism of Schoenberg, Webern, and Berg remained a lifelong obsession. But as the state's attitude toward experimentation and modernism began to relax, younger composers explored developing aspects of the Western avant-garde (total serialism, electronic music, minimalism). The music of the so-called Darmstadt School (Pierre Boulez, Bruno Maderna, Nono, Karlheinz Stockhausen), though officially prohibited, became highly influential. Denisov, a protégé of Shostakovich, operated what was essentially an underground lending library of scores by Western modernist composers. The music of the new Polish avant-garde (Witold Lutoslawski, Krzysztof Penderecki), while condemned by the Composers' Union, found its way into the musical vocabularies of young Soviet composers.

In the 1960s and 1970s, hidden beneath the uniformity of official Soviet music, an unprecedented stylistic diversity began to emerge. Composers such as Shnittke, Pärt and Sofiia Gubaidulina developed highly personal means of composition, taking their inspiration from sources in the West as well as the Soviet republics, including minimalism, early music, folk traditions, religious music, and the increasingly eclectic Western avant-garde. Since the Composers' Union, headed by the hard-liner Khrennikov for four decades, sometimes tolerated and sometimes vilified these composers, their official standing was never clear. Many of their works remained unpublished and unperformed in the Soviet Union. Their creators, however, were allowed to work extensively in the area of film music, and many of them (Shnittke, Denisov, Gubaidulina, Pärt – like

Shostakovich and Prokofiev in an earlier period) produced works of exceptional quality.

As the USSR was atheistic from the outset, religion was synonymous with rebellion. Any music with a religious component inevitably took a stance against the state. In their search for spiritualism in music, some composers looked to the early music movement, which came late to the USSR but nonetheless made its mark. Medieval and Renaissance music went hand-in-hand with religious interests, as much of it came from the liturgical traditions of Western Europe. From this archaic music and contemporary minimalism, Pärt created spare, otherworldly works that evoked a powerful spiritualism. Gubaidulina, a Russian Orthodox believer, combined folk influences from Russia, the Caucasus, and Asia – including microtonal elements, officially frowned upon – with religious sentiment.

Shnittke, who, like Pärt, had experimented with serialism and other modernist methods, developed a polystylistic rather than synthetic technique. Often described as postmodern, this music eschews any single aesthetic and erases historical and generic boundaries. His first symphony, which premiered (1972) not in Moscow but in the 'closed' city of Gorkii (Nizhnii Novgorod), was never played again in the Soviet Union. Though little known in Russia, his works were received enthusiastically in the West.

Performers in the USSR enjoyed an elevated status. Unlike composition, performance could not be accused of anti-democratic tendencies or decadent style and was not held to the same subjective criticism by the state. Soviet performers' high level of skill was known around the world and became a source of national pride. Highly privileged Soviet virtuosos trained like Olympic athletes, with iron discipline and fanatical attention to technique. The Tchaikovsky Competition, established in 1958, served as a Cold War cultural battleground, pitting Soviet musicians against their Western counterparts, usually with a favourable outcome for the former.

Soviet music suffered greatly from the emigration of some of its most talented composers and performers. The reasons for their departure included lack of artistic freedom, an aversion to the ideals of socialism, musical isolation from the West, and curtailed career opportunities.

Those who left in the early years of the Soviet Union included composers Sergei Rakhmaninov and Prokofiev (who repatriated in the mid-1930s) and performers (Vladimir Horowitz, Fedor Shaliapin). With rare exceptions, the music of émigré composers was banned in the Soviet Union, slandered by the Composers' Union, and disgraced in the media. The loss of the internationally renowned Stravinskii was a particular source of irritation. He had been in the West since the outbreak of World War I and adamantly rejected the Soviet state and its cultural policies, despite a celebrated return visit in 1962. During the post-Stalinist period, many major performers emigrated (Vladimir Ashkenazii [Ashkenazy], Gidon Kremer, Mstislav Rostropovich, Galina Vishnevskaia), as did numerous composers (Shnittke, Pärt, Gubaidulina, Volkonskii, and Leonid Khrabovskii [Hrabovskii]).

Although Soviet composers experienced obstacles unknown to their Western contemporaries, they enjoyed some distinct advantages. The Soviet patronage system, while subjecting new compositions to a review that was tantamount to censorship, provided substantial material benefits for select composers. It also allowed for an unusual degree of collaboration between composers and performers. Shostakovich's works were championed by David Oistrakh, Rostropovich, and Vishnevskaia. Later composers such as Shnittke and Gubaidulina came to international prominence largely because superlative performers (Kremer and Iurii Bashmet) programmed their compositions in concerts around the world.

See also: Ashkenazii, Vladimir; Bashmet, Iurii; Caucasus; censorship; classical music, post-Soviet; Denisov, Edison; folk music; Gubaidulina, Sofiia; Khachaturian, Aram; Khrennikov, Tikhon; Kremer, Gidon; Nizhnii Novgorod (Gorkii); Oistrakh, David; opera, Soviet; orchestras, Soviet and post-Soviet; Pärt, Arvo; piano performance, Russian/Soviet; *Pravda*; Prokofiev, Sergei; Rostropovich, Mstislav; Russian Orthodoxy; Shnittke, Alfred; Shostakovich, Dmitrii; Socialist Realism; Stravinskii, Igor; Tchaikovsky Competition; Thaw; unions, creative, Soviet; Vishnevskaia, Galina

Further reading

Edmunds, N. (ed.) (2004) *Soviet Music and Society under Lenin and Stalin: The Baton and Sickle*, New York: RoutledgeCurzon.

Egorova, T. (1997) *Soviet Film Music: An Historical Survey*, Amsterdam: Harwood Academic Publishers.

Maes, F. (1996) *A History of Russian Music: From Kamarinskaya to Babi Yar*, Berkeley, CA: University of California Press.

Schmelz, P. (2005) 'Andrey Volkonsky and the Beginnings of Unofficial Music in the Soviet Union', *Journal of the American Musicological Society*, 58, 1: 139–207.

Schwarz, B. (1972) *Music and Musical Life in Soviet Russia*, Bloomington, IN: Indiana University Press.

Taruskin, R. (2005) *The Oxford History of Western Music*, New York: Oxford: Oxford University Press.

Tsenova, V. (ed.) (1997) *Underground Music from the Former USSR*, Amsterdam: Harwood Academic Publishers.

SUNGHAE ANNA LIM

classical musicians/performers, post-Soviet

The main innovation in post-Soviet performance, in comparison to its Soviet predecessor, has been its emergence onto the world market. Accordingly, Russian performers have had opportunities to perform abroad and have experienced the necessity to do so for economic reasons. This new mobility has had several consequences. Russian performance schools are no longer isolated. Conservatory graduates no longer have to wait for an order from above, but can take the initiative themselves and enter international competitions and audition for orchestral, chamber, and theatrical openings worldwide. Thus Russian musicians have gained top spots in orchestras and opera houses abroad; indeed, their status at home now depends on success abroad. Certain Russian musicians are contracted to perform primarily outside of Russia, and give only guest performances in their homeland. These include cellists Natalia Gutman and Ivan Monigetti, violinist Vadim Repin, pianist Evgenii Kissin, and particularly

opera singers, notably Sergei Leiferkus, Olga Borodina, Vladimir Galuzin, Elena Prokina, and Dmitrii Khvorostovskii. The Russian public receives these performers with the same deference they showed to émigré performers during the Soviet era, who began to give guest performances only during perestroika, such as cellist Mstislav Rostropovich and singer Galina Vishnevskaia, violinist Gidon Kremer, and pianists Vladimir Ashkenazy, Valerii Afanasev, and Aleksandr Toradze. Some of these performers have returned to live in Russia.

The dissolution of the economic structure supporting Soviet-era musical institutions has created a need for more pragmatic projects; as a result, stylistic spheres in classical music have become polarized. While retaining its traditional form, the academic mainstream also has been cultivating a modernized, commercial profile, featuring star performers with light programmes in concerts meant to appeal to a wide audience. Behind such popular concert projects have been violinist Vladimir Spivakov and violist Iurii Bashmet, both of whom also continue to perform in concerts with a more serious repertoire. Traditionalism is epitomized in performances by representatives of the older generation: violinist Viktor Tretiakov and pianists Eliso Virsaladze, Grigorii Sokolov, and Mikhail Pletnev. Sokolov rarely performs and has earned a reputation as the most mysterious and esoteric of Russian performers, his annual concert appearances enjoying near-sacral status.

A new phenomenon, virtually banned in the Soviet Union, is the performance of early music on authentic instruments, which rapidly gained popularity in the 1990s. Among its founders and stars, including those who in the 1960s and 1970s advocated performance on authentic instruments, are pianist, harpsichordist, and organist Aleksei Liubimov, violinist Tatiana Grindenko, violist and choir director Anatolii Grindenko, and younger violinists Nazar Kozhukhar, Andrei Reshetin, and harpsichordist Iurii Martynov. Also experiencing new freedom and thus new expansion is contemporary music, which has a following all its own. Among its leaders are Liubimov and Grindenko, as well as percussionist Mark Pekarskii. Particularly important in performances of contemporary music is the Moscow Union of Musicians, which includes pianist Polina Osetinskaia, violist Andrei Dogadin, violinist Ilia Goff, singers Andrei Slavnyi, Marat Galiakhmetov, and Tatiana Kuindzhi, cellist Oleg Vedernikov, brought together by pianist Aleksei Goribol in exquisite, original concert projects in both capitals, provincial cities, and abroad.

See also: Ashkenazii, Vladimir; classical music, post-Soviet; Gutman, Natalia; Kissin, Evgenii; Kremer, Gidon; Liubimov, Aleksei; Pletnev, Mikhail; Rostropovich, Mstislav; Spivakov, Vladimir; Vishnevskaia, Galina

KIRA NEMIROVSKAIA

closed city

A closed city, called a 'box' in popular parlance, is a top-secret military research centre constructed as a town. The bureaucratic Soviet term for the closed city was the abbreviation ZATO (*zakrytoe administrativno-territorialnoe obrazovanie* [closed administrative-territorial formation]). Such towns, with coded names not indicated on geographical maps, usually had direct air communication with Moscow. Entrance, residence, and employment were under strict KGB control. A typical closed city is Cheliabinsk-70, founded in 1955 as a nuclear weapons research centre and in 1992 renamed Snezhinsk. Other Soviet/Russian closed cities are Arzamas-16 (Sarov), Baikonur, Krasnoiarsk-45 (Zelenogorsk), and Krasnoiarsk-26 (Zheleznogorsk).

See also: Arzamas-16 (Sarov); Baikonur; defence industry

TATYANA LEDENEVA

club (kruzhok)

An organized circle or club of people voluntarily united to pursue common interest activities. In the USSR, such clubs were located at Houses of Culture and organized leisure time for working people and developed amateur arts, fitness, and sports. There were Marxist clubs to educate Soviet citizens, both Party and non-Party members, in the spirit of Communist ideology. Various clubs were organized at schools or vocational schools in special subject areas and for entertainment; convened after classes, they were run by teachers, invited experts, or parents in order to provide children with social opportunities around a common interest, and to educate and entertain children according to their skills levels and interests.

See also: educational system, Soviet; fitness

ELENA OMELCHENKO

coats

Russia's climate makes coats for all seasons an important part of any Russian's wardrobe. Bought to last, coats are treated with care. A fur coat (*shuba*) is commonly worn not merely for luxury or show, but as an everyday winter coat, mostly for women. Russians value fur coats for their warmth, waterproofing adequate for snow, and roominess; they leave room for several layers of clothing. The fur can vary from relatively inexpensive rabbit to mink or sable that sells for prices comparable to those in the West, although they are produced domestically. Fur hats are even more common than fur coats; they can be worn with various different styles of coat. Thick, domestic-made sheepskin coats, made of material similar to that seen in men's hats in the West (as well as in Russia) and dyed black, are also common. Fake fur is jokingly called 'fish fur' and most Russians consider wearing fur a good thing. Many Russians wear fur-lined or, more commonly, thick wool-lined suede coats called *dublenka* (sing.) – a warm and less expensive alternative to the *shuba* as a winter coat, though not waterproofed.

In spring and autumn, Russians of both sexes wear leather jackets and coats much more than do Americans and most Europeans. In the summer, they wear raincoats similar to those worn in Europe and the United States, ranging from nylon rain jackets and coats to trench coats. These are often imported from countries with lower prices, such as China or Turkey, and they are a ubiquitous part of clothing markets where cheap imported items are sold. Central European imports are also fairly common.

For all the variety in styles of Russian coats, one rule holds fast: coats are always dark, because of the muddy streets in spring and fall, and slushy streets and street-blackened snow in winter. The beige trench coat commonly seen in Europe and the United States is rarely seen in Russia.

See also: fashion industry, post-Soviet; fashion industry, Soviet; headgear; market

KAREN EVANS-ROMAINE

Cold War (Kholodnaia voina)

A global confrontation between the United States and the Soviet Union, the Cold War (1946–89) also involved NATO, the Warsaw Pact, and other alliances. It grew out of disagreements among members of the Grand Alliance (the USA, Great Britain, the Soviet Union, and China) toward the end of World War II and acquired its name in the spring of 1946, when the United States (Truman Administration) adopted the strategy of 'containment' of the Soviet Union. On the Western side, there were growing American and British fears of Soviet expansion in the Middle East (Turkey and Iran), the Far East (China and Korea), and in Europe (Germany, Poland, Czechoslovakia, the Balkans). On the Soviet side, there was the determination to create a security buffer consisting of Communist satellites and spheres of influence so as to challenge US–British global hegemony. In 1947, the Cold War acquired openly ideological dimensions with the US proclamation of the Truman Doctrine and the Marshall Plan, and the Soviets' Zhdanov Doctrine of 'two camps'. In 1948–49, military-political blocs came into existence: NATO and the Soviet bloc – Eastern European countries, minus Tito's Yugoslavia. Germany and Korea became divided countries. After the Communist victory in China (October 1949) and the outbreak of the Korean War (June 1950), the Cold War escalated dangerously. The ensuing intense arms race included nuclear weapons and massive conventional deployments in Europe, the Balkans, and the Far East. Both sides used propaganda and cultural technologies and means (printed media, cinema and theatre, radio) to mobilize the Cold War. The process culminated in state 'anti-cosmopolitan' campaigns, mass arrests and executions in the Soviet bloc, and in McCarthyism in the United States.

During 1953–63 the Cold War was punctuated by limited 'détente', acute crises, and the spread of confrontation into the Third World (Indonesia, Indochina, Arab Middle East, Sub-Saharan Africa, Cuba, and Latin America). The bipolarity of the Cold War became pronounced as Great Britain and France lost great power status, and two superpowers, the USA and the USSR, emerged. During this decade the USA abandoned plans to 'roll back' Soviet domination in Europe, and the post-Stalin leadership in Moscow promoted 'peaceful coexistence'. Though the two sides opened limited channels of negotiation, cultural and scientific exchanges, the nuclear and conventional arms race continued to escalate, generating fear and mistrust, and dominating the international agenda of all Cold War protagonists. The Suez crisis (1956), the Berlin crisis (1958–61), and especially the Cuban missile crisis (October November 1962) evoked the spectre of nuclear annihilation. The Soviet Union and China supported 'movements of national liberation' and revolutionary elements in the Third World, trying to destabilize and destroy European colonial empires and US-led alliances and pacts. The bipolar rivalry peaked during the Cuban crisis; both superpowers realized that they had to develop rules of engagement and avoid direct clashes.

In the same decade, the Cold War involved more proxy conflicts and secondary players; members of NATO (1949) and the Warsaw Treaty Organization (1955), and especially the Third World clients of superpowers attempted to pursue autonomous goals and to regain diplomatic freedom. The end of the Sino-Soviet friendship in 1960, after a decade of alliance, signalled the demise of the monopolistic Communist movement and the emergence of a 'third force' in the Cold War – a development parallel to the Vietnamese Communists' decision (1961–63) to launch a war to reunify Vietnam, which led to indirect Soviet and Chinese, and direct US involvement. This period saw the rise of psychological warfare between East and West, and the use of militant ideological slogans (Kennedy's Cold War liberalism, the radicalism of Mao, Castro, and Che Guevara, and Khrushchev's Communist rhetoric). Anti-colonialism, anti-racism, and scientific utopian schemes dominated the contested ideological and cultural field.

The period from 1963–79 introduced 'détente' in Europe and in US–Soviet relations, accompanied and gradually overshadowed by intensifying instability and rivalry in the Third World. Western Europe, shattered by the student movement and New Left radicalism, sought stable relations with the East, while the USA, torn culturally and politically over the Vietnam War, sought to improve relations with the USSR and China. Richard Nixon's trip to Beijing (1971) and superpower summits in Moscow (1972), Washington (1973) and Vladivostok (1974) significantly reduced international tension. Détente arrangements included agreements recognizing the division of Germany; territorial change after World War II (especially between Poland and West Germany); arms control (partial Test-Ban Treaty in 1963, Nuclear Non-Proliferation Treaty in 1968, Strategic Arms Limitation Talks (SALT) I and Anti-Ballistic Missiles Treaty in 1972, SALT II in 1979); the Helsinki Final Act on security and cooperation in Europe (1975); and cooperation in health, agriculture, space, and culture. Trade and commerce between Western Europe and the Soviet bloc countries, as well as state-regulated cultural-scientific exchange, expanded throughout these years.

Yet Cold War dynamics remained basically unchanged and even acquired momentum. The Soviet Union reached strategic parity with the US, but continued to build up nuclear and conventional forces; it developed global power-projecting capabilities and immediately used them in Africa to support revolutionary elements and pro-Soviet clients. In Angola (1974–75) and the Horn of Africa (1977), the Soviet and Cuban military played the role of 'international policemen', previously reserved for European powers and the USA. After 1975, Cold War mistrust and confrontation prevailed again. The Carter Administration, seeking to reform American foreign policy, pushed for international observation of human rights and expressed sympathies for political 'dissidents' in the Soviet Union and Eastern Europe. In the USA, fears of Soviet–Cuban 'penetration' in Africa and Soviet military build-up provided ammunition for neoconservative critics of the Carter Administration. In autumn 1979, Western European NATO members responded to the Soviet build-up with the deployment of a new generation of medium-range missiles and cruise missiles. In December 1979, Soviet troops occupied Afghanistan; the USA, seeing a strategic threat to the Persian Gulf's oil reserve, responded with sanctions and suspended détente arrangements and agreements.

In 1980–83, US–Soviet confrontation reached a new high. The militantly ideological Reagan Administration assisted Islamic fundamentalists fighting in Afghanistan; announced the Strategic Defense Initiative (1983) and funded 'smart weapons' designed to nullify Soviet military superiority in Europe; deployed Pershing missiles in Europe; and tried to undercut Soviet revenues from oil and gas sales. Under American terms, the USSR had to withdraw from the Third World, observe human rights' agreements, and accept American military superiority. The Soviet Union, with a stagnant economy, the decline of Communist ideology, and an aged leadership, had limited capacity to respond to this challenge: the Solidarity movement in Poland (1980–81) had almost shattered Soviet domination in Eastern Europe; Soviet interventions in the Third World had failed to produce the expected spread of 'socialism'; and the occupation of Afghanistan had become a 'Soviet Vietnam' (though lacking a large-scale domestic protest). After 1985, Mikhail Gorbachev, the new, dynamic Soviet leader, saw the Cold War as a disabling risk and obstacle to domestic reforms. After two failed summits in Geneva (1985) and Reykjavik (1986), in Washington, Reagan and Gorbachev agreed (November 1987) to eliminate medium-range missiles. Glasnost, the repudiation of Communist ideology in the USSR, and growing personal trust between the leaders prepared for the peaceful end of the Cold War (1989). As Gorbachev proclaimed 'new thinking' and nonuse of force, anti-Communist nationalist movements in Eastern Europe and the USSR became powerful political entities. Soviet non-involve-ment led to the fall of the Berlin Wall (November 1989) and the collapse of Communist regimes in Eastern Europe. At the Malta summit, US President George H. W. Bush and Gorbachev recognized the end of the Cold War and negotiated on the basis of 'common human values'.

The Cold War had a profound impact on social and cultural developments in the second half of the twentieth century. Global ideological confrontation and the danger of nuclear annihi-lation inspired numerous artists and cultural trends. Conflicts between 'modernism' and 'traditionalism' in art also acquired Cold War dimensions, the former becoming synonymous with the West, and the latter appropriated by Soviet cultural orthodoxy. McCarthyism under-cut the 'socialist left' and created a decade-long conformist climate in the USA. In the Soviet Union, Stalin's needs for a solid Cold War 'home front' fuelled state-supported Russian chauvinism and anti-Semitism. At the same time, while generating xenophobia and con-formism, Cold-War dynamics planted the seeds of rapid socio-cultural change. Beatnik culture in the US and the Thaw generation in the Soviet Union spearheaded resistance to Cold-War conformism. Rival camps carried out social reforms and supported cultural and intellectual efforts to demonstrate the relative advantages of 'socialism' or 'capitalism'. Cold War needs accelerated awareness of racial discrimination and a gender revolution in the West. The 'Sputnik effect' enhanced the role of students and intellectuals in American society; simulta-neously, nuclear physicists (e.g. Andrei Sakharov), cybernetic specialists, and other sci-entists began to influence the Soviet ideological climate. A limited but growing exposure to the world through cultural and scientific exchange (e.g., the Moscow Youth Festival,1957, and the American exhibition, 1959), the electronic media revolution, and Western broadcasting produced an 'enlightened' generation of Soviet intellectuals who dreamed of reintegrating the USSR into Europe. Cold War interaction pro-duced contradictory results: a conservative backlash in the USA during the 1970s brought Reagan to power; at the same time, intellectual ferments of the 1950s and 1960s inspired

Gorbachev and some of his advisers to repudiate the Stalinist legacy and develop 'new thinking'.

See also: anti-Semitism; Brezhnev, Leonid; Communist ideology; defence industry; East Bloc countries; Gorbachev, Mikhail; Khrush-chev, Nikita; perestroika and glasnost; propa-ganda, Soviet and post-Soviet; Sakharov, Andrei; Stalin, Iosif; World War II (Great Patriotic War)

Further reading

Gaddis, J. (1996) *We Now Know: Rethinking Cold War History*, New York: Oxford University Press.

Hixson, W. L. (1997) *Parting the Curtain. Propa-ganda, Culture, and the Cold War, 1945–61*, New York: St. Martin's Press.

Odd, A. W. (2005) *The Global Cold War: Third World Interventions and the Making of Our Times*, Cambridge: Cambridge University Press.

VLADIMIR ZUBOK

collective farms

Initially, in the 1920s, collective farms were formed as voluntary agricultural producers' cooperatives. In 1929, Stalin initiated a cam-paign of mass collectivization: all peasants were forced to transfer their household, land, agri-cultural implements, livestock, and even poultry to the newly formed collective farms, called *kol-khozy*, an abbreviation for *kollektivnoe khoziaistvo*. (In 1930, after Stalin's infamous article 'Dizzy from Success', peasants were allowed to keep poultry and later some cattle in personal own-ership, on their individual plots.) According to the highest estimates, the property of 10–12 per cent of peasant households – the wealthiest, called *kulaks* ('fists') – was completely confiscated and 380,000 wealthy peasants families were exiled in 1930–31 to remote regions of the Soviet Union. By February 1930, 60 per cent of all households were united into collective farms. Unwilling to transfer their cattle to collective farms, peasants slaughtered them: in 1929–33, the cattle population fell by more than half. Yet peasants were legally bound to their land, since internal passports were issued in 1930 only to urban residents, and peasants were prohibited from relocating to the cities without special permission.

Procurement prices for agricultural products were extremely low, virtually symbolic. *Zagotzerno*, the state grain procurement organization, bought grain from collective farms for 7 rubles per 100 kg and sold it to the state mills at 104 rubles. Another 7 rubles were left with *Zagotzerno* to cover expenses, and 90 rubles were paid as a turnover tax to the state to finance industrialization.

In 1953, after Stalin's death, procurement prices for agricultural products were raised substantially, so that for the first time since collectivization collective and state farms were able to cover costs and even to make some profit. At the same time, collective farms were merged, and the poorest collective farms were transformed into state farms, or *sovkhozy*, an abbreviation for *sovetskoe khoziaistvo*: state property was considered to be superior to collective property, and state farms were able to get government subsidies, while collective farms could get only loans that they could not repay. In 1940, there were 237,000 collective farms (*kolkhozy*) and 4,000 state farms (*sovkhozy*); in 1965, there were 47,000 and 12,000 respectively, and in 1985, there were 26,000 and 23,000 respectively. The average collective farm in the 1980s had about 500 employees.

In 1965, all social guarantees enjoyed by workers on state farms (pensions, maternity leave, etc.) were extended to the members of collective farms, and their minimal level of remuneration was raised to the level of wages of workers on state farms. Yet differences among collective and state farms persisted – the former enjoyed greater freedom in the distribution of net income, and their efficiency (measured in output per unit of capital, land labour) was noticeably higher. In the 1990s, state and collective farms were formally reorganized into partnerships, joint stock companies, etc., but in essence remained collective and state farms. The share of individual land plots in total agricultural output increased from 25 per cent in the late 1980s to 50–55 per cent in 2000; the share of agricultural enterprises (old collective and state farms) fell from 75 per cent to about 40 per cent; the share of independent farms increased from 0 to 5 per cent.

See also: economic system, Soviet; economic system, post-Soviet; privatization

TATIANA SMORODINSKAYA

comedians

The satirical comic stage monologue (stand-up comedy) has been a popular form of entertainment in Russia since the beginning of the twentieth century, and live and televised performances by the best-known comedians still attract large audiences today. In the post-Stalinist USSR, stage comedy was a genre that frequently straddled the border between official and unofficial culture; 'approved' comedians such as Arkadii Raikin, who had his own theatre in Leningrad, were no less loved than more daring and semi-underground comedians, such as Mikhail Zhvanetskii, who performed in much smaller, often impromptu settings and sometimes drew the censor's disapproving scrutiny.

The figure of the stage comedian in Russia is most directly traceable to that of the *estrada konferanse* (variety stage emcee), who would read monologues between acts. One can trace the figure even further back, to satirical circus clowns and the *raeshnik* (barker) of traditional Russian folk carnivals. The best-known comedian of the 1920s and 1930s was Vladimir Khenkin, who began in the pre-Revolutionary cabaret tradition and was a significant influence on those who followed, including Raikin – one of the most famous stars of the comedic stage from the late 1930s to the 1980s. During the Thaw, many comedians, some still active and well known today, emerged from the tradition of amateur and student performance, to find lasting fame in sold-out theatres and televised concerts. During Stagnation, when public satire again became politically risky, those comedians who nevertheless continued to write and perform pointed miniatures (especially Zhvanetskii, a former writer for Raikin) became cult figures; homemade copies of their performances were as ubiquitous as similar recordings of bard singers. Comedians who wrote and performed their own material – *avtory-ispolniteli* (author-performers) – were especially well regarded by the highly literate public.

Throughout perestroika, the satirical monologue was a prominent medium for socio-political commentary, and comedians such as Mikhail Zadornov, Gennadii Khazanov, Grigorii Gorin, Evgenii Petrosian, Zhvanetskii, and others were highly visible participants in the culture-wide, multi-media reassessment of the Soviet past and present. Whereas public satire had previously been allowed to target only apolitical human foibles, isolated aspects of Soviet society, or negative elements of life in the West, in the late 1980s satirists engaged directly with the state and its policies. Zadornov, for example, became famous for his impersonations of Mikhail Gorbachev. In the post-Soviet period, many of the 'classics' of the comedic stage monologue are still prolific, as are comedians of a slightly younger generation, such as Mikhail Evdokimov, Efim Shifrin, and Klara Novikova.

See also: bards; perestroika and glasnost; Raikin, Arkadii; Stagnation; stand-up comedy; Thaw; Zhvanetskii, Mikhail

Further reading

Graham, S. (2004) 'Mikhail Mikhailovich Zhvanetsky', in M. Balina and M. Lipovetsky (eds) *Dictionary of Literary Biography*, vol. 285: *Russian Writers Since 1980*, Detroit, MI: Bruccoli Clark Layman, pp. 357–64.

Mesropova, O. (2003) 'Old Bags and Bald Sparrows: Contemporary Russian Female Stand-Up Comedy', *Russian Review*, 62, 3: 429–39.

Stites, R. (1992) *Russian Popular Culture: Entertainment and Society Since 1900*, Cambridge: Cambridge University Press, especially pp. 166–8.

SETH GRAHAM

communal apartment (kommunalka)

Communal apartments emerged as a result of revolutionary residential redistribution, begun in 1917, to requisition apartments of the wealthy so as to provide for the needs of the poor. Lenin's formula (echoing that of Friedrich Engels) defined a wealthy apartment as one in which the number of rooms equalled or exceeded the number of people permanently residing there. Accordingly, all available living space, regardless of its quality, location, and sometimes even of the presence of wall partitions, was divided into equal slices of floor area corresponding to the norm of 10 square metres (108 sq. ft.) per adult and child up to 2 years of age, and 5 square metres (54 sq. ft.) for each child aged from 2 to 12. By 1924, this norm had decreased to 8 square metres (86 sq. ft.), regardless of age. By the end of the 1920s, about 60 per cent of the population lived in communal apartments. Conflicts between total strangers forced to share rooms, kitchens, bathrooms, and toilets were described in Soviet literature by many writers; the most vivid example is Mikhail Zoshchenko's short story *Nervnye liudi* (*Nervous People*, 1924). One of the blockbusters of *samizdat* in the 1970s was Mikhail Bulgakov's story *Sobache serdtse* (*Heart of a Dog*, 1925), which describes a clash between a noble professor, Preobrazhenskii, who occupies a seven-room apartment, and the nasty housing committee members trying to expropriate some of his rooms. The professor's eventual victory contributed to the popularity of the story, and later, of the film by Vladimir Bortko (1988). Communal apartments started to wane during the mass housing development of the Khrushchev era. The All-Union Conference of Builders, Architects, and Construction Industry Workers (1954) emphasized standardization and industrial construction methods, and promised each family a private apartment. The newly acquired joy of privacy could be seen as early as in 1952 in Aleksandr Laktionov's painting *Pereezd na novuiu kvartiru* (*Moving to a New Apartment*) and in many films of the 1960s, such as Anatolii Efros's *Visokosnyi god* (*Leap Year*, 1961). Later, the monotony and sameness of the new housing were satirized in Eldar Riazanov's *Ironiia sudby* (*The Irony of Fate*, 1975). The 1980s, when the poorly built concrete-slab 'khrushcheby' (from *trushcheby*, slums) started to crumble, saw the onset of a certain nostalgia for the *kommunalka*, the majority of which had been in better built nineteenth-century buildings. Some films of the

1980–90s, such as Andrei Konchalovskii's *Blizhnii krug* (*The Inner Circle*, 1991) and Regis Wargnier's *Vostok–Zapad* (*East–West*, 1999), presented the *kommunalka* as a place of suffering, mutual spying, and betrayal. Others, such as Mikhail Kozakov's *Pokrovskie vorota* (*Pokrovskie Gates*, 1982), Pavel Chukhrai's *Vor* (*The Thief*, 1997), and Aleksei German's *Khrustalev, mashinu!* (*Khrustaliov, My Car!*, 1998) showed the *kommunalka*, though still terrifying, through a nostalgic haze.

See also: housing, Soviet and post-Soviet

VLADIMIR PAPERNY

Communist ideology

Inspired by the ideas of Karl Marx and Friedrich Engels, Communist ideology provided the foundation of the 1917 Bolshevik Revolution and the establishment of the Soviet Union. The theory of Marxism states that as capitalist society matures, conflict between the class of owners and the class of workers becomes irreconcilable, and the inevitable result is a 'social revolution'. The revolution replaces private ownership with collectivist ownership, abolishes the division of society into classes, and liberates all oppressed workers by ending the exploitation of labour.

Class struggle is the dynamic force that moves society through stages of history. The term 'class' refers to a group of people within society who share the same social and economic conditions. Communist doctrine explains social classes in terms of their relationship to the means of production.

Marx and Engels's theory of economic determinism contends that all legal, political, and cultural institutions (superstructure) reflect the economic structure and production relations of the society (base). As a result, the people who own the means of production (land, raw materials, tools and machines, labour, and money) dominate not only the economic system, but the social and political systems as well. Political ideologies or philosophies advocated by rulers serve as rationalizations of the existing order.

According to Marx and Engels, all of human history may be reduced to five historical stages. The law of dialectics states that each stage

(thesis) generates its opposite (antithesis), leading to a reconciliation of opposites (synthesis). In other words, each historical stage is the negation of the previous stage. The final stage, communism, is preceded by a period of socialist transformation, in which the means of production are seized from the capitalist class and a temporary, absolute rule by the workers is imposed to prevent any attempts to sabotage the new government.

Leninism

Leninism developed as a result of Vladimir Lenin's efforts to modify the doctrines of Marx and Engels to fit Russian conditions. Lenin believed that the working class on its own would not develop the revolutionary consciousness needed to overthrow the Tsar. As a result, Lenin proposed that a small party of professionals serve as the vanguard of the working class by spreading the revolution and accelerating historical change.

At the beginning of the twentieth century, the Bolsheviks, led by Lenin, advocated immediate and violent revolution to bring about the downfall of capitalism and the establishment of an international socialist state. This seizure of power, rather than economic reform within the framework of capitalism, was an essential component of Leninism. Communist Parties around the world were encouraged to begin revolutions in their own countries.

Another central tenet of Leninism was the notion of the dictatorship of the proletariat, which was equated with rule by the Communist Party. Rather than withering away, the socialist state needed to be strengthened against internal and external enemies.

Lenin's idea of *partiinost* (party-mindedness) meant that academic disciplines were expected to support the Party and its cause. Literature, science, and the arts were required to correspond to the Party's perception of reality or be denounced as idealist or subjective.

Stalinism

The ideology of Marxism-Leninism, coupled with a cult of personality, was used by Stalin to maintain absolute power. Breaking away from

Lenin, Stalin argued that the building of social-ism could be accomplished in the Soviet Union without Communist revolutions in Western Europe. As a result, Stalin's primary goal came to be the building of a true Communist system within the Soviet Union. The emphasis on the revolutionary transformation of a single country departed radically from Marxist internationalism and from the theory of 'permanent revolution', which stressed the necessity of world revolution. Under Stalin's leadership, Communist Parties all over the world were expected to give their loyalty to the Soviet Union as the Workers' Fatherland, and were to accept the leadership of the Communist Party of the Soviet Union.

According to the doctrine of capitalist encir-clement, hostile capitalist countries surrounded the Soviet Union. This justified a programme of forced development of heavy industry and the collectivization of agriculture in order to build socialism. The withering away of the Soviet state was indefinitely delayed, given the condition of capitalist encirclement.

Khrushchev

Nikita Khrushchev denounced the methods of Stalin and called for a return to the principles of Lenin. He launched a full-scale campaign against the cult of personality, arguing that the leader of the Communist Party should not act tyrannically or be worshipped.

Khrushchev also declared an end to Stalin's doctrine of 'capitalist encirclement', on the basis of the rise of the world socialist system and the Soviet Union's enhanced position as a great power. Instead, Khrushchev advanced a doc-trine of 'peaceful coexistence' with Western nations, based on the avoidance of nuclear war while continuing the uncompromising ideologi-cal and economic competition between Com-munist and capitalist states.

Brezhnev

Leonid Brezhnev supported a policy of détente – that is, a relaxation of tensions between the Soviet Union and Western countries, which led to the Nuclear Non-Proliferation Treaty in 1970, Strategic Arms Limitation Talks in 1971, and the signing of the Anti-Ballistic Missile Treaty in May 1972. Détente also resulted in the signing of the 1975 Helsinki Accords on human rights. But even during détente, sig-nificant unease remained between the United States and the Soviet Union.

Brezhnev initiated the Brezhnev Doctrine, which declared that when a threat arises to socialism in any Communist country, that threat could be considered a danger to all Communist countries. Thus, Soviet forces could cross the border into any country to bolster a threatened socialist regime. This doctrine was the rationale for the Soviet invasion of Czechoslovakia in 1968. This foreign policy position rested on appeals to 'socialist internationalism' and 'fra-ternal assistance', evolving naturally from Lenin's commitment to an eventual interna-tional workers revolution, and to Khrushchev's continued support for 'wars of liberation'.

Communist ideology provided a set of concepts for understanding and interpreting the world. Ideology was the language through which the Party informed the populace about current pro-grammes, new initiatives, and official directives. The ideological principles of Communism created a justification for the refusal to share power, for forced collectivization and industrialization, and for the support of revolutionary war.

Marxist-Leninist ideology underwent modifi-cations as successive Soviet leaders manipulated it for their own purposes. The basic core ideas, however, remained relatively constant until the revolutionary challenges ushered in by Mikhail Gorbachev's perestroika and glasnost initiatives.

See also: Brezhnev, Leonid; Communist Party; cult of personality (kult lichnosti); Gorbachev, Mikhail; internationalism; Khrushchev, Nikita; Lenin, Vladimir Ilich; partiinost; perestroika and glasnost; philosophy, Soviet (Marxist-Leni-nist); Stalin, Iosif

Further reading

Furet, F. and Furet, D. (1999) *Passing of an Illusion: The Idea of Communism in the Twentieth Century*, Chicago, IL: University of Chicago Press.
McLellan, D. (ed.) (1988) *Marxism: Essential Writings*, Oxford: Oxford University Press.

VICKI L. HESLI AND JAMES KRUEGER

Communist Party

After Stalin's death, the Communist Party of the Soviet Union (CPSU) remained the nation's sole political party. Although Communist Parties across the East bloc claimed to be the vanguard of the working class, in fact most Party members worked for the state in mostly bureaucratic white-collar positions; they were army officers and civil servants, managers of scientific institutions, and so forth. Despite having 18.9 million members by 1988, the CPSU failed to bring its structure closer to the 'people'. Formally the Party's highest decision-making entity was its Congress, which met every five years. In fact, power in the Party was concentrated in the Politburo and the Secretariat, and particularly in the hands of the Secretary General. The secretive development of CPSU policy (the so-called generalnaia liniia [general line]) persisted from the Thaw period (1956–64) until the Party's demise in the last years of perestroika (1987–90). The accusation levelled by anti-Communist politicians that the CPSU was merely an organized band that had usurped state power bore a striking resemblance to reality.

The main event in the history of the Party after Stalin's death was the 20th Party Congress (14–25 February 1956); there the Party for the first time accepted responsibility for mass repressions of the 1920s and 1930s. Nikita Khrushchev delivered a 'secret speech', the contents of which were revealed to the Soviet public only thirty years later; this speech marked the end of the Stalin era in Soviet history as a period of mass terror. The declared intention of moving from the Stalinist 'cult of personality' to 'collective leadership' was not realized, however, for the structure and the organizational principle of the Party, 'democratic centralism', remained in essence the same as it had been under Stalin. Between 1953 and 1955, Khrushchev won the battle with Stalin's immediate followers for the leadership of the Party and the state and initiated the so-called Thaw.

The 22nd Party Congress of October 1961 proclaimed, along with a 'return to Leninist norms', the achievement of communism in the Soviet Union within the next twenty years. The following three decades witnessed the Party's gradual decline, however. Although Party membership continued to grow, the structure of its leadership, which sought to keep full control of state and society, did not change. The gradual erosion of the CPSU's power began in two directions, the first of which was outside the borders of the USSR. After the secret speech of 1956, the Communist Parties of China, Albania, and Romania slowly moved beyond the CPSU's reach. After the suppression of the Hungarian uprising (1956) and of the Prague Spring (1968), the relatively liberal Communist Parties of Europe which had been CPSU satellites began to turn away. Their emancipation from the CPSU led to a movement known as 'euro-communism', which attracted a large percentage of Italian, Spanish, and French communists.

In October 1964, Khrushchev handed over power within the Party to a group headed by Leonid Brezhnev (1906–82). In the years of 'gerontocracy' under Brezhner's leadership (1964–82) and those of Iurii Andropov (1982–84), and Konstantin Chernenko (1984–85), the Party leadership increasingly acquired grotesque features, and it could exercise only limited control in the country's economic and cultural life. Attempts to exert such control included those of Mikhail Suslov (1902–82; Politburo member since 1966), chief Party ideologist and successor of Stalin's cultural leader Andrei Zhdanov (1896–1948), to tighten ideological control, including a revision of de-Stalinization, new encouragement of a cult of leaders, and right wing-conservative chauvinism. Although according to the Constitution of 1977 the CPSU was the 'leading and organising force of Soviet society', towards the end of the 1960s autocratic power in the CPSU was again concentrated in the hands of the Secretary General.

After Chernenko's death in April 1985, Mikhail Gorbachev (b. 1931) was elected Secretary General. His election took place in a traditional secret voting process, during which the plenary session of the Central Committee chose the candidate proposed by the members of the Politburo. While failing to organize the CPSU along democratic lines, Gorbachev proceeded to reform the state structure of the USSR; however, his first steps toward 'democratization' and 'openness' (glasnost) brought about an even greater diminishment of the CP's role as a governing party. At the same time, some of the most active Party members succeeded in gaining both greater political influence and control of many of Russian economic and natural resources. This combination of new power and influence brought about the leadership of the first president of the Russian Federation, Boris Yeltsin, who expelled from the Kremlin the first and last president of the USSR, Gorbachev.

Yeltsin allowed the co-existence of multiple parties in the Russian Federation and thus undermined the legitimacy of the Communist Party, and membership no longer helped advance people's careers. The short period during which the CP's activities were prohibited – after a failed attempt of 19–21 August 1991 to remove Gorbachev and re-establish the USSR – led to the emergence of several competing communist parties in Russia. The largest of these, the Communist Party of the Russian Federation (CPRF), chaired by Gennadii Ziuganov, forms a small fraction in the Russian Duma. The new party *Edinaia Rossiia* (United Russia), in existence since 2000, is acquiring some external features of the CPRF and sometimes reverts to Soviet organizational models. At the same time, since the end of the 1990s Russia has witnessed a growing interest in the Communist history of the USSR, as well as the emergence of a number of Communist social and political organizations, such as the *Natsional-Bolsheviki* (National Bolsheviks).

See also: Andropov, Iurii; Brezhnev, Leonid; Coup, August 1991; cult of personality; Duma; East Bloc countries; economic system, Soviet; economic system, post-Soviet; Gorbachev, Mikhail; Khrushchev, Nikita; natural resources; perestroika and glasnost; political parties, post-Soviet; Stagnation; Stalin, Iosif; Thaw; United Russia; Yeltsin, Boris

Further reading

Avtorchanov, A. (1959) *Stalin and the Soviet Communist Party: A Study in the Technology of Power*, Munich: Institute for the Study of the USSR.

Graham, L. (1967) *The Soviet Academy of Sciences and the Communist Party, 1927–1932*, Princeton, NJ: Princeton University Press.

Mawdsley, E. and White, S. (2000) *The Soviet Elite from Lenin to Gorbachev: The Central Committee and its Members, 1917–1991*, Oxford: Oxford University Press.

Nor-Mesek, N. and Rieper, W. (1987) *Politburo: Leading Organs of the Central Committee of Communist Party of the Soviet Union and Leading Party Organs of the Republics*, Frankfurt-am-Main: ISOS, Institut für Sowjet-Studien.

GASAN GUSEJNOV

Communist Youth League (Komsomol)

Komsomol is the abbreviation for the 'communist union of youth', generally called the Communist Youth League in English; it also had the acronym *VLKSM* (All-Union Lenin Communist Youth League). The Komsomol was established in 1918 by the Communist Party for 14–28-year-olds. Komsomol members were expected to be politically conscious, vigilant, and loyal to the Communist cause. The Komsomol quickly expanded: with 22,100 members at its inception, in 1941 it had more than 10 million, and in the 1980s more than 42 million members. The overwhelming majority of Soviet youth joined the Komsomol, and the few nonconformists refusing to do so were regarded as black sheep. All members had to observe the rules, attend meetings, and pay monthly membership dues. Violation of these rules often resulted in expulsion from the Komsomol, followed by a ruined career and, during Stalin's purges, by imprisonment and exile.

The history of the Komsomol is embodied in a series of ideological campaigns and mass youth projects promoted by Party authorities, such as a campaign against illiteracy and a competition for best industrial worker (*udarnik*) in the 1920s and 1930s. During World War II the organization engaged in the mobilization of youth. Post-war priorities included industrial restoration of the country and recruiting man-power for large-scale industrial projects, such as factory construction and *tselina*, the Virgin Lands Campaign. The last such project was the construction of BAM, the Baikal-Amur Railroad, in the 1970s and the 1980s.

The organizational structure of the Komsomol duplicated that of the Communist Party.

The primary units existed at industrial enterprises and educational institutions, on collective farms, and in army divisions. Komsomol committees elected at general membership meetings carried out the management of such units. Each unit reported to its local district committee, which in turn answered to the city or oblast committee. The highest body was the VLKSM Central Committee.

Komsomol activity encompassed all spheres of social life: work and study, maintenance of order, community volunteer work (such as clean-up Saturdays at work and school, called *subbotniki*), and leisure (sports, arts and entertainment). The Komsomol's objective was to maintain a mythological image of a positive hero that would appeal to youth. Komsomol congresses were arranged as typical Communist-style shows with banners, anthems, reports, greetings, amateur and professional performances, and awards.

Two novels hold a special place in Komsomol mythology: Nikolai Ostrovskii's *Kak zakalialas stal* (*How the Steel Was Tempered*, 1934) and Aleksandr Fadeev's *Molodaia gvardiia* (*Young Guard*, 1946). The hero of the former, Komsomol member Pavel Korchagin, fights in the Red Army during the Civil War, participates in railroad construction, and finally, blind, severely ill, and bed-ridden, becomes a writer. The characters of the latter novel are participants in the underground resistance in one of the southern towns of Russia under German occupation. Both novels were in the secondary school curriculum, and their characters' names were given to streets, steamships, and cultural centres. The Komsomol owned a network of periodicals (including the newspaper *Komsomolskaia Pravda* and the journal *Iunost* [Youth]) and a number of large publishing houses (including Molodaia gvardiia).

From the 1960s till the 1980s, Komsomol carried out administrative functions along with ideological ones: The Komsomol committee's consent was obligatory for placement at work, graduate study, or travel abroad. The decline of the Komsomol began in the mid-1980s. It dissolved in the early 1990s with the fall of the Soviet Union.

See also: Communist Party; subbotnik; tselina

Further reading

(1965) *Slavnyi put leninskogo komsomola: Ukazatel literatury*, Moscow.
(1966–68) *Istoriia VLKSM: Zhivaia letopis*, Moscow.
(1969) *Leninskii komsomol: Ocherki po istorii VLKSM*, Moscow.

ALEXANDER LEDENEV

complaints book (kniga zhalob)

Kniga zhalob i predlozhenii (book of complaints and suggestions) was used in the USSR to record complains to authorities about inefficiency, violations of established rules and standards, or failure to fulfil work obligations. Complaints books were first introduced at railway stations and shipyards, then in shops and service enterprises (e.g., dry cleaners, shoe repair and tailor shops), and exist to this day. Recorded complaints are sent to higher authorities for investigation and may result in penalties: in Soviet times employees could be denied a holiday or monetary bonus or could lose their jobs. Nowadays privately owned small businesses providing a service could be fined or deprived of their licence.

SVETLANA TITKOVA

Conceptualism, art

An art movement that began in the United States, Europe, and Latin America in the 1960s, Conceptualism privileged the concept of art over its execution in order to reexamine art's validity. With strong interest in linguistics, Conceptualist artists addressed the structuring of realities through language.

Conceptualism appeared in Russia in the early 1970s and continued to be a major factor in nonconformist art until the USSR's collapse. Russian Conceptualism is distinguished by a concentration on the particular uses of language in the USSR and the realities of everyday life there. While Conceptualism in the West requires the viewer's intellectual engagement for its success, Russian Conceptualism additionally requires a knowledge of Soviet history, politics, culture, etc.

Artists such as Ilia Kabakov, Vitalii Komar and Aleksandr Melamid, Irina Nakhova, Dmitrii Prigov, and Svetlana Kopystianskaia dealt specifically with the constant presence of official language in the daily environment. Their use of text in art also recalls the early Soviet avant-garde. In these artists' works, Soviet propaganda is placed in a new context in order to highlight its function in shaping perception. For Kabakov, even the banal exchanges of communal apartment life become loaded with existential concerns.

Russian Conceptual artists initially worked in small, easy-to-conceal albums, drawings, and paintings. Another favoured format was the performance, in which the concept drives the action, which becomes the artwork. During perestroika, the artists switched to large-scale installations and paintings that quickly attracted international attention.

See also: art, nonconformist; Kabakov, Ilia; Komar and Melamid; Nakhova, Irina; Prigov, Dmitrii

Further reading

Ross, D. (ed.) (1990) *Between Spring and Summer: Soviet Conceptual Art in the Era of Late Communism*, Boston, MA: Institute of Contemporary Art.
Tupitsyn, M. (1995) 'On Some Sources of Soviet Conceptualism', in A. Rosenfeld and N. Dodge (eds) *Nonconformist Art: The Soviet Experience 1956–1986*, New York: Thames and Hudson.

KRISTEN M. HARKNESS

Conceptualism, literary

A global artistic movement, Conceptualism reached Russia in the early 1970s. Taking root in Moscow's nonconformist art world, it developed into an original school in both visual arts and literature. Its leading literary exponents include the poets Dmitrii Prigov and Lev Rubinshtein and the prose writer Vladimir Sorokin. Conceptualist writing has an investigative

bent; it focuses on the often unconsciously absorbed ideas underlying everyday human behaviour, on the ways culture and language operate in human society and in which they shape our consciousness. Russian Conceptualist literature has focused chiefly on the fossilized official forms of Stagnation-era Soviet culture and on behavioural and verbal stereotypes of Soviet citizens. Conceptualism registers individual writer-investigators' profound alienation from their verbal environment in works that reproduce the consciousness of individual characters (Prigov), fragments of everyday speech (Rubinshtein), or clichéd discourses of literary genres (Sorokin). Their recognizable forms are ruptured through being stretched to the limits of the absurd (Prigov), through contrapuntal juxtaposition (Rubinshtein) or seamless incorporation of verbally and physically transgressive elements (Sorokin). Although Conceptualist writers encountered extreme difficulties with publishing their work well into the early 1990s, they are now recognized among the leading figures of the Russian literary world.

See also: art, nonconformist; Prigov, Dmitrii; Rubinshtein, Lev; Sorokin, Vladimir; Stagnation

Further reading

Epstein, M., Genis, A. and Vladiv-Glover, S. (1999) *Russian Postmodernism: New Perspectives on Post-Soviet Culture*, New York: Berghahn Books.

VITALY CHERNETSKY

constitutions

The three constitutions (1936, 1977, and 1993) that structured first Soviet and then Russian politics in the modern era all established a strong, centralized executive system and generated a great deal of controversy for failing to deliver to its citizens the promises made on paper.

The Stalin Constitution, as it is commonly called, became law on 5 December 1936. It revised the federal structure of the USSR by granting more power to Moscow to rule over the eleven union republics of other autonomous regions. The 1936 constitution also granted basic civil rights to the Soviet population. According to the language of the document, all Soviet citizens enjoyed universal suffrage and were entitled to benefits such as free secondary education and the right to work. This aspect of the Stalin Constitution has generated a great deal of debate ever since, for the government largely ignored these rights, and many critics have viewed the Stalin Constitution as mere propaganda. Other scholars have argued that the 1936 constitution allowed Soviet citizens to become familiar with a new political language and eventually opened up avenues for complaints to the authorities.

The 1977 or Brezhnev Constitution replaced Stalin's. It also contained contradictory messages and did not differ substantially from the 1936 version. While some scholars have argued that the document enshrined de-Stalinization by acknowledging that legal norms existed, for many Soviet citizens these rights once again existed only on paper. The constitution became known above all for Article Six, which stated that the Communist Party was 'the leading and guiding force of the Soviet society' and 'exists for the people and serves the people', statements many viewed as hollow. The most significant political aspects of the document only emerged after Mikhail Gorbachev successfully passed major amendments in the late 1980s. These changes provided for freer elections and abolished the special position of the Communist Party. The Brezhnev Constitution therefore became the unintended means by which Gorbachev hastened the USSR's political collapse.

After 1991, little consensus existed on the formal means to govern the Russian Federation. The battle over a new constitution led to the first serious political crisis of the Yeltsin era. Facing an impasse over the basic structure of the government, Yeltsin dissolved parliament in September 1993, an act he admitted violated the still-functioning Soviet constitution. His opponents holed themselves up in the White House and pledged to resist any document that granted extraordinary presidential powers. Yeltsin responded by ordering an attack (4 October 1993) that killed at least 150. Afterwards, Yeltsin oversaw ratification of a new constitution in December 1993 and established a 'super-presidential' system that remains in force. For many Russians, however, the image of the smoldering White House remained a powerful symbol for the ineffectiveness of the Russian governing system in general and the Yeltsin Constitution in particular.

See also: Brezhnev, Leonid; Communist Party; Duma; Gorbachev, Mikhail; propaganda; Russian Federation; Stalin, Iosif; Yeltsin, Boris

Further reading

Davies, S. (1997) *Popular Opinion in Stalin's Russia: Terror, Propaganda, and Dissent, 1934–1941*, Cambridge: Cambridge University Press.
Getty, J. A. (1991) 'State and Society under Stalin: Constitutions and Elections in the 1930s', *Slavic Review*, 50, 1: 18–35.
Remington, T. (2001) *The Russian Parliament: Institutional Evolution in a Transitional Regime, 1989–1999*, New Haven, CT: Yale University Press.
Sharlet, R. (1992) *Soviet Constitutional Crisis: From De-Stalinization to Disintegration*, Armonk, NY: M. E. Sharpe.

STEPHEN M. NORRIS

corporate governance

Corporate governance involves overseeing the power and responsibility of corporate entities. It addresses the concerns of those who provide capital to companies, particularly regarding the risk associated with investing in a firm, evaluating its capital allocation policies, and monitoring how its capital is managed over time. Corporate governance also includes enterprise issues such as the composition and responsibilities of boards of directors, the necessity for companies to disclose accurate, consolidated, and timely information using international standards and verified by independent auditors, and a charter stipulating relationships between the board and senior management.

Russia's problems of nondisclosure and nontransparency have made the country one of the riskiest for investment. In the early 2000s, leaders in government, business, and nongovernmental organizations realized that change was needed if Russia were to attract investment to invigorate its emerging market economy. Their efforts resulted in the Code of Corporate Conduct, promulgated in 2002 by the Federal Commission for the Securities Market. Although voluntary, it was largely supported by Russian law and was based on standards developed by international groups including the Organization for Economic Cooperation and Development and the World Economic Forum. The code initially applied to large publicly owned companies, but was expected to be adopted by other firms when they needed to acquire outside financing. The code was based primarily on the Anglo-American model of agency theory, which recognizes the primacy of the rights of all shareholders, rights that had suffered flagrant abuses throughout the 1990s. Corporate governance concepts and practices, including the provisions of the code, became more widespread in the early 2000s, particularly among large firms, but were still foreign to many companies. Although the Anglo-American model provided a quick start for corporate governance, the system might well evolve to better reflect the unique Russian context.

See also: economic system, post-Soviet; privatization

Further reading

Jesover, F. (2001) 'Corporate Governance in the Russian Federation: The Relevance of the OECD Principles on Shareholder Rights and Equitable Treatment', *Corporate Governance: An International Review*, 9, 2: 79–88.
McCarthy, D., Puffer, S. and Shekshnia, S. (eds) (2004) *Corporate Governance in Russia*, Cheltenham: Edward Elgar.

DANIEL J. MCCARTHY AND SHEILA M. PUFFER

corrective labour institutions (ispravitelno-trudovye uchrezhdeniia)

This term refers to camps and colonies where prisoners are forced to perform what is usually unskilled, manual labour with the professed goal of re-education. In pre-revolutionary Russia these institutions originated in the notorious tsarist system of *katorga* (forced labour). Under Stalin, the camp system would become known as the GULag (*Glavnoe upravlenie ispravitelno-trudovykh lagerei* [Main Administration for Corrective Labour Camps]). Although officially created to rehabilitate prisoners, the GULag was in reality an important part of the national economy designed to provide cheap labour. Of the estimated 25 million prisoners of the Stalinist period, 3.6 million were sentenced to the labour camps for so-called 'political' crimes, of which the vast majority of prisoners were innocent.

The camps were located across the country, even in the Far North, an area rich in mineral deposits and timber, but with a severe climate: wintertime temperatures fall below −60 degrees Fahrenheit (−37 Celsius). Clothing, shelter, and medical care were completely inadequate for the prisoners, who were often forced to work up to fourteen hours a day, seven days a week, usually in mines, quarries, or cutting timber. Food was allocated according to productivity. Those unable to meet the often impossible norms were put on starvation rations. More than 1.6 million perished, almost half of them in the first two years of World War II.

When it was revealed after Stalin's death in 1953 that the camps were not profitable, many were closed, and the majority of prisoners were released. Labour camps remained the preferred form of incarceration, but their economic function was now secondary to isolation and punishment. Conditions in the camps remained poor, particularly with regard to basic hygiene, medical care, nutrition, and treatment by the guards. The camp population, which was drastically reduced in the 1950s, again increased in the Brezhnev period. Many political prisoners in the 1970s were active dissidents, such as Andrei Siniavskii, Iulii Daniel, and Anatolii Marchenko.

The post-Soviet government has attempted to improve life in the camps (now called 'correctional colonies' [*ispravitelnye kolonii*] and bring it up to European standards. Their goal is both rehabilitation and public security (Oleinik 2003: 49)). Physical abuse is officially prohibited, although there are still reports of it, particularly from the early 1990s. Rewards and punishments are tied to behaviour, rather than production norms. Work is voluntary and remunerated, but job shortages make it impossible for some prisoners to purchase necessities. Basic living conditions have not improved. Inmates are housed in large communal cells, which are severely overcrowded. Diseases such as AIDS and tuberculosis are rampant, and food shortages are common. Although they are mainly the result of funding shortfalls rather than official malice, these problems reflect the public priorities of a nation with a long history of disregard for the human rights of its inmates.

See also: GULag

Further reading

Applebaum, A. (2003) *Gulag: A History*, New York: Doubleday.

Jakobson, M. (1993) *Origins of the GULAG: The Soviet Prison Camp System 1917–1934*, Lexington, KY: The University Press of Kentucky.

Oleinik, A. (2003) *Organized Crime, Prison and Post-Soviet Societies*, trans. S. Curtis, Burlington, VT: Ashgate.

LAURA KLINE

Cossacks

Descended from Tatars or runaway serfs, Cossacks (a Tatar word for horsemen) settled in steppes along the Don and, later, the Dnieper, Terek, and Ural Rivers. Known for their brutal treatment of opponents, Cossacks formed an equestrian society whose service and loyalty Russian tsars purchased in exchange for concessions of land, immunity from taxes, and limited independence. From Ivan the Terrible on, tsars engaged Cossack warriors, most notably Yermak, to protect and extend the Russian empire along its frontiers, and, later, to ensure internal security. Cossacks rebels, including Stenka Razin and Emilian Pugachev, threatened the very existence of the state.

The courage and independence of these horsemen, festooned in cartridge belts and armed with sabres, were romanticized in Russian literature from Pushkin, Gogol, and Tolstoi to Sholokhov; in music from Mussorgskii to Shostakovich; and in painting, particularly by Repin. Stalin considered Cossacks a dangerous aberration and enemy of collectivization. Persecution of Cossacks continued almost until the 1990s, when Yeltsin reinstated their special status. Today over 4.5 million people (excluding émigré communities) identify themselves as Cossacks. The centre of Cossack culture is the city of Rostov-on-Don, where the revitalization of Cossack culture includes the reintroduction of ceremonial costumes, religious rites of Eastern Orthodoxy, Cossack unions, and military units of conscripted Cossack reservists.

See also: Sholokhov, Mikhail; steppe; Tatars; Yeltsin, Boris

Further reading

Ure, J. (2002) *The Cossacks: An Illustrated History*, New York: Overlook Press.

VLADIMIR STRUKOV

costume design, theatre

Stalin's death in 1953 prompted hope for the rejuvenation of Soviet theatrical design, which, apart from a short period of great innovation during the 1920s (subsequently condemned as decadent and bourgeois), was bleak and predictable. The sole exceptions were the lavish costumes designed by Simon Versaladze for the Bolshoi Theatre. The Thaw allowed for supervised experimentation: as new theatres such as the Sovremennik, Taganka, Bronnaia, and BDT opened, a number of talented young designers emerged: Valentin Dorer, Valerii Levental, David Borovskii, Oleg Sheintsis, and Georgii Aleksi-Meskhishvili. This short period of theatrical flowering was followed by years of stagnation, during which any attempt at innovative creativity was curbed. Despite the absence of restrictions in post-Soviet Russia, no new major talent in theatrical costume design has yet emerged. Instead, various designers largely attempt to revive the long-suppressed avant-garde traditions of the 1920s, as exemplified by the work of Pavel Kopelevich and of the successful and inventive costume designer Ksenia Shimanovskaia, both members of the generation of 40–50 year-olds.

See also: Malaia Bronnaia Theatre; Sovremennik Theatre; Taganka Theatre; Thaw; theatre, post-Soviet; theatre, Soviet; Tovstonogov Bolshoi Drama Theatre (BDT)

REGINA KOZAKOVA

Coup, August 1991

On 18 August 1991, Soviet Union Vice Pre-sident Gennadii Ianaev and other members of the Soviet government announced a takeover of Mikhail Gorbachev's presidential power. The *putsch* (coup) was precipitated by the crisis-like downturn in the Soviet economy and by the prospect of the break-up of the Soviet Empire. The coup plotters forcibly detained Gorbachev at his summer home in the Crimea, and ordered Soviet security forces to take control of Moscow. Boris Yeltsin, President of the Russian Soviet Federated Socialist Republic (RSFSR), con-demned the coup and rallied resistance around the Russian parliament building.

The coup failed because of strategic mistakes: the plotters failed to arrest Boris Yeltsin, and did not ensure the army's and KGB's compliance with their orders. Refusing to fire on civilians, army units defected to the resistance. The lea-ders of many republics and foreign states also opposed the coup plotters by not recognizing the new government. Additionally, the per-estroika, glasnost, and *demokratizatsiia* (democra-tization) reforms that had taken hold in Russia and other parts of the Soviet Union contributed to the coup's failure. People opposed any possibility of a return to dictatorship.

In the aftermath of the attempted coup, Gorbachev never recovered his authority, for his own ministers had orchestrated the plot. By contrast, Yeltsin's unyielding resistance to the hard-line members of Gorbachev's government increased his popularity. With the crisis resolved, Yeltsin, as the legitimately and popu-larly elected President of the RSFSR, filled the power vacuum. Yeltsin also banned the activities of the Communist Party in the Russian Federation and confiscated Party property.

See also: Communist Party; economic system, Soviet; Gorbachev, Mikhail; perestroika and glasnost; Russian Federation; Yeltsin, Boris

Further reading

Suny, R. (1998) *The Soviet Experiment*, Oxford: Oxford University Press.

VICKI L. HESLI AND JAMES KRUEGER

crime

Crime is a socially dangerous action (or non-action) for which the Criminal Code of the Russian Federation stipulates a corresponding punishment. The Code distinguishes not only among various degrees of crime – petty, mid-dling, serious, and especially heinous – but also among categories: crimes against an individual; economic crimes; ones against public safety and social order; against state authorities, against the military; and against peace and the safety of humanity.

Incommensurate responses to the degree of social danger represented by a given crime remain a key characteristic of Russian society and its law enforcement system. Torture or abuse of suspects at police stations, which is widespread in post-Soviet Russia, is but one form of illegal practices among representatives of power-wielding authorities towards delin-quency.

For many years, theft has been the most frequent type of crime (with more than 150,000 instances already recorded in the beginning of 2005). Until 2003, when new amendments to the Criminal Code mitigated the terms, even minors were sentenced to three or more years of imprisonment for petty larceny. Until a similar amendment was introduced in 2004, drug users and petty drug dealers also received unreason-ably long sentences. Currently, more than 40,000 convicts are in prison on drug charges.

The 'especially heinous' and 'serious' degrees of crime constitute the largest percentage of crimes. They include murder (more than 100,000 sentenced in 2005), robbery (more than 50,000 in 2005), and brigandage (more than 80,000 in 2005). Russia's high level of crime is directly connected to the economic and social problems of large segments of the population today. Crimes against an individual often are committed against battered women: according to 2003 data, annually 14,000 women are killed by their husbands; up to 2,000 commit suicide. In 2003, over 140,000 crimes committed by minors or with their participation were registered – a number unlikely to decrease in the near future, according to Iakov Gilinskii, a leading Russian sociologist. Major factors contributing to this phenomenon include young people's participation in local conflicts, an increase in adolescent victims, hazing in the army, and the steadily expanding gap between incomes and opportunities of the super-rich minority and of the impoverished majority of the population.

Crimes committed by organized criminal groups constitute a separate category. In recent years the media increasingly have reported on criminal groups' involvement with government and power structures. According to an estimate of independent experts (INDEM Fund), the scale of corruption in Russia represents a national threat, for the annual turnover of bribes currently totals approximately 40 billion dollars.

Since the Chechen War began, acts of terrorism have become common in Russia, the two largest and deadliest being the hostage crisis in a Moscow theatre (*Nord-Ost*, 2002) and the capture of a school in the North Ossetian city of Beslan (2004). The Chechen War, which started in 1994, generates additional crimes on the part of insurgents as well as federal forces. According to the evidence of human rights organizations such as Helsinki Watch and Memorial, major crimes committed by federal forces in Chechnia include the practice of 'filtration camps', kidnapping, and executions without trial.

The question of capital punishment for major crimes, including terrorism, remains under discussion in Russia. Though the moratorium on carrying out the executions, *de facto* since 1996, is currently in effect, Russia has yet to ratify Protocol No. 6 of the European Human Rights Convention. More than 60 per cent of the country's population supports the death penalty.

See also: corrective labour institutions; economic system, post-Soviet; Helsinki Group; human rights organizations; Memorial; militia (police); *Nord-Ost*; prison system, Soviet and post-Soviet; War, Chechen

ELENA OZNOBKINA

Crimea

An autonomous republic in the south of Ukraine, the Crimea (*Krym*) is situated on the Crimean peninsula (26,100 sq km) jutting out into the Black Sea and the Sea of Azov. The population of the Crimea is 2.03 million people (2001), of which 58.3 per cent are Russian, 24.3 per cent are Ukrainian, and 12 per cent are Crimean Tatar. the official languages of the autonomous republic are Russian, Ukrainian, and Crimean Tatar. since the first millennium BC, many ethnic groups and cultures have left traces of their presence on the peninsula (e.g., Cimmerians, Scythians, Greeks, Romans, Slavs, Karaites, and Italians). The Crimea became part of Russia in 1783, when the Russian Empire annexed the peninsula from Turkey, but was transferred to the Ukrainian SSR in 1954. In 1944, when the peninsula was liberated from the Nazi invaders, the Crimean Tatars were accused of collaboration with the enemy and deported en masse to Central Asia. They began to return to their ancestral homeland during perestroika. The Crimea is known for its machine engineering, agriculture, winemaking, and food-processing industry. The region's natural beauty and mild climate have made it a traditional holiday destination for millions of tourists. The sea ports of varying strategic and economic importance include Kerch, Feodosiia, Yalta, Sevastopol, and Evpatoriia. The capital of the Crimea is Simferopol.

See also: Central Asia; Tatars; Ukraine; World War II (Great Patriotic War)

ELENA BARABAN

Cuban missile crisis

See: Cold War

cult of personality (kult lichnosti)

First identified as anathema to Marxism-Leninism by Marx and Engels, the 'cult of personality' played an important role in Stalinism and post-Stalinism for two diametrically opposed reasons. In the Stalin era, it was usual for party leaders, including Stalin himself, to engage in elaborate rituals of denial that the Stalinist system, complete with its equally elaborate rituals of devotion to the leader, constituted a cult. The word *kult* appeared in Stalinist discourse only to denote religion and the fight against it. In the Khrushchev era, on the other hand, the politics of de-Stalinization required that the Stalin era be redefined as the 'era of the cult of personality' (*epokha kulta lichnosti*). The term, directly attached to Stalin in the title of Khrushchev's secret speech of February 1956 and in the Communist Party Central Committee resolution 'On the Consequences of the Cult of Personality', issued in July of the same year, sounded both scientific and de-personalized. It lent an objective, generalizing air to the personal attacks on Stalin, and when the latter abated (between 1956 and 1961, and again during the Brezhnev era), the use of the term effectively silenced further debate or historical revelations about Stalinism, in line with the new, conservative party policy on the Stalinist past.

See also: Brezhnev, Leonid; Communist Party; Khrushchev, Nikita; Stagnation; Stalin, Iosif; Thaw

POLLY JONES

D

dacha

A simple residence usually located well outside the metropolitan area of large cities, the dacha represents a return to nature, the opportunity for outdoor exercise as well as rest, and offers the lure of fresh produce, opportunities for picking wild berries and mushrooms, and a community of friends and neighbours. The dacha developed from workers' cooperatives, which required participants to tend their own plots and were intended as a partial solution in times of inadequate food supply. Most families have extensive garden plots at their dachas, and each summer weekend, from early May well into September, witnesses a huge exodus of people laden with building and gardening equipment, weekend provisions and supplies, to the dacha and then back to the city to resume the work week. Those who do not have to spend the summer in the city, such as pensioners and children out of school, often remain at the dacha for months. Older dachas tend to be simple wooden affairs suited only to summer habitation, most with no plumbing and some with no electricity. With the development of a more well-to-do middle class, many families have renovated their dachas, while the newly affluent have built deluxe structures resembling castles, which can function as year-round residences ironically called 'cottages' (*kotedzhi*).

See also: housing, Soviet and post-Soviet; vacations, Soviet and post-Soviet

DAVID J. GALLOWAY

Dagestan

A crossroads of civilizations since ancient times, Dagestan is the largest, southernmost Republic of the Russian Federation, located on the eastern slopes of the Caucasus bordering the Caspian Sea. Some forty distinct languages are spoken within a population of about two million. In a conversion movement beginning in the seventh century, Islam became the dominant faith. Imam Shamil led a united opposition to annexation into the Russian Empire in the Caucasian War, a conflict inspiring important works by Lermontov and Tolstoi in the nineteenth century. Dagestan's own rich literary tradition, particularly in poetry, was revived in works by Avarian poet Rasul Gamzatov (1923–2003).

See also: Caucasus; Islam

BYRON LINDSEY

dairy products

Traditional Russian cuisine includes many cultured dairy products, which are considered beneficial to one's health. *Smetana* is a kind of sour cream, traditionally made of the top cream skimmed off soured non-pasteurized milk. It is used as a garnish for soups, in cooking, or eaten in a glass with sugar or jam at breakfast. *Prostokvasha* (literally 'simply soured') is soured clotted milk, similar to buttermilk. *Riazhenka* is sour clotted milk that has been baked. In the post-Soviet period, yogurt (*iogurt*) has become popular and is now produced domestically.

Cheese forms an important part of the Russian diet. Russian cheeses, except for *tvorog*, are generally hard and mild. Similarly hard, mild European cheeses such as Jarlsberg, Gouda, and Emmenthal, have become popular in post-Soviet Russia. *Tvorog* is pot cheese, made from *prostokvasha* that has been heated, sieved, and pressed. It is eaten alone, often with sugar or jam, and used widely in cooking. *Tvorog* forms the basis for a number of sweets: *syrnik* is a small, thick pancake, made primarily of *tvorog* and flour; *vatrushka* is a light, open, sweet roll, filled with sweetened *tvorog*. *Plavlenyi syr* refers to a variety of soft processed cheese spreads, served on bread or used in cooking.

Some dairy products popular in Russia come from bordering countries. *Kefir*, often drunk at breakfast, is a drink made of fermented cow's milk, originally from the Caucasus. *Kumys* is fermented mare's milk, mildly alcoholic, from the Tartar and Central Asian regions. Before the Revolution it was used to treat tuberculosis.

In the late Soviet period, *sgushchennoe moloko* (sweetened condensed milk), commonly called *sgushchenka*, was a prized foodstuff in times of shortages (*defifsit*), and often included in *zakazy*.

Certain Russian regions are associated with milk products: Vologda is traditionally famed for its high-quality sweet butter. *Mozhaiskoe moloko* (Mozhaisk milk) is sterilized, long-lasting milk, sold in bottles.

See also: Asian cuisine; Caucasian cuisine; *Kremlevskii paek (zakaz)*

MICHELE BERDY

Dal, Oleg Ivanovich

b. 25 May 1941, Liublino, Moscow region; d. 3 March 1981, Kiev

Actor

Dal became an actor initially against the wishes of his working-class family. His first film was alongside other recent acting school graduates Andrei Mironov and Aleksandr Zbruev in *Moi*

mladshii brat (My Younger Brother, 1962), Aleksandr Zarkhi's adaptation of Vasilii Aksenov's 1961 novel *Zvezdnyi bilet* (*Ticket to the Stars*). A star of Moscow's Sovremennik and Malyi Theatres in the 1960s and the 1970s, Dal was most noted in film for his performance as the Fool in Kozintsev's *Korol Lir* (*King Lear*, 1971), whom he played as a Russian 'holy fool' who knows the fundamental truth of the world, and who helps a deranged Lear regain his sanity.

See also: holy fool; Kozintsev, Grigorii; Malyi Theatre; Mironov, Andrei; Sovremennik Theatre; Zarkhi, Aleksandr

DAVID GILLESPIE

dance

In the Soviet Union, dance culture was well developed, but restricted by various ideological taboos. Classical ballet dancers from the Bolshoi and Mariinskii (former Kirov) Theatres topped the national lists of stars. In the 1930s, choreographer Igor Moiseev developed a new genre, combining ethnic dance with ballet and created his famous Ensemble of Folk Dance, which today continues to enjoy triumphs worldwide. Dozens of professional dance ensembles that subsequently emerged in the Soviet Union followed his example: the Moldavian Jok; the Virskii Ukrainian Dance Ensemble; the Georgian State Dance Company, founded by Nina Ramishvili and Iliko Sukhishvili, and others.

Professional dance schools, such as the Moscow, St. Petersburg, and Perm choreographic schools, were extremely selective and produced first-class performers. Rigorous ballet training made Soviet rhythmic gymnasts and figure skaters virtually unbeatable. Soviet parades featured remarkable, technically challenging gymnastic performances that blended dance and acrobatics; circus acrobatic performances are also distinguished by strong balletic technique. However, certain genres of choreography were banned as symptomatic of bourgeois Western culture. Soviet theatres excluded modern dance performances and plotless avant-garde ballets from repertoires. Popular Western dances, such as swing, rock-n-roll, and all kinds of 'exotic dancing', such as belly dancing and striptease, were prohibited.

Social dancing included ethnic dances, ballroom dances, and constantly changing contemporary trends in club dancing. In the Soviet era, public dance parties were called *tantsy* (dances); they were organized at clubs, houses of culture, parks, youth camps, and schools, under the strict supervision of the authorities, who oversaw not only security issues, but also music selection and 'moral standards in performance' (maintaining 'appropriate' distance from one's partner, not making overly suggestive body movements, etc.). Adults had opportunities for social dance primarily in restaurants, often with a live band. Whereas major family celebrations in large cities took place in restaurants, in villages weddings and other festive occasions usually were scheduled in the summer months, so that the party could be outdoors or in a local club. Particularly popular in Russian social dancing were pseudo-folk dances, such as the Russian *barynia*, the Gypsy *tsyganochka*, and the Caucasian *lezginka*. Among ballroom dances the waltz prevailed, but in the 1960s, young people preferred more 'democratic', less structured dances, such as the twist and the shake, to partner dances.

Soviet authorities did everything possible to keep the influx of capitalist culture at bay. When Igor Moiseev's dance company performed a rock-n-roll number during its first US tour (1958) fearing Soviet censorship, it announced it as 'a parody'. Authorities accepted Soviet ballroom dancing, which in the 1960s was considered a form of sport, largely to offset young people's enthusiasm for new Western dances. During the Stagnation era, the standard European (waltz, tango, foxtrot) and Latin American (cha-cha-cha, rumba) ballroom dance programmes were 'enriched' by a 'Soviet' programme, which included the polka, *rylio* (Lithuanian swing), *sudarushka* (a slow Russian lyrical dance), and other artificially created dances.

During and after perestroika Soviet youth could openly learn and dance disco, rock-n-roll, and break dance, which in the 1980s symbolized breaking away from the totalitarian past. In 1985, the first international ballroom dancing competition took place in Moscow. Numerous discotheques and night clubs appeared across Russia. Classes in club, sport, hip-hop, Latin American, and belly dancing are offered in all major cities and enjoy enormous popularity. However, without the former support of the government or trade unions, the financial burden now falls solely on participants or their parents.

See also: amateur cultural activity; ballet, Soviet; Bolshoi Theatre; Caucasus; censorship; folk dance; Georgia; Gypsy/Roma; Lezgins; Lithuania; Mariinskii Theatre; Moiseev, Igor; Moldova; perestroika and glasnost; Stagnation; Thaw; Ukraine; unions, professional; wedding ceremony

Further reading

Belova, E. (1997) *Russkii balet: Entsiklopediia*, Moscow: Bolshaia Rossiiskaia entsiklopediia, Soglasie.

Bogemskaia, K. G. (1999) *Samodeiatelnoe khudozhestvennoe tvorchestvo v SSSR: ocherki istorii, konets 1950-kh–nachalo 1990-kh godov*, St. Petersburg: Izd-vo Dmitrii Bulanin.

Sheremetyevskaya, N. (1960) *Rediscovery of the Dance: The State Academic Folk Dance Ensemble of the USSR under the Direction of Igor Moiseyev*, Moscow: Novosti Press.

TATIANA SMORODINSKAYA

Daneliia, Georgii Nikolaevich

b. 25 August 1930, Tbilisi, Georgia

Film-maker and screenwriter

Daneliia graduated from the Higher Courses for Film-makers in 1959. His first feature, *Serezha* (co-directed with Igor Talankin, 1960) established the key conflict of most of his films: the protagonist resisting his fate. While the heroes of his early films succeed in escaping the forces controlling their lives (*Ia shagaiu po Moskve* [*I Walk Around Moscow*, 1963]; *Tridtsat tri* [*Thirty-Three*, 1965]; *Ne goriui* [*Don't Grieve*, 1969]; and *Mimino*, 1977), his later films are about characters at the mercy of fate (*Osennii marafon* [*Autumn Marathon*, 1979], *Slezy kapali* [*Tears Were*

Falling, 1982]; *Kin-Dza-Dza*, 1986; *Passport*, 1990; *Nastia*, 1993; and *Fortuna*, 2000). Many of Daneliia's films carry paradoxical subtitles – *Thirty-Three: Non-Scientific Science Fiction, Autumn Marathon: A Sad Comedy* – and grotesquely mix reality and fantasy. At Mosfilm Studios, Daneliia was the artistic director of the Experimental Creative Unit (1965–69) and the head of the Experimental Unit of Comedy and Musical Films (*Eksperimentalnoe obedinenie komediinykh i muzykalnykh filmov*, 1975–87). Since 1987, he has headed the film studio Ritm (Rhythm) in Moscow.

ALEXANDER PROKHOROV

Daniel, Iulii Markovich

(pseudonym Nikolai Arzhak)

b. 15 November 1925, Moscow; d. 30 December 1988, Moscow

Prose writer, poet, translator

Under the pseudonym Nikolai Arzhak, in the 1960s Daniel illegally published four short stories abroad: *Govorit Moskva* (*This is Moscow Speaking*), *Ruki* (*Hands*), *Chelovek iz MINAPA* (*The Man from MINAP*), and *Iskuplenie* (*The Atonement*). When the authorities discovered Daniel's true identity, he was arrested, put on trial with Andrei Siniavskii, and sentenced to five years of hard labour in 1966. His trial was widely followed in the West; it marked the end of the Thaw in Soviet culture.

Considered anti-Soviet by the authorities in the 1960s, Daniel's prose is marked by black humour and social satire. For example, in *Govorit Moskva*, Daniel describes 'Public Murder Day', when Moscow residents are legally permitted to commit murder. While serving his sentence, Daniel wrote a small collection of poetry that was published abroad after his release in 1971.

See also: censorship; Siniavskii, Andrei; Thaw

Further reading

Dalton, M. (1973) *Andrei Siniavsky and Iulii Daniel': Two Soviet 'Heretical' Writers*, Würzburg: Jal-Verlag. (Transcripts and commentary on the trial.)

Daniel, Iu. (1969) *This is Moscow Speaking, and Other Stories*, trans. S. Hood, H. Shukman, and J. Richardson, New York: Dutton. (Includes all four stories listed above.)

ERIKA HABER

day care, Soviet and post-Soviet

In the Soviet Union, day care and the pre-school education programmes that it provided were government-subsidised and virtually universal, a socio-economic fact that allowed the vast majority of women of child-bearing age to be employed in full-time jobs or studying in higher education. In the mid-1980s, some fifteen million children between 1 and 7 years of age were enrolled in childcare (Lokshin, 2004: 1095). Indeed, pre-school education as a field was very important in the Soviet Union, so much so that the Academy of Pedagogical Sciences included the Scientific Research Institute of Pre-school Education.

The *iasli* (nursery school) was for small children from 2 months to 3 years who were usually divided into three groups with the under-1 year of age group further subdivided. *Detskii sad* (pre-school and kindergarten) was for children from 3 to 6 who were generally divided into four groups according to age, with the oldest group being a preparation-for-school group. Both the *iasli* and *detskii sad* were financed by the national budget; indeed, over a quarter of total public expenditure on education went to pre-school programs. For families sending their children to pre-school establishments, over three-quarters of the cost of nursery schools and pre-school/kindergarten was government and/or employer-subsidised (the *iasli* fell under the purview of the Ministry of Health, while the *detskii sad* was under the Ministry of Education) with the cost to the family being determined by such factors as salary, number of children, and additional income sources such as pensions or alimony. Thus pre-school education for children throughout the Soviet Union was both highly affordable and accessible.

After the 1991 collapse of the Soviet Union, reforms in Russia beginning in 1992 resulted in a drop in the GNP and a concomitant drastic decline in the number of government-funded childcare establishments. Many state-supported programmes have disappeared and fewer enterprises can afford to provide day-care services. Private childcare has emerged but is extremely expensive and beyond the reach of most Russian families. While many women dropped out of formal employment in order to stay at home with their pre-school-aged children, significant numbers of women do continue to be engaged in the labour force. While roughly one-third of children from ages 3 to 7 attend state pre-schools/kindergartens, it appears that in Russia, the informal care of pre-school children by a network of non-working family members has become the substitute for the childcare programmes formerly provided by the Soviet government.

See also: economic system, Soviet; economic system, post-Soviet; educational system, Soviet; educational system, post-Soviet; families; pedagogy, Soviet; women

Reference and further reading

Ispa, J. (1994) *Childcare in Russia: In Transition*, London: Bergin and Garvey.
Kerr, S. (2005) 'Demographic Change and Russia's Schools', in B. Eklof, L. Holmes and V. Kaplan (eds) *Educational Reform in Post-Soviet Russia: Legacies and Prospects*, London: Frank Cass.
Lokshin, M. (2004) 'Household Childcare Choices and Women's Work Behavior in Russia', *The Journal of Human Resources* xxxix, 4: 1094–115
Pearson, L. (1990) *Children of Glasnost: Growing up Soviet*, Seattle, WA: University of Washington Press.
Weaver, K. (1971) *Lenin's Grandchildren: Pre-school Education in the Soviet Union*, New York: Simon and Schuster.

TERESA L. POLOWY

DDT

Since its first incarnation in 1980, the rock band DDT has evolved into a cultural phenomenon with a wide following that spans at least two generations and two political eras. Iurii Shevchuk, DDT's charismatic vocalist and composer, combines elements of the bard tradition with a post-Soviet flair for musical innovation and web marketing. His poetic lyrics reflect a romantically utopian world-view, but hit hard at their often topical targets, e.g., the spiritual impoverishment of consumer culture, the Russian government's war in Chechnia. The music ranges from hard rock to lyrical ballad to folk-inflected fusion. Fans follow the band at www.ddt.ru.

See also: bards; popular music, Soviet; popular music, post-Soviet; rock music; War, Chechen

YVONNE HOWELL

death

Death was understood by both the artistic avant-garde and the young Soviet state as a technological problem. 'The old are to be killed', wrote Vladimir Maiakovskii in 1920, 'skulls turned into ashtrays'. 'Burning Human Corpses is winning over more and more adherents', cheerfully declared an architectural magazine in 1925. This attitude changed dramatically when Lenin died in 1924: the decision was made to preserve his body. The first wooden mausoleum built on Red Square was a temporary structure designed to grant all those unable to come to Moscow for the day of the funeral a chance 'to bid farewell to their beloved leader'. This mausoleum was replaced first by a more solid wooden structure, and then, in 1930, by one of stone, built to last. From 1924 until the collapse of Communism, at least twice a year (1 May and 7 November) Politburo members stood on Lenin's tomb to greet the columns of official demonstrators. The use of the founding father's grave as a meeting place for the tribe was a constant feature of many traditional societies.

Subsequently, the Soviet position on death oscillated between two attitudes: death devoid of any human dimension, simply a problem of disposal, and death as a symbolic event. The first was instrumental in establishing the system of terror (GULag) under Stalin and in winning the Second World War. Technologically inferior, the Soviet army relied on its practically unlimited supply of people. As a result, Soviet war dead outnumbered German by about ten to one. On the other hand, Stalin's death in 1953 was understood rather symbolically. Millions of people were mourning the loss of a stern father. His funeral in Moscow resulted in a stampede and many deaths. In contrast, Vladimir Vysotskii's funeral in 1980 was a genuine expression of people's love and demonstrated a high degree of self-organization by an enormous crowd. In the post-Brezhnev period, as the ruling class was getting older, state funerals became a form of public spectacle. Three successive leaders, Brezhnev, Andropov, and Chernenko, all died within three years (1982–85) and became a stock of macabre jokes as well as of poet Timur Kibirov's mock-nostalgic poem *Zhizn K. U. Chernenko* (*The Life of K. U. Chernenko*). The post-Soviet era is marked by the rise of criminal behaviour and its acceptance by the society. In the words of one Russian businessman, it is often cheaper to hire a hitman than to pay a debt. A wave of contract killings rolled over the country from the early 1990s. In addition to business people, its victims included priest Aleksandr Men (1990), TV journalist Vlad Listev (1995), and politician Galina Starovoitova (1998). Criminal slang found its way into President Putin's public speeches. *My budem mochit ikh v sortire* (*We'll rub them out in a john*) he said of the Chechen insurgents.

Many traditional Russian funeral rituals have survived from at least the sixteenth century, especially in rural areas. They include ritualized crying and weeping, kissing the deceased on the mouth, and holding memorial services on the third, ninth, twentieth and fortieth days after the death (these are presumed to be stages of parting of the soul with the body). The twentieth century added a new element to these traditions: a glass of vodka is sometimes left on a grave as a farewell gift.

See also: Andropov, Iurii; Brezhnev, Leonid; crime; GULag; Kibirov, Timur; Lenin, Vladimir Ilich; Lenin Mausoleum; Listev, Vladislav; Men, Aleksandr; Putin, Vladimir; Starovoitova, Galina; Vysotskii, Vladimir; World War II (Great Patriotic War)

Further reading

Conquest, R. (1990) *The Great Terror: A Reassessment*, New York: Oxford University Press.

Haynes, M. and Husan, R. (2003) *A Century of State Murder?: Death and Policy in Twentieth-Century Russia*, London: Pluto Press.

Kostomarov, N. I. (1860) *Ocherk domashnei zhizni i nravov velikorusskogo naroda v XVI i XVII stoletiiakh* (Essays on Everyday Life of the Russian People in the 16th and 17th Centuries), St. Petersburg: Tipografiia Karla Vulfa.

Pridemore, W. A. (ed.) (2005) *Ruling Russia: Law, Crime, and Justice in a Changing Society*, Lanham, MD: Rowman & Littlefield.

VLADIMIR PAPERNY

defence industry

In Soviet times the defence industry was referred to as *voenno-promyshlennyi kompleks* or VPK (the military industrial complex) and after 1991 as *oboronno-promyshlennyi kompleks* or OPK (the defence industrial complex). In both Soviet and post-Soviet times the VPK/OPK has played a key role in the national economy and hi-tech industrial production, providing the basis for armed forces maintenance and modernization through state defence orders and federal target programmes.

The Soviet VPK was a centralized structure consisting of state-owned enterprises and organizations under the auspices of nine defence-related ministries, supervised by the Council of Ministers' Military-Industrial Commission (later Committee). Until 1991, the Soviet defence industry matched the West in technological development and even surpassed it in such areas as space programmes. While many civilian industries, such as nonferrous metallurgy, concentrated exclusively on military orders, the VPK produced such consumer items as televisions, washing machines, and photo and audio equipment.

After the disintegration of the USSR, Russia inherited 60 per cent of the Soviet VPK enterprises and 70 per cent of the scientific research organizations. In the 1990s the Russian OPK underwent a grave crisis: government investments decreased by 90 per cent; key business links dissolved; technologies were lost, and deliveries terminated. Spontaneous privatization, as a result of which only 28 per cent of the 660 OPK units remained in state ownership, led to radical conversion. Production of consumer goods constituted 50 per cent of OPK industrial output.

In the early twenty-first century, the OPK shows signs of recovery, with new industrial holding groups including the MAPO MiG military aircraft group comprising twelve enterprises and the AVPK Sukhoi military aircraft group with five enterprises. Cutbacks in Russian defence spending have virtually decimated the land systems sector, reducing annual tank production for export from more than 1,000 to fewer than 100.

The naval industry has been identified as a major growth area for foreign sales, with several new releases expected over the next few years. The St. Petersburg-based Rubin Central Design Bureau is one of the world's leaders in conventionally powered submarine design.

Annual industrial output in 2001 doubled that in 1997, though it still approximates 80 per cent of Soviet output. The OPK portion of Russian manufacturing output is 27 per cent; in hi-tech space and aviation equipment and industrial explosives – 100 per cent; in shipbuilding and radio-electronic devices – 90 per cent; in communications facilities – 70 per cent; and in hi-tech medical equipment – 60 per cent. Government investments cover only 20 per cent of OPK financial needs, a gap responsible for widespread layoffs and impeding the industry's critical comprehensive modernization. As one of the world's top five exporters of military hardware, Russia sells military equipment to 76 countries, including China, India, Korea, Greece, Algeria, the United Arab Emirates, Kuwait, and Syria. Several major Russian government-run enterprises operate in foreign markets: Rosvoorouzhenie, the arms export company for new equipment; PromExport, the arms export company for surplus equipment;

Rossiiskie Technologii, the export company for military technology; and Aviaexport, the civil aviation exports company. The OPK exports military aircraft (75 per cent), anti-aircraft rocket and artillery systems, armoured carriers, motorcycles, ammunition, small-arms weapons, semi-finished carbonaceous steel items, industrial explosives, binoculars and monoculars, sports and hunting weapons with cartridges. In 2003, Russian military exports were estimated at $4.8 billion out of a total of $134.4 billion.

See also: Arzamas-16 (Sarov); aviation, Soviet and post-Soviet; Baikonur; closed city

Further reading

Brindikov, A. (2003) 'O formirovanii i razvitii oboronno-promyshlennogo kompleksa Rossii', *Federal Reference Book* 12, Moscow: Rodina-PRO, pp. 283–90.

Dmitriev, (2004) 'Eksport oruzhiia – realnost i perspectivy', *Federal Reference Book* 15, Moscow: Rodina-PRO, pp. 109–14.

Nozdrachov, A. (2003) 'O tendentsiiakh razvitiia oboronno-promyshlennogo kompleksa Rossii', *Federal Reference Book* 12, Moscow: Rodina-PRO, pp. 303–6.

Sanches-Andres, A. (2004)

TATYANA LEDENEVA

Demidova, Alla Sergeevna

b. 29 September 1936, Moscow

Actress

Demidova established her reputation as a major dramatic actress in the 1960s and 1970s at the Taganka Theatre, most importantly as Gertrude in Liubimov's 1971 *Hamlet* and as Ranevskaia in Efros's 1975 production of Chekhov's *Vishnevyi sad* (*The Cherry Orchard*), both opposite Vysotskii. Her emblematic screen appearances as Lisa in Tarkovskii's *Zerkalo* (*The Mirror*, 1975) and the maverick revolutionary Maria Spiridonova in Karasik's *Shestoe iiulia* (*The Sixth of July*, 1968) tempered the characters' emotional severity with a subtle ironic detachment. Whether or not they were overtly masculinized, as was her Commissar in *Sluzhili dva tovarishcha* (*Two Comrades Served Together*, 1968), Demidova's performances offered her viewers a complex, ambivalent model of post-utopian femininity.

See also: Taganka Theatre; Tarkovskii, Andrei; Vysotskii, Vladimir

BORIS WOLFSON

democratic reform movement (demokraty)

The term 'democratic movement' came into use in the Soviet Union with the appearance of the dissident movement (1965). Though some famous dissidents avoided the latter rubric to emphasize the non-political character of the human rights movement, dissident activities served as the basis for the formation of the democratic movement at the end of the 1980s till the beginning of the 1990s. During perestroika, within the Communist Party itself there emerged the 'democratic platform of the CPSU', which gave impetus to the creation of 'People's Fronts' in various regions of the USSR (1988).

The democratic movement of the late 1980s took the form of social protests and affected wide strata of the population: the slogans 'All power to the Soviet' and 'All power to the people' appeared at numerous meetings. The common ground for all participants of the democratic movement was a critical attitude towards the totalitarian past, a yearning for the destruction of the old system of power and for the establishment of a Western-type democratic base. Theoreticians of the democratic movement of that time, Iurii Afanasev and Len Karpinskii, believed that the democratic movement must have both a stable centre and a ramified capillary structure that would 'wash' all cells of the market economy that was emerging. In their view, the united democratic movement had to be constructively radical.

In 1989, the first free elections of deputies to the First Congress of Peoples' Deputies of the USSR took place in Russia. An important role in its work was played by the Interregional Group – the opposition to the majority of the Congress (its members included Boris Yeltsin, Iurii Afanasiev, Gavriil Popov, and Andrei Sakharov). At the Special Third Congress of Peoples' Deputies (1990), the CPSU itself initiated the historically important decision to rescind Article 6 of the Constitution of the USSR proclaiming the leading role of the CPSU in state government. That decision marked the beginning of the chain reaction of democratic socio-political reforms.

One of the first organized structures of the democratic movement became the radical Democratic Union (1988). The events of the 1991 Coup gave a new impetus to the establishment of a multiparty system. The leaders of the democratic movement, called 'democrats of the first wave', and representatives of the progressive part of the Soviet Party and economic *nomenklatura* (establishment), headed by Yeltsin, came to power. By the autumn of 1991 there were twenty parties and a whole series of movements in the country calling themselves 'democratic'. The most famous were the Democratic Party of Russia (1990); the influential, mass sociopolitical movement Democratic Russia (1990); the Democratic Movement of Reforms (1991); and the Party of Economic Freedom (1992).

Though at this time the movement for democratic reforms in Russia did not coalesce into an organized united front, in 1991 the majority of democrats resolutely rose in opposition to Mikhail Gorbachev and in support of Yeltsin, which led to the establishment of the sovereignty of the Russian Federation and, soon after (December 1991), the disintegration of the USSR. The political crisis in the autumn of 1993 (the conflict between Russian President Yeltsin and the Supreme Council of the Russian Federation, which culminated in the armed attack on Parliament) led to a weakening of civic support for the democratic movement. During 1993, in connection with the first elections to the State Duma, the first so-called 'party of power' appeared in Russia. It was the movement Russia's Choice – representing united democratic forces, which became the ideological support for Yeltsin's new regime.

Many democratic forces adopted a radically critical stance to the so-called 'Chechen campaign' initiated in 1994. As a result, a new 'party of power', Our Home is Russia, headed by Viktor Chernomyrdin, was created before the 1995 elections to the State Duma. The same year saw the formation of a new democratic party, Iabloko, headed by Grigorii Iavlinskii. After the elections, only four influential political forces remained in Russia: Communists, moderate reformers who supported state power, 'The Party of Power', and democrats; subsequently, the authority of the latter significantly diminished.

In 1999, a new movement called the Union of Rightist Forces (SPS, a party since 2000) emerged, which united the country's liberal-democratic forces shortly before parliamentary elections to the State Duma. Many perceived Vladimir Putin's ascent to power as a defeat of the democratic movement. The contemporary technology of political power gradually has become more and more widely practised since the election of Putin to the presidency received the name 'managed democracy'. The process is characterized as one in which those in power rely on administrative resources and manipulative election technologies, as well as the artificial creation of new political forces, such as the 'party of power' called United Russia (*Edinaia Rossiia*) and the political youth movement Ours (*Nashi*). Such strategies encounter counteractions from oppositional democratic parties and civil society: the rise of new democratic civic unions (for example, Committee 2008, speaking in support of honest elections) and new youth movements (for example, the First Free Generation and We).

At present, the Russian democratic movement in its early 1990s form no longer exists. Consequence-laden economic reforms have worsened citizens' material conditions, and the masses associate democracy with the deterioration of material well-being, the destruction of their habitual way of life, and the collapse of a great state power. Certain features of the institutionalization of reforms contributed to these perceptions: the reforms' reliance not on broad popular support, but on official administrative resources. After the defeat of the democratic parties Iabloko and SPS at the 2004 elections, there arose the question of forming a new democratic movement, of uniting various political, democratically-oriented forces. In 2005, social polls showed that approximately 30 per cent of voters were ready to vote for a refurbished version of democrats.

See also: Communist Party; Coup, August 1991; dissident; Gorbachev, Mikhail; perestroika and glasnost; political structure, Soviet; Putin, Vladimir; Sakharov, Andrei; Union of Rightist Forces; United Russia; Yeltsin, Boris

Further reading

Kaplan, V. and Morozov, B. (1998), 'Toward a Multi-Party System 1985–93', in N. Schleifman (ed.) *Russia at Crossroads: History, Memory and Political Practice*, London: Routledge, pp. 173–226. Cambridge University Press.
Urban, M. *et al.* (1997) *Rebirth of Politics in Russia*, Cambridge: Cambridge University Press.

ELENA OZNOBKINA

denim

The Soviet Union began to produce denim clothes in 1975, under the ninth Five-Year Plan, dedicated to the rise of mass consumption. The Ministry of Light Industry decided to produce 35.6 million metres of denim and 17 million pairs of blue jeans that year, and 53.2 million metres of denim and 20 million pairs the following year. Soviet jeans were of poor quality, however, and in 1976 newspapers raised *dzhinsovaia problema* (the 'jeans problem'). In 1978, a new denim fabric, *orbita* (orbit), the 56th experimental attempt in textiles and the first wholly cotton fabric, went into production. Some of the previous failures contained a high percentage of wool. Though the Ministry of Light Industry repeatedly tried to produce a pair of jeans acceptable to young people, the inferiority to Western equivalents persisted, and Western brands, both real and knock-off versions, were among the most prized items on the black market.

See also: black market; five-year plan

DJURDJA BARTLETT

Denisov, Edison Vasilevich

b. 6 April 1929, Tomsk; d. 24 November 1996, Paris

Composer

Denisov, Sofiia Gubaidulina, and Alfred Shnittke form the trio of world-renowned composers of the post-Shostakovich generation. Although Gubaidulina's and Shnittke's music is better known abroad, Denisov now enjoys the reputation of leader and mentor to the Russian composers whose careers began in the 1960s. The primary link between Russian and Western composers, he, as well as his vast private library, enabled many contacts. Denisov not only introduced Gubaidulina and Shnittke to the West, but also rekindled interest in the officially anathematized avant-garde of the 1920s, including the music of Roslavets and Mosolov.

Denisov's first major work, a chamber cantata titled *Solntse inkov* (*The Sun of the Incas*, 1964), introduced his music to Western listeners. He found his own musical language in *Peinture* (1970) for orchestra, inspired by the artist Boris Birger. As critics have noted, the influence of Boulez, Ligeti, and Messiaen are perceptible in Denisov's works, which also bear the imprint of Glinka and Mozart. Among his series of concertos, the *Violin Concerto* (1977) is considered the best. His non-liturgical five-movement oratorio, *Requiem* (1980), based on Francisco Tanzer's (1921–2003) cycle with the same title, promotes a vision of human life from birth to death.

See also: classical music, post-Soviet; Gubaidulina, Sofiia; Shnittke, Alfred

Further reading

Kholopov, Y. and Tsernova, V. (1994) *Edison Denisov*, Chur, Switzerland: Harwood.
McBurney, G. (2001) 'Denisov, Edison', in S. Sadie (ed.) *The New Groves Dictionary of Music and Musicians*, 2nd edn, vol. 7, Oxford: Oxford University Press, pp. 203–4.

DAVID GOMPPER

Desiatnikov, Leonid Arkadievich

b. 16 October 1955, Kharkov, Ukrainian SSR

Composer

Born in Kharkov, Desiatnikov has lived in St. Petersburg (Leningrad) since 1972. He became one of the best-known Russian composers of the 1990s and the most prominent representative of the Petersburg branch of contemporary music culture. He studied at the Leningrad Conservatory with Boris Arapov and Boris Tishchenko. His major works – such as the song cycle *Dichterliebe und Leben*, a composition for strings and voice, *The Leaden Echo*, the suite *Sketches to the Sunset*, and the violin concerto *Russian Seasons* – reveal his style as a unique mixture of postmodernism and post-Romanticism, irony and lyricism, Russian and European musical traditions. Desiatnikov's intellectual approach is obvious both in his delicate work with different musical models and with the poetic word. He has set to music the verse of Gavrila Derzhavin, Fedor Tiutchev, Gerard Manley Hopkins, Daniil Kharms, Nikolai Oleinikov, and Oleg Grigoriev. His symphony *The Rite of Winter 1949* is based on the text of a Soviet–English textbook.

In 2004, Desiatnikov completed his opera *Deti Rozentalia* (*Rosenthal's Children*), with a libretto by Vladimir Sorokin, commissioned by the Bolshoi Theatre; its opening in 2005 caused an uproar. He owes his Russian and European fame to close association with distinguished performers such as Alexei Goribol and Gidon Kremer, and to his intensive work in film music in the 1990s.

See also: Bolshoi Theatre; classical music, post-Soviet; Kremer, Gidon; music in film; Sorokin, Vladimir; Tishchenko, Boris

KIRA NEMIROVSKAIA

desserts

Traditional Russian desserts include *prianik*, a dry, heavy spice cake, made in moulds and often filled with jam, nuts, or caramelized condensed milk. The cities of Tula and Viazma remain famous for their intricate *prianik* moulds and traditional recipes. *Ponchik* is a yeast doughnut that is deep-fried and sprinkled with sugar and spices. *Krem* (custard) is a thick cream dessert, flavoured with fruit syrup or chocolate; *zhele* are soft fruit jellies. *Morozhenoe* (ice cream) and *zefir* (meringues) are also traditional desserts. *Tort* is a cake, either *biskvitnyi* (sponge cake), *pesochnyi* (shortcake), or *sloenyi* (made of puff pastry); popular cakes include *Prazhskii*, or Prague cake (chocolate with a chocolate cream filling) and *Ptiche moloko*, 'Bird's Milk' ('bird's milk' being something rare from the world of fairy tales), a light cake made with gelatine layers resembling marshmallow. *Keks* is denser cake, shaped as small loaves or muffins. *Napoleon* is a cake made of puff pastry filled with cream; originally intended to celebrate the centenary of the victory in the War of 1812, it had a triangular form resembling Napoleon's three-cornered hat. Other common desserts include *trubochka*, a thin waffle shaped as a cone and filled with whipped cream; *ekler* (éclair), a light pastry filled with whipped cream; *pirozhnoe* (pastry); *pechene* (cookie); *triufel* (truffle); and *pirozhnoe 'kartoshka'* (pastry 'potatoes' made of sugar, cookie crumbs, cocoa and butter). Russian desserts are usually served with tea.

See also: dining, Russian; dining, Soviet; zephyr

MICHELE BERDY

detective fiction (detektiv)

The first detective stories in Russia date back to the 1860s (Sokolovskii, Stepanov, Timofeev). In the 1870s and 1880s, tales of crime and investigation drew on the traditions of both the Western mystery (Gaboriau) and Russian realism (Dostoevskii). With a detective as the main character, they focused on exploring the criminal's psychology (Shkliarevskii). Although classics of detective fiction (Collins, Gaboriau, Conan Doyle) and masters of adventure novels (Stevenson, Dumas, Haggard) were important sources of inspiration for Russian detective writers at the turn of the century, the most prominent influences on the *detektiv* were crime stories about Nat Pinkerton, written by American author Allen Pinkerton and his numerous imitators. Soviet writers published fiction *à la Pinkerton* in the 1920s. By the end of the decade, however, stories about 'Red Pinkertons' (Marietta Shaginian, Mark Maksim) were criticized as unsuitable for instilling socialist ideology in the masses. Under Stalin, severe ideological constraints on literature marginalized the genre. The 1930s' stories about the police's (*militsiia*) struggle against the enemies of Soviet power (Lev Sheinin, Lev Ovalov) share some characteristics with the police procedural, but draw once again on the adventure novel rather than on classical mysteries. Related to the *detektiv*, novels about military intelligence appeared after World War II (Iulian Semenov), and in the 1950s, thanks to the increase in translations of Western mysteries, the Soviet mystery novel began to develop rapidly. From the 1960s through the 1980s, the most prominent detective writers (Arkadii Adamov, the brothers Arkadii and Georgii Vainer, Nikolai Leonov, Aleksandr and Olga Lavrov) placed more emphasis on the deductive abilities of militia investigators than on the pursuit of criminals. The Soviet *detektiv* featured a collective victory over evil, depicting criminals as loners influenced by alien anti-socialist views. Explanations for why crime persisted in a supposedly fair social system, nonetheless, remained unconvincing. The policies of glasnost, the abolition of censorship (1989), and the rise of private publishing caused a 'detective boom' in the late 1980s. Hundreds of translated detective novels flooded the book market, while Russian detective authors, freed from the fetters of Soviet ideology, explored the detective genre anew. By the mid-1990s, the popularity of domestic authors, with their phenomenal output of action thrillers, mysteries, *militseiskii detektiv* (police detective stories), historical mystery novels, and *ironicheskii detektiv* (the ironic detective novel), surpassed that of translated detective fiction. Non-existent in the Soviet period, gangster sagas have flourished since the 1990s, idealizing mafia types fighting corrupt police (Andrei Konstantinov, Aleksandr Belov). The most successful post-Soviet detective authors are Viktor Dotsenko, Aleksandra Marinina, Andrei Kivinov, Boris Akunin, and Daria Dontsova.

See also: Akunin, Boris; Marinina, Aleksandra; *Mesto vstrechi izmenit nelzia* (*The Meeting Place Cannot Be Changed*); militia (police); perestroika and glasnost

Further reading

Nepomnyashchy, C. (1999) 'Markets, Mirrors, and Mayhem: Alexandra Marinina and the Rise of the New Russian *Detektiv*', in A.-M. Barker (ed.) *Consuming Russia*, Durham, NC: Duke University Press.

Olcott, A. (2001) *Russian Pulp*. Lanham, MD: Rowman and Littlefield.

ELENA BARABAN

developed socialism

Leonid Brezhnev introduced the concept of developed socialism (*razvitoi sotsializm*), also known as mature socialism (*zrelyi sotsializm*), at the 24th Communist Party Congress in 1971 as a new stage in the construction of Communism. Unlike Nikita Khrushchev's 1961 CPSU Programme, which predicted the full-scale construction of Communism by 1980, Brezhnev's concept postponed the achievement of Communism for at least fifty years. Developed socialism promised intensive economic development, improvement in living standards, and the liberalization of the political system to encourage popular political participation. The term remained the ideological guiding principle until Gorbachev's ascent to power in 1985.

See also: Brezhnev, Leonid; Communist Party; Krushchev, Nikita; Stagnation; Thaw

MARKO DUMANČIĆ

dictionaries

Dictionaries began to appear with some regularity during the Petrine Period (1700–25),

when Russia's burgeoning intercourse with Western countries created a need for language standardization and translation manuals. From its earliest format of trilingual columns, dictionaries in Russia systematically became more sophisticated and diverse in content: linguistic, terminological, bilingual, phraseological, dialectical, etymological, normative, orthographic, encyclopedic, biographical, and specialized (e.g., vocabulary of specific authors, not unlike concordances to complete works). However, the most famous dictionary of Russian continues to be the *Tolkovyi slovar zhivogo velikorusskogo iazyka* (*Reasoned Dictionary of the Living Russian Language*; Moscow, 1861–67) by Vladimir Dal (1801–72), which first contained over 200,000 words, at least twice as many as any dictionary before it. Dal's system of 'nesting' words according to the basic roots of the language at first made the dictionary difficult to use. However, Baudouin de Courtenay revised the third (1903–10) and fourth (1912–14) editions to make the format more accessible. Most linguists concur that no one has improved on Dal's collecting of dialects and regionalisms. Beginning in the 1990s, Dal's dictionary began to appear in Russian bookstores, book fairs, and sidewalk stalls; it remains available wherever one can buy books in Russia.

In the twenty-first century, publishing houses have begun to reprint editions of classics such as Max Vasmer's four-volume *Etimologicheskii slovar russkogo iazyka* (*Etymological Dictionary of the Russian Language*), as well as hundreds of varieties of dictionaries, including specialized topics such as Russian morphology, lexicon, and dialects; Church Slavonic; moral and ethical, feminist, gender-related, archaeological, anthropological linguistic, and soviet ideological/political terminology. Almost all dictionaries have become readily available on numerous American and Russian web sites.

CHRISTINE A. RYDEL

Dinamo

The first sports association in the country, Dinamo was established in 1923 to unite the employees of law enforcement bodies. Dinamo's highest achievements were in football (soccer) and ice hockey. The team's traditional colours are blue and white, with the letter 'D' as a logo. Dinamo's best football player was Lev Iashin.

See also: Iashin, Lev; soccer

ALEXANDER LEDENEV

dining, Russian

Russian cuisine is hearty and rich, shaped by the country's geography, history, climate, and economics. The Russian dinner table is famous for many traditional delicacies: smoked sturgeon and salmon, black and red caviar, marinated and salted mushrooms, and shots of vodka. Russian cuisine was basically formed more than a hundred years ago in the period of 1840 till the 1880s, as the empire was established. Regional dishes became national: *pelmeni* (Siberian dumplings), Ukrainian *borsch* (beet soup), chicken Kiev, Far East humpback salmon, and beef Stroganov.

Everyday family dining in Russia is plain and plentiful, comprising four courses: *zakuski* (appetizers), *pervoe* (first course), *vtoroe* (second/main course) and *sladkoe* (dessert). Dining at the Russian table is called *zastole*, which starts with a shot of cold, straight vodka or glass of wine, and follows with appetizers.

Appetizers can range from simply a slice of hearty dark bread, cold salads, various pickled vegetables or salted herring, to more elegant fare, such as smoked salmon, salami, cold meats, and the Russian delicacy, caviar. The first course provides the most common everyday dish, soup; the favourites include *borsch* (served with a dollop of sour cream), *shchi* (cabbage soup made with beef bones, potatoes, and onions), *rasolnik* (made from pickled vegetables), *okroshka* (cold soup made from *kvas*), and mushroom soup. Many soups are served with sour cream. The second, main, course consists of a meat dish, or sometimes fried or grilled chicken or fish, typically accompanied by rice or potatoes. The fish served is usually salmon, sturgeon, pike, or herring. Desserts include cakes, sugared doughnuts (*ponchiki*), chocolate, and ice cream.

Russian crêpe-like pancakes, *bliny*, stuffed with meat, fish, butter, or sour cream, may be served as a main course; or they may be filled with preserves (*varene*), fruit, or chocolate, and served for dessert.

Russians are not big vegetable eaters, though potatoes and cabbage are virtually *de rigueur*. There are different ways of cooking potatoes: boiled, mashed, fried with onions, or as potato pancakes (*draniki*). Cabbage is pickled, stuffed, brined, boiled in soups, and stewed as a popular side dish with tomato puree, onion, salt, pepper, and a little sugar. Most families try to make home preserves as a standby food in the form of pickles from summer vegetables, grown or gathered at the dacha: cucumbers, tomatoes, and mushrooms.

Russian dinners are accompanied by a variety of alcoholic and non-alcoholic drinks, particularly vodka, wine, and mineral water. Tea (*chai*) comes after every meal, served with sugar or preserves. Traditionally coffee has been served less often.

The contemporary dining scene incorporates many different foreign cuisines, most unavailable during the Soviet era. Since the beginning of the 1990s, a wide variety of restaurants has appeared: European cuisine may be found in Italian pizzerias, German eateries, French restaurants, and Irish bars. Expensive Chinese, Japanese, and Korean eateries offer Asian food, with sushi bars popular as status symbols. Other options include American diners, Australian pubs, and Mexican eateries. Many new Russian restaurants, varying dramatically in price and atmosphere, have also appeared.

See also: appetizers; beef Stroganoff; bliny; caviar; dacha; desserts; drinks, alcoholic; drinks, non-alcoholic; fish dishes; kvas; meat dishes; mushrooms; pelmeni; soups; varene; vodka

ELENA SKIPETROVA

dining, Soviet

Soviet cuisine (1917–91) was influenced by historic events that resulted in a mixture of ethnicities, their cooking habits, and their dining traditions. Dishes from Georgia, Central Asia, and other Caucasian republics became staples of Soviet meals, whose most common everyday fare included *pelmeni* (dumplings) from Siberia, *borsch* (beet soup), lard, chicken cutlets (*kotlety po-kievski*), and *vareniki* (dumplings) from Ukraine, chicken soup with noodles from Russia, *syirniki* (cottage cheese patties) from the Baltic countries, beef Stroganov from Odessa, and so-called 'diet dishes' (boiled or steamed foods) from German and Jewish cuisine.

Throughout the Soviet era tea was a standard drink, as was vodka. Soviet republics also produced wine from acres of vineyards in Georgia, Moldova, and the Crimea. Popular white wines were and remain the Anapa Riesling, Tsinandali, and Gourdzhuani; reds are Georgian Saperavi, Mukuzani, Kindzmarauli, and Khvanchkara (reportedly, Stalin's favourite).

In the 1960s and the 1970s such national products as river fish, marinated vegetables, and dry mushrooms disappeared, replaced by European meat dishes: cutlets, beefsteaks, hamburgers, schnitzel, and non-traditional marinades and canned fruit and vegetables. Innovations of the 1970s and the 1980s included poultry products, sausages, and semi-prepared foods as an alternative to two-course meals.

In the 1980s, professional cooks became interested in the national traditions of Soviet republics. Typical dishes of Georgian cuisine, distinguished by its spiciness, are *shashlyk* (skewered meat), *kharcho* (spicy meat soup), *khachipuri* (hot bread with melted cheese), *baklazhan* (eggplant), *chakhokhbili* (steamed dumplings) and *tolma* (meat and rice in vine leaves). Other favourites from USSR satellites include Uzbek, Ukrainian, and Mongolian fare, with pilaf the most popular Uzbek meal.

See also: appetizers; Caucasus; Central Asia; dining, Russian; drinks, alcoholic; Odessa

Further reading

Genis, A. and Vail, P. (2002) *Russkaia kukhnia v izgnanii*, Moscow: Nezavisimaya gazeta.
Pokhlebkin, V. (1998) *Natsionalnye kukhni nashikh narodov*, Moscow: Tsentrpoligraf.

ELENA SKIPETROVA

dissident

It is not exactly clear who coined the term 'dissidents', and when, to describe a diverse, fragmented group of Soviet political activists who from the 1960s until the 1980s challenged the Soviet authorities by appealing to the rule of law and constitutional freedoms. When the dissident movement (*pravozashchitnoe dvizhenie*) started, however, is clear: on 5 December 1965 – which marked the official celebration of the twenty-ninth anniversary of the Soviet Constitution – about 200 people gathered in Pushkin Square in Moscow, demanding a free and open trial for two writers, Andrei Siniavskii and Iulii Daniel, charged with dissemination of anti-Soviet propaganda in *samizdat*. One of the signs that protesters carried at this landmark event reflected the general attitude of the dissident movement: 'Respect the Soviet Constitution!' Embracing the general message of Khrushchev's famous 'secret speech', 'On the cult of personality and its consequences' (1956), the dissidents built their legal resistance movement around existing juridical norms and practices. Challenging the authorities, dissidents openly demanded that the Soviet government observe its own rules. A conscious appeal to Soviet law produced a revolutionary effect: freedom of speech and freedom of association, granted by the Constitution, became a matter of practice rather than an example of political rhetoric.

The year 1968 was another important milestone in the history of Soviet dissidents. Commemorating the twentieth anniversary of its Universal Declaration on Human Rights, the United Nations declared 1968 the Year of Human Rights. In the USSR, this appeal stimulated the appearance of the first uncensored political periodical. Initially compiled and typed by the Moscow dissident Natalia Gorbanevskaia, from 1968–83 the *Chronicle of Current Events* was the cornerstone of the dissident movement. The bulletin contained information about arrests, transcripts of court hearings, political analysis and commentaries, and documents addressed to the authorities.

Unlike Soviet underground art or the unofficial ('second') culture, the dissidents' political activity was unusually public: meetings and demonstrations were accompanied by campaigns to sign 'open letters' to the Soviet and Party authorities, and later to international organizations and mass media. Circulated as a form of *samizdat* yet deliberately aimed at the authorities, these petitions constituted a hybrid form of political participation that blurred the border between the public and the private, the official and unofficial.

Traditionally, Soviet dissidents are associated with their opposition to existing political practices and with their strong emphasis on political freedoms. Other important issues actively supported by dissidents included the right of religious groups to exercise freedom of conscience, the right of Soviet Jews to emigrate to Israel, and the right of ethnic groups to cultural or political autonomy and even independence.

The Soviet invasion of Afghanistan in 1979 symbolically undermined any remaining hope among dissidents for productive dialogue with the Soviet authorities. In turn, the arrest and exile of the prominent scientist and human rights activist Andrei Sakharov in 1980 effectively marked the end of the dissident movement itself. In the 1980s, lack of a strong organizational structure, coupled with the emigrations and arrests of its leaders, left the dissident movement in a state of disarray. Neither dissidents' infrequent attempts to reclaim their moral and political authority during perestroika (1985–91) nor post-Soviet reforms produced any significant impact on the emerging political culture.

The dissidents' moral and legal opposition to the authoritarian regime continued a long-lasting tradition of uneasy relations between the Russian intelligentsia and Russia's power-holders; and despite their virtual disappearance from the post-Soviet political scene, dissidents still retain moral authority in a situation where norms and traditions of a civil society are still taking shape.

See also: censorship; Daniel, Iulii; intelligentsia; Khrushchev, Nikita; Sakharov, Andrei; samizdat; Siniavskii, Andrei

Further reading

Alexeyeva, L. (1985) *Soviet Dissent: Contemporary Movements for National, Religious, and Human Rights*, trans. C. Pierce and J. Glad, Middletown, CT: Wesleyan University Press.

Bukovsky, V. (1979) *To Build a Castle: My Life as a Dissenter*, trans. M. Scammell, New York: Viking Press.

Hopkins, M. (1983) *Russia's Underground Press: The Chronicle of Current Events*, New York: Praeger.

Lourie, R. (2002) *Sakharov: A Biography*, Hanover, NH: Brandeis University Press/University Press of New England.

Oushakine, S. (2001) 'The Terrifying Mimicry of Samizdat', *Public Culture*, 13, 2: 191–214.

Shatz, M. (1980) *Soviet Dissidents in Historical Perspective*. Cambridge: Cambridge University Press.

SERGUEI A. OUSHAKINE

Dodin, Lev Abramovich

b. 14 May 1944, Novokuznetsk

Theatre director

Artistic director of the Malyi (Small) Drama Theatre in St. Petersburg since 1983, Dodin trained at LGITMiK under Boris Zon. The Malyi largely comprises his former students, hence boasts consistency in its methods of character development in the style of Stanislavskii. Critics refer to the company as 'a collection of naturalities' (*nabor naturalnostei*) because Dodin selects actors on their general compatibility with national stereotypes.

After his successful productions of *Dom* (*The House*, 1980) and *Bratia i sestry* (*Brothers and Sisters*, 1985), based on of Fedon Abramov's rural prose, Dodin focused on staging novels. Without a prepared script, his actors painstakingly work through the novel using the étude method, whereby cast and script both emerge in the process of experiencing the original text.

Most of Dodin's prose adaptations, embracing works by Iurii Trifonov (*Starik* [*The Old Man*, 1988]), Sergei Kaledin (*Gaudeamus*, 1990), and Dostoevskii (*Besy* [*The Possessed*, 1991]), as well as his Chekhov stagings, including *Vishnevyi sad* (*The Cherry Orchard*, 1994) and *Diadia Vania* (*Uncle Vania*, 2003), focus on Russia's destiny and national mentality.

See also: St. Petersburg State Academy of Theatre Arts; theatre, Soviet; Trifonov, Iurii

DASHA KRIJANSKAIA

Dolina, Larisa Aleksandrovna

b. 10 September 1955, Baku,
Azerbaidzhan SSSR

Jazz and pop singer

A graduate of the Gnesin Moscow Music
School, Dolina is an accomplished improvisational jazz singer, but best known as a pop
singer. Named People's Artist of Russia in 1998,
in 2002 she became a member of the President's
Commission on Culture and Art.

See also: jazz; popular music, post-Soviet

MICHELE BERDY

Dolukhanova, Zara Aleksandrovna

b. 1918, Moscow

Mezzo-soprano

After studying in Moscow, Dolukhanova made
her debut with the Yerevan opera in Armenia.
Her reputation, however, rests on her advocacy
of the solo song repertoire, from the Italian
baroque and German *Lieder* to Russian romances.
She played a vital role in the development of
contemporary song, performing works by leading
Soviet composers, most notably Shostakovich's
From Jewish Folk Poetry, Op.79, which premiered
in 1955. The effortless richness of her voice, an
impeccable sense of style, and a gift for
communicating in any language won her an
appreciative audience; she was the first singer to
be awarded a Lenin Prize (in 1966).

See also: awards, cultural, Soviet; Shostakovich,
Dmitrii

PHILIP ROSS BULLOCK

Domostroi

The *Domostroi* is a sixteenth-century household
instruction manual that prescribes, among other
topics, the proper rules of a household. It is
probably not of native Russian origin, but based
on a European model; however, the text
provides an interesting view of life in Old
Russia. It contains instruction on relations with
clergy ('How One Should Invite Priests and
Monks to One's House to Pray'), household
management ('How to Teach Your Servants to
Run Errands'), as well as rules of behaviour,
particularly marital relations.

See also: traditions and customs

Further reading

Pouncy, C. (1995) *The Domostroi*, Ithaca, NY:
Cornell University Press.

DAVID J. GALLOWAY

Dontsova, Daria

(née Agrippina Arkadievna Vasileva)

b. 7 July 1952, Moscow

Detective fiction writer

The queen of pulp fiction during the 2000s,
Daria Dontsova challenges the supremacy of
Boris Akunin in this lucrative domain. After
graduating in journalism from Moscow State
University (1974), Dontsova worked as a translator, a correspondent for periodicals, and a
teacher of French and German (1985). Diagnosed as fatally ill with breast cancer, she wrote
her first *detektiv*, *Krutye nasledniki* (*Cool and Tough
Heirs*) while in hospital recovering from three
operations (1998). With more than 65 titles to
her name (2005; all published by EKSMO), her
productivity shows no signs of abating. A ubiquitous presence on numerous TV shows, she
grants countless interviews and publishes books
in various 'light' genres that sell like proverbial
hotcakes (e.g., *Kulinarnaia kniga lentiaiki* [*A Lazy
Women's Cookbook*, 2005]).

Dontsova's *detektivy* only faintly resemble
Western mystery and crime novels. Labeled
'ironic detective fiction', they formally fall into
four series, each identified by the investigator in
question. Permeated with humour, they focus
less on crime than on human relationships
(especially love), travel, and consumerism,
invariably offering the Leibnizian reassurance
that everything in life works out for the best. As
Dontsova herself has noted, her works function
as medicine against depression. Her savvy

choice of titles (relying on commonplaces from folklore or pop culture and humorously unexpected juxtapositions invoking animals) psychologically tap into readers' needs: *Ukha iz zolotoi rybki* (*Fish Soup from a Gold Fish*), *Lampa razyskivaet Alladina* (*Lamp Seeking Aladdin*), *File iz zolotogo petushka* (*Fillet of Golden Cockerel*). Prizes: Voted Russian Writer of the Year (2001, 2002, 2003); Book of the Year in the 'bestseller' category; Person of the Year from the Internet-portal RAMBLER (both in 2003).

See also: Akunin, Boris; detective fiction; literature, post-Soviet

HELENA GOSCILO

Doronina, Tatiana Vasilevna

b. 12 September 1933, Leningrad

Stage and film actress, theatre director

After graduating from the studio school of the Moscow Art Theatre (MKhAT, 1956), Doronina soon became the star of various theatres in Leningrad and Moscow. As a member of MKhAT (1983–), she was a driving force behind the troupe's split into a Chekhov and a Gorkii MKhAT, and was put in charge of the latter (1986). On screen, Doronina gained lasting popularity in contemporary melodramas, such as '*Tri topolia*' *na Pliushchikhe* ('*Three Poplars*' *at Pliushchikha*, 1967) and *Machekha* (*The Stepmother*, 1973) – huge hits with viewers, if not critics. More recently, she has made news as the executive director of the patriotic, pro-Soviet half of MKhAT. People's Artist of the USSR (1981).

See also: Moscow Art Theatre

PETER ROLLBERG

Dovlatov, Sergei Donatovich

b. 3 September 1941, Ufa, Russia; d. 24 August 1990, New York

Writer

An émigré prose writer whose fiction reflects his personal experiences, Dovlatov's witty, anecdotal, and laconic authorial voice, coupled with the understated quality of his prose, earned him a distinct place in contemporary Russian literature. Unable to publish his stories at home because of their subject matter – prison camps, the nonconformist intelligentsia, and Russia's repressive political system – Dovlatov allowed their publication in the West. Under resultant harassment by the KGB, he emigrated in 1978.

In America, he published ten books of fiction in Russian, which were translated into many languages, establishing his reputation as one of the most significant Russian writers abroad. His collections, *Zona* (*The Zone*, 1982), *Nevidimaia kniga* (*The Invisible Book*, 1977), *Zapovednik* (*The Sanctuary*, 1983), *Nashi* (*Ours: A Family Album*, 1983), are elegant and lively, coloured by irony and colloquialisms.

From 1979 to 1983 Dovlatov edited *Novyi amerikanets* (*The New American*), a Russian-language newspaper. Since glasnost, Dovlatov's prose has appeared in Russia, gaining him recognition.

See also: literature, émigré

Further reading

Ryan-Hayes, K. (1992) 'Narrative Strategies in the Works of Sergei Dovlatov', *Russian Literature* 45, 153: 155–78.

TATYANA NOVIKOV

drama, post-Soviet

Following the end of perestroika and the dissolution of the Soviet Union in 1991, Russian society was seized by an identity crisis similar to that following the Bolshevik Revolution in 1917. With the collapse not only of political and social support systems, which made day-to-day life hard, but also of the national symbolic and mythological framework, which made finding psychological orientation in the new circumstances nearly impossible, the nation's populace struggled to define the country it inhabited. Everything 'Soviet' looked irrelevant, but nothing stable arose to replace it. Appropriately, two of the most successful plays from the early post-Soviet period – Daniil Gink's *Lysyi brunet* (*Bald Brunet*, 1991) and Aleksei Burykin's *Nizhinskii* (1993) – featured characters suffering from schizophrenia. Equally revealing is critics' dismissal of both plays as 'non-existent'. This perhaps natural critical myopia engendered the myth that no playwrights in post-Soviet Russia were writing anything worthwhile.

By mid-decade, however, most of the playwrights who laid the groundwork for a new play boom in the 2000s were already active. Nikolai Koliada, a prolific author of gritty plays that attracted international attention, in 1993 established an influential playwriting course in Ekaterinburg. Elena Gremina's *Za zerkalom* (*Behind the Mirror*, 1994), starring opera diva Galina Vishnevskaia at the Moscow Art Theatre, was a rare, at that time, commercial production of a contemporary play. Nadezhda Ptushkina, debuting with *Pri chuzhikh svechakh* (*By the Light of Others' Candles*, 1995) and following with *Ovechka* (*The Little Lamb*, 1996), created a sensation with clever, accessible studies of women in conflict. Olga Mukhina's *Tanya-Tanya* (1996) and *U* (*YoU*, 1997) announced the arrival of a major new voice. Mikhail Ugarov's understated portraits of eccentric people from bygone eras – including *Pravopisanie po Grotu* (*Orthography According to Grot*, 1993), *Oborvanets* (*Deadbeat*, 1995) and *Golubi* (*Doves*, written 1988, produced 1997) – were given small productions but attracted substantial critical attention. The first of Koliada's pupils to achieve popularity was Oleg Bogaev, with *Russkaia narodnaia pochta* (*The Russian National Postal Service*, 1997), a comedy about a lonely pensioner.

By the turn of the century, several new writers had become established and contemporary drama was a major literary trend. Some of the key playwrights were Evgenii Grishkovets, with his sentimental monologues, Maksim Kurochkin, with prodigiously inventive dramas on mythical themes, and Koliada's student Vasilii Sigarev, with the dark social exposés *Plastilin* (*Plasticine*, 2001) and *Chernoe moloko* (*Black Milk*, 2002), widely staged in England and the United States. The Presniakov brothers, Oleg and Vladimir, from Ekaterinburg, achieved fame at home and abroad with episodic plays eclectically mixing comedy and drama – *Terrorism* (2002), *Plennye dukhi* (*Captive Spirits*, 2003) and *Izobrazhaia zhertvu*

(*Playing the Victim*, 2003). The brothers Viacheslav and Mikhail Durnenkov from Toliatti penned witty send-ups of modern Russian society, as in *Kulturnyi sloi* (*The Cultural Layer*, 2003). Two Moscow houses, The Centre for Directors and Playwrights (founded 1998) and Teatr.doc (founded 2002), were instrumental in promoting new plays. The Centre helped launch the careers of Sigarev and the Presniakovs, while the first major success at Teatr.doc, devoted primarily to documentary drama, was Ivan Vyrypaev's *Kislorod* (*Oxygen*, 2002), a two-actor piece loosely based on the Ten Commandments.

See also: drama, Soviet; Gremina, Elena; Grishkovets, Evgenii; Koliada, Nikolai; Kurochkin, Maksim; Moscow Art Theatre; Mukhina, Olga; perestroika and glasnost; theatre, post-Soviet; theatre, Soviet; Ugarov, Mikhail; Vishnevskaia, Galina

JOHN FREEDMAN

drama, Soviet

Like other arts in the totalitarian state, Soviet drama was under the constant scrutiny of censors, since it was seen as a powerful ideological tool for glorifying the Soviet lifestyle and criticizing those who did not follow accepted policy.

Rejecting old religious and moral values as inappropriate for builders of the new society, post-revolutionary Soviet playwrights sought new themes and protagonists. Efforts to recreate the grandeur of the revolutionary struggle on stage led to new characters: revolutionary fanatics who would sacrifice their lives and family members for the sake of the Revolution. This trend was vividly presented in Konstantin Trenev's *Liubov Iarovaia* (1926), Boris Lavrenev's *Razlom* (*Break-up*, 1927), and Vsevolod Ivanov's *Bronepoezd 14–69* (*Armoured Train No. 14–69*, 1927).

Juxtaposed to ideologically charged mainstream plays, Mikhail Bulgakov wrote some of the best works of the mid-1920s and early 1930s, addressing such issues as the transformation of human relationships during historic turbulence in his *Dni Turbinykh* (*Days of the Turbins*, 1925)

and *Beg* (*Flight*, 1926–28), and the battle between artists and ideological leaders in *Kabala sviatosh* (*A Cabal of Hypocrites*, 1930).

Themes introduced in the early 1930s and 1940s that came to dominate Soviet drama until the end of the Soviet era included the cult of Vladimir Lenin and plays promoting industrialization that depicted ideologically strong factory directors and workers who dedicated their lives to the nation's economic prosperity. The heroic deeds of Soviet military commanders, soldiers, and simple civilians during World War II were memorialized in hundreds of patriotic plays.

A new generation of talented playwrights emerged during the Thaw; playwrights worked within the ideological framework of Socialist Realism but focused more on the psychological development of their characters, family relationships, love, friendship, and the search for happiness than on class struggle and industrialization. Such plays as Aleksei Arbuzov's *Irkutskaia istoriia* (*It Happened in Irkutsk*, 1959) and *Moi bednyi Marat* (*My Poor Marat*, 1964), Viktor Rozov's *Vechno zhivye* (*Alive Forever*, 1956) and Aleksandr Volodin's *Piat vecherov* (*Five Evenings*, 1959) are Soviet masterpieces from this period.

Popular plays of the 1960s and 1970s celebrated love and romance of representatives of different ages and social groups, including Leonid Zorin's *Varshavskaia melodiia* (*A Warsaw Melody*, 1967), Mikhail Roshchin's *Valentin i Valentina* (1971), and Arbuzov's *Staromodnaia komediia* (*An Old-Fashioned Comedy*, 1976). Challenging the generally optimistic spirit of Soviet drama, Aleksandr Vampilov introduced rebellious and alienated characters who struggled with the Soviet bureaucracy in plays such as *Utinaia okhota* (*Duck Hunting*, 1967) and *Proshlym letom v Chulimske* (*Last Summer in Chulimsk*, 1972). Vampilov's plays inspired a new wave of playwrights such as Liudmila Petrushevskaia, Aleksandr Galin, and Nina Sadur, who were looking for new forms of self-expression. Petrushevskaia depicts the absurdity of Soviet life with comic and tragic overtones, and the effects of spiritual emptiness, lack of love and understanding between people, and alcoholism in plays such as *Chinzano* (1973), *Uroki muzyki* (*Music Lessons*, 1973), and *Moskovskii khor* (*Moscow Chorus*, 1988).

See also: alcoholism; Arbuzov, Aleksei; censorship; cult of personality; Lenin, Vladimir Ilich; Petrushevskaia, Liudmila; Rozov, Viktor; Sadur, Nina; Socialist Realism; theatre, Soviet; Thaw; Vampilov, Aleksandr; World War II (Great Patriotic War); Zorin, Leonid

Further reading

Glenny, M. (ed.) (1989) *Stars in the Morning Sky*, London: Nick Hern Books.

Mikhailova, A. (ed.) (1979) *Classic Soviet Plays*, Moscow: Progress Publishers.

Reeve, F. (ed.) (1968) *Contemporary Russian Drama*, New York: Pegasus.

Segel, H. (1979) *Twentieth-Century Russian Drama: From Gorky to the Present*, New York: Columbia University Press.

Yershov, P. (1956) *Comedy in the Soviet Theatre*, New York: Frederick A. Praeger Publishers.

OLGA PARTAN

drinks, alcoholic

According to a medieval Russian chronicle, in the tenth century, Grand Prince Vladimir said, 'Drinking is the joy of Russia and we cannot live without it'. Indeed, Russians enjoy drinking perhaps more than any other nation in the world. Medieval Russians did not have distilled drinks and drank mead and beer. Distillation of alcohol from rye or wheat began in the sixteenth century, and thereafter vodka – grain alcohol diluted with water, usually to 80° proof – became Russia's national drink. Generally Russians drink vodka or other alcoholic beverages with meals. On social occasions glasses are always raised together, accompanied by a toast. Vodka is also traditionally consumed with a wide variety of appetizers (*zakuski*).

Russians also adopted alcoholic beverages from other countries, both hard liquors and wines. Brandy is popular and drunk during a meal. Any brandy is called *koniak* (cognac), but few can afford French cognac, preferring instead to drink less expensive brandies from former Soviet republics, particularly Armenia, Georgia, and Moldova, or the even less expensive brandy from the Russian republic of Dagestan. Less common are the Georgian grape vodka, *chacha*, and Ukrainian *gorilka*, grain vodka flavoured with honey and, often, pepper.

Georgia, Moldova, and the Crimea are traditional suppliers of wines to Russia, although since the transition to a market economy, wines from all over the world are readily available. Crimea produces predominantly sweet dessert wines, while Georgia and Moldova export dry table wines. Crimea is also famous for its sparkling wines or champagne, which most Russians prefer semi-sweet or sweet.

In summer, many Russians make various *nastoiki* (vodka flavoured with fruit, berries, or herbs) and *nalivki* (fermented fruit and berry drinks). In the countryside, poor peasants often resort to *samogon* (moonshine), though its production is illegal even for personal consumption.

The beginning of the twenty-first century witnessed a tremendous growth in the popularity of beer, which can be of high quality and is beginning to be exported.

See also: vodka

Further reading

Christian, D. (1990) *Living Water: Vodka and Russian Society on the Eve of Emancipation*, Oxford: Oxford University Press.
Goeben von, R. and Milne, B. (1999) *Vodka*, New York: Friedman/Fairfax.
Pokhlebkin, V. (1992) *A History of Vodka*, trans. R. Clarke, London: Verso.

KONSTANTIN KUSTANOVICH

drinks, non-alcoholic

Russians traditionally have made non-alcoholic drinks from fruit. *Kompot* is made by boiling fresh or dried fruits with sugar; *mors* is made from fresh berry juice and sugar mixed with water. *Limonad* is any variety of fruit-flavoured carbonated water. *Kisel* is a fruit jelly-drink made with cornflour. Served at funeral dinners, it is also a traditional dessert, and occurs in various idioms and expressions, such as *kiselnye berega i molochnye reki* ('*kisel* shores and milk rivers'), which means 'paradise on earth'.

Kvas is a mildly alcoholic drink made of stale black bread, a fermenting agent, sugar, and malt. It can also be made with fruit or flavoured. During the Soviet period, it was sold at stands in reusable glasses or mugs, or dispensed into the customer's jar or container from small trailers fitted with spigots. *Med* or *medovukha* is a drink made of fermented and spiced honey, yeast, and hops. *Sbiten* is a hot drink made from honey, spices, hops, and a variety of herbs. *Gogol-mogol* is a rich drink made of egg yolks mixed with sugar, traditionally served to children.

At the table, Russians drink mineral water (*mineralnaia voda*); particularly popular are the carbonated varieties *Narzan* and *Borzhomi*. Other brands with high mineral levels are consumed at the bathhouse (*bania*) or for medicinal purposes. In the Soviet period, coin-operated machines on the street dispensed carbonated water in reusable glasses.

By far the most popular non-alcoholic drink is tea, drunk throughout the day in various strengths. The traditional way to make tea is to steep tea leaves in boiling water without a net or other strainer; the result is a very strong tea called *zavarka*, which is mixed with boiling water to adjust the tea's strength. Tea is drunk for warmth and to quench thirst, by itself, with sweets, or after dinner.

See also: bania; dining, Russian; dining, Soviet; kvas

MICHELE BERDY

dublenka

A coat made by sheepskin tanning, with the leather outside and the fur inside. Today sheepskin coats are very popular winter wear in Russia, having replaced the widespread Soviet thick woollen coat with fur collar. Supremely comfortable, warm, and wind-resistant, sheepskin is lighter than fur and not as expensive, warmer than down, and more durable than cloth.

Fashion specialists believe that the sheepskin coat originated in Russia. Sheepskin crafting existed during the era of Peter the Great, when the *dublenka* was called a Romanov short fur coat. Russian soldiers during the war of 1812 also sported short sheepskin coats.

In the 1950s, the Russian sheepskin coat became fashionable and was imported into the European fashion world by designers of Moscow's House of Fashion The famous Russian couturier Slava Zaitsev made a collection of sheepskin coats and traditional Russian boots, called *valenki*.

See also: coats; felt boots; Zaitsev, Viacheslav

ELENA SKIPETROVA

Dudintsev, Vladimir Dmitrievich

b. 16 [29] July 1918, Kupiansk, Ukraine; d. 23 July 1998, near Moscow

Writer

A prosaist trained in law who worked for newspapers and wrote stylistically traditional fiction that took risks. Dudintsev's Thaw novel, *Ne khlebom edinym* (*Not by Bread Alone*, 1956), which dramatizes an inventor's struggle with the Soviet bureaucracy for acceptance of his metallurgical invention, caused a sensation. During Stagnation he published only two collections of works (1959, 1962), but made his mark again with the perestroika novel *Belye odezhdy* (*White Robes*, 1987) – an account of scientists' persecution during the late 1940s under the impact of Lysenko's influence. Dudintsev wrote the screenplay for the film version. State Prize (1988).

See also: literature, perestroika; literature, Thaw; science and technology

HELENA GOSCILO

Duma

The State Duma is the lower house of Russia's bicameral national parliament, the Federal Assembly (*Federalnoe sobranie*). Elections for the State Duma were held in December of 1993, 1995, 1999, and 2003. In these elections, half of the seats were filled by the winners in 225 single-member electoral districts (a plurality system), while the other 225 seats are filled by candidates listed on party lists according to the share of the vote received by that party nationally – a proportional representation system (PR). A party had to win at least 5 percent of the nationwide PR vote in order to receive any of the 225 PR seats in the Duma. In May 2005, President Putin signed a new law for elections to the State Duma that introduced a pure proportional-representation system and established the threshold for party-list representation at 7 per cent of the vote.

The primary role of the State Duma is to make laws. In the legislative process, bills must receive majority support in the State Duma and Federation Council, and be signed by the president. The Duma also approves the president's nominee for prime minister, conducts votes of no confidence in the government, appoints and removes the chair of the state bank, state auditors, and the chair of the office for human rights. When a party associated with the president has a majority in the Duma, as Putin's United Russia did after the 2003 elections, the president has the votes needed to pass his legislative agenda.

The head of the Duma is the Speaker, and the leadership organization within the Duma is the Council of the Duma. The Council of the Duma is composed of the Speaker and one representative from each of the registered deputy groups in the parliament. Each deputy, with the exception of the Speaker, Deputy Speakers, and leaders of deputy groups must serve on one of the standing committees of the Duma.

See also: political parties, post-Soviet; political structure, post-Soviet; Putin, Vladimir; United Russia

Further reading

Remington, T. (2001) *The Russian Parliament: Institutional Evolution in a Transitional Regime, 1989–1999*, New Haven, CT: Yale University Press.

VICKI L. HESLI AND JAMES KRUEGER

Dumbadze, Nodar Vladimirovich

b. 14 July 1928, Tbilisi; d. 14 September 1984, Tbilisi

Writer

One of the best Soviet Thaw writers, the Georgian Dumbadze gained fame among Russian readers with his novels *Ia, babushka, Iliko i Illarion* (*Granny, Iliko, Illarion, and I*, 1960) and *Solnechnaia noch'* (*Sunny Night*, 1962), depicting wartime life in a Georgian village. His invariably auto-biographical, first-person narratives combine drama and gentle humour, especially evident in the novel *Zakon vechnosti* (*The Law of Eternity*, 1978) and the novella *Kukaracha* (1984).

See also: Georgia; Thaw

ALEXANDER LEDENEV

Dunaevskii, Maksim Isaakovich

b. 15 January 1945, Moscow

Composer

Son of composer Isaak Dunaevskii, Maksim was born in Moscow and studied at the Moscow Conservatory with Tikhon Khrennikov and Dmitrii Kabalevskii – the two official masters of Socialist Realism in music. Yet Maksim Dunaevskii bypassed conventional aspects of Soviet music, to continue his father's traditions, writing music for film (mostly musical comedies) and original musicals. His most popular works include soundtracks for the musical mini-serials *D'Artanian i tri mushketera* (*D'Artagnan and the Three Musketeers*, 1978) and *Mary Poppins, do svidaniia!* (*Goodbye, Mary Poppins!*, 1983). He composed a new arrangement of his father's music for the film *Deti capitana Granta* (*Captain Grant's Children*, 1936) for its 1987 television remake. Since 1992, Dunaevskii has lived in the United States.

See also: Khrennikov, Tikhon; music in film; musicals, Russian/Soviet; Socialist Realism

KIRA NEMIROVSKAIA

Durov Animal Theatre

The Durov Animal Theatre was founded in 1912 by Vladimir Durov (1863–1934), a circus performer, clown, and animal trainer who used a method devoid of punishment and cruelty. He was the model for the stranger in the short story *Kashtanka* (*Chestnut*) by Anton Chekhov. The popular theatre, most commonly known as Durov's Corner (*Ugolok Durova*), has been variously called *Ugolok dedushki Durova* (Grandfather Durov's Corner), *Strana Chudes dedushki Durova* (Grandfather Durov's Wonderland) and *Teatr Zverei imeni V. L. Durova* (The V. L. Durov Animal Theatre). Since 1978, it has been headed by Durov's great-granddaughter, Natalia.

See also: circus

MICHELE BERDY

Durov, Lev Konstantinovich

b. 23 December 1931, Moscow

Actor

Featured in films since the mid-1950s, and sub-sequently in countless supporting roles, Durov has also appeared in television serials, including *Ognebortsy* (*Firefighters*, 2004), *Novyi russkii romans* (*A New Russian Romance*, 2005) and *V ritme tango* (*To the Rhythm of the Tango*, 2005). He has also been supporting actor in two of the most important films of the Stagnation years, Vasilii Shukshin's *Kalina krasnaia* (*The Red Snowball Tree*, 1973) and Elem Klimov's *Proshchanie* (*Farewell*, 1982), in the latter playing a character who embodies the fears and doubts of the ordinary citizen faced with massive social upheaval. He has also directed for television and lent his voice to children's cartoons.

See also: film, animation; film, television; Klimov, Elem; Shukshin, Vasilii

DAVID GILLESPIE

Dvorzhetskii, Vladislav Vatslavovich

b. 26 April 1939, Omsk; d. 28 May 1978, Gomel

Russian film and stage actor

Son of actor Vatslav Dvorzhetskii (1910–93), he was born during his father's political exile to Siberia. After earning a medical degree, Dvorzhetskii studied acting and worked at the Omsk District Drama Theatre. His stunning performance as the sadistic general Khludov in Aleksandr Alov and Vladimir Naumov's screen version of Bulgakov's *Beg* (*Flight*, 1970) shot Dvorzhetskii to stardom. The only other role in his prolific career of comparable quality is that of the disturbed astronaut Burton in Andrei Tarkovskii's *Solaris* (1972). The hypnotic, burning gaze of Dvorzhetskii's huge eyes, appearing more Martian than human, and his strange, 'foreign' mystique brought him numerous roles in second-rate genres. Dvorzhetskii died of a heart attack during a concert tour.

See also: Alov and Naumov; Tarkovskii, Andrei

PETER ROLLBERG

Dykhovichnyi, Ivan Vladimirovich

b. 1947, Moscow

Director, actor

Trained at the Shchukin School, Dykhovichnyi worked at the Taganka Theatre during the 1970s, later studying with Tarkovskii at the Moscow Higher Courses for Screenwriters and Directors. Dykhovichnyi's best-known film is *Prorva* (released in the West as *Moscow Parade*), controversial in the early 1990s because of its mixed aesthetic admiration for and indictment of high Stalinism. His less successful *Kopeika* (*The Kopeck*) depicts Russian society of the past 30 years through the successive owners of a *Zhiguli* car. Since 1999, Dykhovichnyi has worked as senior director at the television station RTR.

See also: Taganka Theatre; Tarkovskii, Andrei

RIMGAILA SALYS

Dzhigarkhanian, Armen Borisovich

b. 3 October 1935, Yerevan, Armenia

Stage and film actor

Dzigarkhanian attended a Russian high school in Yerevan and studied at the Sundakian Academic Theatre in Erevan, graduating in 1958. In 1967, he moved to Moscow, where at the Lenkom Theatre and Maiakovskii Theatre he demonstrated an awesome versatility in the classical and contemporary repertory, ranging from Shakespeare and Tennessee Williams to modern Russian authors. He became one of the most employed actors in both Armenian and Russian cinema, moving effortlessly from trivial entertainment to sophisticated art. His credits include leads in the psychological drama *Zdravstvui, eto ia!* (*Hello, It's Me*, 1966) and the darkly sarcastic comedy *Gorod Zero* (*Zero City*, 1989). People's Artist of the USSR in 1985.

See also: Lenkom Theatre; Maiakovskii Theatre

PETER ROLLBERG

E

East Bloc countries

The East Bloc countries comprised six East and Central European communist nations: Bulgaria, Czechoslovakia, East Germany, Hungary, Poland, and Romania. These states came under the dominance of the USSR as World War II was nearing its final stages. By 1945, the advancing Red Army had liberated most of German-occupied Eastern Europe. Once occupied by Soviet troops, these six states and their ruling Communist Parties gradually became politically subordinate to Moscow's policies.

From the outset, however, Soviet control over the region proved to be volatile. In 1948, communist Yugoslavia, under the leadership of Marshal J. B. Tito, refused to comply unconditionally with the Kremlin's directives. Arguing that there were many roads to socialism, Yugoslavia became the first Communist country to distance itself from the USSR and by 1961 it had become the founder of the Non-Aligned Movement. Albania also successfully broke relations with the Soviet Union by 1962, aligning itself instead with the People's Republic of China.

Bulgaria, Czechoslovakia, East Germany, Hungary, Poland, and Romania, tied by military and economic alliances, remained under Soviet domination until 1989. In 1949, the Soviet Union and its satellite states in Central and Eastern Europe established the Council for Mutual Economic Assistance (Comecon). For four decades the Comecon served as a framework for cooperation among the planned economies. In 1955, when the NATO alliance accepted West Germany as a member state, the USSR established the Warsaw Pact, a military equivalent of the Comecon. Even though the Warsaw Pact declared that relations among the signatories were based on total equality, mutual noninterference in internal affairs, and respect for national sovereignty and independence, the USSR used the organization to impose its will on its western neighbours. In 1956, Imre Nagy, Hungary's Communist Party leader, withdrew Hungary from the Warsaw Pact, ending the country's alliance with the Soviet Union. The Red Army invaded, brutally crushing the Hungarian resistance; 200,000 refugees escaped to the West following the invasion. Czechoslovakia was similarly occupied in 1968 after Czechoslovak Party Secretary Alexander Dubček refused to discontinue the country's liberalization policies. Though Dubček assured Soviet leadership that Czechoslovakia would not leave the Warsaw Pact, Warsaw Pact troops invaded Czechoslovakia, ending the so-called Prague Spring and the country's democratic experiment. The invasion led Soviet leader Leonid Brezhnev to announce the Brezhnev Doctrine as the formal Soviet policy regarding the East Bloc countries, whereby the Warsaw Pact countries had the right to intervene in the internal affairs of Communist nations whose actions threatened the international Communist movement.

In 1989, Mikhail Gorbachev proposed the so-called Sinatra Doctrine, which abandoned the Brezhnev Doctrine and guaranteed the USSR's non-interference in the internal policies of its Warsaw Pact allies. Gorbachev's doctrine had dramatic effects across East Bloc countries, since the local Communist regimes could not count on Soviet military might to protect them from mounting popular protests, which eventually ousted Communist governments from power in 1989.

See also: Brezhnev, Leonid; Gorbachev, Mikhail; perestroika and glasnost; Stagnation; Thaw

MARKO DUMANČIĆ

Easter, Orthodox

Easter (*Paskha*), described in the Orthodox liturgy as 'the feast of feasts', is the most important religious holiday for Russian Orthodox Christians. Easter observance, described extensively in memoirs and literature, was the religious form to which Russians clung most tenaciously and which the Soviet government fought most strenuously. With the revival of Orthodoxy in Russia after 1991, Easter has resumed its centrality.

After a service that lasts till dawn, Russian Orthodox eat the contents of Easter baskets containing the foods from which they have abstained for seven weeks: sausage (*kolbasa*), smoked meats, hard-boiled eggs, and the traditional Easter desserts of *kulich* (a cylindrical sweet yeast cake) and *paskha* (pyramid-shaped crustless cheesecake). Even otherwise non-observant Russians often go to cemeteries a week after Easter to share the paschal feast with their departed relatives in graveside picnics.

The Russian Orthodox Easter service is a liturgical masterpiece. Composers including Petr Tchaikovsky and Sergei Rachmaninov have written Easter music and incorporated it into their orchestral compositions.

See also: holidays, Russian Orthodox; Lent; Russian Orthodoxy

NADIESZDA KIZENKO

economic system, post-Soviet

Gorbachev's reforms in the second half of the 1980s paved the way for the transition from a centrally-planned to a market economy. The 1987 Law on Soviet State Enterprises introduced many market-oriented reforms. Gorbachev's initiatives of perestroika and glasnost encouraged the creation of cooperatives, small businesses, and joint ventures to help alleviate the gross inefficiencies of state organizations, and the 1990 New Enterprise Law dismantled the Soviet central industrial ministries. Market-oriented reforms accelerated when Yeltsin became president of Russia in late 1991 after the break-up of the Soviet Union. In early 1992, the government freed most prices from state control, cancelled many state orders to enterprises, and cut off most subsidies, forcing enterprises to seek new customers and become self-sustaining. Rampant inflation ensued, with prices rising in 1992 by 2,400 per cent, wages by 1,200 per cent, and incomes by 900 per cent compared to 1991. The black market still constituted a major segment of the economy.

Privatization of the economy, with government ownership of enterprises moving into private hands, began with the 1992 Law on Privatization of State and Municipal Enterprises, which allowed managers, other employees, and the public to own shares in enterprises. Abuses resulted and large holdings of shares ended up in the hands of senior enterprise managers, government officials, and other well-connected members of the *nomenklatura*. This rapid process of privatization without the development of a supporting infrastructure has often been referred to as shock therapy.

There was little new investment and many managers stripped company assets to enrich themselves; industrial production in 1994 declined from 1993 by 20 per cent. Still, privatization appeared to be somewhat successful in the mid-1990s, with substantial growth in the number of small businesses. GDP increased slightly during 1997, and inflation seemed under control at 11 per cent. Additionally, the 1996 Joint Stock Company Law established rules to strengthen shareholder rights, while the Law on Securities Market, passed the same year, included measures to protect minority shareholders. Such laws sought to increase investor confidence and attract funds to Russian enterprises.

However, foreign investment was minimal, and many managers spirited company profits to personal accounts abroad. This capital flight was estimated by the World Bank to have totalled over $88 billion between 1993 and 1996, while another study estimated $140 billion between 1992 and 1997. Also, the profits of many enterprises came primarily from loans to the government through investing in securities at annual interest rates that reached 200 per cent. In 1996, the oligarchs, who had become wealthy by acquiring many of the country's most valuable enterprises in the natural resources sector, continued buying government securities. Many loans were linked to their support for President Yeltsin's re-election and the interest income was often sent offshore. The loans, which constituted over 15 per cent of Russia's GNP, however, became worthless when the government defaulted on its debts in August 1998. Because the loans also accounted for 35 per cent of bank assets, many banks also failed. GDP and industrial output declined by 5 per cent relative to 1997, and inflation rose by more than 80 per cent. The government's debt exceeded $150 billion, and the default caused the IMF to postpone a $4.3 billion installment of its $22 billion economic package. The seemingly prosperous economy turned out to be a house of cards.

Although an economic disaster when it occurred, the country's 1998 financial crisis had an unexpected positive outcome. The subsequent devaluation of the ruble made foreign goods too expensive for most Russian consumers, who turned to Russian products, and domestic and foreign companies increased investments in plants and equipment. GDP grew strongly in 1999, with monthly increases of 6 to 11 per cent during the year over 1998. Exports increased, with Russia building a trade surplus with the US of nearly $4 billion. Foreign direct investment rose by 4.5 per cent compared to a decline of more than 6 per cent in 1998.

The decade ended with the state becoming more involved in the economy compared to the early years of developing a market economy. The government's enormous debt to the banks and the oligarchs, coupled with the devaluation of the ruble, had made the economy highly dependent upon the government's action – a situation that seemed to portend a return to the centuries-old tradition of strong, central governmental control of the economy and business.

With the resignation of President Yeltsin in 2000 and the appointment of Vladimir Putin as acting President, an opportunity arose to introduce clearer economic policies. Putin set the objective for Russia to become a member of the World Trade Organization, which required that the country be designated a market economy by WTO members. The US and Britain did so in the early 2000s, partly because government expenditures accounted for only 42 per cent of 2000 GDP, down from 54 per cent in 1950. The 2000 figure was slightly lower than that of Britain and France, but higher than that of the USA and Japan.

Putin's election in 2001 seemed to provide the stability critical for the business community, foreign investors, and the Russian people. Still, the excesses of the oligarchs and corrupt government officials during the 1990s continued to limit foreign investment and incurred the wrath of Russian citizens, especially when 25 Russians appeared on *Forbes* magazine's 2004 list of the world's billionaires, while 20 per cent of Russians lived below the poverty line. Many Russians and foreigners hoped that Putin would address such economic inequities by dealing with such issues as taxation, business legislation, property rights, and infrastructure. He did, in fact, present plans that included a government-run industrial policy. He also slashed the personal income tax rate from 30 to 20 per cent, and pledged to protect property rights while requiring companies to adopt international accounting standards. He clearly hoped to attract investment and improve the country's GDP of $190 billion, which was only 2 per cent of the US GDP. In 2002, total foreign investment increased to $20 billion, though direct investment was only $4 billion. The biggest investors were Germany, Cyprus (offshore Russian funds), Britain, and the USA. Russian investment abroad also totalled $20 billion, half of which was in the USA; however, only a small percentage was direct investment.

The economy continued to make strong progress in 2003 as real disposable income rose 20 per cent compared to the previous year. Industrial production rose 7 per cent, while investment increased 12.5 per cent as world oil prices tripled to over $30 a barrel. Revenue from crude oil, refined petroleum, and natural gas rose to almost $74 billion in 2003, as opposed to $25 billion in 1994. Nearly half of the petroleum output was exported, but exports accounted for nearly 80 per cent of revenues because domestic petroleum prices were highly subsidised. Small businesses numbered more than 882,000, slightly below the 2000 high. However, private property reforms progressed slowly, and the government still owned more than 90 per cent of the land.

In 2004, industrial production continued to grow at nearly 7 per cent during the first half, and the stock market reached a high of 785 in April. Problems were still apparent, however, with the economy dangerously dependent on petroleum and other natural resources, while the industrial sector was very weak. Government officials estimated that Russia needed $200 billion of new investment to accomplish Putin's goal of doubling GNP by 2014. The stock market was also tied closely to petroleum and other raw materials, and fell by almost 30 per cent in June, but fared better than during the 1998 crash, when it plummeted to 37. Graft and corruption prevailed, although Putin had committed to dealing with those seemingly intractable problems through such initiatives as improving corporate governance and clarifying private property rights. Finally, the spectre of renationalization of some enterprises or industries was raised when oligarch Mikhail Khodorkovskii, the CEO of Yukos Oil, was jailed and put on trial in mid 2004 on charges of fraud and tax evasion. Thus, although during the early 2000s substantial progress had been made toward strengthening the economy, much remains to be accomplished if Russia is to have a fully functioning market economy.

See also: Gorbachev, Mikhail; nomenklatura; oligarkh; perestroika and glasnost; privatization; Putin, Vladimir; shock therapy; Yeltsin, Boris

Further reading

Aslund, A. (1995) *How Russia Became a Market Economy*, Washington, DC: The Brookings Institute.

Puffer, S. and Associates (1996) *Business and Management in Russia*, Cheltenham: Edward Elgar.

Puffer, S., McCarthy, D., and Naumov, A. (2000) *The Russian Capitalist Experiment: From State-Owned Enterprises to Entrepreneurships*, Cheltenham: Edward Elgar.

Randall, L. (2001) *Reluctant Capitalists: Russia's Journey Through Market Transition*, New York: Routledge.

Shleifer, A. and Treisman, D. (2000) *Without a Map: Political Tactics and Economic Reform in Russia*, Cambridge, MA: MIT Press.

SHEILA M. PUFFER AND DANIEL J. MCCARTHY

economic system, Soviet

The Soviet economic system rested on two main principles: (1) state ownership of all means of production (all industrial property and virtually all land); and (2) central planning of production and consumption. First put into practice in 1928, when the first five-year plan was implemented, these principles remained in force until the late 1980s.

Each enterprise received a plan, which included a mix of economic inputs (labour and raw materials), capital investments, a schedule for completion, and prices for wholesale and retail trade. The plans were generated centrally, based on the previous performance of enterprises, their potential, and economic demands. Industrial enterprises, educational and food service establishments, hospitals, research institutes, and even the police were all subject to such planning.

Five-year plans coincided with five-year periods falling between regular gatherings of the Communist Party Congresses. There, party leaders – members of the Politburo – reported on the results of the previous five-year plan (whose production targets were invariably met and surpassed), and outlined production goals for the next five-year plan. These production goals were then passed to the Council of Ministers, where they were elaborated, and sent to GOS-PLAN, the State Planning Agency. GOSPLAN devised a set of detailed production targets for each sector of the economy, and, starting in 1957, for each geographic unit. GOSPLAN's imperative was to balance inputs and outputs, production targets, and necessary resources. Once the ministries received these plans, they divided them into quotas to be met by each enterprise, and forwarded them to enterprise directors for review and suggestions.

The planning process presupposed a great deal of feedback at all levels about the availability of resources and an assessment of existing productive capacities, resulting in a significant degree of bargaining about the feasibility of plans. Once enterprises obtained quotas from the ministries, their administration and sometimes even rank-and-file workers would draft precise plans. These detailed how they would fulfil quotas received from the ministries and what resources they would need. Drafts were forwarded back to the ministries and to GOS-PLAN, which, in turn, revised its master plan according to the drafts, and sent it to the Politburo and Central Committee of the CPSU for approval. After the plan was officially passed, it was again distributed among individual enterprises for implementation.

If a plan was fulfilled or surpassed the quotas, enterprise administrators and workers received bonuses. Therefore, it benefited enterprises to underreport their productive potential to the ministries at the planning stage in order to receive a lower quota. Yet, at the same time, quotas were usually set on the basis of enterprises' past performance. Successfully meeting one's quota meant that the bar would be raised in the next five-year plan. Constant pressure to increase outputs made enterprises value quantity much higher than quality, leading to the production of inferior goods that could hardly compete internationally. Often enterprises manipulated reports to inflate their achievements.

There were other problems in the planning process as well. Although matching plans were generated for suppliers that produced spare parts, in reality, parts and other materials required for production often arrived only a few days before the deadline for meeting quotas. This situation led to 'storming' (*shturmovshchina*) – a last-ditch effort to produce the maximum possible by the deadline. In an attempt to get supplies in time and to fulfil the plan, enterprise directors regularly engaged in second-economy dealings. Specifically, there was a widespread system of semi-legal reciprocal relations among managers, which helped procure supplies, materials, and equipment, enabling enterprises to achieve production targets set by planners.

Fear of supply shortages also encouraged hoarding. The country's leadership tolerated *blat* and other informal practices because they were indispensable to the functioning of the centrally planned economy. The pervasiveness of *blat*, however, undermined the basic ideological principles of the Soviet regime, and was thus subversive for the system as a whole.

Central planning also created difficulties for consumers. Low-quality goods and shortages of most consumer goods and many foodstuffs were endemic to the Soviet economy. The state responded to shortages with rationing and closed distribution. Rationing was a system of hierarchically differentiated access to consumer goods; they were exchanged for ration cards, distributed through the workplace. Rations varied for different categories of labourers. Originally, Russia's tsarist government introduced rationing as a response to the economic crisis during World War I, but it continued until 1918. Reintroduced in 1929, officially abolished in 1935, then briefly reintroduced during World War II, rationing was unofficially practised even in the post-rationing period by local officials. They benefited from ordering local stores to hold produce and consumer goods intended for general consumers so as to give them to officials, their families, and their inner circles. In addition, the state systematically made access to goods and services a reward for loyalty and service to the regime. The privileged – particularly the Party, the cultural elite, and exemplary workers, known since the Stalin era as Stakhanovites – had access to a network of closed-distribution stores, cafeterias, hospitals, and health resorts. Although ordinary citizens were aware of these special establishments, in most cases their physical locations were masked behind inconspicuous facades and strictly guarded. Luxury foods, drinks, imported clothing, and high quality consumer goods were also unavailable to the general public, but accessible to the privileged at reduced cost in special stores, called by the commercial name *berezki* ('little birch trees'). They enjoyed many privileges free of charge, including dachas, apartments, cars, and holidays. Thus the salaries of Party officials were irrelevant as indicators of their well-being. This was the situation of so-called 'ruble inequality', in which the rubles of the elite were worth more than those of ordinary citizens.

Ordinary consumers, ineligible for these privileges, procured restricted goods and services through a mixture of *blat* and bribery. A system of barter and favours developed, covering commodities from *defitsit* chocolates and theatre tickets to officially free services, such as medical procedures and college admissions. These exchanges, stemming from shortages, produced further shortages, both by diverting resources from the formal economy and by providing numerous opportunities for personal gain to managers and workers in state enterprises, making them dependent on the continuation of the practice.

Another systemic reason for chronic shortages of consumer goods was the Soviet economy's priorities, which valorized development of and investments in heavy industry, including defence (group A), at the expense of light and food industries (group B). By the early 1960s, group A accounted for more than 70 per cent of the economic output. To support rapid industrialization, from the late 1920s steel was deemed a priority, with fewer resources devoted to consumer goods and services. Industrialization proceeded at a rapid pace during the 1930s, maintained high growth rates until the 1960s, after which the economy stagnated at a gradual rate slowed only by massive oil exports in the 1970s and 1980s.

Although the Soviet planned economy may be credited with swiftly turning an agrarian country into the second-largest world economy and a leading steel producer, with a military capacity that rivalled that of the USA, this feat was achieved at a staggering cost to human lives, resources, and the environment. Since the criterion of success for enterprises was neither the optimal use of resources nor economic efficiency, but fulfilment of the plan and appeasement of superiors, industries had no incentives to conserve resources or produce more efficiently. The 'soft budget' constraints of Soviet enterprises gave virtually unlimited access to credit and state subsidies. The whole system was geared toward extensive economic development, which often led to wasteful consumption of natural resources, raw materials, land, labour, and capital. The ultimate result was inefficiency, low productivity, and irreparable environmental damage.

See also: blat; Communist Party; GOSPLAN; shortages (defitsit)

Further reading

Gregory, P. and Stuart, R. (2001) *Soviet and Post Soviet Economic Structure and Performance*, 7th edn, Boston, MA: Addison Wesley.
Grossman, G. (1977) 'The "Second Economy" of the USSR', *Problems of Communism*, 26(5): 25–40.
Kornai, J. (1992) *The Socialist System: The Political Economy of Communism*, Princeton, NJ: Princeton University Press.
Lane, D. (1985) *Soviet Economy and Society*, New York: New York University Press.

ALYA GUSEVA

educational channels

Educational channels were well developed on Soviet television. The first such channels were established in the earliest years of Soviet television and continued to develop in the late Soviet period, during perestroika, and in the early 1990s. Produced at the Shabolovka special education department of Gosteleradio USSR, education programmes were devoted to all spheres of science and knowledge – mathematics, chemistry, biology, languages, arts, and music – and for both children and adults.

In the early 1990s, there was a state-sponsored educational channel, *Rossiiskie universitety* (Russian Universities). In 1994, six hours of that channel's evening broadcasting were given to a new private company, NTV, and, in 1996, NTV programming took over the channel. Since then, national Russian television has had no educational channel, with the exception of the independent Moscow company *Shkolnik TV* (Schoolkids' TV), established in 1999. Access to this channel, which features programmes on history, culture, ecology, and human rights, as well as classic films and performances, is provided free by the Moscow city administration to Moscow schools. Over 17 million people in 150 Russian and CIS cities watch Shkolnik TV programmes on cable.

See also: NTV; television, Soviet

NADEZHDA AZHGIKHINA

educational stipends, Soviet/post-Soviet (stipendiia)

A state allowance given out monthly to full-time students of higher and specialized secondary educational institutions. Stipends are granted to students according to their academic progress and participation in public and research work as demonstrated by exam results. The size of the stipends depends on the field of specialization and years of education. Highly successful students receive stipends named after outstanding scientists, writers, and sponsors. Post-Soviet stipends are divided into two categories: academic, paid to students with high exam marks (4 or 5); and social, given to orphans, disabled students, students from large or single-parent families, etc.

See also: academic year, Soviet and post-Soviet; educational system, post-Soviet; educational system, Soviet

ALEXANDER LEDENEV

educational system, post-Soviet

The post-Soviet period in Russian education brought changes first away from central control, then back toward a reinvigorated government vision of education as a tool for developing social capital and helping to spur the country's economic growth. Problems abounded in the early 1990s: many schools were privatized, financial resources were used inefficiently, and children's health deteriorated badly. State curricular standards were imposed for the core academic subjects, and a single state exam for entrance to tertiary education was created. At the start of the new century, the government launched a set of new initiatives to modernize the educational system and enable students to learn new skills, such as creative problem solving and collaborative effort, seen as essential for Russia's future economic competitiveness.

The establishment of the post-Soviet government of Russia in late 1991 brought immediate surface changes for the education system. Yeltsin's Decree Number 1 addressed education and suggested it would be a priority for his administration.

The Law on Education (1992) was controversial, however, because it did not initially ensure the right to a full secondary education. Rampant inflation, beginning in 1992, and consequent budget cuts made further progress virtually impossible for almost a decade. Economic conditions resulted in rapid differentiation within the school system: many state schools became specialized 'lycées' or 'gymnasia' (some of which charged fees), and expensive private schools opened to serve the emerging elite of New Russians. Many former Soviet vocational schools and tertiary institutions were either privatized or changed their names and missions to serve the new economy; schools of business, and law proliferated. The state sought to maintain order by establishing curricular standards, reserving Federal control over basic subjects (Russian language and literature, mathematics, natural sciences). Regional and local authorities were allowed to determine curricula for history, social sciences, the humanities, and non-Russian languages.

Difficult economic conditions brought a number of problems. Many Russian teachers were paid only sporadically in the 1990s; meagre budgets forced school directors to scrounge resources for needed repairs. In higher education, professors openly solicited 'tutoring' fees (bribes) to ensure that students would pass entrance exams. Interlinked social ills (alcoholism, smoking, drugs, family disintegration, sexual abuse, environmental degradation, poor diet, and psychological stress) boosted pupil illness, school absences, and poor performance. Declining births and movement of rural residents to the cities left a multitude of substandard rural schools with few students; maintaining teachers in these schools put serious strain on budgets.

At the start of the new century, the state began to reassert central oversight and control. The Russian economy gradually stabilized, and the government began to define Russia's future in terms of increased participation in a global and interconnected economic system. Russian students began to participate in international studies of academic achievement (TIMSS and PISA), and their performance in these exams, surprisingly, was not as good as had been expected. The old 'command and control' approach to preparing human capital was seen as ineffective in preparing the flexible problem-solvers that the economy demanded.

The government's response to these new indications of lowered educational performance was a series of programmes to modernize the educational system. A government programme of 2000 sought to make development of human capital a state priority. In 2001, a concept paper on the modernization of education stressed accessibility, quality, and merit as important goals. A paper on social and economic development (2003) demonstrated that these views on the importance of the 'new economy' were centrally held within the government.

One key approach was to increase funding for general education, and to improve the transparency of how money flowed through the system (earlier increases in school funding disappeared or were redirected as they made their way from federal to regional to local levels). Teachers' salaries were improved, but still lagged seriously behind salaries for other workers. Talented younger teachers continued to leave the system for more lucrative work in other sectors. State support for universities was a subject for prolonged debate in the early 2000s, with many in the government arguing for a kind of triage of institutions – the most competitive would continue to receive state funding, the weakest would be allowed to wither away, and those in the middle would be encouraged to develop new foci or privatize their operations.

The government sponsored a number of efforts to improve students' academic performance and enable them to develop the sorts of complex, collaborative problem-solving skills seen as critical for Russia's economic future. Some experimentation with alternative models for school teaching and organization continued, and the state supported a network of 'federal experimental sites' via an annual competition. A new emphasis on measuring the outcomes of education resulted in the first-ever common standardized test for entrance to higher education, the *Edinyi gosudarstvennyi ekzamen* (Unified State Exam). (The exam was also intended to remove the incentive for professors to supplement their own incomes with the 'tutorial bribes' noted above.) Considerable effort was invested in the creation and distribution of new textbooks, of which some were truly novel and others represented merely a repackaging of old content.

An interesting aspect of these efforts to modernize the educational system was a new emphasis on the use of information and communication technologies (ICTs) as a tool for change. A government initiative known as 'E-Russia' (2002) advocated the importance for Russia's economic future of the emerging ICT sector generally, and a related document known as 'E-Education' (2001) indicated how technology might be used within the education system. An 'E-Learning Support Project', funded by the government and the World Bank, was launched in 2005 to help create electronic resources for teaching and learning, train teachers and administrators in the use of new-generation educational materials, and create networks of resource centres first in seven pilot regions, and eventually throughout the nation. The frankly economic intent of the project was balanced by an awareness of the need to provide adequate support for teachers as they develop new approaches to teaching and new ways of measuring student success.

See also: economic system, post-Soviet; New Russians; privatization; Soros Foundation; Yeltsin, Boris

STEPHEN T. KERR

educational system, Soviet

Education made major contributions to the Soviet state by establishing conditions of general literacy and enabling the construction of a modern industrial economy. It was conspicuously powerful in addressing issues of mass social development, while less successful in fulfilling individual needs. Tensions existed over the scope of vocational vs. academic instruction, the place of national culture and history in a centralized curriculum, the place of ideological preparation, and the extent of access to study at the tertiary level. As the Soviet era came to a close, these tensions became extreme, and new approaches to the organization and conduct of schooling began to emerge.

Early Soviet education faced immediate and daunting challenges: developing literacy among the still mostly peasant population, rebuilding the country after years of war, and helping children who had grown up as orphans during this period. Efforts in the 1920s and early 1930s saw considerable variety in school organization, curriculum, and pedagogy, but under Stalin's leadership, the system quickly became highly regimented and remained so until the collapse of the USSR.

Children entered the system through day care facilities and kindergartens (which were run by factories and farms as a service for working parents). Children began first grade at the age of 7, a year later than in many countries. For much of the Soviet era, the state guaranteed only an incomplete secondary education (through grade eight); further secondary (ending at grade ten) or vocational education was widely available. Entrance to tertiary education (whether a general university or a specialized vocational institute) was competitive. Vocational education was offered at two levels: unspecialized (through a *professionalno-tekhnicheskoe uchilishche*, professional-technical academy or PTU) and specialized (through *srednee spetsialnoe uchebnoe zavedenie*, specialized secondary educational institutions). The system also included networks of special schools (*spetsshkoly*, for gifted and privileged students) and schools for the disabled and handicapped.

The Soviet curriculum was generally well designed, integrated, and (as experienced by students) intense. Sciences were taught at multiple levels, so that a student would have some chemistry in each of four years, physics in five, and so forth. While parents complained that their children were overburdened with large amounts of reading and homework, the system was remarkably effective in serving a command-administrative economy. While national differences among the peoples of the USSR were nominally recognized via distinct curricula, only the largest nationality groups had anything like a complete curriculum available in their native tongue; most made do with an early smattering of native language and culture.

The educational system was hierarchically organized. Union-level ministries sent orders to ministries at the republic level, which controlled regional and city education offices, which controlled individual schools. At the school level, the *direktor* (school principal or head teacher) organized all aspects of school life, aided by a *zavuch* (assistant principal/deputy for instruction), and the teachers. Teachers were technically employed to teach a certain number of lessons per week, often fewer than they would have in the West, but often taught more than the assumed minimum to enhance earnings.

Class sizes sometimes exceeded forty pupils, and textbooks, lab equipment, and other supplies were often in short supply. The physical condition of schools, especially toward the end of the Soviet era, was often very poor; many schools lacked basic amenities such as central heating and indoor plumbing. Extracurricular activities – sports and children's clubs – were not under the auspices of schools, but were located elsewhere in the community.

Relatively little research or development work was conducted on the educational system. *Akademiia pedagogicheskikh nauk SSSR* (the Academy of Pedagogical Sciences of the USSR) developed curricula and addressed some problems, but most of its work was not valued by teachers. The small amount of statistical data collected about the system consisted mostly of numbers of students enrolled in various types of institutions. Almost no information was gathered on student success or on barriers to learning.

Reforms over the entire Soviet period sought to find the right balance among academic and vocational subjects, and increasing labour shortages created pressure to deliver labour-ready 'cogs' to the military-industrial complex. A final Soviet reform in 1983–84, led by Mikhail Gorbachev, moved the start of school down to age 6. In addition to increased efforts at labour training and improved ideological indoctrination, the reform also introduced a new subject, *informatika* (computer technology and programming) into the curriculum.

Coming at the start of perestroika, this reform coincided with the emergence of a movement of 'educational innovators', including teachers, psychologists, and public intellectuals, all of whom pushed for more radical changes in the system. Teachers were urged to discard the dominant model of impersonal and harsh collectivism, and to work more directly with pupils and parents, practising a 'pedagogy of cooperation'. New and more creative approaches to pedagogy were devised and promulgated both through official teachers' newspapers and informal 'Eureka' clubs for teachers in many cities. A few school directors emerged as models of more democratic practice. Some educational entrepreneurs offered consulting services to schools and regions interested in changing their models of education.

The end of the Soviet era brought both radical change and disintegration. In the late 1980s, a small cadre of progressive reformers and experts came together to form the *Vremennyi nauchno-issledovatelskii kollektiv 'Shkola'* (Ad Hoc Research Committee on the School). Through a series of position papers, proposals, and models, they substantially influenced the direction of discussion about education in ways that stressed 'democratization, humanization, and humanitarization (i.e., reintroduction of subjects from the humanities)'. In 1990, Eduard Dneprov, leader of that group, became Minister of Education for the RSFSR (and later for post-Soviet Russia). He pushed for further basic changes in curriculum, pedagogy, and teacher preparation, for decentralization of the system and more flexible funding models.

But by the end of 1991, deteriorating conditions in schools, low teacher salaries, incipient inflation, and an increasing gap between what schools offered and what the economy was coming to demand led many young people and teachers to leave schools and seek their fortune in the market. Schools increasingly were staffed by an aging, almost entirely female force of teachers.

See also: administrative structure, Soviet; Gorbachev, Mikhail; pedagogy, Soviet; perestroika and glasnost

STEPHEN T. KERR

Efremov, Oleg Nikolaevich

b. 1 October 1927, Moscow; d. 24 May 2000, Moscow

Actor, director

Efremov became a star shortly after his stage debut in 1949. He helped found the Sovremennik

Theatre in 1956, leading it until 1970, when he became chief director at the Moscow Art Theatre, which he ran until his death. As an actor on stage and in the popular films *Zhivye i mertvye* (*The Living and the Dead*, 1964), *Beregis avtomobilia* (*Watch Out for Cars*, 1966) and *Tri topolia na Pliushchikhe* (*Three Poplars on Pliushchikha*, 1968), Efremov was the symbol of an entire generation. His heroes had complex, tragic fates but never lost their charm, humour, and generosity. As a director, he favoured plays with a strong commitment to civic values.

See also: Moscow Art Theatre; Sovremennik Theatre

JOHN FREEDMAN

Efros, Anatolii Vasilevich

(né Natan Isaevich)

b. 3 July 1925, Kharkov; d. 13 January 1987, Moscow

Stage director

One of the greatest directors of the second half of the twentieth century, Efros did much of his work during the Stagnation era. His philosophical art addressed existential issues of life and death instead of affirming the regime, engaging in anti-Soviet opposition, or purveying a social message. In the mid-1960s, as his works increasingly diverged from official social optimism, he fell out of favour with the authorities.

A graduate of GITIS, Efros took over and transformed the *Tsentralnyi detskii teatr* (Central Children's Theatre) in 1954; under his direction, young actors including Efremov, Durov, and Tabakov launched their careers. In 1963, he did the same with the *Teatr Leninskogo komsomola* (Lenin Komsomol, or Lenkom, Theatre), but was removed from his post in 1967 for directorial 'distortions', his philosophical contemporary treatment of the classics. He moved to the *Teatr na Maloi Bronnoi* (Malaia Bronnaia Theatre), where he remained for seventeen years, securing the theatre's enormous popularity. In 1975, Iurii Liubimov invited him to direct Chekhov's *Cherry*

Orchard at the Taganka Theatre. Nine years later, Efros became director of the Taganka when Liubimov stepped down under tumultuous circumstances. Many Taganka actors loyal to Liubimov refused to work with Efros, who died of a heart attack in 1987.

Moving away from the lyricism of his early stagings, such as Viktor Rozov's *V poiskakh radosti* (*In Search of Happiness*, 1957) and *V den svadby* (*On the Wedding Day*, 1964), Efros portrayed lonely human beings forsaken by God and the universe, emphasizing the absurdity of the human condition. Through the interplay of rhythms, lights, and continuous motion of actors on stage, Efros grasped the secret of expressing the fragile precariousness of life. He excelled at Molière's *Don Juan* (1973), Gogol's *Zhenitba* (*The Marriage*, 1975), and Turgenev's *Mesiats v derevne* (*A Month in the Country*, 1977), portraying characters who longed for a higher calling but ended up betrayed by mundane reality.

A former student of Stanislavsky's protégée, Maria Knebel, Efros steadfastly followed the étude method, which allowed actors to produce spontaneous, immediate emotions contributing to the director's trademark floating (*plavaiuschee*) *mise en scène*. Stage movement reflected characters' emotional changes, while the director's casting principle was determined by the actor's psychological/emotional type. Performances resembled ballets amidst minimalist sets, with leitmotifs providing unity.

Efros's best late productions include Shakespeare's *The Tempest* (1983) and Molière's *Le Misanthrope* (1986), staged at the Taganka Theatre.

In addition to his stage works, Efros directed a number of films, the most significant of which is *V chetverg i bolshe nikogda* (*On Thursday and Never Again*, 1977).

See also: Durov, Lev; Efremov, Oleg; Lenkom Theatre; Liubimov, Iurii; Malaia Bronnaia Theatre; Rozov, Viktor; Russian Academy of Theatre Arts; Stagnation; Tabakov, Oleg; Taganka Theatre

DASHA KRIJANSKAIA

Eifman, Boris Iakovlevich

b. 22 July 1946, Rubtsovsk

Choreographer, director

After graduating as a dancer from the Kishinev School of Choreography in Moldova, in 1972, Eifman received a diploma from the Choreography Department at the Leningrad Conservatory. He subsequently worked for the Leningrad Malyi Theatre before founding The New Ballet of Leningrad in 1977. His company, now touring the world as the Eifman Ballet of St. Petersburg, has a distinct reputation created by the more than forty works by Eifman that the company performs. Fusing classical ballet vocabulary with contemporary ballet, his choreography favours expressive, athletic, and emotionally charged actions, which allow dancers to probe the characters' psychology. Following the tradition of narrative ballet, Eifman has explored plots from classical literature in Tolstoi's *Anna Karenina* (2004); Dostoevskii's *Idiot* (1980); and Bulgakov's *Master and Margarita* (1987), among others. During the 1990s, Eifman's ballets often took the form of dramatic biography, which allowed him to investigate the dark, psychologically charged side of the creative personality, as in the ballets *Nizhinskii*; *Tchaikovskii: The Mystery of Life and Death*; *The Red Giselle* (based on the life of dancer Olga Spessivtseva); and *Don Juan and Molière*. Eifman received two Golden Mask (*Zolotaia maska*) awards in 1997 and 1999.

See also: ballet, post-Soviet; ballet, Soviet

TATIANA SENKEVITCH

Ekaterinburg

At Ekaterinburg in south-central Russia, a few kilometres into Asia, Lenin's Bolsheviks brutally assassinated Tsar Nicholas II and his entire family on 16 July 1918, just one of many notable events in the history of a large provincial city founded in 1724 by order of Tsar Peter the Great and named after his wife Ekaterina. The USSR made the city into a top secret centre of strategic research institutes called Sverdlovsk after Iakov Sverdlov, who supposedly ordered the 1918 assassination. Sverdlovsk's rocket base shot down an American U2 reconnaissance aircraft in 1960. The city regained its original name in 1992.

See also: Urals

EDWARD ALAN COLE

Ekho Moskvy (Echo of Moscow)

Ekho Moskvy (Echo of Moscow) is a popular independent radio station (91.2 FM) founded in 1990. Its current director is Aleksei Venediktov. The station was part of embattled tycoon Vladimir Gusinskii's Media-Most empire when a court decision in 2001 placed the station under the authority of the government-controlled natural gas company Gazprom. The nation's pre-eminent news station, famous for unbiased information on political, social, and economic issues (and the only independent broadcaster to stay on the air during a 1991 attempted hardline coup against President Gorbachev), it is broadcast in thirty-nine regions with over 2 million listeners. It is considered the news station for educated listeners. Its trademark is live interviews with call-in questions.

See also: censorship; Coup, August 1991; Gusinskii, Vladimir; radio, post-Soviet

VLADIMIR STRUKOV

Elagina, Elena Vladimirovna

b. 4 July 1949, Moscow

Artist

A graduate of the literature department of the Orekhovo-Zuevo College of Education (1975), from 1964 until 1976 Elagina worked in the studio of the sculptor Ernst Neizvestnyi. She studied with Alisa Poret, a student of Pavel Filonov's, and worked as an illustrator for the magazine *Znanie i sila* (*Knowledge and Strength*, 1969–78). From 1979 to 1989, Elagina was a member of the Collective Action Group and participated in many performances. Since 1990, she and her husband, Igor Makarevich, have been occupied with the mythology of the Soviet epoch – the history of its signs and symbols. Anonymous mass-produced texts of the Stalin era regularly underlie their installations, whereby under the guise of modest restorers of earlier art they select visual equivalents for the texts so as to revive their latent spontaneous, immediate impact. Their works emanate the atmosphere of a romantic fairy tale with an unhappy ending.

NATALIA KOLODZEI

emigration (emigratsiia)

Political emigration has always had a special meaning in Russian history due to what the historian Sergei Solovev has described as the alternating dominance of the population's habit of dispersal and the government's efforts to catch, settle, and secure. The Old Russian, Solovev maintains, was always escaping something or somebody – Tatar or Lithuanian masters, oppressive taxation, an evil provincial governor, or a local bureaucrat. The list of famous Russians trying to escape from tsarist Russia includes Prince Andrei Kurbskii, whom some consider the first Russian political émigré. A protégé of Ivan the Terrible, he became critical of his sovereign's despotism, and in 1564 defected to Lithuania. Aleksandr Pushkin's attitude towards Russia alternated between patriotism and a strong desire to leave. 'It was the devil's work to get me born in Russia with soul and talent!' he wrote to his wife in 1836. He might have become a political émigré, but his attempts to get an exit visa, on the pretext of poor health, failed. In 1847 Aleksandr Gertsen (Herzen) left Russia after internal exile and harassment for his political activity. His journal, *The Bell* (*Kolokol*), which he published together with his lifetime friend Nikolai Ogarev from 1857 till 1867 in London and Geneva, was smuggled into Russia and helped the emergence of the revolutionary movement. (In 2002, Aleksandr Shlepianov attempted to revive *Kolokol* in London, but the enterprise was short-lived.)

Emigration from the Soviet Union started immediately after the Bolshevik Revolution of 1917. The so-called First Wave of emigration comprised mostly political leaders, and members of the aristocracy and the intelligentsia. Some, despite their strong opposition to the Bolshevik regime, refused to leave what they felt was their ailing country. The feeling is expressed in Anna Akhmatova's short poem of 1917 *Kogda v toske samoubiistva* (*When in a suicidal gloom* . . .), in which the speaker shuts her ears to the 'shameful speech' of a voice that calls her to leave her 'gloomy and sinful country' forever. Some members of the intelligentsia were forced to leave: by Lenin's secret decree of 1922, about 200 prominent philosophers and scholars (Pitirim Sorokin and Nikolai Berdiaev among them) were rounded up, loaded on a ship, which later became known as 'the philosophers' ship', and sent to Europe. The so-called Second Wave of emigration included POWs and those who left with the retreating German army during World War II.

The Third Wave started in the early 1970s and peaked at the decade's end. Its representatives fall into four main categories: those forcibly expelled from the country (Solzhenitsyn, Vladimir Bukovskii); defectors (Baryshnikov, Godunov); those whose citizenship was revoked while they were travelling abroad (Brodskii, Rostropovich, Aksenov, Galich, Viktor Nekrasov); and those who gave up their Soviet citizenship in order to reunite with relatives (real or invented) in other countries, mostly in Israel. There is an ongoing debate in the Russian émigré community on whether Russian culture of the diaspora is superior or inferior to the mainland's and whether there are one or two Russian cultures. The question is complicated by the absence of homogeneity in the Russian émigré community. People are divided by the country and language of their residence, by income, by the degree of assimilation to the new culture, and by the strength of their ties with Russia. Numerous attempts to establish a single platform or a single publication that would reach the whole community invariably have failed. In 1981, Olga Matich brought together all practising Russian émigré writers at a conference in the University of Southern California, Los Angeles. She managed to establish a dialogue between writers with dramatically different political and aesthetical positions, such as Aksenov, Aleshkovskii, Dovlatov, Korzhavin, Limonov, Nekrasov, Siniavskii, Sokolov and Voinovich. What is sometimes called the Fourth Wave includes people who left Russia after the collapse of the Soviet Union (mostly for non-political reasons), embraces various categories, and is scattered throughout the United States, Europe, and Israel.

Parallel to the four waves of emigration, there were several waves of repatriation. The first resulted from the New Economic Policy (NEP) of the early 1920s, which ended the Civil War and instigated a degree of economic stability, and it included the writer Viktor Shklovskii. The second started in the mid-1930s, when it became clear that the Bolsheviks were there to stay. It included Aleksei Tolstoi who, after repatriation, became the official Soviet writer; the singer Aleksandr Vertinskii, who had been applying for a Russian visa since 1937 and in 1943, finally received permission to return; and the poet Marina Tsvetaeva, who after her return in 1939 could not assimilate and committed suicide in 1941. Many repatriates were imprisoned and/or executed, Tsvetaeva's husband Sergei Efron among them. The tragic story of a family of repatriates from France comprises the plot of a Russian–Ukrainian–Bulgarian–Spanish–French film, *East–West* (1999). Members of the Third Wave also included repatriates, the most outspoken being Eduard Limonov, who, after publishing an autobiographical novel, *Eto ia, Edichka* (*It's me, Eddie*, 1983), about his unhappy experiences in New York, returned to Russia and formed the National Bolshevik Party; and Aleksandr Zinovev, who had emigrated after publishing his satirical novel *Ziiaiushchie vysoty* (*The Yawning Heights*, 1976) in the West, but, disillusioned with the West, returned to Russia in 1999 and declared the Soviet period the zenith of Russian history.

See also: Aksenov, Vasilii; Aleshkovskii, Iuz; Baryshnikov, Mikhail; Brodskii, Iosif; Dovlatov, Sergei; Galich, Aleksandr; Godunov, Aleksandr; Korzhavin, Naum; Limonov, Eduard; literature, émigré; Nabokov, Vladimir; Nekrasov, Viktor; Rostropovich, Mstislav; Siniavskii, Andrei; Sokolov, Sasha; Solzhenitsyn, Aleksandr; Voinovich, Vladimir; Zinovev, Aleksandr

Further reading

Khotin, L. (ed.) (1981–90) *Abstracts of Soviet and East European Émigré Periodical Literature Quarterly*, Pacific Grove, CA: G. Gezen.

Limonov, E. (1983) *It's Me, Eddie*, trans. S.L. Campbell, New York: Random House.

Matich, O. and Heim, M. (eds) (1984) *The Third Wave: Russian Literature in Emigration*, Ann Arbor, MI: Ardis.

Nabokov, V. (1999) *Speak, Memory: An Autobiography Revisited*, New York: Alfred A. Knopf.

Zinik, Z. (1987) *The Mushroom-Picker*, trans. M. Glenny, New York: St. Martin's Press.

VLADIMIR PAPERNY

employment record (trudovaia knizhka)

The employment record, or *trudovaia knizhka*, is a state-issued document that records a person's education, training, credentials, employment, promotions, and demotions. Stored in the personnel department (*otdel kadrov*) of the person's current employer, it is accessible to authorized persons. Employment not registered in this 'booklet' is illegal. At retirement age, one's pension and other state-provided benefits are calculated on the basis of the employment record, which the Soviet state also used to control employment and the lack thereof, as well as for taxation. In post-Soviet Russia its role has become symbolic, as more and more citizens are paid unofficially in cash and rely on their personal savings rather than meagre state pensions.

VLADIMIR STRUKOV

Encyclopedia, Soviet

The *Bolshaia sovetskaia entsiklopediia* (*Great Soviet Encyclopedia*) is the largest and most comprehensive encyclopedia in Russian, launched by the Soviet government in 1925 to replace the popular pre-Revolutionary *Brockhaus and Efron Encyclopaedic Dictionary*. The Soviet Encyclopedia State Publishing House was established for this purpose. The original 65-volume edition (chief editor Otto Schmidt) was published in 1926–47,

with a second edition of 51 volumes (chief editors Sergei Vavilov and Boris Vvedenskii) – considered biased and incomplete – issued in 1950–58. Under the editorship of the Nobel Prize winner academician Aleksandr Prokhorov, the third and last, 30-volume edition of 1969–78 (the Red Edition) was translated into English. Shortened versions are the *Malaia sovetskaia entsiklopediia* (*Small Soviet Encyclopaedia*) and the one-volume *Sovetskii entsiklopedicheskii slovar* (*Soviet Encyclopaedic Dictionary*). Between 1957 and 1990 the annual *Ezhegodnik Bolshoi sovetskoi entsiklopedii* (*Yearbook of the Great Soviet Encyclopedia*) was released. The first online edition, an exact replica of the text and graphics of the 3rd edition, was published by Rubricon.ru in 2000. Since 2003 the third edition is available on CD.

Further reading

Prokhorov, A. M. (ed.) (1974–83) *Great Soviet Encyclopedia*, New York: Macmillan, London: Collier Macmillan, 31 volumes, 3 volumes of indexes. Trans. of *Bolshaia sovetskaia entsiklopediia*, 3rd edn (Moscow, 1969–78).

ALEXANDER LEDENEV

environment

Environmental protection (*okhrana prirody*) was not significantly developed in the USSR. During construction of large-scale industrial projects, environmental issues were of minimal concern at best, and industrial enterprises were built in dangerous proximity to natural 'treasures', such as a pulp and paper mill on the shore of Lake Baikal and an oil refinery on the banks of the Volga River.

Environment protection in the 1950s and the 1970s tended towards practical application rather than large-scale scientific research, manifested in the authorities' struggle with poaching – mainly in fishing, for caviar was in demand on the black market and abroad. Scientific research on the rational use of nature began later, and the term 'ecology' was introduced only at the end of the 1980s.

The Russian Federation pays more attention to environmental issues. In 1991, it signed the

Kyoto Protocol, which limits emissions of carbon dioxide into the atmosphere. The environmental situation regarding the majority of territories in Russia, however, is dire: practically all major rivers are heavily polluted (especially the Volga River, on which there are many large cities and industrial enterprises). For many years, the level of noise and air pollution in Moscow, St. Petersburg, and Ekaterinburg has equalled that in the largest European cities. Northern Russian territories (the tundra and forest-tundra), where most of the natural deposits are extracted, present specific environmental hazards: non-ferrous metallurgy on the Kolskii peninsula and in the Norilsk region leads to a catastrophic level of soil and air contamination; the oil and gas industry in Western Siberia leads to degradation of deer pastures and pollution of the Ob River; gold mining in the Magadan oblast caused irremediable damage to topsoil; and pulp and paper mills in the Arkhangelsk oblast have decimated forests.

Another large problem is the pollution of water basins. The coastal waters of the Azov and the Black Sea are contaminated by drainage from large metallurgical and ship-repair plants and oil tankers. The Caspian and the Okhotsk Seas suffer from oil spills. Chemical weapons have remained sunk on the bottom of the Baltic Sea since World War II. Major ecological catastrophes include the Chernobyl disaster (1986) and several accidents at the radiochemical complex Maiak in the Cheliabinsk oblast (1949, 1957, 1967), whose total radioactive contamination far surpasses that from Chernobyl. The islands of Novaia zemlia on which nuclear weapon tests were conducted are also heavily contaminated.

Probably the only positive aspect of Soviet nature conservation was its excellent maintenance of nature preserves. The first of these, Belovezhskaia Pushcha (now in Belarus) and Askania-Nova (now in Ukraine), were established in Russia at the beginning of the twentieth century. After the October Revolution, the state took over the conservation of natural zones; the first Soviet preserve (Arkhangelskii) was founded in 1919. The USSR attributed great significance to nature preserves, creating scientific research stations and tourist retreats on their territories. At present the most popular nature preserves are the Solovetskii museum-preserve, the Baikal preserve, and 'Chernye zemli' (Black Lands) in the Kalmykia republic.

Against the background of the ongoing current macroeconomic crisis, the civic position of the population on the issues of environment is passive. At best, there are protests against growing amounts of everyday waste and struggle for the increase of the so-called 'Chernobyl' benefits. The 'green' movement in Russia is mostly represented by international organizations, such as the WWF and Greenpeace, though attempts to bring the issues of environment protection to the level of an entire party's political programme also have been made, though weakly. In 2004, a political organization called the All-Russian Green Party (*Vserossiiskaia partiia zelenykh*) was created, but has no representatives in the Russian parliament.

See also: Baikal; Chernobyl; defence industry; Duma; Ekaterinburg; Far North; health; Moscow; natural resources; political parties, post-Soviet; science and technology; Siberia; St. Petersburg; Urals; Volga region; World War II (Great Patriotic War)

IVAN TITKOV

Eralash

Television series

Eralash was founded in 1974 after director Alla Surikova suggested that the Gorkii Film Studio create a children's version of an adult satirical broadcast *Fitil*. Playwright Aleksandr Khmelnik and director Boris Grachevskii were hired to institute a series that by the early twenty-first century constituted over 170 broadcasts and twelve shows per annum by 2000. Short (10-minute), combined scenarios involving children in a multitude of adventures or mishaps define the 'mixed-up' aesthetic of *Eralash* (Mishmash). Humorous conflicts between misbehaving youngsters and peeved adults are orchestrated with zany melodies and prefaced by unsophisticated, animated titles; they are sometimes concluded with a teacherly finale.

See also: *Fitil*

DAVID MACFADYEN

Erenburg, Ilia Grigorievich

b. 14 (27) January 1891, Kiev; d. 31 August 1967, Moscow

Writer

Novelist, journalist, and memoirist who enjoyed wide popularity. Before World War II, he lived abroad and wrote satirical novels, notably *Neobyknovennye pokhozhdeniia Khulio Khurenito (The Extraordinary Adventures of Julio Jurenito,* 1922). Upon returning to Russia in 1941, he became a war correspondent and published anti-war novels that garnered Stalin Prizes. His novel *Ottepel (The Thaw,* 1956) heralded a period of liberalization and fundamental social changes subsequently referred to as the Thaw. Erenburg's memoirs *Liudi, gody, zhizn (People and Life,* 1961–66) introduced Russia to modern European culture.

See also: literature, Thaw; Thaw

TATYANA NOVIKOV

Ernst, Konstantin Lvovich

b. 6 February 1961, Moscow

Television and film producer

The son of a prominent biologist, Ernst studied biology at Leningrad University and worked as a research biochemist until 1988, when he joined the editorial staff of the TV news magazine *Vzgliad* (Viewpoint). Named general producer of Channel 1 in 1995 and its general director in 1999, Ernst jettisoned 'completely bad shows' and revived the channel's 'brand'. In 2002, he joined about thirty founding members of the 'Industry Committee', a media advocacy organization. Ernst has produced ten feature films, including the 2004 supernatural blockbuster *Nochnoi dozor (Night Watch),* and has co-written the television series *Starye pesni o glavnom (Old Songs about Important Things).*

See also: television channels; television, post-Soviet; television, Soviet; *Vzgliad* (Viewpoint)

TIMOTHY D. SERGAY

Erofeev, Venedikt Vasilievich

b. 24 October 1938, Kandalaksha Station, Murmansk region; d. 11 May 1990, Moscow

Writer

The inimitable voice of besotted Venichka animates Venedikt Erofeev's *samizdat* classic *Moskva-Petushki (Moscow Stations,* 1969), a compelling literary testament of the era of Brezhnevian Stagnation.

Erofeev's own story was as mysterious and tied to his time as that of his namesake hero. Born in the Arkhangelsk district above the Arctic Circle, he spent time in an orphanage after his father's arrest in 1945. Despite hardship, Erofeev completed high school with a gold medal in 1955 and entered Moscow State University, only to be expelled in 1956. Expelled also from Pedagogical Institutes in Orekhovo-Zuevo (1960) and Vladimir (1962), Erofeev did odd jobs. He had one son, Venedikt, born 1966, by Valentina Zimakova. Alcoholic, lacking documentation, Erofeev settled in Moscow in 1977 with his second wife, Galina Nosova. He suffered from throat cancer, for which he underwent operations in 1985 and 1988. He died of complications in 1990.

Always on the margins, fiercely independent, Erofeev was largely self-taught. He kept numerous notebooks, but few finished works survived. After the novel *Moskva-Petushki,* he produced a piece on Vasilii Rozanov (1973), the play *Shagi komandora (Footfalls of the Commander,* 1985), and a compilation of quotes from Lenin (1988). Another novel, *Dmitrii Shostakovich* (1972), was apparently lost, and the play *Dissidents, or Fanny Kaplan (Dissidenty, ili Fanni Kaplan,* 1991), remained unfinished. Erofeev's style tends to the aphoristic and paradoxical. He exploits unexpected conjunctions and utilizes all manner of ready-made textual material. His writing is most lyrical in *Moskva-Petushki,* a work that, in the words of Vladimir Muravev, 'brought Soviet everyday life into dialogue with world culture'.

See also: literature, Stagnation; samizdat

Further reading

Frolova, N. *et al.* (1991) 'Neskolko monologov o Venedikte Erofeeve', *Teatr* 9: 74–118.

Ryan-Hayes, K. L. (ed.) (1997) *Venedikt Erofeev's Moscow-Petushki: Critical Perspectives*, New York: Peter Lang.

ANN KOMAROMI

Erofeev, Viktor Vladimirovich

b. 19 September 1947, Moscow

Writer

Born to parents working in the Soviet diplomatic corps, Erofeev enjoyed the privilege of considerably more exposure to Western culture than most of his peers. A literary critic by training, he secured his place on the literary map by participating in 1979 in the underground almanac *Metropol* as both co-editor and contributor of fiction. Expelled from the Writers' Union, he became one of the prominent figures of the cultural underground. Subsequent years proved extremely productive for Erofeev the writer; while his works remained unpublished, he frequently read them publicly to crowds of intellectual devotees. He finally broke into print during perestroika. He extended his success in the short story with his 1990 novel, *Russkaia krasavitsa* (*Russian Beauty*), which attracted significant international attention, and his literary essays. It is the short stories that showcase Erofeev at his best as a stylist. His fiction often combines postmodernist playfulness with attention to transgressive sexuality, as exemplified by his story *Zhizn's idiotom* (*Life with an Idiot*), made into an opera by Alfred Shnittke and a film by Aleksandr Rogozhkin. Recent (semi-)autobiographical works include *Khoroshii Stalin* (*The Good Stalin*, 2004), which he calls a novel.

See also: *Metropol*; Rogozhkin; Aleksandr; Shnittke, Alfred

VITALY CHERNETSKY

Estonia

At 45,226 square kilometres of mostly flat and swampy territory, Estonia is the smallest of the three Baltic states, with an archipelago of over 1,500 islands, the two largest being Saaremaa and Hiiumaa. The area has been inhabited for approximately 11,000–13,000 years, but the forebears of the current inhabitants, the Finno-Ugric tribes, likely arrived 2,000–3,000 years ago. Throughout its history, Estonia has been dominated by foreign powers. Teutonic knights first conquered and Christianized it at the beginning of the thirteenth century; it then came under the control of its Lithuanian neighbours. Denmark, Sweden, Poland and Prussia all laid claim to this land at various times until it was incorporated into the Russian Empire in 1721.

Following the 1917 October Revolution, Estonia fought a brief war for independence, which it secured on 2 February 1920 and maintained until 1940, when it was occupied by the Soviet Union under the secret terms of the Hitler–Stalin non-aggression pact. Germany's invasion of the USSR in 1941 resulted in Estonia's occupation by the Nazis until 1944, when it was reoccupied by the Soviet Union – a fact unacknowledged by most Western governments. Agitation for independence persisted, and in November 1988, the republic's soviet declared sovereignty. On 20 August 1991, Estonia became a fully independent country in what was known as the 'Singing Revolution'. Ethnic Estonians make up approximately 68 per cent of the population of 1.33 million (2005). Russians, by far the largest minority at around 26 per cent, reside mostly in the capital, Tallinn, and in the industrial areas in the northeast. Though a resource-poor country, Estonia has reserves of oil shale, limestone, peat, phosphorus, and timber. On 1 May 2004, Estonia became a member of the European Union, two months after joining NATO. The country plans to adopt the euro in 2007. Estonia's currency is the kroon, and the official language is Estonian.

See also: Baltic Sea region; Stalin, Iosif; World War II (Great Patriotic War)

ANDREW GUSTAFSON

estrada

See: popular music, post-Soviet; popular music, Soviet

ethnic minorities (malye narody)

Conquest and annexation of neighbouring territories and populations, and the subsequent
migration of the new subjects, as well as of
Russians and Ukrainians to the new peripheries,
redrew the ethnic map of the Russian and Soviet
empires. This migration, sometimes voluntary,
sometimes forced through deportation, especially
in the twentieth century, led to both intermixing
and dispersion of ethnic groups.

The USSR was a country of unparalleled
ethnic complexity, a self-contained migration
space, with movement in and out severely
restricted. The migration that has taken place
among the successor states of the Soviet Union
is more than a by-product of the decolonization
process: the disintegration of the USSR cut off
certain ethnic groups from their territories of
settlement and transformed them into new
ethnic minorities, raising the question of repatriation. Seventeen per cent of all ethnic
Russians remained outside the newly created
Russian Federation.

According to the 2002 census, Russians constitute 80 per cent of the nation's population; the
rest are ethnic minorities whose populations
vary from over one million (Tatars, Ukrainians,
Bashkirs, Chuvash, Chechens, and Armenians)
to a few hundred. Russians and other Slavs have
always dominated not only numerically but also
politically, economically, and culturally. The
condition of ethnic minorities reveals itself in
various ways.

In the USSR there was a notion of the Great
Russian 'elder brother' and junior 'younger
brothers'; this ideology served to legitimize
Russians' ruling position. Russians also preserved the status of a 'great people', while other
ethnic groups were called *malye narody* (minor
peoples). Historical chauvinism was part of
Soviet propaganda (for example, in Sergei
Eisenstein's films). Russian was the official state
language, and the Cyrillic alphabet was used for
languages that did not have their own. Secondary,
elementary, and eventually pre-school education
was conducted in Russian; in the 1960s, systematic education in the native languages of
ethnic minorities was stopped, and schools of
these populations were either closed or converted to teaching in Russian. Languages other
than Russian were displaced from the spheres of
social communication and mass media.

The names of ethnic minorities reflect their
position; the name given by the Russian coloni-
zer replaced the original (compare, for example,
Mordva vs. Moksha, Chechen vs. Nokhchi,
Iakut vs. Sakha, etc.). Soviet nationality policy
often suppressed old ethnic conflicts through a
stronger colonial power; the state was centralized in spite of the official declaration of its
federative structure. The political inventory
listed all ethnic groups in the form of a hierarchy, granting more privileges to people of
some ethnicities than others, despite economic
and social circumstances. Recognition of an
ethnic minority was a matter of an arbitrary
decision by the state, which often manipulated
ambiguous scientific data. The aftermath of the
Soviet empire affected the Russian population
as well; it is difficult to differentiate between the
dictatorship of Moscow and the colonial policy
of the Moscow centre.

Linguistically, languages of the ethnic minorities belong to the following families: Caucasian (Abkhaz, Chechen), Uralic-Yukaghir
(Saami, Vepsi), Altaic (Chuvash, Bashkir),
and Chukchi-Kamchatkan or 'Paleosiberian'
(Koriak).

The majority of ethnic groups are Eastern
Orthodox (Udmurt, Karel, Saami); some are
Orthodox Old Believers (Komi, Nagaibaks) –
both are a result of Russian and Soviet imperial
domination. Other well-represented religions
include Islam (Tatars, Bashkirs, Cherkes), Judaism (Jews and Gorskii Jews), Buddhism (Kalmyks, Tuvins, Buriats), and traditional beliefs
(Chukchi, Koriaks, Nanaitsy).

A geographical approach to the system-
atization of ethnic groups reveals the difference
between the Russian majority and ethnic minorities. The latter occupies a specific territorial
mandate, while the former embraces the principal patria. Russians are not a majority all over
the Russian territory, however: exceptions
include Dagestan, Chechnia, and Tatarstan.
Some territories bear the names of the ethnic
groups historically associated with them; yet
these labels can be grossly misleading. On the
other hand, some 'ethnic' territories preserve
heritage rather than reflect current population
numbers: for example, Evenks constitute 14 per

cent of the population of the Evenk autonomous *okrug* (territory).

In terms of occupied territory, correspondingly, ethnic minorities can be divided into three groups: those occupying a defined area (such as the Transcaucasian states, the Republic of Bashkorstan, etc.); ethnic groups connected with territories outside the USSR and the Russian Federation (Bulgarians, Germans, Poles, etc.); and dispersed ethnicities (such as Gypsies (Roma) and Jews). The Soviet government attempted to place the last of these symbolically on the map by ignoring historical and cultural contexts: the Jewish autonomous oblast in the Far East contains very few people registered as Jewish; it was more a message to Soviet Jewry than any sort of homeland. Ethnic groups that were not allowed administrative and cultural autonomy were and still are placed at the bottom of the ethnic hierarchy, since they do not have social institutions to protect their interests.

Another approach is to view ethnic minorities as those whose ethnic genesis is connected with the territory of modern Russia (Evenks) or with other territories (Germans), or simply by their geographical relation to the centre: peoples of northwestern Russia (Vepsi, Karelians, Saami), of the Volga region (Udmurts, Mordvinians, Chuvash), of the north Caucasus and Dagestan (Cherkes, Kabardinians, Osetians), of western Siberia (Nentsy, Khanty, Mansy), of eastern Siberia (Iakuts, Kets, Evenks), of northeastern Asia (Chukchi, Aleuts, Koriaks), and of the Amur and Sakhalin regions (Nanaitsy, Ulchi, Oroks). This approach, however, entirely ignores the linguistic and cultural distribution of these peoples.

The migratorial approach emphasizes causes of egression: colonial expansion (Ukrainians, Belorussians), relocation or deportation (Germans, Crimean Tatars), and expatriation (Kazakhs, Tatars). Migrations of both Russians and non-Russians facilitated the Soviet goal of russification, since non-Russians removed from their ethnic territories became an easier object for linguistic and cultural transformation. Russians had access to educational and cultural institutions in their mother tongue no matter where they lived, while non-Russians living beyond the boundaries of their ethno-territorial formations lacked this privilege and thus were predetermined to assimilation.

The minorities also differ in their response to Russian domination. Armenians, whose national existence was threatened by neighbouring Muslim states, were the most russophilic of all Soviet ethnic groups. They remain one of the largest minorities residing on the territory of the Russian Federation after the dissolution of the USSR, ignoring migratory opportunities. For Belorussians, incorporation into the Russian empire provided a relief from a stronger oppression; for Komis, Mari, Iakuts, and other tribes of eastern Russia, conversion to Orthodoxy and assimilation represented a social and cultural promotion.

Minorities that resisted Russian and then Soviet rule were usually historical nations or remnants of such nations. Their resistance focused on defence or restoration of various national institutions such as statehood, church, religion, culture, or language. For example, immediately after World War II, intellectuals in Central Asia began to rediscover their national past, lost partially because of two alphabet changes (from Arabic to Latin in 1928, and from Latin to Cyrillic in 1939). After Stalin's death some political figures were rediscovered and rehabilitated (such as the great Turkic conqueror Timur, who acquired a pan-Turkic significance), and some socio-political phenomena were reconsidered (such as the Basmachi movement of 1920–28).

Historically, in the 1990s and later, anthropologists and policy-makers tended to separate existing ethnicities into even smaller sub-groups; for example, the Koriaks split into Alutortsy and Kereks. This tendency, on the one hand, shows that the so-called *malye narody* still undergo ethnic development, which leads to processes of both assimilation and dissimilation; on the other hand, it reveals their attempt to overcome artificially imposed and enforced ethnic boundaries.

The post-Soviet Russian government has been involved in ethnic clashes both inside (Chechnia) and outside the modern state: the Abkhaz-Georgian conflict, which had lasted for decades, became aggravated during perestroika and later turned into a full-scale war.

See also: administrative structure, Soviet Union; Armenia; Bashkorkostan (Bashkiria);

Belarus; Buddhism; Caucasus; Central Asia; Chechnia; Chukchi; Dagestan; Evenki; Far East; Far North (Krainii sever); Georgia; Gypsy/Roma; Iakutia (Sakha); Islam; Jews; Judaism; internationalism; Karelia; Kazakhstan; Koriak; Mordva; Old Believers; Ossetia; perestroika and glasnost; propaganda, Soviet and post-Soviet; religion and spiritualism, non-traditional; Russian Orthodoxy; Saami (Lopars, Lapps); Siberia; Tatars; Ukraine; Volga region; War, Chechen; World War II (Great Patriotic War).

Further reading

Khazanov, A. (1995) *After the U.S.S.R. Collapsed: Ethnic Relations and Political Process in the Commonwealth of Independent States*, Madison, WI: University of Wisconsin Press.

VLADIMIR STRUKOV

Etush, Vladimir Abramovich

b. 6 May 1922, Moscow

Actor

A brilliant comic actor, Etush is known to broader audiences primarily from his screen roles, especially in Leonid Gaidai's blockbusters: the greedy dentist Shpak in *Ivan Vasilevich meniaet professiiu* (*Ivan Vasilievich: Back to the Future*, 1973) and the lewd bureaucrat, Comrade Saakhov, who wraps his sexual designs in Soviet ideological clichés uttered with a hilarious composite Caucasian accent in *Kavkazskaia plennitsa* (*Kidnapping Caucasian Style*, 1966). Etush's most profound and long-lasting contribution to Russian culture lies in the sphere of teaching. For many decades he has been the 'keeper of the flame' at Moscow's Shchukin Theatrical School, which is rooted in the legacy of Evgenii Vakhtangov. In his capacity of professor and School director (1986–2002), Etush has overseen the training of several generations of actors and directors, including major artistic figures who continue to define the face of Russia's theatre and cinema.

See also: Gaidai, Leonid

DAN UNGURIANU

Evenki

This ancient ethnic group (known as *Tungusy* before 1931) of the Mongoloid anthropological type has inhabited the Siberian and Far Eastern *taiga* between the River Enisei in the west and the Sea of Okhotsk in the east since the Paleolithic era. In 2004, the Evenki population in Russia numbered 29,900. The administrative area is the Evenki Autonomous Okrug, a territory of 2 million square km in the Krasnoiarsk Krai; its capital is Tura. One-third of the population speaks the Evenki language, the most widely used of the Manchu-Tungusic languages in Siberia. Lacking ethno-cultural unity, the Evenki are divided into three groups: northern, southern, and eastern, based on language and type of reindeer breeding.

See also: ethnic minorities; Far East; Siberia; taiga

TATYANA LEDENEVA

Evstigneev, Evgenii Aleksandrovich

b. 9 October 1926, Nizhnii Novgorod; d. 4 March 1992, Moscow

Actor

Acting for the Sovremennik (Contemporary) Theatre from 1957 until 1970, Evstigneev made his screen debut in 1957 and developed a reputation for his versatility in both comic and dramatic roles. He acted in more than seventy films. Among his most popular roles: the bureaucratic summer camp director in *Dobro pozhalovat, ili postoronnim vkhod vospreshchen* [*Welcome, or No Trespassing*, 1964]; the engineer Vorobev in *Stariki-razboiniki* [*Old Men-Robbers*, 1972]; Pleishner in the immensely popular TV serial based on Iulian Semenov's wartime thriller, *Semnadtsat mgnovenii vesny* (*Seventeen Moments of Spring*, 1973).

See also: *Semnadtsat mgnovenii vesny* (*Seventeen Moments of Spring*); Sovremennik Theatre

JOSEPHINE WOLL

Evtushenko, Evgenii Aleksandrovich

b. 18 July 1933, Zima, Russia

Writer

Poet, major representative of the post-Stalin generation, an icon for Russia's youth, and a liaison to the West during the cultural policy of the Thaw. Evtushenko's long autobiographical poem *Stantsiia zima* (*Winter Station*, 1956) received widespread attention, for it examined the past and its values while envisioning alternatives for the future. His topical, fresh, and daring poetry was rich in descriptive detail, slang, and innovative verse forms. The publication of *Babii Yar* (1961), which treats the Nazi massacre of Ukrainian Jews and attacks latent Russian anti-Semitism, brought Evtushenko international acclaim.

Evtushenko's poetry was regularly published, and his trips abroad were viewed as contributing to Russia's more open relations with the world. His widely known *Nasledniki Stalina* (*The Heirs of Stalin*, 1963) denounced Stalin's legacy. In his cycle of poems *Bratskaia GES* (*The Bratsk Station*, 1965), Evtushenko viewed the enormous Siberian power plant against the backdrop of Russian history and human fate. Later works include films such as *Detskii sad* (*Kindergarten*, 1983) and *Pokhorony Stalina* (*Stalin's Funeral*, 1990), in which he acted as well as directing, and experiments in prose, such as the novel *Iagodnye mesta* (*Wild Berries*, 1984). Evtushenko now teaches at the University of Tulsa, Oklahoma.

See also: anti-Semitism; literature, Thaw; poetry, Soviet; slang

Further reading

McVay, G. (1977) 'An Interview with Yevgeny Yevtushenko', *Journal of Russian Studies* 33: 13–18.

TATYANA NOVIKOV

Ezhov, Valentin Ivanovich

b. 21 January 1921, Samara; d. 8 May 2004, Moscow

Screenwriter

A student of Aleksandr Dovzhenko at VGIK (class of 1951), Ezhov was influential in creating the new poetic cinema of the Thaw. His screenplay for Grigorii Chukhrai's *Ballada o soldate* (*Ballad of a Soldier*) brought international renown to Soviet cinema and won an Oscar for best screenplay (written with Chukhrai, 1962). Ezhov wrote masterful melodramas about individuals separated by historical circumstances and collaborated with such filmmakers as Georgii Daneliia (*Tridtsat tri* [*Thirty-Three*, 1965]), Larisa Shepitko (*Krylia* [*Wings*, 1966]), Vladimir Motyl (*Beloe solntse pustyni* [*White Sun of the Desert*, 1969]), Andrei Konchalovskii (*Dvorianskoe gnezdo* [*Nest of Gentlefolk*, 1969], and *Sibiriada*, *Siberiade*, 1978), and Sergei Bondarchuk (*Krasnye kolokola* [*Red Bells*, 1982]).

See also: All-Russian (All-Union) State Institute of Cinematography (VGIK); *Beloe solntse pustyni* (*White Sun of the Desert*); Bondarchuk, Sergei; Chukhrai, Grigorii; Daneliia, Georgii; film, Soviet – Thaw period; Konchalovskii, Andrei; Motyl, Vladimir; scriptwriters; Shepitko, Larisa

Further reading

Ezhov, V. and Chukhrai, G. (1966) *Ballada o soldate*, New York: Harcourt, Brace & World.

ALEXANDER PROKHOROV

F

Fabergé

The best-known jewellery company in pre-Revolutionary Russia. Established in 1842 in St. Petersburg, under Karl Fabergé's leadership, the House of Fabergé gained lasting fame by transforming conventional jewellery into pieces of fantasy with the aid of exquisite craftsmanship. Despite the diversity of the Fabergé workshop's production, the 1884 success of the first Easter egg for Tsarina Maria, wife of Tsar Alexander III, was to determine the company's future direction. Intricate design frequently inspired by other works of art characterizes Fabergé eggs, which fit into the palm of the hand and contain a surprise. The Fabergé name notwithstanding, the eggs were created by Mikhail Perchin and Henrik Wigström.

IRINA MAKOVEEVA

families

Contemporary Russians continue to envision themselves as a huge extended family. The autocratic tsar, addressed and regarded as the father of the Empire, provided a role model for all Russian fathers. Mother Russia, the bounteous earth, offered a prototype for Russian mothers.

Marx and Engels's writings inspired early twentieth-century Revolutionary leaders to formulate alternatives to the patriarchal family: The 1917 constitution of the Soviet Union granted all women and men full citizenship, including the rights to work and vote, and the right to an individual identity. The leadership assumed that with equal rights for women, the family would eventually disappear. In the 1920s, socialization of household chores and the rearing of children by society, as well as free unions based on love, were discussed as potential state projects. Mass dislocations and widespread poverty forced consideration of more immediate and practical measures, and by the 1930s families had gained new legitimacy in their prime function of child-rearing. At the same time, construction of a statewide network of nurseries, kindergartens, schools and after-school programmes ensured collectivism, providing education and socialization of children with working parents. For those estimated 2 million abandoned, neglected, and orphaned children, hundreds of custodial homes opened to provide full-time care.

In the Soviet Union the family occupied an ambivalent position: a personal refuge that provided escape from the demands of collectivism, it was also charged with and complicit in raising children to identify with the Communist Party. To ensure them a place in Soviet society, parents, who were legally responsible for their children, often conformed to state pressures.

With state collectivization of peasant holdings in *kolkhozy* (collective farms), large, extended families fragmented into smaller, nucleated units, similar to urban families. Although in the countryside and cities alike the average age at first marriage has hardly changed since 1849 (20.9 for women; 21.5 for men), birth rates plummeted over the course of the twentieth century. In 1939, the average size of a Russian family was 4.3, while in 1989 it was 3.2, and 3.0 in 2003.

Three family types are prevalent in the Russian Federation: (1) married couples with one or two children (nuclear families), about 70 per cent; (2) single parents – overwhelmingly mothers – with one or more children, 15–20 per cent; and (3) married couples with or without children living with one set of parents or other relatives, approximately 15 per cent. Between 1981 and 2001 marriage rates in Russia fell; divorce rates rose. The 2003 census recognized for the first time several million unmarried cohabiting adults by recording them as a separate household category.

Russia is an aging society; currently death rates exceed birth rates. Elderly women, popularly called *babushki* (grandmothers), occupy an important place in families. They are often the major child caretakers, cooks, and cleaners, and their meagre pensions can make the difference between poverty and a subsistence income.

Contemporary Russians remain united by kinship terms, but the re-introduction and increasing use of *gospozha* and *gospodin* (madame; monsieur) may ultimately effect a change. Other potential changes might proceed from popularly voiced desires for retraditionalizing gender roles, although young men seem to prefer a stay-at-home wife, while young women favour egalitarian families. Russian families are also diversifying along class lines; the 1990s saw a rise of poverty among women and children and an increased abortion rate. At the same time some women who left the labour market because their husbands' income was more than sufficient opted to have two or more children.

See also: babushka; collective farms

Further reading

Geiger, H. (1968) *The Family in Soviet Russia*, Cambridge, MA: Harvard University Press.

Makarenko, A. (1967) *The Collective Family: A Handbook for Russian Parents* (orig. *A Book for Parents*, 1937), Garden City, NY: Anchor Books.

Markowitz, F. (2000) *Coming of Age in Post-Soviet Russia*. Urbana, IL: University of Illinois Press.

FRAN MARKOWITZ

fan (bolelshchik)

The word *bolelshchik* derives from the verb *bolet*, which means both 'to be ill' and 'to support fanatically', hence the Russian slang synonym '*fanat*'. Most Russian fans organize around sports clubs and support local soccer and hockey teams; however, individual athletes and other sports also have their fans. Moscow soccer clubs Spartak and TsSKA enjoy strong support from various social groups throughout Russia. Traditionally these red-whites and red-blues are uncompromising opponents, ready to burst into violence. Young fans give their opponents slang nicknames: *miaso* (meat) refers to Spartak, *koni* (horses) to TsSKA.

See also: Spartak; sport clubs and teams; TsSKA

ALEXANDER LEDENEV

Far East (Dalnii vostok)

The Russian Far East (*Dalnii vostok*) covers an area of 7.3 million sq km along the Pacific Ocean. It includes the Amur River, which borders with China; the Kamchatka peninsula; the oblasts of Magadan and Sakhalin; the Primorskii and Khabarovsk *krais*; Iakutia (Sakha); the Jewish Autonomous Oblast; and the Chukchi and Koriak autonomous *okrugs*. The population of 9.2 million people (76 per cent urban) is distributed unevenly. The largest cities are Komsomolsk-on-Amur, Khabarovsk, and Vladivostok. The rural population is settled mainly along the Lena, Amur, Kolyma, and Indigirka Rivers. Besides the Russian majority there are about fifteen ethnic minorities (including Chukchi, Koriak, Itelmen, Eskimo, Aleut, Iakut and others), traditionally involved in fishery, hunting, and reindeer breeding.

The Far East, rich in such natural resources as coal, gas, iron, nonferrous metal ores, gold and diamonds, timber, and furs, comprises mountains, taiga, tundra, and swampland. Though it is Russia's most important fishing area (primarily salmon and crabs), its severe climate and permafrost, remoteness, and lack of transportation infrastructure present major economic problems, particularly in the north.

See also: Chukchi; ethnic minorities; Far North; Iakutia (Sakha); Kamchatka; natural resources; taiga; tundra

TATYANA LEDENEVA

Far North (Krainii sever)

The expression 'Far North' creates confusion, because it includes not only regions in the Far North of the Russian Federation, but also southern and Far Eastern ones. The Soviet government coined the term to identify areas demanding special federal attention because of their great industrial importance, geographical remoteness, severe climate, and low population density. The list of such areas is annually defined by governmental decree and invariably includes the Arctic and Pacific Ocean islands, the continental part of Russia located to the north of the Polar Circle, the Republics of Altai (which nears the southern border of the Russian Federation), Karelia, Komi, Tyva, and Sakha (Iakutia); the Chukchi Autonomous Okrug; the oblasts of Arkhangelsk, Chita, Irkutsk, Kamchatka, Khabarovsk, Krasnoyarsk, Magadan, Murmansk, Tomsk, and Tiumen; Primore [Marine] Krai (capital: Vladivostok); and Sakhalin Island.

These areas are inhabited mainly by native ethnic minorities. The 8 per cent of Russians residing in the Far North supply 25 per cent of national income and 60 per cent of hard currency income. Two-thirds of the nation's natural resources are extracted in these regions: they produce 90 per cent of gas, 75 per cent of oil, and most of the Russian Federation's supplies of gold, nickel, copper, and diamonds.

To attract labour to such remote and economically important regions, the Soviet government assembled a list of financial and social privileges: higher wages, an earlier retirement age, reimbursement of moving costs, guaranteed accommodation during and after the contract period, and other perquisites. Most of these benefits disappeared with the end of the Soviet Union, however, so that some Russians living in the Far North are experiencing difficult conditions and are economically unable to resettle. Currently, the Duma is discussing the possibility of following the USA's example and settling these areas with millions of Chinese, Vietnamese, and Koreans, for the Russian population is now leaving such areas.

See also: Chukchi; Iakutia (Sakha); Magadan; Primorskii krai

TATYANA LEDENEVA

fashion industry, post-Soviet

After the fall of socialism, the 350 Soviet textile companies were merged into the state concern Rostekstil (Russian Textiles) in 1991 and survived by producing commissioned goods for foreign companies. In the early 1990s, a number of new fashion businesses were established by domestic entrepreneurs who knew the mass market well. They had begun their careers under socialism, when their entrepreneurial activities were still illegal. One of them was Anatolii Klimin, the owner of clothing company Tom Klaim, who successfully sold showy, inexpensive clothes to young, middle-income women. Another was Aleksandr Panikin, director of the leading knitwear company Paninter.

While these new fashion companies catered to the masses, newly-rich Russians were interested only in the best-known Western fashion brands. The most prestigious global fashion houses, starting with Gianni Versace in 1994, opened shops in Moscow and, in the space of a couple of years, transformed the city into an important site of consumption on the global fashion map. Viacheslav Zaitsev, the only fashion designer who after the fall of the Soviet Union owned a fashion house that served local celebrities and middle-class professional women, lost many of his customers after the Western brands arrived.

Some local designers, including Valentin Iudashkin, Igor Chapurin, Tatiana Parfenova, Nina Donis, and Iuliia Dalakian became well known through the media presentation of their collections at such bi-seasonal events as Russian Fashion Week and Moscow Fashion Week. Strong competition from leading Western fashion houses whose allure attracted newly-wealthy consumers had the effect of slowing down the development of Russian fashion. New Russian fashion designers still need to establish a wider client base and invest in production and distribution lines, as their output remains small, and more often than not consists of unique, artistically crafted pieces.

See also: economic system, post-Soviet; fashion industry, Soviet; Iudashkin, Valentin; Zaitsev, Viacheslav

DJURDJA BARTLETT

fashion industry, Soviet

After the Bolshevik Revolution of 1917, the Soviet government tried to control dress and fashion by merging art with industry. Throughout the 1920s, artists and designers produced prototypes in experimental laboratories within state artistic institutions and industrial establishments. However, the textile and clothing industries had been seriously damaged and disorganized by the Revolution and Civil War, and were unable to put these artistic prototypes into mass production.

The first five-year plan brought an end to artistically driven dress projects and started to reorganize the textile and clothing industries. In 1935, the state-controlled House of Fashion (*Dom mody*) was founded in Moscow to deliver prototypes of dresses to textile companies throughout the country. Additional Houses of Fashion were set up at lower administrative levels in the late 1940s, establishing central control of clothes production under the auspices of the All-Union House of Fashion.

In the 1950s, Khrushchev tried to replace excessively decorative Stalinist aesthetics with clean and simple lines to improve the quality of mass-produced clothes. However, clothes were still of poor quality and in insufficient supply. During the Brezhnev era, the All-Union House of Fashion grew, ultimately employing sixty-five fashion designers. Some of them designed prototypes for industry, while others, such as Viacheslav Zaitsev, produced fashion-conscious collections that were presented at the socialist

fashion congresses held annually in various East bloc capitals, and at the International Fashion Festival in Moscow (1967), where Western and socialist fashion paraded together. The role of the All-Union House of Fashion became symbolically very important for the regime because of its ability to perpetuate representational dress. The gap between its smart prototypes and the poor quality clothes available in the shops continued throughout the Brezhnev period.

Under Gorbachev, the Ministry of Light Industry tried to introduce change through perestroika reforms and to shake up the Soviet fashion industry. But bureaucratic inertia at the lower levels was too great, and the fashion changes that perestroika initiated were, as in previous periods, merely representational.

See also: Brezhnev, Leonid; economic system, Soviet; East Bloc countries; fashion industry, post-Soviet; five-year plan; Gorbachev, Mikhail; Khrushchev, Nikita; perestroika and glasnost; Zaitsev, Viacheslav

DJURDJA BARTLETT

fashion magazines

Russian fashion magazines reflected the regime's ambivalent relationship towards fashion. The programmatic journal *Atele* (*Atelier*), begun in 1923 by a group of Bolshevik-leaning avant-garde artists, attempted to rehabilitate fashion by connecting it to art and industry. Only one issue of *Atele* was published, but in the late 1920s *Iskusstvo odevatsia* (Art of Dressing) and *Zhenskii zhurnal* (Women's Journal) followed similar political and aesthetic approaches. In contrast, the westernized NEP-era journals, such as *Poslednie mody* (The Latest Fashions), literally copied the latest Western fashion trends. Diversity among fashion magazines ended with the advent of Stalinism. Stalin-era magazines *Modeli sezona* (Fashions of the Seasons) and *Zhurnal mod* (Fashion Journal), which served the *nomenklatura*, presented prototypes of smart dresses from the All-Union House of Fashion.

From the 1960s, those magazines introduced the emerging professional middle classes to the same aesthetics, overlooking the modesty in dress that was still the official ideology advocated in popular magazines such as *Rabotnitsa* (Working Woman).

In 1987, the Russian version of the German fashion magazine *Burda*, much appreciated for its sewing patterns, appeared in Russia. The Soviet response was the revival of *Zhurnal mod* (with *Modeli sezona* as its supplement) in 1989. Although these magazines reflected changes in fashion, they still published only dresses designed by the All-Union House of Fashion. The Russian version of *Cosmopolitan* appeared in post-Soviet Russia in 1994, followed by *Elle* and *Harper's Bazaar* in 1997, and *Vogue* in 1998. Aiming to conquer new markets, these magazines finally brought Western fashion to Russia.

See also: *Burda*; nomenklatura; perestroika and glasnost

DJURDJA BARTLETT

fast food

The absence of Western-style fast food in the Soviet Union did not prevent anyone from eating quickly and inexpensively, in numerous Soviet establishments known either as snack bars (*zakusochnaia*) or by the main dish they served: For example, an establishment serving crêpes (*bliny*) was known as a *blinnaia*, and one serving buns (*pyshki*) as a *pyshechnaia*. Such cheap eateries could be dirty and unpleasant, offering poor service and unsavoury food. Slightly more expensive cafeterias known as *stolovaia* offered seating and wider selections.

The Russian fast-food market was revolutionized in 1990 when McDonald's opened on Pushkin Square in Moscow. An immediate success, it served more than 30,000 people on its first day. Since then, both Russian and foreign companies have opened many other fast-food establishments in Russia. McDonald's continues to lead the market, but such Russian competitors as *Russkoe Bistro* and *Rostik's* attract customers. Major cities also have chains of street kiosks that sell everything from crêpes (such as *Teremok*, the *Little Tower*) to hot dogs (*Stop Top* and *Stardog!s*) or baked potatoes (*Kroshka-Kartoshka, Potato Bud*). Accused of substandard

sanitary practices, they are an omnipresent feature of many Russian cities.

In the late 1990s there appeared many restaurant chains that capitalized on growing feelings of nationalism (*Ëlki-Palki*) and the market for non-Western, particularly non-American, so-called ethnic cuisine (*Ëlki-Palki, Shesh-Besh, Iakitoriia*). These restaurants, generally with sit-down service and thus technically not fast-food establishments, appeal to customers through folksy interiors and staff uniforms.

See also: dining, Russian; dining Soviet

DAVID HUNTER SMITH

Federal Security Service (FSS/FSB)

Federal Security Service (*Federalnaia sluzhba bezopasnosti*) of the Russian Federation. On 20 December, following the October 1917 Revolution, a VChK (*Vserossüskaia chrezvychainaia komissiia*, All-Russian Emergency Commission, commonly called the *Cheka*), headed by Feliks Dzerzhinskii, was formed in order to fight counter-revolution and sabotage. Its emblem was a sword and shield, symbolizing the defence of the revolution and the struggle with its enemies. In February 1918, the VChK obtained special emergency powers from the Bolshevik government; terror became its main weapon.

In 1922, the VChK was transformed into the GPU (*Gosudarstvennoe politicheskoe upravlenie*, State Political Department) as part of the NKVD (*Narodnyi kommissariat vnutrennikh del*, People's Commissariat of Internal Affairs), and in 1923 into the OGPU (United State Political Department) as part of the Soviet of People's Commissariat of the USSR. In the early 1920s, the OGPU's chief task was the liquidation of all underground political groups inside Russia and of émigré organizations abroad seen as committed to the overthrow of the Communist regime. One of the most successful foreign operations by the OGPU was the creation of an organization under the code name 'Trest', which helped to expose the plans of anti-Soviet émigré groups and foreign intelligence services.

After Stalin came to power, the OGPU's primary goal became the struggle against his perceived opponents in the party leadership, in the form of a wide-scale campaign to search for and expose 'enemies of the people'. All problems arising from mistakes and the inadequate qualifications of Soviet officials in the process of industrialization were ascribed to acts of sabotage, in fake cases based on testimonies and confessions obtained by force. The OGPU was also assigned the task of suppressing peasants' resistance to collectivization. The physical extermination and exile of the most productive peasants (*raskulachivanie*) led to hunger in Povolzhe and Ukraine, which cost millions of lives. In the 1930s the organs of state security gained control of correctional institutions, launching the system of labour correctional camps (GULag).

After the murder of the First Secretary of the Leningrad Communist Party Committee Sergei Kirov in 1934, the NKVD forces began a campaign against the rest of Stalin's opponents, both real and imaginary. In August 1936, a trial was staged against the old Bolsheviks Lev Kamenev and Grigorii Zinovev, which was supposed to prove their connections with Stalin's major opponent – Lev Trotskii. By 1937–38, the scale of political repressions, initiated and organized by the NKVD, had sharply increased. The terror was called *ezhovshchina*, after the surname of the newly-appointed head of the NKVD, Nikolai Ezhov, who replaced Genrikh Iagoda. The repressions of these years affected all levels of the Party and State apparatus, as practically the entire generation of those who had spearheaded the Bolshevik Revolution in 1917 was eliminated. At the same time, the Red Army lost several thousands of its commanders, including the major part of the military highly ranked officers (see the trial of Mikhail Tukhachevskii, 1937). *Ezhovshchina* reached its peak in March 1938, with the trial of Nikolai Bukharin. The campaign of repressions targeted NKVD members themselves, including its leaders, who were accused of standard political crimes, such as 'treason' and 'counter-revolutionary activity'. Iagoda and Ezhov were executed, as was Lavrentii Beria (1953), who had replaced Ezhov in 1938 and become one of the most sinister heads of the Soviet security services.

During World War II, the state security's main efforts were concentrated against sabotage, emergencies at industrial enterprises and railroads, exposure of the German intelligence service, and suppression of anti-Soviet activities. At the beginning of 1943 a People's Committee on State Security (NKGB) was formed within the NKVD, comprising a 'fourth department', which dealt with sabotage and partisan movement on the territories occupied by Germans. In addition, a department of counter-intelligence was established under the name SMERSH (abbreviation for *smert shpionam* [death to spies]), with the goal of exposing traitors in the army and German intelligence service members and collaborators on the liberated and occupied territories. In the post-war period, the Soviet intelligence service became one of the most powerful in the world. Secret service operations played an important role in the creation of Soviet nuclear weapons. The NKVD/KGB had a ramified intelligence network in the US, Great Britain, and other countries of Western Europe.

At certain times throughout the 1930s and early 1950s, the organs of state security achieved independent political power over the Party and the State apparatus, but after Stalin's death (March 1953) became subordinated again to the Party. The new leadership of the CPSU conducted reforms and purges in the secret service. A Committee of State Security (KGB) was formed, answerable to the Council of Ministries of the USSR (1954–91), and responsible for intelligence, counter-intelligence, the fight against economic sabotage, and anti-Soviet activity (which generally turned into a prosecution of dissidents). Though in 1961 Khrushchev claimed that all activities of the KGB were under the strict control of the Party and government, and that there were no political prisoners in the USSR, arrests of anti-Soviet dissidents continued until perestroika. Those persecuted for dissidence in the 1970s and 1980s included such famous writers and human rights activists as Andrei Sakharov, Aleksandr Solzhenitsyn, Andrei Siniavskii, Iulii Daniel, and Sergei Dovlatov.

Khrushchev's removal from power and his replacement by Leonid Brezhnev in 1964 brought no significant changes in the activities or the staff of the KGB. Efforts were made to strengthen the struggle against 'ideological sabotage' during the leadership of Iurii Andropov (1967–82), who created the 'fifth department of the KGB' and instituted a network of such departments in every workplace and educational institution; its mandate was to organize counter-intelligence work to eliminate acts of ideological sabotage on home territory.

After the collapse of the Soviet Union, the organs of state security in the Russian Federation underwent reorganization and several changes in name. In 1995, President Boris Yeltsin signed the law 'On the Organs of the Russian Federation's Federal Security Service', which led to the formation of the FSB (*Federalnaia sluzhba bezopasnosti* [*Federal Security Service*]). The FSB is one of the few current Russian power structures dating from the early Soviet period, its emblem of the sword and the shield, plus the image of the founder, Dzerzhinskii, a left-over from the days of the VChK-KGB. Officers of the FSB informally call themselves 'chekisty'.

After Vladimir Putin (a former KGB officer and an ex-director of the FSB, 1998–99) was elected president of the Russian Federation in 2000, the influence of the FSB in Russian life has steadily risen. In mass culture, the image of intelligence service officials occupies an honorary place – in blockbuster films, television serials, bestselling books, and even thematic restaurants promoting the activities of the FSB/KGB. In the mass media, the possibility of restoring Dzerzhinskii's monument (dismantled after the August coup of 1991) is periodically discussed.

See also: Coup, August 1991; dissident; Daniel, Iulii; Dovlatov, Sergei; GULag; Khrushchev, Nikita; perestroika and glasnost; Putin, Vladimir; Sakharov, Andrei; Siniavskii, Andrei; Solshenitsyn, Aleksandr; Stalin, Iosif; World War II (Great Patriotic War); Yeltsin, Boris

Further reading

Albats, E. (1994) *The State within a State: The KGB and its Hold on Russia – Past, Present, and Future*, trans. C. A. Fitzpatrick, New York: Farrar, Straus, Giroux.

Andrew, C. M. (1999) *The Sword and the Shield: The Mitrokhin Archive and the Secret History of the KGB*, New York: Basic Books.

Barron, J. (1984) *KGB Today: The Hidden Hand*, London: Hodder & Stoughton.

Knight, A. W. (1996) *Spies without Cloaks: The KGB's Successors*, Princeton, NJ: Princeton University Press.

Knightley, P. (1990) *The Master Spy: The Story of Kim Philby*, New York: Vintage Books.

YURI ZARETSKY

Fedoseev, Vladimir Ivanovich

b. 5 September 1933, Leningrad

Conductor

Vladimir Fedoseev graduated from the Gnessin Institute in Moscow (1957) and then studied at the Moscow Conservatory (studio of Leo Ginzburg). His first success came in 1971 after he was invited by Evgenii Mravinskii to guest conduct the Leningrad Philharmonic Orchestra. In 1974, Fedoseev became artistic director and chief conductor of the Moscow Radio Symphony Orchestra (now the Tchaikovsky Great Symphony Orchestra), which he still leads. In 1997, Fedoseev was appointed Chief Conductor of the Vienna Symphony Orchestra. Since then he has become one of the most acclaimed conductors in Europe. He has conducted such orchestras as the Bavarian Radio Symphony Orchestra, the Leipzig Gewandhaus Orchestra, the Berlin Philharmonic, the Zurich Tonhalle Orchestra, and has been a regular guest conductor at the Zurich Opera. Fedoseev is known both as an expert in the Russian repertoire and in monumental European symphonism (Beethoven, Mahler).

See also: Moscow Conservatory; Mravinskii, Evgenii

KIRA NEMIROVSKAIA

felt boots (valenki)

From the verb *valiat* (to felt), *valenki* are traditional Russian winter boots without outer soles, formed by hand from felted wool (from a sheep or a goat). Traditional designs are bulky, recalling wrapped peasant footwear. Warm and practical in powdery snow, *valenki* become soggy in slush. This 'Russian national footwear' is still popular, especially in Siberia, though in parts of the country *valenki* have disappeared.

See also: footwear

SIBELAN FORRESTER

feminism

Feminism in Russia has a long and complex history dating to the early nineteenth century. Before the October Revolution, feminists spanned a broad social spectrum and included upper-class women, male liberals, women in medicine, social revolutionaries, and terrorists. After the Revolution, equal rights for women were decreed by law and women's issues were advanced through the Women's Section of the Communist Party (*Zhenotdel*, 1919–30). Under Stalin, many of the laws passed in the 1920s concerning women (the right to an abortion, to divorce, to child support) were reversed, gender equality was declared to have been achieved, and the Women's Section was abolished. Attention to women's issues revived under Khrushchev, with the establishment of the Soviet Women's Committee (*Komitet sovetskikh zhenshchin*, 1956–91, renamed the Women's Union of Russia [*Soiuz zhenshchin Rossii*] in the post-Soviet era). State feminism left a mixed record of successes and failures, including the infamous 'double burden' of work and domestic duties and a scarcity of women in the highest positions of political power.

In this context, Russian women are highly suspicious of the term and generally refuse to identify themselves as feminists, even those working to improve the status of women through political organizing and activism. In 2000, more than 2,500 women's organizations (registered and grass-roots) existed in Russia, addressing such issues as domestic violence, rape, sex trafficking, women's health, and women in politics (Melnikova, 2000: 180). By contrast, academic feminists have embraced the

term, bringing such phrases as 'gender studies' (*gendernye issledovaniia*) and 'women's rights' (*prava zhenshchin*) into mainstream discourse. The two major centres of academic feminism are the Moscow Centre for Gender Studies (*Moskovskii tsentr gendernykh issledovanii*, founded in 1990 by Anastasiia Posadskaia, Natalia Zakharova, and Natalia Rimashevskaia), and the St. Petersburg Centre of Gender Issues (*Peterburgskii tsentr gendernykh problem*, founded in 1992 by Olga Lipovskaia). Like many of the NGOs and businesses practising feminism, these centres and others like them in Ivanovo, Rostov, Saratov, Murmansk, and Tver, often receive Western funding. Prominent feminists include Alevtina Fedulova, the first chair of Women's Union of Russia; the journalist Nadezhda Azhgikhina; and the former Minister of Culture, Natalia Dementeva.

For most Russians, however, 'feminism' brings to mind only one name: that of Mariia Arbatova, the self-styled feminist whose television programme *I Myself* (*Ia sama*, 1996—) and prolific writings have shaped popular perceptions of feminism in the post-Soviet era. Her candid portrayals of love affairs, motherhood, and her liberal values have made Arbatova a controversial figure; her fame and originality underscore some of the features that distinguish Russian feminism from its Western counterparts.

See also: Arbatova, Mariia; Krushchev, Nikita; literature, women's; political parties, post-Soviet; Stalin, Iosif; women

Further reading and reference

Melnikova, T. (2000) *Zhenskoe dvizhenie v Rossii*, Moscow: Mysl.

Noonan, N. and Nechemias, C. (2001) *Encyclopedia of Russian Women's Movements*, Westport, CT: Greenwood Press.

Racioppi, L. and See, K. (1997) *Women's Activism in Contemporary Russia*, Philadelphia, PA: Temple University Press.

Sperling, V. (1999) *Organizing Women in Contemporary Russia*, Cambridge: Cambridge University Press.

ANDREA LANOUX

figure skating

Russia adopted figure skating immediately after its origins at the end of the nineteenth century. The first Russian champion was Nikolai Panin-Kolomenkin, who won the 1908 Olympics in the special section of ice-pattern drawing (later eliminated). He opened the first Russian school of figure skating in Petrograd and wrote the first figure-skating manual. Soviet figure skating reached its peak in the 1960s and 1970s. Liudmila Belousova and Oleg Protopopov established a new Russian style in pair figure skating based on lyrical ballet choreography rather than on complicated jumps and throws. Their 'Dreams of Love' performance earned them a gold medal at the 1964 Winter Olympics. Russian domination in world figure skating gradually extended to all four categories: female singles, male singles, pairs, and ice dancing. The Russian figure skating school is characterized by a combination of technical complexity, high speed, and choreographic virtuosity. Figure skating gained special status among Russians, who considered it a synthesis of sport and ballet, and leading figure skaters could be compared to television and movie stars. The brightest star of Soviet sports was Irina Rodnina, performing in pairs with Aleksei Ulanov, and then with Aleksandr Zaitsev. Her unique record in the history of figure skating shows three consecutive Olympic titles, ten wins at World Championships, and eleven supreme titles at European tournaments (1969–80). Her most popular number was 'Kalinka', performed at every post-tournament show. For two decades Rodnina's private life made headlines in the Russian mass media. Other cult figures include the figure skating pair Ekaterina Gordeeva and Sergei Grinkov; in ice dancing, the pair Liudmila Pahkomova and Aleksandr Gorshkov; male figure skaters Aleksei Iagudin and Evgenii Pliushenko; and female skaters Oksana Baiul, Irina Slutskaia, and Maria Butyrskaia. Russian coaches Stanislav Zhuk, Elena Chaikovskaia, and Tatiana Tarasova became authorities in world figure skating.

See also: Rodnina, Irina

Further reading

Brennan, C. (2002) *Champions on Ice: Twenty-Five Years of the World's Finest Figure Skaters*, Plattsburgh, NY: McClelland & Stewart.

ALEXANDER LEDENEV

Figurina, Elena Nikolaevna

b. 4 November 1955, Ventspils, Latvian SSR

Painter

Self-taught as an artist, Figurina began exhibiting at the end of the 1970s and quickly achieved recognition within Leningrad's community of nonconformist artists; since perestroika, she has exhibited in Western Europe and the United States as well. Her paintings depict childlike figures in elemental landscapes. Making full use of the colouristic richness of oil paint, Figurina employs simple compositional elements that communicate primal emotions of ecstasy, wonder, fear, and isolation. Mythical and biblical situations are sometimes suggested, but these are made intimate and familiar by the directness and apparent simplicity of her technique.

See also: art, nonconformist; perestroika and glasnost

JANET E. KENNEDY

film, animation

Starting in the 1930s, animated film in the Soviet Union achieved a popularity equal to that in the United States. In the post-Soviet era, the influx of Western imports has resulted in a more problematic status for Russian animation; yet nostalgia for Soviet culture helps to maintain respect for this art form.

Almost all Soviet animated films produced between 1936 and the late 1950s were children's films created at Moscow's *Soiuzmultfilm* [Soviet Animated Film] studio. The few animated films predating 1936 extant today were made at small, independent studios either as artistic experiments or as propaganda. Many early film-makers, such as Valentina and Zinaida Brumberg, Ivan Ivanov-Vano, Olga Khodataeva, Aleksandr Ivanov, and Mikhail Tsekhanovskii, were instrumental in founding Soiuzmultfilm and in creating a school for the studio's next generation of animators and directors.

After Stalin's death, many restrictions on Soiuzmultfilm were relaxed. Film-makers moved away from the production of Disneyesque, multicultural folk tales (such as Babichenko's *Bratia Liu* [*Brothers Liu*, 1953] and Atamanov's *Alenkii tsvetochek* [*The Scarlet Flower*, 1952]). Some directors began to experiment with other themes and media, producing films not intended for children (e.g., Fedor Khitruk's *Istoriia odnogo prestupleniia* [*Story of a Crime*, 1962], Andrei Khrzhanovskii's *Steklliannaiia garmonika* [*Glass Harmonica*, 1968]). This new group of directors produced animated films on topics that exposed social ills, posed questions about the nature of art, and criticized bureaucracy. By the 1960s, even the directors of children's films did not always work in the approved Disney-like style but were free to experiment with different art forms and themes, and even managed to include in their cartoons subtexts intended for adults (e.g., Atamanov's *Balerina na korable* [*Ballerina on a Ship*, 1969]). Soiuzmultfilm's other innovations included the creation of a stop-motion animation department. Inspiration was found in previously forbidden Western and pre-Revolutionary Russian art and culture, and since cartoons were still largely marginalized and viewed by the authorities as less important than other media, animation developed as an avenue for social commentary.

While Soiuzmultfilm produced its animated films for cinemas (another studio, Ekran [Screen], was the television arm of animation production in Soviet Russia), many of Soiuz-multfilm's most popular productions of the 1960s and 1970s were widely televised and became important touchstones of popular culture for several generations of Russian viewers. Products of this 'Golden Era' of animation include Kachanov's *Cheburashka* films (1969–74), Kotenochkin's *Nu, pogodi!* (*Just you wait!*) series (1969–86), Kovalevskaia's *Bremenskie muzykanty* (*The Musicians of Bremen*, 1969), and Khitruk's

Vinni Pukh (*Winnie the Pooh*) films (1969–72). These classic animated films continue to be shown on Russian television and delight the current generation of young viewers.

In the post-Soviet period Soiuzmultfilm has been plagued by legal and financial difficulties. The realities of the marketplace have forced many who remain in the field to leave the major studios and create their own smaller production companies. Today these animation companies fill several niche markets, from advertising (e.g., Aleksandr Tatarskii's Pilot Studios) to contract work for international studios (e.g., Christmas Films, which produces films for British television). Ironically, in the post-Soviet period, without a state-funded and state-mandated national animation studio, a dichotomy has developed: Russian television is inundated with Western and Japanese cartoons to the exclusion of new Russian animation, while at the same time Russian animated film directors are gaining international acclaim for their work. A striking example of this recognition is the Oscar awarded to Aleksandr Petrov for his 1999 film *The Old Man and the Sea*.

See also: Cheburashka; film studios; film, children's; Khitruk, Fedor; Kotenochkin, Viacheslav; *Nu pogodi!* (Just You Wait!); Petrov, Aleksandr

Further viewing

Films By Jove (1995) *Stories From My Childhood* series (DVD and VHS).
Films By Jove (1997) *Masters of Russian Animation* series (DVD and VHS).
Films By Jove (2001) *The Adventures of Cheburashka and Friends* (DVD).

BELLA GINZBURSKY-BLUM

film, auteur

'Auteur film' is defined as the evidence of a director's individual style, thought or general creativity in the finished product of a film, over and above the demands or expectations of the script, the studio, or the audience. Given the monolithic structure of the Soviet film industry, it is little wonder that the world had to wait until the death of Stalin and the erosion of Socialist Realist criteria for any concept of an 'auteur' to emerge. In the Soviet Union and post-Soviet Russia, it is above all identified with the work of Andrei Tarkovskii, who throughout the 1960s and 1970s resisted temptations to conform or be subject to ideological dictates. Despite official disapproval of his work, Tarkovskii insisted on the artist's right to express his own feelings and thoughts. Consequently, his films often repeat the same message, but are still packed with memorable visual images and spiritual insights. They also subvert the genres they adopt. *Ivanovo detstvo* (*Ivan's Childhood*, 1962) is a war story, but is more about the spiritual development of the boy Ivan than the war itself. *Andrei Rublev* (1966) outlines the artistic evolution of the fourteenth-century icon painter, set against a particularized, palpable historical and political background, but also functions as an allegory of the artist in any totalitarian society, including that of the Soviet Union in the mid-1960s. Both *Soliaris* (*Solaris*, 1972) and *Stalker* (1979) are ostensibly science-fiction parables about man and the technological future, but both significantly alter their literary source material to make a statement not about man and science, but about man and his soul, not confronting extra-terrestrial civilizations, but at home on earth, affirming his roots, love, and spiritual belonging. In later films made abroad, such as *Nostalgiia* (*Nostalgia*, 1983, shot in Italy) and *Zhertvoprinoshenie* (*The Sacrifice*, 1986, shot in Sweden), Tarkovskii challenged the accepted confrontational East–West notions based on the Cold War by foregrounding the need for hope through spiritual community and personal sacrifice.

A worthy successor to Tarkovskii in the post-Soviet era is Aleksandr Sokurov, whose films challenge both audience expectations and cinematic conventions. In both *Molokh* (*Moloch*, 1999) and *Telets* (*Taurus*, 2000) he demystified history and its leading players with prosaic portraits of Hitler and Lenin. In *Russkii kovcheg* (*Russian Ark*, 2003) he created a 90-minute digital one-take exploration of the last three hundred years of Russian history, as well as a double-edged reflection of the relationship of Russia and the West in the rooms of St. Petersburg's Hermitage Museum.

After the collapse of the Soviet Union, Kira Muratova has continued, in a much more forthright and often harrowing manner, her examination of human relationships and the relationship of the individual to the collective. Films such as *Tri istorii* (*Three Stories*, 1996) and *Vtorostepennye liudi* (*Minor People*, 2001) defy logic and challenge the reader to construct meaning from the various aesthetic possibilities on the screen, and *Chekhovskie motivy* (*Chekhovian Motifs*, 2004) adapts the Russian literary tradition in a wry and startlingly new way.

See also: Cold War; Hermitage; Muratova, Kira; Socialist Realism; Sokurov, Aleksandr; Tarkovskii, Andreii

Further reading

Gillespie, D. and Smirnova, E. (2004) 'Alexander Sokurov and the Russian Soul', *Studies in European Cinema* 1, 1: 57–65.
Johnson, V. and Petrie, G. (1994) *The Films of Andrei Tarkovsky: A Visual Fugue*, Bloomington, IN: Indiana University Press.
Taubman, J. (2004) *Kira Muratova*, London and New York: I. B. Tauris.

DAVID GILLESPIE

film, children's

The Soviet government always considered cinema for children and adolescents a major part of its Marxist enlightenment project. Stalinist culture established the film genres for young audiences: adventure (*Dzhulbars*, Shneiderov 1935), science fiction (*Kosmicheskii reis* (*Space Flight*, Zhuravlev 1936)), and fairy tale (*Novyi Gulliver* (*New Gulliver*, Ptushko 1935)). In 1936 a studio for the production of films targeting children and youth was established: Soiuzdetfilm, since 1948 called the Gorkii Studio.

During the Thaw, the USSR allotted special attention to children's cinema. New values of the era, such as anti-monumentalism, spontaneity, and individualism, brought children and adolescents to the centre of cinematic iconography. The child's world became the ideal sphere, where a communist utopia in all its innocence could reject the cynical adult world. Children's idealism, in turn, served as a model for adults: such an adult child is exemplified in the character of Lenin, whose adolescent behaviour makes him the prophet of communism in Thaw-era films.

Thaw-era cinema inherited some genres from Stalinism, including adventure (*Kortik* [Dirk, Mikhail Shveitser and Vladimir Vengerov 1955], *Na grafskikh razvalinakh* [*On the Count's Ruins*, Vladimir Skuibin 1958], *Voennaia taina* [*Military Secret*, Mechislava Maevskaia 1958]) and fairy tale (*Starik Khottabych* [*Old Genie Khottabych*, Gennadii Kazanskii 1956], *Ilya Muromets*, Aleksandr Ptushko 1956). In the 1960s, the school film emerged as the major genre of children's cinema (*Moi drug Kolka* [*My Friend Kolka*, Alexander Mitta and Aleksei Saltykov 1961], *A esli eto liubov?* [*But What If This Is Love?*, Iulii Raizman 1961], *Dozhivem do ponedel'nika* [*We'll Make It Till Monday*, Stanislav Rostotskii 1969]). The school film's distinctive feature is the conflict between the individual and the community, in which the individual and communal voices are equally valid. These films also addressed multiple audiences: on the one hand, they targeted children and adolescents; on the other hand, they communicated to adult audiences the era's cultural conflicts.

In the 1960s, Soviet film-makers interested in individual expression beyond ideological prescriptions started making auteur films, which technically were still listed as films made for youth. In 1960, Mosfilm established a new creative unit, Iunost (Youth), to make films for young audiences. *Iunost* opened its production with Andrei Tarkovskii's debut *Katok i skripka* (*The Steamroller and the Violin*, 1960). Auteur film-makers of the decade who made films for children include Aleksandr Mitta and Rolan Bykov. In the 1970s, Sergei Solovev became the major director to hide his subjective poetic vision under the guise of cinema for youth (*Sto dnei posle detstva* [*A Hundred Days After Childhood*, 1975], *Spasatel* [*Lifeguard*, 1980]).

In the 1970s television films and mini-series for children gradually displaced children's cinema, which Gorkii Studio phased out from its production schedules as non-profitable, switching to more lucrative action blockbusters and detective-thrillers. In 1986, the reformist leadership of the Film-makers' Union convened to discuss the disastrous condition of Soviet cinema for young audiences and to revive this dying branch of the film industry. No plans established at this meeting were fulfilled, because ideological cinema for children died with the Soviet Union. Post-Soviet children and teens watch Western entertainment, such as Hollywood and Disney films. The recent attempt by Angel Film studio to create a Russian equivalent of the teen flick (*Zaimemsia liuboviu* [*Let's Make Love*, Evstigneev 2002]) demonstrates the dominance of Western genre models among Russian film-makers and moviegoers.

See also: Bykov, Rolan; Mitta, Aleksandr; film, animation; film, Soviet – Thaw period; Solovev, Sergei; Tarkovskii, Andrei

Further reading

Arkus, L., Vasileva, I. and Margolit, E. (2002) 'Detskoe kino v SSSR', in *Noveishaia istoriia otechestvennogo kino*, vol. 4. St. Petersburg: Seans, pp. 98–105.

ALEXANDER PROKHOROV

film, comedy

Soviet comedy grew out of Lev Kuleshov's parody of America *Neobychainye prikliucheniia Mistera Vesta* (*The Amazing Adventures of Mr West*, 1924), Vsevolod Pudovkin's farce *Shakhmatnaia goriachka* (*Chess Fever*, 1925) or Iakov Protazanov's *Protsess o trekh millionakh* (*The Case of the Three Million*, 1926). These narratives and Boris Barnet's *Devushka s korobkoi* (*The Girl with the Hat-Box*, 1927) reflect prejudices of the New Economic Policy.

In the 1930s, Stalinist policy is evident in Ivan Pyrev's rural tales, which equated happy communities and Communism: *Bogataia nevesta* (*The Wealthy Bride*, 1937) and *Traktoristy* (*The Tractor Drivers*, 1939) present musical romances between farm workers, a form Pyrev continued to favour as late as 1949–50, in *Kubanskie kazaki* (*The Kuban Cossacks*), which collapses a personal flirtation into the unification of two farms. His contemporary Grigorii Aleksandrov's most celebrated films emphasize collective bonding amidst competition; *Veselye rebiata* (*The Happy-Go-Lucky Guys*, 1934) features jazzman Leonid Utesov as a cowherd, while *Tsirk* (*The Circus*, 1936) showcases Soviet 'tolerance' in a fantastic plot of an American performer finding sanctuary in the USSR to avoid persecution at home as the mother of a black child. *Volga-Volga* (1938) offers more light-hearted fare, as two village teams compete for a prestigious music prize.

Mikhail Kalatozov's *Vernye druzia* (*True Friends*, 1954) marks Stalin's death and the rebirth of a gentler, more contemplative laughter as the narrative shows three aging men try to preserve the innocence of their boyhood. These quieter gags would become romantic in Iurii Chuliukin's *Devchata* (*The Girls*, 1961), set among young adults working in snow-dappled lumber camps. Together these films echo work by Eldar Riazanov, especially his parodies of bureaucratism in *Karnavalnaia noch* (*Carnival Night*, 1956). Riazanov's comedies often define their decade: *Beregis avtomobilia!* (*Look Out for the Car!* [socialism queried, in 1966]), *Ironiia sudby* (*The Irony of Fate* [personal dignity counters Stagnation, in 1975]), and *Zabytaia melodiia dlia fleity* (*Forgotten Melody for a Flute* [the death of Soviet values, in 1987]).

Two equally prominent directors of comedies are Leonid Gaidai and Georgii Daneliia. The latter's *Ia shagaiu po Moskve* (*I Stroll Around Moscow*, 1963) dramatizes a youthful writer's adventures in noisy Moscow. Movement accelerates in the work of Gaidai, who represents a zanier aspect of Russian cinema with *Kavkazskaia plennitsa* (*Captive Girl of the Caucasus*, 1967), which relies on slapstick to expose local corruption. Gaidai's highly physical humour perhaps was a reaction to the sociopolitical tedium under Brezhnev and it remained a constant in his œuvre, as evident in his *Dvenadtsat stulev* (*The Twelve Chairs*, 1971) and *Ivan Vasilevich meniaet professiiu* (*Ivan Vasilevich Changes Jobs*, 1973). The latter revolves around a time machine shuttling between Soviet apartments and the court of Ivan the Terrible. Gaidai worked with clowns, for instance, Iurii Nikulin, who after movies such as *Brilliantovaia ruka* (*The Diamond Arm*, 1969) became a household name.

Perestroika and the end of the Soviet era witnessed a penchant for bitter satire, epitomized in the work of Iurii Mamin (*Bakenbardy* [Sideburns, 1990]), *Okno v Parizh* [*Window to Paris*, 1993]. In such comedies by Aleksandr Rogozhkin as *Osobennosti natsionalnoi okhoty* (*Peculiarities of the National Hunt*, 1995), 'traditional' Russian values under pseudo-capitalism as a hunting expedition become an alcohol-sodden picnic. Pavel Lungin's *Svadba* (*The Wedding*, 2000) shows a similar disarray, accompanied by alcohol, in village life. Youth comedies, such as Denis Evstigneev's *Zaimemsia liuboviu* (*Let's Make Love*, 2002) and Ruslan Baltser's *Dazhe ne dumai!* (*Don't Even Think about It!*, 2003) laugh at adults' failings.

See also: Daneliia, Georgii; film, Soviet – Thaw period; Gaidai, Leonid; Kalatozov, Mikhail; Lungin, Pavel; Mamin, Iurii; Nikulin, Iurii; perestroika and glasnost; Riazanov, Eldar; Rogozhkin, Aleksandr; Stagnation; Utesov, Leonid

Further reading

Prokhorov, A. (2003) 'Cinema of Attractions versus Narrative Cinema: Leonid Gaidai's Comedies and Eldar Riazanov's Satires of the 1960s', *Slavic Review* 62.3: 455–72.

DAVID MACFADYEN

film directors, 1950s and 1960s

From the mid-1950s until the late 1960s, film directors, along with the other cultural producers of the Thaw, engaged in the gradual destalinization of Soviet culture. In the 1950s, Soviet cinema remained, above all, an ideological institution, while the film-makers timidly tried to abandon the rigidity of the Stalinist film canon. Although Soviet film-makers did not openly embrace the European concept of *auteur*, they practised an Eastern bloc version of auteurism in their work: they used Soviet ideological cinema to artistic ends. In the 1950s, Alexander Alov, Vladimir Naumov, Grigorii Chukhrai, Mikhail Kalatozov, and Marlen Khutsiev articulated a new cinematic language opposed to the monumentalist aesthetics of

Stalinist cinema. Influenced by Italian neorealism, the film-makers of the 1950s favoured melodramatic plots through which they attempted to articulate new cultural values: anti-monumentalism, the cult of the individual, and a focus on the emotional aspects of human nature. At the same time, the new film-makers considered themselves the heirs of the Soviet montage tradition.

The surviving film-makers of the 1920s, above all, Grigorii Kozintsev, Sergei Iutkevich, Leonid Trauberg, and Boris Barnet, made pictures inspired by their own artistic interests rather than the demands of official propaganda. Young Soviet film-makers such as Alov and Naumov revived avant-garde era forms of collective authorship. Not unlike avant-garde film-makers, the new directors emphasized metaphoric editing, favoured poetic screenplays, and rejected the domination of heavy-handed propagandistic scripts. As in avant-garde films of the 1920s, in the films of the 1950s the cameraman played a crucial role in the success of a picture. Critics started listing directors of photography, such as Sergei Urusevskii, Jonas Gritsius, and Vadim Iusov, as directors' prime co-authors. The new cinema of the 1950s also introduced a new generation of scriptwriters (Feliks Mironer, Valentin Ezhov), who collaborated with the directors instead of dominating the film-makers' work, as often happened in Stalinist cinema.

In the late 1950s and 1960s, two Stalin-era film-makers, Ivan Pyrev and Mikhail Romm, played key roles in liberalizing Soviet cinema. Pyrev refurbished the biggest Soviet studio, Mosfilm, hired new film-makers (Alov and Naumov, Rolan Bykov, Grigorii Chukhrai, Leonid Gaidai, Eldar Riazanov), and established the Organizing Committee of the Film-makers' Union, which, under Pyrev's leadership, served as an organization protecting film-makers' interests. Romm trained a new generation of Soviet film-makers (Tengiz Abuladze, Georgii Daneliia, Alexander Mitta, Andrei (Mikhalkov)-Konchalovskii, Gleb Panfilov, Andrei Tarkovskii, Larisa Shepitko, Vasilii Shukhin).

Directors of the 1960s absorbed the heritage of Soviet montage, neorealism, and European art cinema of the 1950s. Like European *auteurs* of the 1960s, the young Soviet film-makers, above all Tarkovskii and Sergei Paradzanov, made metaphysical fragmented plots, visual ambiguity, and reflexivity key elements of their individual cinematic styles. A strong connection with contemporary Russian poetry became a hallmark of the new cinema: the film-makers often collaborated with poets as their scriptwriters (Gennadii Shpalikov, Evgenii Evtushenko). The uncompromising film-maker emerged as the new cultural hero, whose confrontations with cultural authorities over censorship and the shelving of films became a canonical rite of passage. The young cinema challenged established norms and traditions: during the decade, two female film-makers (Larisa Shepitko and Kira Muratova) started their careers.

While art films brought international critical acclaim to the young Soviet cinema, the film-makers of the 1960s also made Soviet cinema a highly profitable commercial enterprise. Gaidai, Daneliia, Elem Klimov, and Riazanov offered moviegoers a wide range of comedies, while Edmond Keosaian and Vladimir Motyl transformed the Civil War film from an ideological vehicle into an action thriller. In 1963, Chukhrai abandoned directing to revive the profession of the producer. He established the Experimental Creative Unit at Mosfilm studio in order to introduce market relations into the Soviet film industry. The end of the Thaw brought economic and stylistic experimentation in cinema to an abrupt halt. The 1960s generation returned to power at the Fifth Congress of the Film-makers' Union in 1986 and was instrumental in dismantling Soviet culture during perestroika.

See also: Abuladze, Tengiz; Alov and Naumov; Bykov, Rolan; Chukhrai, Grigorii; Daneliia, Georgii; Evtushenko, Evgenii; Ezhov, Valentin; film, Soviet – Thaw period; film studios; Gaidai, Leonid; Iusov, Vadim; Kalatozov, Mikhail; Khutsiev, Marlen; Klimov, Elem; Kozintsev, Grigorii; Motyl, Vladimir; Muratova, Kira; Panfilov, Gleb; Paradzlanov, Sergei; Riazanov, Eldar; scriptwriters; Shepitko, Larisa; Shukshin, Vasilii; Tarkovskii, Andrei; Thaw; Urusevskii, Sergei

Further reading

Thaw Cinema CD-ROM (2002) Intro. Margolit, E., Artima Studio, Washington/Pittsburgh: Ford Foundation/NCEEER/University of Pittsburgh REES.

Prokhorov, A. (ed.) (2001) *Springtime for Soviet Cinema: Re/Viewing the 1960s*, Pittsburgh, PA: Pittsburgh Russian Film Symposium.

Woll, J. (2000) *Real Images: Soviet Cinema and the Thaw*, London: I.B. Tauris.

ALEXANDER PROKHOROV

film, documentary

Soviet documentary films were expected to chronicle everyday life in polarized terms for the edification of the masses: socialism as ideal, and capitalism as wholly negative. Facts and events that did not fit Communist ideology were often ignored. When reality fell short of expectations, it was frequently embellished with scenes of events that never occurred, such as recreational episodes in Leonid Varlamov and Boris Nebylitskii's *Moguchii potok* (*Powerful Stream*, 1939) about the construction of the Fergana Canal. Sometimes actors played ordinary people, such as the old peasant and his granddaughter in Sergei Iutkevich's *Ankara – serdtse Turtsii* (*Ankara, the Heart of Turkey*, 1933). Thus the borderline between documentary and feature films became blurred. The situation has been further complicated by forays into the documentary genre by prominent film-makers who treat it not as reportage, but as self-expression by different means. This approach has historical precedents in the experimental nature of early Soviet documentaries, exemplified by Dziga Vertov and Aleksandr Medvedkin, and today Aleksandr Sokurov might arguably serve as its best representative. Even Mikhail Romm's famous *Obyknovennyi fashizm* (*Ordinary Fascism*, 1965), heavily based on archival footage, was edited according to the principles of silent film montage. Conversely, frames from old feature films are sometimes used in modern documentaries to represent a newsreel allegedly recreating the atmosphere of a bygone epoch, as in Evgenii Tsymbal's *Dziga i ego brat'ia* (*Dziga and his Brothers*, 2002).

Given this symbiosis of genres, it is unsurprising that, after the almost complete withdrawal of state support in the early 1990s, which reduced documentary production to 30–40 per cent of late Soviet-era levels, the art of documentary film-making has been searching for a new identity, reflected in the quality of the annual documentary festival 'Russia' in Ekaterinburg (established in 1988). The perestroika period suddenly inspired filmgoers to rush to cinemas to watch such films as *Legko li byt molodym?* (*Hello, Can You Hear Us?*, 1987) by Iuris Podnieks, *Vlast solovetskaia* (*Solovki Power*, 1988) by Marina Goldovskaia, *Zhili-byli sem Simeonov* (*Seven Simons*, 1989) by Gerts Frank and Vladimir Eisner, and *Tak zhit nelzia* (*Can't Live Like This*, 1990) by Stanislav Govorukhin. These offerings' overt and long overdue criticism of the Soviet regime signified only a brief revival of the documentary genre. Though lack of funding and the consequent independence allow documentary film-makers the freedom to discuss serious issues in considerable depth, documentary film remains in decline. To rectify this state of affairs the Russian government has increased investments in documentary film-making (77.2 million rubles in 2000, as opposed to 6 million in 1998) and the Guild of Film and Television Documentary Makers in 2000 established *Lavr* (Laurel), a prize for the best documentary of the year.

Further reading

Dolmatovskaia, G. and Kopalina, G. (eds) (1991) *Vzryv: Bytie i byt dokumentalnogo kino v kontse vos'midesiatykh*, Moscow: NII kinoisskusstva.

—— (eds) (1995) *Posle vzryva: Dokumentalnoe kino 90-kh*, Moscow: NII kinoisskusstva.

Dzhulai, L. (2001) *Dokumentalnyi illiuzion*, Moscow: Materik.

ANDREI ROGATCHEVSKI

film, educational (nauchno-populiarnoe kino)

In the Soviet Union, *nauchno-populiarnoe kino* (educational film), also called *nauch-pop*, was a genre of non-fictional film about science, the arts, nature, travel, ethnography, history, or distinguished personages, usually for a non-specialized audience. The distinction between *nauchno-populiarnoe kino* and *dokumentalnoe kino* (documentary film) was somewhat blurred, especially by the end of the Soviet period. In general, documentaries were informative, but not necessarily educational. Educational films, largely made at specialized studios (separate or part of larger film studios), were overseen by a scholarly consultant and intended to educate or enlighten audiences and popularize some aspect of an academic discipline.

The films were shown on television; in specialized cinemas; as shorts before feature films in cinemas; and in schools, institutions of higher learning, and state enterprises and organizations. In particular, Soviet nature, travel, and ethnographic films demonstrated a high level of technical and artistic mastery. By the late Soviet period, films in this genre were generally less tendentious politically and had a strong authorial point of view.

In the 1990s, government funding for educational films was severely cut back, and television stations largely took over the production of non-fictional programming, especially in new genres such as reality shows and magazine-format talk shows. Since 2000, state and other financing have been available, and studios now produce more films for television. Today, however, *nauchno-populiarnoe kino* is virtually a moribund film genre.

See also: educational system, Soviet; film, documentary; film, television; television, post-Soviet; television, Soviet

MICHELE BERDY

film, festivals and prizes

In the Soviet Union, film prizes were awarded mainly at three international festivals: one in Moscow, one in Tashkent (with an emphasis on Third World cinema), and an All-Union film festival that rotated among republic capitals. Since the USSR collapsed, only the Moscow International Film Festival (established in 1935, biannual since 1959, annual since 1999) has survived, albeit with less prestige. During the 1990s, new film festivals emerged in reverse proportion to the number of films produced by the struggling industry, with the All-Union festival replaced by at least three similar and competing festivals: Sochi's *Kinotavr* (Cinetaur, est. 1990); Anapa's *Kinoshok* (Cine-Shock, est. 1992), which focuses on films from the CIS and the Baltic republics; and St. Petersburg's *Vivat, kino Rossii* (Long Live Russian Cinema!, est. 1993). Numerous new international festivals classified by theme or production type include *Zolotoi vitiaz* (Golden Knight, est. 1992), which concentrates on religious, particularly Russian Orthodox, motifs, such as *Liki liubvi* (Visages of Love, est. 1995) and *Zakon i obshchestvo* (Law and Society, est. 1998). The production type, *Poslanie k cheloveku* (Message to Man, est. 1989), is awarded for documentaries, short feature films, and animation. The *St. Anna* festival (est. 1993) targets student work and debuts, while *Chistye grezy* (Pure Daydreams, est. 1998) recognizes small-budget pictures.

The closest equivalent to the American Oscar in prestige and scope is the Russian Nika prize, originally established in 1987 as the Cinematographers' Union annual prize and in 2001 transferred to the auspices of the Russian Academy of Cinematography. In 2002, director Nikita Mikhalkov established the *Zolotoi orel* (Golden Eagle) prize, under the auspices of another Academy of Cinematography, following disagreements with the administration of the Nika: criticism targeted a perceived arbitrariness in giving one category multiple awards and granting last-minute ad hoc awards in previously unannounced categories. In 2003, Aleksandr Rogozhkin's broadly acclaimed *Kukushka* (*The Cuckoo*, 2002) won the Nika, while what some see as the nationalist Golden Eagle went in 2005 to Vladimir Khotinenko's *72 metra* (*72 Metres*, 2004), perceived by many critics as a poor film.

See also: Mikhalkov, Nikita; Rogozhkin, Aleksandr

Further reading

Beumers, B. (ed.) (1999) *Russia on Reels*, London and New York: I.B. Tauris.

ANDREI ROGATCHEVSKI

film, Georgian

In the 1920s, Georgian film-makers – David Rondeli [Tsagareishvili], Mikhail Kalatozov [Kalatozishvili], and Otar Chiaureli – quickly earned a reputation for daring camerawork that highlighted Georgia's dramatic landscape in films that served revolutionary themes. After Khrushchev repudiated the cult of personality – to which Chiaureli had contributed three notoriously adulatory films – Georgia's Rustaveli Studio emerged as one of the most productive and innovative of republic cinemas, its films receiving national distribution and admiration.

From the late 1950s until the early 1990s, directors such as brothers Eldar and Georgii Shengelaia, Mikhail Kobakhidze, Georgii Daneliia, Tengiz Abuladze, and Otar Ioseliani drew on Georgian culture for lyrical explorations of their country's national past, often despoiled by modernity, or humorously contrasted the rigidity of a hypertrophied bureaucratic society with the wayward desires of individuals. In Ioseliani's *Zhil pevchii drozd* (*There Once Lived a Singing Blackbird*, 1970), for instance, the musician-hero drifts through life, refusing to adjust to a modern society that ultimately avenges itself on him in a shocking finale; in Eldar Shengalaia's more farcical *Golubye gory* (*Blue Mountains*, 1984), made on the eve of perestroika, the old world of lazy, time-serving officials literally collapses. Georgian cinema's distinctive blend of irony and pathos yielded a new genre, dubbed 'philosophical' comedy, and its affinity for absurdity and surrealism expressed itself most brilliantly in Abuladze's 1984 investigation of tyranny, *Pokaianie* (*Repentance*).

See also: Abuladze, Tengiz; Daneliia, Georgii

JOSEPHINE WOLL

film, Kazakh

From 1942–44, Russia's primary film-makers (Eisenstein, Vertov, and Pudovkin) were evacuated with Mosfilm and Lenfilm to the then Kazakh capital of Almaty, where they continued their work. At the end of World War II, having created a fully equipped studio in Kazakhstan, they returned home.

Kazakh national cinema began with Aimanov's first feature film, *Poema o liubvi* (*A Love Poem*, 1954). The 1960s generation of Kazakh film-makers produced epic and national narrative genres, such as Sultan Khodjikov's *Kyz-Zhibek*, 1971). Retrospective historical films recalled troubled distant and not so distant pasts: Mazhit Begalin's *Sledy ukhodiat za gorizont* (*Footsteps Disappear on the Horizon*, 1965), Abdulla Karsakbaev's *Trevozhnoe utro* (*A Troubled Morning*, 1968) and Shaken Aimanov's 1971 *Konets atamana* (*The End of the Ataman*). Late 1970s Socialist Realist films, more ideologically correct, lost artistic quality: Aleksei Sakharov's 1979 *Vkus kheba* (*The Taste of Bread*) about a collective farm.

The second generation of Kazakh film emerged in the 1980s with Russian film-maker Sergei Solovev's class for young Kazakh directors at VGIK (All-Union State Institute of Cinematography). Once back in Almaty, they produced low budget films known as Kazakh New Wave. Contemporary reality replaced past epic events: Rashid Nugmanov's 1988 *Igla* (*The Needle*) and 1993 *Dikii Vostok* (*The Wild East*).

Although separated by twenty years, the two generations of film-makers share a theme: growing up 'Kazakh'. The first filmed grandparents raising 'orphans' in the ancestral *aul*: Aimanov's 1967 *Zemlia otsov* (*The Land of Our Fathers*). Images of ancient stone etchings, steppes and mountains, and the national Kazakh dombra create an ethnoscape.

The second generation – Abai Karpykov's 1989 *Vlyublennaya rybka* (*A Small Fish in Love*), Darezhan Omirbaev's 2001 *Zhol* (Zhol) – rejects the past and depicts urban life that invaded the steppes. Serik Aprymov's 1989 *Konechnaya ostanovka* (*The Last Stop*) exposes dying post-Soviet village life in a quasi-documentary style that recalls French New Wave. The film depicts the death of tradition and orphans who struggle to find meaning in their wasteland.

Satybaldy Narymbetov's 2002 *Molitva Leily* (*Leila's Prayer*) reduces tradition to a young goat girl's dress and the close-knit but shrinking multi-ethnic community, in which the effects of Soviet nuclear blasting have destroyed village life. The protagonist Leila's expected infant is the result of rape, not love; yet in spite of life's blows and the harsh, inhospitable environment, Leila still says her Muslim prayer to save her nation, her child, and herself.

In Guka Omarova's 2004 *Shiza* (*Schizo*), young 'Shiza' (Mufta) is led astray by his mother's lover, a motorcycle-riding Russian thug, but finds a new family with a young Russian widow and her fatherless son.

Kazakh audiences and government became tired of depictions of destitute *auls*. In Aprymov's 2004 *Okhotnik* (*The Hunter*), recalling Kyrgyz director Tolomush Okeev's 1973 *Lyutyi* (*The Fierce One*), a horse-borne nomad hunter (surrogate father) takes a young misfit into the mountains to learn 'true' Kazakh ways of hunting, loving, even breathing.

By 2004, Kazakh film was investing in American-Kazakh action-packed, sensational historical canvases that incite patriotism, such as the Hollywood-made blockbuster *Kochevniki* (*The Nomad*), commissioned by President Nursultan Nazarbaev and co-directed by Ivan Passer, Talgat Temenov, and Sergei Bodrov and shot in Kazakhstan. Bolat Kalymbetov's low-budget 2004 film *Sardar* depicts more credibly a four-teenth-century fight for Kazakh independence against invaders.

Kazakhfilm is now the best equipped Central Asian film studio.

See also: All-Russian (All-Union) State Institute of Cinematography (VGIK); Central Asia; film, post-Soviet; Kazakhstan; Socialist Realism; Solovev, Sergei

Further reading

Abikeyeva, G. (2003) *The Heart of the World: Films from Central Asia*, Almaty: Complex.

JANE E. KNOX-VOINA

film, literary adaptation (ekranizatsiia)

A cinematic work that derives from a literary text. The film declares its connection to the original in one of three ways: through an identical title (e.g., Sergei Bondarchuk's *Voina i mir* [*War and Peace*, 1965–67]); through documentation in the film credits (e.g., Nikita Mikhalkov's *Ochi chernye* [*Dark Eyes*, 1987]); or through the film's narrative structure (e.g., Aleksandr Sokurov's *Spasi i sokhrani* [*Save and Protect*, 1989]). Although popular literary sources have attracted film-makers from the earliest days of cinema, the relationship between the two arts perpetually remains ambiguous.

On the one hand, literature provides the obvious initial source in cinematic literary adaptations. On the other, in its use of litera-ture, cinema invariably strives to 'overcome' its precursor. The two media aspire to different ways of viewing and presenting the same objects, thereby creating disparate images. Maia Turovskaia (1990) suggests that literary adaptation is an aesthetic struggle with the original rather than a reproduction of it. For instance, when transferred to the screen, the verbal description of objects can distort the original author's intent: e.g., Chekhov's abundant objects, when 'faith-fully' projected on screen, absorb the characters, and the result violates the Chekhovian spirit.

Neia Zorkaia (1991) classifies adaptations into three major types: *kinolubok* (including most film adaptations from the first decade of the twen-tieth century), illustration (e.g., Aleksandr Zarkhi's 1967 *Anna Karenina*), and interpretation (e.g., Grigorii Kozintsev's 1964 *Hamlet*). *Kinolubok*, a term based on Russian folk 'comics', erases the original author's individuality. In general, *kinolubok* is cinema without cinematic devices. While this kind of adaptation treats the original text aggressively, illustration follows the literary text, striving for cinematic analogues. Unlike *lubok*, illustration attempts to recreate details of everyday life. The third mode, interpretation, crucially differs from *lubok*-style adaptation and illustration. It entails the cinematic embodiment of a literary work, an interpretation of the author's style and ideas through cinematic means. According to Zorkaia, creative inter-pretation oriented toward the original source is essentially *auteur* cinema.

Whereas early cinema employed well-known literary texts to ensure popular success, while simultaneously seeking legitimation via the 'prestigious' medium of literature, contemporary cinema – now cured of its inferiority complex – adapts classics for different purposes. Thaw-era cinema, Andrei Shemiakin (1996) claims, interpreted literature for the spectator, who expected the screen to reflect and elucidate happenings in the country and people's understanding of them. Recent celluloid versions of Fedor Dostoevskii's novel *The Idiot* – Roman Kachanov's highly irreverent film *Daun Haus* (*Down House*, 2001) and Vladimir Bortko's respectfully faithful adaptation, *Idiot* (2003) – illustrate contradictory tendencies in post-Soviet culture: the attempt to separate itself from the past and to reaffirm national loyalty to earlier values.

Further reading and references

Rifkin, B. (1994) *Semiotics of Narration in Film and Prose Fiction: Case Studies of 'Scarecrow' and 'My Friend Ivan Lapshin'*, New York: Peter Lang.

Russian Studies in Literature (2004) 40, 2–3 (Spring–Summer).

Shemiakin, A. (1996) 'Dialog s literaturoi, ili opasnye sviazi', in V. Troianovskii (ed.) *Kinematograf ottepeli*, Moscow: Materik.

Turovskaia, M. (1990) 'Ob ekranizatsii Chekhova', *Kinovedcheskie zapiski* 5: 25–44.

Zorkaia, N. (1991) 'Russkaia shkola ekranizatsii', in N. Zorkaia (ed.) *Ekrannye iskusstva i literatura*, Moskva: Nauka.

IRINA MAKOVEEVA

film, post-Soviet

Russian cinema of the 1990s and early 2000s developed in the context of specific sociopolitical millennial changes: the collapse of the Soviet Union and its institutions, the resultant ideological void, and the transition from a totalitarian centralized system to a market economy. Directors demythologized former Soviet icons and the Stalinist past. They satirized Russia's newly acquired Western values and vices, redefined national identities, re-negotiated gender roles, explored Russia's new imperial ambitions and its past legacy, and exposed the mismanagement and catastrophic pollution of Soviet industry.

Film production fell from its peak of 300 films in 1990 to fewer than thirty films in 1996 because of a loss of state subsidies, need for capital, marketability, high costs of the latest technology, competition with incoming foreign (particularly, American) films, and, most importantly, audiences' preference for television and videos over out-of-date cinema theatres. Financial considerations motivated a turn to European (particularly French and German) co-producers and sponsors, which necessitated adapting to foreign viewers.

Two generations of cinematographers competed in post-Soviet cinema. Older Soviet *auteurs* (who came of age during the Thaw) took advantage of their already established popularity and status, developing their signature styles in a freer artistic environment: Kira Muratova, Nikita Mikhalkov, Vadim Abdrashitov and Aleksandr Mindadze, Sergei Solovev, Marlen Khutsiev, Aleksandr Mitta, Aleksei German, Eldar Riazanov, and Petr Todorovskii, among others.

The competing younger directors explored new themes and innovative techniques: Valerii Todorovskii, Karen Shakhnazarov, Aleksei Balabanov, Aleksandr Zeldovich, Vladimir Khotinenko, Aleksandr Rogozhkin, Aleksei Uchitel, Pavel Lungin, and many others. Unlike the 'Soviet' generation, they took viewers, theatres, and advertisements – the commercialization of the industry – into account. Newcomers 'coming of age' during glasnost and understanding the importance of self-supporting films, proposed a new Association of Low-Budget Film Studios.

Films by female directors noticeably increased during the 2000s, including Vera Storozheva's *Nebo, samolet, devushka* (*Sky, Plane, Girl*, 2003) and Renata Litvinova's *Boginia: kak ia poliubila* (*Goddess: How I Fell in Love*, 2004). With her pseudo-semi-documentary *S dnem rozhdeniia* (2001), *S liuboviu, Liliia* (*With Love, Lilia*, 2002) and *Trebuetsia niania* (*Babysitter Required*, 2005), Larisa Sadilova became an important presence among the generation aged 40-plus.

Urban crime thrillers and action films, by male directors, dominated the post-Soviet screen: Balabanov's *Brat* (*Brother*, 1997) and *Brat-2* (*Brother-2*, 2000); Boris Giller's *Chek* (*Check*, 1999), Stanislav Govorukhin's *Voroshilovskii strelok* (*Sharp Shooter*, 2000), and Lungin's *Oligarkh* (*The Tycoon*, 2002). Balabanov's criminal comedy *Zhmurki* (*Dead Man's Bluff*, 2005) portrayed young 1990s bandits as today's successful businessmen.

The new (anti-)heroes displaced Homo Sovieticus, whose representatives now became psychologically ill mutants (Muratova's *Tri istorii* [*Three Stories*, 1997]), genderless freaks and pedophiles (Balabanov's *Pro urodov i liudei* [*About Freaks and People*, 1998]), and disposable or paralyzed cripples or expendable corpses (Muratova's *Tri istorii* and *Vtorostepennye liudi* [*Minor People*]). Soviet types were also replaced by cheap swindlers and petty thieves operating in a new economic and social system, as in Muratova's *Nastroishchik* (*Piano Tuner*, 2004).

In various modes that treated different historical periods, Zeldovich's *Moskva* (*Moscow*, 1999), Mikhail Brashinskii's *Gololed* (*Black Ice*, 2003), Shakhnazarov's *Vsadnik po imeni smert* (*A Rider Named Death*, 2004), and Valerii Todorovskii's *Moi svodnyi brat Frankenshtein* (*My Stepbrother Frankenstein*, 2004) reflected an emotional bankruptcy that reduces life to a nightmare. These apocalyptic visions were carried to an extreme in Ilia Khrzhanovskii's *Chetyre/4* (*Four*, 2004), in which wild dogs inhabit a 'post-human' industrial town, four young female clones struggle for identity, and toothless old women chew lifeless dolls made of bread. Rejecting conventional uses of space, the director shot his heroine at the very edge of an empty field, a metaphorical no-man's land.

Other apocalyptic films depicting chaos were Konstantin Lopushanskii's *Russkaia simfoniia* (*Russian Symphony*, 1994) and Abdrashitov's psycho-sociological drama *Magnitnye buri* (*Magnetic Storms*, 2003). In the latter, whose title suggests the Russian male's proclivity for sporadic, spontaneous violence, those storms unleash nightly brutal fights between factory workers; the young hero wanders through bunker-like zones and is 'crucified' at work, his arms outstretched in vices.

'Killer-thrillers' dominated perestroika and the early 1990s. That genre subsequently yielded to a dizzying diversity of genres and subgenres: romantic comedies, retro-dramas, epic dramas, melodramas, monodramas, docu-dramas, American-style blockbusters, war films, national films, historical costume dramas, literary adaptations, and documentaries. The last, in black and white, portrayed what Soviets would have called 'unvarnished reality': Vitalii Manskii's *Chastnie khroniki: monolog* (*Private Chronicles*: Mono-

logue, 1999), Galina Dolmatovskaia's *Zhenshchina na mavzolee* (*Woman on the Mausoleum*, 2002), and Aleksei Muradov's *Zmei* (*The Serpent*, 2002), which captured a day in the life of a small-town military executioner.

An important trend in post-Soviet film was the ideological delineation of otherness and the reconstruction of a 'national identity', at odds with Soviet mythology, yet located in the village – the traditionally perceived source of 'Russianness'. Rogozhkin's *Osobennosti natsionalnoi okhoty* (*Peculiarities of the National Hunt*, 1995) and several sequels, Khotinenko's *Musulmanin* (*Moslem*, 1995), and Lungin's *Svadba* (*Wedding*, 2000) belong to this tendency. Lungin also tackling the issue of New Money and its influence in the provinces.

These and similar films favoured past traditions, rituals, legends, myths, an authentic Russian language peppered with four-letter words, panoramic tracking shots of country landscapes, and portraits of 'quintessential' Russian peasant women: the roles played by Nina Usatova in Khotinenko's *The Moslem* and Nonna Mordiukova in Denis Evstignev's *Mama* (1999), and the old female villagers in Gennadii Sidorov's *Starukhi* (*Little Old Ladies*, 2003) and Lidiia Bobrova's *Babusia* (*Granny*, 2003). Friendship, drinking, brotherhood, and Russian folklore appear as elemental in Sergei Ovcharov's *Skaz pro Fedota-streltsa* (*The Tale of Soldier Fedot*, 2002), Valerii Surikov's *Kostroma* (*Kostroma*, 2002), and Sergei Bodrov Sr.'s *Medvezhii potselui* (*The Bear's Kiss*, 2002). While the village may remain the stronghold of authenticity, in *The Moslem* villagers' Russian faith yields to materialism and intolerance: their river ultimately proves not a source of baptism or renewal, but a flood of American dollars from a rich bureaucrat's gigantic briefcase.

Historical costume dramas became a popular post-Soviet genre, conveying nostalgia for national heritage and empire, as in Sergei Tarasov's *Kniaz Iurii Dolgorukii* (*Prince Yurii Dolgorukii*, 1998), Gleb Panfilov's *Romanovy, ventsenosnaia semia* (*The Romanov Family*, 2000), Svetlana Druzhinina's *Vtoraia nevesta imperatora* (*The Emperor's Second Bride*, 2001), and Vitalii Melnikov's film about a martyred but benevolent noble Tsar lost, *Bednyi, bednyi Pavel* (*Poor, Poor Pavel II*, 2003). Two major films devoted to the tsarist era that elicited considerable controversy were Mikhalkov's *Sibirskii tsiriulnik* (*Barber of Siberia*, 1998) and Aleksandr Sokurov's *Russkii kovcheg* (*The Russian Ark*, 2002), while films examining the Soviet period included Mikhalkov's Oscar-winner, *Utomlennye solntsem* (*Burnt by the Sun*, 1994), and Sergei Livnev's *Serp i molot* (*Hammer and Sickle*, 1995).

Adaptations of literary classics affirmed the status of Russian high culture and satisfied Russian spectators' clamour for pre-revolutionary luxury and expansiveness, as evidenced in Iurii Grymov's *Mu-Mu* (1998), based on Ivan Turgenev's story, Aleksandr Proshkin's costume drama, *Russkii bunt* (*The Captain's Daughter*, 2000), adapted from Aleksandr Pushkin's novel about the Pugachev rebellion, and Semen Gorov's musical comedy, *Vechera na khutore bliz Dikanki* (*Evenings on a Farm near Dikanka*, 2001), which brought Nikolai Gogol's early collection of stories to TV.

Several films devoted to the portrayal of World War II that extended the Soviet convention of depicting both the heroism and the human frailty of the era included Nikolai Lebedev's *Zvezda* (*The Star*, 2002) and Rogozhkin's highly original *Kukushka* (*The Cuckoo*, 2001), with its multi-lingual dialogue and reliance on shamanism. The decade of bombings, kidnappings, and ruthless killings in the Caucasus reverberated in Bodrov Sr.'s prize-winning *Kavkazskii plennik* (*Prisoner of the Mountains*, 1996), Abdrashitov's *Vremia Tantsora* (*Time of the Dancer*, 1997), Rogozhkin's *Blokpost* (*Checkpoint*, 1999) and Natalia Piankova's *Marsh Slavianki* (*Slav's March*, 2003). Balabanov's *Voina* (*War*, 2002), the most virulently pro-Russian, anti-Chechen portrayal of the Russo-Chechen war, could not have contrasted more with Roman Kachanov's *DMB* (*Demobbed*, 2000), a comedy about the antic escapades of three army recruits.

During this period, the trope of the road or journey, signifying transition to a new future, flourished. Real-life constant upheaval, transformations, and mobility (recalling Tom Tykwer's post-Communist Berlin-generation in *Run Lola Run*) transferred to the screen in 'on the move' films by young Russian directors and actors who won prizes at festivals: Balabanov's *Brat*, Filipp Iankovskii's *V dvizhenii* (*Moving*, 2003), and Petr Buslov's *Bumer* (*Bimmer*, 2003). Uchitel's *Progulka*

(*The Stroll*, 2003), with spontaneous performance by young non-professionals, combined a view of the new St. Petersburg with a glimpse of youth's new morality.

By the twenty-first century, the Soviet industrial wasteland had transformed into revitalized, brightly-lit cities, at least in Russia's metropolitan centres. While portraying the spiritual emptiness of a mercantile new world, 'glossy' films advertised luxurious apartments, country mansions, chic restaurants, clubs, and bars, and European furniture, clothes, and goods for the newly-rich Russian consumer, whose affluence was unimaginably remote from the poverty of the provinces.

The sense of loneliness and alienation in the new Russia bred what one could call family films, which narrated the search for parental bonds. The narrator in Pavel Chukhrai's retrospective *Vor* (*Thief*, 1996) struggles with memories of a father missing in war and the reality of his Stalin-like replacement. Boris Khlebnikov's *Koktebel* (2003), Andrei Zviangintsev's *Vozvrashchenie* (*The Return*, 2003), Bodrov Jr.'s *Sestry* (*Sisters*, 2001), Evstigneev's *Mama* (1999), Sokurov's *Otets i syn* (*Father and Son*, 2002) and Vladimir Mashkov's *Papa!* (2004) all seek to restore the broken family, the microcosm of post-Soviet society. Whatever the aesthetic quality of post-Soviet cinema, its productions attest to the embrace of multiple genres, styles, and aesthetics.

See also: Abdrashitov, Vadim; Balabanov, Aleksei; families; film, Soviet; German, Aleksei; Khotinenko, Vladimir; Khutsiev, Marlen; Litvinova, Renata; Lungin, Pavel; Mashkov, Vladimir; Mikhalkov, Nikita; Muratova, Kira; nationalism ('the national question'); New Russians; Riazanov, Eldar; Rogozhkin, Aleksandr; Shakhnazarov, Karen; Sokurov, Aleksandr; Todorovskii, Petr; Todorovskii, Valerii; War, Afghan; World War II (Great Patriotic War)

Further reading

Beumers, B. (1999) *Russia on Reels: The Russian Idea in Post-Soviet Cinema*, London and New York: I. B. Tauris.

Drozdova, M. (1994) 'Beyond Glasnost', in M. Brashinsky and A. Horton (eds) *Russian Critics on the Cinema of Glasnost*, Cambridge: Cambridge University Press, pp. 123–46.

Knox-Voina, J. (2004). 'On the Road in Russia: Sochi and Moscow Film Festivals', *Russian Review*, Jan.: 138–43.

Larsen, S. (1999) 'In Search of an Audience: The New Russian Cinema of Reconciliation', in A. M. Barker (ed.) *Consuming Russia*, Durham, NC: Duke University Press, pp. 192–216.

—— (2000) 'Melodramatic Masculinity, National Identity, and the Stalinist Past in Postsoviet Cinema', in H. Goscilo (ed.) *Studies in 20th Century Literature*, Vol. 24, No. 1, pp. 85–120.

JANE E. KNOX-VOINA

film, Soviet – Stagnation period

In film, the period of Stagnation arguably begins with the shelving or failure to release three films destined to become classics: Andrei Tarkovskii's *Andrei Rublev*, Aleksandr Askoldov's *Kommissar*, and Andrei Konchalovskii's *Asia Kliachina*. A new generation of talented young film-makers got into trouble trying to do what only a few years earlier had been possible: to experiment with style and offer a personal, at times critical, view of the Soviet present or past. Kira Muratova's *Korotkie vstrechi* (*Brief Encounters*, 1968) was quickly buried, and her second feature, *Dolgie provody* (*A Long Goodbye*, 1971) was banned outright, as was Sergei Paradzhanov's stylized mytho-poetic film, *Saiat Nova* (*Tsvet granata* [*The Colour of Pomegranates*], 1970). *Rublev*'s convoluted and tortuous path through the cinema bureaucracy to the screen from 1966 to 1971 reflected the increasing censorship and conservatism in the film industry. Careers were stunted (Muratova) or destroyed (Askoldov). The persecution and imprisonment of Paradzhanov was an international scandal in the 1970s. From the late 1960s to the early 1980s approximately one hundred films were shelved.

The Thaw also saw its share of censorship and bureaucratic meddling, most famously in the case of the forced re-editing of Marlen Khutsiev's *Zastava Ilicha* (*Lenin's Guard*), released as *Mne dvadtsat let* (*I Am Twenty*, 1964). But the lively public discussions and arguments over films among film-makers, critics, and even cinema bureaucrats that had characterized the

Thaw gave way in the late 1960s to official pronouncements or official silence and unexplained shelving of films. Stylistic or thematic experimentation was officially out as the romantic idealism of the Thaw gave way to the pragmatism of the 1970s, the commercialization of film, and new calls for Socialist Realism and movies for the masses. But the cinema bureaucracy in the 1970s was not the ideological and political monolith of Stalinist times. Problematic films were still allowed to be produced, only to be shelved or not released until later. Paradoxically, Stagnation also produced some of the most un-Soviet films made during Soviet times, such as Tarkovskii's idiosyncratic and highly autobiographical *Zerkalo* (*Mirror*, 1975). Surprisingly, *Zerkalo* was not banned outright, yet it barely appeared on the screen.

Russian critic Neia Zorkaia adopts the nineteenth-century writer Aleksandr Gertsen's phrase to characterize the Stagnation period as an 'epoch of external slavery and internal freedom' (*epokha naruzhnogo rabstva i vnutrennego raskreposhcheniia*). She argues that in some ways film-makers were finally free of the Thaw's idealistic belief in 'socialism with a human face' and could begin to address the question of individual human fate and moral responsibility, as does Vasilii Shukshin, the writer-film-maker is his *Kalina krasnaia* (*Snowball Berry Red*, 1973), seen by over 60 million viewers.

While many directors internalized the increasing political conservatism and produced films that could pass the gauntlet of censorship, some also found ways to challenge Soviet ideology through the development of a sophisticated, allegorical Aesopian language to say what could not be articulated directly. Literary adaptations such as Grigorii Kozintsev's *Korol Lir* (*King Lear*, 1971), Andrei Konchalovskii's *Diadia Vania* (*Uncle Vania*, 1970), Nikita Mikhalkov's *Neokonchennaia pesa dlia mekhanicheskogo pianino* (*Unfinished Piece for Mechanical Piano*, 1977) were a particularly fruitful way of offering a critique of a decaying Brezhnevian society that had lost its Communist beliefs and ethical moorings. The increasingly popular science fiction genre also provided a distancing effect that allowed for a serious critique of contemporary Soviet 'civilization', as in Tarkovskii's *Solaris* (1972) and *Stalker* (1979) – the latter film, in the eyes of many, eerily foreshadowing the Chernobyl disaster.

Stagnation-era films also engaged Russian and Soviet history as well as the question of nationhood and the awakening of a national consciousness. Many of these are also literary adaptations. Sergei Bondarchuk's four-part adaptation of Tolstoi's *Voina i mir* (*War and Peace*, 1964–67) bridges the Thaw and Stagnation periods, as does Tarkovskii's *Andrei Rublev*. The 1970s brought big, wide-screen, commercially successful Second World War epics – Iuri Ozerov's *Osvobozhdenie* (*Liberation*, 1968–71), Stanislav Rostotskii's *A zori zdes tikhie* (*The Dawns Are Quiet Here*, 1972), Bondarchuk's *Oni srazhalis za rodinu* (*They Defended the Motherland*, 1975), and Aleksandr Alov and Vladimir Naumov's *Tegeran-43* (*Teheran-43*, 1980). Yet another, revisionist trend in Second World War films began, in which the concepts 'hero' and 'enemy' are complex and heroics give way to moral questioning and human suffering. The best 'war' films of the 1970s include Aleksei German's *Proverka na dorogakh* (*Trial on the Road*, banned in 1971, released in 1985) and his follow-up, *Dvadtsad dnei bez voiny* (*Twenty Days Without War*, 1976), and Larisa Shepitko's *Voskhozhdenie* (*The Ascent*, 1977). The 1980s and the glasnost period witnessed few war films of note, with the exception of Elem Klimov's heart-wrenching tale of German atrocities, *Idi i smotri* (*Come and See*, 1985).

The Revolution, Civil War, and the 1920s were revisited by Russian film-makers (Mikhalkov in *Raba liubvi* [*Slave of Love*, 1976], Vladimir Motyl in the cult classic *Beloe solntse pustyni* [*White Sun of the Desert*, 1969]) and by talented young VGIK-trained directors from the Central Asian republics (Ali Khamraev in *Sedmaia pulia* [*The Seventh Bullet*], 1972, Uzbekfilm) and Eldor Uzarbaev in *Transsibirskii ekspress* (*Trans-Siberian Express*, 1977, Kazakhfilm). There were many such 'Easterns' – action films modelled on the Hollywood Western.

The late 1960s and early 1970s saw a flowering of cinema in the republics, where, far away from Moscow, film-makers were freer to explore, often in stunning visuals, their own land, culture, and history. The spare and hauntingly beautiful *Nevestka* (*Daughter-in-Law*, 1972) by the Turkmen director Khodzhakuli

Narliev and the Kirghiz director Tolomush Okeev's *Nebo nashego detstva* (*The Sky of our Childhood*, 1966) and *Liutyi* (*The Fierce One*, 1973) remain classics to this day. In particular Ukraine and Georgia developed their own film styles and schools with internationally-known directors – Vadim Ilienko, Paradzhanov, Tengiz Abuladze, and Otar Ioseliani. The Thaw, in fact, gave way to Stagnation more slowly and imperceptibly in the republics, thus defying easy categorization.

The official end of Stagnation in cinema is easier to date – 1986, with the release of Abuladze's *Pokaianie* (*Repentance*) and the Fifth Congress of the Union of Film-makers, which elected a new liberal leadership and established a commission to 'unshelve' all banned films. But the seeds of glasnost were planted much earlier in the many slice-of-life films, melodramas, comedies, and tragicomedies that attempted to take an honest look at contemporary social problems. The youthful heroes of Thaw films gave way in the 1970s to middle-aged 'heroes' and, more often, tired 'heroines' juggling work, family, and bureaucracy in films by such directors as Georgii Daneliia, Eldar Riazanov, and Iurii Raizman. Failure of love, divorce, betrayal, generational conflict between parents and children – collectively, these phenomena create an implicit indictment of the larger society. The true precursors of glasnost, however, were a series of allegorical films by the team of Vadim Abdrashitov and Aleksandr Mindadze, which pointed to the moral bankruptcy of the Soviet system and foreshadowed its demise.

The final paradox of Stagnation is that, for all the bureaucratic control, censorship, pressure, and hardships suffered by film-makers, the Soviet film industry produced, particularly in the 1970s, many of the most popular and beloved Soviet films: Leonid Gaidai's zany comedies, including *Brilliantovaia ruka* (*The Diamond Arm*, 1968); Riazanov's *Ironiia sudby ili s legkim parom* (*The Irony of Fate*, 1975), still screened on Russian television every New Year's Eve and the Soviet Cinderella story; and Vladimir Menshov's *Moskva slezam ne verit* (*Moscow Doesn't Believe in Tears*, 1980). The collapse of the Soviet film industry during perestroika and the early post-Soviet period, and recent attempts to create a viable commercial

Russian film industry, have created a sense of nostalgia for the highly professional and successful cinema of the Stagnation era.

See also: Abdrashitov, Vadim; Abuladze, Tengiz; All-Russian (All-Union) State Institute of Cinematography (VGIK); Askoldov, Aleksandr; Bondarchuk, Sergei; censorship: Daneliia, Georgii; film, Georgian; film, literary adaptation; film, Soviet – Thaw period; Gaidai, Leonid; German, Aleksei; Klimov, Elem; Konchalovskii, Andrei; Mikhalkov, Nikita; Mindadze, Aleksandr; Muratova, Kira; Paradzhanov, Sergei; Riazanov, Eldar; Shepitko, Larisa; Shukshin, Vasilii; Tarkovskii, Andrei

Further reading

Golosvkoi, V. (2004) *Mezhdu ottepeliu i glasnostiu: Kinematograf 70-kh* (Between Thaw and Glasnost: The Cinema of the 70s), Moscow: Materik.

Lawton, A. (1992) *Kinoglasnost: Soviet Cinema in Our Time*, Cambridge: Cambridge University Press, Chapter 1.

Zorkaia, N. (1999) 'Istoriia sovetskogo kino, Glava sedmaia. Semidesiatye: Protivostoianie dukha' (History of Soviet Cinema, chapter 7, The Seventies: Spiritual Resistance), special insert to newspaper *Pervoe sentiabria* (September 1), No. 30 (August).

VIDA JOHNSON

film, Soviet – Stalin era

Cinema from 1929–53 was inextricably tied to Stalinist policies. On the eve of this period a union-wide congress pronounced the need for clear ideology within film-making to expand industrial projects within industry and agriculture. In the shift from silent experimentation (of Eisenstein, Vertov *et al.*) towards an aurally persuasive and simpler form of politicized cinema, Nikolai Ekk's *Putevka v zhizn* (*The Road to Life*, 1931) played a key role, even if virtually no cinemas were equipped with speakers or projectors that recognized soundtracks. This tale of homeless children after the Civil War suggested

that progressive politics could be helped by cohesive networks of friends and committed colleagues.

Associated metaphors marked the 1930s, as in the Vasilev brothers' *Chapaev* (1934). The screen version of Dmitrii Furmanov's martial novel attained a statewide, mythological status and garnered prizes at several film festivals: Moscow (1935), Paris (1937) and Venice (1946). The film relies on friendship and fidelity to shape a story of national and ideological power; it transformed a Civil War combatant into a figure of progressive socialist realism. Films of the period needed to justify the losses incurred in war and revolution by placing people in a new, revised understanding of history.

Exceptions included Aleksandr Dovzhenko's classic *Zemlia* (*The Land*, 1930), in which the slow, graceful undulations of the landscape conveyed a harmonious relationship with nature, rather than its modern, industrial manipulation or insistence upon dialectical progression. Successful propaganda needed to be striking, nonetheless, and the 1930s usually had an eye on Hollywood's most profitable genres, such as the musical, where a different kind of harmony was at work. Ivan Pyrev's rural tales equated happy communities with Communism: *Bogataia nevesta* (*The Wealthy Bride*, 1937) and *Traktoristy* (*The Tractor Drivers*, 1939) both offered musical romances between farm workers. As late as 1949–50, Pyrev was still making these politicized pastorals: in *Kubanskie kazaki* (*The Kuban Cossacks*) two farms are united through the flirtation of their directors.

His contemporary Grigorii Aleksandrov's most celebrated musicals, *Veselye rebiata* (*The Happy-Go-Lucky Guys*, 1934), *Tsirk* (*The Circus*, 1936) and *Volga-Volga* (1938), combine music, romance, and ideology. The first, with a cowherd protagonist (played by Leonid Utesov), strives to entertain audiences while manipulating them. *The Circus* showcases an American performer who finds happiness in the USSR, as opposed to persecution in the racist US as the mother of a black child. Her scheming manager is German – a symbol for cinema's worries about impending hostilities in the late 1930s. *Volga-Volga* highlights the spirit of competition so central to Soviet success as we follow two village teams pursuing a prestigious music prize.

Patriotism and peace, crucial during this period, marked Vladimir Petrov's *Petr Pervyi* (*Peter the Great*, 1937–38), which begins with chaotically edited footage of a battle at Narva, with figures flying in and out of illimitable, elemental snow or darkness. Peter, however, brings order, and in his concluding speech emphasizes how the collective labours of both rulers and the people will enable a better future for the fatherland and later generations.

In modern adventure films of the late 1930s, a calm finale after chaos or commotion was also a prerequisite. Sergei Gerasimov's *Semero smelykh* (*The Valiant Seven*, 1936) showed brave, singing Pioneers as they headed off across the Arctic wilderness to help a sickly Eskimo. Despite months of turmoil, they perform acts of selflessness, for the promise of a warm southern holiday and their awareness of their social duty assure and inspire them in difficult times. The fact that Stalin himself embodied this assuredness is clear in Aleksandrov's *Svetlyi put* (*Radiant Path*, 1940). The title's confident, ideological linearity dictates the heroine's story: a rural girl discovers both community among people (not nature) and greater fulfilment as she moves closer to a meeting with Stalin.

The balance between a sense of security and risk (sometimes in the form of military daring) was exemplified in Mikhail Kalatozov's *Vasilii Chkalov* (1941). A devil-may-care pilot, Chkalov symbolizes the triumph of Soviet engineering, the staggering breadth of its triumphs, and, most importantly, an everlasting respect for one's Georgian superior – here, a Communist representative obviously modelled on Stalin.

During the war, film production was evacuated to safer Central Asia, and newsreels became the order of the day, though the war inspired contemporary classics both bellicose (Leo Arnshtam's *Zoia*, 1944) and beautiful: *Dva boitsa* (*Two Warriors*), in which flirting amid bombed-out buildings demonstrated that normal human relations were both possible during destruction and necessary for national victory. In *Zoia*, a teenage girl's brutal murder was intended to inspire outrage that would endure. Even before the hostilities ended, many films, such as Purev's *V shest chasov vechera posle voiny* (*At 6 PM After the War*), were already

falsifying battles, trying again to conflate actuality with a polished national history.

Victory brought back a grim reminder of art's duties, most notably in Zhdanov's attacks on cinema, the most significant victim of which was Eisenstein's *Ivan the Terrible* (Part Two), shelved for years as a result. Films stolen from the Germans helped to bridge several years of low Soviet output as the Cold War began. In Aleksandrov's *Vstrecha na Elbe* (*Meeting on the Elbe*, 1949), the new political tensions were manifest. The old oppositions created by German adversaries were now transmuted into a bellicose patriotism in the face of American imperialism. The film's final words summed up its agenda: 'Russian-American Friendship is the most important question that stands before mankind today'. Correspondingly clumsy rhetoric of the late 1940s, as in Mikhail Chiaureli's *Padenie Berlina* (*The Fall of Berlin*, 1949), hinted at both the creative limits and impending demise of cultic cinema. Indeed, cinema's 'varnishing' of Stalin's self-glorification and the tedium of 'conflictless' plots would disappear within a few years.

See also: Communist ideology; film, comedy; Gerasimov, Sergei; Kalatozov, Mikhail; Socialist Realism; Stalin, Iosif

Further reading

Gillespie, D. (2003) *Russian Cinema*, Harlow: Longman.

Kenez, P. (1992) *Cinema and Soviet Society, 1917–53*, Cambridge: Cambridge University Press.

Leyda, J. (1973) *Kino: A History of Russian and Soviet Film*, London: George Allen and Unwin.

Taylor, R. and Spring, D. (eds) *Stalinism and Soviet Cinema*, London: Routledge.

DAVID MACFADYEN

film, Soviet – Thaw period

For cinema, the post-Stalinist Thaw (roughly 1953–67) offered greater opportunities and latitude both thematically and stylistically than had been available under Stalin. After years of homogenized historical spectacles and blatant Cold War propaganda, when the few movies purporting to portray contemporary Soviet life replaced its reality with a fictitious, sugar-coated simulacrum, movies exemplified – and helped to encourage – the psychological, social, and cultural shifts associated with the Thaw.

The industry itself flourished. The regime subsidized studio expansion, better equipment, renovated cinemas, and a dramatic increase in the number of full-length features. The cultural xenophobia that had locked Soviets away from their European counterparts gave way, not just for film professionals, who were able to see foreign films relatively easily, but even for the public: Moscow hosted its first international film festival in 1959. Dozens of young men and women who had trained with highly skilled if often morally compromised film-makers entered the profession and made movies that enriched, challenged, and sometimes subverted the official dogmas.

Certain bedrock notions endured, among them faith in cinema's didactic influence and discomfort with pure entertainment. But film-makers and film audiences alike hungered for more realistic, less embellished portraits of Soviet life, for more complex characters, for plausible conflicts that did not move inexorably toward pat resolutions. Thus early Thaw-era movies replaced the larger-than-life supermen of late Stalinist films, who never doubted or deviated from their course of action, with ordinary men and women, fallible, ambivalent and uncertain. Grigorii Chukhrai's *Sorok pervyi* (1941, made 1956) and Alov and Naumov's *Pavel Korchagin* (1956) spurned the tenacious stereotype of protagonists who gave absolute priority to their public roles as Soviet citizens. Although the heroine of the first performs her revolutionary duty, and the hero of the second sacrifices his life to the revolutionary cause, neither does so without a terrible awareness of the costs involved. In those movies, as in the series of war melodramas that followed, the private emotions of individuals, relegated for so long to marginal or secondary status, regained legitimacy, and the genuine landscapes and artifacts of everyday life became part of cinema's *mise-en-scène*.

Letiat zhuravli (*The Cranes Are Flying*, 1957), one of the most popular and aesthetically satisfying early Thaw films, illustrates the changes occurring in the industry. The action takes place during World War II, a national trauma that until 1956 had been depicted with emphasis on the frontlines and the military leadership. By contrast, this film concentrates on the personal drama of Veronika, a young woman whom the war deprives of her parents, her home, and her beloved Boris; instead she marries Boris's weak, exploitative cousin, and spends years harshly condemning herself for that decision. Tatiana Samoilova's asymmetric beauty and Aleksei Batalov's quirky intellectual features brought a different look to the screen, as did the film's cinematographer, Sergei Urusevskii, who used hand-held cameras, cranes and dollies, short-focus optics and chiaroscuro with a lyrical freedom reminiscent of the 1920s. And director Mikhail Kalatozov violated one of Soviet cinema's ten commandments: he refused to condemn Veronika for her choices, compelling viewers to reach their own judgements.

By the end of the 1950s an official cultural policy that oscillated unpredictably between relaxed censorship and increased repressions damaged the idealism of the early Thaw. Many films reflected that disillusionment, questioning the very concept of heroism by spotlighting characters who lack hope, barely communicate with one another, and feel alienated from their own families and from society: Alov and Naumov's *Mir vkhodiashchemu* (*Peace to Him Who Enters*, 1961), Shepitko's *Krylia* (*Wings*, 1966), Khutsiev's *Iulskii dozhd* (*July Rain*). Seeking a cinematic form that retained veracity yet could plausibly justify a happy ending, film-makers introduced innocent protagonists: children, whose age protects them from the corruption of adults and whose lack of subterfuge authenticates their vision of the world, and teenagers, honest about their fears and tentative about their hopes.

The men and women graduating from the All-Union State Institute of Cinematography (VGIK) in the early 1960s came of age during the Thaw, and their first films reflect its relative freedom. Georgii Daneliia and Igor Talankin's *Serezha*, Mikhail Kalik's *Chelovek idet za solntsem* (*Man Follows the Sun*), Andrei Tarkovskii's *Ivanovo detstvo* (*My Name Is Ivan*), Elem Klimov's *Dobro pozhalovat, ili postoronnim vkhod vospreshchen* (*Welcome, or No Trespassing*) all took risks in portraying

Soviet life through children's eyes; yet these films received national (if sometimes limited) distribution. By 1965, Brezhnevite repression had begun to edge out the real, though inconsistent, tolerance of the Khrushchev years. The censors banned several completed films and scuttled a range of projects and scripts because of their subjects – the cult of personality, the Holocaust – or because of their treatment of acceptable subjects: of five short films planned to commemorate the 50th anniversary of the Bolshevik Revolution, for instance, all based on vetted texts, only three were produced, and two of the three were banned for years because of their ambiguous depiction of revolutionary values.

The Thaw did not reject all aspects of Stalinist society. Rather, it signified a cleansing of the excrescences Stalinism grafted onto a legacy of utopianism. The ideal of the collective continued to hold sway for years, as did revolutionary idealism, stripped of revolutionary clichés and with the addition of psychological insight. The cult of labour replaced the cult of personality; the pluck of ordinary men and women superseded the hypertrophied valour of the leader. And when it ended, it did so gradually: the process of internalizing constraints imposed from outside took time. Well into the 1970s the central Russian studios and the thriving studios in the republics continued to produce films that suggested a distrust, if not outright rejection, of core Soviet myths, as well as numerous science fiction and adventure films, thrillers, comedies, and melodramas that reflected the 'feminization' of Soviet life. But standardization of style and circumspect choice of theme became more prevalent, while personal and even idiosyncratic film-making dwindled. By the late 1960s Soviet cinema, like the society it mirrored, preferred equilibrium to instability, and security to the risks and rewards of creativity. The Thaw, and its cinema, were over.

See also: All-Russian (All-Union) State Institute of Cinematography (VGIK); Alov and Naumov; Batalov, Aleksei; Chukhrai, Grigorii; Daneliia, Georgii; Kalatozov, Mikhail; Samoilova, Tatiana; Tarkovskii, Andrei; Thaw; Urusevskii, Sergei; World War II (Great Patriotic War)

Further reading

Prokhorov, A. V. (2002) *Inherited Discourse: Stalinist Tropes in Thaw Culture*, PhD dissertation, University of Pittsburgh.

Woll, J. (2000) *Reel Images: Soviet Cinema and the Thaw*, London and New York: I. B. Tauris.

JOSEPHINE WOLL

film studios

The Soviet film industry had relied on the state to finance and distribute films. Film studios, such as Mosfilm and Lenfilm, would act as both producer and distributor: they would employ scriptwriters, directors, actors, and technical personnel, provide all the facilities for making the film, and take charge of distribution.

Mosfilm was organized in Moscow in 1924 as the 'Factory of Goskino'. In 1927, construction of new facilities began on Lenin (Sparrow) Hills in the southwest of the city. The studio was named 'Mosfilm' in 1936. Mosfilm occupies 35 hectares and contains thirteen pavilions. In the Soviet period, it accommodated seven production units (called creative units [*tvorcheskie obedineniia*]), one of them experimental. After the collapse of the Soviet Union, Mosfilm was partly privatized, and producer Vladimir Dostal became its general director (1987–98). He was succeeded by film-maker Karen Shakhnazarov.

Lenfilm is the oldest studio in the country, organized in 1917; it changed its name several times until it became Lenfilm in 1934. From 1986 to 1996, Lenfilm was headed by Aleksandr Golutva, who moved on to the Ministry of Culture. In 1996, Lenfilm became a private corporation, and the studio has since been fully modernized; it is run by film-maker and producer Viktor Sergeev.

Moscow's Gorkii Studio is the third largest studio in Russia. Founded in 1924 as *Mezhrabpom*, since 1963 it has specialized in films for children and youth, producing among others the popular children's programme *Eralash*. In the 1990s the Gorkii Studio was under changing management: Sergei Livnev (1995–98) produced young directors, while Vladimir Grammatikov (1998–2002) returned to the production of children's films. Currently the studio is managed by Stanislav Ershov.

The studios of the former Soviet republics (Dovzhenko Studio, Kiev; Odessa; Tbilisi; Almaty; Tashkent) have reverted to the respective independent republics. Other regional studios continue to work at a very low production level, such as the Sverdlovsk studio in Ekaterinburg.

While the studios were partly or fully privatized after the collapse of the Soviet Union and of national film production, many new production and distribution companies have appeared. The network of cinemas was refurbished and expanded in the latter part of the 1990s and is partly owned by distribution companies (such as Karo). Sergei Selianov's St. Petersburg-based company, STV, produces a mix of art-house and commercial cinema. Sergei Chliants's Moscow-based company Pygmalion promotes young directors' work. CineMax was founded by Roman Borisevich in 2000 and specializes in debut films (e.g. *Koktebel*, 2003). The studio Slovo, headed by Elena Iatsuro and Sergei Melkumov, specializes in art-house films. Vladimir Dostal's Dom Film produces large commercial projects and television serials. Sergei Gribkov's Top Line produces young film-makers (e.g. Roman Baltser). Nikita Mikhalkov's TriTe (managed by Leonid Vereshchagin) prioritizes the production of Mikhalkov's projects. Television channels actively produce television serials and feature films: ORT's film production arm is headed by Konstantin Ernst and Aleksandr Maksimov (*Nochnoi dozor* [*Night Watch*, 2004]); RTR's film production is run by Valerii Todorovskii, while Igor Tolstunov is the head of production at NTV/STS. REN TV specializes in television serials, but also produces art-house films (including *Vozvrashchenie* [*The Return*, 2003]).

See also: Ekaterinburg; *Eralash*; Ernst, Konstantin; film, Georgian; Georgia; Kazakhstan; Kiev; Livnev, Sergei; Mikhalkov, Nikita; NTV; Odessa; privatization; Selianov, Sergei; Shakhnazarov, Karen; television channels; Todorovskii, Valerii; Ukraine

BIRGIT BEUMERS

film, television

The television film emerged as a distinct genre in the 1970s out of Soviet production practices and critics' discussions about the nature of films made for television broadcasting. In the late 1950s, critics thought that the television film would be short (under one hour) and low-budget. Subsequently, under the influence of East German and Polish productions, the low-budget mini-series became the dominant model of cinema made for television. In the 1970s the television film became a separate type of television programme. Eldar Riazanov's *Ironiia sudby ili s legkim parom* (*Irony of Fate*, 1975) became the first successful television film. Originally conceived by Riazanov as a film for theatrical release, *Irony of Fate* was not approved for production because only films with a serious ideological theme at its centre could get funding for a two-episode production. Riazanov received financing from television, and the film established important conventions of the television film genre: a chamber atmosphere, highly conventional, inexpensive *mise-en-scène*, a plot evoking fairy-tale-like wish fulfilment, and episodic structure, with vaudevillian interpolations of song performances. The television film, operating on a relatively low budget, was screened on holidays, usually before and after the official evening news programme *Vremia* (Time).

The television film established a liberal niche in the ideologically orthodox atmosphere of late Soviet cinema and television. While the longer mini-series and longer films for theatrical release were ideologically conservative, the two-episode-long television film was not long enough for a serious television production and did not have the status of a multi-episodic film for theatrical release. The ideological parameters of the television film were not well defined and allowed double-voiced messages and taboo topics to find their home in the Aesopian discourse of these films. Through the narrative stance of the fairy tale for adults, these films delivered an ironic parable for Soviet viewers, experienced in reading between the lines and seeing through disguising images. Mark Zakharov, who usually collaborated with Grigorii Gorin, made the most successful television films: *Obyknovennoe chudo* (*Ordinary Wonder*, 1978), *Tot samyi Miunkhgauzen* (*That Very Same*

Munchhausen, 1979), *Dom, kotoryi postroil Svift* (*The House that Swift Built*, 1983), *Formula liubvi* (*The Love Formula*, 1984). In addition to Zakharov and Riazanov (*O bednom gusare zamolvite slovo* [*Say a Word for the Poor Cavalryman*, 1980]), Konstantin Bromberg also worked productively in the genre (*Charodei* [*Magicians*, 1982]). With the gradual disappearance of ideological censorship during perestroika, the television film, with its Aesopian language, became superfluous in the new commercial media culture. Zakharov's *Ubit drakona* (*To Kill the Dragon*, 1988) was the last gasp of this fine mode of visual irony.

See also: film, Soviet – Stagnation period; perestroika and glasnost; Riazanov, Eldar; television, Soviet; Zakharov, Mark

ELENA PROKHOROVA AND ALEXANDER PROKHOROV

film, World War II

From 1941 until 1945, newsreels and documentaries dominated Soviet screens, although from their Central Asian evacuation location the studios managed to produce about fifty feature films about the war. Most focus on the home front and on partisan warfare, showcasing female protagonists who respond to graphically-detailed Nazi brutality with extraordinary valour and self-sacrifice (*Zhila, byla devochka* [*Once There Lived a Little Girl*], 1944; *Ona zashchishchaet rodinu* [*She Defends the Motherland*, 1943]; *Raduga* [*The Rainbow*], 1944).

From the Nazi surrender until Stalin's death in 1953, 'artistic documentaries' like *Kliatva* (*The Vow*, 1946) and *Padenie Berlina* (*The Fall of Berlin*, 1950) overlooked Soviet defeats in favour of victories and ignored rank-and-file soldiers in order to spotlight brilliant Kremlin and military HQ leadership.

Nikita Khrushchev's de-Stalinization campaign liberated artists to portray relatively truthfully the actual experiences of Soviet men and women during and after the war. The characters in *Letiat zhuravli* (*The Cranes Are Flying*), *Dom, v kotorom ia zhivu* (*The House I Live In*, both 1957), *Ivanovo detstvo* (*Ivan's Childhood*, 1962), *Mir vkhodiashchemu* (*Peace to Him Who Enters*, 1961), *Krylia* (*Wings*, 1966) and many other films do not

always behave with stoic dignity and they manifest profound emotional and psychological scars.

During the culturally repressive Brezhnev years, personally authentic depictions of the war yielded to screen representations which were more rhetorical and ritualistic, if sometimes quite effective visually. Several films used the war theme as a 'safe' prism to examine timeless (hence implicitly timely) issues of honour, dignity, cruelty, among them Elem Klimov's *Idi i smotri* (*Come and See*, 1985), exceptionally disturbing both because of the relentless horrors naturalistically depicted on screen and because of the blighted innocence of the young protagonists. Aleksei German's *Proverka na dorogakh* (*Roadcheck*, 1971, released 1986) portrayed a Soviet POW suspected of collaboration with the Nazis, a 'traitor' who eventually turns hero – an unconventional characterization that put the film on the shelf until glasnost.

After the dissolution of the USSR in 1991 film-makers generally avoided World War II as both setting and theme, until two contrasting films appeared: Nikolai Lebedev's 'neo-patriotic' *Zvezda* (*The Star*, 2002), about a heroic if doomed sniper unit sent behind Nazi lines, and Aleksandr Rogozhkin's sweetly pacifist *Kukushka* (*The Cuckoo*, 2002), where the war brings together a Finnish soldier, a Russian soldier and a Lapp woman in an unlikely triangle.

See also: Brezhnev, Leonid; film, Soviet – Thaw period; German, Aleksei; Klimov, Elem; Krushchev, Nikita; Rogozhkin, Aleksandr; Stagnation; Thaw; World War II (Great Patriotic War)

JOSEPHINE WOLL

Finno-Ugric

Peoples of the Uralic language family who speak Finno-Ugric languages. Linguistically they divide into five branches: (1) Balto-Finnish (Finn, Izhor, Karelian, Veps, Vod, Estonian); (2) Saami; (3) Volga-Finnish (Mordva, Mari); (4) Perm (Udmurt, Komi, Komi-Permiak); and (5) Ugric (Hungarian, Khanty, Mansi). Larger subgroups have political autonomy. Karelians (population, according to the 2002 census: 93,344) live in the republic of Karelia (Russia, capital: Petrozavodsk) and in Tver oblast; Estonians live in Estonia (population 925,000) and the neighbouring Leningrad and Pskov oblasts of Russia (population 28,113); Mordovians (population 843,350) in the republic of Mordva and neighbouring Volga regions of Russia; Mari (population 604,298) in the republic of Mari-El (capital: Ioshkar-Ola); Udmurts (population 636,906) in the republic of Udmurtia (capital: Izhevsk), including an ethnic subgroup in northern Udmurtia, the Besermian (population: 3,122); Komi (population 293,406) in the republic of Komi (capital: Syktyvkar), Komi-Permiaks (population: 125,235) in the Komi-Permiak autonomous okrug (Perm oblast, capital: Kudymkar); Khanty (population: 28,678) and Mansi (population: 11,432) in the Khanty-Mansiisk autonomous okrug (capital: Khanty-Mansiisk).

Finno-Ugric peoples (excluding Hungarians) live predominantly in the north of European Russia. Those without political autonomy in Russia include Finns (population 34,050) and Izhors (population 327) in Leningrad oblast and Karelia; Veps (population 8,240) in the Leningrad and Vologda oblasts and southern Karelia; and Saami (population 1,991) in Murmansk oblast.

Except for Finns, Estonians, and Hungarians, Finno-Ugric peoples use the Cyrillic alphabet. Estonians and Finns are Protestants; others converted to Orthodoxy after Russian colonization, while maintaining some pagan rituals. In southeastern Estonia and western Pskov oblast live the Setu – Estonians who adopted Russian Orthodoxy.

See also: administrative structure, Soviet Union; Karelia; Mari; Mordva; Saami

SERGEI TARKHOV

Firsova, Elena Olegovna

b. 21 March 1950, Leningrad

Composer

Trained at the Moscow Conservatory under Aleksandr Pirumov and Iurii Kholopov, Firsova

writes in a style much indebted to the composers of the Second Viennese School, Olivier Messiaen, and Pierre Boulez, to whose works her mentor, Edison Denisov, introduced her. She composes using fragmentary material as building blocks, and her larger orchestral works and concertos rely on textures frequently associated with chamber music. Her œuvre includes six chamber concertos, two operas, and numerous vocal works, many of which are set to the poetry of Osip Mandelshtam (1891–1938). Firsova teaches at the Royal Northern College of Music in Manchester, United Kingdom.

See also: Denisov, Edison; Moscow Conservatory

DAVID GOMPPER

fish dishes

Fish figures prominently in Russian cuisine, since fish traditionally have been abundant in rivers and lakes, permitted on some days of the many religious fasts, and can be prepared in a variety of ways and preserved through salting, drying, and smoking. In the Soviet period, the government expanded ocean fishing, introduced many new varieties to the table, and promoted seafood as a source of protein when the meat and poultry industries could not keep up with demand. Although fish entrees are rarely special holiday fare, they are virtually always included as part of the appetizer course. In post-Soviet Russia, crustaceans, such as lobster, have become popular and prestigious, and there is a boom in sushi bars.

Fish is a part of the appetizer course, *zakuski* (usually in smoked varieties); salads; soups; and in baked dumplings, *pirozhki*. As a main course, it is most commonly fried or baked, traditionally with sour cream, cheese, or mayonnaise. It is also boiled or braised (*pripushennaia ryba*). Firm-fleshed fish such as sturgeon is grilled on skewers as *shashlyk*. Fish dishes from Jewish cuisine, such as *forshmak* (minced fish cutlets), are also widespread.

Boiled shrimp (*krevetki*) are a traditional accompaniment to beer and are served in beer halls (*pivnye*), as are *vobla* and other dry-cured or jerked (*vialenye*) fish and crustaceans. Cured herring (*seld, seledka*) is a traditional appetizer and used in a number of salads. Crab sticks (*krabovye palochki*) and their imitations, made of fish, quickly entered post-Soviet cuisine and are used in a number of salads.

See also: appetizers; dining, Russian; dining, Soviet; drinks, alcoholic; holidays, Russian Orthodox; Lent; pirog/pirozhki; salads; soups; vobla

MICHELE BERDY

Fitil

Fitil (The Fuse) was a satirical *kinozhurnal* (cinemagazine) shown before theatrical feature films, like a newsreel, from 1962 until 1993. Its editor-in-chief was the poet Sergei Mikhalkov (father of film directors Nikita Mikhalkov and Andrei Konchalovskii). 'Issues' of *Fitil* typically included an animation, a documentary subject, and a live-action, narrative short. Though its satirical take on isolated aspects of contemporary Soviet society frequently tested the boundaries of the politically permissible, it was never censored by the authorities. In 2004, Nikita Mikhalkov announced his intention to resurrect *Fitil* as a television programme. It now runs on RTR, the Russia channel.

See also: *Eralash*; Mikhalkov, Nikita; television, post-Soviet

SETH GRAHAM

fitness (fizicheskaia kultura)

The term literally means the culture of being in good shape and refers to fitness education and training. Fitness education originated in Russia in the 1830s, when gymnastics training was included in the military school curriculum. Beginning in 1871, gymnastics was taught in secondary schools (gymnasiums). After 1917, fitness training was proclaimed a priority in order to ensure universal military preparedness. In the early Soviet period, *fizicheskaia kultura* replaced sports, dismissed as 'bourgeois enter-

tainment'. The widely used abbreviation *fizkultura* referred not only to team sports and Spartan school discipline, but also to a way of life. The terms *sport* and *fizkultura* have different cultural implications: Russians generally respect sports, but usually deem *fizkultura* as dull and ineffective. This attitude stems from the old Soviet tradition of obligatory morning exercises (*zariadka*), led by radio and television exercise programmes. Vladimir Vysotskii ridiculed this practice in his songs. In post-Soviet Russia *fizkultura* is primarily associated with school classes, while in everyday life the English term 'fitness' now dominates, reflecting the fashion for Western-style training and referring to both aerobics and workouts in gyms.

See also: fitness test (GTO)

ALEXANDER LEDENEV

fitness test (GTO)

The abbreviation GTO (*gotov k trudu i oborone*) literally means 'ready for labour and defence' and denotes a series of fitness tests. Established in the USSR in 1931, the nationwide GTO programme aimed to promote sports and physical fitness. It consisted of regular competitions in track and field, gymnastics, swimming, shooting, and cycling. Those who successfully passed the corresponding tests received gold and silver badges. The GTO badge became an emblem of the model young Soviet citizen, as evident in the GTO badge-wearing hero of a Samuil Marshak poem memorized in Soviet primary schools. In the 1950s, the system was updated: requirements were reconsidered and programmes for different age categories established. From the 1950s to the 1970s, GTO programmes were an obligatory part of physical training in primary schools. Upon revision for the last time in 1972, the GTO tests became set of recommendations for five age groups, from ages 10 to 60.

See also: educational system, Soviet; fitness; sports education; sports, Soviet

ALEXANDER LEDENEV

five-year plan (piatiletka)

The five-year plan (*piatiletka*) was the basic planning programme for the economic development of the entire USSR beginning in April 1929, though the Communist Party officially back-dated the decision one year, to 1928. Lenin developed the prototype in 1920, as a plan for the electrification of the country, and in 1921 he institutionalized it as the government planning agency known as GOSPLAN. Under Stalin, the system was applied to the whole country, ensuring that every significant economic decision was governed by the politics of state socialism. Economists sometimes refer to it as a 'command economy'. In theory, a Party Congress approved five-year goals that GOSPLAN, in consultation with the USSR Council of Commissars (subsequently Ministers), translated into comprehensive five-year production quotas for every branch of the economy. The planning process continued downward to the shop committee level, where each worker received yearly production norms for each year of the plan.

Under Stalin, regimentation and coercion ruled to the extent that *vypolnenie* (fulfilment) of the production norms did not guarantee a worker's or a plant manager's security: *perevypolnenie* (over-fulfilment) was the real norm. Such expectations provided incentives for corruption and falsification, while practical economic considerations compelled the regime to turn a blind eye to the existence of a *chernyi rynok* (black market). Although economic historians no longer believe the official statistics that presented a story of nearly unqualified success during the decade prior to World War II, there is no doubt that by 1938, in the sense that most of the country's wealth was generated by industrial output, the USSR was an industrialized economy.

The salient features distinguishing the five-year plans of the 1930s proved to be permanent. The system was ideal for fighting and winning World War II, but disastrous for agriculture and consumers. It also resisted innovation, which disrupted planning assumptions; beginning in 1946, GOSPLAN rebuilt devastated regions of the USSR with obsolete pre-war designs. After Stalin's death in March 1953, Nikita Khrushchev won a four-year power struggle, with a Party mandate to serve consumer needs, address the problems of agriculture, expand planning to seven years, and decentralize planning. Some ideas, such as the widespread distribution of *dachas* (summer cottages), proved successful, but most were failures, and even threatened the Party elite, who removed Khrushchev from power in 1964.

Economic problems continued under Leonid Brezhnev, and a new defect of five-year planning emerged: the plan's inability to fix prices and thus to know how much anything cost. GOSPLAN resorted to borrowing Western prices and subjecting them to a 'socialist factor'. Unfortunately, for military costs, GOSPLAN borrowed CIA estimates, thus infecting the American agency with the same disease. Brezhnev died in 1982, having achieved negative economic growth; after two even more ineffective successors, Mikhail Gorbachev took over, with a mandate to save the economy. The logic of events unfolded, and five-year planning, which had done more than anything else to ruin the USSR, vanished along with it.

See also: black market; Brezhnev, Leonid; Communist Party; dacha; economic system, Soviet; Gorbachev, Mikhail; GOSPLAN; Krushchev, Nikita; Lenin, Vladimir Ilich; perestroika and glasnost; Stagnation

EDWARD ALAN COLE

fiziki-liriki (scientist-poets)

Fiziki-liriki refers to a 1959 poem by Boris Slutskii that crystallized in memorable shorthand the intellectual divide between what he called 'physicists' and 'lyricists'. In the West, this divide had been articulated in C.P. Snow's influential Rede lecture 'The Two Cultures and the Scientific Revolution' (1959), in which he suggested that the specialized discourse and worldview of the hard sciences is no longer understandable to humanists. In Russia, the hard sciences in general, but physics in particular, enjoyed a spectacular ascendancy in the years following the launch of the first sputnik (1957). Young people earnestly debated the relationship between the brave new world of science and the so-called lyrical worldview of the arts and humanities. In retrospect, the debate between 'physicists' and 'lyricists' evidenced not a divide, but the existence of a consensual, collective romanticism about the future world, one in which the spectacular successes of contemporary sciences and the emotional beauty embodied in the humanities would finally be integrated. This worldview infused the popular genres of Soviet science fiction, bard songs, and films with physicist protagonists. The ideal student and future professional of this era was an intrepid scientist, a passionate explorer of new frontiers of knowledge, but also an amateur poet, more often than not with a guitar slung over his shoulder and a classic of world literature in his backpack. Post-Soviet realities imply that, as in the West, the original premise of the debate – that scientists and humanists might speak the same language – will dissolve in the wake of relentless technical advancements and specialization in the hard sciences and the prestige of the social sciences over traditional humanities. However, Slutskii's poem and the cultural moment it defined still serve as a symbolic signpost in the landscape of post-Soviet nostalgia.

See also: bards; science and technology; science fiction; Slutskii, Boris; Strugatskii, Arkadii and Boris

YVONNE HOWELL

Fokin, Valerii Vladimirovich

b. 28 February 1946, Moscow

Theatre director

As staff director at Moscow's Sovremennik Theatre (1971–85), chief director at the Ermolova Theatre (1985–91), founder of the Meierkhold Centre in Moscow in 1991, and artistic director of the Aleksandrinskii Theatre in St. Petersburg since 2002, Fokin has alternated between traditional and experimental styles. Influenced by Jerzy Grotowski, he first worked in Poland in 1976 and has often worked in Europe and Asia since. At the Meierkhold Centre he collaborated with composer Aleksandr

Bakshi, staging the innovative works *Numer v gostinnitse goroda* NN (*A Hotel Room in the Town of NN*, 1994), based on Gogol's *Mertvye dushi* (*Dead Souls*), and Gogol's *Shinel* (*The Overcoat*, 2004).

See also: music in theatre; Sovremennik Theatre

JOHN FREEDMAN

folk art

The long-established traditions of Russian folk art – originally objects peasants made both for use at home and work and for decoration – underwent a renaissance after the 1861 emancipation of the serfs. The tsarist government and wealthy individuals set up various *kustar* (handicraft) industries to provide employment to peasants in order to stabilize the economic trauma resulting in part from emancipation. The development of an industrial 'Russian folk style' was used for luxury goods that enjoyed great popularity on the market.

Russian folk art first came to the serious attention of artists and art critics in the 1870s. In 1873, Vladimir Stasov, prominent art critic and chief champion of the artists' movement called the Itinerants, published *Russian Folk Ornament*, an extensive illustrated study of folk art. It was not until the late 1880s, however, that folk motifs were valued both for their artistic merit, and because they served as signifiers of Russian national identity.

The early twentieth-century avant-garde turned to folk art as a marker of national identity and as inspiration for the exploration of art's formal properties. Natalia Goncharova and Mikhail Larionov are famous for integrating the flat images of *lubok* (popular cartoon-like prints) and icons, as well as the highly decorative motifs of folk art, into Neoprimitivism. Their adoption of folk forms was a response in part to the search for authenticity, but also to the European avant-garde's preoccupation with the representation of space in painting. Kandinskii also turned to the brilliant colours and patterns of Russian folk art in the late 1890s.

After the Revolution, folk art was adopted as a common denominator useful for emphasizing class solidarity. The form of *lubok* was repeated in propaganda posters; schools offering specialized training in folk arts were established; and workshops for producing toys, carpets, jewellery, and other traditional crafts were set up to provide employment. Museums of folk art were established.

Folk art suffered from over-production and lack of inspiration from the 1940s through the 1960s. In the 1970s, it again attracted the attention of artists, this time of Nonconformists. The use of folk art forms was seen as a mark of authenticity and integrity. Through reference to folk art, nonconformist artists subtly declared both allegiance to the avant-garde and a belief in art devoid of the stamp of ideology. Leonid Purygin's art makes many clear references to Russian folk art, particularly the decorative patterning and 'primitive' figuration of *lubok*. These 'primitive features' were also exploited in the work of Elena Figurina, Natalia Nesterova, and Arkadii Petrov.

Unfortunately, in the late 1990s and the early twenty-first century, notwithstanding efforts at preservation, the economic changes sweeping the country have devastated Russian folk art centres. Despite these difficulties, certain forms of folk art not only survived, but flourished under the new market economy and are successfully sold, particularly in places frequently visited by foreign tourists. The best-known genre, the wooden nesting doll called *matreshka*, continues to be mass-produced not only in its traditional form, painted with the face and clothing of abstract Russian peasant beauties, but in popular variations featuring the faces of famous athletes and well-known historical and political figures. Whereas early *matreshki* depicted specifically Russian writers, historical personages, and literary characters, current models include famous foreign personalities. Items of folk art sold all across Russia in souvenir kiosks, in the gift departments of large stores, at outdoor souvenir markets, and simply on tables in the street include hand-painted wooden Easter eggs; handmade blue and white Russian china named after its place of origin, Gzhel; birch-bark carved boxes, barrettes, and frames; enamelled porcelain jewellery called Rostov *finift*, colourful wool Pavlovo-Posad shawls; delicate Vologda lace; hand-painted Zhostovo trays decorated with bouquets of bright flowers against a black background; and various household wooden items decorated in the style of Khokhloma (a combination of red, gold, and black). Lacquered boxes painted with miniature folk scenes in various styles, made in villages including Fedoskino, Mstera, Kholui, and the most famous centre, Palekh, are popular gifts for both Russians and foreigners. Another unique folk art form is the Bogorodskoe carved wooden toy, which depicts humorous scenes from peasant life and has a wooden ball on a string that makes the toy move.

See also: art, nonconformist; Figurina, Elena; Nesterova, Natalia; Petrov, Arkadii

Further reading

Hilton, A. (1995) *Russian Folk Art*, Bloomington, IN: Indiana University.
Salmond, W. (1996) *Arts and Crafts in Late Imperial Russia: Reviving the Kustar Art Industries, 1870–1917*, Cambridge: Cambridge University Press.

KRISTEN M. HARKNESS

folk costume

The basic materials for Russian traditional dress were wool, flax, and hemp. Flax dominated in the northern and central provinces, and hemp in the southern. Winter clothing, shoes, belts, and hats were made from leather decorated with fur.

Men wore a shirt (*rubakha*) and trousers (*shtany*). The basic summer garments for unmarried men and women were long woven shirts (married men wore trousers). Men and women wore woven belts from multicoloured wool or cotton and *lapti* woven from linden-tree bark on their feet. Peasants wrapped their legs with pieces of fabric (*onuchi*) and tied *lapti* around their legs with woven ropes (*obory*). Cossacks and Siberian peasants wore leather shoes.

Standard wear for women comprised a shirt (*rubakha*) and a drop-waist (*poniova*) or sleeveless dress (*sarafan*). Typical female shirts had inserts (*rubakha s polikami*) at the shoulders, gathered at the neck with full sleeves. In the Russian north, a linen dress with a decorated hem (*podol*) might have been worn over the shirt. Around the hips women wore an apron-like garment named *poniova*, which consisted of three panels of plaid wool gathered on a rope with an opening in the front, and elaborately decorated with wool embroidery and ribbons. Skirts appeared in the traditional costume only in the second half of the nineteenth century, under the influence of city fashion.

Unmarried women wore their hair uncovered in a single braid tied with a colourful ribbon or a glass bead decoration at the end (*kosnik*). Married women covered their hair with a scarf, while men sported round or cylindrical hats made from felt. Winter hats were sewn from sheepskin.

Embroidery around the neck, along the neckline, on the upper part of the sleeves, around the wrists and on the hem always decorated male and female clothing, originally to provide magical protection for the labourer's body. The embroidery, mainly in red and black wool and flax, was more elaborate on women's clothing. Multicoloured embroidery appeared in the eighteenth century. Silver and golden threads decorated scarves and leather shoes, especially in the north.

See also: folk dance

YELENA MINYONOK AND
JEANMARIE ROUHIER-WILLOUGHBY

folk dance

Russian folk dances have always been accompanied by song. In the Russian south and southwest, musical instruments, typically fiddles and drums, also were played as accompaniment.

The circle dance (*khorovod*) was the most archaic type of dance form, performed during yearly cycle ritual periods. In western Russia, *khorovods* were performed from Christmas (7 January) to Epiphany (19 January); in the North, from Easter to Trinity (the seventh Sunday after Easter); and in the south from Trinity to St. Peter and Paul Day (12 July). Both men and women danced the *khorovod*, moving at a moderate tempo in a clockwise or counterclockwise direction. Sometimes the dancers held

hands; sometimes they moved separately. In the centre of the *khorovod* two or three dancers might interpret the content of the accompanying song, whose content varied. One common topic was farm labour, for example, about the process of growing, reaping, spinning, and weaving flax. *Khorovod* dance songs also might describe family relationships in a comic way, for example, of a husband catching his wife with another man. Romance also provided the content of *khorovod* dances, for example, a teenage girl in the middle of a dancing circle would choose between two suitors and end the song with a kiss. Winter circle dances were performed indoors; spring circle dances on hills outside villages; summer circle dances near rye fields and in the village centre. The most complicated figures performed by the largest number of participants (up to 400) were found in the Russian north.

Another popular dance, with a faster tempo, was the *pliaska*, typically at a folk wedding. It also was popular on the first day of sending the livestock to the field, at the beginning and end of the harvest, and at other socially important events. Like the *khorovod*, the *pliaska* was accompanied by singing or by musical instruments. Usually it was danced by one or two women (or a woman and a man, or two men) in front of the singers. Women danced these fast dances with arms raised, holding their bodies straight, and not moving their hips or shoulders. Men performed jumping and kicking movements as well as rhythmic clapping on their feet and knees.

From the end of the nineteenth century, dances accompanied by special short comic songs (*chastushki*) became widespread. These dances were performed to special tunes (*semenovna, podgornaia, tsyganochka, barynia*) played on an accordion or balalaika. In these dances women or men sang a solo (the last lines of a *chastushka* could be sung as a duet). *Chastushki* were interspersed with an instrumental interlude during which women (or men) danced.

Beginning in the twentieth century, partnered dances such as the *podyspan, krakoviak*, and the waltz spread throughout Russia.

See also: folk costume; folk music

YELENA MINYONOK
AND JEANMARIE ROUHIER-WILLOUGHBY

folk music

Russian instrumental folk music is closely tied to folk singing. The oldest examples of instrumental folk music are strictly functional: shepherd's calls, played on wind instruments (horns, pipes, etc.). Much of the oldest music is also connected with rituals, such as weddings. Instrumental compositions based on wedding songs were often called 'marches'. They not only accompanied wedding feasts but also the pre-wedding rituals, including the wedding 'train'. In many southern and western Russian traditions, such 'marches' involved laments by the bride and her female relatives. Wedding music could involve any number and combination of instruments, including violins, various kinds of horns (*dudka, rozhok, sopel, zhaleika*), plucked string instruments (*gusli*), cymbals, guitar, mandolin, balalaika, accordion, drums, and wooden spoons.

Similar ensembles of various instruments were associated with *skomorokhi* – wandering professional musicians and actors similar to the medieval troubadours of Western Europe. Earliest records of *skomorokhi* date from the eleventh to the seventeenth centuries. The 'professionalization' of instrumental folk music was recorded in later research expeditions as well: traditional folk music reserved a special place for virtuosi, performers of music 'for listening' or 'for oneself', non-functional music, such as variations on a well-known melody, performed by a soloist. The most widespread form of traditional music-making was dance music, which could be performed on a wide variety of instruments, both with and without vocalists. Later dance music became part of the urban folk tradition, such as the *Korobochka* (Box), *Iablochko* (Little Apple), and *Kadril* (Quadrille). Vocal music accompanied by the accordion (*akkordeon, baian*) or guitar was a late development in folk music, uniting peasant and urban traditions in what came to be called 'new lyricism' or 'romances'.

Russian professional music began to absorb folk music in the second half of the eighteenth century. The operas of Evstignei Fomin incorporated folk music as an exotic element, while the virtuoso folk solo tradition was echoed in Ivan Khandoshkin's violin compositions on folk themes. In the nineteenth-century classical repertoire, folk music became one of the most important sources of historical themes and part of the texture of classical music, both in the form of authentic quotations of folk music and as imitations of folk melodies, as in the music of Mikhail Glinka. Tchaikovsky continued Glinka's experiments, for example, the finale of his Second Symphony quotes a folk dance melody. Borodin and Rimskii-Korsakov's operas contain imitations of *skomorokhi* music. Stravinskii's *Petrushka* contains quotations of popular themes in urban folk music, and his *Rite of Spring* imitates traditional shepherd calls.

The first folk instrument orchestra was founded in 1888 by Vasilii Andreev. Andreev's Great Russian Orchestra (Velikorusskii orkestr), which toured in the 1900s and 1910s, gained enormous popularity in Russia and abroad. It formed a new style of 'souvenir' Russian folklore: the academic reworking or imitation of folk songs. The artificiality of this kind of ensemble can be seen in the grouping of solo instruments, such as balalaikas and accordions, in orchestral style – contrary to the folk tradition of ensembles of soloists. In the Soviet era, folk orchestras became a major part of official musical culture, since they combined elements of 'national' folk culture with the seriousness of a classical orchestra. Folk instrument departments were established in conservatories, music institutes, and music schools. An artificial professional subculture developed into a powerful virtuoso school that enjoys success and continues to develop in the post-Soviet era as well, no longer as part of the official culture, but for the tourist and entertainment industries. One of the more original developments is the St. Petersburg Terem Quartet, which creates brilliant humorous folk remakes of classical compositions.

See also: folk dance; folk song; romance

Further reading

Gippius, E. (ed.) (1987) *Narodnye muzykalnye instrumenty i instrumentalnaia muzyka. Sbornik statei*, 2 vols, Moscow.
——— (1987–88) *Narodnye muzykalnye instrumenty i instrumentalnaia muzyka*, 2 vols, Moscow.

KIRA NEMIROVSKAIA

folk mythology

Folk mythology continues to shape everyday Russian life and culture in an attenuated form. The coherent stories or systems still found by collectors in the early twentieth century survive mainly in printed editions; their remnants combine with idiosyncratic creations in Russian superstitions, such as the prohibition on shaking hands across a threshold or clinking glasses when toasting a dead person's memory. Many Russians feel the pathos of losing a system of beliefs associated with a traditional, perhaps idealized, way of life, and erased by industrialization and modernization. Even educated urban Russians know many details of folk mythology, which is widely recognizable in graphic art or stories by authors such as Nina Sadur and Tatiana Tolstaia, as well as in television advertisements, food packaging, or the kitsch of kindergarten (*sadik*) decorations.

Christian saints overlaid traditional Slavic deities (as Saint Paraskeva-Piatnitsa took over attributes of the goddess Mokosh) in *dvoeverie* (double-belief), a more or less harmonious integration of two belief systems. The Russian Orthodox Church calendar likewise subsumed traditional festivals such as midsummer *Kupala* or Yuletide masking. Fragmentary records of pre-Christian pagan belief attract Russian neo-pagans and enrich the cultural archeology of the Moscow-Tartu school. On the other hand, Russian villagers believed in domestic and field spirits until at least the nineteenth century. Spirits were named for the places they inhabited; the further from hearth and home, the more unpredictable and potentially malevolent. The spirits demanded respectful behaviour (sometimes recalling British folklore about brownies – if you thank them, they stop doing your housework and fly away). Some Russians still toss coins in corners and say the proper words to ingratiate themselves with the *domovoi* (house spirit) of a new apartment. *Domovoi* (and sometimes his wife, *domovikha*) could appear as a grey or black cat, though the shape varied by village and region, and might foretell a death in the household with certain sounds or unwonted appearances. *Dvorovoi* was the yard or stable spirit; the more distant included *bannik*, the tricky spirit of the *bania* (bathhouse), and *leshii* (or

his wife, *leshikha*), the forest spirit, who might lure cattle into the woods or disorient a solitary traveller. The dangerous water spirit, *vodianoi*, dragged down swimmers or horses at a ford, and the *rusalka* was, variously, a seductive mermaid or the wraith of a jilted girl who had drowned herself and took revenge by luring men astray and tickling them to death. *Domovoi* and *leshii* were often euphemistically called '*khoziain*' ('master' or 'owner/landlord') of their respective realms; in some parts of Russia, *domovoi* reputedly looked like the man of the house.

Folk mythology also includes human professions: millers, blacksmiths, midwives, and shepherds were rumoured to have connections with magic, and a sorcerer (*koldun*) or witch (*vedma*) might heal a terrible illness (often with traditional herbal remedies) but could also be dangerous, commanding a set of devils (*cherti*), unlike the benign healer (*znakhar*). Even someone without other magic powers might 'spoil/jinx' another with an envious or covetous glance, causing illness or upset that would require treatment by a specialist.

See also: folk tales; superstitions, Russian

Further reading

Ivanits, L. (1989) *Russian Folk Belief*, Armonk, NY: M. E. Sharpe.

SIBELAN FORRESTER

folk song

Russian folk song (*narodnaia pesnia*) falls into two categories: a traditionally learned anonymous song or one of known authorship, accepted by the Russian folk (*narod*). Ancient songs were created to while away winter nights, accompany major rites of passage (such as lamentations for marriage, departure, or death), or mark agricultural and religious events. Singing was entertaining or purgative, but also useful; loud, chest-voiced songs helped coordinate movement while peasants mowed, reaped, churned butter, or wove, while softer songs calmed animals or lulled babies.

Literate collectors have compiled folk songs since the anthology of the 1780s, attributed to Kirsha Danilov. Songs formed part of a complex traditional matrix: different ages, sexes, and ranks had their own repertoire, often for specific seasons or events. The eighteenth century brought increasing 'contamination' from Western Europe and importation of new instruments, such as the accordion and seven-stringed guitar. The railroad increased ethnic mixing and shifts in class and taste, especially after 1861. Poets such as Nikolai Nekrasov and Apollon Grigorev imitated the folk style or, like Aleksei Koltsov and Sergei Esenin, 'rose' from peasant origins to write songs accepted and adopted by the folk. Jewish and Gypsy orchestras offered popular entertainment, and the accordion and clarinet displaced native instruments. Ritual songs for weddings and funeral lamentations remained more stable, sung publicly in many Russian villages until the end of the 1920s and collectivization.

In the USSR, traditional folklore was transformed by the appearance of 'fakelore' – both command performances on Socialist Realist themes by genuine folk artists, and a homogenized version of Russian and other Soviet ethnicities' folk songs and dances in performance by amateur groups, schools, and professional choirs or folk ensembles. A huge population in prison and labour camps heard the *blatnye pesni* or thieves' songs, whose minor key and melodic energy recall Gypsy song. High mortality and shifting population in the camps kept most singers and composers anonymous, allowing formation of another genuine folk song tradition. Thieves' songs influence post-Soviet popular music, much as rap or gangsta music does in North America.

A post-Soviet industry of folklorists and ethnographers seeks out elderly villagers and collects songs along with other folklore, and some village singing groups travel to perform traditional songs at festivals. This practice may run against the preferences of the villagers themselves, who interpret 'narodnye' to mean 'popular' and prefer the movie ballads of their youth to 'real' wedding laments or *Kupala* ritual songs. Some educated amateurs work to create authentic reproduction performances of folk songs for museums or schools. Well-known folk performers include singer Zhanna Bichevskaia, the ensemble Sirin, and the instrumental *Terem* ('women's quarters') quartet.

See also: Gypsy music

Further reading

Miller, F. (1990) *Folklore for Stalin: Russian Folklore and Pseudofolklore of the Stalin Era*, Armonk, NY: M. E. Sharpe.

Olson, L. (2004) *Performing Russia: Folk Revival and Russian Identity*, New York and London: Routledge.

Reeder, R. (trans., ed.) (1993) *Russian Folk Lyrics*, Bloomington, IN: Indiana University Press.

SIBELAN FORRESTER

folk tales

Thematically and structurally Russian folk tales (*narodnye skazki*) parallel their Western counterparts, while preserving some unique features. Taxonomists largely concur that major categories of folk tales comprise 'magic' tales or 'wonder tales' (*volshebnye skazki*), tales of everyday life, legends, and animal tales.

By far the best known are Russian wonder tales, which typically describe the transformation of the hero or heroine, most commonly from poor younger brother/sister to tsar/tsar's wife, after overcoming multiple obstacles or tests. The wondrous aspect in these tales may be a magical item that facilitates the quest, such as a ring, or a supernatural agent, who bestows gifts or information critical for success. Antagonists may be family members (an evil stepmother or wicked older brother) or supernatural villains (Koshchei the Deathless, a witch or a dragon.)

Tales of everyday life often concern relations between the sexes (notably, husbands and wives), differences based on economic standing (the poor versus the rich) or between humans and the supernatural (often the devil). These tales frequently present women negatively, as wicked, unfaithful, or deceitful wives, eventually punished for their transgressions, often in the form of spousal thrashing. Other subtypes feature a contest with the devil, in which peasants' victories invariably result from deception rather than innate ability or supernatural intervention.

The richest type is the animal tale, where humans figure rarely, if at all, and animals are anthropomorphized to the degree that they speak among themselves and have marriages resembling those of humans. However, their behaviour is almost always based firmly in the real world, so that predators such as foxes and wolves consistently pursue, devour or attempt to mislead their natural prey. Plots in these tales usually hinge on animals' clever deception of one another, to the ruin or death of the victim.

Legendary tales or legends feature named historical or religious figures, such as Ivan the Terrible or Saint Nicholas. Neither type of figure is portrayed realistically or even properly in terms of religious belief; Christian figures may act simply as supernatural helpers and display little motivation based on Christian values. Unlike the wonder tale, legends relegate magic to a minor role, though some saints' miracles approximate magical acts.

The most famous collection of folk tales remains that of Aleksandr Afanasev (1826–71), who did not collect the tales but merely assembled and edited them.

See also: folk mythology; superstitions, Russian

Further reading

Afanasev, A. (1973) *Russian Fairy Tales*, trans. N. Guterman, New York: Pantheon.
—— (1984) *Narodnye russkie skazki*, Moscow: Nauka.
Haney, J. V. (1999) *The Complete Russian Folktale*, New York: M.E. Sharpe.

DAVID J. GALLOWAY

Fomenko, Petr Naumovich

b. 13 July 1932, Moscow

Stage director

A major Moscow-based director, Fomenko views playfulness as the essence of the human condition and malleability of form as a fundamental law of the universe. Accordingly, his productions emphasize the histrionic nature of life, with the focal character juggling various guises. From 1972 to 1981, Fomenko worked at Leningrad Comedy Theatre, where major productions included Giraudoux's *La guerre de Troie n'aura pas lieu* (1973), Molière's *Le Misanthrope* (1975), Ostrovskii's *Les* (*The Forest*, 1979, 2003 remake in La Comédie Française).

In 1993, he founded the Fomenko Studio (*Masterskaia Petra Fomenko*), the company comprising his former GITIS students. Here he has developed a new manner: quick pace and an ethereal touch – the signature style of his current productions. Through skillfully choreographed whispers and rustles, steps and flutters, the characterization of actors in his excellent troupe reveals Fomenko's loving, slightly ironic view of the characters.

Current productions of the Studio include Ostrovskii's *Volki i ovtsy* (*Wolves and Sheep*, 1992), Boris Vakhtin's *Odna absoliutno schastlivaia derevnia* (*One Absolutely Happy Village*, 2000), and Chekhov's *Tri sestry* (*Three Sisters*, 2004). Major productions outside the Studio include Ostrovskii's *Bez viny vinovatye* (*Guilty Without Guilt*, Vakhtangov Theatre, 1993) and Pushkin's *Pikovaia dama* (*Queen of Spades*, Vakhtangov Theatre, 1996).

See also: Russian Academy of Theatre Arts; Vakhtangov Theatre

DASHA KRIJANSKAIA

footwear

Russian traditional footwear is unisex and meant for two seasons: felt boots or *valenki* for walking in the snow, and summer *lapti*, woven from birch (or other) bark over knit socks and tied around the ankle.

Today the styles have changed, but the principle remains the same: a combination of beauty and weather-adapted practicality. Russians wear boots (*sapogi*) for rain, snow, and slush for three seasons of the year; less heavy boots are called by the French term *demi-saison* (*demisezonnye*). Women's boots and summer sandals (*bosonozhki* [barefooters]) are distinguished by their style, in which beauty often wins over practicality: high heels are seen on all kinds of women's footwear, and young women wear high-heeled shoes and boots even in snow and on ice.

More and more footwear is imported from countries with cheaper wares, such as Turkey and China. Those who can afford more expensive imports prefer Italian footwear. Athletic shoes, part of the uniform of lower-level gang members, as well as athletes and young people, are often imported from US major firms; their imitations come directly from China.

See also: felt boots; folk costume; tapochki (slippers)

KAREN EVANS-ROMAINE

Freindlikh, Alisa Brunovna

b. 8 December 1934, Leningrad

Actress

Freindlikh graduated from the Leningrad Theatrical Institute in 1958 and immediately found success on the stage. One of the principal stars of Leningrad's Lensovet Theatre from 1961–83, she performed in both musical and dramatic pieces. Freindlikh's film career includes prominent roles in Eldar Riazanov's *Sluzhebnyi roman* (An Office Romance, 1977) and *Zhestokii romans* (A Cruel Romance, 1984), and in Andrei Tarkovskii's *Stalker* (1980). Since 1983 she has been a leading performer at the Bolshoi Dramatic Theatre (BDT) in St. Petersburg. People's Artist of the USSR (1981).

See also: Riazanov, Eldar; Tarkovskii, Andrei; Tovstonogov Bolshoi Dramatic Theatre (BDT)

EMILY D. JOHNSON

FSB

See: Federal Security Service (FSS/FSB)

G

Gabriadze, Rezo

(né Revaz Levanovich Gabriadze)

b. 29 June 1936, Kutaisi, Georgian SSR

Marionettist, film-maker, writer, artist

Gabriadze grew up in Kutaisi (western Georgia), and graduated from the Philological and Journalism Faculty of Tbilisi State University. In the 1960s and 1970s, he worked in the Georgian film industry, with more than thirty films to his credit. In 1981, he built the 48-seater Tbilisi Marionette Theatre, which became one of the city's cultural landmarks. Gabriadze went into exile during the civil war (1992–94) that followed the collapse of the Soviet Union and Georgia's declaration of independence. He worked in Europe and served as artistic director of the Obraztsov Puppet Theatre in Moscow (1994–95). In 1995, he returned to Tbilisi, rebuilt his theatre, and started touring with the troupe in Europe and the United States. Works that have earned him international renown include his *Battle of Stalingrad* with puppets, which had its premiere in Dijon, France, in 1996 and has toured internationally. An accomplished artist and sculptor, Gabriadze has exhibited his works throughout Europe. For his work in film, he was awarded the Grand Prize at the International Moscow Film Festival and the Nika Prize. His other honours include the USSR State Prize (1989), Commander of the French Republic Award, and the Golden Soft (1997), Golden Mask (1997), and Triumph Prize (1997).

See also: awards, cultural, post-Soviet; film, Georgian; Georgia; Obraztsov, Sergei

CATHARINE NEPOMNYASHCHY

Gabrilovich, Evgenii Iosifovich

b. 17 [29] September 1899, Voronezh; d. 5 December 1993, Moscow

Screenwriter

Gabrilovich wrote for Iulii Raizman (*Mashenka*, 1942; *Urok zhizni* [*Lesson of Life*, 1955]) and Mikhail Romm (*Chelovek #217* [*Person No. 217*, 1945] and *Ubiistvo na ulitse Dante* [*Murder on Dante Street*, 1956]). Subsequently he worked with younger directors, most prominently Gleb Panfilov (*V ogne broda net* [*No Crossing Under Fire*, 1968], *Nachalo* [*The Debut*, 1970]), and Ilia Averbakh (*Monolog* [*Monologue*, 1973]). Lyricism and nuanced psychological portraiture distinguish Gabrilovich's films, including those with a distinctly political agenda, such as the Lenin trilogy he scripted for Sergei Iutkevich and the much-heralded anniversary film directed by Raizman, *Kommunist* (*The Communist*, 1958).

See also: Panfilov, Gleb; Romm, Mikhail

JOSEPHINE WOLL

Gachev, Georgii Dmitrievich

b. 1 May 1929, Moscow

Literary critic, cultural theorist

Born into a musical family, Gachev developed the partly esoteric hypothesis of 'national representations of the world'. Beginning with his book *Zhizn khudozhestvennogo soznaniia* (*The Life of Artistic Consciousness*, 1972), he considers his contribution to be a reconstruction of national mental complexes 'Cosmo-Psycho-Logos', which are responsible for the organic unity of independent national cultures. Sharing organic conceptions of the life of civilizations put forth by Oswald Spengler and Lev Gumilev, Gachev thinks that the high point of Russian culture was court culture of the nineteenth century. The Soviet regime has starved contemporary Russia so much, according to his theory, that the cultural and historical rebirth of Russia is possible only if the country is reduced in size.

Gachev's main works could be published only after perestroika. Among them are *Mentalnosti narodov mira. Skhodstva i razlichiia (Similarities and Differences in the Mentalities of Nations of the World)*, *Nationalnye obrazy mira (National Representations of the World)*, *Obrazy Indii: Opyt ekzistentsialnoi kulturologii (Images of India: An Attempt at an Existentialist Theory of Culture)*, *Russkii Eros. Roman mysli s zhizniu (Russian Eros: The Affair between Thought and Life)*, and *Amerika v sravnenii s Rossiei (America in Comparison with Russia)*.

See also: perestroika and glasnost; philosophy, Soviet (Marxist-Leninist)

GASAN GUSEJNOV

Gaft, Valentin Iosifovich

b. 2 September 1935

Film and theatre actor, writer

Trained at the MKhAT (Moscow Art Theatre) School Studio, Gaft worked in several Moscow theatres before joining the Sovremennik Theatre in 1969. Some of his best film roles have been in Riazanov comedies: Sidorin in *Garazh* (*The Garage*, 1979), Colonel Pokrovskii in *O bednom gusare zamolvite slovo (Put in a Word for the Poor Hussar*, 1980), the leader of the bums' collective in *Nebesa obetovannye (Promised Heavens*, 1991). Whether hero or villain, a Gaft character is usually distinguished by his intelligence and humanity, such as the colonel in *Ankor, eshche ankor! (Encore, Another Encore!*, 1992). Gaft also wrote well-known parodies of his friends, including actors, poets, and directors, collected

and published in 2000 and 2004. People's Artist of the RSFSR (1984).

See also: Moscow Art Theatre; Riazanov, Eldar; Sovremennik Theatre

RIMGAILA SALYS

Gagarin, Iurii Alekseevich

b. 9 March 1934, Klushino, Gzhatsk (Gagarin), Smolensk region; d. 27 March 1968, Vladimir region

Cosmonaut

Gagarin became a national treasure and international celebrity on 12 April 1961, when he orbited the Earth for 108 minutes. During the flight, Gagarin monitored onboard systems, ate, drank, and watched the sun rise over North America. Born into a collective farmers' family, he became a fighter pilot and cosmonaut trainer. Tragically lost in an airplane crash on 27 March 1968 during a training flight, Gagarin was buried at the Kremlin wall in Moscow's Red Square. After his death, 12 April was declared Cosmonauts' Day, in his honour.

See also: space programme and exploration

TATYANA LEDENEVA

Gaidai, Leonid Iovich

b. 30 January 1923, Svobodnyi, Amur region; d. 19 November 1993, Moscow

Film director

Gaidai started his career as a stage actor in the Irkutsk Regional Drama Theatre. In 1955, he graduated from VGIK, where he studied in Grigorii Aleksandrov's workshop. Gaidai revived slapstick as a genre of Russian cinema, which after the experiments of the 1920s had virtually disappeared from Soviet cinema under Stalin. The film-maker introduced a Soviet analogue of the Three Stooges, *Trus, Balbes,*

Byvalyi (Coward, Booby, and Savvy), who have remained Russian viewers' favourite characters. His comedies of the 1960s, *Operatsiia 'Y' i drugie prikliucheniia Shurika (Operation Y and Other Adventures of Shurik*, 1965), *Kavkazskaia plennitsa ili novye prikliucheniia Shurika (Captive of the Caucasus, or the New Adventures of Shurik*, 1966), and *Brilliantovaia ruka (The Diamond Arm*, 1969) were the decade's most popular films. In the 1970s, Gaidai switched to film adaptations, among which the most popular were *Dvenadtsat stulev (The Twelve Chairs*, 1971) and *Ivan Vasilevich meniaet professiiu (Ivan Vasilevich Changes Profession*, 1973). According to surveys, Gaidai's comedies of the 1960s remain Russian viewers' favourites.

See also: All-Russian (All-Union) State Institute of Cinematography (VGIK); film, comedy

ALEXANDER PROKHOROV

Gaidar, Arkadii Petrovich

b. 9 (22) January 1904, Lgov, Kursk guberniia; d. 26 October 1941, Kanev, Ukrainian SSR

Writer

Gaidar volunteered for the Red Army and became a regiment commander at the age of 16. He began publishing in 1925 and found his vocation in children's literature by telling stories of the front-line camaraderie and romanticism of revolutionary struggle (*RVS*, 1926). A good example of this thinking can be found in his *Skazka o voennoi taine (Tale of the Military Secret*, 1935). In this story, the peaceful Soviet motherland is subjected to a sneak attack by bourgeois forces. As their fathers and older brothers are killed, little children have to join the battle. One such child, Malchish-Kibalchish, is captured and tortured, but remains true and does not reveal the great military secret. His bravery gives the Red Army time to ride to the rescue. The novel *Timur i ego kommanda (Timur and his Squad*, 1940) made Gaidar famous. A captivating account of an altruistic pioneer enterprise gave birth to a mass movement of *timurovtsy* all over the Soviet Union. Gaidar died in combat during World War II.

See also: literature, children's; Pioneer organization; Second World War (Great Patriotic War)

ALEXANDER LEDENEV

Gaidar, Egor Timurovich

b. 19 March 1956, Moscow

Economist, politician

Grandson of writer Arkadii Gaidar (Golikov), Egor Gaidar has a Doctor of Economics degree (1990) from Moscow State University. A Marxist economist promoted to editor of economic sections in the main Communist Party periodicals *Kommunist* (1987–90) and *Pravda* (1990), Gaidar entered politics as a member of the 'reformist' government of Yeltsin–Burbulis: from 1991 till 1994 he served as First Deputy Prime Minister, Minister of Economic Development, and Minister of Finance. He is considered the 'father' of economic 'shock therapy' in Russia. Gaidar was a deputy of the State Duma (1994–95; 1999–2003) and is co-founder and co-chairman of the political parties Democratic Choice (Demokraticheskii vybor Rossii) and the Union of Rightist Forces (SPS), as well as Director of Moscow's Institute of Transitional Economy.

See also: Duma; economic system, post-Soviet; political parties, post-Soviet; privatization; shock therapy; Union of Rightist Forces; Yeltsin, Boris

ALEXANDER DOMRIN

Galich, Aleksandr Arkadievich

(né Aleksandr Arkadievich Ginzburg)

b. 19 October 1919, Ekaterinoslav; d. 15 December 1977, Paris

Poet, singer-songwriter, novelist, playwright, screenwriter

A respected member of the Soviet literary establishment in the 1940s and the 1950s,

Aleksandr Galich achieved popular acclaim and official censure during the 1960s and 1970s for his unofficial, intractably anti-Soviet songs.

After a number of his official plays were banned in the late 1950s, Galich gradually shifted to writing outspoken songs that were both anti-Stalinist and highly critical of Soviet society as a whole. Addressing taboo themes such as the GULag and anti-Semitism with uncompromising clarity, Galich earned recognition as the conscience of his generation. These songs, along with works by other bards, circulated extensively by *magnitizdat* (through amateur tape recordings).

In 1968, a rare public concert at a Novosibirsk song festival caused a furore that eventually led to Galich's exclusion from the Writers' Union and the Cinematographers' Union in 1971–72; deprived of any means of earning a living, Galich was ultimately forced to emigrate (1974). In the West, he toured widely, worked for the radio station *Radio Svoboda*, and co-edited the journal *Kontinent*. He died from an electric shock, under what some considered suspicious circumstances, in his Paris apartment.

See also: anti-Semitism; bards; GULag; samizdat; unions, creative, Soviet

RACHEL S. PLATONOV

games

The most popular sports in Russia traditionally were soccer and hockey, which men of all ages played either informally or in organized teams. Almost every yard in Russian towns contained an improvised space for soccer or ice hockey. Basketball and volleyball were secondary school requirements, which guaranteed their popularity. Volleyball, badminton, and ping-pong were favourite leisure activities on beaches, in the country, or at vacation facilities. Among traditional Russian outdoors games, only *gorodki* (a form of skittles or 'Russian bowling') has survived in the contemporary period.

During Yeltsin's presidency, the Russian political elite had to learn to play tennis, Yeltsin's favourite sport; this was problematic, owing to Russia's harsh climate and dearth of enclosed courts. Subsequently, 'politically useful' sports changed according to Putin's tastes: downhill skiing and Asian martial arts (*vostochnoe edinoborstvo*), such as judo. New Russian businessmen prefer paintball, billiards, tennis, and downhill skiing. Children favour soccer, hockey (played only by boys), various ball games (for example, *vyshibaly*, *shtander*), hide-and-seek (*priatki*), tag, and role-playing (daughters–mothers, Cossacks–brigands, etc.). Girls jump rope; boys engage in snowball fights.

Table games range from chess and backgammon (*nardy*) to checkers (*shashki*) and Russian dominoes (also called *goat* [*kozel*]). *Loto* (bingo), word games, *morskoi boi* (sea battle), *krestiki-noliki* (noughts-and-crosses), and puzzles of all kinds help to pass the time during long winter nights for people of all ages. Various card games are popular, including *durak* (fool), *ochko* (similar to blackjack), *preferans* (preference), patience, etc. In the 1970s and 1980s many young people were fascinated with the American game of Monopoly, unavailable in the Soviet Union; lucky players used games smuggled in from abroad, while the majority used home-produced copies. Now a Russian version of Monopoly is readily available and very trendy.

After perestroika, two major developments took place in the Russian game business: legalization of gambling and advances in the Internet. Casinos and slot machines (*igrovye avtomaty*) proliferate in major Russian cities. Gambling is controlled by criminal structures and causes myriad social problems. The Internet offers endless kinds of computer games: new ones (such as Tetris and various flash games), as well as electronic versions of familiar games. Virtual reality is growing into a serious addiction in Russia for children and teens in big cities, where the Internet is readily available.

See also: basketball; chess; crime; fitness; hockey; Internet, Russian; Putin, Vladimir; soccer; sport clubs and teams; sports education; sports, post-Soviet; sports, Soviet; Tetris; toys; Yeltsin, Boris

TATIANA SMORODINSKAYA

Gamzatov, Rasul Gazmatovich

b. 8 September 1923, Tsada, Dagestan; d.
3 November 2003, Moscow

Poet

Gamzatov made his poetic debut in Avar, a
Dagestani language, in 1943. His father, the
highly regarded poet Gamzat Tsadasa, was his
first mentor. The first collection of Gamzatov's
poems in Russian appeared in 1947. One of the
most prolific Soviet poets, Gamzatov published
over twenty books of short love lyrics, long narrative poems, ballads, epigrams, and philosophical octaves, in both Russian and Avar.
Awarded the USSR State Prize in 1952 and the
Lenin Prize in 1962, Gamzatov was fortunate in
his Russian translators, Naum Grebnev and
Iakov Kozlovskii.

See also: poetry, Soviet

ALEXANDER LEDENEV

Gandlevskii, Sergei Markovich

b. 21 December 1952, Moscow

Poet and prose writer

Gandlevskii explores everyday life in his verses,
whose formal metre and rhyme link him to a
pre-Soviet Russian poetic tradition. Part of the
cultural underground during Stagnation,
Gandlevskii was not an active political dissident,
though he wrote outside the official network of
the Writers Union. First published in Russian
literary journals in the late 1980s, in 1996 he was
awarded both the Little Booker Prize and the
Anti-Booker Prize. In addition to poetry, he also
has written dramas, critical essays, and a novel.

See also: awards, literary, post-Soviet; dissident;
Stagnation

JENNIFER RYAN TISHLER

garderob

A cloakroom in theatres, museums, and other
public buildings where visitors are expected to
leave their coats and any other articles of outer
clothing (hats, scarves, etc.), as well as large
bags. Visitors are given a token with a number
on it (*nomerok*), which, upon leaving, they
exchange for their clothing.

Although hardly different from a cloakroom
in American or particularly Western European
public buildings, the *garderob*, with its strict staff
and rules, became an emblem for harsh and
petty Soviet authority. The cloakroom and its
rules are the subject of parody in, most
famously, Mikhail Zoshchenko's satirical story
Prelesti kultury (*The Charms of Culture*).

DAVID HUNTER SMITH

Garin, Erast Pavlovich

b. 28 October [10 November] 1902,
Riazan; d. 4 September 1980, Moscow

Actor, director

Garin debuted in 1922, rising to fame in
Vsevolod Meierkhold's productions of Nikolai
Erdman's *Mandat* (*The Warrant*, 1925), Nikolai
Gogol's *Revizor* (*The Inspector General*, 1926), and
Aleksandr Griboedov's *Gore ot uma* (*Woe from Wit*,
1928). His comic talent combining fragile
eccentricity, psychological subtlety, and emo-
tional warmth in such film classics as Gogol's
Zhenitba (*The Marriage*, 1937), Anton Chekhov's
Svadba (*The Wedding*, 1944), Evgenii Shvarts's
Kain XVIII (*Cain the 18th*, 1963) and *Neobykno-
vennoe chudo* (*An Uncommon Miracle*, 1965), assured
his undying popularity. As a film and theatre
director he often collaborated with his wife,
Khesia Lokshina.

See also: theatre, Soviet

JOHN FREEDMAN

Genis, Aleksander Aleksandrovich

b. 11 February 1953, Riga

Writer

Critic and essayist Genis emigrated to the
United States in 1977 and embarked on a

productive collaboration with Petr Vail. Their co-written articles on contemporary Russian literature and émigré life appeared in such émigré journals as *Kontinent* (*The Continent*), *Vremia i my* (*Time and Us*), *Ekho* (*The Echo*), and *Chast rechi* (*Part of Speech*). Their books, marked by incisiveness and irreverent irony, include *Rodnaia rech* (*Native Tongue*), *Poteriannyi rai* (*Paradise Lost*), *Russkaia kukhnia v izgnanii* (*Russian Cuisine in Exile*), *Amerikana* (*Americana*), and *Shestidesiatye – Mir sovetskogo cheloveka* (*The 60s – Inside the Soviet Mind*). Since the end of their collaboration (1990), Genis has been prolific and successful on his own, publishing *Amerikanskaia azbuka* (*American ABCs*), *Vavilonskaia bashnia* (*The Tower of Babel*), *Ivan Petrovich umer* (*Ivan Petrovich is Dead*), *Trikotazh* (*Knit*) and others. His highly original 'philological novel', *Dovlatov i okrestnosti* (*Dovlatov and Environs*), was short-listed for the 1999 Booker Prize. A talented painter knowledgeable about Japanese art, Genis also has authored and hosted radio programmes on Radio Liberty since 1984.

See also: literature, émigré; Vail, Petr

ALEXANDER BURRY

Georgia

Georgia (Sakartvelo in Georgian), located in Western Transcaucasia, borders Russia in the north and the Black Sea in the west. Two-thirds of its area of 69,700 sq. km consists of mountains in the north (the Greater Caucasus, including Mt. Shkhara 5068 m, Mt. Kazbegi 5033 m). Of Georgia's 25,000 rivers, the main ones are the Rioni in the west and the Mtkvari (Kura) in the Central and Eastern parts. Georgia's climate is subtropical in the west and Mediterranean in the east, with temperatures varying according to elevation. the population (2005) is 4,677,000, the majority of whom live in the lowlands. The largest cities are Tbilisi – 1,050,000; Kutaisi – 178,000; and Batumi – 119,000. Georgians constitute 70 per cent of the nation's population; Armenians – 8 per cent; Russians – 6 per cent; Azeris – 5.7 per cent; Ossetians – 3 per cent; Abkhaz – 2 per cent; the remainder are Greeks, Jews, Kurds, and Tatars.

The Georgian language belongs to the Kartvelian or South Caucasian group; the Georgian alphabet dates back to the fifth century. The majority of ethnic Georgians are Orthodox Christians (65 per cent).

Proto-Georgian tribes first appeared in approximately 1000 BC, and are reflected in Greek myths about the Golden Fleece and Prometheus. In AD 337, Georgia adopted Christianity and thus became the second nation, after Armenia, to adopt Christianity as a state religion. Bagrat III (975–1014) founded the Georgian state, which under the rule of David IV the Builder (1089–1125) and Tsarina Tamara (1184–1212) entered its Golden Age. Georgians participated in the Crusades, and Georgian scholars were famous in the monasteries of Palestine and Greece. In 1220, Georgia was occupied by Mongols, later by Turks and Persians. In the fifteenth century, the nation disintegrated into many princedoms, and in the sixteenth and seventeenth centuries it was captured by Ottoman Turks. Irakli II united the eastern Georgian regions of Kartli and Kakhetia and in 1783 signed the Treaty of Georgievsk with Russia, according to which Russia took his kingdom under its protection. In 1801, Russia annulled the treaty and annexed its territory. Western Georgia became part of the Russian Empire in 1803–64 during the Turkish and Persian wars.

In May 1918, Georgia was declared independent; however, when the Bolsheviks, supported by the Red Army, instigated a military uprising in 1921 and overthrew the Menshevik government, Georgia became one of the Soviet republics. In the Soviet period, industrial enterprises arose, illiteracy was eliminated, and Georgian culture and science flourished. After World War II, Georgian nationalism and economic corruption increased. In April 1991, Georgian state independence was restored. The Civil War of 1990–92, in which Abkhazia and South Ossetia attempted to secede, destroyed the economy and prompted a profound economic crisis, which led to rampant corruption and the impoverishment of the population. As a result, this nation, previously the richest Soviet republic, became the poorest post-Soviet state.

Georgia, with a primarily agricultural economy, produces citrus fruit, tea, hazelnuts, grapes, cheese, mineral water, and alcoholic beverages (cognac and grape vodka called *chacha*). Georgia has the oldest winemaking tradition in the world and produces 500 different types of wine. Industrial production in Georgia includes manganese and copper mining, machinery and metal works, oil refining, chemical industries, and re-export of fuel through oil and gas pipelines throughout its territory. Georgia is also famous for tourism, particularly in the Soviet period, when Black Sea beaches, ski resorts, mountain lakes, caves, waterfalls, and ancient cave cities, castles, fortresses, and early (fifth–seventh-century) Christian churches attracted numerous foreign and Soviet tourists (up to 170,000 annually in the early 1980s).

Rich and versatile Georgian cuisine became very popular in Russia and penetrated into most Russian kitchens and restaurants. Georgian crafts include ornate silver daggers, drinking horns with elaborate metalwork, jewelry, and wool carpets.

Georgia is famous for its polyphonic men's choir singing, table songs, and folk dances. Georgian poets, film-makers, artists, composers, singers, and musicians made an important contribution to Soviet and world culture.

See also: Armenia; Caucasus; economic system, post-Soviet; film, Georgian; vacations, Soviet and post-Soviet

SERGEI TARKHOV

Gerasimov, Sergei Appolinarevich

b. 8 [21] May 1906, Kundravy, Cheliabinsk region; d. 28 November 1985, Moscow

Actor, director, scriptwriter, film industry administrator

Gerasimov began his career as an actor with FEKS (Factory of the Eccentric Actor) in 1924. He appeared in films by Vsevolod Pudovkin and Fridrikh Ermler and all of Grigorii Kozintsev and Leonid Trauberg's silent films. He ran the Central Documentary Film Studio between 1944 and 1946 and taught at VGIK for decades; his pupils include directors Sergei Bondarchuk, Lev Kulidzhanov, and Tatiana Lioznova, and actresses Nonna Mordiukova and

Liudmila Gurchenko as writer and director. His most important films include *Semero smelykh* (*The Brave Seven*, 1936), *Molodaia gvardiia* (*The Young Guard*, 1948), *Tikhii Don* (*Quiet Flows the Don*, 1958) and *Zhurnalist* (*The Journalist*, 1967).

See also: All-Russian (All-Union) State Institute of Cinematography (VGIK); arts administration and management, Soviet and post-Soviet; Bondarchuk, Sergei; film, documentary; Gurchenko, Liudmila; Kulidzhanov, Lev; Lioznova, Tatiana; Mordiukova, Nonna

JOSEPHINE WOLL

Gerdt, Zinovii Efimovich

b. 21 September 1916 Sebezh, Vitebsk region, Belorussian SSSR; d. 18 November 1996, Moscow

Actor

Though Gerdt rarely appeared as a leading actor, his humour and wisdom made him a favourite with audiences. His role as an unselfish and uncompromising magician in Petr Todorovskii's film *Fokusnik* (*The Magician*, 1967) mirrors Gerdt's own personality. His ability to extract the humane essence from an 'insignificant' personage and to illuminate its tragic existence – a possible corollary to the actor's long-time work as a puppeteer – ensured his memorable performance as the goose thief Panikovskii in Mikhail Shveitser's *Zolotoi telenok* (*The Golden Calf*, 1968). Gerdt's role as the idealistic owner of a disintegrating theatre in Petros Sevastikoglou's allegorical film *Veter nad gorodom* (*Wind Over the City*, 1996) was his last.

See also: Shveitser, Mikhail; Todorovskii, Petr

IRINA MAKOVEEVA

Gergiev, Valerii Abissalovich

b. 2 May 1953, Moscow

Conductor

Gergiev studied with Ilia Musin at the Leningrad Conservatory. In 1977, while still a student, he was appointed to the Mariinskii Theatre as Temirkanov's assistant and in 1996 rose to the position of Artistic and General Director. Gergiev has made the Mariinskii Opera Company one of the world's best, primarily by developing an extensive repertoire of Russian and Western operas and by working with the world's leading opera houses. His international tours, extensive recordings (on the Phillips label), and recent appearance in the final scene of Sokurov's film *Russkii kovcheg* (*Russian Ark*, 2002) have brought him worldwide acclaim.

See also: Mariinskii Theatre; opera, post-Soviet

DAVID GOMPPER

German, Aleksei Iurevich

b. 30 June 1938, Leningrad

Director, screenwriter

German is the controversial and uncompromising director of four films that represent a profound cinematic reflection of Stalinism and World War II. By focusing on the everyday experiences of ordinary men and women caught up in historical tragedies, German undercuts the stylistic and ideological clichés of traditional Soviet films. In *Proverka na dorogakh* (*Trial on the Road*, completed 1971, released 1986), German raised the sensitive question of Soviet treatment of returning POWs. *Dvadtsat dnei bez voiny* (*Twenty Days without War*, 1976), a remake of Georgii Chukhrai's *Ballada o soldate* (*Ballad of a Soldier*, 1959), emphasizes the devastating effects of war on the lives of ordinary soldiers and civilians far from the front. *Moi drug Ivan Lapshin* (*My Friend Ivan Lapshin*, completed 1983, released 1985) describes the tragic combination of brutality and idealism among rank and file Stalinists on the eve of the Great Terror. *Khrustalev, mashinu!* (*Khrustalyov, My Car!*, 1998) is a nightmarish vision of the paranoia and senseless brutality of Stalinism's last days. In recent years German has been working on an adaptation of Boris and Arkadii Strugatskii's science fiction novel *Trudno byt bogom* (*Hard to Be a God*).

See also: Chukhrai, Grigorii; film, Second World War; Strugatskii, Arkadii and Boris

ANTHONY ANEMONE

Ghiaurov, Nicolai

b. 1929, Velingrad, Bulgaria; d. 2 June 2004, Modena, Italy

Opera singer

Like that other great Bulgarian bass, Boris Christoff, Ghiaurov was one of the world's leading performers of the title role in Musorgskii's opera *Boris Godunov*, and of Mephistopheles in Gounod's *Faust*. Cultural and political ties between Bulgaria and the Soviet Union facilitated his studies at the Moscow Conservatory between 1950 and 1955, after which he enjoyed the sort of international career denied to many Soviet artists. His rich and powerful voice, supported by impeccable technique, was heard to best effect in the Russian and Italian operatic repertoire, the traditional forte of the Slavic singer. He was married to Italian soprano Mirella Freni.

See also: Moscow Conservatory

PHILIP ROSS BULLOCK

Giatsintova, Sofia Vladimirovna

b. 23 July [4 August] 1895, Moscow; d. 12 April 1982, Moscow

Stage and film actress, theatre director

Following private acting lessons, Giatsintova was invited to join the troupe of the Moscow Art Theatre (MKhAT) at the unprecedented age of 15; in 1938, she switched to Lenkom Theatre. In plays by Shakespeare and Ibsen, Giatsintova demonstrated an astonishing ability to convey subtle psychological nuances. She enhanced her reputation as an original, inventive stage director, with credits including productions of Ostrovskii's *Bespridannitsa* (*Dowryless Girl*) and Turgenev's *Mesiats v derevne* (*A Month in the Country*).

Giatsintova attained late screen fame embodying patriotic mothers in monumental Stalinist pictures, such as *Kliatva* (*The Oath*, 1946) and *Padenie Berlina* (*The Fall of Berlin*, 1950). People's Artist of the USSR (1955).

See also: Lenkom Theatre; Moscow Art Theatre

PETER ROLLBERG

Gilels, Emil Grigorevich

b. 6 [19] October 1916, Odessa; d. 14 October 1985, Moscow

Pianist

One of Russia's most famous pianists, Gilels achieved prominence through a virtuoso technique coupled with a rich sonority rarely heard even today. His repertory covered works of the nineteenth and twentieth centuries, from Beethoven and Brahms to Scriabin and Rachmaninoff. He studied with Genrikh Neigauz (Heinrich Neuhaus) at the Moscow Conservatory and taught there intermittently from 1936 (promoted to the rank of professor, 1952) until 1981. He performed worldwide in concert tours starting in 1955, the year he made his American début with Tchaikovsky's First Concerto. He made recordings that helped to set the highest standard and establish the reputation of Russian pianists as the best in the world. People's Artist of the USSR 1954. USSR State Prize (Stalin Prize) 1946, Lenin Prize 1962.

See also: Moscow Conservatory; Neigauz, Genrikh; piano performance, Russian/Soviet

DAVID GOMPPER

Ginkas, Kama

b. 7 May 1941, Kaunas, Lithuania

Theatre director

After graduating from Tovstonogov's directing class at LGITMIK, Ginkas worked at Krasnoiarsk's Young Spectator Theatre, where he quickly fell out of favour with the authorities for his innovative works. In 1979, with no financial backing, he created *Pushkin and Natalie* – a piece regarded as a turning point in his career. Since 1981, Ginkas has worked regularly in various Moscow theatres, and since 1988 at the Moscow Young Spectator Theatre (MTIuZ), where his wife, Genrietta Ianovskaia, was appointed artistic director.

In his works, Ginkas skilfully combines elements of psychological character building with aggressive formal means. He prefers to work within small theatre spaces that allow him to violate the so-called fourth wall between the audience and the stage to such an extent that provocative, albeit playful, situations threaten to turn the production into a reality show. The histrionic consorts with the heartbreaking in Ginkas's essentially grim outlook on human beings as trapped between existence and death, history and the universe.

Major productions include Dostoevskii-based productions, *Notes From the Underground* (1988), *We Play Crime* (1991), *K.I. From Crime*; literary-historical works, *The Execution of the Decembrists* (1995), *Pushkin. Duel. Death* (1999); and Chekhov-based productions, *The Black Monk* (1999), *The Lady with the Lapdog* (2001), and *Rothschild's Fiddle* (2004).

See also: Pushkin, Aleksandr; St. Petersburg State Academy of Theatre Arts; Tovstonogov, Georgii; Young Spectator Theatre

DASHA KRIJANSKAIA

Ginzburg, Evgeniia Semenovna

b. 10 December 1904, Moscow; d. 25 May 1977, Moscow

Writer

Evgeniia Ginzburg is one of the few Soviet women to have authored a memoir about the Soviet camp system under Stalin that was widely read. Circulated in *samizdat* and *tamizdat* in the 1960s and 1970s, it was not officially published in the Soviet Union until 1989. *Krutoi marshrut* (A Harsh Route, but translated into English in two volumes entitled *Journey into the Whirlwind* and

Within the Whirlwind) describes with novel-like structure and vividness the heroine's fifteen-year ordeal in the GULag.

See also: corrective labour institutions; samizdat; tamizdat

NATASHA KOLCHEVSKA

Ginzburg, Lidiia Iakovlevna

b. 5 (18) March 1902, Odessa; d. 15 July 1990, Leningrad

Critic, scholar, literary theorist, fiction writer, memoirist

Prolific, multi-talented, and long-lived, Ginzburg studied the cultural meanings of human behaviour. She wrote book-length studies of psychological fiction and Russian lyric poetry, and her essay collections include memoirs of avant-garde poets, unusual pieces of short fiction, and bold, analytic studies of literary culture. Ginzburg inspired younger writers with her idiosyncratic wit, fierce integrity, and acute powers of observation (she tellingly admired Tolstoi, Proust, and Pushkin-era poet Viazemskii). She kept notebooks of her memories and observations for decades, and in the 1980s they began to be published to great acclaim.

See also: Pushkin, Aleksandr

STEPHANIE SANDLER

GITIS

See Russian Academy of Theatre Arts

glasnost

See perestroika and glasnost

Glavlit

Acronym for the Main Administration for Literary and Publishing Affairs (*Glavnoe upravlenie*

po delam literatury i izdatelstv). This all-union institution was the main official arm of Soviet censorship. Established in 1922, Glavlit evolved in the course of the Soviet period into an enormous bureaucracy, employing some 70,000 people to screen, in advance of dissemination, the contents of all mass media in the USSR and of all foreign publications brought into the USSR. Glavlit also exercised post-publication censorship powers. The acronym remained in use into the late 1980s, even after the institution was renamed the Main Administration for Safeguarding State Secrets in the Press (*Glavnoe upravlenie po okhrane gosudarstvennykh tain v pechati*).

See also: censorship

CATHARINE NEPOMNYASHCHY

Glazunov, Ilia Sergeevich

b. 10 July 1930, Leningrad

Artist

One of the most renowned Russian artists of the twentieth century, Glazunov graduated from the Repin Institute of Art, Sculpture, and Architecture in Leningrad (1957). A vocal opponent of modernist experiments, Glazunov follows the traditions of classic Russian art. His pictures illustrate a wide range of Russian themes: historical events; national character; personalities in classical literature, and the beauty of the Russian countryside. As a leading Russian portraitist and illustrator of Russian literature (Dostoevskii, Leskov, Ostrovskii, Blok, Goncharov), he produced portraits of various foreign dignitaries, monarchs, and presidents, including Indira Gandhi, Kurt Waldheim, John Paul II, and King Juan Carlos of Spain. In the perestroika era, Glazunov exhibited his monumental works *Eternal Russia, A Hundred Centuries, Great Experiment,* and *Mysteria of the 20th Century.*

Founded by Glazunov in the early 1960s, the patriotic club *Rodina* (Motherland) became one of the first havens of Russian ethnic identity and its self-consciousness. In 1986, he established and headed the Russian Academy of Art, Sculpture, and Craftsmanship, and was the art supervisor of the restoration of the Great Kremlin

Palace (1996–99). An honorary member of Royal Academies of Arts of Madrid and Barcelona, he is the recipient of numerous awards, including the Jawaharlal Nehru international prize and the 'Picasso Golden Medal' – a UNESCO award for contributions to world culture.

Further reading

Glazunov, I. (2004) *Rossiia raspiataia* (Crucified Russia), Moscow: Olimp.

Novikov, V. (2005) *Ilia Glazunov. Russkii geniii* (Ilia Glazunov: Russian Genius), Moscow: Eksmo, Algoritm.

http://www.glazunov.ru/

ALEXANDER DOMRIN

Glinka State Central Museum of Musical Culture

Founded in Moscow on 11 March 1912, this important museum houses rare manuscripts, musical instruments, and artifacts from the history of world music. Among other noteworthy collections, the museum contains major archives of Mussorgskii, Rachmaninoff, Rimskii-Korsakov, Anton and Nikolai Rubinshtein, and Tchaikovsky.

VALERIA Z. NOLLAN

Gluzskii, Mikhail Andreevich

b. 21 November 1918, Kiev; d. 15 June 2001, Moscow

Stage and film actor

Gluzskii belonged to the Central Theatre of the Red Army and later to the Sovremennik Theatre, but excelled most as a versatile supporting film actor. With more than 130 roles to his credit, he is one of the most familiar faces on the Soviet screen. Predominantly cast in parts requiring a headstrong temper, such as military, Party, and state leaders, his ability to transform himself allowed him to also portray reflective intellectuals – most prominently as Professor Sretenskii in *Monolog* (*Monologue*, 1972). In later years, Gluzskii's performances subverted the stern screen image that had emerged over

decades, for example, in *Ostanovilsia poezd* (*The Train Halted*, 1982). People's Artist of the USSR (1983).

See also: Communist Party; Sovremennik Theatre

PETER ROLLBERG

Goblin

(né Dmitrii Iurevich Puchkov)

b. 20 August 1961, Kirovograd, Ukrainian SSR

Translator, screenwriter

Dmitrii Puchkov, universally known by his pseudonym, Goblin, is a well-known translator of English-language films into Russian. He is most famous for his 'funny translations' (*smeshnye perevody*), which strive not for fidelity but for comic effect, substituting the original English script with an entirely different Russian one, replete with Russian criminal jargon, references to iconic Soviet films, and various other elements of Soviet and post-Soviet reality. Puchkov also replaces music from the original soundtrack with music that is either incongruous or ironically appropriate to the action on screen. His efforts in this mode include the *Lord of the Rings* trilogy and *The Matrix*. The *perevod ot Goblina* (Goblin translation) has developed into a genre with many imitators and impostors. Puchkov is also appreciated for his 'correct' translations of English-language films. Before he launched this career, Puchkov worked as a policeman and at various odd jobs.

See also: slang

DAVID HUNTER SMITH

Godunov, Aleksandr Borisovich

b. 28 November 1949, Iuzhno-Sakhalinsk; d. 18 May 1995, Santa Monica, CA

Ballet dancer

Trained at the Riga ballet school in Latvia, where he was Mikhail Baryshnikov's classmate,

Godunov came to Moscow in 1977 to dance with the *Young Ballet of Russia*. A year later he became a principal at the Bolshoi Theatre, and after winning the international ballet competition in Moscow in 1980, Godunov performed leading male roles in *Swan Lake*, *Don Quixote*, *The Carmen Suite*, and others. His technical skills, coupled with his striking stage presence, prompted Maia Plisetskaia to offer him the role of Vronskii in the ballet *Anna Karenina* and the film version of the ballet.

In 1979, during the Bolshoi's North American tour, Godunov requested political asylum in the US. His wife's decision to return to the Soviet Union, after 73 hours of negotiations from an Aeroflot plane detained at John F. Kennedy Airport in New York, made headlines during the tenuous Soviet–American relationship during the Carter and Brezhnev administrations. After defecting, Godunov unsuccessfully attempted to establish himself at the American Ballet Theatre, then under Mikhail Baryshnikov's directorship, and later founded his own touring company. Like his Russian predecessors, Nureev and Baryshnikov, Godunov turned to television productions and movies, trying to perform dramatic roles in feature films. Of the approximately dozen entries in his filmography, his most successful and promising appearance was in the movie *Witness* (1985).

See also: ballet, Soviet; ballet dancers, Bolshoi Theatre; Baryshnikov, Mikhail; Nureev, Rudolf; Plisetskaia, Maia

TATIANA SENKEVITCH

Gogoberidze, Lana Levanovna

b. 13 October 1928, Tbilisi, Georgian SSR

Film director, scriptwriter, actress, politician, diplomat

One of the most interesting and successful Georgian film-makers of the generation that came of age during the post-Stalin period, Gogoberidze made her debut in film as an actress in *Mtsvervalta dampkrobni* (*Pokoriteli vershin*

[*Conquerors of the Peaks*, 1952]), the first Georgian colour film. She made her debut as a director with *Gelati* (1958) and as a scriptwriter with the film, *Erti tsis kvesh* (*Pod odnim nebom* [*Under One Sun*, 1961]), which she also directed. The most acclaimed of the twelve films directed by Gogoberidze over the course of the following three decades is *Ramodenime interviu pirad sakitkhebze* (*Neskolko interviu po lichnym voprosam* [*Some Interviews on Personal Matters*, 1979]), a lyrical exploration of a woman journalist's struggle to balance her personal and professional lives. In the 1990s, Gogoberidze turned to politics, serving as Chairperson of the Majority in the Georgian Parliament (1995–99) and, since 1999, as Ambassador of the Republic of Georgia to the Council of Europe.

See also: film, Georgian

CATHARINE NEPOMNYASHCHY

Golden Ring (Zolotoe koltso)

The Golden Ring (*Zolotoe koltso*), one of the oldest and most popular tourist routes in Russia, is a chain of ancient Russian settlements extending northeastward from Moscow and encompassing the historic nucleus of modern Russia. The most prominent towns and villages compose the Golden Ring, which begins and ends in Moscow, include Vladimir and neighbouring Suzdal, Sergiev Posad (Zagorsk in Soviet times), Pereslavl-Zaleskii, Rostov, Yaroslavl, Kostroma, Rybinsk, Uglich, and Aleksandrov. These picturesque sites bore witness to important events in Russian history and contain unique monuments of Russian architecture from the twelfth to eighteenth centuries. Some thirty of these monuments are in the UNESCO Worldwide Heritage list.

The Golden Ring project was launched in the 1960s by the Soviet government, anxious to preserve and present Russia's unique cultural and architectural heritage to the world and to promote tourism, in order to attract much-needed hard currency. This enterprise entailed not only the restoration of historic buildings, but also a capital project to refurbish the infrastructure and amenities of these historic towns and provide modern roadways with suitable rest stops. To initiate the process, the Soviet government launched a major project in 1969 to construct a hotel and information centre on the outskirts of the historic town of Suzdal, restore and transform its historic centre, and provide a range of amenities, services, restaurants, and shops to accommodate the anticipated tourist trade, following America's Colonial Williamsburg model. The analogous development of other historic towns constituting the Golden Ring followed suit. Today some towns on the Golden Ring have developed a brisk tourist trade for domestic and foreign visitors, particularly Suzdal and the Russian Orthodox pilgrimage centre, Sergiev Posad, while others, and most of the roadside stops, have fared less well in the post-Soviet era.

See also: architecture, wooden; Russian Orthodoxy; Russian Orthodox churches; vacations, Soviet and post-Soviet

Further reading

Komech, A. (1991) *The Golden Ring: Cities of Old Russia*, New York: Abbeville Press.

Senkevitch, A. Jr (1979) 'Suzdal: Soviet Union Implements Plan to Revitalize Medieval City as Major Tourist Center', *American Preservation*, 2 (Dec–Jan.), 20–7.

ANATOLE SENKEVITCH

Goldovskaia, Marina Evseevna

b. 15 July 1941, Moscow

Cinematographer, writer, documentary filmmaker, producer, professor

Goldovskaia trained in the 1960s at VGIK as a cinematographer, then earned Kandidatskaia (1967) and Doktorskaia (1987) degrees in art history. A professor in the Journalism Department of Moscow State University (1966–94), since 1995 she has been a professor at the University of California, Los Angeles School of Film and Television. At the same time, she has made some thirty documentary films and worked as director of photography on fifty television programmes in Russia, Europe, and the United States. She is the author of a number of books, including an autobiography, *Marina Goldovskaia: Zhenshchina s kinoapparatom* (*Marina Glodovskaia: Woman with a Camera*).

Two films made during the glasnost period, *Arkhangelskii muzhik* (*A Real Peasant from Arkhangelsk*, 1986), about the end of collective farming in Russia, and *Vlast solovetskaia* (*Solovki Power*, 1988) documented the human toll of both past Soviet policies and present upheavals – social, economic, and political. The latter film was the first major exposé of Soviet concentration camps. In the 1990s Goldovskaia's films, including *Oskolki zerkala* (*The Shattered Mirror*, 1993), *Povezlo roditsia v Rossii* (*Lucky to Be Born in Russia*, 1994), *Dom s rytsariami* (*The House on Arbat Street*, 1993), and *Vozvrashchenie korolia* (*The Prince Is Back*, 1999), record, in her trademark cinema vérité style, the realities and absurdities of life in post-Soviet Russia. USSR State Prize (1989).

See also: All-Russian (All-Union) State Institute of Cinematography (VGIK); collective farms; corrective labour institutions; film, documentary; Moscow State University; Solovki

VIDA JOHNSON

Goluboi ogonek (Blue Fire)

One of the most popular television programmes in the Soviet Union, it first aired in 1962. Like the hors d'œuvres and bottle of Soviet champagne that decorated every festive table in the Soviet Union, the programme accompanied all national holidays. It brought together the common favourites of a disparate population: attractive television hostesses, sports stars, actors, singers, outstanding scientists, and winners of socialist competitions. The studio layout, in which guests were seated at tables set in a modestly festive manner, was deliberately reminiscent of a family gathering.

IRINA MAKOVEEVA

Gorbachev, Mikhail Sergeevich

b. 2 March 1931, Privolnoe

Politician

Mikhail Gorbachev was the last General Secretary of the Communist Party of the Soviet Union (CPSU). He became a member of the Central Committee of the CPSU in 1971 and joined the CPSU Secretariat as Agriculture Secretary in 1978. In 1980, Gorbachev became a full member of the Politburo as the protégé of Iurii Andropov. With the death of Konstantin Chernenko, Gorbachev, the youngest member of the Politburo, was appointed General Secretary in March 1985. He served as General Secretary of the CPSU for six years, instituting reforms in the soviet system that ultimately led to its dissolution in 1991.

Mikhail Gorbachev served as the first and only president of the Soviet Union. He was elected to the position of USSR President in March 1990 not by direct popular election, but rather by the deputies of the USSR Congress of People's Deputies.

When Gorbachev first became CPSU General Secretary in 1985, he attempted to liberalize and stimulate the Soviet system by continuing Andropov's policy of retiring aged comrades of Leonid Brezhnev and Chernenko from top leadership posts. Gorbachev also deepened Andropov's efforts to combat alcoholism and improve labour discipline, and scaled back Soviet military and economic assistance programmes abroad. When Gorbachev became dissatisfied with the meagre results of these early reform attempts, he initiated more radical ones.

Major components of Gorbachev's reform effort included *glasnost* (openness), *perestroika* (restructuring), *demokratizatsiia* (democratization), and new approaches to foreign policy. Under glasnost, censorship was dramatically reduced, dissidents were released from prison, and religious freedom was officially endorsed. Perestroika represented an effort to reform the nation's economic system. Gorbachev legalized individual entrepreneurship and small cooperative businesses, although the state sector remained dominant and resistant to serious modifications.

The *demokratizatsiia* reforms led to competitive elections with secret ballots that presented the voter with multiple candidates. Elections to a new USSR Congress of People's Deputies in March 1989 heralded the defeat of many old party bosses by more reformist candidates. Subsequent elections at the republic level gave many regional leaders the legitimacy to challenge Soviet rule and demand greater autonomy or independence. These beginnings of democratic reform within the central governing institutions of the Soviet Union represented one of Gorbachev's most lasting transformations.

Gorbachev also initiated a 'new thinking' in foreign policy. During his tenure as General Secretary, Gorbachev met with sitting US Presidents (Reagan and Bush) and signed the START I and Intermediate Nuclear Forces (INF) treaties. He unilaterally withdrew Soviet troops from Eastern European countries and scaled back Soviet aid to communist regimes around the world. He was awarded he Nobel Peace Prize in 1990.

After an attempted coup in August 1991, Gorbachev was never able to recover his authority. Gorbachev resigned as Soviet president on 25 December 1991, and the USSR ceased to exist. Since leaving office, Gorbachev has served as head of the International Foundation of Socio-Economic and Political Studies based in Moscow.

In 1953, Mikhail Gorbachev wed Raisa Maksimovna Titarenko (1932–99). Raisa Gorbacheva was the only Soviet first lady to appear with her husband at public events.

See also: alcoholism; Andropov, Iurii; Brezhnev, Leonid; Communist Party; Coup, August 1991; dissident; Gorbacheva, Raisa; Nobel Prize winners, non-literary; perestroika and glasnost

Further reading

Galeotti, M. (1997) *Gorbachev and His Revolution*, New York: St. Martin's Press.
Gorbachev, M. (2000) *Gorbachev*, trans. G. Shriver, New York: Columbia University Press.

VICKI L. HESLI AND JAMES KRUEGER

Gorbacheva, Raisa Maksimovna

b. 5 January 1932, Rubtsovsk, Altai region;
d. 20 September 1999, Münster, Germany

Social activist, wife of USSR President M.S. Gorbachev

A graduate of the Moscow State University Philosophy Department with a *kandidatskaia* in sociology, Gorbacheva became an associate professor there (1978–85). As the 'first lady of the USSR', she initiated the creation of the Soviet Fund for Culture and several charity organizations to help children with leukemia. She received recognition only after her death (from leukemia). In Russia's mass consciousness she remains a symbol of perestroika, a period of energetic social activity and hopes for a genuine renewal and improvement of life. An honorary chairwoman of the international association Hematologists of the World for Children, honorary professor of several European, American, and Asian universities, in 1988 she received the Women for Peace award.

See also: academic degrees; Gorbachev, Mikhail; Moscow State University; perestroika and glasnost

YURII ZARETSKY

Gorkii

See Nizhnii Novgorod [Gorkii]

Gorkii Park (Park Kultury i otdykha imeni Gorkogo)

Built in 1928, Gorkii Park (*Park Kultury i otdykha imeni Gorkogo*) was given the name of the writer Maksim Gorkii in 1932. The emergence of the idea of a park of culture coincided with the government's and the population's striving for tradition, stability, and festivity, which culminated in Stalin's claim of 1935, 'Life has gotten better, life has gotten merrier'. Architects A. V. Vlasov, K. N. Melnikov, and L. M. Lissitskii

participated in the planning of the park, which replaced the All-Russian Agricultural Exhibition of 1923. The park has become Muscovites' favourite recreational spot, serving as an amusement park in summer and a skating rink in winter. Its name acquired an additional meaning after the 1981 publication of Martin Cruz Smith's spy thriller *Gorky Park*.

VLADIMIR PAPERNY

Goskino

State Committee for Cinematography (*Gosudarstvennyi komitet po kinematografii*). Goskino was founded in 1963 to supervise film production both financially and ideologically. It was subordinated to the USSR Council of Ministers, thus had ministerial status. From 1972 to 1986, Goskino was headed by Filipp Ermash. After the dissolution of the USSR Goskino briefly became Roskomkino before reverting back to Goskino in 1996. From 1992 to 1999, its chairman was film historian Armen Medvedev. In 2000, Goskino merged with the Ministry of Culture. After administrative reorganization in 2004, the responsibilities for cinematography were delegated to the Federal Agency for Cinematography and Culture (*Federalnoe agenstvo po kinematografii i kulture*).

See also: arts administration and management; censorship

BIRGIT BEUMERS

Gosplan (Gosudarstvennyi planovyi komitet [State Planning Committee])

The all-union governmental body for economic planning (1921–91). Originally established as the 'general planning commission' (the name changed in 1948, but the acronym was retained), Gosplan was intended to increase national economic efficiency through careful planning, economic projections, and crisis prevention. The initial plan was to supplement and correct market spontaneity through governmental regulation. In the Stalin era, however, the committee became a totalitarian body prescribing five-year and annual plans and monitoring their implementation in every economic area. In 1992, the bureaucratic body, comprising 3,000 employees, was disbanded as inadequate to the needs of a transition market economy. Part of its regulatory functions passed to the Ministry of Trade and Economic Development.

See also: economic system, Soviet; five-year plan

TATYANA LEDENEVA

Govorukhin, Stanislav Sergeevich

b. 29 March 1936, Berezniki

Film director, actor, scriptwriter, and poet

Govorukhin is an adept of high-quality popular cinema. In the 1970s and 1980s, he made adventure films, based on works by Daniel Defoe, Mark Twain, and Agatha Christie. In 1979, he wrote the script for the blockbuster *Piraty XX veka* (*Pirates of the Twentieth Century*) and made his biggest hit, the five-episode television police series *Mesto vstrechi izmenit nelzia* (*The Meeting Place Cannot Be Changed*), which featured Vladimir Vysotskii. After the collapse of the Soviet Union Govorukhin abandoned genre cinema for politically engaged films. His three-part documentary cycle decried Russia's social and moral degradation. Govorukhin's 1999 film *Voroshilovskii strelok* (*The Voroshilov Sharpshooter*) angered critics with its alleged attack on the intelligentsia. As a member of the Duma and a one-time presidential candidate, Govorukhin is actively involved in Russian politics.

See also: Duma; film, documentary; *Mesto vstrechi izmenit nelzia* (The Meeting Place Cannot Be Changed)

ELENA PROKHOROVA

Gradskii, Aleksandr Borisovich

b. 3 November 1949, Kopeisk, Cheliabinsk oblast

Rock musician, composer, singer

One of the first Russian rock band leaders, Gradskii was trained in classical music at Moscow's Gnessin Institute. He graduated in 1974 with a diploma of opera and chamber singer and later studied composition at the Moscow Conservatory. Yet in the early 1960s he was also the soloist in a few Moscow underground rock bands and finally founded his own group, *Skomorokhi* (The Troubadours). In 1974, Gradskii composed the soundtrack for Andrei Konchalovskii's film *Romans o vliublennykh* (*Lovers' Romance*) which brought him wide popularity in the USSR and abroad. In the late 1970s Gradskii changed roles, from rock band leader to solo singer with guitar; his image combines those of rock musician and bard. Gradskii is also known as a classical tenor; his concert programmes often include opera arias and romances. Evgenii Svetlanov invited him to sing in Rimskii-Korsakov's opera *Zolotoi petushok* (*The Golden Cockerel*) at the Bolshoi Theatre (1988).

See also: bards; Bolshoi Theatre; Konchalovskii, Andrei; Moscow Conservatory; rock music; Svetlanov, Evgenii

KIRA NEMIROVSKAIA

Grand Dramatic Theatre

See: Tovstonogov Bolshoi Drama Theatre

Granin, Daniil Aleksandrovich

(né German)

b. 1 January 1918, Volyn, Russia

Writer

Granin's literary career started after World War II, in which he served at the front. Most of his novels describe the work and moral searchings of Soviet engineers, scientists, and petty officials: *Iskateli* (*Those Who Seek*, 1955), *Sobstvennoe mnenie*

(*Personal Opinion*, 1956), *Posle svadby* (*After the Wedding*, 1958), *Idu na grozu* (*Into the Storm*, 1961), *Kartina* (*The Picture*, 1979), and *Zubr* (*The Bison*, 1987). In collaboration with Ales (Aleksandr) Adamovich, Granin wrote *Blokadnaia kniga* (*A Book of the Blockade*, 1979), about Leningrad's travails during World War II. In the post-Soviet period Granin has produced short stories, the essay *Strakh* (*Fear*, 1997), and a novel about Peter the Great.

See also: World War II (Great Patriotic War)

ALEXANDER LEDENEV

Grebenshchikov, Boris Borisovich

b. 27 November 1953, Leningrad

Rock musician

Singer-songwriter, rock musician, film composer, artist, writer, Grebenshchikov is a lifelong resident of St. Petersburg. As leader of Akvarium, one of Russia's most influential rock bands, which he founded in 1972, Grebenshchikov authored the lyrics and composed the music for most of Akvarium's songs. A mathematician by education, in the early 1980s he emerged as the leader of the Leningrad/St. Petersburg rock music scene and an inspiration for the Russian hippie movement. A participant of *mitki* and other nonconformist art movements, he has participated in many collaborative projects with Russian and Western rock musicians and other creative artists.

See also: Akvarium; art, nonconformist; mitki; rock music

VITALY CHERNETSKY

Grekova, I.

(pseudonym of Elena Sergeevna Venttsel)

b. 21 March 1907, Tallinn, Estonia; d. 15 April 2002, Moscow

Writer

Grekova, like Natalia Baranskaia, depicted women's problems during the 1960s through the 1980s. *Vdovii parokhod* (*A Ship of Widows*, 1979)

describes communal apartment neighbours after World War II. Grekova's typical protagonists are female scientists balancing career and family, as in *Damskii master* (*Ladies' Hairdresser*, 1963). *Letom v gorode* (*Summer in the City*, 1962) alludes to the consequences of Stalin's criminalization of abortion.

See also: literature, women's

BENJAMIN SUTCLIFFE

Gremina, Elena Anatolievna

(née Elena Anatolievna Grebneva)

b. 20 November 1956, Moscow

Playwright, screenwriter

Gremina debuted in 1984, but significant success came in 1994 with *Za zerkalom* (*Behind the Mirror*), about Catherine the Great's affair with a man half her age, produced at the Moscow Art Theatre. *Sakhalinskaia zhena* (*The Sakhalin Wife*, 1996), about a woman convict entering a prisoner colony, helped overturn the myth that Russian drama was dead in the 1990s. A tireless activist for the promotion of new dramatic writing, she is co-founder, with husband Mikhail Ugarov, of the experimental playhouse Teatr.-doc and frequently collaborates on teleplays with him. She is the daughter and sister, respectively, of screenwriters Anatolii Grebnev and Aleksandr Mindadze.

See also: drama, post-Soviet; Mindadze, Aleksandr; Moscow Art Theatre; theatre, post-Soviet; Ugarov, Mikhail

JOHN FREEDMAN

Gribov, Aleksei Nikolaevich

b. 31 January 1902, Moscow; d. 26 November 1977, Moscow

Russian stage and film actor

Gribov studied at the school of the Third Studio at the Moscow Art Theatre (MKhAT) and joined the theatre's troupe in 1924. He became famous for his inventive, witty, and sometimes daringly original performances, particularly in satirical plays, including *Mertvye dushi* (*Dead Souls*), based on Nikolai Gogol's novel, in which he played the moody boor Sobakevich, and in *Selo Stepanchikovo i ego obitateli* (*The Village Stepanchikovo and Its Inhabitants*). In this adaptation of Fedor Dostoevskii's work, he was the pretentious Foma Opiskin. Gribov's most memorable film roles also were in adaptations of Russian classics, especially Gogol and Chekhov. People's Artist of the USSR (1948).

See also: Moscow Art Theatre

PETER ROLLBERG

Grigorovich, Iurii Nikolaevich

b. 2 January 1927, Leningrad

Choreographer

The leading choreographer of the Soviet era, Iurii Grigorovich enjoyed an unprecedented thirty-year tenure at the helm of Moscow's Bolshoi Ballet. A soloist with Leningrad's Kirov Ballet from 1946–64, he created his first important works for that theatre (*Kamennyi tsvetok* [*Stone Flower*, 1957]; *Legenda o liubvi* [*Legend of Love*, 1961]). Grigorovich and his ballets were soon transferred to the more prestigious Bolshoi, where the choreographer developed a recognizable style rich in heightened emotion and dramatic intensity. Like other Soviet choreographers, Grigorovich mainly adapted literary works to the ballet stage. His *Spartak* (*Spartacus*, 1968) remains one of the Soviet ballet's most gripping and lasting works.

See also: ballet, Soviet; ballet dancers, Mariinskii Theatre; Bolshoi Theatre; choreographers, Soviet; Mariinskii Theatre

TIM J. SCHOLL

Grishkovets, Evgenii Valerievich

b. 17 February 1967, Kemerovo

Playwright, actor

Grishkovets debuted in Kemerovo at the Lozha (theatre box) Theatre, which he co-founded in

1991. He developed his self-proclaimed genre of 'new sentimentalism' in *Kak ia sel sobaku* (*How I Ate a Dog*, 1997), an ironic, heartfelt monologue about the adventures of a bewildered Soviet sailor. He continued developing his trademark befuddled hero in the monologues *Odnovremenno* (*At the Same Time*, 1998) and *Drednouty* (*Dreadnoughts*, 2001), which he staged and performed himself. Plays written for multiple actors include *Zima* (*Winter*, 2000) and *Osada* (*The Siege*, 2003). His first novel, *Rubashka* (The Shirt), also written in a naïve, personal voice, appeared in 2004.

See also: drama, post-Soviet; theatre, post-Soviet

JOHN FREEDMAN

Grossman, Vasilii Semenovich

(né Iosif Solomonovich)

b. 29 November [12 December], 1905, Berdichev, Ukraine; d. 14 September 1964, Moscow

Writer

Grossman graduated from Moscow State University's Department of Physics and Mathematics, worked as a chemical engineer in the Donbass region, and in 1934 became a professional writer, focusing on historical, revolutionary, and industrial themes. A war correspondent during World War II, he authored the patriotic novel *People are Immortal* (*Narod bessmerten*, 1942). His essay *The Hell of Treblinka* (*Treblinskii ad*) about the extermination of Jews in a Treblinka death camp was distributed at the Nuremberg Trials as part of evidence for the prosecution. Grossman's fiction about war conceives of the latter as life in extreme circumstances. The fullest expression of this view is his major, two-part work, *Life and Fate* (*Zhizn i sudba*, 1948–60).

See also: literature, World War II; Moscow State University; World War II (Great Patriotic War)

YURII ZARETSKY

Gubaidulina, Sofiia Asgatovna

b. 24 October 1931, Chistopol, Tatar
Autonomous Republic, USSR (now Russia)

Composer

After the death of her avant-garde composer-colleague and contemporary Alfred Shnittke in 1998, Gubaidulina became the most prominent surviving representative of the once semi-underground world of Soviet 'unofficial' music. During the Stagnation era, Gubaidulina's mystical, philosophical, and unconventional music was regarded with suspicion and hostility by the official Soviet musical establishment, hence rarely performed in Russia. After the collapse of communism, however, the West quickly discovered her music, which frequently employs untraditional instruments and ensembles, and she began spending most of her time outside Russia. In 1992, she moved to Germany.

The child of a Russian mother and Tatar father, Gubaidulina spent her early years in Kazan, where she studied piano at the Conservatory. In 1954, after her graduation, she went to Moscow to study composition at the Moscow Conservatory. The Thaw era, for the first time in decades, permitted composers to experiment with foreign techniques such as serialism, which had been effectively banned under Stalin. After graduating from the Moscow Conservatory in 1959 and doing graduate work in composition there, Gubaidulina remained in Moscow, supporting herself primarily by writing film scores. Her film work taught her how to convey specific emotions with brevity and limited musical resources. Many of her compositions also include a strong visual element. A good example is *Offertorium* for violin and orchestra, composed in 1979–80, as an elaborate response to a theme from J. S. Bach's *Musical Offering*. It incorporates various kinds of symbolism to represent sacrifice and transformation.

Gubaidulina has worked in a wide variety of genres, techniques, and styles, from tonality to serialism and electronics. Her many vocal works have set texts from highly diverse sources, ranging from Rainer Maria Rilke to T.S. Eliot and Omar Khayyam. She has avoided identifying herself exclusively with any method or school, and has shown little interest in politics or in the nationalism that has figured so prominently in the Russian musical tradition.

See also: classical music, post-Soviet; Moscow Conservatory; Shnittke, Alfred

Further reading

Campbell, K. (1997) 'A Russian Composer's Path to Freedom', *Christian Science Monitor*, 27 August.

HARLOW ROBINSON

Gubenko, Nikolai Nikolaevich

b. 17 August 1941, Odessa, Ukrainian SSR

Actor

A graduate of the acting (1964) and directing (1969) departments of the All-Union State Institute of Cinematography (VGIK), Gubenko has acted at Moscow's Taganka Theatre (1964–68; 1980–). After a split in the Taganka (1993), Gubenko was elected artistic director of *Sodruzhestvo akterov Taganki* (Community of Taganka Actors), which has its own theatre. Apart from playing in numerous movies, from 1971–88 he also directed six films, including *Podranki* (*Wounded Game*, 1977) and *Zapretnaia zona* (*Forbidden Zone*, 1988), and wrote the screenplays for five of them. After a stint (1989–91) as the USSR Minister of Culture, from 1999 till 2003 he was a deputy of the State Duma and Chairman of the Committee for Culture and Tourism. In May 2002, he was expelled from the Russian Communist Party, of whose Central Committee he had been a member (1995–97).

See also: All-Russian (All-Union) State Institute of Cinematography (VGIK); Communist Party; Duma; Taganka Theatre

ALEXANDER DOMRIN

GULag

The Main Directorate for Corrective Labour Camps (*Glavnoe upravlenie ispravitelno-trudovykh lagerei*, 1930–60), created within the system of

OGPU (*Obedinennoe gosudarstvennoe politicheskoe upravlenie* [United State Political Department]), later NKVD (*Narodnyi komissariat vnutrennikh del* [People's Commissariat of Internal Affairs]) and MVD (*Ministerstvo vnutrennikh del* [Ministry of Internal Affairs]). After the publication of Aleksandr Solzhenitsyn's *Arkhipelag GULag* (*Gulag Archipelago*, 1973), the GULag as a punitive system became a symbol of lawlessness and forced slave labour in Soviet society, equated with the camps and prisons of the NKVD and the totalitarian Stalinist regime as a whole. The regime operated through mass arrests, shootings, and deportations, which collectively created a pervasive fear of power among the populace. Special departments of the GULag united the corrective labour camps located in various regions of the country, which had their own names: Karlag in Kazakhstan, Dalstroi in the Far East, Solovetskii USLON on Solovki Islands, Bereglag on the Kolyma River, Gorlag near Norilsk, Luglag, and so forth. The network of camps covered all of the northern, Siberian, Central Asian and Far Eastern areas of the Soviet Union, with camps particularly concentrated in the European section.

Camps carried out the task of 'exploiting' natural resources with the use of prison labour. Prisoners worked under unimaginably gruelling conditions; elemental human rights were ignored, and severe punishments meted out. Among the projects relying on prison labour were the construction of canals (such as the White Sea–Baltic and the Moscow–Volga Canals), railroads (such as the Baikal–Amur Railroad, BAM), and industrial and other objects. This work was conducted in regions with the harshest climates in the country.

Prisoners of special camps lived under the worst conditions. They comprised Trotskyites, Mensheviks, members of the Socialist-Revolutionary Party, anarchists, nationalists, White Army emigrants, and members of anti-Soviet organizations and groups. With one square metre as their allotted living space, they were chosen for the most taxing work, and any resistance or revolt was suppressed without mercy.

During the time of the purges (the 'Great Terror'), despite frequent recourse to the death penalty and an increase in prisoners' mortality rate, the number of prisoners in the GULag exceeded two million in the spring of 1938. The number of prisoners and camps grew after World War II, owing to the Soviets' expatriation and internment of former Soviet prisoners of war and sundry citizens. By 1950, there were more than 2,600,000 people 'serving time' in the GULag. In the final years of Stalinism, the use of prison labour to fulfil economic tasks became standard practice; in 1949 the system supervised by the Ministry of Internal Affairs accounted for more than 10 per cent of industrial production in the USSR.

Nikita Khrushchev approved several resolutions that enabled the transfer of the GULag archive from the MVD to the State Archive of the Russian Federation; it eventually became available to scholars. However, the burial places of those executed (and in many cases even the very fact of execution) were kept in strict secrecy until the early 1990s. Today the exact number of the GULag's victims remains uncertain. Scholars estimate that between 1930 and 1953 more than 52 million people were sentenced, of which 20 million were interned in the camps. Approximately 1 million were shot, while others died under torture or committed suicide; 6 million were exiled. Aspects of the GULag have survived to this day: Russia's unreformed penitentiary system continues to subject individuals to extreme and sometimes arbitrary forms of suppression.

See also: archives; BAM (Baikal–Amur Railroad); crime; corrective labour institutions; economic system, Soviet; Federal Security Service (FSS/FSB); Khrushchev, Nikita; Shalamov, Varlam; Solovki; Solzhenitsyn, Aleksandr; Stalin, Iosif; White Sea Canal; World War II (Great Patriotic War)

Further reading

Applebaum, A. (2003) *Gulag: A History*, New York: Doubleday.

Solzhenitsyn, A. (1974) *The GULAG Archipelago, 1918–1956*, London: Collins Harvil.

ELENA OZNOBKINA

GUM

Spanning the eastern side of Moscow's Red Square, GUM (the acronym for *Gosudarstvennyi universalnyi magazine*, or 'State Department Store') is Russia's largest and most famous department store. Originally built in 1890–93 by architect Aleksandr Pomerantsev as the 'Upper Mall' (*Verkhnie torgovye riady*), GUM, with its three parallel arcades and curved glass ceiling, combines decorative features of Russian ecclesiastical architecture with the grand functional structure of a nineteenth-century train station. From the first five-year plan until 1953, GUM functioned as office space, but thereafter was refurbished and converted back into a massive shopping mall. Privatized in the early 1990s, GUM has thrived as a top-class shopping centre and celebrated its 100th anniversary in 1993.

See also: Red Square

BETH HOLMGREN

Gundareva, Natalia Georgievna

b. 28 August 1948, Moscow; d. 15 May 2005, Moscow

Actress

A very popular actress on stage and screen, and more recently television, especially in *Peterburgskie tainy* (*Petersburg Secrets*, 1994) and *Salomeia* (2001), Gundareva is well known for films including *Sladkaia zhenshchina* (*A Sweet Woman*, 1976), (*Osennii marafon* (*Autumn Marathon*, 1979)), *I zhizn, i slezy, i liubov* (*Life, Tears, and Love*, 1983) and *Sobachii pir* (*The Dogs' Feast*, 1990). However, she may be best remembered as the eponymous heroine of *Lichnoe delo sudi Ivanovoi* (*The Personal Case of Judge Ivanova*, 1985), where she gives an emotionally convincing performance as a divorce lawyer confronting the breakdown of her own marriage, and all its ramifications.

DAVID GILLESPIE

Gurchenko, Liudmila Markovna

b. 12 November 1935, Kharkov, Ukrainian SSR

Actress, writer, singer

Even before graduating from VGIK (1958), Gurchenko won fame as the sassy, energetic club worker Lena Krylova in one of the Thaw's first comedies, *Karnavalnaia noch* (*Carnival Night*, 1956), a film rebroadcast on Soviet television to celebrate New Year's Eve for many years. In addition to roles in musical comedies, Gurchenko played dramatic heroines with subtlety and sensitivity, most notably the factory director Anna Georgievna in *Starye steny* (*Old Walls*, 1974) and the waitress Vera in *Vokzal dlia dvoikh* (*Station for Two*, 1983). Gurchenko is also widely known as a singer, having produced two popular albums, *Pesni voiny* (War Songs) and *Liubimye pesni* (Favourite Songs).

See also: All-Russian (All-Union) State Institute of Cinematography (VGIK)

JOSEPHINE WOLL

Gusinskii, Vladimir Aleksandrovich

b. 6 October 1952, Moscow

Businessman, media magnate, founder of the first non-state Russian television channel

A graduate of the Institute of Petrochemicals and Natural Gas (1973) and the State Institute of Theatrical Art (1980), during perestroika Gusinskii formed the consulting firm Most. He headed Most Bank (1989), which subsequently was transformed into Most Group (1992) – a holding company and bank that was the main depository for Moscow municipal funds. Gusinskii also established the closed joint-stock company Media-Most (encompassing radio, TV, and publications, such as *Ekho Moskvy, Segodnia*, NTV, *Itogi*). Arrested for fraud on 13 June 2000, and but released three days later, Gusinskii now lives in Israel, affiliated with

NEWSru.com, American Central European Media Enterprises, Ma'ariv Holdings of Israel, and RTV International.

See also: Ekho Moskvy; journalists, post-Soviet; perestroika and glasnost, television channels; television, post-Soviet

ELENA SKIPETROVA

Gutman, Natalia Grigorevna

b. 14 November 1942, Kazan, Russia (USSR)

Cellist

A protégée of both Mstislav Rostropovich and Sviatoslav Richter, Natalia Gutman studied for fifteen years with Galina Kozolupova. Her career was launched when she took first prize in the 1967 Munich ARD Competition in the piano/cello duo category. She has performed with the Vienna Philharmonic and Berlin Philharmonic, the London Symphony and Concertgebouw Orchestra, and teaches at the Hochschule für Musik in Stuttgart. Alfred Shnittke dedicated both his First Cello Sonata and First Cello Concerto to her; she premiered his Concerto Grosso no. 2 (1985) with her late husband, violinist Oleg Kagan. Richter called her 'the incarnation of truthfulness in music'.

See also: Rikhter, Sviatoslav; Rostropovich, Mstislav; Shnittke, Alfred

SUNGHAE ANNA LIM

gymnastics

Gymnastics traditionally has been one of the most popular sports in Russia. It originated at the end of the eighteenth century as part of physical training in Russian military educational institutions. In 1881, the Russian Gymnastic Society was established in Moscow, with Anton Chekhov among its founders, and national championships were introduced at the beginning of the twentieth century. Gymnastics, together with track and field, traditionally forms the basis of physical education at Russian schools. Russian gymnasts achieved their greatest success in the second half of the twentieth century. The 1952 Olympic debut of the USSR team brought individual and team victories for both male and female gymnasts. Soviet athletes dominated world gymnastics from the 1950s till the 1980s, winning more than 300 Olympic medals, half of them gold. These achievements would have been impossible without considerable state support and a network of specialized sports schools. The best gymnasts received government grants and great mass-media attention. Among the most popular Soviet and Russian gymnasts are Larisa Latynina, Liudmila Turishcheva, Svetlana Khorkina, Nikolai Andrianov, Dmitrii Bilozerchev, and Aleksei Nemov. In the 1970s Belarussian Olga Korbut won international fame with her complicated moves (including her loop on the parallel bars and her somersault on the balance beam), bringing gymnastics to a new level of complexity and popularity all over the world.

Besides traditional gymnastics, parallel sports, including acrobatics, trampolining, and artistic gymnastics developed in the USSR and Russia. Artistic gymnastics, with its combination of sports and balletic choreography, enjoys special popularity in Russia. It came to the USSR in the 1930s, and its basic elements were developed by the leading stars of Soviet ballet. Today medals in artistic gymnastics at world championships are generally awarded almost exclusively to Russian, Belarussian, and Ukrainian athletes. The brightest star of twenty-first century Russian artistic gymnastics is Alina Kabaeva.

See also: sports education; sports, Soviet

Further reading

Marten, P. (2004) Sportivnaia gimnastika, St. Petersburg: AST.
Ryan, J. (2000) Little Girls in Pretty Boxes, New York: Warner Books.

ALEXANDER LEDENEV

Gypsy/Roma

Roma or Gypsies settled in Russian territory at approximately the end of the seventh century. Roma tribes were neither repressed nor exiled in Russia, unlike in Western Europe. Some were made serfs, others left free to choose their estate affiliation. Several ethnic groups of Roma remain in Russia to the present day. Roma in Russia adopted Orthodoxy, but did not assimilate into Russian society, preserving their language, culture, traditions, and lifestyle. The assumption that Roma came from India is based on the fact that the Roma language is Indic, sharing features with Sanskrit. Gypsies in Russia speak various dialects of the Roma language and use the Cyrillic alphabet. Traditionally, Roma were nomadic tribes, with men often working as blacksmiths and tinsmiths, and women as fortune-tellers and sorceresses. Most gypsies wandered about the countryside in groups called tabors, and participated in fairs, selling horses, dancing, singing, fortune-telling, and demonstrating performing bears.

Roma all over the world achieved fame as exciting musicians and dancers; in Russia, gypsy choirs were particularly successful. The first gypsy choir was created by Count A.G. Orlov-Chesmenskii in the Moscow suburb of Pushkino (1774). Gypsy choirs performed in restaurants, at private parties, fairs, and markets, and were very popular among the aristocracy and the merchant class. Their repertoire consisted of gypsy folk songs, Russian folk songs, romances, and Russian classics performed with a gypsy flavour. Russian literature, following the Romantic tradition established by Aleksandr Pushkin, depicted gypsies as free spirits, people unspoiled by civilization, temperamental, independent, and proud. That myth still exists in the national cultural consciousness and finds its reflection in contemporary Russian cinema, poetry, and popular music.

After the Bolshevik Revolution of 1917, the Soviet government made an attempt to change the Roma lifestyle and settle gypsies in permanent places of residence, but with only modified success. Soviet propaganda accused Gypsy choirs of being 'out of touch', 'nonproletarian', and 'kitschy', for gypsy music was associated with bourgeois culture and dismissively labelled *tsyganshchina*. This word has several meanings. The first is associated with the anti-socialist restaurant atmosphere surrounding gypsy-music performances, at which 'immoral' female singers accept money from wealthy patrons. The second meaning is associated with inauthentic Roma music or pseudo-gypsy songs performed by Russian singers. In the fight against *tsyganshchina*, the Soviet state encouraged 'authentic' gypsy art and in 1931 created the State Romani Theatre, which was under complete state ideological control. During World War II, 500,000 Roma, along with millions of Jews, were exterminated by the Nazis.

In contemporary Russia, the traditional fascination with gypsy music and performance coexists with distrust, prejudice, and suspicion. Gypsies, who, often sell fake cigarettes and cosmetics or rob and deceive naïve and simple-hearted customers while telling their fortunes, are considered dangerous by Russians. Roma are also blamed for various illegal operations, such as drug trafficking and smuggling. Yet gypsy songs and music remain extremely popular among Russians: Gypsy performers star in stage performances, concerts, and television programmes and sing and play at expensive restaurants. Various recordings of gypsy songs or Russian romances performed by gypsy musicians remain bestsellers today.

See also: folk song; Gypsy music; Jews; Pushkin, Aleksandr; romance; Russian Orthodoxy; Slichenko, Nikolai

Further reading

Crowe, D. (1995) *A History of the Gypsies of Eastern Europe and Russia*, New York: St. Martin's Press.

Lemon, A. (2000) *Between Two Fires: Gypsy Performance and Romani Memory from Pushkin to Postsocialism*, Durham, NC: Duke University Press.

Slichenko, N. (1984) 'From Campfire to Footlights: Gypsies in the Theater', *UNESCO Courier*, 10: 26–8.

TATIANA SMORODINSKAYA

Gypsy music (tsyganskaia muzyka)

Gypsy music has been popular in Russia since the nineteenth century. Russian gypsies adapted Russian folk songs to their musical traditions, modified their intonation and performed them with great success in Russian. Authentic Gypsy songs, with their passionate and sensual overtones and associated with a romanticized sense of freedom, always fascinated Russian listeners. In the Soviet era, Gypsy music was associated with 'decadent' bourgeois values, as a result the term *tsyganshchina* was coined. It refers to *tsygane* (Gypsies or Roma), and, like all Russian terms ending in *-shchina*, has a pejorative connotation. The second meaning of this term refers to the performance style itself, specifically to inauthentic, stylized Gypsy music performed by Russian singers. In the fight against *tsyganshchina* the Soviet state encouraged 'authentic' Gypsy art and created the State Romani Theatre, which was under complete state ideological control. In the 1970s and 1980s Gypsy singers, dancers, and musicians gained great popularity. The Romen Trio, Valentina Ponomareva, Lialia Chernaia, Nikolai Slichenko, and others were participants in major festive events on television and at official concerts. Gypsy musicians are virtuoso violin and guitar performers, such as the Kolpakov Trio, world famous masters of the Russian seven-string guitar.

See also: Gypsy/Roma; internationalism; popular music, Soviet; Slichenko, Nikolai

TATIANA SMORODINSKAYA

Hall of Columns (Kolonnyi zal Doma soiuzov)

Built in 1780–90 by Matvei Kazakov as *Blagorodnoe sobranie* (Noble Assembly), the Hall of Columns, famous for its crystal chandeliers and white Corinthian columns, is a part of the House of Unions (*Dom soiuzov*). Pushkin, Lermontov and Tolstoi danced at balls in the Noble Assembly; Tchaikovsky, Rimskii-Korsakov, Rakhmaninov, and Liszt performed there. Lenin's funeral took place in the Hall in 1924, the event immortalized by Vladimir Maiakovskii in the poem 'Vladimir Ilich Lenin': '*Vovek takogo bestsennogo gruza eshche ne nesli okeany nashi kak grob etot krasnyi k domu soiuzov plyvushchii na spinakh rydanii i marshei.* ('Never before was such a priceless load carried by our oceans as this red coffin to the House of Unions, floating on the backs of weeping and marches' [trans. Paperny]). Subsequent funerals of many prominent political figures, including Stalin, took place in the Hall. Because of its excellent acoustical qualities, it has also become a venue for musical performances.

VLADIMIR PAPERNY

hammer and sickle

In Russia, 'sickle and hammer' (*serp i molot*), has been the main Soviet state emblem since 1923, a symbol of the power of labour, the solidarity of workers and peasants, and the glory of Communism. The emblem was introduced at the 5th Congress of Soviets (10 July 1918) and was first represented in the state seal of the Council of People's Commissars (26 July 1918). The hammer and sickle became part of the flag of the USSR, together with the red star, in 1923. Thereafter it appeared on flags and crests of other Soviet republics and was officially confirmed as the state's main emblem in the Russian (RSFSR) constitutions of 1937 and 1977. The representation of the hammer and sickle was defined in detail by the decree on the State flag of the USSR (19 August 1955). It was then reproduced on all documents, army and railroad workers' uniforms, as a logo for transportation systems on posters, and on medals.

The most famous representation of the hammer and sickle in sculpture is on Vera Mukhina's famous statue 'Worker and Peasant' (*Rabochii i krestianka*, 1935), known internationally as the logo of the Soviet-founded Moscow film company Mosfilm. Dozens of Soviet enterprises, places of recreation, and other institutions are named after this emblem. In the 1930s, twin boys would sometimes be given the names 'Molot' (hammer) and 'Serp' (sickle). During and after perestroika, the emblem became a favourite target of cartoonists; humorous verses (*chastushki*) about the hammer and sickle that proliferated during the Thaw and Stagnation eras were published only then.

See also: chastushka; constitutions; perestroika and glasnost; Stagnation; state symbols, Soviet; Thaw

Further reading

Lahusen, T. (1997) *Socialist Realism without Shores*, Durham, NC: Duke University Press.

Patrick, M. (1933) *Hammer and Sickle*, London: Mathews & Marrot.

Taylor, B. (1991–92) *Art and Literature under the Bolsheviks*, 2 vols, London: Pluto Press.

GASAN GUSEJNOV

hazing (dedovshchina)

Known in the Soviet/Russian Army as *dedovshchina* (from *ded* – grandfather). Army service in Russia is obligatory, and conscripts enlist for two years. The newest recruits usually undergo systematic, organized bullying by more experienced soldiers. The violence, physical abuse and moral humiliation often lead to suicide, murder, mental breakdowns, and desertion of the victimized soldiers. *Dedovshchina* continues to be a major problem in the contemporary Russian army, though seldom acknowledged by military officials.

TATIANA SMORODINSKAYA

headgear

The hat is an obligatory part of most Russians' outerwear for at least half the year, and often longer. Russian hats and scarves are designed to last for frequent use in cold winters and snow. Common hats are the fur hat (*shapka* or *shapka-ushanka*), the simple leather or woollen cap (*kepka*), made of cotton in the summer variant, and, mostly for older women, a woollen headscarf (*platok*).

The fur hat (*shapka*) is the classic and most prestigious Russian hat for both sexes. It can be made with fur as inexpensive as rabbit and as expensive as mink or sable. Fur hats, like fur coats, are valued for their warmth and natural waterproofing. The relative status of various kinds of fur hats is described in Vladimir Voinovich's satire on the Soviet Writers' Union, *Shapka* (*The Fur Hat*). Men's fur hats usually come with ear flaps and are called *shapka-ushanka*; however, it is a sign of pride not to use the ear flaps, keeping them tied instead. Thus one often sees only children or dwellers in extreme cold with the ear flaps tied under their chins.

In less severe weather, the favourite hat among many, particularly working-class, men is a simple cap (*kepka*) of leather or wool. The *kepka* was part of Vladimir Lenin's political image and is immortalized in statues of Lenin that still stand in some cities; today it is also associated with Moscow Mayor Iurii Luzhkov. A larger version of the cap, colloquially called an *aeroport* (airport), is associated with Caucasians selling various wares at markets.

The classic Cossack hat, the tall, sheepskin *papakha*, is an emblem of the Cossacks; it can also be found in the Caucasus. It is also part of the uniform for Russian generals.

The most common headgear worn by Russian peasant women today, and sometimes by urban Russian women, is the elaborately decorated, domestically manufactured woollen scarf, *platok*. Traditionally hand-woven, today the *platok* is primarily produced in specialized factories; the scarves are decorated in flower patterns and bright colours and are considered an emblem of Russia. Some women prefer a plainer alternative: fluffy white or grey woollen scarves, also produced in special factories today (although some are undoubtedly still hand-crocheted), are popular among Russian women as well. Both flowered and plain scarves are wrapped under the chin and around the neck and tied in front or in the back, thus covering the head and hair entirely. Accordingly, the *platok* is commonly worn in Russian Orthodox churches, where women are required to cover their heads and preferably their hair. Some women use the *platok*, in either the flowered or the plain variant, as a Russian fashion alternative and drape it over their shoulders as a shawl.

See also: Caucasus; coats; Cossacks; Lenin, Vladimir Ilich; Luzhkov, Iurii; market (rynok); Russian Orthodoxy; unions, creative, Soviet; Voinovich, Vladimir

KAREN EVANS-ROMAINE

health

Like many scarce commodities, health has been greatly valued in Russia, both before and after the Soviet period. A philosophy of personal exercise, known as physical culture (*fizkultura*), was strongly emphasized in the Soviet era to maintain a healthy workforce. In a society plagued by industrial pollution and environmental destruction, public emphasis was also placed on ecological purity, which was believed to have pronounced health benefits. Sponsored trips to such spa locations were and are highly prized.

In a society where technological medical solutions were prohibitively expensive or simply unavailable, health beliefs and practices have tended to be strongly traditional. Folk beliefs figure prominently in many people's lives. Avoiding exposure to cold, and even to cold beverages, is often justified to avoid infection; Russians likewise may avoid power lines or close exposure to television sets or computer monitors.

Vodka figures prominently in many folk remedies for various ailments, as do teas and herbal remedies. Occasionally occult practices hold sway, from folk shamanism (*znakharstvo*) to white magic and ESP. Water from springs, particularly sacred springs, is prized for its confluence of religion and purity.

Versions of medical therapies are also widely available, including easily accessible antibiotics, probiotic formulations, and even bacteriophage, with associated indications, primarily for treatment of infections and promotion of general health. Even traditional physicians make many of these therapies available.

Unfortunately, despite the considerable energy focused on personal health, Russian society is marked by a dramatic decline in life expectancy and quality, related primarily to alcoholism, tobacco use, malnutrition, atherosclerosis, and the rising tide of infectious disease. The remarkable decline in health, termed *katastroika* by some, did not begin with the fall of the Soviet Union, but arose in the context of the Cold War.

See also: Cold War; fitness; medical system; perestroika and glasnost; shamanism

SAMUEL BROWN

Helsinki Group

The Moscow Helsinki Group (MHG) is the oldest network non-governmental organization in Russia and one of the largest. It was created by an independent public group headed by the physicist and public activist Iurii Orlov (1976) to establish control over the execution of the humanitarian sections of the Final Act of the Helsinki Agreement. Members of the group were Liudmila Alekseeva (who later became its chairwoman), Mikhail Bernshtam, Elena Bonner, Aleksandr Ginzburg, Petr Grigorenko, Aleksandr Korchak, Malva Landa, Anatolii Marchenko, Vitalii Rubin, and Anatolii Shcharanskii. From its first days MHG was persecuted; various members were arrested and sentenced to imprisonment and exile, while others were forced to emigrate. At present MHG serves as a resource centre for hundreds of regional non-government organizations, rendering organizational, informational, and educational assistance and other support. The major activities of MHG encompass monitoring, education, legal programmes, and support of civil coalitions. MHG's annual reports on the state of human rights in Russia serve as an alternative to official publications on the topic.

See also: democratic reform movement; dissident; human rights organizations; Sakharov, Andrei

ELENA OZNOBKINA

Hermitage

The State Hermitage Museum, in St. Petersburg, is the best-known museum in Russia and one of the leading museums in the world. Its particular strength is Western European art from the pre-Renaissance to the avant-garde, but it also boasts valuable collections of Egyptian and Asian artefacts, Greek and Roman antiquities, and exhibits related to Russian history and culture. The Hermitage houses three million items dating from the Stone Age to the present day, displayed in six buildings: the former royal residence (the Winter Palace, 1762, designed by Francesco Bartolomeo Rastrelli), the Small Hermitage (1775, architects Iurii Veldten and Jean Baptiste de la Mothe), Grand Hermitage (1782, architect Veldten), the Hermitage Theatre (1783, architect Giacomo Quarenghi), the New Hermitage (1852, architect Leo von Klenze), and, since 1999, the Eastern Wing of the former Russian Army General Headquarters (1827, architect Carlo Rossi). The museum dates back to 1764, when Catherine II acquired the collection of Johann Ernest Gotzkowski and ordered the construction of a private picture gallery that she called her 'hermitage'. The museum grew rapidly, as the Romanov family continued to acquire art all over the world. Inspired by galleries in Munich, Nicolas I opened the Hermitage to the public in 1852.

During World War I, the Hermitage housed a hospital; in 1917, the Winter Palace was briefly the seat of the Provisional Government. The Bolsheviks' storming of the Winter Palace (25 October [7 November] 1917) marked the beginning of the Revolution. Subsequently the Hermitage became a state museum. In 1941, a large part of its collection (over one million items) was evacuated to Sverdlovsk (now Ekaterinburg). The museum was hit during the Siege of Leningrad by two bombs and thirty shells, but all damaged halls were subsequently restored. Under the leadership of the current director, Mikhail Piotrovskii, the Hermitage has become a world-class museum, equipped with cutting-edge technology and conducting a range of educational programmes. Its international reputation was further bolstered by Aleksandr Sokurov's 2002 experimental film, *Russian Ark*, which explores 200 years of Russian history with the Hermitage as a backdrop.

See also: Ekaterinburg; St. Petersburg; Sokurov, Aleksandr; World War II (Great Patriotic War)

MARIA RUBINS

hero-cities

An honorary title awarded to twelve Soviet cities for the courageous acts of their citizens in World War II (the Great Patriotic War). In 1942, the title was given to Leningrad (St. Petersburg), Odessa, Sevastopol, and Stalingrad (Volgograd); later the cities of Kerch, Kiev, Minsk, Moscow,

Murmansk, Novorossiisk, Smolensk, and Tula received that designation.

See also: Kiev; Moscow; Odessa; St. Petersburg

JENNIFER RYAN TISHLER

Historical Museum and the Upper Retail Arcade

See: Red Square

historical novel

As one of Russian literature's most popular genres, the historical novel of the Soviet period was frequently used for two contradictory purposes: to promote Soviet ideals, and to express, in a disguised form, resistance to official Soviet ideology. Since the Socialist Realist historical novel focused primarily on the legacy of revolution throughout Russian and Western history, it most frequently cast the historical narrative of Soviet officialdom in epic form: Petr Proskurin's *Sudba* (*Fate*, 1972), and Aleksei Ivanov's *Vechnyi zov* (*Eternal Call*, 1970–76). Liberal writers considered the historical novel a possible outlet for airing their dissatisfaction with current political pressures. Often burying their critical messages in multi-layered historical narratives, such authors as Natan Eidelman, Bulat Okudzhava, Iurii Davydov, Iurii Trifovov, and Igor Efimov camouflaged contemporary issues with elaborated historical contexts. They provided their readership with an alternative vision of the most decisive periods of Russian and world history, while demonstrating interconnectivity between past and present.

During the early days of the Thaw, interest in historical fiction waned, transferred to published non-fiction that pertained only to the most recent history, such as repressions of the Great Terror and forgotten or misinterpreted events of World War II. Esteem for the historical novel revived in the 1970s, when the historical biographical novel enjoyed considerable popularity. The literary series *Zhizn zamechatelnykh liudei* (Lives of Remarkable People), established in

1933 under the leadership of Maksim Gorkii, was employed by liberal writers as an outlet for hidden attacks on Soviet ideology. ZhZL's list of personae included not only politically acceptable representatives of the past, but also political rebels, such as nineteenth-century philosopher Petr Chaadaev, who inspired Aleksei Lebedev's *Chaadaev* (1965), and the Decembrist Mikhail Lunin, whose biography prompted Natan Eidelman's *Lunin* (1970). Both narratives achieved canonical status among the liberal intelligentsia, owing to their emphasis on the value of individual resistance to corruption.

The 1970s also witnessed the establishment of a series of historical biographies entitled *Plamennye revolutsionery* (Ardent Revolutionaries) by Politizdat, the publishing house of the Communist Party's Central Committee. Under the auspices of *Plamennye revolutsionery*, historical biographies of revolutionaries were written, paradoxically, by writers known for their liberal views and even those under serious suspicion by Soviet authorities. Important examples include Igor Efimov's *Svergnut vsiakoe igo* (*Topple Every Yoke*, 1977), on the history of the English revolution and its independent thinker John Lilburn; Bulat Okhudzhava's *Glotok svobody* (*Sip of Freedom*, 1969), on the Decembrist Pavel Pestel; and Iurii Trifonov's *Neterpenie* (*Impatience*, 1973), on the populist revolutionary Andrei Zheliabov. At the core of these narratives were issues regarding the complicated relationship between free-thinking individuals and oppressive states, the price of freedom and equality, and the use of violence in the realization of utopian dreams.

Although such historical novels were directed toward readers from the Soviet intelligentsia, the attraction of works written by Valentin Pikul made this genre popular for mass culture as well. Such novels as *Baiazet* (1961) and *Perom i shpagoi* (*With Quill and Sword*, 1972) were often criticized by respected literati for their low artistic quality, the presentation of history as a series of detective stories and scandals, and their deviation from historical facts for the sake of sensationalism. Pikul nevertheless remained extremely popular, garnering a broad readership during the Stagnation years.

An alternative use of historical prose during the late 1970s and 1980s is exemplified in Okudzhava's works. His primary conviction –

that historical fact is merely a trigger that allows the author to create allegorical narratives – made possible a free interpretation of historical realia. The intelligentsia prized his historical novels for their concern with the individual's survival in history. Among the most popular were *Puteshestvie diletantov* (*Journey of Dilettantes*, 1976) and *Svidanie s Bonapartom* (*Meeting with Bonaparte*, 1983).

With glasnost, non-fiction once again became readers' major focus, far surpassing interest in the historical novel. The most innovative development in this genre of the post-Soviet period may be attributed to Vladimir Sharov. His quasi-historical novels *Sled v sled* (*Step for Step*, 1991) and *Do i vo vrema* (*Before and During*, 1993) represent a postmodern twist on Russian history: his narratives are not restrained by chronological boundaries, but rather take advantage of a multi-layered plot with fictional elements dominating over historical data. Boris Akunin's original blend of the historical novel and the detective novel has gained immense popularity, while interesting experiments in historical narratives are currently being pioneered by Faina Grinberg and Ivanov.

See also: Akunin, Boris; censorship; detective fiction; intelligentsia; Okudzhava, Bulat; perestroika and glasnost; Pikul, Valentin; Thaw; Trifonov, Iurii; World War II (Great Patriotic War)

Further reading

Platt, K. (1997) *History in a Grotesque Key: Russian Literature and the Idea of Revolution*, Stanford, CA: Stanford University Press.

Rzhevsky, N. (1983) *Russian Literature and Ideology: Herzen, Dostoevsky, Leontiev, Tolstoy, Fadeev*, Urbana, IL: University of Illinois Press.

Wachtel, A.B. (1994) *An Obsession with History: Russian Writers Confront the Past*, Stanford, CA: Stanford University Press.

MARINA BALINA

hockey

Russia has been producing ice hockey legends since the mid-twentieth century, when Canadian

(NHL-style) hockey superseded ball hockey (an early variant of bandy) in the Soviet Union. The first official games of the 'new' hockey were played in December 1946, launching a two-month season in which seven teams contended for the championship. The Soviet hockey league expanded significantly over the years, dominated throughout by Moscow teams (Dinamo, Krylia Sovetov, Spartak, and especially TsSKA).

Despite poor-quality equipment and a dearth of indoor training facilities, and within a decade of winning their first world championship (1954), the Soviets had become a formidable force in international competition. They won every World Championship between 1963–71, and every Olympic gold medal – with the exception of a stunning defeat by Team USA in 1980 – between 1964–92 (the last of these as the Unified Team). This commanding record was bolstered, however, by the fact that in most cases the Soviets' opponents were officially amateur teams; and that, until perestroika, players were prohibited from leaving the USSR to play in the NHL. Against other professional teams (as in the Summit Series against Team Canada in 1972, and in Canada Cup tournaments between 1976–91), the Soviet team proved itself equal to, but not vastly better than, its foreign counterparts. Since the early 1990s, the Russian national team has been powerful but not dominant in international competition.

In 1989, Aleksandr Mogilny became the first Soviet hockey player to defect in order to play in the NHL. Since then, the number of Russian hockey players in the NHL has increased steadily and their impact has been tremendous. In 2004, history was made once again when for the first time Russian players were chosen first and second overall in the NHL draft.

See also: Bure, Pavel; Dinamo; Kharlamov, Valerii; perestroika and glasnost; Spartak; sport clubs and teams; sports, Soviet; Tretiak, Vladislav; TsSKA

RACHEL S. PLATONOV

holidays, post-Soviet

After the collapse of the Soviet Union, with the resulting economic and social changes, official

Russian ideology regarding official state holidays experienced a crisis in values. For some years, old Soviet holidays had co-existed with both pre-revolutionary Orthodox holidays and newly-declared official holidays. Every state-initiated attempt to change historical symbols, and holidays in particular, meets with sharply negative reactions from Russian citizens. The 'holiday calendar' continues to be a forum for political experimentation, beginning with Yeltsin's presidency in the 1990s and in effect during the new century.

The Day of the Great October Socialist Revolution (celebrated on 7 November), considered the main Soviet holiday, has lost its official association with the Bolshevik Revolution, and in 1996 by the order of the Russian president was renamed the Day of Harmony and Reconciliation (*Den soglasiia i primireniia*), symbolizing Russia's national and ideological unity. In 2005, that holiday was moved to 4 November, timed to the liberation of Russia from Polish-Lithuanian and Swedish troops by a Russian volunteer corps led by Prince Dmitrii Pozharskii and Kozma Minin in 1612.

Constitution Day, introduced as a state holiday by Stalin in 1936, was celebrated on 5 December. After the adoption of the so-called Brezhnev Constitution in 1977, the holiday was moved to 7 October. Since 1994, after the adoption of the latest version of the constitution by the Duma in 1993, the holiday was celebrated on 12 December. However, in 2005, Constitution Day was pronounced a working day, and Russians no longer perceive it as a holiday.

International Women's Day (*Mezhdunarodnyi zhenskii den*), celebrated on 8 March, has existed as an official holiday since the first days of the Soviet state. Originally not considered a holiday, but a purely political symbol, in 1965, it was pronounced a day off work. In the post-Soviet era, its celebration is perceived ambivalently: some consider it a manifestation of Soviet 'quotas' enforcing the participation of women in state policy. Others still perceive it as a welcome holiday and tribute to one's female friends, relatives, and co-workers, to whom both men and other women traditionally give gifts.

On 10 February 1995, the Duma adopted a federal law on 'days commemorating Russia's military achievements and victories'; this law changed the previously existing Soviet Army and Navy Day (*Den Sovetskoi armii i voenno-morskogo flota*), celebrated on 23 February but considered a working day, to an official holiday from work, called Defenders of the Fatherland Day (*Den zashchitnika Otechestva*). To most Russians, this holiday is considered the male counterpart to International Women's Day, marked with gift-giving to one's male relatives, friends, and co-workers.

Another important Soviet holiday left in the contemporary Russian calendar is 1 May, International Workers' Solidarity Day (*Den mezhdunarodnoi solidarnosti trudiashchikhsia*). The traditional Soviet holiday demonstration on Red Square, greeted by Communist leaders from the rostrum of the Lenin Mausoleum, was held for the last time on 1 May 1990. In 1992, the holiday was renamed Spring and Labour Holiday (*Prazdnik vesny i truda*). In the post-Soviet era, this holiday has assumed various forms, from a day of pro-Communist political demonstrations to the unofficial observation of the summer season, when many citizens open up their dachas and begin summer planting.

According to the 112th article of the Russian Federation Labour Code, official state holidays and days off work are the following: 1–5 January (New Year holidays), 7 January (Orthodox Christmas), 23 February (Defenders of the Fatherland Day), 8 March (International Women's Day), 1 May (Spring and Labour Holiday), 9 May (Victory Day, continued from Soviet times and commemorating the capitulation of Berlin and the end of World War II for the Soviet Union), 12 June (Russia Day, a new Russian state holiday, also called Independence Day, commemorating the day in 1990 on which the Russian Federated Soviet Socialist Republic declared sovereignty from the Soviet Union), and 4 November (the Day of Harmony and Reconciliation).

In addition to these official holidays, there are unofficial but popular Russian holidays that existed in the Soviet era, such as the Old New Year (14 January, New Year's Day according to the Russian Orthodox Calendar), and Students' Day (25 January, also called St. Tatiana's Day). These have been supplemented by newly celebrated unofficial Western holidays, particularly Halloween (31 October) and St. Valentine's Day (14 February).

Major Russian Orthodox Church holidays, banned in the USSR, now are being widely celebrated. In addition to Christmas, pronounced a state holiday, Russians observe the Baptism of Christ (*Kreshchenie Gospodne*, 19 January), Orthodox Easter (calculated differently from Western Easter and thus celebrated on a different Sunday), Pentecost or Whitsun (*Troitsa*, or Trinity, celebrated forty days after Easter), and Transfiguration (*Preobrazhenie Gospodne*, 19 August, also called Our Saviour of the Apples, *Iablochnyi Spas*). Some ancient Russian holidays, which go back to pagan traditions and were adjusted to Christianity, are still celebrated, particularly Shrovetide (*Maslenitsa*, the week before the beginning of Lent) and St. John's Day (*Den Ivana Kupala*, 23 June).

There is, finally, a large number of professional holidays, celebrating various professions but not allowing days off work, many of which are carryovers from the Soviet era, including Cosmonauts Day (*Den kosmonavtiki*, 12 April, commemorating Gagarin's first space flight in 1961), Radio Day (7 May), Marines' Day (*Den vozdushno-desantnykh voisk*, 2 August), and Militia Day (*Den militsii*, 10 November). Some holidays and commemorative days were introduced after perestroika, for example: Prosecutors' Day (*Den rabotnikov prokuratury*, 12 January, since 1995), Fishermen's Day (*Den rybaka*, second Sunday in July, since 1988), Pushkin Day (*Den Pushkina*, 6 June, since 1998, commemorating the poet's birthday), and Nature Preserve Day (*Den zapovednikov*, 11 January, since 1997).

A phenomenon particular to the celebration of official Russian holidays is the notion of the 'movable feast': days around holidays are shifted in order to maximize the length of weekends. For example, if 1 May falls on a Sunday, 2 May is generally also considered a day off work; if those two days fall on a Tuesday and Wednesday, then the previous Saturday is often declared a working day, so that it 'substitutes' for Monday and many Russian citizens can take a four-day weekend from Sunday through Wednesday. If 8 March, a single-day holiday, falls on a Thursday, then Sunday may 'substitute' for Friday, in order to create a three-day weekend on Thursday through Saturday, with

Sunday beginning a new work week. Such 'substitutions' are often declared with little advance notice, and workers listen carefully for such announcements on the news.

See also: Brezhnev, Leonid; Communist ideology; Communist Party; constitutions; Duma; Gagarin, Iurii; holidays, Russian Orthodox; holidays, Soviet; Lent; Maslenitsa; militia (police); Pushkin, Aleksandr; Putin, Vladimir; Stalin, Iosif; World War II (Great Patriotic War); Yeltsin, Boris

ELENA OMELCHENKO

holidays, Russian Orthodox

Until October 1917, Russian Orthodox holidays and imperial anniversaries were the only legal holidays in the Russian empire. The Bolsheviks sought to replace them with secular ones. After the 1988 celebrations of the millennium of Christianity in Rus, however, the post-Soviet government again began to promote Russian Orthodox celebrations.

Some key Russian Orthodox holidays are common to Christian Europe: the Annunciation, Christmas, Candlemas (*Sretenie*), Good Friday, and Easter. Russian Orthodox specificities of these feasts include the blessing of apples at Transfiguration (6 August), the blessing of pussy willows on Palm Sunday, and the blessing of water on Theophany (6 January).

Some saints' days had a military significance both in imperial Russia and after 1991. Cossacks have a particular veneration for the holiday of *Pokrov*, the Intercession of the Mother of God (1 October). St. Nicholas and St. Aleksandr Nevskii are the patrons of the Russian navy, St. Dimitrii and the Archangel Michael the patrons of the armed forces, and St. George the patron of both the cavalry and the city of Moscow. The beheading of St. John the Baptist (11 September) commemorates Orthodox soldiers slain in battle. Schoolchildren celebrate St. Tatiana's Day (12 January). Native Russian saints include St. Vladimir and St. Olga, St. Seraphim of Sarov, and St. Sergii of Radonezh.

The canonization of Soviet-era martyrs, particularly Nicholas II, was hotly contested in the late 1990s. Icons of the Virgin Mary are widely venerated and have their own national holidays as well. After 2004, the traditional celebration of the Kazan Icon (4 November) acquired fresh significance as a substitute for the 7 November commemoration of the 1917 Revolution.

See also: Christmas, Orthodox; Easter, Orthodox; Russian Orthodoxy

Further reading

Smith, K. (2002) *Mythmaking in the New Russia: Politics and Memory in the Yeltsin Era*, Ithaca, NY: Cornell University Press.

NADIESZDA KIZENKO

holidays, Soviet

Most Soviet holidays were created as instruments through which culture could be shaped by Communist ideology. That is not to say that Soviet holidays were not widely popular. In fact, some Soviet holidays, such as International Women's Day, continue to be celebrated throughout much of the former Soviet world. Other Soviet holidays have been reinterpreted in accordance with post-Soviet values.

One of the first tasks of any revolutionary government is to remake the national culture to reflect the new official values. Soviet holidays not only were established to reflect Communist values, but also were timed to replace traditional holidays usually celebrated at a particular time of year. For example, the Anniversary of the October Revolution (7 November) was used to cement Soviet identity through the celebration of a key event in Soviet history, while the New Year celebration (1 January) was used to transfer the symbolism of Christmas onto a secular, international holiday.

Holidays that originated in Europe or the United States reflected Soviet internationalism. Internationalist holidays included May Day (1 May) and International Women's Day (8 March). May Day is a European holiday that has pagan roots, but it was adopted by the international labour movement to celebrate workers. It was celebrated with an enormous military-artistic parade in Red Square and smaller parades in the centres of other Soviet cities. Women's Day is a pre-Revolutionary socialist holiday that originally advocated universal women's suffrage in the United States. In the Soviet Union it came to be an occasion when men and boys were expected to give presents to women and girls. Soviet Army Day (23 February) was the inverse, a celebration of men honouring their service to the country.

Other Soviet holidays celebrated particular aspects of Soviet culture. Lenin's birthday (22 April) was an important commemorative holiday, established by Stalin after Lenin's death. After World War II, one of the Soviet Union's most important holidays, Victory Day (9 May), not only celebrated the end of a tragic war that took millions of Soviet lives, but also offered an opportunity to demonstrate military prowess, patriotism, and the 'friendship of the Soviet peoples'.

In addition to these national holidays, the Soviet Union celebrated a number of other days honouring people in a particular profession, such as teachers. Since the Soviet Union was conceived of as a workers' state, these days celebrating different kinds of workers were important to Soviet national culture.

See also: Communist ideology; holidays, post-Soviet; internationalism; Red Square; World War II (Great Patriotic War)

Further reading

Binns, C. (1979–80) 'The Changing Face of Power: Revolution and Accommodation in the Development of the Soviet Ceremonial System: Part I & II.', *Man* 14/15:170–87.

Lane, C. (1981) *The Rites of Rulers: Ritual in Industrial Society – The Soviet Case*, Cambridge: Cambridge University Press.

LAURA ADAMS

holy fool (iurodivyi, iurodivaia)

In the Orthodox tradition, a 'fool for Christ' or 'holy fool' was someone who pretended to be feeble-minded so as to be mocked by others, thus attaining greater humility. This 'foolishness', however, allowed the holy fool to criticize authority with impunity. Russian holy fools who exercised this subversive function include Saints Nikolai of Pskov and Vasilii the Blessed (Vasilii blazhennyi), who mocked Ivan the Terrible, and Kseniia of St. Petersburg. Images of the holy fool in Russian culture include Nikolka in Aleksandr Pushkin's *Boris Godunov*, Prince Myshkin in Fedor Dostoevskii's *Idiot*, Aleksandr Solzhenitsyn's Matrena and Ivan Denisovich, and Vasilii Perov's painting *The Holy One*; the term has also been extended to composer Dmitrii Shostakovich. The holy fool serves as a model for protagonists of recent women's prose, such as Svetlana Vasilenko's *Little Fool* (*Durochka*, 1998).

See also: Russian Orthodoxy; Shostakovich, Dmitrii; Solzhenitsyn, Aleksandr; Vasilenko, Svetlana

NADIESZDA KIZENKO

Holy Trinity-St. Sergius Monastery (Troitse-Sergieva Lavra)

Monastery and important Russian Orthodox spiritual centre located northeast of Moscow, in Sergiev Posad (Zagorsk in the Soviet era). Founded in 1340 by St. Sergius of Radonezh, his small wooden Church of the Holy Trinity rapidly grew into a monastery that became the spiritual centre of Muscovite Russia and the pillar of its politico-cultural identity. Its principal landmarks include the Trinity Cathedral (1422–23), containing the tomb of St. Sergius and a unique iconostasis; the Church of the Holy Spirit (1476–77); the five-domed Cathedral of the Assumption (1559–85); the Muscovite Baroque Refectory with the Church of St. Sergius (1692), and the monumental Baroque belfry (1740). The Theological Seminary, founded in 1742 and expanded into the Moscow Theological Academy (1814), remains Russia's principal seminary and a place of pilgrimage. In 1744, the monastery was designated a lavra (the highest category of Orthodox monasteries), and in 1993 it made the UNESCO World Cultural Heritage List.

See also: icon (ikona); Russian Orthodoxy

TATIANA SENKEVITCH

homelessness

Homelessness in the Soviet Union and in Russia has proved a widespread and lasting phenomenon. Although both the 1977 and the 1993 Constitutions guarantee all citizens the right to housing, authorities have never been able to meet demand. From the late 1920s to the mid-1980s the government denied the existence of homelessness as a large-scale problem. The post-Soviet Russian government, by contrast, has acknowledged it, and has redefined homelessness as a social, not criminal, issue, but has taken few steps to address it.

Determining the number of homeless in Russia today is problematic, but estimates generally range from three to five million. Most official statistics define homelessness as 'rooflessness', though others try to include the 'concealed homeless', counting all those living in overcrowded or otherwise inadequate conditions. Given the numerous cases of people living with friends, in other unregistered communal arrangements, or in hostels, as well as those unable to escape domestic violence for lack of other living arrangements, these figures are likely considerably higher.

The introduction of the *propiska* (residence permit) system in the 1930s gave the homeless some degree of negative formalization as a group. Undesirable residents were often not issued a *propiska* in an attempt to drive them out of certain areas. Some citizens lost their housing while serving prison sentences, thereby losing their *propiska*. Still others were unable to obtain one after graduating from an orphanage. In addition, many are registered at residences where they cannot live for various reasons. All these citizens, particularly those living on the street, are referred to by the semi-official acronym 'BOMZh', meaning 'without fixed abode' (*Bez opredelennogo mesta zhitelstva*).

In the Soviet Union, nearly all social benefits were distributed by regional or municipal authorities. Since these were responsible only to citizens officially residing within their region or municipality, BOMZhi (plural) were *de facto* denied access to such services and rights as medical treatment and, importantly, offers of employment and housing. The reluctance of most authorities to issue a *propiska* to someone without employment or housing created a Catch-22 situation: it was virtually impossible to escape the status of BOMZh. Moreover, that status not only violated passport laws, but was also considered proof of social parasitism (*tuneiadstvo*) and could bring a sentence of up to ten years of corrective labour.

Although officially renamed and revamped, most elements of the *propiska* system remain in place today and continue to pose the same hurdles for the homeless. By most estimates, homelessness increased dramatically in the mid-1990s, owing to many factors, including the disappearance of the Soviet social safety net, a large influx of refugees and forced migrants from other Soviet republics, the privatization of the real estate market, and the many subsequent brokerage scams organized by profiteers.

See also: communal apartment; constitutions; corrective labour institutions; housing, Soviet and post-Soviet; passport; propiska

Further reading

Beigulenko, Y. (1999) 'Homelessness in Russia: The Scope of the Problem and the Remedies in Place', in P. Kennet and A. Marsh (eds) *Homelessness: Exploring the New Terrain*, Bristol: Policy Press.

Höjdestrand, T. (2003) 'The Soviet-Russian Production of Homelessness. Propiska, Housing, Privatisation', in *Anthrobase*. Available at: http://www.anthrobase.com/txt/H/Hoejsdestrand_T_01.htm

Matthews, M. (1993) *The Passport Society: Controlling Movement in Russia and the USSR*, Boulder, CO: Westview Press.

Stephenson, S. (2000) 'The Russian Homeless', in S. Hutton and G. Redmond (eds) *Poverty in Transition Economies*, London: Routledge.

DAVID HUNTER SMITH

homosexuality

As supported by documentary evidence, Russians have been engaging in homosexual activities throughout their history, and for a long time this behaviour was more tolerated by the Russian society than by those in the West. Sodomy was first criminalized by Peter the Great, but prosecutions were rare. However, as in the West, we can speak of a development of a homosexual identity and a distinct subculture, especially in metropolitan centres, only in the second half of the nineteenth century, coinciding with the rise of medical discourse about homosexuality.

During the early twentieth century, after the 1905 relaxation of censorship, depictions of gay and lesbian love in Russian poetry and prose mushroomed; its leading male exponent was Mikhail Kuzmin, and its chief female representative, Sofia Parnok. The Bolshevik Revolution temporarily decriminalized sodomy, but homosexuality continued to be treated as a medical problem, and increasingly, as a 'bourgeois perversion'; it was recriminalized by Stalin in 1934. The sodomy law was used on a number of occasions against prominent cultural figures (such as Sergei Paradzhanov). Although female homosexuality was never punishable by law, lesbians were routinely subjected to punitive psychiatry. Unmentionable in public discourse until glasnost, in Soviet-era public consciousness, homosexuality was connected with the prison system, especially with male rape as a symbolic act of humiliation.

The fledgling Russian lesbian and gay rights movement dating from the late 1980s has gone through many fits and starts. Although the sodomy law was repealed in 1993, and homosexuality is discussed with some frequency in the mass media, Russian attitudes to it remain intolerant. In large cities and on the Internet, however, the gay and lesbian subculture has been growing slowly but steadily. In contemporary Russian literature, Evgenii Kharitonov pioneered gay self-expression in *samizdat* during the 1970s, and a number of younger authors, most notably Yaroslav Mogutin, continue in his footsteps. Director Roman Viktiuk and the late Timur Novikov's New Academy of Fine Arts engage homosexual themes and aesthetics in theatre and art, respectively. The 2004 film *Ia liubliu tebia* (*You I Love*) evidences a growing acceptance of homosexuality.

See also: corrective labour institutions; Internet, Russian; Novikov, Timur; Paradzhanov, Sergei; samizdat; sex and sexuality; Viktiuk, Roman

Further reading

Healey, D. (2001) *Homosexual Desire in Revolutionary Russia: The Regulation of Sexual and Gender Dissent*, Chicago, IL: University of Chicago Press.

Kon, I. (1995) *The Sexual Revolution in Russia: From the Age of the Czars to Today*, New York: The Free Press.

Moss, K. (ed.) (1996) *Out of the Blue: Russia's Hidden Gay Literature: An Anthology*, San Francisco, CA: Gay Sunshine Press.

Schluter, D. (2002) *Gay Life in the Former USSR: Fraternity without Community*, New York: Routledge.

VITALY CHERNETSKY

honorary titles

The Soviet Union developed an extensive hierarchical system of honorary titles, in recognition of distinguished accomplishments by workers in all spheres. Cultural figures, such as actors or musicians, for example, could be awarded the title of Honoured Artist of the USSR or People's Artist of the USSR. Stakhanovite labourers and women performing prodigious reproductive feats also received the titles of Hero of Socialist Labour and Hero-Mother, respectively. Apart from the prestige of official recognition, recipients enjoyed access to various social benefits, such as larger apartments or the purchase of a car. Analogous but less prestigious titles could be awarded by republican and regional authorities. The Russian Federation has preserved a similar system of honorary titles.

See also: mother-heroine; Stakhanovism

DAVID HUNTER SMITH

hotels

With the rise of internationalism and increased efforts to promote cultural exchange and tourism in the post-war period, the Central Committee of the Communist Party allocated ever greater resources to the construction of hotels. Their design and scope differed from those of the emblematic luxury hotels of the late Imperial era, such as the *Metropol* and *Natsional*. Plans for construction between the late 1950s and early 1970s focused on: (1) aggressively increasing the total number of rooms; (2) diversifying kinds of accommodation so as to supplement hotels with camp sites, motels, and large but modest 'complexes' near resort centres on the Black Sea coast; and (3) expanding the number of Soviet cities open to servicing foreign guests, including, in particular, the capitals of the Central Asian and Baltic republics. The flow of tourists during this period rapidly outpaced the rate at which new hotels were developed. Consequently, visitors often returned home with tales of unexpectedly shared bedrooms or long nights in cramped lobbies and corridors. Also common were complaints about the poor service, the staff's inability to observe basic sanitary norms, the presence of KGB bugs in rooms, and frustrating encounters with *dezhurnye* (desk personnel on every floor), whose job it was to monitor guests' movements. Most often, Soviets were denied access to hotels, since the latter were primarily designed to house Western travellers, journalists, trade delegates, and diplomatic representatives. For the same reason, hotels became notorious sites of intrigue and forbidden fruit. American jazz, prohibited elsewhere, streamed out of bars where foreigners drank expensive, imported alcohol. Black marketeers bought and sold clothes, jewellery, and other goods, as well as illegally exchanging currency with foreign guests. And prostitutes, whose presence Soviet officials repeatedly denied, made a living off the steady influx of visitors to the country, a phenomenon captured in Petr Todorovskii's milestone film *Interdervochka* (*Intergirl*). Since the fall of Communism, many notable Soviet hotels from the 1960s and later, such as Moskva and Minsk, have been privatized, renovated or (symbolically) demolished.

See also: *Interdervochka*

Further reading

Drane, J. (1965) *Pilgrimage to Utopia*, Milwaukee, WI: Bruce Publishing.

Kunin, V. (1991) *Intergirl: A Hard Currency Prostitute*, trans. A.W. Bouis, New York: Bergh Publishing, Inc.

Nikolaevskaia, T. (2000) *Isskustvo zhit 1903–2003*, Moscow: Studiia DiF.

Thompson, K. (1959) *Eloise in Moscow*, New York: Simon and Schuster.

Wharton, A.J. (2001) *Building the Cold War: Hilton International Hotels and Modern Architecture*, Chicago, IL: University of Chicago Press.

SHAWN SALMON

House of Recordings (Dom zvukozapisi)

Also known as GDRZ (*Gosudarstvennyi dom radioveshchaniia i zvukozapisi*, State House of Radio Broadcasting and Sound Recordings), *Dom zvukozapisi* was founded in 1938 as a centre for radio and gramophone recordings. It received the Grand Prize for the first stereo recordings at the 1959 Industrial Exhibition in New York.

See also: April Factory; recording studios

OLGA ZASLAVSKY

housing, Soviet and post-Soviet

According to the Soviet model, urban housing was a form of social welfare: state-owned living space was distributed for free according to a per capita norm. Monthly fees for housing and utilities did not exceed a small portion of the family budget and did not cover the real cost of state-subsidised communal services. Access to housing, among other goods, depended on one's social position. Employers often provided housing for their employees (so-called *vedomstvennoe zhile*). Thus, people used but did not own what was given to them. Administrative control over residents' rights and population mobility was maintained with residence permits (*propiska*).

Most urban households occupied either a room in a communal apartment (*kommunalnaia kvartira*) in which several families, each with its own room, shared a common kitchen, bathroom, and toilet; or a separate apartment (*kvartira*); barracks and workers' dormitories were a common option for factory workers. Most of the urban population suffered from housing shortages and lived in overcrowded conditions, with neither privacy nor prospects of changing their situation. Although a separate apartment for each family was proclaimed the goal of state housing policy as early as the 1930s, and was later confirmed as the purpose of a large-scale housing construction programme launched by Khrushchev in the 1950s, it was never achieved. Even by the end of the 1980s, the number of those on apartment waiting lists varied among cities from 10 to 30 per cent of the population. Placement on the waiting list (*ochered*) was available to those whose living conditions were below the sanitary norm (*c.* 5 sq m per person) and to several segments of the population, including shock workers (*udarniki*), Heroes of the USSR, disabled persons, and families with many children. Beginning in the late 1950s, people could invest their money in construction by joining 'housing construction cooperatives'; another opportunity was to exchange living quarters with others (*obmen*).

As a result of Khrushchev's housing programme, low quality mass construction helped alleviate the housing problem by relocating some former occupants of communal apartments to tiny separate flats in poorly designed and constructed four- and five-storey buildings made mostly of prefabricated panels. Initially intended as a temporary solution, those buildings (*krushcheby*, a play on the word *trushcheby* [slum]) deteriorated severely over the decades, yet still accounted for nearly a quarter of all housing in Moscow in the early 1990s. During the Brezhnev era, suburban 'microdistricts' (*mikroraiony*) made of huge nine- to sixteen-storey apartment complexes contributed to the creation of unattractive cityscapes that made the outskirts of all Soviet cities look alike. The plot of Eldar Riazanov's popular film *Ironiia sudby* (*The Irony of Fate*, 1977) is structured around the confusion of virtually indistinguishable districts, street names, buildings, furniture, and interior decoration in the flats located in two different cities.

Shortages of living space, and of consumer goods and services, influenced the mentality and daily routine of Soviet citizens: in spite of the shortages, the dehumanizing uniformity of mass-produced items, and cramped housing, they had to adapt their living environment to normal domestic tasks; to attempt a sense of privacy, psychological security, and self-realization in a personal space; and to establish at least rudimentary domestic comfort (*uiut*). Do-it-yourself home improvements were ubiquitous in those homes where people did not completely abandon the idea of domesticity, as some did. Rooms held multiple functions: the 'large room' (not infrequently the only room, excluding the bathroom and kitchen) could serve as living room, study, and bedroom, sometimes for several family members.

While not realized in urban apartments, domesticity found its specifically Russian expression in the cultural phenomenon of the dacha: a small private house in the environs of the city or in the countryside, usually built on a small agricultural lot and inhabited mostly during the summer. As a result of a dacha-construction boom in the 1980s, more than one-third of Russian urban families had dachas, where they could try to create an environment to their taste.

Following two decades of stagnation in housing construction, the early post-Soviet housing situation (1994) is evidenced in figures on the distribution of various types of housing. Per 1000 households, an individual house was home to 248 Russian households (599 in rural areas); an individual apartment was home to 618 households; and a communal apartment to 49 households. In St. Petersburg, where the share of communal apartments was always higher than elsewhere, 224 households of every thousand were in communal apartments in 1994. The average living space allotment in Russia was 10.8 sq m, that is, around one-fifth of the average figure for the United States. Yet these quantitative data do not show the significant qualitative changes occurring in post-Soviet housing.

The privatization of housing has led to the emergence in the 1990s of a real estate market and, correspondingly, to the appearance of a class of owners, not simply residents, of premises. In the market economy, though the underprivileged sector of the population still needs low-cost housing, since the late 1990s there have been no shortages of goods, including housing; for many citizens, the only shortage is of money. New opportunities have contributed to considerable changes in cultural values: post-Soviet domesticity is a marked cultural trend, evident in the demand for numerous illustrated magazines and TV programmes on interior decoration, as well as in the booming market in construction, home-improvement, interior-decorating materials, and furniture. The success of IKEA and similar chains in Russia attests to this boom. The reform of the system of communal services (*ZhKH*, an abbreviation for *Zhilishchno-kommunalnoe khoziaistvo*) aimed at privatization and marketization of this branch of the economy forms part of current Russian economic policy. The Housing Code of the Russian Federation, enacted on 1 March 2005, serves as the legal basis of the post-Soviet situation in Russian housing.

See also: Brezhnev, Leonid; byt (everyday life); communal apartment; dacha; economic system, post-Soviet; economic system, Soviet; Krushchev, Nikita; privatization; propiska

Further reading

Brumfield, W. and Ruble, B. (eds) (1993) *Russian Housing in the Modern Age: Design and Social History*, Cambridge: Cambridge University Press.
Lovell, S. (2003) *Summerfolk: A History of the Dacha, 1710–2000*, Ithaca, NY: Cornell University Press.
Sosnovy, T. (1954) *The Housing Problem in the Soviet Union*, New York: Research Program on the USSR.
Utekhin, I. (2004) *Ocherki kommunalnogo byta* (Essays on Everyday Life in Communal Apartments), 2nd edn, Moscow: OGI.

ILIA UTEKHIN

human rights organizations

Human rights organizations are an important element of contemporary Russia's emerging civil society. Not united into one structure, they may act individually or jointly. According to the Moscow Helsinki Group, of the approximately 700 human rights organizations in Russia, 300 function regularly, while 100 have regular public office hours. The most famous include the Moscow Helsinki Group, Memorial, the Centre for Assistance in Reforming Criminal Justice, the Defence of Glasnost Fund, Soldiers' Mothers, Civil Control (St. Petersburg), Rights Defence Centre (Perm). Human rights organizations look after the state, its decisions, and actions of its officials, they also see to violations of the Russian laws, European conventions, international pacts, UN decisions.

Many human rights organizations specialize in certain problems, such as defending citizens from abuse by law-enforcement personnel; defending prisoners' rights, human rights in Chechnia, or the rights of refugees, women, soldiers, and children; and protecting freedom of speech or the environment. Violation of human rights in Russia remains an everyday problem: for example, the Moscow Committee for Civil Rights annually receives up to 15,000 letters of complaint. Few new human rights organizations have appeared in recent years, and some experts detect a crisis in their development – in the areas of personnel, finances, and ideology. Largely financed by American and European private and state funds, the organizations often lack sufficient resources to implement fundamental changes. Russian state and private funding is negligible and the majority of Russians approach these organizations' work sceptically.

See also: Helsinki Group; Memorial; perestroika and glasnost

ELENA OZNOBKINA

humour and satire, literary

In the Soviet period, Russian humour and satire were treated as a single literary mode and the terms were used near-synonymously. Humour, like satire, was regarded as essentially utilitarian, with the goal of developing the reader's social and political consciousness. After Stalin's death, humour and satire recovered some of their critical potential and writers tested the limits of acceptability. These limits proved to be inflexible during the last decades of the Soviet regime, but a number of significant works were written and published in *samizdat* and in the West.

Andrei Siniavskii (pseudonym Abram Terts) was not primarily a satirist, but his short novel *Sud idet* (*The Trial Begins*, 1956) is a 'phantasmagoric' (his term) satire on Stalinism. Vasilii Aksënov's *Stalnaia ptitsa* (*The Steel Bird*, written 1965, published 1977) and *Ostrov Krym* (*The Island of Crimea*, 1981) are allegories of Soviet history, the first focusing on Stalinism, the second on the Brezhnev period. Fazil Iskander's epic cycle *Sandro iz Chegema* (*Sandro of Chegem*) includes a number of satirical tales, including *Piry Valtasara* (*The Feasts of Belshazzar*, 1979), which portrays Stalin and his retinue in nocturnal revelry. His *Kroliki i udavy* (*Rabbits and Boa Constrictors*, 1980) is an extended beast fable; the rabbits (the passive Soviet people) live symbiotically with the boa constrictors (Stalinists), who hypnotize and devour them.

An early example of Russian postmodernism, Venedikt Erofeev's *Moskva-Petushki* (*Moscow to the End of the Line*, 1977) satirizes late Soviet culture, in which constant inebriation is the only possible *modus vivendi*. Sasha Sokolov's *Shkola dlia durakov* (*School for Fools*, 1976) is narrated by a schizophrenic boy whose innocence casts Soviet reality into sharp relief. In *Palisandriia* (*Astrophobia*, 1984), Sokolov moves from narrative experimentation to grotesque. Aleksandr Zinoviev is an extraordinarily prolific satirist of the post-Stalin period. His long, rambling *Ziiaushchie vysoty* (*The Yawning Heights*, 1976), *Svetloe budushchee* (*The Radiant Future*, 1978) and *Zheltyi dom* (*The Madhouse*, 1980) are trenchant indictments of Soviet culture. Sergei Dovlatov is the author of several satires of Soviet culture, including *Kompromiss* (*The Compromise*, 1981) and *Nashi* (*Ours*, 1983); these are collections of related character sketches and anecdotes. Perhaps the best-known satirist of this period is Vladimir Voinovich, often compared to Gogol, whose novels *Zhizn i neobychainye prikliucheniia soldata*

Ivana Chonkina (*The Life and Extraordinary Adventures of Private Ivan Chonkin*, 1969) and *Pretendent na prestol* (*Pretender to the Throne*, 1979) earned him acclaim. Many consider his *Ivankiada* (*The Ivankiad*, 1976), *Antisovetskii Sovetskii Soiuz* (*The Anti-Soviet Soviet Union*, 1986), *Moskva 2042* (*Moscow 2042*, 1987), *Shapka* (*The Fur Hat*, 1988) and *Monumentalnaia propaganda* (*Monumental Propaganda*, 2002) seminal works of the contemporary period. Evgenii Popov's *Dusha patriota* (*Soul of a Patriot*, 1989) ushered in the post-Soviet period as one of the first major works of Russian satire written in the absence of censorship. Viktor Pelevin's popular *Omon Ra* (1992), *Zhizn nasekomykh* (*The Life of Insects*, 1997), and *Generation P* (1999), are famous examples of postmodernist satire.

See also: Aksenov, Vasilii; censorship; Erofeev, Venedikt; Iskander, Fazil; Pelevin, Viktor; poetry, ironic; Siniavskii, Andrei; Sokolov, Sasha; Voinovich, Vladimir

KAREN RYAN

humour and satire, Soviet

In the Soviet Union, humour and satire simultaneously functioned in support of and in opposition to the Communist regime. As a tool of government propaganda, satire served to promote Communism and to mock deviations from the Communist Party line. Within the context of Soviet dogma, critics tended to differentiate between satire and humour, while stressing the social importance of the former. According to Soviet theory, satire deals with phenomena harmful to society, whereas humour focuses on socially innocuous facts. In accord with this interpretation, state-sanctioned satire attempted to dominate various forms of mass media (including satirical journals, such as *Krokodil*) and the performing arts. Among the most prominent officially-approved themes were phenomena that 'detracted' from the progress of the socialist state, including the shortcomings of Soviet society (such as alcoholism, bureaucracy, and the black market), as well as the 'negative influences' of international capitalism. In an attempt to deliver pure propaganda or to camouflage the latter as entertainment, in the early 1960s, the Soviet government launched a variety of humorous and satirical television and radio shows, such as the radio program *S dobrym utrom* (Good Morning), as well as the television shows *Kabachok 13 stulev* (The 13 Chairs Café) and KVN (Club of the Sunny and Smart). While the government generally intended these shows as propaganda, until the late 1970s the majority of Soviet citizens viewed these humorous performances as venues for entertainment, punctuated with understated irony.

Unable to express overtly dissident views under the pressure of Soviet censorship, many satirical writers and performers resorted to messages coded in so-called Aesopian language. This oblique satire allowed the authors to allude to certain facts instead of stating them openly. Subtle satire of this sort stood in opposition to official Soviet culture and was welcomed by Soviet audiences, as evidenced by Mikhail Zhvanetskii, who from the 1970s on enjoyed vast popularity for delivering his cleverly disguised anti-government criticism as a stand-up comic on the stage. Aesopian humour became the key to the so-called '16th page' of *Literaturnaia Gazeta* (Literary Gazette), which published humorous and satirical works by Viktoriia Tokareva, Andrei Bitov, Mikhail Mishin, and Arkadii Arkanov (this humorous section was later renamed *Klub 13 stulev* [*The 13 Chairs Café*]). The more overtly oppositional satirical works of bards such as Vladimir Vysotskii and Aleksandr Galich were censored and were clandestinely distributed primarily in the form of *samizdat* or *magnitizdat*. The predominant tone of these satirists was that of irony, scepticism, and disillusioned pessimism. Borrowing from the overall literary and artistic tonalities of the Stagnation era, Russian satirists often portrayed the lonely individual amidst a malevolent and hostile society.

The late 1970s and early 1980s witnessed a tightening of censorship that led to the disappearance of some satirical and humorous shows, along with conversion of others into 'harmless' humour or party-approved satire. For example, the prominent humour festival 'Iumorina', held since the early 1970s in Odessa, was banned in 1976 for deviations from the Party line. Many comedy theatres (including various *estrada* shows) that had opened for amateur innovations during the Thaw came under the Communist Party's close scrutiny. In the context of intensified censorship, humour expressing opposition to state dogma blossomed in underground, unofficial, private forms, such as the genre of *anekdot* (joke). *Anekdoty* as a form of expression and entertainment were exchanged in small private gatherings at home, in the workplace, and even in lines at grocery stores. This genre peaked in the 1970s and early 1980s, during the era of Stagnation. Circulated exclusively via word-of-mouth, this form of unofficial Soviet culture targeted prominent political figures and institutions, as well as the general shortcomings of Soviet life.

Although official and unofficial forms of humour and satire seemingly stood in opposition to one another, at various moments in Soviet history these two discourses shared certain constituent tonalities. The harmony between these two conflicting constructs was most noticeable during times of ideological transition. For example, the Thaw legitimized de-Stalinization, thereby openly promoting formerly underground anti-Stalinist satire. Similarly, Gorbachev's glasnost witnessed the renaissance of bold political and social humour. In the late 1980s, satire in film, music, and popular culture became a ubiquitous form of re-evaluating the Soviet past. Social criticism acquired a key role in the cinematic works of Eldar Riazanov, Iurii Mamin, Nikita Mikhalkov, as well as plays performed in the Satire, Sovremennik, and Satyricon Theatres. Themes that formerly were strictly confined to private joke-telling now became public: on the stand-up comedy stage, in state-supported publications (for example, in *Ogonek* and *Literaturnaia gazeta*), and on radio and television. Iurii Nikulin dedicated a large part of his television show *Klub Belyi Popugai* (White Parrot Club) to political jokes. In the same vein, television shows such as *Anshlag* (Full House) and *Gorodok* (Little Town) targeted prominent personalities and provided satirical discussions and interpretations of Soviet history. Satirical and humorous shows, programmes, and festivals banned during the period of Stagnation were reinstated. Moreover, the *anekdot* (joke or humorous anecdote) found overwhelming popularity in various printed collections, book series, and Internet sites.

Soon after the collapse of the Soviet Union, both the official pro-Soviet and unofficial anti-Soviet forms of satire lost their *raison d'être*. Many contemporary critics (and satirists themselves) perceive humour and satire in post-Soviet Russia as vulgar and decadent. Some satirical genres have virtually disappeared from the Russian cultural scene (for example, the journalistic feuilleton). Others have dramatically changed their satirical frameworks (stand-up comedy, *anekdot*), focusing on an array of themes that are crucial for present-day Russia (such as the New Russians, the mafia, and post-Soviet unemployment). Today's humorous and satirical genres are often a form of escapism that delineates problems without attempting to propose any concrete solutions.

See also: alcoholism; bards; Bitov, Andrei; black market; bureaucracy; censorship; comedians; Communist Party; Galich, Aleksandr; Gorbachev, Mikhail; joke; *Kabachok '13 stulev'* (*The 13 Chairs Café*); *Krokodil*; *Literaturnaia gazeta* (Literary Gazette); Mikhalkov, Nikita; New Russians; Nikulin, Iurii; *Ogonek*; perestroika and glasnost; Riazanov, Eldar; samizdat; Satire Theatre; Satyricon Theatre; Sovremennik Theatre; Stagnation; stand-up comedy; Thaw; theatre, Soviet; Tokareva, Viktoriia; Vysotskii, Vladimir; Zhvanetskii, Mikhail

Further reading

Briker, B. and Vishevskii, A. (1989) 'Iumor v populiarnoi kulture sovetskogo intelligenta 60-kh – 70-kh godov', *Wiener slawistischer Almanach* 24: 147–70.

Draitser, E. (1998) *Taking Penguins to the Movies: Ethnic Humor in Russia*, Detroit, MI: Wayne State University Press.

Horton, A. (1993) *Inside Soviet Film Satire. Laughter with a Lash*, Cambridge: Cambridge University Press.

Ryan-Hayes, K. (1993) *Russian Publicistic Satire under Glasnost: The Journalistic Feuilleton*, Lewiston, NY: The Edwin Mellen Press.

Vishevsky, A. (1993) *Soviet Literary Culture in the 1970s: The Politics of Irony*, Gainesville, FL: University Press of Florida.

OLGA MESROPOVA

I

Iabloko (Apple)

Political party

Formed as a federal party by Grigorii Iavlinskii, Iurii Boldyrev, and Vladimir Lukin to participate in the first Duma elections of 1993. Its official platform was the establishment of a democratic regime with rule of law, a social welfare state, an effective market economic system, and civil society. A liberal-centrist party of urban and rural intelligentsia, in the 1993–99 parliamentary elections Iabloko received between 7.86 per cent (highest, 1993) and 5.93 per cent (lowest, 1999) of votes. As a one-man (Iavlinskii's) party under a dominant figure, Iabloko has been progressively losing not only its co-founders and other key figures (Boldyrev, Lukin, Igrunov), but, more importantly, a large segment of its electorate. In 2003 it failed to clear the 5 per cent threshold and lost its representation in the State Duma.

See also: Iavlinskii, Grigorii; political parties, post-Soviet

ALEXANDER DOMRIN

Iakobson, Leonid Veniaminovich

b. 15 January 1904, St. Petersburg; d. 17 October 1995, Moscow

Russian dancer, choreographer, and ballet director

Upon graduation from the Leningrad Ballet School in 1926, Iakobson began dancing with the Leningrad Ballet (the later Kirov), performing mostly character and grotesque roles. His most famous full-length ballets include *Spartacus* (Kirov, 1956; Bolshoi, 1962), *The Bedbug* (Kirov, 1962), and *The Twelve* (Kirov, 1967). His more than 130 choreographic compositions rarely gained popular success owing to his penchant for an innovative ballet language at odds with traditional classical technique. Best at choreographing short pieces, in 1970 he established the company Choreographic Miniatures in Leningrad. His celebrated production of *The Rodin Tryptich* set the Rodin marble groups from the Hermitage Museum into motion to the music of Debussy and Berg. After his death, his disciple Askold Makarov became the company's artistic director.

See also: ballet dancers, Bolshoi Theatre; ballet dancers, Mariinskii Theatre; ballet, Soviet; Bolshoi Theatre; Hermitage Museum; Mariinskii Theatre

TATIANA SENKEVITCH

Iakobson (Jakobson), Roman Osipovich

b. 11 October 1896, Moscow; d. 18 July 1982, Cambridge, Massachusetts

Linguist, literary scholar

One of the major Russian Formalists and a founding member of the Prague Linguistic Circle, Iakobson ranks among the most significant

Russian scholars of the twentieth century, a seminal figure in structuralism and semiotics. In his youth, he was close to Russian avant-garde poets and painters (Vladimir Maiakovskii referred to him in a poem as 'Romka'), and much of his early writing is connected to their norm-breaking ethos. In 1920, Iakobson left Russia for Czechoslovakia, where he spent extremely fruitful years until the Nazis invaded, whereupon he fled to Scandinavia, then to the USA, eventually receiving professorships in Slavic and linguistics at Harvard and MIT (held concurrently).

Beginning in 1956, Iakobson began visiting the USSR, causing wariness both in Russia, where his scholarly methodology and émigré status were officially unacceptable, and in the West, where he was seen as a Soviet sympathizer (on these grounds Vladimir Nabokov refused to collaborate with him on a translation of the Russian epic *Slovo o polku Igoreve* (*The Lay of Prince Igor*). However, Iakobson found a receptive audience among a new generation of Russian scholars. On his final trip to the USSR (1979), he gave a now legendary lecture at the highly conservative Moscow State University. Editions of his works were published posthumously in Moscow: on linguistics in 1985 and on poetics in 1987.

Throughout his career, Iakobson aspired to give humanistic study scientific rigour. One of his most famous essays was based on medical research (*Two Aspects of Language and Two Types of Aphasic Disturbances*, 1956) and another (*Baudelaire's "Les Chats"*, 1962) was co-authored with the celebrated anthropologist Claude Lévi-Strauss. Iakobson's work continues to be studied, especially in Russia, where his conviction in the inseparability of linguistics and poetics is more widely accepted than in the West.

See also: Moscow State University; Nabokov, Vladimir; structuralism; Tartu-Moscow School

Further reading

Jakobson, R. (1962–88) *Selected Writings* (eight volumes to date), The Hague: Mouton de Gruyter.

MICHAEL WACHTEL

Iakovlev, Egor Vladimirovich

b. 14 March 1930, Moscow; d. 18 September 2005, Moscow

Journalist

A vivid representative of the 'Thaw generation' (*shestidesiatniki*), Iakovlev worked as a Komsomol leader and secretary of the Sverdlov raikom (district Party committee) in 1954–55. He subsequently moved to the newspapers *Za sovetskuiu torgovliu* (For Soviet Trade) and *Moskovskaia pravda*, and the Moscow region newspaper *Leninskoe znamia* (Leninist Banner, from which he was fired for 'incorrect coverage of Soviet agriculture'). From 1966 until 1968, Iakovlev was editor-in-chief of the magazine *Sovetskaia pechat* (Soviet Press, later called *Zhurnalist* [Journalist]). Fired for liberal articles published in that magazine, he worked in Prague at the magazine *Problemy mira i sotsializma* (Problems of Peace and Socialism), in *Izvestiia*, and at APN (*Agentstvo politicheskikh novostei*, Agency of Political News). In August 1986, he became editor of the newspaper *Moskovskie novosti*. When he made it one of the most radical perestroika-era publications, opponents called him '*prorab perestroiki*' (slave of perestroika) and '*zapadnik*' (Westernizer). Elected as a deputy to the USSR Supreme Soviet in 1989, he became a member of the liberal block Inter-regional. After 1991, Iakovlev worked in television, as head of the Ostankino TV station. In 1992, he founded the democratic weekly newspaper *Obshchaia gazeta* (General Gazette), which he headed until 2001. Iakovlev was respected as a talented editor and a sharp writer and thinker. Many journalists consider him their teacher.

See also: journalism; journalists, post-Soviet; perestroika and glasnost; sixties generation; television, post-Soviet; Westernizers

NADEZHDA AZHGIKHINA

Iakovlev, Iurii Vasilevich

b. 25 October 1928, Moscow

Actor

In films since 1956, Iakovlev had his major screen breakthrough in 1958 with his portrayal of Prince Myshkin in Ivan Pyrev's adaptation of Dostoevskii's novel *The Idiot*. Popular and critically acclaimed for his sensitive portrayals of troubled individuals, such as Stiva Oblonskii in *Anna Karenina* (1967), he had his most memorable roles in comedies. In Leonid Gaidai's *Ivan Vasilevich meniaet professiiu* (*Ivan Vasilevich Changes Jobs*, 1973) he plays a time-travelling Ivan the Terrible to hilarious effect, and in Eldar Riazanov's *Ironiia sudby* (*The Irony of Fate*, 1975), his portrayal of the pompous Ippolit brings out his character's increasing self-awareness and painful acceptance of loneliness.

See also: film, literary adaptation; Gaidai, Leonid; Riazanov, Eldar

DAVID GILLESPIE

Iakovleva, Elena Alekseevna

b. 5 March 1961, Novograd, Ukraine

Actress, talk-show host

Iakovleva hosts the talk show *Chto khochet zhenshchina?* (What does a woman want?) on the television channel RTR. Her best-known post-Soviet role is that of the intellectually gifted and socially inept police detective Kamenskaia in the eponymous TV series shown from 1999–2003, based on Aleksandra Marinina's detective novels. Her prominent roles include that of a prostitute with an international clientele in the glasnost-era film of 1989, *Interdevochka* (*Intergirl*), and the post-Soviet TV series in 1994, *Peterburgskie tainy* (Petersburg Secrets). A graduate of GITIS (1984), she has acted at Moscow's Sovremennik Theatre in Moscow since 1984, where, among other roles, she played Eliza Dolittle (1994) in the Russian version of Bernard Shaw's *Pygmalion*. Iakovleva's awards include a *Nika* in 1989 for best actress and in 1992 for best supporting actress.

See also: *Interdevochka*; Marinina, Aleksandra; Sovremennik Theatre; television channels

SUSMITA SUNDARAM

Iakutia (Sakha)

Iakutia, known as the Republic of Sakha since the collapse of the Soviet Union, is the largest autonomous republic of the Russian Federation. In 1632, Russian explorers built a fort called Iakutsk on the Lena River, the region's main transport artery, controlling the territory's rich fur, gold, and logging. The nomadic Sakhas, the second largest indigenous Siberian people, continued to fish, and to breed and hunt horses and reindeer. Some converted to Orthodox Christianity; others remained shamanistic and animistic. They remained a majority until Stalin's collectivization in 1934, which forcibly resettled large numbers of Russians to work in the mining industry. After 1951, when diamond, coal, lead, oil, and gas mining began on a large scale, Russians started coming voluntarily to the area. By 1989, almost 90 per cent of the mining industry staff was Russian. The split between Russian cities and mining industry, on the one hand, and Sakhas in the countryside and agriculture, on the other, has fostered an increasing Sakha national consciousness. Since 2000, Iakutia's well-preserved plant and animal life has made it a favourite location for international wildlife and hunting expeditions.

See also: Far East; natural resources; Russian Orthodoxy; Siberia

NADIESZDA KIZENKO

Iankilevskii, Vladimir Borisovich

b. 15 February 1938, Moscow

Artist

Iankilevskii's artistic notoriety began with his participation in the scandalous 1962 Manezh show in Moscow, after his graduation from the Moscow Secondary Art School (1950–56) and the Moscow Polygraphic Institute (1957–62). His abiding interest in the oppositions of female/male and biological/technological principles and his focus on the surface of the artwork are already apparent in his 1962 pentaptych, *Atomnaia stantsiia* (*Atomic Station*). Iankilevskii's paintings, drawings, and multi-media installations (including *Liudi v korobkakh* [*People in Boxes*, 1990]) have enjoyed international acclaim. In New York from 1990 until 1992, Iankilevskii currently lives and works in Paris.

See also: Manezh exhibition of 1962

ANN KOMAROMI

Iankovskii, Oleg Ivanovich

b. 23 February 1944, Moscow

Actor

One of Russia's best-known faces and voices, Iankovskii has been in films since 1968. Filmed by Tarkovskii in the cerebral *Zerkalo* (*Mirror*, 1974) and *Nostalgiia* (*Nostalgia*, 1983), he has also gained popularity through his committed performances of vulnerable masculinity, especially in Roman Balaian's *Polety vo sne i naiavu* (*Flights in Dreams and in Reality*, 1983). A star of some of the major films of perestroika, including Mikhail Shveitser's *Kreitserova sonata* (*The Kreutzer Sonata*, 1987) and Mark Zakharov's *Ubit drakona* (*To Kill a Dragon*, 1988), he was also praised for his performance as the Machiavellian court intriguer von Pahlen, plotting against Tsar Pavel in Vitalii Melnikov's *Bednyi bednyi Pavel* (*Poor, Poor Pavel*, 2003).

See also: Balaian, Roman; Shveitser, Mikhail; Tarkovskii, Andrei; Zakharov, Mark

DAVID GILLESPIE

Ianshin, Mikhail Mikhailovich

b. 20 October [2 November] 1902, Smolensk; d. 17 July 1976, Moscow

Theatre and film actor

Ianshin studied at the Second Studio school of the Moscow Art Theatre (MKhAT), joining its main troupe in 1924. The role of Lariosik in Bulgakov's *Dni Turbinykh* (*The Days of the Turbins*, 1927) brought him name recognition, which he

subsequently solidified with seminal performances in plays by Aleksandr Ostrovskii and contemporary Soviet authors. Ianshin's innate gift for satire made him an ideal choice for pompous Chekhovian characters, such as Telegin in *Diadia Vania* (*Uncle Vania*) and Simeonov-Pishchik in *Vishnevyi sad* (*The Cherry Orchard*). On screen, Ianshin's grotesque portrayal of Tsar Pavel I in the Tynianov adaptation *Poruchik Kizhe* (*Lieutenant Kizhe*, 1934) stands out. People's Artist of the USSR (1955).

See also: Moscow Art Theatre

PETER ROLLBERG

iashchik

Iashchik means 'box' in Russian, and refers to a secret research institution in the Soviet Union that worked for the defence industry. Instead of having public names, these institutes were usually listed as post office box numbers. Soviet scientists employed in *iashchik* usually had access to secret information and were therefore forbidden to travel abroad or have contact with foreigners. One such institution in the Stalin era was described in Aleksandr Solzhenitsyn's novel *V kruge pervom* (*The First Circle*).

See also: closed city; Cold War; defence industry; iron curtain; Solzhenitsyn, Aleksandr

TATIANA SMORODINSKAYA

Iashin, Lev

b. 22 October 1929, Moscow; d. 21 March 1990, Moscow

Soccer player (goalkeeper)

Lev Iashin played for Dinamo 1949–71. He won five national titles, the Olympic gold in 1956, and the European championship in 1960. In 1963, he won the European Player of the Year award and, in 2000, FIFA hailed him as the 'World's Best Goal Keeper of the Century'. Iashin was known for his shot-stopping unparalleled by any other goalkeeper. He saved over 150 penalties and made 207 shutouts during his career. Iashin's name is given to a symbolic goalkeepers' club for those who had 100 or more shutouts.

See also: Dinamo; soccer

ALEXANDER LEDENEV

Iavlinskii, Grigorii Alekseevich

b. 10 April 1952, Lvov

Economist, politician

Late perestroika economic advisor to Yeltsin and Gorbachev, co-founder of the Iabloko Party, and the most prominent non-Communist, non-nationalist, pro-democratic opposition leader, Iavlinskii ran for the Russian presidency in 1996 and 2000. He denounces post-Soviet 'periphery capitalism' characterized by the transfer of natural resources to a monopolistic oligarchy, and he vociferously opposes the Chechen War and unfair tax loopholes. Called 'Mr. No' for avoiding all compromises or coalitions that would result in them, such as his refusal to join the Yeltsin governments, which he considered illegitimate, Iavlinskii has earned a steady, if modest, electorate and a reputation for integrity. His reputation was further enhanced when he joined a courageous few attempting to negotiate in the 2002 Dubrovka Theatre hostage crisis.

See also: Gorbachev, Mikhail; Iabloko; terrorist acts; War, Chechen; Yeltsin, Boris

AVRAM BROWN

Ibragimbekov, Rustam

b. 5 January 1939, Baku, Azerbaidzhan

Writer, producer, director

A graduate of VGIK and a member of the Union of Film-makers, Ibragimbekov has written numerous film and television scripts, plays,

and prose with exotic ethnic settings, such as Vladimir Motyl's 1970 comedy *Beloe solnste pustyni* (*White Sun of the Desert*) and Iulii Gusman's 1977 *V odin prekrasnyi den* (*One Fine Day*). His ten-year collaboration with Nikita Mikhalkov resulted in such films as *Urga* (*Close To Eden*, 1991), *Utomlennye solntsem* (*Burnt By the Sun*, 1994), and *Sibirskii tsiriulnik* (*The Barber of Siberia*, 1998). He authored the script – commissioned by President Nazarbaev – about invaders' epic conquest for the Hollywood Kazakh blockbuster *Kochevniki* (*Nomad*, 2004).

See also: All-Russian (All-Union) State Institute of Cinematography (VGIK); *Beloe solnste pustyni* (*White Sun of the Desert*); film, Kazakh; film, Soviet – Thaw period; Mikhalkov, Nikita

JANE E. KNOX-VOINA

icon (ikona)

Orthodox Russians believe that God reveals Himself through the *ikona* (icon), a religious painting on wood; therefore artists should not change any aspect of icon tradition. In iconography (the art of icon painting), artists must follow canonical rules that govern materials, form, colours, and images. A door to eternity, the icon dispenses with earthly norms of time and space; instead, its two-dimensional composition adopts reverse perspective: all of the lines intersect upon the observers, who are swept into another world. Icons depict scenes from the lives of Christ, Mary, the saints, and the Church; however, they may not show God the Father because He has never shown himself to humans. Russians especially love icons of Mary, often viewed as 'miracle-working'.

Before icon painters begin their task, they must fast and pray to become worthy instruments of God's revelation. All of their materials – brushes, paints, wood – must be blessed. In general, icon painters are anonymous, except for the brilliant St. Andrei Rublev (1370–1430), best known for his icon the *Troitsa* (*Old Testament Trinity*). In the eastern tradition, the first icon, known as the *Spas nerukotvornyi* (*Saviour Not Made by Human Hands*), came about when the ailing ruler, Abgar of Edessa, sent an emissary to ask Jesus to heal him. Taking pity on Abgar, Jesus washed His face and wiped it with a towel, upon which His image remained. When Abgar touched the towel, he was healed.

Every Russian Orthodox church has an *ikonostas*, a barrier separating the nave from the sanctuary where the priest celebrates the Eucharist. Icons on the *ikonostas* follow a specific order that tells the complete story of Christ's Incarnation. Atop the Royal Doors that open to the sanctuary, two icons depict the Annunciation; the evangelists appear on four panels below. Above the doors appear icons of the Last Supper. The row above (*chin* or *deisis*, row of prayer) has Christ in Glory in the centre, with Mary on His right and John the Baptist on His left. To Mary's right stand the Archangel Michael and then St. Peter; on John's left are the Archangel Gabriel and then St. Paul. They and various apostles and saints all bow their heads and extend their hands in prayer. The row above depicts the twelve feasts of the church year; the next one up shows a row of prophets with Our Lady of the Sign in the centre. The top row depicts Adam, Moses, and other Old Testament Patriarchs, the physical ancestors of Christ.

Taste for western art resulted in a decline in iconography in the seventeenth century; however, in the nineteenth century, when experts restored lost icons, interest in the ancient images reawakened. Throughout the Soviet period, many icons were destroyed; but during glasnost and after the fall of the Soviet Union, icon painting once again came into its own. Icon schools opened around the country, with several prominent new iconographers/teachers; arguably the most notable of them is Archmandrite Zinon (Teodor), formerly of the Pskov Cave Monastery.

See also: perestroika and glasnost; Russian Orthodoxy

Further reading

Baggley, J. and Temple, R. (1995) *Doors of Perception: Icons and Their Significance*, Crestwood, NY: St. Vladimir's Seminary Press.

Ouspensky, L. (1992) *Theology of the Icon*, vols I and II, trans. A. Gythiel, Crestwood, NY: St. Vladimir's Seminary Press.
Ouspensky, L. and Lossky, V. (1989) *The Meaning of Icons*, trans. G. E. H. Palmer and E. Kadloubovsky, Crestwood, NY: St. Vladimir's Seminary Press.

CHRISTINE A. RYDEL

ideological education, Soviet

The official ideology of the USSR is known under several names: the 'doctrine of Marx', 'Marxism' (throughout the entire Soviet period), 'the teachings of Lenin-Stalin' (1930s–53), and 'Marxism-Leninism'. Its basis was the doctrine that conceived class struggle as the chief motor of historical progress, and the inevitability of the eventual emergence of a communist society as a goal of mankind's social development. The main motto of Soviet ideology was Lenin's formula: 'Marx's doctrine is powerful because it is true'. The central authority of Soviet ideological education was the Communist Party. Its educational programmes covered Party structures and society as a whole; ideological education within the Party was structured according to the principle of a 'Party study programme' based on the history and theory of 'Party construction'. Up to the mid-1950s, *A Short Course in the History of the All-Russian Communist Party (Bolsheviks)*, written under Stalin's editorship, had the status of an 'encyclopedia of basic knowledge in Marxism-Leninism'. Subsequently, this volume continued to be fundamental in the ideological education of Soviet citizens, for it served as the core of all later works on the history of the Soviet Communist Party. That history constituted one of the main disciplines in the system of secondary and higher education, the others being Marxist-Leninist philosophy (in its subdivisions – 'dialectical' and 'historical materialism', known respectively as *Diamat* and *Istmat*), scientific communism (*nauchnyi kommunizm*), and, from the 1960s, Marxist-Leninist aesthetics and socialist political economy.

The transfer of ideology assumed the form of brief overviews of so-called 'primary sources', which were used in seminars at institutions of higher education, evening classes, Marxist-Leninist universities, and so forth. Among the compulsory texts taught in this manner was the *Communist Manifesto*, parts of Marx's *Capital*, articles by Lenin and Stalin, and the Communist Party's instructive resolutions and programmes. The Party's Central Committee and its regional Central Committees, as well as regional committees for ideology, were officially entrusted with ideological education. The most influential Party ideologists after Stalin were Andrei Zhdanov (1896–1948) and Mikhail Suslov (1902–82). One of the main tasks of ideological education was the adjustment of the Communist Party's history to each subsequent phase of internal changes in the Party and its doctrine. Thus, between 1956 and 1964, references to Stalin disappeared from most documents associated with ideological education; from 1965 the same happened with references to Nikita Khrushchev. References to fundamental political decisions were distorted or removed (for example, the elimination of the Polish state in 1939–40). The Soviet information agency, TASS, was responsible for continuously updating items in documents, newspapers, magazines, radio, and television pertaining to ideological education.

The system of ideological education extended even to foreign states. Subscribers or purchasers of books with ideological content, such as the *Great Soviet Encyclopedia*, received booklets advising them to cross out references or excise pages no longer deemed suitable for the updated version.

Resistance to ideological education took various forms, from political *samizdat* literature to cultural or religious internal exile. Because of the totalitarian nature of ideology and governance, experimental movements in Soviet culture (for example, Sots-Art) assumed forms that parodied Soviet ideology. After the collapse of the USSR and the system of Soviet ideological education, the latter's weakened structures currently are receptive to different formations of ideas. Post-Soviet indoctrination relies on many Soviet clichés, but cannot be called a system because it is fractured into competing movements (geopolitics, conspirology, new chronology, and others).

See also: censorship; Communist ideology; Communist Party; Communist Youth League; cult of personality; developed socialism; dissident; democratic reform movement; educational system, Soviet; Encyclopedia, Soviet; ITAR-TASS; Khrushchev, Nikita; pedagogy, Soviet; perestroika and glasnost; philosophy, Soviet (Marxist-Leninist); political structure, Soviet; propaganda, Soviet and post-Soviet; samizdat; Scientific Communism; Short Course; Sots-Art; Stagnation; Stalin, Iosif; Thaw

Further reading

Gusejnov, G. (2004) *Soviet Ideologemes in Russian Discourse of the 1990s*, Moscow: Tri Kvadrata.

Leonhard, W. (1974) *Soviet Ideology, Maoism, and Humanist Marxism*, trans. E. Osers, New York: Holt, Rinehart and Winston.

Platt, K. and Brandenberger, D. (eds) (2005) *Epic Revisionism: Russian History and Literature as Stalinist Propaganda*, Madison, WI: University of Wisconsin Press.

Robinson, N. (1995) *Ideology and the Collapse of the Soviet System: A Critical History of Soviet Ideological Discourse*, Aldershot: Edward Elgar.

GASAN GUSEJNOV

Idushchie vmeste (Marching Together)

A patriotic youth organization

Its optimistic message of morality and action for young people echoes that of the Soviet-era Komsomol. Formed in 2000, in reaction to the perceived societal breakdown of the post-Soviet period, the group promotes self-improvement, idealism, patriotism, and respect for one's elders. It has staged rallies in support of Russian President Vladimir Putin, distributed patriotic literature and the Russian classics, and has sponsored drives to collect – and destroy – books viewed as anti-Russian. In 2002, Idushchie vmeste backed an unsuccessful lawsuit against the writer Vladimir Sorokin for allegedly pornographic material in his novel *Goluboe salo* (Blue Lard). The organization's official website is at www.idushchie.ru

See also: Communist Youth League; Putin, Vladimir; Sorokin, Vladimir

JENNIFER RYAN TISHLER

Ilenko, Iurii Gerasimovich

b. 18 July 1936, Dnepropetrovsk, Ukraine

Cinematographer, director, writer

After graduating from VGIK in 1961, Ilenko made his name as Sergei Paradzhanov's cinematographer on *Teni zabytykh predkov* (*Shadows of Forgotten Ancestors*, 1965), a stunningly beautiful film set in the Carpathian mountains. That same year Ilenko directed his own film, *Rodnik dlia zhazhdushchikh* (*A Spring for the Thirsty*), a stylized treatment of the sensitive theme of eroding Ukrainian national culture. Angry authorities banned the film; it was not released until 1987. Ilenko's subsequent films include the award-winning *Belaia ptitsa s chernoi otmetinoi* (*White Bird with a Black Mark*, 1972) and *Lebedinoe ozero. Zona* (*Swan Lake: The Zone*, 1990), a documentary about the 1986 Chernobyl nuclear disaster.

See also: All-Russian (All-Union) State Institute of Cinematography (VGIK); Chernobyl; Paradzhanov, Sergei

JOSEPHINE WOLL

Ilinskii, Igor Vladimirovich

b. 24 July 1901, Moscow; d. 13 January 1987, Moscow

Actor, director

Ilinskii's long career on stage and screen began in 1918, and within a decade he was the most famous comic actor of Soviet silent film, where he excelled in physical comedy and playing hapless heroes. He successfully made the transition to talkies, creating legendary roles in the musical comedies *Volga-Volga* (1938) and *Karnavalnaia noch* (*Carnival Night*, 1956). In both, Ilinskii played villainous bureaucrats whose obsolete ideas and methods are challenged by a heroine representing the new spirit of the age.

SETH GRAHAM

Infante, Francisco

(aka Francisco Infante-Arana)

b. 4 June 1943, Vasilevka village, Saratov oblast

Artist

Son of a Russian mother and a Spanish immigrant who fled from the Spanish Civil War in 1936, Infante graduated from the Stroganov Art School. In 1966, he joined the group *Dvizhenie* (Movement), led by Lev Nusberg. Tension developed between Nusberg and Infante, and in 1970 Infante officially left the group and, together with his wife, Nonna Goriunova, and an engineer, Valerii Osipov, organized the group ARGO (*Avtorskaia Rabochaia Gruppa*, Authors' Working Group). In the summer of 1975, he created a kinetic construction for the Soviet section of the exhibition *Sviaz – 75* (Mail and Long Distance Connections – 75) in Moscow's Sokolniki Park. The feud between Infante and Nusberg over the years grew stronger and spilled out in many mutually incriminating publications and unpublished manuscripts. In 1996, Infante received the State Prize for Art.

See also: Nusberg, Lev

VLADIMIR PAPERNY

informal organizations (neformaly)

Informal youth organizations

The term 'informal youth organizations' was introduced by Komsomol bureaucrats during perestroika to define self-organized youth groups that materialized in opposition to the formal Soviet Komsomol and Pioneer youth and children's organizations. During perestroika, open criticism of Komsomol construction sites and construction brigades, as well as Komsomol's infrastructure, came to light. The trend toward glasnost (openness) appeared in the first youth television projects geared toward young people, such as *Vzgliad* (Viewpoint) and *Dvenadtsatyi etazh* (The Twelfth Floor). The appearance of *neformaly* cast doubt on the role of the Communist Party and Communist-led perestroika as the only correct paths of development for Soviet society.

These informal organizations were divided into 'positive' (espousing ideas acceptable to the Communist Party), 'neutral' (organized around subcultures such as skateboarders and heavy metal fans), and 'negative' (fascists, racists, and 'pro-capitalist groups' – punks and skinheads). In the 1990s, the *neformaly* movement began to decline. The Komsomol broke up, making opposition to it superfluous. Informal organizations found another rival: teenage criminal gangs, called *gopniks*.

See also: Communist Party; Communist Youth League; crime; perestroika and glasnost; *Vzgliad*; youth culture

ELENA OMELCHENKO

intelligentsia

The concept of the intelligentsia, largely defined by its separation from the *narod* (folk) and by its purported stance of political and ethical opposition to the state, has played a significant role in modern Russian intellectual history. Yet the social group designated by the term is difficult to define precisely, partly because its composition has shifted over time and partly because its relationship to the level of education, political sympathies, and class allegiance of its members has been complex from the beginning. While the term was popularized in Russia during the 1860s by the minor writer Petr Boborykin, its origins are often traced to the reign of Catherine the Great in the latter half of the eighteenth century, to the appearance of such educated critics of the regime as the satirical journal editor Nikolai Novikov and the writer Aleksandr Radishchev. Most scholars, however, trace the emergence of the intelligentsia as a distinctive group to the 1830s and 1840s, as the hierarchical Russian class structure began to deteriorate. While the early intelligentsia has been identified with the *raznochintsy* or people of indeterminate social rank (often the sons of priests who attained an advanced education), in fact,

the majority of the intelligentsia in the early decades came from the nobility. In the second half of the nineteenth century, the *intelligent* became a stock character in literature, closely allied with the 'superfluous man'. Among the most famous portrayals of the intelligentsia are those in Ivan Turgenev's *Rudin* and *Otsy i deti* (*Fathers and Sons*), and Fedor Dostoevskii's *Prestuplenie i nakazanie* (*Crime and Punishment*) and *Besy* (*The Demons*).

The contours of the intelligentsia became even more blurred during the Soviet period, and some commentators, including Aleksandr Solzhenitsyn, argue that the intelligentsia ceased to exist in any meaningful sense. While the figure of the *intelligent* as an ineffectual 'bourgeois' character incapable of mustering sufficient revolutionary zeal took root in early Soviet literature, the Soviet cultural and political establishment succeeded in co-opting the term, claiming the revolutionary intelligentsia as its forebears. The official use of the term came to embrace all Soviet citizens with a post-secondary education, with a distinction drawn between the 'creative' and the 'technical' intelligentsia.

Especially during the decades after Stalin's death, the intelligentsia played an important role in the political opposition. Leading dissidents appeared from the ranks of the intelligentsia, and just as the lack of opportunity for legal civic activism in the nineteenth century fuelled the growth of the revolutionary intelligentsia, so Soviet repression and censorship fostered a group identity among those who passed along illicit literature and gathered around the proverbial kitchen table to air nonconformist political views. The figure of the *intelligent* again became a stock character in post-Stalin Soviet literature, both official and unofficial. The eponymous protagonist of Boris Pasternak's *Doctor Zhivago* (1957) provided a role model for post-Stalin intellectuals who avoided active participation in the system by taking menial jobs as yard keepers or janitors. The works of Iurii Trifonov and Andrei Bitov, on the other hand, portray the dilemma of the later Soviet intellectual who achieved stature within the system, trapped between generous state subsidies of intellectual and creative life and the ethical imperative to resist the abuses perpetrated by the same state.

In *The Russian Intelligentsia* (1997), Andrei Siniavskii contends that the Soviet intelligentsia and its successor were seduced by power and therefore failed in their traditional role as a moral opposition. The commercialization of culture in the post-Soviet period, the end of state support for the arts, and the attendant eclipse of high culture by popular literary and cultural forms have posed an even more devastating threat to the intelligentsia's function and sense of group identity in recent years.

See also: Bitov, Andrei; dissident; economic system, post-Soviet; economic system, Soviet; Pasternak, Boris; Siniavskii, Andrei; Solzhenitsyn, Aleksandr; Trifonov, Iurii

Further reading

Pipes, R. (ed.) (1961) *The Russian Intelligentsia*, New York: Columbia University Press.

Sinyavsky, A. (1997) *The Russian Intelligentsia*, New York: Columbia University Press.

Solzhenitsyn, A. (1975) 'The Smatterers' (*Obrazovanshchina*), in A. Solzhenitsyn, *From under the Rubble*, Boston, MA: Little Brown.

CATHARINE NEPOMNYASHCHY

Interdevochka

Film

Based on a best-selling novel by Vladimir Kunin, first published in 1988 in the journal *Avrora*, *Interdevochka* addressed the formerly forbidden issue of foreign currency prostitution (payment for prostitution in hard currency). Petr Todorovskii directed the 1989 film adaptation, a Soviet–Swedish co-production. It attracted 44 million viewers, and the female lead, Elena Iakovleva, received the Nika Prize for best actress. The book's detailed descriptions of foreign luxury items, reflected in the film, contributed to its success, but also prompted accusations of luring girls into prostitution. The tragic finale renders the film script inherently moralistic: the West appears as the source of materialistic temptation, to which the innocent Russian soul falls prey.

See also: Iakovleva, Elena; Todorovskii, Petr

KARIN SARSENOV

internationalism

Inspired by Marx and Engels's slogan, 'Workers of the world, unite!', Communist ideology embraced internationalism, the notion of *druzhba narodov* (friendship of peoples). The Soviets promoted international cooperation because they believed that the 'brotherhood of nations' could overthrow capitalism. Since the Soviet Union itself was a multi-national state, its ideology foregrounded the idea of friendship of the (Soviet) peoples. While internationalism and friendship theoretically promoted tolerance, in practice Russians *vis-à-vis* other nationalities and republics assumed the role of 'elder brother' or 'the first among equals'. That attitude bred resentment within the Soviet Union and in other parts of the socialist world.

See also: Communist ideology

LAURA ADAMS

Internet, Russian

The history of the Russian Internet can be divided into three periods: 1989–93, 1994–98, and 1999–present, each reflecting a change in both technological developments and societal structure.

The first Internet connection was established in Moscow in 1989; Soviet scientists were its initiators and first users. In 1991, the first provider, 'Relcom', appeared, serving over 3,000 users. In 1994, the '.ru' domain officially replaced '.su', symbolically marking the transition from the USSR to Russia, as well as the passage from erratic to more extensive Internet use. Web technology reached professionals and Internet enthusiasts: Major universities were linked, and a reliable e-mail system became a reality. In 1995, the first on-line newspaper (*Uchitelskaia gazeta*, the Education Newspaper) appeared, and the first Internet cafés opened in St. Petersburg in 1996.

Although the Internet remained an unaffordable commodity for the majority of Russians, the number of users steadily increased, and in 1996–98 still more advanced technology offered new services: the first personal web pages (such as that of politician Boris Nemtsov); on-line conferencing; digital art exhibitions (for example, Aleksei Shulgin began to use the Internet as his distribution system and then introduced its codes into his art); search engines ('rambler.ru' and 'yandex.ru', the latter enabling users to surf the web using Russian morphology). Internet advancement during this period depended heavily on the financial support of Western organizations such as the Soros Foundation. The monetary crisis of 1998 slowed developments, but only temporarily. In 1999, the free national e-mail service www.mail.ru became available. It celebrated widespread computer literacy and both commercial and non-commercial Internet use.

In the 1990s, the Internet was a symbol of change, a stimulus to intellectual growth and democratization. In the new millennium it became a tool of political and social manoeuvring, as well as a new market and entertainment arena. In 1999, the Internet proved to be the fastest medium for news delivery, particularly with the emergence of www.lenta.ru, an accessible 24-hour news agency. At the same time the Russian Internet became more self-reflexive, often raising important social issues: the statistical engine SpyLOG was introduced, and Vladimir Sorokin's novel *Goluboe salo* (Blue Lard) was illegally published online. The novel's appearance prompted the first Internet scandal. This lawsuit and others helped to draw public attention to problems of copyright, authorship, and originality. In 2000, Vladimir Putin's official interactive web page was posted, eulogizing the achievements of Russia's democracy; simultaneously, however, the State commenced registration of web resources and activated a system of web perlustration. The State also sponsored educational projects and further proliferation of the Internet, such as the posting of Russian literary classics on the web. The Russian Internet began to cater to ever more facets of society, including Russian speakers living outside the country (www.ukraine.ru). In response, the people embraced the Internet in the form of Masiania, a character in a series of online flash animation cartoons, created by the www.mult.ru art studio, who became a national heroine.

See also: Masiania; Nemtsov, Boris; Sorokin, Vladimir; Soros Foundation

Further reading

www.nethistory.ru

VLADIMIR STRUKOV

Ioseliani, Otar

b. 2 February 1934, Tbilisi, Georgian SSR

Director, writer

After having studied at the Tbilisi Conservatory and the Mathematical-Mechanics Department of Moscow State University, Ioseliani graduated from VGIK in 1965. He followed his first feature film, *Giorgobistve* (*Listopad* [*Leaf-fall*, 1968]), with *Iko shashvi mgalobeli* (*Zhil pevchii drozd*; *Once Upon a Time a Singing Blackbird Lived*, 1970), and *Pastorali* (*Pastoral*, 1975), all of them tragi-comic dramas set in scrupulously observed Georgian society. Based in Paris since 1984, Ioseliani continues to lament the passing of age-old moral and cultural traditions in films shot all over the world: *Les favoris de la lune* (*Favourites of the Moon* [*Favority luny*, 1984]) in Paris; the documentary *Un petit monastère en Toscane* (1988) in Italy; *Et la lumière fut* (*And Then There Was Light*, 1989) in Senegal; *Brigands* (1996) back in Georgia.

See also: All-Russian (All-Union) State Institute of Cinematography (VGIK); film, Georgian

JOSEPHINE WOLL

iron curtain (zheleznyi zanaves)

A political metaphor referring to the fire protection barrier which prevents the spread of fire from the stage to the audience. In its contemporary designation the iron curtain was an insurmountable wall which existed between the free Western world and the Communist East bloc (1946–89). The expression has been in use since Winston Churchill's Fulton speech

(5 March 1946), seen as a starting point for the Cold War. The expression had also been used earlier: at the end of World War II, Count Ludwig Schwerin von Krosigk, and then Josef Goebbels, used the phrase to describe how Stalin would separate Eastern Europe from the rest of Europe. In turn, the Germans borrowed the phrase from the Queen of Belgium, who in 1914 spoke of the 'bloody iron curtain' between her country and Germany.

In Russia, Vasilii Rozanov in his *Apokalipsis nashego vremeni* (*The Apocalypse of Our Time*, 1917) used the term iron curtain to describe a wall erected between Russia and her past: he wrote of an iron curtain descending upon Russian history. In 1930, *Literaturnaia gazeta* published an article by Lev Nikulin entitled 'Iron Curtain' (*Zheleznyi zanaves*), in which the author explained why an iron curtain is in the interests of the bourgeoisie, not the Soviet people.

See also: Cold War; East Bloc countries

GASAN GUSEJNOV

Iskander, Fazil Abdulovich

b. 6 March 1929, Sukhumi, Georgia

Writer

Iskander speaks both Abkhaz and Russian but writes only in Russian. He began publishing poetry in 1957 and short stories in the 1960s. His first novella, *Sozvezdie kozlotura* (*The Goatibex Constellation*), which appeared in 1966, parodies Soviet science, politics, and society. Iskander is best known for his prose collections *Sandro iz Chegema* (*Sandro of Chegem* and *The Gospel According to Chegem*, 1973–88, collected final version, 1989). Written over the course of thirty years and collected in several volumes, these satirical stories make up an epic novel that chronicles the lives of the inhabitants of a fictional Abkhaz village. Iskander also contributed to and helped to publish abroad the illegal liberal literary almanac *Metropol* (1979). *Kroliki i udavy* (*Rabbits and Boa Constrictors*, 1982) represents a marked departure from Iskander's earlier works in its thinly veiled caricatures of Soviet writers and politicians.

See also: *Metropol*

Further reading

Haber, E. (2003) *The Myth of the Non-Russian: Iskander and Aitmatov's Magical Universe*, Lanham, MD: Lexington Books.

ERIKA HABER

Islam

Islam, the second largest religion in the Russian Federation, spread to the region beginning in the seventh century. Islam holds that Allah is the only god and that Muhammad is his messenger. Important Islamic religious texts include the Qur'an, which Muslims believe to be the literal transcription of Allah's revelations to Muhammad, and the Sunna, the account of Muhammad's life. Shari'a, or Islamic law, derives from these two books and establishes rules and norms for all aspects of life.

A Muslim's core duties are listed in the five pillars of Islam: belief in Allah, whose messenger is Muhammad; praying five times daily; performing a religious pilgrimage to Mecca (*hajj*); giving alms; and fasting during the holy month of Ramadan. These practices, especially the *hajj*, were difficult or impossible to follow in the Soviet Union. Most Muslims, however, continued to observe Islamic practices for rites and rituals such as circumcisions, weddings, and funerals. Additionally, though public daily prayer was limited, people gathered on festival days such as Uraz-Bayram, which marks the end of the Ramadan fast, and the sacrificial feast of Qurban-Bayram.

The majority of Muslims in the former Soviet Union live in the North Caucasus, the Volga-Urals region, and Central Asia. The type of Islam practised by different communities varies greatly. Islam is divided into two main branches, Sunni and Shi'a. Most Muslims in the region are Sunni, with fewer than 10 per cent Shi'a (Ro'i 2000: 56). The largest concentration of Shi'a Muslims in the region lives in Azerbaidzhan. Additionally, Sufism is practised in some areas of the North Caucasus and Central Asia.

During the early Soviet period, Bolsheviks viewed Muslims as potential allies. Under Stalin, however, governmental policy reduced Muslim power through widespread propaganda and the liquidation of legal, educational, and financial institutions. Waves of mosque closures and arrests of Muslim clergy followed the new restrictions on religious groups introduced in 1929, requiring religious organizations to register with local authorities. Some Muslims continued to practise Islam in unregistered mosques or with other unofficial groups. These unregistered groups, though small, were quite widespread and especially on festival days held services in private homes, cemeteries, or officially closed mosques.

During World War II, the Soviet government relaxed restrictions on Islam, allowing selected Muslims to go on the *hajj* for the first time since 1929 and permitting limited publication of Islamic literature. From the early 1940s until the break-up of the Soviet Union, the Council for the Affairs of Religious Cults oversaw regional religious boards, or Muftiates, established to regulate the activities of Islamic groups. Religious repression increased during Khrushchev's anti-religious campaign, beginning in 1960: operating mosques and active clergy were reduced further. Despite the less hostile climate under Brezhnev, mosque closures continued.

Removal of many religious restrictions during perestroika and glasnost allowed for open observance of Islamic holidays and ceremonies, and many Islamic institutions of worship and education opened. The numbers of operating mosques and religious schools substantially increased, and Soviet Muslims had greater contact with Islamic countries outside the Soviet Union. Despite improvements in the treatment of religious organizations, opposition continued as concerns about Islam as a political threat surfaced in the 1980s and 1990s. The Islamization of the conflict in Chechnia and fears of religiously justified terrorism probably remain a factor in shaping regional attitudes regarding Islam.

Especially in the first post-Soviet years, many mosques opened and the training of Islamic clergy increased. Additionally, more religious printed materials became available from both internal and external sources. The 1997 Law on Freedom of Conscience and Religious Association solidified the distinction between official and unofficial religious practice. The law distinguishes between registered religious organizations and unregistered groups, the latter having a number of restrictions regarding operating schools, distributing literature, and owning property.

The collapse of the Soviet Union and the dismantling of the religious supervisory boards decentralized Islam in the Russian Federation. A number of groups have emerged in an attempt to provide overall leadership and direction, including the Central Board of Muslims in Russia and European Countries of the Commonwealth of Independent States and the Russian Council of Muftis. While these groups compete for overlapping areas of influence, Islamic communities remain without clear centralized leadership.

See also: Azerbaidzhan; Central Asia; Chechnia; Khrushchev, Nikita; perestroika and glasnost

Further reading

Hunter, S.T. (2004) *Islam in Russia: The Politics of Identity and Security*, New York: M.E. Sharpe.

Kappeler, A., Simon, G., Brunner, G. and Allworth, E. (eds) (1994) *Muslim Communities Reemerge: Historical Perspectives on Nationality, Politics, and Opposition in the Former Soviet Union and Yugoslavia*, trans. C. Sawyer, Durham, NC: Duke University Press. (Original work published in 1989.)

Pilkington, H. and Yemelianova, G. (eds) (2003) *Islam in Post-Soviet Russia: Public and Private Faces*, London: RoutledgeCurzon.

Ro'i, Y. (2000) *Islam in the Soviet Union: From World War II to Gorbachev*, London: Hurst & Company.

Yemelianova, G. (2002) *Russia and Islam: A Historical Survey*, New York: Palgrave.

JENNIFER B. BARRETT

ITAR-TASS

News agency

ITAR-TASS stands for *Informatsionnoe telegrafnoe agenstvo Rossii-Telegrafnoe Agenstvo Sovetskogo Soiuza* (Information Telegraph Agency of Russia-Telegraph Agency of the Soviet Union). The largest news agency of its kind, it has the status of Russia's central state information agency. Its century-long history adds weight to its reports covering the end of the Russian empire, the 1917 Revolution, World War II, and modern transformations in society.

The St. Petersburg Telegraph Agency (SPTA), the predecessor of ITAR-TASS, began to operate in 1904. The project to launch SPTA was approved by the last Russian Tsar Nicholas II, who ordered that St. Petersburg be renamed Petrograd, turning SPTA into the Petrograd Telegraph Agency (1914). When the Bolshevik government (*Sovnarkom*) decreed that PTA become the central government information agency, it moved to Moscow, where it merged with the government's press bureau, and was renamed the Russian Telegraph Agency (1918).

The Telegraph Agency of the Soviet Union (TASS), founded in 1925, assumed the main functions of the RTA as the country's central information agency. TASS comprised the news agencies of all the Soviet republics: RATAU (Ukraine), BELTA (Belorussia), UZTAG (Uzbekistan), etc. After the collapse of the Soviet Union and the proclamation of sovereignty by democratic Russia, the news agency was named the Information Telegraph Agency of Russia (1992).

ITAR-TASS has a widespread net of correspondents and more than 130 offices in Russia and abroad. Its editorial desks process information from correspondents, check and analyse facts, and translate them into five foreign languages. On a daily basis, the agency offers forty-five news streams for its subscribers. ITAR-TASS also cooperates with more than eighty foreign news agencies.

See also: journalism; journalists, post-Soviet

ELENA SKIPETROVA

Iudashkin, Valentin

b. 14 October 1963, Bakovka, Moscow oblast

Designer

Iudashkin founded his own workshop in 1987. His fashion house opened in 1991 on Moscow's Kutuzovskii Prospect. Iudashkin uses exclusive fabrics and rich decorative Russian bead embroidery, which is world-famous. His collections centre on historical themes that define the choice of style and form, colour and material. The 'Fabergé' collection (1991) was particularly noteworthy for the dresses made in the shape of Fabergé eggs. Apart from his haute couture collections, Iudashkin has designed the Russian team's Olympic uniforms (1994, 1996), as well as uniforms for the staff of Moscow's Ukraina Hotel and Aeroflot's international fleet.

See also: Fabergé; fashion industry, post-Soviet

BIRGIT BEUMERS

Iurskii, Sergei Iurevich

b. 16 March 1935, Leningrad

Actor, director, writer

An accomplished director and author of fiction and non-fiction, Iurskii is known mainly as a talented actor who combines intellectualism with improvisation. His paradigmatic role in this respect is that of the Improviser in the film *Malenkie tragedii* (*Little Tragedies*, 1979) based on several of Aleksandr Pushkin's works. Iurskii rose to prominence in Georgii Tovstonogov's Bolshoi Drama Theatre in Leningrad. In 1979, he relocated to Moscow. His most famous screen role is Ostap Bender in *Zolotoi telenok* (*The Golden Calf*, 1968). Also particularly significant is his work in the cult television series *Mesto vstrechi izmenit nelzia* (*The Meeting Place Cannot Be Changed*, 1979), starring Vladimir Vysotskii. Iurskii is among those Soviet-era stars who made a successful transition to the post-Soviet era, especially in theatre.

See also: *Mesto vstrechi izmenit nelzia* (The Meeting Place Cannot Be Changed); Tovstonogov Bolshoi Drama Theatre (BDT)

DAN UNGURIANU

Iusov, Vadim Ivanovich

b. 20 April 1929, Klavdino, Russia

Cinematographer

After graduating from VGIK in 1954, Iusov shot films for directors as different as Andrei Tarkovskii and Georgii Daneliia, finding an appropriate visual vocabulary for each. Iusov shot Tarkovskii's first three films, *Ivanovo detstvo* (*My Name Is Ivan*, 1962), *Andrei Rublev* (1966/ 1971) and *Solaris* (1972). He worked with Georgii Daneliia on *Ia shagaiu po Moskve* (*I Walk Around Moscow*, 1963), *Ne goriui!* (*Don't Burn Up!*, 1969) and a Russian version of *Huckleberry Finn* entitled *Sovsem propashchii* (1973). He became head of VGIK's cinematography department in 1983. Post-Soviet films include *Prorva* (*Moscow Parade*, 1992) and *Kopeika* (*The Kopeck*, 2002) both by Ivan Dykhovichnyi.

See also: All-Russian (All-Union) State Institute of Cinematography (VGIK); Daneliia, Georgii; Dykhovichnyi, Ivan; Tarkovskii, Andrei

JOSEPHINE WOLL

Ivan Kupala

The holiday of Ivan Kupala, called either *Ivanov den* (Ivan's Day) or *Ivanova noch* (Ivan's Night) is celebrated on 24 June, the Saint's Day of St. John the Baptist. Originally a pagan holiday to celebrate the summer Equinox, it blended with the Church holiday after the acceptance of Christianity. Traditional rituals included burning a straw effigy, jumping through bonfires, gathering certain medicinal herbs, communal bathing in rivers and lakes, and fortune-telling. It corresponds with similar celebrations elsewhere in northern Europe (Germany, Scandinavia).

See also: holidays, post-Soviet; holidays, Russian Orthodox

MICHELE BERDY

Ivanov-Vano, Ivan Petrovich

b. 9 February 1900, Moscow; d. March 20, 1987, Moscow

Animation director

A pioneer of Soviet animation and a recipient of many international awards, Ivanov-Vano started film work in 1927 and directed over thirty animated films over almost sixty years. His career encompasses the entire scope of Soviet animation, from his early days making political propaganda films through his founding membership and long career in Soiuzmultfilm studio, making didactic, full-length Disneyesque films in the 1930s and 1940s and moving to newer stylistic forms in subsequent years. His most important films include *Konek-gorbunok* (*The Humpbacked Horse*, 1947), *Prikliucheniia Buratino* (*The Adventures of Pinocchio*, 1959), *Vremena goda* (*Seasons*, 1969), and *Skazka o tsare Saltane* (*Tale of Tsar Saltan*, 1984).

See also: film, animation

BELLA GINZBURSKY-BLUM

Ivashov, Vladimir Sergeevich

b. 28 August 1939, d. 1995, Moscow

Russian stage and screen actor

Ivashov studied at the Soviet State Film School VGIK under Mikhail Romm, graduating in 1963. While still a student, he was cast in the lead role of Alesha Skvortsov in the World War II drama *Ballada o soldate* (*Ballad of a Soldier*, 1959), portraying a young soldier of unfailing moral intuition. None of Ivashov's subsequent roles in a variety of genres – from literary adaptation to contemporary drama – came close to the inspired acting of that debut. During the crisis of the Russian film industry in the early 1990s, Ivashov fell upon hard times and was forced to accept jobs such as a construction worker to make ends meet. People's Artist of the RSFSR (1980).

See also: All-Russian (All-Union) State Institute of Cinematography (VGIK); Romm, Mikhail

PETER ROLLBERG

izba

The Russian peasant hut, constructed of wood logs. The large clay or brick stove (*pech*) dominates the main (sometimes only) room and is used for cooking, heating, and sleeping space, as it features a sleeping bench on top usually reserved, as the warmest in the dwelling, for the grandparents. Other family members sleep on pallets or shelves (*lavki*) lining the walls of the *izba*, which contains an icon and icon lamp, hung in the 'beautiful corner' (*krasnyi ugol*) facing the southeast. Upon entering, visitors first bow to the icon. For roofing, huts in the south use thatch, and long planks in the north. A 'white' *izba* has a permanent chimney; otherwise it is termed 'black', and smoke exits through a temporary hole in the roof or out the door. Despite the simplicity of construction, many huts are decorated with ornate woodcarving on shutters, window-frames, and ridgepoles. Though some aspects of life in the *izba* changed during the twentieth century, many peasant houses remain in use today, normally with electricity but limited or no plumbing.

DAVID J. GALLOWAY

Izmailovo Exhibition

The strong social impact of the 1974 Bulldozer Exhibition compelled authorities to allow an exhibition of nonconformist artists' work in Moscow's Izmailovo Park in autumn of that year. This exhibition became a symbol for artistic freedom. Sixty painters of different ages and styles, independent of any ideological, artistic, political, or commercial dogma, had the unique opportunity to meet one another and show their paintings to the public. Many later became international celebrities. The Izmailovo Exhibition was followed by two 1975 exhibitions in Moscow's VDNKh/VVTs, at the Beekeepers' and Culture Pavilions.

See also: art, informal; art, nonconformist; Bulldozer Exhibition; VDNKh/VVTs

TATYANA LEDENEVA

J

Jakobson, Roman

See: Iakobson [Jakobson], Roman Osipovich

jazz (dzhaz)

The official Soviet attitude towards jazz alternated between enthusiastic acceptance and total rejection. As the music of an exploited ethnic minority, it had to be supported, but as entertainment for the rich – *muzyka tolstykh* (fat people's music), as writer Maksim Gorkii called it – it had to be rejected. The official Communist party newspaper *Pravda* defended jazz even in the midst of Stalin's terror: 'We need jazz, and we are not going to let bourgeois aesthetes push it off our stage' (December 1936). Yet Nikita Khrushchev attacked it during the Thaw: 'Jazz is the kind of music that causes nausea and colic' (December 1963). The early stars of Soviet jazz came from Jewish backgrounds: Valentin Parnakh, Aleksandr Tsfasman, and Leonid Utesov. Modernist poet Valentin Parnakh came to Moscow from Paris in 1922 and, despite the fact that he did not know much about music, established his Eccentric Jazz Band, which ended up performing on the stage of Vsevolod Meerkhold's theatre. Aleksandr Tsfasman's AMA Jazz Band was the first to make a jazz recording, the first to perform live on radio, and the first to appear in sound film. Utesov, born in Odessa, always insisted (half-jokingly) that Odessa, not New Orleans, was the birthplace of jazz, and that jazz improvisation came from Odessa's Jewish weddings. A new era in Soviet jazz began with three important events: the 1955 Moscow performance of Gershwin's *Porgy and Bess* by a visiting American troupe; the 1957 Moscow Youth Festival; and the 1959 American exhibition in Moscow, where the Soviet people had a chance to see, hear, and touch previously banned objects of 'bourgeois culture'. An important channel of information became the daily programs of the *Voice of America Jazz Hour* hosted by Willis Conover, who acquired cult figure status among young Russians. American jazz was an important symbol for the young writers of the Thaw. Jazz and jazz musicians featured in Vasilii Aksenov's novels and short stories. In 1967, Aksenov was a special reporter for *Iunost* (Youth) magazine at the Tallinn Jazz Festival. Jazz musicians who emerged in the 1960s include saxophonist Georgii Garanian (who in 1992 received the title of People's Artist of Russia), saxophonist Aleksei Kozlov (the leader of the Arsenal group), trumpeter and pianist German Lukianov (also known for his poetry), and saxophonist Aleksei Zubov (aka Zoubov), currently living in Los Angeles. During the 1970s many Soviet jazz musicians emigrated to the US, but few reached the level of recognition they had hoped for. One notable exception is trumpeter Valerii Ponomarev, who joined the famous American band Art Blakey and the Jazz Messengers in 1977 for four years, and later became its guest soloist.

See also: Aksenov, Vasilii; Kozlov, Aleksei; literature, Thaw; Odessa; *Pravda*; Thaw; Utesov, Leonid

Further reading

Aksenov, V. (1967) 'Prostak v mire dzhaza, ili ballada o tridtsati begemotakh' (Simpleton in the World of Jazz or the Ballad of Thirty Hippos), *Iunost*, 8.

Batashev, A. (1972) *Sovetskii dzhaz* (Soviet Jazz), Moscow: Muzyka.

Medvedev, A. and Medvedeva, O. (eds) (1987) *Sovetskii dzhaz: Problemy, sobytiia, mastera* (Soviet Jazz: Problems, Events, Masters), Moscow: Sovetskii kompozitor.

Starr, F. S. (1994) *Red and Hot: The Fate of Jazz in the Soviet Union 1917–1991*, New York: Limelight Editions.

VLADIMIR PAPERNY

Jews

For most of the tsarist era, Jews in Russia remained distinctly apart from the dominant culture, rarely participating in the development of broader Russian movements in art, literature, music, or philosophy. In the second half of the nineteenth century, however, Jewish intellectuals responded to the openings created by the Jewish Enlightenment and Russia's newly liberalized political environment. Jews began inserting themselves into the cultural environment of the Russian Empire, with scores of individual Jews actively participating in shaping *fin-de-siècle* Russian culture.

The Russian Revolutions of 1917 accelerated the linguistic and cultural assimilation of Jews in all areas of Russian culture. From literature and architecture, to photography, film, and painting, Jews emerged as some of its foremost producers and consumers. Despite the increasingly hostile atmosphere toward Soviet Jews in the late Stalinist (1948–53) and Stagnation (1968–85) eras, Jews continued to occupy an important place in Russian culture. In post-Soviet Russia, global Russian Jewry has played a significant role in putting Moscow and Russian culture firmly on the world's cultural map.

The Communist Revolution and the relaxation of tsarist-era laws discriminating against Jews allowed this highly-educated, quickly urbanizing population to participate in Russian revolutionary culture. Such celebrated writers as

Isaac Babel and Eduard Bagritskii helped shape Russian literary fiction in the 1920s and 1930s, and Vasilii Grossman and Ilia Erenburg played a central role in the development of Russian journalism of the 1940s and 1950s. Jews likewise were the foremost founders of the Soviet film and photography industries, two new cultural technologies that became central to Soviet culture. Arkadii Shaikhet's photographs adorned the cover of the illustrated magazine *Ogonek*, and his colleague Maks Alpert served as photo editor of *Pravda* and propagated Socialist Realism in photography. Evgenii Khaldei and Dmitrii Baltermants photographed World War II for the Soviet population, showing how Jews created the visual record of both the building of Soviet society and its violent destruction. In painting and drawing, El Lissitskii, Natan Altman, and Isaac Brodskii actively defined the visual arts in the 1920s and 1930s, through the avant-garde movement and then Socialist Realism – the art form that dominated the Russian cultural scene for several decades. In all cultural fields, Jews were both establishing and challenging Russian cultural conventions.

Jews also traditionally propagated Russian culture as émigrés. At the turn of the twentieth century, Russian Jewish émigrés created global Yiddish culture, and in the 1930s, Shimon Dubnov and Iulii Gessen wrote the history of Russian Jewry in Russian. With the mass emigration of Jews from Russia that began in the 1970s, such writers as Zinovii Zinik and such nonconformist artists as Vitalii Komar and Aleksandr Melamid have created new styles of Russian literature and art as multilingual, multicultural émigrés.

In the twentieth century, Jews were most visible in Russian culture during the inter-war period (1918–41). But even after the devastation of World War II and the anti-cosmopolitan campaign of late Stalinism – with its destruction of Yiddish culture and its attempts to exclude Jews from positions of Soviet cultural authority – Jews continued to shape Russian culture. During the Thaw (the late 1950s–early 1960s), named after an Erenburg novel, Jews participated in the new wave of Soviet film, winning international awards and expanding photography as a visual medium. In 1961, Baltermants became photo editor of *Ogonek*, a post he likely would not have occupied ten years earlier during late Stalinism. One of the most notorious moments in Thaw-era culture was Khrushchev's visit to the 1962 Manezh exhibition, which showcased many artists of the new generation (the so-called nonconformists), among whom were many Jews. Two of the most important exhibitors at the Manezh, Ilia Kabakov and Ernst Neizvestnyi, had taken Khrushchev's political and economic liberalization to the cultural sphere and pushed the boundaries of Soviet art.

Starting in the 1970s, many of these Jewish nonconformists left the Soviet Union with the initial wave of refuseniks, with many more emigrating in the late 1980s and 1990s. The youngest generation of non-conformists, such as Komar and Melamid, ended up building their careers as shapers of Russian culture almost entirely as émigrés. As émigrés, and unlike the generation that came of age during Stalinism, they made Jewishness an integral part of Russian culture. The new non-conformists made criticism of official Soviet culture and the incorporation of Jewish themes integral parts of global Russian art, literature, and photography.

But émigrés no longer have a monopoly on the cutting edge of Russian culture. Post-Soviet Russia, and Moscow in particular, has been the site of a significant cultural flowering in the past fifteen years. Some Jewish émigrés from the United States and Israel have returned to Moscow and St. Petersburg (e.g., the journalist Masha Gessen, whose family left the USSR in the 1970s), in order to be at the forefront of Russian culture. Aleksandra Paperno, who spent several years in New York training at the Pratt Institute, now lives in Moscow and is exhibited in the hottest galleries in Moscow. This dual trend – making the Jewishness of Russian culture visible and making Moscow the centre of global Russian culture – hit the art market in 2005 when Nina Kurieva founded the Ulei Gallery, which imports the art of Russian Jewish émigrés from Paris, New York, and elsewhere 'back' to Moscow. In the same year Moscow hosted the international convention of the World Union of Progressive Judaism for the first time in the organization's history, a sign that Moscow is also becoming a centre of Jewish religious culture. In film, theatre, and other

spheres of culture, Jews are pushing the boundaries of Russian culture and simultaneously developing a particularly Jewish culture in Russia, the likes of which have not been seen since before World War II.

With a Jew as Vladimir Putin's prime minister, Jewish religious and cultural institutions springing up every day across the country, and a Jewish population that makes it the third largest Jewish community in the world, Russia is once again becoming a centre of Jewish culture, and Russian a language of global Jewish culture. At the same time Jews are continuing their role as trend-setters of Russian culture.

See also: art, nonconformist; emigration; film, Soviet – Stalin era; film, Soviet – Thaw era; Judaism; Kabakov, Ilia; Komar and Melamid; Khrushchev, Nikita; literature, émigré; Manezh exhibition of 1962; Neizvestnyi, Ernst; *Ogonek*; *Pravda*; Putin, Vladimir; refuseniks; Socialist Realism; Stagnation; Stalin, Iosif; Thaw; World War II (Great Patriotic War)

Further reading

Gitelman, Z. (2003) *Jewish Life After the Soviet Union*, Bloomington, IN: Indiana University Press.

Lvov-Rogachevsky, V. (1979) *A History of Russian Jewish Literature*, Ann Arbor, MI: Ardis.

Nakhimovsky, A. (1991) *Russian-Jewish Literature and Identity*, Baltimore, MD: Johns Hopkins University Press.

Nathans, B. (1999) *Beyond the Pale: The Jewish Encounter with Late Imperial Russia*, Berkeley, CA: University of California Press.

Shrayer, M. (2006) *Anthology of Jewish Russian Literature*, London: M. E. Sharpe.

Slezkine, Y. (2004) *The Jewish Century*, Princeton, NJ: Princeton University Press.

DAVID SHNEER

joke (anekdot)

The *anekdot* (joke) was one of the most ubiquitous forms of Soviet popular culture. Soviet political *anekdoty* are the best-known thematic variety, but *anekdoty* about everyday situations (gender relations, drinking, going to the doctor, etc.); ethnic groups such as Jews, Armenians, and Chukchi; and *anekdoty* satirizing specific, mass-culture texts were no less widespread. Although its heyday came to an abrupt halt with the end of Soviet censorship in the late 1980s, the *anekdot* remains popular today, both as an object of nostalgia and as a productive oral genre.

The genre in its modern, urban form is a descendant of the traditional folk *anekdot*, itself a comic offshoot of the folk tale. The contemporary *anekdot* can also be traced to the so-called literary *anekdot*, a written genre popular in the nineteenth century that narrated a whimsical event in the life of a famous figure. The combined influence of these two generic forebears is detectable in the twentieth-century *anekdot*, especially its political variant, in which real-life personalities appear in humorous situations.

The clandestine sharing of political *anekdoty* emerged as a popular pastime, mainly among the urban intelligentsia, with the aggressive politicization of public and private life after the October Revolution of 1917. Under Stalin, thousands were imprisoned for telling such jokes. The *anekdot*'s popularity peaked during Stagnation, due to the combined effects of widespread cynicism, renewed (though no longer lethal) state intolerance of free expression, official attempts to construct a cult of personality around Leonid Brezhnev, and a series of films and television programmes that lent themselves to oral satire. Prominent among 'intertextual' *anekdoty* were cycles featuring characters from the films *Chapaev* and *Semnadtsat mgnovenii vesny* (*Seventeen Moments of Spring*), whose protagonists became modern-day versions of the traditional Russian folkloric fool. By the 1970s, joke-telling within trusted circles of confidants had become a form of private entertainment akin to reading *samizdat* literature, listening to the BBC and Voice of America on short-wave radios, and enjoying homemade recordings of bard music.

Since the *anekdot*'s potency and appeal were heavily determined by its status as a political taboo, its cultural currency fell precipitously after the end of censorship. Still, the socio-political and cultural novelties of post-Soviet life quickly began to engender new *anekdoty*, including a large cycle about the nascent moneyed class known as the New Russians (*novye russkie*). The reassertion of state influence on the mass media under Vladimir Putin has been a more recent stimulus for popular oral satire. The *anekdot* has also become a popular Internet genre among Russophones worldwide.

See also: bards; Brezhnev, Leonid; Chukchi; folk tales; Jews; Putin, Vladimir; samizdat; *Semnadtsat mgnovenii vesny* (*Seventeen Moments of Spring*); Stagnation

Further reading

Draitser, E. (1998) *Taking Penguins to the Movies: Ethnic Humor in Russia*, Detroit: Wayne State University Press.
Siniavski, A. (1984) 'The Joke Inside the Joke', trans. O. Matich, *Partisan Review* 51, 3: 356–66.
Yurchak, A. (1997) 'The Cynical Reason of Late Socialism: Power, Pretense and the *Anekdot*', *Public Culture* 9: 161–88.

SETH GRAHAM

journalism

The first Russian newspaper, *Sankt-Peterburgskie vedomosti* (The St. Petersburg News), launched in January 1703 by Peter the Great's decree, was devoted to state resolutions. The Russian press not only came under strict control and censorship, but was established to promote governmental ideas and proposals. The history of censorship in Russia is as long as the history of journalism, though Russian journalism has a strong tradition of heated public debate and exchange of opinion among statesmen and public figures. Before the 1917 Revolution, journalism addressed a wide audience, was respected as literature with lofty civic goals, and had high standards, even while its writers waged a constant battle against censorship.

The revolution introduced the concept of media as a tool for education and propaganda. Talented journalists and authors not in tune with the new regime found themselves in exile, and many who remained were repressed. Regulated at the highest governmental and

Party levels, media shaped mass opinion and presented role models, ideals, and images of enemies. Despite the media's propagandistic role, the USSR continued pre-revolutionary traditions inasmuch as the best Soviet authors wrote for the newspapers, worked in radio broadcasting, and were leaders in the media, including Mikhail Bulgakov and Ilia Ilf and Evgenii Petrov. During World War II, many prominent writers served as war correspondents, including Vasilii Grossman, Boris Pasternak, and Ilia Erenburg.

After setbacks to journalistic freedom in the immediate post-war years under Stalin's campaign against so-called 'cosmopolitans' (a code word for Jews), the Thaw infused Soviet journalism with new life. New periodicals appeared, including the literary journals *Iunost* (Youth) and *Molodaia gvardia* (the Young Guard). The era of Stagnation provided a challenge to free speech; writers became adept at Aesopian language. Despite the challenges of tight censorship, some outstanding writers produced courageous work, embracing investigative reportage and editorials that provided new perspectives on current events. Among newspapers of this era, the *Literaturnaia gazeta* (Literary Gazette) was particularly popular. At this paper Arkadii Vaksberg, Evgenii Bogat, Iurii Rost, Iurii Shchekochikhin, Olga Chaikovskaia, and others became favourites among Russian intellectuals. Anatolii Agranovskii at *Izvestiia*, as well as Inna Rudenko and Vasilii Peskov at *Komsomolskaia pravda*, also earned educated readers' respect.

After the collapse of the Soviet Union in 1991, the idea of journalism as art, craft, and civic duty suffered amid the complexities of the new society. Media gradually became big business, and talented journalists were thrown together with newcomers to the profession who lacked training, writing skills, and a sense of professionalism. Television became the most popular medium, taking over that role from newspapers. In recent years it also has become the most closely watched and embattled of the media; the takeover of Vladimir Gusinskii's Independent Television Station, NTV, is the clearest example. The magazine *Itogi*, owned by the same company and initially a partner of *Newsweek*, suffered the same fate. In the post-Soviet era, the Union of Russian Journalists, the nation's largest professional organization, established special awards and campaigns to protect and promote journalistic integrity and courage, as well as the dignity of the profession.

See also: *Literaturnaia gazeta* (Literary Gazette); NTV

NADEZHDA AZHGIKHINA

journalists, post-Soviet

Post-Soviet journalists represent very different trends, backgrounds, ideas, and practices. Many outstanding journalists came to post-Soviet media from the Soviet era, and some of them realized their potential and ideas even after the disappearance of ideological pressure. All leaders of perestroika publications, including Vitalii Korotich, Egor Iakovlev, and Aleksandr Chakovskii, belonged to the Soviet *nomenklatura* and realized the hopes of their youth as members of the 1960s generation only after Gorbachev came to power. New editors, such as Vitalii Tretiakov (*Nezavisimaia gazeta*, Independent Newspaper), Sergei Parkhomenko (*Segodnia*, Today), Dmitrii Muratov (*Novaia gazeta* [New Newspaper]), Vladimir Sungorkin (*Komsomolskaia Pravda* [Komsomol Truth]), and Pavel Gusev (*Moskovskii komsomolets* [Moscow Komsomol Member]) also had Soviet journalistic backgrounds. The best writers and radio and television journalists, such as Valerii Arganovskii, Iaroslav Golovanov, Arkadii Vaksberg, Anatolii Rubinov, Iurii Shchekochikhin, Otto Latsis, Iurii Chernichenko, Natalia Ivanova, Tatiana Ivanova, Inna Rudenko, Vladimir Pozner, and Alla Iaroshinskaia were active before and during perestroika.

Even younger journalists, whose careers rose rapidly during and after perestroika, began practising journalism during the Soviet era: Artem Borovik (*Sovetskaia Rossiia*, Soviet Russia, *Ogonek*, Little Flame, and his own *Sovershenno sekretno*, Top Secret); founder of the first advertising newspaper *Extra M*; Aleksandr Kavernzev; *Ogonek* stars Nina Chugunova and Aleksandr Terekhov; Vladimir Iakovlev (son of Egor Iakovlev and founder of the newspaper *Kommersant*

[Businessman]); Evgeniia Albats; Natalia Gevorkian; television journalists Vlad Listev, Vladimir Molchanov, Irina Zaitseva, Kirill Nabutov, Kira Proshitinskaia, and Tatiana Maksimova all had Soviet training and experience. Newcomers to Russian journalism after the collapse of the USSR included dissident journalists and previously repressed writers: Aleksandr Solzhenitsyn, Aleksandr Zinovev, Andrei Siniavskii, Maria Rozanova, Vladimir Maksimov. On the other hand, some journalists of the same generation (e.g., Aleksandr Prokhanov) agitated for past Communist values.

Some new figures came to journalism from other fields: Aleksandr Minkin had a background in the theatre, Evgenii Kiselev and Sergei Dorenko in foreign languages, Svetlana Sorokina studied at a forest institute, and Vladimir Solovev studied physics. They were all attracted to the media by its energy and sense of change.

Many bright young journalists entered the profession after the Soviet era. Iuliia Latynina is one of Russia's best economic analysts; Anna Politkovskaia devoted her talent to Chechnia and was given the International Women's Media Foundation Courage Award. At the same time, many of the old standards of journalistic ethics underwent change during recent years; some editors prefer 'hot' news to social reportage, ads to investigation, rumour to fact. Some journalists adhere to traditional standards, while others follow the methods of *kompromat* (compromising material) and scandal.

Many newcomers attracted by perestroika and the market economy, especially in the regions, are not as successful as those mentioned above. Average salaries of journalists in Russia are low (around $100 per month), not enough to survive on, and this figure takes into account the high salaries of leading Moscow television journalists and lower ones at local newspapers; such low pay provides opportunities for the manipulation of journalists by regional and local authorities.

Journalism is becoming a women's profession: twenty years ago, Russian journalists were split evenly by gender, while today almost 89 per cent of journalists are women, especially in regional and local media, where they receive low salaries for great responsibilities. Journalists face poverty and lack of respect on the one hand and the dangers of the profession on the other. Since 1992, more than 250 journalists have been killed, the majority not in Chechnia and other sites of war, but in the midst of regular investigations.

Russian journalists number around 150,000 today, including print media, radio, television, and Internet correspondents and photo-journalists; more than 50,000 are members of the Russian Union of Journalists. This union is the nation's largest and the oldest media professional organization; it fights for freedom of expression, protection of journalists and their families, support for the families of murdered journalists, and the preservation of professional standards and ethics. The Russian Union of Journalists has branches in all Russian regions and carries out activities in Russia and abroad. At the same time, the journalistic community faces problems maintaining professional solidarity. Journalists in the provinces feel isolated from those at the national level; their lives differ dramatically from the lives of their colleagues in the capitals, and they are subject to stronger pressure from regional and local authorities and thus need support in professional and ethical issues. For ten years the Union has awarded the Golden Pen (*Zolotoe pero*) to the best journalists; it is the most prestigious award in the profession.

See also: censorship; Central House of Journalists; Chechnia; Iakovlev, Egor; journalism; Kiselev, Evgenii; *Kommersant*; Korotich, Vitalii; Listev, Vladislav; Minkin, Aleksandr; *Moskovskii komsomolets*; *Ogonek*; periodicals, post-Soviet; periodicals, Soviet; Prokhanov, Aleksandr; Siniavskii, Andrei; Solzhenitsyn, Aleksandr; Tretiakov, Vitalii; unions, creative, post-Soviet; War, Chechen; women journalists

NADEZHDA AZHGIKHINA

Journalists' Union Building

See: Central House of Journalists

Judaism

Judaism, a monotheistic religion practised by some Jews, is an integral part of Jewish life and culture. It has a long history in Russia, and the widespread international Chabad-Lubavitch movement has its roots in White Russia (now Belarus). Jews in the region have experienced anti-Semitism from tsarist times to the present day.

Judaism holds that there is one omnipotent, omniscient god, who chose the Jewish people to keep his commandments. Within Judaism, important religious texts include the Hebrew Bible (*Tanakh*) as well as other sacred writings. The Torah, comprising the five books of Moses, is the first section of the Hebrew Bible and the principal guiding text for Judaism. The word Torah is sometimes used to describe all of Judaism's religious teachings. The Talmud, composed of the Mishnah and the Gemara, expands on the Torah through discussions of the interpretation and application of Jewish law.

Religious Jews gather to worship and study at synagogues under the religious leadership of a Rabbi. Prayer services are offered daily, and special services are held on Saturday (the Jewish Sabbath) and other holy days. Under Jewish law, Jewish identity is matrilineal: a child born to a Jewish mother is also Jewish, regardless of the father's identity. Conversion to Judaism is possible, though not traditionally encouraged.

Judaism has several major branches, including Orthodoxy, Conservatism, Reconstructionism, and Reform. While all branches share some characteristics, each branch differs in dogma and practice. For example, some types of Judaism require that followers keep a kosher diet, eating only food that is prepared following Jewish dietary laws, while others consider diet an individual decision.

During the relatively liberal period of New Economic Policy (NEP), from 1921–28, restrictions on religion somewhat relaxed, and the number of synagogues in operation increased. By 1929, however, harsher religious laws were introduced. Under Stalin, many synagogues and almost all other outlets of Jewish culture were closed down or appropriated for other uses. As one of the few types of Jewish organizations officially tolerated throughout the Soviet period, the synagogue acquired greater importance in Jewish cultural life. While the lack of prayer books was a problem and regular attendance at synagogues may not have been high, many people gathered there on holy days such as Yom Kippur (Day of Atonement) and Pesach (Passover). In addition to the officially acknowledged practice of Judaism, small prayer groups (*minyanim*) met regularly at private residences, especially to observe Jewish holy days. Institutions of Judaism began to re-emerge following easing of religious restrictions during perestroika and glasnost, when synagogues reopened and literature became more widely available.

Waves of mass emigration have contributed to a declining Jewish population in the former Soviet Union. In the early 1970s, Jews began to leave the Soviet Union for Israel and Western countries, especially the United States. Not only decreasing numbers but also a long history of Soviet and Russian acculturation may hamper the revival of Judaism and Jewish culture.

Jews living in Central Asia and the Caucasus were also affected by state restrictions on religion, but to a lesser extent. Bukharan, Georgian, and Mountain (mostly from Azerbaidzhan, Chechnia, and Dagestan) Jews are characterized by less Soviet or Russian assimilation and closer bonds between religious, family, and social life. Some members of these groups have moved to post-Soviet Russia.

The present state of Judaism in Russia is related to its historical context. Soviet nationalities policy defined Jews as an ethnic, rather than religious, group. 'Jewish' nationality was listed in the 'nationality' category (the so-called 'Point 5') of the internal passport, and several efforts were made to resettle Jews in an autonomous region. A survey collected in Russia and Ukraine in 1992–93 and 1997–98 indicated that very few Jews in Russia equate Jewishness with practising Judaism. Correspondingly, the same survey suggested that many self-identified Jews did not follow strict traditional religious practice.

See also: anti-Semitism; Belarus; Jews; passport; perestroika and glasnost

Further reading

Buwalda, P. (1997) *They Did Not Dwell Alone: Jewish Emigration from the Soviet Union 1967–1990*, Washington, DC: The Woodrow Wilson Center Press.

Chervyakov, V., Gitelman, Z. and Shapiro, V. (1997) 'Religion and Ethnicity: Judaism in the Ethnic Consciousness of Contemporary Russians', *Ethnic and Racial Studies* 20, 2: 280–305.

Gitelman, Z. (2003) 'Thinking about Being Jewish in Russia and Ukraine', in Z. Gitelman, M. Glants, and M. I. Goldman (eds) *Jewish Life After the USSR*, Bloomington, IN: Indiana University Press.

Gitelman, Z., Glants, M. and Goldman, M. I. (eds) (2003) *Jewish Life After the USSR*, Bloomington, IN: Indiana University Press.

Goluboff, S. L. (2003) *Jewish Russians: Upheavals in a Moscow Synagogue*, Philadelphia, PA: University of Pennsylvania Press.

Kornblatt, J. D. (2004) *Doubly Chosen: Jewish Identity, the Soviet Intelligentsia, and the Russian Orthodox Church*, Madison, WI: University of Wisconsin Press.

Ro'i, Y. (ed.) (1995) *Jews and Jewish Life in Russia and the Soviet Union*, Ilford: Frank Cass & Co. Ltd.

Weinberg, R. (1998) *Stalin's Forgotten Zion: Birobidzhan and the Making of a Soviet Jewish Homeland*, Berkeley, CA: University of California Press.

JENNIFER B. BARRETT

K

Kabachok '13 stulev' (The 13 Chairs Café)

The first and the only sitcom on Soviet television, *The 13 Chairs Café*, took place in a cosy pseudo-Polish café, in which the same characters (called Pan and Pani) met every week. In addition to humorous miniatures, actors would lip-synch foreign songs that were not accessible otherwise to Soviet audiences. The programme was received with great enthusiasm and immediately made all its actors, most of whom came from the Satire Theatre, famous. It became one of the most popular and long-lasting programmes on Soviet television (reportedly, Leonid Brezhnev never missed a single episode). The programme ended after 150 episodes in 1981 due to political unrest in Poland. It was directed by Georgii Zelinskii, Spartak Mishulin, and Inna Marusalova.

See also: Brezhnev, Leonid; television, Soviet

TATIANA SMORODINSKAYA

Kabakov, Ilia Iosifovich

b. 30 September 1933, Dniepropetrovsk

Artist

Co-founder of Moscow Conceptualism, 1970s nonconformist art that examined, thereby deflating, Soviet ideologemes, Kabakov emigrated in 1988. Acclaimed internationally and in post-Soviet Russia for 'excavating' Soviet civilization, Kabakov has allegorized totalitarianism's aesthetic allure in his installations since the mid-1980s. His *Krasnyi vagon* (*Red Wagon*, 1991), leading nowhere, entices us aboard with optimistic Stalinist songs and vistas. Other installations, such as *Chelovek, uletevshii v kosmos iz svoei kvartiry* (*The Man Who Flew into Space from His Apartment*, 1986), which features a catapult, a shattered communal apartment ceiling, and commentary by Kabakov's personae (the hero's remaining flatmates and a culturologist), reflect multifaceted responses to ideological and social pressures. A *Chevalier de l'Ordre des Arts et des Lettres* and recipient of the Max Beckmann Prize (and many others), Kabakov was judged by *ARTnews Magazine* (December 1999) one of the 'Ten Best Living Artists'.

See also: Conceptualism, art

AVRAM BROWN

Kadochnikov, Pavel Petrovich

b. 29 July 1915, Bikborda, Russia;
d. 2 May 1988, Leningrad

Russian film actor and director

A graduate of the Theatre Institute in Leningrad (1935), Kadochnikov achieved lasting popularity as a romantic lead in the musical comedy *Anton Ivanovich serditsia* (*Anton Ivanovich Is Angry*, 1941) and the spy adventure *Podvig razvedchika* (*The Intelligence Agent's Quest*, 1947), among others. Portraying the childlike Vladimir Staritskii in Eisenstein's *Ivan Groznyi* (*Ivan the Terrible*, 1943–46), Kadochnikov added tragic grandeur to an initially one-dimensional portrait. His later film roles mostly served as star vehicles and rarely presented genuine artistic challenges. In 1965, the actor debuted as film director; his critically underrated *Snegurochka* (*Snow Maiden*, 1969) was a fine attempt to avoid the sugar-coating typical of the fairy-tale genre. People's Artist of the USSR (1979).

See also: St. Petersburg State Academy of Theatre Arts

PETER ROLLBERG

Kafelnikov, Evgenii Aleksandrovich

b. 18 February 1974, Sochi

Tennis player

Kafelnikov was the first Russian awarded the Grand Slam title (French Open 1996 – both in men's singles and in doubles). His other major achievements were at the Australian Open 1999, the 2000 Olympics, and the 2002 Davis Cup (with Marat Safin and Mikhail Iuzhnyi as teammates). In May 1999, Kafelnikov made No.1 in the ATP rating. His numerous wins (26 single and 27 pair titles in the ATP tour) made tennis very popular in Russia and gave tremendous impetus to its development. Kafelnikov presented Maria Sharapova, then a little girl, with her first tennis racket, thereby encouraging her future tennis career.

See also: sports, post-Soviet

ALEXANDER LEDENEV

Kaidanovskii, Aleksandr Leonidovich

b. 23 July 1946, Rostov on Don;
d. 3 December 1995, Moscow

Actor, director

A graduate of the Shchukin Theatre Institute in Moscow (1969) and the Moscow Institute

for Scriptwriters and Film Directors (1984), Kaidanovskii studied under Andrei Tarkovskii and Sergei Solovev. His most memorable screen appearances include the White Army Captain Lemke in Nikita Mikhalkov's *Svoi sredi chuzhikh, chuzhoi sredi svoikh* (*At Home Among Strangers*, 1974) and the title role in Tarkovskii's *Stalker* (1979). As a film director, Kaidanovskii excelled at the adaptations of philosophical fiction by Camus (*Jonas*, 1984), Borges (*Gost* [*The Guest*, 1987]) and Lev Tolstoi (*Prostaia smert* [*A Simple Death*, 1985]). His best achievement is arguably *Zhena kerosinshchika* (*The Kerosene Seller's Wife*, 1988), about the diverging fates of two brothers in the last years of Stalin's regime.

See also: Mikhalkov, Nikita; Solovev, Sergei; Tarkovskii, Andrei

ANDREI ROGATCHEVSKI

Kalatozov, Mikhail

(also credited as Mikhail Kalatozishvili)

b. 29 December 1903, Tbilisi; d. 26 March 1973, Moscow

Director

Kalatozov began his career in Georgian cinema in 1923. His Georgian documentary *Marili Svanets,* (*Sol dlia Svanetii* [*Salt for Svanetia,* 1930]) introduced his major theme: the confrontation between humans and nature, and showcased the film-maker's metaphoric and expressive editing style. During the Stalin era, he became a key film-maker and industry administrator, from 1945–48 overseeing all of Soviet feature film production. In the 1950s, he began collaboration with cameraman Sergei Urusevskii. Their films, *Letiat zhuravli* (*The Cranes Are Flying*, 1957), *Neotpravlennoe pismo* (*The Unsent Letter*, 1960), and *Ia Kuba* (*I Am Cuba*, 1964) achieved international acclaim and became milestones of destalinization. His last film, the Soviet–Italian co-production *Krasnaia Palatka* (*Red Tent*, 1970), starring Sean Connery, dramatized the failed polar expedition of the Italian explorer Umberto Nobile.

See also: film, documentary; film, Georgian; film, Soviet – Stalin era

ALEXANDER PROKHOROV

Kaliagin, Aleksandr Aleksandrovich

b. 25 May 1942, Malmyzh, Kirov oblast

Actor

A versatile actor, artistic director, and educator, Kaliagin worked in various theatres in Moscow, becoming director of the Et Cetera Theatre in 1993. Collaborating with outstanding directors, he ingeniously performed a number of remarkable roles in cinema and theatre (including plays by Shakespeare, Molière, and Chekhov). The television drag comedy *'Zdravstvuite, ia vasha tetia!'* (*Uh, hello?!*) brought him instant popularity. As president of Russia's Theatre Union since 1996, he founded the Moscow Theatre Festival. Since 1983 he has held the title of National Artist of Russia.

VLADIMIR STRUKOV

Kalmykia (Kalmyk)

A republic in the Russian Federation inhabited by the Kalmyk ethnic group. The Kalmyks have inhabited the territory between the Volga and the Don rivers since ancient times. In the seventeenth and eighteenth centuries they were colonized by Russia; however, in 1935–43 and 1957–90 Kalmykia attained the status of an autonomous republic. Since 1990 the independent Republic of Kalmykia, it covers a territory of 76,100 sq km, with its capital in Elista. The native population (317,100 in 1998), which calls itself the *halmg*, speaks the Kalmyk language. The economy traditionally was agricultural.

Since 1993, Kalmykia has engaged actively in business and developed an infrastructure and a well-organized management system headed by market-style reformer Kirsan Ilumzhinov. Today this republic, although within the Russian Federation, has its own constitution, which theoretically should not contradict the constitution of the Russian Federation, but, in fact, does. The principal law of Kalmykia is the Steppe Code (1994).

See also: ethnic minorities

TATYANA LEDENEVA

Kamchatka

A peninsula in northeastern Russia covering a territory of 370,000 sq km, Kamchatka is surrounded by the Pacific Ocean, the Sea of Okhotsk, and the Bering Sea. The capital city, Petropavlovsk-Kamchatskii (Petropavlovsk-on-Kamchatka), is the largest port in the region. The land, consisting of tundra, sparse birch, and coniferous forests, is famous for hot mineral springs (including Pauzhet geothermic electric power station), geysers, and over sixty volcanoes (twenty-eight active), the highest of which is Kliuchevskaia Sopka (Spring Hill, 4750 m). The population of 367,000 (83 per cent urban) includes the Koriak ethnic minority.

Kamchatka numbers among Russia's most important fishing regions. The Kamchatka River (758 km) is a salmon spawning-ground. The west coast is famous for crab-fishing. In addition to the fish industry, the peninsula has deposits of coal, oil, and gold.

See also: Koriak

TATYANA LEDENEVA

Kancheli, Giya

b. 10 August 1935, Tbilisi, Georgia (USSR)

Composer

Georgia's most important living composer, Kancheli lived and worked in Tbilisi until his emigration to Berlin in 1991 (since 1994, he has lived in Antwerp). Recognized for its spiritual quality, his music uses extreme contrasts, tone colour, and time suspensions to create myriad emotional landscapes. In his scores one hears the influences of Georgian folk music, American jazz of the 1950s and the 1960s, the polystylistics of Alfred Shnittke, and echoes of Igor Stravinskii, Dmitrii Shostakovich and George Crumb. Kancheli is known for his large-scale works, but his œuvre also contains many chamber works as well as music for films. Recognized (at times grudgingly) by the Soviet cultural establishment, he has enjoyed particular popularity since the advent of glasnost.

See also: Shnittke, Alfred; Shostakovich, Dmitrii; Stravinskii, Igor

SUNGHAE ANNA LIM

Kaplan, Anatolii Lvovich

b. 28 December 1902 (10 January 1903), Rogachev, Belarus; d. 30 July 1980, Leningrad

Artist

Kaplan studied at the Leningrad Art Academy (1921–26) and joined the Artists' Union when it was established in 1939. One of the few Jewish artists tolerated by Soviet authorities, Kaplan preserved the world of his childhood in his paintings, works on paper, and prints. Life of Jews in the *shtetl* was his principal theme. During the late 1930s, he began the first of his large series of illustrations to the stories of Sholem Aleichem. Commissioned by the State Ethnographic Museum in Leningrad to create a series of lithographs depicting life in the Jewish Autonomous Region of Birobidzhan (1937), Kaplan portrayed the traditions of the Jewish people of a bygone era.

See also: anti-Semitism; Jews; unions, creative, Soviet

NATALIA KOLODZEI

kapustnik

A *kapustnik* (skit) is a cabaret-type humorous performance based on subjects of special concern to the theatre community and the current socio-political situation. The name derives from the name of a cabbage pie (cabbage means *kapusta*) traditionally served during Lent.

In the nineteenth century, *kapustniks* were organized by and for actors as private parties during Lent, when theatres were closed. The parties organized by the actor Varlamov, the so-called Varlamov *kapustniks*, were the most prominent in St. Petersburg, while in Moscow the most renowned were those organized by the Moscow Art Theater (MkhAT). The private *kapustniks* at the Leningrad Comedy Theatre were at their best in the 1950s, 1960s, and 1970s, and the *kapustnik* theatre, *Chetvertaia stena* (The Fourth Wall), had enormous success with Russian audiences in the 1990s. Since the mid-1990s, the *Vserossiiskii festival teatralnykh kapustnikov 'Veselaia koza'* (The Merry Goat All-Russian Kapustnik Festival) has been held in Nizhnii Novgorod.

See also: Moscow Art Theatre

DASHA KRIJANSKAIA

Karachentsev, Nikolai Petrovich

b. 27 October 1944, Moscow

Actor

A graduate of MKhAT, Karachentsev has worked in the Lenkom Theatre since 1967. He became famous after a leading role in Lenkom's romantic rock opera production *Juno and Avos*. Excellent in the dramatic and musical repertoire (e.g. Laertes in *Hamlet*), he has enjoyed a successful cinematic career in feature and animation films, notably as the bon vivant in comedies and period and costume dramas, such as the adaptation of Lope de Vega's *El Perro del Hortelano*; on television (*Dose detektiva Dubrovskogo*, Detective Dubrovskii's Dossier); and radio. Karachentsev holds the title of the National Artist of Russia since 1989.

See also: Lenkom Theatre; Moscow Art Theatre; rock opera

VLADIMIR STRUKOV

Karelia

Karelia is a large republic of Russia bounded by Finland, the White Sea, and a line running midway across Lakes Onega and Ladoga, to arch over the Leningrad Region north of St. Petersburg. Named for the Finnic-speaking people who originated the famous Kalevala epic, Karelia has belonged, by turns, to Novgorod, Moscow, Sweden, and Russia. In 1940, the USSR seized Karelia from Finland, which had claimed it in 1918. The Valaam Monastery and the Kizhi Museum are in Karelia, and Petrozavodsk, the capital and cultural centre is a beautiful historic city founded by Tsar Peter the Great in 1703.

See also: church architecture, Russian Orthodox; Lake Ladoga; Moscow; Novgorod; St. Petersburg

EDWARD ALAN COLE

Karelin, Aleksandr Aleksandrovich

b. 19 September 1967, Novosibirsk

Wrestler

The most titled Russian athlete in the history of Greek–Roman wrestling, having won more first-rank national and international competitions, including Olympic and world championships, than any other Russian wrestler, the heavyweight wrestler Karelin became Olympic champion in Seoul (1988), but participated in no tournaments during the following twelve years. The winner of two more Olympic gold medals (1992, 1996) and nine world championships, Karelin served three times as standard-bearer of the Russian Olympic team. In 1997, he was awarded the rank of Hero of Russia. His Siberian origin, physical power, and seeming invincibility have made Karelin a symbolic figure in Russian sports, the embodiment of the nation's physical power. In 1999, he turned to politics as a prominent member of the ruling Edinstvo (Unity) Party.

See also: political parties, post-Soviet; sports, Soviet

ALEXANDER LEDENEV

Karmen, Roman Lazarevich

b. 16 November 1906, Odessa; d. 28 April 1978, Moscow

Journalist, cinematographer, director, scriptwriter

Karmen covered the Spanish Civil War, creating (with Boris Makaseev) nearly two dozen film chronicles as well as two feature-length films. Between 1941 and 1945 Karmen ran the front-line film units, himself shooting footage of the Nazi approach to Moscow, Leningrad under siege, and Berlin in defeat; he filmed the Nuremberg Trials after the war (*Sud narodov*, [*Trial of Nations*, 1946]). Always a passionately committed Communist, Karmen made films about Vietnam, India, China, Cuba, and Chile, as well as the first wide-screen Soviet film, *Shiroka strana moia . . .* (*My Land Is Wide*, 1958).

See also: World War II (Great Patriotic War)

JOSEPHINE WOLL

kasha

Russian *kasha* can refer to virtually any grain cooked into a porridge. Numerous proverbs attest to the centrality of *kasha* in Russian life. In Soviet times, owing to chronic shortages of meat, fresh vegetables and fruit, *kasha* remained a staple in most households and public eating establishments; it also became emblematic of Soviet economic failures. Its varieties are popularly ranked in a hierarchy ascending from thin GULag gruel, barley grits, wheat, rice, millet, and oat porridges to the most favoured buckwheat, rich in protein and iron. Today *kasha* is positively associated with traditional Russian dishes, and as the main food during Russian Orthodox fasts.

See also: GULag; holidays, Russian Orthodox; Lent; proverbs; shortages

YVONNE HOWELL

Kasparov, Garri Kimovich

b. 13 April 1963, Baku, Azerbaidzhan SSR

Chess grandmaster

A graduate of the Azerbaidzhan Institute of Foreign Languages, Kasparov became the 13th world chess champion and a cult figure for the Russian liberal-thinking intelligentsia when at the age of 22 he defeated Anatolii Karpov, a favourite of the pro-government Russian Chess Federation. Having successfully defended his title five times (three of them against Karpov), Kasparov remained the top chess authority until 2000. In 1996, 1997, and 2003 he played chess with computer programs (Deep Blue, X3DFritz). He formally ended his professional chess career in 2004, and joined Russian politics as a leader of the pro-democratic opposition group *Komitet 2008: Svobodnyi vybor* (Committee 2008: Free Choice), promoting open and fair presidential elections.

See also: chess

ALEXANDER LEDENEV

Katiusha

Composed in 1938 by Matvei Blanter, with lyrics by Mikhail Isakovskii, *Katiusha* has a catchy melody and an endearing plot. The song describes the separation of Ekaterina (diminutive form: Katiusha) from her soldier. *Katiusha* became not only a favourite among soldiers and civilians during World War II, but also soldiers' affectionate nickname for a type of rocket battery. The West subsequently misattributed the song to Russian peasants.

TIMOTHY M. SCHLAK

Kazakhstan

A country in Central Asia that was the second largest republic in the USSR, Kazakhstan shares borders with Russia, China, Kyrgyzstan, and Uzbekistan. It also borders the Caspian Sea. In 2004, Kazakhstan had a population of about 15 million, just over half of whom were ethnic Kazakhs, a predominantly Sunni Muslim ethnic group who speak a Turkic language called Kazakh. Russians make up about one-third of the population and live mostly in large cities and in the northern part of the country. Since 1997, Astana has been the capital of Kazakhstan, but Almaty (formerly Alma-Ata), the Soviet-era capital, continues to be the country's first city, with a population of more than one million.

The Russian Empire began to expand into the territory of Kazakhstan in the eighteenth century. During the nineteenth century, the Russian government permitted farmers to settle on Kazakh lands, sparking intermittent rebellions by the Kazakhs. Although officially part of the Soviet Union since 1920, the Kazakh Soviet Socialist Republic was formed only in 1936. When Stalin's policies in the 1930s forced the nomadic Kazakhs to settle and collectivize their herds, many Kazakhs resisted by slaughtering their animals, and hundreds of thousands died from famine or in flight to China. During the 1950s, the Virgin Lands Campaign (*tselina*) brought hundreds of thousands of people, mainly from Russia and Ukraine, to farm the vast steppes of Kazakhstan. Kazakhstan became the site of the world's first space launch in 1957 from the Baikonur Cosmodrome.

When Kazakhstan became independent from the Soviet Union in December 1991, the government pursued a plan of moderate economic liberalization and cosmetic democratization. Kazakhstan's autocratic president, Nursultan Nazarbaev, managed to stay in power for many years by retaining substantial control over parliament and the media, and by policies that made Kazakhstan the most prosperous of the post-Soviet Central Asian states – largely through lucrative deals with Western oil companies that tapped the country's vast reserves.

Taking into account the large and possibly irredentist Russian population in Kazakhstan, the Nazarbaev government was careful in managing Kazakh nationalism. Kazakhstan has maintained good relations with Russia, China, and many Western countries

See also: Baikonur; Central Asia; Kyrgyzstan; tselina; USSR; Uzbekistan

LAURA ADAMS

Kazakov, Iurii Pavlovich

b. 8 August 1927, Moscow;
d. 29 November 1982, Moscow region

Writer

Trained in both music and literature, Kazakov began his writing career in earnest in 1952. Hailed as a 'new voice' in Russian fiction, he published prolifically from 1958 until 1973, mainly short stories. Following the models of such nineteenth-century classical Russian realist authors as Ivan Turgenev and Anton Chekhov, his lyrical narratives feature isolated characters, misfits, and malcontents who flee cities to search for goodness, truth, and beauty in the Russian countryside amidst its old wooden architecture. His evocative descriptions of nature move the readers as well as the characters that Kazakov sensitively depicts with psychological acuity and deep sympathy.

See also: architecture, wooden; literature, Soviet

CHRISTINE A. RYDEL

Kenzheev, Bakhyt

b. 2 August 1950, Chimkent, Kazakh SSR

Poet, writer

One of the 'Moscow' group (along with Aleksei Tsvetkov, Aleksandr Soprovskii, and Sergei Gandlevskii) of poets that emerged in the 1970s, Kenzheev was unable to publish in the USSR and emigrated to Canada in 1982. His poetry is marked by a virtuosity that infuses the exploration of historical and cultural landscapes with intimate, light elegance.

See also: Gandlevskii, Sergei; Kazakhstan; poetry, Soviet

YVONNE HOWELL

KGB

See Federal Security Service

Khachaturian, Aram Ilich

b. 24 May [6 June] 1903, Tbilisi, Georgia;
d. 1 May 1978, Moscow

Composer

An Armenian, Khachaturian, along with Prokofiev and Shostakovich, was one of the most important composers from the 1930s till the 1960s. His compositions bridged European and Eastern traditions, introducing Armenian folksong, much of it based on the *ashugh* tradition – that of the troubadour poet-musicians who wandered through Armenia from the seventeenth to the nineteenth centuries – into Western forms. His *Piano Concerto* (1936) and *Violin Concerto* (1940, composed for David Oistrakh) helped to establish his international career, buttressed by such popular orchestral works as the *Tanets s sabliami* (*Sabre Dance*) from the ballet *Gayane* (1942) and *Waltz* from *Masquerade* (1941).

The first Soviet composer in the country to write film scores, Khachaturian maintained a lifelong interest in cinema. After enduring hardships under the repressive Zhdanov Decree of 1947, he returned to composing with a trio of *Concerto-Rhapsodies* for violin (1961), cello (1963), and piano (1968).

See also: Armenia; classical music, Soviet; folk music; music in film; Oistrakh, David; Prokofiev, Sergei; Shostakovich, Dmitrii

Further reading

Yuzefovich, V. (1985) *Aram Khachaturyan*, New York: Sphinx.

DAVID GOMPPER

Khakamada, Irina Mutsuovna

b. 13 April 1955, Moscow

Politician

Born into a family of Japanese Communists who defected to the USSR in 1939, Khakamada graduated from Moscow's Patrice Lumumba Friendship of Peoples International University.

She holds the academic degree of Candidate of Economics. Khakamada was elected to the Duma in 1993, 1995, and 1999. In 1997–98, she was head of the government Committee for the Support and Development of Small Businesses. In the 2003 parliamentary elections, she and her party, the Union of Rightist Forces, suffered devastating defeats. In 2004, she ran for President and received 3.84 per cent of the vote. At present, Khakamada is the leader of the 'Free Russia Democratic Party'.

See also: academic degrees; Duma; political parties, post-Soviet; Union of Rightist Forces

ALEXANDER DOMRIN

Khamatova, Chulpan Nailevna

b. 1 October 1975, Kazan

Actress

A graduate of the Russian Academy of Theatre Arts (RATI), Khamatova worked in the Russian Young Spectators' Theatre, and at the Sovremennik Theatre (since 1998). One of the most talented actresses of the 'new wave', she was acknowledged as a 'rising star' (*chulpan*) in Russian cinema after her debut in Vadim Abdrashitov's film *Time of the Dancer* (*Vremia tantsora*, 1997). Her roles in Valerii Todorovskii's film *Land of the Deaf* (*Strana glukhikh*, 1998) and Bakhtier Khudoinazarov's original tragi-comedy *Moon Daddy* (*Lunnyi papa*, 1999) brought her international fame, increased by her appearance in Wolfgang Becker's *Good Bye, Lenin!* (Germany, 2003). Often appearing in television productions, Khamatova is active in charity work to help children suffering from hematological diseases. Recipient of prestigious theatre awards and the Russian State Prize (2004).

See also: Abdrashitov, Vadim; awards, cultural, post-Soviet; Russian Academy of Theatre Arts; Sovremennik Theatre; Todorovskii, Valerii; Young Spectator Theatre

YURII ZARETSKY

kharakteristika (reference)

The *kharakteristika* (reference) was a document attesting to the social and political qualities of a Soviet citizen. A reference from a place of work or study was required at all stages of a Soviet citizen's biography beginning with secondary school, for a university or job application or a trip abroad. It usually required a so-called 'triangle' of signatures – from the supervisor, the leader of one's Party unit, and the chair of the trade union at the place of employment. For professional visits abroad, an application to a position in the *nomenklatura*, or by request from judicial bodies, a reference had to be confirmed by higher Party representatives (from the regional secretary of the Communist Party) and the so-called *pervyi otdel* (first department) – the KGB's workplace representative. A positive reference had to end with the obligatory formula 'politically literate, morally firm' (*politicheski gramoten, moralno ustoichiv*). The absence of such a formula meant that the reference was negative.

See also: Communist Party; nomenklatura; unions, professional

GASAN GUSEJNOV

Kharlamov, Valerii Borisovich

b. 14 January 1948, Moscow; d. 27 August 1981, near Moscow

Hockey player

A legend of Soviet hockey of the 1970s, Kharlamov was famed for his skating and stick-handling skills. Of relatively small stature, he was a creative, agile left-winger who outsmarted and outskated opponents. As a member of TsSKA and Team USSR, he won eleven Soviet, seven European, and eight World Championships, and two Olympic gold medals (1972 and 1976, with Vladislav Tretiak). Kharlamov decided to retire from play after the 1981–82 season, but was killed in an automobile accident before the season had begun.

See also: hockey; Tretiak, Vladislav; TsSKA

RACHEL S. PLATONOV

Khazanov, Gennadii Viktorovich

b. 1 December 1945, Moscow

Comedian

Khazanov started his acting career in amateur theatres, and graduated from the State Institute of Circus and Stage Art (*Gosudarstvnnoe uchilishche tsirkovogo i estradnogo iskusstva*). Beginning in 1973, he worked as a comedian at *Moskontsert* (the Moscow concert organization). Monologues of a culinary school student, of a sincere and shy 'little man' (written by Lion Izmailov and Iurii Volovich), and of a brave parrot who cannot stop telling the truth (*Arkadii Khait*) brought him wide fame. Khazanov became one of the most popular Soviet performers: he read Aleksandr Ivanov's poetic parodies, humorous and satirical works by Semen Altov, Viktor Shenderovich, Mikhail Gorodinskii, and Grigorii Gorin, and acted in several film, theatre, and television productions. Often criticized by Soviet cultural authorities for his sharp satire, in 1997 he became an artistic director of Moscow's *Teatr Estrady* (Variety Theatre), and subsequently an ardent supporter of Putin's policies. Recently Khazanov started working as a host on NTV. People's Artist of the Russian Federation (1994), Russian State Prize (1995).

See also: comedians; NTV; Putin, Vladimir; stand-up comedy

TATIANA SMORODINSKAYA

Kheifits, Iosif Efimovich

b. 17 December 1905, Minsk; d. 24 April 1995, St. Petersburg

Film director, screenwriter

Kheifits joined the Soviet film industry in 1928, forming a 'Komsomol directing brigade' at Lenfilm studio with his long-time associate Aleksandr Zarkhi. The duo landed early hits with the moderately Stalinist *Deputat Baltiki* (*Baltic Deputy*, 1937), about an elderly biologist who supports the Bolshevik government during the Civil War, and *Chlen pravitelstva* (Member of the Government, 1939), the story of a simple peasant woman who becomes an administrative leader. After he began to direct on his own during the Thaw, Kheifits won international recognition with sensitive Chekhov adaptations, most famously *Dama s sobachkoi* (*The Lady with the Dog*, 1959). His prolific career spanned sixty years and featured numerous contemporary melodramas distinguished by fine acting and precise social and cultural detail. People's Artist of the USSR (1964).

See also: film, literary adaptations; Thaw; Zarkhi, Aleksandr

PETER ROLLBERG

Khitruk, Fedor Savelevich

b. 1 May 1917, Moscow

Animator, director

Khitruk is the creator of numerous animated adaptations of folktales and children's stories, including Buratino and A.A. Milne's Winnie-the-Pooh stories, the latter featuring the voice of actor Evgenii Leonov. The films inspired a huge cycle of *anekdoty* (jokes) about Pooh and his partner, Piatachok (Piglet). Khitruk also made animated films not specifically for children, touching on social and philosophical themes, including *Istoriia odnogo prestupleniia* (*Story of One Crime*) and *Ostrov* (*Island*), which won the Palme d'Or prize at Cannes in 1973. Khitruk is considered a master of the cut-out and collage animation techniques.

See also: Buratino; film, animation; folk tales; joke; Leonov, Evgenii

SETH GRAHAM

Khodorkovskii, Mikhail Borisovich

b. 26 June 1963, Moscow

Businessman

A former Komsomol leader, Khodorkovskii became the richest *oligarkh* in post-Soviet Russia and head of Menatep Bank and Yukos Oil. After establishing his own bank and holding company, Menatep, he obtained control of Yukos Oil during the 1995 'loans for shares' scandal. A philanthropist who openly compared himself to Andrew Carnegie, Khodorkovskii amassed a fortune estimated at $8 billion. He raised the government's ire in 2003 by criticizing the Kremlin's role in an oil deal. In response, the Kremlin launched a campaign against him that culminated with his arrest (25 October 2003) for tax evasion, a charge for which he was found guilty in 2005 and sentenced to nine years. Ultimately, Khodorkovskii's rise and apparent fall perfectly encapsulate the 'wild capitalism' of the Yeltsin years and the growing 'managed capitalism' of the Putin era.

See also: oligarkh; Putin, Vladimir; Yeltsin, Boris

STEPHEN M. NORRIS

kholodets

Meat in aspic, served cold. Also known as *studen* or, if made with fish, *zalivnoe*. *Kholodets* is a labour-intensive, though inexpensive, appetizer typically served on festive occasions, especially at New Year. A traditional dish, it has also been a feature of urban Russian cuisine since the early twentieth century.

See also: appetizers; meat dishes

SETH GRAHAM

Kholopov, Iurii Nikolaevich

b. 14 August 1932, Ryazan; d. 24 April 2003, Moscow

Musicologist

A music theorist and musicologist, Kholopov studied at the Moscow Conservatory, where he taught from 1960 until his death. As a teacher he helped to overturn traditional approaches to theories of musical form entrenched during the anti-Formalist campaign under Stalin. In the

more than thousand publications that solidified his international reputation, he tried to solve problems associated with contemporary harmony by evoking earlier models, particularly from the medieval period, to establish links between music across the centuries.

See also: Moscow Conservatory

DAVID GOMPPER

Khotinenko, Vladimir Ivanovich

b. 20 January 1952, Slavgorod, Altai Province

Film director, producer, screenplay writer, and actor

Khotinenko studied film-making under actor and director Nikhita Mikhalkov; a chance meeting with Mikhalkov inspired the former architect to change professions. Khotinenko's style, however, significantly differs from that of his teacher. Unlike Mikhalkov, Khotinenko prefers smaller canvases. The award-winning director's protagonists are often disenfranchised intellectuals struggling to find their place in post-Soviet society: the poet Makarov in the 1993 film of the same name or an out-of-work poet in the 1999 film *Strastnoi bulvar* (*Strastnoi Boulevard*). Khotinenko's films, often set in Russia's provinces, typically present an opposition between (Western) rational thinking and a Russian belief in the irrational, with the latter emerging as morally superior.

SUSMITA SUNDARAM

Khrennikov, Tikhon Nikolaevich

b. 28 May 1913, Elets, Russia

Composer

Khrennikov's reputation as Secretary of the Union of Composers (from 1948–91) has overshadowed his status as a composer. Elected deputy to the Supreme Soviet, the Soviet Union's figurehead parliament, in 1974, Khrennikov was reviled by the intelligentsia for his acceptance of the Party's crusade against 'formalism', reflected in the bland lyricism of his own music. Khrennikov's memoirs, *Tak eto bylo* (*That's How It Was*, 1994), however, argue that he managed to support Soviet composers more effectively than did other artistic unions. His operas, often based on leading works of Soviet literature, include Maksim Gorkii's propagandistic *Mat* (*Mother*, opera 1952–57) and Ilf and Petrov's more politically ambiguous *Zolotoi telenok* (*The Golden Calf*, opera 1984–85). Khrennikov has also composed orchestral works, ballet music, songs, and chamber works, as well as incidental music to Shakespeare's *Much Ado about Nothing* (*Mnogo shumu iz nichego*, 1935–36) for the Vakhtangov Theatre. People's Artist of the USSR (1963).

PHILIP ROSS BULLOCK

Khrushchev, Nikita Sergeevich

b. 17 April 1894, Kalinovka, Kursk oblast;
d. 11 September 1971, Moscow

Khrushchev's gravestone, by the sculptor Ernst Neizvestnyi, consists of two conjoined blocks of marble, one black and one white. The contradictions of Khrushchev's character, so aptly captured in this memorial, became the paradoxes of his era; both were fatally divided between conservatism and radical populism.

The son of a peasant family, Khrushchev worked as a mining engineer in Ukraine from a young age, and then as a political commissar during the Civil War. Thereafter, he moved up the Party ranks quickly and took up administrative posts in the Ukrainian and Moscow Party organizations before joining the Politburo in 1939. After wartime and post-war work in Moscow and Ukraine, Khrushchev was prominent enough to be one of several contenders to succeed Stalin after his death in 1953.

Underestimated by his colleagues, Khrushchev deftly manoeuvred in the period of 'collective leadership' (1953–55), to outflank both Viacheslav Molotov and Georgii Malenkov, his main rivals after Lavrentii Beria's violent ousting. Party policies over the ensuing decade were indelibly marked by Khrushchev's impulsive,

utopian leadership style, and by the complexity of the Stalinist legacies bequeathed to him.

Khrushchev was genuinely persuaded of the pragmatic – if not the moral – necessity to break with Stalinism. The Party covertly encouraged de-stalinization from the earliest days after Stalin's death, but only with the decision to give the 'secret speech' at the end of the Twentieth Party Congress (25 February 1956) did anti-Stalinism become explicit. Khrushchev played the leading role in the behind-the-scenes discussions, and the drafting and authorization of the speech. Later, his decisions to allow publication of anti-Stalinist literature by Aleksandr Solzhenitsyn and Evgenii Evtushenko, among others, again propelled de-stalinization forward. Nevertheless, his harsh treatment of Soviet, Polish, and Hungarian 'dissenters' after the Secret Speech betrayed a fondness for the authoritarianism under which he had grown up, as did his summary treatment of the 'anti-Party group' of his rivals in 1957. The same streak of authoritarianism could be felt in 'anti-parasite' legislation and other methods of community surveillance and policing that Khrushchev encouraged during the supposedly 'liberal' 1960s.

Other areas of domestic and foreign policy were likewise affected by these contradictory impulses to voluntarism and to liberalization. Khrushchev tackled stagnant agricultural production by liberalizing treatment of farmers, yet also by forcing through the – ultimately unsuccessful – mass planting of corn and the cultivation of the 'Virgin Lands'. Foreign policy saw overtures to the West – marred, however, by a utopian belief in communism's superiority, evident in the one-upmanship of the space race and also in the near-fatal Cuban Missile Crisis.

The Khrushchev era, like its leader, was complex, characterized by sober retrospection and utopian projections of the communist future, by philistinism and aesthetic experimentation, and by conservatism and radicalism. However, these paradoxes were politically unsustainable. Through his repeated swings between conservatism and radicalism, Khrushchev ultimately squandered support on both sides of the political spectrum. Removed from office through the bloodless coup against him in late October 1964, he was ignored by the Party until his death, and buried with little fanfare in 1971.

See also: Cold War; cult of personality; Communist Party; Evtushenko, Evgenii; Neizvestnyi, Ernst; political structure, Soviet; Solzhenitsyn, Aleksandr; Stalin, Iosif; Thaw

POLLY JONES

Khrzhanovskii, Andrei Iurievich

b. 30 November 1939, Moscow

Animator

One of the most controversial directors at Soiuzmultfilm studios, Khrzhanovskii made animated films that often pushed the boundaries of Party acceptability. His first, *Zhyl byl Koziavin* (*Once There Lived Koziavin*, 1966), tells the story of a ridiculous apparatchik, while his most controversial film, *Steklliannaia garmonika* (*The Glass Harmonica*, 1968), was shelved for its blatant political allegory. As do several of his other films, the latter lyrically portrays art as a counterbalance to autocratic rule. His most important works include animated films of Pushkin's drawings, poetry, and prose writings.

See also: censorship; film, animation; film studios; Pushkin, Aleksandr

BELLA GINZBURSKY-BLUM

Khutsiev, Marlen

b. 4 October 1925, Tbilisi, Georgia (USSR)

Director, writer

Khutsiev's first film, *Vesna na Zarechnoi ulitse* (*Spring on Zarechnaia Street*, 1956), co-directed with Feliks Mironer, initiated a successful if controversial career. His 1959 *Dva Fedora* (*Two Fedors*) ran into official problems because of its supposedly 'dark' view of post-war Soviet reality. His portrait of Soviet youth, *Zastava Ilicha* (*The Ilich Gate*, 1961) provoked Nikita Khrushchev's fury in March 1963; cuts and revisions delayed the film's release (as *Mne dvadtsat let* [*I am Twenty*]) by over a year. Subsequent films include *Iulskii dozhd* (*July Rain*, 1967), about

increasingly disaffected young intellectuals, and *Beskonechnost* (*Infinity*, 1991). Khutsiev has also been a prominent member of VGIK's faculty for many years.

See also: All-Russian (All-Union) State Institute of Cinematography; Khrushchev, Nikita; film, Soviet – Thaw period

JOSEPHINE WOLL

Khvorostovskii, Dmitrii Aleksandrovich

b. 16 October 1962, Krasnoiarsk

Opera singer

Baritone Khvorostovskii's remarkable early trajectory took him from music school in Siberia to the Mariinskii (Kirov) Theatre in St. Petersburg, and then to victory in the BBC Singer of the World competition in 1989. Judicious in his choice of repertoire and engagements, Khvorostovskii enjoys continued popularity with audiences and critics, both in Russia and abroad. His elegant *bel canto* serves him well in Mozart as well as more traditional Russian and Italian operas. An accomplished recitalist, he is as suited to Shostakovich and Sviridov as to Tchaikovsky and Rakhmaninov and folksongs.

See also: folk music; Mariinskii Theatre; opera singers, Mariinskii Theatre; Shostakovich, Dmitrii

PHILIP ROSS BULLOCK

Kibirov, Timur Iurevich

(né Zapoev)

b. 15 February 1955, Shepetovka, Khmelnitskaia oblast, Ukraine

Poet

Kibirov's highly allusive works mix the Russian classics with Soviet and post-Soviet high and low culture to create a distinctive, amusing, and surprisingly harmonious poetic idiom. He was first 'discovered' and encouraged by Lev Rubinshtein and Dmitrii Prigov, with whom he is often compared. Yet his favoured genres (lyric and epistle) and metres (the basic nineteenth-century repertoire), as well as his avowedly moral stance (citing Aleksandr Pushkin, he insists that poetry should 'awaken virtuous feelings') make him less a conceptualist than a traditionalist. Kibirov has won numerous prizes and is among the most popular poets writing today.

See also: Conceptualism, literary; Prigov, Dmitrii; Rubinshtein, Lev

MICHAEL WACHTEL

Kiev

Located on hills over the Dnieper River, Kiev (population: 251,400 in 2005) is the capital of Ukraine and its second largest industrial centre (after Kharkov). Founded in 482 A.D. by Eastern Slavic tribes, Kiev became the capital of Rus in 882 AD and remained the major political, economic, religious, and cultural centre for Eastern Slavs until invading Tatars and Mongols destroyed it in 1240. Incorporated into Lithuania in 1362, Poland in 1569, and Russia in 1654, in 1917–20 it became the capital of the People's Republic of Ukraine, in 1934 of the Ukrainian Soviet Socialist Republic (of the USSR), in 1991, of Ukraine, which gained independence from the Soviet Union.

The most famous of Kiev's many impressive architectural monuments are the Golden Gate (1037), Sofia Cathedral (eleventh century), the Kiev-Pecher Monastery (Kievo-Pecherskaia Lavra, eleventh–eighteenth centuries), Vydubetskii Monastery (eleventh–eighteenth centuries), St. Andrew's (Andreevskaia) Church (1767), St. Vladimir's (Vladimirskii) Cathedral (1896), St. Cyril's (Kirillovskaia) Church (twelfth century), Mariinskii Palace (1755), the main building of Kiev University, and the opera and ballet theatre (1901). Kiev was levelled in World War II. Houses on its main street (Kreshchatik) were rebuilt (1947–54) in Stalinist style. Today Kiev has eighteen colleges and universities, thirteen theatres, and thirty museums.

See also: church architecture, Russian Orthodox; Russian Orthodoxy; Soviet Union; Ukraine; World War II (Great Patriotic War)

SERGEI TARKHOV

Kim, Iulii Chersanovich

b. 23 December 1936, Moscow

Writer

Kim is known as a poet, bard, playwright, actor, and dissident. Orphaned by his parents' repression in 1938, he was raised by relatives. After studies at Moscow's Pedagogical Institute, he taught in schools in Kamchatka and Moscow. In the 1960s his satirical, lyrical and humorous adventure songs (e.g., *Otvazhnyi kapitan* [*The Intrepid Captain*]) were widely circulated on cassettes. Okudzhava privately viewed Kim as the rightful heir to his own 'lyre'. Kim's protest activities necessitated the use of a pseudonym, Iu. Mikhailov, under which he composed song lyrics used in some fifty films (*Bumbarash*, *The Twelve Chairs*) and forty plays. He has written the screenplays for several films and over twenty original plays.

See also: bards; dissident

TIMOTHY D. SERGAY

kinetic art

An art movement (1962–76) founded by Lev Nusberg, also known as *kinetizm*, *kintez* (from 'kinetism' and 'synthesis'), *kiberromantizm*; members sometimes called themselves *kinety*. Participants included (at different times) Francisco Infante, Viacheslav Koleichuk, Galina Bitt, Natalia Prokuratova, Viktor Buturlin, Viktor Stepanov, Aleksandr Grigorev, and others. The group's philosophy may be summarized as follows: People have vices – aggression, greed, hunger for power; they are incurable; eventually they need to be replaced by artificial bio-cybernetic systems. The role of the artist is not to make pretty pictures, but to work on creating these bio-cybernetic systems. The group's greatest public success was decorating the city of Leningrad for the 50th anniversary of the October Revolution (1967). Former members of the movement do not agree on its role and on the chronology of events.

See also: art, Soviet; Infante, Francisco; Nusberg, Lev

VLADIMIR PAPERNY

Kino

Rock band

Formed in Leningrad in 1982, Kino (Cinema) became one of the country's most popular groups, largely because of the romantic, defiant image of its singer, Viktor Tsoi, whose songs expressed the restlessness of Soviet youth during a time of profound change. Kino initially attracted fans by performing at small clubs, festivals, and apartment-concerts, and releasing cassette albums. Like many other groups, Kino was allowed to record on the state label and tour freely only during perestroika. Though the band broke up following Tsoi's death in a 1990 automobile accident, its music is still immensely popular, even among young fans.

See also: rock music; Tsoi, Viktor

SETH GRAHAM

Kio, Igor Emilevich

b. 13 March 1944, Moscow

Circus magician

Son of the renowned magician Emil Teodorovich Kio (1894–1965), Igor Kio entered the Soviet circus ring at the age of 15, performing many of his father's classic tricks and, over the course of his thirty-year career, introducing original, fast-paced, and often elaborate displays of illusion. Kio became well known after his brief marriage to Brezhnev's daughter Galina Brezhneva (1929–98) in 1962, and his frequent appearances in the circus, the theatre, and on television secured his popularity throughout the

Soviet Union. In 1989, Kio resigned from the Union of State Circuses and established his own creative association, 'Igor Kio's Illusion Show', to promote his performances and those of other independent artists. People's Artist of Russia (2003); Meritorious Artist of Georgia.

See also: Brezhnev, Leonid; circus

MIRIAM NEIRICK

Kirkorov, Fillip Bedrosovich

b. 30 April 1967, Varna, Bulgaria

Singer

A Bulgarian-born popular singer and musical producer, Kirkorov studied at Moscow's Gnesin Music School. He began his career in the late 1980s, and his talent and charismatic stage persona earned him an invitation to the Alla Pugacheva Theatre of Song. By 1991, Kirkorov began producing his own stage shows. In these eclectic performances, his repertoire ranges from sentimental romances to tango, alternates between disco and hip-hop rhythms, and relies heavily on remakes of popular Latin American and Western hits. Kirkorov's 1994 marriage, now defunct, to Russian pop diva Alla Pugacheva attracted media attention and boosted his popularity.

See also: popular music, post-Soviet; popular music, Soviet; Pugacheva, Alla

OLGA PARTAN

Kirov Theatre

See Mariinskii Theatre

Kiselev, Evgenii

b. 15 June 1956, Moscow

Television anchor, journalist

A graduate of Moscow State University's Asia and Africa Institute, Kiselev joined television in

1987 as anchorman for the news programme *Vremia* (Time). From 1990, he worked for *Tele-Sluzhba Novosti*, then anchored the news programme *Vesti* on RTR. In September 1991, he returned to ORT and launched the analytical news programme *Itogi* (Summing Up). In 1994, he moved with *Itogi* to NTV, where he also created the show *Geroi dnia* (Hero of the Day). He was Director of NTV from 1993, General Director from February 2000. After the handover of Vladimir Gusinskii's shares to Gazprom in 2001 Kiselev left NTV to join TV6. After the dissolution of TV6 in 2002, he established TV Spectrum, which was taken off the air in June 2003. Since September 2003 Kiselev has been editor-in-chief of the weekly newspaper *Moskovskie novosti* (Moscow News) and can be heard on the radio station *Ekho Moskvy* (Echo of Moscow).

See also: censorship; *Ekho Moskvy* (Echo of Moscow); Gusinskii, Vladimir; journalism; journalists, post-Soviet; *Moskovskie novosti* (Moscow News); NTV; radio, post-Soviet; television channels

BIRGIT BEUMERS

Kissin, Evgenii Igorevich

b. 10 October 1971, Moscow

Pianist, composer

Kissin began to play piano and to improvise at the age of 2 and entered Moscow's Gnesin School of Music four years later. His performances at the age of 12 of Chopin's two piano concertos in the Great Hall of the Moscow Conservatory have become legendary. Kissin developed smoothly from a child prodigy into an internationally acclaimed artist. He made his Western European debut with Herbert von Karajan and the Berlin Philharmonic in 1987, and his American debut with Zubin Mehta and the New York Philharmonic in 1990. He subsequently moved permanently to New York. A musician with an impeccable technique, he is often called the last great Romantic pianist.

See also: classical musicians/performers, post-Soviet; Moscow Conservatory; piano performance, Russian/Soviet

SUNGHAE ANNA LIM

Klimov, Elem Germanovich

b. 9 July 1933, Stalingrad (Volgograd), Russia; d. 26 October 2003, Moscow

Film director

Elem Klimov graduated from the State Film Institute in Moscow in 1964. Like other filmmakers of the new generation, he attempted to jettison the constraints of Socialist Realism. During the next twenty years Klimov shot six feature films that were either shelved or released only after censorship and delays. Elected chairman of the Union of Soviet Film-makers in 1986, he immediately established a Conflict Commission charged with releasing hundreds of shelved films. Paradoxically, during the last seventeen years of his life he created no new films. His last film, *Idi i smotri* (*Come and See*, 1985), is a breathtaking account of a boy's experience during the German occupation of Belarus in 1943.

See also: censorship; unions, creative, Soviet

YANA HASHAMOVA

kliukva

Kliukva, literally a cranberry, is a derogatory term for an artistic portrayal of any kind that purports to be true to life, but actually betrays ignorance of the original: for example, a staging of nineteenth-century court life in which behaviour and language do not conform to the era. Although the expression *razvesistaia kliukva* (spreading chestnut) has been dated by scholars to a play parodying foreign misconceptions of Russia staged in 1910, in Dmitrii Ushakov's dictionary (*Tolkovyi slovar russkogo iazyka*, 1935–40), it is attributed to a nineteenth-century French author called a 'superficial Frenchman' (*poverkhnostnyi frantsuz*) who allegedly described someone sitting 'in the shade of a majestic cranberry'. Today the meaning has been extended to indicate not so much ignorance of the original as insincerity with commercial ends: a desire to portray clichés about 'authentic' Russia to please foreign viewers by confirming their stereotypes. This accusation has been levelled particularly against films supposedly shot for foreign audiences rather than domestic viewers.

KAREN EVANS-ROMAINE

Klub kinoputeshestvennikov (The Film Travellers' Club)

Television programme

The travel-adventure documentary series *Klub kinoputeshestvennikov* (The Film Travellers' Club) is the longest-running programme in the history of Russian television. The Sunday-evening show premiered in 1960 (under a slightly different name) and marked its forty-fourth anniversary on the air in 2004. For most of its run it was hosted by 'adventurer' Iurii Senderevich. During the Soviet period, *Klub* was a primary form of exposure to foreign countries for the vast majority of Soviet citizens, who were not allowed to travel abroad. This fact was satirized by Mikhail Zhvanetskii in a monologue with the same title as the show.

See also: television, Soviet

SETH GRAHAM

kniga zhalob

See complaint book

Kobzon, Iosif Davydovich

b. 11 September 1937, Chasov Iar, Ukraine

Singer

Kobzon holds a degree from the Gnesin Musical Institute in Moscow, where he studied in 1958–62. The singer's fame as one of the most effective performers of Soviet pop culture (*estrada*) rests on his ability to authentically convey patriotic values along with romantic pathos and sentimentality. Kobzon's songs particularly appeal to military and working-class audiences, but usually are dismissed and ridiculed by intellectuals. During numerous concert tours Kobzon appeared as a steadfast Soviet loyalist who, for instance, actively supported interventionist troops in Afghanistan. After the break-up of the USSR, Kobzon embarked on a successful business career, widely reputed to be a godfather of the Russian mafia. In 1997, he was elected to the Russian parliament. People's Artist of the USSR (1987).

See also: Duma; economic system, post-Soviet; popular music, Soviet; War, Afghan

PETER ROLLBERG

Koliada

A pagan god celebrated at the winter equinox, after the Christianization of Rus, *Koliada* became the personification and celebration of Christmas, heavily overlaid with pagan rituals: carols (*koliadki*), mummery, celebration of the sun and fertility, special food (*kutia*, a porridge made of grain, fruit, and meat, also served at funerals), and, in some areas, mock funerals. Carollers go from house to house, singing songs and asking for gifts and food. The tradition, partially maintained in some rural areas during the Soviet period, is being revived in the post-Soviet era. The Russian Orthodox Church condemns the rituals as largely pagan.

See also: holidays, Russian Orthodox; traditions and customs; Russian Orthodoxy

MICHELE BERDY

Koliada, Nikolai Vladimirovich

b. 4 December 1957, village of Presnogorkovka, Kustanaiskaia oblast

Playwright

After a short acting career, Koliada wrote his first play in 1986, and subsequently became a favourite of the Sovremennik Theatre and the director Roman Viktiuk. By 2004, Koliada had written ninety plays. His plain-talking, low-life characters reflected the chaos and dissolution of Russian society in the 1990s. *Rogatka* (*Slingshot*, 1989) examined the intimacy arising between an Afghan War veteran and his impudent male nurse; *Persidskii siren* (*Persian Lilac*, 1995) posited an unlikely love story between two God-forsaken pensioners. Since 1993, Koliada has taught at the Ekaterinburg Theatre Institute, guiding to prominence such playwrights as Oleg Bogaev and Vasilii Sigarev.

See also: drama, post-Soviet; Ekaterinburg; Sovremennik Theatre; Viktiuk, Roman; War, Afghan

JOHN FREEDMAN

Kolyma

Located in extreme northeastern Siberia, Kolyma is associated with two words: gold and GULag. The discovery of gold there in the 1920s provided a rationale for development in this frigid, forbidding landscape, inhabited only by nomadic, indigenous peoples. Kolyma thus became one of the most feared destinations in Stalin's system of GULags, or prison camps. It is unknown how many prisoners, who worked in extreme conditions, perished there; their bodies were dumped into unmarked mass graves that are still discovered from time to time. Though Kolyma is not an island, prisoners referred to the rest of Russia as 'the mainland', an idea reinforced by the fact that convicts arrived in Kolyma not by land, but by sea from Vladivostok to Magadan, the gateway city. Many survivors have attested to the horrors of forced labour in Kolyma; perhaps the best known, and certainly the most talented, was Varlam Shalamov, whose *Kolymskie rasskazy* (*Kolyma Tales*) describe the harrowing lives of prisoners who exist at the edge of survival. Evgeniia Ginzburg's memoir *Krutoi marshrut* (*Journey into the Whirlwind* and *Within the Whirlwind*) details her arrest, interrogation, and life as a prisoner in the region, the second volume devoted to life in Magadan after her release.

DAVID J. GALLOWAY

Komar and Melamid

Komar, Vitalii

b. 11 September 1943, Moscow

Melamid, Aleksander

b. 14 July 1945, Moscow

Artists

Painters and performance artists Komar and Melamid, who always co-signed their canvasses, were the co-founders in the late 1960s of an amalgam of Dadaism and Socialist Realism that they called Sots-Art. Expelled from the Union of Soviet Artists in 1974, they moved to New York in 1978 and currently live and work there. A combination of Soviet pop and conceptual art, Sots-Art is widely considered a forerunner of 1980s Soviet postmodernism. The duo's projects include painting, performance, public sculpture, installations, photography, and most recently, poetry and music. Divergent interests in recent years have led to the amicable dissolution of their partnership. Their shared and individual works hang in museums throughout the United States and Europe.

See also: postmodernism; Sots-Art

NATASHA KOLCHEVSKA

Kommersant

The first independent financial daily in post-Soviet Russia and winner of numerous journalistic awards, *Kommersant* (*Businessman*) is viewed by many as Russia's leading daily newspaper. Founded (1989) by *Ogonek* correspondent Vladimir Iakovlev, it took its name from the pre-Revolutionary newspaper published from 1909–17. It is widely read in the business sector and among the educated elite for its analysis of financial markets, detailed coverage of political events, and international scope. Taking into account its weekly magazines on government, money, foreign cars, and other topics, its circulation hovers around one million. It is available in major Russian cities and online.

See also: *Ogonek*; periodicals, post-Soviet

ANDREA LANOUX

Komsomol

See Communist Youth League

Konchalovskii (Mikhalkov-Konchalovskii), Andrei Sergeevich

b. 20 August 1937, Moscow

Writer, screenwriter, film-maker, producer (theatre and opera)

Konchalovskii graduated from the Moscow Conservatory in 1959 and earned a degree in directing from VGIK (studio of Mikhail Romm) in 1964. From the beginning of his career Konchalovskii's films received recognition not only at home, but at international festivals, culminating in a Cannes special jury prize for *Sibiriada* (1978), his lush, sweeping epic of twentieth-century Russia. His second feature, *Asino shchastie* or *Istoriia Asii Klachinoi, kotoraia liubila, da ne vyshla zamuzh* (*Asia's Happiness*, or *The Story of Asia Kliachina, Who Loved but Never Married*, 1967), a 'documentary comedy' released only in 1988, was banned at first, most likely for its realistic depiction of impoverished village life. Konchalovskii then turned to literary adaptations of Ivan Turgenev's *Dvorianskoe gnezdo* (*Nest of Gentlefolk*, 1969) and Anton Chekhov's *Diadia Vania* (*Uncle Vanya*, 1970). He was also a prolific screenwriter, co-scripting some of the major films of the 1960s and 1970s, including *Andrei Rublev* (1969) with Andrei Tarkovskii, and *Raba liubvi* (*Slave of Love*, 1976) with his brother, Nikita Mikhalkov.

Konchalovskii moved to Hollywood in 1980 and made six films, the best being *Maria's Lovers* (1983) and *Runaway Train* (1985). Since the 1990s he has worked both in Russia and the West, earning an Emmy for directing a television mini-series of *The Odyssey*. However, his recent attempts to make 'Russian' films reflecting on the Stalinist past in *The Inner Circle* (1992), on present-day village life in *Kurochka riaba* (*The Chicken Riaba*, 1997), or his *Dom durakov* (*House of Fools*, 2003), set in Chechnia, have not been as well received as his films from the 1960s and 1970s. Throughout, Konchalovskii has been a versatile film-maker, working in a variety of film styles, but with one overarching theme: the human spirit tested in times of adversity.

See also: All-Russian (All-Union) State Institute of Cinematography; Chechnia; Mikhalkov, Nikita; Moscow Conservatory; Romm, Mikhail; Tarkovskii, Andrei

VIDA JOHNSON

Kondrashin, Kirill Petrovich

b. 21 February (6 March) 1914, Moscow; d. 8 March 1981, Amsterdam

Conductor

Kondrashin studied conducting at the Moscow Conservatory (1932–36). Appointed conductor at Moscow's Malyi Theatre (1936), then at the Bolshoi Theatre (1943), he performed with Van Cliburn at the 1958 Tchaikovsky Competition. Under his leadership of the Moscow Philharmonic (1960–75), the orchestra broadened its repertory, premiering and subsequently recording many contemporary works (on Angel/Melodiia). Known for his vivid interpretations of Prokofiev, Shostakovich and Rachmaninov, in 1978 Kondrashin emigrated to Holland to pursue artistic freedom, and in 1979 was appointed director of Amsterdam's Concertgebouw. His collected articles on conducting, *O dirizherskom iskusstve* (*On the Art of Conducting*), were published in Moscow and Leningrad in 1972.

See also: Bolshoi Theatre; Malyi Theatre; Moscow Conservatory; orchestras, Soviet and post-Soviet; Prokofiev, Sergei; Shostakovich, Dmitrii

DAVID GOMPPER

Kondratev, Pavel Mikhailovich

b. 18 November 1902, Saratov; d. 26 April
1985, Leningrad

Artist

In the 1920s and the 1930s, Kondratev studied
with Mikhail Matiushin, Kazimir Malevich, and
other luminaries of the Russian avant-garde.
For nonconformist artists in Leningrad during
the 1970s and the 1980s, Kondratev offered a
link with this modernist past. Like Malevich, he
rejected traditional perspective in favour of a
dynamic, non-Euclidean conception of space in
which distinctions between internal and external
ceased to exist. Kondratev's philosophical
approach to painting was similar to that of Vladimir Sterligov; both considered painting a
medium through which individual consciousness
became part of a 'living' universe.

See also: Sterligov, Vladimir

JANET E. KENNEDY

Konenkov, Sergei Timofeevich

b. 28 June [10 July] 1874, Karakovichi,
Smolensk oblast, Russia; d. 9 October
1971, Moscow

Sculptor

A graduate of the Moscow School of Painting,
Sculpture and Architecture (1896) and of the
Petersburg Academy of Arts (1902), in his creative work Konenkov reflected critical stages in
Russian history while adhering to his major
theme of human aspirations to freedom. His
early works engaged the theme of revolution
and he participated in the execution of the
Soviets' plan for monumental propaganda. Disillusioned with Bolshevism, he emigrated to the
United States (1924), where he created sculptural portraits of outstanding Russian contemporaries. Riding the wave of rising
patriotism, he returned to the USSR in 1945. At
the end of his life he took up fairy-tale and folk
subjects. Member of the Academy of Arts of the
USSR (1954), People's Artist of the USSR

(1958), Hero of Socialist Labour (1964), Laureate of Stalin and State Prizes of the USSR
(1951).

YURI ZARETSKY

kopeika

Kopeika is the smallest division of the *ruble* (100
kopeks of a *ruble*). Discontinued in the 1990s
during the period of high inflation, it was reintroduced in 1998, with the revaluation of the
ruble after the economic collapse of that year.
Kopeika is used in expressions to mean money in
general, parallel to 'penny' in English.

Kopeika is also the slang term for the first *Zhiguli* Model 1 car (VAZ-2101), released in 1970,
the first affordable car in the USSR. In the
1970s it conferred prestige on its owner; by the
late 1980s and 1990s, when more expensive
Soviet cars and foreign cars appeared, it became
associated with a lower- or middle-class owner.
Remembered nostalgically, the *Kopeika* is the
hero of Ivan Dykhovichnyi's eponymous film
(2001).

Since 1998 it has been the name of a grocery
chain in and around Moscow.

See also: cars, Soviet and post-Soviet; Dykhovichnyi, Ivan; monetary reform; money; slang

MICHELE BERDY

Kopelian, Efim Zakharovich

b. 13 April 1912, Belarus; d. 6 March
1975, Leningrad

Actor

In 1935, Kopelian completed studio courses at
the Bolshoi Drama Theatre in Leningrad and
was invited to join the professional troupe of the
theatre, where he played until his last days. He
is also known for his roles in about sixty Soviet
movies, including *Crime and Punishment* (1969),
Nikolai Bauman (1968), *Oshibka rezidenta* (*The Resident's Mistake*, 1968), and *Sudba rezidenta* (The
Resident's Fate, 1970). Though he technically

did not appear in the cult multi-series film of the 1970s, *Semnadtsat mgnovenii vesny (Seventeen Moments of Spring*, 1973), the movie's tremendous success is partly due to Kopelian's voice behind the screen.

See also: *Semnadtsat mgnovenii vesny (Seventeen Moments of Spring)*

ALEXANDER DOMRIN

Kopystiansky, Svetlana Grigorevna

b. [specific date unknown] 1950, Voronezh

Artist

As a dissident artist in Moscow (1978–88), Kopystiansky rejected the state-sanctioned style of Socialist Realism, inspired, instead, by the works and ideology of such artists as Tatlin and Malevich, the film-makers Eisenstein and Vertov, the theatre director Vsevolod Meierkhold, and the poet Velimir Khlebnikov. In 1988, she emigrated with her artist-husband Igor Kopystiansky to New York, where they have resided ever since. She works in different media, including oil painting, video and photographic projects, and experimental representational arrangements. Kopystiansky has exhibited to great acclaim in many international exhibitions, including the Venice Biennale (1988; 1995), the Sydney Biennial (1992), Documenta 11 (2002), and Solomon R. Guggenheim Museum's exhibition *Russia!* (2005).

See also: art, nonconformist; art, post-Soviet; art, Soviet; dissident; Socialist Realism

KATIA KAPUSHESKY

Koriak

The Koriak (the word means 'working with reindeer') are an ethnic group (population 9,000) living in the Russian Arctic. These partly settled, partly nomadic people of the Arctic Mongoloid anthropological type inhabit the Koriak Autonomous Okrug, the north of the Kamchatka peninsula. The capital is Palana. Population density is 0.1 people per square km. Main occupations are reindeer and dog breeding, hunting, and fishing. The typical settled dwelling is a semi-dugout with funnelled roofing; the nomadic Koriaks live in a portable tent, called an *iaranga*. The Koriak language belongs to the Chukchi-Koriak group of the Paleo-Asian family. The Cyrillic alphabet was introduced in the 1930s. Most Koriak practise Orthodox Christianity.

See also: ethnic minorities; Kamchatka

TATYANA LEDENEVA

Korolenko, Psoi

(né Pavel Eduardovich Lion)

b. 26 April 1967, Moscow

Poet, composer, singer

Lion's stage name Psoi, a rarely used and odd-sounding name from the Orthodox Church calendar, is coupled with the last name of the Russian writer Vladimir Korolenko (1853–1921), the protagonist of Lion's doctoral dissertation. After his first appearances in Moscow in the mid-1990s, Psoi gained acclaim among young Russian intellectuals who appreciate his play with stereotypes of Soviet and post-Soviet mass culture and mentality, as well as his attempts to integrate various genres and stylistic sources. These range from French chanson to Jewish folklore and *klezmer* traditions into performances for club and university audiences in Russia and the United States. His postmodernist lyrics in Russian, Yiddish, French, English and a macaronic mixture of these are rich in literary and cultural associations and sometimes shocking in their obscene vocabulary and provocative message. Lion also uses his stage name in his journalism and cultural criticism. His CDs include *Shliager veka* (*Hit of the Century*, book + CD, 2003); *Pesn Pesnei Psoia Korolenko* (*Psoi Korolenko's Song of Songs*, 2002); *Fioretti* (2001), *Pesnia pro Boga* (*Song about God*, 2000).

ILIA UTEKHIN

Korolev, Sergei Pavlovich

b. 12 January 1906[7], Zhitomir, Ukraine;
d. 14 January 1966, Moscow

Engineer

Known as the founder of the Soviet space programme and involved in rocket research prior to World War II, Sergei Korolev fell victim to the purges and went through the Stalinist prison system. However, his extraordinary energy, intelligence, and managerial abilities resulted in his appointment as head of the first Soviet rocket development centre. Korolev led the development of several generations of ballistic missiles, launch vehicles, military and communications satellites, interplanetary probes, and manned spacecraft. He died at the height of his career. The secret nature of the Soviet space industry explains the authorities' belated, posthumous recognition of his contribution to the space programme.

See also: space programme and exploration

TATYANA LEDENEVA

Korotich, Vitalii Alekseevich

b. 26 May 1936, Kiev

Journalist

After graduation from the Kiev Medical Institute in 1967, Korotich worked as a doctor (1959–66), wrote poems in Ukrainian, and developed into an outstanding representative of youth culture and literature of the 1960s *shestidesiatniki*. He was editor-in-chief of the Ukrainian-language journals *Ranok* and *Vsesvit* (1978–86). In spring 1986, he was named editor-in-chief of the magazine *Ogonek* (Little Flame, 1986–91) and transformed it from a Soviet rag to a symbol of perestroika – an avant-garde emblem of democratization and independent journalism. Elected deputy to the Supreme Soviet, he served there, 1989–91. In 1991–98, he was a visiting professor at Boston University. Since 1999, he has worked as editor-in-chief at the Kiev newspaper *Bulvar* (Boulevard).

Korotich has published more than twenty books of poems, prose, and essays in Russian and Ukrainian, translated into many languages. A member of the Russian PEN club and the writers' democratic movement Aprel (April), he has won the Ukrainian State Prize, the Lenin Komsomol prize, and various journalistic awards.

See also: journalism; journalists, post-Soviet; *Ogonek*; sixties generation

NADEZHDA AZHGIKHINA

Korzhavin, Naum Moiseevich

(né Naum Moiseevich Mandel)

b. 14 October 1925, Kiev

Poet

Outspoken and popular, Korzhavin was arrested in 1947 while a student in Moscow's Gorkii Literary Institute. After imprisonment and internal exile, he returned to Moscow in 1954 and became a highly acclaimed poet, though much of his work could not be published. Following numerous confrontations with the authorities, Korzhavin emigrated to Boston in 1973. Since his triumphant return to Moscow in 1989 (at the personal invitation of Bulat Okudzhava), he divides his time between America and Russia. Korzhavin writes poetry, literary criticism, drama, and essays on social and moral themes. His deft use of language and his striking clarity make him an excellent satirist.

See also: Literary Institute; Okudzhava, Bulat

MICHAEL WACHTEL

Kosolapov, Aleksandr Semenovich

b. 16 April 1943, Moscow

Artist

Often considered a member of the Sots-Art movement founded by Komar and Melamid,

Kosolapov graduated from the Stroganov Art school as a sculptor. He emigrated to the US in 1975. Many of his conceptual art pieces provoked strong negative reaction from the public and corporations. In 1980, Coca-Cola threatened him with a lawsuit for using its logo with the image of Lenin. Religious fanatics destroyed his painting *This is My Blood*, which showed Jesus with the Coca-Cola logo at the show *Ostorozhno, religiia (Danger, Religion)* in 2004 in Moscow. Its companion piece, *This is My Body*, shows Jesus with McDonald's logo, and was destroyed by fanatics at the show *Art-Moscow* in 2005. Public protests led to the removal of his installation *Icon-caviar* from the show *Russian Pop Art* at the Tretiakov Gallery in 2005. All this negative publicity only helped to promote the artist's work.

See also: Komar and Melamid; Sots-Art; Tretiakov Gallery

VLADIMIR PAPERNY

Kotenochkin, Viacheslav Mikhailovich

b. 20 June 1927, Moscow;
d. 20 November 2000, Moscow

Animator

One of Russia's best-known animation directors, Kotenochkin began his apprenticeship at Soiuzmultfilm in 1946. Subsequently he worked as an animation artist under such directors as Ivanov-Vano, Atamanov, and Tsekhanovskii. In 1962, he began directing animated films, ranging from Russian folk and literary tales to Soviet didactic films. In 1968, Kotenochkin was asked to direct a new film on the moralistic theme of protecting the young and helpless, and his creation, *Nu, pogodi! (Just You Wait!)*, ran for eighteen episodes and became the most popular Soviet cartoon series.

See also: film, animation; film, children's; Ivanov-Vano, Ivan; *Nu, pogodi! (Just You Wait!)*

BELLA GINZBURSKY-BLUM

kotlety

The Soviet equivalent of hamburger, a staple of public eateries, *kotlety* are fried or steamed cutlets made of ground meat (usually, a combination of beef and pork, not to mention the poultry, fish, or vegetable varieties), mixed with bread, milk, and onion. If cooked properly, these tender and succulent patties are an excellent dish easily adaptable for mass production. However, it fell victim to the workings of the Soviet food industry, since its meat content tended to shrink and deteriorate in quality. The adulterated greyish *kotlety* became the Soviet Big Mac in reverse, representing a rather unpalatable symbol of failures in the Soviet gastronomic industry.

See also: meat dishes

DAN UNGURIANU

Kozakov, Mikhail Mikhailovich

b. 14 October 1934, Leningrad

Film and theatre actor, stage manager

Kozakov worked at the Maiakovskii Theatre (1956–59), the Sovremennik (1959–70), the Moscow Art Theatre (1971–72), the Malaia Bronnaia (1972–81), and the Lenkom Theatre (1986). Among his best stage roles are Hamlet, Chamberlain in *Golyi korol (The Naked King)* and Aduev-senior in *Obyknovennaia istoria (A Common History)*. On screen he played in *Chelovek-amfibiia (Amphibian Man*, 1961) and *Vsia korolevskaia rat (The Whole Royal Army*, 1971). Kozakov's comic talent shone through in *Zdravstvuite, ja vasha tetia! (Hello!*, 1975). As a film director he made the enormously popular *Pokrovskie vorota (Pokrovsky Gates*, 1982). Kozakov is now artistic director and actor in his own theatre in Moscow – the Mikhail Kozakov Russian Theatre. People's Artist of Russia.

See also: Lenkom Theatre; Maiakovskii Theatre; Moscow Art Theatre; Sovremennik Theatre

IRINA UDIANSKAYA

Kozin, Vadim Alekseevich

b. 21 March 1903, St. Petersburg;
d. 19 December 1994, Magadan

Popular singer and songwriter

A popular tenor known for his renditions of old romantic ballads and gypsy songs, Kozin also composed some 300 songs and had a prolific recording career that began in the 1920s. During World War II he entertained Red Army troops and performed with Marlene Dietrich at the Teheran Conference in 1943. Arrested in 1944, he spent eight years in the Kolyma camps, possibly for homosexuality. He remained in Magadan after his release. Kozin's recordings were banned until the mid-1980s, although he continued to compose and perform. In 1985, Melodiya released the first compilation of his most popular songs. The most recent releases of his songs are *Pismo iz Magadana* (*Letter from Magadan*, 1997) and *Zolotye rossypi romansa* (*Golden Grains of Romances*, 2000).

See also: corrective labour institutions; GULag; homosexuality; Kolyma; romance; World War II (Great Patriotic War)

SHARON A. KOWALSKY

Kozintsev, Grigorii Mikhailovich

b. 9 [22] March 1905, Kiev; 11 May 1973, Leningrad

Director, writer

For twenty years Kozintsev made films with his co-founder of the Factory of the Eccentric Actor, Leonid Trauberg, most notably *Pokhozhdeniia Oktiabriny* (*The Adventures of Octobriana*, 1924) and the 'Maksim Trilogy', three films about the revolutionary awakening of its eponymous hero (*Iunost Maksima* [*Maksim's Youth*, 1935], *Vozvrashchenie Maksima* [*Maksim's Return*, 1937] and *Vyborgskaia storona* [*The Vyborg Side*, 1939]). Subsequently Kozintsev filmed several significant and internationally acclaimed screen adaptations of literary classics, turning *Don Quixote*, *Hamlet*, and *King Lear* into commentaries on his

own contemporary society. He taught at VGIK for nearly fifty years.

See also: All-Russian (All-Union) State Institute of Cinematography

JOSEPHINE WOLL

Kozlov, Aleksei Semenovich

b. 13 October 1935, Moscow

Jazz musician, saxophonist, music arranger, and bandleader

Born in Moscow, Kozlov graduated from the Moscow Architectural Institute, with a PhD thesis on watch design. He established several jazz clubs: Molodezhnoe (Youth, 1961), Ritm (Rhythm, 1968), Pechora (1969), and Arkadiia (Arcadia, 1994), and in 1973 founded the jazz-rock band Arsenal. One of Arsenal's recordings ('With Our Own Hands') was reissued by East Wind Records in the US in 1984. In 1994, Kozlov was invited as a 'jazz clinician' to the Jazz Department of Oklahoma City University. Member of the Composers' Union of Russia, he holds the title of People's Artist of Russia.

See also: jazz

VLADIMIR PAPERNY

Kozlovskii, Ivan Semenovich

b. 11 [24] March 1900, Marianovka, Ukraine; d. 21 December 1993, Moscow

Opera singer

Born into a peasant family in the village of Marianovka, Kiev region, tenor Kozlovskii was a soloist at the Bolshoi Theatre, 1926–54. He performed exclusively in Russian in bel canto style. He performed a total of thirty-five roles from Russian, Italian, French, and German opera, some of which appeared in twenty recordings, primarily on the Soviet label Melodiia; he was particularly celebrated for his performances of Lenskii in Tchaikovsky's *Eugene*

Onegin, Vladimir Igorevich in Borodin's *Prince Igor*, and the Duke of Mantua in Verdi's *Rigoletto*. Kozlovskii also recorded numerous Russian romances, Russian and Ukrainian folk songs, German Lieder, and English and French arias. Since the 1990s, the availability of select CDs and videos has made Kozlovskii recordings more accessible to Western listeners.

See also: Bolshoi Theatre; opera singers, Bolshoi Theatre; romance

OLGA ZASLAVSKY

KPRF

See Communist Party

krasnaia kniga

See Red Book

Kremer, Gidon Markusovich

b. 27 February 1947, Riga, Latvia

Violinist

Born of German parents, Kremer studied with David Oistrakh at the Moscow Conservatory (1965–73), winning various prizes, including the Tchaikovsky Competition (1970). An inspirational performer with a virtuoso technique, he had his Western debut in London (1975), followed by New York (1977), before emigrating to Germany in 1980. Although he performs the traditional repertoire, Kremer strongly advocates contemporary music, and many works have been written specifically for him, by Arvo Pärt, Alfred Shnittke and Edison Denisov, among others. He has also promoted the music of Astor Piazzolla. In 1996, Kremer founded Kremerata Baltica, an ensemble of young musicians from the Baltics, and established a chamber music festival at Lockenhaus in Austria in 1981. He has more than 300 recordings to his name.

See also: classical music, post-Soviet; Denisov, Edison; Moscow Conservatory; Oistrakh, David; Pärt, Arvo; Shnittke, Alfred; Tchaikovsky Competition; violin performance, Russian/ Soviet

DAVID GOMPPER

Kremlevskii paek (zakaz)

Kremlevskii paek (Kremlin ration) was an allocation of food sold at low prices to members of the government, the *nomenklatura*, and the social elite during the Soviet period. Instituted after the revolution to supplement the standard ration, it developed into a complex system of perquisites. The highest officials had delicacies delivered to their doors, while lower-ranking officials went to special shops to pick up an order (*zakaz*) of food that varied according to rank. *Zakazy* of scarce goods were also made available at market prices in the workplace before holidays. *Kremlevskii paek* may refer to the meals in cafeterias in Party buildings and function as a metonym for the privileges of Soviet power.

See also: Communist Party; economic system, Soviet; holidays, Soviet; Kremlin; nomenklatura; shortages

MICHELE BERDY

kremlin (kreml)

The word 'kremlin' (*kreml*) means simply 'fortress' or 'citadel'. It is thought to derive from either the ancient Greek word *kremnos*, meaning a steep hill above a ravine, or the Slavonic term *kremnik*, the term employed in the early Russian chronicles, meaning thick coniferous forest, which yielded the likely material from which the original citadel was constructed. Although the word today is usually associated only with the Moscow Kremlin, the term was generically applied to mean citadel or central fortress in medieval Russian cities, particularly capitals of principalities. Kremlins were usually situated on a promontory at a strategic point along a river and separated from the surrounding parts of the city, at first by wooden and later stone or brick walls with ramparts, moats, towers, and battlements. During the Middle Ages, a kremlin served as an administrative and religious centre and offered protection against military attacks. A kremlin thus constituted a city in itself, containing palaces for princes and bishops, government buildings, churches, marketplaces, and munitions stores. Houses were typically clustered close to the kremlin, and townspeople took refuge in it in times of crisis or invasion. As cities grew, so did kremlins, which would be surrounded by a cluster of dwellings and non-residential buildings erected just beyond the fortress walls. As these clusters expanded to form a 'suburb' (*sloboda*), new walls would sometimes be built to surround them. (*Kitai-gorod*, the commercial quarter just south of the Moscow Kremlin, from which it is separated by Red Square, is a good example of this.) The main streets tended to radiate from the core of the kremlin to the outside walls, with lesser streets crossing them in spider-web fashion. Neighbourhoods would form between and along streets, divided by function, with most trades clustered by type. Well-known kremlins, of which Moscow's is the most famous, still preserved in part or in whole, include those in Smolensk, Yaroslavl, Vladimir, Nizhnii Novgorod, and Astrakhan.

See also: Moscow; Nizhnii Novgorod (Gorkii)

ANATOLE SENKEVITCH

Kremlin (Moscow)

The Moscow Kremlin is Russia's mythic refuge, linking the modern nation to its legendary past; the historical, spiritual and political heart of the nation's capital; and Moscow's most famous landmark and tourist attraction. Today's walled triangular territory is bounded on the south by the Moscow River, on the east by Red Square, and on the southwest by the Alexandrine Gardens and *Manezh* (Manège) Square.

Like all Russian kremlins, Moscow's began as a modest wooden outpost. As the kremlin expanded, the city of Moscow rapidly sprang up around it. In 1366 Moscow Prince Dmitrii

Donskoi ordered that the wooden walls and towers be replaced by a fortified white limestone wall to protect the fortress from fire and attack. By the end of the century, the kremlin teemed with churches, monasteries, and manors housing the Grand Prince's retainers and the local nobility. During the reign of Ivan III (1462–1505), the Kremlin was transformed into an imposing fortress city, befitting its role as the seat of the newly-unified Muscovite state. It is largely this fortress city, built by Italian architects recruited by Ivan III, that stands in Moscow today.

The cathedrals, towers, and palaces erected in Cathedral Square (*Sobornaia ploshchad*), the first great public space in the Muscovite state and the place where coronations and all the associated ceremonial rituals of state took place, became the preeminent site of Ivan III's grand reconstruction project. The impressive Cathedral of the Assumption (*Uspenskii sobor*), the first of Ivan III's Kremlin projects, was built in 1475–79 by the Milanese architect Ridolfo Fioravanti to replace the collapsed earlier cathedral as the seat of the Russian Orthodox Church. Fioravanti's cathedral, used for tsars' coronations and the burial of metropolitans and patriarchs, was a nuanced Renaissance reinterpretation of its venerable twelfth-century namesake in the ancient town of Vladimir. The Cathedral of the Annunciation (*Blagoveshchenskii sobor*), where the tsars were christened and married, was built (1484–89) by masters from Pskov, whose picturesque design owed more to Russia's architectural past than to Ivan's vision of a modern kremlin. The ornate Cathedral of the Archangel Michael (*Arkhangelskii sobor*), the most Italianate of the Kremlin cathedrals and the burial place for Muscovite princes and tsars (except Boris Gudonov) from the fourteenth to the late seventeenth centuries, was built (1505–8) by the Venetian architect Alevisio di Montagna. The 266ft Ivan the Great Bell Tower was erected by the Italian architect Marco Bono (1505–8) for the Kremlin's Assumption, Archangel, and Annunciation Cathedrals, that lacked their own belfries.

The Palace of Facets (*Granovitaia palata*) on the west edge of Cathedral Square was built (1487–91) for Ivan III by Italian architects Marco Ruffo and Pietro Antonio Solario. Used continuously for formal ceremonies and important state receptions, it is the oldest secular building in the Kremlin complex. The Patriarch's Palace and Cathedral of the Twelve Apostles (*Patriarkhalnyi dvorets i sobor Dvenadtsati Apostolov*), framing the entrance to Cathedral Square, was begun in 1640 by Patriarch Nikon, whose ecclesiastical reforms caused an irreparable schism in the Russian Orthodox Church. The palace now houses the Museum of Seventeenth-Century Life and Applied Art.

Successive rulers left their mark on the Kremlin's architectural ensemble. Peter the Great commissioned the construction of the Kremlin Arsenal in 1701. Catherine the Great added the imposing neoclassical Senate Building (1776–88), designed by renowned Moscow architect Matvei Kazakov. The building, which once housed Lenin's quarters and Stalin's study, has been the official residence of the Russian President since 1991. Nicholas I commissioned his favourite architect, Konstantin Ton, to design the Great Kremlin Palace (*Bolshoi Kremlevskii dvorets*, 1838–49) in the officially sanctioned Russo-Byzantine style. The monumental palace was used principally for state and diplomatic receptions and official ceremonies.

The Bolsheviks' choice of Moscow as their capital in March 1918 returned the Kremlin to pre-eminence, and during Soviet rule it experienced its second life as a great centre of power. However, the only substantial architectural additions made by the Soviet regime were the 1934 Presidium and the modernistic State Kremlin Palace. Built in 1959–61 as the Palace of Congresses (*Dvorets sezdov*) during the halcyon days of the Thaw to host Communist Party congresses as well as musical and theatrical performances, the stark, 394ft-long glass and marble-faced concrete building was designed by Soviet architect Mikhail Posokhin. The building was sunk some 49 feet into the ground so as not to dwarf the surrounding churches and buildings. The stage of its huge 6000-seat auditorium originally featured a monumental bas-relief head of Lenin, surrounded by gilded rays. Today the once-familiar relief of Lenin is gone, and the palace hosts regular concerts and gala performances.

Although the Soviet state certainly left its mark on the Kremlin, the centuries-old fortress still retains much of the aura of Tsarist Russia, especially in Cathedral Square, where the spirit of Ivan III and his immediate successors looms much larger than those of Stalin or even Lenin himself.

See also: Communist Party; kremlin; Khrushchev, Nikita; Lenin, Vladimir Ilich; Moscow; Russian Orthodox churches; Stalin, Iosif; State symbols, Soviet; State symbols, post-Soviet; Thaw

ANATOLE SENKEVITCH

Kriuchkov, Nikolai Afanasevich

b. 6 [19] January 1911, Moscow; d. 13 April 1994, Moscow

Actor

Kriuchkov trained at TRAM (Theatre of Young Workers), performing there until 1933. He became a national icon after his portrayal of Socialist Realist hero Klim Iarko in Pyrev's 1939 musical *Traktoristy* (*Tractor Drivers*). Kriuchkov was beloved by Russians throughout the Soviet era as 'the boy from our town' (from the 1942 film *Paren iz nashego goroda*), the rough-hewn but handsome, patriotic, musically talented, and charming hero with a sense of humour, who was also just 'one of the guys'. People's Artist of the USSR (1965), State Prize of the USSR (1941).

RIMGAILA SALYS

Krokodil

Newspaper

The satirical newspaper *Krokodil* (Crocodile), founded in 1922, was published weekly until 1932, then thrice monthly until 1992, when it became a monthly. Its peak circulation approached 6 million. During the Cold War, *Krokodil* was known for cartoons satirizing Western society, as well as isolated undesirable elements of Soviet life. It was well regarded among the intelligentsia; composer Dmitrii Shostakovich even based a small song cycle on texts from the newspaper. During perestroika, *Krokodil* became a prominent medium for critical commentary on contemporary domestic issues, and also published excerpts of works by previously banned authors such as Vasilii Aksenov.

See also: Aksenov, Vasilii; Cold War; journalism; perestroika and glasnost; Shostakovich, Dmitrii

SETH GRAHAM

Kropivnitskaia, Valentina Evgenevna

b. 16 February 1924, Moscow

Artist

Nonconformist artist Valentina Kropivnitskaia grew up in the artistic milieu of parents Evgenii Kropivnitiskii and Olga Potapova and in 1950 married fellow artist Oskar Rabin. They formed the core of the Lianozovo School. Beginning in 1965, Kropivnitskaia participated in numerous nonconformist exhibitions at home and abroad. Her works in watercolour or graphite and coloured pencil, including *Na beregu* (On the Lakeshore, 1971), portray a fairy-tale world of quasi-human creatures, where realistic detail competes with pure fantasy. With Rabin and their artist-son, Aleksandr Rabin, Kropivnitskaia left the USSR in 1978 and settled in Paris.

See also: art, nonconformist; Lianozovo School

ANN KOMAROMI

Kropivnitskii, Lev Evgenevich

b. 27 January 1922, Tiumen, Russia; d. 26 May 1994, Moscow

Artist

Lev Kropivnitskii, son of Evgenii Kropivnitskii, brother of Valentina Kropivnitskaia, attended the Moscow Institute of Applied and Decorative Arts from 1939 until mobilization in 1941.

Arrested in 1946 for 'counter-revolutionary activity', he spent eight years in labour camps in Siberia and Kazakhstan. Amnestied in 1954, he returned to Moscow in 1956. Kropivnitskii was prolific and multi-faceted, authoring both figurative and abstract paintings, drawings, graphic works, poems, and articles about art. He organized unofficial artistic events in the Soviet Union and contributed works to over 100 exhibitions in the USSR, Russia, and abroad.

ANN KOMAROMI

Krylov, Porfirii Nikitich

See Kukryniksy

krysha

This term, which translates from Russian as 'roof', refers to protection, originally within the context of organized crime and a system of violent entrepreneurship, contract enforcement, and dispute settlement services to Russian commercial companies and businessmen starting in 1991. The rise of *kryshas* followed the loss of state monopoly on the exercise of power and its inability to protect private businesses. *Kryshas* varied, from those provided by the local police and state security forces acting as private entrepreneurs to legal private protection companies for organized criminal groups. Their practices ranged from the openly extortionist, and thus illegal, to more settled forms of control with a longer-term perspective, such as eventual investment to become a company shareholder.

ALYA GUSEVA

KSP (Klub samodeiatelnoi pesni; amateur song club)

Klub samodeiatelnoi pesni translates as 'amateur song club'. Under the aegis of the Komsomol, KSPs were formed across the USSR in the early 1960s as a forum for, and as an attempt to control, the emerging bard song movement

Throughout the 1960s and the 1980s, KSPs such as Moscow's Menestrel (Minstrel) and Leningrad's Vostok (East) and Meridian (Meridian) sponsored concerts by well-known bards, fostered new talent, and helped to establish and promote amateur song festivals. Many KSPs have remained active in the post-Soviet period, their numbers reinforced by clubs formed in Russian-speaking communities around the world.

See also: amateur cultural activity; bards; Communist Youth League

RACHEL S. PLATONOV

Ktorov, Anatolii Petrovich

b. 24 April 1898, Moscow; d. 30 September 1980, Moscow

Stage and film actor

Ktorov studied with Fedor Fedorovich Komissarzhevskii, subsequently joining the troupe of the prestigious Korsh Theatre and, after its closure in 1932, the Moscow Art Theatre (MKhAT), where he became a cult star, especially in classic comedies. As a film actor, Ktorov gained immense popularity with the role of the elegant fraud, Michael Korkis, in the crude anti-religious comedy *Prazdnik sviatogo Iorgena (St. Jorgen's Holiday*, 1930). His intense portrayal of the old, emotionally restrained Prince Bolkonskii in the monumental Tolstoi adaptation *Voina i mir (War and Peace*, 1965–67) is one of the all-time accomplishments of Russian film history. People's Artist of the USSR (1963).

See also: Moscow Art Theatre

PETER ROLLBERG

Kublanovskii, Iurii Mikhailovich

b. 30 April 1947, Rybinsk

Poet

A poet and author of numerous essays on Russian and emigrant literature, Kublanovskii graduated from the Moscow State University History Department in 1970. He was a member of the unofficial youth art group SMOG. In 1982–91 Kublanovskii lived abroad. Recipient of the Aleksander Solzhenitsyn Prize (2003).

See also: awards, literary, post-Soviet; poetry, post-Soviet

ALEXANDER DOMRIN

Kukryniksy

(pseudonym of a creative collective):

Kupriianov, Mikhail Vasilevich

b. 8 (21) October, 1903, Tetiushi, Tatarstan, Russia; d. 11 November 1991, Moscow

Krylov, Porfirii Nikitich

b. 9 (22) August 1902, Shchelkunovo, Tula oblast, Russia; d. 15 May 1990, Moscow

Sokolov, Nikolai Aleksandrovich

b. 8 (21) July 1903, Moscow; d. 15 April 2000, Moscow

Caricaturists, graphic artists, painters

All three artists studied in Moscow's Advanced Artistic-Technical Studios (*VKhutemas*) between 1921 and 1929, and worked together from 1924, painting, illustrating books, and creating caricatures in periodicals. World War II radically changed the nature of their work. Their posters, such as *We'll mercilessly defeat and destroy the enemy! (Besposhchadno razgromim i unichtozhim vraga!*, 1941), *Pincers in pincers (Kleshchi v kleshchi*, 1941), and *I lost the ring (Poteriala ia kolechko*, 1942), which rely on grotesquerie to vilify Nazism, were published in a million copies. After the war they produced ideologically approved works in satirical magazines, book illustrations, portraits, and landscapes. Recipients of the Stalin Prize (1942, 1947, 1949, 1950, 1951), Lenin Prize (1965), and others.

See also: awards, cultural, Soviet; periodicals, Soviet; World War II (Great Patriotic War)

YURI ZARETSKY

kulich

Kulich is a cylindrical Easter sweetbread rich with eggs and butter, foods forbidden during the strict Lenten fast; it also contains sultanas and almonds. The letters XB (Russian initials for 'Christ Is Risen') appear atop its white icing. *Paskha*, a pyramid of eggs, cream, and farmer cheese, accompanies it.

See also: Easter, Orthodox; Lent

CHRISTINE A. RYDEL

Kulidzhanov, Lev Aleksandrovich

b. 19 March 1924, Tbilisi, Georgia

Director, film industry administrator

After graduating from VGIK (1955), where he studied with Sergei Gerasimov, Kulidzhanov made a number of successful psychological melodramas, including *Dom, v kotorom ia zhivu* (*The House I Live in*, 1957), *Otchii dom* (*My Father's House*, 1959) and *Kogda derevia byli bolshimi* (*When the Trees Were Big*, 1962), the last an affecting if sentimental account of the regeneration of a drunken widower. Although Kulidzhanov continued to make films, he developed a reputation as a conservative industry bureaucrat in the Brezhnev years, acting as First Secretary of the Union of Film-makers from 1965 to 1986, when he was ousted.

See also: All-Russian (All-Union) State Institute of Cinematography; Brezhnev, Leonid; film, Soviet – Stagnation period; film, Soviet – Thaw period; Gerasimov, Sergei

JOSEPHINE WOLL

Kulik, Oleg Borisovich

b. 15 April 1961, Kiev

Artist-actionist, sculptor

A graduate of the Kiev Geological Institute (1982) and a key figure in the Moscow Actionism movement, the Moscow resident Kulik is the founder and chief representative of *Zoofreniia* (literally, 'animal reason'), an avant-garde movement in the arts. Its goal, according to Kulik, is to resolve the problem of differences between man and animal. The distinctive feature of the movement's exhibitions and performances is social provocation, in which the author defines his role as 'an artist–animal', becoming a fish, a bull, and, most often, a dog (1990–2001). One of his performances as Kulik-dog, conceived as a classic work of the late twentieth century, took place at an exhibition in the Historical Museum (2004). Kulik's individual exhibitions and activities have attracted audiences on the major stages of international centres of contemporary art.

See also: art, post-Soviet; Brenner, Aleksandr; Moscow Actionism

YURI ZARETSKY

Kultura channel

An advertisement-free state TV channel emphasizing top-quality cultural programming, Kultura (Culture), along with the channel Rossiia, Radio Rossii, and radio station Maiak, is the most important subsidiary of the National State TV and Radio Broadcasting Company (*Vserossiiskaia gosudarstvennaia televizionnaia i radio-veshchatelnaia kompaniia*). Raisa Gorbacheva's brainchild, it was established and started broadcasting in 1997. Its founders included Russia's leading cultural and art personalities, such as the academic Dmitrii Likhachev and the musician Mstislav Rostropovitch. The channel endeavours to draw a broad public's attention to the creative work of specialists in science, culture, and the arts, to assess the results of their activities, and to establish conditions for an efficient dialogue between them and society. Laureate of

TEFI (1998) – the most prestigious award of the Russian Academy of TV – Kultura TV has been a constant participant in the European Broadcasting Union, the largest professional association of national broadcasters in Europe, North Africa, and the Middle East. The channel cooperates with the largest European channels, such as the BBC, RAI, ARTE, Beta-film, Granada, Telemondis, and Discovery.

See also: Gorbacheva, Raisa; Likhachev, Dmitrii; radio, post-Soviet; Rostropovich, Mstislav; television, post-Soviet

ELENA SKIPETROVA

Kunstkamera

Founded in St. Petersburg by Peter the Great in 1714, the Kunstkamera is the first and oldest museum and research centre in Russia. Despite its critical contribution to the development of Russian science and museums, the Kunstkamera is mostly known for its collections of human 'monsters' (*urody*) and anatomical specimens, which have been the objects of fascination and horror for several generations of Russian schoolchildren. Such twentieth-century writers as Dmitrii Merezhkovskii and Yurii Tynianov used popular eighteenth-century legends of the Kunstkamera as a 'chamber of horrors' in literary works critical of the Petrine legacy in Russian history and culture.

ANTHONY ANEMONE

Kupriianov, Mikhail Vasilevich

See Kukryniksy

Kuravlev, Leonid Viacheslavovich

b. 8 October 1936, Moscow

Actor

After graduating from VGIK (1960), Kuravlev appeared in the first two films directed by Vasilii

Shukshin, as the appealingly cocky trucker Pashka Kolokolnikov in *Zhivet takoi paren* (A Boy Like That, 1964) and as Stepan, the son whose homesickness spurs him to break out of jail only months before his sentence is to end, in *Vash syn i brat* (Your Son and Brother, 1966). Other comic roles: Shura Balaganov in *Zolotoi telenok* (The Golden Calf, 1970) and Miloslavskii in *Ivan Vasilevich meniaet professiiu* (Ivan Vasilevich Changes Profession/Back to the Future, 1973); among his best dramatic roles is that of Arkadii in *Nachalo* (The Debut, 1970).

See also: All-Russian (All-Union) State Institute of Cinematography; Shukshin, Vasilii

JOSEPHINE WOLL

Kurekhin, Sergei Anatolievich

b. 16 June 1954, Murmansk; d. 9 July 1996, Petersburg

Composer, pianist, actor

Sergei Kurekhin was born in Murmansk and spent his childhood in the Crimea. In 1971, his family moved to Leningrad, and Kurekhin entered the Mussorgskii Music College, where he studied jazz piano. Later he studied at the Leningrad Institute of Culture, but never completed his education at either institution. In the late 1970s Kurekhin was known mostly as a member of famous jazzman Anatolii Vapirov's projects. In 1980, he moved to rock, collaborating with Akvarium, Kino, Auktsion, and others. In 1984, he created Pop-Mekhanika, which was more than ensemble; it was a genre in itself. Pop-Mekhanika performances represented a kind of actionist art, combining the efforts of many rock, jazz, pop, classical musicians, artists (such as Timur Novikov and Sergei Bugaev-Afrika), and film-makers. Since the late 1980s Kurekhin has participated in many significant films as composer, actor, or scriptwriter (*Gospodin oformitel* [Mr. Designer, 1988], *Tragediia v stile rock* [Tragedy, Rock Style, 1988], *Dva kapitana-2* [Two Captains II, 1993], *Nad temnoi vodoi* [Over the Dark Water, 1993]).

See also: Akvarium; Kino; jazz; Moscow Actionism; rock music

KIRA NEMIROVSKAIA

Kurnikova [Kournikova], Anna Sergeevna

b. 7 June 1981, Moscow

Tennis player

Based in Florida since the age of 11, Kurnikova has achieved a rank in tennis – number one in doubles and number eight in singles (1999) – eclipsed by her prodigious earnings and exposure as a model. Sports and gossip editors around the world trade in Kurnikova photos and speculation about her private life. She has frequently topped web tallies and 'world's sexiest woman' polls – even inspiring the first major celebrity photo-lure worm-virus (2001) – and is known as a Russian *femme fatale* (albeit a reportedly affable one) of the Internet age.

See also: sports, post-Soviet

AVRAM BROWN

Kurochkin, Maksim Aleksandrovich

b. 7 February 1970, Kiev

Playwright

Kurochkin graduated from Kiev University (1996) with a thesis on pre-Christian Slavic monuments. Between 1992 and 2004 he wrote a dozen plays incorporating the myths of multiple cultures, occasionally employing multiple languages, including Russian (his primary literary language), Ukrainian, and Polish. *Istrebitel klassa 'Medea'* (*'Medea'-Class Destroyer*, 1994) observed soldiers in an outlandish war of the sexes; *Stalowa Wola* (*Steel Will*, 1998) mixed the Polish Middle Ages with the Space Age. In the phantasmagoric *Kukhnia* (*Kitchen*, 2000), which achieved cult status as directed by Oleg Menshikov, Germans from the Nibelung legend morphed into modern Russians as war raged

around them. *Tsurikov*, staged by Mikhail Ugarov as *Transfer* (2003), observed a man visiting his dead father in hell. His works have been adapted to the screen. Winner of the Anti-Booker prize for *Steel Will*.

See also: drama, post-Soviet; Menshikov, Oleg; Ugarov, Mikhail

JOHN FREEDMAN

Kushner, Aleksandr Semenovich

b. 1936, Leningrad

Poet

A leading poet of the Petersburg school, Aleksandr Kushner made his literary debut in the late 1950s, during the Thaw. Along with his near contemporary Iosif Brodskii, he was part of a group of young writers who befriended the poetess Anna Akhmatova in the last years of her life. Deeply moved by his encounters with her, Kushner has throughout his career identified himself with the classical traditions of early twentieth-century Russian verse. Since 1991, he has served as editor-in-chief of *Novaia Biblioteka Poeta* (the New Poet's Library), one of Russia's most respected publishing series. Russian State Prize (1995), Pushkin Prize (2001).

See also: Akhmatova, Anna; awards, literary, post-Soviet; Brodskii, Iosif; poetry, Soviet; Thaw

EMILY D. JOHNSON

Kuzbas

Kuzbas (Kuznetskii basin) is a coal-mining region in the south-east of western Siberia, with Kemerovo (523,000) and Novokuznetsk (563,000) as major centres. It is part of the Kemerovsk oblast of Russia, with an area of 95,500 sq km – mostly taiga, and forest steppe in the south – and a continental climate with strong frost during winter. Kuzbas has the largest industrial agglomeration in Southern Siberia, Leninsk-Kuznetskii – Prokopevsk-

Novokuznetsk-Kaltan. The population is 2,855,000 (2005), with Russians predominating (91.9 per cent), and minorities including Tatars (1.8 per cent), Ukrainians (1.3 per cent), Germans (1.2 per cent), and Chuvash (0.5 per cent). The major economic industry is the mining of coal, iron, zinc, and gold.

SERGEI TARKHOV

Kuzminskii, Konstantin Konstantinovich

b. 16 April 1940, Leningrad

Poet, collector, editor

Born into a family of artists, Kuzminskii studied biology and theatre and earned his living in a variety of ways, from seasonal worker to guide. He began to write poetry in the early 1950s. From the beginning of the 1960s until 1973, Kuzminskii was a central figure in the Leningrad literary underground. Since 1973, he lived in emigration in Western Europe and in the United States, where he edited a nine-volume anthology of Russian poetry of the 1940s–1980s under the title *The Blue Lagoon*. In the 1990s, Kuzminskii immersed himself in study of the early twentieth-century Russian avant-garde. The main quality of his work has been his striving for a *Gesamtkunstwerk* (total art work), in which the author integrates his own text with references to everyday life and commentaries on the works of other authors. Since 2000, Kuzminskii has been active in Runet.

See also: Internet, Russian; literature, émigré; literature, underground

GASAN GUSEJNOV

kvas

A sweet, fermented beverage, sometimes slightly alcoholic, made from rye bread. Widely considered the Russian national drink, *kvas* frequently appears in folk tales. Russians often drink *kvas* after visiting the *bania* (bathhouse).

During the Soviet period it was sold from vending machines and large barrels by street vendors.

See also: bania; drinks, alcoholic; folk tales

SETH GRAHAM

KVN (Klub veselykh i nakhodchivykh)

Klub veselykh i nakhodchivykh (Club of the Sunny and Smart) is the collective name for a form of amateur, competitive troupe comedy popular among Russian students since the Thaw. Teams compete by performing skits and songs before judges. Like sports teams, KVN troupes have nicknames and are closely associated with their cities and universities of origin. Beginning in the 1960s, KVN was televised, then taken off the air for a decade in the mid-1970s for being too satirically daring. KVN is still popular in Russia and among émigrés in Israel, the US, and elsewhere.

See also: amateur cultural activity; kapustnik; Thaw

SETH GRAHAM

Kyrgyzstan (Kirgizia)

Kyrgyzstan (the Kyrgyz Republic) is a country in Central Asia that used to be one of the fifteen republics of the Soviet Union. It shares borders with Kazakhstan, China, Tajikistan, and Uzbekistan. In 2004, Kyrgyzstan had a population of about 5 million, 65 per cent of whom were ethnic Kyrgyz, a predominantly Sunni Muslim ethnic group who speak a Turkic language called Kyrgyz. Bishkek (formerly Frunze) is the capital of Kyrgyzstan, with a multi-ethnic population of more than 800,000.

The territory of today's Kyrgyzstan became part of the Russian Empire in the 1860s. Although officially part of the Soviet Union since the early 1920s, the Kyrgyz Soviet Socialist Republic was not formed until 1936. In the 1930s, the nomadic Kyrgyz faced many hardships, from famine to sedentarization. During this period, many survivors slaughtered their herds and fled to China to escape Stalin's collectivization campaign. During the late Soviet period, Kyrgyzstan was famous for its mountain ranges and for being the home of writer Chingiz Aitmatov.

Kyrgyzstan's territory mostly consists of mountains, and the country lacks natural resources. When Kyrgyzstan became independent from the Soviet Union in August 1991, the government decided on a strategy of liberalizing its economy to attract foreign investment and the support of international donors. The republic's first president, Askar Akaev, was initially in favour of democratization, though subsequently he became increasingly autocratic and was ousted in 2005. Kyrgyzstan has substantial Russian and Uzbek minorities and has been wary of ethnic conflict, such as that which broke out between Kyrgyz and Uzbeks in the Southern region of Osh in 1990. The Akaev government was prudent in balancing the interests of foreign powers, giving in to border claims from China, maintaining friendly relations with Russia, and allowing a US military base to operate near Bishkek.

See also: Aitmatov, Chingiz; Central Asia; economic system, post-Soviet; Islam; Kazakhstan; natural resources; Stalin, Iosif; Tajikistan (Tadzhikistan); Uzbekistan

LAURA ADAMS

L

Lake Ladoga

Lake Ladoga (*Ladozhskoe ozero*) receives its water from numerous rivers, including the Volkov flowing north from Lake Ilmen, and sends its entire outflow into the Neva, thence through St. Petersburg and into the Gulf of Finland. Despite a powerful rotational current, seiches, storms, and icefields, for over a millennium the lake has featured prominently in Russia's cultural history. Important sites include Valaam Monastery and Peter the Great's Schlüsselburg fortress. During World War II, besieged Leningrad received its only supplies via the *Doroga zhizni* (Road of Life), a truck route running around German lines and across the winter ice of Ladoga's southwestern corner.

See also: Karelia; St. Petersburg; World War II (Great Patriotic War)

EDWARD ALAN COLE

Lamaism (Buddhism)

Lamaism is a form of Buddhism predominant in northern inner Asia, especially the Buriat, Tuvan, and Altai regions, with a western version among the Mongolic Kalmyks. Mongolic and Turkic peoples are associated with this regional Buddhism, which combines features of Vajrayāna and especially Mahāyāna Buddhism. The term 'lamaism' is also used for some Tibetan forms, creating debates concerning what areas and schools the term covers. It stems from 'lama', the word for a Buddhist priest, usually of the Gelugpa School. This branch is in turn sometimes called the 'law of virtue' school, founded by the Tibetan lama Tsongkhava [Tsonghapa] in the late fourteenth century. Its followers wear yellow hats, leading to the often misunderstood phrase 'yellow Lamaism' for this branch. Lamaism incorporates aspects of pre-Buddhist, shamanic practice, and is associated with the Mongolic New Year's festival, *tsagaalgan*. This is a celebration of winter's end, newborn livestock and milk products, *tsagaan edeen*, or 'white food'. The popular, mystical and dramatic tsam ritual is also celebrated yearly at Lamaist monasteries.

Lamaism, like other 'paths' of Buddhism, encompasses principles such as *samsara* [*sansara*] and *nirvana* (roughly glossed as states of condemnation and bliss); the idea of a 'wheel of life'; and the concept that life consists of suffering to attain salvation and enlightenment. The path includes psychological training through yoga and meditation, with emphasis on the transfer of knowledge from teacher to student over many years. Sacred texts include the *Ganjur* and the *Danjur*, with regional variations concerning their significance. Texts of the tantra, numbering 2,606, are especially revered and followed, with small regional shrines as well as large temples containing sacred texts for study. A major centre of Lamaism in Russia is the Ivolga monastery in Buriatia, where lamas trained in Mongolia, Tibet, and in Northern India with the exiled Fourteenth Dalai Lama, have spurred a recent revitalization after debilitating repression in the Soviet period.

See also: Buddhism; Buriatia; Siberia

MARJORIE MANDELSTAM BALZER

Lanovoi, Vasilii Semenovich

b. 16 January 1934, Moscow

Stage and film actor

After graduating from the Shchukin Theatre School in 1957, Lanovoi joined the troupe of the Moscow Vakhtangov Theatre, excelling both as an interpreter of the classical and modern repertoire and as a cultured, passionate poetry-reciter. On screen, Lanovoi was defined early on as a noble, ascetic hero and activist, starting with the title role in *Pavel Korchagin* (1956). The real depth of his talent became obvious in the Tolstoi adaptations *Voina i mir* (*War and Peace*, 1966–67) as the coldly handsome Anatole Kuragin, and *Anna Karenina* (1968) as Vronskii. Yet Lanovoi was mostly cast in patriotic super-hits such as *Ofitsery* (*Officers*, 1971) or as the founder of the Soviet secret police, Feliks Dzerzhinzkii. People's Artist of the USSR (1985).

See also: Vakhtangov Theatre

PETER ROLLBERG

Latvia

The Republic of Latvia (capital: Riga) is located on the Baltic Sea. Its area covers 64,589 sq km, mostly low hills with lowlands along the shore and sand dunes. The major river is the Dau-gava. There are more than 3,000 lakes in Latvia. Swamps cover 10 per cent of its territory.

Baltic tribes populating the area in early medieval times converted to Christianity after their defeat by Teutonic knights (thirteenth century). In 1238 a Livonian Order was created with the capital in Wenden (now Cēsis). After the Livonian war (1558–83) the territory was divided between Denmark and Poland. The region of Vidzeme (Livonia) became part of Sweden in 1629. In the eighteenth century many territories became part of the Russian Empire (including Riga and Vidzeme). In 1918, Latvia became an independent state, in 1940, a Soviet Socialist Republic, and in 1991 independent again.

The Latvian population is 2,290,000 (2005), including 56,000 non-citizens: 59 per cent is Latvian, 29 per cent Russian, 4 per cent Belor-ussian. The official language is Latvian, with Russian still used in large cities. Some 300,000 are Protestant, 500,000 Catholic (in the east), and 100,000 Russian Orthodox. The largest cities are Riga (743,000), Daugavpils (112,000), and Leipāja (85,000). Latvia's economic production includes engineering, radio, electro-technical equipment, pulp and paper, wood-working, petrochemical and chemical, pharma-ceutical and light industries, cattle breeding and dairy, bacon pig breeding, and fishing. Major exports are wood, textiles, and electrical appliances. Amber handicrafts and jewellery are Latvian trademarks. Other popular handicrafts include items of wool and flax, ceramics, and wooden toys.

A popular tourist destination, Latvia is famous for medieval architecture (palaces and castles), a windmill museum, and sandy beaches in Jūrmala, Vidzeme, and Kurzeme. The resort town of Sigulda, with beautiful valleys, caves, and castles, is called the Latvian Switzerland. Riga's old downtown features buildings by German architects (fourteenth–eighteenth centuries) and a famous cathedral (1211). National dishes and drinks include honey, black Riga bread, chocolate of the Laima factory, and a drink called black balsam. Latvia is also famous for a cheese festival, choral festivals, and the midsummer holiday Ligo.

SERGEI TARKHOV

Lavrov, Kirill Iurevich

b. 15 September 1925, Kiev, Ukraine

Stage and film actor

Son of famous actor Iurii Lavrov (1905–80), Kirill Lavrov joined the Lesia Ukrainka Russian Theatre in Kiev in 1950 and the Grand Dramatic Theatre in Leningrad in 1955. His screen image of manly stoicism and dignity was defined by numerous blockbusters, including *Zhivye i mertvye* (*The Living and the Dead*, 1964) and *Neitralnye vody* (*Neutral Waters*, 1969), while his por-trayal of Ivan Karamazov in the three-part Dostoevskii adaptation *The Brothers Karamazov* (*Bratia Karamazovy*, 1967–69) revealed a potential for intellectual complexity. Lavrov excelled in roles of Soviet officials, often uniformed, irradiating patriotism, Communist loyalty, and paternalist warmth. People's Artist of the USSR (1972).

See also: Communist Party; Tovstonogov Bolshoi Drama Theatre

PETER ROLLBERG

Lavrovskii, Leonid Mikhailovich

b. 5 [18] June, 1905, St. Petersburg;
d. 27 November 1967, Paris

Dancer, choreographer, teacher

Director of the Kirov Ballet from 1938–44 and head choreographer of the Bolshoi Theatre, 1944–56, and 1960–64. Lavrovskii's fame as a choreographer derives mostly from his 1940 production of Prokofiev's *Romeo and Juliet*. A work that essays the main trends of Soviet ballet of the inter-war years, Lavrovskii's ballet is a careful adaptation of a literary monument that aims to approximate the author's poetry in movement terms. The brilliant 1954 film adaptation of his ballet, with Galina Ulanova in the lead role, reveals the similarity of this approach to the aesthetics of early cinema, with its reliance on exaggerated facial expressions and stylized pantomime to advance the narrative.

See also: ballet dancers, Mariinskii Theatre; ballet, Soviet; Bolshoi Theatre; Prokofiev, Sergei; Ulanova, Galina

TIM J. SCHOLL

Lebed, Aleksandr Ivanovich

b. 20 April 1950, Novocherkassk;
d. 28 April 2002, Krasnoiarsk region

General, politician

In the 1980s and early 1990s, General Lebed participated in the Soviet Union's main military conflicts including the war in Afghanistan (1981–82). In 1992–95, he was a commander of Russia's 14th division in Moldova, as a peacekeeping force between the nationalist government of Chisinau and the unrecognized Transdniester Republic. Lebed came in third in the first round of the 1996 presidential elections. He was known for his deep voice, gruff manner, and direct, laconic speech. As Secretary of the Security Council in 1996 under Yeltsin, he was responsible for the questionable Khasaviurt agreements with Chechen President Aslan Maskhadov. In May 1998, Lebed was elected Governor of Krasnoiarsk region. He died in a helicopter crash.

See also: War, Afghan; Yeltsin, Boris

ALEXANDER DOMRIN

Lebedev, Evgenii Alekseevich

b. 15 January 1917, Balakovo, Saratov district; d. 9 July 1997, St. Petersburg

Russian stage and screen actor

Son of a priest and a graduate of the Moscow Theatre College (1940), Lebedev became a star in Georgii Tovstonogov's Grand Dramatic Theatre (BDT) in Leningrad, which he joined in 1956. His legendary stage performances included the title role in *Istoriia loshadi* (*Story of a Horse*) after Lev Tolstoi's short story *Kholstomer* (*Strider*), the old traditionalist Bessemenov in Maksim Gorkii's *Meshchane* (*The Petit-Bourgeois*), and the eponymous fascist dictator in Bertolt Brecht's play *Arturo Ui*. Lebedev's inimitable, at times excessive, emotionality is also characteristic of his more than seventy film roles, most of them scene-stealing supporting parts. People's Artist of the USSR (1968).

See also: Tovstonogov Bolshoi Drama Theatre

PETER ROLLBERG

Lebeshev, Pavel Timofeevich

b. 15 February 1940, Moscow;
d. 23 February 2003, Moscow

Director of photography

Lebeshev graduated from VGIK, but he received his professional training through practice with his father, director of photography Timofei Lebeshev. Before graduating he had already filmed the blockbuster *Belorusskii vokzal* (*Belorussian Railway Station*, 1970). Lebeshev excelled in subordinating the image to the over-all sense of the film. His camerawork demon-strates a mastery of light and colour, while his frames followed the compositions of visual art. Lebeshev has shot over fifty films, repeatedly working with Nikita Mikhalkov and Sergei Solovev, as well as Georgii Daneliia, Roman Balaian, Dmitrii Meshkiev, and Sergei Bodrov.

See also: All-Russian (All-Union) State Institute of Cinematography (VGIK); Balaian, Roman; Bodrov, Sergei; cameramen; Daneliia, Georgii; Mikhalkov, Nikita

BIRGIT BEUMERS

legal system, post-Soviet

Following the collapse of the USSR, the Soviet legal system ceased to exist, for all of the ex-Soviet Republics became politically indepen-dent. Nonetheless, many of the old Soviet laws, or local legislation adopted by the former Soviet Republics during the Soviet era, remained in force until repealed. Some of this legislation remains in force to this day. There has been extensive reform of the legal system, however, particularly in economic law and the criminal code.

In the Russian Federation during the early 1990s, a new legal system, which focused on democracy and the market economy, was cre-ated from scratch. A new constitution was adopted and new state bodies were created that had not existed in Soviet times, such as the Constitutional Court, which has the task of monitoring laws to ensure that they comply with the Constitution; the Federal Securities Commission; and the Anti-Monopoly Authority.

In quite a short time (1990–95), Russia adop-ted an entirely new framework of laws aimed at implementing the market economy: a new civil code, new customs regulations, and new corpo-rate laws. The development of a securities market led to the adoption of securities legisla-tion, and the permissible circulation of foreign

currency required the introduction of hard cur-rency legislation. The abolition of state mono-poly on foreign trade encouraged the involvement of the private sector in interna-tional trade, which, in turn, required the adop-tion of new customs regulations. Due to the colossal process of privatization, extensive pri-vatization laws had to be adopted. During the Soviet era Russia did not have a proper taxation system; thus a new tax system and state tax authority had to be elaborated in response to the development of private business.

Crucial changes were also made to the Rus-sian criminal code. A new Criminal Code and Criminal Procedures Code were adopted, and the rights of defence attorneys were extended to allow them to collect evidence for the defence. Jury trials were introduced, initially on an experimental basis, for the most severe offences. Russian criminal law was also extended to include many types of offences unknown to Soviet jurisprudence, such as tax evasion, ter-rorism, and hostage-taking. Due to the admis-sion of the Russian Federation to the Council of Europe, the country introduced a moratorium on the death penalty, while introducing life imprisonment for the most severe offences. Acquittals appear to be becoming more and more common, particularly in jury trials; how-ever, this is still subject to very strict state con-trol, and the highest judicial authorities frequently overturn acquittals made by the lower courts.

Post-Soviet law in Russia partially duplicates foreign legal concepts; in some cases entire branches of law are based on legal models developed in other countries. Russia adopted the concept of challenging decisions made by federal and local authorities, which was con-ceptually impossible under Soviet rule. Sig-nificantly, the importance of case law as a source of law is increasing, particularly in cases relating to civil law and business.

The post-Soviet legal system in Russia has thus undergone rapid change. Often new legis-lation has not been subjected to sufficient scru-tiny before being passed into law; as a result, sometimes conflicting and even contradictory laws apply to the same issue. The drafting of new laws is far from perfect, although the most recently adopted laws are relatively detailed and correct. In addition, Russian ministries and other state authorities are entitled to introduce secondary legislation, sometimes in conflict with federal laws. Russian judges do not yet have enough commercial experience to handle complicated business disputes and, particularly in remote areas, may be greatly influenced by the local authorities. It is no secret that Russia has the reputation of being one of the most corrupt nations in Europe, and the possibility of getting a fair trial in Russia is debatable.

See also: constitutions; crime; legal system, Soviet; privatization

DMITRY GRAVIN

legal system, Soviet

The Soviet legal system, as in the case of most continental European countries, formed a part of the so-called continental (or codified) legal systems based on Roman law. The Soviet legal system was based on so-called codes, that is, a series of laws combined in a single 'book'. Case law was not recognized as a source of law. Although each union republic had its own legal system, each was based on fundamentals established for the entire USSR, and therefore the legal systems of republics were generally quite similar.

The Soviet legal system was aimed at protecting the interests of the Soviet state and the Communist Party, whose leading role was directly specified in the Constitution. The civil and criminal courts were structured in accordance with the Soviet administrative system. Civil law courts mostly dealt with disputes between individuals. Since all assets were state-owned, civil courts did not consider disputes between legal entities (companies), for which there were special 'arbitration courts'. (This term is misleading, for such courts had nothing to do with 'arbitration' as a type of dispute resolution performed by a non-governmental forum. Soviet arbitration courts were state courts aimed at resolving only disputes between companies.)

The Soviet police (*militsiia*) oversaw public order, while the Office of the Prosecutor was responsible for enforcing general compliance with laws. The Soviet criminal system did not recognize the institution of court investigations, which existed in pre-Soviet Russia but was abolished shortly after the October Revolution of 1917. Any offences were investigated by so-called 'special bodies': the police were responsible for investigating most crimes against property or public order, the Office of the Prosecutor for investigating the most serious crimes (many of them punishable by the death penalty), and the state security service (KGB) for investigating crimes against the state. Very often the investigation was biased. Although a defence attorney was admitted to the proceedings, his role in preparing defence arguments and collecting evidence in favour of the accused was tightly restricted or even made impossible. Although the presumption of innocence formally existed in the USSR, in reality this concept was rarely applied.

The Soviet legal system did not employ jury trials, though this institution had existed in Russia before the 1917 Revolution. Although it allowed for the involvement of ordinary citizens in civil and criminal cases, which were heard by a panel consisting of one professional judge and two laypeople (not lawyers), the latter, while officially possessing a voice equal to that of the judge, in fact played an extremely limited role. They were not involved in findings on matters of fact, and the judge alone always determined the sentence.

There were no complete acquittals in the USSR, although partial acquittals were relatively frequent. Cases did not always end up before the court; very often, if the prosecutor believed that there was insufficient evidence of the crime after some investigation, the case was stopped at the investigation stage and did not go to a court hearing. A similar approach was often taken during the court hearing: if a lack of evidence became obvious to the judge, he or she would not acquit the accused, but would refer the case back to investigators for 'further investigation'. The reason for this was ideological, intended to avoid a subversion of state authority: since the investigation ended with one state official (the prosecutor) approving the charge, another state body (the court) could not reverse this finding. The adversarial process was nothing but a formality. Although the state formally provided an attorney for those who were unable to pay for one, since there was no jury system, the role of the counsel for the defence was minimal.

The death penalty was reserved for the most serious crimes against the state, some murders, large-scale embezzlement of state property, and other serious crimes; however, terms of imprisonment were generally shorter than in many other European countries. Penalties did not include life imprisonment; the maximum term of imprisonment was fifteen years.

Civil law procedures were more adversarial, since they almost always involved a dispute between individuals or sometimes between entities and individuals, but not between individuals and the state, as in criminal cases. Judgements (and in criminal cases, sentences) were subject to appeals and further appeals, which could last for years.

The Communist Party had a very strong influence on the Soviet legal system. A candidate for appointment to the position of judge or an executive position in any part of the legal system had to be a member of the Communist Party. Officially, judges were elected by the people, but in fact they were appointed by the state, since voters had no choice regarding whom to elect: there was only one candidate proposed for each judicial position.

See also: administrative structure, Soviet Union; Communist Party; constitutions; crime; Federal Security Service; legal system, post-Soviet; militia (police)

DMITRY GRAVIN

Lemeshev, Sergei Iakovlevich

b. 27 June [10 July] 1902, Staroe Kniazevo, Tver province; d. 26 June 1977, Moscow

Opera singer

Born into a peasant family, tenor Lemeshev studied at the Moscow Conservatory and with Konstantin Stanislavskii before making his debut in 1931 at the Bolshoi Theatre after a few years in the provinces. He never performed outside the Soviet Union, where he rapidly achieved a popularity normally associated with movie stars, even assuming the lead role in the film *Muzykalnaia istoriia* (*A Musical Story*, 1940). His rise from humble origins only added to his allure. Most famed for his subtle and intelligent performances of Tchaikovsky, Lemeshev sang Lenskii in *Eugene Onegin* more than 500 times, a role he recorded alongside Galina Vishnevskaia in 1956.

See also: Moscow Conservatory; opera, Soviet; opera singers, Bolshoi Theatre; Vishnevskaia, Galina

PHILIP ROSS BULLOCK

Lenin, Vladimir Ilich

(né Vladimir Ilich Ulianov)

b. 22 April 1870, Simbirsk [Ulianovsk]; d. 21 January 1924, Moscow

Politician

Vladimir Ilich Ulianov, better known as Lenin, studied law at the University of Kazan until he was expelled for revolutionary activities. After the assassination of Tsar Alexander II in the spring of 1881, the government executed suspected revolutionaries, including Alexander Ulianov, Vladimir Lenin's older brother. Lenin himself was arrested in 1895, imprisoned, sent to Siberia until 1900, and then into exile outside of Russia. When Lenin disagreed with other members of the Russian Social Democratic Labour Party over party organization and membership, two factions emerged in 1903: the Bolsheviks (from the Russian word for 'majority') led by Lenin and the Mensheviks (from the word for 'minority'). The Bolsheviks, led by Lenin, advocated building an organization of professional revolutionaries who would lead the proletariat in bringing about the downfall of capitalism and the establishment of an international socialist state. When the tsar abdicated in March 1917, Lenin returned to Russia and emphasized the need to seize power through violent, forceful means.

After the Bolshevik overthrow of the Provisional government in October 1917, Lenin agreed to the Treaty of Brest-Litovsk with Germany, which pulled Russia out of World War I. In December 1917, the Cheka (*Chrezvychainaia kommissiia* [Extraordinary Commission], the secret police organization) was created to suppress opposition to Bolshevik rule. Groups in Russia who shared the goal of ousting the Bolsheviks organized the White Army and Civil War ensued from 1918 to 1921. This period of War Communism resulted in the rapid expansion of government authority over the economy.

Lenin equated Marx's notion of the dictatorship of the proletariat with rule by the Communist Party. Marx believed that the dictatorship of the proletariat is necessary in the period of transition between capitalist and communist society. According to Lenin, the state could not be expected to wither away; rather, the socialist state needed to be strengthened against internal and external enemies.

Another principle that can be attributed to Lenin's writings is the idea of *partiinost* (party-mindedness). This means that disciplines such as philosophy and the social sciences should support the Party and its cause. The final major principle in Leninism was the theory of imperialism. According to Lenin, imperialism was the highest stage of capitalism. Colonies provided raw materials and abundant, cheap labour supplies. Once all colonial territories were annexed, the only way to acquire new territory was through war. The rivalry of colonial countries would become more and more intense, leading to imperialist wars.

In the aftermath of the Civil War period, the New Economic Policy (NEP) restored capitalist policies to revive the economy. The role of the market in the economy was re-emphasized; light industry was returned to private hands, and tsarist civil servants were reinstated to the bureaucracy. While NEP represented a betrayal of the Bolsheviks' philosophy of radical social and economic transformation, it did result in impressive growth. Lenin's death in 1924 prevented him from witnessing the success of the programme. Lenin's body remains on permanent display in Moscow.

See also: Communist Party; economic system, Soviet; internationalism; Lenin Mausoleum; partiinost; philosophy, Soviet (Marxist-Leninist)

Further reading

Service, R. (1985) *Lenin: A Political Life*, London: Macmillan.

VICKI L. HESLI AND JAMES KRUEGER

Leningrad

See St. Petersburg

Leningrad

Rock group

Arguably the most popular band among post-Soviet Russia's youth, comprising fifteen rotating members, masterminded by lead singer, composer, and self-proclaimed Conceptualist Sergei Shnurov (Shnur). Under the endlessly inventive, versatile Shnurov's management, from the late 1990s Leningrad embraced the individual and collective persona of a foul-mouthed macho hooligan, flaunting his boozing, drug-steeped, crime-associated antisocialism. *Épatage* is Leningrad's banner. Its raucous, aggressive violation of all sacrosanct values in a lexicon consisting chiefly of obscenities – showcased in such albums as *Pulia* (Bullet, 1999), *Mat bez elektrichestva* (Obscene Language without Electricity, 1999), *Dachniki* (Dacha Dwellers, 2000), and *Dlia millionov* (For Millions, 2003) – prompted Mayor Luzhkov to ban the group's performances in Moscow. The ultimate postmodernist borrower, Leningrad drew on rock, rap, reggae, and ska, to produce parodies and pastiches of sundry musical and cultural styles, most notably in its inspiredly antic pseudo-opera, *Babarobot* (2004); the work hilariously parodied Vladimir Vysotskii, the conservative, pro-Putin group Idushchie vmeste (Marching Together), and clichés of Soviet ideology. Films targeting young audiences, such as Natalia Pogonicheva's *Teoriia zapoia* (Theory of the Drinking Binge, 2002), Petr Buslov's *Bumer*

(Bimmer, 2003), and Andrei Proshkin's *Igry motylkov* (Moth Games, 2004) integrated Shnurov's compositions into their soundtracks, and the savvy, entrepreneurial Shnurov (trained in engineering and theology) played roles in several films, most memorably Ilia Khrzhanovskii's *4* (2004).

See also: film, post-Soviet; Luzhkov, Iurii; music in film; popular music, post-Soviet; rock music; Vysotskii, Vladimir

HELENA GOSCILO

Lenin Mausoleum

Aleksei Shchusev designed the Lenin Mausoleum in Red Square in 1924. In 1930, the original wood pyramid was replaced by one in red granite (for Communism), and black labradorite (for mourning). The symbolism increased as one descended to the glass coffin holding Lenin's body: designs of red flames against a black background evoked Hades. In the Soviet era, visits to the shrine were *de rigueur*. In 1953, Stalin's body was displayed next to Lenin's, then removed by Khrushchev in 1961. After 1991, some viewed the preserved corpse as a source of Russia's problems, and a movement began to bury it elsewhere.

NADIESZDA KIZENKO

Lenkom Theatre

Founded as the amateur *Teatr rabochei molodezhi* (TRAM, Theatre of Working Youth) in 1927, the theatre turned professional in 1933 and was renamed *Teatr imeni Leninskogo Komsomola* (Lenin Komsomol Theatre) in 1938, to become officially shortened in 1990 to Lenkom. It rose to prominence under Ivan Bersenev (1938–51), who cultivated star actors in productions of the classics. Anatolii Efros staged six major productions there from 1964 to 1967, when he was fired for ideological reasons. Mark Zakharov's term as chief director, beginning in 1973, brought the theatre mass popularity with matinee idols Evgenii Leonov, Oleg Iankovksii, and

Inna Churikova in flashy, spectacular entertainments ranging from tragedy to musicals.

See also: Efros, Anatolii; musicals, Russian/Soviet; Zakharov, Mark

JOHN FREEDMAN

Lent (Velikii Post)

Lent is the most significant of the Orthodox Church's fasting periods. For the seven weeks before Easter, observant Russian Orthodox Christians abstain from meat, fish, dairy products, alcohol, and sexual relations. The texts and music of such Lenten services as the Great Canon of St. Andrew of Crete and the Liturgy of Presanctified Gifts have inspired Russian writers, including Aleksander Pushkin, Fedor Dostoevskii, and Boris Pasternak. Nikita Mikhalkov's film *Sibirskii tsiriulnik* (*The Barber of Siberia*, 1998) depicts Russian Lenten observances: the *bliny*-eating week of Mardi Gras (*Maslenitsa*) and Forgiveness Sunday.

See also: bliny; Easter, Orthodox; Maslenitsa; Mikhalkov, Nikita; Pasternak, Boris; Russian Orthodoxy

Further reading

Schmemann, A. (2001) *Great Lent*, New York: St. Vladimir's Seminary Press.

NADIESZDA KIZENKO

Leonov, Evgenii Pavlovich

b. 2 September 1926, Moscow;
d. 29 January 1994, Moscow

Actor

Leonov worked in both theatre and film, initially as a comic actor of great subtlety in *Tridtsat tri* (*Thirty Three*, 1966) and *Zigzag udachi* (*Zigzags of Fate*, 1968), then as an equally talented dramatic actor in such melodramas as *Belorusskii vokzal* (*Belorusskii Station*, 1971). His round face and chunky body seemed especially well suited to represent, sometimes seriously and sometimes satirically, a 'man of the people', such as the ignorant but supremely self-confident janitor in the 1981 'sad comedy' *Osennii marafon* (*Autumn Marathon*) by Daneliia. He made over fifty films and 'voiced' a large number of popular cartoon characters, the most famous of which is Winnie the Pooh (*Vinni-Pukh*).

JOSEPHINE WOLL

Leontev, Valerii Iakovlevich

b. 19 March 1949, Ust-Usa, Komi ASSR, Russia

Pop singer

Graduate of the Department of Directing at the Leningrad Institute of Culture, known for his diversity, expressiveness, and ability to synthesize various styles and genres. Extravagant costumes contributed to the theatricality of his stage performances. He played in several films. The peak of his creative work was the grandiose show *Po doroge v Gollivud* (*On Route to Hollywood*, 1996). Since the 1980s, Leontev has frequently toured abroad. People's Artist of Russia (1996), recipient of numerous prizes.

See also: popular music, post-Soviet

YURI ZARETSKY

Leshchenko, Lev Valerianovich

b. 1 February 1942, Moscow

Singer, teacher

A graduate of the State Institute of Theatre Arts (GITIS), the bass-baritone Leshchenko sang at the Moscow Operetta Theatre, and from 1970 was a soloist at the USSR Gosteleradio (State Radio and TV), singing classical romances, arias, etc. Many composers wrote music specifically for him. His popularity grew throughout the 1970s and the 1980s, and he was a successful member of the Soviet establishment. A teacher at the Gnesin Russian Music Academy,

Leshchenko was named People's Artist of the RSFSR (1983).

See also: operetta; radio, Soviet; romance; Russian Academy of Theatre Arts

YURI ZARETSKY

Leshchenko, Petr Konstantinovich

b. 3 June 1898 near Nikolaev, Ukraine; d. 16 July 1954, Bucharest, Romania

Singer

Born into a family of peasants, Leshchenko achieved international fame with his velvety baritone, enhanced by his guitar-playing and dancing. He performed primarily in Bucharest, but also in Paris, the Middle East, Riga, and Odessa. Leshchenko debuted in 1930; together with the composer and accompanist Oscar Strok, he performed Russian folk songs and gypsy songs. In the course of his almost 25-year vocal career, Leshchenko also performed his own songs, as well as romances and popular Soviet songs by composers including Dunaevskii. Although he sang only in Russian and occasionally in Ukrainian, Leshchenko achieved international recognition with performances of dance-like melodies to tango and foxtrot rhythms. CD recordings of his complete repertoire recently have revived his popularity.

See also: Dunaevskii, Maksim; Gypsy music; romance

OLGA ZASLAVSKY

Lezgins

Lezgins (also called Lezgiars, Lezghi, Lezgi, Lezgian, and Kiurinsty) are peoples of the Nakhsko-Dagestan group of the Caucasian language family. Of the 411,535 Lezgins living in Russia (2002), 336,698 reside in southern Dagestan and 178,000 in northeastern Azerbaijan, 14,000 in Kazakhstan, and 10,000 in Turkmenistan. Lezgins are Sunni Muslims.

Main occupations include agriculture (particularly growing grapes), cattle breeding, and handicrafts, including rugs, jewellery, and linens. A very popular dance called the *lezginka* made their name famous throughout the former Soviet Union.

See also: Caucasus; Dagestan; Islam; Kazakhstan; Turkmenistan

SERGEI TARKHOV

Lianozovo School

The so-called Lianozovo School comprised a group of artists and poets including Evgenii Kropivnitskii and his pupils Valentina Kropivnitskaia and Oskar Rabin (Kropivnitskii's daughter and her husband), Genrikh Sapgir, and Igor Kholin. With them, artists Olga Potapova (Kropivnitskii's wife), Lidiia Masterkova, Vladimir Nemukhin, and Nikolai Vechtomov, along with poets Vsevolod Nekrasov and Ian Satunovskii, formed the core group. From the late 1950s until 1965, the group regularly gathered in Rabin and Kropivnitskaia's room at the railroad workers' barracks in Lianozovo outside Moscow. Significant as one of the first unofficial avant-garde groups in the post-Stalin USSR, the Lianozovo School did not feature a specific method or agenda.

See also: Kropivnitskaia, Valentina; Masterkova, Lidiia; Nekrasov, Vsevolod; Rabin, Oskar

ANN KOMAROMI

libraries

The first libraries in Russia date from the eleventh–twelfth centuries and were housed in monasteries. Secular libraries appeared during the eighteenth century, at the Academy of Sciences (1714) and at Moscow University (1756). The first Russian public library opened in St. Petersburg (1814), while in Moscow the first public library was established only in 1862, as part of the Rumiantsev Museum. Starting in 1782, a number of public provincial libraries started operating in regional centres. During the Soviet era, libraries were partly transformed into institutions of communist agitation and propaganda; many old libraries lost a significant share of former holdings, various 'dangerous' books and publications were removed, and 'special collections' (*spetsfondy*) were created in large libraries for printed matter banned by censorship on account of either the information it contained or its ideological and political nonconformity with Soviet orthodoxy.

A vast network of libraries proliferated during the Soviet period. They were divided into universal (*universalnye*), scholarly, public, university, educational-institutional, and departmental (*vedomstvennye*) libraries. In 1990 the USSR boasted 1,331,000 libraries, containing a total of 21,439 million books and print items (*pechatnye edinitsy*). After the collapse of the Soviet Union and the economic crisis of the 1990s, the majority of libraries lost their minimal level of financing and stopped acquiring most new books; only recently have they renewed acquisition of new publications.

At the beginning of the 1990s previously closed 'special holdings' were opened. By 2003, 509,000 libraries with a total of 1,007 million books and publications were operating in Russia. To use libraries, one must register: for public libraries, by presenting one's passport; for scholarly libraries, by showing either a document certifying one's degree or academic title or a special letter from an organization requesting access to library materials. Non-public and departmental libraries may be used only by those with special permission and documents certifying their professional occupation. Unlike in most Western libraries, most books are kept in closed depositories to which readers' access is prohibited (for fear of theft or damage). A library normally consists of a circulation department (where books can be checked out), reading rooms (from which many publications cannot be checked out), a reference-bibliographic department, an alphabetic and system catalogue, and photocopy centres. In large libraries the reading rooms are divided according to discipline: natural sciences, humanities and social sciences, and technology. There are also more narrowly specialized departments that hold items such as musical scores, manuscripts, geographical maps and atlases, foreign language publications, and special collections. The number of items lent at any one time to users of the reading rooms is limited to five to ten.

The largest libraries in Moscow are the Russian State Library, INION RAN (*Institut nauchnoi informatsii po obshchestvennym naukam Rossiiskoi Akademii Nauk* [Institute of Scholarly Information in the Humanities and Social Sciences of the Russian Academy of Sciences]), BEN RAN (*Biblioteka po estestvennym naukam Rossiiskoi Akademii Nauk* [Natural Sciences Library of the Russian Academy of Sciences]), the Moscow State University Research Library, the All-Russian State Library of Foreign Literature (*Vserossiiskaia gosudarstvennaia biblioteka inostrannoi literatury*), the State Public Historical Library (*Gosudarstvennaia publichnaia istoricheskaia biblioteka*), and the Sechenov Central Medical Research Library (*Tsentralnaia nauchnaia meditsinskaia biblioteka imeni I. M. Sechenova*). The largest libraries in St. Petersburg are the Russian National Library, the Library of the Russian Academy of Sciences, the St. Petersburg University Library, and the Polytechnic Institute Library.

See also: Academy of Sciences; Moscow State University; Russian National Library; Russian State Library; St. Petersburg State University

SERGEI TARKHOV

Liepa, Maris-Rudolf Eduardovich

b. 27 July 1936, Riga; d. 26 March 1989, Moscow

Dancer, actor, choreographer

Liepa began to study dance at the Riga Ballet School (1947–53) and continued at the Moscow Choreography School (1953–55). He became a soloist of the Latvian Theatre of Opera and Ballet (1955–56) then worked in the Nemirovich-Danchenko Opera Theatre in Moscow (1956–60) before establishing himself as a soloist at Moscow's Bolshoi Theatre. Liepa's dancing style, encompassing both technical proficiency and a nuanced penetration into the character, brought him to the fore of contemporary ballet productions in the 1960s and 1970s. His major

roles at the Bolshoi Theatre, performed in the contemporary classical ballets choreographed by Iurii Grigorovich, included Farkhad in *The Legend of Love* (1965) and Crassus, his most acclaimed role, in *Spartacus* (1968). Liepa made a significant contribution to the development of the film-ballet, a genre that gained popularity in the Soviet Union in the 1970s. His role in the film *Galatea*, with Ekaterina Maksimova in the title role (directed by Aleksandr Belinskii, 1977), was among his most prominent performances. Recipient of various State and international awards, including the Lenin Prize in 1970 and the Nijinski Prize in Paris, 1971. In 1987–89, he led the Theatre of the Contemporary Musical Drama in Moscow.

See also: ballet, Soviet; Bolshoi Theatre; Grigorovich, Iurii

TATIANA SENKEVITCH

Likhachev, Dmitrii Sergeevich

b. 28 November 1906, Petrograd;
d. 30 September 1999, St. Petersburg

Scholar, politician

Dmitrii Likhachev was an academic, a literary historian and critic, a leading specialist in Old Russian literature, and a senior deputy in the Soviet parliament. His numerous works on Old Russian literature are highly influential – if at times controversial – in Russia and the West. Often called the 'conscience of Russia', Likhachev was widely respected in both Soviet and post-Soviet Russia and has been described by some as a Sakharov-like figure in the realm of Soviet culture. In 1975, Likhachev's refusal to sign a petition condemning Sakharov resulted in his being beaten up by KGB agents outside his apartment.

Arrested by Soviet authorities in 1928, Likhachev served part of his term at the White Sea Canal and later at the Solovki labour camp. Upon returning to academic life, he maintained a low profile politically. His longest professional position was that of senior research fellow at the Institute of Russian Literature in St. Petersburg, a post he held from 1938 until his death.

Likhachev's prolific writings range from commentaries on the medieval Russian epic *Slovo o polku Igoreve* (*The Lay of Igor's Campaign*) to discussions of gardens and Pushkin's works. During the glasnost era Likhachev served as head of the National Cultural Fund under Gorbachev; he continued to advise the first Russian president, Boris Yeltsin, in a similar capacity. When Russian astronomers discovered the 'small planet' No. 2877, they named it after Likhachev.

See also: Federal Security Service; Gorbachev, Mikhail; perestroika and glasnost; Sakharov, Andrei; Solovki; White Sea Canal; Yeltsin, Boris

SUSMITA SUNDARAM

limitchik (limita)

During the Soviet period, temporary residence permits were granted by quota (*limit*) in major cities to workers from the provinces (*limitchik* – male; *limitchitsa* – female; *limita* – plural) in return for fulfilment of the most unqualified and lowest-paying jobs. They were required to work in a particular factory or enterprise, and sometimes at a specific job, for a specific period (usually five years) to receive the permit, and were usually provided with dormitory rooms. *Limita* can be used as a derogatory term meaning 'outsider riff-raff'.

See also: propiska

MICHELE BERDY

Limonov, Eduard Veniaminovich

(né Eduard Veniaminovich Savenko)

b. 22 February 1943, Dzerzhinsk

Writer

An autodidact, Limonov earned his living as foundry worker, bookseller, tailor, furniture remover, and butler. One of the best underground poets of his generation (*Russkoe* [*All That Is Russian*, 1979]; *Moi otritsatelnyi geroi* [*My Negative*

Hero, 1995]), he sold typescripts of his collections. Forced into exile in 1974 because of his independent lifestyle, he described his experiences as an émigré in the United States (*Istoriia ego slugi* [*His Butler's Story*, 1987]) and France (*Ukroshchenie tigra v Parizhe* [*Taming the Tiger in Paris*, 1994]) in a cycle of autobiographical short stories and novels, the first of which, *Eto ia – Edichka* (*It's Me, Eddie*, 1979), caused a scandal because of its obscene language, graphic (including homoerotic) sex scenes, and openly anti-American stance. The autobiographical series continued, covering Limonov's childhood and youth in Kharkov and Moscow (*Podrostok Savenko* (*Savenko the Raw Youth*, 1983)); *Moskva maiskaia* (*Moscow in May*, unpublished). Limonov's attempts to escape the autobiographical mode in fiction, from *Palach* (*The Executioner*, 1986) to *316, punkt B* (*Article 316-B*, 1998), have been less successful.

Limonov is also a prolific political journalist, always in opposition to the regime of whatever country he resides in (*Ubiistvo chasovogo* [*The Murder of a Sentinel*, 1993]; *Anatomiia Geroia* [*The Anatomy of a Hero*, 1998]; *Moia politicheskaia biografiia* [*My Life as a Politician*, 2002]). His return to post-Communist Russia (with dual Russian/French citizenship), involvement with the National Bolshevik Party (which he founded in 1993), and editorship of the party's newspaper, *Limonka*, which attacked the establishment, eventually landed him in jail (April 2001–June 2003) on charges of conspiring to overthrow the government. His testimony about the post-Soviet GULag (*V plenu u mertvetsov* [*A Captive of the Dead*, 2003]; and *Po tiurmam* [*From One Prison to Another*, 2004]) is the most significant human rights document since Solzhenitsyn's exposé of the Communist penitentiary system.

Further reading

Rogachevskii, A. (2003) *A Critical and Biographical Study of Russian Writer Eduard Limonov*, Lewiston, NY: Edwin Mellen Press.

Ryan-Hayes, K. (1993) 'Limonov's *It's Me, Eddie* and the Autobiographical Mode', *The Carl Beck Papers* (No. 1004), Pittsburgh, PA: University of Pittsburgh.

ANDREI ROGATCHEVSKI

lines

See queue

Lioznova, Tatiana Mikhailovna

b. 20 July 1924, Moscow

Film and television director

For over thirty years Lioznova has worked at the Gorkii Film Studio. Her popular melodrama *Tri topolia na Pliushchikhe* (*Three Poplar Trees on Pliushchikha*, 1967) propelled actress Tatiana Doronina to stardom as a Soviet sex symbol and the epitome of Russian femininity. But Lioznova's place in Russian culture rests on her twelve-episode television spy thriller, *Semnadtsat mgnovenii vesny* (*Seventeen Moments of Spring*, 1973), which has retained its cult status in post-Soviet Russia. Despite their genre diversity (from social drama to political thriller to musical), Lioznova's films are invariably about people with troubled identities, 'at home among strangers'.

See also: Doronina, Tatiana; *Semnadtsat mgnovenii vesny* (*Seventeen Moments of Spring*)

ELENA PROKHOROVA

Listev, Vladislav

b. 10 May 1956, Moscow; d. 1 March 1995, Moscow

Journalist

A well-known television journalist who promoted a Western style and journalistic standards in television during perestroika, Listev was also a television producer. Trained as an athlete, he worked as a coach, served in the Soviet Army, and enrolled in the journalism department of Moscow State University as a veteran. After graduation in 1982, he worked as editor of radio programmes at the foreign desk at Gosteleradio USSR, the Soviet Union's radio and television division. In 1987 he moved to the youth programmes desk at Central Television (*Tsentralnoe televidenie*) and became one of the initiators and leaders of the new, critical, highly respected television programme *Vzgliad* (Viewpoint). In the 1990s, Listev worked as an emcee for the new game show *Pole chudes* (Field of Miracles, the Russian version of the American game show *Wheel of Fortune*). He also hosted the political programme *Tema* (Theme).

Listev created a new style in television journalism; his image resembled Larry King's in the United States, and he worked according to the trends and formats of American television. He made significant contributions to the thematic and visual modernization of Soviet and Russian television. In 1991 he became executive producer of the newborn independent TV company ViD, and its president in 1993. He was the first general director of ORT (*Obshchestvennoe rossiiskoe televidenie* [Public Russian Television], Channel 1). His plan to control and even eliminate advertisements in state-owned television faced strong resistance from media and advertising companies. He was shot to death near his apartment. His murder profoundly disturbed Russians, for whom he had become a symbol of democratic and media reform. The investigation of his murder continues, with no arrests or prosecutions to date. A few months after his death, *Medved* (Bear), the first monthly 'men's magazine' in Russia, appeared, masterminded by Listev and launched by his wife, Albina.

See also: journalism; journalists, post-Soviet; *Vzgliad*

NADEZHDA AZHGIKHINA

literary criticism

In the Soviet Union literary criticism, as a professional reader's tool for analysis and evaluation of writing, followed public policy. During the Thaw, Stagnation, and perestroika, it proved a controversial means of assessing aesthetic, philosophical, and socio-political practices. Discussion and resolutions taken at the Second Congress of Soviet Writers (1954) led in 1956 to the establishment of a monthly journal of literary criticism, *Voprosy literatury* (Literary Issues). During the relatively relaxed atmosphere of the Thaw, literary criticism of a liberal-democratic cast began to thrive.

Critics concerned with similar issues and espousing similar views grouped around thick journals. The liberal-democratic *Novyi mir* group of Vladimir Lakshin, Igor Vinogradov, and Natalia Ilina opposed the hard-line Communist orthodoxy of *Oktiabr* (October) and *Ogonek* (Little Flame) and the 'soilnik' (*pochenichestvo*) nationalism of *Molodaia gvardiia*. *Novyi mir* had the support of equally liberal colleagues, such as Stanislav Rassadin and Benedikt Sarnov at the aesthetically pluralistic *Iunost* (Youth), and those who wrote for a variety of periodicals – Lev Anninskii and Igor Zolotusskii. Though vastly dissimilar in their ideological and aesthetic stances, they all belonged to the *shestidesiatniki*, the 'sixties set', a term coined by Rassadin.

When the period of Stagnation succeeded the Thaw and official ideology came to dominate literary criticism, the more gifted critics took refuge in research. In light of the 1972 resolution by the Communist Party Central Committee, 'On Literary Criticism', a journal of literary criticism called *Literaturnoe obozrenie* (Literary Review) was established the following year, supplementing its literary criticism with aesthetic criticism.

The advent of perestroika split literary critics, encouraged the besieged-fortress mentality, and provoked a civil war in literature. During perestroika literary criticism took centre stage in readers' minds as a reflection of larger political battles, and a number of critics, including Lev Anninskii, Vladimir Lakshin, Natalia Ivanova, and others, acquired prominence as public figures. The dramatic upsurge in the print runs of thick journals was due chiefly to their publication of previously banned pieces and secondarily to the commentaries provided by literary critics. In 1993, yet another periodical of literary criticism and literary studies came into being: *Novoe literaturnoe obozrenie* or NLO (New Literary Review), released by a publishing house with the same name, which issued a steady stream of books authored by literary critics.

In 1998, critics in Moscow founded their own professional organization: the Academy of Modern Russian Literature (acronym ARS'S), with four chairpersons taking turns at the helm every two years – Aleksandr Arkhangelskii, Natalia Ivanova, Andrei Vasilevskii, and Sergei Chuprinin. Today, the Internet also provides an excellent and widely read forum for critics, as can be seen in such Internet journals as *Russkii zhurnal*, *Topos*, and others, as well as in the frequently used *Zhurnalnyi zal* (Journal Room).

After perestroika, literature no longer held centre stage in public life; thus the readership of criticism published in thick journals declined, while that of purely journalistic writing rose. The emergence of new dailies and weeklies, the proliferation of television channels, and the appearance of independent radio stations deflected a good deal of public attention from books and literary monthlies, bringing to prominence the new figure of the critic-cum-journalist.

While topical criticism, which rapidly reacts to everyday events and examines the societal changes that reflect them, did not disappear, new critics, including Andrei Nemzer, Arkhangelskii, Aleksandr Ageev, Boris Kuzminskii, and others elaborated a new approach to materials, one independent of ideology. The critic of the early 1990s was typically well educated, witty, and more interested in cool-headed cultural-studies investigation than value-freighted bombast.

Genres underwent radical change as critics assumed a variety of roles, often publishing under one or more pseudonyms. Readers became accustomed to negotiating new modes of writing as the intricate allegories of the totalitarian past ceded to ludic metaphors, insider allusions, and polemical word associations. Marginal genres entered the mainstream: jet-setter commentaries, marginalia *à propos*, rhymed epigrams, humorist columns on 'behaviour', and even doggerel. Under the influence of audio-visual culture, photo op events reign supreme in today's Russia, for the 'event' has supplanted the literary 'product'. Book launches attract more attention than the new books themselves; the cultural significance of literary works pales beside morbid curiosity about authors' private lives; and literary reputations are determined by writers' and critics' public image. This atmosphere has transformed criticism in periodicals such as the newspaper *Nezavisimaia gazeta* (Independent Newspaper) into personalized, informal jibes.

The emergence of glossies, the 'deliterarization' of the media, and changes in the nation's overall cultural code inevitably have affected literary criticism. Radical changes in critical genres have led to a significant decrease in seminal articles in thick literary monthlies; profiles of writers, and cultural, political, and poetic analyses in the context of modern and, more broadly, twentieth-century Russian literature, have given way to the essay. The substantial review has been replaced by the paragraph-long mini-review, in essence a promotional notice that combines information about the release of a new periodical with evaluative judgements condensed into a single epithet, interjection, or sentence.

Having lost its ideological function, criticism no longer shapes public thought. It has retained, however, its diversity, analytical and stylistic virtuosity, and passion for debate. The *raison d'être* of the Academy of Modern Russian Literature is enhancing the status of Russia's literary criticism. Experts in this diverse group rate new books, write columns for periodicals, compose brief yet substantive critiques of new publications, and sit on literary-prize panels. In 1998, ARS'S instituted its own annual literary prize, named after Apollon Grigoriev. The only critics' prize in Russia, it is awarded for the year's outstanding literary work. Literary critics, chosen by lottery, take turns sitting on the panel of judges. The community of professional critics sees as its objective the improvement of 'serious' writers' and literature's authority, even as the book market is expanding dramatically, while the influence of literature and its readership are shrinking. Since consumer demand now overwhelmingly favours popular fiction, literary critics and 'prestigious' literary awards have little impact on readers' choices. Literary criticism as a profession is becoming a rarity, replaced by the newspaper journalist and literary manager (literary agent, publisher, PR agent).

Further reading

Chuprinin, S. (1989) *Kritika – eto kritiki: problemy i portrety* (Criticism is the Critics: Problems and Portraits), Moscow: Sovetskii pisatel.

Ivanova, N. (1996) 'Mezhdu. O meste kritiki v presse i literature' (Betwixt and Between. On the Place of Criticism in the Press and Literature). *Novy mir* 1. Reprinted in Ivanova, N. (2003) *Skrytyi siuzhet. Russkaia literatura na perekhode cherez vek* (The Hidden Plot. Russian Literature at the Turn of the Century), St. Petersburg: BLITS.

Prozorov, V. (ed.) (2002) *Istoriia russkoi literaturnoi kritiki* (A History of Russian Literary Criticism), Moscow: Vysshaia shkola.

Skarlygina, E. (ed.) (2004) *Kritika 50–60-kh godov XX veka* (Criticism in the 1950s–60s), Moscow: Agenstvo KRPA/Olymp.

NATALIA IVANOVA

Literary Institute

Literary courses opened after 1917 to involve new social groups in writing. The most famous of these, the Gorkii Institute of World Literature, was named after Soviet writer of humble origins Maksim Gorkii. Located in Moscow in the former home of nineteenth-century leftist writer Alexander Herzen, it is parodied as 'Griboedov's House' in Mikhail Bulgakov's *Master i Margarita* (*The Master and Margarita*). Similar institutions exist in other major Russian cities. By the 1950s the Moscow Institute offered on-site and correspondence courses in creative writing, literary criticism, and translation; enrolment by 1970 was about 700 students. Soviet-era institutes supported a planned artistic economy: instructors included well-known writers, and many students, including Iurii Bondarev and Vladimir Soloukhin, graduated into prominent literary careers. The Literary Institutes now offer MFA-like programmes.

See also: *Master i Margarita* (*The Master and Margarita*); Soloukhin, Vladimir

SIBELAN FORRESTER

literary museums

More literary museums and literary estates exist in Russia, from its westernmost borders to Siberia and the Russian Far East, than in any other country. This phenomenon arose out of the respect that Russians have harboured for their writers, at least until the fall of the Soviet Union. The post-Soviet period has seen the interest of most Russians (apart from intellectuals) shift dramatically from high to popular culture and from written to other media. The post-Soviet era also has ushered in mixed blessings: museums have opened in honour of writers hitherto ignored for political reasons, but lack of state funding has caused hardships for both old and new establishments. In the post-Soviet period (as of 1997) approximately 109 apartments, homes, and estates of writers function as museums. Pilgrims from Russia and abroad continue to visit some of the most popular literary shrines.

During the Soviet era, the government paid nearly slavish homage to writers deemed ideologically orthodox. The state, which granted them special perquisites during their lifetime, turned their dwellings into museums after they died. Soviet era writers relatively unknown in the West, such as Nikolai Ostrovskii, Fedor Gladkov, Aleksei Tolstoi, Konstantin Fedin, Aleksandr Fadeev, and even the commissar of education, Anatolii Lunacharskii, all had their own museums. Before perestroika and glasnost, Russia had no official museums dedicated to writers who had emigrated, perished in the purges, or not conformed to the dictates of Socialist Realism. Thus, the problematic Nobel laureates Ivan Bunin, Boris Pasternak, and Aleksandr Solzhenitsyn had not been honoured, in contrast to the government apologist Mikhail Sholokhov. The world-famous Vladimir Nabokov and Anna Akhmatova were neglected, along with Mikhail Zoshchenko, Marina Tsvetaeva, and Andrei Belyi (Boris Bugaev). In the post-perestroika period, devotees have established museums to Tsvetaeva (5), Akhmatova (2), Bunin (2), Nabokov (1), Zoshchenko (1), Pasternak (1), and Bulgakov (1).

The Soviet government founded and maintained most of the museums honouring classic Russian writers of the eighteenth and nineteenth centuries; the government either restored or rebuilt their apartments and homes. On the territories of European Russia, Siberia, and the Russian Caucasus are located the museums of Sergei Aksakov (3), Anton Chekhov (7), Nikolai Chernyshevskii (3), Fedor Dostoevskii (6), Nikolai Gogol (1), Ivan Goncharov (1), Mikhail Lermontov (4), Nikolai Leskov (1), Mikhail Lomonosov (2), Nikolai Nekrasov (3), Mikhail Saltykov-Shchedrin (2), Fedor Tiutchev (2), Lev Tolstoi (4), and Ivan Turgenev (2). Top

honours, however, belong to Aleksandr Pushkin, Russia's most beloved writer, with thirteen museums. Tourists may visit the St. Petersburg apartment in which Pushkin died after his ill-fated duel, and in the Leningrad region, one may relive the adventures of characters in his story 'The Stationmaster' (*Stantsionnyi smotritel*) and walk about the very post house that Pushkin visited and used as inspiration for his story. Pushkin House, the premises of the Academy of Sciences Institute of Russian Literature, also contains a fine museum dedicated to the history of Russian literary life.

See also: Academy of Sciences; Akhmatova, Anna; literature, Soviet; *Master i Margarita* (*The Master and Margarita*); museums-estates; Nabokov, Vladimir; Nobel Prize winners, literature; Pasternak, Boris; perestroika and glasnost; popular culture, Soviet; Pushkin, Aleksandr; Sholokhov, Mikhail; Socialist Realism literary classics; Solzhenitsyn, Aleksandr; St. Petersburg

CHRISTINE A. RYDEL

literary research institutions

Literary research institutions in Russia have three main functions: (1) to serve as repositories of archives, illustrative materials, and artifacts related to literature; (2) to display and publish those materials in exhibitions, journals and printed editions; and (3) to facilitate and promote the study of original literary materials. The main such institution in Russia is known as *Pushkinskii dom* (Pushkin House). Founded originally in 1905 in St. Petersburg as a memorial museum and repository of artifacts related to poet Aleksandr Sergeevich Pushkin, Pushkin House was incorporated into the Academy of Sciences and by 1930 was transformed into a centre for scholarly research devoted to Russian literature, called the Institute of Russian Literature of the Soviet (now Russian) Academy of Sciences (Pushkin House or IRLI).

Since 1927 the institute has occupied the building of the former St. Petersburg Customs House (designed and built by Giovanni Luchini between 1829 and 1832) on the Tuchkov (now Admiral Makarov) Embankment. Its staff has grown to hundreds, including scholars, archivists, bibliographers, and museum workers employed in preserving, displaying, publishing, and studying the vast collections.

Publications have included descriptions of archival materials (*opisi*), journals, and academic collected works with textological commentaries – the latter being the main form of the institute's scholarly work since before World War II. Publications include the series *Literaturnoe nasledstvo* (Literary Heritage, since 1933), and the journal *Russkaia literatura* (Russian Literature, since 1958). The Institute is divided into a number of sections (*otdely*), including Old Russian Literature, Eighteenth-Century Literature, Modern Russian Literature, Pushkin Studies, Manuscript Division, Literary Museum, and research groups (such as the Dostoevskii Group, the Turgenev Group, etc.).

With proper permission Russian and foreign scholars can obtain access to the collections and library of the Pushkin House, and the Literary Museum serves foreign and Russian tourists and schoolchildren alike.

Pushkin House has a counterpart in Moscow – the Maksim Gorkii Institute of World Literature of the Russian Academy of Sciences (IMLI), founded in 1932, a scholarly research centre for the study of both Russian and foreign literatures.

See also: Academy of Sciences; Literary Institute; literary museums; Pushkin, Aleksandr

ANGELA BRINTLINGER

literature, children's

Children's literature occupied a unique position in Soviet culture. Contemporary evaluations of literary production for children during the Soviet years reveal two major contradictory trends in interpretation: children's literature is viewed as a distinct part of the Soviet propaganda system, as well as one of the most liberal domains of creative literary expression in the Soviet Union. The Russian critic Marietta Chudakova explains this special status of children's literature as a direct result of the limitations that the socialist realist method imposed on creative writing during the Soviet period.

Soviet literature for adults suffered from compulsory didacticism and stylistic 'infantilism', which were required devices in literature for children; therefore, Soviet writers viewed children's books as a more appropriate domain for the application of these governmentally imposed literary standards. Writers' works were obligated to address ideologically 'correct' themes, such as collectivism, internationalism, and class solidarity, and to do so in the most engaging and innovative ways. Thus literary experimentation with form and plot was somewhat limited, but not precluded. Therefore, although children's literature was appropriated by the government and subordinated to the pedagogical demands of the political moment (thereby controlled and regulated), the actual body of texts produced under the general rubric of this literature was extremely diverse. Thus, politically correct texts on the history of revolutionary class struggle, such as *Iunost Mashi Strogovoi* (*The Youth of Masha Strogova*) by Mariia Prilezhaeva, co-existed with engaging but politically neutral historical narratives that exposed Soviet children to major periods in world civilization, such as in *Pismo grecheskogo malchika* (*The Letter of a Greek Boy*) by Solomon Lure. This relative freedom did not save Soviet children's literature from its own 'purges', manifested in governmental attacks on children's poetry written by Kornei Chukovskii, Samuil Marshak, and Vladimir Maiakovskii in the 1920s, in the fairy tale 'war' of the late 1920s–early 1930s, in the obscurantist campaigns against *Detgiz* (Children's State Publishing House) in 1937, and in the children's periodical *Mursilka* in 1946, to name but a few.

Liberal changes within Soviet society after the Twentieth Party Congress affected children's literature. Although the compulsory set of themes, such as Lenin's life, the glorious Soviet past, and the life of children's political organizations, such as the Young Pioneers, still remained prevalent, new trends became visible in both the creation and the interpretation of literature for children. Thus, the study of the sociological and psychological dimensions of children's literature – initiated in the 1920s but later declared 'bourgeois propaganda' and abandoned during the Stalin years – experienced a revival during the 1950s and 1960s. A leading role in this campaign was assumed by the publishing house Detskaia literature (Children's Literature), formerly known as Detgiz (Children's State Publishing House, 1933). In 1950, under the auspices of this publishing house, Dom detskoi knigi (House of Children's Books) was established, and became a centre for the study of children's literature in Soviet Russia and Soviet republics. Two of the most important enterprises initiated by this centre were the series *Zolotaia biblioteka russkoi klassiki dlia detei* (Golden Library of Russian Classics for Children) and *Biblioteka mirovoi literatury dlia detei* (Library of World Literature for Children), which introduced Soviet children to the best works of Russian and foreign authors in translation. Another significant initiative that promoted interest in publications for children was the establishment of *Nedelia detskoi knigi* (Children's Book Week Festival), devised by the Soviet children's writer Lev Kassil in 1943. In 1965, publication of the scholarly journal *Detskaia literatura* (Children's Literature, originally established in 1932 but discontinued in 1941) was renewed, thus recognizing the unique dimensions of children's literature as a scholarly subject.

The 1960s and 1970s demonstrate an important shift in children's literature toward stylistic diversity, since this period united several generations of writers for children. Sergei Mikhalkov, Agniia Barto, Elena Blaginina, Valentin Kataev, Leonid Panteleev, and Nikolai Nosov, whose formative years coincided with the most restrictive period of Soviet literary history (the 1930s), continued to be active. Often referred to as works of the realist tradition in writing for children, their texts presented young readers with a cautious but perceptible mixture of fantasy and reality. Thus, Sergei Mikhalkov, a very controversial figure in the Soviet literary establishment, is known as the creator of the popular character *Diadia Stepa* (*Uncle Stepa*). Uncle Stepa first entered Soviet children's literature in 1936 as a man of incredible height who uses his 'gift' to help people. Mikhalkov made him a folkloric, good-natured giant, and while entertaining his young audience, he stressed Soviet values, such as respect for authorities, by having Stepa become a militiaman (*Diadia Stepa – militsioner*, 1954). Nosov exposed his

young readers to social and moral codes of behaviour by creating a society of Lilliputians in his *Prokliucheniia Neznaiki* (*The Adventures of Neznaika [Notknow]*, 1954), thus combining realism with imaginative play and fantasy. In popular culture, his heroes and situations were considered so real that when his last story, *Naznaika na Lune* (*Neznaika on the Moon*, 1964–66) appeared, it was read by adult audiences as a masked satire on the Soviet political struggle with the West.

One of the most significant achievements in children's poetry that could be attributed to the liberal politics of the Thaw was the rebirth of 'playful' poetry, which demonstrated a direct connection to the interrupted tradition of Russian avant-garde literature (Daniil Kharms, for example). Although these innovative experiments are typically attributed to the 'generation of the sixties' (Irina Tokmakova, Iunna Morits, Genrikh Sapgir, Eduard Uspenskii), it was poet and translator Boris Zakhoder who spearheaded this movement. His *Mokhnataia azbuka* (*Furry ABCs*, 1958) surprised both young and adult audiences with its free interplay of rhymes and images, as well as the extreme dynamism of the verses. Impressively courageous in his experimentation with language, Zakhoder created new words with only contextual meaning, as in the Futurist practices of the 1920s. Furthermore, Zakhoder's work as a translator earned him nearly legendary popularity among both children and adults. His insistence that his translations were actually a free retelling de-emphasized expectations of linguistic accuracy and promoted unlimited creativity in the author's treatment of characters. Zakhoder was instrumental in introducing his Russian readers to Western canonical characters such as *Winnie the Pooh* (A. A. Milne, 1960), Mary Poppins (P. L. Travers, 1968), *Peter Pan* (J. M. Barrie, 1972), and *Alice in Wonderland* (Lewis Carroll, 1972).

The 1960s and the 1970s also witnessed experiments in prose. Works by Viktor Dragunskii and Uspenskii are among the most popular stories of the time, though these writers differ in their treatment of themes and choice of characters. Dragunskii used a semi-autobiographical approach, choosing a real person (his son, Deniska) as his protagonist.

Curious and adventurous, Deniska discovers the world as moral but comical, full of surprises but friendly. Dragunskii's stories focus on family dynamics, addressing for the first time a new generation of parents who enjoy family life, and love each other and their children. They represent a significant thematic shift from the juxtaposition of children and parents in early Soviet children's literature, as well as in the literature of the early post-World War II years, with its focus on incomplete families, survival and hardship, and the obligatory image of schoolmates and the school collective as a surrogate family. Dragunskii's younger contemporary, Uspenskii also focused on the formation of moral actions, but through the use of the fairy tale genre: his 'alternative' family is composed of characters taken from real life (dogs, cats, the boy Uncle Fedor, the mailman Pechkin) and products of his creative imagination (the damaged toy Cheburashka, the righteous crocodile Gena, the mean Old Woman Shapokliak). The author's tendency to create characters consumed by a single passion (e.g., the Old Woman Shapokliak is obsessed with the perfection of the 'art of scandal', the bureaucrat Pechkin – with the letter of the law) raises his texts to the level of social critique of the adult world. The interesting twist in Uspenskii's narratives also characterizes the prose of such writers among the 1960s' generation as Iurii Koval, Viktor Goliavkin, and Vladimir Zhelesniakov: in their treatment of moral choices and in the distinction between good and evil they provide for their young audiences, goodness and compassion are no longer associated with politically correct behaviour. In fact, most frequently a character with visible shortcomings and mischievous in behaviour, but possessing a curious, active mind, is granted moral triumph.

The dilemma of moral choices in teenage life was introduced into Soviet children's literature in the 1970s and 1980s by Anatolii Aleksin. The years of Stagnation, with its widespread cynical scepticism regarding Soviet ideals, made moral education one of the most controversial topics examined in children's literature. Aleksin's stories *Pozdnii rebenok* (*Child of Their Old Age*, 1968), *Moi brat igraet na klarinete* (*My Brother Plays Clarinet*, 1967), *Bezumnaia Evdokiia* (*Crazy Eudacia*, 1976), and *Dnevnik zhenikha* (*Groom's Diary*, 1980) mod-

ified the popular Soviet genre of '*shkolnaia povest*' (school novella), for his characters challenged the dogmatic notion of the happy world of Soviet childhood. By privatizing conflicts and relegating ethical issues to the much narrower world of the child's immediate family, the author emphasized the role of the family rather than of the state as the major component of children's upbringing, thus increasing the value of children's and adults' personal responsibility for their moral choices.

The economic hardships of the 1990s negatively affected children's publications, since private publishing houses were driven by market demands. However, commercial interests promoted an increased interest in the domain of literary translation and ultimately placed children's reading in Russia on par with that of the West. Thus, Russian children were finally introduced to Nancy Drew mysteries, and even the world of Harry Potter, though the number of such translations often outweighed their quality. At the present time, children's literature in Russia is experiencing a slow but steady revival. Three major trends may be discerned: the reintroduction of pre-revolutionary and émigré children's literature (Lidiia Charskaia, Klavdiia Lukashevich, Sasha Chernyi), which was abandoned during the Soviet years; reprints of the best Soviet books (including series such as *Uchennye Rossii – detiam* [Russian Scholars Write for Children]); and translations of contemporary Western children's literature.

See also: literature, Stagnation; literature, Thaw; Uspenskii, Eduard

Further reading

Balina, M. and Rudova, L. (2005) 'Russian Children's Literature: Changing Paradigms', *Slavic and East European Journal* 49, 2: 186–303.

Chudakova, M. (1990) 'Skvoz zvezdy k terniiam', *Novyi mir* 4: 145–6.

Oinas, F. J. (1978) 'The Political Uses and Themes of Folklore in the Soviet Union', in F. J. Oinas (ed.) *Folklore, Nationalism and Politics*, Columbus, OH: Slavica.

Ronen, O. (2000) 'Detskaia literatura i sotsialisticheskii realizm', in E. Dobrenko and H. Guenther (eds) *Sotsrealisticheskii kanon*, St.

Peterburg: Akademicheskii proekt, pp. 969–79.

Steiner, E. (1999) *Stories for Little Comrades: Revolutionary Artists and the Making of Early Soviet Children's Books*. Seattle, WA: University of Washington Press.

MARINA BALINA

literature, classical

The term 'classical' has connotations specific to the Russian cultural context, as opposed to that of Western Europe. It designates neither the period of classical antiquity nor its revival in the seventeenth century, but rather the highest point in the development of Russian literature, which is generally recognized as roughly coinciding with the nineteenth century. However, there is no single strict definition of the chronological boundaries of Russian classical literature. In the narrowest sense, it is circumscribed by the time of Aleksandr Pushkin's (1799–1837) literary activity, also referred to as the 'Golden Age', when the national literary canon was established and the literary language codified. In the broadest sense, the framework of Russian classical literature can encompass the period from Catherine the Great's reign, immortalized in Gavrila Derzhavin's elaborate odes, through the greatest poets and novelists of the nineteenth century, most importantly Pushkin, Mikhail Lermontov, Nikolai Gogol, Ivan Turgenev, Ivan Goncharov, Fedor Dostoevskii, and Lev Tolstoi, to end with Anton Chekhov and perhaps even such poets and writers of the *fin-de-siècle* (known as the Silver Age) as Aleksandr Blok and Andrei Belyi.

Although there was a rich native tradition of religious, historical, epic, and some fictional writing before Peter the Great reoriented Russia towards Western Europe, classical literature is primarily a result of the creative assimilation of Western models, which were subsequently revised or subverted and filled with original content. Since there was no national tradition of philosophical or social discourse and government censorship was quite severe, literature in the nineteenth century often assumed roles far beyond the realm of pure aesthetics. The nineteenth-century Russian public regarded literature as a source of knowledge and instruction, an attitude that endowed the writer with near-prophetic status and established for literature the highest authority among the arts (this situation continued through the Soviet period, earning Russians a reputation as the world's 'best-read nation').

Throughout the twentieth century, the classical literary canon was a constant point of reference, although treated in diverse ways. While Futurists and avant-garde authors vigorously dismissed classical literature in their manifestos, their texts are punctuated by allusions to nineteenth-century writers. The Soviet educational and cultural establishment ostensibly adopted a position of veneration of the classical legacy, while excluding everything ideologically unpalatable. Thus grotesque, experimental or expressionist writing was downplayed by Soviet literary criticism in favour of a simpler, realist style (the history of misinterpretation of Gogol's works is the best example). Moreover, the religious musings of Tolstoi and Dostoevskii (as well as the latter's insights into the depth of the human subconscious) were ignored, and classical writers whose ideological position contradicted Communist thinking or conservative morals (e.g., Nikolai Leskov) were given short shrift or distorted. As a result, the vision of classical literature promoted in Soviet schools was fragmentary and mythologized. Émigré intellectuals (most notably the circle of Dmitrii Merezhkovskii and Zinaida Gippius) also proclaimed the goal of preservation of the classical literary legacy, which served as a foundation for their national and cultural identity. A much less rigid and at times playful attitude to the classical tradition was characteristic of some younger émigré writers (e.g., Vladimir Nabokov, Gaito Gazdanov, Boris Poplavskii) and of some dissident authors of the later Soviet period (e.g. Abram Terts's *Strolls with Pushkin*). The collapse of ideological controls in the late 1980s unleashed widespread correction and re-writing of the history of Russian classical literature, but, under the influence of the prevailing postmodernist discourse, this has often been done in a light or ironic manner. The results of such revision are as different as Iurii Druzhnikov's debunking of the Pushkin myth in a series of semi-documentary sketches and the remakes of the three fundamental classical novels penned by a mysterious author (*Anna Karenina* by Lev Nikolaev, *Crime and Punishment* by Fedor Mikhailov, and *Fathers and Sons* by Ivan Sergeev).

Despite the political and ideological changes in Russian society, classical literature has remained at the core of the school curriculum, and continues to provide material for contemporary theatre, film, and visual art.

See also: educational system, Soviet; literature, émigré; Nabokov, Vladimir; pedagogy, Soviet; Pushkin, Aleksandr; Siniavskii, Andrei

Further reading

Cornwell, N. (ed.) (1998) *A Reference Guide to Russian Literature*, London: Fitzroy Dearborn.

Kelly, C. (2001) *Russian Literature: A Very Short Introduction*, Oxford: Oxford University Press.

Mirsky, D. (1949) *History of Russian Literature*, New York: Knopf.

Moser, C. (ed.) (1992) *The Cambridge History of Russian Literature*, Cambridge: Cambridge University Press.

Terras, V. (1991) *A History of Russian Literature*, New Haven, CT: Yale University Press.

MARIA RUBINS

literature, émigré

Many writers took part in the mass emigration during the years following the October 1917 Revolution. This so-called first wave of emigration was followed by a second wave during the 1940s, consisting primarily of World War II refugees, and a third wave of mostly Jewish émigrés in the 1970s and 1980s. During most of the Soviet period émigré writers remained unpublished and virtually unknown in their native country, causing some to speak of the existence of two separate Russian literatures. Émigré writers became widely published in Russia only during glasnost, when the two literatures began to merge.

The first wave émigrés included many well-known, established writers, such as the poets Konstantin Balmont, Viacheslav Ivanov, Zinaida Gippius, Igor Severianin, the prose writers Ivan Bunin, Dmitrii Merezhkovskii, Aleksandr Kuprin, Aleksei Remizov, Nadezhda Teffi, Ivan Shmelev, and Boris Zaitsev. There were also promising younger writers who left Russia at an earlier stage in their careers, among them the poets Marina Tsvetaeva, Vladislav Khodasevich, and Georgii Ivanov. Others, younger still, began their careers in emigration. The best known were the prose writers Vladimir Nabokov, Mark Aldanov (in age actually closer to the older generation), Nina Berberova, Gaito Gazdanov, and the poet Boris Poplavskii. Many literary critics and scholars also emigrated, among them Roman Jakobson, Yulii Aikhenvald, Georgii Adamovich, Konstantin Mochulskii, Petr Bitsilli, and Dmitrii Sviatopolk-Mirskii, who wrote an influential history of Russian literature in English. Several well-known philosophers close to literature – for example, Nikolai Berdiaev, Lev Shestov, and Nikolai Losskii – were among the intellectuals expelled from Russia in 1922.

Life was very difficult for the émigrés, who, deprived of their former status and audience, needed to begin their career anew in an alien milieu with a drastically reduced circle of readers. Nevertheless, a thriving cultural life soon sprang up in the cities where émigrés settled, especially in what became the capitals of the Russian diaspora, Berlin and Paris. By 1920 the first Russian publishing houses had opened, most of them in Berlin. Soon Russian journals and newspapers appeared, bookstores opened, and writers' organizations formed. Despite formidable obstacles, many excellent literary works appeared, with some writers producing their best work. Khodasevich and Tsvetaeva published their best verse collections in the 1920s, while Georgii Ivanov rose to an entirely new level of poetic achievement in the 1930s. Aldanov, who had published little before exile, wrote many highly regarded historical novels. Bunin, Merezhkovskii, Zaitsev, Teffi, and other established prose writers wrote works that equalled or surpassed their earlier writings. Younger prosaists, most notably Nabokov, wrote original and striking works, while poetic groupings in Paris, Berlin, and Prague produced a distinctive body of poetry. In general, émigré writers and critics, who considered themselves the preservers of Russian literary tradition, espoused classical restraint in poetry and realism in prose. Innovative, experimental writing, like Tsvetaeva's poetry, was not therefore widely appreciated.

The most vital period for first-wave émigré literature was the 1920s and early 1930s, its high point the award of the Nobel Prize in literature to Bunin in 1933. The later 1930s marked a decline, as doubts about sustaining literature in exile increased and the worldwide economic and political situation deteriorated. Some writers found it more difficult to write. Khodasevich abandoned poetry entirely for literary criticism and Tsvetaeva turned increasingly to prose. The crisis drove a few writers back to the Soviet Union. Kuprin, terminally ill, returned to his homeland in 1937, where he died in 1938. Tsvetaeva followed her husband and daughter back in 1939 and committed suicide in 1941.

World War II marked the collapse of the Russian diaspora as it had existed. Many émigrés fled the Nazis, mostly for the Western hemisphere. Some Jewish writers and those who aided them perished in Nazi concentration camps. The rest of the literary emigration was sharply split between those who opposed the fascists and those who supported them as potential destroyers of the hated Soviet Union. After the war the cultural and publishing centre of emigration shifted to the United States, although many of the older generation, poor and ill, remained in Europe. Several younger writers rebuilt their lives in America. Nabokov, who began writing in English in 1939, won international acclaim as an American writer. Berberova's stories and memoirs also expanded her reputation beyond the Russian milieu.

The end of the war also brought about the second wave of Russian emigration, comprising primarily displaced persons from the western republics of the Soviet Union and the Baltic states. Within the second wave there were relatively few writers and none as famous as some of the first-wave exiles. There were, however, a number of talented writers, particularly poets, such as Iurii Ivask, Igor Chinnov, Ivan Elagin, Nikolai Morshen, and Dmitrii Klenovskii.

The third wave of emigration, during the 1970s and 1980s, consisted primarily of Jews, although not all the writers who left under this pretext were in fact Jewish. A circumstance that contributed to the third wave was a shift in policy toward prominent dissidents, whereby exile abroad replaced imprisonment. The first to benefit from this policy was the Leningrad poet Iosif Brodskii, whose conviction in 1964 on the charge of parasitism had aroused an international outcry and who was allowed to emigrate to the United States in 1972. In 1987, he won the Nobel Prize for literature and in 1991 became American poet laureate. Another internationally known writer who was imprisoned and later allowed to emigrate was Andrei Siniavskii, who for his fiction adopted the pseudonym Abram Terts. He was permitted to leave for France in 1973. The most famous literary dissident to be exiled abroad was Aleksander Solzhenitsyn, whose *Odin den Ivana Denisovicha* (*One Day in the Life of Ivan Denisovich*) marked the pinnacle of the Thaw period, but whose later novels could only be published abroad. After the first part of his *Arkhipelag GULag* (*The Gulag Archipelago*) was published in Paris, Solzhenitsyn, by then a Nobel laureate (1970), was forcibly deported from the Soviet Union in 1974. He eventually settled in the United States, where his critique of Western democracies made him a controversial figure.

Other well-known writers pressured to emigrate during the Brezhnev period were Vasilii Aksenov, one of the most popular prosaists of the Thaw period, but whose later, more experimental works and nonconformist activities aroused official disapproval, and the satirist Vladimir Voinovich, whose novel *Zhizn i neobychainye prikliucheniia soldata Ivana Chonkina* (*The Life and Extraordinary Adventures of Private Ivan Chonkin*) had appeared in 1975 in the West. Both left the Soviet Union in 1980. Some third-wave writers could not be published at all in the Soviet Union due to their experimental style or taboo subject matter. These include Eduard Limonov, whose sexually and linguistically unbridled novel *Eto ia – Edichka* (*It's Me, Eddie*) caused a sensation, and Sasha Sokolov, whose love of stylistic play and intricate plotting placed his works beyond the Soviet mainstream. Aleksandr Zinovev was forced to emigrate in 1978, two years after the publication abroad of his philosophical satire, *Ziiaiushchie vysoty* (*Yawning Heights*). One of the most popular third-wave writers, Sergei Dovlatov, a journalist in the Soviet Union, was able to publish his humorous short stories only after he emigrated in 1978.

During the glasnost and early post-Soviet periods, the artificial barrier dividing Soviet and émigré literature collapsed. Already in the 1950s, after the death of Stalin, selective publication of some first-wave émigrés, such as Bunin, had begun, but it was only under glasnost that the effort began to bring émigré writers into the mainstream of Russian literature. In the years following the collapse of the Soviet Union virtually all significant émigré writers have been published and some, such as Dovlatov, have gained great popularity. Many critical and reference works, especially on the first emigration, came out in the 1990s. Literary research institutes and libraries opened sections devoted to Russia abroad, and entire periodicals, such as *Diaspora*, were devoted to the emigration. Surviving first-wave writers, such as Boris Zaitsev and Irina Odoevtseva, were invited back to Russia, while among third-wave writers the very term émigré became obsolete. Some who had been in exile, such as Solzhenitsyn and Limonov, returned to Russia and became centrally involved in literary and political polemics. Others, such as Tatiana Tolstaia and Voinovich, alternated between living in Russia and abroad, while some non-émigré writers resided outside of Russia for long periods, teaching or on grants.

Further reading

Glad, J. (1999) *Russia Abroad: Writers, History, Politics*, Washington DC and Tenafly NJ: Hermitage and Birchbark.

Karlinsky, S. and Appel, Jr., A. (eds) (1977) *The Bitter Air of Exile: Russian Writers in the West 1922–1972*, Berkeley, CA: University of California Press.

Pachmuss, T. (ed.) (1981) *A Russian Cultural Revival: A Critical Anthology of Émigré Literature before 1939*, Knoxville, TN: University of Tennessee Press.

Poltoratzky, N. (ed.) (1972) *Russkaia literatura v emigratsii: sbornik statei*, Pittsburgh, PA: University of Pittsburgh..

Struve, G. (1956) *Russkaia literatura v izgnanii*, New York: Izdatelstvo imeni Chekhova.

EDYTHE C. HABER

literature, foreign, in translation

In Soviet Russia, the value of foreign literature in translation was viewed in two different ways. As a governmental enterprise, the translation of foreign literature became a showcase for demonstrating to the Western liberal intelligentsia the 'democratic' and 'tolerant' policies of the Communist regime toward the bourgeois West. By publishing such classic nineteenth-century Western authors as Honoré de Balzac, Johann Wolfgang von Goethe, and Charles Dickens, Soviet cultural authorities attempted to prove to the Western world that these authors' 'bourgeois' origins could be overlooked in view of the artistic merit of these works, thus demonstrating that the Soviet government was able to recognize great achievements in world civilization. For ordinary Soviet citizens, foreign literature in translation became the only possible window onto the Western world, given that travel to the West was tightly controlled and that the pre-Revolutionary educational system, with its emphasis on foreign language education, had been abolished. Some Soviet-era writers considered translation a possible escape from the restrictions of Socialist Realism. Such writers as Boris Pasternak and Anna Akhmatova were able to continue to work productively as translators despite the caveats constricting their original creative work. Thus contemporaries often judged their translations, such as Pasternak's renditions of Goethe's *Faust* and Shakespeare's tragedies and sonnets, as valid original contributions to literature.

The officially recognized vehicle for the publication of foreign literature was the journal *Inostrannaia literatura* (*Foreign Literature*, 1955–present). Founded before the October Revolution, it was replaced in the early post-Revolutionary years with *Literatura mirovoi revoliutsii* (Literature of World Revolution, 1931–32), and later with *Internatsionalnaia literatura* (International Literature, 1933–43). Heavily censored in its selection of Western writers, this journal concentrated on sympathizers with the Soviet cause, such as Romain Rolland, Henri Barbusse, Anatole France, Louis Aragon, and Pablo Neruda. However, it also introduced Soviet readers to such writers as John Dos Passos, Ernest Hemingway, and Marcel Proust. Although half of this journal's editorial board perished in the Stalinist Terror, the journal was reestablished in 1955, as a result of the Thaw's renewed interest in publishing foreign literature in translation. Throughout the Soviet era, *Inostrannaia literatura* remained the only official source of foreign literature for Soviet readers. It was obliged, however, to include representative works by authors from East Bloc countries, as well as Asian and African writers from political entities sympathetic to the Soviet cause. The only writers from the West deemed acceptable by Soviet censors were those who depicted 'the woes of international capitalism'. Yet under this guise, many provocative works from twentieth-century literature found their way to Soviet readers during the Thaw. Thus Jean-Paul Sartre's play *The Respectful Prostitute* was published in *Inostrannaia literatura* (1955), but only after its title was changed to the more neutral *Lizzy*. In 1958, William Faulkner was translated by Ivan Kashkin, one of the leading authorities in the Soviet school of translation, and in 1959 the famous translator from the French, Nora Gal, introduced to Russians Antoine de Saint-Exupéry's *The Little Prince*. Erich Maria Remarque's works were published in translation in 1955–65, although he was criticized for his pessimism. A general practice that permitted *Inostrannaia literatura* to publish works by controversial writers was the inclusion of an introduction by a renowned specialist, who would outline the political 'shortcomings' of the authors, who included Franz Kafka, Albert Camus, and Graham Greene, among many others.

With the advent of perestroika, the market for translations changed significantly, for commercialized literature gradually trumped literature by serious writers. The demand for detective novels and Western celebrities' scandalous memoirs had a negative impact on the quality of translations. *Inostrannaia literatura*, however, continues its mission by introducing contemporary readers to seminal works by Western writers such as Milorad Pavić, Thomas Pynchon, and Umberto Eco. In addition, a handful of new publishing houses continue to assert their place in Russian book markets: *Ex Libris* is well known for its reprints of recognized translations of Western classics, while *Inostranka* specializes in translated editions of the most recent works of world literature.

See also: Akhmatova, Anna; censorship; East Bloc countries; economic system, post-Soviet; internationalism; Pasternak, Boris; perestroika and glasnost; Socialist Realism; Stalin, Iosif; Thaw

Further reading

Chukovskii, K. (1964) *Vysokoe iskusstvo: O printsipakh khudozhestvennogo perevoda*, Moscow: Iskusstvo.

Friedberg, M. (1977) *A Decade of Euphoria: Western Literature in Post-Stalin Russia, 1954–64*, Bloomington, IN: Indiana University Press.

——(1997) *Literary Translation in Russia: A Cultural History*, University Park, PA: The Pennsylvania State University Press.

MARINA BALINA

literature, perestroika

Literature of perestroika, alternatively called literature of glasnost, refers to Soviet literary output under Mikhail Gorbachev (1985–91), whose attempts to liberalize and modernize Soviet society revealed the weaknesses and contradictions of the system. The policy of glasnost, introduced at the Twenty-Seventh (and last) Congress of the Communist Party of the Soviet Union (1986), ushered in a profound reevaluation of the past and present Soviet economy, politics, and ideology. Contrary to Gorbachev's expectation of a renewed and reenergized Socialist state, however, perestroika reforms and the policy of glasnost resulted in the official demise of the Communist Party of the Russian Federation on 23 August 1991 (after the failed coup engineered by the highest officials of the Gorbachev administration) and the subsequent disintegration of the Soviet Union on 26 December 1991.

Unique for Russian literature, Gorbachev's 'thaw' ushered in a virtual flood of previously unavailable material – novels, plays, poetry, memoirs, and critical, historical, and philosophical monographs by Russian, Soviet, Western, and émigré authors, written before the Revolution, during the 1950s or late Stagnation, or after Gorbachev came to power. The new literary production under glasnost may be loosely divided into: works written during Khrushchev's Thaw, revised or continued under Gorbachev, and focusing on 'blank spots' in history, i.e. events and personalities erased from the official pages of Soviet histories; 'publicistic' literature of glasnost – fiction by established authors, written under Gorbachev and describing the ills of Soviet society; and works by alternative writers, with careful attention to form, a penchant for revealing the sexual and psychological 'underground' of characters, and deliberate avoidance of direct social messages.

Clearly, the widely used terms 'literature of perestroika' and 'literature of glasnost' embrace a score of different styles, periods, and positions. The word glasnost, however, points to this literature's common denominator. What had been impossible to voice before now had a broad forum, what had been formerly suppressed now could appear, and what had been often concealed under the guise of legends or fantasy now emerged in harsh and openly proselytizing statements about the dire state of Soviet society.

'Publicistic' prose of glasnost offered the Soviet reader direct expressions of dissatisfaction with social problems and an examination of failed promises in the myth of a Communist state. As was common in the works of Khrushchev's Thaw, novels written during perestroika that deal with 'blank spots' in history (such as Anatolii Rybakov's *Deti Arbata* (*Children of the Arbat*, 1987), Vladimir Dudintsev's *Belye odezhdy* (*White Garments*, 1987), and Anatolii Pristavkin's *Nochevala tuchka zolotaia* (*A Golden Cloud Spent the Night*, 1987)) trace the roots of the hardships experienced by Soviet society to the time of Stalin. Vasilii Grossman's novel *Zhizn i sudba* (*Life and Fate*, 1988) portrays life in the camps and provides explicit comparisons between Nazism and Stalinism. Sergei Zalygin's *Posle buri* (*After the Storm*, 1980–85) and the writings of the playwright Mikhail Shatrov, on the other hand, also question the wisdom of early Soviet policy before Stalin. Soviet readers viewed all the above works as major cultural events of glasnost and perestroika.

Overall, affinity with the ideals of the first Thaw was a notable feature of these works, partly because most of them were begun under Khrushchev. Yet these novels went much further in their overt criticism of the Soviet

system, tracing various threads in the intricate web of lies and injustices that led to the collapse of social and moral ideals. Three major areas of concern in publicistic fiction were the following: (1) how and why it all went wrong (the historical perspective); (2) the catastrophic situation in the country (the contemporary perspective); and (3) the possibility of regeneration (the future-oriented perspective). In his novel of the Stagnation period *I dolshe veka dlitsia den* (*The Day Lasts More Than a Hundred Years*, 1980), for example, Chingiz Aitmatov had addressed troubling social issues in the language of fantasy through plots and legends of science fiction. In his contribution to the publicistic literature of glasnost, *Plakha* (*The Execution Block*, 1986), Aitmatov discusses the same issues, but directly. The novel offers an almost journalistic portrayal of the ills of contemporary Soviet society, including drug production and trafficking, the break-up of families, lawlessness and cynicism both in the city and country, the plundering of the environment, the wholesale extermination of wildlife, even the murder of innocent children. Similarly, such writers as Valentin Rasputin in *Pozhar* (*Fire*, 1985), Viktor Astafev in *Pechalnyi detektiv* (*A Sad Detective Story*, 1986) or Vasilii Belov in *Vse vperedi* (*Everything Is Ahead of Us*, 1986) shared a vision of Soviet society in which the spirit of consumerism and indifference is pervasive and where ties with tradition are lost. According to these writers, the senseless use of technology has violated intergenerational continuity and brought about the disintegration of family life and social accord. Most works in the publicistic vein place the blame for the cultural impoverishment of the nation on intellectuals, proponents of Western influences and urban values.

If the literature of Stagnation only warned of the dire consequences of the loss of tradition, publicistic literature examined those consequences as established fact. Publicistic writers saw the moral decline of their nation as part of the general process of humanity's moral degeneration. The recurrent image of Doomsday, the nuclear end of the world found in these works was only an extreme expression of the overwhelming despair with which publicistic literature viewed Soviet reality. The openly nationalistic flavour of some publicistic prose and of public statements by such well-established and respected authors as Rasputin, Astafev, and Belov found a platform in such conservative journals and newspapers as *Nash sovremennik* (Our Contemporary), *Molodaia gvardiia* (The Young Guard), *Literaturnaia Rossiia* (Literary Russia), *Moskva* (Moscow) and *Pravda* (Truth). On the other side of this 'battle of the journals' stood such liberal publications as *Literaturnaia gazeta* (Literary Gazette), *Ogonek* (Flame), *Izvestiia* (News), *Znamia* (Banner), *Novyi mir* (New World) *Iunost* (Youth), *Oktiabr* (October), *Knizhnoe obozrenie* (Book Review), *Ural*, and *Volga*.

These liberal journals served as a safe haven for the works of alternative literature that appeared during perestroika. The term 'alternative' signalled a clear difference between this literature and that of Socialist Realism, village prose, and glasnost publicistic prose. Notably, the alternative current was not altogether absent from the literary scene during Stagnation; intermittently, a handful of 'alternative' texts were allowed to see print in the decade before glasnost. The prose of Vladimir Makanin, Sergei Esin, Anatolii Kim, and others had ignored the conventions of officially sanctioned literature, creating a world metaphorically complex, peopled with characters lost in the uncertainties of everyday existence, and plagued by guilt and moral confusion. The alternative literature of the Moscow school and of its fellow travellers planted the seeds of the new avant-garde, or post-modernism – terms widely used to describe Russian alternative prose of the 1990s. It is precisely pre-glasnost alternative prose that attempted to articulate the concerns of an aesthetic underground through heightened attention to the myth-creating propensities of language, a focus on the previously hidden aspects of human experience, and a desire to give voice to marginalized segments of Soviet society, such as women and homosexuals.

During perestroika this preoccupation with language becomes the sole driving force of the alternative trend. Viktor Erofeev, Zufar Gareev, Viacheslav Petsukh, Sergei Chetvertkov, Valeriia Narbikova, Larisa Vaneeva, Liudmila Petrushevskaia, Tatiana Tolstaia, Nina Sadur, Evgenii Popov, and Aleksandr Ivanchenko are just some of the alternative writers who engaged in the deconstruction of mythologies of the Soviet state by transgressing traditional norms of writing. Illicit sex, deviant sexual practices, bodily functions, and violence for the sake of pleasure were in the foreground of this fiction; investigation of the power of language was its motivating force.

Literature of glasnost and perestroika marked a change of course for Soviet society and for its artistic production. As a result of the newly found openness in expression, the mythical history of the Soviet Union was replaced by efforts to establish facts instead of self-promoting fictions, and in the process the myths nurturing the idea of a Communist society were exposed as illusion.

Further reading

Brown, D. (1993) *The Last Years of Soviet Russian Literature: Prose Fiction, 1975–1991*, Cambridge: Cambridge University Press.

Epshtein, M. (1995) *After the Future: The Paradoxes of Postmodernism and Contemporary Russian Culture*, Amherst, MA: University of Massachusetts Press.

Goscilo, H. and Lindsey, B. (eds) (1990) *Glasnost: An Anthology of Russian Literature under Gorbachev*, Ann Arbor, MI: Ardis.

Lahusen, T. and Kuperman, G. (eds) (1993) *Late Soviet Culture: From Perestroika to Novostroika*, Durham, NC: Duke University Press.

Laird, S. (1999) *Voices of Russian Literature: Interviews with Ten Contemporary Wrtiers*, Oxford: Oxford University Press.

Lapidus, G. (1995) *The New Russia: Troubled Transformation*, Boulder, CO: Westview Press.

Peterson, N. (1997) *Subversive Imaginations: Fantastic Prose and the End of Soviet Literature, 1970s–1990s*, Boulder, CO: Westview Press.

NADYA PETERSON

literature, Soviet

Post-Stalinist Soviet literature was shaped by the cultural conditions inhering in late socialism and by the need to situate itself in relation to what preceded, in both the tsarist and earlier Soviet periods. In its broadest sense, Soviet literature includes all literary works written in the USSR throughout the country's 74-year history, whether published in their country of origin or not. From the time of its inception in the wake of the Bolshevik Revolution (1917), Soviet literature simultaneously tried to define itself by acceptance of or resistance to institutional ideology and aesthetic subordination to state ideology, and by the domination of the Russian literary tradition and Russian-language publishing over the multi-ethnic literature of the Soviet empire. Soviet literary works may be broken down into those published officially in the USSR, those written 'for the drawer', and those circulated in *samizdat* or published in *tamizdat* (abroad, beyond the range of the Soviet censorship).

The first decade of Soviet literature was a period of extraordinary vitality. Many of the more prominent writers of the pre-Revolutionary period had fled Russia in the wake of the revolution, clearing a space for newly emerging talents forged by the experience of revolution and civil war. Three major groups vied for dominance at this time: the Futurists, the Proletcult, and the Fellow Travellers, the last of which produced impressive works of ornamental prose and satire. The early years of Soviet literature also saw the rise of the novel as the dominant form of Soviet literature: e.g., Fedor Gladkov's *Tsement* (*Cement*) and Mikhail Sholokhov's *Tikhii Don* (*Quiet Flows the Don*).

Under Stalin, the decree of 23 April 1932 abolished all independent writers' groups and established the Soviet Writers' Union. At the First Congress of the Union in 1934, Socialist Realism, defined as 'the representation of reality in its revolutionary development', was declared the only acceptable method for a Soviet writer. Henceforth writers were to portray reality through the prism of Communism's inevitable victory. Writers straining against the confining requirements of the Socialist Realist master plot would define the basic tensions of the post-Stalin period.

Reaction against the stultifying restrictions of late-Stalinist culture began almost immediately after the dictator's death. Among the first harbingers of change was the December 1953 publication of Vladimir Pomerantsev's article *Ob iskrennosti v literature* (*On Sincerity in Literature*) in the journal *Novyi mir* (*New World*). In the article Pomerantsev called for an end to 'varnishing reality', especially in the portrayal of the collective

farm, in literature. Ilia Erenburg's novel *The Thaw*, which was to give a name to the ensuing period of cultural relaxation, followed in 1954. In December of that year the Second Congress of the Soviet Writers' Union convened, supplying a forum for emboldened liberal voices. Vladimir Dudintsev's novel *Ne khlebom edinym* (*Not by Bread Alone*, 1956), published in *Novyi mir*, which was becoming the premier journal of the Thaw, created a stir by criticizing the bureaucratization of Soviet society.

Yet the most exciting literary events of the 1950s signalled the appearance of a new generation for whom the defining moment was Khrushchev's 'secret speech' (1956), which revealed the abuses of the Stalin years. They would come to be known as 'people of the sixties' (*shestidesiatniki*). The poets Bella Akhmadulina, Evgenii Evtushenko, and Andrei Voznesenskii declaimed their verses to crowds at public readings, garnering the sort of adulation reserved for rock stars in the West. Emerging young prose writers gathered around the journal *Iunost* (*Youth*) under the editorship of the prominent writer Valentin Kataev, who would himself embark in the 1960s on a new direction in his writing, in what he termed 'mauvism'. Notable among Kataev's young protégés were Vasilii Aksenov, Anatolii Gladilin, and the Abkhazian Russian-language writer Fazil Iskander. While the 'beats' captured the imagination of intellectual youth in the United States, Gladilin in his novel *Khronika vremen Viktora Podgurskogo* (*A Chronicle of the Times of Viktor Podgursky*, 1956) and Aksenov in the novel *Zvezdnyi bilet* (*Ticket to the Stars*, 1961) sketched the hopes, anxieties, and fashions of Soviet young people chafing at the confines of their elders' authority.

Even as constraints on literature eased within the USSR, Soviet writers began to publish abroad in *tamizdat*. Certainly the most notorious example was the publication of Boris Pasternak's novel *Doctor Zhivago* by the Italian publisher Feltrinelli in 1956, whence it went on to become an international bestseller. Originally written for publication in the author's homeland, the novel inadvertently became a foremost work of *tamizdat* when it was rejected for publication by the editorial board of *Novyi mir*. In 1959, a new voice was heard in *tamizdat*, belonging to the anonymous author of a penetrating exposé of official Soviet literature entitled *Chto takoe sotsialisticheskii realism?* (*What Is Socialist Realism?*). The essay was followed over the course of some five years by a series of fantastic fictional works signed with the pseudonym Abram Terts. Not until his arrest in 1965 would the literary critic Andrei Siniavskii be revealed as the author of these works, who had helped other authors – most notably Iulii Daniel, publishing under the pseudonym Nikolai Arzhak – to spirit their works abroad for publication. During the Thaw, uncensored works began to circulate in manuscript (*samizdat*) within the Soviet Union. The first major *samizdat* literary journal, (*Sintaksis* [Syntax]), published by Aleksandr Ginzburg, began its brief run in 1959. The poet Iosif Brodskii's verses were first published there.

The high point of the Thaw was the publication of Aleksandr Solzhenitsyn's novella (*Odin den Ivana Denisovicha*) (*One Day in the Life of Ivan Denisovich*) in *Novyi mir* (1962) through the personal intervention of Khrushchev. Almost immediately afterward and before Khrushchev's ouster in 1964, a new 'freeze' began. In 1964, Brodskii was placed on trial for 'parasitism' (*tuneiadstvo*) in Leningrad and sentenced to exile. The trial of Siniavskii and Daniel for 'anti-Soviet propaganda' in February 1966 marked a symbolic end to the Thaw and the beginning of Stagnation.

Nonetheless, interesting writers managed to publish their works throughout the concluding decades of Soviet rule. Those warranting serious attention belonged to two dominant trends: the more cohesive rural or village prose (*derevenskaia proza*) and the more amorphous urban or intelligentsia prose. Whereas rural prose favoured formulaic structures and thematic and stylistic concerns, urban prose encompassed a diverse group of writers, foremost among them Iurii Trifonov and Andrei Bitov. Even among this group major works could not be published, or could appear only in fragmentary form, as did Bitov's novel *Pushkinskii dom* (*Pushkin House*). Works that did not fit comfortably under these broad divisions included Anatolii Rybakov's moving saga of a Jewish family in the occupied territories during World War II, *Tezhelyi pesok* (*Heavy Sand*, 1978), which made its way into print thanks to the author's clever manoeuvring,

and Iskander's loosely constructed episodic novel, *Sandro iz Chegema* (*Sandro from Chegem*, excerpted in 1973), which could be published in its entirety in the USSR only in 1989.

As controls on literature tightened during Stagnation, more and more works and writers made their away abroad. Among the most notable *tamizdat* works of the period were Venedikt Erofeev's quirky masterpiece *Moskva-Petushki* (translated into English as *Moscow to the End of the Line* and *Moscow Circles*), Vladimir Voinovich's satire *Zhizn i neobychainye prikliucheniia soldata Ivana Chonkina* (*The Life and Extraordinary Adventures of Private Ivan Chonkin*), and Solzhenitsyn's epic fictional and non-fictional accounts of Soviet history, including the novels *Rakovyi korpus* (*Cancer Ward*) and *V kruge pervom* (*The First Circle*) and the monumental exposé of the penal system, *Arkhipelag GULag* (*The Gulag Archipelago*). By the end of the 1970s, Brodskii, Solzhenitsyn, Siniavskii, Voinovich, Gladilin, Aksenov, Aleksandr Zinovev, Sasha Sokolov, and many others were in exile in the West.

Yet even as the 'people of the sixties' were being increasingly squeezed by the system, a new generation of writers was emerging. The 'uncensored' *Metropol* almanac (1979) brought together well-known literary figures and such younger writers as Viktor Erofeev and Evgenii Popov. In 1983, a short story titled *Na zolotom kryltse sideli* (*On the Golden Porch* ...) appeared in the Leningrad journal *Aurora*, marking the beginning of the career of Tatiana Tolstaia, whose sparkling prose would gain her a national and international reputation during glasnost. Tolstaia's focus on the short form, ornamental prose, and marginalized characters proved a bellwether of change.

Mikhail Gorbachev's policy of glasnost in the second half of the 1980s led to the decline and final collapse of Soviet censorship of literature. Side by side with the glasnost blockbusters reclaimed from the past and from the drawer emerged both new talents and older writers who had been held on the margins of literature by the old order. The latter category included Liudmila Petrushevskaia and Vladimir Makanin, as well as Viktor Erofeev and Evgenii Popov. Most notable in the former category was Vladimir Sorokin. Much of the work of these writers could be classified as 'prose noir' (*chernukha*), characterized by a nightmarish preoccupation with the darker sides of Soviet life. The poets of the Conceptualist group – Dmitrii Prigov, Lev Rubinshtein, and Timur Kibirov – also joined the mainstream of published writers during glasnost.

See also: Akhmadulina, Bella; Aksenov, Vaselii; Bitov, Andrei; Brodskii, Iosif; censorship; Conceptualism, literary; Daniel, Iulii; Dudintsev, Vladimir; Erenburg, Ilia; Erofeev, Venedikt; Erofeev, Viktor; Evtushenko, Evgenii; Gorbachev, Mikhail; Iskander, Fazil; Kibirov, Timur; literature, Stagnation; literature, Thaw; Makanin, Vladimir; *Metropol*; Pasternak, Boris; perestroika and glasnost; Petrushevskaia, Liudmila; Popov, Evgenii; Prigov, Dmitrii; Rubinshtein, Lev; Rybakov, Anatolii; samizdat; Siniavskii, Andrei; sixties generation; Socialist Realism; Sokolov, Sasha; Solzhenitsyn, Aleksandr; Sorokin, Vladimir; Stagnation; Stalin, Iosif; tamizdat; Thaw; Tolstaia, Tatiana; Trifonov, Iurii; unions, creative, Soviet; Voinovich, Vladimir; Voznesenskii, Andrei

Further reading

Borden, R. (1999) *The Art of Writing Badly: V. Kataev's Mauvism and the Rebirth of Russian Modernism*, Evanston, IL: Northwestern University Press.

Brown, D. (1978) *Soviet Russian Literature Since Stalin*, Cambridge: Cambridge University Press.

——(1993) *The Last Years of Soviet Russian Literature: Prose Fiction, 1975–1991*, Cambridge: Cambridge University Press.

Brown, E. J. (1982) *Russian Literature Since the Revolution*, Cambridge, MA: Harvard University Press.

Clark, K. (1981) *The Soviet Novel: History as Ritual*, Chicago: University of Chicago Press.

Hayward, M. (1983) *Writers in Russia, 1917–1978*, San Diego, CA: Harcourt Brace Jovanovich.

Lipovetsky, M. (1999) *Russian Postmodernist Fiction: Dialogue with Chaos*, Armonk, NY: M.E. Sharpe.

Maguire, R. (1968) *Red Virgin Soil: Soviet Literature in the 1920s*, Princeton, NJ: Princeton University Press.

Parthé, K. (2004) *Russia's Dangerous Texts: Politics Between the Lines*, New Haven, CT: Yale University Press.

CATHARINE NEPOMNYASHCHY

literature, Soviet Republics

The term 'literature of the Soviet republics' or 'literature of the peoples of the USSR' (*literatura narodov SSSR*) has two distinct meanings. On the one hand, it has been used to refer to the entire history of national literatures of the nations composing the Soviet Union; on the other, it refers specifically to literature written on Soviet territory in all the languages of the Soviet Union during its existence (traditionally counted from the 1917 Bolshevik Revolution, not from the official formation of the USSR in 1922). Moreover, since Russians were an 'unmarked' dominant nation in the USSR, the term 'nationalities' often meant 'all the nationalities except Russian', and the term 'literature of the peoples of the USSR' usually stood for all the national literatures of the USSR except Russian. To confuse things even further, the term 'Soviet literature' has been indiscriminately used to mean both Russian literature of the Soviet period and all the national literatures of the USSR in 1917–91.

The Soviet Union was among the world's most ethnically and linguistically diverse states (in the 1920s, nearly 200 distinct ethnicities were officially counted; in the late 1930s, their number was cut by half). Some of the nations it comprised (such as the Armenians) could boast a literary tradition dating back nearly two thousand years; others had no writing system of their own. The 1920s witnessed an ambitious programme of *korenizatsiia* ('nativization'), promoting the nations' distinct languages and cultures in public life, education, and personnel decisions – a move recently dubbed by historians 'the affirmative action empire' (Martin 2001). The concrete steps of the programme varied according to the status of a particular national unit (from union republics to isolated local soviets), historical and demographic circumstances, and so on. Linguistic and educational policy, however, received most attention. Literary production as such in the languages of the Soviet Union initially was left to its own devices.

Around 1929, a consistent policy was initiated to bring all the distinct national literatures and cultures of the USSR into one orbit, with the gradual elaboration of the 'friendship of peoples' paradigm that took final shape by the mid-1930s, following the First Congress of Soviet Writers. With the proclamation of socialist realism as the only official Soviet style, socialist in content, and national in form, all the diverse national literatures and cultures, which often had little in common with one another, were now supposed to develop in unison, presenting essentially the same content enlivened by their 'picturesque' (ornamental) national form. For this purpose, national cultures were showcased through specially designed festivals (typically brought to Moscow as the main stage for such promotional events, but there were also reciprocal exchanges between republics and other autonomous units) and through an ambitious translation publishing programme. These translations often provided a means of subsistence and an outlet for training formal and stylistic skills for many Soviet writers. The unity was also projected into the past, as national canons of 'progressive' literature were engineered on a cookie-cutter basis. In many cases, earlier writers, such as those in Turkic-language cultures, retrospectively were assigned modern national affiliations based on loose and contradictory criteria. The literary journal *Druzhba narodov* (Friendship of Peoples) was launched in 1939 as a vehicle specifically designed to showcase the development of the USSR's national literatures. The 1930s were also the time of large-scale purges of the non-Russian national intelligentsia, which wiped out leading literary talents or frightened them into conformity. Consequently, by decade's end the literary scene was one of depressing uniformity, characterized by vacuous propagandistic content and ritualized, decorative, 'folksy' form. Collectively, these national literatures formed, to use the apt formulation by the Australian Slavist Marko Pavlyshyn, not a canon but an iconostasis: each of these literatures was represented by a few known figures of writers past and present, officially admired but unread by the larger public.

As a distinct academic discipline within the Soviet educational system, the study of the literatures of the peoples of the USSR fully emerged only after World War II, with special departments created at universities and research institutes. In the development of this discipline, attention to historical discontinuity – the asynchronicity of the synchronous – provided the material for original research. In essence, the more daring scholars within this discipline (such as Moscow State University's H.G. Korogly and R.G. Bikmukhametov) envisioned it as a specific subfield of comparative literature. Frequently, however, 'scholarship' in this field merely supplied lists of names and/or titles, glossing over individual national peculiarities. During the Soviet period, each of the national literatures was supposed to have passed through a stage of 'revolutionary romanticism' followed by 'workers' enthusiasm', before branching out into historical fiction, and so forth. Even after the Thaw, unique local styles, such as the Ukrainian 'chimeric novel' (an indigenous form of magical realism), were explained away – in this particular case, as a local ethnographic version of village prose. At the all-Union level, greater attention was granted to iconic writers from numerically small ethnic groups (e.g., Rasul Gamzatov, an Avar, or Yuri Rytkheu, a Chukchi), writers who translated their own work into Russian (e.g., Chingiz Aitmatov, a Kirghiz, or Vasil Bykaŭ [Bykov], a Belarussian), or those who had entirely switched to writing in Russian (e.g. Fazil Iskander, an Abkhaz). The majority of non-Russian writers, however, were preoccupied with the preservation and development of their national cultures and other related local causes (such as environmentalism) and wrote primarily for audiences who read them in their own language. These nation-specific concerns, however, combined with the indifference of Moscow and of scholars and readers outside the USSR, made these works peculiarly insular and irrelevant to the global spotlight, regardless of their aesthetic quality. Only the literatures of the numerically larger nations or those with strong diasporic traditions received a modicum of attention. For most of the national literatures of the former Soviet Union, no reliable reader guides or unbiased overviews are currently available. In the meantime, the academic discipline of 'literature of the peoples of the USSR' is all but dead in Russia and other ex-Soviet states, while most Russian readers persist in the prejudicial belief that nothing original or innovative can come from the pens of the former 'younger brothers' (the occasional exceptions, such as the attention paid to the Russian-language Ferghana school of poetry in Uzbekistan, only confirm the rule). Still in print, the journal *Druzhba narodov* is little more than a shoestring operation without a consistent policy. The world's attention to recent 'coloured revolutions' and other events in post-Soviet states might yet lead to a greater curiosity about these countries' national literatures.

See also: Aitmatov, Chingiz; Belarus; Bykov, Vasilii; Chukchi; Gamzatov, Rasul; Iskander, Fazil; literature, Soviet; Moscow State University; nationalism ('the national question'); Socialist Realism literary classics; Thaw; USSR; Uzbekistan; World War II (Great Patriotic War)

Further reading

Bikmukhametov, R. G. (1983) *Orbity vzaimo-deistviia*, Moscow: Sovetskii pisatel.

Borozdina, P. A. (1991) *Ocherki istorii literatur narodov SSSR*, Voronezh: Izd-vo Voronezhskogo universiteta.

Lomidze, G. (1983) *National Soviet Literatures: Unity of Purpose*, Moscow: Raduga.

Luckyj, G. (1992) *Ukrainian Literature in the Twentieth Century: A Reader's Guide*, Toronto: University of Toronto Press.

Martin, T. (2001) *The Affirmative Action Empire: Nations and Nationalism in the Soviet Union, 1923–1939*, Ithaca, NY: Cornell University Press.

McMillin, A. B. (1999) *Belarusian Literature in the 1950s and 1960s: Release and Renewal*, Cologne: Böhlau.

Slezkine, Y. (1994) 'The USSR as a Communal Apartment, or How a Socialist State Promoted Ethnic Particularism', *Slavic Review* 53, 2: 414–52.

VITALY CHERNETSKY

literature, Stagnation

The term 'literature of Stagnation' refers to Soviet literature produced between 1968–86, a period characterized by a profound crisis in the entire Soviet system, as confidence in the regime gradually eroded. Economic decline, environmental despoliation, political corruption, and an aging and inept leadership combined to create a widespread sense of deterioration and drift. Under Stalin and Khrushchev, the ability of the Soviet leadership to stimulate productivity and ensure economic welfare led to a congruence of elite and popular values and overall social and political stability. Under Brezhnev, however, a gap emerged between expectations and the capacity of the system to meet them. Stagnation of living standards, declining opportunities for upward mobility, an increase in mortality rates, and the rise of ethno-nationalism contributed to a general feeling of dissatisfaction with the Soviet system. Literature of this period both reflected and contributed to this crisis of confidence in the leadership's ability to find solutions to the country's cultural and sociopolitical problems.

Several important trends within officially sanctioned literature of the time merit particular attention. Village prose – the post-Stalinist thematic orientation in Soviet literature that had a clearly defined ideological, moral, and aesthetic profile – embraced an alienated view of modern society and idealized Russia's patriarchal past. In the period of Stagnation this model was infused with fantasy based on Christian legend and pre-Christian myths. The works of Sergei Zalygin, Valentin Rasputin, Vladimir Drozd, and Vladmir Krupin, for example, celebrate the imagined pre-industrial village as the true ideal. Works by village writers depict the desecration of the environment as directly resulting from the loss of Russian traditional values – reverence and humility toward nature.

Mikhail Bulgakov's last novel, *Master i Margarita* (*The Master and Margarita*, first published 1966–67), became responsible for the 'Bulgakov phenomenon' in the Soviet Union, a virtual cult of the writer that, in the period of stagnation, led to the appearance of a number of novels imitating Bulgakov's Master: Marger Zarin's *Falshivyi Faust* (*The False Faust*, 1981), Natalia Sokolova's *Ostorozhno, volshebnoe!* (*Careful, Magic!*, 1981), and Vladimir Orlov's *Altist Danilov* (*Danilov, the Viola Player*, 1980) are excellent examples of escapist Soviet literature, offering a blend of popular literary genres: mystery, science fiction, and the spy novel. These narratives show the city, not as a source of corruption and evil, à la village prose, but as a magical place where common people's suppressed desires came true and the protagonist assumes the qualities of a superhero, capable of extraordinary achievements.

The works by the 'generation of the forty-year-olds', or representatives of the 'Moscow School' (Anatolii Kim, Ruslan Kireev, Anatolii Kurchatkin, and Vladimir Makanin) generated a lively critical response and discussion. In the fiction of this group of writers, the protagonist is usually an ordinary person, a newcomer from the provinces who has to deal with the pressures of living in a big city. Formally, the work of the Moscow School was characterized by experimentation in style and structure. Most of the writers used fantasy as well as elaborate structural devices to emphasize the disorientation of an ordinary person in a big city. Experiments in form have earned the fiction of the Moscow school yet another name: alternative literature (*alternativnaia literatura*) Alternative modes of thinking and social organization as well as the questioning of the predictability of history and of the human ability to comprehend reality fully were the central issues examined by the writers of the Moscow school. Its writers reassessed the notion that one can know in some concrete sense the moral and psychological nature of another person and the world around; the limits of human perception, the profound moral confusion stemming from the disintegration of former certitudes, and the mind's propensity for mythmaking were its important themes.

In the mid-1970s, the officially sanctioned Soviet literature overall began exhibiting a certain openness to innovation, propelled by a desire to broaden the scope of Socialist Realism. In response to the loosening of the strictures, writers began using utopian motifs and gestures of fantasy to deal in an admissible form with the issues of social imagination and alternative social constructs, with the limitations of the teleological view of history embedded in Marxism-Leninism, and with the constraints on personal freedom that this vision of the world implies. Such different writers as Chingiz Aitmatov in his *I dolshe veka dlitsia den'* (*The Day Lasts More Than a Hundred Years*, 1980), Kim in *Lotos* (*Lotus*, 1980), Makanin in *Gde skhodilos nebo s kholmami* (*Where the Sky Met the Hills*, 1984), and Nikolai Evdokimov (in *Proisshestvie iz zhizni Vladimira Vasilevicha Makhonina* (*An Incident in the Life of Vladimir Vasilevich Makhonin*, 1980)), among others, articulated through the prism of fantasy the crucial issues of the disappearance of tradition

and the search for a national identity, the fear of nuclear war and of ecological catastrophe, and the loss of moral foundations in contemporary Soviet life.

The generation of openly non-conformist poets born in the 1950s – Aleksandr Eremenko, Nina Iskrenko, and Aleksei Parshchikov, among others – contributed to the officially sanctioned move for innovation by introducing modernist and post-modernist poetry into Soviet literature, discussed at length by two important literary periodicals *Literaturnaia gazeta* (The Literary Gazette) and *Literaturnaia ucheba* (Literary Education) in 1982–84.

The dissident movement of the 1970s was chiefly responsible for disseminating works of the 'unofficial' or 'underground' works of Soviet literature. *Samizdat* (self-published literature banned for publication in the USSR) and *tamizdat* (émigré editions smuggled from abroad) became indispensable sources of information for vast numbers of Soviet readers during the period of stagnation. However, efforts to bring 'underground' literature to the surface were swiftly curbed by the authorities. The attempt by a group of twenty-three Soviet writers to produce the independent *Metropol: Literaturnyi almanakh* (*Metropolis: A Literary Almanac*, 1979) resulted in the expulsion of some from the Soviet Writer's Union (Viktor Erofeev and Evgenii Popov), revoking of Soviet citizenship for Vasilii Aksenov, and withdrawal of publishing privileges for all participants.

The underground literary scene in the Stagnation period was based mainly in Leningrad and Moscow. The Leningrad group, influenced by two outstanding poets, Anna Akhmatova and Iosif Brodskii, and represented by Arkadii Dragomoshchenko, Viktor Krivulin, and Elena Shvarts, was known for its modernist orientation. The Moscow underground conceptualist circle included painters Erik Bulatov, Francisco Infante, Ilia Kabakov, Vitalii Komar, Aleksandr Melamid, and Oskar Rabin; writers Evgenii Popov, Igor Kholin, Vsevolod Nekrasov, Dmitrii Prigov, Lev Rubinshtein, Timur Kibirov, and Vladimir Sorokin; and literary critics Boris Groys and Mikhail Epshtein.

The artistic ideology and strategy of the conceptualists, who often combined painting and writing in their creative endeavours, were predominantly inspired by visual art and were aimed at a purposeful demythologizing of prevalent cultural and political clichés. In addition to conceptualists, the underground literature circle in Moscow included Venedikt Erofeev, whose highly influential *Moskva-Petushki* (completed in 1970, first published in 1977), was published abroad and available only in *samizdat* copies during the stagnation period. Another important figure of the underground was Evgenii Kharitonov, whose frank descriptions of gay life in the Soviet Union presaged the flowering of gay culture in post-Soviet Russia.

Thus the literary scene during the period of Stagnation was far from stagnant. Vibrant and receptive to the challenges of modernity, it was chiefly responsible for articulating the issues troubling Soviet society on the eve of monumental changes to come. This period prepared the way for the post-Soviet explosion of creative energies in political and artistic life. By investigating alternative societal structures as models for Soviet society, by questioning the epistemological presuppositions of Marxism-Leninism, and by introducing thematic and stylistic innovations, this literature served as an important prelude and a necessary bridge to the literature of glasnost and perestroika.

See also: Aitmatov, Chingiz; Akhmatova, Anna; Aksenov, Vasilii; Brezhnev, Leonid; Brodskii, Iosif; Bulatov, Erik; Conceptualism, literary; Erofeev, Venedikt; Infante, Francisco; Kabakov, Ilia; Kibirov, Timur; Komar and Melamid; literature, perestroika; literature, underground; *Literaturnaia gazeta* (Literary Gazette); Makanin, Vladimir; *Master i Margarita* (*The Master and Margarita*); *Metropol*; Popov, Evgenii; Prigov, Dmitrii; Rabin, Oskar; Rasputin, Valentin; Rubinshtein, Lev; samizdat; Shvarts, Elena; Socialist Realism; Sorokin, Vladimir; Stagnation; tamizdat; village prose

Further reading

Balina, M., Condee, N. and Dobrenko, E. (2000) *Endquote: Sots-Art and Soviet Grand Style*, Evanston, IL: Northwestern University Press.

Brown, D. (1993) *The Last Years of Soviet Russian Literature: Prose Fiction, 1975–1991*, Cambridge: Cambridge University Press.

Goscilo, H. (ed.) (1993) *Fruits of Her Plume: Essays on Contemporary Russian Woman's Culture*, Armonk, NY: M.E. Sharpe.

Hosking, G. (2001) *Russia and the Russians*, Cambridge, MA: Harvard University Press.

Laird, S. (1999) *Voices of Russian Literature: Interviews with Ten Contemporary Writers*, Oxford: Oxford University Press.

Peterson, N. (1997) *Subversive Imaginations: Fantastic Prose and the End of Soviet Literature, 1970s–1990s*, Boulder, CO: Westview Press.

Shneidman, N. (1989) *Soviet Literature in the 1980s: Decade of Transition*, Toronto: University of Toronto Press.

NADYA PETERSON

literature, Thaw

The term Thaw denotes the period of changes in Soviet life following Stalin's death (5 March 1953), marked by revitalization and relative liberalization in literature and other arts. The progress of these changes was by no means linear and simple; it was impeded by successful counterattacks by literary reactionaries and sudden turnarounds caused by the often moody and erratic Nikita Khrushchev, then First Secretary of the Communist Party and actual head of the government. By the mid-1960s the liberal spirit of the Thaw had declined sufficiently to usher in a new period, known as Stagnation.

The process of de-stalinization started almost immediately after Stalin's death. In April, an article by the poet Olga Berggolts, '*Razgovor o lirike*' (*Talking about Lyrical Poetry*), in the weekly *Literaturnaia gazeta* (Literary Gazette) criticized poetry devoted to fulfilling industrial quotas and called for more attention to love and other subjective emotions in lyrical poetry. An article in December of that year by critic Vladimir Pomerantsev, *Ob iskrennosti v literature* (*On Sincerity in Literature*), became a seminal event in the history of the Thaw. Without naming Socialist Realism, Pomerantsev attacked its role in Soviet literature, particularly its '*lakirovka deistvitelnosti*' (varnishing of reality) and '*bezkonfliktnost*' (conflictlessness). The article criticizes novels that are ideologically correct but lifeless, depicting great achievements of the socialist system rather than real life, real people, and their problems.

Pomerantsev's article appeared in the journal *Novyi mir* (New World), which, under the editorship of poet Aleksandr Tvardovskii, became an important venue for works that reflected the new tendencies – eliminating the legacy of Stalinism in life and the arts.

In 1953 and the first half of 1954, *Novyi mir* also published a novel by Vera Panova and important articles by Fedor Abramov, Mark Lifshits, and Mark Shcheglov, which were written in the new spirit of 'truthfulness'. Other journals followed suit. In February 1954, *Teatr* (Theatre) published the play *Gosti* (Guests) by Leonid Zorin, which touches upon such issues as persecution of innocent people under Stalin, injustice pervading the court system, and abuse of power by Soviet party bureaucrats. The May 1954 issue of another Moscow journal, *Znamia* (Banner), carried the first part of the novella *Ottepel* (*The Thaw*) by Ilia Erenburg, which gave its name to the entire period. Though arguably not a great work of literature, *The Thaw* is programmatic inasmuch as the author demonstrates what could be the subject matter of an honest literary text. Erenburg offers the reader a smorgasbord of topics and conflicts unthinkable in a canonical work of Socialist Realism. He contrasts a talented artist, devoted to his landscapes and living in poverty, with a hack painter who produces portraits of Party bosses and Stakhanovites and is awash in money. Several romantic subplots involve men and women torn by doubts because their feelings – and in the case of one young woman, even sexual desire – are stronger than their notions of propriety and duty to spouse, country, and reason. The novel also contains references to the persecution of Jewish doctors during the last months of Stalin's rule.

The Thaw resulted not only in the regime's tolerance of greater sincerity and subjectivity in literature, but also in increased possibilities for publication. Within two years (1955–56), about a dozen new literary journals had appeared in Moscow, Leningrad, and the provinces, including *Iunost* (Youth), *Molodaia gvardiia* (Young Guard), *Nash sovremennik* (Our Contemporary), *Moskva* (Moscow), and *Druzhba narodov* (Friendship of Peoples). Their very titles reflect the general desire to move away from the legacy of Stalinism and start anew. In 1956, the two volumes of the literary miscellany *Literaturnaia Moskva* (Literary Moscow) came out; they included works by Anna Akhmatova, Boris Pasternak, Marina Tsvetaeva, and Nikolai Zabolotskii – authors whose names had long been out of circulation for ideological reasons. The second volume also featured the strikingly frank short stories by Aleksandr Iashin and Nikolai Zhdanov, which portrayed the harsh reality of life in the Soviet countryside.

These developments did not occur without conflicts or losses. Literary Stalinists – Aleksandr Fadeev, Konstantin Fedin, Nikolai Gribachev, Vadim Kochetov, and Aleksei Surkov – together with scores of hack critics, launched a counterattack accusing the liberal writers, critics, and editors of revisionism, political pessimism, abstract humanism, aesthetic nihilism, and, peculiarly, tendentious portrayals of Soviet life. The word 'cosmopolitanism' – a remnant of the anti-Jewish campaign of the late 1940s and early 1950s – was also often heard from the podiums at official meetings of literary organizations.

The Twentieth Congress of the Communist Party of the Soviet Union (February 1956) rekindled hopes for liberalization. On the last day of the Congress (25 February), at a closed session, Khrushchev delivered what became known as the 'secret speech'. In it he criticized Stalin's 'cult of personality' and held him responsible for the deaths of countless innocent Soviet citizens during the purges. Although the speech was not published at the time, its content was disseminated through Communist and Komsomol cells at all Soviet factories, institutions, and organizations. This new level of openness encouraged further advancement of the Thaw; in August of that year another important novel exposing bureaucrats and party functionaries was published in *Novyi mir*: Vladimir Dudintsev's *Ne khlebom edinym* (*Not by Bread Alone*). In September *Iunost* published the first novel by the young writer Anatolii Gladilin. This work marked the arrival on the literary scene of young writers and poets who belonged to the new, post-Stalin generation, including Bella Akhmadulina, Vasilii Aksenov, Andrei Bitov, Evgenii Evtushenko, Fazil Iskander, Anatolii Kuznetsov, Arkadii and Boris Strugatskii, Georgii Vladimov, Vladimir Voinovich, and Andrei Voznesenskii.

Yet another setback loomed around the corner, however. When the Hungarian uprising of October 1956 was suppressed by the Soviet Army, reactionaries used the uprising to alarm the government by insinuating that liberalization in literature and other arts could lead to the same explosive situation that had preceded the uprising in Hungary. References to the 'Petöfi Circle' – a literary discussion club that became the heart of the uprising – recurred in their diatribes against the liberals and it was quickly appropriated by Khrushchev in his characteristic threats: 'We will not allow another Petöfi Circle here!' Dudintsev's novel and the second volume of *Literaturnaiia Moskva* became targets of reinvigorated attacks by the conservatives.

Thus, the Thaw proceeded at an irregular rhythm, liberalization alternating with constraints. In 1961, the miscellany *Tarusskie stranitsy* (Tarussa Pages), published in Kaluga, introduced the works of such young writers and poets as Boris Balter, Iurii Kazakov, Naum Korzhavin, Vladimir Maksimov, and Bulat Okudzhava. Since their works did not fit the procrustean bed of Socialist Realism, literary functionaries lashed out against the publishers of *Tarusskie stranitsy*; the editors were fired and the printing of the volume was discontinued. The inclusion of Aleksandr Solzhenitsyn's novel *Odin den Ivana Denisovicha* (*One Day in the Life of Ivan Denisovich*) in the November 1962 issue of *Novyi mir* may be considered the symbolic climax of the Thaw. It was the first literary work published in the Soviet Union in which the author, who had spent eight years in Stalin's camps, frankly described the horrors of Stalinism and its labour camps. Significantly, while revealing the harsh truth about Stalinism, Solzhenitsyn did not perform the balancing act of demonstrating his loyalty to the system in general.

Shortly thereafter, the liberals experienced a major blow, which marked the beginning of a slow decline for the process of liberalization. On 7 and 8 March 1963, a humiliating attack took place in the Kremlin during a meeting between top Party and government officials, including Khrushchev, and the *tvorcheskaia intelligentsiia* (creative intelligentsia). Over eight hundred writers, artists, composers, and film and theatre directors were invited to the meeting. The initial amicable atmosphere quickly turned into a personal assault by Khrushchev on Aksenov, Erenburg, Evtushenko, and Voznesenskii. Criticism of Erenburg singled out his recently published memoirs, which attempted to vindicate the early-twentieth-century avant-garde. The young authors took a beating for giving critical interviews abroad. The powerful message to the entire audience was: you follow the Party line, or else.

The occasion demonstrated the limits of the government's tolerance of ideological deviations in arts. After Khrushchev was ousted in October 1964 and replaced by Leonid Brezhnev in the post of First Secretary of the Communist Party, ideological control over cultural production became even tighter. In 1966, writers Andrei Siniavskii and Iulii Daniel were sentenced, respectively, to seven and five years of hard labour for publishing what the establishment called 'anti-Soviet' fiction in the West. For his uncompromising stand against censorship and for publishing his novels abroad, Solzhenitsyn was expelled from the Union of Soviet Writers in 1969, and from the country in 1974.

Thus, the mid-1960s witnessed a halt to the process of liberalization. Any hope for future relaxation of government control was crushed on 20 August 1968, the day Soviet tanks rolled into Prague. This invasion was a tragedy not only for Czechoslovakia, but also for all liberal-minded people in the Soviet Union. It was a clear sign that the Soviet regime was prepared to go to any lengths in maintaining ideological control. The Thaw was over.

See also: Akhmadulina, Bella; Akhmatova, Anna; Aksenov, Vasilii; anti-Semitism; Berggolts, Olga; Bitov, Andrei; Brezhnev, Leonid; Communist Youth League; cult of personality; Daniel, Iulii; Dudintsev Vladimir Erenburg, Ilia; Evtushenko, Evgenii; Iskander, Fazil; Kazakov, Iurii; Korzhavin, Naum; Krushchev, Nikita; *Literaturnaia gazeta*; *Molodaia gvardiia*; *Novyi mir*; Okudzhava, Bulat; Siniavskii, Andrei; Socialist Realism; Solzhenitsyn, Aleksandr; Stagnation; Stakhanovism; Strugatskii, Arkadii and Boris; Thaw; thick journals; Tvardovskii, Aleksandr; Vladimov, Georgii; Voinovich, Vladimir; Voznesenskii, Andrei; Zorin, Leonid.

Further reading

Brown, E. (1982) *Russian Literature Since the Revolution*, Cambridge, MA: Harvard University Press, pp. 192–291.

Chuprinin, S. (ed.) (1989) *Ottepel: 1953–1956*, Moscow: Moskovskii rabochii.

——(1990a) *Ottepel: 1957–1959*, Moscow: Moskovskii rabochii.

——(1990b) *Ottepel: 1960–1962*, Moscow: Moskovskii rabochii.

Gibian, G. (1960) *Interval of Freedom: Soviet Literature during the Thaw, 1954–1957*, Minneapolis, MN: University of Minnesota Press.

Johnson, P. (1965) *Khrushchev and the Arts: The Politics of Soviet Culture, 1962–1964*, Cambridge, MA: MIT Press.

Prokhorov, A. V. (2002) 'Inherited Discourse: Stalinist Tropes in Thaw Culture', PhD dissertation, University of Pittsburgh.

Woll, J. (2000) *Reel Images: Soviet Cinema and the Thaw*, London and New York: I. B. Tauris.

KONSTANTIN KUSTANOVICH

literature, underground

Underground literature refers to writing produced in the USSR and disseminated to readers without being subjected to Soviet censorship. Produced on a small scale before 1953, it grew as a phenomenon during the Thaw, reaching its zenith in the 1970s and 1980s, by which time the methods of publishing underground literature – *samizdat* and *tamizdat* – had become well established and developed. Much of the significant literature of the post-Stalin period existed underground for at least some years: some works initially circulated as underground literature and were later published by the Soviet press, such as Aleksandr Tvardovskii's *Terkin na tom svete* (*Terkin in the Other World*). The majority, however, remained underground until perestroika, such as Aleksandr Solzhenitsyn's *Arkhipelag GULag* (*The Gulag Archipelago*). Underground literature preserved significant traditions of Russian literature, which were largely unacceptable to Soviet censorship, such as novels and short stories containing social criticism and satire. It was also the refuge of important literature and memoirs that recounted the horrors of the Stalinist period. Many works of Russian

literature that otherwise might have been lost, survived the Soviet period in *samizdat*. The authors of underground literature were a diverse group of writers, including official Soviet writers; émigré writers perceived as inimical to the Soviet state; anti-Soviet dissidents; deceased writers lacking official approval; and writers who were unsuccessful in publishing their work officially in the USSR.

Many significant works circulating in *samizdat* in the USSR, especially during the Thaw period, were written by official writers, some of whom hoped to publish their work officially, but found the liberalization of Soviet literature insufficiently quick or extensive. Thus Aleksandr Tvardovskii's *Terkin na tom svete* was read in *samizdat* from 1956 until its official publication in 1962. Many resorted to underground literature when attempts to publish officially failed: when the publication of Aleksandr Solzhenitsyn's *Rakovyi korpus* (*Cancer Ward*) was blocked in the mid-1960s, he allowed the novel to circulate in *samizdat* instead. All underground authors took some risk in permitting their work to appear in *samizdat*, for although *samizdat* itself was not a punishable offence, authors, producers, and distributors of underground literature could be arrested on the grounds of anti-Soviet agitation. In general, *samizdat* publishing was not as dangerous in this regard as *tamizdat*, in connection with which, among others, Andrei Siniiavskii and Iulii Daniel in 1966, and later Solzhenitsyn, were arrested and punished.

In the 1960s many important texts by otherwise official writers existed as underground literature. Anna Akhmatova's *Rekviem* (*Requiem*) appeared in *tamizdat* in Germany, and circulated in *samizdat* in the 1960s. Memoirs by Evgeniia Ginzburg, Lidiia Ginzburg, and Nadezhda Mandelshtam, which describe the Stalinist period and its persecutions, became key texts of underground literature in the post-Stalin period, as did Varlaam Shalamov's *Kolymskie rasskazy* (*Kolyma Tales*), which draw on the author's experience of the GULag at Kolyma. All these works, typically for underground literature of the Thaw period, contain descriptions of the Stalinist terror and the GULag experience, but did not find a place in the limited official project of destalinization. The official writers who produced underground literature in the 1960s included bards. The songs and poems of Aleksandr Galich and Bulat Okudzhava, which often express anti-Soviet sentiments, entered underground literature in written (*samizdat*) and tape-recorded (*magnitizdat*) form.

The recovery of literature composed but not published during the Stalinist past was undertaken to some degree by the official process of destalinization, with its release of previously prohibited works. Where this official process stopped, however, underground literature continued: writers from the past constituted a second significant group of authors of underground literature. The works of authors persecuted by the Soviet regime were available to Soviet readers as underground literature, including some of the later poems of Osip Mandelshtam; novels and stories by Andrei Platonov and Mikhail Bulgakov; and the poetry of Nikolai Gumilev, Vladislav Khodasevich, Nikolai Zabolotskii, Velimir Khlebnikov, and the poets of the OBERIU. Another sphere of literature excluded from Soviet official publications, but represented in underground literature, was the writings of émigré authors. Novels by Vladimir Nabokov and poetry by Marina Tsvetaeva were among the émigré texts of underground literature.

In the 1970s and 1980s, official writers' works circulating in *samizdat* did not focus to such a degree on the experience of the Stalinist era. Many works, however, did contain anti-Soviet material, often in the form of allegory or satire. Vladimir Voinovich's comic and satirical trilogy, *Zhizn i neobychainye prikliucheniia soldata Ivana Chonkina* (*The Life and Extraordinary Adventures of Private Ivan Chonkin*), was initially intended for publication, but after rejection circulated in *samizdat*. Similarly, Andrei Bitov published sections of his novel of the Leningrad intelligentsia, *Pushkinskii dom* (*Pushkin House*), in a Soviet journal, but could publish the entire work only in *samizdat*. In the 1970s it became more common for official writers to publish *tamizdat*, although conditions could become more difficult at home once a writer's work had appeared abroad, and many writers had to deny all knowledge of the publication. In 1972 the Strugatskii brothers, for example, published their satirical science fiction novel *Gadkie lebedi* (*The Ugly Swans*) in Germany, but publicly denied that this was their intention.

Official writers' involvement in underground literature highlighted the fact that in many cases there was little difference between the two spheres. In 1979, some official writers participated in the *samizdat* almanac *Metropol*, and afterwards were restricted in what they could publish; some left the Writers' Union on principle.

Many authors of underground literature were virtually unknown outside the narrow circles of *samizdat* and *tamizdat* readership. They chose to publish their work as underground literature for various reasons: because the work was anti-Soviet and stood no chance of being approved for official publication; because the author was vehemently opposed to the Soviet regime and refused to have anything to do with its institutions; or because the work was not good enough for official publication. During the 1960s underground literature was not strictly delineated from official literature: many young authors circulated quite innocuous work among friends in manuscript form, still hoping that it would be published officially in the future. However, the authorities condemned and made examples of some underground literature. In Leningrad in 1960 Aleksandr Ginzburg produced his *samizdat* journal *Sintaksis* (*Syntax*) and was afterwards arrested and sentenced to a term in the GULag. A few years later in Moscow the group of young writers, SMOG, was persecuted, and a leading figure, Vladimir Batshev, also received a term in a labour camp. Many independent student journals and broadsheets appearing during the Thaw were seized and condemned by the authorities.

When the Thaw ended and the political climate in the USSR became more conservative, underground literature became more self-consciously unofficial and independent of Soviet literature. Underground writers created their own *samizdat* publishing houses, and in 1975–76 two underground literary journals were founded in Leningrad, *Chasy* (The Hours) and *37*, the former appearing regularly for more than ten years. From 1975 onward, writers began to regularly send their work to journals in the West as well. Nevertheless, unofficial writers in the USSR who wanted recognition and a wide readership became frustrated. The narrow circles of *samizdat* and *tamizdat* readers could never replace the general readership of official publishing, and underground writers often became demoralized.

Underground literature by unofficial writers of the post-Thaw period differs more markedly from official literature than was the case during the Thaw. Although some underground writers were explicitly anti-Soviet, others, such as the Leningrad poets Elena Shvarts and Sergei Stratanovskii, became interested in the themes of religion, mysticism, and philosophy, which were outlawed by Socialist Realism. Another characteristic of much underground literature, especially in Moscow, was formal experimentation. In both prose and poetry, writers rejected the highly conservative norms of Socialist Realism and for inspiration looked above all to literary trends at the beginning of the twentieth century. The Moscow Conceptualists were a particular example of this trajectory.

The process of recovering underground authors is ongoing. In the post-Soviet period critics have begun formulating a new canon of literature of the late-Soviet period that incorporates the best of both underground and official literature.

See also: Akhmatova, Anna; bards; Bitov, Andrei; censorship; Conceptualism, literary; Daniel, Iulii; dissident; Galich, Aleksandr; Ginzburg, Evgeniia; Ginzburg, Lidiia; GULag; literature, émigré; literature, Soviet; literature, Thaw; Mandelshtam, Nadezhda; *Metropol*; Nabokov, Vladimir; Okudzhava, Bulat; perestroika and glasnost; samizdat; Shalamov, Varlam; Shvarts, Elena; Siniavskii, Andrei; Socialist Realism; Solzhenitsyn, Aleksandr; Strugatskii, Arkadii Natanovich and Boris Natanovich; tamizdat; Thaw; Tvardovskii, Aleksandr; Voinovich, Vladimir.

Further reading

Aksenov, V. and Bitov, V. (eds) (1979) *Metropol: literaturnyi almanakh*, Ann Arbor, MI: Ardis.

Ivanov, B. (ed.) (2000) *Istoriia Leningradskoi nepodtsenzurnoi literatury*, St Petersburg: Dean.

Kuzminsky, K. (ed.) (1986) *The Blue Lagoon Anthology of Modern Russian Poetry*, Newtonville, MA: Oriental Research Partners.

Maltsev, Yu. (1976) *Volnaia russkaia literatura*, Frankfurt on Main: Posev.

Severiukhin, D. (ed.) (2003) *Samizdat Leningrada*, Moscow: Novoe literaturnoe obozrenie.

Smith, G. S. (1984) *Songs to Seven Strings*, Bloomington, IN: Indiana University Press.

Strelianyi, A. (ed.) (1999) *Samizdat veka*, Moscow: Polifakt.

EMILY LYGO

literature, women's

In some respects, women's literature in the Soviet Union and Russia followed the path of literature in general in the volatile decades after Stalin's death. Khrushchev's speech at the Twentieth Party Congress in 1956 decreased repression and increased possibilities for discussion of social and cultural – if not ideological – issues. Women writers played a small but noticeable role in the burst of energy that marked Soviet cultural life during the Thaw, which ended with Khushchev's removal from power in 1964. With its combination of old stereotypes and new attention to the details of women's lives, Vera Panova's *Vremena goda* (*The Seasons*, 1953) exemplifies this transitional phase between socialist and critical realism. However, in a recurring pattern that dates to the mid-nineteenth century (and continues today), there was also a marked tendency to dismiss women's writing as trivial and excessively preoccupied with everyday life. In this respect, the work of famed wartime poet and film scenarist Olga Berggolts, whose writing even in the post-war period often returned to that war, provides an interesting case study in women writers' loyalty to, and renegotiation of, Socialist Realist and gender stereotypes. One positive aspect of the post-Thaw period was the republication in the Soviet Union, gradual and partial though it may have been, of works by major poets of the previous generation, such as Marina Tsvetaeva and Anna Akhmatova.

In the 1960s, several women writers were prominent among those exposing the consequences of Stalinist policies of the 1930s and 1940s and, to a lesser extent, actively opposing current Soviet power. Beginning in 1962, the synthesis of the personal and the political in Natalia Gorbanevskaia's poetry and journalism challenged the religious and political repression of the Soviet authorities. Memoirs, and specifically those published in *samizdat* and *tamizdat*, written by Evgeniia Ginzburg, a communist and a survivor of the GULag; Nadezhda Mandelshtam, widow of the poet Osip Mandelshtam; and Lidiia Chukovskaia's *Zapiski ob Anne Akhmatovoi* (*Notes on Anna Akhmatova*, published in Paris, 1976–80) and her novel *Sofia Petrovna* (1939–40, published in Paris, 1965) captured a reading public eager to learn of the sins of the Stalinist past from highly literary testimonials. However, dissatisfaction with the opposition's, as well as official Soviet culture's, insensitivity to specifically women's issues led to the creation in the early 1980s of small women's groups in Leningrad, several of them led by women writers with strong feminist and religious convictions: Tatiana Mamonova and Iuliia Voznesenskaia, author of the well-received novel *Zhenskii Dekameron* (*Women's Decameron*, 1987), among others. Like Gorbanevskaia, both emigrated from the Soviet Union in the 1980s. The verse of Olga Sedakova, perhaps the most accomplished poet to emerge from this period, is also rich in religious imagery with a feminine perspective, as is that of her less known though highly innovative contemporary, Elena Shvarts.

Until glasnost, Russian culture's privileging of highbrow and folk forms led to a dismissal of many quintessentially 'women's' preoccupations: the 'double burden' of home and career, maternity, women's mutual support, consumer pleasures, and social services (transportation, kindergartens, hospitals, etc.). Often criticized for its perceived indifference to 'the cursed questions' that traditionally have preoccupied Russia's male writers, women's literature was relegated to the status of a minor genre mired in everyday life. However, even in the 1960s, the work of authors such as Natalia Baranskaia and I. Grekova (pseudonym of Elena S. Ventsel) was widely read and discussed for its portrayal of intelligentsia women in metropolitan centres and the indifference of Soviet cultural and political leaders to their double burden. Written in a traditional critical realist mode, Baranskaia's documentary novella *Nedelia kak nedelia* (*A Week Like Any Other*, 1969) upon first publication in *Novyi mir*, the Soviet Union's most prestigious literary journal, provoked heated debates about the status of Soviet women. Its up-close

chronicling of an ordinary, educated woman's negotiation of the endless pressures of everyday life, and its matter-of-fact exploration of the ubiquitous social exploitation of women by a male-dominated society paying lip service to women's issues, earned it a prominent place in pre-perestroika Soviet literature. Grekova similarly wrote stories, such as *Damskii master* (*The Ladies Hairdresser*, 1963) and *Letom v gorode* (*Summer in the City*), that were stylistically unremarkable but resonated with her professional, urban women readers. Viktoria Tokareva's ironic urban tales, which occasionally invoked the fantastic, also began to appear at this time.

In the 1970s and well into the 1980s, 'women's literature' continued to be regarded with considerable condescension, not least by women writers themselves (Tokareva being a good example). This situation may be partially explained by women writers' internalization of the values of a predominantly male profession. (In 1976 only 1097 of the 7833 members of the Union of Writers were women.) Grekova's novella *Vdovii parokhod* (*Ship of Widows*, 1981), with its unsentimental view of a woman's community, reflects a confrontation with harsh realities ushered in by Mikhail Gorbachev's policy of glasnost in the late 1980s. On the one hand, these years saw improvements in the increase of Russian women writers' participation in professional organizations, and in the legalization of various cultural organizations giving women greater opportunities to serve as activists and leaders both in official institutions such as the Writers' Union and in informal groups and academic venues such as the Centre for Gender Studies at the Academy of Sciences (1990). During the late 1980s, women writers sensed a ready readership and began anthologizing their stories. While collections with such titles as *Zhenskaia logika* (Feminine Logic) and *A Pure Life* (*Chisten'kaia zhizn*) did little to confront gender stereotypes, others, such as *Novye amazonki* (*The New Amazons*), were manifestly intent on embracing a feminist group identity. Many of the stories from these collections made their way into English translations as well, and a number of Russian women prose writers, poets, and playwrights began to attract attention in the West. Plays by and about women figured more prominently on metropolitan stages, including a well-received production of Ginzburg's prison memoir, *Krutoi marshrut* (*Journey Into the Whirlwind*), directed by Galina Volchek at Moscow's Contemporary (Sovremennik) Theatre in the late 1980s, as well as the dramas of Liudmila Razumovskaia and Mariia Arbatova in the 1990s. Arbatova went on to become a major television talk show personality in the mid-1990s.

The major figure to emerge in the post-glasnost period, both in print and on the stage, after many years during which her works were ignored by journal editors and theatre directors alike, was Liudmila Petrushevskaia. Adapting a familiar quote about Nikolai Gogol, Catriona Kelly has asserted that 'most current young Russian women prose writers have come out from under the overskirt of [Petrushevskaia] ... without any doubt the most influential Russian woman writer of the last twenty years' (Kelly 1994: 433). In the late 1980s, her plays – *Tri devushki v golubom* (*Three Girls in Blue*, 1980), *Uroki muzyki* (*Music Lessons*, 1973), *Kvartira Kolombiny* (*Columbine's Apartment*, 1981), *Cinzano* (1973), and others – initially earned public attention with their black humour, sarcasm, and irony; alongside these, there emerged a major corpus of variously ambitious prose works. Petrushevskaia's major concerns and techniques – a bleak view of human nature and of contemporary Russian reality (in contrast to the previous generations' validation of the former and euphemistic approach to the latter); the contempt of her female characters for the men in their lives (as opposed to a long tradition of women valorizing men in both life and art); the debunking of the myth of the selfless, self-sacrificing, and asexual Russian woman; the frank treatment of female sexuality, family dysfunction, and domestic violence; as well as her use of modernist and surrealist narrative techniques such as unreliable narrators and fragmented narratives – have been incorporated into the work of a number of women artists emerging in the 1990s and 2000s.

Among the more interesting recent writers to share Petrushevskaia's dark vision, and her generic diversity, is Nina Sadur. Sadur also uses a variety of linguistic and narrative strategies to examine feminine identity and shifting power relations and occupies a discursive position

somewhere between realist and hyper-realist. In a different vein, which owes as much to late-nineteenth-century Russian ornamentalism as it does to Soviet reality, are the short stories written by Tatiana Tolstaia, who assumes a satirist's stance *vis-à-vis* her protagonists and employs language, imagination, and time to fill her mythic universe. A rich cast of characters and thematic diversity characterize Liudmila Ulitskaia's gynocentric stories and novels. Valeriia Narbikova, whose work has been connected with Conceptualism in its conscious imitation of and quotation from earlier artistic traditions to debunk many of Russian and Soviet society's core myths, is similarly indebted to earlier avant-garde traditions. Other recent writers such as Svetlana Vasilenko and Larisa Vaneeva share with Narbikova an interest in eroticism and in a 'difficult' and fragmented narrative style, while Marina Palei's stories have gained acclaim for their strong effects.

In the 1990s, as cultural tastes in general have shifted to more popular forms, women writers have also been prominent in the genre of the mystery novel (*detektiv*), in which they had previously been little involved. In over twenty smart, gender-stereotype-bending bestsellers written since 1993, Aleksandra Marinina (pseudonym of Marina Alekseeva) has captured the imagination of contemporary readers curious about the mental processes of the demanding female detective (the unfashionable Anastasia Kamenskaia) at the intellectual centre of a team of male policemen that cracks one sordid murder case after another. Daria Dontsova's *detektivy* more than once have made her the country's most popular writer of the year.

Finally, although women have earned increasing recognition, both cultural and financial, for their writing, semi-official awards such as the Russian Booker prize remain out of their reach. Petrushevskaia, Tolstaia, Ulitskaia, and Palei, to name the most prominent of women on the short list, have yet to receive their culture's most prestigious accolade.

See also: Academy of Sciences; Akhmatova, Anna; Arbatova, Mariia awards, literary, post-Soviet; awards, literary, Soviet; Baranskaia, Natalia; Berggolts, Olga; censorship; Chukovskaia, Lidiia; detective fiction; feminism; Dontsova

Daria; Ginzburg, Evgeniia; Gorbachev, Mikhail; Grekova, I.; GULag; Krushchev, Nikita; literature, post-Soviet; literature, Soviet; literature, Stagnation; literature, Thaw; Marinina, Aleksandra; *Novyi mir;* perestroika and glasnost; Petrushevskaia, Liudmila; samizdat; Sadur, Nina; Sedakova, Olga; Shvarts, Elena; Socialist Realism; Sovremennik Theatre; tamizdat; Thaw; Tokareva, Viktoriia; Tolstaia, Tatiana; Ulitskaia, Liudmila; Vasilenko, Svetlana; Volchck, Galina; World War II (Great Patriotic War)

Further reading

Barker, A. (1999) 'The Culture Factory', in *Consuming Russia: Popular Culture, Sex and Society since Gorbachev*, Durham, NC: Duke University Press.

Barker, A. and Gheith, J. (eds) (2004) *A History of Women's Writing in Russia*, Cambridge: Cambridge University Press.

Glas 3 (1992) Moscow: Glas Publishers.

Goscilo, H. (ed.) (1993) *Fruits of her Plume: Essays on Contemporary Russian Women's Culture*, Armonk, NY: M. E. Sharpe.

——(1996) *Dehexing Sex: Russian Womanhood During and After Glasnost*, Ann Arbor, MI: University of Michigan Press.

Kelly, C. (1994) *A History of Russian Women's Writing: 1820–1992*, Oxford: Clarendon Press, Part IV, pp. 337–442.

Ledkovsky, M. *et al.* (eds) (1994) *Dictionary of Russian Women Writers*, Westport, CT: Greenwood Press.

Nepomnyashchy, C. (1999) 'Markets, Mirrors and Mayhem: Aleksandra Marinina and the Rise of the New Russian *Detektiv*', in A. Barker (ed.) *Consuming Russia: Popular Culture, Sex and Society since Gorbachev*, Durham, NC: Duke University Press.

Olcott, A. (2001) *Russian Pulp: The Detektiv and the Way of Russian Crime*, Lanham, MD: Rowman and Littlefield, esp. Chapters 2 and 4.

NATASHA KOLCHEVSKA

literature, World War II

'War prose' is probably the most voluminous genre in Soviet literature, and has been home to many a second-rate but ideologically impeccable writer, at least until perestroika. On the other hand, it is no exaggeration to say that some of the best works of Soviet literature were those devoted to World War II. Viktor Nekrasov's novel *V okopakh Stalingrada* (In the Trenches of Stalingrad, 1947) not only conveyed the horror of front-line combat, but also the psychological make-up of the ordinary soldier; the novel achieved the remarkable feat of both winning a Stalin Prize and gaining international acclaim, especially after its translation into English (under the title *Front-Line Stalingrad*) in 1962. Vasilii Grossman's *Zhizn i sudba* (*Life and Fate;* completed 1961; published abroad 1980; published in the USSR 1988) is also set during the battle of Stalingrad, but encompasses a much grander vision, including the Holocaust, the baneful influence of the commissar on Red Army military planning, and, most provocatively, the spiritual and ideological kinship of the Nazis and the Communists. The work of Belorussian writer Vasil Bykov is exclusively devoted to the war, and his work, spanning over four decades, chronicles the long and bitter victory, but also poses difficult questions of collaboration and political legitimacy in the post-war world.

See also: Bykov, Vasilii; Communist Party; Grossman, Vasilii; Nekrasov, Viktor; World War II (Great Patriotic War)

DAVID GILLESPIE

Literaturnaia gazeta (Literary Gazette)

The first pre-Soviet issue appeared in 1830, with Aleksandr Pushkin's participation; the last, in 1849. Revived by Maksim Gorkii in 1929, the newspaper was published in 1942–44 as *Literatura i iskusstvo* (Literature and Art) under Aleksandr Fadeev's editorship. Under Stalin, literature was considered 'the leader' of all arts; therefore, in 1947 the paper was transformed from a trade publication into a national political newspaper, with Konstantin Simonov as editor-in-chief from 1950–53. From 1960 to the 1980s, a special humorous section titled *The 12-Chair Club*, referencing Ilf and Petrov's satirical novel *Dvenadtsat stulev* (*Twelve Chairs*), was a safe haven for semi-dissident writers and artists using Aesopian language to make fun of the Soviet regime. During Stagnation *Literaturnaia gazeta* functioned as the journalistic bible of the literary intelligentsia.

See also: journalism; Simonov, Konstantin

VLADIMIR PAPERNY

Lithuania

The Lithuanian republic (formerly Lithuania), a country in the northeast of Europe on the coast of the Baltic Sea, is one of the states in the Baltic region. It borders with Kaliningrad oblast (Russia) in the south, Belorussia (Belarus) in the east, and Latvia in the north. Its area is 653,000 sq km, its capital Vilnius.

Most of Lithuanian territory is hilly, with 4400 lakes, 722 rivers (the major one Niamunas [Nemunas]), and 40,000 peat bogs. Woods, predominantly pine and birch, comprise 31 per cent of its territory. There are several large national parks (Aukstaiciai, The Curonian [Kursh] Spit).

Lithuanian tribes, first mentioned in 1009, were united in 1236 by Prince Mindaugas. In the early fourteenth century, the Great Lithuanian principality expanded its territory to the east (into Belorussian and Russian land). In 1386, Lithuanian Prince Jogaila married a Polish princess and became Polish King Wladislaw II Jagiello, just before Lithuanians were baptized. That year Lithuanians were baptized (1387–1413). In the fifteenth century Lithuania expanded its territory further eastward (up to Kursk, Russia) and southward (down to the Black Sea). When Lithuania and Poland united into one Polish–Lithuanian Great Commonwealth in 1569, a process of polonization began. Moreover, at the end of the eighteenth century parts of Lithuania were subsumed by the Russian Empire. In 1918, Lithuania gained independence, with a temporary capital in Kaunas. In 1940, after the invasion of Soviet troops, Lithuania became one of the Soviet republics and regained independence only in 1991 upon the collapse of the USSR.

Lithuania's population is 359,700 (2005): 81 per cent – Lithuanians, 9 per cent – Russians (who live in large cities), 7 per cent – Poles, 1.6 per cent – Belorussians. The official language is Lithuanian. Religious affiliations show 80 per cent – Catholics, 10 per cent – Lutherans, 5 per cent – Orthodox. The largest cities are Vilnius, with 542,000 people, Kaunas – 372,000, Klaipėda – 192,000.

Lithuanian economies include granite and limestone mining, amber industry, engineering (including shipbuilding and repair), electrotechnical, electronic, and chemical goods (fertilizers), metalworking, woodworking, textile, furniture and clothing industries. Popular handicrafts are amber jewellery, ceramic and wooden toys. Agriculture includes cattle-breeding, fishing, poultry, growth of potatoes, beets, flax and vegetables. Major export articles are: construction materials, fabrics and clothing, engineering products, and wood products.

Lithuania is famous for its sandy beaches in Palanga and Nida, balneological resorts, historical and cultural places of interest: Baroque architecture in Vilnius, German seventeenth–nineteenth-century architecture in Klaipėda, castles in Trakai, the old city in Kaunas, churches and cathedrals in Vilnius. The most famous museums are the sea museum in Klaipėda, ethnographic, motorcycle, and cat museums in Šiauliai, an amber museum in Palanga, and one of little demons in Kaunas. Song festivals are very popular in Lithuania. The national cuisine is famous for *cepelinai* (zeppelins); (potatoes stuffed with meat and mushrooms) and *kibinai* (pasty with meat and onions).

See also: Baltic Sea region; Belarus; Latvia

SERGEI TARKHOV

Litvinova, Renata Muratovna

b. 12 January 1967, Moscow

Actress, screenwriter, director

Litvinova is known for her poetic, stream-of-consciousness writing style; her ethereal, mellifluous manner of speech; and her elegant, retro beauty and blonde hair. She studied in the screenwriting department of the State Filmmaking Institute, VGIK. Since 1994 she has collaborated with director Kira Muratova on several films as an actress and writer. Valerii Todorovskii based his acclaimed film *Strana glukhikh* (Land of the Deaf) on a story by Litvinova. Her own directorial debut was the 2004 film *Boginia* (The Goddess).

See also: All-Russian (All-Union) State Institute of Cinematography; Muratova, Kira; Todorovskii, Valerii

SETH GRAHAM

Liube

The rock band Liube appeared in 1989 when Igor Matvienko and Nikolai Rastorguev used the new freedom of perestroika and glasnost to produce their first album, *Atas* (Watch Out), which promoted the group's nationalist and macho appeal. With their nostalgic, patriotic melodies and lyrics, Liube is popular with soldiers, young adults, and the elderly. Rastorguev, whose raucous voice is matched by his public performances in full military uniform, embodies the band's attempts to sound and appear uniquely Russian. The group, whose name and founding musicians come from an infamous industrial suburb of Moscow, profitably exploits nationalist rhetoric without appearing trite.

See also: perestroika and glasnost; rock music

TIMOTHY M. SCHLAK

Liubimov, Aleksei Borisovich

b. 16 September 1944, Moscow

Pianist, harpsichordist, organist

Liubimov began his carrier as a mainstream virtuoso pianist. After studying in the Moscow Conservatory preparatory school and the Conservatory itself (with Genrikh Neigauz and Leonid Naumov), he won international competitions in Rio de Janeiro (1965) and Montreal (1968). However, at the end of the 1960s he began working with contemporary and early music, both of which constituted a kind of musical dissidence at the time. He was closely associated with the ensembles Madrigal, the Moscow Baroque Quartet, and Music – XXth Century, and with musicians including Andrei Volkonskii, Anatolii and Tatiana Grindenko, and Mark Pekarskii. Liubimov also did much for the establishment of both avant-garde and historical performance practices in Russia. In 1988, he founded the Alternative Festival (*Alternativa*), held annually in Moscow, and the Historical and Contemporary Performing Arts Department at the Moscow Conservatory (1997), which he still chairs. In his own solo recitals of the 1990s Liubimov paid as much attention to the baroque and twentieth-century avant-garde as to the standard piano repertoire.

See also: classical musicians/performers, post-Soviet; Moscow Conservatory

KIRA NEMIROVSKAIA

Liubimov, Iurii Petrovich

b. 30 September 1917, Iaroslavl

Director, actor

After graduating from the Vakhtangov Theatre's Shchukin Institute in 1939, Liubimov spent World War II as an emcee in the Song and Dance Ensemble of the NKVD (a precursor of the KGB). He debuted as an actor in 1947, playing Oleg Koshevoi in Aleksandr Fadeev's *Molodaia gvardiia* (*The Young Guard*), and as a director in 1959 with Alexander Galich's *Mnogo li cheloveku nado?* (*Does a Human Being Need Much?*), both at the Vakhtangov.

Liubimov is best known as the founder of the Taganka Theatre, which he opened on 23 April 1964 with Bertolt Brecht's *The Good Person of Setzuan*. For two decades Liubimov's Taganka was considered the 'theatrical conscience' of the Soviet Union, thanks to innovative, dynamic productions in which actors performed live music and addressed the public directly with soul-searching questions and ironic comments. Stripped of his Soviet citizenship while in London in 1984, Liubimov spent four years in exile, primarily in Europe, before returning to Moscow in 1988 to reclaim control of the Taganka in 1989; he weathered a conflict with

Nikolai Gubenko that finally resulted in a schism of the theatre into two independent theatres in 1993. Liubimov has staged over 100 productions worldwide and acted in twenty films, including Ivan Pyrev's *Kubanskie Kazaki* (*Cossacks of the Kuban*, 1950) and Anatolii Efros's *Vsego neskolko slov v chest gospodina de Molera* (*Just a Few Words in Honour of Monsieur de Molière*, 1975).

See also: Gubenko, Nikolai; music in theatre; Taganka Theatre; Vakhtangov Theatre

JOHN FREEDMAN

Liubshin, Stanislav Andreevich

b. 6 April 1933, Moscow

Theatre and film actor, film director

A graduate of the Shchepkin Theatre School (1959), Liubshin worked at theatres including the Sovremennik, Taganka, Ermolova, Malaia Bronnaia, and, since 1980, the Moscow Art Theatre. He played in Marlen Khutsiev's film *Mne dvadtsat let* (*I'm Twenty*; also called *Zastava Ilicha*, 1964), which debuted a whole generation of cinematographers during the Thaw. He created a vivid image of a Soviet scout in Vladimir Basov's film *Shchit i mech* (*Shield and Sword*, 1967), and played in several film adaptations of Chekhov's prose, in the psychologically subtle and restrained manner that is his trademark. Liubshin also directed several feature films. People's Artist of the RSFSR (1981).

See also: Basov, Vladimir; Khutsiev, Marlen; Malaia Bronnaia Theatre; Moscow Art Theatre; Sovremennik Theatre; Taganka Theatre; Thaw; theatre, Soviet

YURI ZARETSKY

Livnev, Sergei Davidovich

b. 16 April 1964, Moscow

Director, scriptwriter, producer

Livnev graduated from VGIK with degrees in cinematography and scriptwriting. In 1988, he co-authored with Sergei Solovev the screenplay for *Assa* (director Solovev, 1988). During the 1990s, he directed two films of his own: *Kiks* (1991) and *Serp i molot* (*Hammer and Sickle*, 1994). Together with Valerii Todorovskii and Igor Tolstunov, Livnev organized one of the first Russian production companies, TTL (1990). In 1995, Livnev became the head of Gorkii Studio and initiated a project to make a series of low-budget films. As part of the project, Livnev produced a thriller, *Zmeinyi istochnik* (*Snake Source*, director Nikolai Lebedev, 1997), and a crime melodrama, *Strana glukhikh* (*Land of the Deaf*, director Todorovskii, 1998).

See also: All-Russian (All-Union) State Institute of Cinematography; film studios; Solovev, Sergei; Todorovskii, Valerii

ALEXANDER PROKHOROV

Losev, Aleksei Fedorovich

b. 10 [22] September 1893, Novocherkassk; d. 23 May 1988, Moscow

Philosopher, philologist, religious thinker, publicist

A follower of Vladimir Solovev, also influenced by Ernst Cassirer and Edmund Husserl, in his youth, Losev was a Christian neo-Platonist. He was close to Pavel Florenskii, with whom he shared an interest in Orthodox mystical practices of *hesichasmus*. In 1930, Losev was deported to a labour camp to work on the White Sea Canal; he returned in 1933, his health badly damaged. In the first twenty years after leaving the camp he had no right to publish his works, but he taught Greek and Latin at Moscow Pedagogical Institute. Losev formed his philosophical doctrine as a young man, basing it on a distinctive diffusion of Orthodox theology, ancient dialectics, and mathematics, and developed it almost exclusively under the mask of ancient history and medieval philosophy and aesthetics. His only point of approximation with Marxism, which proved sufficient to save his life, was Losev's anti-liberalism. In the 1960s–80s he published a multi-volume *Istoriia antichnoi estetiki* (*History of Ancient Aesthetics*), *Estetika vozrozhdeniia* (*Aesthetics of the Renaissance*), and books on Vladimir Solovev, Richard Wagner, and mythology and symbolism. He gradually became a cult figure of the *pochvenniki* ('telluric') segment of the Soviet intelligentsia. Losev himself considered his philosophical work of the last half-century of his life to be 'introductions' to his unwritten philosophical works. His apartment and extensive library are preserved as a museum in the centre of Moscow.

See also: intelligentsia; philosophy, Soviet (Marxist-Leninist); Russian Orthodoxy; Slavophiles; White Sea Canal

GASAN GUSEJNOV

Losev, Lev Vladimirovich

(né Lifshits)

b. 15 June 1937, Leningrad

Poet, scholar

In the Soviet Union, Losev was for many years the editor of a children's journal in the USSR. Losev emigrated to the United States in 1976, received a PhD in Russian literature from the University of Michigan, and began an academic career at Dartmouth College, where he has taught since 1979. His scholarly work focuses on twentieth-century Russian poetry, especially that of his friend Iosif Brodskii. Losev himself began writing poetry seriously (and, he notes, 'unexpectedly') in 1974. Concise, subtle, and cleverly allusive, his verse has earned him Russia's Apollon Grigorev prize.

See also: awards, literary, Soviet; Brodskii, Iosif; poetry, Soviet

MICHAEL WACHTEL

Lotianu (Loteanu), Emil Vladimirovich

b. 6 November 1928, Sokiriany, Ukrainian SSR; d. 18 April 2003, Moscow

Film director

A prominent film-maker of Moldovan descent, Lotianu was educated at Moscow Art Theatre's Acting School and VGIK before working as a director at Moldovafilm and Mosfilm. He began his career with 'ethnic' cinema, drawing on Moldovan and gypsy subjects in *Lautary* (*Lautars*, 1971) and *Tabor ukhodit v nebo* (*The Gypsy Camp Vanishes into the Blue*, 1976, based on an early story by Maksim Gorkii). *Tabor* became the leading blockbuster of the year. His other most acclaimed film – *Moi laskovyi i nezhnyi zver* (*My Tender and Affectionate Animal*, 1978) – is an adaptation of Chekhov's novella *Drama na okhote* (*A Hunting Drama*). The poignant waltz from this film, written by another Moldovan, Eugene Doga, remains among the best loved melodies in the former USSR. Less of a success, Lotianu's *Anna Pavlova* (1983) is noteworthy as the first cinematic tribute to the great dancer. Spectacular and dramatic, marked for their poetic style, musicality, and celebration of feminine beauty, Lotianu's films occupy a distinct place in the culture of the period. Their director has often been dubbed the last romantic of the Soviet cinema.

See also: All-Russian (All-Union) State Institute of Cinematography; Gypsy/Roma; Moldova; Moscow Art Theatre

DAN UNGURIANU

Lotman, Iurii Mikhailovich

b. 28 February 1922, Petrograd; d. 28 October 1993, Tartu, Estonia

Literary historian and theoretician

Lotman was known as a literary historian, cultural historian, structuralist theorist, and the foremost instigator and proponent of the semiotics of culture. A co-founder of the Tartu-Moscow school of semiotics, Lotman advanced sustained theories on structural poetics *Struktura khudozhestvennogo teksta* (*The Structure of the Artistic Text*, 1970), proposed typological generalizations ('The Role of Dual Models in the Dynamics of Russian Culture' (*Rol' dualnykh modelei v dinamike russkoi kultury*), 1977), and excavated layers of Russia's literary, cultural, and intellectual history.

Most innovative were his contributions to the semiotics of culture, in which he extended the notion of text to the way in which a culture organizes its entire cultural production. With startling erudition he analysed previously unexplored facets of Russian culture, including card playing, duelling, and the theatricality of polite society, along with the interrelations among various forms of art. His thick description of aristocratic culture devoted appreciable attention to the situation of women and their contributions to culture (*Besedy o russkoi kulture* [*Conversations on Russian Culture*], 1994). Perhaps his most influential ideas concerned the interpenetration of everyday life and the arts: his biography of Aleksandr Pushkin, for example, demonstrated how the poet designed his social behaviour as a work of art (*Aleksandr Sergeevich Pushkin. Biografiia pisatelia* (*Aleksandr Sergeevich Pushkin: Biography of a Writer*), 1983).

In the 1980s, Lotman moved beyond his structuralist premises, developing a theory of culture no longer based on the distinction between code and utterance, but rather on how messages are embedded in a fluid semiotic environment from which they draw their meaning. In *Vnutri mysliashchikh mirov* (*Universe of the Mind*, 1990) and *Kultura i vzyrv* (*Culture and Explosion*, 1992), his last theoretical works, he proposed ideas on centre and periphery, discursive creativity, and cultural change.

See also: literary criticism; structuralism; Tartu-Moscow School

Further reading

Egorov, B. F. (1999) *Zhizn i tvorchestvo Iu. M. Lotmana*, Moscow: Novoe Literaturnoe Obozrenie.
Schonle, A. (ed.) (forthcoming) *Lotman and Cultural Studies: Encounters and Extensions*, Madison, WI: Wisconsin University Press.

ANDREAS SCHONLE

Lungin (Lounguine), Pavel Semenovich

b. 12 July 1949, Moscow

Film director, screenwriter

Pavel Lungin was born into the family of eminent Russian screenwriter Semen Lungin

(1920–96). Upon graduating from the Department of Applied Linguistics at Moscow State University (1971), Pavel Lungin worked as a programmer and as a section editor at *Literaturnaia gazeta*. He studied scriptwriting at VGIK and wrote his first scenario for the 1976 film *Vse delo v brate* (*It's All about the Brother*). After writing scenarios for a number of films (e.g., *Konets imperatora taigi* (*The End of the Taiga's Emperor*, 1978) and *Nepobedimyi* (*The Unconquerable*, 1983), Lungin turned to directing. He won the Best Director Prize at the Cannes Festival for his drama *Taxi-Blues* (1990). The themes of Russocentrism and anti-Semitism introduced in *Taxi-Blues* are explored in *Luna-Park* (1991) and in *Oligarkh* (*Tycoon*, 2002). Since 1992, Lungin has lived in France. He continues to make motion pictures and documentaries about Russia. With *Svadba* (*The Wedding*, 2000), a melodrama that won the prize for Best Ensemble Movie Cast at the Cannes Film Festival, Lungin has established himself as a superb master of irony and lyricism. The focus of his films is a dramatic encounter of representatives of different classes and worldviews.

See also: All-Russian (All-Union) State Institute of Cinematography; anti-Semitism; Moscow State University; nationalism ('the national question'); oligarkh

ELENA BARABAN

Luspekaev, Pavel Borisovich

b. 20 April 1927, Lugansk; d. 17 April 1970, Moscow

Ukrainian-Russian stage and screen actor

After studies at the Shchepkin Theatre School in Moscow until 1950, Luspekaev worked in theatres in Lugansk, Tbilisi, and Kiev. In 1959, Georgii Tovstonogov hired him at the Grand Dramatic Theatre (BDT) in Leningrad. The actor's legendary fame rests on a supporting role in Vladimir Motyl's cult film *Beloe solntse pustyni* (*White Sun of the Desert*, 1969), a sleeper hit about the Civil War in Central Asia. Luspekaev, already terminally ill, portrayed the melancholy yet physically stalwart loner Vereshchagin, embodying proud, stoic manliness and facing danger and death with a song on his lips: Bulat Okudzhava's *Deviat grammov serdtsa* (*Nine Grams of Heart*). Accomplished Artist of the RSFSR (1965).

See also: *Beloe solntse pustyni* (*White Sun of the Desert*); Motyl, Vladimir; Okudzhava, Bulat; Tovstonogov Bolshoi Drama Theatre; Tovstonogov, Georgii

PETER ROLLBERG

Luzhkov, Iurii Mikhailovich

b. 21 September 1936, Moscow

Politician

Luzhkov became mayor of Moscow in 1992 and won elections in 1996, 1999, and 2003, retaining his post. The populist mayor adopted many controversial policies, such as spearheading large commercial development projects and requiring city residency registration to control immigration. He harboured national political ambitions in the late 1990s, when he helped to found both the Fatherland and United Russia Parties, but his influence waned under President Vladimir Putin. He retained extensive local control, however, and oversaw the redevelopment of Moscow's urban landscape.

See also: Moscow; Putin, Vladimir; Tsereteli, Zurab; United Russia (Edinaia Rossiia); Yeltsin, Boris

BENJAMIN FOREST AND JULIET JOHNSON

M

mafia

See black market; crime; economic system, post-Soviet; krysha; New Russians; privatization; underground economy

Magadan

City and *oblast* (region) in the Russian Far East. A port on the Sea of Okhotsk, the northern city was founded in 1939 during Stalin's drive to exploit the area's rich mineral deposits, particularly gold, using prison labour. Built mainly by inmates, it was the administrative centre for the region's labour camps. After Stalin's death in 1953, most of the camps were closed, and Magadan *oblast* was established, with the City of Magadan as its administrative centre. With a population of 183,000 (2002), Magadan *oblast* occupies nearly 180,000 square miles. Its principal economic activities include mining and fishing.

See also: corrective labour institutions; Far East; natural resources; Stalin, Iosif

LAURA KLINE

Magomaev, Muslim Magometovich

b. 17 August 1942, Baku, Azerbaidhzan

Singer (baritone)

Grandson of a famous Azerbaidzhani composer, Magomaev trained at La Scala in Milan (1964,

1965) and graduated from the Baku Conservatory as a vocalist (1968). His success and variety made him a superstar and idol for several generations, which impeded his operatic development, though his concerts combine a diversity of genres, including operatic arias. Laureate of numerous festivals and competitions, Magomaev received a Golden Disk at the MIDEM awards in Cannes (1969, 1970), and frequently appears on television and radio. People's Artist of the USSR (1973).

See also: Azerbaidzhan; popular music, Soviet

YURI ZARETSKY

Maiak

One of the most popular informational and music radio stations in the USSR and Russia, Maiak was established on 1 August 1964 as 'our answer to western voices' (Aleksandr Iakovlev, chair of propaganda department of the Communist Party Central Committee). The new radio station followed a format that pleased listeners and later would be adopted by many radio stations in the post-Soviet era: it featured five minutes of news and 25 minutes of contemporary music. As a product of the Thaw, Maiak attracted many talented, liberal-minded journalists and writers, musicians and artists. It was allowed to broadcast Western news and was therefore considered *bresh v zheleznom zanavese* (*a hole in the Iron Curtain*). Today Maiak works in long and medium waves, and in FM. It broadcasts throughout Russia and the CIS, and remains a popular state-owned station without advertisements, respected for its news, musical, and analytical programmes, as well as its excellent talk shows.

See also: journalism; journalists, post-Soviet; radio, post-Soviet; radio, Soviet

NADEZHDA AZHGIKHINA

Maiakovskii Theatre

Founded in 1922 as the Theatre of the Revolution under the direction of Vsevolod Meierkhold and renamed the Moscow Theatre of Drama in 1943, it acquired its present name in 1954. Its most illustrious leaders aside from Meierkhold have been Aleksei Popov (1930–35), who specialized in plays by Nikolai Pogodin; Nikolai Okhlopkov (1943–67), a pupil of Meierkhold whose work was characterized by grand-scale, civic themes; and Andrei Goncharov (1967–2001), famed for his highly theatrical, epic style. The great actress Mariia Babanova worked here after leaving Meierkhold in 1927, setting a precedent for consistently high-quality acting, a tradition continued by Natalia Gundareva, Armen Dzhigarkhanian, and others. Sergei Artsybashev was appointed artistic director in 2001.

See also: theatre, Soviet; theatre, post-Soviet

JOHN FREEDMAN

Makanin, Vladimir Semnovich

b. 13 March 1937, Orsk

Writer

Winner of the State Prize for Literature in 2000, Makanin is a philosophically-oriented prose writer lionized by intellectuals. A mathematician who turned to literature during the final years of Khrushchev's Thaw, Makanin debuted with the novel *Priamaia liniia* (*The Straight Line*) in 1967. This work attracted critical attention, though as its sceptical, introspective, apolitical bent fell from favour, leading literary journals rejected his works for years. When the political climate

mellowed in the 1980s, Makanin's short works on timely topics, such as faith-healing in *Predtecha* (*The Forerunner*) and social psychology in *Antilider* (*The Anti-Leader*), drew a sufficiently high readership to warrant regular publication of his works in mainstream publications. Especially notable for their mixture of innovative narrative technique with philosophical issues are Makanin's glasnost-period novellas *Otstavshii* (*Left Behind*), *Utrata* (*The Loss*), and *Laz* (*Escape Hatch*). Critical consensus deems his novel *Andegraund, ili geroi nashego vremeni* (*Underground, or a Hero of Our Time*, 1998) a major work of post-Soviet literature and the culmination of Makanin's œuvre.

See also: literature, perestroika; literature, Soviet; literature, Stagnation; literature, Thaw

BYRON LINDSEY

Makarevich, Andrei Vadimovich

b. 11 December 1953, Moscow

Musician, composer, singer, artist

A graduate of the Moscow Architectural Institute, in 1969, Makarevich founded one of the first, most popular, and long-lasting Russian rock groups, Mashina vremeni (Time Machine). In the 1980s, he began to release solo albums. Makarevich's graphic works are on show at the Central House of Arts in Moscow and have been exhibited abroad. People's Artist of Russia (1998).

See also: Mashina vremeni; rock music

IRINA UDIANSKAYA

Makarova, Tamara Fedorovna

b. 13 August 1907, St. Petersburg; d. 19 January 1997, Moscow

Film actress

Makarova studied with theatre avant-gardist Nikolai Foregger (1892–1939). Following her marriage to director Sergei Gerasimov (1928), for half a century Makarova played both female leads and important supporting roles in his films. She was especially impressive in the Arctic saga *Semero smelykh* (*The Bold Seven*, 1936), the rural pedagogical romance *Uchitel* (*The Teacher*, 1939), and the family drama *Dochki-materi* (*Daughters and Mothers*, 1975). Makarova's screen persona defined the ideal of the modern Soviet woman: matter-of-fact, intelligent, strong-willed, professionally ambitious, socially active, and occasionally sensitive but unsentimental. Her last role was a cliché-defying, sympathetic impersonation of Sofia Andreevna Tolstaia in the biopic *Lev Tolstoi* (1984). People's Artist of the USSR (1950).

See also: Gerasimov, Sergei

PETER ROLLBERG

Makovetskii, Sergei Vasilevich

b. 13 June 1958, Kiev

Actor

Makovetskii has been one of Russia's most versatile and visible actors since the early 1990s, when he drew raves for his performance in the title role in Vladimir Khotinenko's film *Makarov*. Although he has played romantic leads, he is better known as a character actor. He has created several memorable villains in films including Aleksei Balabanov's films *Pro urodov i liudei* (*Of Freaks and Men*) and *Brat-2* (*Brother 2*). In addition to his film work, Makovetskii is a prolific stage actor, having appeared in productions by such directors as Roman Viktiuk and Kamo Ginkas.

See also: Balabanov, Aleksei Oktiabrinovich; Ginkas, Kama; Khotinenko, Vladimir; Viktiuk, Roman

SETH GRAHAM

Maksimov, Vladimir Emelianovich

(né Lev Alekseevich Samsonov)

b. 27 November 1930, Moscow;
d. 26 March 1995, Paris

Writer

Maksimov, whose father was arrested when the boy was 3, spent years in orphanages and

institutions for juvenile delinquents. His novel *Sem dnei tvoreniia* (*The Seven Days of Creation*, 1971) presented such a gritty, disillusioned depiction of Soviet reality that it was rejected by censors and could only appear in *samizdat* and in the West. Repeatedly harassed and incarcerated in mental clinics, Maksimov received permission to leave the USSR in February 1974. He settled in Paris, where he published autobiographical and historical prose and plays and worked as editor-in-chief of the influential quarterly *Kontinent* from its inception (1974) until 1992. During the last years of his life, Maksimov revised some of his staunchly anti-Communist views.

See also: censorship; literature, émigré; samizdat

PETER ROLLBERG

Malaia Bronnaia Theatre (Teatr na Maloi Bronnoi)

Founded in 1946, it now occupies the building on Malaia Bronnaia Street where Solomon Mikhoels's Moscow State Jewish Theatre was located from 1922 to its forced closing in 1948. Led by Andrei Goncharov from 1957–66, the Malaia Bronnaia successfully featured contemporary Soviet and western plays. Anatolii Efros was a staff director from 1967–84, staging several of that era's significant productions of new plays and classics. Sergei Zhenovach (1996–98) and Andrei Zhitinkin (2001–3) had noteworthy tenures as chief director. But Efros, Zhenovach, and Zhitinkin were all fired, fuelling the theatre's reputation as an ill-fated playhouse. In the 1990s and 2000s, the leading actor Lev Durov has also served as chief director.

See also: theatre, post-Soviet; theatre, Soviet

JOHN FREEDMAN

Malyi Theatre

Founded in 1824, but tracing its roots to a Moscow University troupe established in 1756, the Malyi, or small theatre (as opposed to the Bolshoi, or big theatre), is rivalled only by St. Petersburg's Aleksandrinskii as Russia's most storied. In the nineteenth century its reputation as a house of great actors originated with Pavel Mochalov and Mikhail Shchepkin, while its productions of Aleksandr Ostrovskii's plays made an incalculable contribution to Russian drama. After the October Revolution in 1917, the Malyi struggled to redefine itself, eventually becoming the custodian of tradition, a role maintained by Iurii Solomin, who became artistic director in 1988. Some of the great Russian actors of the twentieth century worked at the Malyi, including Igor Ilinskii, Mikhail Tsarev, and Boris Babochkin.

See also: Babochkin, Boris; Bolshoi Theatre; Ilinskii, Igor; Solomin, Iurii

JOHN FREEDMAN

Mamaev Kurgan

Mamaev Kurgan, a hill overlooking Volgograd (formerly Stalingrad), saw fierce combat during the Battle of Stalingrad in 1942–43. In 1967, a large memorial complex commemorating the Soviet struggle against the Nazi invasion opened on the hill. The site features 'Motherland', the largest free-standing statue in the world, designed by Evgenii Vuchetich. It also includes 'the Square of Sorrow' (a mother grieving over a dead soldier), the 'Ruined Walls' (figures carved into replicas of destroyed building), and the nude half-figure 'Fight to the Death' (a soldier with a gun and grenade). The oversized, emotionally powerful monuments glorify the Soviet Union as much as they memorialize the dead.

See also: monuments, Soviet; World War II (Great Patriotic War)

BENJAMIN FOREST AND JULIET JOHNSON

Mamardashvili, Merab Konstantinovich

b. 9 September 1930, Gori (Georgia);
d. 25 November 1990, Moscow

Philosopher and cult figure.

Mamardashvili did not leave many written texts, and the books published after his death were mostly based on transcripts of his public lectures (on Descartes, Kant, and Marcel Proust, among other subjects). In 1955, he graduated from the Department of Philosophy of Moscow State University and in 1970 received a PhD in philosophy from Tbilisi State University (Georgia). He worked as deputy editor-in-chief of the journal *Voprosy filosofii* (Questions of Philosophy) in Moscow (1968–74). In May 2001, a monument to him was unveiled in Tbilisi.

See also: Moscow State University

VLADIMIR PAPERNY

Mamin, Iurii Borisovich

b. 8 May 1946, Leningrad

Film and television director

Having begun his career as a theatre director, since 1976 Mamin has been working at the Lenfilm studio. Though a student of Eldar Riazanov, Mamin approaches comedy differently. His most popular films, in the genre of social satire, came out during perestroika and the early 1990s: *Prazdnik Neptuna* (*Neptune's Feast*, 1986), *Fontan* (*The Fountain*, 1988), *Bakenbardy* (*Sideburns*, 1990), *Okno v Parizh* (*Window to Paris*, 1993). They are all extended anecdotes raised to the level of myths and address issues of Russian identity. Mamin's recent television series, *Russkie strashilki* (*Russian Scary Stories*, 2001), is a parody of the *X-Files*.

See also: film studios; Riazanov, Eldar; television, post-Soviet; television serials

ELENA PROKHOROVA

Mamleev, Iurii Vitalievich

b. 11 December 1931, Moscow

Writer

Author of novels, short stories, and philosophical essays whose works circulated through *samizdat* and audio recordings since the 1960s.

After his emigration to the United States in 1975, Mamleev taught at Cornell University and achieved considerable notoriety through publications in Russian and other European languages. In 1983, Mamleev moved to Paris, and in the early 1990s he returned to Moscow. His fiction is a surreal blend of a metaphysical quest with violence, absurd imagery, and revolting physiological details. The characters are monsters in semi-human disguise, whose simultaneous fear of and fascination with death, combined with solipsism, extreme narcissism, and a lack of any conventional religious or moral sentiment, often lead them to assert their god-like status through gruesome murders, sexual perversion, and necrophilia. Mamleev paints a pervasively negative picture of mankind, since the exclusive focus of his artistic representation and, presumably, the underlying philosophical reflection are on the most destructive and cruel drives, normally relegated to the depths of the subconscious. His narrative persona remains a neutral observer and a matter-of-fact reporter of events. In his philosophical tracts, Mamleev has articulated the so-called 'I-religion', according to which an individual's faith, love and worship are directed solely at his own immortal Personal I.

See also: literature, émigré; samizdat

MARIA RUBINS

Mamonov, Petr Nikolaevich

b. 14 April 1951, Moscow

Musician, songwriter, actor

Mamonov is best known for his highly eccentric lyrics and performance style as the vocalist and songwriter of the legendary avant-garde rock band Zvuki Mu (Moo Sounds) from 1984 to 1990 and the duo Mamonov and Aleksei since 1991. During perestroika, Zvuki Mu collaborated with the British record producer Brian Eno, who called Mamonov a 'poet'. Mamonov has also appeared in several films, including Rashid Nugmanov's *Igla* (*The Needle*) and *Taksi-bliuz* (*Taxi Blues*) by Pavel Loungine

[Lungin], and has written and acted in plays and performance-art pieces in Moscow.

See also: rock music

SETH GRAHAM

Mandelshtam, Nadezhda Iakovlevna

b. 30 October 1899, Saratov; d. 29 December 1980, Moscow

Writer

The best-known and most eloquent 'widow of Russia', a survivor of Stalinism who preserved the work and biography of her husband, the great poet Osip Mandelshtam, Nadezhda Mandelshtam is also read as an astute, provocative commentator on the Soviet era. Born into an educated assimilated Jewish family in Kiev, Mandelshtam initially trained as a theatrical designer in the studio of Aleksandra Ekster. Her subsequent marriage to and nomadic life with Osip, from 1919 until his second arrest and disappearance in 1938, perforce rendered her his secretary and caretaker. After his death, she subsisted as an English teacher and earned her doctorate in linguistics, but primarily devoted herself to memorizing and so archiving her husband's poetry.

The Thaw enabled Mandelshtam's publishing efforts, which ranged from collaborating on a first edition of her husband's works to producing a steady series of ever more provocative memoirs and reflections, three of which were printed in her lifetime (*Vospominaniia* [*Hope Against Hope*], *Mozart i Salieri*, *Vtoraia kniga* [*Hope Abandoned*]). Her first volume of memoirs moved readers with its sharp-tongued narration, trenchant analysis, and dramatic portrait of Osip's martyrdom. Her second volume's more fulsome 'settling of accounts' either awed or outraged readers, who correctly perceived that Mandelshtam had exceeded her role as keeper of her husband's flame.

Further reading

Brodsky, J. (1986) 'Nadezhda Mandelstam (1899–1980): An Obituary', in *Less Than One:*

Selected Essays, New York: Farrar Straus Giroux.

Holmgren, B. (1993) *Women's Works in Stalin's Time: On Lidia Chukovskaia and Nadezhda Mandelstam*, Bloomington, IN: Indiana University Press.

Proffer, C. (1987) 'Nadezhda Mandelstam', in *The Widows of Russia and Other Writings*, Ann Arbor, MI: Ardis.

BETH HOLMGREN

Manezh

The Manezh (Manège), a venerable Moscow landmark that functions as the city's premier exhibition hall, was erected (1817) to house the Imperial Cavalry Riding School and provide a venue for military reviews and festive infantry and equestrian manoeuvres. Commissioned by Alexander I to commemorate the fifth anniversary of Russia's victory over Napoleon, the building was designed by architect Osip Bové and others. It featured a remarkable gabled wood-truss suspension roof designed by French engineer Augustin Bétancourt to span a vast 150ft-wide interior without the use of any intermediate columns. The hall, considered the largest uncolumned interior space in the world, could hold a regiment of 2,000 in addition to visitors and audiences. After 1831, the Manezh was utilized as a concert and presentation hall. In 1867, Hector Berlioz and Nikolai Rubinstein performed there before an audience of 12,000. After the October Revolution, the building was appropriated for use as a Kremlin garage, continuing in that function until 1957, when it became, and remains, the Central Exhibition Hall.

In March 2004, the Manezh was gutted by a fire that destroyed the Bétancourt roof while leaving the massive masonry walls intact. Amidst considerable controversy, Moscow Mayor Iurii Luzhkov relented to calls for restoration, and the refurbished building was completed in a little over a year. The result of raising the roof of the renovated building some 31 inches to accommodate a new roof distorted the building's proportions.

Some years earlier, the underground 'Manezh Mall' (1992–97), the work of sculptor Zurab Tsereteli, was erected in front of the Manezh alongside the Aleksandr Garden and the Kremlin's north-west wall. Conceived as a showpiece of Mayor Luzhkov's ambitious 'grand projects' to de-communize and de-russify the capital in time for its 850th anniversary, the controversial project reduced a complex aimed at evoking the city's ancient bazaars, with their agglomeration of shops, kiosks, and vendor stalls, to a garish extravaganza.

See also: architecture, Soviet and post-Soviet; art galleries and exhibition halls; Luzhkov, Iurii; Moscow; Tsereteli, Zurab

ANATOLE SENKEVITCH

Manezh exhibition of 1962

The former tsarist riding school or Manège (1817–25, designed by Bétancourt and Bové) served as the Moscow Central Exhibition Hall from 1957 until March 2004, when it was destroyed by fire. It was the venue for a number of key exhibitions in the Thaw, notably '30 Years of the Moscow Artists' Union' (1962–63), the scandal which became known as the Manezh Affair. This exhibition, the culmination of artistic de-Stalinization, presented a revisionist survey of Moscow art since the 1920s; it rehabilitated tendencies suppressed under Stalin alongside controversial young artists such as Pavel Nikonov. It was not, as often erroneously described, an exhibition of abstract art, but, on the eve of Khrushchev's official visit, abstract and experimental works by the studio of Elii Beliutin were added to it on a separate floor and removed soon after. Khrushchev's outrage was followed by a series of meetings between party leaders and creative intelligentsia that reasserted the party's ideological control over the arts.

See also: art, abstract; art, Soviet; Beliutin, Elii; Krushchev, Nikita; Manezh; Nikonov, Pavel; Thaw

SUSAN E. REID

Mari

The Mari (meaning 'person', 'man', or 'husband') are an ethnic group (population 644,000) mainly living in the Republic of Mari-El (so named in 1992), located between the Volga River and the Urals, with Ioshkar-Ola as its capital. The Mari population not living in Mari-El is dispersed in the Urals and the Volga Region (Povolzhe). They speak two dialects of the Mari language – which belongs to the Finno-Ugric group and uses the Cyrillic alphabet. *Cheremisy* (the ancient name for Mari) were first mentioned in Russian chronicles in the tenth century. Before incorporation into Russia in the 1550s, Mari territory was the arena of severe struggle between the West and the East, Christianity and Islam. Among religious Mari, Orthodox Christianity predominates, despite many adherents of pagan *Chimarii* belief. Mari's traditional occupation is farming.

See also: ethnic minorities; Finno-Ugric; Russian Orthodoxy; Urals; Volga region

TATYANA LEDENEVA

Mariinskii Theatre

During the Soviet period, the Mariinskii Theatre (known as the Kirov Theatre until 1991) was obliged to yield its Imperial reputation as Russia's leading opera and ballet company to Moscow's Bolshoi Theatre. Since the collapse of the Soviet Union, however, it has regained its status as one of the world's leading houses. The Mariinskii's current house dates from 1860. (The company was originally founded in 1783.) An international competition to build a more up-to-date second stage was announced in 2003.

Although the theatre's operatic repertoire in the 1920s had been strikingly radical (with notable productions of works by Schreker, Prokofiev, and Berg), artistic policy throughout most of the Soviet period was conservative, in terms of both repertoire and production style. Hence, the Kirov staged Petrov's operatic pageant *Petr Pervyi* (*Peter the First*, 1975) and his *Maiakovskii nachinaetsia* (*Maiakovskii Begins*, 1983), whereas Leningrad premieres of operas by

Slonimskii, the city's licensed modernist, took place at the more experimental Malyi ('Small') Opera Theatre. During the Thaw, ballet briefly flourished at the Kirov, where Iurii Grigorovich started his career and produced Prokofiev's *Skaz o kamennom tsvetke* (*The Tale of the Stone Flower*, 1957). An equally memorable Khrushchev-era production was Igor Belskii's version of Petrov's *Bereg nadezhdy* (*The Coast of Hope*, 1959). However, with the defection of Rudolf Nureyev in 1961 and Grigorovich's departure for the Bolshoi, the company began to stagnate. The theatre often struggled to retain its most gifted singers, many of whom gravitated towards the Bolshoi; and dancers Natalia Makarova and Mikhail Baryshnikov followed Nureyev into emigration. A degree of stability was guaranteed by the tenure of Iurii Temirkanov as principal conductor between 1976 and 1988, with Oleg Vinogradov running the ballet between 1977 and 1995.

The theatre's single most influential figure, however, is Valerii Gergiev, who has presided over the company's renaissance since taking over as music director in 1988 and as general director in 1996. The Russian operatic repertoire has been expanded and invigorated, and steps have been taken to develop the Italian repertoire. Most striking of all has been the theatre's commitment to Wagner; between 2000 and 2002 the four evenings of his Ring cycle were performed for the first time since the early 1930s. An academy for young singers, directed by Larisa Gergieva, has also been established, providing the company with a seemingly endless source of impressive voices. The ballet of the Mariinskii Theatre is in equally fine form, with Uliana Lopatkina and Igor Zelenskii leading a distinguished field. As in the Soviet period, dance productions are notable for their poise, elegance, and restraint, particularly in recreations of nineteenth-century classics and the repertoire of the *Ballets Russes*; this revival has led some critics to call the company a 'choreographic museum'. The Mariinskii Theatre has developed a huge international profile through recordings, sponsorship deals, foreign tours, co-productions with London's Royal Opera House and New York's Metropolitan Opera, and collaborations with international directors and choreographers.

See also: ballet dancers, Mariinskii Theatre; Baryshnikov, Mikhail; Bolshoi Theatre; Gergiev, Valerii; Grigorovich, Iurii; Nureyev (Nureev), Rudolf; opera singers, Mariinskii Theatre; Temirkanov, Iurii

Further reading

Ardoin, J. (2001) *Valery Gergiev and the Kirov: A Story of Survival*, Portland, OR: Amadeus Press.

Kovnatskaya, L. (2001) 'St. Petersburg', in S. Sadie and J. Tyrell (eds.) *The New Grove Dictionary of Music and Musicians*, 2nd edn, London: Grove.

Taruskin, R. (1992) 'St. Petersburg', in S. Sadie (ed.) *The New Grove Dictionary of Opera*, London: Macmillan.

PHILIP ROSS BULLOCK

Marinina, Aleksandra

(née Marina Anatolevna Alekseeva)

b. 16 June 1957, Lviv, Ukraine

Detective writer

The author of mystery novels extraordinarily popular with Russian readers, Marinina grew up in Leningrad and in 1971 moved to Moscow. She began writing mysteries in 1992; by the second half of the 1990s, she dominated the bestseller lists, and in 1998, was named Russian writer of the year. After a twenty-year career in the police force, Marinina resigned with the rank of lieutenant colonel (1998) to pursue her literary vocation. Heir to the tradition of classical European mysteries, and frequently compared to Agatha Christie, Marinina presents a crime primarily as a logical puzzle. Her central protagonist is the gifted female detective Anastasiia Kamenskaia, who works at the headquarters of the Moscow Department of Criminal Investigations. Kamenskaia resembles the woman next door in everything except her phenomenal deductive abilities. *Kamenskaia*, the television series produced by Valerii Todorovskii, premiered in 2000 and further popularized this logical prodigy. By unravelling the most intricate of crimes, Marinina's heroine

inspires hope in the victory of justice and stability in Russia.

See also: detective fiction; television, post-Soviet; television serials; Todorovskii, Valerii

Further reading

Nepomnyashchy, C. (1999) 'Markets, Mirrors, and Mayhem: Alexandra Marinina and the Rise of the New Russian *Detektiv*', in A. Barker (ed.) *Consuming Russia*, Durham, NC: Duke University Press.

ELENA BARABAN

market (rynok)

The market (*rynok*) is a part of most Russians' shopping routine. All major and medium-sized cities feature a market building; Moscow has about ten such buildings. Each market building is surrounded by outdoor booths, and there are additional outdoor markets in all cities.

Markets feature fresh food from Russia, the Caucasus, and Central Asia, as well as many packaged grocery items sold in specialized booths: there may be one or more booths for bread, tea, dry goods, and so forth. Many food markets also sell flowers. Because of anti-Caucasian sentiment, often Russian women are employed to sell produce for Caucasian tradesmen.

In addition to food markets, there are specialized, usually outdoor, markets for such items as household goods (*bytovye tovary*), electronics, books (new and used), CDs (usually pirated), clothes, souvenirs, and car parts. Some markets have mixed offerings, for example, both food and clothes.

Market vendors are required to carry a licence issued by the city; however, most markets feature informal, unlicensed trade that is pursued by the authorities.

Market prices vary widely: some items are more expensive at markets, such as produce; some are less, such as some clothing and household items. Items sold inside the market building are usually more expensive than those sold outside.

See also: Caucasus; Central Asia; nationalism ('the national question')

KAREN EVANS-ROMAINE

Marriage Bureau

See Registration of Civil States (ZAGS)

Marxism

See philosophy, Soviet (Marxist-Leninist)

Mashina vremeni (Time Machine)

Rock group

One of the first rock groups to emerge in the USSR, Mashina vremeni, with its ever-evolving style and membership, has exerted a significant influence on generations of rock musicians. The band's name has proven a fitting description for the longest-lasting Russian rock ensemble, often called the 'Russian Beatles'. Formed in 1968 by guitarist Andrei Makarevich in Moscow, the group has released numerous albums, including such collections as *Eto bylo tak davno* (That Was So Long Ago), *Reki i mosty* (Rivers and Bridges), and *Malenkii prints* (The Little Prince).

See also: Makarevich, Andrei; rock music

TIMOTHY M. SCHLAK

Mashkov, Vladimir Lvovich

b. 27 November 1963, Novokuznetsk

Actor, film director, producer, screenwriter

Mashkov achieved his film breakthrough as the murderous seducer Sergei in Valerii Todorovskii's *Katia Izmailova* (1994). As the rough and ready Tolian in Pavel Chukhrai's *Vor* (The Thief, 1997), he cemented his reputation as one of Russian cinema's most bankable stars. In Alek-

sandr Proshkin's *Russkii bunt* (The Russian Rebellion, 1999) and Pavel Lungin's *Oligarkh* (The Tycoon, 2003), he took the leading role of a charismatic leader of men. He has appeared in international films, such as Michael Radford's *Dancing at the Blue Iguana* (2000) and John Moore's *Behind Enemy Lines* (2001). He also wrote, produced and directed *Sirota kazanskaia* (The Sympathy Seeker, 1997) and *Papa* (2005).

See also: Chukhrai, Pavel; Lungin, Pavel; Proshkin, Aleksandr; Todorovskii, Valerii

DAVID GILLESPIE

Masiania

'Masiania' is a cyber project created by Oleg Kuvaev, a St. Petersburg-based new media artist, and launched in 2001 in association with 'mult.ru' flash animation art studio. Clips first distributed on the Internet aired on NTV in 2002. Masiania (derivative of 'Maria') is the heroine of this series of clips, which many perceive as a critique of contemporary Russian culture. Masiania's image, sardonic humour, and flamboyant lifestyle challenge traditional notions of gender, nation, and class.

See also: Internet, Russian; NTV

VLADIMIR STRUKOV

Maslenitsa

'Butter week' (*maslo* means butter), a once pagan celebration to end the winter that was Christianized into the last celebration before the start of Lent. Also called *syrnaia* (cheese), *shirokaia* (lavish) or *razgulnaia* (celebratory) week. In the pre-Revolutionary period, each day of the week had a special name and tradition associated with it. During the entire week, fairs appeared in town squares with puppet shows, ritualized fist-fights, sleigh rides, and bawdy minstrel shows; such celebrations were immortalized in Igor Stravinskii's 1911 ballet *Petrushka*, named for the hero of a puppet show. The tradition of eating *bliny* remained throughout the Soviet period. In the post-Soviet period, *Maslenitsa* fairs have reappeared in cities, sponsored by city authorities and supported by the Church.

See also: bliny; holidays, Russian Orthodox; Lent; Russian Orthodoxy; Stravinskii, Igor

MICHELE BERDY

Master i Margarita (*The Master and Margarita*)

Master i Margarita, written by Mikhail Bulgakov between 1928 and 1940, created an immediate sensation when published in 1966–67, owing to its rollicking humour, unusual form, and bold treatment of taboo issues. A complex work, it combines fantastic satire, connected to the devil's visit to Moscow; a romantic, lyrical story about a persecuted literary Master and his beloved, Margarita; and excerpts from the Master's historical novel about Pontius Pilate.

The novel has a cult following in both popular and high culture in Russia, and especially Moscow. Many of its phrases have entered everyday speech, numerous stage and film adaptations have appeared, yearly festivals are held at one of its locales, a museum has opened in another, and restaurants and cafés bear the names of its characters. The novel's unorthodoxy instantly ignited heated polemics among critics, and fundamental disagreements in interpretation persist, but *Master i Margarita* is now generally recognized as a modern classic.

Further reading

Barratt, A. (1987) *Between Two Worlds: A Critical Introduction to The Master and Margarita*, Oxford: Oxford University Press.

Haber, E. (1975) 'The Mythic Structure of Bulgakov's *The Master and Margarita*', *Russian Review*, 34, 4: 382–409.

Weeks, L. (ed.) (1996) *The Master and Margarita: A Critical Companion*, Evanston, IL: Northwestern University Press.

EDYTHE C. HABER

Masterkova, Lidiia Alekseevna

b. 8 March 1927, Moscow

Artist

Masterkova studied at the Moscow Art School and Moscow State Art College. A dedicated abstractionist, she was associated with the Lianozovo Circle and during the 1960s and early 1970s was one of the significant personalities in the Moscow art world. While her work in the early 1960s included loosely painted watercolours in bright colours, she soon darkened her palette and began to incorporate lace and fabric into her compositions. In the mid-1960s, she opted for abstract compositions created with a palette knife in which dark forms contrasted with a light background. By the early 1970s, these dark forms were still in evidence, but superimposed by collages of white circles bearing the Kabalistic numerals 0, 1, and 9 or by manipulation of India ink or watercolour on wet paper. She exhibited in the first shows of nonconformist art, including the Bulldozer Exhibition of 1974. She emigrated in 1975, and now lives and works in Saint-Laurent-sur-Othain, France.

See also: art, nonconformist; art, Soviet; Bulldozer Exhibition; Lianozovo School

NATALIA KOLODZEI

mat

The lowest register of Russian language, *mat* is previously unprintable profanity, the negative oral counterpart to the sacred written word. Based on core roots referring to sexual organs and copulation (reflected in *ebat/sia*, *khui*, *pizda*), plus two or three other obscene roots (in *bliad*, *mudi*, *manda*), *mat* is a complicated linguistic system all Russians know, and many use, but until recently no one publicly acknowledged. Writer Victor Erofeev calls *mat* 'the GULag of Russian linguistics'. Related to criminal argot and youth slang, Peter the Great's legendary 'minor' (37 words) and 'great' (260 words) improvisations in *mat* testify to this oral art form's use at all social levels.

Uncensored bawdy poetry by the likes of Ivan Barkov and Aleksandr Pushkin gave *mat* a shadowy literary life. In the post-Stalin era, Soviet writers employed *mat* widely to challenge linguistic taboos. While Aleksandr Solzhenitsyn's Ivan Denisovich introduced Soviet readers to thinly veiled profanity in camp jargon, characters such as Iuz Aleshkovskii's Nikolai Nikolaevich exuberantly asserted *mat*'s place in written works via *samizdat*. By the 1990s, literary and scholarly works on *mat* were readily available.

Further reading

Erofeyev, V. (2003) 'Dirty Words', trans. A. Bromfield, *New Yorker*, 15 September.

Uspenskii, B. (1996) 'Mifologicheskii aspekt russkoi ekspressivnoi frazeologii' (1981), in N. Bogomolov (ed.) *Anti-mir russkoi kultury: Iazyk. Folklor. Literatura*, Moscow: Ladomir, 9–107.

ANN KOMAROMI

Matveeva, Bella Petrovna

b. 1961, Troitsk, Cheliabinsk region

Artist

A member of Timur Novikov's New Academy of Fine Arts in St. Petersburg, Matveeva is dedicated to a decorative naturalism focused on the human body, which she depicts in paintings and other media as a highly sexualized aesthetic object. Her lush works are influenced by the patterns and sinuous line of Art Nouveau. Classical elements in her work reflect the New Academy's aesthetic interests, suggesting a nostalgia for the aristocratic 'decadence' of Russia's Silver Age.

See also: Novikov, Timur

KIRSTEN M. HARKNESS

Matveeva, Novella Nikolaevna

b. 7 November 1934, Pushkin, Leningrad region

Poet, bard singer

Matveeva was born into a family of poets; one of her more famous relatives was her uncle Ivan Elagin, an émigré poet in the United States. Her fascination with freedom-loving wanderers, sailors, and gypsies coincided with the spirit of the Thaw generation, assuring her poetry great popularity in the 1960s. One of the first poets who became a bard, in 1966 she released her first album, *Pesni* (Songs), which captured her performance of her own poems/songs as she accompanied herself on guitar. Her lyrics combine simplicity, philosophical depth, and musicality. The author of many verse translations and children's poems, Matveeva lives in Moscow.

See also: bards; sixties generation; Thaw

TATIANA SMORODINSKAYA

Mazurok, Iurii Antonovich

b. 18 July 1931, Kraśnik, Poland

Opera singer

After studying at Moscow Conservatory, Polish baritone Mazurok, who grew up in Ukraine, soon won prizes at competitions in Prague (1960), Bucharest (1961), Moscow (1962) and Montreal (1967). In 1963, he joined the Bolshoi Theatre, where later he became a soloist. His high, lyric baritone, attentiveness to the text, and restrained, almost aristocratic demeanour made him a leading exponent of roles such as Onegin in Tchaikovsky's *Evgenii Onegin* and Prince Andrei in Prokofiev's *Voina i mir* (*War and Peace*). His performance (alongside Elena Obraztsova and Placido Domingo) in Franco Zeffirelli's 1978 Vienna production of Bizet's *Carmen* was just one of many international appearances. People's Artist of the USSR (1976).

See also: Bolshoi Theatre; Moscow Conservatory; opera singers, Bolshoi Theatre; opera, Soviet

PHILIP ROSS BULLOCK

meat dishes

In traditional Russian cuisine that evolved from peasant fare, meat entrées are less complex than salads and soups. Before the Revolution, peasant and low-income families consumed organ meats (liver, heart, kidneys). Game (wild boar, venison, bear) and wild poultry (duck, goose, wood grouse, pheasant) were on both peasant and gentry tables. Traditionally, game and poultry are cooked or served with fresh and dried fruit and berries. Red meats are typically well cooked; only in the post-Soviet period has rare meat been served. Chicken is traditionally fried or stewed; during the Soviet period, the Georgian dish chicken *tabaka* became widespread in restaurants.

Traditionally, beef is stewed with potatoes, onions, and carrots in a dish called *zharkoe*; red meats are also fried or baked, often with onions, potatoes, cheese, sour cream, or mayonnaise. Minced meat dishes are common, including *kotlety*, *pelmeni*, *golubtsy* (cabbage stuffed with meat and rice), and *farshirovannye ovoshchi* (stuffed vegetables).

Given the expense of meat and the difficulty of preserving it, in Russian cuisine pork is cured and smoked or made into *kolbasa* (any variety of minced meat mixed with fillers, garlic, and spices; stuffed into casings; and smoked, cured, or fried). *Kolbasa* also refers to processed meats, such as *doktorskaia kolbasa* (similar to baloney), which were staples during the Soviet period, as were *sosiski* (frankfurters) and *sardelki* (weiners).

Plov, pilaf from Central Asia, and *shashlyk* from Caucasian cuisine are now a basic part of Russian fare.

French cuisine influenced the Russian table at court and among the gentry, introducing rich cream and wine sauces. In the post-Soviet period, there has been a revival of traditional Russian meat recipes, particularly of game and wild poultry.

See also: appetizers; Asian cuisine; Caucasian cuisine; dining, Russian; dining, Soviet; kholodets; kotlety; pelmeni; salads; soups; tabaka

MICHELE BERDY

medical system

Famous for its public health accomplishments and promise of universal coverage, including exceptionally high vaccination rates, the Soviet healthcare system was underfunded and inefficient at providing medical care, except for high-level functionaries and those able to provide hard currency. Alongside the official system existed another system, in which doctors provided higher levels of care or special services in exchange for gifts (particularly cognac, chocolate or other hard currency items) or additional payments, an economic necessity for many cash-strapped but hard-working physicians.

Owing to underfunding, scientific isolation, and an institutional distrust of Western biomedical developments (particularly Lysenko's rejection of biostatistics, the cornerstone of Western clinical medicine), the medical system had fallen significantly behind Western standards by the 1960s, just as medicine began to demonstrate sustained improvement elsewhere. This was not true of the upper-echelon hospitals, which provided European-level care. The low quality did not go uncommented by the masses, but medicine could not compete with military spending during the Cold War arms race. One punning proverb expresses the frustration with the Soviet model of socialized medicine: '*Darom lechitsia – lechitsia darom*', 'Treatment for free is treatment in vain'.

Primary care was provided in polyclinics (health centres based on geography or workplace), with sicker patients referred to hospitals for more specialized care. A given primary care physician covered a given geographical area (in urban areas, a few city blocks); patients did not choose their doctor. The medical system was overstaffed with undertrained physicians, yielding a high per capita density of physicians and the use of physicians in settings where auxiliary medical personnel are used in the US (e.g., ambulances). This surplus also allowed easier access to physicians, in terms of immediate appointments and even house calls, a luxury of which Soviet citizens were sometimes remarkably proud. Physician supply was further extended by the *feldsher*, a healthcare worker analogous to a nurse practitioner or physician's assistant.

When hospitalization was required, certain types of patients were clustered at particular institutions, and infected patients were quarantined in infectious disease dispensaries. The admitting ward (*priemnyi pokoi*) served as the location for acute evaluation in Soviet and Russian hospitals. There, patients would be evaluated by the physician on call (*dezhurnyi*) and triaged to the appropriate subspecialist. Hospitals had substantial excess bed capacity, making prolonged hospital stays both possible and expected.

In distinction to the West, particularly the US, where women were historically denied access to the prestigious medical profession, Soviet medicine was feminized. Though this ostensibly reflected the egalitarian ideals of Soviet society, medicine was a less prestigious discipline, more akin to nursing in the West. Still, though the rank and file were female, higher administrators tended to be male.

The poor pay of doctors was a notorious problem. Often transport engineers (e.g., bus drivers) were better paid than practising physicians. An old joke captures this irony. A nuclear engineer scoffs at a physician friend: 'You guys get paid nothing for your work. Loser.' The physician responds, 'Yeah, sure: in the system we get paid based on the value of the raw materials we use. You work with gold and get paid accordingly. And I get nothing because my raw materials are ... *you*.' As overall funding and pay differential worsened with the end of Soviet rule, more and more physicians quit their posts to work as taxi drivers or street merchants, among other options.

The Soviet system, designed for cheap, easily implemented interventions such as mass vaccination, fared poorly after antibiotics and prior successes limited the effects of infectious disease, a problem they encountered even before the dissolution of the socialist economy. That system and its replacement have proved unable to deal with the scourges of poor diet, alcohol abuse, tobacco abuse, and cardiovascular disease.

Pharmacies and medications were less strictly regulated than in the West. Medications could be dispensed without prescriptions, and pharmacists were able to adjust recommendations as needed to meet exigencies of local supply. Patients often resisted the Soviet-made generics that pharmacies stocked over the more expensive brands. Medications could also be brought by a physician or nurse on a house call.

Perhaps partially deriving from the focus on public health (though Soviet authoritarianism also had its hand here), the medical system was highly paternalistic. Informed consent was neither established nor accepted. Medical decisions were made by the physician without substantial patient input. In fact, many Russian immigrants to the industrial West have found the practice of shared decision-making disorienting, even frightening.

Since the collapse of the Soviet Union, an already fragile healthcare system has had to cope with worse funding along with greater medical need as the population was exposed to considerable socio-economic stress. Municipal hospitals are still charged with caring for patients at the state's expense, but economic realities have forced entrepreneurship and resultant 'private pay services' (*platnye uslugi*), perpetuating the dual nature of Soviet medicine. Private insurance schemes have appeared, though they focus on the rising upper classes and have not yet fundamentally influenced the system.

A private medical system, which services expatriates, employees of international companies, and the *nouveaux riches*, has arisen, providing medical care at international standards, concurrent with the official system. In addition, there is considerable prestige associated with receipt of international medical care, and many affluent families even opt to have children or surgical procedures abroad, e.g., in Germany or Finland.

The public medical system continues to operate under extreme stress. Particularly outside Moscow, shortages of funding are so acute that family members are dispatched to purchase necessary medications for hospitalized patients. Some patients have begun to delay presentation for medical care out of fear that they will be unable to afford payment or from suspicion about the integrity of the medical system. Unfortunately there is no evidence yet that improvements are imminent.

See also: AIDS (SPID); alcoholism; health; sanatoria; shortages; smoking

Further reading

Field, M. G. (1975) *Doctor and Patient in Soviet Russia*, Cambridge, MA: Harvard University Press.

Field, M. G. and Twigg, J. L. (2000) *Russia's Torn Safety Nets: Health and Social Welfare during the Transition*, New York: St. Martin's Press.

SAMUEL BROWN

memoirs

Russian memoirs include a variety of narratives that are based on the authors' recollections of historical and cultural events interwoven with their personal experiences. The memoir is a genre of fluid borders, located between historical, documentary, autobiographical, and literary narration, with an element of personal confession. Therefore, readers expect sincerity and anticipate intimate revelations about the spiritual, emotional, and physical experiences of the authors.

Many prominent nineteenth- and twentieth-century Russian and Soviet authors wrote memoirs that have literary value and provide insights into their contemporaneous cultural surroundings. For example, Lev Tolstoi's *Detstvo* (*Childhood*, 1852), *Otrochestvo* (*Boyhood*, 1854), and *Iunost* (*Youth*, 1857), and Vladimir Nabokov's *Speak, Memory!* (1966) represent a liminal genre between fictional and autobiographical writing. Aleksandr Gertsen's *Byloe i dumy* (*My Past and Thoughts*, 1855–67), written during his exile in Europe, combines autobiographical narrative with sociopolitical and philosophical writing.

Harsh censorship during the Soviet era limited memoirists' freedom of self-expression, restricting this genre and rendering it risky. Only propagandistic, ideologically-charged narratives glorifying the socialist way of life were publishable The most ludicrous examples of such memoirs, which were part of the Soviet school curriculum, were Leonid Brezhnev's two-volume *Malaia zemlia* (*Small Land*) and *Vozrozhdenie* (*Renaissance*, ghost-written), in which the Soviet political ruler portrays himself as a glorious hero of World War II and of Communist labour. Memoirs written by dissidents, which often contained harsh criticism of the Soviet state and presented a view of Russian history that sharply differed from the official line, were banned by the Soviet authorities but were published either in *samizdat* or by foreign publishing houses in *tamizdat*. Such forbidden texts circulated among the Soviet reading public, exposing both distributors and readers to the risk of political persecution.

After the collapse of the Soviet Union and the reduction of ideological censorship, post-Soviet culture has experienced a phenomenal boom of memoirs written by or about celebrities in such diverse spheres as politics, economics, literature, performing arts, science, mass media, sports, etc. Contemporary Russian memoirs compete in popularity with works by leading Russian and Western fiction writers. Overwhelmingly, post-Soviet memoirs and autobiographies have strong confessional elements: the authors disclose damaging details about their lives and the lives of those around them, directly appealing to readers to judge them. Post-Soviet readers, nostalgic for the Soviet past, devour the newly-published memoirs so as to revisit their own past through the reminiscences of their famous contemporaries.

The most notable recent memoirs include *Ukhodiashchaia natura* (*The Evanescent Setting*, 2001), written by the leading Russian theatre critic Anatolii Smelianskii. A brilliant tragic-comic narrative about his work as a literary director of the legendary Moscow Art Theatre, the memoir wittily describes life backstage at this famous cultural institution. Kora Landau, widow of the Nobel Prize-winning physicist Aleksandr Landau, depicts the privileged life of the Soviet scientific elite in her *Kak my zhili* (*How We Lived*, 2003). The corrupt and dangerous world of New Russian capitalism is described by one of the first official Russian millionaires, Artem Tarasov, in his *Millioner: ispoved pervogo kapitalista novoi Rossii* (*The First Russian Millionaire*, 2004). The world-famous ballerina Maia Plisetskaia re-evaluates the hardships of her stardom at the Bolshoi Ballet in her emotional narrative *Ia, Maia Plisetskaia* (*I, Maya Plisetskaya*, 2001). In *Overtaim* (The Overtime, 1998), hockey star Viacheslav Fetisov discusses financial hardships and corruption in the world of Russian sport, and the exodus of leading athletes to the West. Leading Russian politicians have also been prolific memoirists, with Mikhail Gorbachev, Boris Yeltsin, Egor Gaidar, Vladimir Zhirinovskii, and others all publishing popular works describing their political careers and purveying inside stories of Russian politics. The recently published memoirs about the life of President Vladimir Putin, written by his close friends and coworkers, attempt to humanize his persona and demystify his years of work for Soviet intelligence.

A number of common themes appear in many of the post-Soviet memoirs written by Russian celebrities: a discussion of personal, intellectual, or artistic freedom under the totalitarian state or within the narrow framework of Socialist Realism; admissions of sexual promiscuity and heavy drinking that are presented as manifestations of personal freedom and artistic inspiration in a totalitarian state; the authors' struggles with Soviet bureaucracy; encounters with the Soviet secret police; infatuation with Western lifestyles; and reading of literature forbidden by the censors as a source of spiritual and intellectual revelation. Most of these memoirs are written by Russian celebrities who led privileged lives and were cherished by the Soviet state, so their reminiscences are sagas of their ascent to the summit of Soviet prosperity and stardom.

In the post-Soviet era, Vagrius publishing house created a popular line under the title *Moi dvadtsatyi vek* (*My Twentieth Century*) that includes both contemporary Russian memoirs and reprints of works written in earlier decades that were either prohibited in the Soviet Union or were previously published abroad. These include reminiscences by leading military commanders of the White Army who fought against the Bolsheviks during the Civil War and memoirs of Russian writers and artists who emigrated to the West during the most turbulent years of Russian and Soviet history.

The large body of recently published Russian memoirs contains valuable material for the study of Russia's past from anthropological, historical, and cultural perspectives.

See also: Brezhnev, Leonid; censorship; dissident; Gaidar, Egor; Gorbachev, Mikhail; hockey; literature, post-Soviet; literature, Soviet; Moscow Art Theatre; Nabokov, Vladimir; New Russians; Plisetskaia, Maia; publishing houses, Soviet and post-Soviet; Putin, Vladimir; samizdat; Socialist Realism; tamizdat; World War II (Great Patriotic War); Yeltsin, Boris; Zhirinovskii, Vladimir

Further reading

Berberova, N. (1991) *The Italics Are Mine*, London: Chatto&Windus.

Herzen, A. (1982) *My Past and Thoughts: The Memoirs of Alexandr Herzen*, Berkeley, CA: University of California Press.

Holmgren, B. (ed.) (2003) *The Russian Memoir*, Evanston, IL: Northwestern University Press.

Nabokov, V. (1989) *Speak, Memory!: An Autobiography Revisited*, New York: Vintage International.

Plisetskaya, M. (2001) *I, Maya Plisetskaya*, trans. A. Bouis, New Haven, CT: Yale University Press.

OLGA PARTAN

Memorial

An organization founded in 1987 by activists, originally with the aim of constructing a monument to victims of Stalin's repressions, Memorial and its very formation tested the limits of Gorbachev's policies of perestroika. Many noted dissidents, including Andrei Sakharov, assisted in its early work. Memorial has since grown to embrace both the issues of the past (rehabilitation, recognition of camp victims, memorialization and documentation) and the present (providing information on human rights and monitoring rights issues in Russia). Memorial has branch organizations in many Russian cities; the Moscow headquarters contains an archive, library, and information centre.

DAVID J. GALLOWAY

Men, Aleksandr Vladimirovich

b. 22 January 1935, Moscow;
d. 9 September 1990, Semkhoz, Moscow oblast

Russian Orthodox priest, activist, Bible interpreter

Father Aleksandr Men was an intensely popular interpreter of Russian Orthodoxy during the twilight of the Soviet regime. Controversial for his Jewish heritage and ecumenical preaching, he was murdered on his way to church at the pinnacle of his career, perhaps by reactionary forces. His homilies and pastoral activity united prominent dissidents, including Andrei Sakharov and Aleksandr Solzhenitsyn, with simple Orthodox worshippers. His seven-volume history of religion, *Put, Istina, i Zhizn* (*The Way, the Truth, and the Life*) was considered his *magnum opus*, though he is also well known for essays and sermons. He participated informally in movements for freedom of worship and against anti-Semitism and Russian nationalism. His early works were published abroad under pseudonyms, such as Bogolubov, Svetlov, and Pavlov.

See also: anti-Semitism; dissident; Jews; Russian Orthodoxy; Sakharov, Andrei; Solzhenitsyn, Aleksandr

SAMUEL BROWN

Menshikov, Oleg Evgenevich

b. 8 November 1960, Serpukhov

Film actor

Frequently called Russia's 'heart-throb' and leading film star, honoured by Presidents Yeltsin and Putin, Menshikov graduated from Moscow's Shchepkin Theatre Institute. He often portrays dashing but torturously motivated heroes: the cultured musician turned by personal tragedy into NKVD death-dealer Mitia in Mikhalkov's 1994 *Utomlennye solntsem* (*Burnt by the Sun*); the émigré doctor duped into returning, with his French family, to Stalin's Russia in *East/West* (1999); and the embodiment of the 'Russian soul', a cadet who represents a bulwark against Western materialism, in Mikhalkov's nostalgic blockbuster *Sibirskii tsiriulnik* (*The Barber of Siberia*, 1999). Menshikov also produces, directs, and stars in highly successful theatrical productions.

AVRAM BROWN

Menshov, Vladimir Valentinovich

b. 17 September 1939, Baku, Azerbaidzhani SSR

Actor, director, screenwriter, producer

Menshov studied at the Moscow Art Theatre School and VGIK, in the directors' studio of Mikhail Romm. His roles, played over three decades, range from the energetic manager in *Chelovek na svoem meste* (*The Right Man in the Right Place*, 1972) to Timur Bekmambetov's 2004 thriller, *Nochnoi dozor* (*Night Watch*), in which the 'Old Guard' battles post-Soviet dark forces. Menshov won an Oscar for best foreign film for his 1979 *Moskva slezam ne verit* (*Moscow Doesn't Believe in Tears*), about life in Thaw-era Moscow. He wrote, directed, and produced the 2000 *Zavist bogov* (*Envy of the Gods*), also featuring his wife Vera Alentova as a stylish woman of the 1980s during the restrictions of the Andropov era.

See also: All-Russian (All-Union) State Institute of Cinematography (VGIK); Andropov, Iurii; Moscow Art Theatre; Romm, Mikhail; Thaw

JANE E. KNOX-VOINA

Messerer, Asaf Mikhailovich

b. 6 [19] November 1903, Vilnius; d. 7 March 1992, Moscow

Ballet dancer, choreographer, teacher

A graduate of the Moscow School of Choreography, Messerer danced as a soloist at the Bolshoi Theatre until 1954. He was known for virtuoso technical performances in classical ballet productions and, sometimes, ironic interpretations in new Soviet ballet productions of the 1930s. He choreographed several dance numbers, of which *Futbolisty* (Football Players, music by Aleksandr Tsfasman) became very popular. Messerer gained international fame as a pedagogue in classical ballet, teaching classes for leading dancers at the Bolshoi Theatre and working with Maurice Béjart's ballet company in Belgium in the 1960s. His son, Boris Messerer, is a renowned theatre artist in Moscow.

See also: ballet, Soviet; Bolshoi Theatre; choreographers, Soviet

TATIANA SMORODINSKAYA

Mesto vstrechi izmenit nelzia (The Meeting Place Cannot Be Changed)

Television series

This 1979 Soviet television series was directed by Stanislav Govorukhin. The five-episode police procedural, based on Arkadii and Georgii Vainer's novel, *Era miloserdiia* (*The Era of Mercy*, 1976), is set in post-war Moscow and was made in a nostalgic retro style. The continuing popularity of the series is due to the casting of Vladimir Vysotskii in the lead role.

See also: Govorukhin, Stanislav; television serials; television, Soviet; Vysotskii, Vladimir

ELENA PROKHOROVA

Metro, Moscow

Widely regarded as one of the finest technological and aesthetic achievements of official Soviet culture, the Moscow Metro first opened in 1935 and steadily expanded thereafter. It currently comprises more than 170 stations and 250 km of track. The busiest metro system in the world, it transports approximately 8–9 million passengers on each weekday. Initially named in honour of Lazar Kaganovich, the Moscow Communist Party Leader and chief architect of the post-Revolutionary Reconstruction of Moscow project, in 1955 it was renamed in honour of Vladimir Lenin. From the outset, the Soviet authorities were determined to produce the most beautiful metro system in the world and therefore commissioned the nation's finest architects, artists, and designers to work on the project. The stations built during the 1930s boast some of the most innovative architectural and artistic designs, among the most spectacular of which are stations designed by the architect Aleksei Dushkin: Ploshchad Revoliutsii (Revolution Square, 1938), which contains more than eighty life-sized statues by the sculptor Matvei Manizer, charting a history of the Soviet Union from the Revolution to the present day, and Maiakovskaia (1938), featuring a series of ceiling mosaics by the famous Soviet artist Aleksandr Deineka. During World War II, Maiakovskaia station played host to a major banquet in celebration of the 24th anniversary of the Bolshevik Revolution. Notably, this and other metro stations were also deployed as centres of military operation and as public bomb shelters during the conflict. The early post-war period witnessed the production of the most elaborate and baroque of all metro stations, including Komsomolskaia (1952) and Kievskaia (1953). These fantasy spaces, decorated with vast walls of marble and colossal chandeliers, were popularly dubbed 'palaces of the people' and still attract countless tourists to this day.

See also: transportation system

Further reading

Berezin, V. (1989) *Moscow Metro*, Moscow: Planeta.

MIKE O'MAHONY

Metropol

In 1978, during a conversation with Vasilii Aksenov, Viktor Erofeev came up with the idea of publishing an uncensored *almanakh* (literary miscellany) of works by contemporary Soviet authors. Three other writers, Andrei Bitov, Fazil Iskander, and Evgenii Popov, joined in planning and producing the collection, called *Metropol*. The list of the *almanakh*'s authors was very impressive; besides the organizers, it included Bella Akhmadulina, Iuz Aleshkovskii, Fridrikh Gorenshtein, Genrikh Sapgir, Andrei Voznesenskii, and Vladimir Vysotskii. The organizers did not intend to publish dissident writings; the main purpose of this project was to break loose from the fetters of Soviet censorship and create a precedent of a literary publication without the mandatory approval by Glavlit. They also hoped that the controversy would prompt the authorities to relax ideological controls.

The outraged authorities, however, considered the project ideological sabotage and lashed out against the organizers and authors. Popov and Erofeev were expelled from the Union of Soviet Writers. Semen Lipkin and Inna Lisnianskaia rescinded their memberships in protest and, as a result, lost all their membership privileges. Aksenov was forced into emigration. Other authors experienced difficulties with publishing their works. In 1979, the *almanakh* was published in the United States by Ardis.

See also: Akhmadulina, Bella; Aksenov, Vasilii; Aleshkovskii, Iuz; Bitov, Andrei; censorship; dissident; Erofeev, Viktor; Glavlit; Iskander, Fazil; Popov, Evgenii; Stagnation; tamizdat; unions, creative, Soviet; Voznesenskii, Andrei; Vysotskii, Vladimir

Further reading

Erofeyev, V. (1999–2000) 'A Murder in Moscow', trans. P. Carson, *New Yorker* 75(40) (27 Dec–3 Jan): 48–59.
Porter, R. (1994) 'The *Metropol*' Affair', in *Russia's Alternative Prose*, Oxford: Berg.

KONSTANTIN KUSTANOVICH

Miagkov, Andrei Vasilevich

b. 8 July 1938, Leningrad

Actor

Appearing in films since 1965, Miagkov played a naïve and touching Alesha Karamazov in Ivan Pyrev's *Bratia Karamazovy* (*The Brothers Karamazov*, 1968), but is best remembered for his work with Eldar Riazanov in the 1970s and 1980s. Popularity came with his portrayal of the sincere, honest 'little man' who finds love against all odds in *Ironiia sudby* (*The Irony of Fate*, 1975) and *Sluzhebnyi roman* (*An Office Romance*, 1977). He literally finds his voice and rebels in *Garazh* (*The Garage*, 1979), but his 'little man' is dealt a more tragic hand in *Zhestokii romans* (*A Cruel Romance*, 1984).

See also: Riazanov, Eldar

DAVID GILLESPIE

migration, post-Soviet

In spite of Western fears, the opening of Soviet borders did not result in mass departures. Rather, inbound migration has dominated the post-Soviet period. Ethnic conflicts, coupled with dramatically aggravated living conditions for ethnic Russians in the countries of the former Soviet Union, have turned the Russian Federation into a 'migration magnet'. According to figures presented by the US Migration Policy Institute, it has attracted a cumulative net of 3.7 million people between 1989 and 2002. Emigration from Russia to countries outside the CIS and the Baltic States is dominated by ethnic Germans and Jews, who take advantage of generous migration policies in Germany, Israel, and the United States. According to official statistics, approximately 100,000 people have left Russia every year since 1990. In spite of the modest size of this 'fourth wave', the emigrants' high educational level has created anxiety about 'brain drain' in Russia and a noticeable Russian presence in Western academia and culture.

Another issue of concern is the trafficking of women for sexual exploitation. This illegal and therefore undocumented form of travel is estimated to involve tens of thousands of women from the former Soviet Union and Eastern Europe every year. Russian women in prostitution are especially numerous in Israel and Turkey. Matchmaking agencies have promoted the myth of the family-oriented Russian bride, and have added marriage to the technologies of migration. Americans dominate among the male customers: since 1993 an estimated 75,000 Russian women have arrived in the United States on fiancée visas.

The melodramatic potential of the vulnerable Russian bride has been exploited in Western films, e.g. *Birthday Girl* (2001), *The Russian Bride* (2001), and *Last Resort* (2000). Although marriage to a foreigner still counts as a major achievement among large sections of the female population, Russian cinema tends to present the phenomenon in bleak colours. The emblematic perestroika production *Interdevochka* (*Intergirl*, 1989) ends in the tragic death of the marital migrant, while *Nash amerikanskii Boria* (*Our American Boria*, 1992) shows a marriageable foreigner as one of many scarce items for which women queued in early transition Russia.

See also: economic system, Soviet; economic system, post-Soviet; *Interdevochka*; Todorovskii, Petr; vacations, Soviet and post-Soviet; women

KARIN SARSENOV

Mikhalkov, Nikita Sergeevich

b. 21 October 1945, Moscow

Director, actor, screenwriter

The younger son of Sergei Mikhalkov (author of the Soviet anthem), Mikhalkov graduated from the Shchukin Theatre School (1966) and VGIK (1971), where he studied directing under Mikhail Romm. Mikhalkov as director specializes in stylish recreation of various epochs, including the nineteenth century (*Neokonchennaia pesa dlia mekhanicheskogo pianino* [*An Unfinished Piece for Player Piano*, 1976] and *Oblomov* [1979]), the Russian Civil War (*Svoi sredi chuzhikh, chuzhoi sredi svoikh* [*At Home among Strangers*, 1974] and *Raba liubvi* [*A Slave of Love*, 1975]), and Stalin's purges – in the Oscar-winning *Utomlennye solntsem* (*Burnt by the Sun*, 1994). He also depicts tense family dramas, including *Piat vecherov* (*Five Evenings*, 1978) and *Rodnia* (*Kinsfolk*, 1981). Since *Ochi chernye* (*Dark Eyes*, 1987), a Westernized adaptation of Chekhov's story 'Lady with a Lapdog', Mikhalkov seeks co-productions with Italy and France to sell a heavily mythologized image of Russia to Western audiences (such as *Sibirskii tsiriulnik* [*The Barber of Siberia*, 1998]), while positioning himself as a Russian patriot and Eurasianist (*Urga* [*Close to Eden*, 1991]).

Mikhalkov the actor made a smooth transition from 'the boy next door' image (Kolka in *Ia shagaiu po Moskve* [*I Walk around Moscow*, directed by Daneliia, 1963]) to the authoritative paternal figure (Alexander III in *Sibirskii tsiriulnik*)

Also involved in politics, in 1993 he became President of the Foundation for Russian Culture and in 1997 was elected Chairman of the Filmmakers' Union, and remains a controversial patriot and supporter of the regime, both Yeltsin's and Putin's.

See also: All-Russian (All-Union) State Institute of Cinematography (VGIK); Romm, Mikhail; unions, creative, post-Soviet

Further reading

Beumers, B. (2000) *Burnt by the Sun*, London: I. B. Tauris.
Sandler, A. (ed.) (1989) *Nikita Mikhalkov*, Moscow: Iskusstvo.

ANDREI ROGATCHEVSKI

militia (police)

An official body within the Ministry of Internal Affairs (*Ministerstvo vnutrennikh del*), the Russian militia is responsible for maintaining social order. The Soviet militia was institutionalized by the resolution of the NKVD 'About the Workers' Militia' (*O rabochei militsii*, December 1917) after the October Revolution. It put an end to the utopian revolutionary idea that the army and police would be liquidated along with the old order and their functions delegated to armed citizens. The militia comprised a permanent staff that fulfilled special duties, its organization existing independently of the Red Army, with the functions of the two strictly differentiated. In 1918, a Criminal Investigation Department was established within the militia.

The militia closely collaborated with the ChK (Extraordinary Committee – Bolshevik secret police), particularly in maintaining security in the GULag. Its staff benefited from special educational institutions as well as various structures established to assist its personnel in its work. During the Soviet period the militia underwent multiple reforms and purges of its ranks.

In 1991, Russia adopted a new law, currently in effect, 'About the Militia'. The militia consists of investigators; criminal police; public safety police; district militia officers; a part-time staff; and department guards. The major department media include the radio station *Militseiskaia volna* (Militia Wave), the television section of the Ministry of Internal Affairs, the newspapers *Shchit i mech* (Sword and Shield) and *Opasnyi vozrast* (Dangerous Age), and the magazines *Militia* and *Professional*. The Ministry of Internal Affairs has a Central Museum in Moscow.

The militia's punitive and controlling functions as defined by its duties under Soviet rule (such as defence of the state) did not disappear after the Soviet Union's dissolution, but merely underwent transformation. Iurii Levada's Analytical Centre has reported that during the last ten years approximately 10 per cent of the population has complete faith in the militia, whereas those who mistrust it constitute 35–40 per cent. Though 'stability' and 'law and order' figure prominently among the population's values, Russians (especially the residents of large cities) do not feel safe.

Large-scale corruption among the ranks of the Ministry of Internal Affairs and the struggle against it are perceived by the majority of Russians as a means of solving problems between clans of the power elite, and part and parcel of pre-election agitation. The scope of the militia's power is growing, but society and public organizations have no mechanisms to curb it. Citizens fall victims to the militia's rudeness, extortion, bribes, arbitrary detention, red tape and reluctance to take action, refusal to initiate criminal cases, and such physical abuse as beatings and torture. In areas of local armed conflicts the militia fulfils a special function; members of the special militia units (OMON) regularly are sent to such locales as Chechnia, where they participate in combat as part of the federal forces and inflict casualties.

According to two leading Russian sociologists, L. Gudkov and B. Dubin, currently the militia's work is defined by poorly coordinated and even contradictory goals, established by the government during various periods. These disparate and sometimes incompatible aims represent different layers of political culture, reflecting various historical moments in the existence of the Soviet totalitarian-repressive system of social control.

See also: Chechnia; Federal Security Service; GULag; OMON

Further reading

Istoriia sovetskoi militsii, available at http://www.mvd.ru.

ELENA OZNOBKINA

Mindadze, Aleksandr Anatolievich

b. 28 April 1949, Moscow

Screenwriter

A graduate of the Screenwriters' Department of the All-Union State Institute of Cinematography (VGIK), Mindadze is considered one of Russia's best screenwriters. Co-author of all eight films (1976–2003) by director Vadim Abdrashitov, including *Parad planet* (*Parade of Planets*, 1984), *Pliumbum, ili opasnaia igra* (*Plumbum, or a Dangerous Game*, 1985), and *Sluga* (*The Servant*, 1988), Mindadze was awarded the Order of Honour of the Russian Federation, the State Prize of Russia, and the USSR State Prize (1991). He is the recipient of numerous film festival awards, including the Silver Pegasus (Italy, 1986), Silver Bear (Berlin, 1996), and Nika (Russia, 1988, 1997, 2003). Mindadze holds the title of Honorary Cinematographer of the Russian Federation.

See also: All-Russian (All-Union) State Institute of Cinematography (VGIK); scriptwriters

ALEXANDER DOMRIN

Minkin, Aleksandr Viktorovich

b. 26 August 1946, Moscow

Journalist

One of the most popular writers and investigators in the Moscow press since the beginning of perestroika, journalist, art and theatre critic, Minkin graduated from GITIS in 1984 as a theatre critic. In 1978–79 and 1992–96 he worked as writer and columnist for *Moskovskii komsomolets* (*MK*), in 1987–92 as a columnist for *Moscovskii novosti* (Moscow News), in 1990–91 as a columnist for the magazine *Ogonek*, and in 1996–99 as a columnist for *Novaia gazeta* (New Paper). In addition, he worked for *Litsa* (People) magazine in 1997 and *Izvestiia* in 1995. Currently he writes for *MK* and other newspapers. In *Novaia gazeta* and *MK* he reported on several scandals and conducted investigative reporting on high-level corruption, oligarkhs, the war in Chechnia, and terrorism.

See also: journalism; journalists, post-Soviet; *Moskovskie novosti*; *Ogonek*; oligarkh; Russian Academy of Theatre Arts; terrorist acts; War, Chechen

NADEZHDA AZHGIKHINA

Mir

The space station Mir (Peace; World) was launched on 20 February 1986 and was submerged in the Pacific Ocean on 23 March 2001. Designed to demonstrate space achievements of the USSR during the Cold War, it later became a symbol of international collaboration. During the fifteen years it orbited the Earth, the station was visited by 100 astronauts from twelve countries.

See also: space programme and exploration

TATIANA SMORODINSKAYA

Mironov, Andrei Aleksandrovich

b. 7 March 1941, Moscow; d. 16 August 1987, Moscow

Actor, theatre director

A very popular light actor and theatrical director, Mironov made his debut in 1962. Mironov's finest performances are in Leonid Gaidai's comedy *Brilliantovaia ruka* (*The Diamond Arm*, 1968), co-starring Anatolii Papanov, and in Alla Surikova's parodic Western *Chelovek s bulvara kapuchinov* (*The Man from the Boulevard des Capuchins*), one of the most popular films of 1987. He also played a memorable Ostap Bender, again opposite Papanov, in Mark Zakharov's 1977 television adaptation of *Dvenadsat stulev* (*The Twelve Chairs*), and proved that he could develop more serious roles in Aleksei German's *Moi drug Ivan Lapshin* (*My Friend Ivan Lapshin*, 1984). Mironov was at the height of his fame when he died in 1987.

See also: Gaidai, Leonid; German, Aleksei; Papanov, Anatolii; Zakharov, Mark

DAVID GILLESPIE

Mironov, Evgenii Vitalievich

b. 29 November 1966, Saratov, Russia

Actor

Trained at the Saratov Theatre School and a graduate of the MKhAT (Moscow Art Theatre) School-Studio (1990), Mironov is a member of the Tabakerka troupe working under theatre director Oleg Tabakov. His acclaimed dramatic roles include Lopakhin in Nekrosius's production of *The Cherry Orchard*, Hamlet for Peter Stein, and the Pretender in Donnellan's version of *Boris Godunov*. Although he is an engaging comic screen actor (Poletaev in *Ankor, eshche ankor!* [*Encore, Another Encore!*, 1992]), the versatile Mironov's strongest film performances have been in dramatic roles, where he typically plays a troubled, sensitive young hero (Sasha in *Liubov* [*Love*, 1991]), Ivanov in *Musulmanin* (*The Muslim*, 1995), Prince Myshkin in *The Idiot* (2002), Gregor Samsa in *Prevrashchenie* (*The Metamorphosis*, 2001). In 1996, he was named Russian Artist of Merit and received the Russian State Prize.

See also: Moscow Art Theatre

RIMGAILA SALYS

Mironova, Mariia Andreevna

b. 28 May 1973, Moscow, Russia

Actress

A graduate of the State Institute of Cinematography (VGIK), Mironova has acted in the basic repertoire of the Lenkom Theatre since 1996. Her readiness to experiment on stage was evident in her role of Nina in the avant-garde production of Chekhov's *Seagull* (*Chaika*), directed by Andrei Zholdak. After her first major screen role in Pavel Lungin's film *The Wedding* (*Svadba*, 2000), she appeared in numerous films and TV serials. A third-generation actress, Mironova has inherited the best features of her famous father, Andrei Mironov, including nuance and the ability to create a believable character.

See also: All-Russian (All-Union) State Institute of Cinematography (VGIK); Lenkom Theatre; Lungin, Pavel; Mironov, Andrei; theatre, post-Soviet

YURI ZARETSKY

Mitki

Influential Leningrad underground art and literary group, organized in 1983 around the artists Vladimir Shinkarev and Dmitrii Shagin. In art and life, the Mitki exhibit a culture of gentle humour and camaraderie that contrasts with the optimism and forced heroism of Socialist Realist art and literature that was still the official norm of production in the 1980s. The artists Olga Florenskaia and Aleksandr Florenskii and the writer and film director Viktor Tikhomirov form the creative core of Mitki. The group lacks a manifesto and an overt political agenda. Their view is embodied in the earthy central character of Mitka (a diminutive of Dmitrii), visually depicted as a dishevelled, bearded man in a blue and white striped navy shirt. Demonstrating the influence of Russian folktales, stories about the blundering bumpkin Mitka are filled with wry, self-deprecating humour that often pokes fun at the Russian condition.

Although primarily known as artists – in graphics, installations, and canvas painting – Mitki have also published collections of prose, remarkable for its absurd style, language play, and neologisms. The group held their first public exhibition in January 1987; their ten-year retrospective in 1993 was housed at the Marble Palace of the State Russian Museum.

See also: art, nonconformist; folk tales; Socialist Realism

Further reading

Dibdin, M. (1994). 'St. Petersburg in Winter', 7: 66–71.

JENNIFER RYAN TISHLER

Mitta, Aleksandr Naumovich

(né Rabinovich)

b. 28 March 1933, Moscow

Film director, screenwriter, and pedagogue

Mitta studied architecture and then film-making with Mikhail Romm at the Soviet State Film School VGIK, graduating in 1960. After starting out with children's films, he revealed his true artistic potential in the bittersweet *Gori, gori, moia zvezda* (*Shine, Shine, My Star*, 1970) about a quixotic artist during the 1918–21 Civil War. Mitta landed box-office hits with the Soviet–Japanese melodrama *Moskva, liubov' moia* (*Moscow, My Love*, 1974), the fine Pushkin adaptation *Skaz pro to, kak tsar' Petr arapa zhenil* (*The Tale of How Tsar Peter Married off His Moor*, 1976), and the opportunistic disaster movie *Ekipazh* (*Flight Crew*, 1980) about selfless Soviet pilots and their loving women. In the 1990s, Mitta taught film-making in Hamburg and Moscow. Accomplished Artist of the RSFSR (1974).

See also: All-Russian (All-Union) State Institute of Cinematography (VGIK)

PETER ROLLBERG

Mnatsakanova, Elizaveta Arkadevna

(née Elisabeth Netzkowa)

b. 31 May 1922, Baku

Poet

Mnatsakanova is an outstanding practitioner of visual poetry. Her hand-made books include calligraphic illustration, ornamental page borders, and coloured imagery as visual counterpoint to her intensely musical poetry. Mnatsakanova creates highly structured long poems. Paronomasia, repetition, foreign words, and careful formal arrangement on the page are key features of her poems, which suggest tales of death and eternal life, of transformation and enduring love. Her work first appeared in

Apollon-77 in Paris, and several books have been published in Vienna, where she has lived since 1975. *Vita Breve* was published in Perm in 1994; *Arcadia* appeared in Moscow in 2004, when the poet also won the St. Petersburg Andrei Belyi Prize for her poetry.

See also: poetry, post-Soviet

STEPHANIE SANDLER

Moiseev, Igor Aleksandrovich

b. 8 (21) January 1906, Kiev, Ukraine

Ballet dancer, choreographer

A graduate of the Moscow School of Choreography (1924) and the University of Dance (1933), Moiseev worked as a ballet dancer and choreographer at the Bolshoi Theatre until 1939. He founded and was the continuous director of the State Folk Dance Ensemble of the USSR (1937), with its repertoire of several hundred folk dances: choreographic pictures, suites, poems, and novellas. An outstanding artist and innovator in dance, he created the new genre of folk-dance theatre. Today the Moiseev Theatre defines the development of all folk-stage choreography not only in Russia, but abroad. The recipient of multiple awards, including the Lenin Prize (1967), five Stalin/ State Prizes (from the 1940s to the 1990s), and the Oscar Prize in Dance (1961, 1974), Moiseev was also named People's Artist of the RSFSR and USSR (1953).

See also: awards, cultural, Soviet; ballet dancers, Bolshoi Theatre; Bolshoi Theatre; dance; folk dance

YURI ZARETSKY

Moldova (Moldavia, Moldava)

A landlocked country in south-eastern Europe situated between the rivers Prut and Dniester, with Chisinau (Kishinev) as its capital, Moldova (meaning 'people') is part of the historical region of Bessarabia. Its area is 33,843 sq km of mostly flat land with some hills and deep valleys; a warm, temperate climate; and a population of 636,000. From 1349 until 1504, the territory of Moldova was part of the Moldova principality, which in 1456 became a vassal of the Ottoman Empire. From 1484 until 1513 the Ottoman Turks conquered and ruled all of its territory. In 1812, Bessarabia was annexed by the Russian Empire. Although in October 1917 the regional council declared the autonomy of Bessarabia and, in January 1918, the independence of the Moldova people's democratic republic, Moldova was occupied by Romanian troops and a month later became part of Romania. The left bank of the Dniester River became an autonomous Moldavian republic within the Ukrainian SSR in 1920. After Soviet troops took over the territory of Bessarabia in 1940, a new Moldavian Soviet Socialist Republic with a capital in Kishinev was formed.

In 1991, Moldavian SSR became an independent state called the Republic of Moldova. The declaration of independence from Moldova by five regions on the left bank of the Dniester River with a predominantly Russian and Ukrainian population that feared its intentions to join Romania led to armed conflict. The self-proclaimed *Pridnestrovskaia Moldavskaia respublika* (Trans-Dniester Moldavian Republic), with Tiraspol as its capital, however, is not recognized by the international community. Regions of Moldova populated by the Gagauz (a Turkic minority) also declared independence, and the Gagauz republic peacefully received autonomous status and is now called Gagauz Yeri.

The population of Moldova numbers 4,455,000 (2005); its ethnic composition is as follows (1989): 64.5 per cent Moldavian, 13.8 per cent Ukrainian, 13 per cent Russian, 3.5 per cent Gagauz, 2 per cent Jewish, 1.5 per cent Bulgarian, and Roma. The state language is Moldavian, which uses the Latin alphabet, and the predominant religion is Eastern Orthodox; 41 per cent of the population lives in cities.

The economic crisis of the 1990s led to the closure of most large industrial enterprises, and resultant unemployment and impoverishment of the population, 25 per cent of which was forced to seek jobs in Romania, Ukraine, and Russia. Moldova is an agrarian country. Along with cattle breeding, Moldovans grow grain crops, vegetables, fruits, nuts, sunflower, beets, tobacco, and grapes. During the Soviet era, Moldova produced famous wines and cognac. The country's major architectural attractions are underground monastic cloisters and medieval Turkish fortresses. Moldova is famous for its songs (*doinas*), dances (Jok is a world-famous folk dance company), handicrafts (carpet-making and ceramics), and winemaking. Its culture is very similar to that of Romania.

See also: administrative structure, Soviet Union; CIS (SNG); USSR

SERGEI TARKHOV

Molodaia gvardia (Young Guard)

Monthly journal

A monthly established in Moscow in 1922 under the aegis of the Komsomol, *Molodaia gvardiia* covered political, social, cultural, and literary affairs as part of the Soviet propaganda system addressed to young people. After a wartime hiatus, the journal became popular during the Thaw era and became associated with the Slavophilic tradition. Its opponent was the journal *Iunost* (Youth), as well as 'urban' and youth prose of the 1960s and 1970s. *Molodaia gvardia* followed the same mild nationalism characteristic of the journals *Moskva* (Moscow) and *Nash sovremennik* (Our Contemporary) and the newspaper *Literaturnaia Rossiia* (Literary Russia) during the Stagnation era; during perestroika its position turned reactionary. The journal promoted village prose and published historical essays on the Russian past as well as polemical essays. The height of its circulation was in the 1970s at 59,000. The journal was awarded the Order of the Red Banner of Labour.

See also: Communist Youth League; nationalism ('the national question'); perestroika and glasnost; periodicals, Soviet; propaganda, Soviet and post-Soviet; Stagnation; Thaw; thick journals; village prose

NADEZHDA AZHGIKHINA

Molokhovets, Elena Ivanovna

(née Elena Ivanovna Burman)

b. 28 April 1831, Arkhangelsk;
d. *c*. 12 December (?)1918, St. Petersburg

Author of the 'culinary encyclopedia' *Podarok molodym khoziaikam* (*A Gift to Young Housewives*), first published in 1861 and frequently reissued in updated editions to the present day. The book was subtitled 'How to reduce domestic expenses,' and included over 4,000 Russian and other recipes, as well as suggestions on preparing a variety of nutritious meals economically, preserving foods, and even butchering meat and making homemade wines and liqueurs. As the title suggests, it was a common gift for new wives.

SETH GRAHAM

monastic life (monastyrskaia zhizn)

Russian monasticism took three forms: (1) eremitic (hermits); (2) semi-eremitic (brothers who left their *sketes* [hermitages] only to assemble for communal services); and (3) coenobitic, i.e. in communities where monks follow canonical hours of prayer. Monastic life began in Russia in 1051 at the Kiev Cave Monastery, one of four monasteries to receive the honorific title of *lavra*, only two of which remain in post-Soviet Russia: the Aleksandr Nevskii *lavra* in St. Petersburg and the Trinity-Sergiev (Troitsko-Sergievskaia) *lavra* near Moscow. Monasteries flourished until the eighteenth century, when secular attitudes stripped them of wealth and power. The nineteenth century celebrated the age of the *starets* (elder), a holy and wise monk who acted as spiritual advisor to his brothers. The Soviet period saw a great reduction in the number of monasteries and convents from 1,498 in 1914 to thirty-one in 1941; the number rose to eighty in 1947. After World War II, 101 monasteries were functioning, but only the Trinity-Sergiev had legal status. By the early 1950s, ninety remained; by the mid-1960s only seventeen were open. After the fall of the Soviet Union, monasteries began to reopen all over the country and continue to flourish at the beginning of the twenty-first century.

See also: Holy Trinity-St. Sergius Monastery; Moscow; St. Petersburg; World War II (Great Patriotic War)

CHRISTINE A. RYDEL

monetary reform

Russia's transition from a planned to a market economy included monetary reform – a set of policies directed at liberalizing prices, allowing them to fluctuate with supply and demand; curbing inflation; and monitoring the money supply to maintain the ruble's purchasing power.

In the centrally planned economy of the Soviet Union, money did not function as a medium of exchange, as it usually does in market economies; rather, it served as a mechanism to control economic activity. Supply was not dependent on monetary prices, as both were determined administratively. Banking was state-owned and non-competitive, and enterprises enjoyed 'soft-budget constraints', which provided them with easy access to credit, irrespective of performance. The criterion for performance was not the efficient use of resources or the satisfaction of market requirements, but fulfillment of the plan. An elaborate black market grew in response to shortages, where prices were settled at higher levels than in the official trade.

In January 1991, the government announced a three-day long exchange of banknotes of large denomination, 50 and 100 rubles (Pavlov's reform). Official reasons for the exchange were the need to reduce the overall money supply, mostly targeting counterfeit and black market cash. Average citizens queued frantically to exchange banknotes, while criminals were able to convert their rubles into hard currency.

In order to eliminate shortages and to legalize at least some black market trade, in January 1992, economic reformers, led by economist Egor Gaidar, introduced price liberalization on most consumer goods. Based on what they had witnessed earlier in Poland, they expected that the rise in prices would stimulate producers to increase supply. That expectation was thwarted because, unlike Poland, Russia lacked a

substantial number of independent producers in industry and in agriculture, which was mostly collectivized. Instead, the liberalization prompted rampant hyperinflation, decline in living standards, and *de facto* devaluation of bank savings. In 1994, the government admitted that it could only compensate lost savings at face value, though by then the value of the ruble had declined to a fraction of its pre-liberalization level.

In July 1993, the government initiated another currency exchange: It invalidated all banknotes printed before 1 January 1993, so as to destroy the 'ruble zone', which, in addition to Russia, included those former socialist republics that had not yet established their own national currencies. The latter's Central Banks continued to provide ruble credits to enterprises under 'soft-budget constraints', thereby undermining Russia's anti-inflationary measures.

The partial nature of banknote exchanges (since only banknotes from certain years were targeted), and the fact that Russia's own Central Bank nevertheless continued to print money further diluted attempts at stabilization. In addition, inconsistent monetary policy had unanticipated effects: persistent wage arrears and non-payments, and barter relations among organizations, including local governments. Periodic bailouts by the state persisted as a serious societal problem.

In 1994, Russia suffered a banking crisis ('Black Tuesday'), after which the government refused to allow the exchange value of the ruble to drop, and artificially maintained it, primarily by spending its hard currency reserves. Moreover, to finance budget deficits, the government initiated several-years-long speculation with state treasury bonds, which yielded over 80 per cent annual interest. So as to pay existing bond holders, the Russian state had to continue issuing new bonds until this financial pyramid finally collapsed in 1998, once again causing panic among bank depositors, bankrupting many banks, including several of the largest ones, and sending ruble exchange value plunging.

In the 1990s the cumulative effect of multiple banknote exchanges, currency devaluation, hyperinflation that destroyed savings, and wage arrears was the loss of trust by millions of Russians in the Russian state, financial institutions, and the national currency.

See also: economic system, post-Soviet; economic system, Soviet; Gaidar, Egor; shortages

Further reading

Aslund, A. (2002) *Building Capitalism: The Transformation of the Former Soviet Bloc*, Cambridge: Cambridge University Press.

Marshall, G. (1994) *Lost Opportunity*, New York: W.W. Norton & Company.

Titma, M. and Tuma, N. (2001) *Modern Russia*, Maidenhead: McGraw-Hill.

ALYA GUSEVA

money

The role of money changed dramatically during the transition from the Soviet Union's command economy to the post-Soviet free-market economy. In the so-called 'shortage economy' of Soviet times, having rubles was less important than having access to scarce goods. The Soviet ruble was non-convertible, access to hard currency (convertible foreign currencies) was highly restricted, and prices were set by the state.

This system began to break down in the late 1980s as Soviet leader Mikhail Gorbachev's perestroika reforms liberalized certain prices and loosened the monetary regime. The struggle between the central and republic governments opened the financial system further as the two sides fought for control. The Russian republic created the Central Bank of Russia (CBR) in July 1990, and in December 1990 declared sovereignty over the banks on its territory. In response, in January 1991 the Soviet leadership instituted a monetary reform that invalidated all 50 and 100 ruble notes in circulation (large bills held mainly by banks). After the subsequent Soviet break-up, the newly independent states continued to use the Soviet ruble as their common currency. This inadvertently created a short-lived currency union known as the 'ruble zone'.

In January 1992, the Russian Federation liberalized most prices, but could not follow through with macroeconomic stabilization policies. This led to a hyperinflation of over 2,500 per cent in 1992, an explosion of barter and inter-enterprise debt, and an increasing use of parallel (e.g., the Ukrainian coupon) and substitute (e.g., the US dollar) currencies among ruble zone members. In early 1993, the CBR began printing new Russian ruble notes, and in July 1993 it announced that all pre-1993 ruble notes would become invalid in Russia. This forced other ruble zone members either to leave or to cede their monetary sovereignty to Russia, and by late 1993 most remaining members had introduced their own currencies. Russia continued to experience episodes of monetary instability after the ruble zone's breakup, most notably in the November 1994 exchange-rate collapse known as 'Black Tuesday'.

In January 1998, the Russian government believed that it had inflation under control and redenominated the ruble. This currency reform removed three zeros from the inflated 1993 Russian ruble notes, making the new 1998 ruble notes worth approximately six to the US dollar. This optimism proved premature, as the financial crisis of August 1998 led to another round of inflation, a fall in the ruble's exchange rate, and the collapse of several large Russian banks.

As a result of this continuous instability, most ordinary Russians did not trust the financial system and did not keep their money in banks. Those who did use banks typically chose the state-owned bank, Sberbank (savings bank), the largest bank in the country and heir to the Soviet-era national savings bank network.

See also: economic system, post-Soviet; monetary reform; privatization

Further reading

Johnson, J. (2000) *A Fistful of Rubles: The Rise and Fall of the Russian Banking System*, Ithaca, NY: Cornell University Press.

Woodruff, D. (1998) *Money Unmade: Barter and the Fate of Russian Capitalism*, Ithaca, NY: Cornell University Press.

JULIET JOHNSON

monuments, post-Soviet

Post-Soviet monuments primarily fall into two categories: transformed Soviet memorials and newly-built sites. Many Soviet-era monuments were removed or destroyed after 1991, but those associated with pre-1917 Russian history and culture or the Great Patriotic War (World War II) were instead transformed into symbols of Russia. Victory Park memorial at Poklonnaia Gora in Moscow is an excellent example. Construction began in 1958, ceased under Soviet leader Mikhail Gorbachev, and was completed by Zurab Tsereteli in altered form (with much of the Soviet imagery removed) in 1995 through the efforts of Moscow Mayor Iurii Luzhkov. The most controversial Soviet-era monuments include the Lenin Mausoleum on Red Square and the statue of Cheka founder Feliks Dzerzhinskii. The entombed body of Lenin remained in its mausoleum despite numerous calls for its burial in the 1990s, while others regularly demanded that the Dzerzhinskii statue, removed to a park outside the New Tretiakov Gallery in August 1991, be returned to Lubianka Square outside the former KGB building.

With a few exceptions, such as the Gulag Museum at Perm-36 or the simple stone monument to the Soviet regime's victims installed by the Memorial society in 1991 in Lubianka Square, newly-built monuments rarely acknowledge Soviet repression. Rather, post-Soviet monuments have focused either on glorifying the Russian nation or on tragic post-Soviet events, such as the sinking of the *Kursk* submarine (2000) and the terrorist siege of Moscow's Theatre on Dubrovka (2002). Positive representations of Soviet history, including the symbolic renaissance of Stalin, became increasingly prominent under President Vladimir Putin. Most newly-constructed monuments also replicate Soviet-era styles and dimensions, such as Tsereteli's unpopular 60m statue of Peter the Great in Moscow.

See also: death; Federal Security Service; Lenin, Vladimir Ilich; Lenin Mausoleum; Luzhkov, Iurii; monuments, Soviet; Poklonnaia gora; Putin, Vladimir; Stalin, Iosif; Tsereteli, Zurab

Further reading

Forest, B. and Johnson, J. (2002) 'Unraveling the Threads of History: Soviet-Era Monuments and Post-Soviet National Identity in Moscow', *Annals of the Association of American Geographers* 92: 524–47.

Smith, K. E. (2002) *Mythmaking in the New Russia: Politics and Memory During the Yeltsin Era*, Ithaca, NY: Cornell University Press.

BENJAMIN FOREST AND JULIET JOHNSON

monuments, Soviet

Monuments were a key concern of the Soviet state from its inception. Lenin's 'Decree on Monumental Propaganda' of 1918 ordered both the dismantling of all Tsarist monuments and the creation of statues to honour a pantheon of Bolshevik and international revolutionary heroes. Scarce resources hampered the realization of Lenin's utopian plan, and the new monuments, whose design drew on the experimental artistic currents of the time, sometimes perplexed viewers.

Monuments erected in the later years of the Lenin era and in the Stalin era continued to reflect lack of available resources, but they became increasingly easy to 'read', as a distinctively 'monumental' style of statuary became the norm. Socialist Realist monuments under Stalin were often figurative, most often depicting Stalin and/or Lenin. Such monuments were extremely common sights in Soviet city centres. The most famous Soviet monument of all, however, was Vera Mukhina's statue of a female agricultural worker and male factory worker, first shown at an international exhibition in Paris, and later moved to VDNKh.

Monuments were big business. Whole factories were dedicated to their manufacture, while sculptors such as Lev Kerbel and Evgenii Vuchetich made a handsome living from monuments. In the aftermath of World War II, these same sculptors were at the forefront of moves to 'export' extravagant Stalinist war memorials to the newly Sovietized Eastern bloc. The erection of war memorials in the Soviet Union itself was hampered by the Stalinist state's silencing of war commemoration before 1953.

The Khrushchev era made several important changes to Soviet monuments, removing all Stalin monuments during de-Stalinization (except in Georgia), vastly increasing the number of Lenin monuments, as part of the renewed cult of Lenin, and putting war memorials back on the political agenda. These memorials, for example, Vuchetich's Mamaev Kurgan complex in Stalingrad, did not depart much from the gigantist, pompous style of Stalinist statuary.

See also: architecture, Soviet and post-Soviet; East Bloc countries; Khrushchev, Nikita; Lenin, Vladimir Ilich; Socialist Realism; Stalin, Iosif; Stalingrad; Thaw; VDNKh/VVTs; Worker and Collective Farm Worker; World War II (Great Patriotic War)

POLLY JONES

Mordiukova, Nonna Viktorovna

b. 25 November 1925, Konstantinovskaia, Donetsk oblast, Ukraine

Actress

Mordiukova debuted in *Molodaia gvardiia* (*The Young Guard*, 1948), before graduating from VGIK (1950). A large woman with typically Slavic features, she often played peasant characters, conveying psychological depth beneath a stolid veneer: Stesha in *Chuzhaia rodnia* (*Alien Kin*, 1956); Sasha in *Prostaia istoriia* (*A Simple Story*, 1960); Dona Trubnikova in the important film *Predsedatel* (*The Chairman*, 1964). She starred as the eponymous heroine of Aleksandr Askoldov's banned film *Komissar* (*The Commissar*, 1967, released 1987). Other major roles include the house manager in *Brilliantovaia ruka* (*The Diamond Arm*, 1969), and Maria in *Rodnia* (*Kinfolk*, 1982).

See also: All-Russian (All-Union) State Institute of Cinematography (VGIK); Askoldov, Aleksandr

JOSEPHINE WOLL

Mordva

The Mordva are an ethnic group living in central Russia. The word *mordva*, of Iranian origin, means 'person' or 'man'. The first historical reference to Mordva dates back to the sixth century; they obtained statehood in the tenth century and voluntarily entered Russia in the fifteenth–sixteenth centuries. The current population of about 1 million lives in the Republic of Mordovia (established 1991, capital Saransk), in the Volga Region (*Povolzhe*), and in other parts of the CIS. Two sub-ethnic groups of Mordva, western and eastern, speak different languages – *Moksha* and *Erzya*, belonging to the Finno-Ugric group of the Uralic linguistic family. Mordva adopted the Cyrillic alphabet in the eighteenth century after embracing Russian Orthodoxy; pre-Christian beliefs are still widespread. Traditional occupations are farming and iron-craft. Sculptor Stepan Erzya (1876–1959) is a national celebrity.

See also: CIS; Finno-Ugric; Volga region

TATYANA LEDENEVA

Morits, Iunna Petrovna

b. 2 June 1937, Kiev

Writer

A prominent poet, artist, memoirist, and translator now living in Moscow, Morits was born in Kiev into a Jewish family. During wartime evacuation and deprivation, she fell ill with chronic tuberculosis. She studied, with interruptions, at the Gorkii Institute of World Literature and began publishing during the Thaw, with periods of silence during the 1960s, in small print runs that sold out quickly. Her verse, especially poetry for children, came to many readers' attention in songs performed by the Nikitins. Always firm about her unwillingness to sell out for literary success, Morits has been more politically outspoken since perestroika. She won the 'Triumf' Prize in 2000.

See also: Nikitins

SIBELAN FORRESTER

Moscow

Russia's largest city, with 10.6 million residents (2005), or 7.4 per cent of the nation's population, Moscow plays the leading role in Russia's cultural and political life. Since the dawn of Russian statehood, Moscow has initiated the tradition of outward flows of Russian culture into distant corners of Eurasia.

A monastic chronicle made the first reference to 'Moscov' in 1147. Initially an insignificant village, Moscow developed during its struggle for liberation from the Tatar-Mongol Yoke, 1237–1480. In 1480, Grand Duke Ivan III of Moscow ended Moscow's allegiance to the Golden Horde and assembled all Russian lands under his rule. This success was followed by an official doctrine of Moscow as the 'Third Rome', inspired by the fall of Constantinople to the Turks (1453). After the collapse of the Roman and the Byzantine empires, Moscow was to replace them as the stronghold of Christianity. The 1472 marriage of Ivan III to Zoe Sophia Paleologus, niece of the last Byzantine emperor, provided an element of legitimacy to this doctrine, and the two-headed eagle of Byzantium was added to Russia's coat-of-arms. The notion of a divine destiny reemerged each time the Russians defended Moscow from invaders, such as in the Time of Troubles (1606–12), the Napoleonic War of 1812, and World War II.

In 1712, the political capital was moved to St. Petersburg, where it remained until 1918. Moscow compensated for the departure of the imperial court and the government, however; the city thrived as the country's top commercial centre. Construction after the fire of 1812 gave Moscow a European look, as boulevards replaced fortification walls. The railroad construction boom from the 1860s till the 1890s enhanced Moscow's geographical location; by 1901, it was the busiest railroad hub in the Russian Empire. In 1897, the population exceeded a million; by 1917, it had surged to over 1.8 million.

Moscow was also an intellectual centre and, together with St. Petersburg, the home for intellectuals who helped to create the Golden Age of Russian culture in the early nineteenth century. Moscow University, the oldest university in Russia, was founded in 1755. The Bolshoi Theatre (built in 1825) and the Conservatory (1886) provided Moscow with a rich cultural life.

During the twentieth century, industrialization proceeded at a rapid pace dictated by five-year plans. By 1960, Moscow boasted 6 million residents. Soviet rule had a grim ideological component, however: the intellectual elite were decimated by Stalinist purges and later repressions. In a ruthless campaign against symbols of the tsarist past, architectural treasures, including some of the greatest Russian Orthodox cathedrals, were destroyed. The subway, first opened in 1935, provided Soviet symbols to replace pre-Revolutionary ones and transported millions of commuters through palatial underground stations. After World War II, Moscow underwent significant changes due to the rapid development of a well-educated workforce carrying out the tasks of the military-industrial complex. In the 1980s, research and development positions outnumbered manufacturing jobs.

The end of the 1950s ushered in major housing projects in the capital. Soviet leaders recognized that this city of specialists required a new social contract to support the defence industry centred there during the accelerating arms race. Soviet leaders feared losing trust among Muscovites. Dissidents appeared as a new phenomenon. Beginning in the 1960s, the capital city enjoyed special privileges: food supply and consumer goods better than elsewhere, as well as new apartments. In 1971, 60 per cent of families were housed in their own (not communal) apartments, 79 per cent in 1981, and 85 per cent in 1991.

By the late 1980s, however, Moscow had become disillusioned with the Gorbachev reforms, seen as too little and too late. In August 1991, crowds of Muscovites flooded the streets and squares and defeated the coup attempt by Communist hardliners. The energy unleashed by Muscovites in August 1991 led to profound changes.

Today Moscow's area is 1,079.9 sq km, including 37.2 sq km in the satellite town of Zelenograd and 40.1 sq km in other settlements in suburban zones. The city is divided into ten administrative districts, with a further subdivision to 125 boroughs (*upravy*). The executive

branch of the Moscow government is represented by the city mayor and his administration;
the legislative is represented by the Moscow
Duma. Muscovites mostly live in apartment
houses, between five and twenty-two storeys
high. Land allocated to residential areas comprises only 24 per cent of the city's territory, a
lower proportion than in other cities of the
world. Over half of all dwellings are in private
ownership, and the rest is leased from the
municipality. The out-of-date housing stock,
Khrushchev-era housing called *khrushchoby*, is
targeted for demolition. The new master plan
(1998) makes explicit the goal of rendering
Moscow a comfortable city in which to live, with
the renovation of the city's historic centre one of
the main tasks. Restoration of the symbols of
Russian Orthodoxy is a high priority. Surviving
architectural drawings made it possible to
rebuild the Cathedral of Christ the Saviour, the
Church of the Virgin of Kazan, and the Resurrection Gates on Red Square, all destroyed
during the Soviet era.

New construction has flourished. A World
War II memorial ensemble was built in the
western part of Moscow on Poklonnaia Gora
(Steep Hill). The city centre has been transformed by both renovations and new architectural projects. Major transportation projects
have been completed, most notably an expanded beltway called the Moscow Ring Highway
(MKAD), stretching for 109 kilometres around
the city. This new freeway (built 2001–4) forms a
'third ring', which stretches 35 kilometres from the
Kremlin and links major traffic-generating sites.

Moscow has entered the first decade of the
twenty-first century as a new global centre. In
the world hierarchy of such centres, Moscow is
not yet on the 'A list' with London, New York,
and Tokyo, but it can be compared with Zurich,
Madrid, Seoul, and Sydney; moreover, Moscow
is now ranked as the world's second most
expensive city, after Tokyo. The spending
power of the city's businesses and residents is
large; over 1.5 million families belong to the
new entrepreneurial middle class. Moscow excels
in the quality of its labour resources; the GNP
per worker is over twice the national average.

See also: Bolshoi Theatre; Cathedral of Christ
the Saviour; Coup, August 1991; defence

industry; Duma; economic system, post-Soviet;
economic system, Soviet; educational system,
Soviet; five-year plan; Gorbachev, Mikhail;
housing, Soviet and post-Soviet; Khrushchev,
Nikita; Luzhkov, Iurii; metro, Moscow; Moscow
Conservatory; Moscow State University; railroads; Russian Orthodox churches; St. Petersburg; Third Rome; transportation system;
World War II (Great Patriotic War); Yeltsin, Boris

Further reading

Colton, T. (1995) *Moscow: Governing the Socialist
    Metropolis*, Cambridge, MA: Belknap Press,
    Harvard University.
—— (1997) *Moscow's 850th Anniversary*, 2 vols,
    Moscow: Moscow Textbooks.
Vendina, O. (1997) 'Transformation Process in
    Moscow and Intra-Urban Stratification of
    Population', *GeoJournal*, 42, 4: 349–63.

YURI MEDVEDKOV AND OLGA MEDVEDKOV

Moscow Actionism

This leading movement in Moscow contemporary art of the 1990s brought to a scandalous public culmination a type of Conceptual
performance, often marked by 'infantilism',
developed in the Soviet nonconformist underground of the 1980s – notably in Odessa,
Leningrad (for example, Vladislav Mamyshev-
Monroe and Timur Novikov – the Actionists'
self-declared enemy in the 1990s), and Moscow
(for example, *Kollektivnye Deivstviia* or Zvezdochetov's *Mukhomor*). Claiming an avant-garde
ancestry epitomized by the Futurists' 'Slap in
the Face of Public Taste', the Actionists exploited the newly-opened media landscape of the
post-Soviet era. The tendency's prime exponents –
Aleksandr Brenner, Oleg Kulik, Anatolii
Osmolovskii, and Avdei Ter-Oganian – shocked
through radical 'actions' with ostensibly political
import, such as, respectively: spray-painting a
dollar sign over a Malevich painting in the Stedelijk Museum; assuming the role of an aggressive, naked man–dog; unfurling an 'Against All
Parties' banner on the Lenin Mausoleum in the
1999 elections; or chopping up Orthodox icons
with an axe.

See also: art, nonconformist; Brenner, Aleksandr; icon; Kulik, Oleg; Osmolovskii, Anatolii; Ter-Oganian, Advei; Zvezdochetov, Konstantin

IVOR STODOLSKY

Moscow Art Theatre (MKhAT)

Founded in 1898 by the theatre practitioners and theoreticians Konstantin Stanislavskii (1863–1938) and Vladimir Nemirovich-Danchenko (1858–1943), MKhAT was based on new theatre ethics and aesthetics and designed to be accessible to all. Stanislavskii's innovative acting method, first developed and practised on the MKhAT stage, significantly influenced the development of modern theatre worldwide.

Stanislavskii and Nemirovich-Danchenko envisioned MKhAT as a cultural institution representing new morality on and off stage. Rejecting old theatre conventions such as excessive theatricality or declamation, they urged actors to engage their emotional memory to achieve psychological truthfulness and verisimilitude on stage. MKhAT was conceived as a collective theatre without stardom or vanity, where all actors would be equals. According to Stanislavskii, all actors should have strict self-discipline and dedication to the acting profession, for theatre should not only entertain, but also become a powerful force in transforming reality, engaging audiences in serious philosophical reflections. MKhAT opened in October 1898 with Aleksei Tolstoi's historical drama *Tsar Fedor Ioannovich*. The December 1898 production of Chekhov's *Seagull* had a sensational success, as Chekhov's dramas, with their depiction of the nuances of human relationships and creation of a unique mood within a play, provided ideal material for MKhAT's acting and directing style. *The Seagull* became MKhAT's artistic emblem and Chekhov's plays such as *The Cherry Orchard, Ivanov*, and *Three Sisters* have remained at the core of MKhAT's repertoire.

By the mid-1930s, MKhAT was one of the leading state theatres. After Stanislavskii and Nemirovich-Danchenko, it was led by an artistic council of prominent actors and directors. In 1970, Oleg Efremov was appointed its artistic director, and rejuvenated the theatre by assigning leading roles to prominent theatre and film stars such as Oleg Borisov, Aleksandr Kaliagin, Innokentii Smoktunovskii, and Anastasiia Vertinskaia. He attracted outstanding theatre directors such as Lev Dodin, Aleksandr Efros, and Kama Ginkas to produce new plays.

By the mid-1980s, MKhAT's huge state-subsidized troupe comprised a small body of stars and a large group of actors who only acted in mass scenes, losing their professional qualifications. Due to a series of internal conflicts, MKhAT split into two independent institutions in 1987: one, under Efremov's artistic leadership, was called the Chekhov MKhAT, while the other, headed by Tatiana Doronina, became the Gorkii MKhAT. After Efremov's death in 2000, renowned actor Oleg Tabakov became the new artistic director of the Chekhov MKhAT. He significantly improved MKhAT's artistic and financial circumstances by refreshing the repertoire, inviting promising young actors, directors and stage designers, and renting out space to restaurants and shops. MKhAT remains one of Russia's leading cultural institutions and continues to promote Stanislavskii's acting method across the globe.

MKhAT's most memorable productions include Gorkii's *The Lower Depths* (1902), Maeterlinck's *The Blue Bird* (1908), Bulgakov's *The Days of the Turbins* (1926), Tolstoi's *Anna Karenina* (1937), Schiller's *Maria Stuart* (1957), Molière's *Tartuffe* (1981), Saltykov-Shchedrin's *The Golovlevs* (1984), Petrushevskaia's *The Moscow Chorus* (1988), and Chekhov's *Three Sisters* (1997).

See also: Borisov, Oleg; Dodin, Lev; Doronina, Tatiana; Efremov, Oleg; Efros, Anatolii; Ginkas, Kama; Kaliagin, Aleksandr; Petrushevskaia, Liudmila; Smoktunovskii, Innokentii; Tabakov, Oleg; theatre, post-Soviet; theatre, Soviet; Vertinskaia, Anastasia

Further reading

Stanislavskii, K. (1967) *Stanislavski on the Art of the Stage*, trans. D. Magarshack, Boston, MA: Faber and Faber.

Worall, N. (1996) *The Moscow Art Theater*, New York: Routledge.

OLGA PARTAN

Moscow Conservatory

Officially known as the Moscow State Conservatory, named after Petr Tchaikovsky, to this day the Moscow Conservatory is one of the premiere institutions of higher learning in the world whose function is to train young musicians for performing careers. As in many conservatories, students are assigned to a studio teacher on their instrument or voice, but are also expected to take history and theory courses to fulfil stringent academic requirements; however, while composers, theorists, and musicologists co-exist at the Moscow Conservatory, the emphasis is on performance, with particular focus on pianists and violinists. Indeed, these two instruments have produced a worldwide professional and pedagogical force equal to none.

The Moscow Conservatory was founded by Nikolai Rubinstein in 1866, four years after its counterpart in St. Petersburg was established by his brother, Anton. The Conservatories in both cities provided Russia with fully professional native musicians and teachers of music, in contrast to an earlier tradition of importing performers from Europe. At the same time, the conservatories were lightning rods for an opposing force, headed by the composer Milyi Balakirev and music critic Aleksandr Serov, against academicism and for nationalism in music. One result of this conflict, which lasted a decade, was a greater sensitivity to folk and indigenous field research.

After the October Revolution (1917), the government nationalized the conservatories and subsumed them under the state system of higher education, establishing graduate departments (1925) and creating three major branches of study: academic, performance, and pedagogical. Today the Moscow Conservatory has seven major departments: Piano and Organ; Orchestral Studies, which includes subdivisions for strings, brass, and percussion, as well as operatic and symphonic conducting; Vocal Studies; Choral Conducting; Composition; Music Studies comprised of music history and theory; and History and Theory of Performance. The Conservatory's music library is one of the world's largest depositories of books and music scores.

The performing facilities, while modest by comparison with other equally rated institutions, include three major concert venues: the Bolshoi (Large) Hall for orchestral concerts, and the Malyi (Small) and Rachmaninoff Halls for chamber and solo recitals. Like the Juilliard's location in New York close to Lincoln Center, and that of the Royal College of Music, across the street from Royal Albert Hall, the proximity of the Conservatory to the Bolshoi Theatre and the Union of Composers, in the centre of Moscow, attracts not only a devoted audience, but a constant series of critical responses in local newspapers and journals.

The Moscow Conservatory has always included a first-rate faculty, and its alumni have gained world recognition since its inception. Certainly, all major Russian musicians have studied at the Moscow Conservatory at some point in their lives.

See also: Bolshoi Theatre; classical music, post-Soviet; classical music, Soviet; classical musicians/performers, post-Soviet; piano performance, Russian/Soviet; St. Petersburg (Leningrad) State Conservatory; Tchaikovsky (Chaikovskii) Competition; violin performance, Russian/Soviet

DAVID GOMPPER

Moscow Nights

See *Podmoskovnye vechera* (Moscow Nights)

Moscow State Institute (University) of Foreign Relations (MGIMO)

One of the most prestigious universities in Russia, this institute was once called the Russian Harvard by Henry Kissinger. MGIMO was established in 1943 as a department of Moscow State University to provide the country with an elite, highly educated diplomatic corps. It underwent a series of reorganizations, merging in the 1950s with the Moscow Institute of Oriental Studies and the Institute of International Trade. MGIMO also provides some of the best foreign language training in the country. Its 1,500 students, 25 per cent of whom are foreigners, major in international relations, business, law, and journalism. Its graduates include many Soviet, Russian, and CIS ambassadors, diplomats, ministers, top businesspeople, heads of political parties, and high-ranking presidential advisers.

TATYANA LEDENEVA

Moscow State University (Moskovskii gosudarstvennyi universitet imeni Lomonosova)

Moscow State University, named after M.V. Lomonosov (*Moskovskii gosudarstvennyi universitet imeni Lomonosova*, or MGU), is the oldest, the largest, and one of the most prestigious universities in Russia. It was established on 25 January 1755, and at present has more than 40,000 undergraduate and graduate students, including foreign students from 150 countries. MGU was always the centre of the nation's intellectual and cultural life, and it takes pride in preserving and developing democratic traditions since its inception. MGU has two campuses in Moscow: the old one on Mokhovaia Street, near the Kremlin and the Russian State (formerly Lenin) Library, and the main campus known by a Stalin-era high rise building on Vorobevy Gory (Sparrow Hills) in the south-west of the city. There are twenty-nine departments, fifteen scholarly research institutions, four museums, a research park, a botanical garden, a publishing house, and the Gorkii Research Library, which has over 9 million volumes in its collection. Eleven MGU graduates and professors have been Nobel Prize Laureates.

See also: educational system, Soviet; Moscow; Nobel Prize winners, non-literary; Russian State Library

TATIANA SMORODINSKAYA

Moscow Times

The *Moscow Times* is a daily English-language newspaper published in Moscow. Dutch entrepreneur Derk Sauer founded the newspaper in 1992. The *Moscow Times* has remained a small newspaper (circulation 35,000), but nevertheless exerts considerable influence on perceptions of Russia in the West, because its readership includes foreign journalists, businessmen, and the diplomatic community. Through its website the newspaper also reaches a far wider audience abroad, including Western government officials who deal with Russia. The newspaper's parent company, Independent Media, publishes four newspapers and more than two dozen magazines. Finnish publishing giant SanomaWSOY Group acquired Independent Media in 2005.

PATRICK HENRY

Moscow Virtuosi (Virtuozy Moskvy)

The Moscow Virtuosi, Russia's leading chamber orchestra, comprises about twenty-five players and performs music ranging from Bach to Alfred Shnittke. Founded in 1979 by violinist Vladimir Spivakov, it immediately became popular within Russia, and also abroad since 1987, when it first toured the United States and Canada. In 1990, the orchestra established a lengthy residency in Asturias (Spain). When several members chose to remain there permanently, Spivakov was forced to hire a new group of younger Russian musicians. The orchestra performs about 100 concerts a year in Russia and abroad. It has recorded more than twenty CDs.

See also: Shnittke, Alfred; Spivakov, Vladimir

SUNGHAE ANNA LIM

Moskovskie novosti (Moscow News)

Newspaper

Associated primarily with perestroika, this international political paper, founded in 1930 and suspended from 1949 until 1956, has appeared in various incarnations. As a Soviet propaganda publication with Western audiences in mind (such as *Sovetskaia zhenshchina* [*Soviet Woman*], *Sovetskii Soiuz* [*The Soviet Union*], and *Golos rodiny* (*Voice of the Homeland*), during the late Cold War (1960–80) it appeared in English and eight other foreign languages, including Arabic. In 1961, it became a weekly, its circulation reaching 150,000 in the 1970s. The paper was taken over by the New Press Agency on 6 July 1980 – just before the Olympics in Moscow – by special decision of the Communist Party Central Committee.

With perestroika, *Moskovskie novosti* became the standard-bearer for glasnost, attracting a million readers weekly. Editor-in-chief Egor Iakovlev (1986–91) was a prominent liberal media leader of the time and a staunch supporter of Mikhail Gorbachev. Almost all Russian and many Western leading writers, politicians, and journalists wrote for *Moskovskie novosti*. In 1990, the paper's offices on Pushkin Square was destroyed in a fire, but the paper continued to appear. Currently it is privately financed, its circulation reduced to 119,500, with distribution in Russia, the CIS, and fifty foreign countries. Since 2004 the editor-in-chief has been Evgenii Kiselev.

See also: Communist Party; Gorbachev, Mikhail; Iakovlev, Egor; journalism; journalists, post-Soviet; Kiselev, Evgenii; *Literaturnaia gazeta* (Literary Gazette); propaganda, Soviet and post-Soviet

NADEZHDA AZHGIKHINA

Moskovskii komsomolets

Newspaper

MK (pronounced 'em-ka') is one of Moscow's leading daily newspapers. Founded in 1919, it functioned for decades as the official news organ for Soviet youth, as indicated by its title ('Muscovite Komsomol member'). During perestroika it was transformed into a popular daily known for its sensationalist, tabloid-style coverage, cutting-edge political reporting, and eclectic content. Running 4–6 pages, with a print run averaging 2.5 million, and its own website, it

continues to attract a broad readership in Moscow and many other Russian cities, as well as in a number of European countries (including Germany and Spain).

See also: Communist Youth League; perestroika and glasnost; periodicals, post-Soviet; periodicals, Soviet

ANDREA LANOUX

Mossovet Theatre (Teatr imeni Mossoveta)

Founded in 1923 as the theatre of the Moscow Municipal Council of Professional Unions (MGSPS), it acquired its present name in 1938. Under Evsei Liubimov-Lanskoi (1925–40), it championed new Soviet plays. Reflecting the trend in Soviet theatre away from contemporary themes in the middle of the century, chief director Iurii Zavadskii (1940–77), left an indelible mark as an interpreter of Goldoni, Shakespeare, Chekhov, and Dostoevsky. Pavel Khomskii's appointment as chief director in 1985 ushered in an era of considered eclecticism. His productions of musicals (*Jesus Christ, Superstar*), frothy comedies, melodramas, and foreign hits (*On Golden Pond*) maintained the theatre's popularity with audiences. Over the years, the troupe has numbered such popular actors as Faina Ranevskaia, Liubov Orlova, Rostislav Pliatt, Margarita Terekhkova, and Sergei Iurskii.

See also: Iurskii, Sergei; Orlova, Liubov; Pliatt, Rostislav; Ranevskaia, Faina; Terekhova, Margarita; Zavadskii, Yurii

JOHN FREEDMAN

mother-heroine (mat-geroinia)

A 1937 decree by the Council of People's Commissars assigned every woman who had given birth to seven children the status of a 'mother-heroine'. She was entitled to monetary aid, but exceedingly strict requirements, including reams of paperwork, limited its practical application to a few token cases. When a special order for mother-heroines was established in 1944, the required number of children increased to ten. The first recipient of the order was Anna Aleksakhina, who had raised twelve children, eight of whom had fought and four of whom were killed in the war. Official (unreliable) Soviet statistics claimed that between 1937 and 1991, when the distinction was abolished, 500,000 women attained mother-heroine status.

VLADIMIR PAPERNY

Motyl, Vladimir Iakovlevich

b. 26 June 1927, Sverdlovsk

Film director

Motyl is best known for the enormously popular *Beloe solntse pustyni* (*White Sun of the Desert*, 1969), about the struggles of a Red Army soldier against Central Asian bandits in the Civil War, with 'Spaghetti' Western influences. Motyl also directed *Nesut menia koni* (*Horses Carry Me*, 1996), an update of Chekhov's novella *The Duel*.

See also: *Beloe solntse pustyni* (*White Sun of the Desert*); Central Asia; Ekaterinburg

DAVID GILLESPIE

Mravinskii, Evgenii Aleksandrovich

b. 4 June 1903, St. Petersburg; d. 21 January 1988, Leningrad

Conductor

Mravinskii was associated throughout his career with the Leningrad Philharmonic, which he conducted for forty-nine years, until his death. He studied composition and conducting at the St. Petersburg Conservatory. His career-defining moment was the premiere of Shostakovich's *Fifth Symphony* on 21 November 1937, which led to a long friendship with the composer. Mravinskii premiered several other Shostakovich symphonies, including the *Seventh* ('*Leningrad*') Symphony (1943). After winning the

National Conductors' Competition in 1938, he was appointed artistic director of the Leningrad Philharmonic that year. Mravinskii also premiered works by Prokofiev, Khachaturian, Sviridov, and other Soviet composers. His 1961 recording of the Tchaikovsky symphonies received particularly high acclaim, but he was comfortable with a wide variety of Western symphonic composers, including Beethoven, Mozart, Brahms, Berlioz, and Mahler. Though he conducted and recorded with other Russian orchestras, he worked with only one foreign orchestra (the Czech Philharmonic), and was known as a diligent, disciplined taskmaster whose interpretations perfectly balanced passion and precision. He left over 200 commercial, studio, and live recordings; many recordings were released only after his death and the break-up of the Soviet Union.

See also: Khachaturian, Aram; orchestras, Soviet and post-Soviet; Prokofiev, Sergei; St. Petersburg (Leningrad) State Conservatory; Shostakovich, Dmitrii

ALEXANDER BURRY

Mukhina, Olga Stanislavovna

b. 1 December 1970, Moscow

Playwright

Mukhina wanted to study screenwriting, but failed to enter the VGIK cinema institute. Her poetic, stream-of-conscious language and dreamy characters caught in the cold grip of reality showed the influence of Anton Chekhov, but were an innovation in Russian drama. *Tanya-Tanya* (1996) was a mellifluous, though ominous, exploration of people torn by love and aimlessness. *U* (*YoU*, 1997), whose title puns on the English pronoun and the Russian letter, was an ambitious overview of three generations of Muscovites plagued by personal uncertainty and social instability. *Liubov Karlovny* (*The Love of Karlovna*, 1992) was a significant early play about lost love. *Letit* (*Flying*, written 2004), an examination of affluent young Russians, ended a seven-year silence.

See also: theatre, post-Soviet

JOHN FREEDMAN

Muratova, Kira Georgievna

(née Korotkova)

b. 5 November 1934, Soroki, Moldova

Film director, scriptwriter, actress

Trained at VGIK under Gerasimov, Muratova is arguably Russia's greatest woman director, that rare Stagnation-era filmmaker who has continued to produce highly original work in the post-Soviet era. Her Soviet-era films were criticized and sometimes 'shelved' or censored for their auteur style and emphasis on individual psychology rather than collectivist ideals. Throughout her career she has addressed moral issues and values, such as personal and family happiness (*Korotkie vstrechi* [*Brief Encounters*, 1967], *Dolgie provody* [*Long Goodbyes*, 1971], *Chekhovskie motivy* [*Chekhovian Motifs*, 2002]), or murder and the meaning of death (*Peremena uchasti* [*A Change of Fortune*, 1987], *Tri istorii* [*Three Stories*, 1997], *Vtorostepennye liudi* [*Minor People*, 2001]), often from a female perspective. Her dark 1989 film, *Astenicheskii sindrom* (*The Asthenic Syndrome*, 1990), diagnosed the parlous psychological state of glasnost society.

See also: All-Russian (All-Union) State Institute of Cinematography (VGIK); censorship; film, Soviet – Stagnation period

RIMGAILA SALYS

museums-estates

Russian museums-estates are carefully preserved cultural landmarks that allow visitors a glimpse into the way of life of the aristocracy, peasants, and tradespeople during a period of approximately two hundred years. As one of the grassroots movements of the 1960s, the drive to recover essential features of imperial Russia extended to the reclamation and preservation of the country residences of major literary and cultural figures. This movement was necessary, because most of the estates were destroyed during the Civil War (1917–22) or fell into a state of ruin due to decades of intentional neglect by the Soviet government. Well-known examples of museums-estates that have been meticulously restored include Lev Tolstoi's Isnaia Poliana, Aleksandr Blok's Bolshoe Shakhmatovo, Ivan Turgenev's Spasskoe Lutovinovo, Petr Tchaikovsky's estate at Klin, and Sergei Rachmaninoff's Ivanovka.

The Russian country estate (*imenie, usadba*) was the centre for the everyday life of the landed nobility and peasants from the time of Peter the Great in the late seventeenth century to the Bolshevik Revolution of 1917. It also represented the site of the development of Russian culture and customs: the estate served as the repository for art works, book collections, china, silver, and furniture that were handed down from one generation to the next. When viewed as a large, aesthetically organized complex of a manor house (*barskii dom*) and numerous outbuildings supported by peasant villages, the estate becomes a well-defined and traditional way of life in suburban and rural Russia. An entire world was encapsulated in it; indeed, the nineteenth-century estate gave the world the finest products of Russia's culture. Dostoevskii noted that Russian literature was 'a literature of landowners'. As part of the daily life on country estates, residents performed plays and musical works and wrote novels and poetry. Residents and visitors learned foreign languages; carried out translations of literary works; discussed intellectual and political ideas; participated in various Russian Orthodox services at the church typically located nearby; and organized schools, day care centres, and charitable events. Country estates were cities in and of themselves, and in the completeness of their way of life they differ from villas, farms, ranches, plantations, and haciendas, which contain some (but not all) of the aforementioned elements. In Russian culture the principles of goodness and harmony are often associated with life on the estates, as juxtaposed with the qualities of chaos and disharmony linked with urban existence and culture.

The country estate witnessed its greatest period of flowering and architectural innovation during the era of Catherine the Great in the eighteenth century. The main houses were often enormous and built according to European neoclassical models; they were integrated into the surrounding countryside by a system of roads, floral and arboreal landscaping, bridges, gazebos, and ponds designed for inspired contemplation.

See also: Russian Orthodoxy; traditions and customs

Further reading

Roosevelt, P. (1995) *Life on the Russian Country Estate*, New Haven, CT: Yale University Press.
Soloukhin, V. (1993) *A Time to Gather Stones*, trans. V. Z. Nollan, Evanston, IL: Northwestern University Press.

VALERIA Z. NOLLAN

mushrooms

While the Slavs in general seem to be among the world's greatest mycophiles, Russians are particularly passionate about their mushrooms. They consume a wide variety of wild fungi, including those considered inedible or even poisonous elsewhere. Moreover, mushroom hunting in Russia is a veritable obsession, which can be viewed as a part of national identity. The culinary use of mushrooms is extremely diverse: they are cooked fresh, dried, marinated (i.e. preserved with the help of vinegar), and 'salted', (i.e., fermented with salt and spices without the use of vinegar, a quintessentially Russian method). The traditional leader or, according to a folk tale, the colonel of all mushrooms is *belyi grib* (white mushroom)/ *borovik* (*Boletus edulis*), followed by members of the boletus family and various agarics that are, in turn, accompanied by a host of irregulars from various families. There are, however, two agarics of a superior rank: *ryzhik* (red-head) (*Lactarius deliciosus*) and *gruzd* (*Lactarius resimus*), which are unsurpassed for salting. The hierarchy of mushrooms was canonized during the Soviet era, when all edible mushrooms were divided into four categories

according to their nutritional value and agro-industrial worth. Historically, mushroom dishes provided an important dietary supplement during the long periods of fasting prescribed by the Orthodox Church, while pickled mushrooms remain a *sine qua non* of the *zakuski* (appetizers) table. However, the Russian love affair with mushrooms cannot be reduced to culinary considerations, as vividly attested in Vladimir Nabokov's autobiographical *Speak, Memory!*, in which mushroom hunting turns into a potent symbol of the lost motherland.

See also: appetizers; Lent; Nabokov, Vladimir; soups

DAN UNGURIANU

music in film

Music has played an unusually important role in the Soviet film tradition. Leading popular and classical composers collaborated with filmmakers from the earliest days of the Soviet film industry. As a student, Dmitrii Shostakovich accompanied silent films on the piano, and later wrote music for more than thirty films (both silent and sound), among them such masterpieces as *Korol Lir* (*King Lear*, 1971) and *Gamlet* (*Hamlet*, 1964) directed by Grigorii Kozintsev. Sergei Prokofiev composed music for eight films, including two collaborations with Sergei Eisenstein (*Aleksandr Nevskii* [1938] and *Ivan Groznyi* [*Ivan the Terrible*, 1942–46]). Aram Khachaturian composed more than fifteen film scores. In the post-Stalin period, distinguished film scores were produced by such composers as Sofia Gubaidulina (*Chuchelo* [*The Scarecrow*, 1982]), Alfred Shnittke (*Komissar*, 1967), Eduard Artemev (more than eighty scores for films, including Andrei Tarkovskii's *Solaris*, 1972), Viacheslav Ovchinnikov (scores for more than forty films, including *Vojna i mir* [*War and Peace*, 1965] by Sergei Bondarchuk) and Edison Denisov. In the post-Soviet era, St. Petersburg composer Leonid Desiatnikov (b. 1955) has achieved particular success (*Kavkazskii plennik* [*Prisoner of the Mountains*, 1996], *Oligarkh* [*The Tycoon*, 2002]).

In most countries, including the United States, composers who write film scores largely inhabit a category quite separate from what is considered 'serious' concert music. Russian film composers have suffered much less from such categorization. One explanation lies in the supreme importance of film among all the arts during the Soviet period. Film possessed an official cultural status at least equal to that of literature, music, and painting. Furthermore, the birth of Soviet Russian culture, including music, coincided almost exactly with the worldwide explosion of the film industry. During the Soviet period, Russian music and film developed side by side, and it was natural that Soviet composers would work in this new medium.

Numerous prominent Russian film directors (Eisenstein, Tarkovskii) also possessed great musical sophistication, and conceived of music's role in film in new and highly theoretical terms. Their intellectual approach to the film score as an art, and their willingness to respect the composer as a collaborator on equal terms, led serious composers to view film music as a worthwhile and unique genre. For composers like Prokofiev, Shostakovich, Shnittke and Gubaidulina, whose music the Soviet government frequently criticized and even banned as elitist or excessively intellectual, the composition of film scores intended for a mass audience and often possessing high propagandistic content proved a way to earn money while satisfying the demands of the Soviet authorities. Their work in the cinema also influenced their music in other genres, heightening their visual sense and ability to convey emotion succinctly.

Songs, both folk and patriotic, have traditionally played a prominent role in Russian film scores. Beginning with Isaak Dunaevskii in the 1930s and 1940s, composers including Andrei Petrov (*Sluzhebnyi roman* [*An Office Romance*, 1977]), Issak Shvarts (*Beloe solntse pustyni* [*White Sun of the Desert*, 1969], *Zvezda plenitelnogo schastia* [*Star of Captivating Happiness*, 1975]), and Dunaevskii's son Maksim (*Tri mushketera* [*Three Musketeers*, 1961]) have created songs that equal or sometimes surpass in popularity the films in which they were featured

See also: *Beloe solntse pustyni* (*White Sun of the Desert*); Bondarchuk, Sergei; Denisov, Edison; Dunaevskii, Maksim; Gubaidulina, Sofiia; Khachaturian, Aram; Kozintsev, Grigorii; Prokofiev,

Sergei; Shnittke, Alfred; Shostakovich, Dmitrii; Tarkovskii, Andrei

Further reading

Egorova, T. (1997) *Soviet Film Music*, Amsterdam: Harwood Academic Publishers.
Frid, E. L. (1967) *Muzyka v sovetskom kino* (Music in Soviet Cinema), Leningrad: Muzyka.

HARLOW ROBINSON

music in theatre

Music became an integral element in Russian dramatic theatre when composer Ilia Sats joined Konstantin Stanislavskii and Vsevolod Meierkhold at the Studio on Povarskaia in 1905, then worked at the Moscow Art Theatre from 1907 until his death in 1912. Meierkhold throughout his career collaborated with composers Aleksandr Glazunov, Dmitrii Shostakovich, Sergei Prokofiev, Vissarion Shebalin and Mikhail Gnesin, as well as with Mikhail Kuzmin, poet, playwright, and composer. But in the middle of the twentieth century others increasingly used the music of Aram Khachaturian, Matvei Blanter and Isaak Dunaevskii as illustrative filler.

This changed when Iurii Liubimov founded the Taganka Theatre in 1964 and forged partnerships with Alfred Shnittke, Edison Denisov, Mikael Tariverdiev and Iurii Butsko. Liubimov's greatest contribution, however, was his use of songs by the actor and bard Vladimir Vysotskii. These songs, often part of a general musical structure created by Vysotskii, Boris Khmelnitskii and Anatolii Vasilev (no relation to the director of the same name) and performed live on acoustic guitar, cut through theatrical conventions by allowing a contemporary poetic voice to address audiences directly. Many of Vysotskii's most famous songs first appeared in Liubimov's renowned production of *Hamlet* (1971).

Beginning in the 1990s, several directors cultivated relationships with particular composers – Kama Ginkas with Leonid Desiatnikov; Robert Sturua with Giia Kancheli; Valerii Fokin with Aleksandr Bakshi; Liubimov with Vladimir Martynov, who also worked with director

Anatolii Vasilev at the School of Dramatic Art. Bakshi and Martynov, though cultivating different styles and aspiring to diverse goals (Bakshi preferred a secular, mythical basis, while Martynov supported the return of music and theatre to a holy space) were similar in that they often raised the profile of the composer to a level equalling the director's. Martynov's *Plach Ierimeiia* (*The Lament of Jeremiah*, 1996) for Vasilev and his music to Dostoevskii's *Bratia Karamazovy* (*The Brothers Karamazov*, 1997), Peter Weiss's *Marat and Marquis de Sade* (1998) and *Idite i ostanovite progress: Oberiuty* (*Go and Stop Progress: The Oberiuty*, 2003) for Liubimov's productions were important accomplishments. Martynov's *Noch v Galitsii* (*Night in Galicia*, 1996), based on poetry by Velimir Khlebnikov, and *Apokalipsis* (*Apocalypse*, 2001) were attempts to fuse musical performance with theatrical elements. Bakshi, the progenitor of what he called the theatre of sound, went further in over a dozen collaborations with Fokin – among them *Sidur misterii* (*The Sidur Mysteria*, 1992), about the sculptor Vadim Sidur, *Nomer v gostinitse goroda NN* (*A Hotel Room in the Town of NN*, 1994), after Gogol; Kafka's *Metamorphosis* (1995) and Gogol's *Shinel* (*The Overcoat*, 2004). Here he developed his method of determining action through sounds, partially assuming the role traditionally occupied by the playwright. Bakshi's masterworks *Polifoniia mira* (*The Polyphony of the World*, 2001, directed by Ginkas and starring Gidon Kremer) and *Iz Krasnoi Knigi* (*From the Red Book of Extinction*, 2003, directed by Ilia Epelbaum and starring Aleksei Liubimov) raised to new heights his brand of theatre in which music and sound replaced the word. Stepan Andrusenko wrote new music to replace the lost score of the legendary Futurist opera *Pobeda nad solntsem* (*Victory over the Sun*, 1997) and, with director Nikolai Roshchin, created *Shkola durakov* (*School of Fools*, 2003), a Bakshi-like mystery-opera rooted in music and sound.

See also: Denisov, Edison Vasilevich; Desiatnikov, Leonid; Fokin, Valerii; Kancheli, Giya; Khachaturian, Aram; Kremer, Gidon; Liubimov, Aleksei; Liubimov, Iurii; Moscow Art Theatre; Prokofiev, Sergei; Shnittke, Alfred; Shostakovich, Dmitrii; Sturua, Robert; Taganka Theatre; Vasilev, Anatolii; Vysotskii, Vladimir

JOHN FREEDMAN

musicals, Russian/Soviet

Broadly speaking, musicals are stage, television or film productions featuring popular-style dance and song, subordinated to a story or dialogue with several performers, designed for light-hearted entertainment. Song and dance are both integral to the plot; removal of either would compromise the whole.

The first Soviet music hall for staging musical-style productions was created in 1923, in Moscow's Aquarium Park. Its most successful production was *Artisty varete* (Variety Performers, 1933), followed by *Pod kupolom tsirka* (Under the Circus Dome, 1934). The first film versions of USSR musicals were comedies directed by Grigorii Aleksandrov in the 1930s: *Veselye rebiata* (The Jolly Fellows, 1934); *Tsirk* (Circus, 1936); *Volga-Volga* (1938), and Ivan Pyrev's *Traktoristy* (Tractor Drivers, 1939). *Under the Circus Dome* became the highly popular film *Circus*, scripted by Valentin Kataev and Ilf and Petrov, with music by Isaak Dunaevskii, whose 'About the Motherland' (co-written with Vasilii Lebedev-Kumach) became one of the most popular Soviet-era songs. Leonid Utesov and his jazz orchestra, after their successful March 1929 variety show in Leningrad's Little Opera Theatre, were invited to participate in *The Jolly Fellows*. Aleksandrov's musicals featured his wife, Liubov Orlova, a blonde, blue-eyed diva who resembled Ginger Rogers and Mary Pickford. In an environment of Stalinist terror, such glamorous and dazzling musicals were both escapist and ideological, proclaiming Soviet communism's superiority over capitalism. Musical comedy was encouraged by Boris Shumiatskii, head of the Soviet cinema industry, whose 1935 decree urged film-makers to produce movies for the masses.

After Stalin's death (1953) the output of musicals declined; neither Nikita Khrushchev nor Leonid Brezhnev approved of them. A famous post-war film musical was Eldar Riazanov's *Karnavalnaia noch* (Carnival Night, 1956), featuring Liudmila Gurchenko and showing how amateur actors transform a New Year's Eve celebration into a dazzling extravaganza of song and dance, with confetti and firecrackers.

Under Mark Zakharov's directorship (1973), Moscow's Lenin Komsomol (Lenkom) Theatre staged the first Soviet musicals in the style of Broadway productions. His famous musicals include *Til* (1974); *Zvezda i smert Khoakina Muretty* (*The Star and Death of Joaquín Murietta*, 1976), and *Iunona i avos* (*Iunona and Perhaps I'll be Lucky*, 1981), the first Russian rock opera, set to lyrics by Andrei Voznesenskii.

In the late 1990s, musicals again became fashionable after the success of a Russian production of the Polish musical *Metro*, staged by the Moscow Light Opera Theatre. Famous post-Soviet musical theatre productions include *Nord-Ost* (2001), *Guby* (*Lips*, 2002) and *Dvenadtsat stulev* (*Twelve Chairs*, 2003), based on Russian literary classics. Various productions of successful foreign musicals, such as *Cats*, *42nd Street*, and *Notre-Dame de Paris*, also enjoy enormous success with Russian audiences.

See also: Brezhnev, Leonid; Gurchenko, Liudmila; Khrushchev, Nikita; Lenkom Theatre; *Nord-Ost*; perestroika and glasnost; Riazanov, Eldar; rock opera; Socialist Realism; Thaw; theatre, post-Soviet; theatre, Soviet; Voznesenskii, Andrei

Further reading

Horton, A. (ed.) (1993) *Inside Soviet Film Satire: Laughter with a Lash*, Cambridge: Cambridge University Press.

Taylor, R. (1999) 'Singing on the Steppes for Stalin: Ivan Pyrev and the Kolkhoz Musical in Soviet Cinema', *Slavic Review*, 58, 1:143–59.

ALEXANDRA SMITH

N

Nabokov, Vladimir Vladimirovich

b. 10 [22] April 1899, St. Petersburg;
d. 2 July 1977, Montreux, Switzerland

Writer

One of the twentieth-century's best stylists, a poet, critic, literary translator, and avid lepidopterist, Nabokov was born in St. Petersburg to a prominent aristocratic family. After the Bolshevik Revolution of 1917, his family fled to Europe, eventually settling in Berlin. After studying French and Russian literature at Trinity College, Cambridge, Nabokov established his literary reputation as one of the foremost émigré Russian writers in Berlin, and later Paris, under the pseudonym Sirin. In 1940, Nabokov escaped the Nazis with his wife Vera and their young son, Dmitrii. This second exile, to the United States, entailed torturous linguistic consequences, as Nabokov had to abandon his native language and start anew as an English-language writer. He taught in turn at Stanford, Wellesley, Harvard, and Cornell, and eventually achieved fame as a novelist in his adopted language. The *succès de scandale* of his 1955 novel *Lolita* and its subsequent adaptation as a motion picture made Nabokov wealthy and allowed him to move to Switzerland and devote himself entirely to writing fiction.

Nabokov started his literary career as a Russian poet and translator. Among his most significant works in translation are his 1922–23 Russian version of Lewis Carroll's *Alice in Wonderland*, and, in the 1960s, a Russian version of his *Lolita* and a strikingly literal English translation of Aleksandr Pushkin's novel in verse *Eugene Onegin* (1964), with extensive commentaries. His Russian-language œuvre includes numerous stories and novels, among them *Zashchita Luzhina* (*The Defense*, 1929–30), *Otchaianie* (*Despair*, 1934), *Priglashenie na kazn* (*Invitation to a Beheading*, 1935–36), and *Dar* (*The Gift*, 1937). Nabokov's most important English fiction – *Lolita*, *Pnin* (1957), *Pale Fire* (1960–61), *Ada or Ardor* (1959–68) – is celebrated as innovative and controversial. He also published English-language poems and stories, as well as a large number of critical essays, lectures, and translations of his own Russian fiction and of other Russian writers and poets. The 1951 and 1966 versions of his memoirs, *Conclusive Evidence* and *Speak, Memory!*, along with the Russian-language version, *Drugie berega* (*The Other Shores*, 1954), bring into focus the complex phenomenon of Nabokov's art, in which protagonists, including the auto-biographer himself, function alongside their unsettling doubles. Nabokov is not just a great stylist, keen observer of detail, master of literary device, creator of tantalizing patterns, and connoisseur of artistic deception, he is also a profound and original thinker, whose metaphysics is offset by scepticism. Time and consciousness, loss and exile are among Nabokov's persistent themes, just as a butterfly is one of his most recurrent motifs. Nabokov's allegiance to lucid individualism and ironic rationality, paradoxically combined with his ultimately unironic pity for beauty and humanistic ethics, contribute to the unresolved tensions that inform his best novels and their tortured, lucidly mad protagonists (e.g. Humbert in *Lolita* or Kinbote in *Pale Fire*). Nabokov is not so much a solver of transcendental mysteries as a 'manufacturer' of secrets and conjurer of aesthetic delights.

See also: literature, émigré

Further reading

Boyd, B. (1990, 1992) *Vladimir Nabokov: The Russian Years; The American Years*, Princeton, NJ: Princeton University Press.

JULIA TRUBIKHINA

Nagibin, Iurii Markovich

b. 3 April 1920, Moscow; d. 17 June 1994, Moscow

Writer

Prosaist and scriptwriter Nagibin was one of the most prolific, successful, and widely published Russian authors during the Thaw. His prose, mainly comprising short stories, lacks social criticism, examines human emotions and interpersonal relations, and treats such topics as nature, love, war, children, art, hunting, fishing, and other sports. His early characters are simple, unpretentious people of various occupations, ages, and social groups; later works limn more complex personalities. Whereas stories such as the youthful *Zimnii dub* (*Winter Oak*, 1953) celebrate spiritual awakening, more mature narratives (*Chuzhaia*, *The Outsider* 1976) offer a darker perspective on life. Many of Nagibin's stories have been made into films.

Based on childhood memories, Nagibin's collection *Chistye prudy* (*Clear Ponds*, 1962) contains narratives set in villages and provincial towns and abounding in nature descriptions. A master of fictionalized biography, Nagibin wrote a cycle about famous writers and composers. In 1987, he published a quasi-autobiography, *Vstan i idi* (*Stand and Walk*), a revealing testament of the Stalin period, followed in 1995 by his bilious *Dnevnik* (*Diary*, 1995).

See also: literature, Thaw

Further reading

Goscilo, H. (1986) 'Introduction', in H. Goscilo (ed.) *Yuri Nagibin: The Peak of Success and Other Stories*, Ann Arbor, MI: Ardis, pp. 9–26.
Porter, R. (1978) 'The Uneven Talent of Jurij Nagibin', *Russian Language Journal* 32, 113: 103–13.

TATYANA NOVIKOV

Nakhova, Irina Isaevna

b. 6 August 1955, Moscow

Artist

Emerging from the Conceptualism that engaged unofficial Moscow artists in the 1970s, Nakhova in her work explores how vision and language function. Part of Apt-Art, Nakhova regularly transformed the space of her apartment via diverse media. In the 1990s, she produced installations that distort both space and intellectual frameworks. Nakhova has treated feminist concerns, compelling viewers to consider sex and gender as they experience her installations. She now lives in New York.

See also: Apt-Art

KRISTEN M. HARKNESS

name day celebration (*imeniny*)

Before the Revolution, Orthodox Christians were named after a saint who was celebrated on or near the day of birth. Traditionally, Russians celebrated a person's name day (*imeniny*), also called Angel Day (*Den angela*), more lavishly than the actual birthday (if it was on a different day). After a person's death, by Church custom a person's date of death and name day (not the actual birthday) are commemorated. While the tradition was not widely observed during the Soviet period, it has been revived since the 1990s.

See also: Russian Orthodoxy; traditions and customs

MICHELE BERDY

names and renaming, Soviet

The tradition of renaming cities and other inhabited areas existed in Russia before the Soviet period, for the enlargement of the Russian Empire was accompanied by a continuous process of absorbing newly-conquered cities and areas. Soviet ideology added new motives for renaming. From 1917 until the end of the 1930s, renaming was intended to draw the Communist future closer, which is why names of prominent Bolsheviks replaced 'tsarist' elements in toponyms (Elisavetpol thus became Kirovabad in honour of Sergei Kirov; Ekaterinoslav became Dnepropetrovsk in honour of Grigorii Petrovskii; Ekaterinburg became Sverdlovsk in honour of Iakov Sverdlov, etc.). In addition, cities could acquire more 'Communist' connotations with the epithet 'Red' (*krasnyi*: Ekaterinodar became Krasnodar, Aleksandrovsk became Krasnopartisansk), or Leninist/Lenin's (Vorobevy gory [Sparrow Hills] became Leninskie gory [Lenin Hills]). Apart from Lenin (Petrograd became Leningrad) and Stalin (Tsaritsyn became Stalingrad), whose names were widely used in Soviet political geography and topography, the main suppliers of names were Maksim Gorkii (Nizhni Novgorod became Gorkii in 1932) and Mikhail Kalinin (Tver became Kalinin in 1931). After 1956, Stalin's name vanished from all geographical names of the USSR (thus Stalingrad became Volgograd), and after 1991, in Russia and other states emerging on former Soviet territory, the names of Lenin, Gorkii, and Kalinin were also erased in a process of general de-Sovietization.

One exception is the city of Kaliningrad (Königsberg before 1946). This toponym emerged after World War II, when Russian names replaced all German names in Eastern Prussia. Kaliningrad therefore continues to bear its name even after 1991, not because it is Soviet, but because it sounds Russian, whereas, by contrast, Tver, which in 1931 became Kalinin, reverted to Tver in 1993.

Apart from toponyms, the cult of a 'new era', traditionally viewed as dating from the October Revolution (1917), encouraged Russian speakers to invent neologisms instead of traditional first names. Most such names emerged in the 1920s and 1930s. Such names include abbreviations like Vilor (Vladimir Ilich Lenin + Oktiabrskaia revolutsiia; Vladilen = Vladimir + Lenin; Marksen = Marx + Engels, etc.). Moreover, people were given the names of abstract revolutionary concepts (Avangard, or Dognat-Peregnat, a combination of the traditional name Ignat with the slogan '*dognat i peregnat Ameriku*' [to catch up with and overtake America]). Toward the end of the 1950s, names of this nature became less common, although some of these abbreviations were still found pleasing to the ear and ceased to be associated with their original creation (e.g., Vladilen and Marlen).

Further reading

Guseinov, G. (2004) *Sovetskie ideologemy v russkom diskurse 1990-kh*, Moscow: Tri kvadrata.

Murray, J. (2000) *Politics and Place-Names: Changing Names in the Late Soviet Period*, Birmingham: Department of Russian, University of Birmingham.

Pospelov, E. M. (1993) *Imena gorodov: vchera i segodnia (1917–1992). Toponimicheskii slovar*, Moscow: Russkie slovari.

Room, A. (1996) *Placenames of Russia and the Former Soviet Union: Origins and Meanings of the Names for over 2000 Natural Features, Towns, Regions, and Countries*, Jefferson, NC: McFarland.

GASAN GUSEJNOV

names, personal

All Russian citizens have three personal names marked on their birth certificates: the first name (*imia*); the patronymic (*otchestvo*), derived from the father's name; and the last name (*familiia*), usually the father's.

The first name can almost always be turned into a standard nickname; in contrast to most Western practice, the standard form of the nickname is commonly used outside the circle of one's family and close friends. For example, an Aleksandr may commonly be called Sasha or Shura not only by friends and family, but also by colleagues and acquaintances of approximately the same age. Affectionate, diminutive forms of the nickname (such as Sashenka or Shurochka) are used within one's intimate circle of family and close friends, occasionally and affectionately outside that circle, and for children. A pejorative form of the standard nickname, with the ending -ka and no infix (Sashka, Shurka), can be used with siblings, close friends, or among children; its use is intended to be either insulting or ironically affectionate.

The patronymic is derived from the father's first name with a suffix: -ovich or -evich for men and -ovna or -evna for women. The combination of name and patronymic (for example, Aleksandr Petrovich or Tatiana Dmitrievna) is the equivalent of Mr. or Ms. in English. It is used in all formal settings, including business transactions; with adult acquaintances with whom one is on formal terms, such as neighbours; with virtually anyone significantly older than the addressor; and instead of professional titles, including Professor, Doctor, and even President. Thus journalists address(ed) President Yeltsin as Boris Nikolaevich and Putin as Vladimir Vladimirovich. Among adults under 50, the use of the first name in its full form and without patronymic (Western practice) is becoming more common in formal work settings: someone called Aleksei Ivanovich by colleagues at work twenty years ago might today be called simply Aleksei (but not necessarily by the nickname, Alesha). Such usage would be impossible in highly formal settings or in place of titles, however.

Like the patronymic, standard Russian last names (ending in -in, -ov/-ev, or -skii) are marked for gender: the first two add the suffix -a and the last changes to -skaia: thus, male Karenin becomes female Karenina, Dostoevskii becomes Dostoevskaia. Children usually receive their father's surname, though in the Soviet era parents occasionally gave children the mother's last name, usually to conceal non-Russian ethnic origins in the face of institutionalized discrimination; in post-Soviet Russia, parents might make the same choice to emphasize a child's non-Russian ethnic origins on the maternal side. A mother may also choose to give a child her last name if the father is not part of the family; however, she must still provide the child with a patronymic. It is less common in Russia than in Western Europe and the United States for a woman to take her husband's last name. Hyphenation of last names upon

marriage was more common among pre-Revolutionary nobility than in Soviet and post-Soviet Russia. The last name was not traditionally used as a form of address in pre-Revolutionary Russia. It was adopted, together with the title Comrade (*tovarishch*), for Party members in the Soviet era. Once again, it has dropped out of common use as a form of address in post-Soviet Russia. Military forms of address have maintained the word Comrade, together with the military rank. Informally, however, Russian men may be called by their last name.

KAREN EVANS-ROMAINE

Namin, Stas

(né Anastas Alekseevich Mikoian)

b. 8 November 1951, Moscow

Musician, producer

Grandson of Anastas Mikoian, Soviet political figure of 1923–76, and the cousin (twice removed) of a creator of the MIG planes, in 1969 Namin became a founding member of the first Soviet rock 'supergroup' Tsvety (Flowers), which reportedly sold 60 million copies of its albums. In 1987, he founded the Stas Namin Centre, which promotes musicians, groups (such as Gorkii Park), and records and releases their albums. In 1999, Namin founded the Moscow Theatre of Music and Drama, which opened with the Russian version of *Hair*.

ALEXANDER DOMRIN

Nash sovremennik (Our Contemporary)

A periodical (originally an almanac, then monthly journal) of the Russian Union of Writers, founded in 1956 in Moscow. The dismissal of Aleksandr Tvardovskii from *Novyi mir* (1970), made *Nash sovremennik* a haven for a large group of *Novyi mir* authors, especially authors of village prose (*derevenshchiki*), such as Viktor Astafev and Vasilii Belov, who joined the journal's editorial board. Since the late 1980s, *Nash sovremennik* has vocally opposed Russian liberal reformers, and its authors' actively patriotic position guarantees growing public support. Since the fall of the Soviet Union, the journal has had the largest subscription rate of all literary journals in Russia.

See also: Belov, Vasilii; *Novyi mir*; thick journals; Tvardovskii, Aleksandr; village prose

ALEXANDER DOMRIN

national anthem, Soviet and Russian

Following the consolidation of Bolshevik power, the socialist 'Internationale' became the national anthem of the Soviet Union. It was replaced in 1944 by the familiar anthem composed by Aleksandr Aleksandrov, with words by Sergei Mikhalkov and Garold El-Registan, personally edited and approved by Stalin. In its original version, the new anthem praised both Lenin and Stalin. As a result of the policy of de-Staliniza-tion following Stalin's death in 1953, the anthem was played without words until 1977, when a revised version, also authored by Mikhalkov, was adopted. Lenin assumed a more prominent role in the revised anthem, while all mention of Stalin was removed. Following the collapse of the Soviet Union, President Boris Yeltsin issued a decree replacing the Soviet anthem with Mikhail Glinka's wordless 'Patri-oticheskaia pesnia' (Patriotic Song). Throughout the 1990s, the communist-dominated Duma regularly attempted to restore the Soviet-era anthem. In December 2000, President Vladimir Putin proposed that Aleksandrov's score be reinstated with new words. Although sharply criticized by Yeltsin and leading liberals, Putin's proposal enjoyed strong public support and quickly passed into law. The words of the new anthem, authored once more by Mikhalkov, became official in the spring of 2001. Religious and broadly patriotic sentiments now replaced communism and the leading role of the Party.

See also: Lenin, Vladimir Ilich; Putin, Vladi-mir; Stalin, Iosif; Yeltsin, Boris

PATRICK HENRY

national myths (narodnye mify)

'National myths' can denote many things, from myths grounded in folklore to historical untruths; here the term refers to ideas or beliefs that Russians hold about themselves. At the root of most national myths is the belief that Russia is incomprehensible and irrational, as famously stated in Tiutchev's 1866 poem, '*Umom Rossiiu ne poniat*' ('Russia cannot be known through reason'). The Russian soul (*dusha*) is steeped in this notion, as is the concept of spiritual anguish (*toska*), both of which privilege a spiritual essence over the material world. Many positive cultural values – friendship, hospitality, generosity, courage, heroism, and depth of feeling – stem from the life of the soul. Less flattering attributes reside here as well: a tendency towards masochism, suffering, fatalism, superstition, compulsiveness, and a cosmic sense of unluckiness or foolishness (as exemplified by the folk hero Ivanushka-dur-achok [Little Ivan the Fool]). Expressions of national character often contain a gendered dimension: strength, loyalty, and sacrifice are often attributed to Russian women, especially in nineteenth-century fiction (as in Pushkin's heroine from his novel in verse *Evgenii Onegin*, Tatiana Larina); Russian men meanwhile are depicted as weak, wavering, and given to vice.

A notorious paradox is Russians' simulta-neous sense of inferiority and superiority to other cultures. Claims of cultural backwardness hark back to Peter I, echoing throughout the nineteenth century in a self-effacing tradition of cultural criticism. The eternal questions 'What is to be done?' (*Chernyshevskii*) and 'Who is to blame?' (*Gertsen*) continue to resonate in the post-Soviet era. Refrains point to an innate pas-sivity, laziness (*oblomov*), and proclivity to bribe-taking or swindling (*chichikov*). Yet the image of Russia as protector and saviour of Europe per-sists at the core of the Russian Idea, expressed by the Slavophiles and Dostoevskii, and realized during two and a half centuries of Tatar inva-sions and again during World War II. A per-ception of being better educated, more worldly, and intellectually superior to (other) Westerners endures, as does a deep pride in classical Rus-sian literature, music, and ballet.

Analogous paradoxes may be traced to Russia's imperial roots, to its multiethnic composition, and to its unique historical position bordering East and West. Russian culture is at once distinctive and universal, singular and all-encompassing. Centuries of authoritarian rule have fostered a deep suspicion of political power as an alien, even enemy force; at the same time, many believe that Russia's vast size and complexity require heavy-handed leadership (*krepkaia ruka nuzhna*). A history of communal social organizations informs a distaste for individualism (hence the spiritualized notion of collectivity, *sobornost*), and centuries of social upheaval allegedly evince the impossibility of gradual change. Russia is thought to be a land of revolution, not evolution, one destined to hardship and extremes.

See also: ballet, post-Soviet; ballet, Soviet; classical music, post-Soviet; classical music, Soviet; folk mythology; folk tales; nationalism ('the national question'); Pushkin, Aleksandr; Russian soul; Slavophiles; superstitions, Russian; toska; World War II (Great Patriotic War)

Further reading

McDaniel, T. (1996) *The Agony of the Russian Idea*, Princeton, NJ: Princeton University Press.
Rancour-Laferiere, D. (2000) *Russian Nationalism from an Interdisciplinary Perspective: Imagining Russia*, Lewiston, NY: E. Mellen Press.
Solov'ev, V. M. (2001) *Tainy russkoi dushy*, Moscow: Russkii iazyk, kursy.

ANDREA LANOUX

nationalism ('the national question')

To appreciate the place of nationalism and of 'the national question' in contemporary Russian culture, one needs to recall the key historical events that led to the current shape of things. Elsewhere in Europe the rise of modern nationalisms is associated with the late eighteenth and early nineteenth centuries and the aftermath of the French Revolution. Similarly, in Russia, Count Sergei Uvarov's 1833 formula of 'orthodoxy, autocracy, and nationality' and the concurrent rise of the Slavophile movement led to a rethinking of the Russian Empire from dynastic

to ethno-national terms. The shift resulted in aggressive russification (*obrusenie*) campaigns, especially after the suppression of the 1863 Polish uprising, and in the restriction of public and educational use of such languages as Lithuanian and Ukrainian (rescinded only after the revolution of 1905). At the same time, 'the national question' was receiving increasing attention in liberal and Marxist circles across Europe, leading to heated debates during the years before World War I and in its aftermath. In Russia, it was a major preoccupation of Lenin, who wrote prolifically on this topic between 1913 and the early 1920s, and also of Stalin, whose first 'scholarly' work was the 1913 article on 'Marxism and the National Question'. The national question, including such issues as the right of nations to self-determination in politics, economics, and culture; the development of native languages; and the distinction between the oppressor-nation nationalism (known as 'great-power chauvinism') and the oppressed-nation nationalism, formed the kernel of the debates at the VIII, X, and XII Congresses of the Bolshevik Party (in 1919, 1921, and 1923 respectively). Nations were recognized as historically transient, yet 'objectively existing', and the situation of historically oppressed nations was analogized to that of oppressed classes. To win their support for the revolutionary cause, an affirmation of their rights was deemed necessary. Therefore, in the 1920s, the Soviet Union became what historians have recently dubbed 'the affirmative action empire', where some form of territorial or cultural autonomy was granted to nearly two hundred ethnic groups, and ambitious programmes of *korenizatsiia* ('nativization') were devised for education and public life, personnel hiring and promotions, and so forth. This policy, however, always remained half-hearted, as neither the Red Army nor the security services were ever 'nativized', and in 1926, Stalin personally attacked Ukrainian communists for trying to pull their national culture 'away from Moscow'. Beginning with the Great Break of the late 1920s and early 1930s, these affirmative action policies were rolled back. Stalin's thesis about the supposed escalation of class struggle in the course of building socialism meant that 'class enemies' were to be identified and 'purged' (i.e., physically eliminated) within each and every ethnic group. In all cases except that of the Russians, these 'enemies' were labelled 'bourgeois nationalists'. Their ranks usually comprised the older intelligentsia and representatives of the arts and the humanities. Their role was compared to that of the 'wreckers' in industry: with their alleged dreams of primordial nationhood, they were accused of sabotaging the construction of modern, socialist nations.

Official policies towards the Russians as the dominant nation were never consistently articulated in the 1920s, and by the early 1930s Russians were again receiving recognition as an ethnic group with a distinct national culture. That process accelerated and intensified during the remainder of the Soviet Union's history. From 1938, Russian language instruction was again mandatory throughout the USSR. Continuity with the historical tradition of the Russian Empire, beginning with the consolidation of Stalinism in the 1930s, was perhaps most visible culturally in such works as Sergei Eisenstein's films *Aleksandr Nevskii* (*Alexander Nevsky*, 1938) and *Ivan Groznyi* (*Ivan the Terrible*, 1944). The nationalities of the Soviet Union were now clearly ranked (with the Russian nation as the 'elder brother'), the very number of officially recognized nationalities halved, and many autonomous units abolished. The years immediately preceding, during, and shortly after World War II saw many ethnic groups rounded up and deported *en masse*. The infamous 'fifth paragraph' of Soviet internal passports registered a person's nationality, now understood as an immutable biological category. Culturally, nationality was relegated to essentially decorative 'form', to be filled with socialist 'content'. As such, this form was to be prized and celebrated (every nation of the Soviet Union was supposed to love the culture, especially the folklore, of every other Soviet nation), but the Russian nation was to be celebrated above all others. 'Bourgeois nationalism' was now redefined as insufficient admiration for Russia.

The early years of the Thaw following the denunciation of Stalinism at the Twentieth Party Congress in 1956 witnessed a reawakening of the intelligentsia throughout the Soviet Union. In many instances younger national intellectuals took up the causes championed by their predecessors in the 1920s. They were soon dismayed, however, by the new russificatory policies of Nikita Khrushchev, such as the 1959 school reform, which discouraged the study of the native language and made it optional. Similarly, the new 1961 Programme of the Communist Party adopted at the Twenty-Second Congress envisioned the withering away of nations as part of the accelerated building of communism. It proclaimed the formation of a new community of 'the Soviet people' (*sovetskii narod*), prompting a steady decline in secondary and higher education, as well as book and periodical publishing, in languages other than Russian. Thus from its outset, the new human rights dissident movement in the USSR engaged the national question, visible in one of the earliest political samizdat texts, Ivan Dziuba's (1965) treatise *Internationalism or Russification?* It criticized Soviet nationality policies by calling for a return to the vision originally advocated in the writings of Marx and Lenin. Attention to the national question led a sometimes uneasy coexistence with other aspects of the dissident movement, for critique of Soviet policies was advocated from both liberal and reactionary, even xenophobic, positions (particularly Igor Shafarevich's notorious treatise on 'Russophobia'). Yet most Russian and russified ordinary citizens of the Soviet Union (like many Western experts) assigned little importance to the national question until the late 1980s. Hence the widespread shocked reaction to the explosive growth of nationalisms that often erupted into armed conflict across the disintegrating Soviet empire.

The post-Communist policies of the Russian Federation on the national question have been eclectic and inconsistent. The early 1990s again saw the proliferation of autonomous units, but now with no differentiation between regional and ethnically defined ones. Just as in the 1930s, the 2000s saw a rollback in this area. What have disturbed many commentators are the blend of tsarist and Soviet legacies, evident in the official state insignia and other recuperations; the *laissez-faire* attitude towards the rise of xenophobia (visible in the escalating gang violence against racially visible ethnic others); and the openly chauvinist tone of educational materials used in Russian schools. The ongoing war in Chechnya and its interpretation in official media and state-backed cultural efforts (such as film-making) arc arguably the most visible aspects of the current troubled state of affairs. Neglectful and/or disrespectful towards ethnic others within it, the Russian state also uses 'the Russian question' as a lever for destabilizing influence in other ex-Soviet nations, and continues to promote internal conflict in other post-Soviet countries in the hope of turning them into firmly tethered client states.

On the cultural and intellectual level, Russia does not appear ready to perform the post-colonial work of mourning over its lost empire, and remains arrested in melancholy longing for an (imagined) unified imperial cultural space. Notably, postcolonial theory more than any other branch of contemporary intellectual inquiry has met with the greatest resistance in post-Soviet Russia. Even the few examples of thoughtful reflection on the personal and political dilemmas of postcolonial russophone cultural hybridity in the face of resurgent nationalisms (such as the fiction of Andrei Volos and Afanasii Mamedov) tend to be filled chiefly with uncomprehending shock at the rise of nationalisms among non-Russian others. One hopes that the trend towards increasing cultural globalization would eventually lead at least to a greater visibility of more critically self-aware Russian reflections on nationalism, and particularly Russian nationalism.

See also: Chechnya; Communist ideology; Communist Party; dissident; Khrushchev, Nikita; samizdat; Thaw; World War II (Great Patriotic War).

Further reading

Brandenberger, D. (2002) *National Bolshevism: Stalinist Mass Culture and the Formation of Modern Russian National Identity, 1931–1956*, Cambridge, MA: Harvard University Press.

Brudny, Y. M. (1998) *Reinventing Russia: Russian Nationalism and the Soviet State, 1953–91*, Cambridge, MA: Harvard University Press.

Dziuba, I. (1968) *Internationalism or Russification?: A Study in the Soviet Nationalities Problem*, London: Weidenfeld & Nicolson.

Martin, T. (2001) *The Affirmative Action Empire: Nations and Nationalism in the Soviet Union,* *1923–1939*, Ithaca, NY: Cornell University Press.

Polian, P. (2004) *Against Their Will: The History and Geography of Forced Migrations in the USSR*, Budapest: Central European University Press.

Slezkine, Y. (1994) 'The USSR as a Communal Apartment, or How a Socialist State Promoted Ethnic Particularism', *Slavic Review* 53, 2: 414–52.

Suny, R. G. (1993) *The Revenge of the Past: Nationalism, Revolution, and the Collapse of the Soviet Union*, Stanford, CA: Stanford University Press.

Suny, R. G. and Martin, T. (eds) (2001) *A State of Nations: Empire and Nation-Making in the Age of Lenin and Stalin*, Oxford: Oxford University Press.

Volos, A. (2001) *Hurramabad*, trans. A. Tait. Moscow: GLAS.

VITALY CHERNETSKY

natural resources

One of the world's richest countries in raw materials, Russia owns the world's largest oil and natural gas reserves (35 per cent of all stores) and accounts for approximately 20 per cent of world production. This abundance has made Russia virtually self-sufficient in energy and a large-scale exporter of fossil fuels. Oil and gas remain Russia's primary hard-currency earners.

Self-sufficient in nearly all major industrial raw materials, Russia has at least some reserves of every industrially valuable non-fuel mineral. It ranks first in the world in deposits of iron ore (27 per cent of the world's reserves), tin, nickel, silver, and diamonds; second in the world in deposits of gold, potassium, and coal; third in the world in deposits of copper, lead, and zinc. Other mineral reserves include uranium, asbestos, platinum, rhodium, palladium, titanium, bauxite, vanadium, manganese, chromium, sulfur, tungsten, cobalt, and precious gems. The total potential value of Russia's explored mineral resources is estimated at US$29 trillion, and of those as yet unexplored exceeds US$140 trillion. Russia's annual share in world raw mineral extraction makes 13–15 per cent.

Russia's land mass and freshwater reserves in lakes are the largest in the world. The annual energy potential of rivers is estimated at 850 billion kilowatt-hours; yet only 23 per cent of this capacity has been put to use. Russia's forest resources, known as the taiga, are larger than America's mainland and constitute 25 per cent of the world's forests. They contain over one-third of the world's timber and numerous animal resources, with annual new wood gain of 700 million cubic metres. The potential gross revenue of the timber industry is estimated at US$110–20 billion; thus far harvesting has never exceeded 7–8 per cent. Russia has enormous fish reserves off its coasts, including salmon, cod, and herring.

See also: taiga

TATYANA LEDENEVA

Naumov and Alov

See Alov and Naumov

Nautilus Pompilius

Rock band

A legendary Russian rock band (1978–97), founded in Sverdlovsk (now Ekaterinburg) under the leadership of Viacheslav Butusov. Their first album, *Pereezd* (The Move, 1983), received only limited circulation; however, their next album, *Chelovek-nevidimka* (Invisible Man, 1985) was well received in Sverdlovsk rock circles. In 1986, Nautilus Pompilius performed at the first Sverdlovsk Rock Club Festival and released the album *Razluka* (Parting), which brought the group wider renown, strengthened further by performances at rock festivals in 1987. Since then Nautilus Pompilius has released more than ten albums, including *Kniaz tishiny* (Prince of Silence, 1988), *Titanik* (1994), and *Krylia* (Wings, 1996). The group broke up in 1997 because of financial difficulties and creative differences; its last album, *Iablokitai* (Apple-China) was released subsequently. In 2001,

Butusov set up a new group, Jupiter (Iupiter). That band's first album, *Imia rek* (Name of Rivers), appeared in 2003. Nautilus Pompilius's music figures importantly in Aleksei Balabanov's 1997 film *Brat* (*Brother*), which introduced the group to a national and international audience.

See also: Balabanov, Aleksei; Ekaterinburg; rock music

IRINA UDIANSKAYA

Nazarenko, Tatiana

b. 24 June 1944, Moscow

Painter

One of the most prominent Moscow painters of the generation that came of age after the Thaw. After graduating from the Surikov Institute in 1969, Nazarenko received a stipend to work in the prestigious Academy of Arts studios. There she produced the first of a series of major history paintings addressing moments of conflict between the authorities and people in Russian history. Her work also includes satirical commentaries on contemporary life, and autobiographical paintings often concerned with themes of loneliness, memory, and the connection between past and present. Appropriating different historical styles and quotations from disparate sources, Nazarenko's work challenged prevailing conceptions of realism and stylistic unity; it has much in common with postmodernism. Nazarenko has been a professor at the Surikov Institute since 1999.

See also: art schools and academies; art, Soviet; postmodernism; Thaw

SUSAN E. REID

Neelova, Marina Mstislavovna

b. 8 January 1947, Leningrad

Film and theatre actress

A graduate of the Leningrad State Institute of Theatre, Music and Cinematography (1969),

Neelova began to work at the Mossovet Theatre in 1972, then at the Sovremennik Theatre in 1973. Among her best theatrical roles are Viola in *Twelfth Night*, Ania in *The Cherry Orchard*, Masha in *The Three Sisters*, and Honey in *Who's Afraid of Virginia Woolf?* Neelova's performances are characterized by spontaneity and passion, ecstatic tenderness, and a disarming feminine charm, combined with touching defencelessness. She has also worked in cinema and television. People's Artist of the RSFSR (1987).

See also: Mossovet Theatre; Sovremennik Theatre

IRINA UDIANSKAYA

Neigauz, Genrikh Gustavovich

b. 31 March [12 April] 1888, Elizavetgrad (Kirovograd), Ukraine; d. 10 October 1964, Moscow

Pianist, teacher

Neigauz was born into a family of musicians. Pianist and conductor Feliks Blumenfeld was his uncle, composer Karol Szimanowski was his cousin. After early training at home, from 1912 until 1914 he studied in Vienna with Leopold Godovsky. In 1915, Neigauz graduated from the St. Petersburg Conservatory, and then began his pedagogical career. Eventually his success as a teacher even exceeded his fame as a pianist; he was known for his lyric interpretations of Chopin and Skriabin. After brief periods working in Tbilisi and Kiev, in 1922 Neigauz moved to Moscow to teach at the Moscow Conservatory; he worked there till the end of his life. Among his many famous students are Sviatoslav Rikhter and Emil Gilels. Neigauz summed up his experience in the book *Ob iskusstve fortepiannoi igry* (*On the Art of Piano Playing*, 1958).

See also: Gilels, Emil; Moscow Conservatory; piano performance, Russian/Soviet; Rikhter, Sviatoslav; St. Petersburg (Leningrad) State Conservatory

KIRA NEMIROVSKAIA

Neizvestnyi, Ernst Iosifovich

b. 9 April 1925, Sverdlovsk

Artist

The most famous dissident sculptor of the late Soviet period, Neizvestnyi was in his teens at the outbreak of World War II, volunteered for service, and in 1945 was severely wounded. After the war he returned to his studies and, in the early years of the Thaw, started to build his reputation. Perhaps best known for his encounter with Nikita Khrushchev at the infamous Manezh exhibition of December 1962, where his controversially 'modern' works drew the Soviet premier's ire, Neizvestnyi nonetheless was not harassed and even attracted some monumental commissions within the Soviet Union. By the mid-1970s, his reputation as a Soviet dissident artist, bolstered by Western critical support for his work, had made his domestic position untenable. In 1976, he left Russia and eventually moved to New York. Although Neizvestnyi was able to exhibit and sell prints, drawings, and small sculptures, his monumental commissions virtually disappeared overnight. Indeed, only upon his return to Moscow during Gorbachev's perestroika did Neizvestnyi return to monumental sculpture, designing monuments to the victims of Stalinist labour camps in Sverdlovsk, Vorkuta, and Magadan.

See also: dissident; Khrushchev, Nikita; Manezh exhibition of 1962; monuments; Thaw

Further reading

Berger, J. (1969) *Art and Revolution: Ernst Neizvestnyi and the Role of the Artist in the USSR*, New York: Random House.
Leong, A. (2002) *Centaur: The Life and Art of Ernst Neizvestny*, Lanham, MD: Rowman and Littlefield.

MIKE O'MAHONY

Nekrasov, Viktor Platonovich

b. 4 [17] June 1911, Kiev; d. 3 September 1987, Paris

After graduating from the Kiev Construction Institute, Nekrasov worked as an actor and theatre artist. A decorated veteran of World War II who was wounded twice, Nekrasov authored one of the most colourful and true-to-life novels about the war, *V okopakh Stalingrada* (*In the Trenches of Stalingrad*), for which he received the Stalin Prize, second class (1946). He wrote stories, essays, and autobiographical prose. Criticized by the Communist Party for his story *V rodnom gorode* (*In [My] Home City*), published in the journal *Znamia* (Banner, 1954), he participated in the initiative to erect a monument to the victims of 'fascism' killed in Babii Iar near Kiev. Upon expulsion from the Communist Party for his liberal views, he emigrated to Paris (1974), where he was chief editor of the émigré journal *Kontinent* until 1982.

See also: awards, cultural, Soviet; Babii Iar; Communist Party; Stalingrad; thick journals; World War II (Great Patriotic War)

YURI ZARETSKY

Nekrasov, Vsevolod Nikolaevich

b. 24 March 1934, Moscow

Poet, literary critic

Nekrasov studied at the Moscow State Pedagogical Institute and first published in the *samizdat* journal *Sintaksis* (Syntax). One of the main representatives of Russian *vers libre*, a predecessor of the neo-avant-garde of the 1980s, Nekrasov is aesthetically close to the poets and artists of the Lianozovo Circle. Between the Thaw and the end of perestroika he published exclusively in *samizdat* and *tamizdat*. Nekrasov's poetry is based on the contrast between the inner form of the word, ideological clichés, and banalities of everyday speech. A representative anthology of Nekrasov's work was first published in Russia in 2002. Nekrasov considers the cultural practices of the neo-avant-garde style that developed in the 1980s and 1990s, and art criticism that was close to this movement, as imitators of the unofficial art of the 1950s and 1970s. Since the end of the 1990s Nekrasov has published literary criticism, both in the form of memoirs and as polemical poetic replies.

See also: Lianozovo School; literary criticism; perestroika and glasnost; samizdat; tamizdat; Thaw

GASAN GUSEJNOV

Nekrosius, Eimuntas

b. 21 November 1952, Pažobrio village, Raseiniu region, Lithuanian SSR

Lithuanian director

Trained at GITIS under Andrei Goncharov, Nekrosius overcame the tenets of the psychological approach to create metaphorical and poetic works that became emblematic of Lithuanian theatre. The text is of secondary importance: with the exception of Chekhov's *Cherry Orchard* (2003), it is usually truncated to free space for visually powerful by-plays created in the process of translation of a literary fragment into a stage metaphor. The action in his works concerns the development of metaphor and image rather than plot. The transformations of images form by-plays, which form an organic whole with the text. Sets and props develop during the rehearsal process to become objectified metaphors. The director makes extensive use of primal elements such as fire, water, ice, and sand; their metamorphoses signify the cosmogony of Nature and the eternal cycle of time as embedded in the ritual of peasant life. Nekrosius's major productions include *The Square* after Eliseeva (1980), Korostylev's *Pirosmani, Pirosmani* (1983), Chekhov's *Uncle Vanya* (1986) (all in the Vilnius Youth Theatre); Shakespeare's *Hamlet* (1998) (all in the festival LIFE) and *Othello* (2000), *The Seasons* by Kristionas Donelaitis (Theatre Menofortas), and *The Cherry Orchard* (2003), with Russian actors. Opera productions include Verdi's *Macbeth* (Teatro Comunale di Firenze and the Bolshoi Theatre, 2002) and Musorgskii's *Boris Godunov* (Teatro Comunale di Firenze, 2005).

See also: Russian Academy of Theatre Arts; theatre, post-Soviet

DASHA KRIJANSKAIA

Nemtsov, Boris Efimovich

b. 9 October 1959, Sochi

Politician

A graduate of Gorkii (now Nizhnii Novogorod) State University (1981), Nemtsov holds the academic degree of Candidate of Physics and Mathematics. He served as deputy of the Russian Supreme Soviet, 1990–93. He held senior positions at the regional (President Yeltsin's 'Representative' in Nizhnii Novgorod oblast, head of its administration, governor) and federal levels (Fuel and Energy Minister; Vice Prime Minister), 1991–98. He was a deputy in the State Duma, 1999–2003. After the devastating defeat of the Union of Rightist Forces in the 2003 parliamentary elections, Nemtsov became Chairman of the Council of Directors of the Oil Company Neftianoi. He is also advisor to Ukrainian President Viktor Yuschenko.

See also: academic degrees; Duma; political parties, post-Soviet; Ukraine; Union of Rightist Forces; Yeltsin, Boris

ALEXANDER DOMRIN

Nemukhin, Vladimir Nikolaevich

b. 12 February 1925, Moscow

Artist

Painter and sculptor, Nemukhin represents Soviet underground nonconformism. An active member of the Lianozovo Group during the 1950s, in 1974 he participated in the Bulldozer Exhibition. In his search for new artistic paths, Nemukhin turned to the traditions of abstract expressionism, to which he still adheres. The theme of a card table with various graphic compositions of the playing cards constitutes a characteristic motif of Nemukhin's painting. His works in other media include porcelain painting and a series of spatial sculptural compositions in bronze and wood.

See also: art, nonconformist

IRINA MAKOVEEVA

Nenets (Samoeds)

Indigenous people living in the far north of European and the north-west of Asian Russia. The Nenets language belongs to the Samodi group of the Ural language family. Nenets are divided into two ethnographic groups: tundra and mountainous. The Nenets population, according to the 2002 census, is 41,302. They occupy three autonomous regions in Russia, created in 1930: the Nenets autonomous okrug in Arkhangelsk oblast (population 7,754; capital: Narian-Mar), the Iamalo-Nenets autonomous okrug in Tiumen oblast (population 26,435, capital: Salekhard), and the Taimur (Dolgano-Nenets) okrug in Krasnoiarsk krai (population 3054, capital: Dudinka). Primary occupations are hunting, fishing, and reindeer herding. They live in tent-like dwellings covered with deerskins and travel in reindeer sleds. Many Nenets worship spirits (of rivers, earth, fire, and sky). Key centres of Nenets culture are Narian-Mar, Salekhard, and Pechora.

SERGEI TARKHOV

neologisms

The perestroika years saw a dramatic and lasting upsurge in Russian neologisms, i.e., new words and collocations, and new or revived meanings for old words. With the easing of censorship and 'Old Church Soviet' stylistic rigidity, neologisms quickly took hold in the media and became common parlance. Many have been dictated by post-Soviet economic and social realities (*rynochnik*, 'advocate of market reforms'; *aktsionirovanie*, 'conversion of state assets into joint-stock companies'). Neologisms are frequently English borrowings (*menedzhment*, 'management'; *grant*), which contemporary Russian-speakers seem to prefer to their old Slavic equivalents (*upravlenie, posobie*). Some Anglo-oriented neologisms represent the absorption of peculiarly English semantics by existing Russian lexicon ('today's *challenges*': '*vyzovy* sovremennosti'). Various strata of slang (youth/student, military, criminal/police, managerial, etc.) have contributed highly coloured neologisms to the mainstream (*vopros na zasypku*, 'a stumper';

zakazat kogo, 'put out a hit on someone'). President Putin's many unguarded public statements have produced a special class of 'Putinisms', notably *zamochit v sortire*, 'to whack someone in the john'. Most neologisms, however, are stylistically neutral and formed from Russian roots and affixes (*adresnyi*, '[of programmes and benefits] targeted'; *rasshivka neplatezhei*, 'clearing of mutual claims').

Further reading

Palazhchenko, P. R. (2004) *Moi nesistematicheskii slovar: Russko-angliiskii, Anglo-russkii*, Moscow: R. Valent.

Shaposhnikov, V. (1998) *Russkaia rech 1990-kh: Sovremennaia Rossiia v iazykovom otobrazhenii*, Moscow: MALP.

Skliarevskaia, G. N. (1998) *Tolkovyi slovar russkogo iazyka kontsa XX veka*, St. Petersburg: Folio.

TIMOTHY D. SERGAY

Nesterenko, Evgenii Evgenevich

b. 8 January 1938, Moscow

Opera singer

Bass Nesterenko studied at the Leningrad (St. Petersburg) Conservatory and spent most of the 1960s at the Malyi ('Small') Opera Theatre and the Kirov (Mariinskii) Opera, before moving to Moscow's Bolshoi Theatre in 1971. His reputation rests largely on performances of classic Russian operas, particularly the title role in Mussorgskii's *Boris Godunov*, with which he debuted in Milan, New York, and Vienna. He is also noted for his interpretations of Verdi. The dark, quintessentially Russian, timbre of his voice suits Mussorgskii's songs, and Shostakovich composed his *Suite on Texts of Michelangelo Buonarroti, Op.145* with Nesterenko in mind.

See also: opera, Soviet; opera singers, Bolshoi Theatre; Shostakovich, Dmitrii; St. Petersburg (Leningrad) State Conservatory

PHILIP ROSS BULLOCK

Nesterova, Natalia Igorevna

b. 23 April 1944, Moscow

Artist

Nesterova graduated from the Surikov Art Academy in 1968. A member of the USSR Union of Artists, Nesterova became representative of the left wing early in her career. Drawing her inspiration from a variety of sources spanning French modernism to the naïve artist Niko Pirosmanishvili, Nesterova works in a realistic manner, though her paintings combine elements of theatre and fantasy. Often her subject matter reflects leisure activities and everyday scenes. Professor of Painting at the Russian Academy of Theatre Arts in Moscow, Nesterova is the recipient of Russia's National Award in Fine Arts, the Triumph Award, and the Silver and Gold Medals of the Russian Academy of Fine Arts. Nesterova is a fully-fledged Academician of the Russian Academy of Fine Arts.

See also: art schools and academies; arts administration and management, Soviet and post-Soviet; awards, cultural, post-Soviet; unions, creative, post-Soviet; unions, creative, Soviet

NATALIA KOLODZEI

Nevskii Avenue (Nevskii prospekt)

Originally called Nevskii Perspectival Road, Nevskii Avenue is St. Petersburg's major thoroughfare. Cutting through the most historical part of the city, it stretches from the Admiralty (1806–23) to the Moscow Railway Station (1851) and then, after a slight turn, to the Aleksandr Nevskii Monastery. Nevskii reflects the Baroque system of city planning implemented according to Peter I's vision for the new Russian capital. The term *prospekt* derived from the urban concept of a perspectival relationship between the Admiralty – the city's focal and symbolic centre – and three major streets, dubbed 'perspectives', radiating from it and creating a 'goose-foot' motif, originally sketched by Peter I. This trident pattern, with Nevskii as its high point, was affirmed by Petr Eropkin's master plan in 1737 for St. Petersburg.

Imposing buildings designed by leading Russian and Western architects bolstered Nevskii's development into a remarkable route to the city centre: A. N. Voronikhin's Kazan Cathedral (1801–11); Jean Baptiste Michel Vallin de la Mothe's St. Catherine's Catholic Church (1761–62) and Market Arcade (1757–85); and Carlo Rossi's innovative Aleksandrine Theatre complex (1827–32). Nevskii Avenue offered a public promenade that accommodated various cultural and commercial activities. Nikolai Gogol's short story 'Nevskii Avenue' (1835) conveys Nevskii's symbolic role in the life of St. Petersburgers, as does Aleksei Uchitel's recent film *Progulka* (The Stroll, 2003).

See also: St. Petersburg

TATIANA SENKEVITCH

Nevzorov, Aleksandr Glebovich

b. 3 August 1958, Leningrad

Television personality and political figure

As the host of the popular television programme *600 sekund* (*600 Seconds*, 1987–93), Nevzorov became a symbol of the glasnost era. The programme's edgy format and exposure of crime and corruption appealed to viewers. Initially praised as a reformer for addressing problems of the Communist system, Nevzorov later was criticized as a reactionary for his nationalist positions. In the wake of the January 1991 Soviet military attack on Vilnius, Nevzorov produced a pro-Kremlin short film called *Nashi* (*Ours*), which accused Lithuania's pro-independence government of fomenting ethnic hysteria. Nevzorov was elected to the State Duma in 1993.

JENNIFER RYAN TISHLER

New Russians (Novye russkie)

A social-cultural phenomenon introduced during perestroika and the period of 'wild capitalism' that ensued. The New Russian is an entrepreneur of the first wave who engaged in invest-

ments with his own capital and rapidly achieved enormous wealth and business success without governmental support. The phenomenon peaked in the mid-1990s. New Russians have a reputation for flamboyantly parading their rapidly acquired wealth, their ostentatious show of affluence and bad manners, both at home and abroad. They are typically identified by raspberry-coloured jackets, gold jewellery (watches, rings, and chains), expensive imported cars, and a unique slang borrowed from the criminal world. In the post-Yeltsin era, New Russians have been mythologized as symbolic figures of early post-Soviet history. They generated the authority of the criminal 'brigade' (*brigada*, whose members were referred to as brothers [*bratki*] in a brotherhood [*bratva*]) and a new class of mid-level entrepreneurs who have emerged from the shadows and established themselves legally as neo-liberal 'lords'. The latter have rejected their criminal roots, both economically and culturally, while the former continue to follow established codes of public image, language, and conduct. Today the New Russian exists primarily in cultural mythology, in the form of jokes (*anekdoty*), stories, popular reading, soap operas, and specialized souvenir stores, the first of which was established on Moscow's Novyi Arbat street.

See also: crime; economic system, post-Soviet; joke; perestroika and glasnost; privatization; slang; Yeltsin, Boris

ELENA OMELCHENKO

new style

See calendars, old and new

Nezavisimaia gazeta (Independent Gazette)

Newspaper

The 12-page daily paper was founded on 21 December 1990 by Vitalii Tretiakov. The independent paper was read by the intelligentsia; many journalists considered it an honour to publish in *NG*, even if the pay was low. In 1992, during the paper crisis, Tretiakov refused to seek state support; a team of journalists split off to form the paper *Segodnia*. In May 1995, *NG* went bankrupt and publication ceased; it resumed after Boris Berezovskii invested in the paper in the autumn of 1995. *NG* has a number of supplements and a print run of *c.* 40,000.

See also: Berezovskii, Boris; periodicals, post-Soviet; Tretiakov, Vitalii

BIRGIT BEUMERS

Neznaika

Neznaika (Know-Nothing) is a character in three enormously popular children's books by Nikolai Nikolaevich Nosov. Know-Nothing is good-hearted but mischievous and something of a braggart. The first book, *Prikliucheniia Neznaiki i ego druzei* (*The Adventures of Know-Nothing and His Friends*, 1954), was followed by *Neznaika v solnechnom gorode* (*Know-Nothing in the Sunny City*, 1958), and *Neznaika na lune* (*Know-Nothing on the Moon*, 1964). Several children's films were based on the original characters in Nosov's books.

See also: literature, children's

MICHELE BERDY

Nikitins

Nikitin, Sergei Iakovlevich

b. 8 March 1944, Moscow

Nikitina, Tatiana Khashimovna

b. 31 December 1945, Dushanbe, Tajikistan

Singers

A popular singer/songwriter duo, Sergei and Tatiana met at Moscow University while studying physics and married in 1968. Their careers took off with director Petr Fomenko's staging of Zinovii Papernyi's play *Chelovek, pokhozhii na*

samogo sebia (The Man Resembling Himself), for which Sergei Nikitin wrote songs based on Mikhail Svetlov's poems. In addition to writing songs based on Russian poetry, Nikitin has written music for films, including *Moskva slezam ne verit* (*Moscow Does Not Believe in Tears*, 1979), and musicals, including *Meri Poppins* (*Mary Poppins*, 1976). In the 1990s, Tatiana Nikitina briefly occupied the post of a Deputy Minister of Culture of Russia. In 1995, Sergei received the title of Honoured Artist of Russia. In 1997, the couple received the *Tsarskoselskaia* (Tsarskoe Selo) award.

See also: Fomenko, Petr; music in film; musicals, Russian/Soviet; popular music, Soviet

VLADIMIR PAPERNY

Nikolaeva, Tatiana Petrovna

(neé Tatiana Petrovna Nikolaeva-Tarasevich)

b. 4 May 1924, Bezhits, Briansk district;
d. 22 November 1993, San Francisco

Pianist, composer

A major representative of the Russian piano school, Nikolaeva studied with Aleksandr Goldenveizer at the Moscow Conservatory and returned to teach in 1959. Famed for her interpretations of Bach, she took first prize at the Leipzig Bach Festival in 1950. Shostakovich was a member of the jury, and, inspired by Nikolaeva's playing, composed his *24 Preludes and Fugues, Op.87* (1950–51). Initial critical reaction was hostile, yet Nikolaeva's advocacy of this daringly abstract work was instrumental in establishing it in the repertoire. A series of recordings in the early 1990s introduced her to Western audiences. She was awarded the USSR State Prize (1951).

See also: Moscow Conservatory; piano performance, Russian/Soviet; Shostakovich, Dmitrii

PHILIP ROSS BULLOCK

Nikonov, Pavel Mitrofanovich

b. 30 May 1930, Moscow

Painter

Nikonov graduated from the Surikov Art Institute, Moscow in 1956 and immediately achieved prominence with his diploma piece, *Oktiabr* (October), an austere painting of the Revolution. It was awarded a silver medal at the Sixth International Festival of Youth and Students (Moscow, 1957). Conservatives condemned his composition *Nashi budni* (Our Workdays, 1960) for its grim portrayal of labour's effects on the working person under Soviet conditions. In its uncompromisingly tough view of contemporary life; expressive use of colour, form, and space, as well as its reduction of detail and narrative, the painting was paradigmatic of what was later dubbed the Severe Style. An intransigent campaigner against Stalinist practices in the art world during the Thaw, Nikonov participated in the preparations for the retrospective exhibition '30 Years of the Moscow Artists Union' at the centre of the Manezh Affair. His painting *Geologi* (*Geologists*, 1962), shown there, was one of the main targets of Khrushchev's ire.

See also: art schools and academies; art, Soviet; Manezh exhibition of 1962; severe style; Thaw

SUSAN E. REID

Nikulin, Iurii Vladimirovich

b. 18 December 1921, Demidov, Smolensk gubernia; d. 21 August 1997, Moscow

Clown, actor

A leading circus clown for fifty years, Nikulin also had a distinguished career as a film actor. In the 1960s and 1970s, he starred in several enormously popular comedies by director Leonid Gaidai. Nikulin's later film work includes acclaimed dramatic performances in Aleksei German's *Dvadtsat dnei bez voiny* (*Twenty Days Without War*, 1976) and Rolan Bykov's *Chuchelo* (*The Scarecrow*, 1982). From 1982 until his death, Nikulin served as the director of the Moscow Circus on Tsvetnoi Boulevard, now named in his honour. A monument depicting Nikulin in full clown costume graces the pavement in front of the circus.

See also: Bykov, Rolan; circus; Gaidai, Leonid; German, Aleksei

EMILY D. JOHNSON

Nizhnii Novgorod (Gorkii)

Nizhnii Novgorod (called Gorkii from 1932–92, after the Soviet writer who hailed from that city), with a population of 134,000 people (2003), is one of the five largest Russian cities. Founded in 1221 at the confluence of the Oka and Volga Rivers ('*nizhnii*' means 'lowland'), it has been nicknamed the third capital and the pocket of Russia. In the summers of 1817–1917 and 1922–30, it hosted the Makariev Fair, the largest annual national trading event. The GAZ automobile association (founded 1932) manufactured GAZ and Gazel trucks, as well as Pobeda and Volga cars there. Krasnoe [Red] Sormovo is a famous train and shipbuilding factory. A well-developed provincial cultural centre, the city has nine universities, five theatres, and three museums. Its sixteenth- and seventeenth-century architecture prompted UNESCO to list it among the world's 100 most valuable historical and cultural centres.

TATYANA LEDENEVA

Nobel Prize winners, literature

During the twentieth century, Russia produced five Nobel Prize winners in literature: Ivan Alekseevich Bunin (1933), Boris Leonidovich Pasternak (1958), Mikhail Aleksandrovich Sholokhov (1965), Aleksandr Isaevich Solzhenitsyn (1970), and Iosif Brodskii (Joseph Brodsky, 1987). The histories of these awards are all politically charged.

The first Russian author to receive a Nobel Prize for literature was also the first exile so honoured. Bunin (1870–1953), who emigrated to France in 1921, was recognized 'for the strict artistry with which he [had] carried on the classical traditions in prose writing'. While Bunin explored many genres, he particularly excelled in the short story, written in lyrical and descriptive prose that preserved the Russian realist tradition commingled with modernist formal and stylistic elements. Nature, mortality, and love are his favourite themes.

The dramatic history of the second Russian Nobel Prize for literature involved official displeasure at the selection of Pasternak for the award in 1958 because his novel, *Doctor Zhivago*, had been published abroad. Pasternak sent a telegram thanking the Nobel committee, but under pressure dispatched a second telegram declining the prize. Though his petitions to the government averted the threat of exile, he was expelled from the Union of Soviet Writers. The Nobel committee commended Pasternak 'for his important achievement both in contemporary lyrical poetry and in the field of the great Russian epic tradition'. Best known in the West for his novel, in Russia he ranks as one of its greatest poets.

Sholokhov (1905–84), the only Russian Nobel Prize winner politically in tune with the Soviet government, received the award in 1965 'for the artistic power and integrity with which, in his epic of the Don, he has given expression to a historic phase in the life of the Russian people'. However, rumours of plagiarism surrounding his novel *Tikhii Don* (*And Quiet Flows the Don*, 1939) cast a shadow on his success.

Five years later, the Nobel Prize was bestowed upon dissident writer Solzhenitsyn, one of Sholokhov's critics, living in the Soviet Union when the prize was announced, and unable to attend the awards ceremony. Solzhenitsyn was the first writer to expose to the world the atrocities of the Soviet labour camps, and, accordingly, his award was 'for the ethical force with which he has pursued the indispensable traditions of Russian literature'. Three years after receipt of the prize, Solzhenitsyn was deported because of the *tamizdat* publication of the first volume of his monumental *Arkhipelag GULag* (*Gulag Archipelago*).

The fifth and last Nobel Prize for literature awarded in the twentieth century to a Russian author went to Brodskii (1940–96) 'for an all-embracing authorship, imbued with clarity of thought and poetic intensity'. Since Brodskii, like Bunin, was an émigré at the time, his award is not officially listed as conferred upon a Russian writer. Like Vladimir Nabokov, who had been considered for a Nobel Prize, Brodskii wrote in both Russian and English and many consider him an American author.

Further reading

Feldman, B. (2000) *The Nobel Prize: A History of Genius, Controversy and Prestige*, New York: Arcade Publishing.
Nobel Lectures in Literature (1969–2003) 5 vols, Singapore: World Scientific Publishing Company.
http://www.nobel.se/literature/index.html

ONA RENNER-FAHEY

Nobel Prize winners, non-literary

One of the earliest recipients of the Nobel Prize for physiology or medicine was Ivan Pavlov (1904), also the first whose work called into question the limit of three scientists per prize. His research on the physiology of digestion was performed at the Military Medical Academy, where scores of physicians-in-training and research assistants of varying skills aided him for a decade in running a laboratory factory for the production of physiological facts. The Nobel Prize committee in effect rewarded a collective discovery, while noting Pavlov's importance as one of the first of a new breed: the scientific manager. The iconic status he acquired under the Soviets rested in no small part on those skills.

The Russian-Jewish Ilia Mechnikov, born near present-day Kharkiv, Ukraine, in 1845, received the Nobel Prize for physiology or medicine in 1908 (with Paul Ehrlich), two decades after he had left Russia to work at the Pasteur Institute in Paris. His theory of phagocytosis, first developed both in Odessa and Messina, provided the first model of organisms' self-defence from foreign microbes at the cellular level.

Subsequently, for half a century Russians received no Nobel Prizes in the sciences. Then, in fairly short succession, no fewer than seven Soviet scientists received awards, beginning with Nikolai Semenov in chemistry (1956; shared with Cyril Hinshelwood). Trained as a physicist, Semenov was a protégé of Abram Ioffe, a student of Wilhelm Roentgen who became one of the first grandees of the Soviet system of science institutes. Semenov became director of his own Institute of Chemical Physics in 1932, not least due to the work he had performed in the late 1920s describing the kinetics of chemical chain reactions. Another four scientists have been designated since Semenov. Nine of the eleven prize winners conducted their award-winning research during the heyday years of Stalinism (mid-1930s to the early 1950s).

The first Soviet award for physics went to Pavel Cherenkov, Igor Tamm, and Ilia Frank (1958). Cherenkov and his supervisor, Sergei Vavilov (d. 1951), discovered the optical analogue to the Mach effect in acoustics. While Einstein famously specified an absolute upper limit to the speed of light in a vacuum, its speed in other media can be considerably slower, and the high-velocity electrons shooting through these liquids were in fact moving faster than the speed of light within the medium, thus exciting the cone of faint blue-frequency radiation observed by Cherenkov. First Frank (also trained as an experimental physicist), and then Tamm (a theorist) were drawn into providing an adequate theoretical explanation for the phenomenon, in papers published in 1937–38.

It can take decades for 'received opinion' to coalesce in the form of the Nobel Prize, as evidenced by the case of Petr Kapitsa (physics, 1978, with Arno Penzias and Robert W. Wilson, who received the other half of the prize for unrelated work on cosmic microwave background radiation). Following an unusual early career at Cambridge University under the patronage of Ernest Rutherford, Kapitsa was retained in 1934 by the Soviet authorities in Moscow, where a new institute was built on his behalf. There, in late 1937 Kapitsa developed exquisite techniques for producing helium at extremely low temperatures and observing its peculiarly non-classical behaviours, such as its ability to flow without friction through the tiniest of capillaries, even at temperatures very close to absolute zero. Kapitsa asked the head

theorist at his institute, Lev Landau, to elaborate a physical explanation for this 'superfluidity', and the theory Landau published in 1941 became the primary basis for the prize awarded in 1962; today he remains the sole individual Russian recipient since Pavlov. His major insight was to provide a quantum mechanical explanation for what were, in essence, collective phenomena (rather than properties of the states of individual atoms).

The ghost of Landau no doubt hovered over the 2003 physics award to Aleksei Abrikosov and Vitalii Ginzburg (along with Anthony J. Leggett). A close colleague of Tamm, Ginzburg drew Landau into discussions about how to describe superconductivity quantum mechanically. The macroscopic equation they introduced in 1950 proved remarkably robust, even after the appearance of the correct microscopic BCS theory in 1957. Ginzburg, a wide-ranging theorist who was perhaps a prize candidate for his contributions to astrophysics, remained in Moscow throughout his career and used the prize as a pulpit to encourage reform of post-Soviet scientific institutions. Abrikosov, on the other hand, had long moved to the United States at the time of the award and had developed his own theory of 'type-II' superconductors amid spirited arguments with his former advisor, Landau. Whereas type-I superconductors exclude magnetic fields up to a certain critical temperature (the Meissner effect), type-II superconductors (usually alloys or combinations of copper and non-metals) violate BCS theory and permit the penetration of magnetic fields. In the mid-1950s, Abrikosov showed mathematically how 'quantum vortices' can permit the external magnetic fields to enter the superconductor without destroying the effect.

Nikolai Basov and Aleksandr Prokhorov (who received the Nobel Prize in physics in 1964, with Charles Townes) developed the maser, the predecessor to the better-known laser. Building on their wartime experience with radio technology, in the early 1950s they designed devices that demonstrated the possibility of generating powerful, focused, coherent microwave radiation by stimulated emission from crystals and other substances.

Even more ubiquitous than lasers in modern society are the various transistor technologies that drive computers and telecommunications. The two technologies were combined in the work of Zhores Alferov (Nobel Prize for physics, 2000, with Herbert Kroemer and Jack S. Kilby), who discovered how to use layers of different kinds of semi-conductors to create a so-called 'heterostructure laser'. Many of the fibre-optic communications we now take for granted are based on properties first observed in these semi-conductor lasers.

Russian Nobel Prize recipients were not confined to science. Originally trained as a mathematician, Leonid Kantorovich (economics, 1975, with Tjalling C. Koopmans) introduced linear programming techniques into economics in the late 1930s, when the Soviet plywood industry asked him to help solve certain dilemmas in production planning. The alacrity with which he generalized these problems in mathematical terms, moving from microeconomic to macroeconomic formulations, eventually won the attention of such Western economists as Tjalling Koopmans, who were developing similar techniques for market contexts.

The Nobel Peace Prize was awarded to Andrei Sakharov (1975) and Mikhail Gorbachev (1990).

See also: Academy of Sciences; Gorbachev, Mikhail; Sakharov, Andrei; science and technology

Further reading

Graham, L. R. (1993) *Science in Russia and the Soviet Union: A Short History*, Cambridge: Cambridge University Press.
http://nobelprize.org
Les Prix Nobel/Nobel Lectures has been published by Elsevier Publishing Company and subsequently World Scientific Publishing Company in series covering each of the award categories.

KARL HALL

nomenklatura

A list of those named to privileged positions by Party and Komsomol committees in the USSR at the city, regional, and oblast levels, as well as the positions themselves. Those in the *nomenklatura*, the *nomenklaturshchiki*, enjoyed perquisites in all aspects of life. The dictatorship of the *nomenklatura* in the Soviet Union was maintained through centralization, unification, and strengthening of central Party control over local Party cadres and managers. All Soviet citizens knew about the *nomenklatura*, and admission to it was considered prestigious and profitable, since those in it were taken care of for their entire lives. The *nomenklatura* of the Party was placed higher than that of the government. With the dissolution of the Soviet Union, the term has been used rarely, but the phenomenon, in essence, remains as a basic functioning principle of the Russian government. During and since perestroika, former members of the *nomenklatura* established themselves in key positions of the government, enterprises, trade unions, banks, and other financial structures connected with governmental monopoly, and in foreign trade. The first joint ventures were led by former Communist Party committee secretaries. The post-*nomenklatura* can be divided into two sectors: economic, established in both government and business; and ideological, established in political structures.

See also: administrative structure, Soviet Union; Communist Party; Communist Youth League; economic system, post-Soviet; economic system, Soviet; perestroika and glasnost; unions, professional; USSR

ELENA OMELCHENKO

Nord-Ost [North-east]

A musical whose title became synonymous with a catastrophic terrorist attack. *Nord-Ost*, with music and book by Aleksei Ivashchenko and Georgii Vasilev, based on Veniamin Kaverin's patriotic adventure novel *Dva Kapitana* (*Two Captains*), about a boy who becomes a heroic aviator, premiered on 19 October 2001. Its success engendered a boom in musicals in Moscow and made it a conspicuous target. In mid-performance on 23 October 2002, 41 men and women from the breakaway republic of

Chechnia seized the Dubrovka theatre and held 800 hostages for 58 hours. Following the government's gas-aided rescue effort, 129 people died. The show reopened on 8 February 2003, but closed only months later, on 10 May. A touring version was revived in 2004.

See also: Chechnia; musicals, Russian/Soviet; terrorist acts; War, Chechen

JOHN FREEDMAN

Norilsk

One of the five northernmost cities in the world, Norilsk, located in Krasnoiarsk Krai (the Far North), has a severe climate. The settlement, founded in 1935 as *Norillag*, is a labour colony in the GULag structure. More than 500,000 convicts passed through it; 10,000 of them perished there. In 1953, it acquired the name Norilsk and the status of a 'closed city', the latter temporarily suspended from 1991–2001. Norilsk is one of the most polluted cities in the world, with a steadily decreasing population of 138,000 (2000). The extraordinarily successful company Norilsk Nickel produces 70 per cent of the world's palladium, 20 per cent of its nickel, and 15 per cent of its cobalt.

See also: closed city; Far North; GULag

TATYANA LEDENEVA

Norshtein, Iurii Borisovich

b. 15 September 1941, Moscow

Animator

Partly owing to artistic clashes with Soiuzmultfilm studio, Norshtein's body of work is small – fewer than a dozen films from 1968 to the present – though influential. His major innovation is the pairing of articulated paper figures and multiplane camera, a technique suited to his melancholy themes. Many of his films, such as *Skazka skazok* (*Tale of Tales*, 1979) deal with mature topics, but his animation for the nightly children's television show *Spokoinoi nochi malyshi*

(*Goodnight, Little Ones*) is his most widely seen work. Another masterpiece is *Ezhik v tumane* (*Hedgehog in the Fog*, 1975). In recent years he has been working on an animated version of Gogol's *Shinel* (*The Overcoat*).

See also: film, animation

BELLA GINZBURSKY-BLUM

Novgorod

One of Russia's oldest cities, Novgorod lies on both sides of the River Volkov near Lake Ilmen, which once carried the commerce between the Baltic and the Black and Caspian Seas. Christianized by Orthodox Kiev, Novgorod rapidly outgrew its nominal vassal status to become the centre of a democratic merchant republic and a vast empire embracing all the cities of the north and uncharted lands in Siberia. It defeated German Crusaders, escaped Mongols, and joined the Hanseatic League. Moscow conquered Novgorod in 1487. Despite Nazi depredations, much of old Novgorod remains, including its ancient cathedral and its restored kremlin.

See also: Kiev; Moscow; Russian Orthodoxy; Siberia

EDWARD ALAN COLE

Novikov, Timur Petrovich

b. 24 September 1958, Leningrad;
d. 24 May 2002, St. Petersburg

Artist

Artist, musician, and influential cultural figure, Novikov was the unofficial leader of the Leningrad/St. Petersburg nonconformist art scene in the 1980s–90s. His early art work was influenced by the avant-garde traditions of Mikhail Larionov. Later, he made a sharp turn to 'neo-academicism', harshly attacking modernist art for rejecting the idea of the beautiful. In the 1990s, he founded the groups Novye khudozhniki (New Artists) and Novye kompozitory

(New Composers), collaborated with Mitki, Viktor Tsoi's rock band Kino, and Sergei Kurekhin's Pop-mekhanika, and contributed to Sergei Solovev's cult film Assa. In 1989, Novikov founded the New Academy of Fine Arts, whose members produce(d) works steeped in homo-eroticism, and in the 1990s he became one of the most internationally exhibited contemporary Russian artists. In his final years he suffered from blindness and other health problems.

See also: art, nonconformist; Kino; Kurekhin, Sergei; Mitki; Solovev, Sergei; Tsoi, Viktor

VITALY CHERNETSKY

Novosibirsk State University

Novosibirsk State University (NGU) was founded in 1959 within the *akademgorodok* (academic town) near Novosibirsk as part of a project to create a major scientific research centre in Siberia. It was founded in large part thanks to the efforts of physicist and mathematician Mikhail Lavrentev. NGU specialized in mathematics and the natural sciences and, particularly in Soviet times, was intended to educate the future scientific elite of the country. Students have traditionally benefited from the large number of leading researchers working in the various institutions of the *akademgorodok*. Currently around 6,500 students study at NGU.

See also: Academy of Sciences; akademgorodok; educational system, Soviet; science and technology; Siberia

DAVID HUNTER SMITH

Novosti Press Agency

See RIA Novosti

Novyi mir

A revered *tolstyi zhurnal* (thick journal) of literature, literary criticism, and political and social commentary, the monthly *Novyi mir* (New World) during the Soviet era took risks by publishing controversial and repressed authors. Aleksandr Tvardovskii, who served as editor-in-chief 1950–54 and 1956–70, championed the publication of Aleksandr Solzhenitsyn's novel *Odin den Ivana Denisovicha* (*One Day in the Life of Ivan Denisovich*), one of the central works of the Thaw. In the 1980s, during glasnost, the journal printed works that had long been banned in the Soviet Union, including Boris Pasternak's *Doktor Zhivago* (*Doctor Zhivago*) and Solzhenitsyn's *Arkhipelag GULag* (*The Gulag Archipelago*). In post-Soviet Russia, *Novyi mir*, like all thick journals, has lost its former status and many subscribers.

See also: Pasternak, Boris; perestroika and glasnost; Solzhenitsyn, Aleksandr; Tvardovskii, Aleksandr; Thaw; thick journals

JENNIFER RYAN TISHLER

nozhki Busha

Literally 'Bush legs', referring to US President George H. W. Bush, this term refers to chicken drumsticks introduced to Russia in the early 1990s as part of a US food-aid package. Popular for relative affordability rather than quality, 'Bush legs' have decimated Russian poultry production and are a frequent source of conflict in US–Russian trade negotiations.

RACHEL S. PLATONOV

NTV

Independent television station

NTV (*Nezavisimoe televidenie* [Independent Television]) was registered in July 1993 and launched in St. Petersburg thanks to the support of *Media-Most* and tycoon owner Vladimir Gusinskii. Given eighteen hours of broadcast time in 1993 by Yeltsin, NTV returned the favour, supporting the President in his 1996 re-election bid. Yeltsin granted the station nationwide status in January 1998, but critical coverage of the Chechnia campaign, the Dubrovka siege, and a penchant for trenchant satire did not appeal to Putin: Gusinskii was arrested and charged with misappropriation of funds in 2000. The national gas company Gazprom acquired his shares, and many employees resigned.

See also: Gusinskii, Vladimir; oligarkh; Putin, Vladimir; television, post-Soviet; television channels; Yeltsin, Boris; War, Chechen

DAVID MACFADYEN

Nu, pogodi! (Just You Wait!)

Directed by Viacheslav Kotenochkin at Soiuzmultfilm studios, this 18-film animated series (1969–95) is one of the best-known creations of Russian popular culture. Writers Aleksandr Kurliandskii, Feliks Kamov, and Aleksandr Khait imbued their scripts with topical humour and cultural cues. The voices of the main characters, Volk (Wolf), played by actor Anatolii Papanov, and Zaiats (Hare), played by voice artist Klara Rumianova, gave the characters their wide appeal. A prototype for *Nu, pogodi!*, directed by Gennadii Sokolskii, appeared in 1968 as a segment in the first episode of the animated series *Veselaia karusel* (*Happy Carousel*).

See also: film, animation

BELLA GINZBURSKY-BLUM

Nureyev (Nureev), Rudolf Khametovich

b. 17 March 1938, near Irkutsk;
d. 6 January 1993, Paris

Dancer, choreographer, and ballet director

Nureyev began to study dance in Ufa, Bashkiria. At what for ballet training is the relatively mature age of 17, he was accepted by the Leningrad Ballet School, where he studied under Aleksandr Pushkin. In 1958, Nureyev became a principal dancer at the Kirov Ballet, where he performed a wide range of leading roles. His formative years in Leningrad were crucial for his later career, ser-

ving as a foundation for his unfailing sense of choreographic language, his understanding of the profound expressiveness of classical form and the intrinsic musicality of dance. Early in his career in the Soviet Union, Nureyev became known for his independent, nonconformist character. While on tour with the Kirov in 1961, he sought and obtained asylum in Paris, and settled in the West.

Nureyev's remarkable artistic presence and his technique, unmatched by Western dancers of the period, made him an instant star in the West. He worked as a permanent guest artist with the Royal Ballet in London, 1962–77, while performing and staging ballets with the Vienna State Opera Ballet, Australian Ballet, the London Festival Ballet, the Royal Danish Ballet, the Royal Swedish Ballet, and the Ballet du XXe Siècle, led by Maurice Béjart. Nureyev's performances had an electrifying effect on the audience and revived the glory of the Russian male-dancing school known to the West through Diagilev's *Ballets Russes* productions. Working as the Artistic Director of the Paris Opéra's Ballet in 1983–89, Nureyev bolstered the company's fading reputation by restaging a number of classical works choreographed by Marius Petipa in pre-revolutionary St. Petersburg.

Nureyev appeared in films and numerous TV programmes, including *An Evening with the Royal Ballet* (1963), *Romeo and Juliet*, with Margot Fonteyn (choreographed by MacMillan; 1966), *Le jeune homme et la mort* (choreographed by Petit; 1966), and *I Am a Dancer* (1972). Recipient of the French *Chevalier de la Légion d'honneur* (1987) and the *Commandeur de l'Ordre des Arts et des Lettres* (1991).

See also: ballet, Soviet; Kirov Theatre

TATIANA SENKEVITCH

Nusberg (or Nussberg), Lev Valdemarovich

b. 1 June 1937, Tashkent, Uzbekistan

Artist

Founder of the Kinetic Art movement. Born in Tashkent, the son of a German victim of the

GULag and a Tatar mother, Nusberg graduated from the Moscow Art School (MSKhSh).
An eye-opening event for Nusberg was the
Picasso exhibition in Moscow (1956). He formed
the Dvizhenie (Movement) group in 1962,
whose members included Francisco Infante and
Viacheslav Koleichuk among others. The aim of
the group was to create 'bio-cybernetic' systems
called *Igrovye Bioniko-Kineticheskie Sistemy* (playful-
bionic-kinetic systems). A charismatic leader,
Nusberg attracted people, but some members of
the group (particularly Infante) found his management style 'totalitarian'. Nusberg emigrated
to the US in 1981, and leads a hermetic life. He
moved from kinetic art to surrealist painting, and
keeps rewriting the history of the movement.

See also: GULag; Infante, Francisco; kinetic art

VLADIMIR PAPERNY

Obraztsov, Sergei Vladimirovich

b. 22 June [5 July] 1901, Moscow;
d. 8 May 1992, Moscow

Actor, director

A graduate of the Department of Painting at the Advanced Artistic Theatrical Workshops (1926) and an artist at the Nemirovich-Danchenko Musical Theatre (until 1930) and at the Moscow Art Theatre (until 1936), Obraztsov debuted in a solo performance with puppets in 1923. He was the artistic director of the Central State Puppet Theatre (1931), later named after him, and developed a theory and methodology of puppet theatre. In approximately sixty years he has mounted more than seventy performances, elevating puppet 'buffoonery' public-square performances to the level of theatre art. Also a screen writer and film director (from 1956), he became a professor at GITIS in 1973 and authored several books on issues of art. Recipient of numerous government awards, including Lenin and State Prizes: People's Artist of the USSR (1954) and Hero of Socialist Labour (1971).

See also: awards, cultural, Soviet; Moscow Art Theatre; Russian Academy of Theatre Arts

YURI ZARETSKY

Obraztsova, Elena Vasilevna

b. 7 July 1937, Leningrad

Opera singer

Mezzo-soprano Obraztsova made her debut with the Bolshoi Theatre in 1963 while still studying at the Leningrad (St. Petersburg) Conservatory. Endowed with a fine dramatic sense and a voice of great, yet disciplined, richness, she soon established herself as one of Russia's major opera singers. Famed principally for her interpretations of the Russian and Italian classics, she was an effective ambassador for Soviet achievements in the cultural field. Her long association with the Bolshoi has been matched by frequent performances in the world's leading opera houses. Although less well known as a recitalist, she notably collaborated with Sviridov in performances of his songs.

See also: Bolshoi Theatre; opera singers, Bolshoi Theatre; St. Petersburg (Leningrad) State Conservatory; Sviridov, Georgii

PHILIP ROSS BULLOCK

Octobrites (oktiabriata)

In 1923 and 1924, *oktiabriata* was the name applied to children born in the year of the October Revolution, but later in the USSR it became an association of school children aged 7–11. It existed under the auspices of a school Pioneer organization and was designed to prepare children for membership in the Pioneers. An *otriad oktiabriat* (a detachment of Octobrites) united pupils in the same class, and was divided into *zvezdochki* (small five-point stars), with five children in each. Octobrites had to wear a badge showing a red star with a portrait of Vladimir Lenin as a child in the centre. Their motto was: 'Octobrites are friendly kids. They help Pioneers, Komsomol members, and Communists, and seek to become young Pioneers.'

See also: Communist Youth League; Lenin, Vladimir Ilich; Pioneer organization

SVETLANA TITKOVA

Odessa

A city in south western Ukraine, on the coast of the Black Sea. Founded in 1794, it became the Russian Empire's biggest nineteenth-century boomtown and one of its most ethnically mixed cities. Home to a prominent Jewish community, the city is known for its unusual vernacular, which mixes Russian, Ukrainian, Yiddish, and other languages. In the early twentieth century, Odessa became a major centre of literature and the arts; among the writers associated with it are Isaak Babel, Yuri Olesha, Ilia Ilf and Evgenii Petrov, and Valentin Kataev. Known as the unofficial comedy capital of the former Soviet Union, the city hosts a humour festival, *iumorina*, every 1 April, and is the home of the leading ex-Soviet writer/performer of stand-up comedy, Mikhail Zhvanetskii. In music, Odessa is famed for its opera and operetta companies, the Stoliarskii Violin School, and the many popular and jazz musicians the city has produced (most notably Leonid Utesov). The Odessa Film Studio remains a major centre of cinematic production, currently best known for the films directed by Kira Muratova. Odessa has also won acclaim for its school of nonconformist art, especially Conceptualism. The city suffered greatly in both world wars, and has generated a large diaspora around the world.

See also: art, nonconformist; Conceptualism, art; film, festivals and prizes; film studios; humour and satire, Soviet; Jews; Judaism; Muratova, Kira; stand-up comedy; Ukraine; Utesov, Leonid; Zhvanetskii, Mikhail

Further reading

Friedberg, M. (1991) *How Things Were Done in Odessa: Cultural and Intellectual Pursuits in a Soviet City*, Boulder, CO: Westview Press.
Herlihy, P. (1986) *Odessa: A History, 1794–1914*, Cambridge, MA: Harvard University Press.
Iljine, N. (ed.) (2003) *Odessa Memories*, Seattle, WA: University of Washington Press.

VITALY CHERNETSKY

Ogonek

Weekly magazine

One of Russia's longest-running and most popular magazines, *Ogonek* (The Little Flame) was founded in 1899 as an illustrated weekly devoted to literature and culture. From the 1920s until perestroika, it retained its basic format, with sections devoted to art, politics, sports, and humour. In the Soviet period it represented the official (conservative) viewpoint and ran unrivalled as the leading family magazine. During perestroika, under chief editor Vitalii Korotich, it took an oppositional stance, openly criticizing the failures of Soviet society, which significantly increased its readership. During the 1990s the format changed, resembling that of *Time* and *Newsweek*. Its popularity has waned somewhat with new competition, yet it retains its reputation as a stalwart of Russian journalism.

See also: journalism; journalists, post-Soviet; Korotich, Vitalii; perestroika and glasnost

ANDREA LANOUX

Oistrakh, David Fedorovich

b. 30 September 1908, Odessa, Ukraine;
d. 24 October 1974, Amsterdam (buried in Moscow)

Violinist, teacher, conductor

One of the greatest violinists of the twentieth century, Oistrakh began studying the violin at the age of 5 with the famous pedagogue Petr Stoliarskii. He came to international prominence when he won first prize in the 1937 Ysaye (Queen Elisabeth) competition in Brussels. In 1953, he began touring Western Europe and, a few years later, the United States. As a professor at the Moscow Conservatory, he taught some of the finest violinists of the next generation. As a performer, he worked closely with the greatest Soviet composers, many of whom (Dmitrii Shostakovich, Aram Khachaturian) wrote concertos expressly for him. His son, Igor (born 1931), is also an excellent violinist, though not as eminent as his father.

See also: Khachaturian, Aram; Moscow Conservatory; Shostakovich, Dmitrii

SUNGHAE ANNA LIM

Okhlopkov, Nikolai Pavlovich

b. 15 May 1900, Irkutsk; d. 8 January 1967, Moscow

Russian stage and screen actor and director

Okhlopkov studied with Vsevolod Meierkhold and joined his teacher's troupe in 1923. In 1930, he became Chief Director of the Moscow Realistic Theatre, and in 1943–66 of the Maiakovskii Theatre. Among his most accomplished productions was *Medea* by Euripides (1961). Okhlopkov gained fame in silent film as an actor and director – for example, with the satirical comedy *Prodannyi appetit* (*The Sold Appetite*, 1928). He became a star of Stalinist cinema, projecting an image of naïve, somewhat cumbersome manliness, humour, and heroism, such as the loudmouth Vasilii Buslaev in Eisenstein's *Aleksandr Nevskii* (1938). Okhlopkov's theatre work was aesthetically complex, preserving and developing some of Meierkhold's principles. People's Artist of the USSR (1948).

See also: Maiakovskii Theatre

PETER ROLLBERG

Okudzhava, Bulat Shalvovich

b. 9 May 1924, Moscow; d. 12 June 1997, Paris

Writer, singer-songwriter, screenwriter

Okudzhava wrote hundreds of poems, a number of short stories, several novels, and two screenplays.

He is widely known as the first of the Thaw-era bards, with a corpus of approximately 200 songs.

In the late 1950s and early 1960s, Okudzhava published both prose and poetry. He also wrote and performed songs, accompanying himself on the guitar. Departing markedly from official norms, these songs were predominantly melancholy, Okudzhava's voice was tremulous, and his guitar technique was unpolished. The songs circulated rapidly via *magnitizdat*.

Beginning in the early 1960s, Okudzhava's works drew criticism for lacking ideological firmness. Subsequently, the uncontrolled popularity of his songs, the publication of his works abroad, and his signing of several letters of protest led to his temporary expulsion from the Communist Party and to an unofficial moratorium on publication. The first official recording of his songs, excluding those commissioned for film and television, was released only in 1976. During the 1980s and 1990s, Okudzhava continued to write verse, while also authoring a Booker Prize-winning autobiographical novel and translating from several languages.

See also: bards; censorship; Communist Party; samizdat; tamizdat; Thaw

RACHEL S. PLATONOV

Old Believers

In what is known as the schism, the Old Believers split from Russian Orthodoxy over seventeenth-century liturgical reforms. Many traditionalists fled persecution and settled in remote areas of Russia and abroad, where they continue to live today. Some groups turned to ordained Russian Orthodox priests to replenish their clergy, while others operated without priests. Old Believers view themselves as the defenders of tradition, purity, and Holy Russia.

See also: Russian Orthodoxy

Further reading

Vorontsova, L. and Filatov, S. (2000) 'Paradoxes of the Old Believer Movement', trans. M. Sapiets, *Religion, State, and Society* 28, 1: 53–67.

JENNIFER B. BARRETT

Old Church Slavonic (Old Church Slavic)

Old Church Slavonic (*Staroslavianskii iazyk*) was the ecclesiastical language of Kievan Rus, which incorporated parts of present-day Russia, Belarus, and Ukraine. Over the centuries, it has evolved and influenced poetry and literature in those countries; it remains the liturgical language of Russian Orthodoxy. Since 1991, as part of the revival of Russian Orthodoxy, many new texts have been composed in Old Church Slavonic; this has become a political issue. Some Ukrainians wish to move to the vernacular to minimize ties with Russia and Belarus; others, particularly in Russia, champion Old Church Slavonic's link with tradition.

See also: Belarus; Russian Orthodoxy; Ukraine

NADIESZDA KIZENKO

old style

See calendars, old and new

oligarkh

Russians use the term *oligarkh* (oligarch) to refer to individuals who built powerful, politically-influential financial-industrial groups (FIGs) in Moscow during the 1990s. The best known included Boris Berezovskii (LogoVAZ), Vladimir Gusinskii (Most Group), Mikhail Khodorkovskii (Menatep/Rosprom/Yukos), and Vladimir Potanin (Interros). In 1996, Berezovskii famously claimed that six of these FIGs controlled 50 per cent of the Russian economy. Most ordinary Russians considered the oligarchs to be criminals and opportunists. Russian President Vladimir Putin curbed the oligarchs' influence after his election in March 2000, forcing Berezovskii and Gusinskii into exile and arresting Khodorkovskii, who was ultimately sentenced to nine years in jail for fraud and tax evasion.

See also: Berezovskii, Boris; economic system, post-Soviet; Gusinskii, Vladimir; Khodorkovskii, Mikhail; privatization; Putin, Vladimir; Yeltsin, Boris

JULIET JOHNSON

olive (olivier)

Salad dish that became an integral part of Russian cuisine and a Soviet festive table. The traditional recipe includes cooked chicken, potatoes, carrots, hard-boiled eggs, canned peas, pickles, and mayonnaise. Lack of certain foods during the Soviet era required flexibility in preparing this dish: for example, bologna frequently substituted for chicken.

See also: salads

IRINA MAKOVEEVA

Olympic Games 1980 (Olimpiada 1980)

The 1980 Olympic Summer Games in Moscow were the first Olympic competition held in a socialist country. Intended to promote friendly international competition, the Games were instead marred by political disagreement. In protest against the 1979 Soviet invasion of Afghanistan, the United States boycotted the Games. Sixty-one other nations eventually joined the boycott, including Canada, China, Israel, Japan, and West Germany, although Great Britain and France were among the eighty countries participating. Soviet dissidents also supported the boycott to draw attention to their struggle for human rights. In retaliation, the Soviet Union boycotted the 1984 Summer Games in Los Angeles.

To prepare for the Games, Soviet authorities closed Moscow to all non-residents. Dissidents, black marketeers, criminals, and other potentially 'disruptive' elements were rounded up and removed to ensure order during the Games. Soviet officials also tried to limit Soviet citizens' contact with foreigners. The Soviet press issued warnings about the subversive threat posed by the international participants, while its propaganda extolled the virtues and benefits of the socialist system. Nevertheless, Muscovites flocked to the Games, filling venues to near-capacity. Soviet athletes dominated the competition, winning eighty gold medals, with East Germany a close second. Despite the small number of participating countries, athletes set numerous world records, including in swimming, high jump, and pole vault.

See also: dissident; sports, Soviet; War, Afghan

SHARON A. KOWALSKY

OMON

Elite law-enforcement units trained to execute special operations under emergency conditions. OMON (*Otriad militsii osobogo naznacheniia* [Special Assignment Militia Units]) wear camouflage uniforms, helmets, and black masks (to preserve anonymity) and carry clubs, tear gas, and other special resources. Competition for acceptance into OMON is high; requirements include an age limit of 30; service in the armed forces, preferably with combat experience; a high school diploma; minimum height of 175 centimetres; and good health. The state also relies on OMON regiments in situations of political conflict: they stormed the press building in Riga (1991) to prevent the printing of democratic publications and broke up demonstrations in Moscow (October 1993). Since 1994, OMON regiments have participated in combat operations in Chechnia.

See also: militia (police)

ELENA OZNOBKINA

opera, post-Soviet

The survival of opera has been one of the more surprising features of post-Soviet cultural life. For many, opera was tainted by its reputation as an exemplary Soviet form. For others, opera was no longer a viable art form in a postmodern world or it was no longer practical to work without the institutional support of Russia's opera houses. Perhaps the most representative instance of the development of Russian opera since 1991 was the career of Shnittke. All three of his completed operas were written during the 1990s and staged outside Russia: *Zhizn s idiotom* (*Life with an Idiot*), with a libretto by Viktor Erofeev (Amsterdam, 1992); *Gesualdo* (Vienna, 1995); and *Historia von D. Johann Fausten* (Hamburg, 1995). The tendency for new operas to be performed abroad dates back to the late 1980s, when subsidized Western theatres with a taste for the avant-garde were able to patronize a generation of illicit Russian modernists in a way they had never done with official Soviet opera. Dmitrii Smirnov's two contrasting operas inspired by Blake stand out in this regard. The large-scale *Tiriel* was premiered in Freiburg in 1989, followed a few months later by his chamber opera, *Zhaloby Teli* (*The Lamentations of Thel*). Economic instability and artistic caution meant that the belated premières of operas written before 1991 still took place overseas; Nikolai Karetnikov's *Til Ulenshpigel* (*Till Eulenspiegel*) was eventually staged in Nantes in 1999. Important post-Soviet operas were also first seen abroad. Tarnopolskii's *Wenn die Zeit über die Ufer tritt* (*When Time Overflows Its Banks*) was written for the Munich Biennale in 1999 and Aleksandr Knaifel's *Alisa v strane chudes* (*Alice in Wonderland*) was commissioned by The Netherlands Opera and performed in Amsterdam in 2001. Russian theatres have neglected even establishment composers. Two new operas by Shchedrin, once the darling of the Soviet Union's most prestigious theatres, premiered abroad: *Lolita* in Stockholm in 1994, and the so-called 'opera for the concert-stage' *Ocharovannyi strannik* (*The Enchanted Wanderer*) in New York in 2002. Post-Soviet Russia, however, has not lacked its own developments. Shchedrin's *Lolita* was revived in Perm in 2003, Shnittke's *Life with an Idiot* has been staged in Moscow and Novosibirsk, and Slonimskii's *Gamlet* (*Hamlet*) ran in several provincial houses in the 1990s. A controversial new opera commissioned by the Bolshoi Theatre from Desiatnikov with a libretto by Sorokin, whose premiere in March 2005 prompted widely publicized protests by the arch-conservative youth group Idushchie vmeste (Marching Together), may be the first indication of a renaissance of Russian opera in its homeland.

See also: Bolshoi Theatre; Erofeev, Viktor; Idushchie vmeste (Marching Together); Shchedrin, Rodion; Shnittke, Alfred; Slonimskii, Sergei; Sorokin, Vladimir; Tarnopolskii, Vladimir

Further reading

Issues of Moscow's *Afisha*

PHILIP ROSS BULLOCK

opera, Soviet

Attempts throughout the Soviet period to establish an operatic repertoire to rival the imperial heritage peaked in the 1930s, yet debates recurred regularly after 1953. Much of the energy of the post-Stalin period was devoted to rediscovering neglected or repressed works. Shostakovich's *Katerina Izmailova* and *Nos* (*The Nose*) were revived in 1963 and 1974 respectively. Prokofiev's operas were also slowly rehabilitated over many decades: *Semon Kotko* and *Povest o nastoiashchem cheloveke* (*Story of a Real Man*) in 1960, *Igrok* (*The Gambler*) in 1963 (in concert) and 1974 (on the stage), and *Ognennyi angel* (*The Fiery Angel*) as late as 1991.

The post-Stalin era began auspiciously with the belated premiere in 1953 of Shaporin's *Dekabristy* (*The Decembrists*), an opera that deftly reconciled lyric and epic, accessibility and modernity. Kabalevskii's *Nikita Vershinin* (1955) was based on a classic novel by Vsevolod Ivanov. Khrennikov's version of another canonical text, Gorkii's *Mat* (*Mother*), was staged simultaneously in Moscow, Leningrad, and Gorkii (now Nizhnii Novgorod) in 1957. Shebalin's *Ukroshchenie stroptovoi* (*The Taming of the Shrew*), first produced in Perm that same year, provided comic intimacy. *Ne tolko liubov* (*Not for Love Alone*), Shchedrin's lyric presentation on love and duty on a collective farm, appeared in 1961 (the 1972 revised version received the USSR State Prize). Several of these became established favourites; they seemed to suggest the possibility of fulfilling the requirements of Socialist Realism while simultaneously pleasing audiences and performers. None of these developments tempted Shostakovich to return to the form; the nearest he came was *Moskva-Cheremushki* (*Moscow-Cheremushki*), an

operetta about the housing shortage, staged in 1959. The trite and stereotypical scores and libretti of Dzerzhinskii's *Sudba cheloveka* (*Fate of a Man*, 1961) and Muradeli's *Oktiabr* (*October*, 1964) sadly recalled an earlier era.

Kholminov's Civil War epic, *Optimisticheskaia tragediia* (*An Optimistic Tragedy*, 1965) is his most famous score, although he also wrote several small-scale works based on Gogol, Chekhov and Dostoevskii for the Moscow Chamber Opera. Slonimskii, one of the Soviet Union's 'licensed modernists', saw his *Virineia* and *Mariia Stiuart* (*Mary Stuart*) staged in 1967 (revised version 1976) and 1981 respectively. However, his version of Bulgakov's *Master i Margarita* (*The Master and Margarita*), written in the early 1970s, had to wait until 1989 for its first performance, and 1991 for its first production. Petrov's *Petr Pervyi* (*Peter the First*) premiered with great pomp at the Kirov (Mariinskii) Theatre in 1975. That much Soviet opera remained a product of its time and culture was demonstrated by the hostile reaction to Molchanov's *Zory zdes tikhie* (*The Dawns Are Quiet Here*), performed by the Bolshoi Theatre in New York in 1975. Shchedrin explored a very different approach to opera in his complex and challenging *Mertvye dushi* (*Dead Souls*, premiered 1977), which daringly set a text without any obviously lyric or epic hero. Given state control over the commissioning and performance of works for the theatre, not all experiments would be so fortunate; operas by Knaifel and serial composer Karetnikov remained unperformed in public during Soviet times, though Karetnikov did manage to arrange a recording of his *Til Ulenshpigel* (*Till Eulenspiegel*) in a remarkable piece of musical *samizdat*. Glasnost and perestroika were perhaps kinder to Denisov, whose *L'écume des jours* (*Foam of the Days*) was staged in Perm in 1989, three years after its premiere at the Opéra-Comique in Paris. The first Soviet performance of his *Quatres filles* (*Four Girls*) took place in 1990, four years after its premiere in Bonn, heralding a period when much operatic innovation would move abroad.

See also: Bolshoi Theatre; Denisov, Edison; Khrennikov, Tikhon; Mariinskii Theatre; *Master i Margarita* (*The Master and Margarita*); opera singers, Bolshoi Theatre; opera singers, Mariinskii

Theatre; perestroika and glasnost; Petrov, Andrei; Prokofiev, Sergei; Shchedrin, Rodion; Shostakovich, Dmitrii; Slonimskii, Sergei; Socialist Realism

Further reading

Schwarz, B. (1983) *Music and Musical Life in Soviet Russia, 1917–1981*, Bloomington, IN: Indiana University Press.

Taruskin, R. (1992) 'Russia: 20th Century', in S. Sadie (ed.) *The New Grove Dictionary of Opera*, London: Macmillan.

PHILIP ROSS BULLOCK

opera singers, Bolshoi Theatre

As the Soviet Union's principal opera house, the Bolshoi Theatre was the natural home for many of the country's finest singers. For the first four decades of the Soviet period, opera at the Bolshoi Theatre was a domestic affair, catering to the tastes of enthusiastic audiences and the demands of the Party. After 1953, the theatre acquired the role of cultural ambassador for Soviet artistic achievements.

Continuity with the imperial and early Soviet tradition was provided by a generation of singers still active in the post-Stalin period. Aleksandr Pirogov was noted for his performance in the title role of Vera Stroeva's 1955 film version of *Boris Godunov*. Mark Reizen, another bass, sang into his nineties. The leading Soviet baritone, Pavel Lisitsian, joined the company in 1940. Two outstanding tenors, Ivan Kozlovskii and Sergei Lemeshev, made occasional but memorable appearances, evoking their heyday in the 1930s.

The generation that came to prominence in the 1950s and 1960s is perhaps the most famous in the theatre's recent history. Mezzo-sopranos Irina Arkhipova and Elena Obraztsova, tenors Vladimir Atlantov and Aleksei Maslennikov, baritone Iurii Mazurok, and basses Artur Eizen, Evgenii Nesterenko, Ivan Petrov, and Aleksandr Vedernikov were all leading members of the company, rewarded with recordings, overseas tours, and nationwide recognition. In her autobiography, Galina Vishnevskaia, for many years

the Bolshoi Theatre's leading soprano, paints a vivid picture of the highs and lows of working in such an environment.

Throughout the 1980s and 1990s, the theatre struggled to maintain its former high standards; the finest Russian singers now tend to appear at St. Petersburg's Mariinskii Theatre. An exception has been soprano Makvala Kasrashvili, who joined the company in 1996. Her appointment as artistic director of the opera in 2002 suggests that the theatre can look forward to a more promising future.

See also: Arkhipova, Irina; Bolshoi Theatre; Kozlovskii, Ivan; Lemeshev, Sergei; Mazurok, Iurii; Nesterenko, Evgenii; Obraztsova, Elena; opera, Soviet; opera singers, Mariinskii Theatre; Vishnevskaia, Galina

Further reading

http://www.bolshoi.ru

The Great Singers of Russia, vol. 1: *From Chaliapin to Reizen*, VAIDVD4257.

The Great Singers of Russia, vol. 2: *From Petrov to Kazarnovskaya*, VAIDVD4258.

PHILIP ROSS BULLOCK

opera singers, Mariinskii Theatre

For much of the Soviet period, the Mariinskii (Kirov) Theatre had difficulty maintaining a consistent vocal tradition, and was relegated to the status of a respectable regional house with casts and productions to match. Talented singers would frequently be recruited by the Bolshoi Theatre in Moscow; for example, Vladimir Atlanov, Elena Obraztsova, and Evgenii Nesterenko all sang with the theatre for several years before moving to the capital. In the 1960s, however, there were signs that the Kirov Theatre was beginning to establish its own operatic identity; soprano Galina Kovaleva, mezzo-soprano Irina Bogacheva, and bass Boris Shtokolov all enjoyed long and loyal careers there.

The renaissance of the Mariinskii Theatre is often attributed to Valerii Gergiev, but more properly should be traced back to Iurii

Temirkanov's reign between 1976 and 1988. Soprano Liubov Kazarnovskaia, mezzo-sopranos Larisa Diadkova and Evgeniia Gorokhovskaia, tenors Iurii Marusin and Konstantin Pluzhnikov, baritone Sergei Leiferkus, and basses Mikhail Kit, Nikolai Okhotnikov, and Aleksandr Morozov were all distinguished members of the company at this time. Several of them have continued to work with Gergiev, and have since been joined by an almost ceaseless flow of new singers, including sopranos Galina Gorchakova and Anna Netrebko, mezzo-soprano Olga Borodina, tenors Vladimir Galuzin and Gegam Grigorian, baritone Nikolai Putilin, and bass Gennadii Bezzubenkov. An academy for young singers has already produced some notable graduates, including tenor Daniil Shtoda. The voices of Gergiev's tenure have been immortalized in many important recordings, largely of Russian repertoire. Life at the Mariinskii Theatre has not suited everybody; sopranos Gorchakova and Elena Prokina have had well-publicized disputes with Gergiev, and some critics have suggested that while the theatre may excel in Russian classics, its singers have yet fully to master the Italian and German repertoires.

See also: Gergiev, Valerii; Mariinskii Theatre; Nesterenko, Evgenii; Obraztsova, Elena; opera, Soviet; opera singers, Bolshoi Theatre; Temirkanov, Iurii

Further reading

http://www.mariinsky.ru/en
The Great Singers of Russia, vol. 1: *From Chaliapin to Reizen*, VAIDVD4257.
The Great Singers of Russia, vol. 2: *From Petrov to Kazarnovskaya*, VAIDVD4258.

PHILIP ROSS BULLOCK

operetta

In the seventeenth and eighteenth centuries, the term 'operetta' denoted stage works shorter than an opera. The genre of musical performances known today as *opérette* and *opéra bouffe* originated in Paris during the Second Empire. Invented by Florimond Ronger, they were developed by Jacques Offenbach, who composed a series of satirical operettas mocking French court and society, including *La Vie Parisienne*, *La Belle Hélène*, *Orphée aux Enfers*, *Barbe-Bleu*. Russian operetta emerged only in the nineteenth century, following the successful 1868 production of Offenbach's opéra-bouffe *La Belle Hélène* by the St. Petersburg Aleksandrinskii Theatre. Subsequently, some companies started specializing in *opérette* and *opéra bouffe*. In 1873, Mikhail Lentovskii opened his Moscow operetta theatre, known as The Hermitage.

Although early twentieth-century Russia saw some operetta productions, the genre was reborn in the 1920s with the New Economic Policy, which enabled a popular entertainment industry. Popular Lecocq's operettas of this period included Vladimir Nemirovich-Danchenko's *Doch Ango* (*La Fille de Madame Ango*, 1920) and Aleksandr Tairov's *Den i noch* (*Day and Night*, 1926). Soviet operetta theatres emerged by the end of the 1920s, including the Moscow Operetta Theatre (1927), which staged hundreds of productions, with tens of thousands of performances. These includied Dmitrii Shostakovich's *Moskva-Cheremushki* (1959), Isaak Dunayevsky's *Volnyi veter* (*Free Wind*, 1947) and *Belaia akatsiia* (*White Acacia*, 1955), Nikolai Strelnikov's *Kholopka* (*The Serf Actress*,1963), and Frederick Loewe's *My Fair Lady* (1965). Boris Aleksandrov's highly popular 1937 operetta, *Svadba v Malinovke* (*Wedding in Malinovka*, 1937), influenced by Ukrainian folk music, became a 1968 film.

Post-Soviet operettas have been overshadowed by musicals, both foreign and Russian. Interesting contemporary productions include *Prodelki kota v sapogakh* (*Tricks of Puss in Boots*) by the Moscow State Academic Children's Musical Theatre, and the three-million-ruble operetta *Tsarevich* (*Prince*), at the St. Petersburg Lensovet Theatre. The latter, featuring Franz Lehar's music, is based on Gabriela Zapolskaia's play about young Tsar Nicholas II's affair with the ballet dancer Matilda Kszesinska.

See also: musicals, Russian/Soviet; opera, post-Soviet; opera, Soviet; Shostakovich, Dmitrii; theatre, post-Soviet; theatre, Soviet

Further reading

Meas, F. (2002) A *History of Russian Music: From Kamarinskaya to Babi Yar*, Berkeley, CA: University of California Press.

ALEXANDRA SMITH

Optina pustyn

Optina pustyn, a monastery with the status of a hermitage, is one of the most important centres for Russian Orthodoxy. Located on the Zhizdra River near Kozelsk, Optina dates from the fourteenth century. Its distinguished visitors and patrons include Nikolai Gogol, Dostoevskii, and Lev Tolstoi. Optina is famous for the nineteenth-century flowering of Orthodox Elders, a line of spiritual leaders known throughout Russia whose legacy has earned a permanent place in world Orthodox theology and wisdom.

See also: monastic life; Russian Orthodoxy

VALERIA Z. NOLLAN

orchestras, Soviet and post-Soviet

The Soviet system in which each regional centre had its own concert hall and symphony orchestra has been maintained in the post-Soviet era. The opportunities for initiative that came with perestroika gave birth to numerous new orchestras. Some of them have found previously unoccupied institutional niches and, like the philharmonics of the Soviet era, receive government support, while also seeking private sponsorship. Other projects are entirely private. The appearance of new orchestras has led to increased specialization in repertoire and style.

Russian orchestras today suffer from financial problems; only those that perform abroad can provide a decent living for their musicians. This situation presents a particular challenge to traditional, large philharmonic orchestras previously oriented toward a 'settled' existence. The possibility for engagements abroad is tied to the charisma of the orchestra's director and his relationship to his musicians. Accordingly, only a few old orchestras have managed to maintain their status, such as Arnold Kats's Novosibirsk Philharmonic and Vladimir Fedoseev's Bolshoi (Great) Symphonic Orchestra. A counter-example is Moscow's State Symphonic Orchestra, whose musicians revolted against director Evgenii Svetlanov: after thirty years of work together, the musicians demanded that the Ministry of Culture remove him from his post. Orchestra members felt that because of his many obligations abroad he 'abandoned' his musicians to their fate. Similar complaints are made about Iurii Temirkanov, who spends more time with his American and British orchestras than with the St. Petersburg Philharmonic, in sharp contrast to his predecessor, Evgenii Mravinskii, who rehearsed daily and meticulously with his orchestra for fifty years and made the ensemble a legend. Fellow St. Petersburger Valerii Gergiev has shown that charisma can decisively transform an orchestra: because of him, the orchestra of the Mariinskii Theatre, which had not previously performed on its own, has become one of Russia's premier orchestras, with an outstanding international reputation and a significant discography.

Among new orchestras, foremost is the Moscow-based Russian National Orchestra, founded as a private project in 1990 by pianist and conductor Mikhail Pletnev. Its success is based on a system resembling that of Western orchestras: the orchestra frequently invites guest conductors from abroad, including principal guest conductors Paavo Berglund and Kent Nagano. The orchestra makes frequent tours in Russia, performing also in provincial cities – a rare occurrence among leading orchestras in post-Soviet Russia.

The post-Soviet era has seen significant growth in the number of chamber orchestras. Many of them were founded by stars, such as Vladimir Spivakov's Moscow Virtuosi (*Virtuozy Moskvy*) and Iurii Bashmet's Moscow Soloists (*Solisty Moskvy*), both established in the Soviet era. Among the newer chamber orchestras, one of the best is Moscow's Musica Viva, directed by cellist Aleksandr Rudin. Also highly respected is the St. Petersburg Camarata, transformed by director Saulius Sondetskis from a student orchestra to the orchestra of the State Hermitage

Museum. Many of its performance projects are in museum spaces. Another successful chamber orchestra is Ekaterinburg's B-A-C-H. The rise in the popularity of chamber orchestras is linked to increasing interest in the performance of ancient music on authentic instruments. Indicative of this growing interest is the founding of Russia's first Baroque orchestra, the Catherine the Great Orchestra.

See also: Bashmet, Iurii; Gergiev, Valerii; Mariinskii Theatre; Mravinskii, Evgenii; Pletnev, Mikhail; Spivakov, Vladimir; Svetlanov, Evgenii; Temirkanov, Iurii

KIRA NEMIROVSKAIA

Orlova, Liubov Petrovna

b. 29 January [11 February] 1902, Moscow; d. 26 January 1975, Moscow

Actress

Orlova acted on stage from 1926 before making her screen debut in 1934. She became famous for the series of musical comedies in which she starred throughout the 1930s, directed by her husband Grigorii Aleksandrov: *Veselye rebiata* (*Happy Guys*, 1934); *Tsirk* (*The Circus*, 1936); *Volga-Volga* (1938 and *Svetlyi put* (*The Radiant Path*, 1940)). Vivacious and sunny, Orlova represented an idealized image of womanhood for 1930s Soviet audiences. She repeatedly played versions of the same character: the woman who reaches enlightenment/success partly through her own efforts, partly thanks to the helpful tutelage of a representative of the Party. Orlova was also known as a talented singer and dancer.

See also: Communist Party; Socialist Realism

JOSEPHINE WOLL

Orthodoxy abroad

Because the Soviet government followed a policy of official atheism and persecuted Orthodox believers with varying degrees of intensity, for much of the twentieth century, churches abroad preserved Russian Orthodox worship and tradition. Seminaries in Paris and New York State trained clergy; monasteries and publishing houses worldwide carried on the rich pre-revolutionary Russian traditions of scholarship and theology. Many Russian Orthodox abroad objected to the persecution of believers and the Soviet State's co-opting of the Church in Russia, particularly when Stalin and Patriarch Sergii (Stragorodskii) signed a concordat during World War II. In 1991, with the reduction of persecution and the recognition of the Moscow Patriarchate as the national church, relations between the Orthodox Church in Russia and abroad entered a new stage.

Orthodoxy abroad dates from the eighteenth century, when Peter I established churches, along with consulates and embassies, in major European and Asian cities. These became the outposts of the empire, serving both diplomats and travelling Russians. Russian missionaries, including St. Herman and St. Innocent of Alaska, also spread Orthodoxy to what was then part of Russian America.

After the Civil War, many Church leaders and clergy, led by Metropolitan Antonii (Khrapovitskii), left Russia. Patriarch Tikhon (Bellavin) authorized their independent administration. The St. Sergius Institute, St. Vladimir's Orthodox Seminary, and Holy Trinity Monastery published luminaries of Orthodox thought, including Georgii Florovskii, John Meyendorff, George Fedotov, Alexander Schmemann, Archbishop Averkii (Taushev), and Bishop Gregory (Grabbe). Orthodoxy is now an established area of academic research.

In 1970, the Orthodox Church in America received its autocephaly from the Moscow Patriarchate. The Russian Orthodox Church outside Russia continues to question the Moscow Patriarchate's right to represent the entire Russian Orthodox church. Disputes include the legacy of communist and post-communist cooperation with the state, ecumenism, and real estate.

See also: emigration; Russian Orthodoxy

NADIESZDA KIZENKO

Osmolovskii, Anatolii Feliksovich

b. 1969 (date unknown), Moscow

Artist, art theoretician, curator

A student at the Advanced Technical School of the Likhachev automobile plant (1987), Osmolovskii was a major member of the Moscow Actionist movement and the leader of the 'E.T.I.' group ('Expropriation of the Territory of Arts', 1990–92). His most famous art action was a performance on Red Square in Moscow (1991). Chief editor of the magazine *Radek* (1993–98), devoted to issues of contemporary culture, politics, and theory, he authored books and magazine articles on the problems of art. As a political artist, he focuses on the absurdity and realities of political culture in contemporary Russia, relying on everything from anarchic hooliganism and provocations to theorizing, revolutionary agitation, and dissemination of blackmail (*kompromat*). From 1999 until 2000, he participated in the electoral campaigns under the slogan 'Against All'. His works were widely exhibited in Moscow and other European capitals.

See also: Brenner, Aleksandr; Kulik, Oleg; Moscow Actionism; Red Square

YURI ZARETSKY

Ossetia

Approximately 335,000 Ossetians, one of the most ancient ethnic groups in the Caucausus, reside in the Republic of North Ossetia (established 1990, capital Vladikavkaz), which is a part of the Russian Federation. The other 67,000 (the former population of South Ossetia) live in Georgia. They speak in two dialects of the Ossetian language, which belongs to the Iranian group of the Indo-European family and has employed the Cyrillic alphabet since the nineteenth century. Most believers are Orthodox Christians, but there are also Moslem and Pagan minorities. Russia colonized Ossetia in 1774. Traditional occupations have been farming on the plain and livestock breeding (sheep, goats) in the mountains. Ossetian customs of hospitality, brotherhood, mutual help, and blood feuds resemble those of other peoples in the Northern Caucasus.

Ossetia's location on the border of Chechnia has rendered it strategically vulnerable: In September 2004, the terrorist act in a school in Beslan, North Ossetia, resulted in 300 deaths, mainly of children.

See also: Caucasus; Chechnia; ethnic minorities (malye narody); Georgia; Islam; Russian Orthodoxy; terrorist acts

TATYANA LEDENEVA

Ostankino Tower

The Ostankino Tower, constructed in northern Moscow in 1967, is a free-standing television and radio tower that is a startling 1,772 feet in height. It was the tallest free-standing structure in the world until 1975, when the CN Tower in Toronto was completed. In October 1993, the tower was taken over during Yeltsin's stand-off with the Duma. A fire swept through the tower in August 2000, resulting in major damage and the loss of three lives. After massive reconstruction, the tower reopened in 2004, boasting one of the most modern broadcasting facilities in the world. High-speed elevators whisk visitors to the top observation deck, some 1,105 feet from the ground, in under a minute. Just below the observation deck, which presents breathtaking panoramic views of Moscow, are the three dining rooms of the popular restaurant *Sedmoe nebo* (Seventh Heaven).

See also: radio, Soviet; Shabolovka; Stagnation; television, Soviet; Yeltsin, Boris

ANATOLE SENKEVITCH

Ovchinnikov, Viacheslav Aleksandrovich

b. 29 May 1936, Voronezh

Composer, conductor

Ovchinnikov, who began composing at the age of 9, studied composition at the Moscow

Conservatory, graduating in 1962. His early works, including three symphonies, caused a sensation, attracting young film directors' attention. Ovchinnikov's reputation mainly rests on the scores for such cinematic masterpieces as Andrei Tarkovskii's *Ivanovo detstvo* (*My Name Is Ivan*, 1962), Andrei Mikhalkov Konchalovskii's *Pervyi uchitel* (*The First Teacher*, 1965), and Sergei Bondarchuk's monumental Tolstoi adaptation *Voina i mir* (*War and Peace*, 1967). Ovchinnikov's characteristic alternation of an intimate, lyrical atmosphere and unabashed pathos is particularly impressive in his scores for the remastered versions of Aleksandr Dovzhenko's silent classics. His other works include the oratorio *Sergii Radonezhskii* (*Sergius of Radonezh*) and piano, violin, and cello concerti.

See also: Bondarchuk, Sergei; Konchalovskii, Andrei; Moscow Conservatory; Tarkovskii, Andrei

PETER ROLLBERG

Ovchinnikov, Vladimir Afanasevich

b. 4 October 1941, Shchuche ozero

Painter

In a deliberately naïve style, Ovchinnikov depicts solemn, nearly identical figures pursuing ordinary working-class lives. Occasionally, his rotund and comical human protagonists are visited by equally rotund angels, whose presence hints at the possibility of another world. Ovchinnikov achieved prominence in the 1970s, when he played an active role organizing studio and apartment exhibitions that bypassed official channels of approval. He was among the organizers of the first major exhibition of nonconformist art in Leningrad, at the Gaz Palace of Culture (1974). Since 1980, he has exhibited in Europe and the United States.

See also: art, nonconformist

JANET E. KENNEDY

P

Pakhmutova, Aleksandra Nikolaevna

b. 9 November 1929, Volgograd

Composer

The reputation of Pakhmutova, one of the Soviet Union's most prominent women composers, rests primarily on some 400 popular songs, many to texts by Nikolai Dobronravov. These reflect the public and private experiences of Soviet citizens in the 1960s and 1970s, from Gagarin's space flight to a vaguely patriotic love of the countryside. Similarly, her songs for the Komsomol deftly express the spirit and appeal of the movement, with little mention of ideology. A staple of the estrada repertoire, her songs have retained a nostalgic allure for those keen to recreate the atmosphere of a lost Soviet past.

See also: popular music, Soviet

PHILIP ROSS BULLOCK

Pamiat

Political organization

Formed in 1985 by artist and photographer Dmitrii Dmitrievich Vasilev, the nationalist organization Pamiat (Memory) became one of the very first proto-parties in the USSR. On 6 May 1987, Pamiat held the first unsanctioned demonstration in Moscow (since the 1920s) and was received by Moscow City Communist Party First Secretary Boris Yeltsin. In the late 1980s, Pamiat split into several organizations (headed by Sychev, Emelianov, Ostashvili, and Barkashov, among others). In the late 1990s, Pamiat relocated to Pereslavl-Zalesskii, outside Moscow. Following Vasilev's death in July 2003, it became marginalized. The influence of Pamiat and its activity in Russia have been greatly exaggerated.

See also: nationalism ('the national question'); political parties, post-Soviet

ALEXANDER DOMRIN

Panfilov, Gleb Anatolievich

b. 21 May 1934, Magnitogorsk

Film director

Panfilov's early films provided early starring roles for his wife, actress Inna Churikova: *V ogne broda net* (*No Ford in a Fire*, 1967) is set in the Civil War, and *Nachalo* (*The Debut*, 1970) is about an actress playing the part of Joan of Arc. *Tema* (*The Theme*, 1979) was banned for its picture of a demoralized writer (played by Mikhail Ulianov) weighed down by compromise. *Vassa* (1983) and *Mat* (*Mother*, 1989) are adaptations of works by Maksim Gorkii, and *Romanovy, ventsenosnaia semia* (*The Romanovs: An Imperial Family*, 2000) is an epic portrayal of the last months of the Russian royal family, culminating in their execution in 1918.

See also: censorship; Churikova, Inna; Ulianov, Mikhail

DAVID GILLESPIE

pantomime

The art of creating an image with the help of body movements, mimicry, and wordless gesture, pantomime is claimed by ballet, dance, drama, and the circus, but also successfully exists as an independent art in the form of short miniatures (Anatolii Elizarov, Aleksandr Zheromskii, Robert Gorodetskii, Vladimir Arkov, E. Konovalov, Aida Chernova and Iurii Medvedev, Natalia and Oleg Kiriushkin, S. Vlasova and O. Shkolnikov, Boris Amarantov) and full-scale plastic theatrical productions (*Eksperimentalnyi teatr-studiia* [Experimental Theatre Studio, Aleksandr Rumnev], *Moskovskii teatr mimiki i zhesta Vserossiiskogo obshchestva glukhonemykh* [Moscow Theatre of Mimicry and Gesture of the All-Russian Society for the Deaf and Mute, Pavel Savelev], *Moskovskii teatr plasticheskoi dramy* OKTAEDR [Moscow Theatre of Drama in Motion, Gedrius Matskiavichus], *Irkutskii teatr pantomimy* [Irkutsk Pantomime Theatre, Valerii Shevchenko]).

In the early twentieth century, pantomime was an important and innovative way to develop and renew the language of scenic expression in the work of directors Nikolai Evreinov, Vsevolod Meierkhold, Aleksandr Tairov, Solomon Mikhoels, Mikhail Chekhov, and others. During the Stalin era, pantomime virtually vanished as an artistic form: pantomime allowed for multiple interpretations, its metaphoric language was difficult to control and censor, and Stalin's aesthetics pronounced it on the border of formalist *formotvorchestvo* (form-creation), while Soviet art promulgated the priority of verbal expression. Even in circus productions, clowns were required to speak. Pantomime continued to exist in classical ballet productions and the individual performances of some stage actors, mostly in comedies.

The successful tours of French mimes in the USSR during the Thaw triggered the rebirth of pantomime. Marcel Marceau's performances in 1961 caused an explosion of interest in pantomime as an autonomous art with its own, self-sufficient language. Pantomime's unlimited expressive potential made it possible, without words, to achieve a depth of philosophical generalization, suggest a wide range of associations, express subtle nuances of emotion, and even address the absurdity of contemporary life. Pantomime therefore became practically a dissident artistic form, attracting many young people. In the 1960s hundreds of studios arose, including Mark Rozovskii's *Nash dom* (Our House), with Ilia Rutberg directing pantomime productions, Robert Liger's *Riga pantomime*, and hundreds of amateur groups throughout the country. In 1975, Matskiavichus directed a pantomime production, *Preodolenie* (Overcoming), devoted to Michelangelo, which made plastic drama a popular new theatrical genre. Eccentric and acrobatic pantomime continued to be an essential part of circus art; performances by famous Russian clowns such as Iurii Nikulin, Oleg Popov, and Andrei Nikolaev were predominantly pantomime numbers. In the 1970s, Leonid Engibarov, 'the clown with sad eyes', revolutionized the art of clownery by introducing poetic and lyrical tones into traditional buffoonery and grotesque sequences. His legacy was later developed by Viacheslav Polunin's clown-mime-theatre, *Litsedei*, Georgii Deliev's mime company, *Maski* (Masks), and others. By the 1980s pantomime was an intrinsic part of avant-garde drama theatre productions (Roman Viktiuk's *Sluzhanki* [The Maids, 1988] and Iurii Liubimov's productions at the Taganka Theatre). Though in the 1990s most plastic theatre companies either became integrated into dramatic theatre or merged with contemporary dance companies, individual mime numbers continue to occupy an important place in Russian show business and the circus.

See also: ballet, post-Soviet; circus; Liubimov, Iurii; Nikulin, Iurii; Polunin, Viacheslav; Popov, Oleg; Rozovskii, Mark; Stalin, Iosif; Taganka Theatre; Thaw; Viktiuk, Roman

TATIANA SMORODINSKAYA

Papanov, Anatolii Dmitrievich

b. 31 November 1922, Vazmae;
d. 7 August 1987, Moscow

Actor

Popular in both comedies and in more serious roles, Papanov joined Moscow's Satire Theatre in 1949 and entered the film world in 1952. His most memorable comic roles have been in *Dvenadstat stulev* (*The Twelve Chairs*, 1977), and *Inkognito iz Peterburga* (*Incognito from St. Petersburg*, 1978). He also provided the wolf's voice for over twenty years in the television cartoon series *Nu, pogodi!* (*Just You Wait!*). He played in Iulii Raizman's *Vremia zhelanii* (*A Time of Wishes*, 1984), and, to poignant effect, a political prisoner in Aleksandr Proshkin's *Kholodnoe leto 53-ego* (*The Cold Summer of 1953*, 1988), his last film.

See also: *Nu, pogodi!* (Just You Wait!); Satire Theatre (Teatr satiry)

DAVID GILLESPIE

Paradzhanov, Sergei Iosifovich

b. 9 January 1924, Tbilisi, Georgia; d. 20 July 1990, Yerevan, Armenia

Film director

One of the most significant cinematic talents of the post-War Soviet Union, Sergei Paradzhanov directed acclaimed films showcasing his highly original painterly and baroque sensibility: *Tini zabutykh predkiv* (*Shadows of Forgotten Ancestors*, 1964), *Sayat Nova* (*The Colour of Pomegranates*, 1969), and *Ashik Kerib* (1988). Born in Tbilisi to Armenian parents, he enrolled briefly at the Tbilisi Railway Engineering Institute, then at the Moscow Film Institute (1946–52), and worked sporadically in the Ukrainian, Armenian, and Georgian film studios. Outspoken and eccentric, in 1947, 1974–77, and 1982 he was imprisoned on charges of homosexuality and speculation.

ANN KOMAROMI

parasitism (tunaiedstvo)

The right to work guaranteed by the Soviet Constitution was de facto the obligation to work for the 'welfare of the Motherland'. The system provided every adult able to work with a job that paid at least a subsistence wage. Anyone unemployed was deemed a criminal, a parasite living off 'other people's' work.

Parasitism was punishable according to Soviet law (article 209 of the Criminal Code of the RSFSR), and was defined as an existence lived at the expense of the collective, demonstrating a lack of moral responsibility and an aversion to and neglect of socially useful labour. Any employable adult who lived four months out of twelve without a job could be prosecuted. The law adopted by the Russian Federation on 5 December 1991 made no mention of 'parasitism', a term now in disuse.

The most famous show-trial for parasitism was that of poet Iosif Brodskii (Nobel Prize laureate, 1987). The first, closed court hearing (February, 1964) in Leningrad ordered Brodskii placed in a forensic psychiatric clinic, which declared him 'able to work and mentally sound'. The second, open trial (March 1964) sentenced him to five years of exile with mandatory physical labour.

See also: Brodskii, Iosif; constitutions; Nobel Prize winners, literature

ELENA OMELCHENKO

Parfenov, Leonid Gennadievich

b. 26 January 1960, Cherepovets

Journalist, producer, director

Russia's witty and politically savvy television anchorman who remained after NTV's takeover and split of staff, Parfenov was one of the few journalists in the state-controlled electronic media not afraid to criticize the authorities. Creator of *Namedni* (The Other Day), NTV's weekly current affairs show that enjoyed consistently high ratings, he was dismissed in June 2004 after refusing to succumb to the demands of the channel's management. The Parfenov scandal amplified the continuous debate over the freedom of speech and the return of censorship in Russia.

See also: censorship; NTV; television, post-Soviet

VLADIMIR STRUKOV

Pärt, Arvo

b. 11 September 1935, Paide, Estonia, 1935

Composer

After studies at the Tallinn Conservatory, Pärt began to write film and theatre music early in his career. He took an interest in serial composition and applied principles of serialism to duration and rhythm, mirroring Pierre Boulez's work a decade earlier. During the 1960s he became enthralled with the polyphonic work of Bach as well as Gregorian chant, which inspired works including his *Credo* (1968) for chorus and orchestra. Pärt's style, with its minimalistic traits, was also influenced by medieval and renaissance music, particularly Notre Dame *organum* and the music of Ockeghem and Josquin.

By 1976, Pärt had created an approach to tonality called *tintinnabuli*. Referring to the ringing of bells, this technique reveals a second set of pitches associated with the central tone, usually notes of the tonic triad. Pärt's works from this period helped to establish his international career. He emigrated with his family to Vienna in 1980, acquired Austrian citizenship, and a year later moved to West Berlin, where he settled.

Today Pärt is best known for his series of works entitled *Fratres*, *Tabula Rasa*, both written in 1977, and his *St. John Passion*, completed in 1982 after his emigration to Berlin. More recent works include *Litany* (1994) and a series of choral works (with and without orchestra) based on various Passion texts.

Further reading

Hillier, P. (1997) *Arvo Pärt*, Oxford: Oxford University Press.

DAVID GOMPPER

partiinost

Partiinost, sometimes translated as 'partisanship', 'party-mindedness', or 'party spirit', was a central requirement of all Soviet cultural production. Novelists, playwrights, poets and philosophers all were exhorted to produce work that supported the Communist Party and defended the ideological interests of the working class. What this meant in more practical terms was hard to pin down and, more often than not, the notion of *partiinost* was used polemically to discredit ideologically unsound works and authors. The concept was introduced by Lenin and endlessly reiterated, notably by Gorkii in his famous 1934 programmatic statement defining the characteristics of Socialist Realism.

See also: Communist Party; Lenin, Vladimir Ilich; Socialist Realism

DAVID HUNTER SMITH

passport

A passport is a government-issued document that remains the major form of identification within Russia ('internal passport'). It indicates a person's name, age, sex, and place of birth; it also contains information on a person's marital and family status, *propiska* (residence permit), and record of military service. In Moscow, since the terrorist attacks of the 1990s, everyone is required to carry a passport at all times and present it to officials on demand. Passport checks on the streets and in metro stations have become commonplace, particularly for young men, especially those of Caucasian appearance.

In both the Russian and Soviet Empires passports were used to restrict the movement of people. In the USSR, passport-holders had to specify their ethnicity (the so-called 'entry number 5'), which allowed for discrimination on those grounds. In 2003, the Russian government stopped issuing passports with the symbols of the Soviet Union.

To travel outside the country Russian citizens must obtain a foreign (external) passport, renewable every five years. Applicants for foreign passports undergo an examination by the FSB (formerly KGB). Sometimes people's applications are rejected for security reasons, whereas in the Soviet era, external passports were used to impede political and economic emigration.

See also: propiska

VLADIMIR STRUKOV

Pasternak, Boris Leonidovich

b. 29 January [10 February] 1890, Moscow;
d. 30 May 1960, Peredelkino, near Moscow

Poet and prose writer

As the eldest son of painter Leonid Pasternak and pianist Rosalia Kaufman, Boris Pasternak came of age in pre-revolutionary Moscow artistic circles. He studied musical composition and philosophy before publishing his first verse collections, *Bliznets v tuchakh* (*Twin in the Clouds*) in 1914 and *Poverkh barerov* (*Over the Barriers*) in 1917. Pasternak's early poetry is indebted to Symbolism and Ego-futurism, as well as to Maiakovskii's verse and persona, against whose rhetoric of self-dramatization Pasternak struggled in his early work. The poetry of *Sestra moia zhizn* (*My Sister Life*), the 1922 collection that established him as a major poet, is dynamic, explosively emotional and rapturously in love with life and nature. Pasternak's vocabulary, rhyme and metonymy, conveying a vision of the unity of being, are highly original and complex, making his poetry difficult for the average reader. In an effort to come to terms with a changed post-revolutionary cultural landscape and respond to the epic register of the era, during the 1920s Pasternak published a series of long narrative poems, such as *Spektorskii*, which addressed revolutionary events, mainly from the perspective of the intellectual or creative individual. As the ideological sky darkened, Pasternak published *Okhrannaia gramota* (*Safe Conduct*), a testimonial to the individuals who had shaped his artistic identity. The title of Pasternak's 1932 collection *Vtoroe rozhdenie* (*Second Birth*) signified both personal and professional rebirth: the love lyrics and Georgian impressions were inspired by his trip to the Caucasus with Zinaida Neigauz, who became his second wife after the disintegration of his marriage to Evgeniia Lure; the language of the collection reflected Pasternak's striving to simplify his poetic diction. Under the repressive conditions of the late 1930s Pasternak ceased original publication, earning his living by translating Georgian poets, Byron, Keats, Verlaine, the major Shakespeare tragedies (now the standard Russian versions), and later *Faust* and Schiller's *Maria Stuart*. When ideological constraints were somewhat relaxed during World War II, Pasternak was able to publish two new verse collections, *Na rannikh poezdakh* (*On Early Trains*) and *Zemnoi prostor* (*Breadth of Earth*), dealing with patriotic themes and communion with the people in simple, transparent language. Although Pasternak had published fiction in his youth, notably *Detstvo Liuvers* (*The Childhood of Liuvers*), prose writing did not come easily to him. Nevertheless, during the reactionary Zhdanov years he quietly began working on the novel *Doctor Zhivago*, a panoramic record of his generation's experiences refracted through the central character of a Moscow doctor and poet who embodied Pasternak's artistic beliefs. Although *Doctor Zhivago* casts the broad net of a nineteenth-century historical novel, its quasi-symbolic figuration of characters, passive central hero, subjective apprehension of historical events and reliance on coincidence subvert nineteenth-century realism and causality, as well as the historical determinism and activist ideals of Socialist Realism. After *Doctor Zhivago* was rejected by *Novyi mir*, the writer allowed Giangiacomo Feltrinelli to publish the novel abroad in 1957, and Pasternak was awarded the Nobel Prize the following year. A vicious government campaign against the writer forced him to decline the award. During his last years Pasternak published the verse collection *Kogda razguliaetsia* (*When the Weather Clears*) and *Avtobiograficheskii ocherk* (*Autobiographical Essay*). *Doctor Zhivago*, the Soviet-era work that irrevocably breached the Iron Curtain, was finally published in Russia in 1988.

See also: censorship; Nobel Prize winners, literature; *Novyi mir*; poetry, Soviet; thick journals; World War II (Great Patriotic War)

Further reading

Barnes, C. (1989–98) *Boris Pasternak. A Literary Biography*, vols 1 and 2, Cambridge: Cambridge University Press.

RIMGAILA SALYS

Patrice Lumumba People's Friendship University

See Russian People's Friendship University

Paustovskii, Konstantin Georgievich

b. 19 May 1892, Moscow; d. 14 July 1968, Moscow

Prosaist

Paustovskii spent his youth in Kiev, where he began to publish prose in 1912. In the 1930s he gained recognition for his series of documentary novellas about industrialization in the remote parts of Soviet Russia. While addressing the politically correct subjects of the time, Paustovskii focused his novellas *Kara-Bugaz* (1932) and *Kolkhida* (1934) on the complex interaction between humans and nature, thereby subsequently gaining a reputation as a forefather of Russian environmental prose. Great popularity came to Paustovskii in the post-World War II years with the publication of his autobiographical novel, *Dalekie gody* (*Distant Years*, 1946). The author surprised his contemporaries with the explicitly personal nature of his narrative, which completely lacked the expected political undertone. In 1956, Paustovskii published his collection of philosophical essays, *Zolotaia roza* (*The Golden Rose*, 1955), which discussed the complexity of the writer's creative process, also without recourse to Soviet rhetoric.

As an organizer and editorial board member, Paustovskii participated in two significant literary initiatives during the early years of the Thaw: the publication of the literary almanacs *Literaturnaia Moskva* (*Literary Moscow*, 1956) and *Tarusskie stranitsy* (*Pages from Tarusa*, 1961). These collections introduced not only works by contemporary authors, but also prose and poetry by writers who had perished or were silenced under Stalinism. When the political climate changed, both publications were discontinued and Paustovskii was heavily criticized in the Soviet press for his role in them. During his lifetime the writer enjoyed immense respect among progressive Soviet intellectuals for his fearless defence of writers such as Vladimir Dudintsev, Iulii Daniel, and Andrei Siniavskii. Nominated for the Nobel Prize in 1965.

See also: Daniel, Iulii; Dudintsev, Vladimir; literature, Thaw; Siniavskii, Andrei; Thaw

Further reading

Ilin, V. S. (1967) *Konstantin Paustovsky: Poeziia stranstvii*, Moscow: Sovetskaia Rossiia.

Levitskii, L. A. (1983) *Vospominaniia o Konstantine Paustovskom*, Moscow: Sovetskii Pisatel.

Slonim, M. (1977) *Soviet Russian Literature: Writers and Problems*, New York: Oxford University Press, pp. 118–22.

Svirski, G. (1981) *A History of Post-War Soviet Writing: The Literature of Moral Opposition*, Ann Arbor, MI: Ardis.

MARINA BALINA

pedagogy, Soviet

Soviet pedagogy was connected to a rich heritage of Russian psychological research. This resulted in a fruitful array of experimental pedagogical approaches, but the centralized nature of Soviet schools and restrictions on local initiative led to overly simplified interpretations of these for most teachers and schools.

Perhaps best known among Soviet educational psychologists was Lev Semenovich Vygotskii, whose work on the socially embedded nature of learning and development influenced two generations of Russian educators. Vygotskii and his school (Luria, Elkonin, Davydov) maintained that development emerges from social activity and the mastery of culturally important psychological tools (literacy, numeracy, artistic forms). Pedagogical models and systems based on this work were developed initially during the Soviet era in such fields as mathematics and are widely used today in Russia under the general rubric of 'developmental instruction'.

Unfortunately, early Soviet educational psychology was ideologically constrained. Vygotskii's own system for monitoring individual children's progress (known as 'pedology') was denounced as bourgeois and suppressed for many years. This general Soviet antipathy towards individual assessment and especially standardized tests resulted in a period of stasis on measuring educational outcomes for much of the Soviet period.

A distinctive feature of the Soviet approach to pedagogy was the differentiation between *vospitanie* (upbringing or character education) and *obuchenie* (instruction or teaching). These were officially seen as inseparable. The Soviet model of upbringing particularly emphasized Leninist ideology and devotion to the collective. An early figure in the development of this approach was Stanislav Teofilovich Shatskii, who stressed the importance of educating children to work for the collective good and introducing them early to physical labour. Perhaps the best known of those working on upbringing was Anton Semenovich Makarenko, an educator charged during the 1930s with creating schools to educate homeless and 'wild' children. His success and publicistic efforts made him a model for others working on upbringing and for Soviet teachers generally.

Later in the Soviet period, alternative images of how young people should be treated began to appear. The work of Vasilii Sukhomlinskii, a Ukrainian school director, stressed the happiness of the individual as a precondition to establishing a successful collectivist orientation. Although his ideas were considered subversive during the late Soviet era, Sukhomlinskii's followers worked with children in both school and non-school settings, and many of them became important figures in the 'social-pedagogical movement' of the 1980s. That decade saw the 'discovery' of a number of unusually creative 'innovator' teachers, whose work was increasingly held up as a model for good pedagogical practice. These included Viktor Fedorovich Shatalov, who developed a system of graphical outlines that allowed students to learn physics more easily. Sofia Nikolaevna Lysenkova created a system of 'intensive education' that allowed first-grade children to make remarkable and rapid progress in mastering reading and writing. Shalva Aleksandrovich Amonashvili, a Georgian psychologist, modelled systems that paid more individual attention to students, encouraged them to work together more productively, and engaged them in meaningful self-governance.

See also: educational system, Soviet; sports education; vocational education

STEPHEN T. KERR

Pelevin, Viktor Olegovich

b. 22 November 1962, Moscow

Writer

Arguably the most talked-about post-Soviet writer, Pelevin is a hybrid: his postmodernist play with Soviet ideological and cultural flotsam recapitulates the failure of Soviet history; however, his earnest philosophizing – not, critics have noted, a postmodernist hallmark – problematizes existence in general. Pelevin's typical protagonist confronts political and existential conspiracy – a conflated worldview suited to the Soviet and post-Soviet experience. In *Spi* (*Sleep*), a vodka drinker fails to decode in time Stolichnaya's '*SoiuzPlodoImport*' trademark – a globe inscribed SPI ('SLEEP!') – eventually succumbing to universal sleep, or late-Soviet 'stagnation'.

In *Omon Ra*, a cosmonaut's subjection to a senseless suicide mission accompanies philosophical speculation on the enslavement of the stars themselves; the hero's eventual resistance becomes both an action movie set-piece and an existentialist revolt against Stoic (philosophical and Soviet) worship of *kosmos*/order. The post-Soviet typology of *Zhizn nasekomykh* (*The Life of Insects*) foregrounds species instinct through mosquito-businessmen who suck blood. In 1999's ambitious *Pokolenie 'P'* (*Babylon*), an adman's initiation into the secret media construction of Russia's governing elite and governing desires condemns post-Soviet pseudo-reform while instantiating analogous metaphysical traps: Schopenhauer's will-to-live, the Buddhist *samsara* (delusion of individuation), and Marx's commodity fetishism.

Further reading

McCausland, G. (2004) 'Viktor Pelevin', in M. Balina and M. Lipovetsky (eds) *Dictionary of Literary Biography*, vol. 285, *Russian Writers Since 1980*, Detroit: Gale.

AVRAM BROWN

pelmeni

Small, navel-shaped Siberian dumplings filled with ground beef and pork, and finely minced onions, *pelmeni* are served in beef or chicken broth, accompanied by sour cream and/or white vinegar. Made in batches of hundreds, in Siberia they are stored in bags in the icy snow, and elsewhere in conventional freezers.

CHRISTINE A. RYDEL

Peltser, Tatiana Ivanovna

b. 6 June 1904, Moscow; d. 16 July 1992, Moscow

Theatre and film actress

Peltser's father, famous actor Ivan Peltser (1871–1959), was her acting teacher. Beginning in 1920, she worked with different troupes, most prominently in the Theatre of Satire (1947–77) and the Theatre of the Lenin Komsomol (Lenkom, 1977–92). She began her career in the classical repertoire, especially plays by Ivan Turgenev and Aleksandr Ostrovskii. Eventually, her forte became comedic roles. Both on stage and on screen, she gained huge popularity with her portrayals of peculiar elderly women with strong personalities, sharp tongues, and golden hearts. While some of Peltser's performances bordered on the grotesque, her characterizations always had psychological depth. People's Artist of the USSR (1972).

See also: Lenkom Theatre

PETER ROLLBERG

pensions

The Soviet state paid particular attention to the social security of its citizens. In 1956 a unified all-Soviet law regarding state pensions was adopted, according to which all working people had the right to receive a pension. In 1964, the law was adopted for collective farm workers. In the USSR, pensions were paid from the government budget, mostly out of contributions that all enterprises were required to make and partially from other income sources. The state was the only employer and it guaranteed social support; people were confident that they would get a modest pension, enough to live independently. The retirement age in the USSR was 55 for women and 60 for men, if they had worked a total of 20 and 25 years respectively. The average old age pension in 1989 totalled 89 rubles a month, 37 per cent of the average wage. Those working in hazardous or hard labour industries or in harsh climatic conditions could receive a pension after fewer years of work; early retirement was also available for doctors, teachers, dancers, flight attendants, and some other professions. In calculating the pension amount the average wage in the past twelve months or any five years out of last ten were taken into account. The total amount of all wages during one's career did not affect pension size. There was a minimal and maximum size of pension, which led to a levelling (*uravnilovka*). Thus no one could influence the amount of retirement payments; that was solely the prerogative of the state. There were also special pensions according to Soviet laws: for mother-heroines, disabled or orphaned children, families breadwinner.

The Russian pension system has been under reform since 1995. Several important legal acts were adopted: on the system of obligatory pension insurance, private pension funds, state pensions, etc. The Russian Pension Fund (*Pensionnyi fond Rossii*) was created, and enterprises were required to contribute 29 per cent of their wage fund as a social tax (later replaced by *Edinyi sotsialnyi nalog* [unified social tax]). Pension reform is one of the most complex and painful issues in Russia today. Current pensions provide barely enough to survive; in some expensive urban areas, such as Moscow, local authorities established additional payments to supplement pensions. State attempts to deprive older people of social benefits in 2005 and replace medical, transportation, and other benefits with monetary compensation met active protests and widespread disapproval. Some current Russian pension problems are not unique: an aging population, the necessity of introducing a fully-funded system instead of a pay-as-you-go system, diversification of investments in pension funds, and encouraging investment through private companies. Yet there are specific post-socialist issues as well: Russians are not used to accepting personal responsibility for their retirement and still expect the government to provide for them.

See also: economic system, post-Soviet; economic system, Soviet

TATIANA SMORODINSKAYA

Peredelkino

A lovely wooded area 12 miles southwest of Moscow, Peredelkino belonged to the Samarin estate before the October Revolution. Stalin seized the land for the Union of Writers (established in 1932) to build state-owned country homes for approved authors. Peredelkino is most closely associated with Boris Pasternak, who wrote there from 1936 until his death in 1960. His home became a museum in 1990; he is buried in the local graveyard. In the post-Soviet period, local authorities have yielded to pressure to develop the area's prime real estate. Writers and their relatives fear the loss of Peredelkino's rich literary heritage.

See also: literary museums; Moscow; Pasternak, Boris; unions, creative, Soviet

CHRISTINE A. RYDEL

perestroika and glasnost

Perestroika, meaning 'restructuring', and glasnost, signifying 'openness', formed the core of Mikhail Gorbachev's reformist policies from 1985 to 1991. Perestroika principally constituted efforts to reform the antiquated planned economic system by incorporating elements of a market economy. Glasnost, as originally conceived, permitted an atmosphere of open examination of the economy, which, Gorbachev believed, could yield the kind of reformist economic policies he desired. Neither policy eventuated as he intended. The restructuring of the Soviet economy did not produce enough reform, and openness was carried to such an extreme that it helped to undermine the Soviet political system.

Restructuring

Restructuring comprised three key domestic economic reforms and one related foreign policy reform. The first dealt with the reform of the Soviet enterprise system. The law on state enterprises, introduced at the June 1987 Communist Party plenum, proposed a shift of managerial decision-making from the central economic ministries to the enterprise level. It constituted a radical shift in formal decision-making authority, giving significantly more power to individual enterprises to determine their fates and become more efficient and profitable. Enterprises could fire workers, if the need arose – a violation of the Soviet social contract, which promised workers jobs in return for support of the centralized political system. In theory, industries could go bankrupt, too. But this was no market system, as the central authorities kept broad controls through the overall central planning mechanism and could create, merge and dissolve enterprises. Most significant, the central structures kept control over pricing, which meant that industries were constrained in what they could charge for their products. It was a fatal flaw, since it prevented enterprises from achieving profitability and continued their reliance on the centre for state orders of their products.

The second part of restructuring concerned agriculture. The policy endeavoured to stimulate farmers to produce efficiently and profitably, while still meeting state demands for their products. In other words, the plan contained the same contradiction between individual stimulus and state constraint that the industrial sector portrayed. At the June 1987 plenum, Gorbachev introduced the notion of the family contract system, which permitted farmers to practise small-scale private farming, a radical notion for a populace that was used to working on collective farms. Larger groups, called contract groups, were also created. Single groups, in contrast with the previous practice, which utilized several specialized groups, would be responsible for the entire production cycle of farming, from ploughing to planting to harvesting. But the state still loomed large in both its planning apparatus and pricing mechanisms, hindering progress. Perhaps even more important in preventing real change in the countryside was lack of ability to own the land on which one farmed, implying that the state could come in to take control of a farm if it did the 'wrong' thing. The fear that Soviet farmers had felt during the harsh, forced collectivization campaign during the 1930s was still palpable in the 1980s. It meant that farmers were reluctant to try much that was innovative. The attitude was so strong that it carried well past the dissolution of the USSR, continuing to hinder progress in agriculture.

A third economic aspect of restructuring dealt with the trade-off between the consumer sector and defence. For true economic reform, Gorbachev needed to restrain defence spending, which swallowed a large proportion of the Soviet budget, and allocate funds to other, more productive parts of the economy, including the manufacture of consumer goods, always in short supply. He attempted to do this through changes in the twelfth five-year plan (1986–90), ordering military industry to increase its production of consumer goods to 65 per cent of total output from 40 per cent. But, instead of yielding the production of consumer products in demand, such as consumer electronics, military industry often used its sophisticated equipment to make low-technology items, such as pots and pans. Not only did the behaviour of military industry fail to produce a revolution in consumer goods, but Gorbachev's reliance on central directives undermined the spirit and letter of decentralization.

Gorbachev conceived of changes in Soviet foreign policy as playing an important role in the success of restructuring. He believed that the creation of a more peaceful international system, particularly improved Soviet–US relations, would create breathing space for perestroika to succeed. This policy, called 'new political thinking', would mean a significantly lessened Soviet military posture that would demonstrate peaceful Soviet intentions and yield less Soviet military spending to permit economic recovery and become engaged in international trade. Among other things, Gorbachev announced the unilateral reduction of Soviet troops in East Europe and Mongolia (1988) and withdrew Soviet troops from Afghanistan (1989), where they had been fighting for ten years. He agreed to asymmetrical reductions in intermediate-range nuclear weapons in Europe and along the Sino-Soviet border (1987), conventional force reductions in Europe (1990), and reductions in nuclear weapons (1991). Moreover, he acquiesced to East European regime changes in 1989. While new political thinking was revolutionary and can be credited as the main factor producing the end of the Cold War, it did not redound to the advantage of economic restructuring as quickly as Gorbachev had hoped. Rather, its effect took time, to be realized only well after he had left power.

Openness

Gorbachev intended glasnost to complement perestroika. The idea was to open up limited debate about the economic and political systems to effect change. Thus, openness became the engine to drive restructuring. Initially, Gorbachev and his compatriots created a tripartite attack on slow-moving Party and government bureaucrats. The first thrust came from top Party leaders, including Gorbachev, who made daring policy proposals and who criticized and replaced high-level Party and government officials. They also pushed through radical changes in the political system, transferring policy-making power to the government from the Party and instituting competitive elections to newly-created bodies at all levels of the political system. The second attack was launched by intellectuals, who could formulate important critiques of the current system and advance ideas about economic reform. Abel Aganbegian, Tatiana Zaslavskaia, and their colleagues in Novosibirsk wrote a number of important economic reform proposals and founded important concepts central to restructuring. The 'human factor' in economic policy was one of these, proposing that human beings respond well to economic and non-economic incentives (such as higher salaries and access to consumer goods), producing more and better products accordingly. The final thrust came from below, where workers and other employers were encouraged openly to criticize their bosses and Party leaders for poor economic performance. Articles in, and letters to editors of, magazines and newspapers reflected this more liberal policy.

It did not take long for openness to expand from its beginnings, for popular dissatisfaction with Party and government officials had been building since at least the mid-point of the Brezhnev regime. Soon many things were open to criticism – even Gorbachev himself. Boris Yeltsin gleefully seized upon the more open political climate to propose even more radical economic reform than Gorbachev's, and Gorbachev's conservative opponents used it to call for restraint. Meetings of the Soviet Communist Party elites, broadcast on Soviet television, showed open dissent within the Party for the first time. Unanimous votes on proposals at Party and government meetings were a thing of the past. Regular members of the Party began to see and criticize corruption at the top of the Party apparatus and, in increasing numbers by 1990, resigned from the Party. Instead of creating support for restructuring in a clear and controlled way, openness created a bifurcated political atmosphere, with Gorbachev, nearly alone, in the middle.

Thus, glasnost had gone too far and perestroika had not gone far enough, though Gorbachev must be credited with introducing and legitimizing basic aspects of democracy and a market economy and, most significantly, bringing an end to the Cold War. The incendiary conditions created by perestroika and glasnost helped lead to a fundamental authority crisis in the USSR. The very structure of the system, led by the Communist Party, was called into question, helping to establish promising directions for change in the new regime that was to follow.

See also: Brezhnev, Leonid; Cold War; collective farms; Communist Party; defence industry; East Bloc countries; economic system, Soviet; five-year plan; Gorbachev, Mikhail; privatization; War, Afghan; Yeltsin, Boris

Further reading

Breslauer, G. (2002) *Gorbachev and Yeltsin as Leaders*, Cambridge: Cambridge University Press.

Goldman, M. (1992) *What Went Wrong with Perestroika*, New York: W. W. Norton.

Gorbachev, M. S. (1987) *Perestroika: New Thinking for Our Country and the World*, New York: Harper & Row.

——(1996) *Memoirs*, New York: Doubleday.

GEORGE E. HUDSON

periodicals, post-Soviet

According to the new Russian media law announcing freedom of the press (December 1991), publications and other media may be founded not only by state institutions and governmental bodies, but also by private ones, by groups of citizens, and even by individuals. Initial analysis showed that in 1992 alone more than 400 new publications appeared, which meant that every day more than one new magazine or newspaper was born. Though many newcomers did not survive market competition, more new publications continued to be launched by various individuals and organizations.

In 2004, in Russia one can find more than 42,000 licensed publications, 17 thousand magazines and 25,000 newspapers. More than 7,000 of the latter are local – the so-called *raionki*, which originated in the 1920s and 1930s as propaganda organs. Some 80 per cent of all publications are established by governmental bodies or associated with state institutions, 20 per cent – by private ones. Private publications are produced mostly in Moscow, other large cities, and regional centres, less in small towns, and only occasionally in villages, often sponsored by local businesses or journalists. The largest players in the press market at the national level (besides the state) are the corporation *Prof-media* (which owns *Komsomolskaia pravda* ['Komsomolka']) and the state gas company, *Gazprom*. They have branches in all regional centres and unite hundreds of regional publications, such as special regional issues of *Komsomolka*, which enjoy an enormous combined circulation. Branch and regional versions also exist for the periodicals *Moskovskii komsomolets* (Moscow Komsomol), *Argumenty i fakty* (Arguments and Facts), and *Ekonomika i zhizn* (Economy and Life). Some regional and inter-regional companies unite regional publications, such as the publishing house *Provintsiia* (The Provinces) and *Zolotoe koltso* (The Golden Ring). Major media holdings work in the regions, uniting various media around well-known names, such as

Krasnoiarskii rabochii (The Krasnoiarsk Worker), *Biznes* + (in Nizhnii Novgorod), *Cheliabinskii rabochii* (The Cheliabinsk Worker), *Stavropolskaia Pravda* (Stavropolsk Truth), and others.

Publications vary widely. Well-known newspapers such as *Moskovskii komsomolets* and *Komsomolskaia pravda* have changed their content radically. *MK* became popular in the late 1980s as the first 'trashy' newspaper; its new style and presentation, featuring sharp and sometimes shocking titles, emphasis on scandals, and use of slang attracted thousands of readers. In the last few years *MK* has become more serious, known for analysis and investigative reporting. Its uniqueness lies in its combination of highly professional texts, published according to two decades of tradition, with a tabloid manner and focus on entertainment. *Komsomolka* turned completely to tabloid practices. *Izvestiia* (News), a respected Soviet newspaper, has changed ownership and leadership many times since perestroika, most recently after the 1 September 2004 tragedy in Beslan, when editor Raf Shakirov was fired after the paper criticized the official version of events. Many readers understood this development as a clear example of renewed censorship. *Izvestiia* was divided twice: some of its journalists established the new publication *Novye izvestiia* (New News), which then underwent further division, and the new publication *Russkii kurer* (The Russian Courier), which appeared in 2000. *Argumenty i fakty*, popular during perestroika, turned into a tabloid. *Pravda* was divided, changed leadership, and lost its influence. But *Sovetskaia Rossiia* (Soviet Russia), fairly liberal in the early 1980s, became a symbol of Communist-leaning opposition under Chikin's leadership. Another pro-Communist opposition newspaper is *Zavtra* (Tomorrow); it replaced *Den* (Day), which was closed after the 1991 coup, but under its new name retained the same team and the same editor-in-chief, writer Aleksandr Prokhanov, as well as the notorious literary critic Vladimir Bondarenko. Liberal opposition in the 1990s was represented by *Izvestiia* (depending on its leadership), the new publication *Kommersant* (Businessman), the also new *Novaia gazeta* (New Paper), *Segodnia* (Today), *Nezavisimaia gazeta* (Independent Paper), and *Itogi* (Conclusions) magazine, among others. *Literaturnaia gazeta* lost its importance and went

through various financial and management problems. *Ogonek*, once Vitalii Korotich departed in 1991, began to lose readers and quality, and after 1995 changed its format and content, taking the German magazine *Focus* as its model. In the late 1990s it again changed its format, and is now part of Video International holding, which also owns tabloids. New quality publications appeared as well – *Sovershenno sekretno* (Top Secret, Artem Borovik's investigative project), *Stringer*, *Ezhenedelnyi zhurnal* (Weekly Magazine), etc.

Thick journals, suffering from lack of finances, were sponsored by Western foundations, particularly Soros. New art and literary publications appeared, including *Novoe literaturnoe obozrenie* (The New Literary Review), oriented toward post-modern philology, criticism, and theory. Women's monthlies such as *Rabotnitsa* (Woman Worker) and *Krestianka* (Woman Peasant) turned to a glossy style, combined with Soviet-era *zadushevnost* (domesticity). Special-interest and science magazines actively seek sponsorship, and many new such periodicals have thus appeared. The oldest professional magazine, *Zhurnalist* (Journalist, published since 1914), remains at the centre of professional discussion and the struggle for the freedom and dignity of journalists in the country. Religious and ethnic publications are developing rapidly, as well. The new trend is in so-called 'alternative publications' established by NGOs in Moscow and other regions, devoted to human rights issues, the disabled, prisoners, the feminist movement, and so forth. Many of them, as well as national and regional mainstream media, also produce Internet versions.

Thousands of entertainment, health, youth, women's, and men's publications have flooded the market, while pornographic publications, which appeared in the early 1990s, now occupy a small niche. Moscow teems with Russian versions of international publications like *Cosmopolitan*, *Good Housekeeping* (*Domashnii ochag*), *Glamour*, *Elle*, *Vogue*, *Men's Health*, *Seventeen*, *Maxim*, *GQ*, *Yes*, and many others. At the same time, new Russian publications such as *Egoist*, *Vodka*, *Molotok* (Hammer), *Otdokhni* (Relax), *Turizm i otdykh* (Tourism and Leisure), *Dosug v Moskve* (Leisure in Moscow), *Trubki i tabaki* (Pipes and Tobaccoes), *Domashnii doktor* (Home Doctor), as well as many new entertainment, health, youth, women's, and family publications are sold in the regions. In comparison with television, the print media enjoy considerably greater formal freedom and are in a position to provide more critical materials and tough investigative reporting. However, Russians read less today than during the Soviet era; the majority prefer local newspapers and national state-owned TV – largely for economic reasons, since the new glossies can be prohibitively expensive.

See also: *Argumenty i fakty*; censorship; journalism, post-Soviet; Korotich, Vitalii; *Literaturnaia gazeta* (Literary Gazette); *Moskovskii komsomolets*; *Ogonek*; *Pravda*; thick journals

Further reading

Vlast zerkalo ili sluzhanka, vol. 2, Moscow: Moscow Union of Journalists.
300 let-300 gazet, Moscow, 2003.

NADEZHDA AZHGIKHINA

periodicals, Soviet

The most important and well-developed part of the Soviet media system, the Soviet periodical press was totally controlled by the state and the Communist Party on all levels. Supervision was centred in Moscow and extended to all Soviet republics, regions, cities, towns, and villages. The system, based on a theory of socialist propaganda originating in Lenin's works and lasting until the collapse of the USSR, was regulated by the Party's ideology department and the CPSU Central Committee's special decree. Soviet publications played an important role in state politics as a means of conveying and promoting all state decisions; they shaped Soviet life and society.

All Soviet periodicals were associated with governmental, Party, or other Soviet institutions: *Pravda* (Truth) was the 'organ' of the Communist Party's Central Committee; *Izvestiia* (News) was the mouthpiece of the Supreme Soviet; *Trud* (Labour) was the voice of officially controlled trade unions; *Selskaia zhizn* (Village Life) represented the Ministry of Agriculture; *Komsomolskaia pravda* (Komsomol Truth) – the

Komsomol (Communist Youth League); *Pionerskaia pravda – young Pioneers* (the Party's children's organization); *Literaturnaia gazeta* (Literary Gazette) spoke for the Union of Soviet Writers, and so forth. Each republic had the same structure, including national and Russian language publications. Each region had its own regional Party and governmental newspapers, and each town and rural area had local newspaper associates with their local Party organization. Even big factories and collective farms, academic institutions and military organizations had their own publications. Regular periodicals were supplemented by many specialized magazines, including literary journals (so-called 'thick journals' [tolstye zhurnaly] such as *Novyi mir* [New World], *Znamia* [Banner], *Sibirskie ogni* [Siberian Lights]), science magazines such as *Nauka i zhizn* (Science and Life), *Khimiia i zhizn* (Chemistry and Life), and specialized periodicals for various industries and professional interests, including *Pchelovodstvo* (Beekeeping), *Voprosy filosofii* (Issues in Philosophy), etc. National women's magazines included *Rabotnitsa* (Female Worker), *Krestianka* (Peasant Woman), and *Mir zhenshchiny* (Women's World, aimed at foreign audiences and published in many languages). Magazines such as *Sovetskii soiuz* (Soviet Union) and *Golos rodiny* (Voice of the Motherland) targeted Western readers and Russian émigrés. The only fashion magazine during the late Soviet era was *Siluet* (Silhouette), published in Tallinn (Estonia); it was in great demand. All publications were officially censored.

Circulation of Soviet publications was inordinately high: in the late 1970s, *Pravda* had a daily circulation exceeding 10 million, *Trud's* was over 20 million. During the 1970s and 1980s, the Russian public read a great deal, with the average family subscribing to from five to seven publications (one Party newspaper; one regional; one youth, children's, or women's; one or two literary, sport, or science magazines, etc.). With some literary magazines in particularly high demand, subscriptions were distributed to the best workers, Party leaders, and other outstanding citizens. The popularity of periodicals may be explained by reasonable subscription prices, the comparatively uninteresting level of TV and radio broadcasts, poorly developed entertainment, and ample leisure time for reading after work. Readers sent thousands of letters to national periodicals every day, and often asked for aid or counsel, believing that newspapers could help them more effectively than did Soviet structures, police, or the courts. Writers for the Soviet press were very popular; readers appealed to them personally and trusted them absolutely.

Soviet publications changed after the Thaw. Some of them managed to attract excellent writers and analysts, who, under official control, produced brilliant examples of Aesopian language (writing between the lines) and sharp ideas. While *Pravda* purveyed propaganda in a poor style, *Izvestiia* published interesting analytical articles by Anatolii Agranovskii and Otto Latsis; *Literaturnaia gazeta* printed extremely popular essays and investigative articles by Evgenii Bogat, Arkadii Vaksberg, Iurii Shekochikhin, Iurii Rost, and others, from which astute readers gleaned information about corruption and legal violations in the Soviet system as a whole. A periodical's liberal orientation often depended on the personality of the editor-in-chief: for example, Mikhail Nenashev turned the organ of the Russian Federation Communist Party, *Sovetskaia Rossiia* (Soviet Russia), in a liberal direction in the early 1980s, making it one of the country's most critical publications; Boris Pankin did the same with *Komsomolskaia pravda* in the 1970s, assembling a strong journalistic team around him. In fact, perestroika values were already reflected and promoted in liberal Soviet periodicals of the 1970s and 1980s. Many new publications appearing since the Thaw, including the journals *Iunost* and *Molodaia gvardiia*, recast old discussions between Westerners (the former) and Slavophiles (the latter).

During perestroika the situation changed; a significant gap appeared between liberal and reactionary publications. Three national weeklies became symbols of a new freedom of speech: *Literaturnaia gazeta*, edited by Aleksandr Chakovskii; *Ogonek* (Little Flame), under Vitalii Korotich from 1986 on; and *Moskovskie novosti* (*Moscow News*), under Egor Iakovlev's leadership. They tackled new themes and printed articles by dissidents and victims of Stalin's terror, stories and works by writers and artists forbidden before perestroika, and open discussions devoted to Russia's past, present, and future. Perestroika witnessed a genuine civil war in journalism and literature, waged between old and new trends, and periodicals played a key role in this war, with the three liberal weeklies in conflict with many 'official' opponents, including *Pravda*. New trends in post-Soviet journalism thus have their roots in Soviet publications of the 1980s.

See also: censorship; Communist Party; Communist Youth League; dissident; Iakovlev, Egor; journalism; journalists post-Soviet; Korotich, Vitalii; *Literaturnaia gazeta* (Literary Gazette); *Novyi mir*; perestroika and glasnost; Pioneer organization; *Pravda*; Shchekochikhin, Iurii; Slavophiles; Stagnation; Thaw; thick journals; Westernizers

NADEZHDA AZHGIKHINA

Pesniary

Folk rock group

Arguably the most significant Soviet band, Pesniary (the Songsters) was formed in 1968 (originally as Liavony) in Minsk by Russian composer, singer, and multi-instrumentalist Vladimir Georgievich Muliavin (1941–2003). Pesniary blended in their compositions the best traditions of Belorussian village music with elements of folk-, art-, and jazz-rock (in the vein of Chicago or the British Gentle Giant and Fairport Convention). In 1976–77, Pesniary became the first Soviet group to twice visit the US with successful concert tours. In 1996, Moroz Records reissued the band's anthology on eight CDs. Since Muliavin's death, Pesniary has been led by Leonid Bortkevich, the band's vocalist during the group's heyday, 1971–80.

See also: folk music; rock music

ALEXANDER DOMRIN

Petrenko, Aleksei Vasilevich

b. 26 March 1938, Kharkov, Ukrainian SSR

Actor

A versatile actor in Leningrad and Moscow theatres from the 1960s, and in films since 1966,

Petrenko has lent his considerable physical presence to a wide variety of roles, from the lackey Oswald in Kozintsev's *Korol Lir* (*King Lear*, 1971) to the semi-crazed Rasputin in Klimov's *Agoniia* (*Agony*, 1974). He also portrayed a Plan-obsessed technocrat in Klimov's *Proshchanie* (*Farewell*, 1981), and Stalin in Kara's *Pir Baltazara, ili noch so Stalinym* (*Balthazar's Feast, or a Night with Stalin*, 1989). Petrenko also played a hapless general in Mikhalkov's *Sibirskii tsiriulnik* (*The Barber of Siberia*, 1999), and a ruthless wartime counter-intelligence officer in Mikhail Ptashuk's *V avguste 1944-ogo* (*In August 1944*, 2000).

See also: five-year plan; Klimov, Elem; Kozintsev, Grigorii; Mikhalkov, Nikita; Stalin, Iosif

DAVID GILLESPIE

Petrov, Aleksandr Dmitrievich

b. 17 July 1957, Yaroslavl

Animator

Petrov's drawn animation has attracted international attention since the beginning of his career. *Korova* (*Cow*, 1989) tells the story about a cow whose calf is taken away to be slaughtered, while the mother cow commits suicide out of despair. *Rusalka* (*The Mermaid*, 1996) is based on the Russian fairytale. In 1999, working in Canada, he completed the drawn animation for an IMAX format (75 mm) film: *The Old Man and the Sea*, based on Hemingway's story, which explores with fine drawings the relationship between man and nature. Petrov won an Oscar in 2000. He lives in Yaroslavl.

See also: film, animation

BIRGIT BEUMERS

Petrov, Andrei Pavlovich

b. 2 September 1930, Leningrad

Composer

A leading member of the Leningrad/St. Petersburg musical establishment, Petrov is an eclectic and prolific composer, the recipient of many official honours. His melodic gift is best displayed in his film scores (many with director Eldar Riazanov) and songs in the romance tradition. During the Soviet period, several of his stage works were performed at the Kirov (Mariinskii) Theatre: the operas *Petr Pervyi* (*Peter the First*, 1975) and *Maiakovskii nachinaetsia* (*Maiakovsky Begins*, 1983), and the ballet *Pushkin* (1978). Petrov's adaptability is evident in the appearance of Christian themes in his orchestral works of the 1990s.

See also: Kirov Theatre; music in film; Riazanov, Eldar

PHILIP ROSS BULLOCK

Petrov, Arkadii Ivanovich

b. 7 April, 1940, Shakhty Komsomolets, Donetsk region, Ukraine

Artist

Petrov moved to Moscow in 1957, graduated from the Moscow 1905 Art College (1963) and the Surikov Art Academy (1969), then joined the Artists' Union in 1971. Inspired by such objects of provincial Russian popular culture as photos, postcards, souvenirs, and plastic bouquets, Petrov staged slightly primitive or naïve figures in landscapes or interior setting. His paintings from the 1990s are experiments with the style of Sots-Art.

See also: art schools and academies; Sots-Art; unions, creative, Soviet

NATALIA KOLODZEI

Petrushevskaia, Liudmila Stefanovna

b. 26 May 1938, Moscow

Writer, playwright, poet

Liudmila Petrushevskaia is an innovative playwright and exceptional prose stylist whose works explore and deftly articulate the experience, sensibility, and speech of the Russian urban everyperson. Petrushevskaia spent her first eighteen years wandering with her Party-affiliated family as they fled arrest during Stalin's successive purges. After returning to Moscow in 1956, she completed a degree in journalism at Moscow State University and worked for Moscow Radio and Moscow Television.

In the 1970s, Petrushevskaia developed simultaneously as playwright and fiction writer, and in both endeavours encountered unofficial critical support and overt censorship. Aleksei Arbuzov supported her writing in his studio, and her early plays (*Cinzano*, *Uroki muzyki* [*Music Lessons*]) were produced, if not published, by studio, student, and amateur theatre groups. The bulk of her fiction did not see print until glasnost. Thereafter Petrushevskaia's critical reputation skyrocketed and her published output greatly increased in both quantity and genre diversity. Her corpus has expanded from *Vremia noch* [*The Time Night*], the stunning novella monologue of a monstrous mother, to poetry, 'fairy tales for adults', juvenile fiction, '*sluchai*' ('chance': urban folklore), and stories 'from another reality'. In much of her drama and various fiction forms Petrushevskaia lets her characters drift through the random turns and banal tragedies of daily life and masterfully 'records' their attempts to strategize, narrate, and communicate.

See also: Arbuzov, Aleksei; drama, post-Soviet; literature, post-Soviet

Further reading

Goscilo, H. (1995) 'Mother as Mothra: Totalizing Narrative and Nurture in Petrushevskaia', in S. S. Hoisington (ed.) *A Plot of Her Own: The Female Protagonist in Russian Literature*, Evanston, IL: Northwestern University Press.

Kolesnikoff, N. (1998) 'The Absurd in Ljudmila Petruševskaja's Plays', *Russian, Croatian and Serbian, Czech and Slovak, Polish Literature*, May 43, 4: 469–80.

Milne, L. (2000) 'Ghosts and Dolls: Popular Urban Culture and the Supernatural in Liudmila Petrushevskaia's *Songs of the Eastern Slavs* and *The Little Sorceress*', *Russian Review*, April, 2: 269–84.

BETH HOLMGREN

Petsukh, Viacheslav Alekseevich

b. 18 November 1946, Moscow

Prose writer, essayist.

Trained as a history teacher, Petsukh was editor-in-chief of the thick journal *Druzhba narodov* (Friendship of Peoples) from 1993–95. He is the author of collections of short stories and novellas, including *Alphabet*, *Central-Ermolaevo War*, *New Moscow Philosophy*. In Petsukh's stories, the history of the Russian state not so much precedes or explains the events of contemporary Russian life as affirms the narrator's view that in Russia, nothing changes. With his philosophical inclinations and a dark sense of humour, Petsukh depicts Russians' reaction to bizarre circumstances of Russian life in order to assert that the Russian soul becomes stronger when tested and is empowered by alcohol, inborn patience, and Russian literature.

See also: literature, post-Soviet

LYUDMILA PARTS

Philharmonic Hall, St. Petersburg

The Grand Philharmonic Hall (*Bolshoi zal filarmonii*) is the most important concert hall for classical music performances in St. Petersburg. It was built in 1839 by architects Pierre Jacout and Carlo Rossi (façade) as the Assembly of the Nobility. At the end of the 1840s it began to function as a concert hall. Until the end of the nineteenth century it was the main Russian stage for guest conductors and performers including Berlioz, Wagner, Liszt, and Schumann. At the turn of the century there were landmark performances of Mahler, Richard Strauss, Schoenberg, and Debussy. Renamed the Petrograd Philharmonic in 1921, the building maintained its traditional function; foreign conductors and performers continued to appear there in the 1920s and 1930s, including Bruno Walter, Arthur Schnabel, and Otto Klemperer. In the late 1930s the flow of great Western conductors and soloists stopped. Evgenii Mravinskii, the brilliant director of the Leningrad Philharmonic in 1938–88, had to replace them all, rehearsing and performing with his orchestra almost daily and virtually never going on tours. Since 1988 the Philharmonic Hall has housed two philharmonic orchestras: the primary orchestra, the St. Petersburg Philharmonic, under the direction of Iurii Temirkanov; and the 'secondary', the St. Petersburg Philharmonic Academic Symphonic Orchestra, under the baton of Aleksandr Dmitriev. The hall also features various recitals, choir concerts, ballet and poetry evenings, jazz events and – rarely – guest orchestra performances.

See also: classical musicians/performers, post-Soviet; Mravinskii, Evgenii; orchestras, Soviet and post-Soviet; Temirkanov, Iurii

KIRA NEMIROVSKAIA

philosophy, post-Soviet

Post-Soviet philosophy, as perhaps no other field in the humanities, suffers from institutional and generational fragmentation. Previously limited to a small number of key universities (in Moscow, St. Petersburg, Ekaterinburg, and Tomsk), the field of professional training of philosophers has radically expanded over the last two decades. Simultaneously, the institutional monopoly of *Voprosy filosofii* (Issues in Philosophy), the main disciplinary journal that defined the field's academic standards and agenda during the last six decades, was challenged by new influential publications of the Institute of Philosophy (The Russian Academy of Sciences, Moscow) and by a broad variety of philosophical journals and anthologies published by departments and faculties of philosophy throughout the country. Having abandoned traditional typologies (official vs. dissident; Slavophiles vs. Westernizers, etc.) and yet not established new disciplinary boundaries and professional standards, post-Soviet philosophy today is a chaotic and contradictory field, often

presented as an example of a 'poli-paradigmatic' approach (*poliparadigmalnost*).

The increased accessibility of philosophical training, however, has not eliminated the overall social marginalization of philosophy caused by the institutional and ideological collapse of Soviet Marxism. As a result, newly emerging discourses and intellectual strategies often attempt to revitalize the privileged position of the intellectual commentator that 'official' philosophy formerly guaranteed.

Thematically, post-Soviet philosophy manifests two major intellectual tendencies: active efforts to revisit the roots of Russian philosophical thought and, as a counterbalance, a strong drive to reunite with intellectual traditions from which Russian philosophers have been isolated for so long. Recent publications of previously banned Russian philosophers (including Vasilii Rozanov, Vladimir Solovev, and Pavel Florenskii) helped to focus the philosophical debates about the role of religious values in contemporary Russian life in general and of Orthodox Christianity in particular. Similarly driven is the interest in the newly discovered legacy of Eurasianism, a philosophical and historical movement developed in Europe in the 1920s and 1930s by Russian émigrés Piotr Savitskii and Nikolai Trubetskoi. Aleksandr Dugin, perhaps the most vocal representative of the new Eurasianism, taking Savitskii's basic premise about Russia's unique geo-cultural combination of European and Asian mentalities, questions the basic ideological and cultural premises of Russia's current attempts to 'join Europe'. This appeal to 'neo-traditionalism' is also used as a major argument in current philosophical debates about Russia's response to globalization (Aleksander Panarin).

If Russian neo-traditionalists' main purpose is to recuperate discursive elements from Russia's past in order to modify the understanding of its future possibilities, then the appropriation and adaptation of 'Western' (mostly French) philosophical traditions to Russian reality undertaken by some Russian philosophers are remarkably grounded in Russian intellectual history. Deconstruction, psychoanalysis, visual and postcolonial studies are employed by such influential philosophers of Russian culture as Valerii Podoroga, Mikhail Ryklin, and Boris Groys above all so as to understand the nature of totalitarianism and the meaning of the Soviet legacy. The main thrust of this philosophical tradition seems to be more ontological rather than political, being defined by the question: How/why did our past become possible?

Further reading

Ab Imperio (2004) 1.

Epstein, M., Genis, A. and Vladiv-Glover, S. (1999) *Russian Postmodernism: New Perspectives on Post-Soviet Culture*, trans., ed. S. Vladiv-Glover, New York: Berghahn Books.

Erjavec, A. (ed.) (2003) *Postmodernism and the Postsocialist Condition: Politicized Art under Late Socialism*, Berkeley, CA: University of California Press.

Scanlan, J. (ed.) (1994) *Russian Thought after Communism: The Recovery of a Philosophical Heritage*, Armonk, NY: M.E. Sharpe.

SERGUEI A. OUSHAKINE

philosophy, Soviet (Marxist-Leninist)

Western accounts of Soviet philosophy have generally treated it as one of the few examples in history of philosophy in a so-called totalitarian system. While Soviet philosophy indeed owed its unique stature largely to the nature of its relationship with politics and ideology, more recent accounts have been sceptical of attempts to reduce Soviet philosophy to mere fulfilment of ideological orders received from above. Instead, they emphasize the debate that occurred within the field and the importance that philosophy had for those who were involved in it.

Most of the basic positions of official Soviet philosophy, however, had already been established by the mid-1930s and remained unchallenged until perestroika. Since these positions were developed from the writings of Lenin, and the later Marx (as well as Engels), Soviet philosophers called their discipline Marxist-Leninist philosophy.

Among these positions, Soviet philosophers made a strong claim to scientific objectivity, while simultaneously claiming to be partisan

supporters of the working class. Unlike the vast majority of their Western contemporaries, Soviet philosophers believed in the project of uniting all knowledge into a single system. As one observer put it, they generally considered their discipline capable of providing a general, integrated view encompassing everything from subatomic particles to international relations. Marxist-Leninist philosophy, then, was not just an academic discipline, but was also said to constitute a 'world-view' (*mirovozzrenie*). The common thread holding this view together was its dialectical materialism. Soviet philosophers considered themselves materialists because they asserted the ontological primacy of matter. They considered their materialism dialectical because they held that the resolution of contradictions in matter was the source of all change in the world and, moreover, that this change occurred by means of the dialectic. Dialectics were said to follow three objective laws that governed all change in everything from history to chemistry.

Dialectical materialism, often abbreviated to '*diamat*', was the subdivision of Soviet philosophy responsible for epistemological and ontological questions. Historical materialism, or '*istmat*', was the other major subdivision of Soviet philosophy and was responsible for social and historical questions.

Since divergence from official positions, when not commissioned by a directive from the Party, carried considerable risk to the author's career, thinkers with more creative minds found safer niches in relatively marginal and thus less ideologically-constrained fields, such as the history of philosophy or logic. As a result, despite the original contributions of a handful of thinkers (most writing during the Thaw), much post-Stalin Soviet philosophy proved a rather banal affair, with constant minute reworkings of seemingly inconsequential positions and copious citations from the 'classics of Marxism-Leninism'. This would seem an inevitable development for a philosophy that was supposed to be always developing, yet at the same time not allowed to challenge any of its central assumptions.

Institutionally, Soviet philosophy was centred in a few universities, most notably Moscow State University and the Institute of Philosophy of the Soviet Academy of Sciences. Students in all Soviet universities, however, were required to take a heavy course-load in such Marxist-Leninist disciplines as dialectical and historical materialism, scientific Communism, and scientific atheism. Important Soviet philosophers in the post-Stalin era, all for vastly different reasons, included Evald Ilenkov, Bonifatii Kedrov, Fedor Konstantinov, Teodor Oizerman, Aleksei Losev, Aleksandr Zinovev, and Merab Mamardashvili.

See also: Academy of Sciences; Communist ideology; Moscow State University; partiinost; perestroika and glasnost; philosophy, post-Soviet; propiska; Thaw

Further reading

Bakhurst, D. (1991) *Consciousness and Revolution in Soviet Philosophy: From the Bolsheviks to Evald Ilyenkov*, Cambridge: Cambridge University Press.

Scanlan, J.P. (1985) *Marxism in the USSR: A Critical Survey of Current Soviet Thought*, Ithaca, NY: Cornell University Press.

van der Zweerde, E. (1997) *Soviet Historiography of Philosophy: Istoriko-Filosofskaja Nauka*, Boston, MA: Kluwer Academic Publishers.

DAVID HUNTER SMITH

photo-art (foto-art)

Photography is one of the most dynamic and flourishing art forms in contemporary Russia. Although from the 1930s photography in Russia had been mostly confined to the style of Socialist Realism, from the late 1980s it has been developing quickly, adopting new technologies and embracing diverse subject matters. One of the first names to emerge in Russian photo-art at the decline of the Soviet Union is Igor Mukhin, who depicted the decay of the political system in two series, *Fragments* and *Monuments*. The extravagant figure of the Russian art world, Vladislav Mamyshev-Monro, attracted public attention by personifying film stars, politicians, and cultural figures of the past, such as Joan of Arc, Marilyn Monroe, Lenin, and Adolf Hitler, to explore self-identification, role models, and urban mythology. Tatiana Antoshina and Olga Tobreluts are two of the most prominent women photo-artists, who in their works subvert

gender roles and playfully reinvent popular examples of classical art and antiquity.

The important task of promoting the Russian photographic heritage and of supporting contemporary Russian photographers and artists is performed by the Moscow House of Photography, organized in 1996. Its endeavours have led to the formation of a collection of works by leading artists and the organization of the Moscow Photo Biennale, which provides intellectual and creative exchange and helps Russian photographers to enter the international art-scene.

See also: Antoshina, Tatiana

KATIA KAPUSHESKY

photorealism/hyperrealism

These terms describe an international art movement that emerged in the United States in the late 1960s and emphasized a painterly style that reproduces the effects of photography. The subject matter was particularly focused on urban street scenes and portraits. Soviet photorealism spans the period of the 1970s and 1980s. Despite its association with the artistic avant-garde, which remained outside the official art scene, photorealism met with official approval thanks to its realistic representation and themes. Prominent Soviet photorealists include Semen Faibisovich, Aleksandr Petrov, Nikolai Filatov, and the artists representing Group 6 (Aleksei Tegin, Sergei Sherstiuk, Evgenii Gorokhovskii, Sergei Geta, Sergei Bazilev, and Igor Kopystiansky).

See also: Petrov, Aleksandr

LARISSA RUDOVA

piano performance, Russian/Soviet (Russkaia fortepiannaia shkola)

Since the late nineteenth century the Russian School of fortepiano has produced numerous dazzling pianists, and arguably has become the world's most advanced in the areas of performance technique and music pedagogy. Dating from the mid-nineteenth-century efforts of Anton Rubinshtein, Petr Tchaikovsky, and Nikolai Rimskii-Korsakov, the era of legendary pianistic interpreters of both Western and Russian classical music focused attention on the musical centres of St. Petersburg and Moscow. With the establishment of the St. Petersburg Rimskii-Korsakov State Conservatory (1862) and the Moscow Tchaikovsky State Conservatory (1866) for advanced work in music theory, performance, and pedagogy, talented students of piano and composition could study with the most gifted professors in Russia.

The turn of the twentieth century saw the rise of such distinguished composer-pianists as Sergei Rachmaninov and Alexander Scriabin, both of whom studied with the composer-pedagogues Sergei Taneev and Anton Arenskii at the Moscow Conservatory. Rachmaninov advanced the work begun by Franz Liszt and exploited more fully than any other composer-pianist the vast resources of the instrument. The innovative composer-pianist Sergei Prokofiev studied at the St. Petersburg Conservatory with Anatolii Liadov and Alexander Winkler. Prokofiev emigrated to Paris in the 1920s, but returned to the Soviet Union in the 1930s. Because the Bolshevik Revolution of 1917 forced many musicians to flee abroad, the early 1920s witnessed major contributions of Russian émigré pianists to the American School. Among the latter are Alexander Ziloti (Siloti), one of the last students of Liszt; Rosina and Josef Lhévinne; and Vladimir Horowitz (Gorovits). In the Soviet Union after World War II, Sviatoslav Rikhter and Emil Gilels (students of the renowned Genrikh Neigauz) toured the country, but also performed abroad. Despite a period of imprisonment under Stalin, Neigauz continued playing until his death in 1964.

Recent products of the Russian School who have been successful on the international concert circuit include the composer-conductor-pianist Mikhail Pletnev (b. 1957) and the pianist Nikolai Luganskii (b. 1972), who studied with the well-known Tatiana Nikolaeva. In the twenty-first century Russian émigrés continue to invigorate American pianism by teaching and performing concerts: examples are Vladimir Leetchkiss, one of the last of Neigauz's students, and Irina Morozova.

Characteristics of pianists typical for the Russian School include a grand, sweeping expressive style buttressed by an extraordinary technique whose standard is 'Rachmaninovian' (*rakhmaninovskaia tekhnika*); efficiency of movement; a clarity of presentation of the melodic line; vast, almost steely reserves of concentration during performance of the most taxing pieces; the ability to articulate the broad structure of a piece; and an originality of interpretation that preserves the canonical qualities of a musical work. These characteristics combine to capture the broad-spiritedness and exoticism of Russian compositions, which have roots in folkloric and Russian Orthodox liturgical music, but also have been influenced by European, Russian gypsy, and Asian ('oriental') styles and motifs.

International piano competitions that take place on a regular basis in Russia are the Tchaikovsky Competition and Rachmaninov Competition, both of which are held in Moscow.

See also: classical musicians/performers, post-Soviet; folk music; Gilels, Emil; Moscow Conservatory; Neigauz, Genrikh; Pletnev, Mikhail; Prokofiev, Sergei; Rikhter, Sviatoslav; Russian Orthodoxy; St. Petersburg (Leningrad) State Conservatory; Tchaikovsky (Chaikovskii) Competition

VALERIA Z. NOLLAN

Pichul, Vasilii Vladimirovich

b. 15 June 1961, Zhdanov [Mariupol]

Film director

Pichul studied with Marlen Khutsiev at the Soviet State Film School VGIK, graduating in 1983. His sensational debut, *Malenkaia Vera* (*Little Vera*, 1988), benefited from Pichul's sober depiction of the everyday plights of a rank-and-file provincial family – alcoholism, generational estrangement, lack of purpose. These dilemmas, to which Pichul was attuned early, anticipated the fiasco of the perestroika experiment. Pichul's subsequent pictures, including the Ilf and Petrov adaptation *Mechty idiota* (Dreams of an Idiot, 1993), were ambitious but disappointing. He fared better with the popular television series *Kukly* (Puppets, 1994–98), poking fun at post-Communist politicians and other prominent figures, satirizing their stupidity and corruption. In the late 1990s, Pichul switched to taboo-breaking documentaries.

PETER ROLLBERG

Piekha, Edita Stanislavovna

b. 31 July 1937, Noyelles sous l'Ens, France

Actress, singer

Film actress and singer Edita Piekha started her singing career as a Polish exchange student in Leningrad in 1955. Her performance with the group 'Druzhba' (Friendship) that year brought her immediate success, and she continued to sing with that ensemble until 1976. She was the first to perform the Soviet 'Twist and Shake' and the first to speak to the audience between songs. With her enticing foreign accent, she came to personify glamour in the Thaw period. She performed regularly until 2003, when she broke her leg.

KARIN SARSENOV

Pikul, Valentin Savvich

b. 13 June 1928, Leningrad; d. 17 July 1990, Riga, Latvia

Writer

Historical novelist, whose fiction covers major events of history from the seventeenth to the twentieth centuy. *Bayazet* (1961) depicts the Russo-Turkish war, *Moonzund* (*Moon Strait*, 1973) World War I, *Perom i shpagoi* (*With Pen and Sword*, 1972) Frederick the Great, and *Bitva zheleznykh kantslerov* (*The Battle of the Iron Chancellors*, 1977) Bismarck. Pikul excels in historical portraiture, and his novels, captivating and rich in detail and propounding patriotism and pride in Russian achievements of the past, enjoy great popularity.

TATYANA NOVIKOV

Pioneer organization

The Pioneer organization, founded on 19 May 1922, was a mass volunteer children's Communist network, uniting children 10–15 years old. With many organizational features and rituals borrowed from the scout movement, its goal was to provide a Communist upbringing for Soviet children – hence wearing the symbolic red triangular tie and badge was obligatory.

Almost every schoolchild in the Soviet Union was a Pioneer, though membership supposedly was an honour, open only to the best. To join the organization, one had to swear an oath: 'I (name, last name), joining the ranks of the All-Union Pioneer Organization named after Vladimir Ilich Lenin, solemnly swear before my comrades to love my Motherland dearly, live, study, and struggle in a manner bequeathed by the great Lenin and taught by the Communist Party, and to hold sacred the Laws of the Pioneers of the Soviet Union'. Those laws mandated faithfulness to the Motherland, the Party, and Communist principles; preparedness to become Komsomol members; development into hero(in)es of struggle and labour; honouring the memory of fallen fighters; and readiness to defend the country. Pioneers were expected not only to excel in academics, sports, and labour, but also to be honest and loyal comrades, championing 'truth', serving as comrades and leaders of the Octobrites (*oktiabriata*), and so forth. The Pioneer motto, 'Be ready!' (*Bud gotov!*) automatically elicited the response 'Always ready!' (*Vsegda gotov!*)

Following a military model, every school had a Pioneer squad (*druzhina*), divided into detachments (*otriady*) and units (*zvenia*). Each squad elected a council and its chair. Komsomol members provided leadership in the Pioneer organization. Rituals included the Pioneer salute, marching in formation with a song, naming a *druzhina* after a Soviet hero, and admitting a veteran or outstanding famous person as an honorary member of a Pioneer organization. The Central Council of the All-Union Pioneer organization and the Central Komsomol Committee (from March 1925) published a mass children's newspaper, *Pionerskaia Pravda* (Pioneer Truth), that explained Party policies in simplified form and reported international and domestic events. Pioneers and schoolchildren were staff correspondents, disseminating information about activities and achievements of Pioneers across the country.

Beginning in 1935 Pioneer 'palaces' and 'houses', overseen by Ministries of Education and Komsomol committees, sprang up nationwide as extracurricular institutions promoting political, educational, and cultural work. Their programmes encompassed propaganda talks and lectures; clubs and circles (*kruzhki*) such as dance ensembles, art studios, theatres, choirs, science clubs, philately, creative writing, etc.; as well as competitions, exhibitions, and holiday celebrations.

Children could spend school vacations at Pioneer camps, usually located outside of cities in the forest or on a lake or seashore. Life in Pioneer camps followed a strict routine, with a timetable for getting up, going to bed, eating, resting, swimming, exercise, and activities and entertainment. The Pioneer campfire functioned as a special symbol of the organization's unity. The most famous Pioneer camps were *Artek* (Crimea) and *Orlenok* (Eaglet, Krasnodar krai).

Despite attempts in the mid-1980s to revamp the Pioneer organization, in the 1990s it ceased to exist as a national structure. Its successor in 1990 became *Soiuz pionerskikh organizatsii: Federatsiia detskikh soiuzov* (The Union of Pioneer Organizations: Federation of Children's Unions), which is independent of political parties and movements, has no ideological agenda, and unites different children's organizations throughout the country. Though the largest, the union has no monopoly, for there are more than 419,000 children's organizations currently registered in Russia, uniting only 10 per cent of all schoolchildren and receiving no state support.

See also: Artek; Communist Party; Communist Youth League; Octobrites; propaganda, Soviet and post-Soviet

ELENA OMELCHENKO

pirog/pirozhki

Pirog/pirozhki are Russian savoury pies of different sizes. The *pirog* can be a large oval or rectangle, while *pirozhki* (singular *pirozhok*) are baked or fried smaller crescents suitable for finger food. Fillings may consist of ground meat, eggs, fish, cabbage, mushrooms, mashed potato and cheese, or rice. The crust depends on the size and filling: plain yeast dough produces a heavier base suitable for a *pirog* with a substantial filling, whereas quick yeast dough is lighter and flakier, but can stand up to a juicy filling. Buttery, flaky sour-cream dough and traditional puff pastry make excellent *pirozhki*.

CHRISTINE A. RYDEL

Piskarev Cemetery

Cemetery and memorial site in northeast Petersburg where nearly one million military and civilian victims of the Siege of Leningrad are buried in common graves. The site was opened to the public in 1960 and includes monuments and a small museum.

See also: St. Petersburg, World War II (Great Patriotic War)

JENNIFER RYAN TISHLER

Pivovarov, Viktor Dmitrievich

b. 14 January 1937, Moscow

Artist, writer

A graduate of the art department of the Moscow Institute of Polygraphy (1962) and a member of the USSR Union of Artists, Pivovarov worked for twenty years as an illustrator of children's books. That experience influenced his conceptual albums and paintings. In his art, which is associated with Moscow Conceptualism, Pivovarov combines written texts and fantastic imagery composed around fictional characters. From 1975–82, he created a series of twelve albums, including *Tears, Face*, and *Projects for a Lonely Man*, which explore the mundane Soviet existence represented by a fictional 'everyman'. These albums were intended to be read as well as seen, engaging the viewers' memories, emotions, and dreams. Many of Pivovarov's works break down pictorial space by destroying logical connections. He emigrated in 1982 and now lives and works in Prague.

NATALIA KOLODZEI

Pletnev, Mikhail Vasilevich

b. 14 April 1957, Arkhangelsk

Composer, conductor, pianist

Pletnev was born into a musical family, and his extraordinary talent was identified early. Four years after he entered the Moscow Conservatory (1974) he won the Gold Medal at the Tchaikovsky International Piano Competition. In 1990, with private sponsorship, he established the highly acclaimed Russian National Orchestra. Pletnev's repertoire focuses on the major classical and romantic works. His interpretations of Rachmaninov's works have earned him particular distinction. His compositions include orchestral and chamber music. Pletnev has recorded as a pianist and conductor for Deutsche Grammophon and Virgin Classics.

See also: orchestras, Soviet and post-Soviet; Tchaikovsky (Chaikovskii) Competition

VALERIA Z. NOLLAN

Pliatt, Rostislav Ianovich

b. 13 December 1908, Rostov on the Don; d. 30 June 1989, Moscow

Theatre and film actor

A student of famous director Iurii Zavadskii, Pliatt joined his teacher's studio theatre in 1928 (renamed Mossovet Theatre in 1943). He excelled in George Bernard Shaw's comedies and Henrik Ibsen's dramas, among others, demonstrating human warmth, intelligence, and a subtle sense of irony. Pliatt's film debut as an unmarried geologist in Tatiana Lukashevich's comedy *Podkidysh* (*The Foundling*, 1939) made him a national star overnight, adored by millions of viewers for his decency and helpless naïveté. One of Pliatt's best-known performances is that

of the courageous, anti-Nazi pastor Schlag in Tatiana Lioznova's television cult series *Semnadtsat mgnovenii vesny* (*Seventeen Moments of Spring*, 1973). People's Artist of the USSR (1961).

See also: Lioznova, Tatiana; Mossovet Theatre; *Semnadtsat mgnovenii vesny* (Seventeen Moments of Spring); Zavadskii, Iurii

PETER ROLLBERG

Plisetskaia, Maia Mikhailovna

b. 20 November 1925, Moscow

Dancer, choreographer, actress

Internationally recognized as one of the greatest modern ballerinas, Plisetskaia possesses outstanding technical skills, ingenious dramatic gift, expressiveness of body position, and a profoundly innovative and individualized approach to classical ballet language. A graduate of Moscow Ballet School (1943), she elaborated her own inimitable interpretation of roles, ranging from the classical to the modern and contemporary repertoires. In such works as *The Carmen Suite* (Bizet-Shchedrin, 1967) and *La Pheadre* (choreographer Serge Lifar) she created a new female type in ballet; her interpretation of the famous *Dying Swan* choreographed by Fokin for Anna Pavlova is her signature piece.

Plisetskaia danced with the Bolshoi Theatre (1943–2000) while performing with leading ballet companies in Europe from the 1980s on. She choreographed and performed the leading roles in *Anna Karenina* (1972), *Chaika* (*The Seagull*, 1980), and *Dama s sobachkoi* (*The Lady with the Lapdog*, 1985), all composed by her husband, Rodion Shchedrin. She played Countess Betsy Tverskaia in the Aleksandr Zarkhi's film *Anna Karenina* (1967).

The recipient of numerous Soviet and international awards, she published her memoirs, *I, Maya Plisetskaya*, in 2001.

See also: ballet, Soviet; ballet dancers, Bolshoi Theatre; Shchedrin, Rodion; Zarkhi, Aleksandr

TATIANA SENKEVITCH

Plotnikov, Valerii Fedorovich

b. 20 October 1943, Barnaul

Photographer

One of the most famous photographers in Russia, Plotnikov was trained as an artist and cameraman, which influenced his artistic style. A master of staged photographic portraits, for thirty-five years he created a picture encyclopedia of the most significant figures in Soviet and Russian cultural history: writers, actors, musicians, poets, film directors, and artists. His photographs of Vladimir Vysotskii, taken over thirteen years, resulted in his latest album, *Vladimir Vysotskii. Taganka* (2004). His works are published in major magazines, such as *Vogue, Cosmopolitan, Ogonek, Domovoi, Ekran, Iskusstvo kino, Teatr*, and others; they have been exhibited at numerous international exhibitions, used for TV, film, and theatre design.

See also: photo-art (foto-art); Vysotskii, Vladimir

TATIANA SMORODINSKAYA

Pluchek, Valentin Nikolaevich

b. 4 [17] September 1909, Moscow; d. 17 August 2002, Moscow

Theatre director

Pluchek acted for Vsevolod Meierkhold and assisted on his 1930 production of Vladimir Maiakovskii's *Bania* (*The Bathhouse*). After directing in many theatres, he became staff director at the Moscow Satire Theatre in 1950, rising to artistic director in 1957, a post he held until 2000. Deploying accessible, broad-stroked satire, he returned numerous neglected plays to the Soviet repertoire, including Maiakovskii's *Bania* (1953, revived 1967), *Klop* (*The Bedbug*, 1955) and *Misteriia-buff* (*Mystery-Bouffe*, 1957); Mikhail Bulgakov's *Beg* (*Flight*, 1977) and Nikolai Erdman's *Samoubiitsa* (*The Suicide*, banned 1982, revived 1987). His landmark production of Beaumarchais's *Zhenitba Figaro* (*The Marriage of Figaro*, 1969) starred film idol Andrei Mironov.

See also: Mironov, Andrei; Satire Theatre; theatre, Soviet

JOHN FREEDMAN

Podmoskove

The environs of Moscow within the boundaries of Moscow oblast. Administratively a separate jurisdiction from the city of Moscow, it has 6.6 million residents, the most among provinces in Russia. Podmoskove functions as the core area of the country. In economic development and in the complexity and diversity of cultural landscapes this province has no equals in Russia. The area of Podmoskove, 46,058 sq km, has over a hundred cities, not counting Moscow. It has high population density and a clustering of cities that is strikingly different from the rest of the national territory. The area size and urbanization (79 per cent) are very similar to a comparable part of the Netherlands, around its poly-nuclear metropolis, Randstad Holland. Podmoskove is well linked by eleven railways radiating from Moscow. In addition, it has two ring railroads. Between 1950 and 1980 all the railroads were electrified; they operate with fast and frequent commuter trains.

Podmoskove is rich in monuments and memorial places that mark every stage in Russia's history. The western sector witnessed the famous Borodino Battle of 1812. It suffered colossal damage during World War II. By the end of the nineteenth century, old monasteries and manor houses were eclipsed by industrial towns. The Soviet era left an exceptionally heavy concentration of military factories along the railroads leading to Nizhnii Novgorod and the Urals. Several of the new towns became prominent centres for applied research and development, including Dubna, Chernogolovka, Zhukovskii, and Zelenograd.

In post-Soviet years, the infusion of transnational investments has added vitality to the cities of Podmoskove. The oblast successfully competes with Moscow in attracting investment because it offers less expensive construction sites, lower taxes, and roads without transportation bottlenecks – a common problem in Moscow. The highways are increasingly turning into major commuting routes for the new middle class, which has adopted a lifestyle with family cars and suburban villas. The labour reserves of Podmoskove are of critical importance for Moscow, considering that in recent decades the country has faced a decreasing population.

See also: administrative structure, Soviet Union; defence industry; Moscow; Nizhnii Novgorod (Gorkii); Urals

Further reading

Hamilton, I. (1976) *The Moscow City Region*, Oxford: Oxford University Press.
Ioffe, G. and Nefedova, T. (1998) 'Environs of Russian Cities: A Case Study of Moscow', *Europe-Asia Studies* 8.

YURI MEDVEDKOV AND OLGA MEDVEDKOV

'Podmoskovnye vechera' (Moscow Nights)

Song

'Podmoskovnye vechera' (Moscow Nights), by lyricist Mikhail Matusovskii and composer Vasilii Solovev-Sedoi, is one of the most popular songs in Russian history, and has also been recorded in several other languages. Originally composed for an obscure 1955 sports documentary and performed by Vladimir Troshin, the song did not attract much attention until Troshin's recording was broadcast on the radio, where it quickly became a listener favourite. Its lasting place in the Russian consciousness was further ensured in 1964, when the melody became the interval signal of radio station Maiak.

See also: Maiak; Troshin, Vladimir

SETH GRAHAM

poetry, ironic

Contemporary Russian irony has its eclectic origins in the absurdism of the late 1920s,

embodied in the *Oberiuty* literary circle; in the 'total' art of Socialist Realism; in the revival of humour during the Thaw; and in the near-total cynicism that enveloped Soviet society when the idealism of the 1960s came to an end. The end of the communist utopia coincided with Russian postmodernism, and irony itself became near total. In the broadest of senses, irony served a wide variety of contemporary poets, ranging from the bards of the 1960s and 1970s (Aleksandr Galich, Bulat Okudzhava, Vladimir Vysotskii) to Iosif Brodskii, as well as younger poets who emerged from Moscow poetry clubs of the 1980s (Ivan Akhmetev, Vladimir Vishnevskii, Igor Irtenev, Vladimir Druk, Vladimir Strochkov, Nina Iskrenko, Iurii Arabov, Aleksandr Eremenko, and others), as an instrument of summing up generational experience and eliminating the hierarchical division between high and low. Some, like Druk, work in stylized kitsch. For others, like Eremenko, irony serves as a sceptical tool of introspection. Irtenev has moved to the genre of political satire, working on the liberal radio station Ekho Moskvy. Apart from others stands Igor Guberman, the best of whose Jewish-Russian ironic quatrains became part of the folklore of the intelligentsia, reminding one of *chastushki* with an authorial twist. In ironic poetry proper an important place belongs to the Conceptualists (Dmitrii Prigov, Lev Rubinshtein, Mikhail Sukhotin, Vsevolod Nekrasov, Timur Kibirov), whose citational, eclectic, and often theatrical experiments derived from the Sots-Art of the 1970s. They ironically deploy Soviet stereotypes and language clichés that come, as Mikhail Epstein put it, from 'the idiotic depths of the collective unconscious' (1995: 34).

See also: Arabov, Iurii; bards; Brodskii, Iosif; chastushka; Conceptualism, literary; *Ekho Moskvy* (Echo of Moscow); Galich, Aleksandr; Kibirov, Timur; Nekrasov, Vsevolod; Okudzhava, Bulat; poetry, post-Soviet; Prigov, Dmitrii; Rubinshtein, Lev; Vysotskii, Vladimir

Further reading

Epstein, M. (1995) *After the Future: The Paradoxes of Postmodernism and Contemporary Russian Culture*, Amherst, MA: The University of Massachusetts Press.

High, J. *et al.* (eds) (2000) *Crossing Centuries: The New Generation in Russian Poetry*, Jersey City, NJ: Talisman House Publishers.

JULIA TRUBIKHINA

poetry, post-Soviet

The venerable Russian poetic tradition sustained a difficult era under Soviet rule, but, despite losses of those who died young or were silenced, poetry stubbornly endured. Remarkable poets emerged, particularly from the underground cultural scenes that flourished after the 1960s. When the Soviet Union collapsed in 1991, poets who had long struggled to get their work published found easier access to the public. Post-Soviet poetry can be seen as a stage beyond the poetry of perestroika because of the virtual end to censorship and the concomitant emergence of dozens of new venues for publication. Poets of the older generations who had been published sporadically or in severely censored form were seen anew by readers. These included Semen Lipkin, Inna Lisnianskaia, Boris Slutskii, Arsenii Tarkovskii, and perhaps especially Iosif Brodskii. The publication of Brodskii's poems in such journals as *Zvezda* (The Star) or in selected and collected poetry volumes only enhanced the émigré and Nobel Prize-winning poet's stature in Russia. Younger poets who had largely been known to one another, through *samizdat* or through publications abroad, also began to see their poems appear in major journals and in separate editions. It did not take long for readers to overcome the shock of seeing volumes of Elena Shvarts or Dmitrii Prigov competing for attention in bookstores, and what had once been all the more desirable because of its inaccessibility quickly seemed another commodity in a rapidly changing post-Soviet culture.

Some critics predicted hard times for poets, and certainly there were economic consequences for anyone who had once found support from the Writers' Union, which increasingly had little to offer even as new members might have swelled its ranks. Poetry, however, flourished beyond all expectations, nourished by the entrepreneurial efforts of new publishers, the generous prizes regularly awarded to genuinely talented poets, occasional foreign grants and subsidies, and the availability of new means to reach readers: salons, bookstores, festivals, competitions, clubs, and, above all, the Internet.

For some poets, this new freedom also posed an unexpected challenge. Their poetic world had been constructed during the Soviet period, with the myths and distortions of that era their principal target. These poets, loosely grouped as Moscow Conceptualists, created poetic texts that mixed slogans and catchphrases with images and rhythms from traditional Russian poetry. The results could be hilarious but also very incisive, particularly in the works of Dmitrii Prigov, Lev Rubinshtein, and Timur Kibirov. For such poets, the demise of Soviet Russia meant the loss of a target for their parody, and their work necessarily lost some of its pungency.

Another group of poets was less directly affected by political change – the loosely grouped Metarealists. Because their poetry reached beyond immediate reality, albeit with less certainty about the plausibility of their quest than had been true of, say, the Russian Symbolists, these poets could continue their search for linguistic purification, transcendence, and solace. They include Olga Sedakova, Ivan Zhdanov, Arkadii Dragomoshchenko, Aleksei Parshchikov, and Elena Shvarts, though several of these poets are so idiosyncratic as to defy genuine membership in any group.

A generation of younger poets, for whom Soviet-era struggles are merely second-hand tales, has also emerged, and the wide range of their themes, formal experiments, and ideas about what poetry can do in the world is impressive, as is their talent. Elena Fanailova, Grisha Bruskin, Aleksandra Petrova, Aleksandr Skidan, Mariia Stepanova, Dmitrii Vodennikov, Polina Barskova, and Maksim Amelin are among those establishing reputations in the twenty-first century.

The post-Soviet period has allowed a reconsideration of the groupings and hierarchies of Soviet poetry. One opposition, émigré vs. native, which seemed crucial before the demise of the Soviet Union, has particularly dwindled in importance. Besides Brodskii, who died in

New York in 1996, dozens of poets have continued to flourish in Jerusalem, Paris, Rome, New York, San Francisco, and elsewhere. They have recreated communities of like-minded intellectuals and creative artists in these cities, and any appraisal of post-Soviet poetry must take into account the hybrid sense of national identity and cultural politics that necessarily results from this vital diaspora. Other lessened divisions originate in a once rigid cultural hierarchy. The bards of guitar poetry, for example, once deemed peripheral, have gained growing respect, and visual poetry, although still far from the mainstream, commands attention through the continued significant work of Elizaveta Mnatsakanova and others. Mnatsakanova is also among those whose work mixes languages, a semiotically interesting formal feature that can signal a poet's life abroad (Mnatsakanova lives in Vienna, Petrova in Rome). Foreign locutions also figure in the work of poets still in Russia (Fanailova, for example), suggesting that the use of quotation and mixed alphabets looks back to the linguistic play of Pushkin's *Eugene Onegin* as much as it looks outward toward contemporary poetic traditions. A number of poets have done significant work as translators, bringing poets as different as John Ashbery, Paul Célan, Michael Palmer, and Charles Simic into Russian culture.

One aspect of post-Soviet Russian poetry radically distinguishing it from that of previous generations is the energized mixing of traditional forms, themes, and rhetorical devices with innovations across the board. For every poem that tries to bring new music to the rhythms of a standard iambic or dactylic beat, there is another that entirely rejects regular rhythm and rhyme. Some poets stubbornly practise one or the other and, particularly in St. Petersburg, a number of poets insist that a conservative adherence to form and theme is the only way to preserve Russian poetry's distinctiveness (for example, Aleksei Purin, poetry editor at the influential journal *Zvezda*). Others answer the beckoning call of free verse, as have Russian poets for decades, and both sides can claim that the other path leads only to perdition. Some of the best poets, as always, show their versatility in all forms, even seeking ways to combine both possibilities in individual poems (in Petersburg,

Viktor Krivulin, Shvarts). A number of significant experimental, visual poets have gained more prominence in the 1990s, although they had been working for many years before (Genrikh Sapgir, Mnatsakanova, Ry Nikonova, Sergei Sigei among them).

Many cultural phenomena once regarded as 'deviant' have taken centre stage in the post-Soviet period, reversing previous cultural hierarchies. Women poets are now more likely to find themselves included in anthologies and invited to poetry festivals, and feminist scholarship has drawn special attention to their work. Among the most celebrated was Nina Iskrenko, who died in 1996, as well as Shvarts and Sedakova. Though women's poetry remains marked in the same way that poetry with gay and lesbian themes strikes many readers as specialized, such conservative labelling is waning, if slowly.

The Internet has made poets more easily accessible, as has the emergence of several new journals and webzines. *Mitin zhurnal* (Mitia's Journal), once a major *samizdat* venue for risky poetry, prose, and translation, maintains a presence on the web and has a publishing enterprise, although it has ceased to publish new issues of the journal. A journal entirely devoted to Russian poetry, *Arion*, has been in publication since 1994. *Vavilon*, a former *samizdat* journal, maintains a strong presence on the web and in print. Some of the highest-profile new journals have increasingly devoted attention to poetry, chief among them *Novoe literaturnoe obozrenie* (New Literary Review). These new journals are notable for their translations of foreign poets and theorists, an important step in the long process of diminishing Russia's intermittent cultural isolation. A crowning achievement of this journalism and scholarship has been the emerging sense that Russia's poetry no longer stands apart from or above its culture. It is fully a part of post-Soviet culture, showing all its stresses, fractures, impulses, and energies.

See also: bards; Brodskii, Iosif; censorship; Conceptualism, literary; Internet, Russian; Kibirov, Timur; Mnatsakanova, Elizaveta; perestroika and glasnost; Prigov, Dmitrii; Rubinshtein, Lev; samizdat; Sedakova, Olga; Shvarts, Elena; thick journals; Zhdanov, Ivan

Further reading

Epstein, M. (1995) *After the Future: The Paradoxes of Post-Modernism and Contemporary Russian Culture*, Amherst, MA: University of Massachusetts Press.

High, J., *et al.* (eds) (2000) *Crossing Centuries: The New Generation in Russian Poetry*, New York: Talisman House.

Janecek, G. (2000) *Sight and Sound Entwined: Studies of the New Russian Poetry*, New York: Berghahn Books.

Polukhina, V. (ed.) (2002) *Russian Women Poets. Modern Poetry in Translation* 20, London: Kings College.

Smith, G. (1984) *Songs to Seven Strings: Russian Guitar Poetry and Soviet 'Mass Song'*, Bloomington, IN: Indiana University Press.

—— (ed.) (1993) *Contemporary Russian Poetry: A Bilingual Anthology*, Bloomington, IN: Indiana University Press.

STEPHANIE SANDLER

poetry, Soviet

Soviet poetry did not remain constant over time, since it was produced according to the official method of Socialist Realism, which changed with the politics of the USSR. In the post-Stalin era, three periods of Soviet poetry are discernible, each characterized by political pressures on, and expectations of, poets and their poetry. The three periods correspond roughly to the following eras: (1) the post-Stalin Thaw (1953–68), when lyric poetry was rehabilitated and grew fashionable, and more experimental new and formerly prohibited works were published; (2) Stagnation (1968–85), during which political control of literature increased, Soviet poetry became repetitive and lacklustre, and increasing numbers of poets eschewed official procedures and published their work in *samizdat* and *tamizdat*; and (3) glasnost under Gorbachev (1985–91), when censorship relaxed again and poetry that did not conform to the strictures of Socialist Realist finally saw print.

Certain elements of Soviet poetry remained constant from 1953 until the late 1980s. The most significant of these was its subjection to censorship. In practice, censorship imposed norms of language, tone, and prosody on Soviet poetry that obtained, with little deviation, throughout the period. The standardized language of Soviet poetry excluded a too high or literary style, on the one hand, and colloquial or sub-normal language, on the other. Poetry had to be optimistic in tone, and could include negative comments only about the USSR's officially approved enemies. Prosody was, for the most part, highly conformist and unadventurous: in Soviet poetry one finds almost exclusively syllabotonic metres, most commonly iambic and trochaic tetrameter and pentameter, and dolniks. The standard stanza form was the quatrain with alternating rhyme, and the post-1953 period saw wide use of the *stolbik* and *lesenka*, which Maiakovskii first popularized. Rhyme was predominantly exact, and often grammatical, which contributed to the banality of many poems. Lastly, the long narrative poem (*poèma*) was not a common form in Soviet poetry; short poems of 20–30 lines dominated the genre. Divergence from these norms was censored: while too little adherence to them was considered symptomatic of Western-style decadence, too much, in the form of innovative or complex form, was branded 'formalism', and remained equally beyond the pale of Soviet poetry.

The Thaw witnessed an efflorescence and liberalization of Soviet poetry. Changes to the overtly politicized, formulaic style of Stalinist-era verses were initiated in 1953 by Olga Berggolts's articles in *Literaturnaia gazeta* (The Literary Gazette), and by a discussion of lyric poetry held at the Leningrad Branch of the Writers' Union. Soviet poetry of the period addressed a wider range of themes, and was notably more depoliticized than had been the case in previous decades. Typical themes included nature, the seasons, the great future, poetry, romantic love, travel, motherhood, and technology. Poems on the theme of war decreased, as this often melancholy theme was officially discouraged.

In the early 1950s, the most famous names in Soviet poetry included Aleksandr Tvardovskii, Nikolai Tikhonov, Mikhail Isakovskii, and Aleksandr Prokofiev, but it was not long before a new generation of poets appeared whose youth, charisma, and boldness in poetry quickly became synonymous with the Thaw. The young Moscow poets Evgenii Evtushenko, Andrei Voznesenskii, Robert Rozhdestvenskii, and

Bella Akhmadulina, and their slightly older counterparts, Bulat Okudzhava and Boris Slutskii, entered the limelight in the 1950s, when censorship relaxed considerably more in Moscow than in Leningrad and the provinces. These poets wrote on topical and sometimes controversial themes, and experimented with more unusual forms reminiscent of the Futurists. They were viewed as 'licensed dissidents', since their poetry was daring, but publication was ultimately controlled by the authorities. Nevertheless, poetry had become exciting, cutting-edge, and a symbol of freedom in the USSR, and these poets became stars: their readings attracted huge crowds, the largest-ever poetry reading being held in 1962 at the Luzhniki Stadium in Moscow attended by over 14,000 people.

The fame and relative freedom of Evtushenko and others contributed to the upsurge in poetry during the Thaw. Literary workshops (LITOs) run by the Writers' Union became very popular and became a particular phenomenon in Leningrad. From them emerged such poets as Aleksandr Kushner, Nikolai Rubtsov, and Viktor Sosnora, who became professional Soviet poets, and others such as Evgenii Rein, Dmitrii Bobyshev, and Anatolii Naiman, who published little until the post-Soviet period. Iosif Brodskii also appeared first in this milieu. The Thaw also witnessed the republication of formerly prohibited poets' works. In 1956, poems by Tsvetaeva and Zabolotskii were published in the almanac *Literaturnaia Moskva* (Literary Moscow), in the 1960s Anna Akhmatova was published again, and an edition of Marina Tsvetaeva came out in 1965. The most significant Thaw publication by an establishment poet was Tvardovskii's *Terkin na tom svete* (*Terkin in the Other World*), published in 1963, which contained not only Tvardovskii's poetic response to de-Stalinization, but also criticism of contemporary Soviet society.

Republication of formerly prohibited poets continued even into the Stagnation period, with an edition of Osip Mandelshtam in 1975. The liberalizing trend, however, did not last, and the late 1960s saw new Soviet poetry once again confined to a narrow range of conservative themes and orthodox forms. Established poets were more restricted in what they could publish than had been the case during the Thaw, and it

became very difficult for young poets to publish at all. As a result, Soviet poetry became for the most part uninteresting. Poems on the theme of the Great Patriotic War returned to the pages of the journals as the USSR attempted to perpetuate a 'siege mentality' in the population. Alongside these offerings were a greater number of explicitly political poems articulating loyalty to the Party and devotion to Lenin. Notable exceptions to the monotony of most Soviet poetry were the first collections of Oleg Chukhontsev (1983), and Rein (1984). Sosnora, Kushner, Iunna Morits, and Akhmadulina also published interesting work during the Stagnation period, but many talented poets chose or were compelled to emigrate, including Brodskii, Bobyshev, Lev Losev, Bakhyt Kenzheev, and Aleksei Tsvetkov.

The near-impossibility of publishing led many young poets in the USSR to turn to *tamizdat* and *samizdat*. Some official poets, too, faced with the prospect of battles with editors and censors to publish compromised versions of their work, also disseminated their work through these channels. In 1979, official poets Akhmadulina, Inna Lisnianskaia, and Voznesenskii contributed work to the *samizdat* almanac *Metropol*. Soviet poetry was becoming more difficult to define, as for some the label 'Soviet' indicated a level of professionalism and status, whereas for others it had come to carry a pejorative meaning, intimating a lack of integrity in the poet's lifestyle and work. The terms 'official', 'unofficial', and 'Soviet' were further blurred by Club 81 in Leningrad (1981). This writers' club, comprising 'unofficial' writers whose work was largely unpublished in the USSR, was given legitimate status by the authorities and it eventually published an anthology, *Krug* (*Circle*, 1985).

Soviet poetry's assimilation of greater stylistic variety accelerated with the liberal reforms after 1985. The Gorbachev period saw less the production of significant new poetry than the retrospective publication of much that had been prohibited for some or all of the Soviet period: for the first time since 1934, there was widespread official acknowledgement and publication of poetry that did not conform to Socialist Realism. Poetry published between 1985 and 1991 is, strictly speaking, Soviet, but the term Soviet poetry now customarily refers to the monolithic corpus of work published before glasnost. It would not normally include, for example, the work of Khodasevich and Gumilev, which was published in the USSR in 1986 for the first time in many years, nor Akhmatova's *Requiem*, and Tvardovskii's *Po pravu pamiati*, which appeared the following year. At the end of the 1980s the work of living émigré poets such as Bobyshev, Brodskii, and Natalia Gorbanevskaia began to return to the pages of Soviet journals, and at the same time poets in the USSR born mostly after 1940 were at last able to publish. Olga Sedakova, Elena Shvarts, Sergei Gandlevskii, Timur Kibirov, and Viktor Krivulin are just a few of the many names that fall into this category.

See also: Akhmadulina, Bella; Akhmatova, Anna; Berggolts, Olga; Brezhnev, Leonid; Brodskii, Iosif; censorship; Evtushenko, Evgenii; Gorbachev, Mikhail; Kenzheev, Bakhyt; Kibirov, Timur; Kushner, Aleksandr; *Literaturnaia gazeta* (Literary Gazette); Losev, Lev; *Metropol*; Morits, Iunna; Okudzhava, Bulat; poetry, post-Soviet; samizdat; Sedakova, Olga; Shvarts, Elena; Slutskii, Boris; Socialist Realism; Stagnation; Stalin, Iosif; tamizdat; Thaw; thick journals; Tvardovskii, Aleksandr; unions, creative, Soviet; Voznesenskii, Andrei

Further reading

Evtushenko, E., Todd, A. and Hayward, M. (1993) *Twentieth Century Russian Poetry*, London: Fourth Estate.

Ivanov, B. I. and Novikov, Yu. V. (1985) *Krug. Literaturno-khudozhestvennyi sbornik*, Leningrad: Sovetskii pisatel'.

Kates, J. (ed.) (1999) *In the Grip of Strange Thoughts: Russian Poetry in a New Era*, Newcastle: Bloodaxe Books.

Lowe, D. (1987) *Russian Writing Since 1953: A Critical Survey*, New York: Ungar.

Smith, G. (ed. and trans.) (1993) *Contemporary Russian Poetry: A Bilingual Anthology*, Bloomington, IN: Indiana University Press.

——(2001) 'Russian Poetry since 1945', in N. Cornwell (ed.) *The Routledge Companion to Russian Literature*, London, Routledge.

Weissbort, D. (ed.) (1974) *Post-War Russian Poetry*, Harmondsworth: Penguin.

EMILY LYCO

Poklonnaia gora

Moscow's Poklonnaia gora (bowing hill), which historian Ivan Zabelin termed 'the most memorable place in Russian history', was the site where Napoleon waited in vain to be presented with the keys to the city in 1812. In the past, travelers approaching Moscow from the West would climb the hill, which once commanded a panoramic view of the capital, to pay homage, or bow, to the ancient Russian capital. (*Poklon* means 'bow'.)

Today's complex on Poklonnaia gora, which opened on the 50th anniversary of the Soviet Union's victory over Nazi Germany in World War II (1995), encompasses the Museum of the Great Patriotic War (1983–95) and the Chapel of St. George the Triumphant Martyr (1993–95), which frame Victors' Square. The Victory Monument obelisk (1995) rises 141.8 metres from the centre of the square to symbolize the 1,418 days of the war; it features a bronze figure of the Victory Goddess Nike and, at its base, a monument of St. George Slaying the Dragon, executed by the sculptor Zurab Tsereteli. Rounding out the complex is the memorial ensemble added in 2005 to commemorate the 60th Anniversary of the Soviet victory in World War II. The monument, executed by Tsereteli and architect Mikhail Posokhin, extends along a central avenue toward the Victory Monument and the Museum of the Great Patriotic War. It comprises a colonnade of fifteen 29-foot memorial bronze columns, or stelae, with ten stelae symbolizing the ten fronts of the military campaign; three commemorating the North, Baltic, and Black Sea fleets, and the remaining two memorializing the partisans and the troops who defended the rear guard. The monument's extravagant design was conceived to evoke the figurative ethos of post-war Stalinist architecture. Plans were recently announced to erect a monument to Winston Churchill, Franklin Roosevelt, and Josif Stalin to honour the three Allied leaders.

See also: monuments, post-Soviet; Moscow; Tsereteli, Zurab; World War II (Great Patriotic War)

ANATOLE SENKEVITCH

Pokrovskii, Dmitrii Viktorovich

b. 3 May 1944, Moscow; d. 29 June 1996, Moscow

Folklorist, conductor, singer, actor, composer

The master of authentic Russian folk singing, Pokrovskii studied folk instruments, playing in a music college and at the Gnessin Institute in Moscow. After graduation, he attended conducting classes at the Moscow Conservatory, where he studied with Boris Khaikin. In the end of the 1960s, he went on his first folklore expeditions to Arkhangelsk region, and became involved in the study of transitional music and traditional vocal performance practices. Since its founding in 1973, the Dmitrii Pokrovskii Ensemble has been the premier ensemble in its field. Pokrovskii and his troupe combined performance and scholarly practice, preparing every new programme as a result of new expeditions. One of their biggest successes was Stravinskii's *Les Noces* (1994) performed in folk style. Pokrovskii worked with many theatre and film directors (e.g., Iurii Liubimov, Lev Dodin, Kama Ginkas, Elem Klimov, Nikita Mikhalkov) either with his ensemble or solo, as a composer or actor.

See also: folk dance; folk music; Ginkas, Kama; Klimov, Elem; Liubimov, Iurii; Mikhalkov, Nikita; Stravinskii, Igor

KIRA NEMIROVSKAIA

police

See militia (police)

political parties, post-Soviet

Political parties in Russia are different from those in established European democracies; in part, as a result of the historical role of the Communist Party in Soviet society and the correspondingly recent establishment of competing parties. Most European political parties formed more than a century ago around cleavages between worker and employer interests and between rural and urban dwellers. In contrast, Russia's political parties emerged in a much later era, becoming legal only in 1990 after over seventy years of repression.

Although Russia has scores of political parties, few have competed in all parliamentary elections since 1993 and fewer still held seats in the State Duma. New parties tend to appear shortly before the elections, and then fade away after electoral defeat. In 1999, twenty-six parties were listed on a ballot for the Duma elections, but only six received enough votes to gain seats through the proportional representation (PR) allocation formula. Only four of the twenty-three parties listed on the ballot in 2003 won PR seats.

The winning party in the 2003 election was *Edinaia Rossiia* (United Russia), formed from a merger of the *Edinstvo* (Unity) and *Otechestvo* (Fatherland) parties in December 2001. President Vladimir Putin welcomed the formation of the new party, and later openly endorsed United Russia for the 2003 parliamentary elections. Led by Putin's Interior Minister Boris Gryzlov, United Russia received 38 per cent of the proportional representation vote in 2003 and came to control the majority of the seats in the Duma. During the 2003 electoral campaign, United Russia benefited from its close association with President Putin and from the support that it received from regional leaders. In addition, its electoral fortunes were helped by abundant, positive media coverage.

The Communist Party came in second place in the 2003 election. Although the Communist Party of the Soviet Union (CPSU) was banned in the aftermath of the August 1991 coup, the Russian Constitutional Court reversed Boris Yeltsin's ban and the Communist Party of the Russian Federation (CPRF) was officially registered in 1993. Led by Gennadii Ziuganov, the official goals of the CPRF include the propagation of socialism and the development of a society with social justice, a collective character, and equality. The Communist Party also supports the restoration of the Soviet Union on a 'voluntary basis' and the establishment of a strong Russian nation.

Although the share of the Duma seats controlled by the Communist Party shrank considerably after the 1999 parliamentary elections (compared with the seats won in the election of 1995), the Communist Party was still the largest single party in the State Duma. In the 2003 elections, however, the vote share won by the Communists dropped further to 13 per cent of the PR vote. As a result, the Communists shrank to a much smaller faction in the Duma.

The Liberal Democratic Party of Russia (*Liberalno-demokraticheskaia partiia Rossii*, LDPR) secured third place in the 2003 party-list voting. The LDRP was founded by Vladimir Zhirinovskii. The political platform of the LDPR, although known for a nationalist orientation that calls for reincorporating former union republics into Russia, also makes significant promises in the area of social welfare. The relatively strong showing of the LDRP in 2003 can be attributed to the continued popular appeal of Zhirinovskii, who has been extremely successful in attracting the support of protest voters.

The Motherland-National Patriotic Union (*Rodina*) came in fourth place in December 2003 with 9 per cent of the PR vote. Rodina, registered in September 2003, offered voters a nationalist-leftist alternative to the Communist Party. Included among the constituent parties was the Party of Russia's Regions (*Regiony Rossii*), the Socialist Unified Party of Russia or Spiritual Heritage (*Dukhovnoe nasledie*), and the Party of National Rebirth (*Partiia natsionalnogo vozrozhdeniia*, also known as the People's Will Party, *Narodnaia volia*).

Rodina's political platform criticized the injustices of the country's current system of exploiting Russia's natural resources. The party ran a campaign that called for social justice and a redistribution of the wealth stolen from the Russian people by a handful of billionaires during the privatization process. The proposed vehicle for this redistribution would be a huge tax on those corporations that control Russia's vast natural resources.

Neither of the two pro-market opposition parties, Iabloko and the Union of Rightist Forces (*Soiuz pravykh sil*, SPS), passed the 5 per cent threshold in 2003. Iabloko has contested every election since 1993. Its 2001 manifesto identified several goals including: establishing a democratic regime with rule of law, an effective market economy system, civil society, and a European framework of a post-industrial strategy.

SPS was formed in 1999 as a centre-right, pro-market coalition composed of smaller parties headed by former prime ministers and current governors. The coalition sought to enhance the representation of the country's developing middle class, entrepreneurs, managers of small businesses, and private farmers. A coalition between Iabloko and SPS might have allowed them to pass the electoral threshold; however, attempts at negotiation failed due to the insistence of Iabloko's leader Grigorii Iavlinskii that the two parties are not ideologically compatible.

The 2003 parliamentary elections supported a new structure in Russia's party system, which could be called a 'one-and-a-half party' system: the 'party of power', United Russia, commands more influence than all other parties combined. Previously, the Communist Party had been able to block initiatives from the president's office. After 1999, this was no longer the case, as Putin could build coalitions of parties in the Duma that would vote affirmatively for his policy priorities. The strength of the United Russia faction in the Duma, together with its lack of ideological rigidity, provides President Putin with a powerful legislative ally that almost without fail supports his policy initiatives.

See also: Communist Party; Coup, August 1991; Duma; Iabloko (Apple); Iavlinskii, Grigorii; nationalism ('the national question'); natural resources; privatization; Union of Rightist Forces (*Soiuz pravykh sil*, SPS); United Russia (Edinaia Rossiia); Yeltsin, Boris; Zhirinovskii, Vladimir; Ziuganov, Gennadii

Further reading

Brown, A. (ed.) (2001) *Contemporary Russian Politics*, Oxford: Oxford University Press.
Remington, T. (2003) 'Putin, the Duma and Political Parties', in D. Herspring (ed.) *Putin's Russia: Past Imperfect, Future Uncertain*, Lanham, MD: Rowman & Littlefield.

VICKI L. HESLI AND JAMES KRUEGER

political structure, post-Soviet

The break-up of the Union of Soviet Socialist Republics (USSR) in 1991 led to the creation of fifteen new independent states. Of these, the Russian Federation is the largest and most politically and economically significant within the world system. This entry describes the political structure of the Russian Federation.

The Presidential system

The Russian Presidency was created in 1991. Presidential power was expanded in the 1993 constitution, giving the president control over the armed forces and foreign policy. The President can call a referendum, make federal laws, issue directives, and under certain circumstances dissolve the State Duma. The President also has the power to legislate by decree, arbitrates disputes between federal bodies and the authorities of regional governments and can declare a state of emergency. Elected by popular vote for a four-year term, the President nominates judges and appoints presidential representatives to the regions.

The Russian presidency is a formidable position, with extensive powers and constitutional prerogatives. In institutional terms, the President of the Russian Federation dominates the Federal Assembly and the constituent administrative units of the federation. The person who holds the position of President has the authority to shape the policy direction of the Russian state. It is for this reason that the extraordinarily strong chief executive position in the Russian Federation has been termed a 'super presidency'.

The Russian Federation has had two presidents. Boris Yeltsin was elected by direct popular vote to this position on 12 June 1991, and won a second term in 1996. Term limits barred Yeltsin from competing in the 2000 election. He resigned after the December 1999 parliamentary elections; Prime Minister Vladimir Putin assumed the position of acting President, and went on to win the presidential election in March 2004 with 52 per cent of the vote. With presidential power transferred to Vladimir Putin early, his victory was all but guaranteed. In this sense Yeltsin picked his successor.

The legislature

The Russian Federation's December 1993 constitution created a bicameral legislature called the Federal Assembly. The lower house of the Federal Assembly, the State Duma, has 450 members, each of whom is elected for a four-year term. Elections for the State Duma were held in December of 1993, 1995, 1999, and 2003.

The Federation Council is the upper house of the Federal Assembly, created for the purpose of representing Russia's eighty-nine administrative regions. The executive and legislative branches of each region appoint a representative to the Council. The Speaker of the Federation Council follows the President and Prime Minister in Russia's constitutional hierarchy.

Bills must receive majority support in the State Duma and Federation Council, and be signed by the President to become law. In addition to its law-making functions, the Duma also approves the President's nominee for Prime Minister, conducts votes of no confidence in the government, appoints and removes the chair of the state bank, state auditors, and the chair of the office for human rights.

The deliberative role of the Federation Council tends to be more limited than the Duma's. Despite this trend, the Federation Council has formal constitutional authority that cannot be ignored. It has the power to approve the President's decrees, impeach the President, and to call presidential elections. The Federation Council also has the power to confirm border changes within the federation, approve the appointment of Constitutional and Supreme Court judges, and the General Prosecutor.

The Prime Minister

While the President is 'head of state', the Prime Minister is the chief executive. The President appoints and dismisses a Prime Minister, but this nomination must be confirmed by a vote taken in the State Duma. The Russian Prime Minister has primary responsibility for economic management, while the President coordinates and oversees all bodies of state power, directs foreign and security policy, and defines the strategic course for the country.

The Prime Minister directs the government through ministries and state agencies. He heads the Council of Ministers, which is responsible for the formulation and implementation of economic and social policy.

In Russia's dual executive system, its Prime Minister is constitutionally accountable to the parliament. No-confidence votes have been held periodically throughout the 1990s and 2000s.

The judicial branch

The Constitutional Court of the Russian Federation, established in July 1991, ensures that all laws and decrees conform to the constitution. The Constitutional Court also resolves jurisdictional disputes between federal or local organs of power, and interprets the federal constitution. The Supreme Court of the Russian Federation is the supreme judicial body for civil, criminal, administrative and other cases under the jurisdiction of courts of general jurisdiction. The Superior Court of Arbitration is the highest court for the resolution of economic disputes.

The Procuracy is responsible for the administration of judicial oversight and for criminal investigations. It is a centralized agency with branches in all sub-national jurisdictions, including cities. The chief of the agency is the procurator general, who is appointed by the president with the approval of the State Duma.

Russia's institutions of internal security

The Federal Security Service (FSB) is the primary successor organization to the KGB in the Russian Federation. In March 2003, the Federal Agency of Governmental Communications and Information (FAPSI) and the Federal Border Guard Service (FSP) were both incorporated into the FSB.

Russian federalism

The Russian state is a federal system separated into eighty-nine different administrative districts. Thirty-two units are defined by ethnoterritorial characteristics. These ethnically based political units are named after the nationality group that has historically inhabited the region. Russia's forty-nine oblasts are comparable to the fifty states in the United States, and not based on an ethno-territorial principle.

In September 2000, Russian President Vladimir Putin created a State Council and announced that it would be an executive body including all governors and heads of republics. The full State Council meets four times a year to discuss important strategic issues.

See also: administrative structure, Russian Federation; Duma; Federal Security Service; Gorbachev, Mikhail; Putin, Vladimir; Russian Federation; Yeltsin, Boris

Further reading

Brown, A. (2001) *Contemporary Russian Politics: A Reader*, Oxford: Oxford University Press.
Remington, T. (2003) *Politics in Russia*, 3rd edn, New York: Longman.

VICKI L. HESLI AND JAMES KRUEGER

political structure, Soviet

The Union of Soviet Socialist Republics (USSR), commonly known as the Soviet Union, had four constitutions, ratified in 1918, 1924, 1936, and 1977. The constitution of 1918 applied only to the Russian Federation. The 1924 constitution established the Soviet Union, which included Russia, Ukraine, Belarus, and the Caucasus. Central Asia entered the USSR shortly thereafter. The Baltic States were incorporated during World War II. The 1936 constitution introduced universal suffrage and a directly elected Supreme Soviet. The 1977 constitution emphasized the guiding role of the Communist Party in Soviet society. Each of these constitutions listed the rights of the people, but these rights could be exercised only if they contributed to the building of socialism.

The Supreme Soviet (national parliament) of the Soviet Union, the highest organ of state authority, consisted of two chambers: the Council of the Union and the Council of Nationalities. Delegates to the Union Council were directly elected from districts throughout the Soviet Union. Delegates to the Council of Nationalities represented national districts, union republics, autonomous republics, and autonomous regions.

Members of the Supreme Soviet served four-year terms. Elections, however, were not competitive. The ballot listed only one person, selected by the Communist Party, for each seat in the Supreme Soviet. Deputies elected to the Supreme Soviet included the political elite, military officers, scientists, prominent writers and artists, and exemplary workers and collective farmers. The Supreme Soviet served as a forum where the regime could announce its programmes. By confirming decisions made by the Communist Party, the Supreme Soviet legitimated the Party's rule.

At the head of the Supreme Soviet was the Presidium, elected at a joint session of both chambers. The Presidium, led by its chairman and composed of vice chairmen from each union republic, functioned as a collegial presidency.

Executive and administrative authority was vested in the Council of Ministers. The Communist Party leadership appointed and dismissed members of the Council of Ministers. The Council of Ministers included those officials who ran the various ministries of government, such as the ministers of agriculture, finance, foreign affairs, and defence. A Prime Minister, who was subordinate to or whose position was held concurrently by the General Secretary of the Communist Party, chaired the Council of Ministers.

The Council of Ministers was a large body, including the Premier (Prime Minister), deputy premiers, over fifty ministers, heads of agencies such as the State Security Committee (KGB) and State Planning Committee (GOSPLAN), and premiers of the union republics. A smaller body, the Presidium of the Council of Ministers, would often act in the Council's name. The Presidium of the Council of Ministers consisted of ten members, most of whom were industrial administrators responsible for coordinating the economy.

The Soviet government comprised two different kinds of ministries: union-republic ministries and all-union ministries, the former concerned primarily with heavy industry and foreign trade. These ministries were centralized and were managed directly from Moscow. The union-republic ministries dealt with matters such as finance, health, and law enforcement, and were subject to the authority of ministries in Moscow and to republic-level governments.

Union republics, the fifteen major administrative divisions of the USSR, replicated the constitutional and legislative structure of the USSR. Each union republic had its own Supreme Soviet, Presidium and Council of Ministers. These were directly subordinate to the USSR Supreme Soviet and Council of Ministries, and were monitored by the republic committees of the Communist Party. Ministries managed at the republic level were either branches of the union-republic ministries centred in Moscow or were specialized agencies in charge of local activities.

The Gorbachev reforms

While Mikhail Gorbachev was General Secretary to the Communist Party (1985–91), the Supreme Soviet adopted amendments to the constitution that established a USSR Congress of People's Deputies, increased the power of the Supreme Soviet and its Chairman, imposed term limits for elected officials, and formed a committee for constitutional oversight. Governments at the union republic level were encouraged to adopt similar democratizing reforms.

The new 2,250-member USSR Congress of People's Deputies, elected in March 1989, was the highest representative governing body in the Soviet Union. The Congress of People's Deputies had authority over the country's most important issues, including constitutional amendments. Some 1,500 deputies were directly elected in multi-candidate elections in districts throughout the country; 750 were elected by official organizations such as the Communist Party and the Academy of Sciences.

A Supreme Soviet was elected in May 1989 from within the membership of the USSR Congress of People's Deputies. Membership consisted of a fifth of the Congress and was divided into two houses, called the Council of the Union and the Council of Nationalities, each of which had 271 members. The Supreme Soviet met in spring and autumn sessions running three to four months. In contrast to the operation of the Supreme Soviet before Gorbachev's reforms, these sessions were marked by passionate debate and were publicly televised. Members of the Supreme Soviet levelled criticism at Party and government officials. The Supreme Soviet elected the Council of Ministers, headed by a Prime Minister.

In March 1990, the USSR Congress of People's Deputies approved amendments to the constitution that created an executive presidency, and immediately elected Gorbachev to the position. He served as the first and only President of the Soviet Union, from March 1990 till December 1991. The Soviet President was granted broad powers and was the Commander-in-Chief of the Soviet armed forces and the head of state. The same constitutional amendment that created the position of the President also created a powerful Presidential Council that assumed the decision-making tasks of the Politburo. Plans were drawn up for a direct popular presidential election to be held in 1994, but the Soviet Union dissolved before this election was held.

See also: administrative structure, Russian Federation; administrative structure, Soviet Union; Belarus; Caucasus; Central Asia; constitutions; Federal Security Service; GOSPLAN; Gorbachev, Mikhail; perestroika and glasnost; Russian Federation; Ukraine.

Further reading

Federal Research Division, The Library of Congress, *A Country Study: Soviet Union (Former)*, http://lcweb2.loc.gov/frd/cs/sutoc.html.
Medish, V. (1990) *The Soviet Union*, Upper Saddle River, NJ: Prentice-Hall.

VICKI L. HESLI AND JAMES KRUEGER

Poloka, Gennadii Ivanovich

b. 15 July 1930, Kuibyshev

Film director

Poloka studied at the State Film School VGIK with Lev Kuleshov and Aleksandra Khokhlova, graduating in 1957. In the popular drama *Respublika ShKID* (The Republic of ShKID, 1966), Poloka created a highly romanticized image of a 1920s school for juvenile delinquents who are educated by an idealistic pedagogue, a representative of classical humanistic principles. *Interventsiia* (*The Intervention*, 1967), challenging stereotypes of the Bolshevik Revolution through a blend of pathos and farce, was shelved and could only be completed during perestroika. Despite continuous harassment from Soviet censors, Poloka retained a peculiar nostalgic loyalty to Communist values, as demonstrated in *Vozvrashchenie bronenostsa* (*The Return of the Battleship*, 1996), a tongue-in-cheek reconstruction of the shooting of Eisenstein's *Bronenosets Potemkin* (*Battleship Potemkin*, 1925). People's Artist of Russia (1998).

See also: All-Russian (All-Union) State Institute of Cinematography; censorship; Communist ideology; perestroika and glasnost

PETER ROLLBERG

Polunin, Viacheslav (Slava) Ivanovich

b. 12 June 1950, Novosil, Orlov oblast

Clown

Polunin graduated from the Leningrad Theatre Institute (LGITMiK) and formed the clown group *Litsedei* (Hypocrites) in 1979. He held the 'Mime Parade' (1982), and founded the *Listedei Litsei* (Lyceum of Hypocrites) in 1987. He organized the 'Congress of Fools' and launched the 'Caravan of Peace', touring in 1989–90. In 1992, he set up the Academy of Fools, but he left Russia in 1993 to work with the Cirque du Soleil in Canada, and subsequently to London, where he has lived since 1994. In the show *Asisyai* he created his prototype, a clown with red fluffy slippers and yellow baggy trousers. *Asisyai* and *SnowShow* have toured the entire world.

See also: circus; St. Petersburg State Academy of Theatre Arts

BIRGIT BEUMERS

Pomore

Running along the northwestern coast of Russia, Pomore ('sea coast') is a loosely defined area with a long tradition of fishing, whaling, native shipbuilding, and a distinctive local folklore. The White Sea freezes in winter; its climate and distance from central Russia made Pomore, like Karelia, a miniature Siberia – a 'cultural refrigerator' and the site of both infamous labour experiments (Solovki, the Belomor Canal) and efforts to support and increase the local population. Special benefits for Soviet residents in the far north included earlier retirement age and higher standard wages. Industries today include fishing, mining, logging, and tourism.

See also: Karelia; Siberia; Solovki

SIBELAN FORRESTER

Popov, Evgenii Anatolievich

b. 5 January 1946, Krasnoiarsk

Writer

Popov's writing was influenced by 'village prose'. His work was first published in *Novyi mir* in 1976 and subsequently banned until perestroika because of his participation in the *Metropol* affair of 1979. His novels *Podlinnaia istoriia 'zelenykh muzykantov'* (*The Real Story of the 'Green Musicians'*, 1999) and *Master Khaos* (*Master Chaos*, 2002), attack the injustices of Soviet and post-Soviet history.

See also: *Metropol*; *Novyi mir*; village prose

DAVID GILLESPIE

Popov, Oleg Konstantinovich

b. 31 July 1930, Moscow

Circus clown

A graduate of the Moscow Circus School (1949), Popov delighted audiences with his innovative clowning throughout forty-five years in the circus ring. He developed a unique clown mask, abandoning the traditional red wig and exaggerated face paint in favour of a more naturalistic appearance, better suited to his portrayal of the Soviet 'everyman'. His most popular routines dramatized the comedic and often poignant episodes in the daily life of this resolutely and, at times, naïvely optimistic character. Popov made his first international appearance in 1956 and quickly won the hearts of world audiences, who knew him, affectionately, as the 'sunny clown'. Popov emigrated to Germany in 1991. People's Artist of the USSR (1969).

See also: circus

MIRIAM NEIRICK

popsa

A term derived from the phrase *pop-muzyka*, which appeared in the 1970s. It is a derogatory word for light pop music, similar to what in the West is called bubblegum music. *Popsa* refers disparagingly to any form of popular culture that is simple and appeals to the lowest cultural denominator.

See also: popular music, post-Soviet; popular music, Soviet.

MICHELE BERDY

popular culture, post-Soviet

The restructuring and the growth of Russian popular culture since glasnost have been marked by two major tendencies: Westernization and an emergence of new popular tastes, evident in the increased production of 'comfortable' art – books, films, theatre, and music that are light and easy to consume. In the 1990s, 'lesser' literary genres such as detective novels, crime, and science fiction reached printings in the millions and became the preferred reading of millions of Russians, including members of the intelligentsia. Boris Akunin, an exceptionally successful writer, achieved an effective balance between the detective genre and a more complex style, with numerous literary and cultural references, to satisfy the taste of both highbrow and lowbrow readers. Placing the crimes and their investigation at the end of the nineteenth century, the writer assuages Russian readers' nostalgia for the past, but does not hesitate to explore issues of social, national, and gender identity pertinent to Russian culture at the turn of the millennium. Aleksandra Marinina and Daria Dontsova, two very popular writers, promoted female detectives; their skilful and captivating narratives struck the right chord with audiences. While Marinina developed an unpretentious and very likable female protagonist, Dontsova utilized fashionable new vocabulary (usually English) and appealing humour. In 2004, Dontsova headed the list of bestsellers alongside authors such as Paulo Coelho and J. K. Rowling.

Sergei Lukianenko, a writer of science fiction and fantasy, topped bestseller lists with his fantasy-thriller *Nochnoi dozor* (*Night Watch*). Although popular TV series have been based on the works of Akinin, Marinina, and Dontsova, the 2004 summer release of the feature film *Nochnoi dozor* (directed by Timur Bekmambetov) was a unique event in Russia: the film grossed an unprecedented $5.3 million in the first week and favourably competed with *Spiderman 2* shown at the same time in cinemas. Watching predominantly Hollywood films in the first half of the 1990s, Russian viewers developed a taste for high-tech cinema with intense action and computer effects, and rewarded the first Russian film that met their Hollywood expectations. Other Russian box-office hits, such as Aleksei Balabanov's *Brat-2* (*Brother-2*) (2000) and Egor Mikhalkov-Konchalovskii's *Antikiller-2* (*Antikiller-2*) (2003), also subscribed to the code of Hollywood action films but offered nationalist and anti-terrorist sentiments. At the beginning of the twenty-first century Russian cinema is becoming financially successful only by following American film style. The most watched films in Russia's cinemas still remain foreign and especially Hollywood films.

At the same time, Russian television has featured more domestically produced programmes, such as soap operas and mini-series, replacing some Latin American and Western productions that were wildly popular in the 1990s. From 1998 to 2004 the most watched Russian TV series was *Ulitsy razbitykh fonarei* (*Streets of Shattered Streetlights*), showing the work of St. Petersburg *militsionery* (policemen). The criminal content of the mini-series *Brigada* (*Brigade*, 2002) similarly captured the attention of Russian viewers. Surprisingly, in 2003, Russian viewers' preferences turned toward productions based on Russian classical literature. The television production of Dostoevskii's *Idiot* (2003) achieved unexpected high ratings and motivated work on future television dramatizations such as *Master i Margarita* (*The Master and Margarita*), *Anna Karenina*, *Mertvye dushi* (*Dead Souls*), and *Besy* (*The Possessed*). Another curious shift in viewers' taste is evident in the emergence of series allowing women to propel the cinematic narrative and become its agents rather than its victims. After *Sex and the City* Russian shows such as *Taksistka* (*Woman Cab Driver*), *Balzakovskii vozrast* (*Prime of Life*), *Ne ssorites, devochki!* (*Don't Quarrel, Girls!*), *Svobodnaia zhenshchina* (*Free Woman*), and *Ia vse reshu sama* (*I'll Make My Own Decisions* [or: *I'll Figure it Out for Myself*]) appeared on Russian TV screens and promoted women's confidence and financial independence. Since the early 1990s Russian television has projected a Western image, offering commercials, talk shows, gossip shows, and mass consumerism.

Russian theatre changed no less than Russian literature, cinema, and television. In addition to the state-funded theatres, small independent theatre groups and independent individual productions called *antreprizy* found their way into Russian stage life. The new small theatres and independent productions easily tour the country and are able to reach wide audiences. While state theatres, with their traditional acting and directing styles, are still representative of Russia's theatrical traditions, Fomenko's workshop, for example, provides an innovative alternative approach. With a new market economy in place, some theatre managers attempt to appeal to the tastes of the newly rich, *novye russkie* (New Russians). *Teatr luny* (Theatre of the Moon) is known to target affluent Russians and to effectively combine state funding with substantial private sponsorship. The importation of Western musicals brought perhaps the most significant change to the Russian theatre scene. Russian productions of the French musical *Romeo and Juliet* and the American *Chicago* became very popular and revealed once again Russian audiences' desire to share the taste of Western viewers.

The Russian music scene also follows Western fashion, while simultaneously promoting original Russian melodies and rhythms. The popular band Ivan Kupala based its songs on folk tunes but modified them electronically with a contemporary beat and offered attractive video clips that combined folk and modern images. Popular bands such as Liube and Leningrad, and singers such as B-2, Filipp Kirkorov, and Zemfira dominate the popular music scene at the beginning of the twenty-first century, replacing rock bands such as Nautilus Pompilius, Mashina vremeni (Time Machine), and Akvarium, which led musical culture during glasnost and the first half of the 1990s. Russian rap is a new phenomenon picking up speed and popularity. Appealing mostly to Russian teenagers, Russian rap culture organized on the Internet and offered many Internet releases, although more and more concerts are being promoted. At the beginning of this century Russian popular culture continues to develop, even though torn between conflicting global and national values; its leaders are driven by talent, spontaneity, freedom, and competition.

See also: Akunin, Boris; Akvarium; Balabanov, Aleksei; detective fiction; film, post-Soviet; Fomenko, Petr; Internet, Russian; Kirkorov, Filipp; literature, post-Soviet; Liube; Marinina, Aleksandra; Mashina vremeni (Time Machine); musicals, Russian/Soviet; Nautilus Pompilius; New Russians; rock music; science fiction; television, post-Soviet; television serials; theatre, post-Soviet; Zemfira

Further reading

Abdulaeva, Z. (1996) 'Popular Culture', in D. Shalin (ed.) *Russian Culture at the Crossroad: Paradoxes of Postcommunist Consciousness*, Boulder, CO: Westview Press.

Barker, A. (ed.) (1999) *Consuming Russia: Popular Culture, Sex, and Society since Gorbachev*, Durham, NC: Duke University Press.

Stites, R. (1992) *Russian Popular Culture: Entertainment and Society since 1900*, Cambridge: Cambridge University Press.

YANA HASHAMOVA

popular culture, Soviet

Before the October Revolution of 1917, forms of Russian popular culture and entertainment in Russia were like those in Europe and the United States. Numerous cultural imports such as tango, jazz, and detective fiction as well as Russian arts, including gypsy songs and urban ballads, were the most popular forms of entertainment. Regulated by the free market, pre-Revolutionary popular culture was different from so-called 'high culture' (classical music, classical and avant-garde literature and fine arts, repertory theatre, ballet, and opera).

From the point of view of Marxism-Leninism, popular culture under capitalism is characterized by commercialism and the cultivation of consumerism, national prejudice, sex, and violence. Disguised as entertainment, mass culture generates conformism; it serves the purpose of inculcating bourgeois values and thus contributes to the oppression of the lower classes in a capitalist society.

Critical of mass culture under capitalism, Bolsheviks sought to create so-called *kultura mass* (culture for the masses), which would enlighten the masses and give all citizens access to all sources of knowledge and opportunities for creative expression. In the USSR, there was to be no opposition between high and low art. All culture was to belong to the masses of working people, regardless of their class or nationality, and serve the purpose of building an enlightened egalitarian society. Although the dichotomy between high and low art was never eliminated in the USSR, the gap between high culture and popular entertainment narrowed. The Soviet patronage of arts made classical ballet, theatre, literature, and music readily available to the majority of people. Thanks to state subsidies, prices of books, tickets to the theatre, opera, cinema, concerts and other cultural events remained remarkably low throughout the Soviet period. By the 1970s, the USSR had the highest rate of cinema attendance in the world. Important factors in shaping Soviet popular culture were the elimination of illiteracy and the development of an educational system that provided free education from kindergarten through high school and, for those admitted, through university and graduate school. By the end of the 1980s, the Soviet Union was issuing editions of the world's classics in large numbers, and every seventh book published in the world was published in the USSR. As a consequence, the USSR was dubbed 'the most well-read country in the world'.

Despite the fact that Soviet popular culture comprised some elements of high culture, the latter often remained little understood by mass audiences. They preferred stage comedies and circus performances to productions of Shakespeare's tragedies; and the 1930s' musical comedies by Grigorii Aleksandrov were more popular than masterpieces by film directors such as Sergei Eisenstein, Vsevolod Pudovkin, and Dziga Vertov.

In the USSR, the distinction between high and low art was in any case less important than the distinction between officially promoted culture and culture which was truly popular within different social groups. Immediately after the Revolution, the state nationalized the entertainment industry and established control over individual and collective expression. The major task of Soviet culture was propaganda in support of Communist ideology that was to ensure the hegemony of the proletariat. Stalin's cultural revolution (1928–32) put an end to the relative creative freedom of the 1920s by tightening censorship and organizing all the arts to ensure adherence to the new method of Socialist Realism, which required artists and writers to promote optimism and reinforce an ideological message of Soviet progress.

The Great Patriotic War (1941–45) consolidated the nation in the struggle against the Nazis and marked a new turn in the development of Soviet culture. From the 1940s to the 1980s patriotic songs, novels, and feature films that celebrated Russia's military heroism were a significant part of Soviet popular culture. After Stalin's death in 1953, Soviet cultural policy became more accommodating of popular tastes. Under Khrushchev and Brezhnev, some cultural forms such as jazz and detective fiction were revived, and many new popular art forms, such as stand-up comedy and game shows, began to develop more fully. In literature, science fiction, mysteries, and spy thrillers overtook the popularity of literary classics. Love songs (Edita Piekha, Alla Pugacheva, Sofia Rotaru), slapstick and lyrical film comedies (Leonid Gaidai, Eldar Riazanov), stand-up comedy (Arkadii Raikin, Gennadii Khazanov), and circus performances were among the favourite arts in Russia. Their distribution was greatly facilitated by the development of television: by the 1980s, almost 90 per cent of Soviet families owned a television set. The questioning of Communist ideology provided the impulse for the rise of political jokes (*anekdoty*), bards' guitar poetry, and rock music, which mostly circulated outside official cultural institutions, through self-made copies of records and tapes (*magnitizdat*).

By the mid-1980s, it was clear that Soviet cultural policy had failed to create an enlightened society loyal to the ideas of socialism. Soviet popular culture was a compromise between the official cultural policy, creative artists, and popular tastes; it was an uneasy balance between, on the one hand, the ideological and didactic functions of popular art forms that the State wished to promote, and on the other hand, the natural tendency of those forms to be pure entertainment. As soon as the grip of censorship relaxed with the advent of perestroika and when censorship was abolished (1989), consumer demand began to shape Soviet popular culture more fully. The fall of the USSR (1991) caused the rapid disintegration of Soviet culture and the rise of new popular entertainment forms characterized by commercialization and the incorporation of American popular culture.

See also: ballet, Soviet; bards; Brezhnev, Leonid; censorship; circus; classical music, Soviet; Communist ideology; detective fiction; educational system, Soviet; film, Soviet – Stagnation period; film, Soviet – Stalin era; film, Soviet – Thaw period; film, World War II; Gaidai, Leonid; Gypsy music; jazz; joke; literature, Soviet; literature, Thaw; perestroika and glasnost; philosophy, Soviet (Marxist-Leninist); Piekha, Edita; Pugacheva, Alla; Raikin, Arkadii; Riazanov, Eldar; samizdat; Socialist Realism (Sotsrealism); Stalin, Iosif; stand-up comedy; television, Soviet; Thaw

Further reading

Edelman, R. (1993) *Serious Fun: A History of Spectator Sports in the USSR*, New York: Oxford University Press.

MacFadyen, D. (2001) *Red Stars: Personality and the Soviet Popular Song, 1955–1991*, Montreal: McGill-Queen's University Press.

Schwarz, B. (1983) *Music and Musical Life in Soviet Russia, 1917–1981*, Bloomington, IN: Indiana University Press.

Stites, R. (1992) *Russian Popular Culture: Entertainment and Society Since 1900*, Cambridge: Cambridge University Press.

ELENA BARABAN

popular music, post-Soviet

After the fall of the Soviet Union, several problems manifested themselves in popular music that remain unresolved. The first and most scandalous involved a group of boys from various children's homes who created *Laskovyi mai* (Tender May), playing feeble, synthesized pop. Taking advantage of the chance to make large sums of money, they resorted to lip-synching, known in Russian as *fanera* (veneer). Established Soviet artists who for decades had toured across Russia waxed indignant, especially when Laskovyi mai suddenly began to alter its membership and several bogus ensembles appeared simultaneously, all claiming to be the 'real thing' on lucrative tours in rural districts. A similar trajectory characterized the career of the male/female ensemble Mirazh, which subsequently spawned several solo careers: those of Tatiana Ovsienko, Natalia Vetlitskaia, and Irina Saltykova.

While these new groups opted for quick profits, others launched careers that benefited from their relationships to established Soviet performers. The children of socialist pop-stars, such as Dmitrii Malikov, Vladimir Presniakov, Filipp Kirkorov and, most famously, Kristina Orbakaite did so to great effect. Orbakaite is the daughter of Alla Pugacheva, who began her career in the mid-1970s and became the most popular singer in all of Eastern Europe. By 2000, she had sold a quarter of a billion records.

Larisa Dolina and Laima Vaikule likewise forged a dignifying link to the past, with its purported disinterest in rapid enrichment. Dolina, who refers to herself as the 'voice of Russia', began her career in jazz, with its long-standing traditions in Odessa, before moving to pop/rock genres and somewhat tawdry 'popular' experiments. The Latvian Vaikule started out singing in Baltic holiday resorts, where state control was less evident, and simultaneously worked with fellow countryman Raimonds Pauls, the Latvian jazz pianist crucial to the Golden Age of Pugacheva's career after the late 1970s. The cabaret atmosphere of such Latvian resorts as Jurmala, though associated by many with tipsy *nomenklatura* on funded getaways, allowed Vaikule to claim continuity with a stable, established past. Ever since the early career of jazzman Leonid Utesov in the 1930s, Russian popular music has nurtured a fondness for costume and 'theatrical or persona changes' (*teatralizatsiia*) between songs and sets; cabaret robustly embraced these shifts, and they were used to explain capricious changes in fashion after 1991. In particular, female performers such as Natasha Koroleva, *Litsei*, Tania Bulanova, and Alena Apina could, and did, argue that music simply was doing what it always had.

The popular music scene demonstrated another tendency: singers such as the Latvian Vaikule and the Ukrainians Koroleva, Anzhelika Varum, and the group Via-Gra all sang in Russian and tried to establish themselves in Moscow, hoping to attract larger audiences and to earn the sort of money inaccessible in the former Soviet republics. Vaikule came to Moscow in the early 1980s and her Russian concerts garnered her huge popularity. Varum, born in Lvov, joined her father in Moscow in the early 1990s and made a career for herself. Though some commentators have lambasted these female singers for appealing to sexuality ('tastelessness'), by comparison with their Western counterparts, they are relatively prudish, limiting their risqué gestures to brief changes into racy costumes before reverting to propriety (hence *teatralizatsiia*).

The pressures of piracy have affected singers' choices in live performance and recordings. According to sundry reports, major Western artists can never sell 1,000 legal CDs in Russia before bootlegs or mp3s flood Russia's market stalls. Pirated sales of software, CDs, DVDs, mp3 discs, and videos in Russia top $1 billion per annum. Well over 80 per cent of all such formats nationwide are pirated; people outside of major cities in Russia may never see legal software or discs. With Russia now having the second largest piracy industry after China, its contemporary musicians are struggling to emerge onto the international music scene, despite the persistence of low production standards and occasionally slavish imitations of Western hits, including exact reproductions of English-language songs with Russian lyrics (*perepevki*) that flout copyright.

Russian chances of winning the Eurovision Song Contest only became even remotely likely in the first few years of the twenty-first century (with Alsu and Tatu); while not competitive in the international sphere, musicians continue to uphold Russian rock's traditionally more serious cultural role. Elder statesmen of the late Soviet Union are still important figures, in particular Boris Grebenshchikov and Viacheslav Butusov, while others, such as Iurii Shevchuk of DDT, perform acoustically with sufficient frequency to evoke memories of bardic traditions from the 1960s and 1970s. That genre, in fact, has been returned into the mainstream through the gentle songs of, for instance, Oleg Mitiaev, whose lyrical tales soothe psyches troubled by modern life.

Despite various problems, however, rock has established some impressive, if not groundbreaking, tendencies in Russian pop-crossovers. That especially holds true of female singer-songwriters, such as Zemfira, Iulia Chicherina, and Iuta. Moreover, some groups from the periphery have managed to avoid Muscovite homogenization – Mummi Troll from Vladivostok – while others have chosen to sing in languages other than Russian, such as Okean Elzy, from Ukraine.

Moscow remains the centre of rock, nonetheless, for it monopolizes trade and offers the largest audiences. Perhaps Moscow's decisive role in rock explains the trend in nostalgic patriotism, showcased in the civic pop songs of Oleg Gazmanov, a close friend of Moscow's mayor, Iurii Luzhkov, and in the latest repertoire of Liube, which recently has favoured retro lyrics lauding soldiers' bravery in the midst of war. Nostalgia also flourishes in the production of prime-time music television shows, with New Year's Eve shows dedicated to long-gone but eternally performed pop classics of the 1930s and 1940s, reworked by today's most popular artists. The most popular group, however, remains the St. Petersburg-based Leningrad, which specializes in outrageous parodies and mockery of musical and ideological clichés.

Russian rock music has difficulties breaking out of the domestic market owing to the language barrier. Yet two healthy and corrective tendencies are well under way. Artists who have lived and worked in London – Tatu, Alsu, and Mummi Troll – have acquired proficiency in English and not only can sing in English, but also have a solid sense of international audiences. Additionally, since 2000, Russian DJs have either vivified the work of mainstream performers with remixes done across distant time zones (e.g., for Valeriia), or have found success in the clubs of Europe, most notably PPK from Rostov. Amateur technical savvy, aesthetic daring, and the ability of sound files to defeat geography promise better things for the development of instrumental dance music from Russia.

See also: bards; DDT; Dolina, Larisa; Grebenshchikov, Boris; Kirkorov, Filipp; Leningrad; Liube; Luzhkov, Iurii; Moscow; nomenklatura; Pugacheva, Alla; Tatu; Zemfira

Further reading

Cushman, T. (1995) *Notes from Underground: Rock Music and Counterculture in Russia*, Albany, NY: State University of New York Press.

MacFadyen, D. (2002) *Estrada?! Grand Narratives and the Philosophy of the Russian Popular Song since Perestroika*, Montreal: McGill-Queen's University Press.

Troitsky, A. (1988) *Back in the USSR: The True Story of Rock in Russia*, London: Faber and Faber.

DAVID MACFADYEN

popular music, Soviet

During the Soviet era, popular music (also known as *estrada* music) was a favourite form of mass entertainment. The Russian term 'estrada' is of foreign origin and means 'elevated platform or stage'. *Estrada* music – catchy, easy-listening tunes with patriotic or sentimental lyrics – was performed by popular singers on stage, radio, and TV. Estrada more broadly refers to a type of performing art comprising concerts (similar to Western variety shows and Russian pre-revolutionary cabarets) and multiple forms of entertainment such as pantomime, comic sketches, circus acts, dancing, and parodies. The music and lyrics of popular Soviet estrada songs combined tradition with innovation, and were strongly influenced by Russian folk songs, urban, sentimental, or cruel romances, gypsy music, and popular Western music.

Soviet popular music was a powerful propaganda tool that, unlike its Western counterpart, was financed, controlled, and censored by the government. The Soviet government sought to build support for the socialist homeland and faith in the Communist system with optimistic melodies and ideologically-charged lyrics. During the Stalin era, many of these songs, such as Isaak Dunaevskii's life-affirming *Shiroka strana moia rodnaia* (Wide Is My Native Country) – originally composed for the film *Tsirk* (Circus, 1936) – became a popular tune and enjoyed the status of a hymn inseparable from everyday Soviet life. Popular stars also sang intimate and sentimental songs that dealt with universal topics such as love, hope, and friendship. During World War II, Klavdiia Shulzhenko's intimate and emotional performances made her a cultural icon, and for generations of Russians her nostalgic 'Little Blue Kerchief' became a musical symbol of loyalty and love. Leonid Utesov was loved for his melodic, humorous, jazz-influenced songs. Lidiia Ruslanova was famous for performing stylized Russian folk songs, while Izabella Iurieva offered passionate renditions of gypsy and Russian romances.

During the Thaw, Soviet pop music was characterized by euphoria and hope for the future, exemplified in such songs as *Pust vsegda budet solntse* (Let There Always Be Sunshine) by Aleksandr Ostrovskii and Lev Oshanin. This period also saw the rise of such popular singers as Edita Piekha, who performed lyrical songs by O. Feltsman and V. Solovev-Sedoi with elegance and tenderness, and Iosif Kobzon, who popularized melodic songs by Aleksandra Pakhmutova and Mikael Tariverdiev.

From the 1970s until the dissolution of the Soviet Union (1991), a new generation of popular music stars was increasingly experimental, eccentric, and often Westernized. The theatrical shows of such stars as Alla Pugacheva, Valerii Leontev, and Laima Vaikule held great appeal for younger generations. At the same time, other popular singers, including Lev Leshchenko, Muslim Magomaev, Sofiia Rotaru, and Valentina Tolkunova, were more conventional: their repertoires were often patriotic and ideologically charged, and their performing styles formal and static. Other talented *estrada* performers included Liudmila Zykina, who specialized in Russian folk songs or their Soviet versions, and the charismatic Nikolai Slichenko, a passionate propagandist of gypsy romances. The last decades of the Soviet era saw the flourishing of VIA: vocal-instrumental ensembles that promoted multi-national musical traditions of the Soviet republics with such groups as the Russian Samotsvety, the Belorussian Pesniary, and the Uzbek Jalla.

See also: gypsy music; Kobzon, Iosif; Leontev, Valerii; Leshchenko, Lev; Magomaev, Muslim; Pakhmutova, Aleksandra; Pesniary; Piekha, Edita; propaganda, Soviet and post-Soviet; Pugacheva, Alla; romance; Shulzhenko, Klavdiia; Slichenko, Nikolai; Socialist Realism; Utesov, Leonid; vocal-instrumental ensemble

Further reading

MacFadyen, D. (2001) *Red Stars: Personality and the Soviet Popular Song, 1955–1991*, Montreal: McGill-Queen's University Press.
—— (2002) *Songs for Fat People: Affect, Emotion, and Celebrity in the Russian Popular Song, 1900–1955*, Montreal: McGill-Queen's University Press.
Stites, R. (1992) *Russian Popular Culture: Entertainment and Society since 1900*, Cambridge: Cambridge University Press.

OLGA PARTAN

poshlost

Poshlost refers primarily to vulgarity, tackiness, and poor taste. It has a secondary meaning that can refer to vulgar or caddish sexual assumptions, double entendres in questionable taste, tired pick-up lines, and cynicism about the possibility of romance or exalted feelings between potential sexual partners. The *poshlyi* person, or *poshliak*, suffers from a lack of taste or borrows thoughts and opinions from others. The term, spelled as 'poshlust', was elegantly summarized by Vladimir Nakobov, who saw its traces in the celebratory commercial images of middlebrow North America. Whether it shows up as sexual innuendo or as self-satisfied mediocrity in the Nabokovian sense, *poshlost* nonetheless requires a certain level of education and culture, so that the offending individual presumably knows better.

SIBELAN FORRESTER

pososhok

Commonly found in the phrase *vypit na pososhok* (to drink one for the road), this term refers to a last alcoholic drink consumed before leaving home or with guests before their departure. The term derives from *posokh* (walking stick), while the custom is said to derive from Cossack tradition.

See also: Cossacks; drinks, alcoholic; traditions and customs

RACHEL S. PLATONOV

postmodernism

Roughly coinciding with the first manifestations of Western postmodernism, the first examples of Russian postmodernism developed in the visual arts and literature during the late 1960s and early 1970s. They embraced such characteristic postmodernist concepts and practices as anti-utopianism, disillusionment with totalitarian systems, and mockery of ideological and cultural simulacra. Russian postmodernists found their antecedents in Vasilii Rozanov, Konstantin Vaginov, Daniil Kharms, Nikolai Oleinikov, and, most importantly, Vladimir Nabokov. Postmodernist experiments were almost entirely excluded from 'official' Soviet culture and belonged to the sphere of underground art (*samizdat*, informal art, Apt-Art). Various critics include the following among the classics of Russian postmodernism: Venedikt Erofeev, as author of the 'narrative poem' *Moskva-Petushki*

(*Moscow to the End of the Line*), the so-called Lianozovo School, the Moscow Conceptualist Circle (Ilia Kabakov, Erik Bulatov, Leonid Sokov, Aleksandr Kosolapov, Grisha Bruskin, Irina Nakhova, Francisco Infante, Viktor Pivovarov, Vladimir Iankilevskii); the founders of Sots-Art (Vitalii Komar, Aleksandr Melamid); conceptualist writers Dmitrii Prigov, Lev Rubinshtein, and Vladimir Sorokin; neo-baroque novelist Sasha Sokolov; gay 'poet of underground Moscow' Evgenii Kharitonov; the author of black-humour poetry, Oleg Grigorev; such performative groups as the Leningrad *Mitki* or Moscow *Kollektivnye deistviia* (Collective Actions).

The first theoretical approaches to Russian postmodernism were suggested – in *samizdat* and *tamizdat* publications – by Boris Grois (Groys, in the article 'Moscow Romantic Conceptualism', in the Paris-based journal *A-Ia* in 1979), Mikhail Epstein (in various manifestoes of new poetry and analytical articles of the 1980s), and, in emigration, by Petr Vail and Aleksandr Genis, Margarita and Viktor Tupitsyn. However, broad critical reflection, including the use of the term 'postmodernism', was delayed in Russia until the years of perestroika, when this layer of culture was gradually legitimized. The heated critical discussion about postmodernism in Russian literary journals, as well as several conferences (the most prominent was 'Postmodernism and We' in 1991), helped separate this trend from the other movements of underground culture, such as the avant-garde, 'high modernism', naturalism (*chernukha*) or anti-Soviet social realism.

In post-Soviet Russia, postmodernism became a meta-transgressive trend, simultaneously a medium for depicting taboo-breaking behaviour (sexuality, obscene language, naturalistically presented violence, cannibalism, scatological gestures, etc. – especially shocking after seven decades of puritanical moral censorship) and itself a form of taboo-breaking behaviour. Russian postmodernists demonstratively undermined the traditional Russian image of the writer as 'the voice of the state' or, alternatively, 'the voice of the people'. Scandalous gestures, clownish self-representation, performatism, emphatic indifference to the social significance of writings – no wonder the cultural establishment of the late Soviet and post-Soviet period perceived these features of Russian postmodernists' artistic behaviour as sacrilege, or at least as acts of anti-cultural hooliganism.

The scandalous assimilation of postmodernism to the post-Soviet cultural scene soon made it a popular catch-phrase and a synonym for everything in vogue. In the 1990s, postmodernist poetics began to affect the mainstream in various media. Most notably, Russian postmodernism 'closed the gap' between 'high' and 'popular' culture – the task traditionally assigned to postmodernism in the West – when the postmodernist, stylized mystery novels of Boris Akunin and the philosophical phantasmagorias of Viktor Pelevin (*Chapaev i Pustota* [*Buddha's Little Finger*] and *Generation'P'* [*Homo Zapiens*]) achieved sensational commercial success. In the 1990s, postmodernist poetics influenced the artistic and literary mainstream and affected *popsa* and journalism (overpowering irony becoming a trademark of new Russian journalism, including on TV). Simultaneously, Western postmodernist theory was widely translated and popularized by such publishing houses and journals as Ad Marginem, Logos, Aleteia, *Novoe Literaturnoe Obozrenie* (New Literary Review), *Kommentarii* (Commentary), *Khudozhestvennyi zhurnal* (Artistic Journal), and others.

The cultural meaning of Russian postmodernism remains different from that in the Western cultural paradigm. In Russia, postmodernism is not opposed to the modernist tradition (as it is in the West). On the contrary, it represents one of its phases. Russian postmodernism simultaneously performs two contrasting functions. On the one hand, it continues the modernist evolution, which had been heavily suppressed, yet not completely eliminated, in Soviet culture: in this aspect, it mostly focuses on the displays of the unconscious in individual and collective existence, thus undermining the rationalist illusion of an orderly and comprehensible world. Attraction to this pole produced such aesthetic formations as 'metarealist' poetry, 'metafiction', 'post-Conceptualism', 'new autobiographism', and 'neo-Baroque'. On the other hand, Russian postmodernism corresponds to the international postmodernist canon insofar as it problematizes and critiques the central discourses of modernity (such as progress, identity, truth, the word, and meaning) by substituting them with an interplay of conflicting non-individual discourses, simulacra, myths, and heterogeneous narratives. The domination of this function shapes different versions of Conceptualism.

The neo-Baroque tendency is represented by various writers, as well as by Leonid Desiatnikov, the late Sergei Kurekhin, Aleksei Papernyi, and Aleksei Rybnikov in music; Novaia Opera and Aleksandr Titel in musical theatre; Kirill Serebrennikov in dramatic theatre; Evgenii Grishkovets, Maksim Kurochkin, Olga Mukhina, the Presniakov brothers, and Nina Sadur in playwriting; Ivan Dykhovichnyi (*Kopeika* [*The Kopek*]) and Aleksandr Zeldovich (*Moscow*) in cinema. In the visual arts, though, only Mikhail Shemiakin (in his works of the 1990s), Konstantin and Larisa Zvezdochetov, Elena Figurina, Bella Matveeva, and a few other artists lean towards neo-Baroque. Indeed, Conceptualism almost exclusively dominates visual art and preserves its small, yet strong presence in literature (Prigov, Rubinshtein, Sorokin, Peppershtein and Anifriev) and cinema (Necrorealism, Peter Lutsik's *Okraina* [*The Outskirts*]).

However, this distinction is rather schematic, since most postmodernist authors unobtrusively juxtapose these two functions in their artistic style and œuvre, if not in any single work. One easily detects the fusion of the modernist philosophy of freedom and 'high culture' with the postmodernist word-and-world game, even in the works of such extremely popular Russian writers (usually defined as postmodernist) as Sasha Sokolov, Pelevin, Tatiana Tolstaia, and Timur Kibirov. In a way, any significant work of Russian postmodernism may be interpreted as postmodernist and modernist at the same time. This 'undecidability' defines Russian postmodernism's uniqueness as a productive fluctuation, a channel for an explosive interaction between modernist and postmodernist cultural, philosophical, and aesthetic paradigms.

See also: Akunin, Boris; Apt-Art; art, informal; Bruskin, Grisha; Bulatov, Erik; Conceptualism, art; Conceptualism, literary; Desiatnikov, Leonid; Dykhovichnyi, Ivan; Erofeev, Venedikt; Figurina, Elena; Genis, Aleksander; Grishkovets,

Evgenii; Iankilevskii, Vladimir; Infante, Francisco; Kabakov, Ilia; Kibirov, Timur; Komar and Melamid; Kosolapov, Aleksandr; Kurekhin, Sergei; Kurochkin, Maksim; Lianozovo School; literature, post-Soviet; Matveeva, Bella; Mitki; Mukhina, Olga; Nakhova, Irina; Pelevin, Viktor; Pivovarov, Viktor; poetry, post-Soviet; popular culture, post-Soviet; Prigov, Dmitrii; Rubinshtein, Lev; Rybnikov, Aleksei; Sadur, Nina; samizdat; Shemiakin, Mikhail; Sokolov, Sasha; Sokov, Leonid; Sorokin, Vladimir; Sots-Art; tamizdat; Tolstaia, Tatiana; Vail, Petr; Zeldovich, Aleksandr; Zvezdochetov, Konstantin; Zvezdochetova, Larisa

Further reading

Balina, M., Condee, N. and Dobrenko, E. (eds) (2000) *Endquote: Sots-Art Literature and Soviet Grand Style*, Evanston, IL: Northwestern University Press.

Berry, E. and Miller-Pogacar, A. (eds) (1995) *Re-Entering the Sign: Articulating New Russian Culture*, Ann Arbor, MI: University of Michigan Press.

Dyogot, E. (1995) *Contemporary Painting in Russia*, Roseville East, NSW: Craftsman House.

Epstein, M. (2000) *Postmodern v Rossii: Literatura i teoriia*, Moscow: R.Elinin.

Epstein, M., Genis, A. and Vladiv-Glover S. (1999) *Russian Postmodernism: New Perspectives on Post-Soviet Culture*, New York and Oxford: Berghahn Books.

Eshelman, R. (1997) *Early Soviet Postmodernism*, Frankfurt am Main: Peter Lang.

Genis, A. (1999) *Ivan Petrovich umer: Stat'i i rassledovaniia*, Moscow: NLO.

Goscilo, H. (1996) *Dehexing Sex: Russian Womanhood During and After Glasnost*, Ann Arbor, MI: University of Michigan Press.

Groys, B. (1992) *The Total Art of Stalinism: Avant-Garde, Aesthetic Dictatorship, and Beyond*, trans. C. Rougle, Princeton, NJ: Princeton University Press.

——— (1993) *Utopia i obmen. Stil' Stalin. O novom: Esse*, Moscow: Znak.

Lipovetsky, M. (1999) *Russian Postmodernist Fiction: Dialogue with Chaos*, Armonk, NY: M.E. Sharpe.

Tupitsyn, V. (1998) *Communal (Post)modernism: Russian Art of the Second Half of the 20th Century*, Moscow: Ad Marginem.

MARK LIPOVETSKY

Pozner, Vladimir Vladimirovich

b. 1 April 1934, Paris

Television journalist, political commentator, author

The son of a Russian émigré father and French mother, Pozner spent his childhood in Paris, New York, and Berlin. After returning to the Soviet Union and entering radio and television, he appeared on American network television via satellite in the 1970s as a spokesperson for the Soviet way of life. In the mid-1980s he hosted the historic 'space-bridge' series, a hallmark of glasnost. He published two best-selling books, collaborated with Phil Donohue, and hosted popular Russian talk shows. Since November 2002, his weekly programme *Times* (*Vremena*) has drawn millions of viewers and won numerous awards for its quality political analysis.

See also: journalism; journalists, post-Soviet; perestroika and glasnost

ANDREA LANOUX

Pravda

Newspaper

A political newspaper, established in April 1912 as the official publication of the Bolshevik Party. Lenin, the paper's *de facto* founder and editor-in-chief, from 1912–14 alone, published more than 300 articles in *Pravda*, presenting his theory of socialist propaganda. The paper's founding was celebrated before the Revolution on 22 April (5 May New Style) 1914 as Workers' Press Day, and after 1922 as Press Day. *Pravda* served as a clear example of a Party newspaper (*partiinaia gazeta*), what Lenin called a 'collective propagandist, agitator, and organizer', aimed at protesting against socio-political ills and educating readers. The original *Pravda* published many letters from readers.

Sponsored by workers' contributions, *Pravda* played a significant role in organizing the workers' movement in Russia. Almost all active participants in the socialist movement wrote for it; writer Maksim Gorkii edited the section on culture. Closed eight times between 1912 and 1914, *Pravda* became the official Bolshevik newspaper in March 1917. During the Soviet era, *Pravda* was the leading propaganda tool, supporting and promoting all Party decisions; publishing all state and Party documents and announcements (such as the appeal to the population in June 1941, after the German invasion of the Soviet Union signalling the beginning of World War II); promoting official Soviet writers and artists; and struggling with 'enemies of the state', dissidents, and 'agents of the West'.

The history of *Pravda* reflected the history of the Soviet state. The newspaper strictly followed the official line, forcing the public to read between the lines to determine the reality behind reported current events. Since the fall of the Soviet Union, circulation has dropped precipitously, from 11 million in 1975 to 65,000 in 2004. The paper began to lose influence on the reading public beginning with perestroika. It was divided and resold several times; in 1990 there were several newspapers entitled *Pravda* in Moscow alone.

See also: censorship; journalism; Lenin, Vladimir Ilich; perestroika and glasnost; propaganda, Soviet and post-Soviet

NADEZHDA AZHGIKHINA

Prigov, Dmitrii Aleksandrovich

b. 5 November 1940, Moscow

Poet, prose writer, visual and performance artist

Prigov is one of the leading representatives of Conceptualism in Russian literature and arts. He has been publishing his writing in *samizdat* and *tamizdat* since the mid-1970s, and in official media since perestroika. An extraordinarily prolific writer, having authored tens of thousands of texts, Prigov brings together in a seemingly unconsidered fashion elements drawn from the widest spectrum of human experiences, which he then usually organizes into subtly subversive quasi-doggerel verse. In his texts, Prigov targets the many possible speaking subjects of

Soviet and post-Soviet reality; however, he artfully dismantles the voices of his imagined personae, pushing his texts ever so slightly toward the realm of the absurd. Prigov's focus is on verbalizing the consciousness of his many appropriated 'selves' – an urban philistine, a poet fascinated by the might of the State as symbolized by the figure of the Policeman, or even a sensuous young woman or a shy gay man – a sideshow of the characters populating daily Soviet and post-Soviet life, portrayed in a mildly grotesque key. In addition to verse, he has authored catalogue-like texts, fiction, plays, and critical essays. In visual arts, he is known in particular for allegorical graphic works and installations.

See also: Conceptualism, art; Conceptualism, literary; samizdat; tamizdat

VITALY CHERNETSKY

Primakov, Evgenii Maksimovich

b. 29 October 1929, Kiev

Politician

A graduate of the Moscow State Institute of Oriental Studies (1953), Primakov has held a number of responsible positions in academia (Deputy Director and Director of the Institute of World Economy and International Relations; Director of the Institute of Oriental Studies), the Communist Party (Candidate Member of the Politburo), and the governments of the USSR (Chairman of the Soviet of the Union of the USSR Parliament), and Russia (Director of the Foreign Intelligence Service; Minister of Foreign Affairs; Prime Minister). From 1999–2001 he headed the faction Fatherland-All Russia in the State Duma. He is currently President of the Russian Federation Chamber of Trade and Commerce.

See also: Duma; political parties, post-Soviet

ALEXANDER DOMRIN

Primorskii krai

Literally the 'Maritime Region', the farthest southeastern part of Russia, between China and the Pacific Ocean, plus several islands in the Sea of Japan. The capital, Vladivostok, was founded in 1860 and its name means, tendentiously, 'Rule the East'. *Primorskii krai* occupies about 166,000 sq km in area, mountainous in parts, with a humid but not intemperate climate. Russians form the majority of a slowly shrinking, ethnically mixed population of over two million; aboriginal peoples constitute a tiny minority. Major industries are mining (coal, various metal ores) and forestry, with shipbuilding and fishing on the coast.

SIBELAN FORRESTER

prisons

Incarceration has existed in Russia since the sixteenth century. Until then, major forms of punishment were the death penalty, corporal punishment, and fines. The Criminal Code of 1903 stipulated several modes of imprisonment: penal servitude, exile, and confinement at a house of correction, fortress, or prison. After the October Revolution of 1917, there gradually arose a system of the GULag, with its network of camps placed under the command of the NKVD (1922). In 1998, administration of the department of prisons was transferred from the MVD to the Ministry of Justice of the Russian Federation; currently the department is called FSIN (*Federalnaia Sluzhba Ispolennii Nakazanii* [Federal Service of the Execution of Punishment]). The transfer has ushered in substantial changes: the new Service is interested in humane reform of the system and in reducing the number of those imprisoned. At present, Russia holds second place (after the United States) in the relative number of prisoners (530 per 100,000 population).

In more than 1,000 institutions there are 763,000 prisoners, including approximately 50,000 women and 15,000 minors; in eleven prison orphanages there are more than 500 children (forced to live in prisons next to mothers who are serving their sentences). Organization of the penitentiary system in Russia remains based primarily on camps, with only eight prisons as such. Historically the most famous prisons include Kresty (an isolation prison; St. Petersburg, 1890), Vladimirskii tsentral (Vladimir Central, 1783), and Butyrka (Moscow, 1771). According to the estimate of the oldest human rights organization, Center for the Assistance of Criminal Justice Reform (www.prison.org), every fourth adult man in contemporary Russia has had some prison experience.

See also: corrective labour institutions; crime; GULag; human rights organizations; prison system, Soviet and post-Soviet

ELENA OZNOBKINA

prison system, Soviet and post-Soviet

According to experts, Russia incarcerated more people during the twentieth century than any other country, and one-quarter of adult Russian men have spent time behind bars. Without question, the prison system has figured importantly in Russian society and culture, sometimes being viewed as a microcosm of life outside the barbed wire.

The contemporary Russian prison system has its roots in the vast network of prisons and camps of the Stalinist period. Millions of Soviet citizens were arrested for belonging to suspect categories (political, religious, economic, etc.), as well as for 'economic crimes', such as damaging factory equipment. In prison many were subjected to psychological and physical torture, deprived of food and sleep, and held in overcrowded, poorly ventilated cells with primitive facilities for personal hygiene. Trials were based on fabricated confessions, and many were sentenced by 'special commissions' without trial. Prison sentences ranged from five to twenty-five years. Camp inmates, known as *zeks* (from the abbreviation 'z/k' (for *zakliuchennyi*, prisoner), used for prisoners working on the White Sea Canal in the 1930s), were forced to perform heavy labour in inhumane conditions, working in mines, construction, agriculture, and logging. Death rates were high, especially in the Far North.

A well-organized criminal underworld, which originated in the tsarist period, flourished under

Stalin. Its members, called *blatnye*, separated themselves from and preyed upon the other prisoners. The *blatnye* were ruled by *vory v zakone* (thieves in law), and were bound together by *vorovskoi zakon* (thieves' law), a complex set of oral rules whose violation was punishable by death. Criminals developed their own jargon, called *fenia*, and used tattoos to display personal information. Believing that criminals were socially closer to the regime than were political prisoners, the Stalinist government gave them the more privileged positions in the camps, and allowed them to victimize the weaker and poorly organized 'politicals'.

After Stalin's death, millions of prisoners were released, and many of the economically unprofitable camps were closed. Measures were also taken to control the *blatnye*, who had become extremely powerful. Nonetheless, the basic structure of the prison system remained intact. Most inmates served their sentences in labour camps; prisons were used primarily for pre-trial detention and as a disciplinary measure. Living conditions were little better than in the Stalinist period, and human rights abuses were common.

During the Stalinist period, information about conditions in the prison system was suppressed; its disclosure could lead to arrest. Only after Khrushchev's 'secret speech' in 1956 was limited public discourse possible. This climate of semi-openness, called the Thaw, ended when the government returned to more conservative policies under Brezhnev. But now the regime found it more difficult to stifle the voices of human rights advocates. These dissidents publicized the proceedings of illegally conducted trials, such as that of poet Iosif Brodskii, and protested against inhumane prison conditions. Some sentences were even commuted owing to the international pressure they solicited. In response, numerous dissidents were falsely diagnosed with mental diseases and confined to the MVD's (Ministry of Internal Affairs) newly-created 'special psychiatric hospitals', where many were tortured with drugs and shock therapy.

In the late 1980s, during Gorbachev's reforms, the Soviet government took the first steps to bring the prison system in line with international standards, including releasing most political prisoners. The Russian Federation has continued this process by passing legislation to make the system more humane, and by affirming rehabilitation as its primary objective. Important changes include transferring the prison system from the MVD (the police) to the Ministry of Justice, and permitting public monitoring of prisons. The success of the latter measure is illustrated by the continued existence of NGOs such as 'Moscow Center for Prison Reform', which publishes detailed information about Russian prisons.

Nevertheless, prison conditions have deteriorated since the collapse of the Soviet Union. With crime rates soaring, Russia has approximately one million people behind bars, making it second only to the United States in its rate of incarceration. One-fifth of those inmates are serving sentences for violent crimes such as murder, and one-quarter for banditry, robbery, or rape. Approximately one-third of prisoners are under 25. Prisoners are held in 191 pre-detention facilities, 731 labour colonies, and 63 educational colonies for minors.

Because the financially strapped government has been unable to provide adequate prison facilities or necessary services, inmates suffer from severe overcrowding, food shortages, poor nutrition, and inadequate health care and sanitation. In 2002, 98,000 prisoners had tuberculosis (including drug-resistant strains), and 36,000 prisoners were HIV-positive. Human rights violations are common, as prisoners, particularly pre-trial detainees, are beaten and even tortured to extract confessions. Many of the approximately 20 per cent of prisoners held in remand prisons, often for up to two years before trial, live in deplorable conditions. Housed in group cells, inmates have had as little as 5 square feet of living space apiece and have had to sleep in shifts; some have died from asphyxia. Recent amnesties, increasing recourse to probation, and the decreased usage of prisons to hold those under criminal investigation have improved conditions somewhat.

The criminal underworld has undergone significant changes since the Stalinist period. The new *tiuremnyi zakon*, or 'prison law', replaced 'thieves' law' in the 1960s, and applies to all prisoners, not just the *blatnye*. Moreover, the *blatnye* now oversee and maintain order for the entire prison population, and constitute a rival authority to the administration. Violence is still common, especially towards lower castes of the prison hierarchy, such as the 'untouchables', who have seriously violated the 'prison law'. However, violence is worse among juvenile prisoners than adults.

See also: Brezhnev, Leonid; Brodskii, Iosef; corrective labour institutions; Gorbachev, Mikhail; GULag; Krushchev, Nikita; perestroika and glasnost; Solzhenitsyn, Aleksandr; Stagnation; Thaw

Further reading

Applebaum, A. (2003) *Gulag: A History*, New York: Doubleday.
Kalinin, V. (2002) 'The Russian Penal System: Past, Present and Future', Lecture at King's College, University of London.
Moscow Center for Prison Reform. www.prison.org.
Oleinik, A. (2003) *Organized Crime, Prison and Post-Soviet Societies*, trans. S. Curtis, Burlington: Ashgate.
Rossi, J. (1989) *The Gulag Handbook*, trans. W. A. Burhans, New York: Paragon House.
Varoli, J. (1999) 'Crime and Punishment', *Russian Life* 42, 6: 37–47.

LAURA KLINE

private property

Private property was forbidden in the Soviet Union from 1917 until 1993. In March 1930, in his article *Golovokruzhenie ot uspekhov* ('Dizzy with Success') Stalin published a rather short list of property and animals a peasant could own without danger of expropriation. In fact, this list remained an informal guaranteed list of so-called *lichnaia sobstvennost* (personal property) tolerated by the state. Even before 1917, the notion of private property was not well developed in Russia. Collective ownership and management of property were favoured among Russian peasants in their collective, the *mir* (world; peace). Aggressive animosity towards individual ownership, paradoxically, was combined with distrust towards the state, which usurped the right to punish for property crimes

in both the pre- and post-Revolutionary eras. Thus, after the collapse of the Soviet Union, all former state-owned property was subject to mass plunder. The first fifteen years of post-Soviet Russia did not increase the assurance that private property has become one of the principles of the new Russian state. That is why the wealthiest private proprietors since 1990s generally invested in countries with a longer tradition of private property than their own.

See also: black market; collective farm; economic system, post-Soviet; economic system, Soviet; money; oligarkh; privatization; shortages; underground economy

GASAN GUSEJNOV

privatization

Privatization is the process of transferring property from the state to private owners. In 1993, the Yeltsin administration began privatizing the vast majority of state-owned enterprises, although the state would remain a shareholder in many. Privatization was a key policy for converting the country from a centrally planned to a market-oriented economy as a way of making the stagnant economy more efficient and productive, thereby stimulating growth. It happened rapidly, in a process sometimes called shock therapy.

The first phase, called voucher privatization, involved issuing vouchers to enterprise managers, employees, and private citizens, which gave them ownership rights in enterprises. The process was managed by Anatolii Chubais, who headed the State Property Commission. The intent was to redistribute ownership into private hands. The enterprises, however, received no new capital in the process. By 1994, nearly 20,000 enterprises had been privatized, including most smaller and medium-sized firms. Over 40 million citizens owned stock, and more than 60 per cent of the labour force was employed in the private sector. At the time, many considered the privatization programme successful.

However, many former state enterprise directors adopted the form of privatization that allowed the majority of shares to be distributed to them and their workers. Additionally, many senior managers bought large percentages of shares very cheaply and eventually became the primary owners of their enterprises, and then stripped the firms of assets to enrich themselves. Enterprises often became destitute and virtually incapable of producing anything of value, or, at best, operated as they had before privatization. Overall, the results of privatization's first stage turned out to be less successful than originally thought.

In mid-1994, the second phase of privatization began, with the objective of attracting capital to the newly privatized enterprises by selling shares at auctions. However, the openness and honesty of the auction process were highly questionable. Ownership of most formerly state-owned enterprises ended up in the hands of senior enterprise managers, well-connected government officials, and the infamous oligarchs, who became extremely wealthy in the process.

The low point of the privatization period occurred during the reelection campaign of President Yeltsin in 1996. Many wealthy oligarchs supported Yeltsin by infusing much-needed money into the government's coffers in the infamous loans-for-shares scheme. When the government defaulted on the loans, triggering the country's financial crash in August 1998, these oligarchs took ownership of many of the country's prized enterprises at a fraction of their true value.

While privatization began with good intentions, the process was grossly distorted, resulting in ownership of key industries concentrated in a small group of enormously wealthy oligarchs. Many other enterprises were controlled by managers from the Communist period, even though they were not necessarily majority owners. These conditions persisted throughout the 1990s and early 2000s, underscoring the need for good corporate governance. In 2004, President Putin commissioned a key government agency to reexamine privatization and rectify the abuses of the previous decade.

See also: Chubais, Anatolii; corporate governance; economic system, post-Soviet; oligarkh; Putin, Vladimir; shock therapy; voucher; Yeltsin, Boris

Further reading

Blasi, J., Kroumova, M., and Kruse, D. (1997) *Kremlin Capitalism: Privatizing the Russian Economy*, Ithaca, NY: Cornell University Press.
Goldman, M. (2003) *The Piratization of Russia*, New York: Routledge.

DANIEL J. MCCARTHY AND SHEILA M. PUFFER

Prokhanov, Aleksandr Andreevich

b. 26 February 1938, Tbilisi, Georgian SSR

Writer

Between 1960 and 1970 Prokhanov worked for the newspaper *Pravda*; at the end of the 1960s he worked as a foreign correspondent for *Literaturnaia gazeta*, reporting from Afghanistan, Nicaragua, Cambodia, Angola, Ethiopia and other 'hot spots'. In his novels and pamphlets, Prokhanov combines critique of American technology and the American way of life with the cult of the Soviet era as a path towards the global establishment of Russia's imperial power; he has denounced perestroika as a conspiracy for the destruction of the Soviet empire. Prokhanov writes apocalyptic political 'fantasy' works and edits the radical-reactionary newspaper *Zavtra* (Tomorrow), in which extreme right-wing ideology blends with the extreme left. His literary style combines elements of early Soviet kitsch with elements of modern Russian pop culture (*popsa*); his work often features conspiracy theories.

See also: *Literaturnaia gazeta* (Literary Gazette); nationalism ('the national question'); perestroika and glasnost; popsa; *Pravda*

GASAN GUSEJNOV

Prokofiev, Sergei Sergeevich

b. 11 [23] April 1891, Sontsovka, Ukraine; d. 5 March 1953, Moscow

Composer, pianist

One of the most important, popular, and influential Russian composers of the twentieth century, Prokofiev spent the first part (1891–1918) of his career in pre-revolutionary Russia, the second (1918–36) mainly in Europe and America, and the third (1936–53) back in the USSR. This unusually cosmopolitan life, with countless appearances as virtuoso pianist in major musical capitals, helped to win his music wide international appeal. Soon after his controversial return to Moscow in 1936, however, Prokofiev fell under suspicion for his foreign connections and alleged 'formalism'. In 1948, he (along with Shostakovich and other prominent composers) came under the Communist Party's attack for ideological and aesthetic shortcomings. Sickness, privation, and the arrest and imprisonment of his foreign-born first wife blighted his last years. Ironically, he died the same day as Iosif Stalin.

A prolific and highly disciplined composer who worked with many distinguished collaborators (Sergei Diagilev, Sergei Kussevitskii, Vsevolod Meierkhold, Sergei Eisenstein, Galina Ulanova, Mstislav Rostropovich, Sviatoslav Rikhter), Prokofiev produced more than 130 works in a wide variety of genres: dramatic music (eight operas, eight ballets, incidental music for theatre), eight film scores, music for symphonic orchestra (seven symphonies, simfoniettas, concertos, suites, overtures, symphonic poems, divertissements), music for solo and chamber ensemble, vocal and vocal-symphonic music (oratorios, cantatas, choruses, songs), and music for solo piano (nine sonatas and numerous major cycles).

Although Prokofiev received his education at the St. Petersburg Conservatory at the height of the modernist movement, his own relationship to modernism was inconsistent. In early works, such as the operas *Liubov k trem apelsinam (Love for Three Oranges)* and *Igrok (The Gambler)* and the *Piano Concerto No. 2*, Prokofiev boldly challenged traditional concepts of form and harmonic and tonal language. In his early years, the Russian musical establishment denounced him as an impudent Futurist. Yet Parisian critics often found his music too traditional, and regarded his stubborn interest in opera as reactionary. By the early 1930s, on the eve of his return to Russia, Prokofiev was retreating to what he called a 'New Simplicity'. Central to this style was melody, as the ballet *Romeo i Dzhuletta (Romeo*

and Juliet) and the *Violin Concerto No. 2*, both composed in 1935, demonstrate.

A complex, immensely talented and contradictory personality with an odd sense of humour and a notable lack of diplomatic skills, Prokofiev, after returning to the USSR, produced numerous large nationalistic works, including the opera *Voina i mir (War and Peace)*, and scores for the epic historical films *Aleksandr Nevskii* and *Ivan Groznyi (Ivan the Terrible)*. Yet perhaps Prokofiev's most beloved scores are the playful, sardonic *Symphony No. 1* ('Classical'), completed during the turmoil of the Bolshevik Revolution, and *Petia i volk (Peter and the Wolf)*, a *Symphonic Fairy Tale for Children*, written in 1936 for the Moscow Children's Musical Theatre.

See also: ballet, Soviet; opera, Soviet; Rikhter, Sviatoslav; Rostropovich, Mstislav; Shostakovich, Dmitrii; Ulanova, Galina

Further reading

Prokofiev, S. (1998) *Selected Letters of Sergei Prokofiev*, ed. and trans. H. Robinson, Boston, MA: Northeastern University Press.
——(2002) *Dnevnik 1907–1918, Dnevnik 1919–1933 (Diary 1907–1918, Diary 1919–1933)*, Paris: SPRKFV.
Robinson, H. (2002) *Sergei Prokofiev: A Biography*, Boston, MA: Northeastern University Press.

HARLOW ROBINSON

propaganda, Soviet and post-Soviet

In the USSR, propaganda was understood as a 'profound explication of the doctrine of Marx-Engels-Lenin-Stalin' (e.g., *Politicheskii slovar*. Moscow: Gospolitizdat, 1940, p. 453). Propaganda was declared an instrument of educational work and a 'matter of life and death' for the Party, since it 'armed' the wider popular masses with the foremost ideological weapons. The need to propagate Marxism-Leninism was asserted in different editions of the Communist Party programme. Each level of Party hierarchy had its own department of propaganda and mass agitation, from the Central Committee to local party organizations. At the early stage of development of Soviet power, propaganda occurred alongside other public educational programmes (such as the 'liquidation of illiteracy', the teaching of Russian to the non-Russian population of the Soviet Union, and the like), and was strongly supported by the state's tools of repression. Towards the end of the 1930s, the Soviet Union championed new techniques of propaganda, aimed at the gradual elimination (in targeted segments of the population) of critical introspection and the ability to take individual social or political decisions. The Communist Party took almost full control of mass media by securing a presence in all newspapers, radio stations, and publishing houses.

Until the 1930s, this propaganda was founded on the idea of a world revolution and the future success of the Soviet Union. As Stalin's power strengthened and he became an authoritarian leader, the central theme took the shape of a narrative of heroism, and a focus on the past replaced its original focus on the future. The appeal to the heroic deeds of the fathers and grandfathers became increasingly important in the process of manipulating public consciousness. Until the beginning of the Thaw (mid-1950s), propaganda activities were accompanied by repressions, which ensured that popular resistance remained low. After a decree on Party propaganda released by the Central Committee on 14 November 1938 in connection with the publication of *A Short Course on the History of the Communist Party*, the main content of Soviet propaganda until the end of the Soviet era comprised the history of the Communist Party and the USSR, which was narrated teleologically.

After World War II (1941–45), the Soviet victory became the major propaganda event in the history of the USSR, and was used to legitimate all difficulties, old and new, faced by the Soviet Union. Another change dating to 1945 was increasing nationalism of Communist propaganda. Indeed, from the 1960s onward, non-Russian regions of the Soviet Union embraced a nationalist rather than Communist ideology.

Thereafter, propaganda presented whatever situation obtained in the country as the best possible achievement or result thanks to the efforts of Party and government. Moreover, the original aim of propaganda was continuously deferred to the indefinite future. In 1961, for example, Soviet propaganda set the date for the successful 'construction of Communism' at 1980. By the end of the 1970s, the Central Committee proclaimed that the Soviet Union was entering a 'historically long-lasting period of developed socialism'. The actual abandonment of the Communist Party's original goals, effectively admitted by this time, turned official propaganda into a source of mass apathy and object of public ridicule: for example, the Olympic Games, which took place in Moscow in the 1980s, were said to have replaced the Communism promised in 1961. At the same time, the vast resources allocated to propaganda maintained and even raised the influence of the propaganda apparatus within the Party and government leadership. 'Propaganda bureaus' now mushroomed also in the so-called 'creative unions' of writers, film-makers, composers, etc. However, the greater the investment in the propaganda machinery, the less effectively it worked. Mikhail Gorbachev, from 1985–91, set new propaganda goals (perestroika, glasnost, democratization), notwithstanding the fact that, once realized in practice, these slogans undermined the original principle of propaganda – the control of public opinion.

Toward the end of the 1980s, Moscow's weakness as the centre of the Soviet Union was used, especially in the former republics of Central Asia and the Caucasus, to call for 'sovereignty' and secession from the empire. In post-Soviet Russia, under Boris Yeltsin's leadership (1991–99), and even more evidently under President Vladimir Putin (2000–), some core methods of Soviet propaganda continue to be implemented (such as the heroic narrative, including a new rewriting of history). The propaganda arsenal has also been expanded, to include such means as ads, and relies on so-called 'political technologists'. By contrast to the propagandists of the Soviet period, such technologists operate with a narrative of threats. The function of repression in the older Soviet propaganda model has been replaced by a description of threats that the population allegedly would have to face should it distrust the currently ruling elite. Long-term political goals have ceded to appeals to a nostalgia for elements of the Soviet past and hopes for Russia's return to superpower status. However, to date, the presence of alternative sources of information, as well as the openness of Russian borders for people and ideas, the absence of a fully controlled system of state repression, and the presence of influential competitors in this field have prevented a renewed indoctrination of the Russian population. Communist propaganda proper has retained some importance for a marginal layer of Russian citizens, which include some Russian youth movements.

See also: censorship; Communist ideology; Communist Party; Communist Youth League; cult of personality; democratic reform movement; developed socialism; dissident; ideological education, Soviet; journalism; perestroika and glasnost; political structure, Soviet; political structure, post-Soviet; *samizdat*; Scientific Communism; Stalin, Iosif; Stagnation; *Short Course*; World War II (Great Patriotic War)

Further reading

Bittman, L. (ed.) (1988) *The New Image-makers: Soviet Propaganda and Disinformation Today*, Washington, DC: Pergamon-Brassey's International Defense Publishers.

Ebon, M. (1987) *The Soviet Propaganda Machine*, New York: McGraw-Hill.

Gorsuch, A. E. (2000) *Youth in Revolutionary Russia: Enthusiasts, Bohemians, Delinquent*, Bloomington, IN: Indiana University Press.

Leighton, M. K. (1991) *Soviet Propaganda as a Foreign Policy Tool*, New York: Freedom House.

Wilson, A. (2005) *Virtual Politics: Faking Democracy in the Post-Soviet World*, New Haven, CT: Yale University Press.

GASAN GUSEJNOV

propiska

A residence permit indicating mandatory government permission to reside at a particular address and stamped in one's internal passport. This practice, traceable to the tsarist regime, was abolished in 1917 but reinstated by Stalin in 1932 as a form of administrative control. It effectively tied individuals to their place of residence and made voluntary geographic mobility extremely difficult. A propiska was necessary to apply for a job, to get married, and to receive medical care and social benefits. In post-Soviet Russia this practice has been challenged as unconstitutional, but it nevertheless persists, albeit in a slightly different form. The propiska is now called 'registration', purportedly mere notification of one's address to the authorities. This registration, however, can amount to permission, as it can be difficult to obtain, particularly in Moscow. There the registration (still commonly called 'propiska') remains in force partially to stem mass movement to the capital. The registration process takes places through the building management and the local police office.

See also: passport

ALYA GUSEVA

Proshkin, Aleksandr Anatolievich

b. 25 March 1940, Leningrad

Director

After graduating from the Leningrad Institute for Theatre, Music, and Cinema, Proshkin became Head of the Central Television Department for Literary and Drama Programmes. In 1968–78 he directed over thirty television biopics – plays representing great figures in Russian culture and science (for example, *Mikhailo Lomonosov*, 1985). Since 1987 he has been a director of feature films at Mosfilm studio. His debut, *Kholodnoe leto 1953 goda* (*The Cold Summer of 1953*, 1987) and, more recently, an adaptation of Pushkin's account of the Pugachev rebellion (*Kapitanskaia dochka* [*The Captain's Daughter*], 1999) explore pivotal moments in Russian history. National Artist of Russia (1989).

VLADIMIR STRUKOV

Protestantism

Protestantism describes a diverse set of Christian groups with theological frameworks distinct from Orthodoxy or Catholicism, including Baptists, Evangelicals, Lutherans, Pentecostals, and Jehovah's Witnesses. While some groups have a short history in Russia, others have a presence dating back several centuries.

Bolsheviks originally treated Protestants mildly, but in 1929 introduced new restrictions on all religious groups. Especially problematic for Protestant groups was the stipulation against religious education of children, and numerous arrests of ministers occurred in subsequent years. After Stalin's death, many religious prisoners were released (1953–57), but harsher governmental opposition to religion under Khrushchev led to arrests and church closures after 1960. Restrictions loosened during perestroika and glasnost. In 1990, all religious organizations were given legal standing.

The 1997 law on Freedom of Conscience and on Religious Associations affected some Protestant groups. It distinguishes between religious organizations and religious groups, requiring confirmation that a group has practised in Russia for at least fifteen years before it may qualify as a religious organization. Religious groups are restricted in missionary activity, including the publication and distribution of literature.

Following the collapse of the Soviet Union, the relationship between Protestantism and Russian Orthodoxy sometimes has been problematic. The chief sources of conflict between the Protestants and Russian Orthodoxy involve proselytism of individuals baptized in the Orthodox Church and of those considered traditionally Orthodox. Fear that some foreign missionaries take advantage of Russia's depressed economy, using money to purchase converts to their faiths, further fosters resentment.

See also: Khrushchev, Nikita; perestroika and glasnost

Further reading

Elliott, M. and Corrado, S. (1999) 'The 1997 Russian Law on Religion: the Impact on Protestants', *Religion, State and Society*, 27, 1: 109–34.
Ramet, S. P. (ed.) (1992) *Protestantism and Politics in Eastern Europe and Russia: The Communist and Post-Communist Eras*, Durham, NC: Duke University Press.

JENNIFER B. BARRETT

proverbs (*poslovitsy*)

A particularly rich Russian folk genre, proverbs (*poslovitsy*) are still encountered frequently and are considered a major aspect of Russians' cultural knowledge: According to Permiakov (1989), 'Every adult Russian language speaker . . . knows no fewer than 800 proverbs, proverbial expressions, popular literary quotations and other forms of clichés'.

Though definitions vary, the Russian proverb is usually a short, grammatically complete sentence that offers advice, usually moral, or a general statement about the world. It often has an internal rhythmic pattern, though rhyme is not always present. Proverbs usually are expressed as two parallel elements, as in 'The quieter you go, the farther you'll get' (*Tishe edesh, dalshe budesh*) or 'No sooner said than done' (*Skazano – sdelano*).

Proverbs impart a folksy flavour to the language, though some come from sources other than the peasantry, such as merchant life or the Bible. Russian proverbs may be variants of Western forms, such as 'Where there's smoke, there's fire' (*Dyma bez ognia ne byvaet*), or render an identical message through unfamiliar analogy, as in 'The first *blin* (pancake) comes out as a lump' (*Pervyi blin komom*), a version of 'if at first you don't succeed, try, try again'. On the other hand, some proverbs may have no analogies in Western European traditions.

Proverbs can describe realia precisely and succinctly. For example, the Russian equivalent of the English warning against 'bringing coals to Newcastle', 'Don't carry your *samovar* to Tula' (*V Tulu so svoim samovarom ne ezdiat*), conveys Tula's hallmark industry as effectively as the English proverb describes Britain's coal centre.

Use of proverbs as wisdom and as part of riddling speech also occurs folk tales. Expressions such as 'the morning is wiser than the evening' (*Utro vechera mudrenee*) and 'speedily a tale is spun, with less speed a deed is done' (*Skoro skazka skazyvaetsia, da ne skoro delo delaetsia*) are both part of the tale structure and independent proverbs.

See also: folk tales

Further reading

Dal, V. (1999) *Poslovitsy russkogo naroda*, Moscow: Olma-Press.

Mertvago, P. (1998) *Dictionary of Russian Proverbs*, New York: Hippocrene.

Permiakov, G. L. (1989) 'On the Question of a Russian Paremiological Minimum', trans. K. J. McKenna, *Proverbium* 6: 91.

DAVID J. GALLOWAY

Provincial Russia

Forty-nine provinces, along with *gubernii*, were introduced in Russia in the first quarter of the eighteenth century in the aftermath of Peter the Great's reforms. Provinces as an administrative division were subsequently terminated and became a pejorative term for a form of sub-culture reflecting regional characteristics of mainstream cultural development. Geographically, politically, and culturally the term relies on the existence of a centre and a periphery; the uneven relationship between the two results in the interpretation of provincial culture as secondary and conservative. In modern usage, *provintsiia* usually implies a type of culture specific to small towns and villages of Central Russia, whereas *glubinka* refers to remote, often isolated and inaccessible areas of the north of the country and the Far East. Provincialism can be generalized as a designating obstinate cultural philistinism.

Three periods in the history of assertion and perception of provincial Russia in the twentieth century can be distinguished: industrial (1930–50); social (1960–80); and cultural (1990–present). All three reflect the impact of Soviet ideology and the State doctrine on the society regarding its geopolitical location

First, industrialization and collectivization radically changed the mode of life of peasants – the bulk of the people in the provinces, who came to towns primarily in search of work. Second, as the Soviet interpretation of Marxist theory emphasized homogenizing social life in the country, the State elaborated programmes intended to benefit local communities. Contrary to that intention, these plans resulted in depopulation, degradation, and the disappearance of villages and small towns. Finally, economic and social changes in post-Soviet Russia corroded viability in the provinces. The gap between the centre and periphery appeared unbridgeable, leading the former to view the latter almost as an alien land with an exotic culture. It was then that the notion of 'Moscow for Muscovites' was coined, thus isolating local communities and making cultural exchange problematic. There have been attempts to revitalize provincial Russia: for example, from the 1960s to the 1980s the State Planning Committee directed university graduates to work in small towns.

Provintsiia and *glubinka* have been objects of academic and governmental study since the eighteenth century, for their role was recognized for military, political and cultural reasons. Traditionally, the political process in the Russian regions is widely portrayed as irremediably corrupt and authoritarian.

From the 1950s to the 1980s, provincial life became the focus of so-called village prose, which became an influential movement in Russian literature and cinema. It reconsidered and redefined provincial life, with an emphasis on Russian traditional peasant culture or the culture of ethnic minorities. In the 1990s and the early twenty-first century, interest in *glubinka* revived. Contemporary cinema, for example, depicts it as the locus of national identity and the embodiment of spirituality.

See also: ethnic minorities; Far East; Far North; Red Belt; Solzhenitsyn, Aleksandr; village prose

VLADIMIR STRUKOV

publication and republication, perestroika

When Mikhail Gorbachev became General Secretary of the Communist Party of the Soviet Union (1985), he was determined to reform Soviet society from above, to make it economically more efficient and politically more accountable. In this cause, he enlisted the liberal intelligentsia for greater openness (glasnost) that would lead to 'democratization'. Among the first signs of this 'literary spring' was the publication of first-wave émigrés Vladimir Nabokov, Evgenii Zamiatin, and Vladislav Khodasevich, to whom the Soviet reader had had no previous official exposure. Much of Anna Akhmatova's poetry had already been published, but her major work, *Rekviem* (*Requiem*), appeared only in 1987; similarly, Andrei Platonov had been known to the Soviet reading public as essentially a writer of witty short stories, but his major novels *Kotlovan* (*The Foundation Pit*) and *Chevengur* were published only in 1987 and 1988 respectively, thus immediately necessitating a reappraisal of his place and significance. Banned works by accepted Soviet writers, such as Iurii Trifonov, Aleksandr Bek, Anatolii Rybakov, Andrei Bitov, Fazil Iskander, Vladimir Dudintsev, and many others, were also a feature of the cultural regeneration of 1986–88. Whereas it could have been possible in these years to argue that this new cultural 'thaw' was simply redressing the cultural balance, and restoring to Russians their cultural heritage, there were more subversive offerings about to be unleashed. In 1988 Boris Pasternak's *Doktor Zhivago* was published, as was Vasilii Grossman's *Zhizn i sudba* (*Life and Fate*), two works that challenged the very political and moral legitimacy of the Soviet state (Grossman had been told at the time of the 'arrest' of his manuscript in 1961 that this novel would not be published for 'two or three hundred years'). An even more outspokenly dangerous work, Grossman's *Vse techet* (*Forever Flowing*), was published in 1989, as were works by implacable ideological enemies such as Aleksandr Solzhenitsyn: *Arkhipelag GULag* (*The Gulag Archipelago*) was published in 1990, and works by other writers thrust into exile by the previous generation of Soviet authorities, such as Vladimir Voinovich, Georgii Vladimov, and Vasilii Aksenov, were also now freely available on bookshelves and in libraries. The role and courage of literary editors, such as Sergei Zalygin in *Novyi mir*, and Grigorii Baklanov at *Znamia*, were crucial in revitalizing literary life, and it was also in these journals that the works of younger writers also appeared, including Evgenii Popov and Sergei Kaledin. By 1990 the publication free-for-all had integrated Soviet literature's past and present, and brought émigrés back into the communal fold. Previously sacrilegious foreign works, such as Orwell's *Animal*

Farm and *1984*, had also been published. By the end of 1991 the Soviet Union had collapsed, and it is difficult to avoid the conclusion that Gorbachev's desire for greater openness had opened the floodgates for previously forbidden ideas, and that literature, as ever in Russia, had played a key role in the evolution and dissemination of free ideas, through which the rulers were challenged by the ruled, and found wanting.

See also: Akhmatova, Anna; Aksenov, Vasilii; Bitov, Andrei; censorship; Communist Party; Dudintsev, Vladimir; Gorbachev, Mikhail; Grossman, Vasilii; Iskander, Fazil; journalism; literature, émigré; literature, perestroika; Nabokov, Vladimir; *Novyi mir*; Pasternak, Boris; perestroika and glasnost; periodicals, Soviet; Rybakov, Anatolii; Solzhenitsyn, Aleksandr; thick journals; Trifonov, Iurii; Vladimov, Georgii; Voinovich, Vladimir

Further reading

Brown, D. (1993) *The Last Years of Soviet Russian Literature: Prose Fiction, 1975–1991*, Cambridge: Cambridge University Press.

Shneidman, N. (1995) *Russian Literature 1988–1994: The End of an Era*, Toronto: University of Toronto Press.

DAVID GILLESPIE

publishing houses, Soviet and post-Soviet

On 21 May 1919 the Communist Party's Central Committee created the first state publishing company, *Gosizdat* (State Publishing). During the 1920s, publishing houses mushroomed: *Moskovskii rabochii* (Moscow Worker) produced propaganda literature, *Molodaia gvardiia* (Young Guard) published books for adolescents, and *Zemlia i fabrika* (Land and Factory) issued fiction and poetry. In 1924 the central publishing house, *Tsentralnoe izdatelstvo*, was established to publish literature in other Soviet languages; at the same time, the children's section of *Gosizdat* was founded in Leningrad. A 1928 Central Committee decree on mass literature pressured publishers to issue more socialist propaganda. During World War II, 40 per cent of all published books were devoted to war and patriotic literature; most were issued by the military publishing house, Voennizdat. New publishing houses proliferated during the 1950s and 1960s, and in the 1960s-70s the prominent publisher Mirovaia literatura (World Literature) released 200 volumes of world literature. Other famous Soviet publishing houses included the literary publishing house Sovetskii pisatel (Soviet Writer), propaganda-producing *Progress, Iskusstvo* (Art), *Nauka* (Science), *Detskaia literatura* (Children's Literature), *Sovetskaia entsiklopediia* (Soviet Encyclopedia), and *Prosveshchenie* (Education). In 1971 some four million items were printed daily in forty-two foreign languages. All published materials were censored; in the late 1980s Glavlit employed some 70,000 censors.

The post-Soviet era witnessed the collapse of the state publishing structure and the emergence of many private publishing houses. Today, many scientific and scholarly books are published by *Nauka, Akademicheskaia kniga* (Academic Book) and *Pleiada* (Pleiades). The successful publishing house *Vagrius* deals in memoirs, foreign fiction, science fiction, and contemporary popular Russian literature by such authors as Viktor Pelevin, Vladimir Makanin, and Liudmila Petrushevskaia. One in five books in Russia is published by the group *AST*, founded in 1990. It produces 800 new books every month, including reference books, fiction, children's literature, fantasy and science fiction, maps, textbooks, art, and business management. Some publishers, including *Moskovskii izdatelskii dom* (Moscow Publishing House, founded 1995), specialize in reprinted literature, as well as history and art books.

See also: censorship; Communist Party; economic system, post-Soviet; economic system, Soviet; Glavlit; Makanin, Vladimir; Pelevin, Viktor; Petrushevskaia, Liudmila; propaganda, Soviet and post-Soviet

Further reading

Bushnell, K. (2001) *Russian Publishing, 2000–2001: Threats to Freedom of Information, But a Record Year for Books: A Report to the 2001 Summer Slavic Librarian's Workshop*, Evanston, IL: Northwestern University Press.
Gorokhoff, B. (2001) *Publishing in the USSR*, Bloomington, IN: Indianapolis University Press.
Kelly, C. (2001) *Refining Russia: Advice Literature, Polite Culture and Gender From Catherine to Yeltsin*, Oxford: Oxford University Press.

ALEXANDRA SMITH

Puchkov, Dmitrii Iurevich

See Goblin

Pugacheva, Alla Borisovna

b. 15 April 1949, Moscow

Singer, composer, producer

Alla Pugacheva is one of the great superstars of Soviet and post-Soviet pop culture; she has maintained phenomenal popularity for over three decades. Her performing style is characterized by theatricality, a combination of comedic and dramatic elements, a blend of tradition and innovation, and constant experimentation with various musical genres.

Pugacheva first achieved broad critical recognition and popularity with her hit *Arlekino* (1975), about a clown who entertains the public while hiding his tears, and she has cultivated a clownish stage persona based on her unruly red hair, extravagant costumes, exuberant energy, and self-mockery. Pugacheva sings about love, hope, and loneliness, with both sentimentality and humour, and combines high and low culture, often using lyrics based on poems by classical poets such as William Shakespeare or Boris Pasternak.

During the post-Soviet era, Pugacheva has continued her artistic experimentation, creating musical pastiches and interweaving jazz with stylized folk tunes, disco with nineteenth-century lyrical love songs, and comic musical vignettes. Her stage persona and private life, with her pop star daughter, Kristina Orbakaite, and (now dissolved) marriage to the singer Filipp Kirkorov, constantly attract media attention.

See also: Kirkorov, Filipp; popular music, post-Soviet; popular music, Soviet

OLGA PARTAN

Pushkin, Aleksandr Sergeevich

b. 26 May [6 June] 1799; d. 29 January [10 February] 1837

Poet, prose writer, historian

Born into an ancient *boyar* (noble) family, Pushkin's maternal great-grandfather was the African Abram Gannibal, baptized as Peter the Great's godson. Pushkin published his first poem at the age of 14, while still a student at the lyceum in Tsarskoe Selo outside of Petersburg. When still in his twenties, Pushkin was recognized as the national poet of Russia. In the course of his career, he wrote important works in virtually every literary genre of the day, increasingly turning to prose fiction and history as he grew older. His sharp wit, irreverence, and political volatility, all of which found expression in his poetry and epigrams, earned him exile (1821–25) and vexed relations with the tsarist authorities to the end of his life. Pushkin was killed in a duel over his wife's honour with the French émigré officer Georges d'Anthès. His major works include the 'novel in verse' *Eugene Onegin*, the play *Boris Godunov*, the narrative poem *The Bronze Horseman* (*Mednyi vsadnik*), the short story *The Queen of Spades* (*Pikovaia dama*) and his one completed (historical) prose novel, *The Captain's Daughter* (*Kapitanskaia dochka*).

It would be difficult to overestimate the importance of the Pushkin cult in Russia to the present day. That cult, which took impetus from the poet's dramatic, premature death, reached its apotheosis in the nineteenth century in Fedor Dostoevskii's 'Pushkin Speech' at the unveiling of the Pushkin monument in central Moscow (1880). Dostoevskii hailed Pushkin as the 'universal man'. Recognizing the political potency of the Pushkin myth, the tsarist government coopted the 1899 centennial of the poet's birth as a source of imperial legitimacy. Throughout the Soviet period, the figure of Pushkin was claimed both by disaffected intellectuals and by the Soviet government. The centenary

commemoration of Pushkin's death by the Stalinist government in 1937, at the height of the purges, with celebrations of Pushkin extending to the farthest and most remote reaches of the Soviet empire, marked the culmination of the Soviet establishment's appropriation of the pre-revolutionary Russian artistic heritage. Despite the exploitation of Pushkin by the Soviet cultural authorities, throughout the Soviet period, writers challenged the 'official' Pushkin. At the 84th anniversary of Pushkin's death commemorated at the House of Writers in Petrograd on 14 February 1921, the poet Vladislav Khodasevich, with gloomy foresight, pronounced Pushkin the 'name [by which] we are to hail one another in the darkness that is descending upon us'. Among the most memorable 'dissonant' literary treatments of Pushkin and the Pushkin cult, none of which could be published in the Soviet Union until the late-glasnost period, are Daniil Kharms's 'Pushkin and Gogol', Andrei Bitov's *Pushkin House*, and Andrei Siniavskii's *Strolls with Pushkin*. The resilience of the Pushkin cult even in the wake of regime change was demonstrated by the government's support for the celebration of the bicentennial of Pushkin's birth (1999). References to Pushkin continue to saturate even burgeoning contemporary popular culture, and the post-Soviet period has witnessed notable interest in unorthodox revisions of the poet, particularly with regard to his African ancestry.

See also: Bitov, Andrei; Siniavskii, Andrei; Stalin, Iosif; unions, creative, Soviet

Further reading

Bitov, A. (1987) *Pushkin House*, New York: Farrar, Straus, and Giroux.

Levitt, M. (1989) *Russian Literary Politics and the Pushkin Celebration of 1880* Ithaca, NY: Cornell University Press.

Nepomnyashchy, C. T., Trigos, L. and Svobodny, N. (eds) (2006) '*Under the Sky of My Africa': Alexander Pushkin and Blackness*, Evanston, IL: Northwestern University Press.

Sandler, S. (2004) *Commemorating Pushkin: Russia's Myth of a National Poet*, Stanford, CA: Stanford University Press.

Sinyavsky, A. (A. Tertz) (1993) *Strolls with Push-kin*, New Haven, CT: Yale University Press.

CATHARINE NEPOMNYASHCHY

Pushkin State Museum of Fine Arts

The Pushkin Fine Arts Museum in Moscow, dedicated to Western art, boasts a vast collection ranging from Roman antiquities to Impressionist and Modernist canvases. The museum was founded by Ivan V. Tsvetaev, Professor of Art History at Moscow University. Its elegant classical building, following a design by Moscow architect Roman I. Klein, opened in 1912 as the Alexander III Museum of Fine Art. After Moscow became the Soviet capital in 1918, the museum acquired works confiscated from private collections and in 1937 was renamed the Pushkin State Museum of Fine Arts. Its most significant holdings came from the Rumiantsev Museum; the superb S. I. Shchukin and A. I. Morozov collections of French Impressionist and post-Impressionist paintings; officially expropriated works from the Hermitage; and private gifts from such Western artists as Marc Chagall, Henri Matisse, and Rockwell Kent. The Pushkin Museum acquired its international reputation during détente with a series of news-making blockbuster exhibitions, enhanced in 1991 by the revelation of the Soviet repositories of war booty. More recently, the Pushkin has entered into a long-term partnership with the Museum of Fine Arts in Houston.

See also: Hermitage; Moscow State University

TATIANA SENKEVITCH

putevka

Official certificate issued to a person who is sent to an institution such as a sanatorium, house of rest, pioneer camp, educational course, or a construction site. In the USSR trade unions were in charge of issuing *putevki* to employees at the workplace for trips to sanatoriums and houses of rest; priority was given to workers in leading branches of industry, Stakhanovites,

industrial innovators, handicapped veterans of World War II and labour, family members of those killed defending the Motherland, and families with many children. Eighty per cent of workers received government-supported *putevki* free of charge, or paid only 30 per cent of their cost. Komsomol *putevki* were special assignments for young people sent to work at economically important locations, such as construction sites. Today the word *putevka* is used by tourist agencies to define vacation packages (for example, a *putevka* to Turkey).

See also: Communist Youth League; Stakhanovism; vacations, Soviet and post-Soviet; World War II (Great Patriotic War)

ELENA OMELCHENKO

Putin, Vladimir Vladimirovich

b. 1 October 1952, Leningrad

Russian president

Vladimir Putin was appointed Prime Minister of Russia in August 1999, became Acting President when Boris Yeltsin resigned in December 1999, and was elected to the Russian Presidency in 2000 with over 50 per cent of the popular vote. He was re-elected in March 2004.

In 1975, Putin joined the Committee for State Security's (KGB) foreign intelligence unit. After resigning from the KGB in 1991, Putin held several positions in St. Petersburg's government. In August 1996, Putin was called to Moscow to work under President Yeltsin. In July 1998, he was appointed director of the Russian Federal Security Service (FSB) and in March 1999, Putin became secretary of the Russian Security Council while keeping his post of FSB director.

Putin has extraordinary authority, partly from the constitution and from enabling legislation, but also from his close ties with the secret police. His career background in the security services has provided him with networks and additional resources for exerting his power. Putin centralized authority through the appointment of presidential envoys charged with overseeing the regional governors. Beginning in 2005, the president of the Russian Federation nominates regional executive-branch heads and regional legislatures approve the nominations. Direct elections of regional executive-branch heads were replaced with a system under which regional legislatures confirm candidates who are nominated by the president. Incumbent republic presidents and oblast governors must request reconfirmation by Russia's national president.

Putin also enjoys cooperative relations with the Duma, first under the coalition government and, after the 2004 elections, under United Russia's majority control of the Duma. Putin prosecuted oligarchs, the wealthy entrepreneurs who took control of Russian businesses during the privatization of state-owned property.

Vladimir Putin enjoys enormous popularity, but the presidential election of 2004, which he won with over 70 per cent of the popular vote, cannot be described as free and fair. The media, particularly television, were extremely biased toward Putin and gave him largely uncritical coverage while limiting coverage of his challengers. It was also alleged that directors of state enterprises and institutions put pressure upon their employees to vote for Putin. In addition, corruption throughout society remains a serious obstacle in Russia's goal of reaching its economic potential.

With regard to foreign policy, the overall goals of Putin's government are to enhance Russia's security, defensive capability, and international trade relations, and to maintain Russia's status and influence in the world arena. Although Putin actively participated in the international anti-terrorism coalition, he has pursued 'multi-polarity' in his foreign policy; his goal being to counterbalance the exceptional international power of the United States by fostering relations between Russia and many other countries. A high priority of Russia's foreign policy is to maintain influence and control in the territory of the former USSR. Under Putin, Russian security forces invaded Chechnia in 1999, after a previous campaign under Yeltsin beginning in 1994; this protracted and continuing conflict represents a challenge to Russian territorial integrity and security.

See also: Duma; Federal Security Service (FSS/FSB); oligarkh; War, Chechen; Yeltsin, Boris

Further reading

Jack, A. (2004) *Inside Putin's Russia*, Oxford: Oxford University Press.

Shevtsova, L. (2003) *Putin's Russia*, rev. edn, Washington, DC: Carnegie Endowment for International Peace.

VICKI L. HESLI AND JAMES KRUEGER

Q

queue (*ochered*)

Spending considerable time standing in queues defined everyday life for an overwhelming majority of Soviet citizens. Visible short-term lines (for food, clothes, toilet paper) combined with invisible long-term lines (for an apartment, furniture, car, books). Waiting in queues evoked the contradictory emotions of equality and inequality, unity and competition. The Soviet elite was excused from lines. War veterans, invalids, and mothers with more than two children (called 'mother-heroines') enjoyed the privilege of being served without lines or in separate ones. Huge lines to pay tribute to Lenin in the mausoleum or to pass packages to imprisoned relatives emphasized the ubiquity of the Soviet queue.

See also: Lenin Mausoleum; mother-heroine; shortages

IRINA MAKOVEEVA

R

Rabin, Oskar Iakovlevich

b. 2 January 1928, Moscow

Artist

A leader of Soviet nonconformist artists, Rabin was educated for two years at the Riga Academy of Arts and for a few months at Moscow's Surikov Institute. He owed his principal artistic formation to Evgenii Kropivnitskii, whose daughter Valentina Kropivnitskaia he married in 1950. Their family formed the centre of the so-called Lianozovo School outside Moscow. From 1965, Rabin organized nonconformist exhibitions in Moscow, including the 1974 Bulldozer Exhibition. His paintings, including *Passport* (1972), have been described as 'socially engaged' and 'expressionist'. Stripped of Soviet citizenship in 1978, Rabin has continued in Paris to develop his distinctive, darkly lyrical approach to everyday objects.

See also: art, nonconformist; Bulldozer Exhibition; Lianozovo School

ANN KOMAROMI

radio, post-Soviet

The end of censorship announced in the Russian Media Law (1991) and the start of market reforms gave birth to new developments in Russian radio. The first independent radio station *Ekho Moskvy* (Echo of Moscow), founded in August 1990, symbolized for many Russians a truly democratic trend in broadcasting. It was established by the Moscow City Council (*Mossovet*), the Moscow State University School of Journalism, and *Ogonek* magazine; financial sponsorship was provided by the conglomerate *Media Most* and since 2001 majority-owned by the state gas company Gazprom. In August 1991, *Ekho Moskvy* was the only source of real news about the coup in Moscow. Today *Ekho Moskvy* remains the only public (not state) news-based radio station and the only independent station among all national electronic media after the closure of all national independent television stations.

The largest state company, *Radio Rossii* (Radio Russia), was established in December 1990 as a branch of VGTRK (*Vserossiiskaia gosudarstvennaia teleradioveshchatelnaia kompaniia*, the All-Russian State Television and Radio Broadcasting Company) and broadcasts 24 hours a day on radio channel 1 (on long, medium, and ultra-short waves). In the 1990s, new independent stations began to appear in medium and FM waves, such as the first women's radio station, *Nadezhda*, which closed in 2000, *Avtoradio* (Auto Radio), *Radio Retro*, *Radio Retro FM*, *Love Radio*, and others, as well as many regional stations. Some of them were joint ventures – the Russian-French *Nostalgie*, *M-radio*, *Serebrianyi dozhd* (Silver Rain), and *Evropa Plus*; the Russian-American *Radio Maximum*, *Radio 7 na semi kholmakh* (Radio 7 on [Moscow's] Seven Hills), and some religious stations. Since the state did not strictly monitor the radio market for some time, it developed at a rapid pace.

After the economic crisis of 1998, the radio market became increasingly monopolistic. In 1998 President Yeltsin signed a special decree to unite the technical complex of state electronic media; this action was followed by the establishment of a state system that included all national television and radio companies and their regional branches. Since then Russian radio listeners can hear stations that are mainly either state-owned or owned by major conglomerates. In the 1990s, Media Most took over several stations, including *Ekho Moskvy* and *RDV* (*Radio Delovaia Volna*), *Otkrytoe radio* (Open Radio), *Sport FM*, *Do-radio*, and *Ekho Sankt-Peterburga* (Echo of St. Petersburg), which after Gusinskii's departure abroad fell under the control of Gazprom.

The largest conglomerate today is *Russkaia Media Gruppa* (Russian Media Group), which received a state prize in science and technology in 2001 for establishing a national broadcasting system. It owns the most popular commercial stations, *Russkoe radio* (Russian Radio), *Monte Carlo*, *Dinamit* (Dynamite) FM, *Russkoe Radio-2*, and the information agency *Russkaia sluzhba novostei* (Russian News Service). Private conglomerates created strong networks. *Russkoe radio* broadcasts in 800 cities in Russia and the CIS, and in six American cities; *Evropa Plus* reaches 300 Russian cities. New media holdings began to appear in large cities with developed media structures: St. Petersburg, Nizhnii Novgorod, Samara, Krasnoiarsk, Tiumen, Ekaterinburg, and others. Small enterprises such as the above-mentioned *Nadezhda* failed, however. Small private companies appeared in many cities and towns and they concentrate mostly on local news. In the early 1990s, the growth in the number of radio stations led to some decline in quality. At many news stations the professionalism of live discussions and even the language of broadcasters worsened.

Currently, more than 1,300 radio stations broadcast in Russia, both state-owned and private. The most popular, according to recent polls, are *Radio Rossii*, *Russkoe Radio*, *Maiak*, *Evropa Plus*, *Ianson*, *Radio 7 na semi kholmakh*, *Ekho Moskvy*, and *Avtoradio*. The state-owned stations *Radio Rossii* and *Maiak*, and the private stations *Russkoe Radio* and *Evropa Plus*, have the largest audiences.

The more or less liberal character of the radio market in Russia is due to the relatively small influence of advertisement strategies in comparison with advertisers' influence on television. Nationally in 1997, it had only 11 per cent of airtime allocated for advertisements, 16 per cent in 2001. Since 1991 many newly established radio stations prefer to broadcast Western music and entertainment programmes. Whereas in the early 1990s the only Russian-oriented station was radio *Nadezhda*, today many stations favour Russian music (*Russkoe Radio*, *Radio Shanson* [Chanson], *Troika*, *Retro*, *Nashe Radio* [Our Radio], etc.). *Evropa Plus* has started special jazz programmes. Many stations broadcast live talk shows, game shows, and serious discussions. The most interesting analytical programmes are featured on *Ekho Moskvy* and *Maiak 24*, featuring interviews with politicians and world leaders, as well as special programmes handled by prominent analysts, journalists, and writers. Russian audiences still listen to the foreign-produced Russian Radio Liberty and Russian BBC, which use Russian journalists and focus on Russian events.

The Russian radio audience is wide and varied. Three-quarters of Moscow residents listen to radio regularly, 15 per cent more than in 1994. Men listen to two–five stations daily, women to two–three. Prime time is 8.30–10.00 a.m., 12.00–4.30 p.m., and 6.00–7.30 p.m. Generally both men and women listen to news, sports, politics, arts broadcasting, and talk shows. Some 97 per cent of the regional audience listen to national and regional radio programmes, and 77 per cent are satisfied with the content of radio stations. The quality of radio programmes has improved during recent years. Since 1997 many stations also broadcast their programmes on the Internet.

See also: censorship; Ekaterinburg; *Ekho Moskvy* (Echo of Moscow); journalism; journalists, post-Soviet; Maiak; Nizhnii Novgorod (Gorkii); *Ogonek*; radio, Soviet

Further reading

Sherel, A. (2004) *Audiokultura 20-go veka*, Moscow: Progress-traditsiia.

(2003) *Spravochnik po televideniiu, radio i pechati v Rossii*, Moscow: Izdanie Maksimova.

Zasurskii, A. N. (2005) *Teleradioefir. Istoriia i sovremennost*, Moscow: Aspekt Press.

NADEZHDA AZHGIKHINA

radio, Soviet

In 1995, Russia celebrated the centenary of radio, first developed by Aleksandr Popov. With the Revolution the radio quickly became a useful propaganda tool, with the first famous radio appeal transmitted to audiences in 1917: the programme, *Vsem! Vsem!* (To All! To All!), created by Vladimir Lenin, broadcast the first Soviet decrees. The first radio stations started in Moscow in 1921; by 1923, there were approximately 300 stations in Russia. Regular radio broadcasting from Moscow started in 1924, and radio stations were established in Minsk (Belarus), Novosibirsk, Astrakhan, Kharkov (Ukraine) and other cities as well. New radio stations appeared in the regions, and beginning in 1927 they all had to pass censorship before going on the air. As part of the state propaganda system, Soviet radio promoted Party decisions and blamed enemies of the nation.

Starting in 1922, Moscow stations began broadcasting abroad in many languages and by 1929, the government foreign broadcasting service, Inoveshchanie, had become one of the Soviet state's most important propaganda tools. By 1930, radio had developed throughout much of the Soviet Union, including Ukraine, Caucasus, Turkmenia, Moldova, and Central Asia, and after 1933, State radio was available to Siberia and the Far East. In 1940, the USSR had 5 million radio points (*radiotochki*). There were three main channels on the standard radio.

World War II provided a new impetus to radio journalism. Established in June 1941, *Sovinformburo* was the central information resource. At the same time, thousands of journalists went to the front to cover developments and write human interest stories and many radio journalists perished in the war. Radio also provided the troops with the opportunity to listen to famous performers and songs, and to send their regards home; more than 5000 families were reunited because of such announcements. Radio also engaged in a propaganda war with Germany: since many German radio stations worked in occupied Soviet territory, appealing to Soviet citizens, Soviet propaganda countered with its own programmes, sending Soviet propaganda to Germans as well. Soviet radio provided critical moral support for Soviet soldiers during the war, and most of the country's famous writers and artists worked for radio programmes and supported the war effort. Thus, World War II is considered the Golden Age of Soviet radio. Wartime radio achievements are commemorated on Radio Day, first celebrated on 7 May 1995, two days short of the 50th anniversary of Soviet victory in the war.

New post-war programmes were dedicated to rural youth, international affairs, socialist competition, and other topics. After Stalin's death, such new programmes as 'Iunost' (Youth) began to appear. The founding of the *Maiak* station (whose theme song, *Podmoskovnye vechera* [Moscow Nights], was named the longest-lasting radio broadcasting theme in the *Guinness Book of World Records*) provided a breath of fresh air to Soviet listeners.

After the war, the national Soviet radio system (*Vsesoiuznoe radio*) consisted of several channels: Channel 1 transmitted state news and some culture programmes. Channel 2, *Maiak*, provided 24 hours of news and music programming. At first, Channel 3, devoted to literature and music, reached only the Moscow region, but in 1982 it became accessible in the Far East and Siberia. Channel 4, which broadcast music, was established in 1972. Channel 5 was addressed to foreigners and the Russian diaspora. Soviet radio broadcast important programmes for children and youth, full-length theatrical and opera productions, and educational programming.

While playing a critical role in transmitting Soviet propaganda, Soviet radio also presented the work of bright and talented writers, broadcasters, and musicians to a wide audience. Even under strict censorship, Soviet radio had high standards of professionalism. Though many Soviet radio professionals left the USSR, a substantial number currently work in new Russian media.

See also: censorship; journalism; Maiak; propaganda, Soviet and post-Soviet

NADEZHDA AZHGIKHINA

radio theatre

Radio theatre is an art form developed for on-air broadcasting. Radio theatre adaptations require special devices, techniques, and superb acting in order to replace visual support in listeners' perceptions. In the Soviet Union, the first radio theatre production was released in 1925 (*Vecher u Marii Volkonskoi* [A Night at Mariia Volkonskaia's], directed by Nikolai Volkonskii, and devoted to the Decembrist uprising of 1825). Prior to the television era, radio in the Soviet Union was the only medium available to wide audiences. Radio drama adaptations could reach every citizen living on the vast territories of the USSR, who never had the opportunity to attend theatres located in major cities. Literary-dramatic broadcasts propagated classical works of world, Russian, and Soviet literature, developed the imagination, and served as a perfect tool of enlightenment. However, the selection of a work or an author for every production was strictly censored.

Radio theatre achieved its highest popularity in the 1940s and 1950s, and continued to be in great demand until the end of the 1980s. The best Soviet actors were invited to record radio theatre plays: Oleg Efremov, Mikhail Ulianov, Evgenii Vesnik, Iia Savvina, Oleg Tabakov, Oleg Borisov, Iurii Iakovlev, Innokentii Smoktunovskii, and Faina Ranevskaia. The professional lives of countless Soviet actors were dramatically extended through radio: for example, Maria Babanova, who played the roles of children and adolescents in her late seventies. Educational radio programmes for children were also designed in the form of radio plays, including *V strane literaturnykh geroev* (In the Land of Literary Heroes), *Radioniania* (Radio Nanny), and *Klub znamenitykh kapitanov* (The Club of Famous Sea Captains). Generations of Soviet citizens grew up listening to the programme *Teatr u mikrofona* (Theatre at the Microphone), which introduced them to classics of world literature. These programmes were broadcast on the waves of the all-union first radio channel, available in every corner of the country, with no additional equipment needed. Veterans of radio theatre in the Soviet Union were Roza Ioffe and Liia Velednitskaia, who directed dozens of productions.

After the collapse of the Soviet Union, radio theatre as a genre almost disappeared. New radio stations started working in live broadcasting, and could not afford to allocate lengthy, uninterrupted spans of time to theatre dramatizations. Yet in recent years several radio stations throughout Russia have made attempts to resurrect the traditions of literary-dramatic broadcasting (*Kultura*, Russia, *Ekho Moskvy*). In 2005, radio *Kultura* recorded Mikhail Lermontov's play *Maskarad*, whose success was guaranteed by the superb work of the actors of Petr Fomenko's renowned theatre, and announced an annual international competition for the best radio play. Though it is unlikely that radio theatre will regain its popularity with wide audiences, archival recordings from the *Gosteleradiofond Rossii* (State TV and Radio Fund of Russia) are now released commercially in various audio formats.

See also: Borisov, Oleg; Efremov, Oleg; *Ekho Moskvy* (Echo of Moscow); Fomenko, Petr; Iakovlev, Iurii; radio, post-Soviet; radio, Soviet; Ranevskaia, Faina; Savvina, Iia; Smoktunovskii, Innokentii; Tabakov, Oleg; Ulianov, Mikhail; Vesnik, Evgenii

Further reading

Gleizer, M. (1990) *Radio i televidenie v SSSR: daty i fakty, 1917–1986*, Moscow: Iskusstvo.
Gurevich, P. and Ruzhnikov, V. (1976) *Sovetskoe radioveshchanie: stranitsy istorii*, Moscow: Iskusstvo.

TATIANA SMORODINSKAYA

Radzinskii, Edvard Stanislavovich

b. September 23, 1936, Moscow

Playwright, historian, television personality

From the 1960s to the 1990s, Radzinskii wrote many of the best Russian plays. His *104 stranitsy o liubvi* (*104 Pages about Love*, 1964) and *Snimaetsia kino* (*A Film Is Being Made*, 1965) explored the romanticism of youth and the weaknesses of the Soviet intellectual. Historical works, such as *Besedy s Sokratom* (*Conversations with Socrates*, 1975) and *Teatr vremen Nerona i Seneki* (*Theatre in the Time of Nero and Seneca*, 1986), probed the effect of state power on the individual. Radzinskii's popular biographies of

Nicholas II (Russia's last tsar), Stalin, and Rasputin were bestsellers in the United States in the 1990s, and his Russian telecasts based on them earned high ratings.

See also: drama, Soviet; television, Soviet

JOHN FREEDMAN

Raikin, Arkadii Isaakovich

b. 10 [24] October 1911, Riga, Latvia;
d. 17 December 1987, Moscow

Actor, comedian, director

A legendary film and comedy theatre performer, Raikin is widely recognized as the father of modern Russian stand-up comedy. He began his career as an actor in Leningrad's *Teatr miniatiur* (Theatre of Miniatures), of which he later became artistic director; the theatre moved in 1982 to Moscow and in 1987 became *Teatr Satirikon imeni A. Raikina* (the Raikin Satirikon Theatre). Raikin was famous for bittersweet, often philosophical, sometimes didactic social commentary. By combining pantomime, dance, verse, and parodic sketches, he created a repertoire of comedic masks and lines that have become part of the Russian vernacular, including his famous coinage *avoska* (from the word '*avos*' ['maybe I'll be in luck'], used for a net shopping bag). In the 1960s and 1970s he worked closely with Mikhail Zhvanetskii. Raikin also starred in many Soviet films, including his 1974 project, *Liudi i manekeny (People and Manequins)*, which he directed.

See also: avos/avoska; comedians; Satyricon Theatre; stand-up comedy; theatre, Soviet; Zhvanetskii, Mikhail

OLGA MESROPOVA

Raikin, Konstantin Arkadievich

b. 8 July 1950, Leningrad

Actor, director

Son of Arkadii Raikin, Konstantin Raikin is a prominent theatre performer and director, and

film actor. He began his acting career in 1971 at the Sovremennik (Contemporary) Theatre. In 1981 he joined his father's comedy theatre (renamed the Satyricon in 1987), and became its artistic director in 1988, introducing innovative approaches to acting and directing. Raikin is known for staging avant-garde repertoire, including Roman Viktiuk's famous work *Sluzhanki* (The Servant Girls) and several plays by Robert Sturua. Among Raikin's best-known film roles are *Mnogo shuma iz nichego (Much Ado About Nothing*, 1971), *Truffaldino iz Bergamo (Truffaldino from Bergamo*, 1976), and *Oshibka Puaro (Poirot's Mistake*, 2001). His famous theatrical roles include Richard III. The recipient of many Soviet and post-Soviet awards (including *Zolotaia maska*, the Golden Mask), in 2001 Raikin became an instructor at the Moscow Art Theatre (MKhAT). He is also a member of the Russian President's Council on Culture and Art.

See also: Moscow Art Theatre; Raikin, Arkadii; Satyricon Theatre; Sovremennik Theatre; Sturua, Robert; Viktiuk, Roman

OLGA MESROPOVA

railroads

Railroads traditionally served as Russia's primary means of communication and transportation. The first railways were built by and for the mining and metallurgical industries in the 1760s in the Urals. The first Russian steam locomotives were built by the Cherepanovs, father and son, serf mechanics at Demidov's factories. The St. Petersburg–Tsarskoe Selo Railroad inaugurated the public railway system in 1837. The next major project, the St. Petersburg–Moscow line, completed in 1851, was then the world's longest (650 km) two-gauge railroad, followed by the world's longest railroad, the Trans-Siberian (7,000 km), built in 1891–1901. Rapid construction of railways in the nineteenth and early twentieth centuries was reflected in literary works (Nekrasov, Blok) and folk songs.

In Soviet times, railroad construction was a primary industrial enterprise, involving both volunteers and GULag convicts. The greatest Soviet project was BAM (Baikalo-Amurskaia

Magistral [Baikal-Amur Railroad], 3,145 km), completed in 1991. The Soviet Ministry of Railroads was a kind of state within the state, operating a wide network of towns, hospitals, schools, shops, etc. The railroad, its attributes (station, locomotive, carriage, etc.) and employees (trackman, conductor) appear in many popular songs, books, and movies. The occupation of engineer was one of the most prestigious in the Soviet professional hierarchy. Vera Panova's popular post-war book, *Sputniki* (*The Train*), describes the story of a hospital train during World War II. In the post-Soviet era, railroads (total length 87,157 km) continue to be the main means of transportation, with 80 per cent of cargo and 40 per cent of passenger transport.

Further reading

Haywood, R. (1969) *The Beginnings of Railway Development in Russia in the Reign of Nicholas I, 1835–42*, Durham, NC: Duke University Press.

Tupper, H. (1965) *To the Great Ocean: Siberia and the Trans-Siberian Railway*, Boston, MA: Little, Brown & Company.

Westwood, J. (1964) *A History of Russian Railways*, London: George Allen and Unwin.

ALEXANDER LEDENEV

Ranevskaia, Faina Grigorevna (Georgievna)

(née Feldman)

b. 27 August [9 September] 1896, Taganrog; d. 19 August 1984, Moscow

Actress

Despite performing few major roles in cinema or theatre, where she rarely stayed in one troupe for long, Ranevskaia is acknowledged as one of Russia's great actresses. She debuted in the provinces in 1915, moving to Moscow in 1931. Asked late in life why she had changed theatres so often, she replied, 'I was seeking art.' Asked if she had found it, she quipped, 'Yes, in the Tretiakov Gallery'. She played classic comic film roles in *Pyshka* (*Boule de suif*, 1934), *Svadba*

(*The Wedding*, 1944), and *Vesna* (*Spring*, 1947). Her witty, caustic and bluntly honest diaries became bestsellers and made her a folk heroine when published in the 1990s.

See also: theatre, Soviet; Tretiakov Gallery

JOHN FREEDMAN

Rasputin, Valentin Grigorevich

b. 15 March 1937, Ust-Uda, Irkutsk oblast, Russia

Writer, journalist, and environmental activist

Rasputin was born in a Siberian village, and his worldview and writings strongly reflect his origins. Although he started out as a journalist, Rasputin broke into the literary world in 1967 with his novella *Dengi dlia Marii* (*Money for Maria*). Three more works quickly followed: *Poslednii srok* (*Borrowed Time*) in 1970; *Zhivi i pomni* (*Live and Remember*) in 1974; and *Proshchanie s Materoi* (*Farewell to Matyora*) in 1976. These four stories documented the hardships of Siberian village life and established Rasputin as one of the best writers of Village Prose. Published in 1985, the novella *Pozhar* (*The Fire*) is a sequel to *Proshchanie s Materoi*. In the mid-1980s, Rasputin began writing polemical articles supporting nationalist causes and conservative politics.

Rasputin is well known for his efforts on behalf of the environment, especially Lake Baikal. Some of his essays on Siberian culture, environment, and history were collected, translated, and published in 1996 as *Siberia, Siberia*.

See also: Baikal; Siberia; village prose

ERIKA HABER

rassol

The brine obtained in the process of *solenie*, the quintessential Russian method of making vegetable and mushroom preserves that should not be confused with marinating. Marinating relies on the use of vinegar, which conserves the product, but at the same time 'kills' it, accounting for the eternal shelf life and uniformity of taste in all marinated products. In contrast, *solenie* represents the process of natural fermentation moderated with salt, which releases the unique taste of a given product, often enhanced with spices (the basic ones are garlic and dill; optional ones include leaves of cherry, horseradish, currant, oak, etc.). The most common *rassols* are cucumber brine and sauerkraut juice. They have numerous culinary uses, being an essential ingredient in such traditional soups as *shchi, rassolnik*, and *solianka*, while also enjoying notoriety as one of Russia's favourite hangover remedies. In the United States, genuine cucumber brine can be found in Jewish deli sections (kosher pickles that contain no preservatives and have to be kept refrigerated).

See also: appetizers; soups

DAN UNGURIANU

RATI

See Russian Academy of Theatre Arts

recording studios

European recording labels prevailed in early twentieth-century Russia. As early as 1903, German companies such as Gramophone and Zonophone owned factories in Riga, which produced records for the Russian market, and the German label Metropol Records owned the April Factory (*Aprelevskaia fabrika*) near Moscow. A British company, also called Gramophone, produced records in Russia under the label *Pishushchii Amur* (Recording Amor), and in 1907 the French-owned Pathé Bros. opened a factory in Moscow.

During World War I, the April Factory (1911–17) produced records for the Russian-owned gramophone society RAOG. Other Russian-owned labels were V. I. Rebikov and Company (*Tovarishchestvo V. I. Rebikov I K°*, 1903–

4) and *Zvukopis* (1911), which issued recordings of the 10-year-old Yasha Heifetz.

Early recordings ranged from gypsy romances to such early twentieth-century opera stars as Fedor Shaliapin (whose first recording in 1902 was with British Gramophone). Writers such as Lev Tolstoi, Leonid Andreev, and others recorded their literary works as early as 1909.

Later known as GDRZ (*Gosudarstvennyi Dom Radioveshchaniiai zvukozapisi* [State House of Radio and Sound Recording]), *Dom Zvukozapisi* (DZ, House of Recording) was founded in 1938 as a centre for radio and gramophone recordings; it released millions of records after the war. Largely confined to works of folk and Soviet songs and classical music, these recordings downplayed popular and classical Western genres and performances, but during the 1950s private groups undertook the unofficial production of Western-influenced music.

Vsesoiuznaia studiia gramzapisi firmy Melodiia (All-Union Studio of the Record Company Melodiia, founded in 1958) encompassed six factories and nine recording studios in several major cities and issued over 150 million records and 12 million cassettes a year. *Melodiia*'s reign ended with the imminent disintegration of the Soviet Union in 1989, to be replaced by its major spin-off, *Russkii Disk*, and numerous new companies. A number of Russian CD recordings have been remastered by Western companies such as Naxos, which also releases new classical Russian recordings. The production of classical CDs by Russian performers in the West far outweighs the production of popular music, which is largely a domestic enterprise.

See also: April Factory (Aprelevskaia fabrika); House of Recordings (Dom zvukozapisi)

OLGA ZASLAVSKY

Red Belt (Krasnyi poias)

The Red Belt (*Krasnyi poias*) is a sociological term that reflects a phenomenon within the Russian electoral system in relation to its geographical distribution. It covers a substantial portion of Central Russia (including the Briansk, Tula, and

Kursk oblasts, to name a few) that was controlled by the Communist Party and hard-line conservatives. The term first appeared after the presidential elections of 1996, when the Communist Party and its leader, Gennadii Ziuganov, won the majority of votes in these regions, as economically they suffered most during Yeltsin's reforms. After a series of aggressive anti-Communist political campaigns, the Red Belt had almost completely disappeared by 1999.

See also: Communist Party; political system, post-Soviet; Yeltsin, Boris; Ziuganov, Gennadii

VLADIMIR STRUKOV

Red Book/Red List (*krasnaia kniga*)

Krasnaia kniga is a list of plants and animals that are either rare or facing extinction. It contains biological descriptions and data regarding distribution, reasons for the decline in numbers, and extinction of particular species. Data collection began in 1949 by The International Union for the Conservation of Nature and Natural Resources (IUCN). The Soviet Red Book was established in the USSR in 1974, and later had its republic-specific versions set up. The Russian Red Book includes anything under threat of disappearance, such as collapsing fortresses, types of fish, and so forth. It is now officially called the IUCN Red List of Threatened Species.

See also: environment

SVETLANA TITKOVA

Red Square (Krasnaia ploshchad)

Although Red Square no longer is the venue for Soviet military parades and demonstrations, its expansive space retains vivid emblems of its layered history. The square was established at the end of the fifteenth century, after Ivan III ordered the demolition of wooden structures outside the Kremlin walls to prevent the tsar's residence within from catching fire. A central market began to form in their place and function

for some time. With the construction of St. Basil's Cathedral, the square continued to function as a market, but also became a place for celebrating church festivals, issuing governmental pronouncements, and accommodating public gatherings.

Moscow's emergence as the capital of a unitary state under Ivan IV (the Terrible) prompted the tsar to erect St. Basil's Cathedral (*Khram Vasiliia Blazhennogo*, 1555–61; official name: Cathedral of the Intercession of the Virgin 'on the Moat' [*Pokrovskii sobor, chto na rvu*]) to commemorate his victory over the Tatar stronghold of Kazan, thereby endowing the cathedral with civic as well as religious significance. Its extravagant decorative exterior of variegated floral designs and bright spiralling onion domes, dating from the seventeenth and eighteenth centuries, masks a far more restrained and disciplined scheme, which focuses on the uniform grouping of eight small, domed chapels around a larger, taller central church surmounted by a small dome resting on an attenuated tent form. This organization is generally assumed to be without precedent and to derive from various numerological associations with Ivan IV's victory at Kazan. Perhaps the cathedral's most striking feature is its small chapels, with so little room to accommodate worshippers that, on special feast days, services were held outdoors on Red Square, using St. Basil's as an outdoor altar. Religious processions staged in the Kremlin's Cathedral Square proceed onto and through columns of worshippers on Red Square, pausing in front of St. Basil's.

The appearance of Red Square changed perceptibly at the end of the nineteenth century with the construction of the Historical Museum and the Upper Retail Arcade, today's fabled GUM. Erected on the site of the former Land Office, the Historical Museum (1875–81) was designed by artist and ardent Slavophile Vladimir Sherwood. His intricate red-brick building, employing an assortment of traditional Muscovite motifs in affirmation of the emerging neo-Russian style, was matched by an interior lavishly decorated with ornate details and an impressive ceiling painting depicting a family tree of all the Russian monarchs from Vladimir and Olga of Kiev to Alexander III, who opened the museum in 1893. Between 1986 and 1997 the museum was closed and underwent a massive restoration programme, with its spires again topped by gilded double eagles dating from tsarist times.

The Upper Retail Arcades *Verkhnie torgovye riady* (1890–93); since Soviet times known as GUM (*Gosudarstvennyi universalnyi magazin*, or State Department Store) were built immediately after the Historical Museum on a site opposite the Kremlin that long had been Moscow's busiest market. The building, erected by the architect Aleksandr N. Pomerantsev in a Victorianized neo-Russian style, was the largest and most fashionable department store when it opened in 1893. Its design evinced a singular fusion of the venerable Paris arcades and the fashionable Parisian *magasin*, with expansive shopping windows opening out onto the pavements of major shopping thoroughfares – in this case, Red Square. The elegant interior comprised three parallel shopping arcades, along which rows of more than thousand shops were spread out on two storeys. Circulation occurred along the cantilevered concrete galleries and connecting bridges overlooking the galleries. Daylight flooded into the arcades through continuous steel-framed, glazed barrel-vaults designed by Russia's leading engineer, Vladimir Zhukov. The building marked the first use of steel and ferroconcrete in Russia.

After the 1917 Revolution, the Upper Retail Arcades complex was nationalized and renamed GUM. Retail activity continued there until 1928, when it was taken over for use by a succession of Soviet administrative entities. The building was restored in 1953 to its original function, though its use was mired in stodgy, ineffectual Soviet retail practices. Since 1991, the complex has been radically transformed into an extravagant shopping mecca, with exclusive foreign shops and designer boutiques filling the resplendent arcades, thus bolstering the conversion of Red Square and its environs into a showcase of fashion and commerce.

The recent reconstructions of the long-demolished Kazan Cathedral (*Kazanskii sobor*, 1636, demolished 1936, reconstructed 1990–93) and Resurrection Gate (*Voskresenskie vorota*, sixteenth century; demolished 1931, reconstructed 1994–95) on their original sites in the northeast corner of the square reflect a concerted effort by Moscow mayor Iurii Luzhkov to reaffirm the innately Muscovite character of Red Square from the seventeenth century and to restore that identity, which had been obliterated by the Stalinist regime. The original Cathedral was built in 1636 in honour of the Kazan Icon of the Kazan Mother of God and to commemorate Tsar Mikhail Romanov's victory over the Poles and Lithuanians in 1612. The original Resurrection Gate was the main entry gate into the trade district Kitai-Gorod and the Tsars' ceremonial entrance to Red Square. Its attached Iberian Chapel, housing the legendary miracle-working Icon of the Mother of God of Iberia (*Iver*), was one of the holiest places in Moscow. Despite the religious and civic importance of both structures, they were torn down by the Stalinist regime as part of its offensive against the Orthodox Church. The Resurrection Gate's chapel was dismantled in the 1920s and replaced by a modern sculpture of a worker as 'the new socialist gatekeeper'. The entire gate was dismantled in 1931 on Stalin's orders, to allow tanks access to the parades on Red Square. The Kazan Cathedral was torn down by the Stalinist regime in 1936, and various structures were erected on the site, including a street café and a public toilet.

With the appearance of the Lenin Mausoleum, the Revolution acquired its ultimate symbol. Red Square was transformed into a site associated preeminently with the revolution, becoming the Soviet Union's principal parade ground for mounting major military parades and demonstrations on major Soviet holidays.

Immediately following Lenin's death in January 1924, Aleksei Shchusev designed a temporary wooden mausoleum, rendered as a bold but simple cube, then a larger mausoleum, still built of wood but this time forming an elaborate stepped ziggurat from whose summit Party officials could gather and make speeches on important Soviet holidays. In 1929, Shchusev replaced the wooden structure with a stone replica, reducing the earlier stepped ziggurat form to a stark mass faced with red granite (signifying Communism) and black labradorite (signifying mourning) and bearing the simple inscription 'Lenin' over its bronze doors. After Stalin's death in 1953, his embalmed body was placed on display alongside Lenin's, but was removed in 1961 on Khrushchev's orders and buried by the Kremlin wall alongside various other important Party functionaries.

Once revered as a veritable cathedral of Soviet socialism, since 1991 the Lenin Mausoleum has become one of Moscow's more curious tourist attractions. Locals tend to regard it either as an awkward reminder of the country's Communist past or as a cherished relic of the good old days, while visitors view it with bewildered fascination. The once-lengthy lines snaking around the square for admission have dropped off considerably. Gone are the honour guards who originally flanked the entrance. A visit today is accompanied by a rather bizarre sense of having entered a place that time forgot. The preserved Lenin, or a facsimile, attired in a snappy pin-striped suit, still lies in the crystal casket, seemingly unaffected by the vast changes that have swept over Russia, transforming the emblem of his once seemingly invincible domain into a site furiously venerating the once-condemned capitalist commodity fetish.

See also: Kremlin (Moscow); Khrushchev, Nikita; Lenin, Vladimir Ilich; Luzhkov, Iurii; Moscow; Russian Orthodoxy; Russian Orthodox churches; Stalin, Iosif

ANATOLE SENKEVITCH

reference

See: kharakteristika

refuseniks (otkazniki)

Soviet citizens wishing to emigrate whom the KGB refused permission to leave the country. For approximately two decades (early 1970s until the late 1980s), several thousand people, from famous dissidents openly defending their rights, to masses of unknowns, lived in limbo. They lost their jobs and risked jail or exile to Siberia. Thanks to international pressure, human rights activist Anatolii Sharanskii was eventually released and flown out of the country. Concert pianist Vladimir Feltsman, who

was not allowed to tour or make recordings during the most productive years of his career, later emigrated. Thousands of professionals who became refuseniks had to work as janitors and caretakers under fictitious names in order to survive.

See also: anti-Semitism; dissident; emigration; Federal Security Service (FSS/FSB)

REGINA KOZAKOVA

Registration of Civil States (ZAGS)

The office for the Registration of Civil States or ZAGS (*Zapis aktov grazhdanskogo sostoianiia*) is a state institution that registers all kinds of acts of civil status: births, deaths, marriages and divorces, name changes, establishment of paternity, and adoptions. Before the Soviet Revolution of 1917, this was the prerogative of religious institutions, but after the revolution state offices were created for this purpose in each administrative division of the country. Each ZAGS records the reported changes of civil states in registry books and issues certificates, and each office holds an archive of all documents issued there. In Soviet times all marriages had to be performed in a ZAGS office, whose employees were notorious for being formal and impersonal. In post-Soviet Russia religious ceremonies have become popular, but a marriage is not legally valid without ZAGS registration.

See also: families; wedding ceremony

TATIANA SMORODINSKAYA

rehabilitation (reabilitatsiia)

Rehabilitation means establishing the innocence of people convicted of political crimes under Soviet rule. The first great wave of rehabilitation occurred in the 1950s under Nikita Khrushchev, the second in the 1980s under Mikhail Gorbachev. Under Khrushchev rehabilitation accompanied de-Stalinization, was secret, and applied mostly to post-war victims of repression. About 625,000 people were rehabilitated. Most did not receive any material compensation. Many Soviet leaders feared rehabilitation, as it raised the question of responsibility for false accusations and convictions. Indeed, Khrushchev used rehabilitation as a political weapon against his opponents. During the 1960s and 1970s, few people were rehabilitated. Gorbachev resumed rehabilitation in order to strengthen reform of Soviet society. The press set the stage for rehabilitation by re-examining Stalinist political repressions. The Politburo set up a commission in late 1987 that reviewed repressions of the 1930s till the 1950s and publicly rehabilitated Stalin's major political opponents. The new civic society Memorial pressured authorities to extend rehabilitation to ordinary citizens. Rehabilitation in the 1980s included reparations for losses and reinstatement of Party membership. After the break-up of the USSR, the Russian parliament extended rehabilitation to victims of repression from 1917 to 1991; these included dispossessed kulaks, persecuted religious dissenters, and dissidents. Rehabilitation did not end in the 1990s. As recently as 2002, many former political prisoners, especially those outside Moscow, still faced long waits for the documents that would allow them to receive social benefits. Moreover, rehabilitation remained controversial both for those who participated in the repressions and for those who feared its disruptive impact on Russia's weak democracy.

See also: Communist Party; democratic reform movement; dissident; Gorbachev, Mikhail; human rights organizations; GULag; Khrushchev, Nikita; Memorial; perestroika and glasnost

Further reading

Adler, N. (2002) *The Gulag Survivor: Beyond the Soviet System*, New Brunswick, NJ: Transaction Publishers.
Iakovlev, A. (ed.) (1991) *Reabilitatsiia: Politicheskie protsessy 30–50-kh godov*, Moscow: Politizdat.
Smith, K. (1996) *Remembering Stalin's Victims: Popular Memory and the End of the USSR*, Ithaca, NY: Cornell University Press.

BARBARA C. ALLEN

religion and spiritualism, non-traditional

Russia has a long tradition of religion and spirituality outside of the official Russian Orthodox Church. While Kievan Rus, the predecessor to the modern Russian state, adopted Eastern Christianity in 988, folk beliefs and rituals survived well into the twentieth century. Attempts to modernize the Russian Orthodox Church in the seventeenth century met with great resistance, resulting in a variety of splinter groups collectively known as Old Believers. Some of these groups developed strong communities independent of the state and the official Church. The Soviet state destroyed the vast majority of Old Believer communities, leaving very small numbers of believers, still surviving today.

The Soviet period also sparked new religious movements, both in response to state-sanctioned atheism and in opposition to the revival and state takeover of the Russian Orthodox Church in 1943. Few groups had large followings, but the mere presence of alternative religious communities made them a threat in the state's eyes. Some foreign religious movements, particularly the Hare Krishnas and the Jehovah's Witnesses, established communities in the Soviet Union in the face of harsh persecution. Sectarians faced job discrimination, police interrogation, arrest, and exile through the early 1980s. Not until the late 1980s, during glasnost, did the state loosen restrictions on religious worship. The Supreme Soviet finally codified freedom of religion in 1990.

The collapse of the Soviet Union resulted in a great increase in the diversity of religious expression. Books, radio, and TV programmes that focused on Eastern spirituality, meditation, hypnosis, and folk religion proved enormously popular. Thousands of foreign missionaries entered Russia after 1990, representing both sectarian Christian organizations such as the Mormon Church, and non-Christian organizations such as the Unification Church (Moonies) and the Church of Scientology. At the same time, homegrown Russian sects formed around charismatic leaders, in particular *Beloe Bratstvo* (White Brotherhood) and *Bogorodichnyi Tsentr* (Mother of God Centre). Among Muslims in the Russian Federation, Islamic sects, including

Wahhabism, have experienced steady growth, in part due to the Chechen conflict and the growth of Muslim fundamentalism among Chechen rebels. While the number of citizens involved in non-traditional religions accounted for only a tiny fraction of the total population in the 1990s, their strong presence in major urban centres and the extensive, largely negative media coverage devoted to new religious movements amplified their presence and fuelled hostility. In particular, the growth in religious pluralism alarmed the Russian Orthodox Church, leading it to organize efforts to combat the perceived threat of new religious movements. A 1997 religious law tightened restrictions on registration for religious organizations and granted special status to the Russian Orthodox Church. Since then, many members of non-traditional religious organizations have faced discrimination and hostility by their neighbours, their employers, and local and federal authorities.

See also: Islam; Old Believers; perestroika and glasnost; Russian Orthodoxy; War, Chechen

Further reading

Balagushin, E. (1999) *Netraditsionnye religii v sovremennoi Rossii*, Moscow: Institute of Philosophy, Russian Academy of Sciences.
Epshtein, M. (1994) *Novoe sektantstvo*, Moscow: Labyrinth.
Kolarz, W. (1961) *Religion in the Soviet Union*, New York: St. Martin's Press.

EMILY B. BARAN

research institutions

Originally the Russian Academy of Sciences, established in St. Petersburg (1724) at Peter the Great's behest, the USSR Academy of Sciences in 1925 became officially involved in the nation's economic and cultural development through a network of specialized research institutions. Soviet policy-makers believed that large research institutes created to serve Soviet industry would provide a more effective industrial research environment than found in capitalist countries. The Academy moved from Leningrad

to Moscow in 1934, but many of its research institutes remained in Leningrad. Stalin's purges had a negative effect on scholarly research; yet by the end of the 1960s the USSR Academy of Sciences comprised 600 research institutes. Currently it includes some 400 institutes, with over 60,000 specialists engaged in various academic fields.

The system of scholarly research that emerged in the Soviet Union in the 1930s consisted of three categories: (1) the USSR Academy of Sciences and the republican academies; (2) the educational institutions; and (3) government ministries. Members of the Academy of Sciences held the USSR's most prestigious academic positions and received generous financial support.

Arguably the most famous literary research institute, the Pushkin House (*Pushkinskii Dom*, founded 1905), established as a centre for researching and collecting materials related to Aleksandr Pushkin and his contemporaries, publishes the journal *Russian Literature* (*Russkaia literatura*, 1958), and from 1995–2003 compiled and published facsimile editions of Pushkin's works and dictionaries of Russian writers. The Institute of Philosophy (1921) publishes the journal *Issues of Philosophy* (*Voprosy filosofii*) and since 1989 it has released forty volumes of significant works by Russian philosophers. The Institute of Linguistic Research (*Institut lingvisticheskikh issledovanii*) publishes dictionaries and the journal *Studies in Linguistics. Acta Linguistica Petropolitana*. The Institute of the History of Material Culture (*Institut istorii materialnoi kultury*), which specializes in archaeology, publishes the journals *Archaeological News* and *Radiocarbon and Archaeology*. The Institute of Oriental Studies (*Institut vostokovedeniia*, founded 1930 in Leningrad, in Moscow since 1950) continues to publish important Eurasian studies findings and translations of classical Japanese and Chinese culture. The Institute of Linguistic Studies (*Institut iazykoznaniia*, founded 1950) incorporates a wide range of studies, including cognitive linguistics, sociolinguistics, translation theory, and linguistic anthropology; its 1995 linguistic encyclopedia received the State Prize.

National politics constrained Soviet science and technology, which was strong in theory but weak in application. Soviet scientists excelled in biology, chemistry, physics, and mathematics, while areas such as genetics, cybernetics, and psychology were often suppressed. Since the collapse of the Soviet Union, some research activities have been commercialized, and financing and management of scientific research remain topics of heated internal political debate.

See also: Academy of Sciences; Pushkin, Aleksandr; philosophy, post-Soviet

Further reading

Adams, M. (2000) *Networks in Action: The Khrushchev Era, the Cold War, and the Transformation of Soviet Science*, Trondheim: Norwegian University of Science and Technology.

Fortescue, S. (1986) *The Communist Party and Soviet Science*, Baltimore, MD: Johns Hopkins University Press.

Graham, L. (1975) 'The Formation of Soviet Research Institutes: A Combination of Revolutionary Innovation and International Borrowing', *Social Studies of Science*, 5, 3: 303–29.

——(2003) 'Science in the New Russia (International)', *Issues In Science and Technology*, 19, 4: 91–2.

ALEXANDRA SMITH

residence permit

See: propiska

restaurants

During the Soviet period, the small taverns (*kabaki*), cafés, and restaurants of the pre-Revolutionary era disappeared, replaced by a few state restaurants, most with large halls and bright overhead lighting. Décor varied slightly, but the tableware was virtually identical in every restaurant across the country. Reserving a table usually required *blat* or a bribe to the doorman. It was common to see a sign on a restaurant door reading *mest net* (no available tables), although the hall would be near-empty.

People generally only dined out when there was an occasion to celebrate. Typically, a table would be reserved along with *zakuski*, which would be on the table upon one's arrival. An evening at a restaurant was a long affair, with drinks, long toasts, stories, and several courses. Live music and a dance floor were common in restaurants; dancing, song requests, and occasionally singing with the band were part of the restaurant experience.

The first private (*kooperativnyi*) restaurant opened in Moscow in 1987. In the post-Soviet era, private cafés and restaurants are ubiquitous, from family-run snack bars in small towns and along highways to extremely elegant and expensive restaurants in large cities serving cuisine from around the world, with foreign chefs, extensive wine cellars, and elaborate décor.

In addition to formal restaurants, in the Soviet era there were many informal establishments, including dining halls (*stolovaia*), cafes, and specialized cafes featuring pirozhki (*pirozhkovaia*), bliny (*blinnaia*), chebureki (*cheburechnaia*), ice cream (*morozhenitsa*), and similar classic light fare. Some of these dining genres have remained in the post-Soviet era and have been joined by Russian fast-food establishments of various kinds.

See also: appetizers; blat; bliny; chebureki; dance; pirog/pirozhki

MICHELE BERDY

rhetoric, Soviet

In the USSR, the concepts of 'rhetoric' and 'Soviet language' were applied to Soviet Russian only at the end of the 1980s. Outside the borders of the USSR, and in unofficial research in the Soviet Union, Soviet rhetoric was studied as an instrument of ideological indoctrination.

In the educational programmes of the Communist Party which prepared journalists and 'agitators', Soviet rhetoric was taught as a compilation of codes for different communicative situations and genres. Contradictions between styles were initially ignored. Thus from the 1920s onwards, Soviet rhetoric had acquired an absurdity reflected in the literature of the time – especially in works by Andrei Platonov, Mikhail Zoshchenko, Mikhail Zamiatin, Ilia Ilf and

Evgenii Petrov, and Mikhail Bulgakov. From the end of the 1920s, Soviet ideologists (and above all Stalin himself) proceeded to bring Soviet rhetoric in harmony with the existing Russian literary language, which resulted in an impoverished and primitive bureaucratic jargon, a so-called 'wooden language'. The concept of 'proletarian culture', which prevailed during the revolution, was replaced with Socialist Realism (1932), which governed Soviet rhetoric throughout the Stalin era. Stalin and his appointed cultural representatives controlled this language.

The official characteristics of Soviet rhetoric are simple language, the contrast between 'ours' and 'theirs', an emphasis on certainty and health, the dissolution of the individual into the collective, and a hypostasis of abstract concepts (such as Party, Communism, and the like). The use of Soviet rhetoric demanded an understanding of subtext, as the exchange of words as labels took the place of the interaction in a dialogue. The evident contradiction between speech and subtext in Soviet rhetoric generated forms of satirical protest. As a result, from the beginning, Soviet rhetoric was accompanied by various genres parodying and ridiculing it, such as jokes, anecdotes, popular verses (*chastushka*), and parodic literature. Because of the existence of satire, it is impossible to apply the concept of 'new speech' as presented in George Orwell's *1984*, Aldous Huxley's *Brave New World*, and Evgenii Zamiatin's *My* (*We*) to Soviet rhetoric.

The generation of Soviet schoolchildren growing up in the 1930s till the 1950s witnessed an increasingly deepening conflict between the stilted bureaucratic jargon of Soviet rhetoric, encoded in literature sanctioned according to the criteria of Socialist Realism, and the language of classical Russian literature and daily speech. By the Thaw era, this conflict had lessened, but sharpened again during the 1965 'literary trials' of Andrei Siniavskii and Iulii Daniel. At the end of the 1970s, an attempt was made to give Soviet rhetoric a 'human face', when a group of writers wrote and published the memoirs of the Secretary General of the Communist Party Central Committee, Leonid Brezhnev, in *Novyi mir*, the most important of the so-called 'thick journals'. The text was supposed to become an authoritative source representing the era of 'developed socialism'. However, by this time the last remnants of trust in Soviet rhetoric had been undermined. During perestroika (1985–90), censorship was gradually abolished, and the official mass media could find a fresh approach to Soviet citizens. The erosion of Soviet rhetoric was by that point unstoppable, and by the mid-1990s, a new and intricate complex of official linguistic practices had emerged in its place.

See also: Brezhnev, Leonid; censorship; chastushka; Communist Party; Daniel, Iulii; developed socialism; joke; journalism; literature, Soviet; *Novyi mir*; perestroika and glasnost; periodicals, Soviet; Siniavskii, Andrei; Socialist Realism; Stagnation; Stalin, Iosif; Thaw; thick journals

Further reading

Fesenko, A. and Fesenko, T. (1955) *Russkii iazyk pri sovietakh*, New York: Rausen Bros.

Graudina, L. K. and Miskevic, G. I. (1989) *Teoriia i praktika russkogo krasnorechiia*, Moscow: Nauka.

Grenoble, L. (2003) *Language Policy in the Soviet Union*, Dordrecht: Kluwer Academic Publishers.

Gusejnov, G. (2004) *Sovetskie ideologemy v russkom diskurse 1990-kh*, Moscow: Tri quadrata.

Hodgkinson, H. (1955) *Doubletalk: The Language of Communism*, London: G. Allen & Unwin

Wodak, R. and Kirsch, F. (eds) (1995) *Totalitäre Sprache – Langue de bois – Language of Dictatorship*, Vienna: Passagen.

GASAN GUSEJNOV

RIA Novosti

Today *RIA Novosti* (The Russian News and Information Agency) is one of the most authoritative Russian state sources of information. Its history dates back to 24 June 1941, when the Soviet Information Bureau (*Sovinformburo*) was founded so as to relay information to the radio and newspapers about developments on the warfront and within the country. In 1961, the Novosti Press Agency (APN, *Agentstvo Pechati Novosti*) succeeded *Sovinformbiuro* and became the monopolist mass media holding entrusted with disseminating propaganda about life in the Soviet Union to foreign countries. Its founders were the USSR Journalists Union, the USSR Writers Union, and the *Znanie* Society. APN had bureaus in over 120 countries. According to its charter, adopted on 3 April 1961, APN's mandate was to foster understanding, trust, and friendship among peoples by regularly publishing information about the USSR abroad. The Agency published sixty illustrated newspapers and magazines in forty-five languages, with a one-time circulation of 4.3 million copies. APN Publishing House produced over 200 books, with a total annual circulation of 20 million copies. Its lines included: 'Science and Technology', 'Sport', 'Culture and Art', and a 'Daily Review' of the Soviet press in English. Reorganized by a decree of USSR President Mikhail Gorbachev, APN became Information Agency *Novosti* (IAN) in 1990. The following year RIA *Novosti* was created from IAN, and today has a wide correspondent network in the Russian Federation and abroad. The agency's Website publishes its main online information in twelve languages, including Russian, the main European languages, and Arabic. In 2005, *RIA Novosti* founded an English-language 24-hour news TV channel, *Russia Today*, which broadcasts Russian news to foreign countries, provides viewers with a Russian perspective on world and domestic events, and strives to show a positive image of Russia abroad.

See also: Gorbachev, Mikhail; literature, Soviet; radio, Soviet; television channels; unions, professional

ELENA SKIPETROVA

Riazanov, Eldar Aleksandrovich

b. 18 November 1927, Samara

Film director, scriptwriter

Riazanov received his training at the Directing Department of VGIK. Upon graduation (1950), he worked on documentary films; his *Ostrov Sakhalin* (Sakhalin Island) received a prize at the Cannes Film Festival in 1955. Since 1956, when

Karnavalnaia noch (*Carnival Night*) won the director critical and popular acclaim, Riazanov has specialized in satirical and lyrical comedies. Many of these count among Russians' favourite films, such as the New Year's classic *Ironiia sudby, ili s legkim parom* (*The Irony of Fate*, 1975). USSR State Prize (1977), People's Artist of the USSR (1984).

See also: All-Russian (All-Union) State Institute of Cinematography; film, comedy; film, documentary

ELENA BARABAN

Rikhter, Sviatoslav Teofilovich

b. 20 March 1915, Zhitomir, Ukraine; d. 1 August 1997, Moscow

Pianist

Rikhter was one of the greatest pianists of the twentieth century. He was self-taught until his first recital in Odessa in 1934. From 1937 until 1944, he studied with Genrikh Neigauz at the Moscow Conservatory. Rikhter's superb interpretations of Bach, Schumann, Prokofiev, Beethoven, Mozart, and Haydn won him international acclaim in the 1950s and the 1960s. In addition to solo recitals, Rikhter also performed chamber music with musicians including David Oistrakh, Mstislav Rostropovich, and Iurii Bashmet. Rikhter received the Stalin Prize (1949), the USSR State Prize (1950), Lenin Prize (1961), State Prize of the Russian Federation (1995) and was awarded the title of People's Artist of the USSR (1961) and Hero of Socialist Labour (1975).

See also: Bashmet, Iurii; Moscow Conservatory; Neigauz, Genrikh; Oistrakh, David; piano performance, Russian/Soviet; Rostropovich, Mstislav

ELENA BARABAN

rock music (rok-muzyka)

Rok-muzyka (rock music) has been popular in Russia for nearly as long as it has in the West, but it became part of the mainstream entertainment industry only during perestroika. Before then, especially during Stagnation, rock was largely an underground phenomenon, which the state attempted to control with an uneven mix of prohibition and cooptation. Consequently, the Russian connotations of the term 'rock music' differ from those elsewhere. The word *rok* not only refers to a musical style, but implies the autonomy of the musicians, and is contrasted with other genres that use similar instrumentation and target similar audiences, especially popular music acts created by an outside producer, and whose members do not compose songs. Due to its markedly independent stance, as well as the erudition and intellectualism of the musicians, Soviet rock was always more lyrics-based and socio-politically and philosophically sophisticated than its Western counterpart. The distinction between rock and other forms of popular music has grown less clear since the end of censorship, and especially since popular culture's commodification in the post-Soviet period, but Russian rock still retains associations acquired during its long history as an unofficial, non-conformist medium.

Rock's cultural presence in Russia began in 1957, when the Seventh International Festival of Youth and Students took place in Moscow. That event, a sign of the Thaw, allowed young Soviet citizens unprecedented contact with their foreign peers, including jazz musicians, writers, and artists. The Festival also first exposed most Russians to electric guitar music and brought the first rock-and-roll records into the country. Since the records were not sold in state-run stores, fans copied them using homemade engraving devices and x-ray prints in place of vinyl (a form of do-it-yourself media reproduction known as *rentgenizdat*, analogous to *samizdat* literature). Records were also brought into the country by Soviets who had lived or travelled abroad, including in other countries of the Eastern Bloc, where the influence and presence of Western culture was more pronounced. Other sources of music and information about rock culture over the next two decades would include the radio stations Voice of America and the BBC, and, in the Baltic republics, Finnish television.

Native Russian rock bands began to form in the wake of Beatlemania, which was as powerful

in the USSR as elsewhere. One of the earliest groups was Tarakany (The Cockroaches), led by Aleksandr Gradskii. Russian rock groups initially sang exclusively in English, and those who could imitate the Beatles most closely were particularly admired. Eastern Europe was a major influence on Russian rock at this stage in its development, both musically and materially. Many groups included students from other socialist nations among their members, and musicians from Poland, East Germany, Yugoslavia, and other East Bloc countries sometimes sold their electric guitars and amplifiers while on tour in the USSR, where such equipment was extremely scarce.

In 1966, the state music industry created the *vokalno-instrumentalnyi ansambl* (vocal-instrumental ensemble, or *VIA*) as a form of official competition for the increasingly popular, but unsanctioned, rock music. VIAs were clean-cut, prefabricated combos that sang upbeat songs about Soviet life. Although VIAs hardly dented underground rock's popularity, they did attract many rock musicians, who chose the stable, paying VIA jobs as the only way to make a living playing music. By the late 1970s, the state had also begun to tolerate a select number of innocuous Western groups for official radio play lists and recordings on the state record label, Melodiia, including ABBA and the Bee Gees.

The best-known Russian rock bands had unofficial status until the late 1980s. Andrei Makarevich's influential band, Mashina vremeni (Time Machine), showed no sign of slowing down when it celebrated its thirtieth anniversary with a national tour in 1999. Boris Grebenshchikov's more experimental, art-rock-oriented Leningrad band, Akvarium (Aquarium), was founded in 1972. Other legendary groups include Kino, led by the idolized Viktor Tsoi; DDT, which earned official disapproval with an early song critical of the Afghan War; and Nautilus Pompilius. These and many other groups reached huge audiences by recording cassette albums that were then copied by fans (in official production called *magnitizdat*) and playing concerts and festivals organized by underground producers and promoters. Beginning in the 1970s, there was also a thriving *samizdat* rock journalism.

Although Soviet cultural authorities had been suspicious of rock music since the 1950s, and the very term was not used officially until perestroika, state crack-downs on rock did not begin in earnest until the late 1960s. One tactic was to open 'beat clubs', and then use the information supplied by musicians on their applications as surveillance dossiers. There were also occasional prosecutions of promoters, musicians, and those who sold musical equipment on the black market. During the last years of Stagnation, with the renewed flare-up of the Cold War, state intolerance of underground rock rose sharply.

With the onset of perestroika, the distinction between official and unofficial culture disappeared. In 1985, the Russian rock group Avtograf (Autograph) appeared via satellite at the Live-Aid benefit concert in England. Akvarium released an album in the West in 1987, as did Petr Mamonov's avant-garde band Zvuki Mu in 1989. Since 1992, Russian rock bands have been free (or forced) to compete on the market not only with one another, but also with foreign acts. Popular rock musicians of the post-Soviet period include Leningrad, Mumii Troll, Zemfira, and Splin.

See also: Akvarium; censorship; DDT; East Bloc countries; Gradskii, Aleksandr; Grebenshchikov, Boris; Kino; Makarevich, Andrei; Mamonov, Petr; Mashina vremeni (Time Machine); Nautilus Pompilius; perestroika and glasnost; popular music, post-Soviet; popular music, Soviet; rock opera; samizdat; Stagnation; Thaw; Tsoi, Viktor; vocal-instrumental ensemble (VIA); War, Afghan; Zemfira

Further reading

Cushman, T. (1995) *Notes from Underground*, Albany, NY: SUNY Press.

Glossop, N. (1998) 'On the Peculiarities of Soviet Rock and Roll', in A. B. Wachtel (ed.) *Intersections and Transpositions: Russian Music, Literature, and Society*, Evanston, IL: Northwestern University Press.

Ramet, S. P. (ed.) (1994) *Rocking the State: Rock Music and Politics in Eastern Europe and Russia*, Boulder, CO: Westview Press.

Troitsky, A. (1987) *Back in the U.S.S.R*, New York: Omnibus.

SETH GRAHAM

rock opera (rok-opera)

The first rock opera widely known in Russia was *Jesus Christ Superstar*, recordings of which infiltrated the USSR in 1971 and quickly became a source of songs for underground rock groups. The genre eventually became one of the forms of rock music acceptable to the state. The first native rock opera was *Orfei i Evridika* (*Orpheus and Eurydice*, music by Aleksandr Zhurbin, lyrics by Iurii Dimitrin), recorded by the group Poiushchie gitary (Singing Guitars) in 1975. The first Russian rock opera to be staged was *Iunona i Avos* (Iunona and Avos), music by Aleksei Rybnikov, with a libretto by poet Andrei Voznesenskii and directed by Mark Zakharov in 1981.

See also: rock music; Voznesenskii, Andrei; Zakharov, Mark

SETH GRAHAM

Rodina (Motherland)

Political party

Registered by the Russian Federation Justice Ministry on 14 September 2003, the Motherland National-Patriotic Union electoral bloc was formed just three months before the 2003 parliamentary elections. Originally headed by the State Duma deputies Chairman of Foreign Relations Committee Dmitrii Rogozin and prominent economist Sergei Glazev, the bloc included twenty-nine parties and organizations that are leftist, patriotic, anti-oligarch, and conservative in orientation. Motherland's success was a big surprise and a major event of the elections. The bloc received 9.02 per cent of votes and became the fourth faction in the State Duma. A split in the bloc in July 2005 might jeopardize their future success.

See also: Duma; nationalism ('the national question'); political parties, post-Soviet

ALEXANDER DOMRIN

Rodnina, Irina Konstantinovna

b. 12 September 1949, Moscow

Figure skater

Trained by Stanislav Zhuk, and later by Tatiana Tarasova, Rodnina made her debut on the international rink in 1969. Rodnina skated with Aleksei Ulanov until 1972, when Ulanov married the skater Liudmila Smirnova and subsequently performed with her. Rodnina then skated with Aleksander Zaitsev, whom she later married. She was an Olympic gold medallist in pairs figure skating in 1972, 1976, and 1980, and ten-time world champion in consecutive years. After ending her career as skater in 1980, she went to the United States as a coach, later returning to Moscow to run her own training school in the late 1990s.

See also: figure skating

BIRGIT BEUMERS

Rogozhkin, Aleksandr Vladimirovich

b. 3 October 1949, Leningrad

Film director and screenwriter

First trained as an art historian and a graphic artist, Rogozhkin turned to film in 1980. In 1982, he graduated from VGIK, where he studied directing under Sergei Gerasimov. Rogozhkin has created several powerful social dramas (*Karaul* [*The Guard*, 1989], *Chekist* [*The Chekist*, 1991]). With *Osobennosti natsionalnoi okhoty* (*Peculiarities of the National Hunt*, 1995) and its sequels, Rogozhkin has established himself as a master of eccentric comedies. Due to its original interpretation of World War II themes, superb camera work and acting, *Kukushka* (*The Cuckoo*, 2002) has become a landmark in Rogozhkin's career and brought the director international acclaim.

See also: All-Russian (All-Union) State Institute of Cinematography; Gerasimov, Sergei; World War II (Great Patriotic War)

ELENA BARABAN

Roma

See Gypsy/Roma

romance (romans)

The preferred lyric genre during the Soviet period was the *pesnia* (song), which included folk song, mass song, and popular estrada numbers. The *romans* (romance), however, was regarded with some suspicion, chiefly because it emphasized personal emotion and private experience. It was also deemed an outdated bourgeois form that had properly died out after the October Revolution. However, the rebirth of lyric poetry after the death of Stalin did much to revive interest in the *romans*, though it never regained its former vitality.

The *romans* has traditionally been divided into various sub-categories such as *gorodskoi romans* (urban romance), *zhestokii romans* (cruel romance), and *tsyganskii romans* (gypsy romance). Difficult to define, such songs celebrate the consequences of uninhibited passions with varying degrees of rancour, melancholy, or nostalgia. State control over publishing, broadcasting, and recording meant that many of the more extreme examples of *romans* survived only in the oral tradition, often among members of the intelligentsia; bards' guitar poetry constitutes the most obvious development of such songs. Official culture accommodated more moderate versions; sanitized and standardized, they were performed by both opera singers and more popular artists. Films were also an important vehicle for transmitting the *romans* in a more acceptable form, just as the musical comedies of the 1930s had done much to promote the mass song. Petr Todorovskii's *Gorodskoi romans* (*Urban Romance*), Andrei Konchalovskii's *Romans o vliublennykh* (*Romance for Lovers*), and Eldar Riazanov's *Zhestokii romans* (*Cruel Romance*) all tellingly combine image, word, and music. Scores by composers such as Andrei Petrov and Mikael Tariverdev contained memorable instances of *romans* lyricism. Aleksandra Pakhmutova showed that the intonations of the *romans* could be creatively adapted to popular song. In the post-Soviet period, the form has been marginalized by pop, rock, and other forms of modern

Western music. Concerts by performers such as Oleg Pogudin still sell out, but most Russians will naturally speak of *starinnye romansy* (old-fashioned romances).

In contrast, classical composers approached the *romans* with rare ambition, most notably by turning to large-scale cycles. The first performance of Dmitrii Shostakovich's *Iz evreiskoi narodnoi poezii* (*From Jewish Folk Poetry*) in 1955 (written in 1948) was crucial in this respect, and his late settings of Blok (1967), Tsvetaeva (1974), and Michelangelo (1975) are among the most significant works of the period. Georgii Sviridov composed ambitious cycles to texts by Blok (1961–63) and Esenin (1977). Another composer of similar folkloric, even nationalist inclination was Valerii Gavrilin, whose *Russkaia tetrad* (*Russian Notebook*) caused a sensation in 1965. Modernists have also been attracted by the *romans*; Edison Denisov in particular set extensive selections of Blok and Pushkin in 1981 and 1982 respectively. For all this, other composers have lamented the passing of an authentic *romans* tradition. Valentin Silvestrov's two-hour cycle, *Tikhie pesni* (*Silent Songs*), dates from 1973–77. Setting Russian and English poets of the early nineteenth and early twentieth centuries, Silvestrov develops a musical language that recalls the amateur *romansy* of the Pushkin period in the context of minimalism. An equally postmodern attitude to the *romans* can be seen in the work of Leonic Desiatnikov.

See also: bards; Denisov, Edison; Desiatnikov, Leonid; intelligentsia; Konchalovskii, Andrei; Pakhmutova, Aleksandra; Petrov, Andrei; popular music, Soviet; postmodernism; Riazanov, Eldar; Shostakovich, Dmitrii; Sviridov, Georgii; Todorovskii, Petr

Further reading

McBurney, G. (1998) 'Soviet Music after the Death of Stalin: The Legacy of Shostakovich', in C. Kelly and D. Shepherd (eds) *Russian Cultural Studies: An Introduction*, Oxford: Oxford University Press.

Redepenning, D. (1995) '"And Art Made Tongue-Tied by Authority": Shostakovich's Song-Cycles', in D. Fanning (ed.) *Shostakovich*

Studies, Cambridge: Cambridge University Press.

Smith, G. (1984) *Songs to Seven Strings: Russian Guitar Poetry and Soviet 'Mass Song'*, Bloomington, IN: Indiana University Press.

PHILIP ROSS BULLOCK

Romanova, Elena Borisovna

b. 1944, Moscow

Artist

Romanova graduated from the Surikov Art Academy in 1969. A member of the USSR (now Russian) Artists' Union, Romanova is best known for her portraiture, which ranges from anonymous children to stars like Alla Pugacheva, and includes self-portraits. Adhering to a naturalistic style influenced by the Northern and Italian Renaissance, Romanova was able to work within Socialist Realism during the Stagnation era to produce psychologically penetrating portraits and lyrical landscapes.

See also: art schools and academies; Pugacheva, Alla; Socialist Realism; Stagnation

KRISTEN M. HARKNESS

Romm, Mikhail Ilich

b. 11 [24] January 1901, Irkutsk; d. 1 November 1971, Moscow

Director, writer, teacher, administrator

Romm began his career by adapting Maupassant's *Boule de Suif* (*Pyshka*, 1934), but he won fame for *Lenin v oktiabre* [*Lenin in October*, 1938] and *Lenin v 1918 godu* [*Lenin in 1918*, 1939]. Several relatively orthodox films followed, until Stalin's death and the ensuing Thaw liberated Romm to make two films of genuine moral concern, the drama *Deviat dnei odnogo goda* [*Nine Days of a Year*, 1962], and a documentary on Nazism, *Obyknovennyi fashizm* [*Ordinary Fascism*,

1966]. His last film, *I vse-taki ia veriu* [*And Still I Believe*, 1976], was completed by a team that included director Elem Klimov, one of Romm's many students at VGIK, who also numbered Tengiz Abuladze, Grigorii Chukhrai, Georgii Daneliia, and Gleb Panfilov.

See also: Abuladze, Tengiz; All-Russian (All-Union) State Institute of Cinematography; Chukhrai, Grigorii; Daneliia, Georgii; film, Soviet – Thaw period; Klimov, Elem; Panfilov, Gleb

JOSEPHINE WOLL

Rossiiskaia gazeta

Newspaper

A daily political newspaper published since 11 November 1990, *Rossiiskaia gazeta* (Russian Paper) currently has a circulation of 411,000. Published in thirty-two Russian cities and CIS countries, the paper employs national and international correspondents, with a network of thirty-eight bureaus in Russia, Asia, and Europe.

RG is the official publisher of state documents such as federal laws, presidential degrees, governmental decisions, Constitutional Court decisions, and the like. As the official governmental mouthpiece, it features only articles that represent the official viewpoint. The most recent (fourth) editor-in-chief is Vladislav Fronin, who brought on staff many well-known journalists from the leading newspapers *Komsomolskaia pravda* (in its original form), *Literaturnaia gazeta*, and *Izvestiia*. Various prominent political and media figures have contributed to *RG*, including Mikhail Gorbachev, Sergei Kapitsa, Evgenii Primakov, and Vitalii Tretiakov. The newspaper was recognized by the Russian Union of Journalists in 2002 for its record-breaking circulation.

See also: Gorbachev, Mikhail; *Literaturnaia gazeta*; Periodicals, Soviet; Primakov, Evgenii; Tretiakov, Vitalii

NADEZHDA AZHGIKHINA

Rostropovich, Mstislav Leopoldovich

b. 27 March 1927, Baku

Cellist, conductor, pianist

Known primarily as a cellist and conductor, Rostropovich studied at the Moscow Conservatory with Semen Kozolupov, and graduated with highest honours. He is a strong advocate for contemporary composers, many of whom, including Prokofiev, Britten, Lutoslawski, and Schnittke, have composed works for him. Unequalled in his technique, he performs with an unusual accuracy of pitch and fullness of tone.

Although, as an accomplished pianist, Rostropovich has accompanied his wife (since 1955), soprano Galina Vishnevskaia, in song recitals, he is best known abroad as a conductor. He made his début in 1968 with *Eugene Onegin* at the Bolshoi Theatre. In 1977 he was appointed music director of the National Symphony Orchestra, where he remained until 1994. He made the first recording of Shostakovich's controversial opera *Lady Macbeth of Mtsensk* in 1979, and has premiered many operas, including Schnittke's *Zhizn s idiotom* (*Life with an Idiot*, 1992).

Because of his anti-Soviet stance and his friendship with, and support of, Aleksandr Solzhenitsyn, Rostropovich (along with Vishnevskaia) was stripped of his Soviet citizenship in 1978; their citizenship was restored by Gorbachev only in 1990. He and Vishnevskaia became naturalized Swiss citizens and have remained abroad.

See also: Bolshoi Theatre; Moscow Conservatory; Prokofiev, Sergei; Shnittke, Alfred; Shostakovich, Dmitrii; Solzhenitsyn, Aleksandr; Vishnevskaia, Galina

DAVID GOMPPER

Rozenbaum, Aleksandr Iakovlevich

b. 13 September 1951, Leningrad

Singer, songwriter

Rozenbaum, known for his virtuoso guitar playing and strong voice, is a prolific bard singer popular since the early 1980s. A trained anesthesiologist, Rozenbaum began composing and performing songs while in medical school, under the influence of songs by Vladimir Vysotskii and Bulat Okudzhava. Rozenbaum first attracted attention with a self-recorded cycle of songs about Odessa, which, like the songs of other bards, circulated in countless homemade copies. Major themes of Rozenbaum's work include Cossack life, especially horses, the Afghan War, his beloved Leningrad/St. Petersburg, and abstract themes such as bravery and self-sacrifice.

See also: bards; Odessa; Okudzhava, Bulat; Vysotskii, Vladimir; War, Afghan

SETH GRAHAM

Rozhdestvenskii, Gennadii Nikolaevich

b. 4 May 1931, Moscow

Conductor

Rozhdestvenskii has a reputation as a maverick musical figure. A highly versatile conductor who studied at the Moscow Conservatory, he has renewed interest in lesser-known works of twentieth-century composers such as Prokofiev, Hindemith, Berg, Schoenberg, Stravinsky, and Poulenc, and has also championed various younger composers, including Rodion Shchedrin and Giya Kancheli. Orchestras he has directed include the Bolshoi Theatre, the Stockholm Philharmonic Orchestra, the BBC Symphony Orchestra, and the Vienna Symphony Orchestra. Brought in to revive the Bolshoi Theatre in 2000, he resigned a year later after his production of the original version of Prokofiev's opera *Igrok* (*The Gambler*) flopped.

See also: Bolshoi Theatre; Moscow Conservatory; Prokofiev, Sergei; Shchedrin, Rodion

ALEXANDER BURRY

Rozov, Viktor Sergeevich

b. 8 [21] August 1913, Iaroslavl; d. 28 September 2004, Moscow.

Playwright, screenwriter

Rozov helped set the more humane, less ideological tone of the Thaw era with his play *Vechno zhivye* (*Alive Forever*, 1954) which, as the film *Letiat zhuravli* (*The Cranes Are Flying*, 1957), won Best Picture at Cannes in 1958. From the 1950s to the 1970s his realistic, psychological plays about young idealists facing the hard realities of life were popular and influential. The typical, so-called 'Rozov hero' in such plays as *V den svadby* (*Wedding Day*, 1963) and *Traditsionnyi sbor* (*The Class Reunion*, 1966) was a prudently independent young man disturbed by moral paradoxes.

See also: film, Soviet – Thaw period; theatre, Soviet

JOHN FREEDMAN

Rozovskii, Mark Grigorevich

b. 3 April 1937, Petropavlovsk-Kamchatskii

Theatre director, dramatist

A journalist by education, Rozovskii founded and ran the amateur studio *Nash Dom* (Our House) at Moscow State University from 1958 until it was closed by the authorities in 1969. He participated in Aleksei Arbuzov's playwriting studio in the 1970s, and his dramatization of Lev Tolstoi's *Istoriia loshadi* (*The Story of a Horse*) was staged by Georgii Tovstonogov at Leningrad's Bolshoi Drama Theatre in 1975. From 1981–83 he staged three shows at the Moscow Art Theatre, the last being the long-running *Amadeus*. In 1983 he founded the small *Teatr u Nikitskikh vorot* (Theatre at the Nikita Gates), where during the course of over two decades he staged dozens of plays, often musicals or prose works in his own adaptations.

See also: Arbuzov, Aleksei; Bolshoi Theatre; Moscow Art Theatre (MKhAT); Moscow State University; Tovstonogov, Georgii

JOHN FREEDMAN

RSFSR

See: Russian Federation

Rubina, Dina Ilinichna

b. 19 September 1953, Tashkent, Uzbek SSR

Writer

Rubina began publishing short stories in the magazine *Iunost* (Youth) in 1971. A graduate of the Tashkent Conservatory (1977), she taught piano while writing plays, novellas, and screenplays. In the mid-1980s, she moved to Moscow, and in 1990 she emigrated to Israel, where she wrote her most significant works, which earned her worldwide popularity with Russian readers. These works include the novels *Vo vratakh tvoikh* (*At Thy Gates*, 1993), *Vot idet Mashiakh* (*Here Comes the Messiah!*, 1996), and the recent, controversial *Sindikat* (*Syndicate*, 2004); the novellas *Kamera naezzhaet!* (*The Camera Zooms In*, 1996), *Vysokaia voda venetsiantsev* (*The Venetians' High Waters*, 1999); and collections of stories, such as *Pod znakom karnavala* (*Under the Sign of Carnival*, 2000) and *Neskolko toroplivykh slov o liubvi* (*Several Hurried Words about Love*, 2003). Rubina's first-person narratives portray Russian émigré existence in Israel and Jewish culture, religion, and history from an ironic perspective. She engages in linguistic games, parody, intertextual allusions, genre experimentation (defining her novel *Sindikat*, for instance, as a 'comic strip'), suffusing her works with the spirit of carnival, and revealing the absurd and grotesque aspects of conventional reality.

See also: literature, Soviet

MARIA RUBINS

Rubinshtein, Lev Semenovich

b. 19 February 1947, Moscow

Poet

A leading Moscow Conceptualist, since 1974 Rubinshtein has written poems on index cards found in public libraries. The poems are built on sequences of words and phrases from different styles of speech or writing, from the prosaic daily details of washing up to sublime reflections on the meaning of life. The juxtapositions can be ironic and the tone is often light; yet the poems meditate on such themes as identity, destiny, and the place of poetry in modern Russia. Taking advantage of the flexible ordering of his poems written on cards, Rubinshtein, especially in performance, emphasizes the seemingly arbitrary progression of his carefully ordered work. Member, Writers' Union, since 1991.

See also: Conceptualism, literary; poetry, post-Soviet

STEPHANIE SANDLER

ruble

The ruble is the main monetary unit in Russia. The word derives from the verb *rubit* (to chop), because it originally denoted a certain amount of silver chopped off an ingot. During the late Soviet period, it was issued in paper bills of one, three, five, ten, 25, 50, and 100 rubles. Because its purchasing power was limited (many goods could only be purchased in special stores for hard currency or certificates), it was colloquially known as *dereviannyi* (wooden). Since the most recent revaluation of 1998 it has been issued as one-, two-, five-, and ten-ruble coins; ten-, 50-, 100-, 500-, and 1000-ruble bank notes. Abbreviated as RUR and now convertible in Russia, ruble can also be used as a metonym for money in general.

See also: economic system, post-Soviet; economic system, Soviet; kopeika; monetary reform; money

MICHELE BERDY

Rukhin, Evgenii Lvovich

b. 2 July 1943, Saratov; d. 24 May 1976, Leningrad

Artist

From 1961 to 1966, Rukhin studied in the Geology Department of Leningrad University and in 1964–65 attended classes at the Higher Technical Art School. One of the most important figures in non-conformist art, in 1974 Rukhin took part in the Bulldozer and the Second Autumn Open-Air Exhibitions in Moscow and at Gaza House of Culture in Leningrad. In 1975, he also participated in the exhibition at Leningrad's Nevskii House of Culture. When it was nearly impossible to export nonconformist art, Rukhin managed to have exhibitions at the Betty Parson Gallery (New York, 1966), the North Carolina Museum of Art (Raleigh, 1975), and the Phillips Collection (Washington, 1976). Starting with his early, more representational canvases and drawing his inspiration from Jasper Johns, Rukhin quickly moved to an interest in canvas texture by layering the paint, a white acrylic that he topped off with oil, collage, and attachments to the painting surface. For the attachments in his earlier works, Rukhin favoured objects discarded by society (furniture fragments, old fabric, locks) that represented a continuity with the past. In later works, Rukhin incorporated everyday objects from Soviet life and placed the objects themselves in the centre of the canvas. His exploration of the essential qualities of form and texture continued until his mysterious death in a fire at his studio.

See also: art, nonconformist; Bulldozer Exhibition

NATALIA KOLODZEI

Ruslanova, Lidiia Andreevna

b. 14 [27] October 1900, Chernavka, Mordovia, Russia; d. 20 September 1973, Moscow

Singer

Born a poor peasant and raised in an orphanage, Ruslanova distinguished herself early as a singer, performing in churches and the furniture factory where she first worked. Ruslanova never pursued formal training, but based her own immensely popular style on that of traditional folk singers and thrilled audiences with her rich

nasal contralto and extraordinary repertoire of Russian folk songs, many of which became her signature pieces (*Valenki* [Felt Boots], *Okrasilsia mesiats bagriantsem* [The Moon Shone Red], *Zlatye gory* [Golden Hills]). The highlights of Ruslanova's career include her performances for the frontline troops in World War II and her concert on the steps of the Reichstag after the Red Army had occupied Berlin.

See also: folk music; World War II (Great Patriotic War)

BETH HOLMGREN

Ruslanova, Nina Ivanovna

b. 5 December 1945, Bogodukhovo, Ukrainian SSR

Film and theatre actress

Ruslanova was raised in an orphanage and worked on construction prior to beginning her training at the Kharkov Theatre Institute and the Shchukin Acting School in Moscow. Though she has worked at the Vakhtangov and Maiakovskii Theatres in Moscow, she is best known for her screen roles. After her debut in Kira Muratova's film *Korotkie vstrechi* (*Brief Encounters*, 1967), she appeared in Georgii Danelia's *Afonia* (1975), Aleksei German's *Moi Drug Ivan Lapshin* (*My Friend Ivan Lapshin*, 1984) and *Khrustalev, mashinu!* (*Khrustalyov, My Car!*, 1998), and numerous other films. Ruslanova became famous for creating sincere emotional and strong female characters, embodying an archetypical image of the Russian woman that borders on folk representation. People's Artist of Russia (1998).

See also: Daneliia, Georgii; film, post-Soviet; film, Soviet – Stagnation period; German, Aleksei; Maiakovskii Theatre; Muratova, Kira; theatre, post-Soviet; theatre, Soviet; Vakhtangov Theatre

TATIANA SMORODINSKAYA

Russian Academy of Theatre Arts (RATI, formerly GITIS)

The Russian Academy of Theatre Arts (RATI, formerly GITIS) is one of the largest theatre schools in Europe, offering undergraduate and graduate education in a wide range of performing arts. First founded in 1878 as a music school under the auspices of the Amateur Society for Drama and Music (*Obschestvo liubitelei muzykalnogo i dramaticheskogo iskusstva*), it was renamed the Philharmonic Society Drama and Music School in 1883 and gained renown as an educational institution in theatre and music. Such famous theatre practitioners as Aleksandr Iuzhin and Vladimir Nemirovich-Danchenko headed its drama department. In 1922 it merged with the State Post-Secondary Theatre Studio (*Gosudarstvennye vysshie teatralnye masterskie*), under Vsevolod Meierkhold's leadership, and was named *GITIS* (State Institute for Theatre Arts), only to be renamed RATI in 1991. Students enrol in one of the Academy's eight departments, which provide training in the disciplines of theatre acting and directing, opera directing, choreography, circus, theatre studies, show business, management, and design.

See also: theatre, Soviet

DASHA KRIJANSKAIA

Russian Federation

The Russian Federation or Russia is the world's largest country by area (17 million square km) and the seventh largest by population (143.7 million in 2004). The population census of 2002 shows that Russians constitute 80 per cent of all residents. In addition, thirty-nine other ethnic groups exceed 100,000. There are six ethnic minorities whose population numbers over a million: Tatars (5.5), Ukrainians (2.9), Bashkirs (1.7), Chuvash (1.6), Chechens (1.4), and Armenians (1.1). Most minorities are fluent in Russian.

Of the eighty-nine territorial units in the Russian Federation, fifty-seven form the Russian settlement belt. More than 82 per cent of the entire population lives in this region, which

Russians developed for grain farming many centuries ago. Today, nearly all cropland is in the Russian settlement belt. Borderlands harbour twenty-one ethno-republics and eleven homelands populated by non-assimilated minorities. Russians outnumber minorities in all but five ethno-republics: Chechnia, Chuvashia, Ingushetia, North Ossetia, and Tyva. The most populous member of the Federation (10.3 million), the federal capital of Moscow is followed by the Moscow region (6.6 million) and by the Krasnodar territory (5.1 million). Two ethno-republics have a population of over 3 million: Bashkortostan and Tatarstan.

Post-Soviet reforms gave ethno-republics new opportunities to shelter their culture from Russification. Concerns on this point occur because better-urbanized Russian provinces lead in social innovations, offering modernity to younger generations. Other mechanisms are also at work: Conscription forces young males to speak Russian during the years of military service, and higher education uses mainly Russian textbooks.

Ethno-republics maintain a careful balance between tradition and change. Typically, partnerships on the federal and international levels are replacing insularity. In the 1990s, conditions deteriorated in Chechnia, as it fell into a vicious cycle of poverty and self-isolation. The trade-offs have been more productive for populous minorities (Tatarstan, Bashkortostan) and those rich in mineral resources (Sakha, Khanty-Mansia, Yamalo-Nenetsia).

Today, all Russia is at a stage of similar trade-offs, catching up with innovations after seventy years of Communist-imposed isolation. The rate of modernization varies by population strata and by regions, largely in proportion to the educational level of the majority. In this respect, cities differ dramatically from villages.

Under the Soviet system, education concentrated on training the workforce for industrialization, a focus that widened the gap between cities and villages in the educational achievements of residents. Graduates of universities and four-year colleges make up a quarter of Russia's urban workers (48.5 million in 2002). The percentage of this stratum is two times smaller among Russia's rural workers (13 million). Graduates from universities and colleges are most strongly represented in the cities of the Central Federal district, where they account for over 29 per cent of the workforce, while fewer than 20 per cent of the population in the cities of the Urals federal district belong to this stratum. Those with a higher education make up the smallest percentage of the population, less than 11 per cent, in the villages of Ural federal district.

Russia has thirteen cities, all of them major cultural centres, with a population of over a million. Collectively, they train half of all college and university students. Nearly a third of the students are concentrated in Moscow and St. Petersburg.

The geographical distribution of human capital favours the Central Federal District of Russia, which is the nation's heartland. Seventeen provinces settled by Russian native speakers form the district that also includes the city of Moscow. In area the Central Federal District exceeds France, while its population (38 million in 2002) slightly exceeds half of that in France. Population densities in seven provinces exceed 50 persons per sq km, a rare distinction for Eastern Europe.

Elsewhere in Russia, nearly three-fifths of provinces populated by Russians have much lower densities, between 50 and 12 persons per sq km. Extremely low densities, fewer than three persons per square kilometre, are in five Russian units of the federation and in thirteen ethno-republics. Those areas rarely can afford enterprises with large-scale operations. The few seaports in Russia are distant from the heartland. Railroads spanning Russia's eleven time zones carry major flows of goods.

Vast territories remain unpopulated, because they are in the inhospitable zones of tundra, taiga or in mountains next to the Caucasus, Mongolia, and China. Permafrost constrains settlement in the northeastern half of the country. Soviet social engineering expanded the network of cities, at the price of agricultural decline. Oversized industrial cities came to the tundra, including Norilsk, Vorkuta, and Monchegorsk. Giant steel mills were built in the Urals, the Kuzbas region, and the Far East, each with abnormally high operating and transportation costs. During the Cold War the Soviet military-industrial complex added over 300 secret cities, in intentionally isolated areas.

During the 1950s, Khrushchev attempted to galvanize Russia's rural life, but failed to heal the wounds in villages devastated by the collectivization campaign of the 1930s. Instead, he instituted a short-lived expansion of grain farming through the cultivation of virgin lands in the southern Urals and Siberia, arid areas with unstable yields. Severe winters and the destruction of topsoil by wind erosion compound the difficulties.

After 1990, Russia's farmland stopped expanding. The depopulation of marginal agricultural lands became common in the Russian heartland and in the periphery. By the beginning of the twenty-first century, Russia's agricultural lands had contracted to 12.9 per cent of the territory. Croplands occupy less than 5 per cent of the territory.

Since 1991 urbanization in Russia has stabilized at 73–74 per cent. The percentages are high enough to trigger changes known as the demographic transition. Natural population growth declined to zero and below. Crude death rates exceeded birth rates. Between 1988 and 2002 the population of Russia decreased by 1.8 million, despite positive net migrations. In the post-Soviet period Russia obtains annually from 0.2 million to 1.9 million new residents, mainly ethnic Russians who flee from the 'near abroad'. In the 1990s, decreases in population led to a shrinkage in Russia's network of cities. Numerous unsustainable urban places were reclassified as villages, a process mainly affecting remote areas in Siberia and the Far East.

Decreases in population forced Russia to improve labour efficiency. The regions of Russia compete with one another to attract labour. Private initiatives in the utilization of human and natural resources have become important; local self-governance and the market economy open doors for new initiatives. Russia's status as a major supplier of oil and natural gas to the world market ensures a large positive foreign trade balance and the flow of money from foreign trade is helping Russia recover from transitional difficulties. Since 1998, private businesses have succeeded in replacing imports in the domestic market of consumer goods. Oil extraction and exports are expanding, and private businesses bring consumer goods to all corners of Russia. The perennial shortages that plagued the Soviet consumer have disappeared. The country's new middle class is growing in numbers and wealth, introducing cities and villages to upscale housing and the family car. The most spectacular construction occurs in Moscow, which benefits from its dual role as the multicultural centre of the federation and the organizer of links to transnational corporations.

Russia is restructuring itself in three directions. It has ceased to be an aggressive empire and focuses on tidying up its domestic affairs, as does any normal nation-state. It has rejected dictatorship in favour of democracy and it has replaced the state command economy with a market economy.

See also: administrative structure, Russian Federation; Bashkortostan (Bashkiria); blizhnee zarubezhe (near abroad); Caucasus; Chechnia; closed city; Cold War; collective farms; defence industry; economic system, post-Soviet; ethnic minorities; Far East; Far North; Krushchev, Nikita; Kuzbas; Moscow; natural resources; Siberia; St. Petersburg; taiga; Tatars; tundra; Urals

Further reading

Smith, G. (1999) *The Post-Soviet States: Mapping the Politics of Transition*, New York: Oxford University Press.

YURI MEDVEDKOV AND OLGA MEDVEDKOV

Russian Museum (Russkii muzei)

Established by special decree of Nicholas II in 1895 in the former Mikhailovskii Palace (architect Carlo Rossi, 1825), this first state museum dedicated to Russian visual art possesses rich collections of Russian folk art, Russian visual art and sculpture of the pre-revolutionary and Soviet periods, and Russia's decorative art collections. In 1992 the museum was declared a treasure of Russia's cultural heritage. The 1990s brought significant changes to the museum by adding a complex of buildings to expand its collections. Today the Russian Museum includes not only the original Mikhailovskii Palace, but also other satellite museums, such as the Mikhailovskii Castle (Vincenzo Brenna, 1801), the Marble Palace (Antonio Rinaldi, 1785), and the Stroganov Palace (Bartolomeo Rastrelli, 1754, which was rebuilt in the early nineteenth century by Andrei Voronikhin). The museum additionally serves as an important research and educational centre: the Russian Centre of Museum Pedagogy and Children's Creativity was established in 1990, leading the country's educational programmes with the creation of the Russian Museum's numerous virtual spaces throughout the country.

See also: art galleries and exhibition halls; folk art

MARINA BALINA

Russian National Library

Second in size and significance among Russian libraries with archival collections, the RNL, founded as the main library of the Russian Empire in 1795, is located in St. Petersburg, with its main building on the corner of Nevsky Avenue and Sadovaia Street. In 1805, it opened a department of manuscripts; from 1810–1917 two copies of all printed materials published within the borders of the Empire were sent to its depository – which explains why the pre-revolutionary collection of the RNL is the most complete in the country. In the 1860s the Hermitage library's collection was transferred to RNL, and the department 'Rossika' (comprising books about Russia published abroad before 1917) was created.

After the 1917 Revolution, the library's holdings were increased by books from liquidated ministries, pre-revolutionary institutions, the Novgorod theological seminary, cloisters, and private collections. The M.E. Saltykov-Shchedrin Library was renamed the Public Library. In the mid-1920s a special fund was opened for books banned by censorship, and the library began to receive foreign publications. In the late 1920s, it again began to receive an obligatory copy of all domestic publications (books, magazines, newspapers, and other printed materials, including items in the various languages of the USSR). In the 1930s, the scholarly reading rooms were separated from general ones, specialized departments were opened, such as those in socio-economics, literature and the arts, natural sciences and medicine, physics and mathematics, chemistry, periodical literature, and cartography. The library did not cease operating even during the siege of Leningrad (1941–44), but evacuated the most valuable collections. In 1992 the library was renamed the Russian National Library (RNL). In 1998 the construction of a new building on Moscow Avenue (*Moskovskii prospekt*), with sixteen reading rooms and a large book depository, was finished; many holdings were transferred there. By 2001 the project of scanning the card catalogue (eight million items) was completed. Currently RNL houses 34,150,000 books and other units (including twenty-four special collections). The library serves 1.5 million readers annually.

See also: censorship; libraries; literature, underground; samizdat

SERGEI TARKHOV

Russian Orthodox churches

Russian Orthodox Church architecture and ecclesiology evolved directly out of Byzantine culture and religion; since Orthodox Christianity represents the foundational influence on Russian architecture and art between the tenth and eighteenth centuries, its theology governs the appearance and sensibilities of the country's churches. The onion-shaped domes, orientation of the altar, arrangement of interior space, absence of pews, omnipresence of icons, ordering of icons of the iconostasis – all these essential features developed according to ancient laws and customs relating to Russian Orthodoxy. The aesthetic principle is strong and pronounced: the Orthodox liturgy engages both the interiors and exteriors of churches in a synaesthetic way, aiming through this multi-sensory experience of beauty to direct the faithful to a higher spiritual realm. The faithful stand in a spacious interior, contemplate the icons, inhale the incense, hear a capella chanting, and physically move to different locations of the church's interior (and sometimes exterior) according to the requirements of the liturgy.

Each Orthodox church must be built in such a way that its altar faces Jerusalem. In order for the church to be consecrated, it must house in a place of honour the relics (or even a small relic) of a saint. The open area of the interior is arranged in the form of a cross, while the movement of people throughout this space is intended to resemble the breathing of a communitarian (*sobornyi*) body: the individual possesses maximum freedom, but within, and answerable to, a larger body of believers. Worshippers light candles in the vestibule (narthex) and central area (nave), venerate icons, kneel or prostrate themselves on the floor, or stand transfixed at the mystery of the Eucharist service that is central to the liturgy. The preparation of the Eucharist takes place behind the closed Royal Doors and Royal Curtains, which separate the nave (Earth) from the altar/altar table (Heaven), symbolic, respectively, of the church militant and the church triumphant. The Royal Doors stand between the two sides of the iconostasis, which can be gilded and as ornate as the specific parish community desires. In the various rows (three is the minimum) of the iconostasis, the icons are strictly arranged according to their theological significance.

Icons cover the walls of Orthodox churches; they are a canonical component of the theology of the faith tradition. A large icon of Christ is painted on the ceiling of the church, and on the ceiling above the altar is an icon of the Mother of God 'embracing' the church community and theologically serving as a conduit between Earth and Heaven. Important icons are encased within ornate silver frames (*oklady*), and larger churches may contain an icon that is considered 'miracle-working'.

See also: architecture, wooden; icon; Russian Orthodoxy

Further reading

Brumfield, W. (2004) *A History of Russian Architecture*, Seattle, WA: University of Washington Press.

Florensky, P. (1996) *Iconostasis*, Crestwood, NY: St. Vladimir's Seminary Press.

Ouspensky, L. (1992) *Theology of the Icon*, Crestwood, NY: St. Vladimir's Seminary Press.

VALERIA Z. NOLLAN

Russian Orthodoxy

One of the world's major religions and Russia's historical faith tradition, Russian Orthodoxy takes 988 CE as its origin in Kievan Russia. According to the legend, under Prince Vladimir the early Slavs were baptized into Orthodoxy after emissaries returning from abroad recommended that religion to him. In the twenty-first century, approximately 70 per cent of Russia's citizens profess some type of affiliation with the Russian Orthodox Church. The church's spiritual and theological head in the early years of the third millennium is Patriarch Alexii II (*Patriarkh Vseia Rusi*) of Moscow.

Russian Orthodox religiosity is characterized by obedience to a hierarchy dating back to the apostles of Christ, the celebration of the Eucharist as central to the church liturgical service, and a monastic tradition that evolved from the Egyptian 'desert dweller' ascetics and Byzantine monks of the first millennium. Its long periods of standing and kneeling prayer, as well as its four major fasting periods and well-developed dietary laws, connect it directly with Judaism as well as ancient Christianity.

Russian Orthodoxy reached its theological heights in the nineteenth century with the writings of such lay theologians as Slavophile Aleksei Khomiakov, the religio-philosophical works of Vladimir Solovev, and the flowering of the elders of Optina pustyn. The spiritual wisdom of the Optina Elders became popular with both intellectuals and the common people, causing friction with the church hierarchy. The most notable of the elders was Amvrosii (Ambrose), who became the prototype for Elder Zosima in Dostoevskii's *Brothers Karamazov* (1881). In addition to these sources of authority for the Orthodox faithful, one of the most significant saints for world Orthodoxy, Serafim of Sarov, lived in Russia at the beginning of the nineteenth century. Major theologians whose writings were seminal for the reaffirmation of Orthodox thought during the late nineteenth and early twentieth centuries include Father Pavel Florenskii, Father Georges Florovskii, and Father Sergei Bulgakov.

After 1917, the Bolsheviks persecuted the clergy and monastics of Orthodoxy in an attempt to eradicate from the new society the essential features of tsarist Russia, including Russian Orthodoxy. In the 1920s, thousands of the Orthodox faithful were exiled to the West, imprisoned in the Soviet Union, or killed. The Orthodox Church as a result split into three groups: (1) the official church, which attempted to coexist with the Soviet regime; (2) the 'catacomb' church, whose members continued practising the traditional faith in the Soviet Union in secret 'underground' communities; and (3) the Church abroad, whose members received the blessing of the church in Russia to form a jurisdiction that would preserve the faith intact until Russia could be freed from Communist rule. This last group organized first in Europe in the 1920s, and in the United States in the 1940s after World War II, under the name of the Russian Orthodox Church Abroad (later renamed the Russian Orthodox Church Outside of Russia). Its current Chief Hierarch is Metropolitan Lavr (Laurus, elected in 2001).

Another challenge facing Russian Orthodoxy in the early twentieth century was the calendar issue. Although the Gregorian (New Style) calendar was adopted in much of the West under Pope Gregory XIII in 1582, the Orthodox Christian world continued to use the Julian (Old Style) calendar. In 1923, as a result of a controversial Pan-Orthodox Congress in Constantinople, some Orthodox jurisdictions adopted the Gregorian calendar. Russia and several other Slavic countries refused to adopt this calendar, considering the jurisdictional representation at the council incomplete; as a result, to this day Russian Orthodox liturgical events remain on the Julian calendar.

After Stalin's death in 1953, the position of the Orthodox Church became somewhat more promising. Despite the continued persecution of religion in the Soviet Union under Khrushchev and Brezhnev, courageous statements of faith appeared: in literature embedded in the writings of Aleksandr Solzhenitsyn and some of the village prose writers (Valentin Rasputin, Vladimir

Soloukhin); and in theology in the writings of, among others, Father Dmitrii Dudko.

In the first decade of the twenty-first century, the Moscow Patriarchate (Church in Russia) and Russian Orthodox Church Outside of Russia seem to be moving towards reunification. Bishops of both branches have held meetings in Moscow and Paris, and relations between the two branches have become warmer and more communicative than was the case in the twentieth century. Perhaps the most significant point of division between them was the question of ownership of what are historically Orthodox church properties in Israel, which the Church Outside of Russia, most notably under Chief Hierarchs Metropolitan Philaret and subsequently Metropolitan Vitalii, had cared for and developed throughout the twentieth century. Another issue was the canonization of the members of the royal family of Tsar Nicholas II, who were assassinated by the Bolsheviks in 1918. The Church Outside of Russia canonized them as Royal Martyrs in 1982, while the Church in Russia did not canonize them until 2000. The settlement of these issues will pave the way for a likely reunification of these branches of traditional Russian Orthodoxy in the future.

Regardless of whether or not this reconciliation of the Russian churches inside and outside of Russia takes place, the church will continue to reassert itself in post-Soviet Russia by developing the monasterial lands, seminaries, and other church properties that were returned to it by the Russian government in the late 1980s and 1990s. It will also, however, have to articulate its position both with respect to the Russian government and to the myriad Christian evangelical groups travelling to Russia on a regular basis and creating new denominational communities. The growing presence of Muslims, the second largest religious group, will also test the vitality of Russian Orthodoxy in the future.

See also: calendars, old and new; emigration; holidays, Russian Orthodox; Holy Trinity-St. Sergius Monastery; Islam; Judaism; Kiev; Lent; monastic life; Optina pustyn; Rasputin, Valentin; Russian Orthodox churches; Slavophiles; Soloukhin, Vladimir; Solzhenitsyn, Aleksandr; village prose; World War II (Great Patriotic War)

Further reading

Florensky, P. (1993) *The Pillar and Ground of the Truth*, Princeton, NJ: Princeton University Press.

Shevzov, V. (2003) *Russian Orthodoxy on the Eve of Revolution*, Oxford: Oxford University Press.

Valliere, P. (2000) *Modern Russian Theology: Bukharev, Soloviev, Bulgakov*, Edinburgh: T & T Clark.

Ware, T. (Bishop Kallistos) (1993) *The Orthodox Church*, New York: Penguin.

VALERIA Z. NOLLAN

Russian People's Friendship University

The Russian People's Friendship University (Rossiiskii universitet Druzhby narodov, RUDN) was founded in Moscow in 1960. From 1962 until 1992, the university bore the name of Patrice Lumumba in honour of the first prime minister of the Congo, assassinated in 1962. (The Belgian government has since admitted complicity in Lumumba's death, and many suspect CIA involvement, as well.) RUDN's mission has been to educate students from Asia, Africa, and Latin America in areas of great demand in their home countries. Despite the pacifist and internationalist rhetoric that has always surrounded the university, RUDN was an important tool in the Soviet Union's international politics: it accepted only students from countries on the 'socialist track'. More than 2,500 international students from more than one hundred countries currently study at RUDN; however, they now constitute a minority of the university's 17,000 students and no longer benefit from the generous scholarships previously offered by the Soviet government.

DAVID HUNTER SMITH

Russian roulette (Russkaia ruletka)

Russkaia ruletka (Russian roulette) seems to have been translated back into Russian from English, since there is no evidence that this game was invented or practised in Russia. Some scholars attribute the origin of the term to an American short story published in 1937 in which a purported Russian officer in the French Foreign Legion describes the practice, in which each of participants in turn, using a revolver loaded with one bullet, spins the cylinder, points the muzzle at his head, and pulls the trigger. Today the term refers to any high-risk undertaking.

MICHELE BERDY

Russians

During World War II, the epithet 'Russian' (*russkii*) was used both in the sense of 'Soviet' – that is, comprising the ethnically non-Russian citizens of the Soviet Empire – and in the meaning of 'Russian, by contrast to other peoples of the Soviet Union' (see, for example, Stalin's speech of 24 May 1945, where he calls Russians the 'leading [*rukovodiashchii*] people'). In the second half of the twentieth century, the notions of 'Russian' and 'from Russia' (*rossiiskii*) were used in several different ways. The epithet 'rossiiskii' was applied to the administration of a territorial unit – i.e., RSFSR. In addition, 'greater Russian' (*velikorusskii*) signified a Russian who was specifically not Ukrainian (*malorossiiskii*) or Belorussian. In the 1960s and the 1970s, the notion of 'Russian by birth/by nationality' became the dominant meaning of 'Russian' (*russkii*): for example, entries in the *Short Literary Encyclopedia* (*Kratkaia literaturnaia entsiklopediia*) distinguished between 'Fedin – Russian Soviet writer' and 'Tsydynzhapov – a Buryat Soviet playwright' (Vol. 9, Moscow, 1975: 411). By contrast, in the language of other peoples of the Soviet Union, 'Russian' (*russkii*) meant 'Soviet'. Thus in Andrei Bitov's book *Uroki Armenii* (*Lessons from Armenia*), an author who introduces himself as Russian is confronted with the imperative to specify more precisely: 'What kind of Russian? A Russian Russian?' (*Kakoi russkii? Russkii russkii?*). After the collapse of the USSR, the epithets '*russkii, rossiiskii*' became a permanent word compound, in which '*rossiiskii*' signifies citizenship (or, in imperial terms, to which power the person is subject), while '*russkii*' denotes ethnic origin. On the other hand, in the former Soviet republics, 'Russians' and 'Russian

speakers' ('*russkoiazychnye*') is the indiscriminate label for all post-Soviet immigrants. At the same time, after the collapse of the USSR, the notion of 'Russia' itself comprises regions and countries that formerly were part of the Russian Empire and the USSR. As new state-building processes have transformed these countries and regions, while the meaning of 'Russian' (*russkii*) has narrowed down independently from these processes, this new, narrower meaning of 'Russian' (*russkii* in some areas of post-Soviet Russia is often perceived as offensive to ethnically non-Russian but Russian-speaking people, such as Ukrainians, Germans, or Tatars living in Kazakhstan).

See also: administrative structure, Soviet Union; Armenia; Belarus; Bitov, Andrei; Caucasus; Central Asia; CIS; ethnic minorities; Kazakhstan; nationalism ('the national question'); Tatars; Ukraine; World War II (Great Patriotic War)

Further reading

Gusejnov, G. (2003) *Materialy k russkomu slovariu obshchestvenno-politicheskogo iazyka XX veka.* Moscow: Tri quadrata, pp. 468–77.

GASAN GUSEJNOV

Russian soul (Russkaia dusha)

Russian soul (*russkaia dusha*) in Russian literature and speech refers to characteristics that purportedly reflect cultural and moral values automatically ascribed to Russians, including openness; sincerity; hospitality; generosity; loyalty; self-sacrifice; the capacity for enduring love, even when not requited; and emotional extremes. When modified by the noun 'enigma' (*zagadka*) or the adjective 'enigmatic' (*zagodochnaia*), it refers to what seem to be illogical, irrational, or contradictory characteristics or behaviour, such as taking risks or jeopardizing health and well-being for the sake of a person, a lofty goal, or pleasure.

MICHELE BERDY

Russian State Library (Rossiiskaia gosudarstvennaia biblioteka imeni Lenina)

The largest library in Europe was founded in 1862 as the Rumiantsev Public Museum. Renamed the Lenin State Library (*Gosudarstvennaia biblioteka imeni Lenina*) in 1925 and the Russian State Library in 1993, it is still referred to in the twenty-first century as the 'Leninka'. It is located in central Moscow and attracts one and a half million visitors each year. Its holdings exceed 43 million items in 247 languages, including 16 million books and brochures, 13 million journals, and half a million manuscripts. It also hosts numerous public events each year, including seminars, conferences, and nearly 300 exhibitions.

The library experienced enormous growth in the period following World War II to the mid-1980s, including the establishment of its reading room system (18 separate halls seating 2,103 patrons) and the construction of an off-site repository in the Moscow suburb of Khimki. The collapse of the Soviet Union and subsequent funding losses sparked a period of crisis for the library, which continued to operate throughout the 1990s amid a crumbling infrastructure and need to restructure salaries for its 2,100 workers; the library was closed for renovations from 2000–2004. The library entered the new century with an online catalogue, Internet stations, and major capital reconstruction, including an upgrade to its basement café.

ANDREA LANOUX

Russian State Museum of Musical Culture

See: Glinka State Central Museum of Musical Culture

Russian State University for the Humanities (Rossiiskii gosudarstvennyi gumanitarnyi universitet, RGGU)

One of Russia's leading universities for the study of the humanities, RGGU was founded in Moscow in 1991 by Iurii Afanasev on the territory of a Soviet Higher Party School (*vysshaia partiinaia shkola*). Previously a Historical-Archival Institute (*Istoriko-arkhivnyi institut*), RGGU has a liberal humanities programme and maintains an international profile through student and faculty exchanges with various international institutions of higher learning, such as the Sorbonne and many American universities. According to the official constitution of the university, its chief goals include providing education aimed at 'universality' and creating an intellectual atmosphere based on a rigorous theoretical foundation.

See also: Moscow

SUSMITA SUNDARAM

Russkoe radio (Russian Radio)

Radio station

Russkoe radio began broadcasting on 2 August 1995 and became the first nationwide station with playlists made up exclusively of Russian-language compositions. Comparable radio stations, in particular *Evropa Plus*, have played both Slavic songs and more fashionable Western material since the post-Soviet media explosion. Like its kindred spirit in musical television, *MuzTV*, *Russkoe radio* considers itself a bastion of cultural protectionism and enjoys sympathetic support from listeners in 700 cities across Russia, the CIS and émigré communities worldwide. Counting synchronous webcasts, the station boasts a potential round-the-clock audience of over 120 million listeners.

See also: radio, post-Soviet; rock music

DAVID MACFADYEN

Rybakov, Anatolii Naumovich

b. 1 [14] January 1911, Chernigov; d. 23 December 1998, New York [buried in Moscow]

Writer

The 1987 publication of Rybakov's most famous work, *Deti Arbata* (*Children of the Arbat*) served as a major signal that the Gorbachev administration was making a political investment in reappraising the Stalinist past. A semi-autobiographical chronicle of several young Muscovites' lives in the early 1930s, the novel intersperses lengthy inner monologues by Stalin with the most explicit descriptions of the purges to have appeared in the Soviet Union up to that point. The book became an international bestseller, and Rybakov, who had been known for his popular young-adult adventure stories and a controversial novel on 'the Jewish question', turned into one of perestroika's most prominent public intellectuals.

See also: anti-Semitism; Gorbachev, Mikhail; Jews; literature, Soviet; perestroika and glasnost

BORIS WOLFSON

Rybnikov, Aleksei Lvovich

b. 17 July 1945, Moscow

Composer

A student of Aram Khachaturian, Rybnikov graduated from the Moscow Conservatory in 1967, and finished its graduate programme in 1969. From 1969 to 1975 he taught at the Moscow Conservatory. He composed several operas and numerous film scores. By 1989, Rybnikov's music had been released on more than 10 million discs. In his rock opera *Iunona i Avos*, staged at Moscow's Lenkom Theatre in 1981, Rybnikov combined elements of 'art rock' with Russian religious hymns. In 1994–95, Rybnikov and his 'Modern Opera' theatre, founded in 1988, toured the United States. People's Artist of Russia (2000).

See also: Khachaturian, Aram; Lenkom Theatre; Moscow Conservatory; rock music; rock opera

ALEXANDER DOMRIN

Rybnikov, Nikolai Nikolaevich

b. 13 December 1930, Borisoglebsk, Voronezh oblast; d. 22 October 1990, Moscow

Actor

Rybnikov made his name in the 1950s playing young men of the same generation as many of his fans. Occasionally he played villains, more often worker-heroes. His portrait of the brash worker, Sasha Savchenko, in *Vesna na Zarechnoi ulitse* (*Spring on Zarechnyi Street*, 1956) struck viewers as fresh and engaging, as did his performances as the tractor-driving Fedor Soloveikov in *Chuzhaia rodnia* (*Alien Kin*, 1956) and as the supremely self-confident rigger Pasechnik in *Vysota* (*Heights*). Other roles include Denisov in *Voina i mir* (*War and Peace*, 1966–67).

JOSEPHINE WOLL

S

Saami (Lopars, Lapps)

Ethnic group living in the far northeast of Europe, primarily in northern Norway (40,000), Sweden (18,000), Finland (4,000), and Russia (1,900), of which 1,769 live in Murmansk oblast. Saami do not possess political autonomy. The Saami language belongs to the Finno-Ugric group of the Uralic language family. Anthropologically Saami differ from neighbouring northern peoples in that they have mongoloid features. Primary occupations are reindeer herding, fishing, and hunting. Saami live in tents consisting of deerskin suspended on a pole, with a fire in the centre. Saami practise shamanism and have preserved some elements of paganism, including the worship of spirits and sacred stones.

Aleksandr Rogozhkin's acclaimed 2002 film *Kukushka* (*The Cuckoo* [*The Sniper*]) familiarized audiences with Saami and selective aspects of their culture.

SERGEI TARKHOV

Sadur, Nina Nikolaevna

b. 15 October 1950, Novosibirsk

Writer

Prose writer and playwright Nina Sadur became known to a wider public during perestroika. After graduating from the drama section of Moscow's Literary Institute in 1983 she wrote for 'the drawer' for a long time, while working as a cleaning lady at the Pushkin Theatre. In 1987, the student theatre of Moscow State University staged her play *Chudnaia baba* (*The Marvellous Old Woman*), and productions soon followed in established theatres. In 1999, Mark Zakharov staged her play *Brat Chichikov* (*Brother Chichikov*) at the Lenkom Theatre. She has published seven collections of plays and prose, beginning with *Chudnaia baba* in 1989. In the cycle of short stories *Pronikshee* (*Touched*, 1990), she transforms her experience in the margins of society into folkloric horrors. Her main protagonists are predominantly female; their refusal to conform to norms and public requirements renders them both vulnerable and empowered. Her most ambitious work from the 1990s is the novel *Sad* (*The Garden*), which uses modernist, destabilizing devices to represent post-Soviet reality. In 2001, Sadur published stories in the pornographic magazines *Pleiboi* (The Russian Playboy) and *Kets shou* (*Cats Show*).

See also: Lenkom Theatre; Literary Institute; Zakharov, Mark

KARIN SARSENOV

Sagalaev, Eduard Mikhailovich

b. 3 October 1946, Samarkand

Journalist, television personality

Sagalaev worked on *Radio Iunost* (Youth Radio, 1980–84) before moving to television, where he produced the ground-breaking perestroika programmes *Vzgliad* (Viewpoint) and *Dvenadtsatyi etazh* (Twelfth Floor) between 1984 and 1988. In

Dvenadtsatyi etazh young people raised critical issues during live satellite links with remote areas of the country, while Party officials responded from the studio. Sagalaev was news editor on central television (1988–90) before moving to VGTRK (1991–92); from 1992–96 at Moscow Independent Broadcasting Corporation (MNVK), where he launched Channel TV6. After a brief stint (1996–97) as head of RTR, he returned to TV6. He heads the National Association of Television and Radio Broadcasters (NAT).

See also: perestroika and glasnost; radio, Soviet; television, Soviet; television channels; *Vzgliad*

BIRGIT BEUMERS

Sakha

See: Iakutia (Sakha)

Sakharov, Andrei Dmitrievich

b. 21 May 1921, Moscow; d. 14 December 1989, Moscow

Physicist, human rights activist

One of the creators of the Soviet thermonuclear bomb (the first tests took place in 1953), Sakharov was also a social activist and winner of the Nobel Peace Prize (1975). As a physicist specializing in theory, he worked under conditions of secrecy, authored fundamental works on the evolution and structure of the universe and the idea of utilizing directed thermonuclear synthesis for peaceful purposes. The youngest academician-physicist at the Academy of Sciences of the USSR (1953), awarded many state prizes, and three times recognized as a Hero of Socialist Labour, he was stripped of all his titles and awards for his public protests against the Soviet invasion of Afghanistan (1980).

He wrote in his autobiography of 'an increasingly acute awareness of the moral problems inherent in his work' as a physicist from 1953–62. In July 1968, he published his work *Progress,*

Coexistence, and Intellectual Freedom in the West and achieved international fame. For his human rights activities, in 1980 he was exiled to Gorkii (Nizhnii Novgorod), where he spent seven years in isolation under the surveillance of the special service. In 1986, he was recalled from exile by special order of Mikhail Gorbachev. In 1989, Sakharov was elected as a People's Deputy of the USSR to the Supreme Soviet, becoming one of the leaders of the oppositional Interregional group of deputies. He authored the draft of the new *Constitution of the Union of Soviet Republics of Europe and Asia* (1989).

In contemporary Russian society, Sakharov symbolizes a democratic mode of development and resistance to political injustice. His legacy is preserved in an archive created by the Andrei Sakharov Fund (1994) and located in the house where he lived in 1972–1979 and 1987–1989 (105064, Moscow, Zemlianoi val, 48-B, apt. 62). One of the first non-state archives, it comprises works, documents, and materials about Sakharov's life.

See also: Academy of Sciences; archives; awards, state and government, Soviet and post-Soviet; Federal Security Service; Gorbachev, Mikhail; Nobel Prize winners, non-literary; perestroika and glasnost; science and technology; War, Afghan

Further reading

Sakharova (1921–1989) Letopis zhizni, nauchnoi i obshchestvennoi deiatelnosti Andreia Dmirtievicha., v 3-kh ch. Ch. 1 (1921–1953). 2002 [Fond Andreia Sakharova] Comp. E. Bonneri dr. Moscow: Prava cheloveka.

Sakharov, A. (1968) *Progress, Coexistence, and Intellectual Freedom*, New York: Norton.

——(1990) *Memoirs*, New York: Alfred A. Knopf.

Sakharova (1921–1989) v 3-kh ch. Ch. 1 (1921–1953). 2002 [Fond Andreia Sakharova] Sost. E. Bonneri dr. Moscow: Prava cheloveka.

ELENA OZNOBKINA

salads

Russian salads are complex combinations of ingredients and part of the appetizer course. A typical holiday table will include at least two and as many as ten different salads. They are also eaten as the first course in a meal at home or in a restaurant. They comprise primarily fresh vegetables; boiled root vegetables; fish, meat, or cheese dressed with oil (traditionally, sunflower oil), mayonnaise, or sour cream; and often include pickled vegetables. Restaurants serve *salat-kokteili* (salad cocktails) – salads comprising many ingredients that are often given opaque names, such as *siurpriz* (surprise) or *firmennyi* (speciality of the house). During the Soviet period, salads from the Caucasus and Central Asia became part of Russian tables, as did salads invented to use the paltry number of products available in a challenged economy (such as a salad made of grated cheese, minced garlic, and mayonnaise). Lettuce did not appear in traditional Russian salads. In the post-Soviet period, Greek salad (*grecheskii salat*) and Caesar salad (*salat Tsezar*) are commonly found on menus.

Ingredients in typical fresh vegetable salads (*ovoshchnye salaty*) include cucumbers, radishes, tomatoes, and/or peppers, dressed in oil or sour cream and garnished with fresh parsley or dill. *Vitaminnyi salat* blends fresh cabbage with other vegetables; *koreiskaia morkov* (Korean carrot) is a salad of finely grated carrots marinated in a spicy oil dressing. Traditional salads made of boiled root vegetables include olivier (*olive*) and beet salad in oil (*vinegret*). Meat salads may include boiled beef, tongue, chicken, or veal, as well as processed meats. Meat and fish salads usually include potatoes or rice.

See also: appetizers; dining, Soviet; olive (olivier); vinegret

MICHELE BERDY

Salakhova, Aidan Tairovna

b. 25 March 1964, Moscow

Artist, gallery owner

After graduating from the Surikov Art Academy (1987), in 1989 Salakhova opened one of Moscow's first privately-owned galleries, Pervaia, with Aleksandr Iakut and Evgenii Mitta. A year later, she exhibited in the Soviet Pavilion at the Venice Biennale and received a special Menzione d'Onore medal, and in 1992 she founded Aidan Gallery in Moscow. Her early works were Neo-Academist in style, devoid of social or political motifs; she largely explored and aspired to visual experiments within the limits of 'traditional' technologies of painting, drawing, and photography. Her later works explore sexuality, Islamic culture, and particularly femininity in the Islamic world. She teaches at the Surikov Art Academy.

See also: art schools and academies; Islam

NATALIA KOLODZEI

samizdat

The term *samizdat* appeared in the 1950s, and mimics the names of Soviet publishing houses. It means literally 'self-publishing', and refers to material published and disseminated in the USSR outside the auspices of the Soviet publishing houses, and not, therefore, subject to censorship. *Samizdat* became integral to Soviet unofficial culture in the post-Stalin period. Although the production and possession of *samizdat* material were not criminal offences, the authorities arrested many who were involved in *samizdat* on charges of anti-Soviet agitation and propaganda. The dissemination of manuscripts and typescripts grew as production methods were developed. In the 1950s, most *samizdat* was handwritten or typed and reproduced using carbon paper; subsequently replaced by blueprint paper, and later by Xerox, when contacts were established with people who had access to photocopiers. Photography and microfilm were also used.

In the 1950s, poetry was the principal genre of *samizdat*, but literary and journalistic prose soon appeared as well. In the 1960s, the most common *samizdat* work was Boris Pasternak's novel *Doctor Zhivago*. Literature circulating in *samizdat* was not always unpublished: sometimes a poem or novel was published once, in a small edition, and copies were made and circulated to compensate for its lack of availability. The 1960s also saw the development of '*magnitizdat*' – electronic, audio *samizdat*. When reasonably priced and readily available cassette players appeared in the USSR, tape-recordings of bards were reproduced and circulated clandestinely.

From the mid-1960s, much political literature appeared in *samizdat*, such as transcripts of trials, beginning with Iosif Brodskii's in 1964, and essays by liberals such as Andrei Sakharov. The year 1968 saw the first edition of the *samizdat* journal *Khronika tekushchikh sobytii* (*Chronicle of Current Events*), which aimed to record human rights abuses in the USSR. The journal provided information about the trials and sentences of dissidents, and the conditions for political prisoners in the GULag and psychiatric hospitals. It lasted almost twenty years.

Samizdat culture became firmly established in Moscow and Leningrad in the 1970s. Moscow publications remained chiefly political, while Leningrad produced primarily literary, philosophical and religious *samizdat*, including two *samizdat* literary and philosophical journals, *Chasy* (The Hours) and *37*. In Moscow, many information bulletins appeared concerning, amongst other issues, the rights of invalids, the right of emigration, and psychiatry in the USSR. There, the historical journal *Pamiat* (Memory) was founded, which aimed to record events not included in official versions of Soviet history. By the 1980s, the Soviet authorities were unable to stop the production of *samizdat*: although in 1981–82 *samizdat* activity was severely punished, with many people arrested, such measures proved futile. By the end of the 1980s *samizdat* represented a diverse range of political views and agendas, including those of neo-Marxists, democratic groups, feminists, and orthodox nationalists.

See also: bards; Brodskii, Iosef; censorship; dissident; GULag; Pasternak, Boris; Sakharov, Andrei; Stagnation; tamizdat

Further reading

Dolinin, V. and Ivanov, B. (eds) (1993) *Samizdat*, St. Petersburg: Nauchno-Informatsionni Tsentr 'Memorial'.

Reddaway, P. (ed.) (1972) *Uncensored Russia*, London: Jonathan Cape.

Severiukhin, D. (ed.) (2003) *Samizdat Leningrada*, Moscow: Novoe literaturnoe obozrenie.

Strelianyi, A. (ed.) (1999) *Samizdat veka*, Moscow: Polifakt.

EMILY LYGO

Samoilova, Tatiana Evgenevna

b. 4 May 1934, Leningrad

Actress

Though she has made fewer than a dozen films, Samoilova remains one of the best-loved actresses of her generation for one role: Veronika in *Letiat zhuravli* (*The Cranes are Flying*, 1957), the enigmatic and lovely young woman who, amid the upheavals of World War II, loves one man but marries another. She starred in another, less successful film made by the same team that created *Cranes*, director Mikhail Kalatozov and cinematographer Sergei Urusevskii, *Neotpravlennoe pismo* (*The Unsent Letter*, 1960), and in a 1967 adaptation of *Anna Karenina* directed by Aleksandr Zarkhi.

See also: Kalatozov, Mikhail; Urusevskii, Sergei; World War II (Great Patriotic War); Zarkhi, Aleksandr

JOSEPHINE WOLL

samovar

Literally, 'self-brewer' or 'self-boiler', the *samovar* was a traditional Russian home's ceremonial centrepiece. A large metal urn with a central column heated by live coals or electric coils, it has a tap on one side for dispensing hot water, and a teapot stand on top. Tea is brewed with loose leaves in the teapot; the strong brew (*zavarka*) is poured into individual cups and diluted to taste with water from the samovar. Kettles have largely replaced samovars, and increasingly popular tea bags may change the way tea is prepared. Many Russians drink fairly weak tea all day, usually with sugar, for warmth, caffeine, quenching of thirst, and social interaction.

SIBELAN FORRESTER

sanatoria (sanatorii)

Sanatoria were the facilities that supplied medical treatment in a resort (*kurort*) setting, analogous to European spas, though officially integrated into the medical system. As with other medical facilities, they were often quite specialized, though some were multi-specialty. The municipal government managed tuberculosis and pediatric *sanatorii*, while trade unions oversaw all other types. Many of the medical therapies *sanatorii* provided focused on rehabilitation and convalescence, and *sanatorii* could be used as bridges from hospital to home. Sanatorium stays could also be recreational. In post-Soviet times, the medical role of sanatoria has declined, though recreational uses persist.

See also: health

SAMUEL BROWN

Satire Theatre (Teatr satiry)

One of Moscow's most popular comedy theatres, the *Teatr satiry* is known for its daring sarcasm, all-star cast, and vibrant performances. The Theatre began in 1924 as a venue for contemporary plays featuring social satire. In 1950, Valentin Pluchek became the theatre's director, enriching its repertoire with classics of European and Russian satire. Plays such as Beaumarchais' *Marriage of Figaro*, along with Vladimir Maiakovskii's *Bania* (*The Bathhouse*), *Klop* (*The Bedbug*), and *Misteriia-Buff* (*Mystery-Bouffe*) have come to symbolize the theatre's emotional and witty style, coupled with exquisite sets and music. Russian television often transmits video recordings of these plays. *Teatr satiry* was home to actors Andrei Mironov and Anatolii Papanov. Current members of the troupe include Aleksandr Shirvindt (artistic director since 2000), Olga Aroseva, Mikhail Derzhavin, Spartak Mishulin, and Natalia Selezneva.

See also: Aroseva, Olga; Mironov, Andrei; Papanov, Anatolii; Pluchek, Valentin; Shirvindt, Aleksandr; theatre, Soviet

OLGA MESROPOVA

Sats, Natalia Ilinichna

b. 14 [27] August 1903, Irkutsk; d. 18 December 1993, Moscow

Director, playwright, producer, writer

Daughter of composer Ilia Sats, she received a musical education and spearheaded the professionalization of Soviet children's theatre.

From 1921 to 1937 she served as artistic director of the Moscow Children's Theatre. Among her collaborators was Sergei Prokofiev, who wrote *Peter and the Wolf* for her company. Arrested and sent to a labour camp in 1937, she subsequently worked in Kazakhstan before returning to Moscow. As artistic director of Moscow's Musical Theatre for Children from its founding in 1964, she commissioned numerous operas and musicals, establishing herself as a leader of the international children's theatre movement.

See also: Prokofiev, Sergei

HARLOW ROBINSON

Satyricon Theatre

This legendary satirical theatre opened in 1939 in Leningrad (under the name of *Teatr estrady i miniatiur*), with Arkadii Raikin as its leading actor and artistic director. Known as 'Raikin's theatre', it was famous for its sharp social commentary, unique repertoire, and revolutionary performances. In 1982, the theatre moved to Moscow and in 1987 it acquired its present name (*Teatr Satirikon imeni A. Raikina*). Led by Konstantin Raikin since 1987, Satyricon has combined elements of philosophical drama, comedic farce, ultramodern performances, and arresting visual imagery. It has featured modernistic interpretations of Kafka, Murdock, Shakespeare, Rostand, and Molière. Robert Sturua and Roman Viktiuk are among the directors who have worked with the theatre.

See also: Raikin, Arkadii; Raikin, Konstantin; Sturua, Robert; theatre, Soviet; Viktiuk, Roman

OLGA MESROPOVA

Savvina, Iia Sergeevna

b. 2 March 1936, Voronezh

Actress

A graduate of the Moscow State University journalism department (1958), Savvina has consistently acted on both stage (the Mossovet

Theatre, the Moscow Art Theatre) and screen. She debuted in Iosif Kheifits's lyrical 1960 adaptation of Chekhov's 'Lady with the Lapdog', playing with great delicacy an artless young woman whose holiday romance turns into a passionate love affair. She starred in *Istoriia Asi Kliachinoi, kotoraia liubila, da ne vyshla zamuzh* (*The Story of Asia Kliachina, Who Loved But Didn't Marry*, 1966), a melodrama mangled by the censors before its release as *Asino schaste* (*Asia's Happiness*) in 1968. Other roles include Anikeeva in the satire *Garazh* (*The Garage*, 1980). USSR State Prize (1983), People's Artist of the USSR (1990).

See also: Moscow Art Theatre; Mossovet Theatre

JOSEPHINE WOLL

science and technology

Russia's science and technology sector has been struggling since its collapse in early 1992 to find its bearings in the new capitalist order. The worst years for post-Soviet science were the early to mid-1990s; the last decade has seen modest progress in funding and organizational reforms.

Since the founding of the Russian Academy of Sciences by Peter the Great in 1725, science and technology in Russia had been a state institution, patterned after Western models, and focused mainly on the state's military-industrial needs, and to a lesser degree on its need to be seen as an equal to the West. Russia had imported various Western industrial innovations, which soon stagnated on Russian soil, leaving Russia chronically 'backward' (Graham 1993). These patterns continued through the Soviet period, during which state-sponsored science provided many educated Russians with enviably stable and socially prestigious employment in thousands of basic and applied research institutions; the other side of the coin was ideological control – as in 'Lysenkoism', the rejection of 'bourgeois' Mendelian genetics, ethnic discrimination in admissions and employment, and the exploitation of imprisoned scientists and designers in the *sharashka* laboratories of the GULag. Soviet science was an indisputable world leader in the so-called 'blackboard' fields of mathematics and theoretical physics, but it was also strong in such 'hardware-oriented' fields as nuclear, plasma and solid-state physics, quantum electronics and liquid helium research. Soviet achievements in nuclear weapons and aerospace sent shudders of fear through the West and led to the arms and space races of the Cold War.

Before 1992, however, the overseers of Russian and Soviet science had never seriously reckoned with considerations of economic efficiency and viability. 'Block-funded' state scientific institutions were allowed to bloat, efforts were duplicated, layers of management and oversight multiplied. The Russian scientific establishment that ran aground on economic reality in early 1992 was by virtually all accounts ineffective, monstrously overstaffed, and over-bureaucratized. The liberalization of prices in January 1992 plunged that establishment into a struggle for financial survival. Researchers had to choose between paying for electricity to run equipment and receiving their meager salaries. Physical plants deteriorated; subscriptions to foreign publications lapsed; travel to conferences became unaffordable. An external 'brain drain' and a far larger internal one decimated the field, as scientists and engineers found jobs unrelated to their training in Russia's new business structures and in government. Science suffered a dramatic loss of prestige, leaving scientists marginalized.

The government eventually responded to the crisis in Russian science. Russia's most viable research institutes were designated for priority funding as 'federal science centres'. There are now 58 such centres, employing 80,000. The Russian Foundation for Basic Research (*Rossiiskii fond fundamentalnykh issledovanii*), modelled on the US-based National Science Foundation, introduced Western-style peer review and competitive funding. Concerned foreign state and private grant-awarding institutions opened offices in Moscow in 1992; chief among these was George Soros's International Science Foundation (active 1993–96). The International Science and Technology Centre, founded by Japan, the US, and the EU, has sought to secure employment for Russia's nuclear and weapons scientists. One beneficiary is Moscow's Kurchatov

Institute, which was made a partner in the $10 billion international thermonuclear experimental reactor project. Foreign funding of Russian research and development climbed steadily through the 1990s, peaking at 16.9 per cent of the total in 1999, the same year that the government began meeting its spending commitments to R&D and the 'brain drain' essentially bottomed out (Dezhina and Graham 2002).

Russia's 'science watchers' remain concerned about low domestic demand for Russian high technology, low research productivity, hyperspecialization, government 'spy mania' targeting scientists for prosecution, and the public's enthusiasm for 'pseudoscience' such as astrology, the occult, and parapsychology. Nevertheless, Russian science and technology are surviving and headed gradually toward a more sustainable balance between their magnitude and their resources. Russia's universities are being better integrated with the research capabilities of the Russian Academy of Sciences. Competitive and project-based funding methods are gaining favour, and there is reasonable hope for productive ties between the worldwide Russian scientific diaspora and its mother country.

See also: Academy of Sciences; Cold War

Further reading

Dezhina, I. and Graham, L. (2002) 'Russian Basic Science After Ten Years of Transition and Foreign Support', Carnegie Endowment, Russian and Eurasian Program, Working Paper No. 24.

Graham, L. (1993) *Science in Russia and the Soviet Union: A Short History*, Cambridge: Cambridge University Press.

Krementsov, N. (1997) *Stalinist Science*, Princeton, NJ: Princeton University Press.

Mirskaya, E. (1995) 'Russian Academic Science Today: Its Societal Standing and the Situation within the Scientific Community', *Social Studies of Science* 25, 4: 705–25.

Schweitzer, G. (1995) 'Can Research and Development Recover in Russia?', *Technology in Society* 17, 2: 121–42.

TIMOTHY D. SERGAY

science fiction (nauchnaia fantastika)

Russian science fiction has a rich but checkered history. It springs as much from Dostoevskii's story 'The Dream of a Ridiculous Man' and Chernyshevskii's novel *What is To Be Done?* as from Jules Verne or H. G. Wells. Early Soviet works by Evgenii Zamiatin, Mikhail Bulgakov, and Aleksandr Beliaev (1884–1942) suggested a genre poised to flourish; Aleksei Nikolaevich Tolstoi's *Aèlita, Princess of Mars* became an early silent film. The cultural politics of the early 1930s, however, displaced science fiction into such genres as literature for children, the historical novel, or literary translation, all possible refuges for writers unwilling to produce on demand Socialist Realism, the Soviet version of the utopia that the genre of science fiction customarily debunks.

Soviet science fiction flowered during the Thaw, following publication of *Tumannost Andromedy* (*The Andromeda Nebula*, 1957) by paleontologist Ivan Efremov (1907–72). Science fiction could risk an oblique critique of society, or at least of an imaginary society, from political as well as technological perspectives: simplistic conflicts of capitalism versus communism on another planet might aesopically conceal a more engaging plot. The science component also fit within the theoretical/philosophical framework of scientific communism, and it could advance technical knowledge; readers often judged new works by the originality of their scientific hypotheses. Authors and readers alike appreciated Eastern European writers Karel Čapek (Czech, 1890–1938) or Stanisław Lem (Polish, b. 1921), whose early novel *Solaris* was adapted in a 1972 movie by Andrei Tarkovskii. Western and especially Anglophone science fiction was also influential, with favourites including Isaac Asimov and Arthur Clarke (more technical, or 'hard'), Robert Heinlein, Ray Bradbury, and Roger Zelazny (more concerned with psychology, or 'soft'). In post-Soviet Russia, cyber-punk and other sub-genres are widely available in translation, often with related video games. The same fans read translations and adaptations of J. R. R. Tolkien's *Lord of the Rings*.

The best-known Soviet science fiction writers are Arkadii (1925–91) and Boris (b. 1933)

Strugatskii, whose 25 novels and numerous other works have been widely translated. The genre exploded during perestroika, both in translation and in original works by local authors. Established authors include Kir Bulychev (pseudonym of Igor Mozheiko, 1934–2003) and Vladislav Krapivin (b. 1938), along with younger authors writing in various styles: Marina and Sergei Diachenko, Aleksandr Gromov, Sviatoslav Loginov, Sergei Lukianenko, Genri Laion Oldi (Dmitrii Gromov and Oleg Ladyzhenskii), Nikolai (Nik) Perumov, Viacheslav Rybakov, and Vladimir Vasilev. As Tolkien's popularity suggests, science fiction in Russia overlaps with fantasy and swords-and-sorcery – these distinctions are less sharply preserved than in Western literary markets, as *nauchnaia* is just one subset of the larger realm of *fantastika*.

See also: literature, Thaw; Strugatskii, Arkadii and Boris; Tarkovskii, Andrei; Thaw

Further reading

Clowes, E. (1993) *Russian Experimental Fiction: Resisting Ideology After Utopia*, Princeton, NJ: Princeton University Press.

Grebens, G. (1978) *Ivan Efremov's Theory of Soviet Science Fiction*, New York: Vantage Press.

Howell, Y. (1994) *Apocalyptic Realism: The Science Fiction of Arkady and Boris Strugatskii*, New York: Peter Lang.

SIBELAN FORRESTER

Scientific Communism (Nauchnyi kommunizm)

Scientific communism is a special ideological discipline, which in Soviet times proclaimed itself the chief science of social systems – a Soviet variant of political science. *The Encyclopedic Dictionary of Philosophy* (1983) defined it as follows: 'Scientific communism is one of the three components of Marxism-Leninism (along with the philosophy of dialectical and historical materialism and a proletarian political economy); it reveals the general laws, modes, and forms of the proletariat's class struggle, socialist revolution, and the building of socialism and communism.' The terms also designated Marxism-Leninism in general. Scientific communism focused primarily on the worldwide historical mission of the proletariat and elaborated a theory of the proletarian socialist revolution and the dictatorship of the proletariat as the means of constructing socialist society.

Basing its theory on the works of the 'classics' of Marxism-Leninism (Marx, Engels, and Lenin), scientific communism purportedly offered a scientific way of eliminating human exploitation and replacing it with an economically and socially equitable organization of society. In the 1960s scientific communism became a required discipline in Soviet higher educational institutions, which created joint departments of Marxist-Leninist philosophy and scientific communism. Moscow University established a department of scientific communism during the 1980s. University students throughout the USSR could graduate with a major in scientific communism until 1991, when such units were transformed into departments of political science.

The 1970s witnessed attempts, particularly by the Soviet philosopher Evald Ilienkov, to interpret scientific communism as a supremely humanistic philosophy in its emphasis on human worth. During that decade heated polemics arose about the relationship between scientific communism and sociology. Sociologists were accused of representing a bourgeois science on account of their admiration for Western sociology and their departure from Marxist principles. Proponents of scientific communism demanded that sociology deal exclusively with applied research, while scientific communism serve as a methodological basis. Scientific communism significantly held back the development of objective social science, which became possible only after perestroika. Currently scientific communism remains the official ideological basis for the work of the Communist Party of the Russian Federation.

See also: Communist ideology; Communist Party; philosophy, Soviet, Marxist-Leninist

ELENA OZNOBKINA

scientific organizations (nauchnye obshchestva)

The importance of scientific societies in Russia reflected both the prestige accorded science and technology in Soviet culture and the dependence of Russian science on the financial and ideological will of the State. Soviet science was organized in three institutional pyramids (Academy of Sciences, universities, military-industrial complex), all supported and controlled by the State. There were no non-governmental research institutes. Soviet science was large, reliably funded (in priority areas), and prestigious in the popular imagination. Thousands of researchers participated in the activities of their professional associations (conferences, publications), but ultimately the structure of Soviet science ensured the State's control of professional scientists' aspirations. When the Soviet Union collapsed, much of the prestige and most of the funding for science disappeared. However, since 2000 the pared-down scientific establishment has shown signs of recovery, amidst such structural changes as the rise of private, independently funded research institutes. Russian scientists have become adept at securing internal as well as international funding according to the peer review system. Independent scientific societies in many fields have revived. They actively promote young researchers through award competitions, and facilitate local and international scholarly contacts.

See also: Academy of Sciences; defence industry; science and technology

YVONNE HOWELL

scriptwriters

The role of scriptwriters in post-Stalinist Russo-Soviet cinema hinges on the privileged place of verbal discourse in Soviet culture. Since script-writing in its finest manifestations has always been regarded as a form of high art, akin to high-brow writing of plays and literature, it traditionally has been subject to close supervision and state censorship. Many of Russia's best or politically influential writers and playwrights gladly collaborated with film-makers, while the best scriptwriters were viewed as important literary figures – not just industry employees, but artists with high-culture status. Starting in 1973, in fact, new screenplays were published in the thick-journal-style periodical *Kinostsenarii*. The current crisis of the scriptwriter as a creative identity is closely connected with ongoing changes in the role of the verbal arts and the literary canon in post-Soviet Russian culture.

During the Thaw, a new generation of scriptwriters participated in the de-Stalinization of Soviet culture: Valentin Ezhov, Feliks Mironer, Iurii Ilenko, Andrei Konchalovskii, and above all Gennadii Shpalikov came to be known as authors of poetic screenplays that provided narrative material for a new type of cinema. Their scripts were anti-monumental, fragmented, dealt with an individual's dramas and choices, and were often motivated by poetic metaphors rather than either official ideology or cause-and-effect relations. Not surprisingly, poetry became an important common denominator for the era's scriptwriters. While Shpalikov authored both poetry and screenplays for key films of the era (*Mne dvadtsat let* and *Zastava Ilicha* [*I Am Twenty* and *Lenin's Guard*], *Ia shagaiu po Moskve* [*Walking the Streets of Moscow*]), important poets (Evgenii Evtushenko) and innovative prose writers (Vasilii Aksenov, Iurii Nagibin, Vladimir Tendriakov) wrote screenplays for Thaw films. Screenplay-writing was also an economic niche for politically problematic figures, such as Nikolai Erdman and Mikhail Volpin. For a while Aleksandr Galich managed to combine a career as an official Soviet scriptwriter with that of a dissident guitar-bard. A lot of Soviet scriptwriters graduated from the School of Scriptwriters, which opened in Moscow in 1960, and was later reorganized into the Two-Year School of Scriptwriters and Film-makers (1964).

During the Brezhnev era, the Soviet script-writers' guild became more diverse in its ideology and production practices. The repressive political atmosphere of the 1970s triggered a rich tradition of double-voiced screenplays, often ironizing the stifling atmosphere of late Soviet culture (Aleksandr Adabashian, Grigorii Gorin, Anatolii Grebnev, Aleksandr Mindadze, Alexander Volodin, Valerii Frid and Iulii Dunskii). An ambiguous parable became a common form of screenplay (Revaz Gabriadze, Rustam Ibragimbekov, Gorin). Many script-writers who had started their careers during the Thaw (Grebnev's *Iiulskii dozhd* [*July Rain*], Semen Lungin's *Dobro pozhalovat ili postoronnim vkhod vospreshchen* [*Welcome or No Trespassing!*]) adjusted their writing to the hostile political cli-mate while dealing with Thaw-generation issues of individual identity, personal choice, and the moral dilemmas of a person trapped in a police state. Natalia Riazantseva and Iurii Klepikov, who had begun their work during the late Thaw, became prominent as writers confronting such implicitly political issues as the individual hero who does not belong in the community, and the role of privacy in social life.

While paying lip service to ideological com-mandments, the cinema of the 1970s functioned as a fully-fledged commercial industry. Such scriptwriters as Stanislav Govorukhin, Valentin Chernykh, Viktor Merezhko, Frid and Dunskii, Vladimir Valutskii, and Eduard Volodarskii authored a wide variety of market-oriented screenplays that turned into such blockbusters as *Piraty dvadtsatogo veka* (*Pirates of the Twentieth Century*, 1979), *Moskva slezam ne verit* (*Moscow Does Not Believe in Tears*, 1980), *Rodnia* (*Kinfolk*, 1981), *Ekipazh* (*The Crew*, 1980), *Zimniaia vishnia* (*Winter Cherry*, 1985), *Svoi sredi chuzhikh, chuzhoi sredi svoikh* (*At Home Among Strangers*, 1974).

The last days of Soviet culture and per-estroika brought brief fame to such scriptwriters as Sergei Livnev (*Assa*), Aleksandr Kabakov (*Nevozvrashchenets* [*Defector*]), Mariia Khmelik (*Malenkaia Vera* [*Little Vera*]), Sergei Popov (*Astenicheskii sindrom* [*Asthenic Syndrome*]), Vladimir Vardunas (*Prazdnik Neptuna* [*Neptune's Feast*]), and Mariia Zvereva (*Zashchitnik Sedov* [*Defence Counsel Sedov*]). In the age of swift political changes, the journalist (Kabakov) or the writer-politician (Ales Adamovich) would often turn to writing screenplays for politically topical films.

Post-Soviet scriptwriters comprise an eclectic community that includes seasoned veterans, such as Valutskii, Volodarskii, Petr Todorovskii, and a diverse new generation of scriptwriters. Most importantly, many young scriptwriters are also successful entrepreneurs (Valerii Todor-ovskii, Livnev). Such author-film-makers as Aleksei Balabanov or Aleksandr Rogozhkin usually write their own scripts. Among the most

important *auteur*-oriented scriptwriters of the 1990s are Iurii Arabov, Mikhail Konovalchuk, Nadezhda Kozhushanaia, Irakli Kvirikadze, Renata Litvinova, Petr Lutsik and Aleksei Samokhvalov, and Valerii Zalotukha. Among scriptwriters working for popular audiences the most successful are Arif Aliev (*Mama* [1999], *Zaimemsia liuboviu* [*Let's Make Love*, 2002]) and Oleg Danikov, who writes scripts for Dmitrii Astrakhan's melodramas.

Many Russo-Soviet film-makers collaborate regularly with the same scriptwriters. Often the film-maker is married to his scriptwriter (Aleksei German and Svetlana Karmalita, Ilya Averbakh and Natalia Riazantseva), but more often these are male creative unions: Marlen Khutsiev and Mironer, Eldar Riazanov and Emil Braginskii, Vladimir Khotinenko and Valerii Zalotukha, Vadim Abdrashitov and Mindadze, Aleksandr Sokurov and Arabov.

See also: Abdrashitov, Vadim; Adabashian, Aleksandr; Aksenov, Vasilii; Arabov, Iurii; Balabanov, Aleksei; bards; Brezhnev, Leonid; dissident; Evtushenko, Evgenii; Ezhov, Valentin; film, Soviet – Thaw period; Galich, Aleksandr; German, Aleksei; Govorukhin, Stanislav; Ibra-gimbekov, Rustam; Khotinenko, Vladimir; Khutsiev, Marlen; Konchalovskii, Andrei; Litvi-nova, Renata; Livnev, Sergei; Mindadze, Alek-sandr; Nagibin, Iurii; perestroika and glasnost; Riazanov, Eldar; Rogozhkin, Aleksandr; Sokurov, Aleksandr; Tendriakov, Vladimir; Thaw; Todorovskii, Petr; Todorovskii, Valerii

ALEXANDER PROKHOROV

Sedakova, Olga Aleksandrovna

b. 26 December 1949, Moscow

Poet and essayist

Sedakova is a leading Russian poet of consider-able international acclaim. She has studied and taught at Moscow State University and was involved with the Tartu-Moscow School. Seda-kova officially emerged on the literary scene in 1986 with the *tamizdat* publication of her first book, *Vrata, Okna, Arki* (*Gates, Windows, Arches*).

Since then she has published widely, in various literary genres, including not only poetry, but essays and literary scholarship, both in Russia and abroad, in translation.

Sedakova's verse, spiritual and philosophical, has been termed metarealist. Her literary influences include Aleksandr Pushkin, Velimir Khlebnikov, T. S. Eliot, and Rainer Maria Rilke.

See also: Moscow State University; poetry, post-Soviet; tamizdat; Tartu–Moscow School

ONA RENNER-FAHEY

Selianov, Sergei Mikhailovich

b. 21 August 1955, Olonets, Karelian oblast

Director, producer

Selianov graduated from VGIK in 1980. His films, from *Den angela* (*Angel's Day*, 1980, rel. 1988) to *Vremia pechali eshche ne prishlo* (*The Time for Sorrow has Not Yet Come*, 1995) juxtapose corruption in the city with the sincerity and naïveté in the countryside. *Russkaia idea* (*The Russian Idea*, 1995) was commissioned by the British Film Institute. The montage film traces the concept of the Russian idea in Soviet films made between the Revolution and 1948. In 1992, Selianov organized CTB, one of Russia's most successful film production companies, which has produced films by Balabanov, Rogozhkin, and Bodrov.

See also: All-Russian (All-Union) State Institute of Cinematography; Balabanov, Aleksei; Bodrov, Sergei Sergeevich; Rogozhkin, Aleksandr

BIRGIT BEUMERS

Semenov, Iulian Semenovich

(né Iulian Liandres)

b. 8 October 1931, Moscow; d. 5 September 1993, Moscow

Writer, journalist

A graduate of the Institute of Oriental Studies, Semenov started his career with journalistic reportages from around the globe. He soon became one of the most popular detective and spy thriller writers of the Brezhnev era, combining ideological correctness with titillating details. Semenov's unusual freedom of travel and access to closed archives earned him the reputation of a 'KGB man'. By the mid-1980s he had sold over 12 million copies of his works, popularized through their adaptation for television and cinema, e.g., *Semnadtsat mgnovenii vesny* (*Seventeen Moments of Spring*, 1969), a novel about the Soviet super-agent and counterpart of James Bond, Colonel Isaev-Shtirlits. Semenov's best-sellers include a novel about Moscow police, *Petrovka-38* (1963), and a political thriller, *TASS upolnomochen zaiavit* (TASS Is Authorized to Announce, 1979). In 1986, Semenov became the President of the International Association of Political Detective Novel and started publishing the newspaper *Sovershenno sekretno* (Strictly Confidential).

See also: detective fiction; *Semnadtsat mgnovenii vesny* (*Seventeen Moments of Spring*)

ELENA PROKHOROVA

Semnadtsat mgnovenii vesny (Seventeen Moments of Spring)

Tatiana Lioznova directed this 1973 twelve-episode spy thriller television serial based on a novel by Iulian Semenov. It features a Soviet super agent, Colonel Isaev-Shtirlits, who works under cover in Nazi Germany and single-handedly prevents a separatist agreement between Americans and Nazis. Despite its monumentalism and Cold War message, the series became a cult text of popular culture and continues to be broadcast on all major television channels. The theme of the collapsing Third Reich resonated with late Soviet viewers, and quotes from the serial became part of Russian urban folklore.

See also: Lioznova, Tatiana; Semenov, Iulian; television serials; television, Soviet

ELENA PROKHOROVA

Seventeen Moments of Spring

See *Semnadtsat mgnovenii vesny*

severe style (surovyi stil)

Term coined retrospectively in 1967 by critic Aleksandr Kamenskii (Kamenskii 1969: 13) to designate a new, dour, and expressive mode of painting and sculpture associated with the Thaw (also translated as 'austere' or 'tough' style). Never a conscious movement, it referred initially to a few landmark works produced between 1957 and 1962, and identified at the time with the 'contemporary style': Pavel Nikonov, *Nashi budni* (*Our Workdays*, 1959–60), Nikolai Andronov, *Kuibuishevskaia GES* (*The Construction of the Kuibuishev Hydroelectric Station*, 1957), Edgar Iltner, *Muzhia vozvrashchaiutsia* (*The Husbands Return*, 1957), Viktor Popkov, *Stroiteli Bratskoi GES* (*The Constructors of Bratsk*, 1960–61), Tair Salakhov, *Remontniki* (*Maintenance Men*, 1960), and sculpture by Dmitrii Shakhovskoi. In their search for truth and intensity of expression, these works broke with the cheerful depictions of contemporary reality, meticulous detail, and smooth finish associated with Stalinist art. Models included Soviet art of the 1920s, especially Aleksandr Deineka, and contemporary 'progressive' international trends, such as Italian Neo-Realism. Controversial at the time of its formation, it rapidly became a new, heroic official idiom.

See also: art, Soviet; Nikonov, Pavel; Thaw

Further reading

Kamenskii, A. (1969) 'Realnost metafory', *Tvorchestvo* 8: 13–15.

SUSAN E. REID

sex and sexuality

Russian sexual mores and behaviour have been shaped by complex historical developments both in the remote past and in the twentieth century. Russian Orthodoxy has always considered any manifestation of sexuality outside marriage a great sin, and this notion has deep roots in the nation's psyche. A brief period in the 1920s witnessed an unprecedented sexual revolution: women were given equal rights with men; marriage and divorce became mere formalities; and abortion was legalized. But in the 1930s, under Stalin, the new 'religion', Communist ideology, reintroduced moral values strikingly similar to those dictated by the Orthodox Church. The Party and the government did everything possible to desexualize the population and to redirect the human need for love to the only love that was encouraged at the time: for the Party and its leaders. Only after Stalin's death did the Party somewhat relax its unrelenting control over personal lives.

While the population heeded official propaganda and developed a sanctimonious attitude toward sex, many factors in Soviet life encouraged promiscuity. World War I, the Civil War, the Stalin purges, and World War II widowed millions of women and brought a significant demographic disproportion between the male and female population. Many single women had few hopes of long-lasting relationships and were willing to settle even for a fleeting affair. The horrors of the wars and purges, abounding in rape and violence, devalued the human body and stripped sexual contact of deep psychological significance. The effects of global cataclysms were supplemented by conditions of everyday life that engendered temptations and provided opportunities to fulfill them.

The housing shortage brought people together in large communal apartments. Sharing a kitchen, bathroom, toilet, and the apartment halls, neighbours were forced into routine intimate contact fraught with temptations. Relations at work played an even greater role in fostering promiscuity. Since salaries and work conditions were relatively standard, people often stayed with the same employer from their youth until retirement. Coworkers developed strong bonds, and affairs between them were not uncommon. Because of strict holiday schedules spouses had to take their holidays at different times, spending three to four weeks away from each other. For many, a holiday included sexual gratification free from any responsibility. Another unique feature of the Soviet system was the temporary transfer of city workers to the countryside, usually for a month, to help with the harvest, which presented ideal conditions for fleeting relationships as well. Chances for romance also arose during frequent business trips of designers and engineers to client factories in remote cities, required by the system of centralized industrial production. These relatively long absences from home weakened family ties and created a psychological environment of anonymity that helped ease the conscience.

The heightened susceptibility to sexual temptation among Soviet citizens was caused in part by the Soviet socio-economic system that virtually eliminated the excitement and rewards of personal initiative; sex and drinking were the only activities that provided some sense of freedom and independence. In addition, affairs helped citizens forget the hardships of daily life: long queues, cramped and dirty communal apartments, fights with one's spouse, and problems with the children.

Yet many barriers stood in the way of unbridled sexual activity. Traditional values still dominated the consciousness of many Russians. Crowded living conditions created a problem in finding a place for intimacy. Ignorance about sexual matters also contributed to keeping people in check. Literature that could educate the population about the rich palette of sexual relations was not available. The fear of unknown and potentially embarrassing situations topped by the fear of unwanted pregnancy and venereal disease, as well as lack of privacy, could significantly reduce young people's sexual drive.

One of the major obstacles to carefree sex was lack of readily available quality contraceptives. The Pill revolution never reached the USSR. The Pill was believed to have serious side effects, and most women shunned it. Use of IUDs often resulted in complications and infections. Soviet-made male prophylactics – the only kind available in Soviet drugstores – were of such poor quality that few men used them. Besides, the common macho attitude toward sex placed all responsibility for birth control on women. For these reasons, with the exception of a twenty-year period from 1936 till 1955, when the law forbade it, abortion was the main method of birth control.

The era of glasnost and perestroika in the late 1980s and early 1990s brought tremendous changes to Russian society in general and to sexual practices in particular. The abolition of censorship opened the gates to a flood of publications about sex and eroticism. Naked bodies and often graphic portrayals of sex became almost mandatory in films, theatre performances, and television shows. At the same time the country was undergoing a severe economic crisis. In this atmosphere of social and economic chaos many traditional values lost their validity. The cult of money replaced the previous cult of culture. A study conducted in the mid-1990s showed that the most popular occupation among female Moscow secondary school students was that of hard-currency prostitute. 'Help wanted' ads unabashedly sought young, pretty women *bez kompleksov* (with no hang-ups). Many destitute families disintegrated, and thousands of children became homeless and were exposed to sexual exploitation and victimization. The average age of sexual initiation has significantly dropped while drug use, rape, and the number of AIDS cases have grown dramatically. These changes have been more drastic in big urban centres than in the provinces.

The beginning of the twenty-first century has been marked by a return to relative stability in the economy and in society as a whole. The wild capitalism of the early 1990s, characterized by violence and extreme social vices, has given way to a society that is more benign and less violent, albeit still corrupt. Individuals' sex lives are determined strongly by personal factors, such as family or peer influence, rather than by governmental control. Among teenagers, the permissive attitude toward sex approaches that of their peers in the West. Yet early sex in Russia is still connected with deviant behaviour, such as drug use, drinking, and rape.

See also: AIDS (SPID); communal apartment; Communist Party; families; homosexuality; housing, Soviet and post-Soviet; *Interdevochka*; mother-heroine; queue; perestroika and glasnost; Russian Orthodoxy; women; youth culture

Further reading

Kon, I. (1995) *The Sexual Revolution in Russia: From the Age of the Czars to Today*, New York: The Free Press.

Kon, I. and Riordan, J. (eds) (1993) *Sex and Russian Society*, Bloomington, IN: Indiana University Press.

Maddock, J. W. *et al.* (eds) (1994) *Families Before and After Perestroika*, New York: The Guilford Press.

Stern, M. with Stern, A. (1980) *Sex in the USSR*, ed. and trans. M. Howson and C. Ryan. New York: Times Books.

KONSTANTIN KUSTANOVICH

shabashnik

A worker who performs temporary construction, repair, or other labour. During the Soviet period, such a job, called *shabashka*, was off the books and well paid. Today the term refers to any kind of Russian moonlighter, working off or on the books, usually doing temporary and/or rush jobs. Foreign workers from the 'near abroad' (countries of the former Soviet Union) doing similar work are usually called *gasterbeitery* (*Gastarbeiter*, German for 'guest worker'). The word is derived from *shabash* – Sabbath; the original meaning of *shabashka* was 'time off', which presumably evolved to mean work done during time off from one's regular job.

See also: blizhnee zarubezhe (near abroad); economic system, post-Soviet; economic system, Soviet

MICHELE BERDY

Shabolovka

A broadcasting tower and television centre located on the street of the same name in Moscow, Shabolovka was built in 1919–22 by Russian engineer and inventor Vladimir Shukhov, and is also known as Shukhov's tower. Pioneered for the purpose of radio broadcasting, Shabolovka transmitted signals from the radio-telegraphic station in Moscow in 1922 for the first time in the USSR. It subsequently began to transmit television signals from Moscow's television centre, functioning as the main TV and radio transmitting centre from 1938 until 1967,

when the television tower at Ostankino was built.

The filigree tower has a unique construction, consisting of six metal hyperboloid sections on top of each other instead of the nine originally planned. At the time it was built, the tower could be implemented only on a reduced scale because of a shortage of steel. It is 160m tall instead of the envisioned 350m.

ELENA SKIPETROVA

Shagal, Mark

See Chagall, Marc

Shakhnazarov, Karen

b. 8 July 1952, Krasnodar

Director, scriptwriter, writer and television host

Trained at Igor Talankin's Director's Studio at VGIK, Shakhnazarov directed his diploma film, *Shire shag, maestro* (*Step It up, Maestro*) in 1975, having joined Mosfilm Studio in 1973. He received the Festival of Young Cinematographers prize for his first full-length feature, *Dobriaki* (*Kind Men*), in 1980 and subsequently established a reputation with *My iz dzhaza* (*We're from Jazz*, 1983) and *Zimnii vecher v Gagrakh* (*Winter Evening in Gagra*, 1985). His *Kurer* (*Courier*, 1986) brought him prominence among the glasnost generation. His later films developed apocalyptic themes: *Gorod Zero* (*City Zero*, 1988), which won several prizes, including the Golden Hugo in Chicago; *Tsareubiitsa* (*Assassin of the Tsar*, 1990), *Den polnoluniia* (*Day of the Full Moon*, 1998) and the 3-million dollar meandering take on terrorism, *Vsadnik po imeni smerti* (*The Rider Named Death*, 2004). As director of Mosfilm since 1998, Shakhnazarov advocates the imposition of quotas on American films shown in Russia.

See also: All-Russian (All-Union) State Institute of Cinematography

JANE E. KNOX-VOINA

Shalamov, Varlam Tikhonovich

b. 18 June [1 July] 1907, Vologda; d. 17 January 1982, Moscow

Writer, poet

Although Shalamov wrote poetry, his fame rests on his primary output: 145 short stories known collectively as *Kolymskie rasskazy* (*Kolyma Tales*), based on his seventeen-year odyssey through the Stalinist forced-labour camps.

In 1929, Shalamov was sentenced to three years in the camps for attempting to distribute copies of Lenin's *Testament*. Rearrested for the same crime in 1937 and sent to the hellish camps of Kolyma, he spent the next fourteen years there. He worked in the mines, and was often near death from starvation and disease. After his release in 1951, he began writing his *Kolyma Tales*. Harshly critical of the Soviet regime, these stories could not be published in the Soviet Union during Shalamov's lifetime, but circulated in *samizdat* and were printed abroad.

Kolyma Tales are among the most pessimistic works of labour-camp fiction. In a series of concise episodes linked together by thematic and mnemonic association rather than chronological progression, Shalamov presents the GULag as an inferno from which there is no physical or psychological escape. Subjected to severe abuse and privation, prisoners quickly shed the fragile trappings of civilization, retreating to primitive survival instincts. Moral boundaries blur, and common assumptions about human nature come into question. The result is a disturbing document that testifies not only to the personal tragedies of the Stalinist repressions, but to the anguish of living in a world where religious and philosophical frameworks have collapsed in the face of human evil.

Since the publication of his stories in the Soviet Union in the late 1980s, Shalamov's reputation has continued to grow, both at home and abroad, as one of the most powerful voices to emerge from the catastrophes of twentieth-century Russia.

See also: corrective labour institutions; Kolyma; Lenin, Vladimir Ilich; samizdat

LAURA KLINE

shamanism

Shamanism is a widespread complex of religious and medical beliefs and rituals, centred on a community or family shaman, who is usually perceived to be a mediator among spiritual and human worlds for specific purposes. The mediation is often dramatic, culminating in a seance through which shamans describe themselves as negotiating with mystical forces. The shamanic seance has been variously portrayed, depending on the cultural context and perspectives of observers and participants. While early Russian Orthodox missionaries saw shamans and their seances as fearful examples of wild, frenzied truck with the devil, more recent analyses have stressed the poetry, artistry, and effectiveness of shamanic curing. Scholars debate the psychological condition of a shaman during seances, querying whether trance (sometimes called ecstasy) or other techniques are key to a shaman's altered consciousness. Some suggest that the frequent, rhythmic dancing and drumming of seances can stimulate natural morphine, endorphins in the brain, influencing shamans, their patients, and other séance participants. Others theorize that community healing, group therapy, and empathy are key to the success of the seances.

Shamans historically have been the doctors, pharmacists, psychologists, priests, leaders, and entertainers of their communities. Their persecution in the Soviet period led to losses of curing knowledge and practice, as well as to the loss of talented male and female healers. Predominant among indigenous peoples of the North, Siberia and the Far East, as well as in Central Asia, shamanic practice today is often combined with other, more recent religious forms. Origins of the word 'shăman' are debated, with a leading theory tracing it to the Tungusic (Altaic family) language. Shamanic chants, poetry and legends are a rich resource for understanding elaborate cosmologies and symbolism in Eurasia. Shamanism has been declared moribund many times in the last few centuries, but it lives to be reincarnated and reinvented among some believers in each generation.

See also: Central Asia; Far East; Far North; Russian Orthodoxy; Siberia

MARJORIE MANDELSTAM BALZER

Shchedrin, Rodion Konstantinovich

b. 16 December 1932, Moscow

Composer

Shchedrin graduated from the Moscow Conservatory in 1955 and taught composition there between 1965 and 1969. A prolific composer, Shchedrin is considered one of the pre-eminent Russian composers of the latter half of the twentieth century. From 1973–90 he was also head of the Composers' Union of the Russian Federation, succeeding Shostakovich. Shchedrin's work endeavours to unify disparate elements – classical, folk, and popular. He uses materials borrowed freely from many sources, and he is considered a postmodernist in the truest sense. *Zapechatlennyi angel* (*The Sealed Angel*, 1988, from text by Nikolai Leskov) for mixed choir and reed pipe continues the rich choral tradition embodied in Rachmaninov's *Vsenoshchnoe bdenie* (*Vespers*, 1915) and confirmed by Shnittke's *Concerto for Mixed Chorus* (1984–85). Shchedrin is married to ballerina Maia Plisetskaia. Since 1992 he has lived in both Moscow and Munich. USSR State Prize (1972), Lenin Prize (1984), Russian State Prize (1992), Shostakovich Prize (1993).

See also: Moscow Conservatory; Plisetskaia, Maia; Shnittke, Alfred; Shostakovich, Dmitrii; unions, creative, Soviet

DAVID GOMPPER

Shchekochikhin, Iurii Petrovich

b. 9 June 1950, Kirovobad; d. 3 July 2003, Moscow

Journalist, writer, politician

Shchekochikhin was one of the sharpest investigators of corruption in the late Soviet and post-Soviet media. He began his career at the age of 17 as a writer for *Moskovskii komsomolets*. He established telephone hotlines for teenagers and covered teenage crime and youth issues in *MK* and *Komsomolskaia pravda*, where he was named chair of the youth department in the 1970s. As a columnist, member of the editorial board, and chair of the investigative department of *Literaturnaia gazeta* he published famous articles and investigations on corruption and crime. Because of his articles he was elected deputy to the Supreme Soviet USSR for 1989–91 and to the Russian State Duma (representing the Iabloko Party) for 1995–2001, where he served as deputy chair of the Duma Defence Commission. From 1996 he was deputy editor of *Novaia gazeta*, publishing articles on corruption, politics, and Chechnia, where he also was a correspondent. Shchekochikhin also wrote several books of prose and journalism, as well as scripts for four films and six dramas. He died suddenly under unclear circumstances. He was granted the Legend of Russian Journalism prize and the Artem Borovik prize posthumously in 2004.

See also: Chechnia; Duma; journalism; *Literaturnaia gazeta* (Literary Gazette); *Moskovskii komsomolets*

NADEZHDA AZHGIKHINA

Shemiakin, Mikhail Mikhailovich

b. 4 May 1943, Moscow

Artist, sculptor, stage designer, theorist

Shemiakin grew up in occupied East Germany, and returned to Russia in 1957. Expelled from the Special High School of the Repin Academy of Art in Leningrad for failing to observe Socialist Realist norms, from 1959 until 1971 he worked as a labourer in various capacities. In 1967, he developed his philosophy of Metaphysical Synthesism, dedicated to the creation of a new form of icon-painting based on the study of religious art of all ages and peoples. Drawing for inspiration on a variety of sources, Shemiakin works in a broad range of media and on themes ranging from the theatrical to the philosophical, creating series such as *Carnival in St. Petersburg*, *Still Life*, *Metaphysical Heads*, *Angels of Death*, *Cocoons* and *The Death of Kings*. In 1971, Shemiakin emigrated to France and since 1981 he has lived and worked in New York.

Shemiakin's monuments include *Peter the Great* in St. Petersburg, *Children-Victims of Adults' Sins* in Moscow, and *Cybele: Goddess of Fertility* in New York. Shemiakin has five honorary doctorates and is a founder of the Institute of the Philosophy and Psychology of Art.

See also: Socialist Realism

NATALIA KOLODZEI

Shenderovich, Viktor Anatolevich

b. 15 August 1958, Moscow

Writer, political commentator

Scriptwriter, stand-up comedian, author of satirical prose, and political commentator on the radio station *Ekho Moskvy* (Echo of Moscow). Russia's top political satirist, Shenderovich is best known as the creator of *Kukly* (Puppets), the weekly satirical television show inspired by Britain's *Spitting Image* and broadcast by NTV for over five years: grotesque latex puppets of Russia's political and business elite quarrelled and conspired against each other in uproarious sketches. His other satirical project, *Itogo*, produced together with poet Igor Irteniev, ceased in the aftermath of NTV's imposed reorganization.

See also: *Ekho Moskvy* (Echo of Moscow); NTV; television, post-Soviet

VLADIMIR STRUKOV

Shepitko, Larisa Efimovna

b. 6 January 1938, Artemovsk, Ukraine; d. 2 July 1979, Kalinin oblast, Russia

Film director, scriptwriter, actor

Along with Kira Muratova, recognized as the leading woman film director in the Soviet Union and one of the major directors to emerge during the Thaw period. Married to Elem Klimov, a prominent director in his own right. Her 1963 debut film, *Znoi* (*Heat*), based on a novella by Chingiz Aitmatov, launched the new cinema of

Kyrgyzstan. Shepitko's second feature, the 1966 *Krylia* (*Wings*), an incisive, unvarnished look at a female war veteran's troubles in readjusting to post-war life, received harsh official criticism. Her next film, *Rodina elektrichestva* (*Motherland of Electricity*), based on a story by Andrei Platonov, was banned and released only during perestroika, and led to long-term problems with censorship. Sheptiko's final work, the 1976 *Voskhozhdenie* (*The Ascent*), a harrowing war drama set in Nazi-occupied Belarus, based on a novel by Vasil Bykov, received worldwide acclaim. She perished in a car accident while shooting a film based on Valentin Rasputin's *Proshchanie s Materoi* (*Farewell to Matyora*), later completed by her husband.

See also: Aitmatov, Chingiz; Belarus; film, Soviet – Thaw period; Klimov, Elem; Kyrgyzstan; Muratova, Kira; perestroika and glasnost; Rasputin, Valentin

VITALY CHERNETSKY

shestidesiatniki

See sixties generation (shestidesiatniki)

Sheverdnadze, Eduard Amvrosevich

b. 25 January 1928, Mamati, Georgian SSR

Politician

Eduard Sheverdnadze held the position of First Secretary of the Georgian SSR Communist Party in 1972 until he was called to Moscow in 1985 to serve as Foreign Minister of the Union of Soviet Socialist Republics (USSR). He resigned in early 1991 to protest what he perceived to be an impending dictatorship. Prior to his resignation, he was a close ally of Mikhail Gorbachev and a major architect of Gorbachev's 'new thinking' in foreign policy which involved increased cooperation with the West and a scaling back of Soviet military commitments abroad. Returning to Georgia, Shevardnadze became president of the country in 1992. He resigned in 2003 amid allegations of election fraud in both the 2000 presidential and 2003 parliamentary elections. While president, Sheverdnadze sought help from the Russian Federation to resolve Georgia's civil war and secessionist movement in Abkhazia.

See also: administrative structure, Soviet; Caucasus; Communist Party; Georgia; Gorbachev, Mikhail

VICKI L. HESLI AND JAMES KRUEGER

Shilov, Aleksandr Maksovich

b. 6 October 1943, Moscow

Artist

A graduate of the Surikov Moscow Art Institute (1973), Shilov is a realist who quickly denounced all modernist experiments. Though landscapes, still lifes, and graphics figure among his numerous works, portraits are his main genre. His portraits of contemporaries include people of different social positions, ages, intellect, character, and appearance: for example, his grandmother (1977), the cosmonaut Gagarin (1980), the machine-gunner Shokhin (1987), and an anonymous homeless person (1993). Shilov's collection of paintings and graphic works (reportedly valued at tens of millions of dollars [1996]), of which he made a present to the state, is exhibited in the Moscow State Art Gallery (Shilov Gallery). People's Artist of the USSR (1985), member of the Russian Academy of Art (2001).

See also: Academy of Arts; art galleries and exhibition halls; art schools and academies; Gagarin, Iurii

YURI ZARETSKY

Shirvindt, Aleksandr Anatolievich

b. 19 July 1934, Moscow

Actor

Born into an artistic family, Shirvindt became a popular actor both at Moscow's Satire Theatre and in numerous supporting roles in film. He also worked as an author and director for several famous comic duos in the 1960s (L. Mirov and M. Novitskii, M. Mironova and A. Minaker), and created a famous comedian duet of Veronika Mavrikievna and Avdotia Nikitichna (two old women played by two young male actors V. Tonkov and B. Vladimirov) which was a hit in the 1970s. His comic duet with Mikhail Derzhavin, another popular actor from the Satire Theatre, expanded the boundaries set by their Soviet precursors in the 1940s and 1960s and based their subtle humour on well-hidden subtexts. They became popular through their improvised sketches depicting how the intelligentsia encounters the absurdity of Soviet reality. Shirvindt is now the artistic director of the Satire Theatre.

See also: Satire Theatre

GASAN GUSEJNOV

shliager

A hit song in the genre of light popular music. During the Soviet period, *shliager* (from the German, *Schlager* [hit]) referred to any popular song, from films or singers' repertories. The songs did not necessarily reflect sales of albums. Today the term has largely been replaced by the English word *khit* (hit).

See also: popular music, post-Soviet; popular music, Soviet

MICHELE BERDY

Shnittke, Alfred Garrievich

b. 24 November 1934, Engels; d. 3 August 1998, Hamburg, Germany

Composer

Among the most prominent Soviet/Russian composers of the post-Stalinist period, Shnittke came from an unusually cosmopolitan background that is reflected in his highly sophisticated, intellectual, deeply spiritual, and eclectic music. Born to a father who had emigrated from Frankfurt in 1926 and a mother descended from Germans who had settled in Russia in the 1700s, after World War II Shnittke lived briefly in Vienna while his father worked as a correspondent for a Soviet newspaper. After the family returned to Moscow in 1948, Shnittke was enrolled in a special musical school. In 1953, he entered the composition department at Moscow Conservatory, where he remained as student, graduate student, and instructor for almost twenty years, until 1972.

Harshly criticized and largely ostracized by the official Soviet musical establishment in the 1970s and early 1980s for writing music considered excessively complex, individualistic, and pessimistic, Shnittke quickly gained wide international recognition during glasnost. In the late 1980s, he moved to Germany.

Shnittke composed in a wide variety of genres, from symphonies to operas, film scores, concerti, and oratorios. His many works for chamber ensemble include sonatas for various solo instruments, string quartets, and piano pieces. In much of his music, especially after 1968, Shnittke employed a technique variously called 'eclectic', 'polystylistic', or 'pluralistic'. He blended seemingly disparate musical styles and traditions from different eras, often inserting direct quotations from works of classical composers (he was especially fond of the Germanic masters) into his own compositions, but deforming and deconstructing them through the lens of postmodernism. Many of Shnittke's works use tape, amplification, and electronic effects. Serialism (the twelve-tone system devised as an alternative to conventional tonality by Arnold Schoenberg) also figures prominently, although Shnittke most often leavens serialist technique with tonality.

See also: Moscow Conservatory; perestroika and glasnost

Further reading

Ivashkin, A. (1996) *Alfred Schnittke*, London: Phaidon.

Shnittke, A. and Ivashkin, A. (eds) (2002) *A Schnittke Reader*, Bloomington, IN: Indiana University Press.

HARLOW ROBINSON

shock therapy

In the early 1990s, the Yeltsin government sought ways to make a swift transition to a market economy and the privatization of most state-owned enterprises. Thus, Jeffrey Sachs and Andrei Shleifer of Harvard University, along with Anatolii Chubais and other government officials, created a programme often referred to as shock therapy. The government seemed convinced that private ownership and a market economy had to be implemented swiftly to prevent the Communists from reimposing a centrally planned economic system. Measures were carried out quickly, but the institutions and legal infrastructure essential for a market economy were not created. The government stopped ordering goods from most state-owned enterprises and also cut subsidies dramatically, forcing enterprise managers to seek new customers, develop new products, become competitive, and be self-sustaining by earning profits. Additionally, in January 1992, the government freed prices, allowing enterprise managers, rather than central ministries, to set them. Shock therapy has been criticized as having been a too-rapid method of instituting such dramatic change, but also defended as crucial for moving to a market-oriented economy.

See also: Chubais, Anatolii; Communist Party; economic system, post-Soviet; economic system, Soviet; privatization; Yeltsin, Boris

Further reading

Sachs, J. and Pistor, K. (eds) (1997) *The Rule of Law and Economic Reform in Russia*, Boulder, CO: Westview Press.

DANIEL J. MCCARTHY

Sholokhov, Mikhail Aleksandrovich

b. 11 [24] May 1905, Kruzhilin, Russia; d. 1984, Veshenskaia, Russia

Writer

Noted for his depiction of the Don Cossacks, Sholokhov lived most of his life in the Don River region. His first published book was a collection of stories, *Donskie rasskazy* (*Tales of the Don*, 1926). Sholokhov achieved distinction with the publication of *Tikhii Don* (*And Quiet Flows the Don*, 1928–40), a historical epic about the Cossacks from before World War I until 1922. Rich in detail and artistically powerful, it became the most widely read novel in Russia. Sholokhov's second major novel, *Podniataia tselina* (*Virgin Soil Upturned*, 2 vols, 1932, 1960), deals with the collectivization of agriculture.

A celebrated establishment writer who received many honours and prizes, Sholokhov was a member of the Communist Party Central Committee. His unfinished novel *Oni srazhalis za rodinu* (*They Fought for Their Country*, 1942) portrays Russians' experiences during World War II. Awarded the Nobel Prize in 1965, Sholokhov produced no literary work after 1969.

See also: Communist Party; literature, Soviet; Nobel Prize winners, literature; World War II (Great Patriotic War)

Further reading

Ermolaev, H. (1982) *Mikhail Sholokhov and His Art*, Princeton, NJ: Princeton University Press.

Stewart, D. H. (1967) *Mikhail Sholokhov: A Critical Introduction*, Ann Arbor, MI: University of Michigan Press.

TATYANA NOVIKOV

Short Course

The *Short Course on the History of the All-Union Communist Party* (*Bolsheviks*) (*Kratkii kurs istorii vsesoiuznoi kommunisticheskoi partii bolshevikov*) resulted from a collaboration of historians and writers commissioned by the Central Committee. The latter wanted to wrap up the Party Purges with a work recognizing Stalin as Lenin's only heir, and all the other 'Old Bolsheviks' as traitors to the Revolution. Stalin himself wrote much of the history and edited the remainder so heavily that, after the initial 1938 printing, the new interpretation was known simply as his *Short Course*. The *Short Course* remained the sole interpretation of Soviet history until 1956, when Khrushchev desacralized it.

EDWARD ALAN COLE

shortages (defitsit)

Chronic shortages of most consumer goods were an endemic problem of the Soviet economy. They were a result of both insufficient production and inadequate distribution of goods. The problem of shortages came to the forefront with the move from a market to a planned economy at the end of the 1920s, when almost all consumer goods (clothing, shoes, food, and housing) fell into short supply. It was further aggravated in the 1930s by the disastrous collectivization efforts in the countryside and several famines. Shortages persisted with variable intensity (less in Moscow than in smaller regional towns) until the price liberalization following the break-up of the Soviet Union in 1991. While the Soviet economic system emphasized the development of the military-industrial complex at the expense of light and other consumer industries, shortages also demonstrated another fundamental problem with central planning – the Kremlin's inability to effectively organize production and distribution. While markets regulate excess demand by raising prices, in the Soviet Union prices were rigidly determined by GOSPLAN, the state planning agency, without adequately reflecting the supply–demand relationship. Shortages resulted in an elaborate informal economy, widespread *blat*, and corruption, as ordinary people tried to compensate for their inability to obtain consumer goods through the state distribution channels.

See also: blat; economic system, Soviet; GOSPLAN

ALYA GUSEVA

Shostakovich, Dmitrii Dmitrievich

b. 12 [25] September 1906, St. Petersburg;
d. 9 August 1975, Moscow

Composer, pianist

Considered by many not only the greatest
Soviet composer but one of the greatest composers of the twentieth century, Shostakovich
achieved early fame with the premiere of his
Symphony No. 1 in 1926, and remained a dominant and highly publicized figure in Soviet
music and culture for the remainder of his
prolific and politically charged career. Despite
his frequent and bruising conflicts with Communist Party officials and censors, most notably
in official and press campaigns against his
'formalist' work in 1936 and 1948, Shostakovich's many nationalistic works (especially his
Seventh ['*Leningrad*'] *Symphony*, written in the
early days of the Nazi assault upon the USSR
in 1941), his endurance, growing international
stature, and willingness to represent the
regime at home and abroad earned him a
chestful of decorations: Deputy to the
Supreme Soviet of the USSR, Hero of
Socialist Labour, People's Artist of the USSR,
laureate of the Lenin and State Prizes. After
his death, Shostakovich's name was also
added to the official title of the Leningrad/St.
Petersburg Philharmonic, and to its concert
hall in the centre of St. Petersburg, where he
was born and lived until moving to Moscow
during World War II.

A brilliant pianist, Shostakovich as a student
at the Petrograd Conservatory accompanied
silent films and initially contemplated a career as
a virtuoso. But by the late 1920s, he was
devoting most of his energy to composing in a
wide variety of genres and fields. He wrote incidental music for numerous avant-garde stage
productions, as well as three ballets and two
operas, the madcap experimental comedy *Nos*
(*The Nose*) and the satirical tragedy *Ledi Makbet
mtsenskogo uezda* (*Lady Macbeth of the Mtsensk District*). First performed in 1934, *Lady Macbeth*
enjoyed enormous success with audiences, but
was abruptly banned in 1936 on Stalin's
orders as obscene and excessively dissonant.
Shostakovich and his music were attacked in
Pravda in an infamous article titled 'Chaos

instead of Music' (*Sumbur vmesto muzyki*). These
events led Shostakovich to abandon his promising career in opera and to cultivate a somewhat
more accessible and traditional musical language.

After restoring himself to official favour with
his *Symphony No. 5* in 1937, Shostakovich continued to produce large symphonies at regular
intervals. Several of his fifteen are highly
unconventional in form, and four incorporate
verbal texts, notably the controversial *Symphony
No. 13*, subtitled *Babii Yar*, first performed in
1962 and set to Evgenii Evtushenko's poem by
that title.

Shostakovich wrote more than thirty scores
for films, including classics of Stalinist propaganda as well as Shakespearian adaptations –
Gamlet (*Hamlet*) and *Korol Lir* (*King Lear*) – directed
by Shostakovich's longtime friend and collaborator Grigorii Kozintsev. Alongside his very
'public' symphonies, concerti, cantatas, overtures, marches and songs, Shostakovich produced a large body of chamber music, including
a provocative cycle of fifteen string quartets and
works for solo piano. In much of this more 'private' music, Shostakovich seems to express 'dissident' sentiments of self-doubt and
introspection that have led to extensive and
controversial speculation over his somewhat
schizophrenic identity as an official Soviet
composer.

See also: Evtushenko, Evgenii; Kozintsev,
Grigorii

Further reading

Fay, L. (2000) *Shostakovich: A Life*, Oxford:
Oxford University Press.
Shostakovich, D. (2001) *Story of a Friendship: The
Letters of Dmitry Shostakovich to Isaak Glikman*,
trans. A. Phillips, Ithaca, NY: Cornell University Press.
——(2004) *Testimony: The Memoirs of Dmitri Shostakovich*, ed. S. Volkov, New York: Limelight.
Wilson, E. (1994) *Shostakovich: A Life Remembered*, Princeton, NJ: Princeton University
Press.

HARLOW ROBINSON

Shukshin, Vasilii Makarovich

b. 1929, Srostki, Russia; d. 1974, Kletskaia, Russia

Writer, screenwriter, film actor, director

Shukshin's work deals with existential themes; his often ironic and somewhat humorous stories deal with unusual situations in everyday life. They are economical, with lively dialogue, local colour and idiom. Shukshin's characters are country folk – simple, uncompromising, and eccentric individuals searching for truth, values, and liberty. Shukshin's restless hero-philosopher is often captured in transition, trying to adjust to a new environment and grappling with questions of life and death, freedom, and beauty.

Shukshin's collections *Selskie zhiteli* (*Village Dwellers*, 1963), *Tam, vdali* (*There, in the Distance*, 1968), and *Besedy pri iasnoi lune* (*Conversations under a Clear Moon*, 1974) met with great success. His novel *Ia prishel dat vam voliu* (*I Came to Bring You Freedom*, 1971) focuses on the peasant insurgent Stepan Razin.

As a director, writer, and actor who graduated from Moscow's foremost film-making institute, VGIK, Shukshin made prizewinning movies including *Zhivet takoi paren* (*There Lives Such a Fellow*, 1964) and his most famous, *Kalina krasnaia* (*Snowball Berry Red*, 1974), which portrays an uprooted criminal seeking spirituality in the Russian countryside.

See also: All-Russian (All-Union) State Institute of Cinematography

TATIANA NOVIKOV

Shulzhenko, Klavdiia Ivanovna

b. 24 March 1906, Kharkov; d. 17 June 1984, Moscow

Singer

Starting out as a stage actress in Kharkov, Shulzhenko made her singing debut in Moscow music halls in 1929. In the late 1930s, she performed as a soloist with various jazz ensembles, one of which was directed by her husband, Vladimir Koralli. During World War II, the singer gave numerous concerts at the front and acquired legendary fame with her romantic, bitter-sweet song *Sinii platochek* (*The Little Blue Handkerchief*, 1942). After the war, Shulzhenko continued with concert tours and recordings of popular songs, many of them featuring patriotic themes conveyed in an emotional, often touchingly artless manner. In later years, she frequently appeared on television. People's Artist of the USSR (1971).

See also: popular music, Soviet; World War II (Great Patriotic War)

PETER ROLLBERG

Shvarts, Elena Andreevna

b. 17 May 1948, Leningrad

Poet, prose writer, essayist, translator

A prolific writer known for her innovative poetry, Shvarts graduated from the Leningrad Theatre Institute in 1973. During the 1970s and 1980s, she was an important figure on the underground literary scene, particularly with the group Club 81, and in 1979 became the second recipient of the unofficial Andrei Belyi Prize for literature. The mid-1980s were a significant time in Shvarts's career: she wrote what would become one of her most celebrated pieces, the poetic cycle on the nun Laviniia, and her first book of poetry, *Tantsuiushii David* (*Dancing David*), appeared in *tamizdat*. After glasnost, Shvarts could publish in Russia and has continued to do so actively. An extensive two-volume collection of her work and a book of her memoirs were published in 2002 and 2004, respectively. In 2003, Shvarts was awarded the $50,000 Triumph Prize.

Shvarts's poetry is recognized for its diversity, intense introspection, and unorthodox versification. She draws her imagery from numerous world religions, mythologies, and cultures; yet, the universalism of her verse notwithstanding, Shvarts's native city and its traditions also figure prominently in numerous poems. The poets Marina Tsvetaeva and Velimir Khlebnikov rank among her influences.

See also: poetry, post-Soviet; poetry, Soviet; tamizdat

ONA RENNER-FAHEY

Shveitser, Mikhail Abramovich

b. 16 March 1920, Perm; d. 2 June 2000, Moscow

Director, scriptwriter

Although he graduated from VGIK, where he worked with Sergei Eisenstein, in 1944, Shveitser made his first important films during the Thaw: *Chuzhaia rodnia* (*Alien Kin*, 1956) and *Tugoi uzel* (*The Tight Knot*, 1957), the latter heavily censored and released as *Sasha vstupaet v zhizn* (*Sasha Embarks on Life*). Versatile in both comic and dramatic genres, Shveitser frequently adapted works of literature for the screen and for television: Lev Tolstoi's *Resurrection* (*Voskresenie*, 1960–61); Valentin Kataev's popular novel, *Time, Forward!* (*Vremia, vpered!*, 1965); Chekhov stories; Ilf and Petrov's beloved comic novel *The Golden Calf* (*Zolotoi telenok*, 1968), and Pushkin's *Little Tragedies* (*Malenkie tragedii*, 1980).

See also: All-Russian (All-Union) State Institute of Cinematography; film, Soviet – Thaw period

JOSEPHINE WOLL

Siberia

Russian territory in Asia, extending from the Urals to the Far East. The word 'Siberia' originally referred to the name of the ancient Tatar capital on the Tobol River. Russia colonized Siberia in the sixteenth and seventeenth centuries. Of primary importance in this process was not the government, but the private initiative of merchants (the Stroganov brothers) and Cossacks who founded the first Russian settlements. A fur tax was imposed upon approximately 100 native ethnic groups, which provided 25 per cent of the national income in the eighteenth century. Despite governmental protection, by the early twentieth century,

two-thirds of ethnic minorities had disappeared. The construction of the Trans-Siberian Railroad (1891–1905), which allowed 20 million peasants to move to Siberia, opened a new chapter in its history.

Modern Siberia is a huge area of 10 million sq km (larger than the entire territory of the United States), with a sparse population of 22 million people (a tenth of the US population), divided by the Enisei River into East and West Siberia. The majority of the population is concentrated in large cities (Novosibirsk, Krasnoiarsk, Omsk, Tomsk, Tiumen), and along the rivers Ob, Irtysh, Lena, Enisei. The unofficial capital of Siberia is Novosibirsk. Thirty-one ethnic minorities reside in Siberia, including Buriats, Sakha (Iakuts), Chukchi, Koriaks, Nentsy, and Evenki. Living conditions are hard: a severe, sharply continental climate with winter temperatures as low as minus 48 degrees Celsius; tundra and taiga covering most of the territory; poor infrastructure; and a low standard of living. To combat constant population outflow from Siberia, the Russian government is prepared to invite labour from China, Korea, and Vietnam.

Constituting 18 per cent of the Russian population, Siberia provides about 50 per cent of national income. The Siberian industrial region, where 70 per cent of Russian natural resources are concentrated, is the main supplier of Russian oil (70 per cent), natural gas (90 per cent), and coal (80 per cent). Siberian deposits of diamonds and nonferrous metal ores are the largest in the world.

Since the seventeenth century Siberia has been a major place of exile for political, religious and criminal prisoners, who made up 5 per cent of Siberian population.

The history of Siberia and its social, moral, and ecological problems are exposed in the prose of Anatolii Ivanov (*Vechnyi zov* [*Eternal Call*]), Valentin Rasputin (*Proshchanie s Materoi* [*Farewell to Matyora*]), Viacheslav Shishkov (*Ugrium-reka* [*Ugryum River*]), and Sergei Zalygin (*Na Irtyshe* [*On the Irtysh*]).

See also: Buriatia; Chukchi; Cossacks; ethnic minorities; Evenki; Far East; GULag; Iakutia (Sakha); Kolyma; Koriak; Magadan; Nenets

(Samoeds); Norilsk; Rasputin, Valentin; taiga; tundra; Urals

Further reading

Bobrick, B. (1992) *East of the Sun: The Epic Conquest in Tragic History of Siberia*, New York: Poseidon Press.

Rasputin,V., Winchell, M., and Mikkelson, G. (1996) *Siberia, Siberia*, Evanston, IL: Northwestern University Press.

Wood, A. (1991) *The History of Siberia: From Russian Conquest to Revolution*, London: Routledge.

Wood, A. and French, R. A. (1990) *The Development of Siberia: People and Resources*, New York: St. Martin's Press.

ALEXANDER LEDENEV

Simonov, Konstantin Mikhailovich

b. 18 [28] November 1915, St. Petersburg; d. 28 August 1979, Moscow

Writer

Six-time winner of the Stalin Prize for literature, prose writer, playwright, journalist, and poet, in 1967 Simonov was awarded the Lenin Prize, the Soviet Union's highest literary honour, and was named a Hero of Soviet Labour (1974).

Primarily known for his war poetry, journalism, fiction, and film and TV documentaries on World War II, Simonov wrote a war-trilogy, *Zhivye i mertvye* (*The Living and the Dead*), his major work. His *Zhdi menia i ia vernus* ... (*Wait for me and I'll return* ... , 1941) remains arguably the most famous and popular poem of the era. Simonov was at the centre of the Soviet literary establishment, serving as editor of both *Literaturnaia gazeta* and *Novyi mir*. His memoirs of life under Stalin, *Glazami cheloveka moego pokoleniia: razmyshleniia o I. V. Stalina* (*Through the Eyes of a Man of My Generation: Thoughts on Joseph Stalin*, 1990), were published posthumously.

See also: awards, literary, Soviet; journalism; World War II (Great Patriotic War)

ANGELA BRINTLINGER

Simonov, Ruben Nikolaevich

b. 20 March [1 April] 1899, Moscow; d. 5 December 1968, Moscow

Actor, theatre director

Born in Moscow to Armenian parents, Simonov was a leading actor (1921–68) and the artistic director (1939–68) of the Vakhtangov Theatre. His acting and directing were characterized by vivid theatricality and festivity interwoven with psychological truthfulness. He advocated synthetic, improvisational performances, intermixing dramatic passages with singing, dancing, and elaborate stage designs. Simonov earned a reputation as a gifted performer of both romantic and comedic roles, such as Benedick (Shakespeare's *Much Ado About Nothing*, 1936) and Khlestakov (Gogol's *Revizor* [*The Inspector General*], 1939). His directing repertoire included such diverse productions as Hervé's operetta *Mademoiselle Nitouche* (1944) and Lev Tolstoi's drama *Zhivoi trup* (*The Living Corpse*, 1962). People's Artist of the USSR (1946).

See also: Vakhtangov Theatre

OLGA PARTAN

Siniavskii, Andrei Donatovich

(aka Abram Tertz/Terts)

b. 8 October 1925, Moscow; d. 25 February 1997, Paris

Writer, critic, scholar

Siniavskii was one of the most controversial and gifted literary figures in Russian culture of the latter half of the twentieth century. After receiving his *kandidatskaia* in Russian literature (1952), he was appointed to the prestigious Gorkii Institute of World Literature (IMLI). During the Thaw period, articles he published in the premier literary journal, *Novyi mir* (The New World), established his reputation as a liberal voice in Soviet letters.

Concurrently with his official activities, Siniavskii pursued an illicit career, smuggling his works abroad for publication under the pseudonym Abram Tertz. In 1965, six years after the publication of his first *tamizdat* work (the essay 'What is Socialist Realism?') in the West, Siniavskii's identity was uncovered by the KGB and he was arrested. In February 1966, he was placed on trial for 'anti-Soviet activity' with his co-defendant, Iulii Daniel, whom Siniavskii had helped spirit his works out of the USSR for publication under the pseudonym Nikolai Arzhak. While it was a foregone conclusion that the writers would be found guilty, both pleaded innocent, and the protests surrounding their trial and conviction to terms in hard labour camps are widely recognized as the beginning of the Soviet dissident movement. After serving the bulk of his seven-year term in a camp in Mordovia, Siniavskii emigrated with his family to France in 1973. He taught at the Sorbonne until his retirement in 1996 and died of cancer the following year. His major works include the prison memoir *Golos iz khora* (*A Voice from the Chorus*, 1973) the autobiographical novel *Spokoinoi nochi* (*Goodnight*, 1984), and the literary meditation *Progulki s Pushkinym* (*Strolls with Pushkin*, 1975).

Throughout his career, Siniavskii's resistance, first to the Soviet, and later to the émigré and post-Soviet cultural mainstreams, and his transgressive aesthetic stance made him a target of attack. His most contentious work was *Strolls With Pushkin*, a seemingly innocuous study of Russia's national poet, which Siniavskii wrote while in the labour camp and sent out in letters to his wife. The free-flowing metaphors – Abram Tertz's stock in trade – and the light-hearted approach to Pushkin enraged straitlaced Russian nationalists at home and abroad, just as the writer's fantastic fictions had infuriated the Soviet government. While Siniavskii's writings remain relatively little known to the general Russian reading public, he is recognized in avant-garde literary circles as a cultural figure of the first magnitude.

See also: academic degrees; Daniel, Iulii; Federal Security Service; Literary Institute; literary research institutions; *Novyi mir;* prisons; Pushkin, Aleksandr; tamizdat; Thaw

Further reading

Kolonosky, W. (2003) *Literary Insinuations: Sorting out Sinyavsky's Irreverence*, Lanham, MD: Lexington Books.

Nepomnyashchy, C. (1995) *Abram Tertz and the Poetics of Crime*, New Haven, CT: Yale University Press.

Sandler, S. (1992) 'Sex, Death and Nation in the *Strolls with Pushkin* Controversy', *Slavic Review* 51, 2: 294–308.

CATHARINE NEPOMNYASHCHY

Sitkovetskii, Aleksandr Vitalevich

b. 5 April 1955, Moscow

Rock musician

A founding member of two famous Soviet rock bands: *Vysokosnoe leto* (Leap-Year Summer, with Chris Kelmi, 1972–79) and Avtograf (Autograph, 1979–89), Sitkovetskii was born into a family of classical musicians. Technically, Avtograf was one of the most sophisticated Moscow groups, playing a Soviet equivalent of 'art' or 'progressive' rock. In March 1980, the band participated in the first official rock festival in Tbilisi and received second prize. After the band's dissolution, Sitkovetskii and his fellow musician Leonid Gutkin emigrated to the US, where they founded the musical studio Red Sunset. A reunion tour in June 2005 ended with a triumphant concert at the Olympic Stadium in Moscow.

ALEXANDER DOMRIN

Sitnikov, Aleksandr Grigorevich

b. 20 February 1945, Iva, Penza Region, Russia

Artist

Muscovite Sitnikov graduated from the Surikov Art Academy in 1972. A member of the USSR Union of Artists, early in his career he became representative of the left wing. His paintings, which draw upon a variety of sources – from

Surrealism to Egyptian art – are brightly coloured and heavily layered, combining colour with surreal symbolical imagery. Recurrent subjects in his art include his family, self-portraits, or composers Dmitrii Shostakovich and Alfred Shnittke, as well as allegorical and mythological motifs. His canvases feature the interplay of colours and their connotations, while geometrical, sensual, emotional, and rational elements create an intellectual playground containing signs and symbols of civilization. Recipient of Russia's National Award in Fine Arts (2001).

See also: art schools and academies; Shnittke, Alfred; Shostakovich, Dmitrii

NATALIA KOLODZEI

sixties generation (shestidesiatniki)

Meaning roughly 'people of the sixties', the term *shestidesiatniki* is applied to members of a generation, born in the mid-1930s, who reached maturity in the late-1950s and early 1960s. The phrase 'children of the Twentieth Party Congress', commonly synonymous with *shestidesiatniki*, underscores the significance of this political milestone for the generation. At the Congress (1956), Nikita Khrushchev gave his 'secret speech' denouncing Stalin and the cult of personality, which ushered in the Thaw – a period of relative liberalism in political, social, and artistic life.

Shestidesiatniki is not simply a chronologically defined concept, however: it is not a universal appellation for all members of one generation, nor does it automatically exclude those born somewhat earlier or later. Rather, the term refers particularly to writers and other cultural figures whose creative activity flowered during the Thaw, and it connotes shared values, attitudes, and ideals. These included a rejection of the oppressive dogmatism and prescriptiveness of the Stalin regime; an emphasis on sincerity and a rejection of falsity; a well-developed sense of individual responsibility; and an overarching spiritual maximalism.

The poets Bella Akhmadulina, Evgenii Evtushenko, Robert Rozhdestvenskii, and Andrei Voznesenskii are often called the 'official' *shestidesiatniki*. All challenged the literary status quo to some degree, Evtushenko and Rozhdestvenskii through openly publicistic verse, Akhmadulina through unexpected treatment of familiar themes, and Voznesenskii through technical experimentation. For reciting their poetry to large audiences, they were also known as the 'loud poets' or 'stage poets'. Their popularity reflected a mass interest in poetry that was also expressed in annual 'poetry days' (instituted in 1955) and in lively, well-attended poetry readings (held in Moscow, for example, at the Polytechnic Museum and spontaneously at the then-new monument to Vladimir Maiakovskii). Aside from these 'official' representatives, the term *shestidesiatniki* is also applied to many other cultural figures, albeit with varying degrees of consistency. These include poets Aleksandr Kushner, Iunna Morits, Rimma Kazakova, and Naum Korzhavin; bards Vladimir Vysotskii, Bulat Okudzhava, and Novella Matveeva; prosaist Vasilii Aksenov; critics Lev Anninskii and Stanislav Rassadin, and many more.

Though some of the *shestidesiatniki* were openly critical of the Soviet regime, a cautious navigation of the boundaries of acceptable public discourse was more common. During perestroika, this circumspection engendered scorn among younger generations, who came to view the *shestidesiatniki* as a retarding force in artistic and socio-political development. The significance of the *shestidesiatniki* continues to be debated in the post-Soviet period.

See also: Akhmadulina, Bella; Aksenov, Vasilii; bards; censorship; cult of personality; Evtushenko, Evgenii; Korzhavin, Naum; Krushchev, Nikita; Kushner, Aleksandr; literature, Thaw; Matveeva, Novella; Morits, Iunna; Okudzhava, Bulat; perestroika and glasnost; Stalin, Iosif; Thaw; Voznesenskii, Andrei; Vysotskii, Vladimir

Further reading

Anninskii, L. (1991) 'Shestidesiatniki, semi-desiatniki, vosmidesiatniki ... K dialektike pokolenii v russkoi kulture', *Literaturnoe obozrenie* 4: 10–14.

Brown, D. (1977) '"Loud" and "Quiet" Poets of the Nineteen Sixties', in B. A. Stolz (ed.) *Papers in Slavic Philology 1*, Ann Arbor, MI: University of Michigan Press.

Vail, P. and Genis, A. (2001) *60-e – mir sovetskogo cheloveka*, Moscow: Novoe literaturnoe obozrenie.

RACHEL S. PLATONOV

slang

The term slang and its close synonyms, jargon and argot, have all been imported into Russian (*sleng*, *zhargon*, *argo*), where they refer, like their foreign originals, to the dynamically evolving, often insular, and even 'secret' language patterns of various social groupings or 'subcultures', defined by such markers as professions, classes, age groups, and avocations. The study of Russian slang dates to at least the 1840s, when the great lexicographer Vladimir Dal compiled four dictionaries of the secret patois of Petersburg thieves and provincial wool-beaters, horse rustlers, and the itinerant hucksters known as *ofeni*, from which term Russian derives its only apparently 'native' word for slang, *fenia* (Bondaletov 2004). Soviet ideology discouraged the study and lexicography of slang, which was supposed to fall naturally into disuse under socialism (Filin 1979: 24; Shlyakhov and Adler 1999: v).

With the end of the Soviet Union came a resurgence of interest in slang, particularly the 'thieves' cant' (*blatnaia muzyka*, *vorovskoi zhargon*) traditionally linked with the very concept of slang in Russian culture. 'Thieves' cant' seemed to burst into the mainstream of 1990s urban life along with the post-Soviet rise in crime and crime reportage in the newly 'yellowed' Russian press, as businessmen at all levels paid one *bratva* ('gang') or another to provide them with a *krysha* (lit., 'roof', 'protection') against the *otmorozki* ('thugs') of rival gangs, meanwhile taking care to *zariazhat* ('grease') government inspectors and politicians with either *chernyi nal* ('cash') or more sophisticated forms of *otkat* ('kickbacks').

Soviet literature, of course, had never been cleansed of slang, but the language of Soviet newspapers, radio, and television had been kept relatively antiseptic, generic, and neutral. Beginning with glasnost, stylistic uniformity in the media fell off sharply, and many slang and colloquial forms rushed from the linguistic 'periphery' to the centre. As with neologisms in general, the marked activation of slang in post-Soviet Russia was largely in response to the proliferation of new social realities, which demanded new language even where 'old' terms were still serviceable. Managerial and business slang, for instance (*menedzhment*, *venchurnyi* ['venture'], *brend* ['brand']), was adopted directly from English, a process no doubt aided by American consultants and the 'Chicago School' economic thinking of figures like Egor Gaidar, whose speeches were so jargonized that many Russians found them unintelligible. Various lexicographers (A.L. Burak, M.A. Grachev, V.M. Mokienko, T.G. Nikitina, R.I. Rozina, Harry Walter *et al.*) have produced admirable dictionaries in recent years of both generally adopted Russian slang (*obshchii zhargon*) and specific subcultural slangs (student slang, naval slang). Meanwhile, the prominent culturologist and lexicographer of Russian slang, Vladimir Elistratov, has been arguing that the 'boom' in slang, substandard colloquialisms and *mat* (obscenities) that began during perestroika was strongly exaggerated and mythologized by the media, and in reality has subsided and entered a period of stabilization.

See also: crime; economic system, post-Soviet; Gaidar, Egor; Gorbachev, Mikhail; mat; neologisms; perestroika and glasnost

Further reading

Bondaletov, V. (2004) *V. I. Dal i tainye iazyki v Rossii*, Moscow: Flinta.

Elistratov, V. (2000) *Slovar russkogo argo*, Moscow: Russkie slovari. Available at http://slovari.gramota.ru/portal_sl.html?d = elistratov.

——(2001) 'Kak govorit sovremennaia rossiiskaia molodezh?' Text and audio at http://sonoteka.libfl.ru/ra/tcommande.php3?cote = MSU0000027.

——(n.d.) 'Varvarizatsiia iazyka, ee sut i zakonomernosti', text at http://www.gramota.ru/mag_arch.html?id = 12.

Filin, F. (1979) *Russkii iazyk: Entsiklopediia*, Moscow: Sovetskaia entsiklopediia.

Shlyakhov, V. and Adler, E. (1999) *Dictionary of Russian Slang and Colloquial Expressions*, 2nd edn, New York: Barron's.

TIMOTHY D. SERGAY

Slavophiles

The Slavophiles were an informal group of six aristocratic, idealistic, and educated Russian men, Europeanized yet religiously Orthodox, who hosted salons devoted to the nationalism emanating from Europe in the 1840s. In particular, they sought to answer Peter Chaadaev's 1836 assertion that Russia had no past, present, or future. Slavophiles replied that Russia had been true to itself until it adopted European civilization in the eighteenth century, and that its unique virtue of *sobornost* (collectivity) could save Europe itself from materialism and individualism. Aleksei Khomiakov was the most famous Slavophile, followed by Ivan and Petr Kireevskii, the brothers Ivan and Konstantin Aksakov, and Georgii Samarin. Their opponents were the Westernizers, who embraced European values in a spirit of progressiveness.

See also: Russian Orthodoxy; Westernizers

EDWARD ALAN COLE

Slichenko, Nikolai Alekseevich

b. 21 December 1934, Belgorod, Russia

Singer, actor, director

A graduate of the Advanced Courses for Directors at the State Institute of Cinematography (GITIS, 1972), Slichenko was an actor in the musical-dramatic gypsy theatre Romen (from 1951), and in 1977 became its artistic director. His production of *My – tsygane* (We're Gyspies, 1976) became the theatre's trademark. Slichenko acquired international fame as a performer of gypsy romances, in which he applied passion and temperament to lyrics from Russian poetry. He aspires to the preservation of genuine gypsy art, attempting to draw attention to the unique culture and life of Roma in Russia and abroad.

Slichenko appeared in several feature films and was recognized as People's Artist of the USSR (1981), recipient of the USSR State Prize (1987), and the Moscow City Award (2001).

See also: awards, cultural, post-Soviet; awards, cultural, Soviet; Gypsy/Roma; Gypsy music; romance; Russian Academy of Theatre Arts

YURI ZARETSKY

Slonimskii, Sergei Mikhailovich

b. 12 August 1932, Leningrad

Composer, pianist, teacher

Son of the writer Mark Slonimskii and relative of the musicologist Nikolai Slonimskii, Sergei Slonimskii is best known as a composer whose ecumenical interests have resulted in compositions for a wide range of media and musical forces; his influences include the European avant-garde and folk music. This stylistic universality corresponds to the pluralism that is part of the St. Petersburg tradition. Many works involve 'instrumental theatre', the use of instrumentalists for theatrical effects. For example, his non-traditional opera *Master i Margarita* (*The Master and Margarita*, 1970–72) not only replaces the conventional opera orchestra with solo instrumentalists specifically paired to each singer, but expands the range of musical idioms that serve to highlight the plot of Mikhail Bulgakov's text. He has taught composition at the St. Petersburg (Leningrad) State Conservatory since 1967. People's Artist of Russia (1987).

See also: *Master i Margarita* (*The Master and Margarita*); St. Petersburg (Leningrad) State Conservatory

DAVID GOMPPER

Slutskii, Boris Abramovich

b. 7 May 1919, Slaviansk, Donbass region; d. 22 February 1986, Tula

Poet

Slutskii published his first book of poems in 1941, after graduating from Gorkii Literary Institute. A volunteer in World War II, he was badly wounded. His main books of verse are

Pamiat (*Memory*, 1957), *Vremia* (*Time*, 1959), *Segodnia i vchera* (*Today and Yesterday*, 1961), *Rabota* (*Work*, 1964), *Sovremennye istorii* (*Modern Histories*, 1969), *Godovaia strelka* (*Year Clockhand*, 1971), *Dobrota dnia* (*Kindness of the Day*, 1973), and *Sroki* (*Terms*, 1984). One of his main motifs is abhorrence of great people and monuments, and a deep interest in ordinary people and their everyday duties and joys.

See also: Literary Institute; World War II (Great Patriotic War)

ALEXANDER LEDENEV

Smekhov, Veniamin Borisovich

b. 10 August 1940, Moscow

Actor, director

Smekhov is mainly associated with Moscow's Taganka Theatre, where he memorably played the role of Woland in Iurii Liubimov's adaptation of Bulgakov's fantastical novel *Master i Margarita* (*The Master and Margarita*). He has also played the part of Athos in the television films *D'Artanian i tri mushketera* (*D'Artagnan and the Three Musketeers*, 1978), and its sequels, *Mushketery 20 let spustia* (*The Musketeers 20 Years Later*, 1992) and *Taina korolevy Anny, ili mushketery 30 let spustia* (*The Secret of Queen Anne, or the Musketeers 30 Years Later*, 1993), all directed by Georgii Iungvald-Khilkevich.

See also: film, television; Liubimov, Iurii; *Master i Margarita* (*The Master and Margarita*); Taganka Theatre

DAVID GILLESPIE

smoking

Tobacco smoking in Russia has a long and ongoing history. The genus *Nicotiana* includes approximately thirty species. Though all are considered 'tobacco', common smoking tobacco is *N. tabacum*. A hardier species, *N. rustica*, is well known in Russia as *makhorka*. More pungent in flavour, *makhorka* represented the poor man's

tobacco, smoked in hand-rolled cigarettes. A common source for the paper used in home-made cigarettes at times of scarcity was newsprint, as it was both strong and thin enough to roll into cigarettes, leading to fabled shortages of newspaper in the early Soviet period. *Makhorka* is also made into snuff.

Papirosy, longer, wider cigarettes with tobacco in cardboard tubes without filters were smoked commonly into the 1970s, at which time traditional filtered cigarettes became more popular. Bulgarian cigarettes enjoyed popularity in the 1970s, and while Cuban cigars, so coveted in the West, were cheap, they had few fans. The *Belomorkanal* (White Sea Canal) brand is still popular and, abbreviated *Belomor*, has become synonymous with *papirosy*.

Pipe smoking has a relatively limited following in Russia and is considered pretentious. Cigar smoking, another affectation, is primarily popular among the so-called New Russians (*novye russkie*).

Despite considerable cultural nostalgia, smoking represents a critical public health problem. Worldwide, the burden of disease is rising and soon tobacco smoke will be the leading cause of preventable death. Russia has made several abortive attempts to limit the use of tobacco legislatively, but with little result. Companies offer hard currency and local jobs, and demand remains high throughout all age groups (Ministry of Health estimates in 2001 suggested that 10 per cent of primary school children actively use tobacco, as do three-quarters of young adult males).

See also: health; New Russians

SAMUEL BROWN

Smoktunovskii, Innokentii Mikhailovich

b. 28 March 1925, Tatianovka, Tomsk oblast; d. 3 August 1994, Moscow

Actor, scriptwriter

Smoktunovskii, one of the most beloved actors of his generation, performed in dozens of plays and more than ninety films. He first came to prominence with his portrayal of the clever, charming, cynical physicist Kulikov in *Deviat dnei odnogo goda* (*Nine Days of a Year*, 1962), and consolidated his reputation with his Hamlet (1964), for which he won international acclaim and a Lenin Prize at home. He handled comedy as adroitly as tragedy, most notably as Detochkin the car thief in *Beregis avtomobilia* (*Watch for the Car*, 1966), and acted in two or three films every year until his death. He was also a star of the Moscow Art Theatre.

See also: Moscow Art Theatre

JOSEPHINE WOLL

Smolnyi

Built in St. Petersburg in 1808 by Giacomo Quarenghi as the first Russian school for girls from noble families, Smolnyi became the symbol of Bolshevik power in 1917. During the October Revolution, it served as the headquarters of the Military Revolutionary Committee, and afterwards it was the seat of the first socialist government led by Vladimir Lenin. During the Soviet era, Smolnyi housed the Leningrad City and Regional Committee of the Communist Party, thus embodying the most important power structure of the region. In popular slang, the word Smolnyi meant 'highest authority', thus proving that, in the Soviet context, political power overruled civil authority. This fact may have contributed to the decision of Anatolii Sobchak, St. Petersburg's first mayor, to convert Smolnyi into the seat of the city's government in 1991, thereby replacing the political stigma attached to the building with a new meaning. Today Smolnyi houses St. Petersburg's City Government and Administration. The only remnant of the building's former revolutionary glory is the Lenin Memorial Museum (including Lenin's study and his small private quarters), which opened in 1927 and remains the oldest Lenin museum in the country.

See also: Communist Party; Lenin, Vladimir Ilich; Sobchak, Anatolii; St. Petersburg

MARINA BALINA

soap opera (mylnaia opera)

In the mid-1960s Russian television worked with Polish studios to create television series, some of which were over twenty episodes long. These efforts, together with the fact that the British *Forsyte Saga* was broadcast later in the decade, helped the development of television series in the 1970s, such as *Teni ischezaiut v polden* (*Shadows Disappear at Noon*, 1970) and *Semnadtsat mgnovenii vesny* (*Seventeen Moments of Spring*, 1973). Political leanings changed in the following decade, however, and it was the imported Brazilian soap *Rabynia Isaura* (*Isaura the Slave*) in 1988 that dragged Russian television into international (or homogenized) notions of primetime soaps. By the early 1990s, the meagre budget of national television stations, plus the public's desire for long, unhurried narratives, led to the bulk purchase and repeated broadcasting of series from Mexico, such as *Simply Maria* (*Prosto Mariia*) or *The Wealthy Weep Too* (*Bogatye tozhe plachut*), and slightly dated (and thus cheaper) American equivalents, in particular *Santa Barbara*. Debate over worsening quality and foreign influence has gradually led to the development of first-rate, often nostalgic, domestic series in the 2000s: *Ostanovka po trebovaniiu* (*Request Stop*), *Granitsa* (The Border), and *Uchastok* (*The Police District*).

See also: *Semnadtsat mgnovenii vesny* (*Seventeen Moments of Spring*); television, serials; television, Soviet; television, post-Soviet

DAVID MACFADYEN

Sobchak, Anatolii Aleksandrovich

b. 10 August 1937, Chita, Russia; d. 20 February 2000, Svetlogorsk, Kaliningrad oblast, Russia

Politician

A political figure with legal training and vocal proponent of democratic political reform, Sobchak served as chairman of the Leningrad city soviet in 1990–91, and led the campaign to rename the city St. Petersburg. Elected mayor of St. Petersburg in June 1991, Sobchak expressed ambitious dreams for Petersburg to become a global centre of tourism and finance, but detractors accused him of ignoring the city's shrinking manufacturing base and crumbling transportation system. He lost his bid for reelection in 1996. Sobchak was campaigning on behalf of presidential candidate Vladimir Putin when he suffered a fatal heart attack.

See also: Putin, Vladimir; St. Petersburg

JENNIFER RYAN TISHLER

soccer

As a spectator sport, soccer exploded in Russia during the 1890s when the most popular teams in Moscow often drew attendances of over 12,000. The first bona fide Russian club created was actually in St. Petersburg, however, the *Krukhok liubitelei sporta* (Amateur Sports Club); others leaned heavily on expatriate British players working in the area. British industrialists also formed teams from their Russian employees and by 1912 a national tournament was held; the nation joined FIFA and played Olympic qualifying games in the same year. After World War I, the cultural significance of Moscow–Leningrad derbies was instituted and by the early 1930s urban competitions across Russia were involving over one hundred registered teams.

The New Economic Policy had allowed money to determine the loyalty of players and the development of a star system. Disconcerted by the commercialization of soccer, the Soviets created a state-monitored, professional league system in 1936, in which two Moscow teams quickly dominated: Dinamo and Spartak. The construction of Dinamo Stadium in 1928 pre-dated this new, grander scale for the game; originally housing 35,000 seats, it was given floodlights in 1940. The stadium became a symbol for the reconstruction of Soviet soccer after World War II, and by the 1945 season Dinamo had toured Great Britain. Nonetheless, Stalin's inward-looking policies made international fixtures increasingly problematic. As the Red Army began pilfering the best players from other clubs, the construction of a powerful

'amateur' team for the Olympics looked feasible. Indeed, the Soviets won the gold medal in Melbourne (1956) and Seoul (1988), and the bronze medal in 1972, 1976, and 1980. The USSR won the European Championship in 1960, but success in the World Cup has always eluded both the USSR and Russia.

See also: Dinamo; Spartak; sports clubs and teams; TsSKA

DAVID MACFADYEN

social stratification, post-Soviet

Social stratification in post-Soviet societies is patterned along a different line than during the Soviet era, when Communist Party membership and other non-economic factors were important preconditions for one's belonging to groups with access to privileges and resources. Ideology no longer plays a role, the main line of social stratification today being economic, based on wealth. Whether 'classes' have been formed in full after 1991 and whether they are stable entities are questionable, but the segregation into oligarchs or super-rich, business people and entrepreneurs, those in the government sector (who sometimes turn out to be the working poor), and 'social outcasts' is a current reality. In post-Soviet Russia very deep social divisions emerged quickly. The main question, then, is how 'wealth' was acquired or distributed, for people did not become 'rich' or 'poor' entirely arbitrarily.

Sociologically speaking, 1991 may be seen to mark a successful economic revolution and property reform, carried out by technocratic elites, industrial managers, and, partially, the Communist *nomenklatura*, i.e., those groups that had accumulated considerable power and access to resources under socialism, and were invested in conserving it and ensuring its transfer to their children. Private property was prohibited in the USSR, and means of production (factories, plants) and natural resources belonged to the 'people'. With the transition to a market economy, what previously had been under public ownership turned into private wealth. State-owned enterprises were privatized by the government, and members of the privileged groups often used their connections with industry, finance, and international partners to purchase them, sometimes at 'discount prices' and to enrich themselves in the emerging capitalist system. They opened banks, stock exchanges, and other ventures typical of a market economy.

In the mid-1990s, more than 60 per cent of Russia's millionaires and about 70 per cent of the new political elite were former members of the Communist *nomenklatura*. More than one-third of the successful entrepreneurs had held economic positions in the Party. The new super-rich, who currently own Russian natural resources and industry, and often are assumed to have criminal connections, constitute less than 1 per cent of the population. Their extravagant lifestyle, ownership of villas and even castles in France and Spain, purchase of soccer clubs in Britain, and so forth, became a source of profound social alienation.

Children of members of the Communist bureaucracy or managerial elites, as well as some educated professionals, were also likely to take advantage of the opportunities in the new economy. Many became bankers and stock-brokers, the core of a subclass of young businesspeople running trading and investment markets in Moscow and St. Petersburg. These young urbanites are highly visible in the social scene of the larger cities; they also make up the group that, according to sociological polls, is best poised to evade taxes successfully. They are ardent supporters of the free market and low taxes in general, for in the ideology of new liberalism taxes impede economic efficiency. They often view state-funded and largely female jobs in education, healthcare, childcare, and social services as 'non-productive' and hampering 'economic growth'.

Those employed in the government sector, which ensures social reproduction and without which no nation can exist, proved to have poor gains in the new system. They are mostly rural women, rural men over 35, urban women over 40, and urban men over 50, i.e., those whose lack of flexibility stems from education, occupation, age, regional differences in job opportunities, etc. In the 1990s, they often suffered from inflation, infrequent wage adjustments, and delays in pay. The 'working poor' is a new

post-Communist phenomenon. They may be employed in education, science, or health, and often have dependants. For them, full employment might not guarantee basic necessities, while the various consumer goods that are now available are far beyond their means.

At the lowest end of the low-income group are single-parent families, most of which are headed by women, elderly people without relatives, and the unemployed. While pensions and allowances shrank under inflation, the socialist welfare system, which was not designed to deal with the realities of the market, was of little help in coping with the injustices of the new system.

In the post-socialist era, gender has become a contributing factor in segregating people into those who score high or low on the scale of economic success. In the post-Soviet labour market, globalization granted some professionals an increase in wages; in return, it demanded a different type of work contract. The new arrangement is based on the idea of an autonomous and competitive, risk-taking 'global' worker, who must constantly market his or her abilities, proving that he or she is needed, and be the entrepreneur of his or her own potential. This is how capitalist competition, which is about who can better sell himself or herself, is created. It brings profound changes into the life of those participating in it, for one's fate depends on one's necessity to the system. At the same time, post-Soviet radical economic and social reforms, carried out with the advice of such proponents of neo-liberal economics as the World Bank and the International Monetary Fund, included a partial dismantling of the system of social service delivery. When receiving money in the form of Western loans, enterprises were required to direct their social services elsewhere, as these were impeding economic efficiency. Thus with the change in social policy, part of care-work was relegated from the state to the private sphere. In households with a perceived lack of time, care may be provided by hired domestic workers, who are usually low-income females, but most often it comes from wives, who thereby become less competitive in the labour market. It is known that women were less likely than men to take extra jobs, go into private enterprise or change occupations, and some previously dual career households changed into households with a male breadwinner.

With time, as post-Soviet society became aware of the social cost of the transition, the government embarked on some policies to mitigate social and economic disparities.

See also: Communist ideology; economic system, post-Soviet; economic system, Soviet; families; health; New Russians; nomenklatura; women

Further reading

Burawoy, M. (2000) 'Marxism after Communism', *Theory and Society*. 29, 2: 151–74.
Gapova, E. (2002) 'On Nation, Gender and Class Formation in Belarus … and Elsewhere in the Post-Soviet World', *Nationalities Papers* 30: 4.
Gerber, T. P. (2000) 'Membership Benefits or Selection Effects? Why Former Communist Party Members Do Better in Post-Soviet Russia', *Social Science Research*, 29: 25–50.
King, L. and Szelenyi, I. (2004) *Theories of the New Class: Intellectuals and Power*, Minneapolis, MN: University of Minnesota Press.
Kliamkin, I. and Timofeev, L. (2000) *Tenevaia Rossiia. Ekonomiko-sotsiologicheskoe issledovanie*, Moscow: RGGU.
Piirainen, T. (1997) *Towards a New Social Order in Russia: Transforming Structures and Everyday Life*, Dartmouth: Aldershot.

ELENA GAPOVA

social stratification, Soviet

Social stratification in a society that scholars define as 'state socialism' or 'organized socialism', unlike in market economies, was based on factors other than economic status. In most societies the major category according to which people are stratified is class, defined in general in terms of ownership, wealth, and access to resources. Marxism maintained that differences between the classes, as well as between the interests of different classes, are antagonistic in character and that all of human history had been the history of struggle between the classes of the exploiters and the exploited. Thus it was

the Bolsheviks' revolutionary goal to eliminate these divisions as the root cause of inequality. Socialism posits the absence of classes, with group owning private property and living off the 'exploitation of others'.

The socialist transformation of the 1920s and 1930s abolished private property, and the society that eventually formed was called a proletarian dictatorship (*diktatura proletariata*), or a workers' state. Industrial workers (proletariat) were deemed the most advanced revolutionary group, having true collectivism and class consciousness. The 'avant-garde' of the revolutionary proletariat was the Communist Party. All other social groups (peasants, intelligentsia, and petty merchants, who still existed up to the early 1930s) were viewed as less class conscious because of their social position. The Communist Party introduced a strong 'affirmative action' policy on behalf of workers and peasants to give them access to higher education and professions which required it, thus recruiting their future elites from the previously less privileged groups.

The socialist economy and society in general developed such that by the 1960s, the dictatorship of the proletariat reformed into 'the state of all people' (*gosudarstvo vsego naroda*), officially consisting of workers, collectivized peasants employed in socialist agriculture, and the 'working' (*trudovaia*) intelligentsia. These groups were differentiated according to the kind of work they performed, but the differences among them were considered 'non-antagonistic', as they lived off their own work instead of the exploitation of others, contributed to the 'building of Communism' or a society of complete equality and well-being, and received their resources from the state. In 1961, at the XXII Party Congress, the Programme of the Communist Party of the Soviet Union, also called the Programme for the Building of Communism, was adopted. It became the normative text of the classless society, which defined the social goal for which the Soviet Union was officially striving as 'Communism':

Communism is a classless social system with one form of public ownership of the means of production and full social equality of all members of society; under it, the all-round development of people will be accompanied by the growth of the productive forces through continuous progress in science and technology, all sources of public wealth will gush forth abundantly, and the great principle, 'From each according to his ability, to each according to his needs', will be implemented.

Although Communist or classless society was yet to be achieved, socialism was characterized by a largely equal distribution of wealth and resources – the exception being the privileges enjoyed by the ruling apparatus. The existing income differentiations were not large enough to sustain economic inequality. Nevertheless, social stratification into those less and more privileged did exist, stemming from factors other than economic wealth. These factors were sometimes more difficult to overcome than economic inequality.

There are several major concepts of social stratification in later Soviet society, as well as in those socialist societies that followed the Soviet model. A general view of socialist stratification takes into account privileges granted to various groups. According to Milovan Djilas, who belonged to the top Communist elite in Socialist Yugoslavia and after his defection argued that the Communist bureaucracy (*nomenklatura*) constituted the socialist 'new class'. This group's power remained unchallenged and its members suppressed and exploited all others for their own benefit.

Hungarian sociologists George Konrad and Ivan Szelenyi, who studied privileges in the distributive system of socialism, found that it is the intellectuals who received most benefits, and not the workers in whose name the socialist Revolutions had been fought. They argue that state socialism created a special place for intellectuals, who were, in fact, its ruling class with its own interests. A planned economy required professionals capable of organizing production and distribution, as well as ideologues who could justify the social order; eventually these new elites accumulated considerable power and became invested in 'conserving' it and passing it on to their children.

Whatever the true 'ruling class' was, it is possible to view Soviet social stratification as status-based. As in the planned economy, privileges

and access to valuable goods and services were made possible through a centrally controlled distribution system, they became tied to one's non-monetary status in the same way as in market societies they are about wealth. In conjunction with the perpetual deficiency of goods this contributed to the rise of the Soviet phenomenon of *blat*, or exchange networking, and to the growth of an unofficial, or shadow, economy. One's position in the distribution hierarchy, be it official or unofficial (i.e. a sales assistant, ticket master, car mechanic, etc.) involved unequal access to goods and privileges and thus was accompanied by a different degree of prestige, which technically was not related to money, but to the very possibility of access. For example, as tickets to the opera or ballet at the Bolshoi Theatre were cheap, anyone could technically afford them, but it is only if one was a Communist boss or had *blat* (connections) that one could really get them. This is the explanation for the notorious 'high status of culture' in socialist societies, where access to it depended upon one's position in the social hierarchy.

See also: blat; Communist Party; defence industry; economic system, Soviet; five-year plan; intelligentsia; nomenklatura; philosophy, Soviet (Marxist-Leninist)

Further reading

Burawoy, M. (2000) 'Marxism after Communism', *Theory and Society* 29, 2: 151–74.

Djilas, M. (1983) *The New Class: An Analysis of the Communist System*, New York: Harcourt Brace Jovanovich.

King, L. and Szelenyi, I. (2004) *Theories of the New Class: Intellectuals and Power*, Minneapolis, MN: University of Minnesota Press.

Konrad, G. and Szelenyi, I. (1979) *Intellectuals on the Road to Class Power*, New York: Harcourt Brace Jovanovich.

Ledeneva, A. (1998) *Russia's Economy of Favours: Blat, Networking and Informal Exchange*, Cambridge: Cambridge University Press.

Piirainen, T. (1997) *Towards a New Social Order in Russia: Transforming Structures and Everyday Life*, Dartmouth: Aldershot.

The Programme of the Communist Party of the Soviet Union (Draft) (1961) New York: Crosscurrents Press.

ELENA GAPOVA

Socialist Realism (Sotsrealizm)

Established in 1932 (reportedly, by Iosif Stalin himself), socialist realism was officially introduced at the First Congress of the Union of Soviet Writers in 1934 as the exclusive representational system of Soviet literature. The authority of the method was quickly extended to all other arts, thus making socialist realism the sole legitimate method of artistic creation in the country; it retained its exclusive status to the very end of the Soviet era. For more than fifty years, all officially endorsed production in literature, music, the visual and performing arts was, by default, 'socialist realist'.

The introduction of socialist realism – part of a broad institutional reform in the aftermath of Stalin's 'cultural revolution' (1928–32) – complemented the structural transformations already under way. With its resolution of 23 April 1932, the Party had intervened decisively into what it considered a fragmented, discordant, and ideologically porous cultural sphere by officially dissolving all (formally) independent artistic associations in the country. They were to be replaced by artistic unions directly sponsored and controlled by the state. Membership in them was demanded of all cultural workers sympathetic to the Communist cause. Organized on the model of the industrial enterprise, each union was to operate on a general 'plan' of artistic production (sanctioned by the Party and the Ministry of Culture and coordinated with the country's five-year plan), commissioning projects from its individual members in accordance with specific Party directives. Socialist realism was to be the method of cultural production, the code through which the regimented unity of artistic labour was to translate into an ideal unity of the aesthetic realm.

Stalinist culture witnessed the convergence of two conceptual currents issuing from the artistic and intellectual debates of the 1920s: one leading toward the aestheticization of reality, the other toward the politicization and 'instrumentalization' of aesthetics. In this sense, socialist realism is perhaps best understood as the normative and institutional framework of this convergence. On the one hand, the code of socialist realism prescribes a politically engaged artistic text, whose immediate function is to 'educate the working people in the spirit of socialism'. To this instrumental inflection, on the other hand, Andrei Zhdanov's speech at the First Congress of the Soviet Writers adds the significant demand for the artist to provide a truthful depiction of reality 'in its revolutionary development'. The latter, much-quoted phrase provides the key to the so-called 'romantic' aspect of socialist realism: its appeal to a kind of artistic vision that captures an essential (and imperatively 'better') reality beyond, and yet through, the immediately given.

To the extent that it treats the artistic text as a medium for the manifestation of a singular and unchangeable truth about the world – a secular sacred of sorts – socialist realism is more akin to the religious art of distant pasts than to contemporaneous Western modernist movements. And, as in religious art, in the culture of socialist realism the aesthetic sphere is characteristically segregated: on one side, there is the sphere of craftmanship (artistry on the level of pure skill), and on the other – the realm where artistic concepts become indistinguishable from ideological-ethical norms.

To this second realm belong the four guiding principles of socialist realism: *partiinost* ('party-mindedness'), *ideinost* ('idea-mindedness'), *klassovost* ('class-mindedness'), and *narodnost* ('people-mindedness'). In their coordinated unity, they set the conditions for optimal ideological clarity between the representing subject and the represented world. By the same token, an optimal artistic text is one in which these four principles operate simultaneously.

Partiinost holds a privileged position among the four. Derived from Lenin's article 'Party Organization and Party Literature' (1906), *partiinost* is, most generally, the consciousness that every artistic act is necessarily a political one – that it is, overtly or covertly, 'tendentious'. More specifically, *partiinost* calls for an art that implements the 'tendency' of Marxism-Leninism; it enjoins the artist to assume the vantage point of this authoritative knowledge (i.e., the vantage point of the Party) in order to achieve a truthful representation of reality. Only this position affords the 'romantic' vision of the world and, at the same time, sanctions it as objective and 'realistic'.

Where *partiinost* provides the cardinal world-view underlying every socialist-realist work of art, *ideinost* supplies its topical content in accordance with the newest tasks of socialist construction (and the corresponding Party slogans). *Ideinost* is the point where the artistic text is supposed to turn into convincing, engaging representations the guiding ideologemes of the present day.

Similarly to *partiinost*, *klassovost* refers both to an inalienable property of every form of art – its class origin and class allegiance – and to a positive imperative for socialist-realist art, as it prescribes awareness of the ongoing class struggle and the progressive, historically unique role of the proletariat in it. The principle of *klassovost* lost some of its importance and normative stringency after the Soviet Constitution of 1936 declared the end of class antagonism in the country and consecrated the henceforth harmonious coexistence of the three principal social groups: the proletariat, the peasantry, and the intelligentsia.

This meant, among other things, a new prominence for the principle of *narodnost*. During the 1930s, *narodnost* stood primarily for the idea that art should be accessible to the masses, that it should immerse itself in the life of the common people, and draw on their language and traditions; in the multinational Soviet state, this amounted to a sanction for cultural diversity within ideological uniformity. After the late 1930s, the rising tide of Russian nationalism significantly altered this particularist/pluralist cultural agenda. The notion of *narodnost* now featured an avowal of the Russian people's grand mission in the world and their exclusive position among the other Soviet nationalities. *Narodnost* thus circumscribed the paradoxical conceptual space in which 'Russian' came to stand for everything quintessentially 'Soviet'.

The ideologues of socialist realism declared it to be the legitimate heir of all progressive tendencies in world culture through the ages. For the arts of pictorial and verbal representation, it was understood that all progressive artistic forms and texts were, by definition, 'realistic' (i.e., truthful). In this conflation of political and critical judgments, Aeschylus, Michelangelo, Cervantes, Rembrandt, Pushkin, and Goya were grouped together as some of the great realists of the past. As its closest kin, socialist realism recognized nineteenth-century Russian critical realism, represented in art by the school of the so-called *peredvizhniki* (Itinerants, including Ilia Repin, Vasilii Surikov, Nikolai Kramskoi, and Vasilii Shishkin), and in literature by such writers as Nikolai Nekrasov, Nikolai Ostrovskii, Nikolai Chernyshevskii, and Mikhail Saltykov-Shchedrin. A point of climactic confluence for all previous 'realisms', socialist realism set cultural workers of all spheres to the task of 'studying from the classics'. This education was to be one in craft, rather than in 'spirit'. For where socialist realism parts ways with all its predecessors and designates its special space in cultural history is, avowedly, in the unique vision of the world it affords. For any previous age, a realist representation could be, at best, critical, having for its immediate object a historical reality to which inequality and oppression seem hopelessly innate. Only socialist realism makes possible a deeply positive, knowingly optimistic reflection of reality that is, at the same time, 'realistic', as it places the creative subject face-to-face with a social world in which the contradictions of earlier human history are being effectively resolved.

The artists' 'classical' education was, therefore, to be complemented by emulation of existing paragons of the socialist-realist method. Paradoxically, such paragons were already at hand when Socialist Realism was introduced. At the First Congress of the Union of Soviet Writers, literary works of the recent and not-so-recent past were cited as canonical instantiations of the method. The other arts established similar canons for themselves, recruiting not only the heritage of realism of the post-revolutionary period, but also some of that era's indisputably modernist achievements, such as the art of Aleksandr Deineka and the cinematic masterpieces of Vsevolod Pudovkin and Sergei Eisenstein. After 1937, annual state prizes awarded for artistic achievements gave official form to this process of cultural legitimation. From today's perspective, Socialist Realism is most readily associated with cultural artifacts from the Stalinist period. Among others, the literary works of Aleksandr Fadeev and Konstantin Simonov, the paintings of Aleksandr Gerasimov and Arkadii Plastov, the sculptures of Vera Mukhina, the dramaturgy of Vsevolod Vyshnevskii, and the films of Ivan Pyrev and Mikhail Chiaureli have become emblematic of the method.

In that it is prone to substitute ideological codes for artistic ones (politics for poetics), Socialist Realism presents the cultural historian with a challenging task. It seems that, in order to identify a text as 'Socialist Realist', one must proceed not so much from the concrete properties of the text at hand, as from its reception and status in official Soviet culture. Thus, during Stalinism, when cultural politics in the Soviet Union is at its most regimented and monolithic, it is still possible to categorize as 'socialist realist' all legal cultural production in the country. This equation is increasingly more problematic for subsequent Soviet history. The relatively liberal political climate of the Thaw period (1956–64) gave rise to an artistic culture of liberated self-expression, mild experimentation, and tolerated non-conformism, which enjoyed legality, yet contrasted considerably with the heritage of earlier Socialist Realism. During the Stagnation years (1968–86), the conservative 'freeze' in cultural politics went hand in hand with the incursion of new genres and themes, a heightened awareness of Western styles and forms, and ever-greater orientation toward popular taste and entertainment value. These developments, together with the formation of viable undergrounds in art, literature, and music, further problematized the place of Socialist Realism. Beginning in the late 1970s, some of its theorists called for a broader, more liberal framework that could accommodate the heterogeneity of the cultural process in the Soviet Union. In one of its terminal definitions, Socialist Realism appeared as a 'historically open aesthetic system for the truthful representation of reality' (Dmitrii Makarov), avowedly permitting a multiplicity of individual styles and approaches within a general humanist commitment. Far from effecting an actual liberalization of the method, such capacious formulations portended its obsolescence.

See also: censorship; Communist Party; five-year plan; Gerasimov, Sergei; literature, Soviet; Sholokhov, Mikhail; Simonov, Konstantin;

Socialist Realism literary classics; Stagnation; Thaw; unions, creative, Soviet

Further reading

Bown, M. C. (1998) *Socialist Realist Painting*, New Haven, CT: Yale University Press.

Clark, K. (2000) *The Soviet Novel: History as Ritual*, Bloomington, IN: Indiana University Press.

Günther, H. and Dobrenko, E. (eds) (2000) *Sotsrealisticheskii kanon*, Sankt-Peterburg: Akademicheskii proekt.

James, C. V. (1973) *Soviet Socialist Realism: Origins and Theory*, New York: St. Martin's Press.

Paperny, V. (2002) *Architecture in the Age of Stalin: Culture Two*, Cambridge: Cambridge University Press.

Robin, R. (1992) *Socialist Realism: An Impossible Aesthetic*, Stanford, CA: Stanford University Press.

PETRE MILLTCHOV PETROV

Socialist Realism literary classics

The classical canon of Socialist Realist literature was based on literary works written before the official declaration of the Socialist Realist method in 1934 at the First All-USSR Writers' Congress. Due to their focus on the depiction of revolutionary struggle for a better socialist future, works chosen as models to be emulated included *Mat* (*Mother*, Maksim Gorkii, 1906); *Chapaev* (Dmitrii Furmanov, 1923); *Zheleznyi potok* (*The Iron Flood*, Aleksandr Serafimovich, 1924); *Tsement* (*Cement*, Fedor Gladkov, 1925); *Razgrom* (*The Rout*, Aleksandr Fadeev, 1927); and *Podniataia tselina* (*Virgin Soil Upturned*, Mikhail Sholokhov, 1928–60). These works became part of compulsory reading lists in schools and universities. Throughout the Soviet period, Socialist Realism's leading principles of *partiinost* (recognition of Party leadership in the arts), *klassovost* (class-consciousness), *narodnost* (accessibility of art to the people), and *ideinost* (ideological commitment) retained their importance as evaluative tools of governmental censorship.

The years immediately following World War II contributed to this canon with works on the USSR's struggle against Nazi Germany and collective efforts to rebuild life after the war.

Depiction of the Party's strong leadership remained crucial for works by Aleksandr Fadeev, Boris Polevoi, Semen Babaevskii, and Vsevolod Kochetov. The de-Stalinization of Soviet society in the mid-1950s ushered in new trends in Soviet classics, including criticism of Stalin as a political and military leader, as seen in Konstantin Simonov's *Zhivye i mertvye* (*The Living and The Dead*, 1959–71). In such novels, the focus shifted from the collective experience to that of the individual, and introduced formerly 'forbidden' topics, such as the fate of World War II prisoners (Mikhail Sholokhov's *Sudba cheloveka* (*The Fate of Man*, 1953)) and the controversy of collectivization (Sergei Zalygin's *Solenaia piad* [*Salt Valley*, 1968]). Such countertrends became standard for even the most canonical Socialist Realist novels of the post-Stalinist period, such as Grigorii Markov's *Sibir* (*Siberia*, 1973) and Petr Proskurin's *Sudba* (*Destiny*, 1972). Finally, new Soviet classics of the 1970s turned their attention to the controversies of human relationships and survival in the chaotic world of Soviet history (Iurii Bondarev's *Bereg* [*The Shore*, 1975] and Anatolii Ananev's *Gody bez voiny* [*Warless Years*, 1973–83]). Today the classics of Socialist Realism are rarely read, except by literary scholars.

See also: Socialist Realism

Further reading

Brown, D. (1978) *Soviet Russian Literature Since Stalin*, Cambridge: Cambridge University Press.

Clark, K. (1981) *The Soviet Novel: History as Ritual*, Chicago, IL: University of Chicago Press.

Dobrenko, E. (2001) *The Making of the Soviet Writer: Social and Asthetic Origins of Soviet Literary Culture*, Stanford, CA: Stanford University Press.

Gibian, G. (1960) *The Interval of Freedom: Soviet Literature During the Thaw, 1954–1957*, Minneapolis, MN: University of Minnesota Press.

Parthé, K. (2004) *Russia's Dangerous Texts: Politics between the Lines*, New Haven, CT: Yale University Press.

MARINA BALINA

Soiuz pravykh sil

See: Union of Rightist Forces (Soiuz pravykh sil; SPS)

Soiuzpechat

Founded in 1930, Soiuzpechat had the formidable task of distributing periodicals across the entire territory of the Soviet Union. To accomplish this, it both created a nationwide network of kiosks for retail of individual periodicals and developed a system of distribution to individual and institutional subscribers. At the time of its inception, television was non-existent and radio still in its infancy; thus the distribution of periodicals was crucial to the Soviet Union's ability to mobilize its population. In 1994, Soiuzpechat was privatized, reorganized, and renamed Rospechat, though it retains and uses the Soiuzpechat brand name for certain of its services.

See also: journalism; journalists, post-Soviet; periodicals, post-Soviet; periodicals, Soviet

DAVID HUNTER SMITH

Sokolov, Nikolai Aleksandrovich

See: Kukryniksy

Sokolov, Sasha

(né Aleksandr Vsevolodovich Sokolov)

b. 6 November 1943, Ottawa, Canada

Sokolov is a leading avant-garde writer of the late and post-Soviet era. Born in Canada to a military diplomat, Sokolov grew up in Moscow and became a journalist. His stories appeared in various Russian magazines in the 1960s and 1970s.

His postmodernist novel *Shkola dlia durakov* (*A School for Fools*, 1976) could not pass censorship in the Soviet Union because of its extravagant narrative style. It appeared in the West after Sokolov's 1975 emigration and brought him swift worldwide acclaim. Viewing the world through the consciousness of a schizophrenic boy, this plotless, dialogue-free novel merges different voices and obliterates the boundary between life and death. The novel, in which identities are fluid and time is suspended, is remarkable for its linguistic virtuosity and varied stylistic organization.

Sokolov's other novels, full of invention and verbal fireworks, also experiment with style and form. *Mezhdu sobakoi i volkom* (*Between Dog and Wolf*, 1980) is an ambitious and complicated work, set in remote hunting and fishing areas of the upper Volga. His mock-epic, *Palisandria* (*Astrophobia*, 1985), narrates the fantastic adventures of a grotesque personage, parodies various literary genres, and subverts history and its laws.

See also: emigration; Volga region

Further reading

Canadian-American Slavic Studies, special Sokolov issue, 21 (1987).

TATYANA NOVIKOV

Sokov, Leonid Petrovich

b. 11 October 1941, Mikhalevo, Tver region

Artist

Sculptor and artist who often works with the ready-made. Sokov graduated from the Stroganov Art School in 1969, and emigrated to the US in 1979. The most noticeable quality of his sculptures and objects is humour, in the tradition of Russian folk toys. He often juxtaposes characters from Russian and American mythologies (Stalin embracing Marilyn Monroe, the Russian bear fighting the American eagle). His works have been acquired by Museum of Modern Art, New York; Centre George Pompidou, Paris; Solomon R. Guggenheim Museum, New York; Pushkin Museum of Fine Art, Moscow; Tretiakov Gallery, Moscow, and others.

VLADIMIR PAPERNY

Sokurov, Aleksandr Nikolaevich

b. 14 June 1951, Podorvikha, Russia

Film-maker

Sokurov is one of Russia's most significant contemporary film-makers. His career spans over twenty-five years and has registered the decline of the Soviet Union and the difficult years of transition. In ten feature films and twice as many documentaries Sokurov has demonstrated a lasting interest in the human condition. A disciple of Andrei Tarkovskii, Sokurov is famous for camera work, which has moved away from the montage used in his early films; he has utilized long silent takes that scrutinize characters' subjective states and transient imagery. Sokurov's elegies *Moskovskaia elegiia* (*Moscow Elegy*, 1986–87), *Sovetskaia elegiia* (*Soviet Elegy*, 1989), and *Prostaia elegiia* (*Simple Elegy*, 1990) invite viewers to look at and reflect upon real-life subjects, Andrei Tarkovskii, Boris Yeltsin, and Vytautas Landsbergis, respectively.

Sokurov's warm voiceover reveals the director's most personal thoughts and feelings. Thematically some of his feature films (*Molokh* [*Moloch*, 1999] and *Taurus* [2001]) are centred on the grotesque and paradoxical role of the leader in human history, Hitler and Lenin respectively. *Mat i syn* (*Mother and Son*, 1997) and *Otets i syn* (*Father and Son*, 2003) explore the core of family love and relations. *Russkii kovcheg* (*Russian Ark*, 2002), a technological sensation, filmed in a single 90-minute continuous shot, unveils 300 hundred years of Russian history and culture as reflected in the rooms of the Hermitage.

See also: Tarkovskii, Andrei

YANA HASHAMOVA

Solomin, Iurii Mefodievich

b. 18 June 1935, Chita

Theatre and film actor and director

Upon graduation from the Shchepkin Theatre school (1957), Solomin joined the troupe of the Moscow Malyi Theatre, where he excelled in classical Russian plays such as Aleksei Konstantinovich Tolstoi's *Tsar Fedor Ioannovich*. He became a cult star as Bolshevik double agent Pavel Koltsov in the suspenseful television miniseries *Adutant ego prevoskhoditelstva* (*Aide to His Excellency*, 1970). Solomin's portrayal of writer-ethnographer Vladimir Arsenev in Akira Kurosawa's Oscar-winning epic *Dersu Uzala* (1975) was a remarkable performance, distinguished by natural decency and tact – characteristic features of Solomin's art. The actor served as Minister of Culture of the Russian Federation in 1990–92. His brother, Vitalii Solomin (1941–2002), was a successful theatre and film actor. People's Artist of the USSR (1988).

See also: Malyi Theatre

PETER ROLLBERG

Solonitsyn, Anatolii Alekseevich

(né Otto Alekseevich Solonitsyn)

b. 30 August 1934, Bogorodsk, Gorkii oblast; d. 11 June 1982, Moscow

Actor

Solonitsyn is best known for his association with Andrei Tarkovskii for over more than a decade. He made his film debut playing the eponymous fourteenth-century icon painter *Andrei Rublev* in 1966, was one of the scientists beset by self-doubt in *Soliaris* (*Solaris*, 1972), featured in *Zerkalo* (*Mirror*, 1974), and again played one of the leads in the science-fiction allegory *Stalker* (1979). However, arguably his best, and certainly most sinister, role is as the black-clad wartime collaborator Portnov in Larisa Shepitko's *Voskhozhdenie* (*The Ascent*, 1976), in a performance that combines menace with considerable intellectual depth. Honoured Artist of the RSFSR (1981).

See also: Shepitko, Larisa; Tarkovskii, Andrei

DAVID GILLESPIE

Soloukhin, Vladimir Alekseevich

b. 14 June 1924, b. Olepino, Vladimir region; d. 5 April 1997, Moscow

Poet, prose writer, essayist

As a village prose writer (*derevenshchik*), Soloukhin celebrates the peasant life of rural Russia and the essential features of pre-revolutionary Russian culture: a Russian Orthodox piety, admiration for native folklore, respect for the monarchy, and love for Russian literature and language. These sensibilities are sharpened when viewed against the background of the systematic destruction by the Soviet government of these features of imperial Russian culture. Soloukhin's patriotism permeates his work as a programmatic effort to preserve a way of life that was rapidly disappearing during his peasant boyhood in the 1920s and 1930s. In the 1960s he emerged as an activist for the preservation of cultural and historical landmarks.

Soloukhin's writings manifest a linguistic sophistication and broad erudition. His prose fiction presents Russian country life at its most idyllic, while his essays comment with wit and elegance on socio-political and religious issues. His documentary novel *Pri svete dnia* (In Broad Daylight, 1992) became a part of the process of demythologizing Lenin. His numerous works include *Zapiski iz russkogo muzeia* (Letters from a Russian Museum, 1966), *Olepinskie prudy* (The Ponds of Olepino, 1973), and *Vremia sobirat kamni* (*A Time to Gather Stones*, 1980).

See also: folk tales; nationalism ('the national question'); Russian Orthodoxy; village prose

VALERIA Z. NOLLAN

Solovei, Elena Iakovlevna

b. 24 February 1947, Moscow

Actress

Raised in East Germany in a Soviet military family, Solovei became one of the most stylish actresses in Soviet cinema. A graduate of the All-Union State Institute of Cinematography

(VGIK, 1970), she achieved fame through leading roles in three films by Nikita Mikhalkov: *Raba liubvi* (*Slave of Love*, 1975); *Neokonchennaia pesa dlia mekhanicheskogo pianino* (*Unfinished Piece for Mechanical Piano*, 1977); and *Neskolko dnei iz zhizni Oblomova* (*Oblomov*, 1979). In 1991, Solovei and her family emigrated to the United States. She lives in New York and occasionally plays minor roles in Russian and American movies and series (including *The Sopranos*), and in the theatre. Honoured Artist of the Russian SSR (1981).

See also: All-Russian (All-Union) State Institute of Cinematography

ALEXANDER DOMRIN

Solovev, Sergei Aleksandrovich

b. 25 August 1944, Kem, Karelian oblast

Film director

Solovev graduated from VGIK in 1968. From 1994–97 he was chairman of the Russian Filmmakers' Union. His films include adaptations of classical literature, such as *Stantsionnyi smotritel* (*The Stationmaster*, 1972), *Chernyi monakh* (*The Black Monk*, 1987), *Tri sestry* (*Three Sisters*, 1994), and *O liubvi* (*About Love*, 2004); and films dealing with adulthood in times of change: *Sto dnei posle detstva* (*One Hundred Days after Childhood*, 1974), and *Chernaia roza – emblema pechali* . . . (*Black Rose Is the Symbol of Sorrow* . . . , 1989), and *Nezhnyi vozrast* (*A Tender Age*, 2000). *Assa* (1988), starring figures of the Leningrad underground movement and featuring the music of Viktor Tsoi, was groundbreaking for representing rock music as an alternative lifestyle rather than a source of destruction.

See also: All-Russian (All-Union) State Institute of Cinematography; film, literary adaptation; Karelia; rock music; Tsoi, Viktor; unions, creative, Soviet

BIRGIT BEUMERS

Solovki

A monastery transformed into a prison camp on the Solovetskii islands on the White Sea, Solovki entered popular consciousness as the 'first' Soviet prison camp, though other camps operated simultaneously. Administered by the secret police under the acronym SLON (*Severnye lagery osobogo naznacheniia* or Northern Camps of Special Significance), Solovki began operating in 1923. It was the destination for many early opponents of the Soviet regime, which did not hide it from public view, but propagandized it as a place of reform instead of brutal punishment. The monastery was reopened in the 1990s and restoration begun. Its history as a prison camp has been documented in Marina Goldovskaia's film *Vlast solovetskaia* (*Solovki Power*, 1988).

See also: Goldovskaia, Marina; White Sea Canal

DAVID J. GALLOWAY

Solzhenitsyn, Aleksandr Isaevich

b. 11 December 1918, Kislovodsk

Writer

Prose writer, Nobel Prize winner, and prominent opponent of the Soviet regime who exposed Stalin's labour-camp network. A captain of artillery during the war, Solzhenitsyn was arrested in 1945 for anti-Stalinist comments and spent eight years in labour camps and three years in exile in Central Asia.

Released in 1956, Solzhenitsyn returned to European Russia and worked as a mathematics teacher. He became an instant celebrity in 1962 with the publication of his novella *Odin den Ivana Denisovicha* (*One Day in the Life of Ivan Denisovich*), in A. Tvardovskii's journal *Novyi mir*. Based on Solzhenitsyn's own experiences, this first depiction of Stalin's concentration camps caused a major sensation in Russia and abroad. His criticism of repressive government policies soon ended Solzhenitsyn's period of official favour, making further publication of his works at home impossible. His open letters and statements became internationally known, leading to his open harassment by the authorities. The publication abroad of Solzhenitsyn's novels *V kruge pervom* (*The First Circle*, 1968) and *Rakovyi korpus* (*Cancer Ward*, 1968), capturing his experiences in camp and in exile, made him world famous but intensified the persecution campaign against him. Solzhenitsyn was expelled from the Writers' Union and prevented from travelling to Stockholm to accept the Nobel Prize in 1970.

In 1971, his historical novel *Avgust chetyrnadtsatogo* (*August 1914*) appeared in Paris as part of *Krasnoe koleso* (*The Red Wheel*), a planned multivolume epic on World War I and the 1917 Revolution. The 1973 release in Paris of *Arkhipelag GULag* (*The Gulag Archipelago*), a documentary-literary history of the Soviet penal camp system and an indictment of repression in Russia, created an international furor. In 1974, Solzhenitsyn was vilified in the Russian press, arrested, charged with treason, and deported from the Soviet Union.

After spending two years in Zurich, Solzhenitsyn moved to the United States, where he continued to work on his historical cycle. He published parts in book form as *Lenin v Tsiurikhe* (*Lenin in Zurich*, 1975), revised all his earlier works, wrote additional sections to *Krasnoe koleso*, and in 1978 began publication of his collected works. *Borolsia telenok s dubom* (*The Oak and the Calf*, 1980) is Solzhenitsyn's autobiographical account of his battle with the totalitarian regime.

Perestroika in the late 1980s made Solzhenitsyn's work accessible to Russian readers. His Russian citizenship was restored in 1990, and Solzhenitsyn finally achieved acclaim at home. In 1994, he moved back to Russia and remains one of the most significant personalities in Russian literature.

See also: Central Asia; corrective labour institutions; GULag; Nobel Prize winners, literature; *Novyi mir;* perestroika and glasnost; thick journals; Tvardovskii, Aleksandr; unions, creative, Soviet

Further reading

Mahoney, D. J. (2001) *Aleksandr Solzhenitsyn: The Ascent from Ideology*, Lanham, MD: Rowman and Littlefield Publishers.

Pearce, J. (1999) *Solzhenitsyn: A Soul in Exile*, Grand Rapids, MI: Baker Books.

Rothberg, A. (1971) *Aleksandr Solzhenitsyn: The Major Novels*, Ithaca, NY: Cornell University Press.

Scammell, M. (1984) *Solzhenitsyn: A Biography*, New York: W. W. Norton.

Thomas, D. M. (1998) *Aleksandr Solzhenitsyn: A Century in His Life*, New York: St. Martin's Press.

TATYANA NOVIKOV

song, Soviet popular

One of the most popular forms of entertainment in the Soviet Union, song was often linked to Communist propaganda. The ideological struggles of 1921–32 were evident in the campaign of the Russian Association of Proletarian Musicians (RAMP) for proletarian music. In 1930, according to State Musical Publishing House researchers, 44 per cent of songs performed in Red Square marches commemorating the October Revolution were 'petit-bourgeois'. Lev Nikolaevich Lebedinskii, a RAMP leader, categorized some songs as the backbone of the masses' musical life. His commentary used the term 'song for the masses' and singled out two examples glorifying the Red Cavalry's victorious past: 'Budennyi's Cavalry' (*Marsh Budennogo*, 1920, composed by Dmitrii Pokrass) and 'They wanted it to destroy us … ' (*Nas pobit, pobit khoteli …* , composed by Aleksandr Davidenko). The latter song featured words by prominent proletarian poet Demian Bednyi. Despite cultural figures' attempts to influence popular taste, such pre-revolutionary urban genres such as gypsy romance and cruel romance continued to flourish. The influence of gypsy song is felt in Mikhail Isakovskii and Matvei Blanter's 'Katiusha' (1938), which became popular during World War II.

Under Stalin, Pavel German and Valentin Kruchinin produced songs of everyday life that remained popular for several decades. Their 'Brick Factory Song' (*Kirpichiki*, 1923) tells of a working-class girl and her boyfriend Semen, who return to revamp a brick-making factory destroyed in World War I. The song ends happily, with Semen as the factory director, and

Klavdiia Shulzhenko often performed it at workers' clubs with great success. Shulzhenko's World War II career compares to Vera Lynn's success in England. Her ballads glorify wartime comradeship; and Leonid Utesov called her famous song 'Little Blue Kerchief' (*Sinii platochek*, 1940–42), composed by Jerzy Peterburgskii, with lyrics by Iakov Galitskii and M. Maksimov, 'the symbol of every frontline soldier's love'. Isaak Dunaevskii, recipient of the 1941 Stalin music prize, created famous Soviet mass songs, including 'Song of the Motherland' (*Pesnia o rodine*) from the film *Tsirk* (*Circus*, 1936) and 'Enthusiasts' March' (*Marsh entuziastov*, 1940).

The most popular post-war *estrada* singers included Muslim Magomaev, Lev Leshchenko, Iurii Guliaev, Maia Kristalinskaia, Iosif Kobzon, and Edita Pekha. Eduard Kolmanovskii's 'Do Russians Want War?' (*Khotiat li russkie voiny*, 1961) and 'Alesha' (1966), were often featured in television and radio programmes promoting the USSR as peace-loving. Many post-war songs focused on urban developments, praising young people's participation in rebuilding the Soviet economy. Iurii Vizbor and Dmitrii Sukharev's 'Aleksandra' (music by Sergei Nikitin) was included in the film *Moscow Does Not Believe in Tears* (*Moskva slezam ne verit*, 1979), while Aleksandra Pakhmutova's 'Do you know what sort of fellow he was?' (*Znaete, kakim on parnem byl?*), with lyrics by Nikolai Dobronravov, celebrated Iurii Gagarin's space travel. In the late 1950s and 1960s, alternative Soviet music known as *magnitizdat* emerged, reaching mass audiences through tape recordings of such prominent guitar-poets ('bards') as Bulat Okudzhava, Vladimir Vysotskii, and Aleksandr Galich.

Alla Pugacheva emerged in the 1970s and remains the best loved performer of all time, selling several hundred million records. The collapse of censorship and political pressures in the late 1980s gave way to extravagant shows with technical, choreographic and musical support, pioneered by Fillip Kirkorov.

See also: Gagarin, Iurii; Galich, Aleksandr; Kirkorov, Fillip; Kobzon, Iosif; Leshchenko, Lev; Magomaev, Muslim; Nikitins; Okudzhava, Bulat; Pakhmutova, Aleksandra; popular music; Soviet; Pugacheva, Alla; samizdat; Socialist Realism; Stalin, Iosif; Vysotskii, Vladimir; World War II (Great Patriotic War)

Further reading

Brooke, C. (2002) 'Soviet Musicians and the Great Terror', *Europe-Asia Studies* 54, 3: 397–413.

Gillespie, D. C. (2003) 'The Sounds of Music: Soundtrack and Song in Soviet Film', *Slavic Review* 62, 3: 473–90.

MacFadyen. D. (2001) *Red Stars: Personality and the Soviet Popular Song, 1955–1991*, Montreal: McGill-Queen's University Press.

——(2002) *Estrada: Grand Narratives and the Philosopher of the Russian Popular Song Since Perestroika*, Montreal: McGill-Queen's University Press.

Rothstein, R. A. (1980) 'The Quiet Rehabilitation of the Brick Factory: Early Soviet Popular Music and Its Critics', *Slavic Review* 39, 3: 373–88.

Smith, G. (1984) *Songs to Seven Strings: Russian Guitar Poetry and Soviet 'Mass Song'*, Bloomington, IN: Indiana University Press.

ALEXANDRA SMITH

Sorokin, Vladimir Georgievich

b. 7 August 1955, Bykovo (near Moscow)

Writer, playwright, scriptwriter

Sorokin started his literary career in the late 1970s, joining a movement in literature and art known as Moscow Conceptualism. His writings rebelled against representational art, in particular, against Russian literature, which for two centuries had served as a conduit for liberal ideas and enjoyed tremendous moral and ideological authority among readers. This rebellion paralleled the postmodernist loathing for any authoritative system, from language and literature to Marxism and Freudianism.

A gifted stylist, Sorokin recreated Russian literary discourses, meticulously reproducing their language, style, and archetypal characters. Halfway through, he would destroy the imitated text by loading it with images of extreme violence, cannibalism, and sundry human excretions. Since his earlier works, such as *Norma*

(*The Norm*, 1994) and *Pervyi subbotnik* (*The First Working Saturday*) subjected Socialist Realism to this kind of sacrilege, he is also placed within the Sots-Art movement. Subsequently he subjected the classical nineteenth-century Russian novel to a similarly blasphemous treatment (*Roman* [*The Novel*, 1994]) and more recent works (*Goluboe salo* [*Blue Lard*, 2002]), assailed all of Russian literature through calculatedly 'disgusting' images of its saints and martyrs: Anna Akhmatova, Iosif Brodskii, Osip Mandelshtam, and others.

Recognized as one of the most important contemporary Russian writers, Sorokin remains a source of continuous controversy and scandal. In 2002, the nationalist youth organization *Idushchie vmeste* (*Marching Together*) filed a lawsuit against him for disseminating pornography. In March 2005, the organization, together with the Russian parliament, Duma, protested against the new Bolshoi Theatre's opera *Deti Rozentalia* (*Rosenthal's Children*), whose libretto was written by Sorokin.

Sorokin's works have been translated into many languages. His plays have been staged both in Russia and abroad.

See also: Bolshoi Theatre; Conceptualism, literary; Idushchie vmeste (Marching Together); literature, post-Soviet; opera, post-Soviet; Sots-Art; theatre, post-Soviet

Further reading

Gillespie, D. (2000) 'Vladimir Sorokin and the Norm', in A. McMillin (ed.) *Reconstructing the Canon: Russian Writing in the 1980s*, Amsterdam: HAP.

Kustanovich, K. (2004) 'Vladimir Georgievich Sorokin', in M. Balina and M. Lipovetsky (eds) *Dictionary of Literary Biography*, vol. 285, *Russian Writers since 1980*, Farmington Hills, MI: Gale.

KONSTANTIN KUSTANOVICH

Soros Foundation

The Soros Foundation, named after George Soros, also known as Open Society Institute,

functioned in Russia for fifteen years until 2003, when it suspended its operations after a dispute over the right to use its premises in Moscow. Its goals were to promote education, civil society, and legal and local government programmes with the help of an elaborate system of grants and scholarships exceeding a total of US$1 billion. The Foundation was a major benefactor of and, often, substitution for the Russian State. It introduced the Internet and created partner organizations in the provinces, supported independent media, and helped develop non-profit organizations.

See   also: provincial   Russia;   scientific organizations

VLADIMIR STRUKOV

Sotkilava, Zurab Lavrentievich

b. 12 March 1937, Suhumi, Georgia

Opera singer, tenor

A graduate of Tbilisi State Conservatory (1965), Sotkilava worked in the Tbilisi Opera and Ballet Theatre named after Paliashvili (1965–74), studying in La Scala in 1966–68. In 1974, he was invited to join the Bolshoi Theatre opera troupe. His repertoire included nearly all tenor roles, as well as Italian, Russian, and Georgian songs. Among his best roles in the theatre are Otello, Arzakan (*Pokhishchenie luny* [*Theft of the Moon*]), Vodemon (*Iolanta*), and José (*Carmen*). Sotkilava is highly regarded for his splendid voice, expressive manner in performance, and boundless charm. People's Artist of USSR (1983), Rustaveli State Prize (Georgia, 1998).

See   also: Bolshoi   Theatre;   opera   singers, Bolshoi Theatre

IRINA UDIANSKAYA

Sots-Art

A style in visual art and literature, Sots-Art developed in the early 1970s and declined with the dissolution of the USSR. Most of its exponents lived in Moscow (many artists eventually emigrated to the USA), had no official recognition, and formed a community known as nonconformists, or *andegraund* (underground). They displayed their works at small private exhibitions and readings. The term itself was coined, by analogy with pop art, in 1972 by the duo of Vitalii Komar and Aleksandr Melamid. Other important figures in Sots-Art include artists Grisha Bruskin, Erik Bulatov, Aleksandr Kosolapov, Dmitrii Prigov, Leonid Sokov, and writers Timur Kibirov, Prigov, Lev Rubinshtein, and Vladimir Sorokin.

Sots-Art undermined Soviet ideological myths by rendering their sacred iconography profane through idiosyncratic use of clichés and images derived from Socialist Realism. Through distortion and incompatible juxtapositions with these images Sots-Artists created an irony of incongruity that desacralized the underlying myth.

Many critics place Sots-Art within the broader movement of Conceptualism; both were part of the general postmodernist rebellion against metanarratives and representative art. At the same time, the persistent revisiting by Sots-Art of the myths that were practically dead also betrays a degree of nostalgia.

Sots-Art is rooted in the urban lore of the mid-1960s, when a growing skepticism toward official Soviet ideology produced hundreds of jokes about the Civil War hero Vasilii Chapaev and Lenin himself. It also has precursors in the works written in the mid- and late 1960s by Vasilii Aksenov, Venedikt Erofeev, and Evgenii Popov.

See also: Aksenov, Vasilii; Bruskin, Grisha; Bulatov, Erik; Conceptualism, literary; Erofeev, Venedikt; Kibirov, Timur; Komar and Melamid; Kosolapov, Aleksandr; Lenin, Vladimir Ilich; Popov, Evgenii; Prigov, Dmitrii; Rubinshtein, Lev; Socialist Realism; Sokov, Leonid; Sorokin, Vladimir

Further reading

Andreeva, E. (1995) *Sots Art: Soviet Artists of the 1970s–1980s*, Roseville East, Australia: Craftsman House.

Balina, M. *et al.* (eds) (2000) *Endnote: Sots-Art Literature and Soviet Grand Style*, Evanston, IL: Northwestern University Press.

Kholmogorova, O. (1994) *Sots-art*, Moscow: Galart.

Tupitsyn, M. (1989) 'Sots Art: The Russian Deconstructive Force', in *Margins of Soviet Art*, Milan: Giancarlo Politi Editore.

KONSTANTIN KUSTANOVICH

soups

Russian cuisine distinguishes hot soups (cooked in beef, fish, or mushroom broths) from cold (chiefly prepared with *kvas*). For example, *okroshka* consists of kvas and such ingredients as chopped boiled beef, scallions, cucumbers, and hard-boiled eggs. Hot *borshch* (beet soup of a distinct red colour) and *shchi* (fresh or sour cabbage soup) also contain such vegetables as potatoes, carrots, and onions. *Rassolnik*, another popular soup, features pickles and pickle juice as its main ingredients. Pickles are also used in *solianka*, which offers a unique combination of beef (or fish), sausage, olives, onions, and lemon. Sour cream completes the taste of most Russian soups.

See also: kvas

IRINA MAKOVEEVA

Soviet Union

See USSR

Sovremennik Theatre

The Sovremennik, or Contemporary, Theatre was founded by graduates of the Moscow Art Theatre school at the beginning of the Thaw in 1956 as a studio intended to inject sincerity and reality into the theatrical process. Although the group was run collectively by Galina Volchek, Igor Kvasha, Oleg Tabakov and others, the undisputed leader was Oleg Efremov. Their debut production of Viktor Rozov's *Vechno zhivye*

(*Alive Forever*), followed by the plays of Evgenii Shvarts, Aleksandr Volodin, Vasilii Aksenov, and others made the theatre a favourite with young audiences. Volchek became chief director in 1972 and, aided by a popular troupe featuring Evgenii Evstigneev, Valentin Gaft, Marina Neelova, and Elena Iakovleva, has maintained the Sovremennik's position as one of Moscow's most beloved theatres.

See also: Aksenov, Vasilii; Efremov, Oleg; Evstigneev, Evgenii; Gaft, Valentin; Iakovleva, Elena; Moscow Art Theatre; Neelova, Marina; Rozov, Viktor; Tabakov, Oleg; Thaw; Volchek, Galina

JOHN FREEDMAN

space programme and exploration

Continuing the legacy of rocketry's Russian grandfather, Konstantin Tsiolkovskii, and numerous Soviet theoreticians, the initial triumphs of Soviet space exploration coincided with the Thaw. Russia's firsts – including the first satellite (Sputnik, 1957), automated Moon impact (1959), and human in orbit (Iurii Gagarin, 1961) – awed and alarmed. Nikita Khrushchev promoted Soviet rocketry as evidence of socialism's superiority; with the idolization of Gagarin and, upon his death and declassification (1966), chief designer Sergei Korolev, space flight became a key new *raison d'être* for the USSR, renovating its post-Stalinist self-image as glamorous gateway to the Cosmos. Fans thronged to cosmonauts' tours; Moscow's hottest ticket in 1983 was the 'space wedding' of cosmonauts Andrian Nikolaev and the first woman in space, Valentina Tereshkova, toasted by Khrushchev himself.

Space flight's connection with national prestige meant that endeavours often remained secret until accomplished; Soviet space's unsung or underexposed failures prompted speculation and rumour. The Baikonur cosmodrome conflagration (1960), which killed 165, was made public only in 1990; in 2002 it was revealed that Laika, the famous first dog in space, who reportedly had died painlessly after a week's orbiting (1957), in fact succumbed to overheating several hours after launch.

The United States similarly connected space exploration to national prestige; with its more centralized NASA and higher prioritization of lunar landing, the US won the Moon race. The Soviet media reaction was mixed, both belittling and celebrating this achievement. Soviet Moon flight efforts were retroactively claimed to have emphasized unmanned exploration; the abortive Soviet counterpart to the Apollo programme was not officially confirmed until 1989.

From the early 1970s, Russia pioneered space station development. Televising cosmonauts as living-room scientist-heroes raised the emotional stakes; a return-flight valve malfunction made the Soiuz-11 trio (1971) – charming national celebrities after their record 23 days aboard the station Saliut-1 – the first humans to die in space, a widely publicized national disaster.

Russian space stations – especially Saliut-6 (1977–82) and Mir (1986–2001) yielded voluminous data in astronomy, Earth climatology, materials and pharmaceutical processing, as well as pioneering experience with telemetry, rendezvous and refueling automation, and space physiology.

Russian space exploration suffered catastrophic budget cuts with the Soviet collapse. As part of the US-Russia contribution to the International Space Station, the US financed Mir's renovation in exchange for the opportunity to collaborate with Russian cosmonauts aboard Mir and to benefit from Russia's record-setting experience with long-duration space flight.

Space flight remains important for Russian national self-perception. Communists with vague views on Stalin and even Lenin claim the legacy of the Party of Korolev and Gagarin. A modern variant of Slavophilism, 'Russian anthropocosmism' deems Russians predestined by national character for life in space. Less exotically, Vladimir Putin has declared (2004) cosmonautics the *sine qua non* of Russian claims to international leadership. Despite the troubled state of post-Soviet capital and educational investment in space science, Russia's space leadership was underscored by US reliance (2003–) on Russian Soiuz rockets for International Space Station work while inspecting and replacing its aging Space Shuttle fleet.

See also: Baikonur; Gagarin, Iurii; Korolev, Sergei; Krushchev, Nikita; Lenin, Vladimir Ilich; Mir; Putin, Vladimir; Slavophiles; Tereshkova, Valentina; Thaw

Further reading

Harvey, B. (1996) *The New Russian Space Programme*, New York: John Wiley.

AVRAM BROWN

Spartak

The trade unions' sports society of volunteers. The official flag of this popular organization is red, with a white band. The Spartak-Moscow soccer team won twelve national titles in the Soviet era and nine titles in the post-Soviet era. Spartak attracts many intellectuals and artists among its fans.

ALEXANDER LEDENEV

Spas nerukotvornyi

The icon of the Saviour Christ Not-Made-by-Hands, called Mandylion in the Byzantine tradition. The original image Not-Made-by-Hands was transferred to a cloth when Christ wiped His face with it. When Abgar, the ruler of Edessa, kissed the cloth, his leprosy was partially cured; the final cure came with the arrival of the disciple St. Thaddeus, in accordance with Christ's words. The third Feast of the Saviour on 16 [29] August celebrates the transfer of the original icon from Edessa to Constantinople in 944. Most icons of Spas nerukotvornyi depict Christ against the background of a cloth, and surrounded by a halo inscribed with a cross and the Greek letters abbreviating His name.

See also: icon; Russian Orthodoxy

MICHELE BERDY

Spivakov, Vladimir Teodorovich

b. 12 September 1944, Ufa, Russia

Violinist, conductor

Educated at the Moscow Conservatory, Vladimir Spivakov emerged as a major violinist of his generation after winning first prize in the Montreal Competition and second prize in the Tchaikovsky and Paganini Competitions. Though fully capable of playing virtuoso repertoire, he tends to favour less flashy classical fare. He founded the Moscow Virtuosi chamber orchestra in 1979, which he conducts (sometimes while soloing on violin), while also leading the Russian National Orchestra since 1999. When not on tour, Spivakov spends his time in Russia, where he figures prominently in musical life and in numerous and varied charities.

See also: Moscow Conservatory; Moscow Virtuosi; Tchaikovsky (Chaikovskii) Competition

SUNGHAE ANNA LIM

sports, post-Soviet

Following the disintegration of the USSR, each of the independent states started its own national competition in individual sport events. A united team represented the CIS at the 1992 Olympics; since then independent teams have represented Russia, Ukraine, Belarus, and other former Soviet republics. In the 1990s, the Russian government significantly decreased its investment in sports clubs and competitions. Although the main system of training through a network of specialized sports schools for young athletes was not abandoned, many of the schools closed and competitions came to depend on private sponsorship. Popular opinion regarding the hierarchy of different sports changed. The previously marginal tennis, martial arts (karate, judo, kickboxing, tae kwon do), and motor sport became both popular and prestigious. These changes were immediately reflected in media coverage and were noted by Russian politicians. President Boris Yeltsin posed in political ads as a tennis player, while President Vladimir Putin's judo training forms part of his public image. At the same time, weightlifting, gymnastics, skating, and even track-and-field – events in which Soviet athletes previously achieved their greatest successes – lost popularity. To promote the development of result-oriented sports, since the 1990s, Russia has employed a system of government stipends and bonuses to finance the best athletes. An important trend in the development of post-Soviets sports is its newly attained professional status and the free movement of athletes between foreign championships. The best Russian athletes frequently represent foreign clubs and teams (especially in team sports). The other side of this process is the internationalization of Russian football, basketball, and ice hockey championships. The biggest Russian stars of post-Soviet sports successfully compete with politicians and celebrities. Charismatic Russian figures in sports include swimmer Aleksandr Popov, wrestler Aleksandr Karelin, tennis players Evgenii Kafelnikov, Marat Safin, and Mariia Sharapova, ice hockey player Pavel Bure, boxer K. Tszyu, figure skaters Evgenii Pliushchenko and Irina Slutskaia, gymnast Alina Kabayeva, basketball player Andrei Kirilenko, and track-and-fielders Elena Isinbaeva and Iurii Borzakovskii. Sports media in post-Soviet Russia are growing fast. The para-Olympic movement is a new feature.

See also: Bure, Pavel; figure skating; gymnastics; hockey; Kafelnikov, Evgenii; Karelin, Aleksandr; Putin, Vladimir; soccer; Yeltsin, Boris

ALEXANDER LEDENEV

sports, Soviet

A sports infrastructure was created in Soviet Russia after the adoption of the governmental decree 'On Pre-Draft Training' in April 1918. Within the framework of general military training, the state was developing forms of physical activity that promoted national defense. So-called 'bourgeois' sports, such as wrestling and boxing, initially were not accepted among Soviet sports, which emphasized technical events (shooting, auto sport, and aviation), gymnastics, track-and-field, and outdoor games (football [soccer], ice hockey, basketball, volleyball). Later the development of a mass sports movement became the primary objective of the State Committee on Physical Culture and Sports (*Gosudarstvennyi komitet po fizicheskoi kulture i sportu*). Officially, the USSR did not promote any professional sports. Physical education became a mandatory discipline in secondary schools and colleges, and its instructors were trained in over 200 colleges. Mass sports developed through a network of sports societies associated with trade unions. A system of sports clubs was formed, the largest being TsSKA, Dinamo, and Spartak. Sports federations, which became members of the corresponding international sports organizations, regulated the development of individual sports.

In the 1960s and the 1980s, sixty-four Soviet federations existed in the USSR, with track-and-field, skiing, football, volleyball, ice hockey, basketball, shooting, gymnastics, and chess federations as the largest. Federations organized training and competitions on different levels – district, city, oblast, republic, and national, and specialized sports schools for young athletes conducted advanced training. In the 1980s, there were about 5000 such schools in the USSR. *Spartakiads*, which were held regionally and nationwide every four years, were the largest national competitions, with up to 90 million participants. In the 1960s, a system of children's sports clubs and mass competitions was established in events including hockey, soccer, skiing, track-and-field, and chess.

A multi-element system of sports ranking evaluated levels of achievement. When an athlete successfully completed a specific base standard, he was given 1st, 2nd, or 3rd rank in an individual sports event. Having a sports rank was prestigious – a bonus in college and job admissions. Anyone achieving a higher degree of sportsmanship was called a 'candidate for master of sports' (*kandidat v mastera sporta*), 'master of sports' (*master sporta*), and 'international master of sports' (*mezhdunarodnyi master sporta*). Outstanding achievements earned the title of 'master of sports emeritus', which usually entailed material benefits.

After World War II, the government became interested in result-oriented sports. The Soviet team, which debuted at the 1952 Olympics in Helsinki, immediately earned multiple awards. At the Olympics, Soviet athletes were particularly successful in gymnastics, wrestling, shooting, weightlifting, boxing, track-and-field, and certain outdoor sports (basketball, volleyball, water polo). Several athletes became cult figures, including boxer Boris Lagutin, weightlifter Iurii

Vlasov, football player Lev Iashin, ice hockey players Vsevolod Bobrov, Valerii Kharlamov and Vladislav Tretiak, gymnasts Larisa Latynina and Olga Korbut, cyclist Viktor Kapitonov, figure skater Irina Rodnina, track-and-fielders Vladimir Kuts, Valerii Brumel, and Valerii Borzov. The national mass media began devoting serious coverage to sports. Over thirty sports newspapers and magazines were published in the USSR. The newspaper *Sovetskii sport* and the weekly *Football-Hockey* were particularly popular.

See also: Dinamo; figure skating; gymnastics; hockey; Iashin, Lev; Kharlamov, Valerii; Rodnina, Irina; Spartak; soccer; sports education; Tretiak, Vladislav; TsSKA; Vlasov, Iurii

Further reading

Kukushkin, G. (ed.) (1975) *Sovetskaia sistema fizicheskogo vospitaniia*, Moscow.
Stolbov, V. (ed.) (1975) *Istoriia fizicheskoi kultury i sporta*, Moscow.

ALEXANDER LEDENEV

sport clubs and teams

In Russia, sport clubs appeared in the middle of the nineteenth century: the emperor's yacht club (1846), sport games club (1860), tennis and cricket club (1868), and others. In the USSR in the 1920s and the 1930s, priority was placed on sports related to military training. Numerous shooting and automobile clubs, as well as aviation and parachute schools, were later merged into a defensive sports organization, the Voluntary Society of Army, Aviation, and Naval Assistance. Mass sports in the USSR were organized mainly through 'voluntary sports societies'. They were formed on a professional basis and included regional subsidiaries and sports teams in individual events. In the 1950s and 1980s, there were seven national sport societies (*Burevestnik* [Petrel], *Vodnik*, *Dinamo*, *Zenit*, *Lokomotiv*, *Spartak* and *Trudovye rezervy* [Labour Reserves]) as well as a united military sports organization – *TsSKA*. Formally, the societies included amateur athletes, but in fact the members' status was different. Owing to a

formidable infrastructure and centralized financing, the societies that represented the army (TsSKA) and police (Dinamo) attained leading positions. Membership in these teams counted as mandatory military service for young men; hence TsSKA and Dinamo had unlimited power to shape their teams, and the athletes were in reality professionals. That explains the dominance of these teams in the most popular sports, football (soccer), ice hockey, and basketball. Their only real competitors during Soviet times were the Spartak, and, to a lesser extent, Torpedo, societies. The Spartak Moscow football club became known as the 'people's team' owing to its mass popularity. In the post-Soviet period, the system of voluntary sports societies collapsed. Sports clubs were reorganized as joint-stock companies and became commercial enterprises, while athletes became officially recognized as professionals. Change of ownership led to a change of certain clubs' names; for example, the Iaroslavl hockey team Torpedo, which used to represent the local motor plant, was renamed Lokomotiv after the joint stock company Russian Railways became its owner. Nevertheless, the names of most sports clubs remain the same and they still trigger the same cultural associations in mass culture.

See also: Dinamo; Spartak; TsSKA

ALEXANDER LEDENEV

sports education

In Russia, sports education is conducted on two levels: preparation of generalist physical education teachers and coaches in individual events, and training of young athletes in specialized sports-oriented schools and extracurricular groups associated with sports societies. In the USSR, the first sports colleges appeared in Moscow (1918) and Petrograd (1919), and later spread across the country. Most students are professional athletes who receive theoretical instruction along with intensive training and competitions. Students have to meet strict standards in several events – not only their major, but two or three minor ones as well.

Physical education is mandatory in schools. A characteristic feature of the Russian sports education system is the wide network of specialized sports schools and boarding schools for young athletes (football and ice hockey players, gymnasts, track-and-field athletes, etc.). Sports schools for young athletes exist together with general education schools and function mostly in the afternoon hours. The students train in individual sports. The most promising young athletes receive both general and special sports education in boarding schools. Athletes successful in competitions train in elite 'schools of advanced sportsmanship' (*shkoly vysshego sportivnogo masterstva*).

In the 1970s and the 1980s, the USSR had about 5,000 sports schools. The main measure of their efficiency was the number of graduates in 'masters of sport' (*master sporta*), athletes who fulfilled the standards. During Soviet times, track-and-field and swimming schools in Leningrad, the gymnastics school in Voronezh, the rowing school in Novgorod, and hockey and figure skating schools in Moscow were especially popular. In the post-Soviet period, the number of sports schools financed by the state has decreased, and private schools have appeared in the newly prestigious sports (figure skating, tennis, and martial arts).

See also: educational system, post-Soviet; educational system, Soviet

ALEXANDER LEDENEV

spravka

A *spravka* (plural *spravki*) is a document issued by an authority to certify any piece of information. Some *spravki*, such as ones certifying good health, one's place of work or one's salary, may have analogies in the various countries of the West. However, in the often bureaucratic Russia and the even more bureaucratic Soviet Union, *spravki* were and are frequently required for many activities that ordinarily in the West would not require them. A *spravka* of good health from a doctor, for example, must often be presented in order to use a public swimming pool. The excessive importance of documentation in the form of *spravki* in daily life became the target of satire at the hands of comedians even in the Soviet era.

DAVID HUNTER SMITH

SPS

See Union of Rightist Forces (Soiuz pravykh sil; SPS)

Stagnation

Stagnation (*zastoi*) refers to the period of economic and social inertia under Leonid Brezhnev, particularly from 1970 until Brezhnev's death in November 1982. Two fundamental factors precipitated economic and cultural stagnation – the Soviet economy's over-reliance on an inefficient system of agriculture and the central government's unwillingness and inability to ameliorate the USSR's industrial sector. By the early 1970s, both the agricultural and the industrial bureaucracies were populated by a firmly entrenched clique of aging technocrats who resisted reforms that might lead to greater efficiency and productivity.

The Soviet Union survived these difficult times relatively unscathed because, as one of the world's producers of fossil fuels, it benefited from high oil prices. These allowed the government to subsidize its bloated agricultural and industrial enterprises without overhauling the nation's hyper-centralized economy. The Soviet Union exported petroleum products at reduced prices to its client states in Eastern Europe and elsewhere in exchange for cheap imports of grain and finished goods. Moreover, petroleum revenue allowed the Kremlin to maintain the social status quo, which included near-universal employment for its citizens and a cradle-to-grave welfare system. One of the drawbacks of this stability, however, was the maintenance of an underperforming consumer goods sector that continued to churn out poor-quality items in chronic undersupply.

Popular attitudes toward daily living conditions gradually worsened. The availability of the basic necessities of life, however insufficient, averted social crisis, but the populace's increased expectations for a better life remained unrealized.

See also: Brezhnev, Leonid; economic system, Soviet; natural resources

Further reading

Hanson, P. (2003) *The Rise and Fall of the Soviet Economy*, London: Longman.

Service, R. (2003) *A History of Modern Russia: From Nicholas II to Putin*, London: Penguin.

Suny, R. (2003) *The Structure of Soviet History: Essays and Documents*, New York: Oxford University Press.

Thompson, W. (2003) *The Soviet Union under Brezhnev*, Edinburgh: Pearson.

CHRISTOPHER J. WARD

Stakhanovism

Stakhanovism took its name from Aleksei Stakhanov, a miner from the Donbas region who, on the night of 30–31 August 1935, hewed 102 tons of coal or fourteen times the quota for a regular shift. Stakhanov's, however, was no regular shift, for local authorities had prearranged many of the conditions necessary for the accomplishment of his record-breaking feat. Nevertheless, a mania for beating individual production records soon swept across all sectors of Soviet industry. Central Party officials, already faced with the problem of increasing worker productivity, approved of and actively encouraged the phenomenon, while doing their best to turn it into a collective rather than individual feat. Factories were assigned Stakhanovite months and 1936 was designated the Stakhanovite year. The movement eventually lost steam and by the mid-1950s the term 'Stakhanovite' no longer had currency.

See also: Communist Party; economic system, Soviet; five-year plan

DAVID HUNTER SMITH

Stalin, Iosif

(né Iosif Vissarionovich Dzhugashvili)

b. 6 December 1878, Gori, Georgia; d. 5 March 1953

Few modern leaders wielded the power of Stalin both in politics and culture. As supreme arbiter of cultural affairs for a quarter of a century, Stalin bequeathed a complex and formidable cultural legacy.

A cobbler's son, Stalin was drawn into the revolutionary struggle at a young age. At 19, he abandoned seminary studies in Georgia to pursue the radical politics of Russian Marxism, which resulted in numerous arrests and periods of exile before the October Revolution in 1917. During the Civil War, Stalin emerged from the background of the Bolshevik Party to become one of its leading political figures. Stalin transformed the position of Party General Secretary into one of immense political and personal power, ultimately liquidating his rivals by 1929 to become the unchallenged Party leader until his death.

In informal meetings with writers and artists, Stalin personally laid the groundwork for the doctrine of Socialist Realism and imbued artists with the role of transforming humanity and serving state objectives. Officially inaugurated in 1934, the policy articulated Stalin's personal fondness for realism and mass cultural sensibilities to produce a uniform culture depicting an idealistic socialist reality. Ending the experimentation and proletarian cultural associations of the 1920s, the newly imposed Party and ideological controls on culture and its producers included the establishment of artists' unions, Party-approved themes, incentives, purges of counter-revolutionary genres such as formalism, and the repression of thousands of artists. In all areas of culture Stalin presided as master-builder, ideological font, omnipotent patron, and ultimate censor.

Stalinist culture yoked conservative and revolutionary impulses to manufacture consent and to forge a new Soviet man. Marked by a system of privileges, a leadership cult, traditional values, a revival of folklorism, and an overarching civilizing mission, Stalinist culture also extensively relied on elements of mass culture, including cinema, radio, public spectacles, and the pro-motion of consumerism and leisure. A product of and reaction to modernization, Stalinist cul-ture aimed to erase distinctions of high and low culture by deploying the state-controlled mass media and the new Soviet artistic canon to pro-pagandize and entertain. Contrasting sharply with the deprivations and repressions of the period, the arts celebrated the optimism and tri-umphalism embodied in Stalin's 1935 pro-nouncement of a better and more joyous Soviet life. The burgeoning Stalin cult and his ubiqui-tous image in the visual arts cemented the cultural system and reinforced Stalin's political power.

Stalinist wartime cultural policies revealed a relaxation of ideological and artistic restraints. To mobilize cultural resources and bolster patriotism, Stalin charged artists to emphasize the role of the motherland and Russia's national history, temporarily replacing the Party's pri-macy and the Stalin cult in the arts. In return for their support of him as a military and cul-tural leader, Stalin also pragmatically initiated a truce with the Russian Orthodox Church in 1942.

Extinguishing hopes of liberalization, Stalin's post-war cultural policies were characterized by a re-tightening of Party Control, Ideological orthodox, an escalation of the Stalin cult, and Russian chauvinism as the main cultural deter-minant evident in the period's stolid literature, cinematic biopics of historical figures, and florid architecture. Stalin simultaneously launched a brutal anti-cosmopolitanism (anti-Semitic) cam-paign, supervised by Andrei Zhdanov, to purge unpatriotic and alien influences in the arts, such as satire, jazz, and modernist tendencies in clas-sical music and literature. The powerful reas-sertion of Party vigilance and cultural witch-hunt persisted until Stalin's death.

Subsequent generations of cultural producers continued to react, both positively and nega-tively, to the Stalinist cultural legacy. Released by Stalin's death and the Khrushchevian Thaw in culture, architecture, for example, rejected Stalinist neoclassicism for the modernist func-tionality of prefab structures. Later, while offi-cial attempts to construct the Brezhnev cult consciously resuscitated Stalinist cultural mechanisms, the Sots-Art movement subverted Socialist Realist techniques and iconography.

Although many original Stalinist cultural artifacts have been destroyed or archived, today Staliniana still serves as a powerful vehicle for nostalgia and patriotism in the post-Soviet cultural landscape.

See also: anti-Semitism; Brezhnev, Leonid; Communist Party; cult of personality; Georgia; journalism; Khrushchev, Nikita; nationalism ('the national question'); propaganda, Soviet and post-Soviet; Russian Orthodoxy; Socialist Realism; Sots-Art; Thaw; unions, creative, Soviet; World War II (Great Patriotic War)

SUSAN CORBESERO

Stalingrad

The Southern Volga city of Tsaritsyn was re-named Stalingrad in 1925 in honour of Stalin's leadership of the Civil War Battle of Tsaritsyn (1918). In the 1930s, the city and its gigantic new factories were important centres of indus-trialization. Its most enduring fame derived from the victory in the World War II battle of Stalingrad (1942–43). As a result of Khrush-chev's campaign of de-Stalinization, the city was renamed Volgograd in 1961, arousing wide-spread popular protest. It remains one of the main sites for the commemoration of the victory in World War II, with an enormous monument to victory erected on the city's Mamaev Kurgan site in 1967.

See also: World War II (Great Patriotic War)

POLLY JONES

Stalinki

See vysotka (high-rise)

stand-up comedy

Also known as *estrada* or monologue comedy, stand-up comedy is one of Russia's most popular forms of entertainment. The genre took its contemporary form in the 1930s and has its roots in the revolutionary satire of the 1920s, short satirical stories, journalistic feuilleton, and the art of the *konferanse* (master of ceremonies). Among the pioneers of Russian stand-up comedy were Vladimir Khenkin, Nikolai Smirnov-Sokolskii, Mariia Mironova, Aleksandr Menaker, and Arkadii Raikin. A distinctive difference between Russian stand-up comedy and its Western counterpart is the former's markedly theatrical nature. Most standard venues for Russian stand-up comedy are professional theatres, *dvortsy kultury* (palaces of culture), and national television channels. Moreover, Russian stand-up comedy displays a literary orientation. Many *estrada* comics read their monologues directly from a script and rarely resort to improvisation. Russian comedy routines also tend to be lengthy, displaying significant stylistic and thematic complexity. The most prominent contemporary Russian stand-up comedians are Mikhail Zhvanetsii, Mikhail Zadornov, Efim Shifrin, Semen Altov, Klara Novikova, Evgenii Petrosian, and Elena Stepanenko.

During the periods of Thaw and Stagnation stand-up comedy presented a unique blend of officially approved discourse and dissident commentary. Many comedians skirted the edge of Soviet censorship in their expression of sharp social satire and ironic worldview. Zhvanetskii, a seminal Russian stand-up comedian, is best known for his dissident Aesopian satire. With the advent of Gorbachev's glasnost, *estrada* comedy's subtle, anti-regime criticism lost its *raison d'être*. The comedy of the early 1990s witnessed a renaissance of undisguised, direct, and bold political humour. In the late 1990s many Russian comedians began to focus their comedy on the private areas of family life and human relationships. The move from sharp social satire to a lighter form of irony with nostalgic undertones has led to what many Russian critics and comedians see as the decline of Russian stand-up comedy.

See also: censorship; comedians; humour and satire, Soviet; perestroika and glasnost; Raikin, Arkadii; Stagnation; Thaw; Zhvanetskii, Mikhail

OLGA MESROPOVA

Stanislavskii Music Theatre

Moscow's Stanislavskii-Nemirovich-Danchenko Music Theatre was established in 1941 with the merger of the Stanislavskii Opera Theatre Studio and the Nemirovich-Danchenko Music Theatre. Effectively the capital's second lyric stage, it played a role in Soviet and post-Soviet music life no less significant than that of the more pompous and monumental Bolshoi Theatre. Rather like the Small ('Malyi') Opera Theatre in Leningrad/St. Petersburg, the Stanislavskii Music Theatre has long enjoyed a reputation for the quality of its acting, the intimacy of its productions, and the breadth of its repertoire. Under the direction of Leonid Baratov in the 1950s and Lev Mikhailov in the 1960s and 1970s, a number of notable operas were staged, including the first performance in December 1962 of Shostakovich's *Katerina Izmailova*, the revised version of *Ledi Makbet Mtsenskogo uezda* (*Lady Macbeth of the Mtsensk District*). The successful rehabilitation of this previously banned work (whose official premiere took place in January 1963) was proof of the company's importance during the Thaw. The theatre's ballet company emerged when Viktoriia Krieger's Moscow Art Ballet merged with the Moscow Art Theatre productions. Under her leadership these productions were unique in their union of balletic technique and Stanislavskii's acting method, allowing for greater freedom and depth of expression. Under the direction of Vladimir Burmeister, the theatre's ballet reached its height in the 1960s. He was succeeded by Aleksei Chinchinadze in 1971–84, followed by Dmitrii Briantsev in 1985.

A fruitful collaboration with Berlin's *Komische Oper* did not prevent a degree of stagnation during the 1970s and 1980s, when Boris Pokrovskii's Moscow Chamber Opera became Moscow's most significant centre for operatic innovation. Matters worsened when conductor Evgenii Kolobov resigned in 1989, taking with him a number of musicians and staff who were later to form Moscow's Novaia Opera (New Opera). However, since 1991 the theatre not only has survived, but has regained some of its former prestige. New productions, a cast of young and talented singers (such as soprano Khibla Gersmava), and a devoted audience make it one of Moscow's most appealing musical venues. The ballet company is also highly regarded and tours extensively abroad. An ambitious reconstruction project was begun in 2003.

See also: Bolshoi Theatre; opera, Soviet

PHILIP ROSS BULLOCK

Starovoitova, Galina Vasilevna

b. 17 May 1946, Cheliabinsk; d. 20 November 1998, St. Petersburg

Politician

A graduate of the Leningrad State University and post-graduate programme at the Institute of Ethnography, Starovoitova held an academic degree of Candidate of History (*kandidatskaia, kandidat istoricheskikh nauk*). In 1989, she was elected deputy of the USSR Supreme Soviet, and in 1990 of the Russian Supreme Soviet. In 1991–92, she was an assistant to President Boris Yeltsin on interethnic relations. Starovoitova was also co-chair of the 'Democratic Russia' movement and held fellowships at the Kennan Institute for Advanced Russian Studies and Brown's University Watson Institute for International Studies. In 1995, she was elected to the State Duma but in 1996 she was disqualified as a presidential candidate for falsification of signatures in her support. She was assassinated in St. Petersburg, and the investigation, which lasted for several years, did not solve the crime.

See also: academic degrees; democratic reform movement; Duma; Yeltsin, Boris

ALEXANDER DOMRIN

State Attestation Commission

Vysshaia Attestatsionnaia Komissia (VAK, the Higher Certification Commission) is the governmental body overseen by the Ministry of Education that certifies the academic degrees of candidate and doctor of sciences/humanities, the academic status of professor, docent (senior lecturer or associate professor), and the rank of senior researcher/scholar. VAK also controls the work of academic councils that award academic degrees. Founded in 1932, it began to work in 1934. VAK members are appointed by the federal Council of Ministers. VAK comprises a Presidium, eleven sections, and seventy-six boards of experts on separate branches of knowledge.

See also: academic degrees; academic titles; Academy of Sciences

ALEXANDER LEDENEV

State Kremlin Palace (Gosudarstvennyi Kremlevskii dvorets)

See: Kremlin (Moscow)

State symbols, post-Soviet

Post-Soviet state symbols represent Russia's confusion about the Soviet past. In 1993, by unilateral decree Boris Yeltsin abandoned state symbols associated with the old regime, replacing them with pre-revolutionary symbols. The resultant confusing mixture of democratic and monarchic symbols did not last long. A succession of Communist-dominated parliaments rejected Yeltsin's provisional symbols and reintroduced some Soviet ones.

The two-headed eagle first appeared in Moscovia in the fifteenth century. It came from Byzantium with Sophia Paleologue, a member of the last Byzantine Emperor dynasty, who became the wife of Tsar Ivan III. It is generally thought that the eagle's two heads symbolize Russia's two equally important parts, the European and the Asian. The coat of arms was first used as a symbol of the RSFSR and later of Russia as a successor of both the RSFSR and USSR.

The three-colour national flag, first introduced by Peter the Great in 1705 as a trade banner, was proclaimed the Russian national flag by Alexander II in 1858. In 2000 Vladimir Putin, seeking a unifying emblem for a divided society, restored the Soviet red flag (now called the Red Victory Flag, to commemorate World War II) as the pennant of Russia's armed forces.

In 2000, with the approval of the Federation Council, Putin replaced the provisional anthem (originally, *The Patriotic Song*, by nineteenth-century composer Mikhail Glinka), which had been in use between 1993 and 2000, with the Soviet hymn. The latter, composed by Aleksandr Aleksandrov during World War II, has become the national anthem. Incorporating the old-new anthem, with its lyrics transformed into socio-political discourse, Putin boosted the rising reactionary tide and provoked fears of emerging neo-totalitarianism among the country's liberals.

See also: Communist Party; Duma; national anthem, Soviet and Russian; Putin, Vladimir; Russian Federation; state symbols, Soviet; World War II (Great Patriotic War); Yeltsin, Boris

VLADIMIR STRUKOV

State symbols, Soviet

The history of Soviet state symbols reveals a gradual rejection of tsarist imagery in favour of new ideology. In 1918, Party symbols were used as state emblems: instead of the double-headed eagle, the state introduced the red shield with a crossed hammer and sickle and rising sun as its new coat of arms. The hammer and sickle represented the unity of workers and peasants; the red colour referred to the blood of workers spilt in their fight for freedom – an idea borrowed from the red banner flown at the Paris Commune. The red colour was also used as the symbol of other state and social organizations: e.g., by young Pioneers, who wore red ties, with the latter representing part of the red banner of the Revolution.

In the same year the five-pointed star was introduced as the emblem of the Red Army and later was added to the state symbols. The star showed the international status of the Bolshevik government, as the five points were representative of the five inhabited continents.

In 1920, the abbreviation RSFSR (for Russian Soviet Federative Socialist Republic) was added, and the shield was framed by a sheaf of wheat draped with a red scroll, bearing the motto, 'Proletarians of all nations, unite!'

In 1922, the emblem of the USSR was created to symbolize a new state. The sheaf of wheat encircled a globe, and the scroll was divided into ribbons, each with the same motto in a different language: it was meant to represent the autonomy of each and unity of all the constituent republics. In 1936–46 the emblem had eleven ribbons, and from 1956 on, fifteen, corresponding to the number of republics.

In 1918, the national flag of the RSFSR was established as a red banner with a blue vertical line and a hammer, sickle, and star. In 1924 the first Constitution of the USSR defined the Soviet flag as a red banner with a hammer, sickle, and star.

The 'Internationale' was used as the national anthem of the RSFSR from 1918, and of the USSR from 1922. In 1944 Stalin commissioned a new hymn with a Russian theme to address the patriotic feelings of the nation, enmeshed in World War II. The music, composed by Aleksandr Vasilevich Aleksandrov (1883–1946), originally was intended as the 'Hymn of the Bolsheviks'. The lyrics were written by Sergei Vladimirovich Mikhalkov (b. 1913) and edited by Stalin himself. The new national anthem replaced the ideology of world revolution with the ideology of Russian nationalism: whereas each constituent republic had its own national anthem, the RSFSR's national hymn was the same as that of the Soviet Union itself.

During Khrushchev-era de-Stalinization, the anthem retained its former melody, but its then-offensive lyrics made it a 'song without words'. The lyrics were revised (eliminating mention of Stalin) in 1977, and the anthem could thus be sung once again.

Soviet state symbols were discarded in 1993.

See also: Pioneer organization; state symbols, post-Soviet; Thaw; World War II (Great Patriotic War)

VLADIMIR STRUKOV

steppe

An ecological zone in Russia characterized by grassland, often having particularly rich soil for agricultural cultivation. The Russian steppe stretches from Ukraine in the west to Mongolia in the east; parts are called black earth (*chernozem*) to describe the fertile, dark soil valuable for crops. However, the steppe's distance from water makes it very dry. Outside of the summer growing season, lack of geographical features to obstruct northern Arctic air masses from moving southwards renders it extremely cold.

See also: Black Earth region; Ukraine

DAVID J. GALLOWAY

Sterligov, Vladimir Vasilevich

b. 18 March 1904, Warsaw; d. 1 November 1973, Peterhof

Painter

In 1926, Sterligov enrolled as a student of Kazimir Malevich at the State Institute of Artistic Culture (GINKHUK) in Leningrad. Later, working as an illustrator of children's books, he was able to pursue painting as a private activity. In the 1960s, his Leningrad studio was a gathering place for those interested in recovering the legacy of Russia's early-twentieth-century avant-garde. During this period, Sterligov developed his unique 'cup-cupolan' system of composition: space was conceived as curved and continuous; the complementary forms of chalice and cupola acted as structuring elements and as symbols of unity.

JANET E. KENNEDY

stiliagi

The *stiliagi* (singular: *stiliaga*) were a loosely organized subculture of jazz lovers active in Soviet cities beginning in the late 1940s. Their name, derived from the word *stil* (style), was first used in state media to denounce them. The *stiliaga* look included a zoot suit and a Tarzan-style haircut (*stiliagi* were sometimes called *tarzantsy*). They favoured traditional jazz, which made them somewhat old-fashioned by the early-1960s, when Soviet youth were beginning to embrace rock music. Interest in the *stiliagi* aesthetic revived during perestroika, when some youths and popular musicians resurrected the name and the look.

See also: jazz; rock music

SETH GRAHAM

St. Petersburg

St. Petersburg was founded in 1703 by Peter I to protect territory regained through war with Sweden (1701–21) to secure access to the Baltic Sea. The city was named after the tsar's patron saint; however, the name soon became identified with St. Petersburg's royal founder, whose equestrian statue (1782), nicknamed the Bronze Horseman, has been an emblem of St. Petersburg ever since. St. Petersburg was the first Russian city built according to a plan (the original design was by Peter I himself) and by predominantly European architects. In 1712, Peter I moved the capital of the Russian Empire from Moscow to St. Petersburg. This controversial decision generated a split in Russian culture and mentality, producing an opposition between the two cities, in which Moscow was perceived as traditional, organic, domestic, and authentic, but also Asian and barbarian, while St. Petersburg was seen as European, rational, and civilized, but also cold, bureaucratic, foreign, and demonic. This opposition was central in the nineteenth-century polemical discourse of the Slavophiles and Westernizers.

After Russia's entry into World War I in 1914, the city's Germanic-sounding name was replaced with its Slavic equivalent, Petrograd. The city remained the capital of Russia until 1918, when the seat of government shifted back to Moscow. All three Russian revolutions – in 1905, February 1917, and October 1917 – began in St. Petersburg. After Lenin's death in 1924, the city was renamed Leningrad ('the city of Lenin'), even though the Bolshevik leader had spent only 72 days there. The original name was restored in 1991.

During the Soviet period, the city was reduced to the status of a provincial centre and suffered considerably from the Stalinist purges of the 1930s and late 1940s till the early 1950s. The blockade by German forces during World War II, which lasted approximately 900 days (September 1941–January 1944), brought starvation, daily air raids, damage and destruction of many buildings, and the loss of two-thirds of its population to the city. Rebuilding the city's historical monuments after the war took decades, the most recent efforts preceding the elaborate tercentenary celebrations in May 2003.

St. Petersburg's unique place in Russian culture is expressed in the 'Petersburg myth', inscribed in literary and non-fictional texts, works of art, and theatrical performances, treating the city not only as a material or aesthetic, but also as a spiritual and even metaphysical phenomenon. In the eighteenth century, folklore presented the new city as a demonic project and its founder as the Antichrist, whereas court literature endorsed the cosmogonic myth, portraying Peter I as a demiurge who had created the city *ex nihilo*, and praising the city's architectural beauty, calling it the 'Northern Palmyra' and 'a window to Europe'. Both currents merged in Aleksandr Pushkin's 1833 narrative poem *Mednyi vsadnik* (*The Bronze Horseman*), which presented the city's contradictions as the eternal struggle of cosmos and chaos, state and individual. Later nineteenth-century writers largely emphasized the negative and mystical aspects of the city. Physiological sketches focused on the underbelly of life in a big, modern metropolis, presenting the Russian capital as the centre of bureaucracy, poverty, and social inequality. Nikolai Gogol's St. Petersburg is a ghostly town that destroys the individual. Fedor Dostoevskii's delirious vision of the city emphasizes its artificial nature, lacking national roots. The ultimate St. Petersburg novel appeared in the early twentieth century: Andrei Belyi's *Petersburg* provides an apocalyptic vision of the imperial capital. Significantly modified after the Revolution, the Petersburg myth survived into the modern period, especially in the poetry and prose essays of Iosif Brodskii and the prose of Andrei Bitov and Tatiana Tolstaia.

See also: Bitov, Andrei; Brodskii, Iosif; Moscow; Pushkin, Aleksandr; Slavophiles; Tolstaia, Tatiana; Westernizers; World War II (Great Patriotic War)

Further reading

(2000) *Moskva-Peterburg: pro i contra: Dialog kultur v istorii natsionalnogo samosoznaniia*, St. Petersburg.

Salisbury, H. (1985) *The 900 Days: The Siege of Leningrad*, New York: Da Capo Press.

Volkov, S. (1995) *St. Petersburg: A Cultural History*, New York: The Free Press.

MARIA RUBINS

St. Petersburg (Leningrad) State Conservatory

The Nikolai Rimskii-Korsakov St. Petersburg State Conservatory is the oldest musical training institution in Russia. Throughout its history it has played a significant role in setting academic tradition, both for establishing schools of composition and for scholarship. It was founded in 1862 by Anton Rubinstein, under the sponsorship of the Imperial Russian Musical Society. Rubinstein directed the Conservatory from 1862–67 and 1887–91, and he taught piano and composition. One of his first students was Petr Tchaikovsky, who graduated with a gold medal (highest honours). In its first decades the Conservatory was guided by the German model of musical instruction; most of the faculty were from Germany and Austria or had studied there. A national school arose at the Conservatory in the 1880s, led particularly by Rimskii-Korsakov (who taught there from 1871–1908), Anatolii Liadov (1876–1914), and Aleksandr Glazunov (faculty member 1899–1905, director 1905–28). These composers also led the so-called Beliaev Circle, named after its sponsor Mitrofan Beliaev, which promoted a distinctly Russian academism in music. Another member of this circle was Maksimilian (Maximilian) Steinberg, who worked at the Conservatory in 1908–46 and, as director of the composition department, was one of Dmitrii Shostakovich's teachers.

The Conservatory's piano school was founded by Rubinstein and Feliks Leshetitskii, the violin school – by Genrik Veniavskii and Leopold Auer, whose students included Efrem Zimbalist and Yasha Heifetz, as well as cellists Karl Davydov and Aleksandr Verzhbilovich. The Conservatory's pre-revolutionary graduates included Sergei Prokofiev (1904–14), who graduated with three diplomas: in piano, composition, and conducting.

In 1918, the Conservatory came under state ownership. Scholar Boris Asafev oversaw the revision of the curriculum in the 1910s and early 1920s; an energetic organizer, he also had a tremendous impact on the establishment (1923) and development of the opera studio.

The Conservatory's structure and curriculum underwent significant changes in the Soviet era. Major figures who founded new schools and directions there included singer Ivan Ershov, conductor Nikolai Malko, pianist Leonid Nikolaev, and organist Isai Braudo. One of the most famous schools was the conducting studio of Ilia Musin (1932–96), whose students included Vasilii Sinaiskii, Arnold Kats, Semen Bychkov, Neeme Järvi, Iurii Temirkanov, Valerii Gergiev, and many other conductors in Russia and abroad. In the 1960s, a circle of composers formed under the leadership of Dmitrii Shostakovich, some of whom later taught there, most notably Boris Tishchenko. Another major composer who taught throughout his career at the Conservatory was Sergei Slonimskii. The Conservatory's scholarly tradition includes music historians Roman Gruber, Mikhail Druskin, Pavel Vulfius, and music theorists Iurii Tiulin, Khristofor Kushnarev, Aleksandr Dolzhanskii, and Ekaterina Ruchevskaia.

Today the Conservatory maintains its historic building (1896) on St. Petersburg's Theatre Square, across from the Mariinskii Theatre; besides classrooms, it has an opera theatre and concert hall. The Conservatory has seven departments: composition, piano, orchestral, vocal, symphonic and choral conducting, music history and theory, and instrumental folk music.

See also: Gergiev, Valerii; Mariinskii Theatre; Prokofiev, Sergei; Shostakovich, Dmitri; Slonimskii, Sergei; Temirkanov, Iurii; Tishchenko, Boris

Further reading

(1962) *100 let Leningradskoi konservatorii, 1862–1962*, Leningrad: Muzgit/Gos.muzykalnoe izd.vo.
(1987–88) *Leningradskaia konservatoriia v vospominaniiakh, 1862–1962*, 2 vols, Leningrad: Muzgit/Gos.muzykalnoe izd.vo.

KIRA NEMIROVSKAIA

St. Petersburg State Academic Capella

The St. Petersburg Capella was established in 1479 as Tsar Ivan III's private choir. In 1701, it was renamed the Court Choir and relocated to St. Petersburg, where it fused traditional Russian music with Western European influences. In 1887–89 its facilities, including the Capella Orchestra and School, were reconstructed by the architect Leontii Benois. Leading Russian composers – Dmitrii Bortnyanskii, Mikhail Glinka, Milyi Balakirev, and Nikolai Rimsky-Korsakov – served as its directors. Since 1974, led by the venerable conductor Vladislav Chernushenko, the St. Petersburg Capella has toured the world. Its repertory includes traditional liturgical music and contemporary church and folk music.

TATIANA SENKEVITCH

St. Petersburg State Academy of Theatre Arts (SPGATI, formerly LGITMiK)

This theatre academy offers undergraduate and graduate education in a wide range of theatre professions; it also functions as a conservatory. It was founded in 1918 when Leonid Vivien's School of Acting and Vsevolod Meierkhold's Stage Direction Courses were established. It came into being as the Institute for Theatre Arts in 1922 and, after a number of mergers and reorganizations, in 1962 it became known as the Leningrad State Institute for Theatre, Music, and Cinema. The Academy adopted its present name in 1993. It offers rigorous training in the departments of acting and directing, show business, set and light design, theatre studies, puppet theatre, television, and theatre management. The Academy prides itself on being one of the top Russian drama schools, actively promoting the Stanislavskii method.

DASHA KRIJANSKAIA

St. Petersburg State University (Sankt-Peterburgskii gosudarstvennyi universitet, SPGU)

Founded in 1819, St. Petersburg State University now has about 25,000 students, 5,000 staff members, and 20 science and humanities faculties. In the nineteenth century it was famous for its divisions in mathematics (Pafnutii Chebyshev), chemistry (Dmitrii Mendeleev), embryology (Ilia Mechnikov), and physiology (Ivan Sechenov). Its famous graduates include writer Ivan Turgenev, poets Aleksandr Blok (who grew up on the university campus, as his maternal grandfather, botanist Andrei Beketov, was then president [rector] of the university), and Nikolai Gumilev, composers Mikhail Glinka and Aleksandr Glazunov, painters Mikhail Vrubel and Nikolai Rerikh, performing arts celebrities Sergei Diagilev and Vasilii Kachalov. Seven professors and graduates of this university are Nobel Prize winners (Ivan Pavlov, Mechnikov, Nikolai Semenov, Lev Landau, Aleksandr Prokhorov, Vasilii Leontev, and Leonid Kantorovich). Vladimir Putin graduated from its law school.

See also: Nobel Prize winners, non-literary; Putin, Vladimir

TATYANA LEDENEVA

Stravinskii, Igor Fedorovich

b. 5 [17] June 1882, Oranienbaum; d. 6 April 1971, New York

Composer

Probably no other composer of the twentieth century has been more thoroughly interviewed, documented, analyzed, idolized, criticized, or imitated than Igor Stravinskii. Born into a highly musical and well-connected family (his father was a famous operatic bass) in St. Petersburg just as the city was entering its most brilliant artistic era, as a young man Stravinskii studied privately with Nikolai Rimskii-Korsakov. But it was his encounter with the impresario Sergei Diagilev that changed Stravinskii's life and led him into the world of ballet, where he achieved his early successes with the scores for *Zhar-Ptitsa* (*The Firebird*), *Petrushka* and *Vesnia sviashchennaia* (*The Rite of Spring*), brilliantly staged in Paris by Diagilev's *Ballets russes* just before World War I. From 1914, Stravinskii lived in Europe, first in Switzerland and later in France. In 1939, he left Europe for the United States, settling in Los Angeles in 1940, where he lived until just before his death.

Since Stravinskii hated to repeat himself, his music continued to absorb and explore new influences and techniques throughout his career. His remarkable early success was strongly connected to Russian folklore, folk music, and the traditions of nineteenth-century Russian musical nationalism, but his treatment of this familiar material grew increasingly unconventional and modernist in form and execution. The premiere of *The Rite of Spring* in Paris on 29 May 1913, with its savage portrayal of pre-historic pagan ritual, created one of the greatest scandals in ballet history, becoming a defining event of twentieth-century cultural history. The score's most innovative feature was its fragmentary, montage-like structure, composed of small units that collided with one another like atoms in a smasher. In Stravinskii's music, complex rhythmic patterns are a more important organizing principle than melody or harmony. Following in the footsteps of his adored model Tchaikovsky, to whom he paid homage in several scores, Stravinskii established ballet as a serious and respectable arena for classical composers. He also developed a close collaboration with Diagilev's disciple, the choreographer George Balanchine, creating several important ballets with him (*Apollon Musagete, Jeu de Cartes, Orpheus, Agon*).

The 'Russian' Stravinskii continued to resurface in later works, but he was eager to shed what he regarded as the limitations of that identity. Increasingly, he cultivated and sought the role of a cosmopolitan artist, not a nationalist. He worked with particular success in a 'neoclassical' style, with its wide-ranging possibilities for finding, reexamining, and reinterpreting musical material and forms from various cultures and eras. Examples include the ballet *Pulcinella* (a gloss on the eighteenth-century style of Pergolesi), the *Concerto for Piano and Wind Instruments* (with strong echoes of Bach and Handel), and the opera *Oedipus Rex* (looking back to Verdi). In such scores as *Symphony of Psalms*, Stravinskii created startling effects by employing unusual ensembles that contrasted with the expectations of a certain genre. He also led the way towards postmodernism, with its eclectic embrace of diverse and incongruous styles.

See also: ballet, Soviet; classical music, Soviet

Further reading

Craft, R. and Stravinsky, I. (2003) *Memories and Commentaries*, London: Faber & Faber.
Cross, J. (ed.) (2003) *The Cambridge Companion to Stravinsky*, Cambridge: Cambridge University Press.
Walsh, S. (2002) *Stravinsky: A Creative Spring: Russia and France, 1882–1934*, Berkeley, CA: University of California Press.

HARLOW ROBINSON

Strizhenov, Oleg Aleksandrovich

b. 10 August 1929, Blagoveshchensk

Film and theatre actor

A graduate of the Shchukin Theatre School in Moscow (1953), Strizhenov became a national superstar with his film debut as Arthur in *Ovod* (*The Gadfly*, 1955), based on Ethel Voynich's novel. The fair-haired actor's striking looks and acting talent made him an excellent choice for chivalrous, romantic roles, among them such internationally recognized achievements as the male lead in Grigorii Chukhrai's Civil War drama *Sorok pervyi* (*The Forty-First*, 1956). Strizhenov's exceptional star power was put to good use in adaptations of classical literature, but also

exploited in films with an underlying propagandistic agenda in which the actor portrayed Soviet spies, officers, and other idealized Communist characters. People's Artist of the USSR (1988).

See also: Chukhrai, Grigorii; Communist ideology; propaganda

PETER ROLLBERG

structuralism

A methodology in the humanities and the social sciences that focuses on the interconnections between, on the one hand, the object being studied and the internal hierarchies of its constitutive elements, and, on the other, larger systems to which that object might be related. Russian and Soviet scholars have distinguished themselves both in helping develop structuralist theory and in applying it with great success to various fields (linguistics, poetics, literary history, anthropology, folklore, mythology, etc.). During the 1920s and the 1930s, the Prague Linguistic Circle, an association of Czechoslovak and Russian scholars (most, such as Nikolai Trubetskoi, Roman Iakobson, Petr Bogatyrev, and Sergei Kartsevskii, lived in emigration in Western Europe) provided the organizational framework for the development of the structuralist paradigm: ultimately, thanks in large measure to Roman Iakobson, and especially his contacts with Claude Lévi-Strauss, the Prague School had a profound influence on post-World War II Western scholarship. Starting in 1960 and continuing into the 1980s, structuralism became one of the twin methodological pillars for the many-sided research activities by the Moscow-Tartu School (Viacheslav Ivanov, Vladimir Toporov, Boris Uspenskii, Iurii Lotman, Zara Mints, Mikhail Gasparov, and others); the other pillar, as was also the case with the Prague School, was provided by semiotics – the study of meaning-bearing signs and sign systems found in various spheres of culture and nature. 'Structural-semiotic' (the accepted designation) studies challenged Soviet dogma by pursuing research into areas that had been nearly abandoned during the Stalin period (verse theory, poetics), by opening the doors to Western scholarly and intellectual discourses in such fields as linguistics, comparative religion (Mircea Eliade), and philosophy (R.G. Collingwood); by recovering the extraordinary legacy of Russian scholarship of the first half of the twentieth century (the Formalists and Young-Formalists, literary scholar and philosopher Mikhail Bakhtin, mythologist Olga Freidenberg, film director and theoretician Sergei Eisenstein, and others); and by actively studying the works of such great Silver Age poets as Osip Mandelshtam and Anna Akhmatova, generally ignored or disparaged in officially approved accounts of twentieth-century Russian literature. Unlike West European structuralism, largely focused on general systems, the comparable trend in the Soviet Union privileged the study of the specific text and its historical-cultural context and treated theory as a tool that could be altered or even abandoned if needed. Ultimately, the impact of Moscow-Tartu structural-semiotic studies was felt in culture no less than in scholarship: they became part of the larger struggle for memory during the late Soviet period and helped prepare the groundwork for the intellectual ferment of the glasnost period.

In the West, by the late 1960s, largely thanks to Jacques Derrida, structuralism began to give way to poststructuralism and its diverse methodologies, especially deconstruction. A different situation prevailed in the Soviet Union and still prevails in today's Russia: although the theoretical militancy of the early years had abated by the late 1970s, the work of the 'structuralists' and 'semioticians' moved from the periphery into the scholarly mainstream, while during the 1990s several Moscow-Tartu scholars, especially Gasparov, Ivanov, and Toporov, became enormously influential figures within Russian culture as a whole. While deconstruction has had some impact, historicism – without discarding the achievements of the structural-semiotic movement – is undoubtedly a more significant presence in contemporary Russian scholarship.

See also: Akhmatova, Anna; Iakobson (Jakobson), Roman; Lotman, Iurii; perestroika and glasnost; Tartu–Moscow School; World War II (Great Patriotic War)

Further reading

Baran, H. (1985) 'Structuralism and Semiotics', in V. Terras (ed.) *Handbook of Russian Literature*, New Haven, CT: Yale University Press, pp. 448–51.

Steiner, P., Baran, H. and Culler, J. (1993) 'Structuralism', in A. Preminger and T. V. F. Brogan (eds) *The New Princeton Encyclopedia of Poetry and Poetics*, Princeton, NJ: Princeton University Press, pp. 1215–22.

HENRYK BARAN

Strugatskii, Arkadii and Boris

Strugatskii, Arkadii Natanovich

b. 28 August 1925, Batumi, Georgia; d. 12 October 1991, Moscow

Strugatskii, Boris Natanovich

b. 15 April 1933, Leningrad

Writers

The writing team comprising the brothers Arkadii and Boris Strugatskii, along with Iurii Gagarin's historic flight, was largely responsible for the spectacular ascendancy of science fiction as a politically challenging but genuinely popular genre during the Thaw and Stagnation under Brezhnev. Their first stories were optimistically construed adventures in interplanetary travel that clearly reflected the *sputnik*-era Soviet enthusiasm for science and technology (*Ulitka na sklone* [*Snail on the Slope*], 1968). In subsequent works, they adroitly exploited the 'what if' premise of their genre to counter official literary depictions of Soviet society (*Skazka o troika* [*Fairytale of the Troika*], 1968). Their books imagined alternative societies where rationality and scientific integrity are not at odds with human rights and freedom. In the 1970s and the 1980s, under increasing censorship, their novels voiced a generation's authentic political and cultural aspirations, combined with a racy plot. Since his brother's death in 1991, Boris Strugatskii has maintained visibility as a liberal public intellectual. The allegorical arguments against preemptive war and government-controlled secret science that an earlier generation espied in their fiction have not lost their relevance for a new generation, and the Strugatskii's novels are continually in print, while an active on-line fan club is devoted to all aspects of Strugatskiana.

See also: fiziki-liriki (scientist-poets); Gagarin, Iurii; science fiction; Stagnation; Thaw

YVONNE HOWELL

Sturua, Robert

b. 31 July 1938, Tbilisi, Georgia

Director

A spiritual disciple of Sandro Akhmeteli, the founder of modern Georgian theatre, Sturua applies intrinsic national qualities to all authors, whether Bertolt Brecht (*The Caucasian Chalk Circle*, 1975), Shakespeare (*King Lear*, 1987) or Carlo Gozzi (*The Serpent Woman*, 1998). As such, his work may be compared to Akira Kurosawa's cinematic adaptations of world literature. Artistic director of the Rustaveli Theatre in Tbilisi, Georgia, since 1979, Sturua often works in Moscow, where he has staged Mikhail Shatrov's *Brestskii mir* (*The Peace at Brest*, 1988), Carlo Goldoni's *Signor Todero Brontolone* (2002), Samuel Beckett's *Krapp's Last Tape* (2002), Shakespeare's *Hamlet* (1998), *The Merchant of Venice* (2000) and *Romeo and Juliet* (2004).

See also: Georgia; theatre, post-Soviet

JOHN FREEDMAN

subbotnik

Subbotnik, from the word *subbota* (Saturday), is voluntary collective work useful to the community, originally scheduled on Saturdays. Lenin considered Communist *subbotniks* the real beginning of Communism. The first *subbotnik* was organized by railway workers on 12 April 1919 to answer Lenin's call 'to work the revolutionary way'. It prompted a mass movement that soon spread throughout the country. During World War II *subbotniks* were transformed into *voskresniks*

(Sunday). Later, *subbotniks* were called Lenin's *subbotniks* and throughout the Soviet period they took place on 22 April (Lenin's birthday). Today this form of volunteer work is used to foster a corporate spirit in companies, universities, or cities.

See also: Communist Party; Communist ideology; Lenin, Vladimir Ilich; World War II (Great Patriotic War)

ELENA OMELCHENKO

superstitions, Russian

Many Russian superstitions resemble Western beliefs – a black cat means bad luck, and not only for village peasants. Poet Aleksandr Sergeevich Pushkin was famously superstitious, reportedly escaping direct involvement in the Decembrist uprising, and thus punishment or exile, when omens dissuaded him from a planned trip to St. Petersburg. Superstitions survive from a more fully elaborated Russian folk mythology, such as belief in the Evil Eye (*sglaz*) and persons with the power, intentional or not, to cast it. Superstitions combine recurring elements with local variations and idiosyncratic additions (like a basketball player's lucky shorts); traditional superstitions mix with contemporary and imported elements. Omens (*primety*) both predict the future and determine behaviour (take the first step with your right, 'lucky' foot). While some are familiar in other traditions, others are specific to Russia: a bachelor who holds out his teacup for a serving without the saucer will remain unmarried. Not 'speaking of the devil' is a prominent concern (paradoxically in a culture with a rich, semi-taboo language of swear words, *mat*). After a slip of the tongue or pen that threatens someone's health or welfare, or an optimistic statement on these subjects, many Russians say or write '*Tfu, tfu, tfu!*' – 'spitting' three times over the left shoulder, into the eye of the demon there, so as not to tempt fate (*ne sglazit*). Interpreting dreams is popular, combining fortune-telling with the pleasure of social ritual. Dream books (*sonniki*) and other such popular works were suppressed in the Soviet Union but are now widely published. Young people may employ love spells or spells to pass examinations. The common nervousness about draughts recalls the belief that witches or sorcerers 'cast' illness onto the wind. To keep off the evil eye (in New Age terms, 'negative energy') a Russian may wear a safety pin upside-down inside her clothes.

See also: folk mythology

SIBELAN FORRESTER

Sverdlovskaia oblast

See: Ekaterinburg

Svetlanov, Evgenii Fedorovich

b. 6 June 1928, Moscow; d. 4 May 2002, Moscow

Conductor, composer, pianist

Svetlanov was born into a family of opera singers. His parents were soloists in the Bolshoi Theatre. As a boy Svetlanov participated in the children's choir, acting in many opera performances. After graduating from Moscow Conservatory, where he studied conducting (with Aleksandr Gauk), composition (with Iurii Shaporin) and piano (with Genrikh Neigauz) and after a few years with Moscow Radio Symphony Orchestra, Svetlanov returned to the Bolshoi (1955). In 1962, he became chief conductor and in 1964 led the tour of the Bolshoi to La Scala, which was the turning point of the theatre's history and brought it worldwide fame. Svetlanov conducted at the Bolshoi until the end

of his life, and, from 1965 on, also the State Symphony Orchestra, which for three decades was known as '*Svetlanov's orchestra*'. The monument to these years is a great cycle of recordings, '*An Anthology of Russian Symphonic Music*', begun in the 1960s and ending with Svetlanov's final days.

See also: Bolshoi Theatre; Moscow Conservatory; orchestras, Soviet and post-Soviet

KIRA NEMIROVSKAYA

Sviridov, Georgii Vasilevich

b. 3 [16] December 1915, Fatezh, Kursk oblast; d. 6 January 1998, Moscow

Composer, pianist

A musical nationalist, Leningrad Conservatory graduate, and student of Shostakovich, Sviridov wrote music in the nineteenth-century endemic tradition of Glinka, Mussorgskii, and Rimskii-Korsakov. His approach to folk music differs from theirs, however, for he believed that the peasantry's music would emancipate and free the composer. Sviridov's output is large, and his greatest legacy is considered his choral works set to words of folk texts or those of twentieth-century Russian poets. Particular significant is his monumental *Pesnopeniia i molitvy* (*Canticles and Prayers*, 1987–97), in the rich tradition of Rachmaninov's *Vsenoshchnoe bdenie* (*Vespers*, 1915).

See also: Shostakovich, Dmitrii; St. Petersburg Conservatory

DAVID GOMPPER

T

tabaka (chicken)

Tabaka enjoys popularity as an entrée in Georgian cuisine. A partially boned and flattened young chicken is weighted down with a heavy implement during cooking. Liberally salted and sometimes spiced with garlic, it is fried in a special skillet. *Satsivi* (walnut) or *tkemali* (sour plum) sauces may serve as garnish.

See also: Caucasian cuisine

CHRISTINE A. RYDEL

Tabakov, Oleg Pavlovich

b. 17 August 1935, Saratov

Actor, director, teacher

A major figure in Russian culture for several decades, Tabakov began his career as one of the founders of the *Sovremennik* (Contemporary) Theatre, which became an important symbol of Khrushchev's Thaw. An extremely prolific actor, he has played over 200 parts on stage and screen, many of which have a comical streak or a touch of soft irony. His best-known roles in film include the SS intelligence mastermind Walter Schellenberg in the cult television series *Seventeen Moments of Spring* (*Semnadtsat mgnovenii vesny*, 1973) and the title role in *Oblomov* (1979), Nikita Mikhalkov's cinematic adaptation of Ivan Goncharov's classic nineteenth-century novel. Tabakov also performs as a voice actor in animation. His tomcat Matroskin (Russian Garfield of sorts) from the *Prostokvashino* series (1978–84)

grew so popular that this cartoon character is often projected onto its creator. In the mid-1980s, recruiting his GITIS students, Tabakov formed a theatre studio nicknamed *Tabakerka* (Snuff Box) in an obvious pun on the founder's last name. Tabakov's marriage to Marina Zudina, a young star of the new company, provided ample food for the budding Russian tabloids. Tabakov also made a comeback in his alma mater, the Moscow Art Theatre, serving as the director of its school (1986–2000) and eventually as its head director (since 2000). In the latter capacity Tabakov has been remarkably successful, balancing financial and artistic considerations. He also has restored the theatre's unique role as the meeting point of tradition and experimentation in contemporary Russian theatre.

See also: Mikhalkov, Nikita; Moscow Art Theatre; Russian Academy of Theatre Arts; *Semnadtsat mgnovenii vesny* (*Seventeen Moments of Spring*); Sovremennik Theatre; Thaw

DAN UNGURIANU

Taganka Theatre

Founded in 1964, Moscow's Taganka Theatre was long famed for its nonconformist tendencies, its bold choice of repertoire, and its tradition of aesthetic and technical innovation. The Taganka was formed on the basis of the Moscow Theatre of Drama and Comedy, and has been directed almost continuously by Iurii Liubimov.

For several decades the Taganka was a bastion of the liberal intelligentsia. Ideals and attitudes characteristic of the Thaw were reflected in the theatre's orientation towards publicistic poetry, seen, for example, in shows based on the works of Andrei Voznesenskii and also in the dynamic, emotionally charged performances of its actors, particularly Vladimir Vysotskii.

During the 1970s, both the Taganka's reputation and its social authority grew. Success at international theatre festivals contributed to the former, while continual clashes with the Soviet authorities contributed to the latter. The next decade brought crisis: Vysotskii died prematurely in 1980, while Liubimov was unceremoniously fired in 1984. Reinstated in 1989, Liubimov has devoted undivided attention to the theatre only since 1997. The Taganka remains popular with spectators, but for a predominantly traditional repertoire that represents a major departure from its avant-garde past.

See also: Demidova, Alla; Efros, Anatolii; Gubenko, Nikolai; Liubimov, Iurii; intelligentsia; Smekhov, Veniamin; Thaw; theatre, Soviet; Voznesenskii, Andrei; Vysotskii, Vladimir; Zolotukhin, Valerii

RACHEL S. PLATONOV

taiga

An ecological zone in Russia characterized by coniferous (evergreen) tree growth. *Taiga* is the Russian word, but it is used to describe such zones worldwide. A band of taiga encircles the northern hemisphere, encompassing large areas of Canada, the Nordic countries, and Russia. In Russia, the taiga lies south of the band of Arctic tundra. Trees in the taiga are well adapted to extreme cold, a short growing season, and heavy snowfall. These vast Siberian forests are part of Russia's tremendous natural wealth, though indiscriminate and illegal lumberjacking present serious ecological consequences to clear-cutting large areas.

See also: natural resources; Siberia

DAVID J. GALLOWAY

Tajikistan (Tadzhikistan)

Tajikistan is a country in Central Asia that used to be one of the fifteen republics of the Soviet Union. It shares borders with Uzbekistan, Kyrgyzstan, China, and Afghanistan. In 2004, Tajikistan had a population of about 7 million, 65 per cent of whom were ethnic Tajiks, a predominantly Sunni Muslim ethnic group that speaks an Iranian language called Tajik. Dushanbe is the capital of Tajikistan, with a multiethnic population of about 800,000.

Most of the territory of today's Tajikistan was taken over by the Russian Empire in the late nineteenth century. The main cities where Tajiks lived – Bukhara and Samarkand – ended up within the territory of the Uzbek Soviet Socialist Republic when the Tajik Soviet Socialist Republic was split off in 1929. To this day, many Tajiks live in Uzbekistan and Uzbeks in Tajikistan. One of the poorest Soviet republics during the Soviet period, Tajikistan remained so after independence, reliant on aid and trade with other former Soviet republics. Tajikistan's territory is mostly mountains and scarce in natural resources.

Tajikistan became independent from the Soviet Union in September 1991. The civil war that broke out the following year continued, off and on, until 1997, resulting in tens of thousands of deaths. Flawed elections were held in 1994, which elevated Emomali Rakhmanov to the presidency. Rakhmanov became increasingly autocratic in the years that followed. The government of Tajikistan had been ambivalent about Russian influence, especially the presence of Russian troops serving as guards on the Tajik border with Afghanistan. However, in 2004, Tajikistan agreed to a number of security measures that strengthened its relationship to Russia.

See also: Central Asia; Islam; Kyrgyzstan; USSR; Uzbekistan

LAURA ADAMS

tamada

Tamada (the toastmaster) organizes ceremonial feasts in Georgia. Usually the most eloquent and witty of those present, he begins with toasts to God, the hostess, other family members, and then friends. He also paces the drinking to avoid inebriation and to preserve an aura of dignity during the festivities. An excellent example of *tamada* occurs in a chapter titled *Belshazzar's Feasts* from Fazil Iskander's novel *Sandro from Chegem* (*Zhitie Sandro chegemskogo*)

See also: Georgia; Iskander, Fazil; tost

CHRISTINE A. RYDEL

tamizdat

Tamizdat, literally 'there-publishing', refers to material written in the USSR, but published in the West. The first *tamizdat* publication – Naritsa's novel *Nespetaia pesnia* (*Unsung Song*) – was published in the émigré journal *Grani* (Borders) in 1960. The journals *Grani*, *Posev* (Sowing), *Kontinent*, and *Sintaksis* (Syntax), the newspaper *Russkaia mysl* (Russian Thought), and the publishing house Ardis were the main organs of *tamizdat* publishing. Literature and journalism were smuggled out of the USSR principally by sailors, who were usually paid for their services; a network of émigrés in Europe and the US coordinated its collection and publication. Some have alleged that the CIA aided *tamizdat* publication, considering it a useful weapon in the Cold War, but Ardis had no links whatever with the government. Authors of *tamizdat* included both official and unofficial writers. Particularly for the latter, this method of publishing was vital for reaching an audience. Some writers published *tamizdat* under a pseudonym, while others did not disguise their identity. *Tamizdat* publications often circulated as *samizdat* in the USSR, or in the *tamizdat* editions sent back to their authors from the West. The most significant *tamizdat* publications included *Doctor Zhivago* by Boris Pasternak, Aleksandr Solzhenitsyn's works, and Nadezhda Mandelshtam's memoirs.

See also: Mandelshtam, Nadezhda; Pasternak, Boris; samizdat; Solzhenitsyn, Aleksandr

EMILY LYGO

tapochki (slippers)

Flat-soled, cloth house slippers, *tapochki* are worn by family members and guests alike. Upon entering homes, Russians remove their outer footwear, which could be muddy or wet from the harsh climate, and don *tapochki*, in order to protect floors and keep feet warm. Hosts keep extra *tapochki* on hand for guests. Visitors to museums must wear *tapochki* that cover their shoes in order to protect the floors because the buildings themselves are considered works of art.

CHRISTINE A. RYDEL

Tarkovskii, Andrei Arsenievich

b. 4 April 1932, Zavrazhie village, near Iurievets; d. 29 December 1986, Paris

Film director, screenwriter, writer

Tarkovskii graduated from VGIK in 1960 (Mikhail Romm's studio). His graduation film was *Katok i skripka* (*The Steamroller and the Violin*), a work typical for the era, about a boy, an aspiring musician, and a labourer who teaches him about life. Despite the conventional theme, the technical virtuosity in camerawork, editing, sound, and music foreshadowed the scrupulous attention to detail and absolute professionalism Tarkovskii was to achieve in all his films. During his career he worked with the best cinematographers (Vadim Iusev, Georgii Rerberg, Sven Nykvist), screenwriters (Andrei Konchalovskii, Fridrikh Gorenshtein), and composers (Viacheslav Ovchinnikov, Eduard Artemiev) of his day.

Tarkovskii emerged onto the national and international scene with his first feature, *Ivanogo detstvo* (*Ivan's Childhood*, 1962), a darkly poetic story of a young scout in World War II; the film earned him the prestigious Golden Lion award at the Venice Film Festival. But it was his second film, *Andrei Rublev* (1966, released 1971) that cemented Tarkovskii's reputation abroad and created what would be career-long problems with the film bureaucracy at home. *Andrei Rublev* is a magisterial, three-hour long, metaphysical, yet starkly naturalistic meditation on the life and the brutal times of the medieval

Russian monk and icon painter Andrei Rublev. Here Tarkovskii fully developed what would become his signature style – long, uninterrupted shots (what he called 'imprinted time') and minimal or complex narratives in which dream and reality or time frames often converge, and where objects seem to be imbued with multiple personal or symbolic meanings (which he often denied). He challenged the increasingly conservative tenets of Socialist Realism, as did his unconventional heroes – often passive and reflective rather than active – and thus his own insistence on the primacy of the spiritual over the material. Tarkovskii ignored contemporary Soviet reality and explored eternal questions of faith, love, duty, and moral responsibility, and the role of the artist in society and history.

Over twenty-five years Tarkovskii made only seven feature films: five in the Soviet Union – *Ivan, Rublev*, the autobiographical *Zerkalo* (*Mirror*, 1975), the futuristic *Solaris* (1972, based on a novel by Stanislaw Lem), and *Stalker* (1979, from the Strugatskii brothers' *Piknik na obochine* [*Roadside Picnic*]); and two in Europe (*Nostalgia*, Italy, 1983 and *The Sacrifice* [*Zhervoprinoshenie*], Sweden, 1986). Despite being made in different countries, with different crews, collaborators, and technical, economic, and logistical support, Tarkovskii's films create a stylistic and thematic whole. Tarkovskii is now recognized at home and abroad as arguably the greatest *auteur* in modern Russian cinema, with the film-maker Aleksandr Sokurov as his worthy disciple.

When in 1984 he refused to return home and decided to stay in Europe to work, Tarkovskii became a 'non-person' in the Soviet Union; however, after his death in 1986 and with the onset of glasnost, he was rapidly recognized anew: he was posthumously honoured at home with retrospectives and re-releases of his films, which during his lifetime were either temporarily shelved or poorly distributed.

See also: All-Russian (All-Union) State Institute of Cinematography; cameramen; Konchalovskii, Andrei; Ovchinnikov, Viacheslav; Romm, Mikhail; Socialist Realism; Sokurov, Aleksandr; Strugatskii, Arkadii and Boris

VIDA JOHNSON

Tarkovskii, Arsenii Aleksandrovich

b. 12 (25) June 1907, Elizavetgrad, Kherson district (now Ukraine); d. 27 May 1989, Moscow

Poet, literary translator, critic

Father of the celebrated film-maker Andrei Tarkovskii, Arsenii Tarkovskii was born into the family of a former Populist. He studied creative writing in Moscow in the 1920s and became a professional literary translator from Turkmenian, Armenian, Georgian, and Arabic. During World War II, Tarkovskii worked as a frontline correspondent and was wounded. His literary fate was quietly tragic: he was admired by his famous older contemporaries (Tsvetaeva, Akhmatova, Pasternak), but had to write in obscurity and isolation, banned from official Soviet literature and unable to publish. His poetry began to appear in print during the Thaw. His first book, *Pered snegom* (*Before the Snow*), highly praised by Akhmatova, came out when he was in his mid-fifties; it was followed by many more. Outside of Russia Tarkovskii is known primarily by the poems his son included in his films *Zerkalo* (*Mirror*) and *Nostalgia*. Tarkovskii's dramatic, minimalist, classically terse verse has been alternatively characterized as 'pantheistic' and 'organic'. Having consciously distanced himself from the Soviet literary elite, he achieved self-realization as a remarkably free Russian (not Soviet) poet under conditions of extreme restrictions. At the time of his death in 1989, Tarkovskii was recognized as the last heir to Russia's high poetic culture of the Silver Age.

See also: Akhmatova, Anna; censorship; Pasternak, Boris; Tarkovskii, Andrei; Thaw; World War II (Great Patriotic War)

JULIA TRUBIKHINA

Tarnopolskii, Vladimir Grigorevich

b. 30 April 1955, Dnepropetrovsk, Ukraine

Composer

A former student of Edison Denisov at the Moscow Conservatory, Tarnopolskii composes music in the European avant-garde tradition, which combines diverse styles, experiments with timbral resources, and exploits devices of postmodernist theatre, including ironic and grotesque elements. Important large works include the opera *Kogda vremia vykhodit iz beregov* (*When Time Overflows Its Shores*, 1999), *Dykhanie ischerpannogo vremeni* (*The Breath of Exhausted Time* for orchestra, 1994), and *Chevengur* (2001) and *Cassandra* (1991) for chamber ensemble.

Tarnopolskii actively promotes contemporary music in Moscow. He co-founded the *Assotsiatsiia sovremennoi muzyki* (Association of Contemporary Music) in Moscow in 1989; in 1993 he founded *Studiia novoi muzyki* (Studio of New Music), an ensemble that performs many works by Russian avant-garde composers, and the *Tsentr sovremennoi muzyki* (Centre for Contemporary Music) at the Moscow Conservatory. In 1994, he founded the annual contemporary music festival *Moskovskii forum* (Moscow Forum).

See also: Denisov, Edison; Moscow Conservatory

DAVID GOMPPER

Tartu–Moscow School

An informal association of Soviet scholars in the humanities who shared an interest in systems theory, structuralism, and semiotics (the study of sign systems), the Tartu–Moscow School arose in the 1960s and quickly won international attention. Researchers associated with the group, including Iurii Lotman, Boris Uspenskii, and Viacheslav Ivanov, contributed to the study of history, folklore, and Asian culture, as well as literature and linguistics. Inclined to view many commonly accepted approaches to cultural inquiry as overly subjective, they worked to introduce scientific standards to the study of the humanities. They argued that scholars needed to move away from evaluation and towards rigorous analysis; instead of labelling movements, phenomena, and texts as progressive or reactionary, good or bad, researchers should focus on understanding their structure and the way they function.

As its name implies, the Tartu–Moscow School represented an amalgamation of two initially distinct scholarly collectives. The Moscow group emerged during the Thaw, when restrictions on the development of Soviet academic life eased and it became possible for scholars to practise previously suspect disciplines and approaches. A circle of linguists associated with the Sector of Structural Typology at the Institute of Slavonic Studies and the Linguistics Section of the Council on Cybernetics developed a new structuralist approach to the study of communicative codes built upon the work of both Western and Russian antecedents (de Saussure, Iakobson).

Learning of the new trend, Iurii Lotman, the chair of the Department of Russian Literature at Tartu State University in Estonia, sensed that it complemented an approach to the study of literary texts that was emerging in Tartu. In the summer of 1964, he invited the Moscow linguists to attend a week-long scholarly gathering at a forest retreat near Tartu. Dubbed the 'First Summer School', this meeting represented the first true Tartu–Moscow event and laid the foundation for a host of projects, including the creation of the landmark Tartu University publishing series *Trudy po znakovym sistemam* (Works on Signs Systems). Follow-ups to the 1964 Summer School were held biannually in Estonia during the late 1960s and early 1970s.

Although at least half of the scholars who participated in the Tartu–Moscow School in the 1960s and 1970s resided in Moscow, the movement's most important ventures were based in Estonia: the republic had a strong democratic tradition and was far from the watchful eye of Moscow. Particularly in the early years, Tartu–Moscow scholars found they could operate with greater freedom there, publishing works by and on cultural figures long out of official favour.

According to most sources, the Tartu–Moscow School slipped into decline in the late 1970s. It is remembered today as perhaps the most important Soviet academic trend of the second half of the twentieth century and a major component of European structuralism.

See also: censorship; Estonia; Iakobson (Jakobson), Roman; Lotman, Iurii; structuralism

Further reading

Lucid, D. (ed.) (1977) *Soviet Semiotics: An Anthology*, trans. D. Lucid. Baltimore, MD: Johns Hopkins University Press.

EMILY D. JOHNSON

TASS

See: ITAR-TASS

Tatars

People of the Turkic group of the Altaic language family, Tatars are Sunni Muslims, as well as a small group of Christians – the Keräşen Tatars. All use the Cyrillic alphabet. In the USSR, Tatars were the sixth most numerous population at 66,488,000 (in 1989). The majority of Tatars resided in the RSFSR (55,221,000), Uzbekistan (5,737,000) and Kazakhstan (2,877,000). Only 26 per cent of all Tatars (1,765,000), however, lived in the autonomous state, Tatar ASSR. In the Russian Federation, Tatars are the second most numerous people (5,554,601 in 2002). Tatars enjoy state autonomy within the Russian Federation, in the Republic of Tatarstan, with its capital in Kazan. Tatars compose 52.9 per cent of the republic's population but represent only 36 per cent of all Tatars living in Russia. Spread throughout the whole territory of Russia, most Tatars live in the Volga region, the Urals, and southern Siberia. Many reside in Moscow (1,661,000) and St. Petersburg (356,000).

Tatars divide into three large groups: the Volga-Ural, Siberian, and Astrakhan Tatars (Crimean Tatars are considered a separate people). The Turkic language-speaking Bulgarian tribes who settled in the Volga region in the seventh–eighth centuries, and founded a Volga-Kama Bulgaria there, were the progenitors of the Volga-Ural Tatars. Tribes speaking Turkic settled on the territory of contemporary Russia during the Mongol conquest in the thirteenth century. The consolidation of Tatars as a people took place in the fourteenth–sixteenth centuries, and they established themselves in the Volga region, the Urals, and southern Siberia, where they reside to this day. Kazan, Askrakhan, Kasimov, Tiumen, and Siberian Tatar khanates existed before Russian colonization from the sixteenth–eighteenth centuries.

Rural Tatars are engaged in agriculture, horse- and sheep-breeding, bee-keeping, and trade. Handicrafts include barrel-making and production of matting, gold and tambour embroidery, wood and stone carvings, artistic weaving, leather and sheepskin treatment, leather mosaics, and woollen handicrafts. Tatar clothing articles encompass embroidered skull-caps (*tiubeteika*), colourful women's headware (*kalfak*), decorated with pearls, coins and gold embroidery, and encrusted leather boots (*ichigi* and *kamzol*). National cuisine is famous for *belesh* (*beliash*) – baked pastry with meat or potato filling; *chak-chak* – sweet pastry balls with honey; *kyzylyk* – horse sausage; *katyk* and *airan* – fermented milk drinks. Major traditional holidays are Kurban-bairam, Uraza-bairam (the end of fasting in Ramadan), and the Sabantui festival (competitions in running, jumping, horse racing, and national wrestling, while serving porridge in a big cauldron). Major centres of Tatar culture in Russia are Kazan, Astrakhan, Kasimov, Moscow, Tiumen, Tobolsk, and Tara.

See also: Crimea; ethnic minorities; Islam; Russian Orthodoxy; Siberia; Urals; Uzbekistan; Volga region

SERGEI TARKHOV

Tatianin den

The feast day of St. Tatiana (25 January), which is celebrated as a holiday for university students and graduates. On 12 January 1755 (25 January, New Style), Empress Elizabeth signed a decree founding Moscow University, the first university in Russia. Now the holiday is traditionally celebrated in all Russian institutions of higher learning, the festivities including an official ceremony during the day followed by a banquet and parties in the evening.

See also: calendars, old and new; holidays, post-Soviet; holidays, Soviet; Moscow State University

JENNIFER RYAN TISHLER

Tatu

Popular music duo

Tatu comprises two girls, Iulia Volkova and Lena Katina, presented in 1999 by producer Ivan Shapovalov. Embracing a more fashionable, dance-oriented aesthetic than usually seen in Russian popular music, Tatu caused outrage with rain-soaked 'lesbian kissing' in the video for *Ia soshla s uma* (All the Things She Said) and were denounced on Western television as 'pedophiliac entertainment'. Drawing heavily upon aspects of Japanese animation, the duo released a highly professional parallel version of their first album in English, produced by Trevor Horn: *200 km/h in the Wrong Lane* (2003) and almost won a Eurovision award.

See also: popular music, post-Soviet

DAVID MACFADYEN

Tchaikovsky (Chaikovskii) Competition

One of the world's most prestigious international music competitions, it takes place every four years at the Moscow Conservatory and is open to pianists, violinists, cellists, and vocalists under 28 years of age. Begun in 1958, from the beginning it was a highly politicized undertaking, with an aura of mystery and notoriety that other competitions lacked. Russians traditionally have dominated – among the most notable are Vladimir Ashkenazii (1962), Gidon Kremer and Vladimir Spivakov (1970), Mikhail Pletnev (1978) – but the infrequent American winners returned home as national heroes. The competition continues to the present day, but without the media fascination it attracted during the Cold War.

See also: Ashkenazii, Vladimir; Cold War; Kremer, Gidon; Moscow Conservatory; Pletnev, Mikhail; Spivakov, Vladimir

MICHAEL WACHTEL

tea glass holder (podstakannik)

A *podstakannik* is a cup-like holder for tea glasses. Russian tea traditionally was served in glasses nestled in a stainless steel or silver holder with a handle; the *podstakannik* absorbs the heat from the hot liquid. The word is formed from the prefix *pod-* ('under') and *stakan* ('glass'). Still seen on trains and ships, *podstakanniki* are also an item of exported Russian kitsch.

DAVID J. GALLOWAY

television channels

The history of Soviet television started in September 1938, when the Leningrad television station opened and the first experimental television programmes were made in Moscow at the Shabolovka television station. In March 1939, the XVIII Congress of the Communist Party was broadcast on television for the first rime in Soviet history, but these innovative experiments only anticipated genuine media. During postwar reconstruction, print media and radio dominated, and television took off only in the late 1960s and 1970s. The Ostankino television station introduced colour in 1967 – the year Central TV began broadcasting round the clock. On 1 October 1967, the satellite *Ekran* (Screen) enabled viewers in Siberia to watch programmes from Moscow in real time. The first programmes for the deaf appeared in 1987. By 1981, 230 million people (88 per cent of the Soviet population) were watching television in forty languages of the USSR, and more than eighty cities had colour broadcasting. The state television system was developed to such an extent that in 1984 there were 126 stations in the country and 85 million TV sets.

As part of the Soviet propaganda system, television was under complete state control and censorship. TV channels (long limited to just three) broadcast official news programmes (the most popular, *Vremia* [Time], first went on the air in 1962), films, programmes devoted to the Soviet Army (*Sluzhu Sovetskomu Soiuzu*, [I Serve the Soviet Union]), five-year plans, and some programmes for youth (*A nu-ka devushki, A nu-ka parni* [Well, Now, Girls! Well, Guys!]) and family

(*Ot vsei dushi* [From the Bottom of My Heart]). Popular among Soviet citizens were comedy programmes, such as *KVN*, many of whose participants later became famous journalists. Regional and national republic stations had similar programming.

Perestroika revitalized Soviet television, offering the first Russian-American TV bridges, conducted by Phil Donahue and Vladimir Pozner, and fresh news programmes, such as *12-yi etazh* (The Twelfth Floor), *Do 16 i starshe* (Up to 16 and Beyond), the Leningrad-based analytical programme *Piatoe koleso* (Fifth Wheel), and the Moscow programme *Vzgliad* (Viewpoint). From 1986–88 the number of live programmes increased threefold.

The 1990s were a revolutionary decade for television. State control collapsed; Russian TV appeared on Channel 2 and presented an opposition of sorts to the official Channel 1; and in 1990 the first, rather primitive advertisement appeared on the newborn channel '2 x 2'. After the collapse of the state radio and television company, *Gosteleradio*, in 1991, new regional and Moscow stations appeared. The Independent TV station NTV was born in 1993. In the mid-1990s television became serious business; new enterprises made money on state-owned TV, including VID, ATV, REN TV, and the advertising companies Video International and Premier SV made billions of dollars. Newcomers, first and foremost businessmen Boris Berezovskii and Vladimir Gusinskii, played a major role in the media and television, especially in 1994–96: they created genuine media empires, including two main TV channels. ORT (*Obshchestvennoe Rossiiskoe televidenie* [Public Russian Television]) was associated with Berezovskii from 1995, and NTV with Gusinskii. In fact, they occupied state channels without any tender, and no one knew how much and whom they paid for its use. This period witnessed media wars, dirty use of technologies and *kompromat* (blackmail) on television; as a result, ethical standards fell and trust in journalists eroded – a situation that persisted into the early 2000s. Television, especially ORT and NTV, played a significant role in Yeltsin's successful presidential election campaign in 1996, becoming an effective propaganda tool in the campaign 'Vote or Lose', and in the 1999 parliamentary elections. The most popular and respected channels competed in blaming one another's politics and politicians. The political reputation of Premier Evgenii Primakov, Moscow mayor Iurii Luzhkov, and the entire *Otechestvo* (Fatherland) Party were destroyed by ORT, which by then supported the new *Edinstvo* (Unity) Party. The name of ORT anchor Sergei Dorenko became a symbol of professional immorality and political servility. Different channels provided a different picture of the first Chechen War in 1995. ORT played a decisive role in Putin's first election (2000) and pro-Putin propaganda.

After Putin's election, the resumed Chechen War, and explosions in apartment buildings in Moscow, the state tightened its control over television; the notion of stability and security replaced the idea of a free press in state policy. The most interesting channel, NTV, which had a brilliant team of journalists, had to change ownership during the state war against Gusinskii's Mediamost empire that occurred in 1999–2001. Gusinskii emigrated, as did Berezovskii.

Independent television no longer exists at the national level in Russia. Channel 1 replaced ORT in 2003; it was included in the official list of 56 strategic entities (such as military factories). Since 2002 it has been under complete state control and presents mostly state propaganda. Channel 2 (*Rossiia*) is an official state enterprise, and the state also owns Channel 6, *Kultura* (Culture) and *Sport*; Channel 6, in turn, replaced the former TV-6, where the old NTV team had worked since 2003. State television began to broadcast the Russian version of *Euronews* in the morning on Channel 6. Channel 3, shared by *TV-Tsentr* (TV-Centre) and Moscow, is affiliated with the Moscow government. The gas company Gazprom became strongly associated with the state after purchasing the former Mediamost stocks that controlled NTV. Since the Gazprom takeover of NTV, its satellite version NTV-Plus, and the entertainment TNT channel, virtually all critical programmes have been cancelled. The state television network is still active in all parts of Russia and successfully competes with new private companies in the regions. Newborn cable channels are becoming increasingly popular in Moscow; in the regions these cable stations are truly independent and sometimes present interesting programmes.

Now, when television is the most popular of the media (indeed, the only one for many Russians), Russia faces 'the revenge' of the old Soviet propaganda system. Many Russians cannot pay for cable or satellite and therefore watch state-controlled Channel 1 or *Rossiia* (Channel 2), which present the state viewpoint. All national channels offer very similar political and analytical programmes; all broadcast many of the same advertisements (80 per cent of the national market is in Moscow), serials, talk shows, and game shows.

Public broadcasting does not exist in Russia; however, the Russian Union of Journalists has initiated a movement for public television in Moscow and the regions.

See also: Berezovskii, Boris; censorship; Communist Party; five-year plan; Gusinskii, Vladimir; journalism; journalists, post-Soviet; *KVN* (*Klub veselykh i nakhodchivykh*); Luzhkov, Iurii; NTV; Ostankino Tower; perestroika and glasnost; political parties, post-Soviet; Pozner, Vladimir; Primakov, Evgenii; propaganda, Soviet and post-Soviet; Provincial Russia; Putin, Vladimir; Shabolovka; *Vzgliad*; War, Chechen; World War II (Great Patriotic War); Yeltsin, Boris

Further reading

Mickiewicz, E. (1988) *Split Signals: Television and Politics in the Soviet Union*, Oxford: Oxford University Press.

Muratov, S. (2001) *TV – evoliutsiia neterpimosti. Istoriia i konflikty eticheskikh predstavlenii* (TV and the Evolution of Intolerance: History and Conflicts in Conceptions of Ethics), Moscow.

——(2001) *Televidenie v poiskakh televideniia* (Television in Search of Television), Moscow.

——(2005) *Teleradioefir. Istoriia i sovremennost* (Tele-Radio-Air: History and Contemporaneity), Moscow.

Tsvik, V. (2004) *Televizionnaia zhurnalistika. Istoriia. Teoriia. Praktika* (Television Journalism: History, Theory, and Practice), Moscow

NADEZHDA AZHGIKHINA

television, post-Soviet

After 1991, the Russian government kept control of two television stations, renaming the Soviet Channel 1/*Central Television* (*Tsentralnoe televidenie*) as *Ostankino* and Channel 2 as *Russian Television* (*RTR*). In 1995, the Yeltsin government turned Ostankino into Russian Public Television, known as *ORT* (*Obshchestvennoe rossiiskoe televidenie*). The station was now 51 per cent state-owned and 49 per cent privately owned. The government turned to advertising revenues and private sponsors to balance the books; for example, Yeltsin supporter Boris Berezovskii proved to be of vital fiscal significance during the re-election campaign. Nonetheless, the maintenance of 9,000 aging transmitters, 8 satellites and 22,000 km of landlines was both complicated and prohibitively expensive. In the mid-1990s, ORT was creating just over 20 per cent of its schedule, mainly news and current affairs; the rest was purchased.

While ORT broadcast across the entire CIS, RTR was designed for Russian audiences. By the mid-1990s it was broadcasting to almost 99 per cent of Russians through 5 satellites and 5,000 transmitters. In more local markets, St. Petersburg garnered Channel 5, which soon reached 90 million people around the country; over 100 local government stations operated on their own wavelengths or by using time on RTR. Virtually none were self-supporting and thus showed many pirated shows or films.

By 1993, *NTV* (Independent Television) was offering an alternative, in particular through its star reporter, Evgenii Kiselev. Multiple feature films, political satire, and anti-government viewpoints made NTV a success. Yeltsin gave the station free rein; NTV returned the favour, supporting the President in his 1996 reelection bid. Yeltsin then granted the station nationwide status in January 1998, but critical coverage of the Chechen campaign was not welcomed by his successor, Vladimir Putin. Owner Vladimir Gusinskii was arrested in 2000; the national gas company Gazprom acquired his shares and many employees resigned.

By late 2001, similar pressure was being applied to *TV-6*, now a final haven for anti-government reporting. Within four months, the Kremlin's Press Minister had intervened. Despite Putin's assertions of a subsequent, open auction to be established for the TV-6 broadcast licence, staff (including Kiselev) moved again, this time establishing *TVS* until its closure, too, in June 2003. Meanwhile, a related conflict had been worsening since October 2002, following the terrorist hijacking of Moscow's *Teatralnyi Tsentr na Dubrovke* (Dubrovka Theatre Centre) during a production of the musical *Nord-Ost* (Northeast). Yet again NTV's leadership was changed following critical coverage. By the summer of 2004, the station had a government-appointed manager.

Today RTR and ORT (often called *Pervyi kanal* [Channel 1]) enjoy a 25 per cent market share. These stations are followed by *NTV* and the comedy-heavy *STS* (10–12 per cent), while highbrow network *Kultura* (3–5 per cent) and *MTV Russia* (1 per cent) define the typical size of any remaining influence. *STS* since 2004 has gradually been increasing its market share thanks to copyrighted remakes of American sitcoms, but long, serialized dramas are the most significant product of post-Soviet television. In 1999, Russian television series occupied less than 10 per cent of primetime line-ups; by 2001–2, they claimed 46 per cent. That figure continues to grow, such that several television stations have regularly been able to subsidize feature film-making.

See also: advertising; Berezovskii, Boris; CIS (SNG); Kiselev, Evgenii; Kultura channel; *Nord-Ost*; NTV; Putin, Vladimir; television channels; television serials; Yeltsin, Boris

DAVID MACFADYEN

television serials

The pioneers of the form were Sergei Kolosov and Evgenii Tashkov, who in the 1960s produced made-for-TV war movies and spy thrillers. The latter genre proved to be the most popular as well as ideologically unproblematic. The decade of the 1970s was the heyday of Soviet serials, whose peak was the twelve-episode spy thriller *Semnadtsat mgnovenii vesny* (*Seventeen Moments of Spring*, 1973). Also popular were historical melodramas (*Vechnyi zov* [*Eternal Call*], 1974–77; *Sibiriada*, 1979), and police procedurals (*Sledstvie vedut znatoki* [*The Investigation Is Conducted by Experts*], 1971–89; *Mesto vstrechi izmenit nelzia* [*The Meeting Place Cannot Be Changed*],

1979). The 1980s witnessed a crisis in television productions, with the exception of Igor Maslennikov's successful adaptation of Sherlock Holmes stories. After the Soviet Union disintegrated, television screens were flooded with American and Mexican soap operas, and new Russian serials appeared only in the mid-1990s, with police drama and gangster sagas leading the market. The success of television series among viewers is especially striking in the context of declining cinema attendance. Many film directors, such as Aleksandr Rogozhkin and Valerii Todorovskii, began directing or producing serials. The former launched *Menty* (*Cops*), the most successful police show of the 1990s. The latter produced a number of recent television hits, e.g., *Brigada* (*Brigade*, 2002) – the Russian answer to *The Sopranos*, and adaptations of Dostoevskii's *Idiot* (2003) and Bulgakov's *The Master and Margarita* (2005).

See also: *Semnadtsat mgnovenii vesny* (*Seventeen Moments of Spring*); *Master i Margarita* (*The Master and Margarita*); *Mesto vstrechi izmenit nelzia* (The Meeting Place Cannot Be Changed); Rogozhkin, Aleksandr; Todorovskii, Valerii

Further reading

Akopov, A. (2000) 'Serial kak natsionalnaia ideia', *Iskusstvo kino* 2: 5–9.

Olcott, A. (2001) *Russian Pulp:* The Detektiv *and the Russian Way of Crime*, Lanham, MD: Rowman & Littlefield Publishers.

Prokhorova, E. (2003) 'Can the Meeting Place Be Changed? Crime and Identity Discourse in Russian Television Series of the 1990s', *Slavic Review* 62, 3: 512–24.

Zorkaia, N. (1994) *Folklor. Lubok. Ekran*, Moscow: Iskusstvo.

ELENA PROKHOROVA

television, Soviet

Soviet television, conceived in the 1940s, became a mass medium only by the 1960s. Moscow's Ostankino TV tower began broadcasting in 1967. The State Committee for Television and Radio (Gosteleradio) oversaw the national channels (Channel 1, founded in 1960;

Channel 3/Educational, founded in 1965; Channel 4/Moscow, founded in 1967; Channel 2, founded in 1982). Though officially charged with promulgating state and Party policies, television broadcast an eclectic content: television films and broadcast theatre performances, which constituted the bulk of television programming, plus game and travel shows. Lack of recording technology in the 1950s and 1960s resulted in considerable live news coverage, achieving a much-valued 'reality effect'. As appointed head of Gostelradio, Sergei Lapin streamlined Soviet television programming of the 1970s both ideologically and formally. The news programme *Vremia* (Time) – which ventriloquized the Party's voice – was broadcast on all channels; live broadcasts and television journalism virtually disappeared; 'talking heads' reading censored scripts delivered the news. Selective domestic and international news coverage reflected the official perspective on events: social unrest and natural disasters occurred only behind the Iron Curtain, domestically, economics and politics thrived.

Yet the 1970s also were the peak of widely popular Soviet television serials, and many programmes were informational rather than propagandistic. Favourite programmes included *Klub puteshestvennikov* (Travellers' Club), *Mezhdunarodnaia panorama* (International Panorama), *Kinopanorama* (Cinema Panorama), and sports and children's programmes. Entertainment embraced variety shows, concerts of classical and popular music, and game and quiz shows (e.g., *KVN*, Club of the Sunny and Smart). As domestic spectacle, television was appealing despite its ideological rigidity and provided access to high-quality theatre, film, and musical productions to viewers in remote corners of the Soviet Union.

Gorbachev's policy of glasnost drastically transformed Soviet television, partly owing to new technologies that competed with television in providing leisure activities (video) or information (foreign radio broadcasts in Russian). The delayed reporting of the Chernobyl nuclear meltdown demonstrated the urgent need for timeliness of news. Live, on-location reporting reappeared, together with investigative journalism and open discussion of formerly taboo topics: economic problems, political corruption,

crime, drugs, AIDS, and prostitution. The format of television programmes also improved. The new talk show *Vzgliad* (Viewpoint) featured young hosts whose lively manner and polemical topics attracted millions of viewers every week. Another new feature was teleports, organized by Vladimir Pozner and Phil Donahue, offering many Soviet citizens their first encounter with an American audience, and treating such polemical issues as politics and sex.

The attempted coup by Communist hardliners in August 1991 revealed flaws in state-controlled television. Instead of reporting the events, all channels broadcast classical music. With the demise of the Soviet empire, monolithic Soviet television ended, and the 1990s witnessed channel privatization, the spread of cable networks, and the rise of media moguls.

See also: *KVN*; Ostankino Tower; perestroika and glasnost; Pozner, Vladimir; television serials; *Vzgliad*

Further reading

Bonnell, V. and Freidin, G. (1995) 'Televorot: The Role of Television Coverage in Russia's August 1991 Coup', in N. Condee (ed.) *Soviet Hieroglyphics: Visual Culture in Late Twentieth-Century Russia*, Bloomington, IN: Indiana University Press, pp. 22–51.

Boretskii, R. A. (1998) *V Bermudskom treugolnike TV*, Moscow: Ikar.

Mickiewicz, E. (1981) *Media and the Russian Public*, New York: Praeger.

——(1988) *Split Signals: Television and Politics in the Soviet Union*, New York: Oxford University Press.

Plakhov, A. (ed.) (1981) *Bolshie problemy malogo ekrana*, Moscow: Iskusstvo, 103–21.

ELENA PROKHOROVA

Temirkanov, Iurii Khatuevich

b. 10 December 1938, Nalchik

Conductor

Since his youth Temirkanov has been connected with Leningrad, where he studied violin at the Conservatory's   Secondary   Special   School

(1953–57) and then conducting at the Leningrad Conservatory (1957–62) with Ilia Musin. At the age of 28, he won first prize at the Second All-Union Conductors' Competition in Moscow. From 1966 until 1972 Temirkanov worked at the Leningrad Malyi Opera and Ballet Theatre, and from 1968 until 1976 he was the chief conductor and music director of the Leningrad Symphony Orchestra. In 1976–88 Temirkanov occupied the same position at the Kirov (now Mariinskii) Theatre. His main achievements there were two Tchaikovsky operas, *Eugene Onegin* (1982) and *The Queen of Spades* (1984), which he directed either musically or scenically. Since 1988 Temirkanov has been the chief conductor and music director of the St. Petersburg Philharmonic. During this period he has divided his time among the St. Petersburg Philharmonic Orchestra and the Royal Philharmonic Orchestra in London, Danish Radio Orchestra, and the Baltimore Symphony. He founded the Arts Square festival in St. Petersburg in 1999. Known for the lyric expressiveness of his conducting and the emotionality and originality of his interpretations, Temirkanov has many honorary posts and awards, including People's Artist of the USSR (1981), the Order of Lenin (1983), and the USSR State Prize (1976, 1985).

KIRA NEMIROVSKAYA

Tendriakov, Vladimir Fedorovich

b. 5 December 1923, Makarovskaia, Vologda region; d. 3 August 1984, Moscow

Writer

Tendriakov came to public attention in the immediate post-Stalin years; his work made a major contribution to the public campaign aimed at modernizing agricultural management. Subsequently, in works such as *Ukhaby* (*Potholes*, 1956) and *Sud* (*The Trial*, 1961), he attacked the mendacious Stalinist mindset that sacrificed human values for impersonal state priorities. In *Chudotvornaia* (*The Miracle-Working Icon*, 1958) and *Apostolskaia komandirovka* (*On Apostolic Business*, 1969) Tendriakov touched on religious themes, suggesting a spiritual vacuum in Soviet society

that Christianity could fill. This vacuum is further explored in such works as *Vesennie perevertyshi* (*A Topsy-Turvy Spring*, 1974) and *Noch posle vypuska* (*The Night after Graduation*, 1974), where Soviet education is found wanting. Spiritual values are the central theme of *Zatmenie* (*The Eclipse*, 1977). As with several other writers, Tendriakov's most interesting work was only published during perestroika. *Khleb dlia sobaki* (*Bread for a Dog*) and *Para gnedykh* (*A Pair of Bay Horses*), both published in 1988, detail the horrors of collectivization. In *Chistye vody Kitezha* (*The Clear Waters of Kitezh*, 1986) and *Na blazhennom ostrove kommunizma* (*On the Blessed Island of Communism*, 1988), Tendriakov reflects on literary and journalistic hypocrisy. Though deeply troubled by his times, he was unable to engage these concerns publicly.

See also: collective farms; educational system, Soviet; perestroika and glasnost; Thaw

DAVID GILLESPIE

Terekhova, Margarita Borisovna

b. 25 August 1942, Turinsk

Actress and director

Margarita Terekhova studied acting at the School of Iurii Zavadskii and became a leading actress of the Mossovet Theatre. Her most significant acting achievements came through her work with the film director Andrei Tarkovskii; she played the mother and Nataliia in Tarkovskii's *Zerkalo* (*Mirror*, 1975). Her role (Milady) in *D'Artanian i tri mushketera* (*D'Artagnan and the Three Musketeers*, TV, 1978) won her fame and the love of the Russian public. In the early 1990s, Terekhova directed a theatre performance based on Garcia Lorca's works. In 2004, she worked on the film *Chaika* (*Seagull*), based on Chekhov's play, as both film director and scriptwriter.

See also: Mossovet Theatre; Zavadskii, Iurii

YANA HASHAMOVA

Tereshkova (Nikolaeva-Tereshkova), Valentina Vladimirovna

b. 16 June 1937, Iaroslavl oblast

Cosmonaut

On 16–19 June 1963 Tereshkova, the first female cosmonaut, nicknamed *Chaika* (Seagull) after her space call-sign, orbited the earth 48 times on spacecraft Vostok-6. A textile factory worker and amateur parachutist before joining the space programme, after the flight, under pressure from Khrushchev, she married cosmonaut Adrian Nikolaev and gave birth to a daughter. The couple split up in 1986, and she later remarried. From 1968 until 1990, Tereshkova represented the Soviet government in various worldwide women's organizations. Since 1990, she has headed the government centre for international scientific and cultural cooperation. A retired Air Force General, she resides in the cosmonauts' Moscow colony, Zvezdnyi (Star City).

Two more women have participated in the Soviet/Russian space programme: Svetlana Savitskaia (flights in 1982, 1984), the first woman in the world to walk in space, and Elena Kondakova (flights in 1994–95 and 1997), a member of the US/Russian STS-84 crew.

See also: space programmes and exploration

TATYANA LEDENEVA

Ter-Oganian, Avdei

b. 2 December 1961, Rostov-on-Don

Artist

A member of the Art or Death group (1988–90), during 1991–93 Ter-Oganian managed the Trekhprudnyi Lane Gallery (jointly with Konstantin Reunov) in Moscow. He created the project *School of Contemporary Art* (1995–98) and in the early 1990s appeared in the disguise of a provincial artist making copies of famous modernistic works in his series *Pictures for a Museum*.

In another series, *Abusive Painting*, Ter-Oganian suggested a new interpretation of modernism, inserting abusive words into museum masterpieces. His recent series, *Radical Abstractionism*, a playful geometrical abstraction, is deconstructed with the use of quotations from the Russian criminal code. Ter-Oganian became a controversial figure after his performance in 1999, when he destroyed icons with an axe (the performance was credited to his project *School of the Young Avantgardist*). Forced into exile by the Russian authorities, in 1999 Ter-Oganian asked for, and in 2002 obtained, refugee status in the Czech Republic. He now lives in Berlin.

NATALIA KOLODZEI

territorial conflicts

After the Civil War (1917–22), the Soviet Union was directly involved in numerous armed conflicts, both on its own territory and beyond. Before World War II, Soviet Russia had undertaken several conquest operations with the goal of reclaiming the borders of the Russian empire, which had shrunk as a result of the revolutions and the Civil War. A 'Combat operation for the liquidation of the Basmachi movement' in Central Asia and Kazakhstan (October 1922–June 1931) secured Russian control over the region as a whole. After the Winter War with Finland (30 November 1939–13 May 1940), the USSR annexed Eastern Karelia. According to the Molotov–Ribbentrop treaty of 1939, the USSR also acquired territories that had been part of Poland and Romania (17–28 September 1939). Officially, the partition of Poland between the USSR and Germany was labelled a 'reunification of the USSR, Western Ukraine, and Western Belorussia'.

Between 1937 and 1950, Red Army units were almost continuously involved in military operations in the Far East, first on Chinese territory and, in 1950–53, in Korea. Soviet border conflicts with China were most visible on Damanskii Island (March 1969) and in the region of Lake Zhalanashkol (August 1969).

In the Soviet Union, several large-scale deportations were undertaken, with the long-term consequences of new bloody conflicts.

From the end of the 1930s to the mid-1940s, the Soviet government deported and resettled hundreds of thousands of people from ethnic minorities from the Far East, the Crimea, the Volga region, and the Caucasus (Crimean Tatars, Chechens, Ingush, Kalmyks, Balkars, Volga Germans, Koreans, Greeks, Meskhetian Turks, and others). Some of them and their descendants returned to their native regions between the 1950s and the 1980s. Because not all those who returned could settle in their ancestral areas, old conflicts resurfaced and new ones began. These conflicts became sharper as the USSR disintegrated.

From 1987 to 2000, between 5 and 7 million people fled from the republics of the USSR and its independent successor states of Central Asia: Uzbekistan, Tajikistan, Kyrgyzstan, Turkmenistan, and Kazakhstan. These included Volga Germans, Crimean Tatars, Russians, and Jews, as well as almost all Meskhetian Turks, who had been deported to Georgia in the mid-1940s. The case of Meskhetian Turks, Muslim inhabitants of Meskheti (Georgia), a region bordering with Turkey, is a typical history of a deported minority in the Soviet Union. In 1944, they were deported to Central Asia. In 1989, a pogrom of Meskhetian Turks occurred in Fergana Valley, Uzbekistan. After their evacuation from Uzbekistan, Meskhetian Turks have been dispersed over a number of other republics of the former Soviet Union. In the 1990s, some of them tried to return to Georgia by claiming an ethnic Georgian origin, but were rejected by the local Armenian population. Nor were they welcomed in other countries (Azerbaijan has its own refugees from Nagorno-Karabakh and Armenia, and Turkey wanted to settle them in underdeveloped Kurdish regions). In February 2004, the International Organization for Migration started a programme for the resettlement of Meskhetian Turks from the Krasnodar region (Russia) to the United States.

Since the 1990s, Kyrgyzstan has been in territorial dispute with Tajikistan over the border in the Isfara Valley area. Tajikistan also disputes most of its borders with China. In the Far East, Japan claims the islands of Etorofu (Iturup), Kunashiri (Kunashir), Shikotan (Shikotan), and Habomai (Khabomai), occupied by the Soviet Union in 1945 and now administered by Russia.

China disputes two sections of the border with Russia.

In Europe, Estonia claims Russian islands in the Baltic, referring to the Peace Treaty of Tartu (1920). Based on the Treaty of Riga (1920), Latvia claims the Abrene (Pytalovo) section of the border, which was ceded to the Russian Federation by the Latvian Soviet Socialist Republic in 1944. There are also ongoing talks over a border dispute with Lithuania concerning oil exploration rights on the border with the Russian enclave of Kaliningrad. There is no official border dispute with Finland concerning Eastern Karelia, but a lively discussion of the subject is regularly held in both countries' press. Adjacent territories of Moldova and Ukraine, including Bessarabia and Northern Bukovina, have been considered by Bucharest as a historical part of Romania; this territory was incorporated into the former Soviet Union following the Molotov–Ribbentrop Pact in 1940. Romania is also in dispute with Ukraine over the continental shelf of the Black Sea, which is expected to hide significant gas and oil deposits. The self-declared Transdniestrian Republic between Moldova and Ukraine, with its predominantly Russian population, is seeking a formal union with Russia, which still has its 14th Army positioned near the capital, Tiraspol. The Russian-speaking population of Crimea (administratively subordinated to Ukraine in 1954) strives for a possible reunification with Russia. The Crimean Tatars demand more political rights and national autonomy and oppose stronger ties with Russia. There is an ongoing dispute between Russia and Ukraine over the Black Sea Fleet assets and bases in Sevastopol.

In the Caucasus, the heaviest of conflicts have no end in sight; they involve both border disputes and armed violence between minority groups. In the southern Caucasus, the conflict between Armenia and Azerbaijan over the Nagorno-Karabakh region has not been resolved since it surfaced in 1988, with Russia as its main mediator. Russia uses the regions of Abkhazia and South Ossetia, whose independence from Georgia is accepted only by Russia, to increase its influence on Georgia. In the Northern Caucasus, the most acute conflict is between Russia and Chechnia. Since 1994, two wars have taken place on Chechen territory, which resulted in a population decline in the region from about 1 million to about 500 thousand inhabitants. Several hundred thousand refugees from the region are now living in the neighbouring republics as well as in central Russia. A massive emigration of the Russian population from the region continues. In 2003–2005, the armed conflict has spread to other Russian republics in Northern Caucasus.

See also: Armenia; Azerbaidzhan; Caucasus; Central Asia; Chechnia; Crimea; East Bloc countries; Estonia; ethnic minorities; Far East; Georgia; Islam; Jews; Karelia; Kazakhstan; Kyrgyzstan (Kirgizia); Latvia; Lithuania; Tajikistan (Tadzhikistan); Tatars; Turkmenistan (Turkmenia); Ukraine; Uzbekistan; Volga region; War, Chechen; World War II (Great Patriotic War)

Further reading

Hughes, J. and Sasse, G. (eds) (2001) *Ethnicity and Territory in the Former Soviet Union*, London: Routledge.
Kaiser, R. (1994) *The Geography of Nationalism in Russia and the USSR*, Princeton, NJ: Princeton University Press.

GASAN GUSEJNOV

terrorist acts

On 1 September 2004, School # 1 in the Northern Ossetian town of Beslan was attacked by an armed group of Chechen terrorists; approximately 1,000 children, parents, and teachers were taken hostage. After a three-day siege, Russian security forces stormed the school, triggering an unexplained explosion that resulted in 334 people dead (including 186 children). In the course of numerous investigations, local officials were accused of corruption in allowing attackers to pass through checkpoints on the Chechen border. During the first days of the siege, Russian officials misinformed the public by underestimating the number of hostages, and failed or were not willing to negotiate with terrorists in order to avoid the armed storming of the building. Nongovernmental organizations, *Materi Beslana* (Mothers of Beslan) and *Golos Beslana* (Voice of Beslan), were formed in an attempt to uncover the real nature of those events, but so far with limited success.

The violence in Beslan was far from the first terrorist assault in Russia. In June 1995, Chechen militants seized hundreds of hostages in a hospital in Budennovsk (southern Russia); in January 1996 they captured 3000 hostages in a hospital in Kizliar (eastern Chechnia). In August 1999, a bomb exploded in an underground shopping centre in Moscow. Explosions of apartment buildings in Buinaksk, Volgodonsk, and Moscow in September 1999 killed over 200 residents. Russian authorities held Chechen terrorists responsible for those explosions, which gave then Prime Minister Putin justification to launch a second Chechen military campaign. In the summer of 2000, two major suicide bombings took place near Groznyi, the Chechen capital, killing dozens of policemen and Russian soldiers. In August 2000, a bomb explosion in a Moscow downtown underpass killed several people. In October 2002, Chechen terrorists held 800 people hostage in the Moscow Theatre during the production of the musical *Nord Ost*. The gas used by the Russian special forces that stormed the building killed not only all of the terrorists but also over 100 hostages.

Suicide bombers continued to attack Russian soldiers, local officials, and civilians in the following years in Chechnia and other regions of Northern Caucasus. In July 2003, suicide bombers blew themselves up at a rock festival in Moscow; in December 2003, another suicide bombing took place near the Duma building in downtown Moscow, followed by yet another in February 2004 on a subway train, killing dozens of people. Just a few days before the Beslan siege, two Russian passenger planes were simultaneously blown up during flight, and a female suicide bomber blew herself up near the entrance of the Moscow subway station Rizhskaia, killing nine and injuring dozens.

See also: Caucasus; Chechnia; *Nord-Ost* (Northeast); Ossetia; territorial conflicts; War, Chechen

TATIANA SMORODINSKAYA

Tertz, Abram

See Siniavskii, Andrei Donatovich

Tetris

Tetris is a video game that ranks among the most popular of all time. It was developed by Russian programmer Aleksei Pazhitnov in 1985 while he was working at the Computing Centre of the Soviet Academy of Sciences. In the game, tetra-minos, or shapes consisting of four squares arranged in different patterns, fall down in turn from the top of the screen. The player must guide the shapes so that the squares form complete horizontal levels when they reach the bottom. The game became instantly popular in Moscow and spread to other cities. Soon discovered by a Western company, in 1986 it was released in the United States, where its success exceeded that in the Soviet Union. Ever since its release, rights to the game have been the subject of much legal wrangling and Pazhitnov has seen very few of the millions of dollars earned by his program.

See also: Academy of Sciences

DAVID HUNTER SMITH

Thaw

The term Thaw denotes the period of changes in Soviet life following Stalin's death (5 March 1953), marked by revitalization and relative liberalization in literature and other arts. The advancement of these changes was by no means linear and simple; it was impeded by successful counterattacks by literary reactionaries and sudden turnarounds caused by the often moody and erratic Nikita Khrushchev, then First Secretary of the Communist Party and actual head of the government. By the mid-1960s the liberal spirit of the Thaw had declined sufficiently to usher in a new period, known as Stagnation.

The process of de-Stalinization started almost immediately after Stalin's death. In April, an article by the poet Olga Berggolts, *Razgovor o lirike* (*Talking about Lyrical Poetry*), in the weekly *Literaturnaia gazeta* (Literary Gazette) criticized poetry devoted to fulfilling industrial quotas and called for more attention to love and other subjective emotions in lyrical poetry. An article in December of that year by critic Vladimir Pomerantsev, *Ob iskrennosti v literature* (*On Sincerity in Literature*), became a seminal event in the history of the Thaw. Without naming Socialist Realism, Pomerantsev attacked its role in Soviet literature, particularly its '*lakirovka deistvitelnosti*' (varnishing of reality) and '*bezkon-fliktnost*' (conflictlessness). The article criticizes novels that are ideologically correct but lifeless, depicting great achievements of the socialist system rather than real life, real people, and their problems. Pomerantsev's article appeared in the journal *Novyi mir* (New World), which, under the editorship of poet Aleksandr Tvardovskii, became an important venue for works that reflected the new tendencies – eliminating the legacy of Stalinism in life and the arts.

In 1953 and the first half of 1954 *Novyi mir* also published a novel by Vera Panova and important articles by Fedor Abramov, Mark Lifshits, and Mark Shcheglov, which were written in the new spirit of 'truthfulness'. Other journals followed suit. In February 1954, *Teatr* (Theatre) published the play *Gosti* (*Guests*) by Leonid Zorin, which touches upon such issues as persecution of innocent people under Stalin, injustice pervading the court system, and abuse of power by Soviet Party bureaucrats. The May 1954 issue of another Moscow journal, *Znamia* (Banner), carried the first part of the novella *Ottepel* (*The Thaw*) by Ilia Erenburg, which gave its name to the entire period. Though arguably not a great work of literature, *The Thaw* is programmatic inasmuch as the author demonstrates what could be the subject matter of an honest literary text. Erenburg offers the reader a smorgasbord of topics and conflicts unthinkable in a canonical work of Socialist Realism. He contrasts a talented artist, devoted to his landscapes and living in poverty, with a hack painter who produces portraits of Party bosses and Stakhanovites and is awash in money. Several romantic subplots involve men and women torn by doubts because their feelings – and in the case of one young woman, even sexual desire – are stronger than their notions of propriety and duty to spouse, country, and reason. The novel also contains references to the persecution of Jewish doctors during the last months of Stalin's rule.

The Thaw resulted not only in the regime's tolerance of greater sincerity and subjectivity in literature, but also in increased possibilities for publication. Within two years (1955–56), about a dozen new literary journals had appeared in Moscow, Leningrad, and the provinces, including *Iunost* (Youth), *Molodaia gvardiia* (Young Guard), *Nash sovremennik* (Our Contemporary), *Moskva* (Moscow), and *Druzhba narodov* (Friendship of Peoples). Their very titles reflect the general desire to move away from the legacy of Stalinism and start anew. In 1956, the two volumes of the literary miscellany *Literaturnaia Moskva* (Literary Moscow) came out; they included works by Anna Akhmatova, Boris Pasternak, Marina Tsvetaeva, and Nikolai Zabolotskii – authors whose names had long been out of circulation for ideological reasons. The second volume also featured the strikingly frank short stories by Aleksandr Iashin and Nikolai Zhdanov, which portrayed the harsh reality of life in the Soviet countryside.

These developments did not occur without conflicts or losses. Literary Stalinists – Aleksandr Fadeev, Konstantin Fedin, Nikolai Gribachev, Vadim Kochetov, and Aleksei Surkov – together with scores of hack critics, launched a counterattack accusing the liberal writers, critics, and editors of revisionism, political pessimism, abstract humanism, aesthetic nihilism, and, peculiarly, tendentious portrayals of Soviet life. The word 'cosmopolitanism' – a remnant of the anti-Jewish campaign of the late-1940s and early-1950s – was also often heard from the podiums at official meetings of literary organizations.

The Twentieth Congress of the Communist Party of the Soviet Union (February 1956) rekindled hopes for liberalization. On the last day of the Congress (25 February), at a closed session, Khrushchev delivered what became known as the 'secret speech'. In it he criticized Stalin's 'cult of personality' and held him responsible for the deaths of countless innocent Soviet citizens during the purges. Although the speech was not published at the time, its content was disseminated through Communist and Komsomol cells at all Soviet factories, institutions, and organizations. This new level of openness encouraged further advancement of the Thaw; in August of that year another important novel exposing bureaucrats and party functionaries was published in *Novyi mir*: Vladimir Dudintsev's *Ne khlebom edinym* (*Not by Bread Alone*). In September *Iunost* published the first novel by the young writer Anatolii Gladilin. This work marked the arrival on the literary scene of young writers and poets who belonged to the new, post-Stalin generation, including Bella Akhmadulina, Vasilii Aksenov, Andrei Bitov, Evgenii Evtushenko, Fazil Iskander, Anatolii Kuznetsov, Arkadii and Boris Strugatskii, Georgii Vladimov, Vladimir Voinovich, and Andrei Voznesenskii.

Yet another setback loomed around the corner, however. When the Hungarian uprising of October 1956 was suppressed by the Soviet Army, reactionaries used the uprising to alarm the government by insinuating that liberalization in literature and other arts could lead to the same explosive situation that had preceded the uprising in Hungary. References to the 'Petöfi Circle' – a literary discussion club that became the heart of the uprising – recurred in their diatribes against the liberals and it was quickly appropriated by Khrushchev in his characteristic threats: 'We will not allow another Petöfi Circle here!' Dudintsev's novel and the second volume of *Literaturnaiia Moskva* became targets of reinvigorated attacks by the conservatives.

Thus, the Thaw proceeded at an irregular rhythm, liberalization alternating with constraints. In 1961, the miscellany *Tarusskie stranitsy* (*Pages from Tarusa*), published in Kaluga, introduced the works of such young writers and poets as Boris Balter, Iurii Kazakov, Naum Korzhavin, Vladimir Maksimov, and Bulat Okudzhava. Since their works did not fit the procrustean bed of Socialist Realism, literary functionaries lashed out against the publishers of *Tarusskie stranitsy*; the editors were fired and the printing of the volume was discontinued. The inclusion of Aleksandr Solzhenitsyn's novel *Odin den Ivana Denisovicha* (*One Day in the Life of Ivan Denisovich*) in the November 1962 issue of *Novyi mir* may be considered the symbolic climax of the Thaw. It was the first literary work published in the

Soviet Union in which the author, who had spent eight years in Stalin's camps, frankly described the horrors of Stalinism and its labour camps. Significantly, while revealing the harsh truth about Stalinism, Solzhenitsyn did not perform the balancing act of demonstrating his loyalty to the system in general.

Shortly thereafter the liberals experienced a major blow, which marked the beginning of a slow decline for the process of liberalization. On 7 and 8 March 1963, a humiliating attack took place in the Kremlin during a meeting between top Party and government officials, including Khrushchev, and the *tvorcheskaia intelligentsiia* (creative intelligentsia). Over eight hundred writers, artists, composers, and film and theatre directors were invited to the meeting. The initial amicable atmosphere quickly turned into a personal assault by Khrushchev on Aksenov, Erenburg, Evtushenko, and Voznesenskii. Criticism of Erenburg singled out his recently published memoirs, which attempted to vindicate the early-twentieth-century avant-garde. The young authors took a beating for giving critical interviews abroad. The powerful message to the entire audience was: you follow the Party line, or else.

The occasion demonstrated the limits of the government's tolerance of ideological deviations in arts. After Khrushchev was ousted in October 1964 and replaced by Leonid Brezhnev in the post of First Secretary of the Communist Party, ideological control over cultural production became even tighter. In 1966, writers Andrei Siniavskii and Iulii Daniel were sentenced, respectively, to seven and five years of hard labour for publishing what the establishment called 'anti-Soviet' fiction in the West. For his uncompromising stand against censorship and for publishing his novels abroad, Solzhenitsyn was expelled from the Union of Soviet Writers in 1969, and from the country in 1974.

Thus, the mid-1960s witnessed a halt to the process of liberalization. Any hope for future relaxation of government control was crushed on 20 August 1968, the day Soviet tanks rolled into Prague. This invasion was a tragedy not only for Czechoslovakia, but also for all liberal-minded people in the Soviet Union. It was a clear sign that the Soviet regime was prepared to go to any lengths in maintaining ideological control. The Thaw was over.

See also: Akhmadulina, Bella; Akhmatova, Anna; Aksenov, Vasilii; anti-Semitism; Berggolts, Olga; Bitov, Andrei; Brezhnev, Leonid; Communist Youth League; cult of personality; Daniel, Iulii; Erenburg, Ilia; Evtushenko, Evgenii; Iskander, Fazil; Kazakov, Iurii; Korzhavin, Naum; Krushchev, Nikita; literature, Thaw; *Literaturnaia gazeta* (Literary Gazette); *Molodaia gvardiia*; *Novyi mir*; Okudzhava, Bulat; Siniavskii, Andrei; Socialist Realism; Solzhenitsyn, Aleksandr; Stagnation; Stakhanovism; Strugatskii, Arkadii and Boris; thick journals; Tvardovskii, Aleksandr; Vladimov, Georgii; Voinovich, Vladimir; Voznesenskii, Andrei; Zorin, Leonid

Further reading

Brown, E. (1982) *Russian Literature Since the Revolution*, Cambridge, MA: Harvard University Press, pp. 192–291.

Chuprinin, S. (ed.) (1989) *Ottepel: 1953–1956*, Moscow: Moskovskii rabochii.

——(1990a) *Ottepel: 1957–1959*, Moscow: Moskovskii rabochii.

——(1990b) *Ottepel: 1960–1962*, Moscow: Moskovskii rabochii.

Gibian, G. (1960) *Interval of Freedom; Soviet Literature during the Thaw, 1954–1957*, Minneapolis, MN: University of Minnesota Press.

Johnson, P. (1965) *Khrushchev and the Arts: The Politics of Soviet Culture, 1962–1964*, Cambridge, MA: MIT Press.

Prokhorov, A. V. (2002) 'Inherited Discourse: Stalinist Tropes in Thaw Culture', PhD dissertation, University of Pittsburgh.

Woll, J. (2000) *Reel Images: Soviet Cinema and the Thaw*, London and New York: I. B. Tauris.

KONSTANTIN KUSTANOVICH

theatre, post-Soviet

Theatre was poised to leave behind the Soviet era even before the Soviet Union was dissolved by the Belovezhskaia Pushcha Pact and the resignation of President Mikhail Gorbachev in December 1991. The great directors Anatolii Efros and Georgii Tovstonogov died in 1987 and 1989, respectively; the influential critic and historian Konstantin Rudnitskii died in 1988.

The loss of such authorities, coupled with rapid social and political change, made the defining attributes of the Soviet theatrical experience obsolete.

The first private, non-governmental production companies since 1917 were founded in Moscow. They included the *Letuchaia mysh* (Bat) Theatre (1989), the Anton Chekhov Theatre (1989), the Meicrkhold Centre (1991), the Roman Viktiuk Theatre (1991), David Smelianskii's Russian Theatre Agency (1992), and the Bogis Agency (1992). Their appearance heralded changes that affected Russian theatre into the twenty-first century. Some actors and directors, who previously had been bound to a single company, began working as freelance artists, while producers chose plays for commercial potential as much as for artistic merit. These developments weakened the tradition of the Russian theatre as a house of art and destabilized the repertory system – a structure by which theatres maintained large repertoires of productions performed several times a month for years or decades. Many argued that the system was outdated and antithetical to the flexibility that modern theatre required; others insisted that it must be preserved as one of the great achievements of the Soviet period.

The 1990s saw the rise to prominence of two directors, Kama Ginkas and Petr Fomenko, who had toiled in relative obscurity for decades, because their artistic visions ran counter to the Soviet model. Ginkas refined a style of provocative, emotionally explosive works based on adaptations of prose by Fedor Dostoevskii, Anton Chekhov and others. He primarily utilized small, unorthodox performance spaces, reflecting a key element of early post-Soviet theatre: its endeavour to communicate intimately with spectators. Fomenko's influential production of Aleksandr Ostrovskii's *Bez viny vinovatye* (*Guilty without Guilt*, 1993) was also performed in two small rooms, but it was the founding of the *Masterskaia Fomenko* (Fomenko Studio) in 1993 that made this director one of the era's central figures. The Studio, incorporating graduates of Fomenko's acting and directing class at the Russian Academy of Theatre Arts (RATI), quickly achieved international fame.

Several established directors remained active, each distinctively exercising Russia's tentative and often chaotic new freedoms. Lev Dodin embarked on a triumphant international career with his Malyi Drama Theatre of St. Petersburg through a series of foreign tours and European co-productions. His grand-scale brand of meticulous psychological realism illuminating social themes epitomized the finest achievements of Soviet-style theatre. Anatolii Vasilev combined high-profile activity in Europe with a hermetic existence in Russia at his School of Dramatic Art (founded in 1987). His laboratory experiments at the School were largely off-limits to spectators until the 2000s, leaving him outside of general trends, though his *Plach Ierimeia* (*The Lament of Jeremiah*, 1996) was a significant public success and effectively displayed the jeweler's precision and mastery of detail, space, and light that distinguished his art. Iurii Liubimov spent the early 1990s shuttling between Europe and his Taganka Theatre in Moscow, but rededicated himself to the Taganka with strong productions of Dostoevskii's *Bratia Karamazovy* (*The Brothers Karamazov*, 1997) and Peter Weiss's *Marat and Marquis de Sade* (1998). His fragmentary, idiosyncratic productions in the 2000s led to claims that his relevance had waned, but few contemporaries matched the legacy he continued to build. Valerii Fokin, after two decades of creating traditional, realistic theatre, began staging innovative experimental works under the aegis of his newly founded Meierkhold Centre.

In the 1990s, the theatre community lacked a sense of common purpose; no significant force or trend unified the many significant productions, directors, and actors. In Moscow, Vladimir Mirzoev irritated traditionalists and achieved fantastic popularity with extravagant productions mixing Oriental philosophy and Freudian psychology. Sergei Artsibashev created intimate pieces employing the scrupulous realism usually associated with cinema. Iurii Pogrebnichko cultivated a unique style of emotionally detached and dryly ironic acting at Okolo Theatre near the Stanislavskii House. Boris Iukhananov and Klim (aka Vladimir Klimov), two former students of Efros and Vasilev, nurtured avant-garde experiments. A number of inventive directors emerged in

St. Petersburg: Grigorii Ditiatkovskii evolved a style of refined realism set in lush, abstract settings; Viktor Kramer, who had worked with the clown Viacheslav Polunin, explored the aesthetics of eccentricity at his *Farsy* (Farces) Theatre; Andrei Moguchii created strange, quirky worlds that bared the theatrical devices behind them; Iurii Butusov, a connoisseur of paradoxes, created extravagant visual images going far beyond the dictates of the text. In short, theatre in the two capitals blended plenitude with heterogeneity.

Theatres in the provinces suffered financially after the centralized Soviet system collapsed, but many generated noteworthy accomplishments, among them: the Omsk Drama Theatre, the *Krasnyi fakel* (Red Torch) Theatre in Novosibirsk, the Young Spectator Theatre in Ekaterinburg, and Sergei Fedotov's *U mosta* (At the Bridge) Theatre in Perm. Working in various cities, the director Evgenii Marcelli elaborated a theatrical aesthetic combining psychological precision with expressive acting. In Ekaterinburg, the playwright and director Nikolai Koliada cleared the way for the most significant trend of the early 2000s, the so-called 'new drama' movement. His assertive advocacy of contemporary drama was a vital counterweight to the dominance on Russian stages of Chekhov, Ostrovskii, Gogol, Dostoevskii, and Shakespeare.

Two Moscow theatres, the Playwright and Director Centre, created by veteran playwrights Aleksei Kazantsev and Mikhail Roshchin in 1998, and Teatr.doc, founded by playwrights Elena Gremina and Mikhail Ugarov in 2002, pursued a policy of promoting new talent. The effect was rapid; Russian theatre entered its first major youth movement since the 1950s and 1960s. These theatres launched or furthered the careers of many writers (the Presniakov Brothers, Vasilii Sigarev, Ivan Vyrypaev, Danila Privalov, Maksim Kurochkin, Natalia Vorozhbit, Iurii Klavdiev), directors (Olga Subbotina, Kirill Serebriannikov, Vladimir Ageev), and actors. By the mid-2000s, most innovative ideas and artists from around Russia were being channelled through these theatres, the Meierkhold Centre, and Praktika, a house founded in 2005. Established venues such as the Moscow Art Theatre, the Sovremennik and, to a lesser extent, the Satirikon hired the individuals discovered by the

small houses in order to capitalize on their growing popularity. That practice enabled many newcomers to infiltrate the mainstream with remarkable speed.

Experiments aside, the economic pressures on average playhouses intensified in the 2000s. Many of the larger theatres chose to concentrate on star-driven, audience-friendly productions. Roman Kozak and Sergei Artsybashev had success with this at the Pushkin Theatre and the Maiakovskii Theatre, respectively. Mindaugas Karbauskis emerged after his debut in 2001 as one of the most talented of the new traditional, realistic directors.

See also: acting schools; Dodin, Lev; drama, post-Soviet; Efros, Anatolii; Ekaterinburg; Fokin, Valerii; Fomenko, Petr; Ginkas, Kama; Gremina, Elena; Koliada, Nilolai; Liubimov, Iurii; Moscow Art Theatre; Polunin, Viacheslav; Satyricon Theatre; Sovremennik Theatre; Taganka Theatre; theatre, Soviet; Tovstogonov, Georgii; Ugarov, Mikhail; Vasilev, Anatolii; Viktiuk, Roman

Further reading

Freedman, J. (1997) *Moscow Performances: The New Russian Theater 1991–1996*, Amsterdam: Harwood Academic Publishers.

——(1998) *Moscow Performances II: The 1996–1997 Season*, Amsterdam: Harwood Academic Publishers.

——(2000) 'The Changing Space of Russian Theatre', *TheatreForum* 17 (Summer/Fall), 3–11.

Sellar, T. and Ross, Y. (eds) (2006) *Theater* Vol. 36, No. 1, Durham, NC: Duke University Press.

JOHN FREEDMAN

theatre, Soviet

Following the 1917 October Revolution and throughout the Civil War (1918–22), theatre experienced the same turmoil as every other sphere of activity in the Soviet Union. Major houses such as the Bolshoi and Malyi Theatres in Moscow and the Mariinskii and Aleksandrinskii Theatres in Petrograd continued to function, but the old repertoires did not reflect the new era's expectations and interests. The Moscow Art Theatre, headed by Konstantin Stanislavskii, toured Europe and the United States from 1922 to 1924 as if considering staying abroad for good. The director Vsevolod Meierkhold began seeking a new aesthetic by producing Vladimir Maiakovskii's *Misteriia-buff* (*Mystery Bouffe*, 1918, restaged 1921), a satire about the 'clean' and 'unclean' members of the new society. Other key directors were Aleksandr Tairov, whose stylish productions made the Kamernyi (Chamber) Theatre famous; Evgenii Vakhtangov, an experimenter whose death at age 39 in 1922 was a great loss; and Nikolai Evreinov, who staged the legendary 1918 outdoor spectacle imitating the storming of the Winter Palace, then emigrated in 1925.

Meierkhold quickly became the standard-bearer for Soviet theatre, his work combining aesthetic innovation and socio-political awareness. After Vladimir Lenin introduced the New Economic Policy (NEP) in 1922, the country stabilized, and growth and experimentation ensued in theatre. Because the state recognized theatre's educational properties, it created many new playhouses, such as those now known as the Mossovet, the Maiakovskii, the Lenkom, and the Young Spectator Theatre (*Teatr iunogo zritelia*). These houses offered images of the new heroes, men and women building a new society, and explored the exotic theme of a society seeking to invent itself almost from scratch. Comedy and satire reigned in the mid-1920s, but soon gave way to drama, melodrama, and heroic epics. The diverse achievements of the 1920s made Moscow one of the world's leading theatrical cities.

After Iosif Stalin consolidated power in 1927, the official Communist Party line was increasingly enforced, with intolerance for deviation. After Socialist Realism was declared the official method of artistic expression in 1934 and the Stalinist purges reached their apogee in 1937, the theatre community was hit hard. Meierkhold's fall from grace – the closing of his theatre in 1938, followed by his arrest in 1939 and his murder in prison in 1940 – was emblematic of an era when thousands of theatre artists were exiled, sent to labour camps or executed. So extensive was this phenomenon that prison theatres, each with a resident troupe, became common in the GULag – something historians began documenting only in the 1990s.

The years of World War II naturally gave rise to a period of heightened national pride, and such writers as Konstantin Simonov supplied the demand for patriotic plays. Nevertheless, most quality theatre from the second half of the 1930s to the mid-1950s was created around the classics. Directors Ruben Simonov and Iurii Zavadskii made reputations crafting quality work with ideologically safe material. Similarly, former actors of Meierkhold, such as Igor Ilinskii, Mikhail Tsarev, and Evgenii Samoilov, found safe haven and productive careers at the traditional Malyi Theatre. Throughout this period, Molière, Beaumarchais, Goldoni, Gozzi, Schiller, Rostand, and Shakespeare were as popular as Anton Chekhov, Maksim Gorkii and Aleksandr Ostrovskii. European comedies and historical chronicles allowed directors to employ what became known as 'Aesopian language', offering circuitous commentary on Soviet life through characters and texts that had no direct relevance to Soviet reality. Working with classics and Soviet writers alike, the director Nikolai Okhlopkov developed an influential style founded on heightened civic pathos and heroic proportions, while Nikolai Akimov elaborated a sophisticated method grounded in fantasy and fairy tale.

The Thaw brought monumental changes in Soviet life and art. In theatre there now was a concerted effort to work on an accessible, human scale. Playwrights Viktor Rozov, Aleksandr Volodin, Leonid Zorin, Eduard Radzinskii, and Aleksei Arbuzov explored the private lives of common people and, in productions by Anatolii Efros, their characters set the tone for the era stretching from the 1950s into the period of Stagnation. In Moscow in 1956 the Sovremennik Theatre was founded on the principle of speaking simple truths in a contemporary intonation, while in Leningrad that year Georgii Tovstonogov became chief director at the Bolshoi Drama Theatre (BDT). His tenure until his death in 1989 established one of the great Soviet-era theatres, steeped in the realistic, psychological tradition developed by Stanislavskii. Another major playhouse appeared in 1964 when Iurii Liubimov, an actor at the

Vakhtangov Theatre, founded the Taganka Theatre, destined to become known as the theatrical conscience of the nation. Some of the great actors of the age emerged from these houses: Innokentii Smoktunovskii, Evgenii Lebedev, Tatiana Doronina, Oleg Efremov, Evgenii Evstigneev, Vladimir Vysotskii, Alla Demidova, and others.

The 1960s and 1970s witnessed the debut of the important directors Petr Fomenko, Kama Ginkas, Lev Dodin, Valerii Fokin, and Anatolii Vasilev. But only Fokin and, to a lesser extent, Vasilev could realize their potential before the relative rush of freedom that followed the onset of perestroika in 1986. Some of the most popular productions from the Stagnation period belonged to the subgenre of 'industrial drama', portraying conflicts caused in the workplace by the rift between individual and state aspirations. None of these plays had lasting value. Noteworthy playwrights in the late-Soviet period included: Aleksandr Vampilov, who explored the lives of embittered outcasts; Liudmila Petrushevskaia, who aimed a withering gaze at the minutiae of Soviet sexual and familial relationships; Nina Sadur, who created quirky characters with a mystical bent; Liudmila Razumovskaia, who plumbed the depths of contemporary tragedy; and Mikhail Roshchin, whose ironic plays walked a fine line between realism and fantasy. To some extent, the liberties of perestroika (censorship ceased to be enforced around 1988) plunged Soviet theatre into crisis. Unable to resolve internal differences, many houses – including the Moscow Art Theatre, the Ermolova Theatre, and the Taganka – underwent schisms that broke them in two. The chief trend in the 1980s was that of the small theatre-studio organized independently of the state. They numbered Mark Rozovskii's *Teatr u Nikitskikh Vorot* (Theatre by the Nikita Gates), Oleg Tabakov's Theatre-Studio, Liudmila Roshkovan's *Chelovek* ('Human') Studio, and Valerii Beliakovich's *Teatr-Studio na Iugo-Zapade* (Southwest Theatre Studio).

See also: Akimov, Nikolai; Arbuzov, Aleksei; Bolshoi Theatre; censorship; Communist Party; Demidova, Alla; Dodin, Lev; Doronina, Tatiana; drama, Soviet; Efremov, Oleg; Efros,

Anatolii; Evstigneev, Evgenii; Fokin, Valerii; Fomenko, Petr; Ginkas, Kama; GULag; Ilinskii, Igor; Khrushchev, Nikita; Lebedev, Evgenii; Lenin, Vladimir Ilich; Lenkom Theatre; Liubimov, Iurii; Maiakovskii Theatre; Malyi Theatre; Mariinskii Theatre; Moscow Art Theatre; Mossovet Theatre; Okhlopkov, Nikolai; perestroika and glasnost; Petrushevskaia, Liudmila; Radzinskii, Edvard; Rozov, Viktor; Rozovskii, Mark; Sadur, Nina; Simonov, Konstantin; Simonov, Ruben; Smoktunovskii, Innokentii; Socialist Realism; Sovremennik Theatre; Stagnation; Stalin, Iosif; Tabakov, Oleg; Taganka Theatre; Thaw; Tovstonogov, Georgii; Vakhtangov Theatre; Vampilov, Aleksandr; Vasilev, Anatolii; World War II (Great Patriotic War); Young Spectator Theatre; Zavadskii, Iurii; Zorin, Leonid

Further reading

Leach, R. and Borovsky, V. (eds) (1999) *A History of Russian Theatre*, Cambridge: Cambridge University Press.

Rudnitsky, K. (2000) *Russian and Soviet Theatre: Tradition and the Avant-Garde*, 2nd edn, trans. R. Permar, London: Thames and Hudson.

Smeliansky, A. (1999) *The Russian Theater After Stalin*, ed. D. Bardby, trans. P. Miles, Cambridge: Cambridge University Press.

JOHN FREEDMAN

thick journals

The so-called 'thick' journals constitute a specific phenomenon in Soviet, perestroika, and post-Soviet literature. As a venue for initial publication of memoirs and new works by contemporary poets, prose writers, critics, and political commentators, during Stagnation thick journals shaped the public's reading tastes and organized literary factions through the editorial boards' careful selection of manuscripts and their ideological slant in literary criticism. Though during perestroika these monthlies exerted an increasing influence on public consciousness, their significance subsequently waned. Literary monthlies became a forum for introducing the reader to new works by accomplished authors and for debuting works of unknown or budding writers. Despite their reduced influence, thick journals continue to play an important role in consolidating the literary mainstream and in providing a meeting ground – a kind of club – for writers of different generations but similar standards, literary beliefs, and social perceptions.

Before and after Stalin's death (1953), the journal *Novyi mir* (New World, 1925) started the process, moulding (unobtrusively at first, then more explicitly) an officially acceptable liberal trend within Soviet literature, despite the pre-print censorship that existed throughout the Soviet era. The readers of ideologically opposed literary monthlies – the liberal *Novyi mir* and the hard-line Communist *Oktiabr* (October, 1924) – became polarized during the Thaw as representatives of two ideological camps. After Party attacks on *Novyi mir*'s editors in 1970, the polemic between the two died down: liberal authors such as Iurii Trifonov moved to the monthlies *Nash sovremennik* (Our Contemporary, 1956) and *Druzhba narodov* (Friendship of Peoples, 1939), which gradually became leaders of Soviet jingoistic nationalism (the former) and liberalism and internationalism 'with a human face' (the latter).

With the advent of perestroika and glasnost, the Communist Party Central Committee appointed new chief editors to the major literary monthlies: Sergei Zalygin to *Novyi mir* and Grigorii Baklanov to *Znamia* (The Banner, 1931). Thick journals became the organizers of the country's socio-political life and the first publishers of previously banned and émigré literature, and, starting in 1989, of underground literature. The monthlies' print runs peaked in 1990: *Novyi mir* sold 2.5 million copies; *Druzhba narodov*, 1.8 million; *Znamia*, one million; *Zvezda* (The Star, 1923), 600,000. These and other thick journals contained not only uncensored prose and poetry, but also articles by political commentators and literary critics that examined the condition of society, the economy, and the State. While breaking political, ideological, and aesthetic taboos, the thick journals were perceived as divided into strongholds of neo-Westernism (*Znamia, Oktiabr, Zvezda, Neva*, 1955) and neo-Slavophilism (*Nash sovremennik, Molodaia*

gvardiia [Young Guard], 1922). In the 1990s, *Novyi mir* opted for a centrist literary and socio-political orientation, though it was the first among the thick journals to repatriate the work of Iosif Brodskii and Aleksandr Solzhenitsyn, both of whom lived abroad and had not been published in their homeland for decades.

After their unprecedented boom at the turn of the 1990s, thick journals steadily lost their influence on public consciousness and the literary process. Subscriptions fell, print-runs dropped drastically, settling at 3,000 (*Druzhba narodov*) to 9,000 copies (*Nash sovremennik*) by 2004. Today thick journals provide at best a testing ground for texts by non-commercial authors in various formats; at worst, a playground for aggressive but increasingly marginal authors. Among the losses suffered by the thick journal corps is the demise of the provincial monthly *Volga*, whose publication was discontinued in 2000 owing to a dramatic drop in the print-run (to under a thousand copies) and lack of financial support.

See also: awards, literary, post-Soviet; awards, literary, Soviet; Brodskii, Iosif; censorship; Communist Party; intelligentsia; literature, perestroika; literature, post-Soviet; literature, Soviet; literature, Stagnation; literature, Thaw; nationalism ('the national question'); *Novyi mir*; perestroika and glasnost; Slavophiles; Solzhenitsyn, Aleksandr; Stalin, Iosif; Tvardovskii, Aleksandr; Westernizers

Further reading

Biul-Zedgenidze, N. (1996) *Literaturnaia kritika zhurnala 'Novyi mir' A.T. Tvardovskogo* (Literary Criticism in Aleksandr Tvardovskii's *Novy mir* (1958–70)), Moscow: Pervopechatnik.

Dubin, B. (2001) *Slovo – pismo – literatura. Ocherki po sotsiologii sovremennoi kultury* (The Word, Writing, Literature. Essays on Contemporary Sociology of Culture), Moscow: NLO.

Eggeling, W. (1999) *Politika i kultura pri Khrushcheve i Brezhneve. 1953–1970-kh* (Politics and Culture under Khrushchev and Brezhnev: 1953 to the 1970s), Moscow: AI-XX. Novoe literaturenoe obozrenie (NLO).

Gudkov, L. and Dubin, B. (1995) *Intelligentsiia. Zametki o literaturno-politicheskikh illiuziiakh* (The Intelligentsia. Notes on Literary and Political Illusions), Moscow: Epicenter; Kharkiv: Folio.

NATALIA IVANOVA

Third Rome

The political doctrine of Moscow as 'the third Rome' was articulated in the sixteenth century in the epistles of Philotheus, a monk of Eleazar Monastery in Pskov; the first record of his communication of this idea to Ivan III is from 1511. From the perspective of Russian Orthodoxy, once Rome itself had fallen to the 'Catholic heresy', and the second Rome – Constantinople – to the Turks in 1453, the centre of world Christianity shifted to the new guardian of the true faith: Muscovy. Philotheus expressed Moscow's messianic role as follows: 'Two Romes have fallen, a third stands, a fourth there shall not be'. Having adopted Christianity from Byzantium in 988, the Russians naturally projected themselves as their spiritual successors. The transfer of Orthodox leadership from Constantinople to Moscow (then emerging as the political and religious centre of the Russian lands) was further reflected in the marriage of Grand Duke Ivan III to the niece of the last Byzantine Emperor, Sophia Paleologus, who brought to Russia the Byzantine state seal, the double-headed eagle. The 1547 coronation of Ivan IV (the Terrible) as the first Russian tsar (a word derived from 'caesar') and the formal establishment of the Russian Patriarchy in 1589 further underscored Moscow's imperial and religious status as the centre of world Christianity. The doctrine of 'Moscow as the third Rome' has become an indelible part of Russia's founding mythology, frequently evoked in a variety of contexts, from nineteenth-century Slavophile discourse to post-perestroika nationalist rhetoric.

See also: nationalism ('the national question'); Russian Orthodoxy; Slavophiles

MARIA RUBINS

Tikhonov, Viacheslav Vasilevich

b. 8 February 1928, Moscow oblast

Film and television actor

Tikhonov's roles embody the thoughtfulness and deliberation of the Russian intellectual; his characters are often strong, but not hardened. Beloved by Soviet audiences for his portrayal of Prince Andrei Bolkonskii in Sergei Bondarchuk's screen adaptation of *War and Peace* (1966–67), Tikhonov achieved cult status following his appearance as the Soviet intelligence agent Isaev-Stirlitz in Tatiana Lioznova's twelve-part television series *Semnadtsat mgnoveniia vesny* (*Seventeen Moments of Spring*, 1973). Stirlitz remains Tikhonov's most famous role; he portrayed the agent as thoughtful, deliberate, chivalrous, and unwaveringly devoted to the Soviet Union. Tikhonov has appeared in over fifty films and television series, including Nikita Mikhalkov's *Utomlennye solntsem* (*Burnt by the Sun*, 1994), and *Berlinskii ekspress* (*Berlin Express*, 2001).

See also: Bondarchuk, Sergei; Lioznova, Tatiana; Mikhalkov, Nikita; *Semnadtsat mgnoveniia vesny* (*Seventeen Moments of Spring*); television, post-Soviet; television, Soviet

JENNIFER RYAN TISHLER

Tishchenko, Boris Ivanovich

b. 23 March 1939, Leningrad

Composer

A student of Galina Ustvolskaia and later Shostakovich, Tishchenko is one of the most original composers to gain prominence in the 1960s. Regarded by many as a second Prokofiev, he is considered Russia's most important symphonist since Shostakovich. His abundant output includes concertos, ballets, symphonies, and a host of chamber instrumental works. Tishchenko's music, like Sergei Slonimskii's, is rooted in St. Petersburg composers' contact with authentic folk culture, and reflects both Western and Eastern folk influences. He teaches at the St. Petersburg Conservatory, where his students acknowledge a Tishchenko School of music. People's Artist of Russia (1987).

See also: Prokofiev, Sergei; Shostakovich, Dmitrii; Slonimskii, Sergei; St. Petersburg Conservatory; Ustvolskaia, Galina.

DAVID GOMPPER

Todorovskii, Petr Efimovich

b. 26 August 1925, Bobrinets, Kirovograd region, Ukrainian SSR

Film director

In the course of his long artistic career, Todorovskii has worked as cameraman, scriptwriter, and composer. His major artistic concern – producing plausible plots about realistic characters in concrete situations – determines his penchant for tragicomedy. Although Todorovskii's films arose out of diverging epochs – World War II (*Vernost* [*Faithfulness*, 1965]), the Stalin era (*Ankor, eshche ankor!* [*Encore, Once More Encore!*, 1992]), the Thaw (*Fokusnik* [*The Magician*, 1967]), Stagnation (*Liubimaia zhenshchina mekhanika Gavrilova* [*The Mechanic Gavrilov's Beloved Woman*, 1981]), perestroika (*Interdevochka* [*Intergirl*, 1989]), and the post-Soviet period (*Zhizn zabavami polna* [*Life is Full of Fun*, 2002]) – they narrate the similar stories of hatred and love, betrayal and loyalty, loss and happiness. Todorovskii's faithfulness to the ideals of the sixties generation (*shestidesiatniki*) permeates most of his films.

See also: perestroika and glasnost; sixties generation; Stagnation; Stalin, Iosif; Thaw; World War II (Great Patriotic War)

IRINA MAKOVEEVA

Todorovskii, Valerii Petrovich

b. 9 May 1962, Odessa

Film director, scriptwriter, producer

Son of a famous film director, Todorovskii inherited his father's talent for telling 'human interest' stories. His film *Liubov* (*Love*, 1991), which explores the theme of first love in the context of Russian anti-Semitism, won the ecumenical prize at Cannes. *Strana glukhikh* (*Land of the Deaf*, 1998), set in post-Soviet crime-infected Moscow, explores the theme of orphanhood. Since 2000, Todorovskii has combined directing with his work as producer of television serials for the television channel RTR. His projects include such recent hits as gangster saga *Brigada* (*The Brigade*, 2002), an adaptation of Dostoevskii's novel *The Idiot* (2003), and a production of Bulgakov's novel *Master i Margarita* (*The Master and Margarita*).

See also: *Master i Margarita* (*The Master and Margarita*); Todorovskii, Petr

ELENA PROKHOROVA

Tokareva, Viktoriia Samoilovna

b. 20 November 1937, Leningrad

Writer

Prose author, scriptwriter, and playwright Viktoriia Tokareva is a prominent exponent of 'women's' literature, a categorization to which she objects. After studying music and acting, she first attracted attention with stories published in the late 1960s; her best-known movie scenarios (*Dzhentlmeny udachi* [*Successful Gentlemen*], 1971; *Mimino*, 1977) date from the 1970s. Tokareva won great popularity in the late Soviet period with realistic, wryly humorous stories about women's lives and loves, in which she avoided tendentious social commentary. Her resigned irony and close observation of her characters' suffering sometimes resembles the late work of Nadezhda Tèffi [Nadezhda Aleksandrovna Buchinskaia, née Lokhvitskaia, 1876–1952]. Tokareva's later fiction examines mother/daughter relationships in an increasingly serious and critical vein.

See also: literature, women's

SIBELAN FORRESTER

Tolstaia, Tatiana Nikitichna

b. 3 May 1951, Leningrad

Prose writer, essayist, TV personality

A prosaist of formidable imaginative power and linguistic virtuosity, during perestroika Tolstaia was the Anglophone Russian writer of choice. She debuted in 1983 with the story *Na zolotom kryl'tse sideli ...* (*On the Golden Porch*) – also the title of her first collection (1987), an instant bestseller. Approximately twenty stories later, Tolstaia stopped writing fiction for almost a decade, though during her extended stay in the United States from 1988, she reviewed books, authored essays, gave highly opinionated interviews, and taught at several universities. After her return to Moscow, she finally completed and published her novel, *Kys* (*The Slynx* 1986–2000; trans. 2003), reissued her stories in various editions, and authored numerous essays. In 2002 she became co-hostess with the film scriptwriter Dunia Smirnova of a popular TV show entitled *Shkola zloslov'ia* (*School for Scandal*), which archly combines interviews with gossipy commentary.

Tolstaia's brief, trope-saturated early stories explore time, imagination, creativity, and desire in a stylistically luxuriant, ornamented prose reminiscent of Gogol, Olesha, and Nabokov. While the unpredictable shifts between irony and lyricism, and the intertextuality of her narrative mode evoke (post)modernism, her works embrace traditional Russian values: idealism, caritas, and faith in the imperishability of art and the supreme power of language (the true hero of her fiction). Myths and folklore endow such dense, compact stories from the 1980s as *Svidanie s ptitsei* (*Date with a Bird*), *Peters*, and *Poet i muza* (*The Poet and the Muse*) with a wealth of layers and cultural associations, while later works, which confront Russia's image in a historical (*Siuzhet* [Plot]) and dystopian context (*Kys*), lack compression and rigorous structure. Winner of the Triumph Prize (2000).

See also: literature, perestroika; literature, post-Soviet; literature, women's

Further reading

Goscilo, H. (1996) *The Explosive World of Tatyana N. Tolstaya's Fiction*. Armonk, NY: M. E. Sharpe.
Tolstaya, T. (2003) *Pushkin's Children: Writings on Russia and Russians*, trans. J, Gambrell, Boston: Houghton Mifflin Co.

HELENA GOSCILO

Tolubeev, Iurii Vladimirovich

b. 1 May 1905, St. Petersburg; d. 28 December 1979, Leningrad

Stage and film actor

Tolubeev studied at the Institute for Stage Arts in Leningrad, graduating in 1929. In 1942, he joined the Leningrad Academic Pushkin Theatre – the former Aleksandrinskii – and soon became one of its stars. In devotional Stalinist films such as *Velikii perelom* (*The Great Turning Point*, 1945), Tolubeev played strong-willed characters intended to be typical representations of the Russian people and their assumed 'natural' pro-Soviet loyalty. The actor, who used his corpulent physique to great comical and tragicomical effect, was superb in literary adaptations, especially as the mayor in *Revizor* (*The Inspector General*, 1952) and Sancho Pansa in *Don Quijote* (1957), displaying enormous emotional and physical drive. People's Artist of the USSR (1956).

See also: St. Petersburg Academy of Theatre Arts

PETER ROLLBERG

Torpedo

Sports club

Soviet sports club established in 1924 by an automobile society. Traditional colours are black and white. Every major motor-car factory in the USSR had its own Torpedo hockey or football team. During the 1960s, the most popular football team, belonging to a Moscow plant, won several national titles. The top, legendary football player was Eduard Streltsov.

ALEXANDER LEDENEV

toska

A notoriously difficult concept to translate, *toska* denotes a troubled state of the soul. It conveys an understanding of the fleeting nature of the material world, a desire for spiritual truth, or an intense longing (as in *toska po rodine*, longing for one's homeland). It is often rendered in English as anguish, depression, boredom, longing, or nostalgia.

ANDREA LANOUX

tost (toast)

A rich and lively tradition, toasting accompanies all social gatherings and follows set conventions. The host or toastmaster (*tamada*) usually opens with a brief toast 'to our meeting' or 'to the guests'. The second toast is often a longer, well-crafted speech, followed by a third 'to the hosts'. Subsequent toasts follow no particular order but can include 'to health', 'to women' (said with men standing), and to various relatives. Because it is considered impolite to drink without toasting, informal toasts ('let's go') and random toasts ('to the linear concept of time') are quite common. 'One for the road' has countless mutations and can last up to several hours.

See also: dining; drinks, alcoholic

ANDREA LANOUX

tourism

See vacations, Soviet and post-Soviet

Tovstonogov Bolshoi Drama Theatre (BDT)

Bolshoi Drama Theatre (BDT), now the St. Peterburg Tovstonogov Bolshoi Drama Theatre, was founded in 1919 by Maria Andreeva, Aleksander Blok, and Maksim Gorkii as a theatre for heroic drama and elevated comedy; its mostly classical repertory corresponded in the 1920s to the heroic image of the revolutionary era. A prolonged crisis in the 1930s and 1940s ended during the Thaw with Tovstonogov's appointment as artistic director in 1956. The theatre quickly became part of the Soviet establishment and achieved fame for its superb ensemble (dominated by male stars) and the novel-like performance style (*spektakl-roman*). Such prominent actors as Oleg Borisov, Tatiana Doronina, Efim Kopelian, Evgenii Lebedev, Pavel Luspekaev, Vitalii Politzeimako, Emma Popova, Innokentii Smoktunovskii, Zinaida Sharko, Sergei Iurskii, and Alisa Freindlikh worked there at various times.

After Tovstonogov's death in 1989, one of BDT's leading actors, Kirill Lavrov, assumed artistic leadership. In the spirit of political change, he has engaged in some cautious innovations by inviting various directors who nonetheless have to comply with the theatre's trademark psychological approach.

See also: Borisov, Oleg; Doronina, Tatiana; Freindlikh, Alisa; Iurskii, Sergei; Kopelian, Efim; Lavrov, Kirill; Lebedev, Evgenii; Luspekaev, Pavel; Smoktunovskii, Innokentii; Thaw; theatre, Soviet; Tovstonogov, Georgii

DASHA KRIJANSKAIA

Tovstonogov, Georgii Aleksandrovich

b. 15 [28] September 1915, Tbilisi; d. 23 May 1989, Leningrad

Director

Although educated during the era of Socialist Realism, Tovstonogov, especially after 1960, was able to merge psychological acting with formal stage approaches such as stylization and montage, thus reviving Meierkhold's legacy. He was interested in recreating the social and psychological essence of groups and individuals. Though his works avoided open political criticism, his revivals of classics were imbued with contemporary social meaning. In casting, Tovstonogov sought exceptional stage personality corresponding to the director's idea of a given character. Thus his major productions had no double casting (the usual practice in the Soviet theatre).

Appointed artistic director at Leningrad's Bolshoi Drama Theatre (now renamed the Tovstonogov Bolshoi Drama Theatre) in 1956, he managed to remain on good terms with the authorities throughout his long career, and retained the post until his death.

Major productions include: Dostoevskii's *Idiot* (1957), Gorkii's *Varvary* (*Barbarians*, 1959), Griboedov's *Gore ot uma* (*Woe from Wit*, 1962), Chekhov's *Tri sestry* (*Three Sisters*, 1965), Shakespeare's *Henry IV* (1969), Tsagareli's *Khanuma* (1972), and Tolstoi's *Kholstomer* (*Story of a Horse*, 1975).

See also: Tovstonogov Bolshoi Drama Theatre; Socialist Realism; theatre, Soviet

DASHA KRIJANSKAIA

toys

Originally toys were the objects of cult and worship. Later varieties included magical, valuable (family heirlooms, collector's items), entertainment for adults (clockwork musical toys, sex toys), handicraft (wooden and clay folk products from Gzhel, Dymkovo, Zagorsk and other regions), and cheap mass-produced toys. Specialized according to social status, toys were intended to train children in important skills along well-defined gender lines: boys were supposed to learn the skills of a hunter, fisherman, cattle-breeder, and soldier, and girls those of a bride, mother, and housekeeper.

The Soviet Union viewed toys as a means of cultivating class consciousness, and the Communist Party paid special attention to them, placing their production and distribution under the control of the Ministry of Education. The Museum of Toys was founded in 1918, and the All-Union Scientific Research Institute of Toys in Zagorsk (Sergiev Posad) in 1932. In 1948, at a republican competition for new toys, toymakers

reproduced the images of Soviet people of different professions, dressing doll-boys and doll-girls in various profession-specific uniforms and outfits: those of pilot, border guard, doctor, miner, militia man, schoolgirl, nurse, collective-farm worker, etc. A special council was created in the RSFSR Ministry of Education to oversee the ideological, pedagogical, and artistic quality of toys produced, to elaborate themes and samples of socialist toys that would fulfil the task of children's Communist upbringing: acquaint them with the achievements of Soviet technology, with peoples of the USSR, and how Soviet people work and relax. In the 1950s, Soviet pedagogues classified toys according to the following categories: toys for creative games (for example, dolls); educational toys (table games, semi-fabricated toys, constructors, building blocks, and others); technical toys (cars, tractors, etc.); toys for active games and sports; and decorative toys and carnival and holiday decorations.

Toys for the New Year tree (Christmas toys) held a special place in the history of Soviet toys. Their production dates from 1934, when Stalin allowed the celebration of the New Year. In the 1950s, these toys were cucumbers, eggplants, tomatoes, carrots, grapes, and strawberries; in the 1960s – corn, spaceships, sputniks. An indispensable item on the Soviet New Year tree was a red five-point star. Stuffed animals and characters from Soviet cartoons enjoyed enormous popularity with Soviet children. With the collapse of the Soviet Union, most toys sold at stores are imported; particularly popular are Barbie, Lego, and characters from American cartoons and films.

See also: educational system, Soviet; folk art; games; holidays, Soviet

ELENA OMELCHENKO

track and field

Track and field in Russia originated with an amateur sportsmen's club established in the St. Petersburg suburbs in 1888. The first national championship was held in 1908, and the Olympic debut of a national team occurred in 1912.

In the second half of the twentieth century Soviet track-and-field athletes had great success: they consistently achieved good results at the Olympics, particularly the female team, which generally won the most medals. Traditionally the most prestigious track-and-field sports in Russia have been jumps (especially high jump) and running disciplines (particularly sprints and medium distances). The most popular Russian athlete of the twentieth century was high-jumper Valerii Brumel, who broke American athletes' long period of championships by beating six world records in 1961–63 and establishing the 'sky' record of 2 m, 28 cm. Other cult figures of Soviet track and field were Valerii Borzov, who won both short-distance races at the 1972 Olympics; triple jumper and three-time Olympic champion V. Saneev; and Ukrainian pole vault jumper S. Bubka, who still holds the world record. The most significant success in Russian track and field at the 2004 Olympics was Iurii Borzakovskii's gold medal in the 800m race and Elena Isinbaeva's victory in pole vaulting.

See also: Brumel, Valerii; sports, post-Soviet; sports, Soviet

ALEXANDER LEDENEV

traditions and customs

Contemporary Russian traditions and customs constitute a blend of old and new rituals, religious and secular holidays, pagan and modern beliefs. The most popular Russian national holidays include New Year, which many celebrate on both 1 and 14 January (the latter was New Year Day in the Julian calendar used in Russia before 1918); 23 February – Soldier's Day, which replaced Soviet Army Day; 8 March – Women's Day (women are usually given flowers, cards, and gifts); 9 May – Victory Day, to commemorate victims of World War II (people place flowers and wreaths on wartime graves, organize ceremonies for veterans); 12 June – Independence Day, the newest holiday, commemorating adoption of the Russian Federation's 1991 Declaration of Sovereignty. Easter, added recently as an official holiday, is widely celebrated with cakes and painted eggs; 7

November is still celebrated as the anniversary of the October Revolution (1917); Shrovetide or Pancake Week (the last week of February) is devoted to the pagan Maslennitsa, when Russians make pancakes and organize activities in parks to welcome spring. Many Russians celebrate Green Saturday (also known as Saturday of Remembrance of the Dead), which precedes Pentecost Sunday, when ancestral graves are visited and decorated with flowers, wreaths or green branches, and the repose of ancestors' souls are prayed for. 1 September is a holiday signifying the start of the academic year; school children bring flowers to their teachers. During Soviet times, St. Nicholas was replaced with the image of Father Frost (*Ded Moroz*) and the Christmas tree is decorated on New Year's Eve (Russians still celebrate Christmas on 7 January, to keep pace with the Julian date for New Year).

Church weddings and baptisms, suppressed in Soviet times, have become widespread again. Newlyweds no longer feel obliged to follow the Soviet custom of visiting the Tomb of the Unknown Soldier.

Several important traditions relate to the death of friends and relatives, who are commemorated nine and forty days after death. A Soviet and post-Soviet tradition is the commemoration of births and deaths of famous Russian writers, especially Aleksandr Pushkin (1799–1837), entailing pilgrimages to the writers' houses and apartments, transformed into museums.

Traditions that are still operative and inseparable from paganism and superstitions include the following: When setting off on a journey, Russians sit for a few moments on a suitcase or chair, indicating the desire to return home. One should avoid a black cat, associated with bad luck, especially if it crosses one's path, and should not shake hands or kiss across the threshold of a home, to avoid arguments or quarrels with the host. On entering a Russian home, visitors take off shoes and put on slippers. Bouquets to friends and relatives must comprise an odd numbers of flowers; an even number is appropriate for funerals and graves. Unsuitable gifts include handkerchiefs, mirrors, and sharp objects. Whistling indoors is avoided, to prevent all the money in the house from flying out of the window.

See also: holidays, post-Soviet; holidays, Russian Orthodox; holidays, Soviet; Pushkin, Aleksandr; superstitions, Russian; tapochki; women

Further reading

Bondarenko, E. O. (1993) *Prazdniki khristianskoi Rusi: russkii narodnyi pravoslavnyi kalendar,* Kaliningrad: Kaliningradskoe knizhnoe izdatelstvo.
Chamberlain, L. (1996) *The Festive Food of Russia,* London: Kyle Cathie.
Sandler, S. (2004) *Russia's Myth of a National Poet,* Stanford, CA: Stanford University Press.

ALEXANDRA SMITH

transportation, inner city

The Soviet period, starting from the 1920s, witnessed a monopoly on public transportation in Russia's cities. During the five-year plans, public transportation served the task of bringing workers, in snowballing numbers, to state-owned factories that rapidly multiplied. Initially, the tram and the trolleybus carried most urban passengers. With the acceleration of urban sprawl in the late 1950s, the bus dominated the city streets. In 2002, the year of the first post-Soviet population census, 1,274 Russian cities had a municipal bus system, 68 cities had trams, and 89 had trolleybuses. These three branches of public transportation usually co-exist in major cities.

The saturation of streets by passenger carriers in Russian cities with over a million residents makes subways necessary, and the first was built in Moscow in 1935, with more lines added over the years. By 1995 six cities enjoyed the benefits of a subway system: Moscow, St. Petersburg, Ekaterinburg, Nizhnii Novgorod, and Samara. Cheliabinsk's plans to build a subway system have run into delays, with the completion date postponed from 2006 to 2010, then to 2020. The subway offers speedier transportation and the best comfort during Russia's long, severe winters.

Because public transportation was important in boosting industrialization, the Soviet state instituted artificially low, state-subsidized passenger fares, which continue and have expanded in the post-Soviet era; they belong to the social safety net that helps people adjust to a market economy. Russian city dwellers take for granted the cheapness of public transportation fares. Surveys in 2001–2003 show that an average family spends less on city public transportation than on either vegetables or dairy products.

Unfortunately, state subsidies mean that bureaucrats control this vital service. Though bureaucrats have to respond to the challenge of radically changed transportation needs in the post-Soviet city, the rule-bound and hierarchical nature of bureaucracy militates against innovation.

Until the 1990s, urban passenger flows were uncomplicated. The city was monocentric, and its workforce was rigidly bonded to state-provided jobs and housing. The state limited earnings, thereby keeping transportation mobility at low levels. This situation permitted Soviet planners to establish corridors in built-up areas and to prescribe public transportation routes.

The post-Soviet city, however, is polycentric, self-organizing, highly dynamic, and transportation-hungry because of the private sector's business activity. The private sector brings multiple jobs and unlimited earnings, which result in record-high transportation mobility. Most businesses are consumer-oriented; they have to optimize accessibility to the customer and thus frequently relocate and change outputs. For the private sector's entrepreneurs and employees, who realize that time is money, wasting time by using inherited public transportation routes is unacceptable. These legacy routes tend to radiate from the city centre (as the subway exemplifies) or from obsolete giant factories. Such routes are of little value for people in the private sector, whose profession requires movement from one booming peripheral borough to another. A mass infusion of automobiles into the city is vital for the private sector: the car mitigates the mismatch between new flows and the legacy routes of public transportation.

The Soviet worker accepted time waste in travel to work because similar and greater waste abounded – in poorly organized state jobs, in food lines, or in the pursuit of scarce consumer goods. Urban public transportation was cheap, but overcrowded, slow, and uncomfortable, but

Soviet overseers of urban transportation could ignore consumer complaints.

At the beginning of the twenty-first century, urban public transportation in Russia continues to operate in the developed space dominated by the physical planning of the Soviet era. Wide streets are few, mainly in more recent and peripheral urban boroughs. In the historical core of the city, vehicles of public transportation crawl and zigzag along one-way streets. In newer urban areas, they run for kilometres along fences that enclose spacious sites allocated to factories. At factory gates, workers are far from their destination, needing to walk a long way inside the vast industrial area to reach the shop floor. Public transportation similarly does not offer door-to-door passenger delivery. Housing complexes built in the Soviet period comprise closely spaced high-rise apartment buildings that public transportation vehicles cannot enter. At best, passengers may expect to find a bus stop at the corner of the complex. Typically, a long walk to a transportation stop is necessary, and most inner-city travel requires transfers or two modes of transportation, with unpredictably long waits at stations and stops.

In the first post-Soviet decades, adjustments in public transportation largely consist of selective amputation. In 1991–2001, the total number of passengers using public urban transportation declined by 3.4 per cent. The number of passengers on municipal buses declined by 24 per cent. The municipal taxicab lost nearly 98 per cent of its passengers. This branch of public transportation has practically disappeared, whereas the tram and the trolleybus showed increases in passengers of 23 per cent and 23 per cent, respectively. These changes result from the competing presence of the family car and the popularity of 'hitchhiking' – flagging down a private car and paying a price agreed upon on the spot.

By the end of the first post-Soviet decade, 2002, the number of family cars in Moscow had risen to 2.4 million, or one car per four residents. In St. Petersburg the ratio became one family car per seven residents. In older areas of Moscow the traffic jams owing to automobile traffic are approaching intolerable levels. Moscow ranks first by number of cars per hundred residents, Kaliningrad ranks second, and

the towns of the Moscow region share third place, with Vladivostok in fourth place and St. Petersburg in fifth.

Russian cities are slow to deploy solutions that in other countries harmonize the benefits of the family car with public transportation. Moscow, haltingly developing street-widening, is making some progress in this direction. Few cities dare to dream about the monorail or multi-level streets that have transformed, for example, booming commercial centres in China or South Korea.

See also: Ekaterinburg; Moscow; Nizhnii Novgorod (Gorkii); queue; shortages; St. Petersburg

YURI MEDVEDKOV AND OLGA MEDVEDKOV

transportation system

The transportation system in the Russian Federation includes the following kinds of transport: railway, motor, pipelines, waterways, and airways. The low density of the population and the economy, their uneven distribution, large distances (10,000 km from west to east, and 4,000 km north to south), the harsh climate in the north and northeast, and the isolation of certain regions – all characteristic of Russia – have made transport the most important means of structuring the enormous space, providing economic, cultural, political, and social reciprocity among its regions, and connecting parts of the country into a united whole.

Economic and cultural space in Russia is extremely dissimilar, and distribution of its population and economy very uneven, with 70 per cent of its inhabitants concentrated in the far west and south, the remaining 30 per cent dispersed in the north and east as multiple, small, isolated centres of pioneer development. Within the developed zone, the transportation network is very dense, and in the undeveloped zone it is minimal and in many areas absent. In general, the density of the transportation network in Russia is low compared to that in the developed countries (31 km of hard-surface motorways and 5 km of railway tracks per 1,000 sq km).

The share of each transport changed throughout the twentieth century; whereas railroad and internal waterway transport prevailed in the early decades, by 2001 railroads were transporting 40 per cent of the cargo, motor vehicles 21 per cent, pipelines 32 per cent, internal waterways 5 per cent, and sea and air 2 per cent. Patterns of passenger transportation likewise changed: in 1940 67 per cent travelled by railroad, 29 per cent by motor, 4 per cent by waterways, whereas in 2001 41 per cent travelled by railroad, 54 per cent by bus, 5 per cent by air, and none by sea or internal waterways. In the past decade Russia's transportation has transformed into an export-oriented and transit system. The major priorities in its development became the expansion of latitudinal international transit corridors from the Asian-Pacific region to Central-Eastern Europe, and the strengthening of export transportation outlets to Europe and Asia.

By the end of the twentieth century railroad transport had become the main mode of transport because its network covered all developed and even several weakly developed regions. The major latitudinal railway direction is Smolensk – Moscow – Urals – Omsk – Novosibirsk – Krasnoiarsk – Irkutsk – Khabarovsk – Vladivostok. The eastern part of the system, called Transsib, is duplicated by the Southern-Siberian Route in the south and the Baikal-Amur Route (BAM) in the north. Major meridian routes pass through Moscow or run parallel to the Urals and the Volga.

In economically developed areas, motor transport prevails over other kinds of transportation in local communications. Currently the network of motorways is the most developed in Russia, its length 5.4 times that of railroads. Extensive road construction in 1960–2000 in the European part of Russia and in the south of western Siberia has provided a framework of main motorways and generally solving the problem of bad roads. However, the absence of direct connecting roads still cuts off many northern areas (Yakutia, the Magadan and Tomsk oblast, the Krasnoiarsk region, and south of the Far East) from neighbouring regions. There are few quality high-speed motorways and few latitudinal motorways (unlike railroads) in Russia; most motorways are radial, leading to Moscow or St. Petersburg. Russia still lags behind developed countries in Europe, Northern America, and Eastern Asia in the number of cars on the road (in 2000, statistics showed 132 motor vehicles per 1,000 people in 2000, compared to 400–750 in developed countries).

Airlines have taken over long-distance transport and regular transport to remote and inaccessible regions. After the collapse of the USSR, 420 small air companies appeared, breaking the Soviet monopoly of Aeroflot. After the financial crises of 1998, their number was reduced to 247 (2001). Large air companies compete with one another particularly in snagging the routes to Siberia and the Far East.

Sea transportation remains the main agent in foreign trade. Of the 43 sea trade ports in Russia, the major ones are Novorossiisk, Nakhodka, St. Petersburg, Tuapse, Vostochnyi, Murmansk, and Vladivostok. The majority of the ports' waters freeze in winter, except for Murmansk and those on the Black Sea and the Sea of Japan. The 'northern delivery' of cargo (diesel fuel, coal, food) to ports of less developed regions in the Far North is executed during a short time of navigation with the help of eleven ice-breakers.

Pipeline transport provides industry and the population with cheap oil and gas fuel. The major route of main pipelines in Russia is from Western Siberia to the consumers in the west and south. The total length of pipelines has increased from 140,000 (1992) to 152,000 km (2001). In 2002 a new pipeline was constructed along the bottom of the Black Sea from Russia to Turkey. There are plans to build several export pipelines on the bottom of the Baltic Sea, from the Tomsk region to China, and from Sakhalin to Japan.

See also: Baltic Sea region; BAM (Baikal-Amur Railroad); Far East; Far North; Moscow; railroads; St. Petersburg; Siberia

Further reading

Lapidus B. M., Pekhterev F. S. and Tereshkina N. P. (2000) *Regionalistika*, Moscow: UMK MPS.

Sergei I. *Transport Rossii* (1998) Moscow: ASMO-Press.

Transport v Rossii (2002) *Statisticheskii sbornik*, Moscow: Goskomstat.

SERGEI TARKHOV

Tretiak, Vladislav Aleksandrovich

b. 25 April 1952, Orudevo

Hockey player

An outstanding goaltender for TsSKA and Team USSR, Tretiak won thirteen Soviet, nine European, and ten World Championships, and three Olympic gold medals (1972 and 1976, with Valerii Kharlamov, and 1984). He was the first Soviet-born player inducted into the Hockey Hall of Fame in Toronto (1989), and was voted 'Best Russian Hockey Player of the Twentieth Century' (2000). Since retiring from play in 1984, Tretiak has served as president of the International Sports Academy (Moscow) and as a goaltending consultant for the NHL's Chicago Blackhawks.

See also: hockey; Kharlamov, Valerii; TsSKA

RACHEL S. PLATONOV

Tretiakov Gallery (Tretiakovskaia galereia)

The State Tretiakov (Tretyakov) Gallery (*Tretiakovskaia galereia*) in Moscow houses the nation's primary collection of Russian art, enabling the public to view many acknowledged masterworks of Russian painting and sculpture from the oldest times to the present. Unlike most Russian collectors of their day, Pavel and Sergei Tretiakov, scions of a wealthy merchant family, preferred Russian to European masterpieces. In 1892, the year of Sergei's death, Pavel presented their collections to the city and people of Moscow. Viktor Vasnetsov's 1903 façade, itself a masterpiece of the Abramtsevo *style moderne*, serves the new and, in the 1990s, greatly expanded building.

The main building houses art through the early-twentieth century. Soviet and post-Soviet art is housed in a separate building, together with the Central House of Artists (*Tsentralnyi dom khudozhnikov*) several subway stops away.

See also: art galleries and exhibition halls; Moscow

EDWARD ALAN COLE

Tretiakov, Vitalii Tovievich

b. 2 January 1953, Moscow

Journalist, scholar

After graduation from the Moscow State University School of Journalism in 1976 Tretiakov worked at the news agency *Novosti* (News, 1976–88) and at the newspaper *Moskovskie novosti* (Moscow News, 1988–90) as columnist and deputy editor-in-chief under Egor Iakovlev. In 1990, he founded the first independent Russian newspaper *Nezavisimaia gazeta*, serving as its editor-in-chief from 1990 to 2001. Since 2001, he has not only been the host of the weekly television programme *Chto delat? Filosofskie besedy* (What Is to Be Done? Philosophical Conversations) on the *Kultura* (culture) channel, but also a professor at the International Journalism Department of the Moscow State Institute of International Relations (MGIMO), a member of the President's Council on Foreign and Defence Policy and of the board of directors of the Russian Association of International Scholars, and head of the survey company 'Vox popoli-t' (Vox Populus/Politics). Recipient of the TEFI Golden Pen and other awards, he has written 2000 articles in Russia and abroad and five books on Russian politics and journalism.

See also: Iakovlev, Egor; journalists, post-Soviet; Kultura channel; *Moskovskie novosti* (Moscow News); Moscow State Institute (University) of Foreign Relations; *Nezavisimaia gazeta* (Independent Newspaper)

NADEZHDA AZHGIKHINA

Trifonov, Iurii Valentinovich

b. 28 August 1925, Moscow; d. 28 March
1981, Moscow

Writer

Trifonov lost his father to the purges in 1937
and his mother to the GULag for years, an
experience central to his most important prose.
His career began with the orthodox *Studenty*
(*Students*, 1950), a novel that barely hinted at the
psychological depth of his 'Moscow trilogy',
novellas revealing fundamental moral collisions
via the details of everyday Soviet life. He
turned to the Terror in *Dom na naberezhnoi* (*The
House on the Embankment*, 1976) and *Vremia i
mesto* (*Time and Place*, 1981), and added a historical perspective in *Starik* (*The Old Man*,
1978). Though branded a conformist by some,
Trifonov managed to extend the boundaries of
what could be published within the Soviet
Union.

See also: GULag; literature, Soviet; Stalin, Iosif

JOSEPHINE WOLL

troika

In traditional Russian songs, *troika*, a form of the
word for 'three', meant a carriage with three
horses, normally used as a symbol of escape:
'*byla by tolko troika, da troika pobystrei*' ('if only I had
a *troika* and a faster one'). A famous passage
from Nikolai Gogol's *Mertvye dushi* (*Dead Souls*)
compared all of Russia to a speeding *troika*. Ironically, after the Bolshevik Revolution, the word
(as a 'threesome' or 'trio') came to signify a
group of three members of the secret police with
the right to investigate, arrest, judge and execute
'people's enemies'. The idea was introduced in
1918 by the decree of the Council of People's
Commissars, *Sotsialisticheskoe otechestvo v opasnosti*
(The Socialist Fatherland Is in Danger), which
gave the ChK (Cheka, the KGB's precursor)
extraordinary powers to fight 'enemy agents,
speculators, burglars, hooligans, antirevolu-
tionary agitators, German spies, saboteurs and
other parasites.' *Troika* is also an academic

grade, the equivalent of C or satisfactory performance.

See also: Federal Security Service

VLADIMIR PAPERNY

Troitskii, Artemii Kivovich

b. 16 June 1955, Iaroslavl, Russia

Music critic, journalist

In his childhood years in Prague, Troitskii grew
interested in rock'n'roll, then banned in the
USSR. After his move to Moscow, he became a
major figure in the Russian rock movement,
becoming the first Russian DJ (1972–74, at
MGU), organizing underground rock festivals,
and participating in various *samizdat* publications about Western music. In the 1990s he
organized the first Moscow jazz festival and
published the first slim history-encyclopedia of
Russian rock music (*Back in the USSR: The True
Story of Rock in Russia*, London: Omnibus, 1987).
For several years he was the editor-in-chief of
the Russian *Playboy*; since 1991, he has worked
as an editor of television music programmes. At
present his main occupation is radio and Internet journalism.

See also: rock music; samizdat

TATIANA SMORODINSKAYA

trophy art (trofeinoe iskusstvo)

Approximately 2.2 million artworks and about 3
million archival files that were removed from
defeated Germany as a form of what the USSR
considered reparation for the damage inflicted
on the USSR by the Nazi regime. Between 1955
and 1969, as a manifestation of its good will, the
Soviet Union returned to the German Democratic Republic the lion's share of the art
objects: more than 1,922,000 pieces of art (or
87.4 per cent of what had been taken) and
almost all archival files. Among the art treasures
were the paintings from the Dresden Art Gallery, with its Raphael's Sistine Madonna, a collection of works from the Berlin National

Gallery, the famous Pergam Altar, and masterpieces by Titian and Botticelli. Most of the remaining artifacts are monuments of numismatics (175,000 coins and medals) and archaeology, as well as approximately 55,000 paintings. Adopted in 1997 (despite two vetoes by President Yeltsin), the Trophy Art Law differentiates between art objects that originally had been looted by Nazi forces (and that can now be returned to their original owners) and other cultural valuables that are regarded as the property of the Russian Federation and not to be returned to former 'aggressor-countries'. The law was upheld in a subsequent decision of the Russian Constitutional Court.

See also: World War II (Great Patriotic War)

ALEXANDER DOMRIN

Troshin, Vladimir Konstantinovich

b. 15 May 1926, Mikhailovskii, Russia

Singer, actor

Troshin is best known for his 1955 recording of the legendary song *Podmoskovnye vechera* (Moscow Nights), which made him a star of the popular music style known as *estrada*. His numerous other hit songs since the 1950s include *Odinokaia garmon* (The Lonely Accordion) and *Rano ili pozdno* (Sooner or Later). An acclaimed performer even before *Podmoskovnye*, as a Moscow Art Theatre-trained stage actor, he received the Stalin Prize in 1951 for his performance as the jester in Shakespeare's *Twelfth Night*. Troshin's many film roles include Lenin, Voroshilov, and Winston Churchill.

See also: *Podmoskovnye vechera* (Moscow Nights); Moscow Art Theatre; popular music, Soviet

SETH GRAHAM

Trus, Balbes, Byvalyi

These comic film characters, a Soviet version of *The Three Stooges*, became phenomenally popular because their adventures eschewed official satirical didacticism and recalled *lubok* (folk cartoon)

narratives. Leonid Gaidai created the heroes for his slapstick short *Pes Barbos i neobychainyi kross* (*Dog Barbos and the Unusual Race*, 1961). Georgii Vitsyn played *Trus* (*Coward*), Iurii Nikulin played *Balbes* (*Dumb Ass*), and Evgenii Morgunov – *Byvalyi* (*The Experienced One*). These three appeared in Gaidai's full-length films *Samogonshchiki* (*The Moonshiners*, 1962), *Operatsiia 'Y' i drugie prikliucheniia Shurika* (*Operation Y and Other Adventures of Shurik*, 1965), and *Kavkazskaia plennitsa ili novye prikliucheniia Shurika* (*Captive of the Caucasus or the New Adventures of Shurik*, 1966). The Soviet Three Stooges made cameo appearances in the comedies of Eldar Riazanov and Evgenii Karelov.

See also: Gaidai, Leonid; Riazanov, Eldar

ALEXANDER PROKHOROV

tselina

This term, generally translated as 'virgin soil', refers to soil that has never been farmed. In 1954–60 the steppes of Kazakhstan, the Volga Region (*Povolzhe*), Southern Siberia, the Urals, and the Far East – in total 42 million hectares, equal to the combined territory of Iowa, Alabama, and Illinois – were intensively tilled for grain crops to combat the Soviet Union's increasing food shortage, caused by Khrushchev's short-sighted agricultural policies. Previously this territory had been used mainly for cattle grazing. This massive endeavour was undertaken by 500,000 Komsomol members, soldiers, and convicts. Besides cultivating, they constructed new state farms (*kolkhozy*), roads, and towns, including Astana, today the capital of Kazakhstan, then called Tselinograd. The project, directed by Khrushchev, caused environmental disasters. Nevertheless, former *tselina* continues to supply 40 per cent of Russia's grain yield, and one-third of the nation's meat and dairy goods.

See also: collective farms; Far East; Kazakhstan; Siberia; Urals; Volga region

TATYANA LEDENEVA

Tselkov, Oleg Nikolaevich

b. 15 July 1934, Moscow

Artist

A highly influential nonconformist artist. After graduating from the Moscow Secondary School of Art in 1953, he studied further at the Art Institute in Minsk and the Repin Academy of Arts in Leningrad, only to be expelled from both institutions. He exhibited at the 1957 Sixth World Youth Festival, and in 1965 staged a solo exhibition at the Kurchatov Institute of Atomic Physics. His unsettling images of de-humanized individuals with often brutal, mask-like features proved highly controversial and in 1970 his solo exhibition at the Central Club of Soviet Architects was closed after just fifteen minutes. Tselkov emigrated to Paris in 1977, where he continues to work as a successful artist.

See also: art, nonconformist

MIKE O'MAHONY

Tsereteli, Zurab

b. 4 January 1934, Tbilisi, Georgia

Sculptor and Painter

Tsereteli is a well-known sculptor who presides over several artistic and cultural organizations in Russia (including the Russian Academy of Arts) and actively supports UNESCO. The favourite artist of Moscow Mayor Iurii Luzhkov, Tsereteli has won several important public art competitions in the city since 1992. As a result, his large, controversial, and much-criticized works dominate Moscow's monumental landscape. These include a 60m statue of Peter the Great on the banks of the Moscow River and the 141.8m central monument in Victory Park (Park Pobedy) at Poklonnaia Gora.

See also: Luzhkov, Iurii; Moscow

BENJAMIN FOREST AND JULIET JOHNSON

Tsoi, Viktor Robertovich

b. 21 June 1962, Leningrad; d. 15 August 1990, near Riga

Musician, songwriter, actor

Tsoi was the leader of the legendary Leningrad rock band Kino from 1982 until his death in an automobile accident. Of Korean heritage, he attended art school before dropping out to devote his time to music. He was a prominent figure in the underground rock scene of the early 1980s, and his defiant, romantic image and lyrics made him a youth icon during perestroika. He also played the lead in Rashid Nugmanov's film *Igla* (*The Needle*). Fans still gather at certain sites in St. Petersburg and Moscow to pay tribute to Tsoi and sing his songs.

See also: Kino; perestroika and glasnost; rock music

SETH GRAHAM

TsSKA

The Central Sports Club of the Army (*Tsentralnyi sportnivnyi klub armii,*) TsSKA is one of the most popular sport clubs in the country. The famous Red Army hockey team won nationals twenty times. The team's charismatic figures were Vsevolod Bobrov, Valerii Kharlamov, and Vladislav Tretiak. In 2005, the TsSKA football team won the UEFA Cup. Club colours are red and blue.

See also: sports clubs and teams

ALEXANDER LEDENEV

Tsvetkov, Aleksei

b. 2 February 1947, Stanislav, Ukraine

Writer

Poet, prose writer, essayist, and journalist Tsvetkov graduated from Moscow State University in journalism and history and completed a Ph.D. in Russian literature at the University of Michigan. In the early 1970s, Tsvetkov was a central figure of the unofficial poetic group *Moskovskoe vremia*. In 1974, he emigrated to the US. His poetry (*Sbornik pes dlia zhizni solo* [*Collection of Plays for Life Solo*, 1978]; *Sostoianie sna* [*Dream State*, 1981]; and *Edem* [*Eden*, 1985], all published by émigré publishing house Ardis) features lyrical and metaphysical notes, with a dose of irony. His knowledge of antiquity informs his recent lyrico-philosophical poem in prose (*Prosto golos* [*Just a Voice*, Moscow, 2002]). Tsvetkov has also worked for radio on Voice of America and Radio Free Europe.

See also: literature, émigré; Moscow State University; poetry, Soviet

ANN KOMAROMI

tundra

An ecological zone in Russia characterized by sparse vegetation, frozen soil, and extremely low temperatures. Tundra may be found in two locations: the polar regions of northern Russia near the Arctic Circle, and in high mountains (termed alpine tundra). The Russian Arctic tundra, which dominates an increasing area of Siberia as one moves eastward, hinders development owing to difficulties in building on the permafrost, a layer of soil that remains frozen in the summer. When the layer above the permafrost melts in springtime, moisture cannot drain away, and marshy areas form; the resulting temperature changes and unevenness in the soil can cause buildings to sink or lean and their foundations to crack.

See also: Siberia

DAVID J. GALLOWAY

Turkmenistan (Turkmenia)

A country in Central Asia that used to be one of the fifteen republics of the Soviet Union, Turkmenistan shares borders with Kazakhstan, Uzbekistan, Afghanistan, and Iran, and borders the Caspian Sea. In 2004, Turkmenistan's population numbered nearly 5 million, 85 per cent of whom were ethnic Turkmens, a Sunni Muslim ethnic group who speak a Turkic language called Turkmen. Ashgabat (Ashkhabad) is the capital of Turkmenistan, with a multi-ethnic population of about 800,000.

The territory of Turkmenistan was taken over by the Russian Empire during the second half of the nineteenth century. The Turkmen Soviet Socialist Republic was set up in 1925, and was the poorest Soviet republic. By the end of the Soviet period, however, the literacy rate in Turkmenistan was 98 per cent and the country had a developed resource extraction sector. Turkmenistan became independent from the Soviet Union in October 1991. Since Turkmenistan is mostly desert, the economy depends on its natural resources, especially its substantial oil and gas reserves. Turkmenistan was also a major cotton exporter until its harvests began to collapse in the early twenty-first century.

Turkmenistan's president-for-life, Saparmurat Niiazov, was elected in 1990 and after independence, began building an elaborate cult of personality, calling himself Turkmenbashi, or leader of the Turkmen. Turkmenistan became an authoritarian state known for its repression and lack of economic reform, with Turkmenbashi determining all governmental policies, many of which were detrimental to the country's educational, cultural, and international status. Even though Turkmenistan's Russian citizens suffered under his rule, relations with Russia remained good because of the pipeline that connected Turkmenistan's natural gas supplies with Russia's consumers.

See also: Central Asia; cult of personality; Kazakhstan; natural resources; USSR; Uzbekistan

LAURA ADAMS

tushenka

Tinned, stewed meat. Particularly during the Soviet period, it was one of the cheapest forms of prepared food, provided as a ration in the armed forces and favoured by students, campers, and travellers. Among the older generation, it is still associated with Lend Lease as one of the products received from the US during and after World War II.

See also: World War II (Great Patriotic War)

MICHELE BERDY

Tvardovskii, Aleksandr Trifonovich

b. 21 June, 1910, Zagore, Smolensk oblast; d. 18 December, 1971, Krasnaia Pakhra, Moscow oblast

Writer, editor

Tvardovskii's reputation rests on his wartime and post-war poetry and on the vital role that his editorship of *Novyi mir* played during the Khrushchev-era Thaw. Despite his 'kulak' background, the soldier hero of his most significant literary work – the wartime serialized poem *Vasilii Terkin* – ensured Tvardovskii's popular appeal and his good reputation in Party circles.

After Stalin's death, Tvardovskii's editorship of *Novyi mir* proved crucial to the Thaw. The publication of caustic criticism of Stalinist literature by Vladimir Pomerantsev and Fedor Abramov cost him the editorship in 1954. Yet he remained one of the most celebrated of Soviet poets, and his own works, *Za daliu dal* (*Distance beyond Distance*) and *Terkin na tom svete* (*Terkin in the Other World*), once published, were hailed as courageous attempts to rethink the Stalinist past. Successful negotiations during his second term as editor to publish Aleksandr Solzhenitsyn's *Odin den Ivana Denisovicha* (*One Day in the Life of Ivan Denisovich*) in *Novyi mir* in 1962 detonated the Thaw's most significant debate about Stalinism. As Solzhenitsyn later argued, though Tvardovskii was too ensconced in Party politics to be a dissident, his ability to move between official and unofficial circles ultimately did much to expand the liberalization of the post-Stalin years.

See also: Khrushchev, Nikita; *Novyi mir*; Solzhenitsyn, Aleksandr; Thaw; thick journals

POLLY JONES

U

Uchitel, Aleksei Efimovich

b. 31 August 1951, Leningrad

Film director

A professional cameraman, Uchitel started his career as a documentary film-maker. His best-known documentary, *Rock* (1987), examines the Soviet underground music movement. Uchitel's critically acclaimed fictional films, often scripted by Dunia Smirnova, reveal his desire to penetrate the façade of Russian cultural and historical myths. His films *Mania Zhizeli* (*Gisele's Mania*, 1995) and *Dnevnik ego zheny* (*His Wife's Diary*, 2000) reconstruct the private lives of the ballerina Olga Spesivtseva and the writer Ivan Bunin, respectively. The film *Kosmos kak predchuvstvie* (*Dreaming of Space*, 2005) investigates the triumphant epoch of Iurii Gagarin through the prism of everyday life in a provincial town. Different in style and content, his *Progulka* (*Stroll*, 2003) resuscitates the old myths as it depicts the incessant wandering of young people around twenty-first-century St. Petersburg.

See also: ballet, Soviet; film, documentary; Gagarin, Iurii; rock music; St. Petersburg

IRINA MAKOVEEVA

U.E.

Short for *uslovnye edinitsy*, or conditional units, usually equal to US dollars (or euros). In post-Communist Russia they have served as price anchors for some services and goods (usually imported) because of the perceived instability of hard currencies. Actual prices in rubles are calculated on the basis of the currency exchange rate on the day of purchase. The U.E. therefore allows for greater price stability.

See also: economic system, post-Soviet

ALYA GUSEVA

Ugarov, Mikhail Iurevich

b. 23 January 1956, Arkhangelsk

Playwright, screenwriter, director, novelist

Ugarov began as an actor, then literary director, in the provinces. After moving to Moscow, he wrote over a dozen subtle, literate plays in the 1990s that often were staged by the Osobniak Theatre in St. Petersburg, but ignored in the Russian capital. His breakthrough occurred in 2002, when he directed *Smert Ivana Ilicha* (*The Death of Ivan Ilich*), his own adaptation of Ivan Goncharov's classic novel *Oblomov*. That same year he and his wife, Elena Gremina, founded Teatr.doc, a basement theatre that had significant influence, showcasing experimental plays in the so-called documentary or verbatim genre.

See also: drama, post-Soviet; Gremina, Elena; theatre, post-Soviet

JOHN FREEDMAN

Ukraine

Situated in Eastern Europe, the Ukrainian Republic covers 603,700 sq km and is the second largest country in Europe after Russia. Ukraine borders on Russia, Belarus, Moldova, Slovakia, Romania, Hungary, and Poland; it faces Georgia, Bulgaria, and Turkey from the sea. The republic's population is 48.5 million, of which 67.2 per cent live in urban areas (2001). Ukraine is a multi-ethnic state. Its population consists of 37.541 million ethnic Ukrainians, 8.334 million Russians, 275,000 Belorussians, 258,000 Moldavians, and ethnic minorities such as Crimean Tatars, Bulgarians, Hungarians, Jews, Poles, and Romanians. Ukrainian is the official language of the republic; 67.5 per cent of the population consider Ukrainian their mother tongue, and 30 per cent – Russian (2001). The largest religious groups are Russian and Ukrainian Orthodox Christians.

The country, with Kiev (2.6 million people) as its capital, consists of twenty-four oblasts and the autonomous republic of the Crimea. The head of state is a president, elected by secret ballot for a five-year term. The supreme council (*verkhovna rada*) is the highest legislative body of the republic.

Ninety-five per cent of the Ukrainian territory is steppe, sparsely covered with forests; the rest is the Carpathian Mountains in the south-west (2061m above sea level) and the Crimean Mountains (1545m above sea level) in the south. The climate is moderate and mostly continental, while the southern coast of the Crimea has a Mediterranean climate. The coldest month of the year is January; the hottest, July. Average winter temperatures are 7–8° C below zero in the north and 2–4°C above zero in the south; average summer temperatures are 18–19°C in the north and 23–24°C in the south. Ukraine's major rivers are the Dnieper, the southern Bug, the Severskii Donets, Dnestr, and Danube. The Dnieper divides the country into left-bank Ukraine (east of the river) and right-bank Ukraine (west of the river). In the south, Ukraine meets the Black Sea and the Sea of Azov.

History

The earliest inhabitation in Ukraine dates back to the Stone Age (*c.* 300,000 BCE). In the first millennium BCE, southern Ukraine was populated by the Cimmerians, tribes of Iranian descent. They were conquered by the Scythians, nomads from Central Asia, whose state lasted until the second century CE. Greek city-states existed on the coast from the seventh century BCE, some of them united into the Bosporan kingdom in the fifth century BCE. The Romans took over the Greek colonies in the first century CE, but had to abandon them to nomadic invaders in the second century. The Sarmatians, the Goths, the Huns, the Khazars, and the Greeks of Byzantium have left traces of their cultures in the Ukrainian south. The Polianians, an advanced Slavic tribe from central Ukraine, founded Kiev in the sixth century CE. The Varangians, warriors from Scandinavia, conquered the Polianians' territories and established the foundations of Kievan Rus, a powerful Slavic state that flourished from the ninth until the twelfth century. Russians, Ukrainians, and Belorussians descend from this state. Orthodox Christianity became the state religion of Rus in 988. In the twelfth century, Rus disintegrated into a number of princedoms that became subjects to the Mongol invasions in the thirteenth century and were conquered by the Grand Duchy of Lithuania and Poland in the fourteenth century. Seceding from the Golden Horde, the Crimean Tatars founded their khanate in the Crimea and in 1458 became vassals of the Ottoman Empire. In the sixteenth century, runaway serfs who called themselves Cossacks (*kozak* means 'a free man' in Turkic) formed their own state, Zaporozhian Sich, on the banks of the Dnieper River. In 1654, Bohdan Khmelnytsky (leader of the Zaporozhian Host, 1648–57) signed the Pereiaslav Treaty establishing an alliance of the Left-Bank Ukraine and Muscovy in their struggle against Poland. By the end of the eighteenth century, Russia had absorbed Ukraine in its entirety and annexed the Crimea from Turkey. In order to crush Ukrainian nationalism, Russian authorities banned Ukrainian in schools and media in the second half of the nineteenth century. After the October Revolution, the Ukrainian struggle for independence resulted in the establishment of the Ukrainian National Republic, the Ukrainian State, and the Western Ukrainian National Republic (1917–22). After the Civil War, the

Ukrainian Soviet Socialist Republic, proclaimed in 1917, was re-established and became part of the USSR (1922). During Stalinist collectivization, 6 million Ukrainians died in a famine (1932–33), and millions were executed or sent to labour camps during the purges (1937–39). According to the Molotov–Ribbentrop Pact (1939), territories in Western Ukraine seceded to Poland in 1920–21 became part of Soviet Ukraine. During World War II, Ukraine was the site of severe battles (Kiev, Odessa, Kerch, Sevastopol). In 1954, in honour of the tercentenary of the Pereiaslav Treaty, the Crimea was transferred from Russian control to Ukrainian jurisdiction. In July 1990, Ukraine declared sovereignty from the USSR and in 1991 gained its independence.

Economy

Ukraine is a developed industrial country. Its major industries are ferrous and nonferrous metals production, coal mining, production of machinery and transport equipment, and chemical production. Ukraine is also a large producer of electric power. With 50 per cent of the territory covered with fertile black soil, Ukraine has always been an important centre of agriculture. During the Soviet period, it had the reputation of being 'the breadbasket of the USSR'. Ukraine grows wheat, rye, barley, maize, buckwheat and other grain, vegetables, and fruit. Tourism is an important part of economy in the Carpathians and in the Ukrainian south. Odessa and the Crimea are traditional holiday destinations for domestic and international tourists. The country's major trade partners are Russia, Belarus, and the countries of Central Europe. Ukraine has a developed infrastructure, an efficient system of railway, roads, and highways. The major sea ports are Odessa, Kherson, Ismail, Mariupol, and Kerch. Ukrainian currency is called the *hryvna*.

See also: Belarus; collective farms; Cossacks; Crimea; economic system, Soviet; Georgia; Jews; Kiev; Moldova; Odessa; Russian Federation; Russian Orthodoxy; Tatars; USSR; vacations, Soviet and post-Soviet; World War II (Great Patriotic War)

Further reading

Harasymiw, B. (2002) *Post-Communist Ukraine*, Edmonton: Canadian Institute of Ukrainian Studies Press.
Hrushevsky, M. (1997–) *History of Ukraine-Rus'*, trans. M. Skorupsky; A. Poppe and F. E. Sysyn (eds), Edmonton: Canadian Institute of Ukrainian Studies Press. 10 vols.
Kubijovyc, V. (ed.) (1984; 1993) *Encyclopedia of Ukraine*, Toronto: University of Toronto Press, 5 vols.
Magocsi, P. (1996) *A History of Ukraine*, Toronto: University of Toronto Press.

ELENA BARABAN

Ulanova, Galina Sergeevna

b. 26 December 1909 [8 January 1910], St. Petersburg; d. 21 March 1998, Moscow

Ballerina

One of the greatest dancers of the twentieth century, Ulanova came from a ballet family and in 1928 joined what later became the Kirov Ballet, where she performed leading roles (Odette/Odile in *Swan Lake*, Aurora in *Sleeping Beauty*, Giselle in *Giselle*) until moving to Moscow to become a soloist at the Bolshoi Ballet in 1944. At the Bolshoi, she became closely identified with the ballets of Sergei Prokofiev (*Romeo and Juliet, Cinderella, The Stone Flower*), and her lyrical performance as Juliet on the 1959 Bolshoi tour of the United States caused a sensation. After retirement in 1960, she taught at the Bolshoi.

See also: ballet dancers, Bolshoi Theatre; Prokofiev, Sergei

HARLOW ROBINSON

Ulianov, Mikhail Aleksandrovich

b. 20 November 1927, Tara, Omsk oblast

Actor, director, writer

Ulianov began his stage and screen acting career in 1950. Among more than fifty film roles, several stand out: the stalwart geologist Dmitrii in *Dom, v kotorom ia zhivu* (*The House I Live In*, 1957), the authoritarian Egor Trubnikov, doggedly determined to revive his collective farm from its post-war ruin (*Predsedatel* [*The Chairman*], 1964); the over-the-hill playwright in *Tema* (*The Theme*, 1979). In 1972 he directed his first film, *Samyi poslednii den* (*The Final Day*), in which he also starred, and he has often played historical figures, such as Marshall Zhukov in *Esli vrag ne sdaetsia* (*If the Enemy Doesn't Surrender*, 1983). In 1987, Ulianov became director of the Vakhtangov Theatre. Lenin Prize (1966), USSR State Prize (1983), People's Artist of the USSR (1969).

See also: Vakhtangov Theatre

JOSEPHINE WOLL

Ulitskaia, Liudmila Evgenievna

b. 23 February 1943, Davlekanovo, Bashkiria (Bashkortostan)

Writer

A novelist and short story writer, Ulitskaia was born in Bashkiria (Bashkortostan, Russian Federation) and received a degree in biology from Moscow State University. Prior to her literary career, which began in her late forties, Ulitskaia worked as a geneticist before becoming the literary director of the Moscow Jewish Theatre. In her interviews, she explains that her writing is a continuation of the study of human nature – merely from a different perspective.

Ulitskaia's lyrical, elegant prose continues the realist tradition in Russian literature, providing deep psychological insight into human relationships and following the characters' spiritual quests. Her œuvre focuses on the historical destiny of the scientific and artistic intelligentsia formed during the Soviet era, and the existential problems of the individual amidst various social surroundings.

Ulitskaia's best-known works include *Sonechka* (1993), a novella that tightly intertwines the heroine's private life with Soviet history, which won her the French Medici Prize; *Medea i ee deti* (*Medea and Her Children*, 1997), a family chronicle that put her on the short list for a Booker Prize; and *Veselye pokhorony* (*The Funeral Party*), a novella based on Ulitskaia's observations of Russian-speaking émigrés in the United States; and *Kazus Kukotskogo* (*The Kukotskii Case*, 2000), for which she became the first female recipient of the Booker in 2001.

One of Russia's most prominent contemporary writers, Ulitskaia has seen her works translated into over twenty languages.

See also: intelligentsia; awards, literary, post-Soviet; literature, post-Soviet

OLGA PARTAN

underground economy

The term describes practices of production and distribution of goods and services that started actively emerging after World War II and became especially pervasive during the period of Stagnation. A classified study conducted in the Soviet Union in 1975 established that about 20 million people took part in various forms of illegal economic activity (Neznansky, 1985: 49). The illegality of the underground economy (also known as the 'second economy' and later as the 'shadow economy') was rooted in two main principles of Soviet socialism. The heavily centralized Soviet economy monopolized not only the material sources necessary for production of commodities, but also the networks of distribution through which goods could be delivered to consumers. Independent production and selling of consumer goods were prohibited.

Despite its planned nature, the centralized economy routinely failed to meet increasing consumer demands (and planned goals). The underground economy was a reaction to this economy of shortages: it diverted material resources originally allocated for planned projects in order to fulfil private needs (e.g. construction, production of clothing and shoes, dental services, etc.). Given the centralized nature of the Soviet economy, underground entrepreneurs could sustain their activity only through close and mutually profitable cooperation with representatives of the official economy.

Bribed party and state officials (*nomenklatura*) could re-allocate the large-scale flow of resources in the 'right' direction. In turn, managers of stores, warehouses, depots, etc. for extra payment could provide underground entrepreneurs with raw materials and goods instead of selling them through official channels. This 'theft of state property', as it was traditionally defined in court documents, was often accompanied by a second, political, charge. Organized production that involved labour of hired workers was considered exploitation for the 'purpose of private enrichment' and was condemned as incompatible with the main principles of the socialist state. When during perestroika private cooperatives (*kooperativy*) and later small enterprises were allowed to exist, the underground economy started its slow and irreversible legalization.

See also: economic system, Soviet; five-year plan; nomenklatura; perestroika and glasnost; shortages; Stagnation; World War II (Great Patriotic War)

Further reading

Humphrey, C. (2002) *The Unmaking of Soviet Life: Everyday Economies After Socialism*, Ithaca, NY: Cornell University Press.
Lovell, S., Ledeneva, A. and Rogachevskii, A. (eds) (2000) *Bribery and Blat in Russia: Negotiating Reciprocity from the Middle Ages to the 1990s*, New York: St. Martin's Press.
Neznansky, F. (1985) *The Prosecution of Economic Crimes in the USSR, 1954–1984*, Falls Church, VA: Delphic Associates.

SERGUEI OUSHAKINE

Union of Rightist Forces (Soiuz pravykh sil; SPS)

Political party

A political party, formed in 1999, when many leading Russian Westernizers and free-market reformers decided to unite their respective parties. Founders included Boris Nemtsov, Irina Khakamada, Egor Gaidar and Anatoloii Chubais. Iabloko and SPS – the successor to another such union party, *Pravoe Delo* (Right Cause) – are the two Russian parties most committed to Western-style constitutional democracy, but SPS has closer associations with Yeltsin-era economic reforms and privatization. Whereas in 1999 SPS won twenty-nine seats in the federal Duma, in the 2003 legislative elections it managed to win only two.

See also: Chubais, Anatolii; Duma; Gaidar, Egor; Iabloko; Khakamada, Irina; Nemtsov, Boris; Westernizers; Yeltsin, Boris

DAVID HUNTER SMITH

Union of Soviet Socialist Republics

See USSR

Union of Theatre Workers

The Union of Theatre Workers of the Russian Federation (STD, formerly VTO) was founded in 1887 to provide Russian actors with professional support and social benefits. Today the Union still serves the same mission, organizing local and international theatre festivals and conferences and providing legal and social services to its members. Union members have access to exclusive holiday spas, clubs, libraries, and retirement homes. The Union consists of seventy-four regional branches located throughout the Russian Federation, and its members include actors, directors, playwrights, stage designers, theatre critics, educators, and other theatre professionals working for musical, drama, and puppet theatres.

See also: theatre, post-Soviet; theatre, Soviet; unions, creative, post-Soviet; unions, creative, Soviet

OLGA PARTAN

unions, creative, post-Soviet

Since the collapse of the USSR, while the creative unions that came into being during the Soviet period have continued to function, all have been tasked with the difficult problem of how to remake themselves from the institutions of control and distribution of privilege they were during the Soviet period into genuine professional organizations in a period when the institutional structure of culture as a whole is undergoing a profound transformation. The degree of success each union has enjoyed in the process of transition has depended on a variety of factors. Not surprisingly, the Writers' Union, the oldest and most powerful of the Soviet unions, left fragmented and deeply divided by battles between reformers and conservatives in the late glasnost period, has suffered the greatest loss of prestige and relevance. The once monolithic and hegemonic union has splintered into 'baby' unions. The struggle for resources pits the better funded and more conservative Fraternity of Writers' Unions (*Sodruzhestvo pisatelskikh soiuzov*) against the more liberal Union of Russian Writers (*Soiuz rossiiskikh pisalatei*), which collaborates with the Russian Pen Centre. The Moscow Writers' Union (*Moskovskii soiuz pisatelei*), is allied with neither of the national unions and works closely with the Moscow Government. The Trade Union of Russian Writers (*Profsoiuz pisatelei Rossii*) was founded in the post-Soviet period to defend writers' rights. Other unions, either because they are younger or more successfully initiated reform during perestroika, have fared better. The Architects' Union, for instance, in a manner consistent with its role in the vanguard of reform during the glasnost period, has adopted a particularly active stance in defending its members' professional interests. Still the overall picture remains disorderly. There are many organizations, but no system, leaving some professionals, including many in the television industry, with no union dedicated to their interests.

See also: perestroika and glasnost; unions, creative, Soviet

CATHERINE NEPOMNYASHCHY

unions, creative, Soviet

The Soviet creative unions (*tvorcheskie soiuzy*) were among the most distinctive of the bureaucratic controls imposed on cultural production by the Soviet government. The basis for the creation of these institutions was laid by the 23 April 1932 decree of the Central Committee of the Communist Party, 'On the Restructuring of Literary and Artistic Organizations' (*O perestroike literaturno-khudozhestvennykh organizatsii*), which announced the liquidation of independent literary groupings and the creation of a single union for all Soviet writers. It called for the establishment of analogous unions for practitioners across the spectrum of the arts. Membership in Soviet creative unions ultimately embraced writers, translators, composers, architects, artists, journalists, film-makers, and scholars and critics of literature and the arts. The Writers' Union and the Unions of Composers and Architects were established in 1932, immediately in the wake of the decree. The All-Union Soviet Artists' Union (1957), the Journalists' Union (1959), and the Cinematographers' Union (1965) came into being only in the post-Stalin period, when the increasingly rigid bureaucratization of Soviet cultural life brought the union structures into their own. The unions regimented Soviet culture by disciplining wayward artists and allotting privileges to those who conformed to the dictates of the cultural authorities. The Writers' Union remained the most powerful of the creative unions, expelling from its ranks many of the most prominent and talented writers of the Soviet period, including Anna Akhmatova, Mikhail Zoshchenko, Boris Pasternak, Andrei Siniavskii, Aleksandr Solzhenitsyn, and Vladimir Voinovich. The 1964 trial and subsequent exile of Iosif Brodskii for 'parasitism' and for claiming the profession of poet without being a member of the Writers' Union dramatically demonstrated the union's hegemony in the sphere of Soviet literature. Voinovich's novella *The Fur Hat* (1988) presents a biting satire on the hierarchy of privilege in the Writers' Union.

During the Gorbachev era, the unions became frontlines in the battle between those seeking to preserve the controls and privileges of the old order and those pursuing the liberalization of Soviet cultural institutions. The latter sought to transform the creative unions into genuinely professional organization designed to protect members' professional interests. The pace of reform varied from union to union;

several new unions arose as a result of the impulse to cultural reform, most notably the Union of Theatre Workers (*Soiuz teatralnykh deiatelei*). With the collapse of the Soviet Union and the attendant loss of government subsidies, the status of all of the unions declined sharply, and the once-powerful Writers' Union fragmented into competing and mutually hostile 'baby' unions.

See also: Brodskii, Iosif; Communist Party; Pasternak, Boris; perestroika and glasnost; Siniavskii, Andrei; Solzhenitsyn, Aleksandr; unions, creative, post-Soviet; unions, professional; Voinovich, Vladimir

Further reading

Condee, N. and Padunov, V. (1988) 'The Frontiers of Soviet Culture: Reaching the Limits?' *The Harriman Institute Forum*, 1, 5 (May): 1–8.

Garrard, J. and Garrard, C. (1990) *Inside the Soviet Writers' Union*, New York: The Free Press.

Nepomnyashchy, C. T. (1994) 'Perestroika and the Soviet Creative Unions', in J. O. Norman (ed.) *New Perspectives on Russian and Soviet Artistic Culture: Selected Papers from the Fourth World Congress for Soviet and East European Studies, Harrogate, 1990*, New York: St. Martin's Press.

Voinovich, V. (1989) *The Fur Hat*, trans. S. Brownsberger, San Diego, CA: Harcourt Brace Jovanovich.

CATHARINE NEPOMNYASHCHY

unions, professional

Unions became legal in Russia in 1905, but were harassed or subject to ban until 1917. When the tsarist government fell in 1917, unions again were legalized and an All-Russian Central Council of Trade Unions formed. At first, members freely elected union leaders. When the Communists came to power, they began taking control of unions. Unions resisted, but by 1922 Communist leaders had succeeded in subordinating unions to the Party and appointing their leaders. Party leaders insisted that unions limit their role to educating workers and stimulating worker productivity. Unions

could not conduct strikes or negotiate wage agreements. In 1933, the government allocated to unions the tasks of inspecting working conditions and distributing social benefits to workers. During World War II, unions helped mobilize the workforce for war production. Trade union bureaucrats were privileged members of the *nomenklatura*, but were not likely to rise to high Party positions.

After Stalin died, trade unions assumed some state planning functions. They acted as the Party's representatives within the workplace, ensuring that management did not exploit workers so much as to cause unrest but their chief role was to stimulate production through incentives and benefits. Soviet unions remained conservative when Gorbachev initiated reform in the 1980s. Their first major crisis came in 1989, as Russian miners went on strike and official unions took the government's side. When subsequently unions underwent reform, the newly-constituted General Confederation of Trade Unions (GCTU) was independent of Party and state and had more autonomy for regional branches. Despite these changes, the new structure's leaders remained loyal to the government during another wave of strikes in 1991. A new body had already begun forming in 1990, the Federation of Independent Trade Unions of Russia (FITUR). The August 1991 coup was a decisive event in the evolution of contemporary Russian trade unions. GCTU was tainted by its association with the coup plotters, while FITUR was not. Unions participated in electoral politics in the 1990s but with mixed results. The unions that backed losing candidates, especially unions of workers dependent on the state budget, concluded that trade unions should stay out of politics. Unions that elected candidates to parliament viewed political participation more positively. These included coalminers and metallurgists.

The state attacked unions' strength in the 1990s. In 1994, Yeltsin's government rescinded unions' authority to administer social insurance, bringing this function under state control and thereby reducing the unions' personnel. But the 1995 Law on Trade Unions gave official recognition to unions as 'social organizations'. In the early twenty-first century, Russian unions represented more than half of workers and had a well-defined national administrative structure. The main obstacles to union strength remained national leaders' hesitation to challenge state policies on labour and inadequate staff at the local level, making it nearly impossible to defend workers in the workplace.

See also: Communist Party; Gorbachev, Mikhail; nomenklatura; World War II (Great Patriotic War)

Further reading

Ashwin, S. and Clarke, S. (2003) *Russian Trade Unions and Industrial Relations in Transition*, New York: Palgrave Macmillan.
Ruble, B. (1981) *Soviet Trade Unions: Their Development in the 1970s*, Cambridge: Cambridge University Press.

BARBARA C. ALLEN

United Russia (Edinaia Rossiia)

Political organization

Political organization that plays an important role in the life of contemporary Russia. Created on 24 December 2003, it has all the formal signs of a party: programme, leader, factions in the State Duma of the Russian Federation and regional legislative bodies. With no clear ideology and an eroded social base, it unconditionally supports President Putin, who is not a formal member of the party. Its platform is expressed in the brief formula, 'We are Putin's party'. United Russia's electorate comprises people who believe that those in power know better than they what should be done and how. As an organization of the Russian bureaucracy (a party of 'bosses'), it exists to provide political service to the current ruling elite.

See also: Duma; Putin, Vladimir

YURII ZARETSKY

Urals

Called *Ural* in Russian, a mountain range in east European Russia and north-western Kazakhstan, forming, together with the Ural River, the traditional boundary between Europe and Asia. The Urals extend for 2,400 km from the Arctic tundra to the deserts of the Caspian Sea. The highest point is 1,895 m. The population consists primarily of Russians, with some Bashkirs, Tatars, Udmurts, and Komi-Permiaks (who populate the Northern Ural region, including the Republic of Komi and the city of Perm). Reached in the early twelfth century by colonists and fur traders from Novgorod, the Urals were colonized in the late sixteenth century. The first ironworks were established in the 1630s, and Peter the Great encouraged metallurgy in the early eighteenth century. From 1929 to 1939, the tremendous industrial development of the Urals was based on iron ore and coking coal. During World War II, industries were evacuated from European regions in the USSR to the Urals. Since then, the metallurgical industry has expanded enormously. Except in the polar and northern sections, the mountains are forested, and lumber is an important industry. Russia's most significant mineral resources are in the Urals: iron ore, coal, copper, manganese, gold, aluminium, potash, oil, and precious and semiprecious stones. Major cities and cultural centres in the Urals include Ekaterinburg, Magnitogorsk, Cheliabinsk, Perm, Berezniki, Nizhnii Tagil, Orsk, Orenburg, Ufa, and Zlatoust. The concentration of industry in the Urals has led to severe environmental problems.

See also: Ekaterinburg; environment; Kazakhstan; natural resources

TATYANA LEDENEVA

Urusevskii, Sergei Pavlovich

b. 23 December 1908, St. Petersburg; d. 12 November 1974, Moscow

Cameraman, artist, scriptwriter, film-maker

Urusevskii and Vadim Iusov were the two most important cameramen in Russian cinema during the second half of the twentieth century. A student of constructivist artist Aleksandr Rodchenko, Urusevskii used a mobile camera and wide-angle lens to create his subjective and expressive visual style. His cinematography departed from the monumental style of Stalinist cinema and evoked the visual culture of the 1920s' Russian avant-garde. He was director of cinematography in Vsevolod Pudovkin's *Vozvrashchenie Vasiliia Bortnikova* (*The Return of Vasilii Bortnikov*, 1952), Grigorii Chukhrai's *Sorok pervyi* ('41, 1956), and Mikhail Kalatozov's *Letiat zhuravli* (*Cranes Are Flying*, 1957), *Neotpravlennoe pismo* (*The Unsent Letter*, 1959), and *Ia Kuba* (*I Am Cuba*, 1964). Urusevskii also directed two films himself: *Beg inokhodtsa* (*Ambler's Run*, 1968) and *Poi pesniu, poet* (*Sing Your Song, Poet*, 1973).

See also: Chukhrai, Grigorii; Kalatozov, Mikhail

ALEXANDER PROKHOROV

Uspenskii, Eduard Nikolaevich

b. 22 December 1937, Moscow

Writer

Eduard Uspenskii is late twentieth-century Russia's most famous children's author. His famous characters Cheburashka and Gena the crocodile debuted in 1966 with the publication of *Krokodil Gena i ego druzia* (*Crocodile Gena and his Friends*), followed in the 1980s by his popular *Prostokvashino* (*Sour Milk*) series. Uspenskii has produced hundreds of children's stories and poems, adapting many of them for television and radio. In recent years, his characters have been used to advertise everything from milk to the Olympics. Uspenskii continues to write and publish in Moscow.

See also: Cheburashka; film, animation; film, children's; literature, children's

EMILY B. BARAN

USSR (Union of Soviet Socialist Republics, Soviet Union)

The Union of Soviet Socialist Republics, a state spanning Eurasia, covered a territory of 22,402,200 sq km, with a population of 290,077,000 in 1991. Its territory extended from East to West over a distance of 10,000 km (about 6,800 miles) and eleven time zones. The capital of the USSR from 1922–91 was Moscow. In 1991, the USSR included fifteen Union republics: the Russian Soviet Federal Socialist Republic (RSFSR), the Ukrainian Soviet Socialist Republic (USSR), the Belorussian Soviet Socialist Republic (BSSR), and the Uzbek, Kazakh, Kirgiz, Tajik, Turkmen, Armenian, Azerbaidzhani, Georgian, Moldavian, Latvian, Lithuanian, and Estonian Soviet Socialist Republics (SSRs).

The USSR was created on 30 December 1922 through the unification of five Soviet Socialist Republics: RSFSR; Ukrainian, Belorussian, and Turkestan SSRs, and the Transcaucasian SFSR (the union of the Armenian, Georgian, and Azerbaidzhani SSRs). In 1924, the Uzbek and Turkmen SSRs were added. In 1929, a new Tajik SSR was separated from the Uzbek SSR. The Kazakh and Kirgiz SSRs were separated from the RSFSR, and the Transcaucasian republic was abolished, its three republics receiving independent status. In 1939, Stalin and Hitler divided spheres of influence in Eastern Europe; as a result, the three Baltic states were incorporated into the USSR. In the spring of 1940, the Karelian-Finnish Moldavian, Estonian, Latvian and Lithuanian SSRs were established; the first of these was abolished in 1956 and recreated into the Karelian autonomous SSR, part of the RSFSR. Many of the republics were divided into *oblasts*, *krais*, autonomous republics and regions (*okrugs*). When the USSR broke up, there were twenty autonomous republics (ASSR), eight autonomous oblasts and ten autonomous *okrugs* established by ethnicity, as well as 129 oblasts and territories (*krais*). Each union republic had its own parliament (Supreme Soviet), government (Soviet of Ministers), and capital. Political power at all levels was in the hands of the Communist Party and its republic branches, whose leaders were First Secretaries of Party Central Committees. The Party's monopoly on state power ended in 1990, when Mikhail Gorbachev introduced the new position of President of the USSR and the institution of the Congress of People's Deputies.

The population of the USSR almost doubled from 1926 to 1989, in spite of enormous losses caused by wars and internal social conflicts that amounted to 64.3 million (Erlikhman, 2004). The male population was significantly lower than the female: in 1989, the difference constituted 16 million people, predominantly among older age groups. The birth rate among Slavic nations in the post-war period decreased, while predominantly rural populations in the Caucasus, the central Volga region, and Central Asia remained high. The infant mortality rate decreased from 182 in 1940 to 24 in 1989 because of medical advances. In 1989, 38 per cent of the population was employed in industry and construction, 19 per cent in agriculture and forestry, and the remainder in service industries and scientific and cultural spheres. Sixty-three per cent of the gross national product was industrial, 16 per cent agricultural, and 21 per cent in service industries. Population distribution was extremely uneven: 90 per cent lived in the main population belt (Leningrad, Kirov, Sverdlovsk, Novosibirsk, Novokuznetsk and the south). Population density throughout the country was very low – 13 per sq km: 35 per sq km in the European territory and 4 per sq km in the Asian territory. Central regions of Russia, Ukraine, Moldavia, Caucasus, and Central Asia were more densely populated, containing 86 per cent of the total population. The rest of the territory was less economically developed and less populated. Thanks to rapid industrialization from the 1930s to the 1960s, the USSR was transformed into an urban state: 66 per cent of the population in 1989 lived in cities, and there were twenty-six cities with a population of over 1 million. The largest Soviet cities were Moscow, Leningrad, Kiev, Tashkent, Kharkov, Baku, Novosibirsk, and Sverdlovsk.

The education level was relatively high: in 1989, 81 per cent of the population had completed a secondary or post-secondary education. From 1990–91, in the USSR there were 991 higher education institutions enrolling 5,162,000 students. Some technical disciplines that had practical applications for the military-industrial complex were very highly developed. Social sciences served the regime and fulfilled Communist Party orders. The theoretical level of those sciences was very low. Many disciplines (sociology, social psychology, political science) were banned or strongly ideologized (philosophy, history, economics) for a long time. The development of science was under the control of the USSR Academy of Sciences, which had a wide network of special institutes, regional divisions, and centres. Every Soviet republic had its own Academy of Sciences (except for the RSFSR, which had smaller divisions), and there were special Academies for agricultural, architectural, economic, artistic, pedagogical, and medical sciences. In the post-war period each ministry and department had its own research institutes, geared toward applied sciences. In 1990 in the USSR there were 134,600 clubs (including palaces of culture and workers' and rural clubs); 747 professional theatres (including fifty-five opera and ballet theatres; 479 drama, comedy, and musical theatres; and 213 children's and youth theatres); 2,471 museums (historical and revolutionary [507], memorial [507], regional history and ethnography [969], natural science [38], art [392], and specialized [58]), which were visited by 215 million people.

There were almost two hundred ethnic groups living in the USSR. The proportion of Slavic peoples (Russians, Ukrainians, Belorussians) was significant and determined the process of russification of many populations in predominantly Russian areas. Even in the republics where the local culture predominated and the use of languages other than Russian was encouraged, Russian was a necessary second language for career advancement. Universal conscription of young men also encouraged the spread of Russian. The smallest native populations were in Kazakhstan (40 per cent) and Kirgizia (52 per cent), and the largest were in Armenia (93 per cent) and Lithuania (80 per cent). Large cities in the Baltic, Transcaucasian, and Central Asian republics were subjected to strong russification campaigns, and Russian engineers and highly skilled workers as well as ideological workers were transferred there.

In the Soviet period, authorities did not tolerate ethnic conflict. Stalin deported ethnic minorities as 'punishment'. Nationalism arose as a result of perestroika and many ethnic conflicts came to the surface, and some developed into ethnic wars and ethnic cleansing. In the Baltic republics anti-Russian feeling intensified, which quickly led to calls for independence. The USSR disintegrated along ethnic lines, and many ethnic antagonisms appeared in those countries that replaced the Soviet Union.

Church and state were separated in 1918, and massive antireligious and atheistic campaigns were initiated; many priests and monks were executed or sent to concentration camps. The majority of churches and monasteries were closed, stripped bare (part of the artifacts were transferred to museums and other cultural preserves), and converted into factories, plants, warehouses, or clubs; monasteries were turned into prisons and colonies. Some major cathedrals in new regional centres, including Moscow, were destroyed. Representatives of Old Believer and non-orthodox Christian beliefs (Islam, Buddhist, Protestant, Catholic, and others) were prosecuted even more cruelly. During World War II, Stalin softened his attitude towards the Orthodox Church: in 1943, a Council on Religious Affairs was created to regulate Church activities, and the majority of the clergy had to work for the KGB. New attacks on the Church took place in the beginning of the 1960s, when Kiev's main monastery, the Kievo-Pecherkaia Lavra, was closed. The restoration of Orthodox churches began in 1988, during the celebration of the millennium of Russia's conversion to Christianity. In 1943, religious authorities over the Muslims of Central Asia, Kazakhstan, and the Caucasus were created and in 1945 two mosques were opened in Uzbekistan. However, the number of Muslim communities decreased from 1820 in 1966 to 751 in 1986. In 1947 there were 162 synagogues in the USSR, in 1966 only sixty-two, and in 1990 only sixty-one. Buddhism in the Lake Baikal region, Tuva, and Kalmykia was eradicated in 1936–37, and all lamas were repressed. Buddhism was restored only in 1946; that year the Ivolga Datsan in Buriatia and the Agin Datsan were reopened. The first Buddhist communities were revived in Tuva, Kalmykia, and Leningrad only in 1988–89.

Under Stalin, heavy and military industries became the cornerstones of the Soviet economy. Agriculture, light industry, and the food industries were considered secondary, and only meagre resources were devoted to them. The population suffered from shortages of food, clothing, footwear, and other consumer goods, which were barely profitable. Social life was regulated by strict Communist dogma, and cultural life served Party and Soviet ideology.

In June 1941, Hitler attacked the USSR. In the course of World War II (called the Great Patriotic War in the Soviet Union), most major cities in the west of the country were destroyed; more than 20 million people perished. However, the Soviet economy was restored by the early 1950s.

Stalin's death in 1953 bought an end to totalitarian terror. The era of Khrushchev's Thaw (1955–64) was marked by the liberalization of society and the de-Stalinization of economics and culture. Mass housing construction began to provide modest apartments for an overcrowded population. Khrushchev's rapid and poorly considered reforms ended in 1964 with his removal from the post of the First Secretary of the Communist Party. His successor, Leonid Brezhnev, undid all reforms, and the invasion of Czechoslovakia in 1968 marked the end of all possible liberalization in the countries of Eastern Europe. The economy was again centralized, the development of light industry was halted, and once again shortages of food and consumer products occurred. Large financial resources from exports were again invested in the development of the military, nuclear, and space industries, and to support foreign Communist Parties and guerilla-style terrorists in Asia, Africa, and Latin America. Nuclear energy became the main source of electric power. Use of large quantities of chemical fertilizers, pesticides, and large-scale irrigation led to catastrophic consequences in environment and public health. The major means of transportation were road, rail, river, and sea, yet highway networks were inadequately developed, and roads were extremely poor. By 1978, economic growth had stopped, the state had accumulated an enormous debt ($6 million), and the stage was set for economic stagnation. Despite the low standard of living, so-called 'developed socialism' in that period guaranteed stable incomes, access to consumer goods at state-regulated prices, and access to free education and medical care. In order to support minimal living standards, large quantities of grain and various consumer goods were imported from the West. Nevertheless, shortages of food and consumer goods increased. The main articles for export from the USSR were natural gas and oil (transported through export pipelines to the countries of Eastern and Western Europe), electricity, wood, non-ferrous metals, weapons, and auto parts; 61 per cent of exports were sent to East Bloc countries.

The war in Afghanistan started by Brezhnev in 1979 deepened the economic and political crisis in Soviet society. After his death in 1982 and the deaths of his elderly successors (the so-called 'five-year plan in four coffins'), Mikhail Gorbachev came to power in 1985. He attempted radical political, economic, and social reforms. Gorbachev's economic reforms (called perestroika, or 'restructuring') were initiated with unexpected ill consequences: salaries rose, but labour productivity did not. Inflation gathered momentum, heated up by the foreign debt (up to $70 million) that had begun in the Stagnation period. Inflation encouraged the spread of a black market under conditions of complete shortages of consumer goods. In 1991, the Soviet economic and political crisis reached a peak. An attempted coup, headed by military and Party conservatives, revealed the weaknesses of Gorbachev's power and that of the Communist Party, as well as the unfeasibility of the Soviet State. The declaration of independence by virtually all Union republics during the weeks following the August 1991 coup led to the collapse and rapid disintegration of the USSR. Formally the USSR came to an end on 25 December 1991. Of the fifteen former Union republics, twelve entered the organization of the Newly Independent States (NIS [*Sodruzhestvo Nezavisimykh Gosudarstv* or SNG]).

See also: administrative structure, Soviet Union; Brezhnev, Leonid; Buddhism; Communist ideology; Communist Party; Coup, August 1991; defence industry; developed Socialism; East Bloc countries; economic system, Soviet; ethnic minorities; Gorbachev, Mikhail; Islam; Krushchev, Nikita; perestroika and glasnost; Protestantism; Russian Orthodoxy; shortages; Stagnation; Thaw

Further reading

Bolshaia rossiiskaia entsiklopediia (2004) volume on *Russia*, Moscow: Nauchnoe izd-vo bolshaia rossiiskaia entsiklopediia.

Erlikhman, V. (2004) *Poteri narodonaseleniia v 20 veke: Spravochnik*, Moscow: Russkaia panorama.
comp. Goskomstat SSSR. *Narodnoe khoziaistvo SSSR v 1990 g. Staticheskii ezhegodnik* (1991) Moscow: Finansy i statistika.
Soviet censuses of 1926, 1939, 1959, 1970, 1979, 1989.

SERGEI TARKHOV

Ustvolskaia, Galina Ivanovna

b. 17 June 1919, Petrograd [St. Petersburg]

Composer

While her early works reflect the direct influence of her Leningrad Conservatory teacher Shostakovich, Ustvolskaia's style developed beyond Shostakovich's neo-classical approach by avoiding the traditional orchestra and relying on sacred texts or Orthodox chants. Her music is characterized by an ascetic style, high emotionality, and abrupt dynamic and textural changes, often taken to extreme limits of expression. Her works include five symphonies, six piano sonatas, and a number of compositions for chamber ensemble.

See also: St. Petersburg (Leningrad) State Conservatory; Shostakovich, Dmitrii

DAVID GOMPPER

Utesov, Leonid Osipovich

(né Lazar Iosifovich Vaisbein)

b. 21 March 1895, Odessa; d. 9 March 1982, Moscow

Jazz musician, bandleader, singer, actor

Born in Odessa, he always half-jokingly insisted that Odessa, not New Orleans, was the birthplace of jazz, and that jazz improvisation came from Odessa's Jewish weddings. In 1929, he established *Tea-Dzhaz* – a theatricalized jazz show. He and his orchestra appeared in many films, most notably in *Veselye rebiata* (*Happy Guys*, a.k.a. *Jolly Fellows*, 1934). His low raspy voice (slightly resembling that of Louis Armstrong) was admired by millions of Russians in live performances, films and recordings. In November 2004, a group of fans installed a homemade memorial plaque on the house where Utesov lived in Moscow.

See also: jazz; Odessa

VLADIMIR PAPERNY

Uzbekistan

A country in Central Asia that used to be one of the fifteen republics of the Soviet Union, Uzbekistan shares borders with Kazakhstan, Kyrgyzstan, Tajikistan, Afghanistan, and Turkmenistan. The Karakalpak Autonomous Republic is located in the north-western part of the country. In 2004, Uzbekistan's population numbered about 26 million, 80 per cent of whom were ethnic Uzbeks, a Sunni Muslim ethnic group who speak a Turkic language called Uzbek. The capital, Tashkent, has a multi-ethnic population of about 2 million.

Most of the territory of today's Uzbekistan was taken over by the Russian Empire in the late nineteenth century. Though the October Revolution (1917) sparked movements for independence, the Uzbek Soviet Socialist Republic came under the control of Moscow in 1924. Uzbekistan was the main cotton-producing republic in the USSR, though the cotton crop required intensive irrigation owing to Uzbekistan's aridness. As a result, much of the river water that normally would flow into the Aral Sea (shared with Kazakhstan) was diverted for farming. Now rapidly drying up, the Aral Sea is considered one of the world's most serious environmental disasters.

Uzbekistan became independent from the Soviet Union in August 1991. In the post-Soviet period it has continued to rely heavily on cotton, but the economy has also been boosted by revenues from oil, natural gas, and gold. Though the government slowly liberalized the economy after independence, most of the key industries remain under government control. The 1992 constitution declared Uzbekistan a secular, democratic republic, but the political system retains the character of an authoritarian state. Soviet-era leader Islam Karimov has persecuted opposition groups and severely restricted civil liberties for the entire population. After a decade of trying to avoid Russian influence, Uzbekistan's government began to build closer relations with Russia in the early part of the twenty-first century.

See also: Central Asia; Kazakhstan; Kyrgyzstan; natural resources; Tajikistan; USSR

LAURA ADAMS

V

vacations, Soviet and post-Soviet

Vacations during the Soviet era were closely linked to health; their purpose was to allow workers to recover from the rigours of their jobs. From the 1920s, Soviet health agencies, together with trade union organizations, operated a network of vacation facilities. A law expanding paid annual leaves in 1968, combined with increasing affordability of air travel, dramatically increased the number of Soviet citizens taking annual vacations away from home.

A continuing shortage of vacation facilities restricted travel opportunities. Those lucky enough to receive a paid voucher from their trade union could spend their holidays at a rest home, which offered room, board, and recreation in natural sites across the country. More formal, medicalized vacations were available through a network of sanatoria, where vacationers were considered patients and followed a regimen of diet and therapy such as mud baths or mineral water cures. More active vacationers used vouchers to engage in tourist travel, which ranged from organized camping excursions to package tours by bus, train, or plane. Travel by ship (on rivers and along the Black Sea) and on tourist trains became increasingly popular in the 1960s and 1970s. Although the state attempted to develop vacation facilities in all parts of the country, the seashore and mountains attracted the most visitors, particularly the Black Sea coast, Crimea, the Caucasus, and the Baltic Sea coast. Travel abroad was highly restricted in the Soviet period, but group tours to Eastern Europe expanded beginning in the 1950s. The most frequently visited countries in 1970 were Poland, Bulgaria, and the German Democratic Republic. Acquiring a place on such a tour required approval from one's workplace and the KGB.

The nature of the voucher system meant that individuals vacationed separately, children often spending their summers at camps. Improved standards of living, combined with the shortage of domestic vacation facilities, especially for families, gave rise to the 'unorganized', or 'wild', vacationer. Families or individuals would travel on their own, usually to popular resort areas along the coast, where they would rent private rooms or camp out, using the public dining and recreational facilities already provided for organized vacationers. In some spots along the Black Sea in the 1970s, wild vacationers outnumbered the organized by two to one. In post-Soviet times, the market replaced the voucher system. Russians now could travel abroad as well as within their country, but costs became much higher and prohibitive to many. Foreign package tours to destinations such as Cyprus or Turkey became more affordable than travel to a Black Sea resort.

See also: Caucasus; Crimea; health; medical system; sanatoria; unions, professional

Further reading

Azar, V. I. (1972) *Otdykh trudiashchikhsia SSSR*, Moscow: 'Statistika'.
Gorsuch, A. E. and Koenker, D. P. (eds) (2006) *Turizm: Travel, Leisure, and Nation-Building in Russia, USSR, and Eastern Europe*, Ithaca, NY: Cornell University Press.

Shaw, D. J. B. (1991) 'The Soviet Union', in D. R. Hall (ed.) *Tourism and Economic Development in Eastern Europe and the Soviet Union*, London: Belhaven Press.

DIANE P. KOENKER

Vail, Petr Lvovich

b. 29 September 1949, Riga

Critic and essayist

Vail worked for the newspaper *Sovetskaia molodezh* (Soviet Youth) in his native Latvia before emigrating to the United States in 1977. He co-wrote various articles on contemporary Russian literature and émigré culture with Aleksandr Genis for *Kontinent* (Continent), *Vremia i My* (Time and Us), *Ekho* (The Echo), *Chast rechi* (Part of Speech), and other émigré journals. Their works include *Rodnaia rech* (*Native Tongue*), *Poteriannyi rai* (*Paradise Lost*), *Russkaia kukhnia v izgnanii* (*Russian Cuisine in Exile*), and *Amerikana* (*Americana*). He is a frequent moderator of the cultural programme on Radio Liberty.

See also: Genis, Aleksander; Latvia; literature, émigré

ALEXANDER BURRY

VAK

See: State Attestation Commission

Vakhtangov Theatre (Teatr Vakhtangova)

The theatre opened in Moscow in 1921 as the Third Studio of the Moscow Art Theatre, and in 1926 was named after its founder, actor and theatre director Evgenii Vakhtangov (1883–1922). He defined his artistic credo as 'fantastic realism' and urged his actors to combine inventive artistic fantasy with psychological 'truthfulness'. Vakhtangov's legendary production of Carlo Gozzi's *Princess Turandot* (1922) became

the theatre's artistic trademark and realization of its aesthetics, and is still staged today, with performances that synthesize vivid theatricality, inventive stage design, elegantly choreographed movement, musicality, optimism, and life-affirming spirit.

OLGA PARTAN

Valdai

Geographical region in north western Russia (Tver and Novgorod oblasts), occupying the Valdai rise, at the watershed of the Volga and western Dvina Rivers. The hilly landscape is covered with both pine and deciduous forests; Valdai also has many lakes and several historical towns. Ostashkov, on the southern bank of Lake Seliger, boasts a number of seventeenth-century churches. Vyshnii (Upper) Volochok is the centre of the textile industry. Torchok is known for its handicrafts; Valdai is famous for its little bells. The area's natural beauty and unspoiled environment account for its traditional role of popular vacation spot, particularly for camping and fishing. Before the Revolution, well-known Russian artists used to work and relax at a local dacha belonging to the St. Petersburg Academy of Arts.

See also: bells; dacha

SERGEI TARKHOV

valenki

See: felt boots

Vampilov, Aleksandr Valentinovich

b. 19 August 1937, Kutulik (near Irkutsk); d. 17 August 1972, Lake Baikal.

Playwright

Vampilov's major plays – *Proshchanie v iiune* (*Farewell in June*, 1966), *Utinaia okhota* (*Duck Hunting*, 1967), *Starshii syn* (*The Elder Son*, 1969) and

Proshlym letom v Chulimske (*Last Summer in Chulimsk*, 1971) – explored the spiritual aspirations and frustrations of quirky people from the Russian countryside. His one-act works, known collectively as *Provintsialnye anekdoty* (*Provincial Anecdotes*) were equally popular. He drowned in a boating accident on Lake Baikal just as he began achieving fame. While many popular writers from the Stagnation period were forgotten after the collapse of the Soviet Union, Vampilov's status rose to that of a classic.

See also: Baikal; drama, Soviet; literature, Stagnation; provincial Russia; Siberia

JOHN FREEDMAN

varene

A staple in many Russian households, *varene* (preserves) is made by boiling fruit, usually berries, with sugar and sometimes water. It is served in small bowls with tea, or as a topping for pancakes. Some believe *varene* has curative powers, especially for the common cold.

LAURA KLINE

vareniki

Vareniki (also known outside Ukraine as *perogi*) are a traditional Ukrainian dish. They are small boiled dumplings that may have a variety of fillings, including mashed potatoes, cottage cheese, blueberries, cherries, fried mushrooms, or boiled ground beef mixed with fried onions. *Vareniki* may be served with fried chopped onions and sour cream.

ELENA BARABAN

Vasilenko, Svetlana Vladimirovna

b. 24 January 1956, Kapustin Iar

Writer

Vasilenko's works attack Soviet society's environmental and moral degradation. *Shamara*

(1989) describes a prison town, while the novel *Durochka* (*Little Fool*, 1998) blends folklore and hagiography in depicting a holy fool's struggle against Stalinism and nuclear holocaust. Vasilenko, a feminist who asserts that women must preserve the world men have almost destroyed, has edited and participated in several anthologies of women's literature.

See also: holy fool; literature, women's

BENJAMIN SUTCLIFFE

Vasilev, Anatolii

b. 4 May 1942, Danilovka village, Penza region

Director

A student of Maria Knebel and a major proponent of Stranislavskian realism, Vasilev moved from the revival of psychological theatre to the iconoclastic revision of theatre practices in general. Although he started with a modified *étude* method, since the late 1970s he has demonstrated no interest in the process of building character and exploring dramatic conflict. Starting with *Pervyi variant Vassy Zheleznovoi* (*The First Version of Vassa Zheleznova*, 1978), he used the Platonic image of tiny dust particles dancing in a sunbeam inside a dark shed to demonstrate the focus of his concept; he endorses a notion of theatre as ephemeral substance which exists only in the moment of creation. In 1987, Vasilev founded his own School for Dramatic Art, where he first experimented with breaking the psychological association of the actor with his character, a technique fully demonstrated in his production of Pirandello's *Six Characters in Search of an Author* (1987). He then began to work with the idea of a text devoid of its narrative function and purified of mundane meaning. In his recent works, the word serves as an auditory sign (Müller's *Medeamaterial*, 2001) or conveys a metaphysical quality (*Mozart and Salieri*, 2000). Since *Don Juan, or The Stone Guest and Other Poems* after Pushkin (1998), words are to be delivered with a particular, affirmative intonation. The 'pulsing sound of the attacking word', as Vasilev describes it, combined with light and music, defines the space between stage game and religious ritual.

See also: theatre, post-Soviet

DASHA KRIJANSKAIA

Vasilev, Konstantin Alekseevich

b. 3 September 1942, Maikop, Russia;
d. 29 October 1976, Vasilevo, Tatarstan, Russia

Artist

Graduate of the Kazan Art School (1961) as a theatre set designer, Vasilev in his works followed Russian symbolist and modernist traditions, focusing on themes from folklore and Russian history that emanate a philosophical and mystical aura: *Northern Legend* (*Severnaia legenda*, 1970), *The Russian Knight* (*Russkii vitiaz*, 1974), *Battle with the Dragon* (*Boi so zmeem*, 1974). He illustrated works of classical Russian literature and Richard Wagner's operatic *Ring* cycle. Modern Russian history appears in his war cycle of 1974, executed with dense symbolism and comprising *Marshal Zhukov*, *The Slavic Woman's Farewell* (*Proshchane slavianki*), and *Nostalgia for the Homeland* (*Toska po Rodine*), among others.

YURI ZARETSKY

Vasilev, Vladimir Viktorovich

b. 4 April 1940, Moscow

Ballet dancer, choreographer, director

A graduate of the Moscow Ballet School (1958), he joined the Bolshoi Theatre ballet as principal dancer and immediately distinguished himself. His technical skill, sustained jumps, and outstanding acting vouchsafed his success in both classical and contemporary repertoires. His style embodied the Russian tradition of heroic male dancing. Vasilev is especially remembered for his interpretation of roles in *Humpback Horse* (*Konek-Gorbunok*, music by Rodion Shchedrin, 1960) and Iurii Grigorovich's version of *Spartacus*

at the Bolshoi (1968, music by Aram Khachaturian). His long-term stage partnership with his wife, Ekaterina Maksimova, a prima ballerina at the Bolshoi Theatre, showcased the elegance of the balletic duet.

Vasilev choreographed several ballets (broadcast on television) and served as General Director of the Bolshoi from 1995 to 2001. National and international prizes include the Marius Petipa Prize (1972, Paris), State Prize (1977; 1991); People's Artist of the USSR (1973).

See also: ballet, Soviet; ballet dancers, Bolshoi Theatre; Grigorovich, Iurii; Khachaturian, Aram; Shchedrin, Rodion

TATIANA SENKEVITCH

vatnik

A water-permeable padded cotton jacket, usually grey, the *vatnik* used to be the basic garment of collective farmers, soldiers, prisoners, and deported convicts in the USSR. As a symbol of the restrictions of Soviet life, the *vatnik* appears in literature, such as Aleksandr Solzhenitsyn's *One Day in the Life of Ivan Denisovich* (1961). Photos of Iosif Brodskii and Iakov Gordin as prisoners or deportees in *vatniki* are famous.

See also: Brodskii, Iosif; coats; collective farms; GULag; Solzhenitsyn, Aleksandr

GASAN GUSEJNOV

VDNKh/VVTs

The Exhibition of Economic Achievements (*Vystavka dostizhenii narodnogo khoziaistva*, 1959–92) was the second incarnation of the All-Union Agricultural Exhibition (*Vsesoiuznaia selskokhoziaistvennaia vystavka*, 1939–59), designed to demonstrate the achievements of forced collectivization from 1927–30. Collectivization resulted in one of the worst famines in Russian history. The show of abundance at the Moscow exhibition was to compensate for the lack of food in the country. In 1959, the regional pavilions of the exhibition were renamed to represent the various spheres of economy: the Azerbaidzhan's pavilion, for example, became Computer Science, while preserving a typical Azerbaidzhan décor. In 1992, VDNKh became the All-Russian Exhibition Centre (*Vserossiiskii vysta-vochnyi tsentr*) and one of the largest swap meets in the world.

See also: collective farms; economic system, Soviet

VLADIMIR PAPERNY

Vertinskaia, Anastasia Aleksandrovna

b. 19 December 1944, Moscow

Actress

Daughter of actor Aleksandr Vertinskii (1889–1957), Vertinskaia achieved early cinematic fame in *Alye parusa* (*Scarlet Sails*, 1961), and sensationally more so in *Chelovek-amfibiia* (*The Amphibian Man*, 1962), where the foregrounding of her youthful sensuality was a breakthrough for Soviet cinema. Subsequently she played the vulnerable, puppet-like Ophelia in Kozintsev's acclaimed *Gamlet* (*Hamlet*, 1964), and the major roles of Liza Bolkonskaia in Bondarchuk's *Voina i mir* (*War and Peace*, 1967) and Kitty in Zarkhi's *Anna Karenina* (1968). A veteran of the Sovremennik and Moscow Art Theatres, she was also in Abdulov's *Bremenskie muzykanty* (*The Bremen Town Musicians*, 2000).

See also: Abdulov, Aleksandr; Bondarchuk, Sergei; Kozintsev, Grigorii; Moscow Art Theatre; Sovremennik Theatre; Zarkhi, Aleksandr

DAVID GILLESPIE

Vesnik, Evgenii Iakovlevich

b. 15 January 1923, Petrograd (St. Petersburg)

Theatre and film actor, theatre director

A graduate of the M.S. Shchepkin Theatre School (1948), Vesnik acted in the Stanislavskii Drama Theatre, the Satire Theatre, and the Malyi Academic Theatre. His life was in many respects typical for his generation: an orphan after his parents fell victim to the Stalinist repressions, he fought and was wounded during World War II. A character actor, master of transformation, Vesnik played over ninety roles in film and over 120 in theatre. Author of more than ten books and several screenplays for radio and TV, he directed productions in Moscow theatres and composed scores for cartoons. People's Artist of the USSR (1989).

See also: Stalin, Iosif; World War II (Great Patriotic War)

YURII ZARETSKY

VGIK (Vserossiiskii Gosudarstvennyi Institut Kinematografii)

See: All-Union (All-Russian) State Institute of Cinematography (VGIK)

Viktiuk, Roman Grigorevich

b. 28 October 1936, Lvov

Stage director

Viktiuk debuted as an actor in Lvov, Ukraine, in 1956 and began directing there in 1965 before becoming chief director of the Moscow State University Theatre (1977–79). From the mid-1970s he worked at numerous Moscow venues, including the Moscow Art Theatre, the Sovremennik, the Vakhtangov Theatre, and the Mossovet Theatre. He gained the reputation of a talented interpreter of contemporary dramatists, especially Liudmila Petrushevskaia and, later, Nikolai Koliada. His all-male production of Jean Genet's *The Maids* (1988) signalled a major style-change for the 1990s, introducing extravagance, sexual titillation, and frank treatment of homosexual themes. In 1990, he founded the Roman Viktiuk Theatre, which was sensationally popular until the mid-90s.

See also: Koliada, Nikolai; Moscow State University; Mossovet Theatre; Petrushevskaia, Liudmila; Sovremennik Theatre; theatre, post-Soviet; Vakhtangov Theatre

JOHN FREEDMAN

village prose

This term refers to a literary mode and perspective on Russia that thrived during the 1960s and 1970s. Its practitioners (*derevenchchiki*) focused on rural themes, discovering in the Russian village the ethical values of centuries-old peasant culture. Ruralists rejected the idealized portrayal of the countryside in *kolkhoz* fiction, giving an honest and depressing picture of the poverty, backwardness, and misery of village life. Village prose suggested that the government's policies of urbanization and industrial progress depleted the spiritual reservoirs of old Russia, while historical and social calamities, such as forced collectivization, were responsible for the disruption of peasants' lives and the devastation of their community.

Believers in the superiority of traditional peasant structures, village prose writers turned to the Russian provinces for character and setting. They favoured such locales as Siberia or the rural north, where the communal spirit of peasant culture still existed and the wealth of old Russia, reflected in the integrity of the common people's worldview, still survived. Nature became a favourite subject, and ecological concerns a common theme.

Leading representatives of village prose include Vladimir Soloukhin, Vasilii Belov, Sergei Zalygin, Fedor Abramov, and Valentin Rasputin. Using local colour, dialect and folklore, they depicted the harsh reality of village life, addressing persistent problems of the peasant experience. Ruralists lamented the city's invasion of the village, warning about the tragic consequences of losing Russia's religious heritage and its traditions. The preservation of Russian churches, religious art, and architectural landmarks was one of their recurrent themes.

See also: Abramov, Fedor; Belov, Vasilii; Far North; literature, Stagnation; literature, Thaw; nationalism ('the national question'); Provincial Russia; Rasputin, Valentin; Russian Orthodoxy; Siberia; Slavophiles; Soloukhin, Vladimir

Further reading

Gillespie, D. (1986) *Valentin Rasputin and Soviet Village Prose*, London: Modern Humanities Research Association.
Parthé, K. (1987) *Time, Backward! Memory and the Past in Soviet Russian Village Prose*, Washington, DC: Wilson Center, Kennan Institute for Advanced Russian Studies.
—— (1992) *Russian Village Prose: The Radiant Past*, Princeton, NJ: Princeton University Press.

TATIANA NOVIKOV

vinegret

A cooked vegetable salad tossed in an oil, vinegar, and dry mustard dressing, *vinegret* is a staple of every Russian cook. Though the ingredients may vary according to the taste of the chef, the basic salad consists of half-inch cubes of potato, beets, carrots, scallions, dill pickles, and canned peas.

See also: salads

CHRISTINE A. RYDEL

violin performance, Russian/Soviet

The illustrious tradition of Russian violin playing is a relatively recent phenomenon. In the eighteenth and early nineteenth centuries, classical music in Russia was performed primarily by musicians imported from Western Europe. The first conservatory in Russia was founded in St. Petersburg only in 1862, followed by the establishment of the Moscow Conservatory in 1866. A distinctive Russian violin school began with the appointment of Leopold Auer (1845–1930) to the St. Petersburg Conservatory in 1868. A Hungarian trained under such legendary violinists as Jakob Dont and Joseph Joachim, Auer taught violin at the Conservatory for forty-nine years.

Although Auer is considered the founder of the Russian School of violin playing, there is no consensus on what the 'Auer technique' meant. His authoritarian method of teaching targeted interpretation rather than technical mastery. Indeed, Auer reportedly accepted only those students whose technique was already flawless. The combination of note-perfect execution and iron discipline became the hallmark of Russian violin playing. Out of this New Russian School of St. Petersburg came an astonishing roster of world-renowned violinists, including Misha Elman, Iasha Heifetz, Nathan Milstein, and Efrem Zimbalist.

After the October Revolution, Auer and many of his finest students emigrated, spreading the legend of the Russian School and profoundly influencing Western musical performance. Some remained in Russia (most prominently Miron Poliakin) and continued the tradition in Leningrad and later in Moscow. A third centre of musical education arose around the pedagogue Petr Stoliarskii (1871–1944) in Odessa. In 1911, Stoliarskii established a private violin school that identified and nurtured children with special musical talent. These children were immersed from an early age in intense musical training to the exclusion of other activities.

Stoliarskii's most famous student was David Oistrakh, who became the Soviet Union's greatest violinist and pedagogue. He taught at the Moscow Conservatory from 1934 to 1974, producing a steady stream of virtuosos comparable to Auer's output a half-century earlier. With the Soviet system's generous training and support systems, his students frequently won international competitions. After Oistrakh's death in 1974, Leonid Kogan became the premiere Soviet violinist, but never achieved Oistrakh's international stature and popularity.

In the post-Soviet era, the Russian violin tradition is continued by virtuosos such as Gidon Kremer, Vladimir Spivakov, Vadim Repin, and Maksim Vengerov; the last two were students of the gifted violinist and teacher Zakhar Bron. This younger generation keeps alive the quintessential Russian style – large tone, commanding technique, soloistic attitude, and emphasis on Romantic repertoire. However, the Russian school is no longer insulated, and many Russian violinists have happily incorporated 'Western' approaches, integrating elements of the early-music movement, contemporary music, and ethnic music into their musical and technical vocabularies.

See also: classical music, post-Soviet; classical music, Soviet; classical musicians/performers, post-Soviet; Kremer, Gidon; Moscow Conservatory; Odessa; Oistrakh, David; Spivakov, Vladimir; St. Petersburg (Leningrad) State Conservatory; Tchaikovsky (Chaikovskii) Competition

Further reading

Campbell, M. (1980) *The Great Violinists*, London: Granada Publishing.

Farga, F. ([1940] 1983) *Geigen und Geiger*, Rüschlikon-Zürich: Albert Müller Verlag, pp. 320–31.

Roth, H. (1987) *Great Violinists in Performance*, Los Angeles, CA: Panjandrum Books.

Schwarz, B. (1983) *Great Masters of the Violin*, New York: Simon and Schuster, Inc., pp. 408–81.

SUNGHAE ANNA LIM

visas and registration

Every Soviet and now Russian citizen is required to have a permanent residence permit (*propiska*). In the USSR, free relocation inside the country was not encouraged and was strictly regulated. One either had to be officially directed to move due to a job transfer or a new professional appointment, or to justify any change in residence by changed family circumstances, such as marriage. It was difficult to obtain a job in a major city without a permanent registration or a permanent registration without an official job assignment. Certain places in the Soviet Union were closed for free travel because of their proximity to borders or for military or other strategic reasons (for example, Arzamas-16, Vladivostok, Magadan, areas bordering Turkey in southern Georgia, etc.). Special permission was needed, obtainable at a local police station based on presented justification for the trip, which could be either a business trip certificate or an invitation from close relatives. In the Russian Federation, the situation with registration continues to be very strict, but mostly in large cities, particularly in Moscow, which historically was and remains the most desirable place to live due to a significantly higher standard of living and more varied career opportunities. Today, however, a Russian citizen moving to a new place can obtain temporary registration while looking for a job or a place to live.

The Soviet Union strictly controlled and restricted international travel. Citizens could travel abroad only on government business or in organized tourist groups, and in most cases only to socialist countries; any potential travellers were required to undergo an examination of their moral and ideological maturity and reliability, so as to receive permission from a special Party 'departure' committee. After the collapse of the Soviet Union, exit visa requirements were removed, and Russian citizens could freely travel abroad. Foreigners visiting the Soviet Union were required to present an exact itinerary in applying for a visa, and to get an obligatory registration stamp on their visa at each hotel in each city. Residence at private homes was generally forbidden to visitors and foreign students before perestroika. Registration with local authorities is still required in the Russian Federation, but it is no longer necessary to present a day-by-day itinerary in order to apply for a visa. Foreigners still need to receive a visa invitation letter from an individual (for private visits) or an official organization (for business or study visits), or a hotel reservation voucher (for tourist visas) in order to receive a visa, however. Visa and registration rules and regulations remain strict and are subject to constant and sudden changes.

See also: closed city; iron curtain; kharakteristika; passport; perestroika and glasnost; propiska; putevka; vacations, Soviet and post-Soviet

TATIANA SMORODINSKAYA

Vishnevskaia, Galina Pavlovna

b. 25 October 1926, Leningrad

Soprano

Often compared to Maria Callas, Vishnevskaia was gifted with a strong, expressive voice. Her penetrating intelligence, coupled with a keen stage sense, allowed her to appear in a wide variety of roles. Her career began in earnest at the Bolshoi Theatre in 1952 and ended in Paris thirty years later in her most famous role, Tatiana in Tchaikovsky's *Evgenii Onegin*. In the 1960s she performed at the Metropolitan, Covent Garden, and La Scala and appeared in the film of Shostakovich's *Katerina Izmailova* (*Lady Macbeth of Mtsensk*, 1966). In 1955, she married Mstislav Rostropovich, with whom she left the Soviet Union for political reasons in 1974. Her life was the subject of an opera composed by Marcel Landowski (1915–99), and she wrote an autobiography titled *Galina: A Russian Story* (1984, in Russian 1991). Today she works at the Galina Vishnevskaia Opera Centre in Moscow, training singers in the transition from the Conservatory to the professional stage.

See also: Bolshoi Theatre; opera singers, Bolshoi Theatre; Rostropovich, Mstislav

DAVID GOMPPER

Vizbor, Iurii Iosifovich

b. 20 June 1934, Moscow; d. 16 September 1984, Moscow

Singer-songwriter, journalist, actor, writer

A teacher by training, Iurii Vizbor achieved fame in the 1960s and 1970s as a prolific figure in many different genres. The author of numerous screenplays, plays, and short stories, and a driving force in establishing the radio station *Iunost* (Youth), Vizbor is nonetheless best known as an actor (for his role as Borman in the television film *17 mgnovenii vesny* [*Seventeen Moments of Spring*], among others), as a founder and active propagandist of the bard movement, and as the author-performer of approximately 250 songs.

See also: bards; radio, Soviet; *Semnadtsat mgnovenii vesny* (*Seventeen Moments of Spring*)

RACHEL S. PLATONOV

Vladimov, Georgii Nikolaevich

(pseudonym of G. N. Volosevich)

b. 19 February 1931, Kharkov, Ukraine; d. 19 October 2003, Frankfurt, Germany

Writer, editor, dissident

Vladimov's most famous work is the novella *Vernyi Ruslan* (*Faithful Ruslan*, 1975), which describes a prison camp's closing from a guard dog's point of view. Vladimov began his career as a Soviet writer but parted ways with Socialist Realism, ceremoniously returning his Writer's Union card in 1977. He emigrated to Germany in 1983, where he spent the remainder of his life, though his citizenship was restored in 2000. His works include the novella *Bolshaia ruda* (*The Great Ore*, 1961), the novel *Tri minuty molchaniia* (*Three Minutes' Silence*, 1969), the novel *General i ego armiia* (*The General and His Army*, 1994–96, winner of the 1995 Russian Booker Prize), and the prose collection *Ne obrashchaite vnimaniia, maestro!* (*Pay No Attention, Maestro!*, 1999, after the story by that title first published in 1983).

See also: Socialist Realism; unions, creative, Soviet

DAVID J. GALLOWAY

Vlasov, Iurii Petrovich

b. 5 December 1935, Makeievka, Donetsk oblast

Weightlifter, writer, politician

Vlasov played an outstanding role in establishing the USSR as a sport superpower in the 1960s. The son of a Soviet diplomat and an intellectual himself, he radically transformed the image of the athlete. At the 1960 Olympics he broke four world records in the heavyweight category and was declared Athlete of the Olympics and Strongest Man in the Universe. Unlike most weightlifters, he was slim and wore glasses. His great erudition and sociability made him a popular public person in Russia. Author of several books of fiction and non-fiction, in the 1990s he was a Russian State Duma member and in 1996 ran for the presidency.

See also: Duma; Olympic Games

ALEXANDER LEDENEV

VLKSM

See Communist Youth League (Komsomol)

vobla

A fish known in English as the Caspian roach, *vobla* is typically sold dried and salted, and eaten as an accompaniment to beer. Before eating a *vobla*, gourmands – often working-class men, according to the stereotype – beat the fish against a table to soften it, then peel off the scales.

See also: fish dishes

SETH GRAHAM

vocal-instrumental ensemble (VIA)

Vokalno-instrumentalnyi ansembl (VIA) is associated with the late-Soviet period, when pop groups appeared in the mid-1960s in schools and higher educational institutions, then as professional groups that performed under the auspices of the state concert organizations. The typically all-male groups normally included guitarists, a drummer, and vocalists, usually dressed in identical suits or folk costumes, who performed a strictly controlled repertory that often included songs reflecting Soviet state values. However, many also performed 'unofficial' concerts and anticipated Soviet rock groups.

See also: educational system, Soviet; folk music; popular music, Soviet; propaganda, Soviet and post-Soviet

MICHELE BERDY

vocational education

Various forms of vocational education (*professio-nalno-tekhnicheskoe obrazovanie*) were instituted immediately after the October Revolution (1917) on the basis of pre-revolutionary craft and trade schools to train workers in agricultural and blue-collar jobs. The current system was instituted in 1959. By the end of the Soviet period it provided training in over 1,000 professions at over 4,000 schools. The training was 2–4 years if the student had an 'incomplete' secondary education (8 years), and 1–2 years if s/he had a 'complete' secondary education (10 years), and included both course work and practical experience. The schools (*professionalno-tekhnicheskoe uchilishche*, in the singular) are still referred to by their abbreviation, *PTU*. Students are colloquially called *PTUshniki*. Although some of the *PTU* were extremely competitive (for example, the schools that trained chefs for the Merchant Marine or personnel for Intourist restaurants and hotels), by the late Soviet and post-Soviet period *PTU* and students were regarded with disdain, stereotyped as lacking intellectual ability and ambition, from working-class or incomplete families.

In the post-Soviet period, the training is 1–3 years (depending on the length of the student's secondary education programme) in state or private schools. Some have been renamed *kolledzh* (college), sometimes with an expanded curriculum.

See also: educational system, post-Soviet; educational system, Soviet

MICHELE BERDY

vodka

Perhaps Russia's most famous export, vodka (diminutive of *voda* [water]) is an unaged, virtually flavourless, clear liquor distilled from wheat, rye, or potatoes, which may be flavoured with herbs, spices, fruit, or peppers. It originated in Poland or Russia during the early fifteenth century and since the seventeenth century has been Russia's favourite national drink. Served chilled and in shot glasses, it is a central part of the *zakuski* (appetizers) table. Vodka was banned from the markets from 1917–36, the prohibition increasing the production of *samogon* (moonshine). Despite attempts to reduce its consumption, vodka has contributed to Russians' alcoholism, though since the collapse of the Soviet Union that consumption has fallen, while that of beer has risen.

See also: alcoholism; appetizers; drinks, alcoholic

DAVID J. GALLOWAY

Voinovich, Vladimir Nikolaevich

b. 26 September 1932, Dushanbe

Writer

Émigré prose writer Voinovich is known as a great satirist. His early stories met with instant success, establishing Voinovich as a gifted young writer of the Thaw. In the late 1960s, he was subjected to pressure for his dissident activities and his satirical novel *Zhizn i neobychainye prikliucheniia soldata Ivana Chonkina* (*The Life and Extraordinary Adventures of Private Ivan Chonkin*, 1969), which circulated in *samizdat*. After its publication abroad, Voinovich was expelled from the Writers' Union, his books were banned, and he was forced into exile in 1980. A brilliant satire on the Soviet system, *Ivan Chonkin* attacks the military, the Communist Party, and the KGB. Its hero, the good-natured simpleton Chonkin, is entangled in grotesquely comic situations. The sequel, *Pretendent na prestol* (*Pretender to the Throne*, 1979) continues to expose the absurdity of the regime.

Voinovich's mock-epic, *Ivankiada* (*Ivankiad*, 1976), is a critique of the official writers' establishment, and his futuristic dystopia, *Moskva 2042* (*Moscow 2042*, 1986), mocks the Communist police state.

The publication of his prose during perestroika quickly made Voinovich popular in Russia.

See also: Communist Party; dissident; Federal Security Service (FSS/FSB); literature, émigré; samizdat; Thaw; unions, creative, Soviet

TATYANA NOVIKOV

Volchek, Galina Borisovna

b. 19 December 1933, Moscow

Stage director, actress

Upon graduating from the Moscow Art Theatre School, Volchek (daughter of the distinguished cinematographer Boris Volchek) joined Oleg Efremov and others to found the Sovremennik Theatre in 1956. She established her reputation as an actress of tough, complex heroines in Viktor Rozov's *Vechno zhivye* (*Forever Alive*, 1956), Aleksandr Volodin's *Naznachenie* (*The Appointment*, 1963), and others. Her infrequent film roles have been memorable, as in Grigorii Kozintsev's *King Lear* (1971) and Georgii Daneliia's *Osennii marafon* (*Autumn Marathon*, 1979). Volchek debuted as a stage director in 1962 and became chief director at the Sovremennik in 1972; since then she has staged some three dozen productions.

See also: Daneliia, Georgii; Efremov, Oleg; Kozintsev, Grigorii; Moscow Art Theatre; Rozov, Viktor; Sovremennik Theatre

JOHN FREEDMAN

Volga Region (Povolzhe)

Territory adjoining the Volga River or economically gravitating to it. The right bank of Povolzhe consists of highlands; its left bank, of lowlands. The area, stretching 680,000 sq km, includes Astrakhan, Volgograd, Samara, Penza, Saratov, Ulyanovsk oblasts, Kalmykia, Mordovia, and Tatarstan. Its population (16.9 million, 73 per cent urban) is predominantly Russian. Povolzhe is an important industrial region, specializing in oil extraction and refining, petro-chemistry, automobile engineering, grain, and wool-meat agriculture. The Volga estuary is Russia's major internal fishery pool; however, its ecological condition has sharply deteriorated in recent years.

See also: Kalmykia (Kalmyk); Mordva; Tatars

TATYANA LEDENEVA

volunteerism

Volunteerism (*obshchestvennaia rabota* or *poruchenie*, lit. 'social work' or 'societal assignment') entails involvement in one of multiple forms of social activities, ranging from editing a *stengazeta* (wall-newspaper, posted on a bulletin board), helping elderly people, or collecting waste, to unpaid work in volunteer police and fire brigades (*druzhiny*), 'comrade' courts, and such forms of civil participation as street, apartment, and parents' committees. Not to be confused either with passive membership in the Party, the Komsomol, trade unions, and other mass organizations and movements, nor with professional work as a functionary in such organizations, volunteerism follows the Party Programme of 1961. The latter emphasized the importance of social activism for the transition to a Communist society, implying 'the gradual transformation of the organs of state power into organs of public self-government'. Supposedly voluntary, *obshchestvennaia rabota* was, in fact, considered a duty, an expression of a Soviet citizen's active social stance (*aktivnaia zhiznennaia pozitsiia*). Correspondingly, not having an assignment or a 'load' (*nagruzka*) would elicit accusations of social inactivity by colleagues or Pioneer, Komsomol, and Party groups, and could even be an obstacle to career progression. Conversely, being an *obshchestvennik* (social activist) elicited tolerance for those neglecting their immediate work or study obligations. Toward the end of the Soviet period, all kinds of independent and genuinely volunteer associations (at that time referred to as *neformalnye obedineniia*, or informal associations) arose that were beyond the organizational and ideological control of the Party and the authorities; people did not regard membership in them as a 'social assignment'.

See also: Communist Party; Communist Youth League; Pioneer organization; unions, professional

ILIA UTEKHIN

Voskresene (Resurrection)

Rock band

Founded by Aleksei Romanov in 1979, this cult band has survived several incarnations and one incarceration: in 1982, Romanov was imprisoned for 'illegal commercial activities'. Justifying its name, the band was resurrected in the 1990s and is creatively more active now than ever before.

ALEXANDER DOMRIN

voucher

A certificate with a face value of 10,000 rubles issued to each citizen of Russia during the mass privatization of 1992–94. Vouchers could be used to directly buy shares of any enterprises to be privatized; placed in investment funds (voucher privatization funds or VPFs), which would use vouchers to purchase shares of privatized companies; or sold for cash to others. Although viewed as a quick and fair method of distributing formerly state-owned property, in reality, voucher privatization did not create millions of real owners, because enterprise insiders managed to remain in control over privatized companies. Specifically, workers neither understood nor valued vouchers and often sold them for cash to the managers of their enterprises, enabling the managers to transform their *de facto* control into *de juro* ownership.

See also: economic system, post-Soviet; privatization.

ALYA GUSEVA

Voznesenskii, Andrei Andreevich

b. 12 May 1933, Moscow

Poet

One of the most popular poets of the post-Stalin era, famous for his original and experimental work, Voznesenskii first published poems in 1958, to an enthusiastic public response. The 1960 publication of his collections *Mozaika* (*Mosaic*) and *Parabola* resulted in worldwide success.

In contrast to the officially endorsed poetry of the Stalin period, Voznesenskii's poetic style was distinguished by inventiveness, bold metaphors, stunning and evocative imagery, and formal play. Linguistically rich, his poetry employed such unorthodox devices as free and internal rhymes, changing metres, creative use of sound associations, assonance, and verbal play.

Voznesenskii's public readings drew immense audiences, and he regularly travelled abroad. His later publications include *Antimiry* (*Antiworlds*, 1964), *Akhillesovo serdtse* (*Achilles' Heart*, 1966), and *Soblazn* (*Temptation*, 1970). In 1978, he received the USSR State Prize.

His apolitical poetry explored human values, technology and civilization, history, and addressed such themes as love, nature, the motherland, and labour. Two musical theatrical productions based on his poems – *Antimiry* and *Avos* – were staged at Moscow theatres.

See also: literature, Thaw; sixties generation

TATYANA NOVIKOV

VTsIOM (Vserossiiskii tsentr informatsii i obshchestvennogo mneniia [Russian Centre for Information and Public Opinion])

The all-Union (since 1992, all-Russian) public opinion research centre, established in 1987 by the Soviet Labour Ministry and the Trade Unions Central Council, was converted in 2003 into an open joint-stock company under full government ownership. It is the nation's leading research company, conducting socio-political, socio-economic, and marketing studies through mass polling, interviews, and focus groups. The centre provides complete surveying and analysis services, from research design to analytical reports. It is guided by the ESOMAR (European Standards Organization for Marketing) ethics code.

TATYANA LEDENEVA

vysotka (high rise)

The term *vysotka* (plural *vysotki*) is an abridged form of the Russian term for a high-rise building, *vysotnoe zdanie* (tall building). It also popularly refers to the seven tall buildings erected by the Stalinist regime in post-war Moscow, often called *Stalinki* (sing: *Stalinka*).

The skyscraper idea, borrowed from late nineteenth-century American architecture, was avidly pursued by Russia's post-revolutionary avant-garde, whose fantasies were embodied in various unrealized projects: Vladimir Tatlin's 1919–20 project for the Monument to the Third International, Leonidov's 1934 competition project for the Commissariat of Heavy Industry Building, and Boris Iofan's design for the Palace of Soviets, which was to be the pre-eminent skyscraper of Stalinist Russia. The grandiose tower, topped by a 328-ft effigy of Lenin, would have soared to a height of 1,400 feet, exceeding that of the Empire State Building. This design served as the conceptual nucleus of the ensuing Stalinist ensemble of the seven *vysotki* erected in post-war Stalinist Moscow.

The ensemble of high rises was conceived to commemorate the 800th anniversary of Moscow's founding (1147) and to present a uniquely Muscovite paradigm for post-war Soviet urban development. Erected on strategic sites visible throughout the city and forming a ring around the centre of Moscow, with the projected Palace of Soviets at its core, the seven tall buildings included the Ukraine Hotel at the intersection of Kutuzov Prospect and the Moscow River to the west; the Leningrad Hotel on Komsomol Square in the northeast; two residential towers, one on Kudrinskii Square northwest of the Kremlin and the other on the Boiler (Kotelnicheskaia) Embankment to the southeast; the

Ministry of Transportation on Red Gate Square in the northeast; the Ministry of Foreign Affairs on Smolensk Square in the heart of the city; and Moscow State University, on Sparrow Hills in the south west of Moscow. The 650-ft, 34-storey Ukraine Hotel was the first *vysotka* to be completed, in 1951; the 787-ft, 36-storey University complex was the last, completed in 1954. An eighth skyscraper, initially planned, was never built. These buildings were designed by the nation's leading architects, and Stalin personally approved key aspects of their design, most notably their crowning spires.

The effect of placing the ring of seven tall buildings around the Palace of Soviets was to imitate on a grander scale the traditional spatial configuration and pyramidal silhouette of medieval Russian kremlins and monasteries, whose enclosing ring of wall towers and cathedral cupolas was dominated by a tall central belfry. That paradigm simultaneously resembled the pyramidal morphology of multiple setback towers and visionary proposals for a 'city of towers' advanced in the 1920s by New York architects Harvey Wiley Corbett and Hugh Ferriss, and Raymond Hood, with the participation of Moscow architect Viacheslav Oltarzhevskii, who conveyed the concept to his Moscow colleagues. These skyscrapers thus manifested a fresh juxtaposition of contemporary and historic strategies.

The break-up of the Soviet Union in 1991 unleashed a real-estate boom with a growing demand for exclusive residences for the new capitalist elite; the *vysotki* and other Stalin-era buildings acquired a new aura of exclusivity, both because they were well-built, previously inaccessible spaces (as apartments for the *nomenklatura*), and because of nostalgia for the Soviet past. New residential buildings emulating Stalinist architecture were erected. Symptomatic of this phenomenon is the recently completed Triumph Palace, a 61-storey pseudo-Stalinist set-back skyscraper, currently Europe's tallest residential building.

The Stalinist *vysotki* still fascinate with their combination of bold exterior architectural forms and extravagant interior décor, characteristic of post-war Soviet buildings. Though intended for the *nomenklatura*, they were widely publicized: on postcards and souvenirs, confectionery wrappers and soft drink labels, and in films as symbols of post-war Stalinist modernity, meant to exemplify both wartime victory and a better, brighter future.

See also: architecture, visionary; housing, Soviet and post-Soviet; Moscow; nomenklatura; oligarkh; Stalin, Iosif; World War II (Great Patriotic War)

Further reading

Proekt Rossiia [*Project Russia*], Issue 24 (2002).
Senkevich, A. with A. A. Chernikhov (2002) 'Russkii neboskryob [Russian skyscraper]', *Ezhegodnoe izdanie Moskovskogo otdeleniia mezhdunarodnoi Akademii arkhitektury* [Annual Edition of the Moscow Branch of the International Academy of Architecture], 1: 86–91.

ANATOLE SENKEVITCH

Vysotskii, Vladimir Semenovich

b. 25 January 1938, Moscow; d. 25 July 1980, Moscow

Actor, poet, singer-songwriter

Vladimir Vysotskii was the first true Soviet superstar, a celebrity who enjoyed near-universal popularity and a wild, extravagant lifestyle. He was a well-known actor, both at the rebellious, pioneering Taganka Theatre and in thirty different productions for television and the silver screen. Yet his overwhelming fame came from his songs; alongside Bulat Okudzhava and Aleksandr Galich, he is recognized as one of the most important Soviet bards.

A talented poet, Vysotskii was not recognized by the official literary establishment. During his lifetime, his works were rarely published, and then only in periodicals. In the early 1960s, Vysotskii began singing his poems and accompanying himself on the guitar. In 1967, his popularity skyrocketed as a result of his first major concert and the release of the film *Vertikal* (Vertical), which featured a number of his songs. Though Vysotskii gave semi-official concerts all across the Soviet Union, most of his fans knew his songs only through crude, home-made tape recordings, a method of dissemination known as *magnitizdat*.

Vysotskii wrote hundreds of songs on a wide range of topics. Themes of love, war, the search for truth, and the courage of ordinary people in extraordinary situations appear frequently. Also prominent are first-person narratives in which Vysotskii expressed the attitudes and concerns of diverse social types (criminals, athletes, soldiers, lorry drivers, and so on). Vysotskii's convincing performances, in which he drew on his training as an actor, inspired widespread belief that these songs were autobiographical.

Vysotskii had a complicated relationship with the Soviet authorities. His unorthodox professional activities and his flamboyant personal life, especially his alcoholism and his marriage to French actress Marina Vlady, were a constant source of irritation. His uncontrollable popularity made him virtually untouchable, however, both during his lifetime and after his premature death from a heart attack. Though virtually ignored by the press, Vysotskii's funeral turned into a spontaneous demonstration. Unable to contain the surge of popular feeling, the authorities eventually responded by co-opting Vysotskii into the official canon. During perestroika, Vysotskii was widely heralded in the Soviet press and was awarded a state literary prize; his works were published and official recordings of his songs released. Numerous audio and video recordings, as well as collections of song texts, are now readily available.

See also: alcoholism; bards; death; Galich, Aleksandr; Okudzhava, Bulat; perestroika and glasnost; samizdat; Taganka Theatre

Further reading

Andreev, Iu. and Boguslavskii, I. (*c.* 1990) *Vladimir Vysotsky: Hamlet with a Guitar*, Moscow: Progress.
Lazarski, C. (1992) 'Vladimir Vysotsky and His Cult', *Russian Review* 51: 58–71.
Leonidov, P. (1983) *Vladimir Vysotskii i drugie*, New York: Russkoe kn-o 'N'iu Iork'.
Soldatenkov, P. (1999) *Vladimir Vysotskii*, Moscow: Olimp.

Tolstykh, V. (1987) 'In the Mirror of Art: Vladimir Vysotskii as a Cultural Phenomenon', *Soviet Review* 28,4: 37–64.

RACHEL S. PLATONOV

Vzgliad (Viewpoint)

Television programme

Vzgliad was a weekly current affairs programme featured on Channel 1 from October 1987 to January 1991. Shown initially on late Friday evenings, *Vzgliad* was the first programme to offer live news coverage and to touch upon sensitive themes, such as the Afghan War, discussed in a programme where Afghan students complained about the new Soviet-supported regime. Anchors came from the foreign section of Radio Moscow: Aleksandr Liubimov, Vlad Listev, Vladimir Mukusev, and Sergei Lomakin formed the *Vzgliad* team under Anatolii Lysenko. *Vzgliad* was continually threatened with closure. In December 1990, the programme was not allowed to cover Foreign Minister Eduard Shevardnadze's resignation. On 9 January 1991, the programme was shut down.

See also: journalism; Listev, Vladislav; perestroika and glasnost; radio, Soviet; Shevardnadze, Eduard; television channels; television, Soviet; War, Afghan

BIRGIT BEUMERS

War, Afghan

The path to the Soviet Union's involvement in the so-called Afghan War of 1979–89 began on 27 April 1978, when the Soviet-backed People's Democratic Party of Afghanistan (PDPA) murdered Prime Minister Muhammad Daoud and many of his supporters. PDPA leader Nur Muhammad Taraki proclaimed himself Prime Minister of the newly-created Democratic Republic of Afghanistan, and the Afghan Marxists now endeavoured to implement a reform programme along the Marxist-Leninist model of their Soviet backers.

The policies of Taraki's regime, which included a poorly conceived plan of land redistribution and persecution of Afghanistan's religious and intellectual elites, were a complete failure. By the second half of 1979, the PDPA found itself battling a nationwide insurgency with the help of Soviet advisors and material provided under the terms of a mutual friendship treaty signed in December 1978.

Soviet concerns over Afghanistan's stability increased after Hafizullah Amin, the leader of a PDPA faction that opposed President Taraki, took power in September 1979. Despite Amin's victory, it was clear to the Kremlin leadership that Amin's government was both unstable and unwilling to heed Soviet advice on how to strengthen its hold on power. Based on the perception that the Amin regime was on the brink of collapse and that an Iranian-style Islamic fundamentalist state might replace the current regime, the Soviet Union sent a group of *spetsnaz* (Special Forces) commandos to storm the Presidential Palace in Kabul on 27 December 1979.

After a bloody struggle, the troops killed President Amin and replaced him with Babrak Karmal, the once-exiled leader of the PDPA's Parcham faction. Large numbers of Soviet forces entered Afghanistan to stabilize the country in the following weeks.

The next decade witnessed an unmitigated disaster that affected the Soviet military as well as the civilian populace of the USSR. As Soviet forces and their Afghan collaborators tried and failed to subdue a strengthening insurgency that, by the mid-1980s, enjoyed support from the United States, any remaining collective faith in the Soviet leadership waned. This scepticism was due partly to the public opposition to the war by such well-known dissidents as Andrei Sakharov, who spoke out against his government's heavy-handed tactics. Among the general populace, the sight of disabled veterans, coupled with growing casualties, added to the unpopularity of the Afghan conflict and prompted further questioning of Soviet-style state socialism.

After years of grinding guerrilla warfare, the Soviet leadership under General Secretary Mikhail Gorbachev became increasingly aware that its efforts to maintain a friendly government in Kabul were in vain. In 1988, the Soviet government signed the Geneva Accords, which allowed the disengagement process to begin.

While the last Soviet troops left Afghanistan in February 1989, the legacy of the Soviet involvement there remains. The civil war that began after the Soviet withdrawal eventually led to the rise of the Taliban, and many Muslims, particularly the anti-Soviet partisan Osama bin Laden, saw it as a Soviet war against Islam. This development, in turn, served to strengthen

Islamic fundamentalism in post-Soviet Central Asia and the independence movement in the breakaway Russian republic of Chechnia, which Russia has been fighting intermittently since the mid-1990s.

See also: Central Asia; Chechnia; dissident; Gorbachev, Mikhail; Islam; Sakharov, Andrei; War, Chechen

Further reading

Kakar, M. (1995) *Afghanistan: The Soviet Invasion and the Afghan Response, 1979–1982*, Berkeley, CA: University of California Press.

Lohbeck, K. (1993) *Holy War, Unholy Victory: Eyewitness to the CIA's Secret War in Afghanistan*, Washington, DC: Regnery Gateway.

MacKenzie, D. (1994) *From Messianism to Collapse: Soviet Foreign Policy 1917–1991*, Fort Worth, TX: Harcourt Brace.

Strayer, R. (1998) *Why Did the Soviet Union Collapse? Understanding Historical Change*, Armonk, NY: M.E. Sharpe.

CHRISTOPHER J. WARD

War, Chechen

The Chechen War (1994–96, 1999–present) is an ongoing conflict between Russia and the Northern Caucasian republic of Chechnia. The two wars have resulted in the deaths of thousands of soldiers, civilians, and journalists. The conflict may be traced back to the nineteenth century, when the Chechens were among the most rebellious of the Caucasian peoples whom the Russians tried to conquer. Daghestani warrior Imam Shamil led a rebellion against the Russian campaigns for a quarter of a century before being defeated in 1859. In the twentieth century, the Chechens fought mostly on the side of the Bolsheviks in the Civil War, and Chechnia, along with its neighbour Ingushetia, was proclaimed an autonomous republic in 1922. In 1944, half a million Chechens and Ingush were deported to Kazakhstan by Stalin for allegedly collaborating with the Nazis. Thousands died along the way, and although in 1957 under Khrushchev the survivors were allowed to return, the deportation left scars that continue to nourish the hatred and resentment Chechens feel for Russia today and inspire their current struggle.

Dzhokhar Dudaev proclaimed Chechnia's independence from the Soviet Union in 1991, and declared himself its first president. Boris Yeltsin, however, never recognized Chechnia as an independent nation. Encouraged by a cabinet that supported a 'small, victorious war' to enhance Russian military prestige, he sent troops into the capital, Grozny, in June 1994. Despite the Russian army's far superior numbers, Chechen fighters ambushed the invaders and inflicted many casualties. The Russians destroyed Groznyi and invaded much of the remaining Chechen territory. However, Groznyi was recaptured in 1996, and Yeltsin signed an armistice in Khasaviurt; thus the first war ended with Russia's defeat. Aslan Maskhadov was legitimately elected Chechen president in 1997, but was unable to rein in separatist fighters. A series of Moscow apartment bombings in late 1999, blamed with little evidence on Chechen fighters, and simultaneous attacks by Wahhabite militants Shamil Basaev and Omar ibn al-Khattab on Dagestan led to renewed hostilities. Yeltsin ordered air strikes, and Russian troops entered Chechnia in October. The war has featured various terrorist acts, such as the October 2002 hostage-taking at the Moscow theatre production of the musical *Nord-Ost*; the assassination in May 2003 of Akhmad Kadyrov, the Russian-installed president of Chechnia; the attack on a school in Beslan during school opening ceremonies in September 2004, and the March 2005 killing of Maskhadov. Russia has relied mostly on air power, with heavy carpet bombing and ballistic missile strikes, in order to minimize its casualties. The conflict continues, although Vladimir Putin has publicly declared the war over. One particularly notorious case of the various Russian atrocities against civilians was the rape and killing of an 18-year-old girl named Kheda Kungaeva by Colonel Iurii Budanov. Budanov was found not guilty by reason of insanity in December 2002, but was then retried and sentenced to a ten-year prison term.

The Chechen War has various implications for both Russia and Chechnia. It underscores the difficulty of defeating an opponent simply through superior numbers. The Russian media have succeeded in portraying its struggle against the Chechen separatists as an aspect of the broader 'war on terror', partly to deflect criticism of and investigation into its wartime conduct. The Chechen separatists, for their part, see it as the continuation of a two-centuries-long programme of Russian imperialism in the North Caucasus. Chechnia's vast supplies of oil are an important factor in Russia's interest there. The conflict has exposed the ineffectuality of the former Soviet Army, whose organization, equipment, leadership and morale have proven inferior to the vastly smaller but better organized Chechen forces. The Chechen War thus diminishes Russia's claims to be a major military player on the world stage.

See also: Caucasus; Chechnia; ethnic minorities; Kazakhstan; *Nord-Ost (North-east)*; Khrushchev, Nikita; Putin, Vladimir; Stalin, Iosif; terrorist acts; Yeltsin, Boris; World War II (Great Patriotic War)

Further reading

Gall, C. and de Waal, T. (1998) *Chechnia: Calamity in the Caucasus*, New York: New York University Press.

Lieven, A. (1998) *Chechnia: Tombstone of Russian Power*, New Haven, CT: Yale University Press.

Politkovskaya, A. (2001) *A Dirty War: A Russian Reporter in Chechnia*, trans. J. Crowfoote, London: The Harvill Press.

—— (2003) *A Small Corner of Hell: Dispatches from Chechnia*, trans. A. Burry and T. Tulchinsky, Chicago, IL: University of Chicago Press.

Tishkov, V. A. (2004) *Chechnia: Life in a War-Torn Society*, Berkeley, CA: University of California Press.

ALEXANDER BURRY

wedding ceremony

The main components of the Russian wedding rites, established in approximately the fifteenth century, include matchmaking, affiancing (*pomolvka*), an all-girls party for the bride (*devich-*nik*), and the actual wedding ceremony. International customs, such as a white dress symbolizing the bride's virginity, combine with a specifically Russian emphasis on the bride's departure from her father's house and her entry into her husband's family household.

In Soviet Russia, weddings were non-religious ceremonies; couples registered their conjugal vows in ZAGS, the recording agency that still keeps track of births, deaths, marriages, and divorces.

Since the civil registration in ZAGS was brief and formal, Soviets organized elaborate wedding receptions in restaurants or at home. Especially outside the urban centres, couples observed ancient customs, which encompassed toasting the bride and groom, encouraging their kisses with cries of *Gorko!* ('bitter', to be sweetened by the couple's kiss), having the first dance, and cutting the wedding cake. As elsewhere, the bride would throw her bouquet to the woman next in line for marriage, and her garter to the man next in line. Weddings in today's Russia, which frequently revert to pre-Soviet traditions, combine elements of both civil and religious ceremonies.

Religious marriage involves Orthodox Church ceremonies and rituals that constitute one of the Mysteries, a sacrament and a martyrdom of mutual self-abnegation. Divorce is discouraged, but allowed when the relationship no longer exists. Priests and deacons are not permitted to remarry.

See also: Registration of Civil States (ZAGS); Russian Orthodoxy

ELENA SKIPETROVA

Westernizers

Westernizers (*zapadniki*) comprised, in relation to the relatively small Russian public of the 1840s, a numerous and socially diverse group of idealistic and educated gentlemen defined by their infatuation with European civilization and, consequently, by opposition to their contemporaries, the Slavophiles. Westernizers, in general, celebrated Russia's adoption of European civilization in the eighteenth century.

Moderates, such as the historian Timofei Granovskii, argued that Russian development followed the European pattern and that Slavophile views were a fantasy; while radicals, such as Aleksandr Gertsen (Herzen) in 1848, reproached Europe for not adopting socialism. In 1856, the official censorship permitted open debate between Slavophiles and Westernizers, which found literary expression in Ivan Turgenev's novels. The fundamental differences in the two groups' ideologies proved paradigmatic, resurfacing in the conflict between Soviet hardliners and Western-oriented liberals during the Soviet period, and between nationalists and 'globalists' in the post-Soviet era.

See also: Slavophiles

EDWARD ALAN COLE

white nights

In June and early July the sun virtually never sets in St. Petersburg, which is located on the 60th parallel. After the long, dark winter, the constant light represents a welcome change. Local residents see the white nights as a time for romantic strolls through the city centre and also for celebrating secondary school and university graduations. Writers and artists have often tried to capture the unique atmosphere and look of St. Petersburg during this period. Since 1993, each summer the city has hosted a lavish programme of cultural events known as the Stars of the White Nights Festival.

See also: St. Petersburg

EMILY D. JOHNSON

White Sea Canal (Belomorkanal)

The White Sea Canal is a system of man-made canals and natural waterways (141 miles/227 km long), connecting the White Sea and Lake Onega in the north-west of Russia. The idea of such an enterprise had existed since the eighteenth century, for the system shortened the Arctic voyage around the Norwegian coast.

Constructed 1930–33, the canal gained notoriety for its use of slave labour under gruelling conditions with primitive tools. Prisoners from Solovki and others arrested specifically for the project were among the over 100,000 employed to complete it. The canal was one of Stalin's favourite projects, who demanded that it be constructed in twenty months. Ironically, the canal, which cost numerous human lives, ultimately saw little use. Although it was celebrated in a special volume in 1934, upon touring it for the first time, Stalin famously pronounced it 'shallow and narrow'.

See also: Solovki; Stalin, Iosif

Further reading

Ruder, C. (1998) *Making History for Stalin: The White Sea–Baltic Canal*, Gainesville, FL: University of Florida Press.

DAVID J. GALLOWAY

women

Women were a special target group for the Bolsheviks. Since Marxism relates the oppression of women to private property, the woman's question was an integral part of the class issue: as soon as classes would be abolished, the revolutionaries believed, the root cause of gender oppression would disappear.

After the Revolutions of 1917, women were declared equal citizens and granted the same rights as men. Accordingly, in 1918, divorce and abortion were legalized (abortion was criminalized in 1936, and legalized again in 1953). But in spite of the new liberal laws, masses of women in largely rural Russia remained 'backward' and tied to the household. Since their emancipation was a key component of the envisioned social transformation, a special women's section of the Communist Party, the Zhenotdel, was created.

The socialist industrialization project needed working hands, and women were enlisted in work outside the home and made visible in public space. As illiteracy was very high, the Soviet government launched a campaign of 'liquidating illiteracy' (*likbez*) through adult education classes. Later, the Soviet-standardized educational system became an important venue for the inclusion of women in the labour force. Economic and cultural goals of the period became inextricably combined, and the advocate of women's emancipation, Aleksandra Kollontai, celebrated the change whereby '[t]he self-centred, narrow-minded, and politically backward female becomes an equal, a fighter, and a comrade'. Around 1929, a consistent policy was initiated to bring women into professions that made them financially independent of men. The system of state-supported childcare, without which women's labour participation would have been impossible, was developed. By the mid-1930s, the women's question was declared solved.

During World War II, 800,000 Soviet women enlisted in the military – more than in any other country. With men away at the Front, women in the rear became the core force of production; they were also responsible for the survival of children, and, later, were intensively engaged in post-war rebuilding and economic development. In 1963, Valentina Tereshkova became the world's first female space pioneer.

Post-war USSR had the highest rates of female labour participation in the world: nine out of ten women of child-bearing age worked. By the 1980s, their ratio among those with college degrees was higher than men's. As the birthrates fell during Stagnation, an extended system of benefits was elaborated to support motherhood. It encompassed free childcare, healthcare, and paid parental leaves. A partially paid leave of three years to take care of a new child and fully paid leaves to take care of a sick child were available for any family member, but usually taken by mothers, and they counted as work time for retirement. Thus Soviet women were more dependent on the socialist state than on men for their livelihood, while the traditional belief that family obligations are women's rather than men's work continued to flourish.

The break-up of the Soviet Union brought women new challenges. In the market system, profit-oriented companies tend to reject women if they insist on parental benefits, while their educational credentials and workforce experience still remain an important factor

when negotiating their status and independent identities.

See also: Communist Party; economic system, post-Soviet; economic system, Soviet; families; feminism; literature, women's; Stagnation; Tereshkova, Valentina; World War II (Great Patriotic War)

Further reading

Ashwin, S. (ed.) (2000) *Gender, State and Society in Soviet and Post-Soviet Russia*, London and New York: Routledge.

Buckley, M. (1989) *Women and Ideology in the Soviet Union*, Ann Arbor, MI: University of Michigan Press.

Nechemias, C. and Kuehnast, K. (eds) (2004) *Post-Soviet Women Encountering Transition: Nation Building, Economic Survival, and Civic Activism*, Washington, DC: Woodrow Wilson Center Press.

Sperling, V. (1999) *Organizing Women in Contemporary Russia: Engendering Transition*, Cambridge: Cambridge University Press.

Wood, E. (1997) *The Baba and the Comrade: Gender and Politics in Revolutionary Russia*, Bloomington, IN: Indiana University Press.

ELENA GAPOVA

women journalists

The Soviet era began as an epoch of women's emancipation, a phenomenon that affected particularly the rural and Muslim areas of the country. Among other possibilities, women could now take employment in the mass media. At the same time, men occupied most leading positions in the state, the Party, and economic organizations – a bias partly related to Stalin's misogyny, which increased after his wife's suicide (1932). However, even after the de-Stalinization of Soviet society during the Thaw and later, an anti-feminist discourse continued to prevail in Russia, despite a cult of women poets such as Anna Akhmatova. Even if formal equality of the sexes was achieved in some instances (for example, the proportion of female members of the Supreme Soviet exceeded women's representation in democratic parliaments of the time), women's actual role in Soviet society was not reflected in such quotas. This paradoxical status led women to increased activity in the mass media. Thus in the human rights and dissident movements, gender equality established itself naturally. Despite considerable resistance both in media management and in society at large, women succeeded in making careers in journalism. As victims of structural discrimination, women have promoted discussion of unlawful aspects of the Soviet state and society. By perestroika (1985), some of the most striking positions in Russian journalism were occupied by women: in the 1980s, Olga Chaikovskaia in *Literaturnaia gazeta* and Tatiana Ivanova in *Ogonek*; in the 1990s, Galina Kovalskaia, Veronika Kutsyllo, Evgenia Albats, Anna Politkovskaia, Svetlana Aleksievich, Natalia Gevorkian, Elena Masiuk, and Elena Tregubova. Female television journalists have attained both popularity and influence: they include Svetlana Sorokina, Tatiana Mitkova, Tatiana Tolstaia, and Dunia Smirnova. When the organizers of the coup against Mikhail Gorbachev (August 1991) gave a press conference, it was a woman – Tatiana Malkina – who asked the pertinent question: 'Do you realize that you have just engineered a government takeover?'

One paradox of the democratization of Soviet society after 1991 was that, with the abandonment of the formal Soviet demand for gender equality, by the mid-1990s women had disappeared almost completely from Russian politics, especially after the assassination of Galina Starovoitova in 1998. As surveys of women's issues in Russian media and society undertaken by Nadezhda Azhgikhina have shown, sexism increased in Russian society during the last years of the twentieth century. Under Boris Yeltsin (1991–99) and Vladimir Putin (since 2000), Russian society has become polarized along gender lines: many socially and politically active women have been driven out of the political and economic spheres. At the same time, in the 1990s and 2000s, women have occupied some key positions in independent electronic and print media. The chief editors of the two most-read Internet sites and the largest, award-winning literary journal in Russia are women: Galina Timchenko at lenta.ru and Elena Bereznitskaia-Bruni at newsru.com. The founder and editor-in-chief of post-Soviet Russia's leading thick journal, *Novoe literaturnoe obozrenie* (The New Literary Review), is Irina Prokhorova.

See also: Akhmatova, Anna; Coup, August 1991; Duma; Internet, Russian; journalism; journalists, post-Soviet; *Literaturnaia gazeta* (Literary Gazette); NTV; *Ogonek*; periodicals, post-Soviet; perestroika and glasnost; Putin, Vladimir; Stalin, Iosif; Starovoitova, Galina; television, post-Soviet; thick journals; Yeltsin, Boris

Further reading

Azhgikhina, N. and Tax, M. (eds) (2000) *Women's Voices and the New European Order*, New York: Women's WORLD.
Barker, A. and Gheith, J. (eds) (2002) *A History of Women's Writing in Russia*, Cambridge: Cambridge University Press.

GASAN GUSEJNOV

work

The Russian work ethic swings between the extremes encapsulated in two proverbs: *rabota ne volk – v les ne ubezhit* (work isn't a wolf – it won't flee into the woods) and *bez truda ne vynesh i rybku iz pruda* (without work you won't even be able to pull a fish out of the pond). Characters in Russian fairy tales, which every Russian knows from childhood, become rich and famous not through hard work, but through lucky happenstance (the aid of such 'magic helpers' as a golden fish, a wolf or horse, the witch Baba Iaga, etc.). Luck is granted not to the hard-working or clever, but to the kind and disinterested. The best-known fairy-tale protagonist, Ivan-durak (Ivan The Fool), refuses to work with his brothers and spends all day sleeping, indifferent to money and material goods, yet one day magically acquires wealth, a beautiful princess, and a kingdom. However, the realization that work is the only rational way to earn money brings the second proverb into play: even a magic fish has to be caught, and certain minimal efforts need to be applied. The Russian mode of work differs from Western European and American norms: instead of committing themselves to a regular, everyday input, Russians prefer to relax and let the work sit for a while, and when it piles up and the deadline is imminent, to work overtime, completing it by a last-minute effort, which is called *avral* (urgent work by the entire personnel on a ship after an alarm). The quality of work might suffer, but it will be finished on time at all costs.

The long period of Soviet rule corrupted Russians' work ethic. Abolition of private property and private enterprise killed labour initiative, and only Stalin's repressive system could make people work hard, under the threat of severe punishment for an unfulfilled plan or lack of discipline. The propaganda of socialist enthusiasm for labour was launched in the 1930s, when heroes of labour exceeding quotas and expectations were highly rewarded (as during the Stakhanovite movement), but after Stalin's death the impetus vanished. Equal pay regardless of productivity led to workers' total demoralization, as reflected in the popular saying of the 1970s, 'They pretend to pay us, and we pretend to work.' Most industrious and entrepreneurial people tried to make money on the side by taking a second job, practising unofficial moonlighting (*khaltura*), working in underground businesses, selling something on the black market, or providing private services (*shabashnik*), which brought extra cash but was illegal and therefore dangerous. Parasitism (*tunaiedstvo*) was a crime in the Soviet Union – it is for this crime that poet Iosif Brodskii was tried in 1964 – but to work hard for personal benefit was also a crime, for everyone had to fit into the socialist labour system like a cog in a readymade machine. After perestroika, one of the major psychological shocks experienced by the majority of the Soviet population was the necessity to find well-paying work without its automatically being made available to all citizens. Moreover, state bureaucracy at all levels, coupled with a hatred of the rich and the more productive and successful, which for decades had settled in the national psyche, to this day continues to hamper the development of small and medium-sized business in Russia. Nevertheless, Russia always had an educated, skilled, and highly qualified workforce, resourceful and creative, and able to work hard under stress, capable of accomplishments of international renown.

See also: black market; Brodskii, Iosif; bureaucracy; collective farms; economic system, post-Soviet; economic system, Soviet; five-year plan; parasitism; perestroika and glasnost; private property; privatization; propaganda, Soviet and post-Soviet; shabashnik; Stakhanovism

TATIANA SMORODINSKAYA

Worker and Collective Farm Worker

Sculpture

This colossal stainless steel sculpture was first designed by Vera Mukhina to adorn the Soviet Pavilion at the Paris International Exhibition in 1937. The work represents two young Soviet workers – one male, one female – symbolizing the industrial and agricultural developments of the 1930s. Constructed on site, the monument dominated the exhibition, strategically positioned directly opposite the German Pavilion. Following the closure of the Paris Exhibition, Mukhina's work was transported back to Russia and re-erected outside the entrance to the VDNKh (All Union Agricultural Exhibition). Here it has become an easily recognizable icon for the city of Moscow. It also functions as the symbol of Mosfilm, a model of the work appearing in the opening sequence to all Mosfilm productions.

See also: Socialist Realism; VDNKh/VVTs

MIKE O'MAHONY

World War II (Great Patriotic War)

Within days of Germany's surprise invasion on 22 June 1941, the Soviet mass media had dubbed World War II on the Eastern Front the Great Patriotic War (*Velikaia Otechestvennaia voina*). The name connected the contemporary struggle to the original 1812 Patriotic War against Napoleon, and suggested the new importance of Russian nationalism in Soviet propaganda. In the post-Soviet period, the war has remained for many Russians the greatest national achievement of the twentieth century. The rituals and rhetoric of the sixtieth anniversary of victory over Germany in 2005 recalled the Soviet state's use of the war as a central legitimizing myth.

In the years immediately after the war, Iosif Stalin, in an effort to strengthen his own claim to having orchestrated victory, suppressed the wartime convention of lauding the individual initiative and personal motivations of Soviet citizens. In 1947, Victory Day (9 May, commemorating the fall of Berlin and German capitulation) ceased to be a national holiday. However, after Stalin's death in 1953, his political heirs, seeking their own legitimizing myths, initiated a 'cult' of the Great Patriotic War. In the 1960s and 1970s, new monuments and rituals honoured individual sacrifices and Soviet military power. Victory Day was reinstated as a national holiday in 1965.

The extent of Soviet losses in World War II – approximately seventy times those suffered by the United States, and forty times those suffered by Great Britain – provides some explanation of the uniquely powerful Russian memory of the war. The concept of the Great Patriotic War to save the *rodina* (birthplace, in both the narrow sense of hometown and in the broad sense of motherland) gave meaning to the sacrifices of the approximately 27 million war dead.

With the advent of glasnost in the late 1980s, Soviet critics, particularly young people, began to question the verities of the war cult, emphasizing, for example, the Hitler-Stalin Pact that precipitated the war. Nonetheless, the war has remained a vital symbol of Russian national strength and sacrifice. By the mid-1990s, Boris Yeltsin's government was co-opting the rituals and monuments of the Soviet cult. In 2005, his successor, Vladimir Putin, celebrated victory as a moment of liberation, ignoring the protests of Eastern Europeans, who view the Soviet victory as the beginning of decades of Communist domination.

See also: East Bloc countries; perestroika and glasnost; Putin, Vladimir; Stalin, Iosif; Yeltsin, Boris

Further reading

Kirschenbaum, L. (2006) *The Legacy of the Siege of Leningrad, 1941–1995: Myth, Memories, and Monuments*, Cambridge: Cambridge University Press.

Krylova, A. (2004) 'Dancing on the Graves of the Dead: Building a World War II Memorial in Post-Soviet Russia', in D. Walkowitz and L. Knauer (eds) *Memory and the Impact of Political Transformation in Public Space*, Durham, NC: Duke University Press.

Schleifman, N. (2001) 'Moscow's Victory Park: A Monumental Change', *History and Memory* 13, 2: 5–35.

Smith, K. (2002) *Mythmaking in the New Russia: Politics and Memory during the Yeltsin Era*, Ithaca, NY: Cornell University Press.

Tumarkin, N. (1994) *The Living and the Dead: The Rise and Fall of the Cult of World War II in Russia*, New York: Basic Books.

LISA A. KIRSCHENBAUM

Y

Yeltsin (Eltsin), Boris Nikolaevich

b. 1 February 1931, Butka

Politician

President of the Russian Federation (1991–2000). Born into a peasant family in a village in Sverdlovsk oblast and educated in construction engineering, Yeltsin joined the Communist Party in 1961 and rose to the position of Sverdlovsk Communist Party First Secretary (1976–85). Made head of the Party in Moscow (1985) upon Mikhail Gorbachev's initiative, Yeltsin campaigned against *nomenklatura* privileges, but was demoted by Gorbachev (1987), who resented Yeltsin's impatience with the Politburo and his own leadership. Yeltsin recovered, to win election to the Congress of People's Deputies in the first free parliamentary elections (1989), and Party attempts to discredit him only reinforced his image as the government's foremost progressive.

As Russia's first popularly elected President (1991), Yeltsin curtailed Party control. His decisiveness aided resistance against Party putschists (1991); his rallying thousands to defend Moscow's White House (then the seat of the Supreme Soviet) crystallized Yeltsin's perceived incarnation of Russia's democratic aspirations in 1989–91. However, his participation in the dissolution of the USSR (1991) without electoral mandate foreshadowed his presidency's insufficient regard for democratic legitimacy. His 'free-market' ideologues' shock price deregulation (initiated in 1992), which reduced the average citizen's living standards, and the corruption associated with his privatization campaign, in which public assets were transferred to former *nomenklatura* monopolists, opened a 'moral and psychological gap' (Reddaway and Glinski, 2001: 242) between the regime and the people. Western analysis meanwhile over-emphasized Yeltsin's indispensability to Russian democracy and supported post-Soviet crony capitalism.

The constitutional struggle of 1993, in which legislators sought executive limitations and the administration sought limitations on parliamentary power, ended when Yeltsin unconstitutionally disbanded the Supreme Soviet on 21 September and called for December elections to a new parliament (the Duma). Vice President Aleksandr Rutskoi compromised parliamentary opposition with a call for armed resistance, to which 'red-brown' (Communist and right-wing nationalist) extremists responded. Yeltsin ordered the shut-down and blockade of the White House, where opposition Supreme Soviet deputies were gathered. On 3 October 1993, opposition forces stormed the Moscow mayor's office building and the Ostankino television station; the following day, Yeltsin ordered the shelling of the White House. He claimed that such an action would prevent a return of totalitarian government – the claimed rationale for his push to adopt the 1994 constitution, which established unlimited presidential power. His administration throughout the 1990s was increasingly characterized by personalization and clannishness.

Initially trailing most candidates, and debilitated by heart disease, Yeltsin did not cancel the 1996 presidential election, as some had advised. However, his victory, though reflecting majority opinion, involved fraud, intimidation, and illegal financing by 'oligarchs'.

Factors of varying legitimacy induced Yeltsin, who reckoned insufficiently with Russian military corruption and Chechen postcolonial enmity, to invade the fractious republic of Chechnia (1994). The resultant war cast a shadow on the rest of his presidency, and at his impeachment proceedings in the Duma (1999) it drew the most votes against him. Yeltsin began grooming Vladimir Putin to succeed him in 1999, and Putin pardoned Yeltsin upon taking over the leadership in 2000.

Yeltsin earned historic acclaim as Russia's first elected leader. Upon resigning, he publicly expressed regret at having initially believed in a speedy transition from Communism to a new order. While Yeltsin's memoirs contrast his claimed practicality with the dreaminess of his faultfinders in the intelligentsia, many believe that his oligarchic 'liberalism' has left a deleterious legacy.

See also: Chernomyrdin, Viktor; Communist Party; Coup, August 1991; Duma; economic system, post-Soviet; Gaidar, Egor; Gorbachev, Mikhail; nomenklatura; oligarkh; Ostankino Tower; Putin, Vladimir; shock therapy; War, Chechen

Further reading

Reddaway, P. and Glinski, D. (2001) *The Tragedy of Russia's Reforms*, Washington, DC: US Institute of Peace.
Service, R. (2003) *Russia: Experiment with a People*, Cambridge, MA: Harvard University Press.
Shevtsova, L. (1999) *Yeltsin's Russia: Myths and Reality*, Washington, DC: Brookings Institution Press.

AVRAM BROWN

Young Spectator Theatre (Teatr iunogo zritelia, TIuZ)

Numerous Young Spectator Theatres were formed throughout the Soviet Union in the 1920s. The Moscow version emerged in 1927, offering children's fare. In later years it was a springboard for such popular actors as Inna Churikova and Liia Akhedzhakova. The theatre's

course changed drastically when Genrietta Ianovskaia became chief director in 1986. Her productions of Mikhail Bulgakov's *Sobache serdtse* (*Heart of a Dog*, 1986), Anton Chekhov's *Ivanov* (1993), Aleksandr Ostrovskii's *Groza* (*The Storm*, 1997) and Agatha Christie's *Witness for the Prosecution* (2001) offered a sophisticated mix of entertainment and cutting-edge drama that, alongside the renowned productions of her husband, Kama Ginkas, brought the theatre (officially called the New Generation Theatre in English) international acclaim.

See also: Akhedzhakova, Liia; Churikova, Inna; Ginkas, Kama; theatre, Soviet

JOHN FREEDMAN

youth culture

The term applies to various types of youth interests and activities united by common characteristics: autonomous organizations and practices, as well as unique symbols, all oriented toward a space free from adult control. Youth culture can be divided into the conventional majority or the mainstream and progressive and/or alternative minorities – a subculture, counterculture, or underground (*andegraund*).

Each underground subculture has its own image, slang, and practices aimed at shocking. Various subcultures have unique names: Europe has had Teddy Boys, mods, skinheads, rastafarians, punks, and goths. The Soviet Union and post-Soviet Russia have boasted *stiliagi*, *KSP-eshniki* (members of amateur song clubs), *Mitki*, *Igroviki*, and others. Thanks to wide press coverage, the behaviour of some subcultures has created panic: some consider these underground cultures a threat to social order, values, and ideology. In the West some commentators saw countercultures as forces prepared to organize mass rebellion against society. In the Soviet Union the press spoke of 'blind followers of the West', ready to betray Communist ideology and opposed to Komsomol and Party identity and loyalty.

In Russia, as abroad, the rise of youth subcultures is connected with plurality; structural changes in the relationship between work and leisure; the rise of the consumer market, particularly service industries for young consumers; and the greater complexity of the youth market. At the beginning of the twenty-first century, there is discussion of the 'death' of subcultures and the formation of ephemeral, mixed identities; the circulation of exotic images of the fashion industry; and the gradual dissolution of authentic subcultures in the youth mainstream. Alongside 'pure' subcultures there are their imitators, tourist variants that populate Moscow's pedestrian zone, the Arbat, and similar areas in other major cities. Confusion of the terms 'youth culture', 'subculture', and 'counterculture' reflects the complex history of their Russian adaptations and the mixture of corresponding phenomena among contemporary Russian youth.

The popular term *tusovka* (slang for 'gathering') refers to alternative groups in Russian cities beginning in the late 1980s with perestroika. They supported a style alternative to the mainstream in music, film, and literature, and were characterized by localization and cliquishness. Although members of a *tusovka* did not necessarily come from privileged circles, they tended to flock toward the centre of a city and were geared to upward mobility; they had nothing in common with youth gangs located in urban outskirts and their territorial fights. *Tusovki* actively ignored governmental power by creating alternative social spaces that helped to alleviate the alienation resulting from social disintegration. The *tusovka* embraces an aesthetic of cynicism and performance (*performansy*).

Counterculture refers to alternative groupings in the Thaw era of the 1960s, which rejected the previous (Stalinist) generation's 'culture of the word'. The context of countercultural protest could be found in radical leftist philosophy, existentialism, neo-Freudianism, utopianism, Romanticism, Eastern mysticism, the Russian avant-garde of the 1920s, and the practices of early hippies and beatniks. Two major subgroupings within the counterculture are the mystical and the political. European counterculture strived for political change, while in America the counterculture pursued a transformation of consciousness through the use of psychotropic substances (the psychedelic underground), Eastern mysticism, and communal (hippie) culture. The rise of performance art and

thousands of rock festivals are associated with the countercultural movement. The loss of faith in the revolutionary transformation of the world led to the dissolution of the countercultural movement and its metamorphosis into the Green movement, feminism, and left-wing terrorist movements.

The cultural underground has manifested itself in musical (rock), political, sexual, narcotic, and ethnic revolutions in the United States and Europe. In the USSR the aestheticized underground took political form, and was associated with risk, since opposition to officialdom required sacrifice and heroism. Underground movements were periodically repressed, as in the case of the 1962 Manezh exhibition, repressed by Khrushchev. Domestic salons and clubs in private spaces – apartment kitchens and dachas – were opposed to the frankly public activity of Western underground movements. Because of the strict regulation of Soviet cultural life, the most interesting works and movements in art, rock music, and literature came from the underground.

See also: amateur cultural activity; Communist ideology; Communist Party; Communist Youth League; journalism, Soviet; Khrushchev, Nikita; Manezh exhibition of 1962; perestroika and glasnost; propaganda, Soviet and post-Soviet; sixties generation; Thaw

ELENA OMELCHENKO

youth literature

Generally speaking, the forces that have shaped Russian youth literature closely resemble those that influenced Russian children's literature. Youth literature during the Thaw was enriched by the period's more liberal approaches to style and theme. While responding to calls for greater realism in literature for teenagers and youth, these works tackled formerly 'taboo' topics such as divorce, youth crime, and the conflicts of teens at home, school, and work. Examples of prose popular with youth include Anatolii Rybakov's adventure stories, the humorous prose of Viktor Dragunskii and Viktor Goliavkin, Liubov Voronkova's novels for girls, and the science fiction of Arkadii and Boris Strugatskii. Anatolii Aleksin's 'psychological' novels, stories, and plays stressed moral questions and character formation at the intersection of the worlds of adults and teenagers.

During perestroika, youth literature was again called upon to reflect the moral crises of the time, though economic neglect and a dearth of new authors had eroded its status. Today the role and content of youth literature are once again being re-evaluated, as is the heritage of Russian youth literature, beginning with the reissue of the best books of the Soviet period and an interest in the neglected literature of pre-Revolutionary and émigré Russia. In addition, commercial forces are driving the production and marketing of popular translations of contemporary Western youth literature.

See also: crime; economic system, post-Soviet; families; literature, children's; perestroika and glasnost; Rybakov, Anatolii; Strugatskii, Arkadii and Boris; Thaw

TERESA POLOWY

Z

Zags

See Registration of Civil States

Zaitsev, Viacheslav (Slava) Mikhailovich

b. 2 March 1938, Ivanovo

Fashion designer

Couturier, fashion designer, painter, and designer of theatrical costumes, Zaitsev was one of the first fashion designers to negotiate a successful transition into the post-Soviet Russian fashion arena. He made a name for himself in the Soviet era and was appointed the artistic director of the Soviet House of Dress Design (*Vsesoiuznyi dom modelei odezhdy*). Popularly known as Slava Zaitsev, the designer stresses Russianness in his design, has a House of Fashion in Moscow, and runs a School of Fashion Design in the capital. He was among the first Russian designers to create a line of perfumes and other beauty products at the invitation of the French company L'Oréal in the early 1990s.

See also: fashion industry, post-Soviet; fashion industry, Soviet

SUSMITA SUNDARAM

Zakharov, Mark Anatolievich

b. 13 October 1933, Moscow

Director, actor, writer

Since 1973, Zakharov has been the artistic director of Moscow's Lenkom Theatre, where he has directed such legendary productions as the rock opera *Iunona i Avos* (*Iunona and Avos*), and Liudmila Petrushevskaia's *Tri devushki v golubom* (*Three Girls in Blue*), staged in 1985, one of the last Soviet productions to be officially banned. Zakharov has worked with many of Russia's most famous actresses and actors, including Inna Churikova and Andrei Mironov. He has also directed several films, including *Dvenadtsat stulev* (*The Twelve Chairs*) and *Tot samyi Miunkhgauzen* (*That Very Munchhausen*). In 1989, he was elected to the Congress of People's Deputies.

See also: Churikova, Inna; Lenkom Theatre; Mironov, Andrei; Petrushevskaia, Liudmila; rock opera

SETH GRAHAM

Zalakavicius, Vitautas

b. 14 April 1930, Kaunas, Lithuania; d. 12 November 1996, Vilnius, Lithuania

Director, scriptwriter, administrator

Lithuania's most prominent director during the Soviet period, Zalakavicius graduated from VGIK in 1956. He consistently made films dealing with Lithuanian history, most notably the prize-winning *Nikto ne khotel umirat* (*No One Wanted to Die*, 1965), a version of a Hollywood Western set in a post-war Lithuanian village where anti-Soviet bands still roam and violence reigns. Subsequent films include two set in Latin America, the revolutionary drama *Eto sladkoe slovo – svoboda!* (*This Sweet Word – Freedom*, 1972), and *Kentavry* (*Centaurs*, 1978), about a CIA plot against the country's leftist president. From 1961–75 and again in the 1980s Zalakavicius headed the Lithuanian Film Studio.

See also: All-Russian (All-Union) State Institute of Cinematography; Lithuania

JOSEPHINE WOLL

Zarkhi, Aleksandr Grigorevich

b. 5 [18] February 1908, St. Petersburg;
d. 27 January 1997, Moscow

Director, scriptwriter

Initially Zarkhi collaborated with Iosif Kheifits on several films, the most prominent including *Deputat Baltiki* (*Baltic Deputy*, 1937), based loosely on the biography of pro-Bolshevik scientist Kliment Timiriazev, and *Chlen pravitelstva* (*Member of the Government*, 1940), the Soviet equivalent of a rags-to-riches story about a battered wife/farmhand who becomes a collective-farm chairwoman and later Deputy of the Supreme Soviet of the USSR. After Zarkhi and Kheifits split up, Zarkhi directed one important Thaw film, *Vysota* (*Heights*, 1957), mixing psychological veracity into his ideological orthodoxy. Subsequently he adapted novels by Lev Tolstoi and Konstantin Fedin for the screen.

See also: collective farms; film, Soviet – Thaw period

JOSEPHINE WOLL

Zarnitsa

Sport

Zarnitsa literally means summer lightning and metaphorically refers to shooting. In 1968, the Zarnitsa patriotic game for teenagers, distantly resembling paint-ball, was launched in the USSR as a part of primary military and physical training. The game was played nationwide in forests or on cross-country terrain. Participants were divided into teams simulating military divisions. The final objective of the game was to capture the rival's headquarters or fighting banner. In spite of its strong military and patriotic character, the game was popular among schoolchildren.

See also: fitness test (GTO); sports education

ALEXANDER LEDENEV

Zasurskii, Iasen Nikolaevich

b. 29 November 1929, Moscow

Professor

Zasurskii is a professor of American Literature and the Media, and since 1965 has been Dean of the Moscow State University Department of Journalism, one of that university's most contradictory and paradoxical departments. On the one hand, this department was pronounced the ideological school for Communist propaganda; on the other, it was a centre for liberal thought and innovative literary and scholarly activity. More than 20,000 journalists have graduated from the department since 1965, and almost all have become well-known editors and authors, from Aleksei Adzhubei (Khrushchev's son-in-law, editor-in-chief of *Izvestiia* from 1959–64) to Vladislav Listev. The department's graduates could be found among both dissidents and Party propagandists in almost equal proportions during the Soviet era.

A vivid representative of the Thaw generation's so-called *shestidesiatniki* (sixties generation), Zasurskii himself provided an interesting example of the independent-minded intellectual who preserved the ideals of his youth: freedom of speech, journalistic integrity, and the dignity of the profession. Zasurskii is the author of several dozen books on contemporary journalism in Russia, the United States, and other countries, and a well-known intellectual and participant in media discussions since 1985, with a critical stance toward media monopolization and state control. He was one of the first to propose the economic independence of the media in the early 1990s, but was ignored.

See also: censorship; Communist Party; journalism, post-Soviet; journalists, Soviet; Krushchev, Nikita; Listev, Vladislav; Moscow State University; propaganda, Soviet and post-Soviet; sixties generation; Thaw

NADEZHDA AZHGIKHINA

Zavadskii, Iurii Aleksandrovich

b. 30 June [12 July] 1894, Moscow; d. 5 April 1977, Moscow

Theatre director

Zavadskii joined Evgenii Vakhtangov's studio in 1915, studying under Vakhtangov and Konstantin Stanislavskii, and acted and directed in the Moscow Art Theatre's Third Studio (1920–24). After stints in the Art Theatre (1924–31), the Red Army Theatre (1936–40) and others, he became artistic director of Moscow's Mossovet Theatre in 1941, remaining there until his death. Under his leadership, it became one of the city's most popular venues, mixing light, dazzling comedy, classical tragedy, and Russian realistic prose. His pupils included numerous major actors (including Vera Maretskaia, Rostislav Pliatt, and Margarita Terekhova) and directors (including Mikhail Levitin, Alexei Borodin, and Jerzy Grotowski).

See also: Moscow Art Theatre; Mossovet Theatre; Pliatt, Rostislav; Terekhova, Margarita; theatre, Soviet; Vakhtangov Theatre

JOHN FREEDMAN

Zeldin, Vladimir Mikhailovich

b. 28 February 1915, Kozlov

Theatre and film actor

Zeldin studied at the Mossovet Theatre school until 1935 and became a star of Soviet cinema with the role of Musaib in Ivan Pyrev's Stalinist musical comedy *Svinarka i pastukh* (*Swineherd and Shepherd,* 1941). On stage, Zeldin gained wide popularity after joining the Theatre of the Soviet Army in 1945. He excelled in contemporary Soviet fare as well as foreign plays, including Neil Simon comedies, displaying elegance, wit, and a fine sense of musical rhythm. His most famous performance is Aldemaro in *The Dancing Teacher* by Lope de Vega, which he also played in a 1952 film adaptation. People's Artist of the USSR (1975).

See also: Mossovet Theatre

PETER ROLLBERG

Zeldovich, Aleksandr Efimovich

b. 4 December 1958, Moscow

Scriptwriter, director

Zeldovich earned a psychology degree from Moscow State University (1980), then completed Higher Courses for Scriptwriters and Directors (1986) as a student of Gleb Panfilov and Aleksandr Mitta.

Based loosely on Isaac Babel's famous Odessa tales, his first feature, *Zakat* (*Sunset*, 1990), a highly stylized, symbolic meditation on human suffering during the Revolution and in general, allied him with a new generation of postmodern Russian filmmakers that arose in the late 1980s. His second feature film, *Moskva* (*Moscow*, 2000), co-written with Vladimir Sorokin, was a visually and aurally stunning, often shocking, end-of-century and end-of-millennium philosophical rumination on 'New Russians' and Moscow and its many shifting images.

See also: Moscow; Moscow State University; Mitta, Aleksandr; New Russians; Panfilov, Gleb; postmodernism; Sorokin, Vladimir

VIDA JOHNSON

zelenyi zmii

Literally 'green serpent', *zelenyi zmii* is the personification of alcohol: 'demon drink'. It can be used to describe the grip of alcohol on an individual or a state of total intoxication (*napitsia do zelenogo zmiia* – to drink oneself into a stupor).

See also: alcoholism; drinks, alcoholic

MICHELE BERDY

Zemfira

(née Zemfira Talgatovna Ramazanova)

b. 26 August 1976, Ufa, Bashkiriia

Rock singer

Pop-rock singer Zemfira was hailed by critics as a symbol of her generation after her 1998 appearance at the Moscow Rock Festival. One of the first performers to address such issues as same-sex love and AIDS, she mesmerized young audiences with her sincerity and unconventional, deglamorized image. Zemfira launched her career with the song '*AIDS*', chanting: 'You have AIDS, and so we're gonna die!' She produces visually compelling music videos and describes her career as a constant search for new means of self-expression.

See also: Bashkortostan; rock music

OLGA PARTAN

zephyr (zefir)

Russian confection somewhat similar to marshmallows and meringue cookies. Made primarily of eggs, sugar, and puree of fruit, typically of apple, *zefir* comes in a variety of flavours, such as vanilla and crème brûlée. One of the most popular versions of *zefir* is covered in chocolate glaze (*zefir v shokolade*).

SUSMITA SUNDARAM

Zharov, Mikhail Ivanovich

b. 27 October 1899, Moscow; d. 15 December 1981, Moscow

Actor

In the 1920s, Zharov worked at the Meierkhold and the Chamber (Tairov's) Theatre, and from 1938 for many years was a leading actor at the Malyi Theatre in Moscow. In cinema, Zharov played over seventy roles, working with Boris Barnet, Grigorii Kozintsev, and Sergei Eisenstein (as Maliuta Skuratov in *Ivan Groznyi*, *Ivan the Terrible*, 1944), among others. Yet in popular consciousness his best roles were associated with playful, contradictory characters, such as the gang leader Zhigan in Nikolai Ekk's *Putevka v zhizn* (*Road to Life*, 1931) or Menshikov in Vladimir Petrov's *Petr Pervyi* (*Peter the First*, 1937–38). Zharov's ironic heroes were icons of unruly Russian masculinity, visible even in his old village detective Aniskin, a Soviet equivalent of Columbo, in a popular series of made-for-TV films.

See also: Malyi Theatre

ELENA PROKHOROVA

Zhdanov, Ivan Fedorovich

b. 16 January 1948, Ust-Tulatinka, Altai region

Poet

A central figure in unofficial late Soviet poetry, Zhdanov is a leading exponent of meta-realism, a loose-knit movement that arose in the mid-1970s. His densely metaphorical and highly complex poems bear the traces of such diverse influences as Russian Symbolism and the later poetry of Osip Mandelstam. Following the publication of his first book, *Portret* (*Portrait*, 1982), Zhdanov became a lightning rod for criticism of 'young poets' in the literary press. Four more collections of poetry followed between 1990 and 1997, when Zhdanov was awarded the Apollon Grigorev Prize. Zhdanov has written little since the late 1990s, as his focus has shifted to photography.

See also: awards, literary, post-Soviet; poetry, post-Soviet

PATRICK HENRY

Zhilinskii, Dmitrii Dmitrievich

b. 25 May 1927, Volnovka, Krasnodar region

Painter

A graduate of Moscow's Surikov Institute, Zhilinskii contributed to the search for new art-historical models characteristic of the Thaw, but where some of his contemporaries looked to the Russian Cézannist tradition, Zhilinskii turned instead to the Middle Ages and the early Renaissance. In Russian icons, the Italian Quattrocento, and the Northern Renaissance, he found a balance between concrete observation of appearances and the conventions and harmony of art. As a teacher at the Surikov Art Institute from 1952 to his dismissal in 1974, he significantly influenced the young generation of Moscow artists of the 1970s such as Tatiana Nazarenko. Honoured Artist, Russian Soviet Republic (*Zasluzhennyi deiatel iskusstv RSFSR*, 1983), named corresponding member of the Soviet Academy of Arts (1978).

See also: art schools and academies; art, Soviet; Nazarenko, Tatiana; Thaw

SUSAN E. REID

Zhirinovskii, Vladimir Volfovich

b. 25 April 1946, Alma-Ata, Kazakh SSR

Politician

A graduate, with honours (1970), of Moscow State University's Institute of Eastern Languages (now the Institute of Asia and Africa) with a specialization in Turkish studies, and of the University's Law School (1977), Zhirinovskii entered political life in 1987. In 1990, he helped form the Liberal Democratic Party of the Soviet Union, subsequently renamed the Liberal Democratic Party of Russia (LDPR), which Zhirinovskii has led with considerable success, claiming top-three finishes in many general elections. Zhirinovskii is known for his outrageous behaviour and ultra-nationalist, sexualized rhetoric, including an expressed desire to expand Russia south to the Indian Ocean, retake Alaska, flood the Baltic States with nuclear waste, and personally ensure Russian women's impregnation. He has also released his own musical album as well as an eau de cologne and a brand of vodka bearing his name. All this, combined with a pro-Kremlin voting record, has helped Zhirinovskii make a successful career as a politician and lobbyist, whose involvement in politics has made him rich. Many doubt Zhirinovskii's serious intention of fulfilling his ultra-nationalist promises, believing instead that he plays the political clown for his own personal benefit. Rumours have circulated that the Kremlin underwrites Zhirinovskii's performances.

See also: Moscow State University; nationalism ('the national question'); political parties, post-Soviet

DAVID HUNTER SMITH

Zhvanetskii, Mikhail Mikhailovich

b. 6 March 1934, Odessa

Writer, comedian

Zhvanetskii has been Russia's most famous satirical comedian since the early 1970s, when he began performing his own material after having spent years writing for the legendary Arkadii Raikin. Zhvanetskii's stage persona – the writer reading monologues, with his Odessa Jewish intonation, from manuscript pages pulled from a tattered briefcase – is universally recognized. During Stagnation, his pointed satire frequently skirted the boundaries of the politically permissible, and he could not perform in large concert halls or publish widely. He became a household name, however, by giving concerts in small venues, which were recorded and circulated in countless homemade copies, like the songs of

Bulat Okudzhava, Vladimir Vysotskii, and other bards. Zhvanetskii's signature themes include bureaucracy, endemic shortages, official corruption, the frustrations and small pleasures of everyday life, and his beloved Odessa. His fame (and skill at double entendres) was such that he never received more than a mild reprimand from the state. In the post-Soviet period, Zhvanetskii has remained popular, performing and publishing prolifically.

See also: bards; comedians; Odessa; Raikin, Arkadii; Stagnation; stand-up comedy

SETH GRAHAM

Zinovev, Aleksandr Aleksandrovich

b. 29 October 1922, Kostroma oblast

Philosopher and writer

A military pilot during World War II, from 1946 till 1954 Zinovev studied at Moscow State University and from 1954 till 1976 was a research fellow at the USSR Academy of Sciences's Institute of Philosophy. The author of numerous scholarly books and articles, following publication in the West of his novel *Ziiaiushchie vysoty* (*The Yawning Heights*, 1976), Zinovev was dismissed from the Academy, deprived of all his titles and decorations, and in 1978 forced to leave the country. In 1999, he returned to Russia as an ardent critic of the West and its aggression against Russian civilization.

See also: Academy of Sciences; Moscow State University; World War II (Great Patriotic War)

ALEXANDER DOMRIN

Ziuganov, Gennadii Andreevich

b. 26 June 1944, Mymrino

Politician

Communist Party Duma faction leader and twice (1996, 2000) presidential candidate,

Ziuganov accused the Yeltsin regime of reducing Russia to a raw-materials appendage of Western capitalism. Aside from emphasizing ecological sustainability, Ziuganov's essentially non-Marxist ideology foregrounds *derzhavnost* – great power concern for Russia's imperial and Soviet territorial legacy; this view treads close to rehabilitating Stalin (as that idea's champion). Characterizing Russia theoretically, Ziuganov draws on Slavophile notions of the people's spiritual unity in Orthodox Christianity. Ziuganov's capacious traditionalism twice rendered him the closest the post-Soviet period saw to a viable opposition presidential candidate.

See also: Communist Party; Duma; nationalism ('the national question'); natural resources; political parties, post-Soviet; Russian Orthodoxy; Slavophiles; Yeltsin, Boris

AVRAM BROWN

Znanie

Scientific society

A public organization in the USSR/Russia for distributing political, scientific, and other information, Znanie (Knowledge) was established in 1947 under the leadership of scientist Sergei Vavilov. Znanie had offices in every administrative territory of the country, with a membership of 3 million in 1990. The organization has sponsored planetaria, scientific and technical centres, lectures on scientific subjects, consultations, and popular brochures in various fields. After 1993, Znanie became less ideologically biased. In the post-Soviet era, its expanded offerings include foreign language courses, club meetings for various hobbies, gardening classes, massage, ethics, rhetoric, and other subjects for the general public. It also publishes a quarterly magazine, *Novye znaniia* (New Knowledge).

See also: science and technology

TATYANA LEDENEVA

Zolotukhin, Valerii Sergeevich

b. 1941, Bystryi Istok, Altai region

Actor

Zolotukhin is best known for his work at the Moscow Taganka Theatre, where he has worked since 1964. He also has had a prolific film career, starting in 1968, and starring in Iosif Kheifits's *Edinstvennaia* (*My Only One*, 1975) and Gennadii Poloka's *Interventsiia* (*Intervention*, 1968) alongside his fellow Taganka actor and friend, Vladimir Vysotskii. His television appearances include the TV film *Brezhnev* (2004) and the Russian television adaptation of Bulgakov's *Master i Margarita* (*The Master and Margarita*, 2004). Most recently, he played in the blockbuster vampire movie *Nochnoi dozor* (*The Night Watch*, 2004). Zolotukhin has written stories and performed songs on film soundtracks.

See also: film, literary adaptation; film, television; *Master i Margarita* (*The Master and Margarita*); Taganka Theatre; Vysotskii, Vladimir

DAVID GILLESPIE

Zorin, Leonid Genrikhovich

b. 3 November 1924, Baku

Playwright, novelist

The characters of Zorin's numerous plays, short stories, and novels capture with sophistication and flair the anxiety-driven sensibility of the post-Stalin cultural elite. At the core of the stylized, controversial *Rimskaia komediia* (*A Roman Comedy*, 1964), the wistful love story *Varshavskaia melodiia* (*A Warsaw Melody*, 1966), and the period drama *Tsarskaia okhota* (*A Royal Hunt*, 1974) are urbane parables about the ambivalent task of negotiating ambition, loyalty, and personal integrity in a world in which language is the ultimate source of authority. The 1982 television version of Zorin's nostalgic comedy *Pokrovskie vorota* (*The Pokrov Gates*, 1974), directed by Mikhail Kozakov and starring Oleg Menshikov, became a cult classic.

See also: Kozakov, Mikhail; Menshikov, Oleg

BORIS WOLFSON

Zverev, Anatolii Timofeevich

b. 3 November 1931, Moscow; d. 9 December 1986, Moscow

Artist

In the 1950s Zverev invented a unique, vigorous artistic style close to figurative touchism. The subjects of his landscapes, portraits, and still-lifes remain recognizable, but are dissolved in a spontaneous play of colours. Zverev excelled at improvisations and was famous for his seemingly off-the-cuff female portraits. A homeless vagabond and alcoholic, he was adored by the Moscow cultural underground and attained international fame at the 1965 Paris exhibition. A posthumous exhibition of his works in Russia prompted interest in his work by the foremost Russian museums.

TATIANA LEDENEVA

Zvezdochetov, Konstantin Viktorovich

b. 22 September 1958, Moscow

Artist

A graduate of the Moscow Art Theatre School (stage design class, 1981), during 1978 to 1984 Zvezdochetov was among the founding members of the Mukhomor group, and from 1982–84 among the organizers of Apt-Art exhibitions. Zvezdochetov is also one of the founding members of the Avant-Garde Club (*Klava*) and is affiliated with Moscow Conceptualism. His works have been exhibited in *Documenta IX*, Kassel, Germany (1992) and in the Russian pavilion of the 50th Venice Biennale (2003). The main character of his early works is *Malchish-Kibalchish* (based on Arkadii Gaidar's ideological children's story), who travelled in the desert and wrestled with anacondas in the jungles. In his later works, the artist invented the history of a fictional tribe, Perdo. Zvezdochetov's witty fictional stories and myths make allusions to Soviet reality and are filled with a sense of conspiracy.

See also: Apt-Art; art, Soviet; Gaidar, Arkadii

NATALIA KOLODZEI

Zvezdochetova, Larisa Iurevna

(née Larisa Iurievna Rezun)

b. 25 June 1958, Odessa, Ukrainian SSR

Artist

After studying at the Ushinskii Pedagogical Institute in Odessa, Ukraine (1975–82), in the mid-1980s Zvezdochetova moved to Moscow, where she took part in Apt-Art exhibitions, such as *Odessa–Moscow*. Drawing for inspiration on a variety of folk art traditions in her work, Zvezdochetova explores elements of kitsch in the everyday objects and symbols of pop culture. Using bright colours, synthetic fabric and velvet, embroidery, collage, and found objects, Zvezdochetova explores the notion of 'beauty' and 'beautiful'. Summarizing and exaggerating popular notions of 'beauty', Zvezdochetova recreates, with mild irony, the world of Soviet petty-bourgeois happiness. She lives and works in Holland.

See also: Apt-Art; art, Soviet; folk art

NATALIA KOLODZEI

Zykina, Liudmila Georgievna

b. 10 June 1929, Moscow

Russian singer

Zykina began her career as a girl during World War II, working in a factory during the day and singing for wounded soldiers at night. In 1947, she joined the prestigious Piatnitskii choir as soloist; in the 1970s, she became the artistic director and lead soloist of the ensemble *Rossiia* (Russia), with which she performed on numerous national and international tours. Her repertoire consists of Russian folk songs, usually accompanied by a grand orchestra dominated by folk instruments such as the balalaika and the baian, as well as pathos-filled songs by Soviet composers, expressing love for the motherland and its nature and people. Zykina's voice is rich, powerful, and uniquely recognizable. People's Artist of the USSR (1973).

See also: popular music, Soviet

PETER ROLLBERG

Index